牛 津
英语联想词典

OXFORD
Learner's Wordfinder Dictionary

英 语 版

〔英〕Hugh Trappes-Lomax 编

商 务 印 书 馆
The Commercial Press
OXFORD
UNIVERSITY PRESS
牛津大学出版社

Originally published by Oxford University Press,
Great Clarendon Street, Oxford

原版由牛津大学出版社出版

序

王 逢 鑫

从功能来看,词典可以分为“查词”词典和“找词”词典。前者的功能是:当读者遇到生词时,它能告诉这个生词的意义、读音和用法,就这个词论这个词。这种词典是读者们非常熟悉的通用词典。后者的功能是当读者萌生某种想法而不知用什么词汇表达时,它能帮助读者通过联想找到所需要的特定单词和相关词汇,提供更广泛的语言知识和文化知识。这种词典是读者们不很熟悉的联想词典。本词典就是一部新颖的联想词典。

这部词典有三个功能:

1. 帮助读者查找所需要的一个特定单词;

2. 帮助读者搜集与某个特定话题领域相关的词汇;

3. 帮助读者通过自由查阅不同的话题领域来扩大词汇量。

这部词典有三个特色:

1. 调动读者的思维能力,发挥联想的作用。词典的23个意义相关的话题领域,提供了大量的生动的语境。查找所需要的特定单词,将孤立的单词置于广泛的语境之中,将相关的词汇放在一起,联系记忆,联系学习,举一反三,学一知三。

2. 集词汇与知识于一体。词汇是知识的载体。词汇系统是知识体系的反映。掌握大量词汇,表明拥有丰富知识。扩大词汇量,表明扩大知识面。学习词汇,离不开联想;获取知识,也离不开联想。在查阅词汇过程中,读者可以系统学习相关知识,增大词汇量,扩大知识面。

3. 熔语言与文化于一炉。在查阅词汇过程中,读者可以全面了解词汇的文化含义,掌握词汇在一定文化背景下的准确意义和用法。将学习英语与学习英语国家的文化结合起来,在扩大语言知识的同时,扩大文化知识。

这部词典的最大特色就是联想。联想是独立思考和原创思维的表现。

一个富于联想和善于联想的人,常常是肯于独立思考和具有创新精神的人。学会使用这部词典有助于培养联想能力。

根据语义学理论,一个核心概念(通常用一个核心词表现)与属于同一范畴的词汇,构成一个领域。语义学家借用物理学的"场"的概念,将这个领域称为"语义场"。而语用学家也有类似的表述,以一个话题为核心(通常也是用一个核心词表现),将与其相关的内容结合在一起,构成一个话题领域。它与语义场有雷同和重叠之处,但各自出发点不同。本词典是在一个话题领域之内、和在不同话题领域之间进行联想。

利用联想查找和扩展词汇,涉及三种方法:辐射联想、推理联想和交叉联想。

辐射的方法是以一个表示话题的核心词为中心,通过分类及其属性、特征、功能和动作,联想与其相关的方方面面的内容。例如:说到"天气"(weather),自然会想到具体的天气状况:晴阴(sunny, cloudy)、冷热(hot, warm, cool, cold)、干湿(dry, wet)、现象(rain, snow, storm, wind, fog);想到气候(tropical climate, temperate climate);想到四季(season, spring, summer, autumn, winter);想到天气预报(weather forecast);想到气象研究(meteorology)。

推理的方法是从一个已知的词出发,利用逻辑关系找出它的反义词、近义词、上义词和下义词等等。例如,利用 cloudy,找到反义词 cloudless;利用 weather,找到近义词 climate;利用 spring,找到上义词 season;利用 season,找到下义词 spring, summer, autumn, winter。

交叉的方法是由一个话题领域联想到另一个话题领域。例如,度假需要知道天气,可以在 holiday 的话题领域,找到与 weather 有关的词汇。天气是电视和广播等媒体经常关注的内容,也可以在 television/radio 的话题领域,找到与 weather 有关的词汇。

学会使用这部联想词典,会培养你的联想能力。常常使用这部联想词典,会使你插上联想的翅翼,在英语的王国里自由翱翔。

王逢鑫

北京大学教授

2003年10月

Author's preface

As a learner of English, you know that building up your stock of words is your biggest task. You probably already have a dictionary to help you do this. So why a new one?

Most dictionaries are 'checking' books: you come across a word, for example when you are reading a book or listening to someone speaking, and you go to the dictionary to check its meaning, its pronunciation or its use.

This dictionary is different: it is a 'discovering' book. It is designed to help you to expand your vocabulary in the directions *you* want – giving you the words you need, to say the things you want to say.

If you glance through the book you will quickly see that it is different from most other dictionaries in two important ways:

- instead of listing words in alphabetical order, it groups them according to their similarities and differences of *meaning* and *use*;
- instead of giving you the word first and then its meaning, it gives you the meaning first *and then the word (or words) that you are looking for.*

This explains the name, **Word*finder***.

Working with students studying English, in Kenya and Tanzania and later in Britain, helped me to see the value of a dictionary of this sort. I am grateful to all my students, as well as to others who have contributed more directly to the creation of this book:

In Edinburgh, Sandra Anderson, Mark Backer-Holst, David Caulton, Penny Hands, David Hill, Michael Meyler and Ingrid Yngstrom were principal contributors. I also want to thank Sheena Davies, Thora Nicholson, Luan Porter, and Elizabeth White; and, for their interest, their tolerance and their support in many different ways, all my colleagues at the Institute for Applied Language Studies in the University of Edinburgh.

In Oxford, Moira Runcie, for her faith in the project, and Sally Wehmeier, Judith Willis and, especially, Margaret Deuter, for their wonderful editorial skills and (apparently) inexhaustible reserves of patience and encouragement, are due abundant thanks.

And to my wife, Jocelyn Nceckei, who has lived with this book from the first idea to the final proof-reading, much more than thanks.

Hugh Trappes-Lomax

Terms, symbols and short forms

AmE	American English
BrE	British English
formal	used in more formal contexts, such as writing a report or speaking at a conference
informal	used in informal contexts, such as a conversation with family or friends
noun, verb, adjective, adverb	the part that a word plays in its sentence (**Note**: these labels are not used in all cases, but only when they are needed for clarity.)
U	an uncountable noun
C/U	a noun that is often countable but can also be uncountable
U/C	a noun that is often uncountable but can also be countable
singular	a noun that is used only in the singular
plural	a noun that is used only in the plural
with singular or plural verb	a singular noun (for example **family**, **government**) which can have a plural verb if you are thinking of the actions, feelings, etc of the individual members of the group
only before a noun	an adjective which comes before a noun, not after a verb like **is** or **seems**
not before a noun	an adjective which comes after a verb like **is** or **seems**, not before a noun
usually passive	a verb that is more common in the passive than the active form
*	an irregular verb (see table on p 516)
abbreviation	a short form of a word
opposite	a word which is opposite in meaning to another word
sb	somebody
sth	something

Contents

Using the dictionary

1 With *Wordfinder*, you can:

- look for a particular word that you want
- collect words that are related to a particular topic area
- expand your vocabulary by looking freely through topic areas

Looking for a word

You know the word 'letter', but you don't know the word for the way that you write your name at the end of a letter. You look at **letter** and you find:

> – your name, written by hand in a special way so that nobody else can copy it: **signature**
> – to put your signature on sth: **sign** (sth)

You want to know the opposite of 'sweet'. You look at **sweet** and you find:

> – having a sharp taste like that of a lemon: **sour** ◦ *These apples are rather sour.*
> – having a sharp unpleasant taste: **bitter** ◦ *bitter coffee*

You know that 'promise' means to say that you will do something that somebody wants. If you do not do what you promise to do, what is the expression for this? You look at **promise** and you find:

> – if you do not do what you promised to do, you **break*** a promise, **go* back on** your **word**, the promise is **broken** ◦ *I can't believe he went back on his word!* ◦ *broken promises*

Collecting words about a topic

You are preparing to give a short talk about holidays. You need to think about the different kinds of holiday that people choose, how they travel, and where they stay. You look up **holiday** and you find:

> **holiday**
>
> **1** time when people do not work
> **2** special days and times which are holidays
> **3** going away on holiday
> **see also** TRAVEL

From this, you choose 'going away on holiday', and you find:

> – a special holiday where you pay for your travel, hotel and some or all of your meals before you leave: **package holiday**
> – a holiday on a large ship: **cruise** ◦ *to go on a round-the-world cruise*
> – a holiday in Africa, looking at wild animals: **safari** ◦ *to go on safari*
> – a journey when you visit a place and return: **trip** ◦ *a trip to the seaside*
>
> – to travel around on holiday carrying your luggage in a bag on your back: **go* backpacking** ◦ *They went backpacking round Europe last summer.*
> – to go on a holiday with a tent: **go* camping**
> – a holiday that you spend doing sports or other outdoor activities: **adventure/activity holiday**
> – a holiday that you spend walking or cycling: **walking/cycling holiday**
> – a holiday that you spend travelling round a place, for example in a car or a bus: **touring holiday**
> – a holiday when you do some work: **working holiday**

Now you want to think about the different ways of travelling. You follow up the suggestion at the beginning of **holiday**, 'see also TRAVEL', and you find:

travel

1 travelling
2 means of transport
3 tickets, passports, money, etc
4 starting a journey, moving and arriving
luggage and packing ⇨ BAG
accidents and crashes ⇨ ACCIDENT
travelling in space ⇨ SPACE²
see also HOLIDAY, HOTEL, CAMP

You look at section 2 to check that you know all the words for means of transport, and how to use them. (Do we say 'with the train', 'on the train', or 'by train'?).

2 means of transport

- using a car, bus, lorry, etc to travel: **by road, car, bus,** etc, **on the bus/coach**
- to go somewhere in a car: **drive***; a journey in a car or other vehicle: **drive** ◦ *We're driving up to Scotland this summer.*
- to travel by getting free rides in other people's cars, lorries, etc: **hitch-hike,** (*informal*) **hitch**; a person who does this: **hitch-hiker** ◦ *We hitched down to Devon.* ◦ *I picked up two hitch-hikers on the way home from Bath.*

- using a bicycle or motorcycle: **by bike, by motorcycle**, etc
- to travel on a motorcycle: **ride*** (sth)
- to travel on a bicycle: **ride*** (sth), **cycle** ◦ *to ride along cycle tracks in the New Forest* ◦ *I usually cycle to work.*

- using a train or trains: **by train, on the train, by rail**
- (used about long journeys) by road or rail: **overland** ◦ *We travelled overland to Delhi and then flew on to Singapore.*

- using an aeroplane: **by air, by plane**
- to travel somewhere by plane: **fly***; a journey by plane: **flight**

- using a boat: **by sea, by boat**
- to travel somewhere in a boat: **sail**; a long journey by sea: **voyage**
- to travel by boat, visiting a number of places, as a holiday: **cruise**; *noun*: **cruise** ◦ *to go cruising in the Mediterranean* ◦ *a river cruise*

- without using a vehicle: **on foot**
- to go somewhere on foot: **walk**

Now you need to think about types of accommodation. In the box at the beginning of keyword **travel** you saw the cross-references to **hotel** and **camp**. Look up **hotel** to find the different types of hotel:

- a place where you stay when you are travelling or on holiday: **hotel** ◦ *a first-class hotel* ◦ *We stayed in a small country hotel.*
- a hotel where you can park your car near your room: **motel**
- a small hotel sometimes in a private house: **guest house**
- a private house where you can spend the night and have breakfast in the morning: **bed and breakfast** (*abbreviation* **B&B**)
- a place (like a cheap hotel) where people can stay when they are living away from home: **hostel** ◦ *a youth hostel* (= a hostel for people who are walking, cycling, etc in the countryside)

Now look at camp and make sure that you know the words there:

- to put up a tent and sleep in it: **camp** (**out**) ◦ *We camped in a field by a stream.* ◦ *We decided to camp out for the night.*
- sleeping or spending a holiday in a tent: **camping** (*noun* U) ◦ *They went on a camping holiday.*
- to spend a holiday living in a tent: **go* camping** ◦ *We're going camping in the South of France this summer.*
- a special place where people camp: **campsite** (*AmE* **campground**)
- a person who camps: **camper**

Looking freely through topic areas

To help you talk about the weather, you look up **weather**, and you find these cross-references:

see also RAIN, SNOW, STORM, WIND

You follow up the cross-reference to SNOW. You read the section on 'enjoying the snow' and you find:

- to move over snow on long, flat, narrow pieces of wood, metal or plastic (**skis**) that are fastened to boots: **ski**; a person who skis: **skier**
- a type of flat board, often with metal strips underneath, that people use for travelling downhill on snow for fun: **sledge**; *verb*: **sledge** ◦ *Let's go sledging!*
- a lump of snow that is pressed into the shape of a ball and used by children for playing: **snowball** ◦ *a snowball fight*
- the figure of a person made out of snow, usually by children: **snowman** (*plural* **snowmen**)

▷more on skiing ⇨ SKI

To find out more about skiing, and to see a picture, you look at the entry for **ski**.

2 Finding your way in *Wordfinder*

Keywords

Words are grouped together under **keywords**, which are arranged alphabetically in the book.

Some keywords just direct you to another keyword. If you look up **able**, you will find:

able
- able to be done ⇨ POSSIBLE²
- having skill ⇨ SKILL

Most keywords have an index which shows you how the words are organized. If you look up **television**, you will find:

television / radio
1 watching television
2 listening to the radio
3 controlling a television or radio
4 television and radio programmes
5 broadcasting

To help you find your way, some keywords have smaller sections with their own headings. Under **television and radio programmes**, you will find four headings:

- news and weather
- information and talk
- stories and plays
- games

If you want to go on to learn some words that are more difficult, you will find a section in some keywords called **MORE**. If you look up **blood**, you will find this group of words:

■ **MORE ...**
- easily upset by the sight of blood: **squeamish** ◦ *I couldn't be a nurse. I'm far too squeamish.*
- full of violence and blood: **gory** ◦ *a gory film*
- involving bloody injuries: **gruesome** ◦ *The battlefield was a gruesome sight.*

Words that are related in meaning

Some words are grouped together because they are related in meaning. For example, if you look up **plane**, you will find **plane** with **aeroplane**. They are *synonyms* (= they mean the same). You will also find **aircraft**. This has a *more general meaning* than **plane** and **aeroplane**.

- any vehicle that can fly in the air: **aircraft** (*plural* **aircraft**) ◦ *a jet aircraft* (= powered by a jet engine)
- a vehicle with wings and one or more engines that can fly through the air: **plane, aeroplane** (*AmE* **airplane**) ◦ *to travel by plane* ◦ *a plane ticket* ◦ *a plane crash* ◦ *a supersonic plane* (= a plane that can fly faster than the speed of sound)

You will also find these *different kinds* of plane:

- a large plane that carries passengers: **airliner**; a very large jet plane that carries passengers: **jumbo (jet)**
- a plane that carries goods: **cargo plane**
- a plane that takes off and lands on the sea: **seaplane**

If you look up keyword **useful/suitable**, you will find the word **convenient** with its *opposite* **inconvenient**. You will also find the related *adverbs* **conveniently** and **inconveniently**.

- suitable or practical for a particular purpose; not causing difficulty: **convenient** (*adverb* **conveniently**); *opposite*: **inconvenient** (*adverb* **inconveniently**) ◦ *When would it be convenient to phone?* ◦ *Have I called at an inconvenient moment?*

Words that are related in use

Some words are grouped together because they are often used in the same sentence or in the same situation.

If you look up **butter**, you will find **spread**, and in the same group **soft** and **hard**. These words will often come up together, so it is useful to learn them as a group.

- to put butter on a piece of bread, etc: **butter** sth ◦ *Shall I help you to butter the sandwiches?* ◦ *buttered toast*
- to put butter, jam, etc, on bread: **spread*** A **on** B, **spread*** B **with** A ◦ *Spread margarine on it.* ◦ *Spread it with margarine.*
- butter which is easy to spread is **soft**; *opposite*: **hard** ◦ *It's too hard to spread.*

If you look up **meet**, you will find **meet** meaning to see and talk to a person for the first time. In the same group you will find the verb **introduce** and the noun **introduction**. This is because people are introduced when they meet for the first time.

- to see and talk to sb for the first time: **meet*** (sb) ◦ *I first met my future husband at a horse race.* ◦ *Where did you two first meet?*
- to tell two or more people who have not met before what each other's names are: **introduce** sb (**to** sb); *noun*: **introduction** ◦ *Have you two been introduced?* ◦ *Pauline – I'd like to introduce you to Andrew from the graphics department.* ◦ *Shall I make the introductions?*

Topic areas

The 23 groups of keywords on this and the following pages will help you to explore an area of vocabulary that you are interested in and to find the keyword that you need.

For example, if you want to find vocabulary for describing people, look at **TOPIC AREA 1**. In this section, you will find a number of ideas connected with this topic, and the keyword where you should look to find the words that you need. So, if you want to know the words that are to do with the way people live, find

how people live their lives	**live**[2]

The keyword that you need is **live**[2].

If you cannot find what you are looking for in these groups of words, there are some suggestions on the right for other related keywords and topic areas.

1 People

the human race and human nature; races and ethnic groups	**people**
society and social groups	**society**, **group**
people as individuals	**person**
the stages of a person's life	**life**, **birth**, **death**, **young / old**
how people live their lives	**live**[2]
babies and children	**baby**, **child**
men and women	**man**, **woman**
male and female	**sex**[1]
personal qualities and ways of behaving	**personality**, **behaviour**, **habit**
some particular qualities or ways of behaving	**brave**, **clever**, **generous**, **honest**, **kind / cruel**, **lazy**, **proud**, **careful**, **sensible**
good and bad behaviour	**right / wrong**[2]
sexual behaviour	**sex**[2]
behaviour that is shared by groups of people	**custom**

- for relationships between people, look at **relationship**
- for some particular kinds of relationship, look at **family**, **friend**, **love**, **marry**
- for being famous, look at **famous**
- for the human body and its parts, look at **TOPIC AREA 2**

2 Your body, personal appearance and clothes

the body as a whole	**body**
parts of the body	**hand / arm**, **leg / foot**, **bone**, **muscle**, **blood**, **skin**, **heart**, **stomach**
head, hair and face	**head**, **hair**, **face**
parts of the head and face	**nose**, **mouth**, **tooth**, **ear**, **eye**
tall or short?	**height**
thin or fat?	**fat / thin / thick**
how heavy?	**weight**
strong or weak?	**strong / weak**
attractive?	**beautiful / attractive**
clothes in general	**clothes**
some particular kinds of clothes	**coat**, **hat**, **shoe**, **trousers**
jewellery	**jewellery**
glasses	**glasses**
fashion	**fashion**

- for looking after your body and your appearance, look at **wash**, **cosmetics**, **exercise**
- for using the bathroom and toilet, look at **bathroom**, **toilet**
- for illness, injury, etc, look at **TOPIC AREA 16**
- for looking after your clothes, look at **wash**, **ironing**

3 Everyday life

washing and using the bathroom getting dressed	**wash**, **bathroom**, **toilet** **clothes**	– for different kinds of entertainment, look at **TOPIC AREA 11**
going to school or work going shopping	**travel**, **school**, **work** **shop**	
cooking and eating and drinking cleaning the house	**cook**, **eat**, **meal**, **drink** **clean / dirty**	
resting and relaxing going to bed and sleeping	**rest**, **entertainment**, **exercise** **bed**, **sleep**	

4 Food and drink

food and eating bread, cakes, etc butter, milk, etc meat and fish vegetables, etc fruits and nuts salt and pepper	**food**, **eat** **bread**, **cake**, **flour** **butter**, **cheese**, **egg**, **milk** **meat**, **bird²**, **fish²** **vegetable**, **potato**, **rice** **fruit**, **nut** **salt/pepper**	– for things that you use when eating and drinking, look at **knife/fork/spoon**, **plate/bowl/dish**, and **cup/glass** – for how food or drink tastes, look at **taste**
drinking and kinds of drink coffee and tea alcoholic drinks drinking in a bar or pub	**drink** **coffee/tea** **alcohol**, **beer**, **wine** **bar/pub**	
meals eating in a café or restaurant cooking	**meal**, **breakfast** **restaurant** **cook**	

5 Where you live

living in a particular place town and countryside	**live²** **town**, **country²**	– for buildings in general, look at **building** – for constructing a house or other building, look at **build** – for keeping a house warm or cool, look at **cold**, **hot**, **fire** – for fuel that is used in a house, look at **coal**, **gas**, **electricity**
houses and flats parts of a house, etc	**house** **floor**, **roof**, **window**, **door**, **stairs**	
walls and fences gardens	**wall/fence/hedge** **garden**	
rooms in a house the kitchen the bedroom the bathroom and toilet	**room** **kitchen** **bed** **bathroom**, **toilet**	
furniture	**furniture**, **chair**, **table**	
being tidy	**tidy**	

6 The natural environment

the world as a whole	**world**
nature and the environment	**nature**, **environment**
the stars and space	**star/planet/moon**, **space[2]**
the sun and sky	**sun**, **sky**
the air	**air**
the shape of the land; land use	**land**
the surface of the earth	**ground**
the countryside	**country[2]**
rivers and mountains	**river**, **hill/mountain**
the sea	**sea**
beside the sea	**beach**

- for the weather in general, look at **weather**
- for some particular kinds of weather, look at **storm**, **snow**, **wind**, **rain**

7 Animals and other living things

being alive	**live[1]**
animals	**animal**
some domestic animals	**cat**, **cow**, **dog**, **horse**, **pig**, **sheep**
some wild animals	**lion/leopard/tiger**, **snake**
fish	**fish[1]**
birds	**bird[1]**
insects and spiders	**insect**, **bee**, **spider**
plants	**plant**
trees	**tree**
flowers	**flower**
grass	**grass**

- for animals and plants on farms, look at **farm**
- for hunting, look at **hunt**
- for animals and plants as food, look at **food**

8 Work, business, industry and technology

all kinds of work	**work**
factory work	**factory**, **industry**
office work	**office**
computers	**computer**
farm work	**farm**
making things	**make**, **design**, **invent**
working with machines	**machine**, **tool**
having a job	**employment**
working in business	**business**
managing a business	**management**

- for resting from work or having a holiday, look at **rest[2]**, **holiday**
- for fuel for machines look at **fuel**, **oil**, **electricity**
- for materials used for making things, look at **material**

9 Money and buying and selling

money in general	**money**
banks	**bank**
paying for things	**pay[1]**, **cheque**
having debts	**debt**
buying and selling	**buy**, **sell**, **price**, **rent**, **shop**
advertising	**advertisement**
money for the work that you do	**pay[2]**
tax	**tax**
insurance	**insurance**

- for a country's money, trade and industry, look at **economy**
- for business, see **TOPIC AREA 8**

10 Education and science

education in general	**education**	– for knowledge and information, look at **know, information**
teaching and learning	**teach, learn**	– for being good at doing things, look at **skill**
examinations	**exam**	
schools and universities	**school, university**	
science	**science**	
mathematics	**mathematics**	
other subjects of study, how people study things, do research, etc	**study**	

11 Leisure, sport, art and music

kinds of entertainment	**entertainment**	– for going on holiday, look at TOPIC AREA 12
having a party	**party**	– for things that interest you or that you enjoy doing, look at **interesting**
children having fun	**play²**	– for acting and actors, look at **act²**
television and radio	**television/radio, video**	– for the people watching a film, play, etc, look at **audience**
films and the cinema	**film, cinema**	– for competitions and words to do with winning and losing, look at **competition, win/lose**
plays and the theatre	**play¹, theatre**	
games	**game**	
some particular games	**cards, chess**	
sport	**sport**	
some particular sports	**athletics, boxing, football, race², ski, swim**	
all kinds of art	**art**	
particular kinds of art	**draw, paint¹, picture, sculpture**	
photography	**photograph**	
music	**music, dance, orchestra, pop/rock, record, sing**	

12 Transport, travel and holidays

transport in general	**transport**	– for driving a vehicle, especially a car, look at **drive**
by air	**plane**	– for fuel for vehicles, look at **fuel**
by sea	**boat**	– for roads, look at **road**
by rail	**train**	– for accidents, look at **accident**
by road	**bicycle, bus, car, lorry, motorcycle, taxi**	
holidays	**holiday**	
camping	**camp**	
going on a journey	**travel**	
buying a ticket	**ticket**	
staying in a hotel	**hotel**	
arriving and leaving	**arrive, leave**	

13 Government and politics

government and politics	**government, politics**	– for countries, look at **country¹**
kings and queens	**king/queen**	–for political and other kinds of power, look at **power**
parliament	**parliament**	
elections	**election**	

14 The law and crime

the law	**law**, **trial**, **police**	– for good and bad behaviour, look at **right/wrong²**
crime	**crime**	
stealing	**steal**	
drugs	**drugs**	
punishment	**punish**, **prison**	

15 Fighting and war

fighting in general	**fight**	– for enemies, look at **enemy**
hitting and kicking	**hit**	
war	**war**	
the armed forces	**army**, **navy**, **air force**	
weapons in general	**weapon**	
guns and bombs	**gun**, **bomb**	

16 Illness and injury

illness, injury and pain	**illness**, **injury**, **pain**	– for problems with teeth, look at **tooth**, **dentist**
accident	**accident**	
mental illness	**mind**	
treatment for illness or injury	**doctor**, **hospital**, **medicine**, **operation**	

17 Religion and beliefs

religion in general	**religion**, **god**	– for the part of you which is not physical, look at **spirit**
some particular religions	**Christian**, **Muslim**, **Jew**	
churches	**church**	– for belief that something is true, look at **true**
priests	**priest**	
astrology (the stars) and magic	**astrology**, **magic**	

18 Language and communication

communication in general	**communication**	– these keywords cover particular kinds of meaning or use of language: **advise/suggest**, **agreement**, **allow**, **and/or/but**, **bet**, **blame**, **cause/effect**, **complain/protest**, **criticism**, **describe**, **encourage**, **example**, **greet**, **if**, **inform**, **insult**, **invite**, **lie¹**, **must**, **need**, **offer**, **order²**, **persuade**, **polite**, **possible¹**, **praise**, **promise**, **question**, **reason**, **request**, **thank**, **warn**, **yes/no**
signs, gestures, etc	**sign**	
laughing and crying	**laugh**, **cry**	
the human voice	**voice**	
language	**language**	
words and meaning	**grammar**, **meaning**, **word**, **name**	
sounds and spelling	**letter²**, **punctuation**	
saying what you think, feel, etc	**say**, **discuss/argue**	
speaking and listening	**speak**, **listen**, **conversation**	
writing and reading	**write**, **read**	
things used for writing	**paper**, **pen/pencil**, **computer**	
means of communication	**telephone**, **post**	
letters, e-mail and faxes	**letter¹**	
meetings	**meeting**	

19 The media and literature

news and information	**news**, **information**	– for producing a book, newspaper, etc, look at **publish**, **print**
books and newspapers	**book**, **newspaper/magazine**	– for libraries, look at **library**
television and radio	**television/radio**	
films and cinema	**film**, **cinema**	
stories, plays, poems	**story**, **play**[1], **poem**, **literature**	

20 Knowing, thinking, feeling, wanting, liking

knowing things	**know**, **understand**, **remember/forget**	– for the five senses, look at **see**, **look/seem**, **show**, **smell**, **taste**, **feel**, **touch**, **hear**, **listen**, **sound**
using your imagination	**imagination**	
thinking and having opinions	**think**, **opinion**	
thinking that sth is certain, possible or probable	**possible**[1]	
feelings in general	**emotion**, **suffer**	
particular feelings	**afraid**, **angry**, **excited**, **forgive**, **happy**, **sad**, **sorry**, **sympathy**, **tired**, **worry**	
wanting and hoping	**want**, **hope**	
making plans, choices and decisions	**intend/plan**, **decide/choose**	
being willing to do sth	**willing**	
trying, avoiding, succeeding, failing	**try**, **avoid/prevent**, **succeed/fail**, **problem**	
liking and disliking	**like**[2], **enjoy**, **prefer**, **dislike**	
describing the good and bad qualities of things	**good**, **bad**, **important**, **useful**, **value**	

21 Situations, actions, events and movement

events and situations	**happen**, **situation**, **luck**	– for giving, getting, keeping, etc, look at **give**, **provide**, **get/obtain**, **borrow/lend**, **have/possess**, **keep**
describing situations	**funny**, **interesting**, **quiet**, **strange**, **surprise**	– for finding, losing and looking for things, look at **find**, **lose**[2], **look for**
actions and behaviour	**action**, **behaviour**, **habit**	– for actions towards other people (such as helping or protecting a person), look at **help**, **protect**, **support**, **trust**, **power**, **duty**, **obey**
ending an action	**stop**	
repeated actions or events	**again**	
beginning, continuing, finishing	**begin**, **continue**, **end/finish**	
ready or waiting	**ready**, **wait**	
changing, growing and developing	**change**, **grow**, **develop**	
movement in general	**move**	
going to a place	**arrive**, **leave**, **come/go**, **enter**, **climb**, **visit**	
ways of moving	**run**, **walk**, **fly**, **jump**, **fall**, **turn**	
speed of movement or action	**fast/slow**	
causing something to move	**put**, **bring/take/carry**, **lift**, **pull/push**, **throw**	
the position of your body	**lie**[2], **sit**, **stand**	

22 Time and place

time in general	**time**
length of time	**long/short[1]**
when?	**before/after, early/late, soon**
how often something happens	**how often**
one thing after another	**first/next/last**
telling the time	**clock/watch**
periods of time	**day, night, week, year, season**
the date	**date**
where a thing or person is	**place[1]**
parts and positions of things	**place[2], direction, right/left, distance**

- for past, present and future, look at **past[2], present[2], future**
- for events and periods in the past, look at **history**
- for modern times, look at **modern**

23 Describing objects and materials; measuring; counting

lines and shapes	**line, shape, angle, circle, straight**
colour	**colour**
surfaces	**surface**
size in general	**size**
big and small	**big/small**
dimensions	**height, long/short[2], wide/narrow, deep, fat/thin/thick**
weight	**weight**
numbers in general	**number**
some particular numbers	**one, two, hundred**
quantities and amounts	**how much/many**
changing quantities or amounts	**increase/decrease**
average amounts	**average**
enough	**enough**

- for different materials that things are made of, look at **material**
- for some particular materials, look at **glass, gold/silver, metal, stone, wood**

able

- able to be done ⇨ POSSIBLE[2]
- having skill ⇨ SKILL

about ⇨ ALMOST

above ⇨ PLACE[2]

abroad ⇨ COUNTRY[1]

accent ⇨ SPEAK

accept

- an invitation ⇨ INVITE
- an offer ⇨ OFFER

accident

1 accidents in general
2 crashes
3 after an accident

things which happen unintentionally ⇨ INTEND / PLAN

1 accidents in general

- an unpleasant event that happens unexpectedly and causes damage, injury or death: **accident** ◦ *I saw a really bad accident* (= traffic accident) *on my way home from work today.* ◦ *to have a nasty/ serious accident* ◦ *She was involved in a serious accident at work.*
- a very bad accident: **disaster** ◦ *a nuclear disaster* ◦ *the Clapham rail disaster* (= a train accident at a place called Clapham)
- if you frequently have accidents, you are **accident-prone** ◦ *I've never known anybody so accident-prone – yesterday she fell down the stairs and today she trod on some broken glass.*
- to stop an accident happening: **prevent** sth; *noun* (U): **prevention** ◦ *People need to be taught how to prevent accidents.*
- a kind of contract (= written agreement) in which, in return for regular payment, a company agrees to pay you a sum of money in case you lose sth, become ill, die, etc: **insurance** (**against** sth) (*noun* U) ◦ *motor insurance* ◦ *accident insurance*

▷ more on insurance and preventing accidents ⇨ INSURANCE, AVOID / PREVENT

2 crashes

- to have an accident in a vehicle: **crash** (sth); *noun*: **crash** ◦ *All of a sudden, I realized we were going to crash.* ◦ *Mum, Dad, I'm sorry – I've crashed the car.* ◦ *We were held up by a crash on the motorway.* ◦ *a train/plane crash*
- to touch sb or sth with a lot of force: **hit*** sb/sth ◦ *He was hit by a lorry as he was crossing the road.*
- to hit sth by accident when you are moving: **bump against/into** sth ◦ *I wasn't looking where I was going and bumped into the door.*
- to move with great force into/against/through sth: **crash/smash into/against/through** sth ◦ *The car skidded and smashed through the shop window.*
- an accident in which two people or things hit each other violently: **collision**; *verb*: **collide** (**with** sb/sth) ◦ *I collided with another pedestrian as I ran down the street.*
- with the front of one car, etc hitting the front of another: **head-on** (*adjective, adverb*) ◦ *She was involved in a head-on collision with another car.* ◦ *We collided head-on.*
- a crash that involves several cars, etc: **pile-up** ◦ *There was a big pile-up involving two lorries and four cars on the M4 last week.*
- to turn over so that the top is at the bottom: **overturn** ◦ *The car hit the lorry and then overturned.*
- to hit sb with a car: **run*** sb **over**, **knock** sb **down** ◦ *A car came speeding round the corner and knocked down an old lady who was crossing the road.*
- a driver who knocks sb down and does not stop to see if they are hurt: **hit-and-run driver**; an accident where this happens: **hit-and-run accident** ◦ *The police are looking for a young man after a hit-and-run accident last night.*
- when a train comes off the railway track, it is **derailed**
- a train crash in which a train comes off the track: **derailment**
- when an aircraft falls from the sky, it **crashes**, **comes* down** ◦ *The plane ran out of fuel and came down in the sea.*

3 after an accident

■ damage

- to make sth useless or not as good as before: **damage** sth; the effect of damaging sth: **damage** (*noun* U)
- a hollow place in the surface of sth that is the result of sth hitting it hard: **dent**; *verb*: **dent** sth ◦ *I bumped into a lamp post in my car and dented the bonnet.*
- pieces from sth that has crashed or been destroyed: **debris** (*noun* U) ◦ *Debris was scattered right across the road.*

■ injury

- physical damage caused to a person or animal, especially in an accident: **injury** (*noun* C/U) ◦ *Ten people were taken to hospital with serious injuries.*
- a condition of extreme weakness caused by damage to the body or by seeing or being part of a bad accident: **shock** (*noun* U); suffering from shock: **in shock** ◦ *Nobody was hurt as a result of the accident but three people were being treated for shock.*
- a person who is killed or seriously injured in an accident: **casualty** ◦ *It was a serious accident, with numerous casualties.* ◦ *the casualty list* (= the list of people hurt in an accident)

▷ more on injuries ⇨ INJURY

accident *contd.*

■ help

– to save sb/sth from sth that is dangerous or unpleasant: **rescue** sb/sth (**from** sb/sth); *noun*: **rescue**; a person who does this: **rescuer** ◦ *Five men have been rescued from a blazing oil platform.* ◦ *I want to thank my rescuers.*

– the official services (fire, police and ambulance) that give help after an accident: **the rescue services**

– a special motor vehicle for taking injured people to and from hospital: **ambulance**

– a piece of cloth supported by two poles that is used for carrying a person who has been injured in an accident: **stretcher**

– a person who has had special training in caring for people who are ill or hurt. They often travel in ambulances and go to people injured in an accident: **paramedic**

– a way of restoring sb's breath to save their life after a bad accident: **kiss of life** ◦ *He was pulled out of the water and given the kiss of life.*

▷ the fire service ⇨ FIRE

▷ the police ⇨ POLICE

accurate ⇨ EXACT/APPROXIMATE

acid ⇨ LIQUID

act[1]

– doing sth ⇨ ACTION

act[2] in a play, film, etc

1 acting
2 people who act
3 being in a play or film
see also PLAY[1], FILM, THEATRE

1 acting

– to perform a part (= pretend to be a different person) in a play or film: **act** (**in** sth) ◦ *She just can't act!* ◦ *to act in a play/film*

– the art or profession of performing in plays or films: **acting** (*noun* U) ◦ *It wasn't a very good play, but his acting was superb.*

– the things that an actor says and does as a particular character: **part**, **role** ◦ *I played the part of the tramp.* ◦ *Hamlet is a difficult part for a young actor.*

– the words that are written for a particular character to say in a play or film: **lines** (*noun plural*) ◦ *to learn your lines*

– the clothes that an actor wears to play a particular character: **costume**

– to wear special make-up in order to look different: **be made up** (**as** sb) ◦ *I didn't recognize him when he was made up as an old man.*

■ practising

– to practise for a play or film: **rehearse** (sth); the time when this happens: **rehearsal**; the last rehearsal, when all the actors wear their costumes: **dress rehearsal** ◦ *Rehearsals have been going on for weeks.*

– to rehearse sth by practising it from the beginning to the end without stopping: **go* through** sth, **run* through** sth; *noun*: **run-through** ◦ *We'll just go through it once more to make sure everything's all right.* ◦ *another quick run-through before the performance*

■ on the stage

– to move onto the stage to join in a play that is being performed: **go*/come* on**, (*formal*) **enter**; *noun*: **entrance** ◦ *The audience cheered when she came on.* ◦ *to make an entrance*

– to leave the stage: **go* off**, (*formal*) **exit**; *noun*: **exit** ◦ *He made a quick exit.*

– a signal which tells an actor when to start doing or saying sth: **cue** ◦ *The words 'Too late' are your cue to go on.*

– to remind an actor of the words that should come next: **prompt** (sb), **give*** sb **a prompt**; the person who helps actors remember the next words: **prompter** ◦ *I forgot my lines and had to be prompted.*

2 people who act

– a man or woman who acts in a play or film: **actor**; a female actor can also be called an **actress**

– a very famous actor or actress: **star** ◦ *a film star*

– a person who acts as a hobby, not as a job: **amateur** (*noun, adjective*); *opposite*: **professional** (*noun, adjective*) ◦ *The play was very good, considering they're all amateurs.* ◦ *a professional actor/actress*

▷ more on actors in films ⇨ FILM

3 being in a play or film

– to perform a particular part in a play: **play** sb/sth ◦ *His ambition is to play King Lear.* ◦ *I play the part of the doctor.*

– to take an important part in a play or film: **star** (**in** sth) ◦ *She's starring in a new play in London.*

– all the actors in a film or play, etc: the **cast** (*with singular or plural verb*) ◦ *She's the youngest member of the cast.*

– a kind of test when a person can show how good they are at acting (often a particular part): **audition**; to do this kind of test: **audition** (**for** sth); to give the test: **audition** (sb) (**for** sth) ◦ *He auditioned for the part of Romeo but didn't get it.* ◦ *They're auditioning for 'My Fair Lady' – are you going to try and get a part?*

– to be seen in a play or film: **appear** ◦ *to appear on television* ◦ *She recently appeared in 'The Importance of Being Earnest'.*

– one occasion when a person appears: **appearance** ◦ *her first film appearance*

– a first appearance in public of an actor: **debut** ◦ *She made her debut in that film.*

– the way that sb acts in a play or film: **performance** ◦ *a brilliant performance by an exciting new talent*

■ MORE ...

– to use words, actions, etc that you have just thought of, not planned or remembered: **improvise**; *noun* (C/U): **improvisation** ◦ *He was good*

at improvising if he forgot his words. ◦ *a brilliant improvisation* ◦ *a clever piece of improvisation*
- to act without speaking, using only actions to communicate: **mime** (sth); *noun* (C/U): **mime** ◦ *to perform a mime* ◦ *The whole story was in mime.*

---

action

> **1** doing sth
> **2** different kinds of action
> **3** doing sth with or for other people
> **4** the order in which things are done
> **5** the time when sth is done
>
> continuing to do sth ⇨ CONTINUE
> doing sth again ⇨ AGAIN
>
> **see also** BEHAVIOUR, HABIT, HAPPEN, WORK

1 doing sth

- to perform an action or actions: **do*** sth ◦ *'What are you doing tonight?' 'I'm going to the cinema.'* ◦ *I wish somebody would do something about that terrible noise.* ◦ *I've got nothing to do.*
- to do things in a particular way: **behave, act**; *noun* (U): **behaviour** (*AmE* **behavior**) ◦ *He was behaving very strangely.* ◦ *He is acting like a child.* ◦ *bad behaviour*
- to do sth (often sth secret and perhaps sth that you should not do): **be up to** sth ◦ *Where are my children? – I bet they're up to something.* ◦ *What are you up to these days?*

- doing a lot: **active** ◦ *an active trade union member* ◦ *to be active in local politics*

- to think that you would like to do sth: **feel* like** sth/doing sth ◦ *I don't feel like studying this evening – let's go out.*
- to feel able to do sth: **feel*/be up to** sth ◦ *I didn't feel up to going to work this morning.*

- to do a piece of work or sth that you have been told to do: **carry** sth **out**, (*formal*) **perform** sth ◦ *The policeman said he was only carrying out orders.* ◦ *to carry out repairs on a car* ◦ *The doctor performed the operation under very difficult circumstances.*
- to plan that an event will take place: **hold*** sth, **put*** sth **on** ◦ *We're holding a farewell party for the summer students.* ◦ *We're planning to put on a special concert to mark James's retirement.*

- to do what is necessary in order to solve a problem, complete a task, etc: **do*** sth **about** sth, **see* to** sth, **deal* with** sb/sth ◦ *You really must do something about your cough.* ◦ *Don't worry about the rest of the cleaning – I'll see to it.*
- to do sth urgently (in order to solve a problem, complete a task, etc): **act** ◦ *There's no time to lose – we need to act now.*

- to say or do sth because of sth that has happened or sth that sb has said: **respond** (**to** sth), **react** (**to** sth); *nouns* (C/U): **response, reaction** ◦ *to respond to criticism* ◦ *'How did she react to your suggestions?' 'She was very sympathetic.'* ◦ *What was his reaction to the news?*

- to start doing sth which you used to do before: **return to** sth/doing sth, **go*/come* back to** sth/doing sth; *noun*: **return** ◦ *When do you have to return to work?* ◦ *I don't want to go back to being unemployed!* ◦ *I'm looking forward to my return to work.*

■ not doing sth
- not to do sth that you were supposed to do: **fail to** do sth; *noun*: **failure** ◦ *He failed to turn up for his interview this morning.* ◦ *your failure to complete the work on time*
- doing nothing; not active: **inactive**; *noun* (U): **inactivity** ◦ *The machines lay inactive for weeks.* ◦ *a period of inactivity*

- to be present but do nothing in a situation: **stand* by, stand* about/around** ◦ *They just stood by and watched while we did all the work.*

2 different kinds of action

- a thing that you do: **action** (*noun* C/U), **act** ◦ *Of course everyone is responsible for their own actions.* ◦ *The noise finally became so bad that they decided to take action.* ◦ *That was a very kind act.*
- a situation in which there is a lot of action or movement: **activity** (*noun* U) ◦ *constant activity*
- something that you do, usually regularly and for enjoyment: **activity** ◦ *The school organizes lots of activities for the students.*
- the actual doing of sth rather than the ideas or theory: **practice** (*noun* U) ◦ *It may be all right in theory but it won't work in practice.*

Note: to describe an action you can use 'of' after **act** but not after **action** ◦ *an act* (not *action*) *of great kindness*

- the things that you have done; the knowledge or skill that you get from seeing or doing sth: **experience** (*noun* U); having a lot of experience of sth: **experienced** ◦ *to have experience in the hotel trade* ◦ *You need to get some experience.* ◦ *Do you think she's experienced enough for this job?*

3 doing sth with or for other people

- to do sth with other people: **take* part** (**in** sth), **join in** (sth), (*formal*) **participate** (**in** sth) ◦ *to take part in a game/play/competition* ◦ *The older children were playing outside but they wouldn't let any of the younger ones join in.*
- a person who takes part in sth: **participant** ◦ *Most of the participants in the course are experienced professionals.*

- taking part in sth: **involved** (**in** sth) ◦ *We still don't know how many people were involved in the robbery.* ◦ *I became involved in politics when I was at university.*
- to try to take part in sb's affairs when you and your help are not wanted: **interfere** (**in** sth); *noun* (U): **interference** ◦ *Don't interfere – it's none of your business.*
- to do sth for sb else: **act on** sb's **behalf** ◦ *We're acting on behalf of the local council.*

4 the order in which things are done

- a number of things that are done in a certain order for a particular purpose: **process** ◦ *a pro-*

action *contd.*

duction process ◦ the process of applying for a new passport
- the actions that you must take in order to do sth in the correct or usual way: **procedure** ◦ *I made a lot of mistakes because I don't know the correct procedure.*
- one action in a sequence of actions: **step** ◦ *The first step is to choose your topic. Next, discuss it with your tutor.*

- the time when you must or may do sth: **turn** ◦ *Whose turn is it?* ◦ *Now it was my turn to show what I was capable of.*
- one after the other: **in turn** ◦ *We went up in turn to collect our prizes.*
- to do sth one after the other: **take* turns** (**at** doing sth) ◦ *The children took turns at riding on the horse.*
- to wait until it is your turn to do sth: **wait your turn** ◦ *There was a long queue, so we just had to wait our turn.*

- something that is most important, that you must do before anything else: **priority** ◦ *This is number one on my list of priorities.*

5 the time when sth is done
- while doing sth: **in the middle of** sth/doing sth ◦ *Don't disturb me now – I'm in the middle of writing some letters.*

- with very little time to prepare sth: **at short notice** ◦ *I can't do this at such short notice; you should have told me about it weeks ago.*
- if you decide to do sth at the moment of doing it, you do it **on the spur of the moment** ◦ *I decided to go to London on the spur of the moment; I hadn't planned to go at all.*
- not planned: **spontaneous** (*adverb* **spontaneously**) ◦ *a spontaneous act of kindness*

- to decide not to do sth until a later time: **delay** sth/doing sth, **put*** sth **off**, **put* off** doing sth ◦ *She always puts things off until the last minute and then she has to hurry to get them finished.*
- to finally do sth after doing other things; to find the necessary time to do sth: **get* around to** doing sth ◦ *I didn't get around to phoning him today; I'll try and do it tomorrow.*

▷ more on delaying sth ⇨ **EARLY/LATE**

- going to do sth very soon: **just about to** do sth, **on the point of** doing sth ◦ *I was just about to leave when the phone rang.*

■ **MORE ...**
- an action that you take because you want to achieve a particular result: **move** ◦ *If you want to be friends again, you have to make the first move.*
- an action that is done for a special reason: **measure** ◦ *The government are taking emergency measures to deal with crime.*

- to use a lot of care and effort in doing sth: **take* the trouble to** do sth ◦ *It was very kind of you to take the trouble to come all that way just for the party.*
- to make a very special effort to do sth: **go* out of** your **way** (**to** do sth) ◦ *He went out of his way to be kind to us.*
- to recognize and use a suitable time to do sth: **take* the opportunity to** do sth/**of** doing sth ◦ *I'd like to take this opportunity to thank you all for coming here tonight.*

actor/actress ⇨ ACT[2]

add
- more of sth ⇨ **MORE[2]**
- numbers ⇨ **NUMBER**

admire ⇨ LIKE[2]

advertisement

1 different kinds of advertisement
2 the work of advertising
see also SELL, INFORMATION

1 different kinds of advertisement
- a piece of information in a newspaper, on television, etc intended to persuade people to buy sth or do sth: **advertisement**, (*BrE informal*) **advert**, (*informal*) **ad**

■ on television or radio
- an advertisement on television or radio is also called a **commercial**
- a time when advertisements are shown on TV: (**commercial**) **break** ◦ *I'll make a cup of coffee during the break.*

■ in newspapers
- small advertisements in a newspaper where people offer to buy or sell things, to employ sb, etc: **classified ads** (*noun plural*), **small ads** (*noun plural*) ◦ *If you want to find a flat you should look in the small ads.*
- the place in newspapers where you can find personal messages: **personal column**

■ other printed advertisements
- a large printed advertisement in a public place, for example on a wall: **poster**
- a large board in the street where advertisements are put: **hoarding** (*AmE* **billboard**)

- a book with a list of things (usually with pictures) that you can buy from a company: **catalogue** (*AmE* **catalog**)
- a small printed piece of paper that advertises or gives information about sth: **leaflet** ◦ *People in the street were handing out leaflets advertising the new shop.*
- a small book with pictures that gives you information about sth: **brochure** ◦ *a tourist brochure* ◦ *our firm's new brochure*

2 the work of advertising
- to put an advertisement in a newspaper, on TV, etc: **advertise** (sth), **place/put* an advertisement in/on** sth; a person who does this: **advertiser** ◦ *I'm going to advertise in our local paper for a cleaner.*

- to use advertising and/or other means to attract people's attention to sth or to give information about sth: **publicize** sth ○ *Friends of the Earth groups have been publicizing the threat to the rain forest*.
- if sb/sth is given a lot of attention by newspapers, television, etc, they get a lot of **publicity** (*noun* U) ○ *The council's plan to ban cars from the town centre has received a lot of publicity in the media.*
- a plan to do a number of things to advertise sth: (**advertising**) **campaign**, **publicity campaign** ○ *Our local school has launched* (= started) *a campaign to make children 'think green'.*

- a company that specializes in advertising: **advertising agency**
- the job of making a company, organization, etc popular with people: **public relations** (*abbreviation* **PR**) (*noun* U, *with singular or plural verb*) ○ *When I'm in Singapore, I'll be doing some PR for my company.*

■ **MORE ...**
- a short phrase that is easy to remember and that is used to advertise sth: **slogan**
- a symbol or design that is used as an advertisement by a company: **logo** ○ *We need a new logo to put on our publicity material.*

- to help to pay for a sports event, concert, etc in order to advertise sth: **sponsor** sth; *noun* (U): **sponsorship** ○ *The football league used to be sponsored by Barclays Bank.* ○ *We're looking for sponsorship for the concert we're planning.*
- a person or organization that does this: **sponsor** ○ *The Edinburgh Festival is supported by several big sponsors.*

advise/suggest

1 suggesting
2 recommending
3 advising sb to do sth
4 advising sb not to do sth
5 making use of advice

1 suggesting
- to tell sb a plan or idea to find out if they agree with it: **suggest** sth, (*formal*) **propose** sth ○ *Krishna suggested a Chinese take-away.* ○ *I suggest we go out for a meal.* ○ *Steve suggested cooking a meal at home.* ○ *It was later proposed that the scheme should be dropped.*
- something that is suggested: **suggestion**, **idea**, (*formal*) **proposal** ○ *Does anyone have any suggestions?* ○ *Do you mind if I make a suggestion?* ○ *I bought this one at Alice's suggestion* (= because Alice suggested it). ○ *I've got an idea – why don't we all go?* ○ *A number of different proposals have been put forward.*

- to have an idea or make a suggestion: **think* of** sth, **come* up with** sth ○ *Can anyone think of a better idea?* ○ *They came up with some really good suggestions.*

- to suggest that sb would be a suitable person for a job, award, etc: **suggest** sb (**for/as** sth), **propose** sb (**for/as** sth), **put*** sb **forward** (**for** sth) ○ *Can you suggest anyone for the job?* ○ *Who do you propose as the new leader?* ○ *Several names have already been put forward.*

- if you think a suggestion is a good idea, you can call it **helpful**, **constructive**, **positive** ○ *a helpful suggestion* ○ *a number of positive/constructive proposals*

■ ways of making suggestions
- to make a suggestion, you can say **How about ...?**; or **What about ...?**; or **Shall I/we ...?** ○ *How about going to the theatre?* ○ *What about a quiet evening at home for a change?* ○ *Shall we have a drink before our meal?*
- a stronger suggestion can be made with **Why don't I/we/you ...?** or **Why not ...?** ○ *Why don't we go and see the new film at the Odeon?* ○ *Why not get a second-hand one and save money?*
- an even stronger suggestion can be made with **Let's ...** or **I know what: let's ...** ○ *Let's ask Kevin if he'd like to come too.* ○ *I know what: let's have a democratic vote on this!*

2 recommending
- to strongly suggest sth; to say that sth would be good idea: **recommend** sth, **recommend** sb **to** do **sth**; *noun* (C/U): **recommendation** ○ *I wouldn't recommend that restaurant.* ○ *The architect recommended demolishing the entire building.*
- to strongly suggest that sb would be a suitable person for a job, award, etc: **recommend** sb (**for/as** sth) ○ *Who would you recommend?*

3 advising sb to do sth
- to tell sb what you think they should do: **advise** sb (**to** do sth); *noun* (U): **advice** ○ *I would strongly advise you to take the job.* ○ *She gave us a lot of useful advice.* ○ *If you want my advice, I'd stay at home.* ○ *Let me give you a piece of advice.*
- to strongly advise sb to do sth by talking and reasoning with them: **try to persuade** sb (**to** do sth); *noun* (U): **persuasion** ○ *I tried to persuade her to go, but she wouldn't listen.* ○ *It took a lot of persuasion, but he finally agreed to come.*

▷ more on persuading sb ⇨ PERSUADE

- help or advice: **guidance** (*noun* U) ○ *We were offered expert guidance.*
- something which you would advise sb to do is **advisable**, **suggested**, **recommended** ○ *It's advisable to book a seat in advance.* ○ *the recommended daily amount of vitamin C*
- a small piece of useful advice: **tip** ○ *a useful tip for removing wine stains*

■ ways of giving advice
- to give sb advice, you can say **you'd better ...** or **you should ...** or **you ought to ...** ○ *You'd better leave it till you're feeling a bit stronger.* ○ *You should really try to cut down on fatty foods.*
- to make your advice sound more personal, you can begin with **I think** or you can say (**If I were you,**) **I'd ...** or **I would ...** (**if I were you**) ○ *I honestly think you ought to say no.* ○ *If I were you, I'd sell it and buy a better one.* ○ *I'd certainly think twice before agreeing.*

advise / suggest *contd.*

4 advising sb not to do sth

- to tell sb that you think they should not do sth: **advise** sb **not to** do sth, **advise** sb **against** sth, **warn** sb **not to** do sth, **discourage** sb (**from** sth); *noun*: **warning** ◦ *We were advised not to go there at night.* ◦ *They advised us against buying a house for the moment.* ◦ *I warned you not to trust him.* ◦ *He ignored all our warnings.*
- to strongly advise sb not to do sth: **try to dissuade** sb (**from** sth/doing sth) ◦ *I tried to dissuade her from going.*
- something which you would advise sb not to do is **inadvisable** ◦ *It's inadvisable to go swimming when you have a cold.*

▷ more on warning ⇨ WARN

■ ways of advising sb not to do sth

- to advise sb not to do sth, you can say **You'd better not ...** or **You shouldn't ...** or **You ought not to ...** ◦ *You'd better not be caught wearing your brother's new jeans!* ◦ *You really shouldn't take these things so seriously.* ◦ *You ought not to listen to such nonsense.*
- to make your advice sound more personal, you can say **I don't think ...** or (**If I were you,**) **I wouldn't ...** or **I wouldn't ...** (**if I were you**) ◦ *If you want my advice about that job, I don't think you should take it.* ◦ *I don't really think you ought to take the money. After all, it's not hers to give.* ◦ *If I were you, I wouldn't give it another thought.* ◦ *I wouldn't go near it, if I were you!*

4 making use of advice

- to ask sb if they would like your advice: **offer** sb (your/some) **advice** ◦ *Can I offer you some advice?*
- to ask sb for their advice on sth: **seek*** sb's **advice, turn to** sb (**for advice**) ◦ *I don't know who to turn to for advice.*
- to take notice of sb's advice: **listen to** sb's **advice** ◦ *I don't know why I bother – he never listens to my advice.*
- to do what sb has advised you to do: **take*** sb's **advice**, **follow** sb's **advice** ◦ *If you take my advice, you'll go and see a doctor.* ◦ *If she'd followed my advice, she wouldn't be in this mess.*
- if you do not take sb's advice, you **ignore** sb's **advice** ◦ *Why did you ignore the doctor's advice?*

■ professional advice

- to go to sb for professional advice: **consult** sb; a meeting where you ask for professional advice: **consultation** ◦ *You'd better consult a doctor.* ◦ *a consultation with a lawyer*
- the advice of a lawyer: **legal advice** (*noun* U) ◦ *We've decided to get legal advice on the matter.*
- a person who gives professional advice: **adviser** (*AmE* **advisor**) ◦ *a government adviser*
- a person who gives professional advice on business, etc: **consultant** ◦ *a management consultant*

- to give professional advice to sb on personal problems: **counsel** sb; *noun* (U): **counselling** ◦ *Several people are likely to need counselling as a result of the disaster.*
- a person who gives professional advice on personal problems: **counsellor** (*AmE* **counselor**) ◦ *a marriage counsellor*

- a person who receives professional advice: **client**

■ **MORE ...**

- a column in a newspaper which gives advice to people who write in with personal problems: **problem page**, **agony column** (*especially AmE* **advice column**)
- a woman who writes the replies to letters sent in to an agony column: **agony aunt** (*AmE* **advice columnist**)

aeroplane ⇨ PLANE

afraid

1 afraid
2 very frightened
3 not afraid
see also WORRY

1 afraid

- the feeling that you have that sth dangerous, painful, etc might happen: **fear** (*noun* C/U) ◦ *a fear of spiders* ◦ *We felt that their fears were not justified.* ◦ *She knew the operation was dangerous but she showed no fear.* ◦ *I was shaking with fear.*
- if you feel fear when you see sb/sth or experience sth, you are **afraid** (*not before a noun*), **frightened**, **scared** ◦ *Don't be afraid!* ◦ *You're not afraid of her, are you?* ◦ *My sister is afraid to ask questions in class.* ◦ *a frightened animal* ◦ *I wasn't frightened of being hurt.* ◦ *When I was a child I was scared of the dark.*
- to feel fear, particularly of sth important: (*rather formal*) **fear** sth ◦ *Most people fear death.*

Note: afraid, frightened and **scared** can be followed by a noun (*afraid of injections*) or by the '-ing' form of the verb (*afraid of flying*) or by the 'to' form of the verb (*afraid to cross the road*).

- a sudden feeling of being afraid: **fright**, **scare** ◦ *I got a nasty fright when that dog came running after me.*

- to make a person or animal frightened: **frighten** sb/sth, **scare** sb/sth ◦ *He really scared me when he started screaming and shouting.*
- a person or thing that frightens you is **frightening**, (*informal*) **scary** ◦ *a frightening experience* ◦ *When I was walking home today I thought I was being followed. It was really scary.*

■ often afraid

- afraid to talk to people that you do not know: **shy** (*adverb* **shyly**); *noun* (U): **shyness** ◦ *Don't be shy! Just go straight up and ask her.* ◦ *She smiled shyly at the cameramen.*
- easily frightened: **timid** (*adverb* **timidly**)

- a person who has no courage and is afraid in dangerous or unpleasant situations: **coward**; *adjective*: **cowardly**

■ showing that you are afraid

- to make a sudden movement because of surprise or fear: **jump** ◦ *The sudden bang made us all jump.*
- to shout sth suddenly, because of being afraid, surprised, etc: **cry out** ◦ *to cry out in fear*

- to make short quick movements which you cannot control, because of being afraid, cold, etc: **shake***, **shiver**, **tremble**; a shaking movement: **shiver** ◦ *She was shivering with fright.* ◦ *His hands were trembling.* ◦ *He gave a shiver of fear.*
- when the hairs of your skin stand up and cause raised spots because you are afraid or cold, you have **goose-flesh**, **goose-pimples** (*AmE* **goose-bumps**)
- to stop suddenly because of fear: **freeze*** ◦ *She froze with terror when she heard the shot.*

2 very frightened

- very frightened: **terrified**, **frightened/scared to death**, (*informal*) **scared stiff** ◦ *I'm terrified of snakes.* ◦ *a terrified child* ◦ *She was scared stiff of going into the cellar.*
- to have a great fear about sth that will happen in the future: **dread** sth; *noun* (U): **dread** ◦ *He dreaded telling his father the truth.* ◦ *to live in dread of sth*

- great fear: **terror** (*noun* U) ◦ *He had a look of terror on his face.*
- a feeling of great fear or shock: **horror** (*noun* U) ◦ *People watched in horror as the car mounted the pavement.* ◦ *a horror film/story* (= one that entertains people by describing frightening things)
- a sudden feeling of fear that makes you do things without thinking carefully about them: **panic** (*noun* C/U); to experience panic: **panic***; *adjectives*: **panic-stricken**, (*informal*) **panicky** ◦ *The noise from the gun made one of the horses panic.* ◦ *I started feeling a bit panicky just before the performance was due to begin.*

- to make sb very frightened: **terrify** sb, **frighten the life out of** sb ◦ *Injections terrify me!* ◦ *You frightened the life out of me when you screamed.*
- very frightening: **terrifying** ◦ *a terrifying scream* ◦ *He told us a terrifying story.*
- a situation that frightens you very much **makes*** your **hair stand on end**, **makes*** your **blood run cold** ◦ *It made my hair stand on end when they started talking about ghosts.* ◦ *Hearing them say my name made my blood run cold.*

3 not afraid

- not afraid: **unafraid**, **fearless** (*adverb* **fearlessly**)
- showing no fear: **brave** (*adverb* **bravely**), **courageous** (*adverb* **courageously**); *nouns* (U): **bravery**, **courage**

▷ more on being brave ⇨ **BRAVE**

- to make sb feel less worried, nervous or frightened: **reassure** sb; the help that you give when you do this: **reassurance** (*noun* U); a thing or person that gives reassurance is **reassuring** (*adverb* **reassuringly**) ◦ *She gave him a reassuring smile.*

■ **MORE ...**

- a feeling of being afraid or nervous in front of an audience: **stage fright** (*noun* U) ◦ *to suffer from stage fright*
- a nervous feeling in your stomach before you do sth: (*informal*) **butterflies** (**in** your **stomach**) ◦ *All actors get butterflies from time to time.*

after ⇨ BEFORE/AFTER

again

beginning again ⇨ **BEGIN**

- another time: **again** ◦ *Sorry, can you say that again please?* ◦ *Let's start again.*
- a second time from the beginning: (**all**) **over again** ◦ *I did it wrong so I've got to do it all over again.*
- one more time: **once more** ◦ *Just once more, then I promise I won't ask you to do it again.*

- to say or do sth again: **repeat** sth ◦ *Can you repeat that please? – I couldn't quite hear what you said.*
- something that you do or that happens again: **repetition** (*noun* C/U) ◦ *yet another repetition of the same song* ◦ *There must be no repetition of last night's behaviour.*
- done or happening many times: **repeated** (*only before a noun*) ◦ *a repeated knocking on the wall*
- not interesting because the same thing is repeated many times: **repetitive** ◦ *It's quite a nice song but very repetitive.*

- many times: **over and over** (**again**), **again and again**, **repeatedly** ◦ *I've said it over and over again but he never listens.*
- many times (in an annoying way): **always** ◦ *She's always talking about her computer.*
- to emphasize that sb/sth is always doing sth, you can say they **never stop** (doing) it ◦ *Why does that dog never stop barking?*

- to cause sth that existed before to be introduced again: **bring*** sth **back** ◦ *They're bringing back all the songs from the seventies.*
- to make sth popular again: **revive** sth; *noun*: **revival** ◦ *The nineties have seen a revival of fashions from the seventies.*
- to begin again or continue after a pause or interruption: (*formal*) **resume**; *noun*: **resumption** ◦ *a resumption of fighting*

Note: some verbs can express the meaning that sth is done again by adding the prefix **re-** ◦ *I'm going to retake my exam* (= I'm going to take it again). ◦ *We haven't got as much money as we thought so we're going to have to rethink our holiday plans* (= we're going to have to plan our holidays again). ◦ *It's too long – I'll rewrite it* (= I'll write it again). ◦ *I'm afraid you'll have to redo this piece of work, it just isn't good enough* (= you'll have to do the work again).

■ **MORE ...**

- if you have to repeat a task from the beginning, you are (*informal*) **back to square one** ◦ *Oh*

again *contd.*

dear, I thought we'd finished but we seem to be back to square one.

– to do sth again from the beginning: **make* a fresh start** ◦ *You've made a bit of a mess of this – you'd better make a fresh start.*

– a repetition of a song or piece of music at the end of a performance: **encore** ◦ *to give an encore* ◦ *She played something by Beethoven as an encore.*
– something which people shout at the end of a show, when they want to hear or see an encore: **encore!**

age ⇨ YOUNG/OLD

agree

– reaching agreement ⇨ AGREEMENT
– in a discussion ⇨ DISCUSS/ARGUE
– agreeing to a plan ⇨ INTEND/PLAN
– having the same opinion ⇨ OPINION

agreement

agreeing on a plan ⇨ INTEND/PLAN
agreeing with sb in a discussion ⇨ DISCUSS/ARGUE
having the same opinion ⇨ OPINION

– to arrange with sb that you or they will do sth: **agree** (**with** sb) (**on/about** sth), **agree to** do sth; *noun* (U): **agreement** ◦ *We've agreed on a plan.* ◦ *They agreed to meet again.*
– a decision that two or more people have made together: **agreement** ◦ *I thought the agreement was to meet at 2.30.* ◦ *It took several hours to work out an agreement which was acceptable to both sides.* ◦ *to come to an amicable* (= friendly) *agreement*
– agreed by everyone: **unanimous** (*adverb* **unanimously**) ◦ *The members of the jury were unanimous.* ◦ *It was a unanimous decision.*

– to fail to reach agreement: **disagree**; *noun* (U): **disagreement** ◦ *The talks ended in disagreement.*
– to end an argument or disagreement: **come* to an agreement**, **reach** (**an**) **agreement**, **settle** sth ◦ *Have management and unions reached an agreement yet?* ◦ *They finally managed to settle the dispute.*
– the end to a disagreement: **settlement** ◦ *The strike lasted several weeks before a settlement was reached.* ◦ *a permanent settlement of the dispute*

■ working to reach an agreement
– to discuss sth in order to try to reach an agreement: **negotiate** (sth); *noun* (C/U): **negotiation** ◦ *The Government is still negotiating with the unions.* ◦ *to negotiate an agreement* ◦ *a negotiated settlement* ◦ *a matter for negotiation* ◦ *pay negotiations*
– a person who negotiates: **negotiator**
– something which can be negotiated is **negotiable** ◦ *The price is negotiable.*
– to talk to two groups of people to try to settle an argument: **mediate**; *noun* (U): **mediation** ◦ *They rejected all our offers of mediation.*
– a person who mediates in an argument: **mediator**

– to suggest sth as a possible plan or idea in a negotiation: **propose** sth; *noun*: **proposal**
– to agree to a proposal: **accept** sth; *noun* (U): **acceptance**
– to refuse to agree to a proposal: **reject** sth; *noun* (U): **rejection**

– an agreement between two people or groups about what each of them will do for the other or others: **bargain** ◦ *'If you babysit for me tonight, I'll do the same for you on Saturday.' 'OK, it's a bargain.'*
– an agreement in which both sides have to give up sth they originally wanted in order to reach agreement: **compromise** (*noun* C/U); *verb*: **compromise** ◦ *a compromise agreement* ◦ *They refused to compromise.*

– something which you agree to give up in order to reach a compromise: **concession** ◦ *to make a concession*
– to reach an agreement unwillingly and without getting what you originally wanted: **climb down**; *noun*: **climbdown** ◦ *The union was forced to climb down and withdraw its original demands.* ◦ *a humiliating climbdown*

■ formal agreements
– a business agreement: **deal** ◦ *We've negotiated a valuable deal.* ◦ *It's a deal!*
– a written agreement, for example in business: **contract** ◦ *to sign a contract*
– a written agreement between two or more countries, for example after a war: **treaty** ◦ *a peace treaty*
– the conditions of an agreement: **terms** (*noun plural*) ◦ *according to the terms of the contract*

– to do what you have agreed to do: **keep*** (**to**) sth; *opposite*: **break*** sth ◦ *I've kept my side of the bargain.* ◦ *to keep to an agreement* ◦ *to break a contract/agreement*
– to make sb do what they have agreed to do: **hold* sb to sth**, **keep* sb to sth** ◦ *She kept him to his word.*

■ **MORE ...**
– to shake hands in order to confirm an agreement: **shake* on** sth ◦ *Let's shake on it.*

aim ⇨ INTEND/PLAN

air

1 the outside air
2 the air inside rooms, buildings, etc
3 putting or keeping air inside sth

see also WEATHER, BREATHE

1 the outside air

- the mixture of gases that surrounds the earth and that people, animals and plants breathe: **air** (*noun* U) ◦ *She threw the ball high up in the air.* ◦ *Can you open the window? There's not enough air in here.* ◦ *pure* (= clean) *mountain air*
- the mixture of gases that surrounds the earth or any other planet: **atmosphere** (*usually singular*); *adjective*: **atmospheric** ◦ *atmospheric pollution*
- the main gases which make up the air are **oxygen** (*noun* U), **carbon dioxide** (*noun* U), **nitrogen** (*noun* U)

- clean cool air, outside or from outside: **fresh air** ◦ *Let's go out for a walk – I feel like a breath of fresh air.*
- outside in the fresh air: **in the open air**; *adjective*: **open-air** ◦ *to go swimming in the open air* ◦ *an open-air swimming pool*
- the movement of air across the earth: **wind** (*noun* C/U) ◦ *a fresh wind* ◦ *The curtains were blowing in the wind.* ◦ *a gust of wind*
- with a lot of wind: **windy** ◦ *a windy day* ◦ *a windy place*

▷ more on wind ⇨ WIND

- when there is a lot of water in the air, it is **humid, damp**; *nouns* (U): **humidity, dampness, damp** ◦ *a hot and humid climate* ◦ *The air was cold and damp.* ◦ *a high level of humidity*
- when the air is dirty, it is **polluted**; *noun* (U): **pollution** ◦ *The air in Los Angeles is badly polluted.* ◦ *an increase in industrial pollution*
- a mixture of fog and smoke in the air of polluted industrial cities: **smog** (*noun* U)

2 the air inside buildings, etc

- when a room has plenty of fresh air, it is **airy** ◦ *a beautiful airy bedroom*
- when a room does not have enough fresh air, it is **airless, stuffy**; *noun* (U): **stuffiness** ◦ *They live in a horrible airless little flat.* ◦ *It's very stuffy in here.*
- a current of air that comes into a room and makes it unpleasantly cold: **draught** (*AmE* **draft**); a place with a lot of draughts is **draughty** (*AmE* **drafty**) ◦ *Could you shut the door, please? There's a cold draught in here.* ◦ *a draughty corridor*
- the air inside a room, etc: **atmosphere** ◦ *I hate the smoky atmosphere in pubs.*

■ keeping the air cool

- to let air into a room to make it fresh: **air** sth ◦ *We opened the windows to air the bedrooms.*
- to allow air to move freely in or out of a room or building: **ventilate** sth; *noun* (U) **ventilation** ◦ *a poorly ventilated building* ◦ *It's a very small room and the ventilation is rather bad.*
- an electrical machine with blades which turn around and keep the air moving in a room: **fan**
- a system that keeps the air in a building or car cool and clean: **air-conditioning** (*noun* U)

3 putting or keeping air inside sth

- to fill sth with air: **blow*** sth **up**, (*formal*) **inflate** sth ◦ *to blow up a balloon*
- a piece of equipment for filling sth with air: **pump**; to use a pump: **pump** air **into** sth, **pump** sth **up** ◦ *to pump up a bicycle tyre*
- something which can be filled with air is **inflatable** ◦ *a small inflatable boat*
- a small device which controls the movement of air into sth: **valve**
- the force of the air which is inside sth: **pressure** (*noun* U) ◦ *Don't forget to check the pressure in your tyres regularly.*

- to close sth so that air cannot get into it: **seal** sth ◦ *a tightly sealed jar*
- when sth is sealed, it is **airtight** ◦ *After you've opened the packet, you should keep the coffee in an airtight container.*

■ **MORE...**

- a space where there is no air: **vacuum**
- something which is operated using air pressure is **pneumatic** ◦ *a pneumatic drill*

---

aircraft ⇨ PLANE

---

air force

see also ARMY, NAVY, PLANE, WAR

- the part of a country's armed forces that uses aeroplanes for fighting: **air force** ◦ *a small but well equipped air force* ◦ *the Royal Air Force* (= the British air force) ◦ *a US air force jet*
- a member of an air force: (*BrE*) **airman** (*plural* **airmen**)

- an aeroplane for use in war: **warplane**
- a warplane that attacks other warplanes: **fighter**
- a warplane that drops bombs: **bomber**
- a powerful exploding weapon that can travel long distances through the air: **missile**
- a group of warplanes: **squadron**

▷ bombs ⇨ BOMB

- an airport for military aeroplanes: **airbase**
- an attack by warplanes: **air raid, air strike**
- a special journey in a warplane: **mission** ◦ *He flew several bombing missions.*

- a person who gives orders to others in the navy, army, air force, etc: **officer**
- the people who operate an aeroplane: **crew** (*with singular or plural verb*)
- the person who controls an aeroplane: **pilot** ◦ *a fighter pilot*

---

alcohol

1 places where people go to buy and drink alcohol
2 drinks made with alcohol
3 drinking alcohol
4 not drinking alcohol
5 making alcohol

alcohol *contd.*

1 places where people go to buy and drink alcohol

– a place in a hotel, restaurant, club, etc where you can buy and drink alcoholic drinks: **bar** ◦ *I'll meet you downstairs in the bar.* ◦ *a theatre bar*
– a building where people go to meet their friends and drink: **pub** (*AmE* **bar**), (*formal*) **public house** ◦ *We're going down to the pub for a drink.*
– a shop where you can buy alcohol: **off-licence** (*AmE* **package store**)

▷ more on bars and pubs ⇨ BAR / PUB

2 drinks made with alcohol

– drinks made with alcohol: (**alcoholic**) **drink** (*AmE* **liquor**) (*noun* U), (*informal*) **booze** (*noun* U) ◦ *We must get some drink for the party.*
– strong alcoholic drinks: **spirits** (*noun plural*) (*AmE* **hard liquor**, *noun* U) ◦ *I never drink spirits, only beer and wine.*

– a drink made from grain: **beer**; a type of light beer: **lager**
– a drink made from grapes: **wine**
– a drink made from apples: **cider**

▷ more on beer and wine ⇨ BEER, WINE

– a strong brown drink made from grain: **whisky** (*AmE* **whiskey**); whisky which comes from Scotland: **Scotch**; a type of whiskey made in the USA: **bourbon**
– a strong dark brown drink made from wine: **brandy**
– a strong colourless drink often drunk with tonic water: **gin**
– a strong colourless drink typically from Russia: **vodka**

Note: beer, **wine**, etc can be used as uncountable nouns: ◦ *Do you like Australian wine?* ◦ *My favourite drink is Scotch on the rocks* (= Scotch whisky with ice). ◦ *There's some beer in the fridge.* If used as countable nouns, the meaning is 'a type of' or 'a glass of': ◦ *This is an excellent brandy* (= a good type of brandy). ◦ *Would you like a beer* (= a glass of beer)*?*

– a drink that people have before a meal: **aperitif** ◦ *Shall we have an aperitif?*
– a strong sweet drink that is usually drunk in small quantities after a meal: **liqueur**
– a drink containing a mixture of alcoholic drinks, fruit juices, etc: **cocktail**
– a mixture of different drinks made in a large container at a party: **punch**

3 drinking alcohol

– to drink alcohol: **drink***, **have a drink** ◦ *He drinks too much.* ◦ *She was sitting in the bar having a drink.*
– to express good wishes before having an alcoholic drink, people sometimes say **cheers** ◦ *They raised their glasses to each other and said 'cheers'.*
– (used about a drink) containing twice as much as the usual amount: **double**, **large** ◦ *a double brandy* ◦ *a large whisky and soda*
– (used about a strong alcoholic drink) served with nothing added: **neat** ◦ *neat vodka* ◦ *No water, thanks. I'll drink it neat.*

■ people who drink a lot of alcohol
– a person who drinks a lot of alcohol is a (**heavy**) **drinker**
– a person who often drinks too much is a **drunkard**
– a person who needs alcohol every day is an **alcoholic**; the medical condition is **alcoholism** (*noun* U) ◦ *the social costs of alcoholism*

■ when people drink too much
– if sb drinks too much, they **get* drunk** ◦ *Peter got really drunk last night.*
– a person who has drunk too much is **drunk**, (*informal*) **pissed**, (*formal*) **intoxicated** ◦ *It was a good party – no one got really drunk.*
– very drunk: **blind drunk**, (*informal*) **plastered** ◦ *'Was he drunk?' 'Absolutely plastered.'*

– a person starts feeling the effects of alcohol when it **goes* to** their **head** ◦ *She only had one drink but it went straight to her head.*
– having drunk too much alcohol, or showing the effects of too much alcohol: **drunken** (*only before a noun*); *noun* (U): **drunkenness** ◦ *I was shouted at by some drunken youths.* ◦ *drunken singing*

– not drunk: **sober** ◦ *I stayed sober last night because I had to drive home.*
– to start to feel normal again after being drunk: **sober up** ◦ *He drank some coffee to try and sober up.*
– the headache that a person may have after drinking too much: **hangover** ◦ *I couldn't do any work this morning; I had a terrible hangover.*

▷ drinking and driving ⇨ DRIVE

4 not drinking alcohol

– containing no alcohol: **non-alcoholic**; a drink which is non-alcoholic: **soft drink** ◦ *I'd better have something non-alcoholic – I'm driving.*
– (used about beer or wine) containing no alcohol or very little alcohol: **alcohol-free**, **low-alcohol** ◦ *alcohol-free wine*

– to drink less alcohol than you normally do: **cut* down** (**on** sth) ◦ *I won't have a drink thanks – I'm cutting down.*
– to not drink alcohol: **keep* off** sth ◦ *The doctor told me to keep off alcohol.*
– a person who never drinks alcohol: **teetotaller** (*AmE* **teetotaler**); *adjective*: **teetotal** ◦ *She never drinks – she's teetotal.*

5 making alcohol

– to change chemically: **ferment**; *noun* (U): **fermentation** ◦ *As a result of fermentation, the sugar changes to alcohol.*

– the main process used in making whisky, gin, etc: **distilling** (*noun* U); *verb*: **distil** sth

– a place where whisky, gin, etc are made: **distillery**

▷ making beer and wine ⇨ BEER, WINE

alike ⇨ SAME

alive ⇨ LIVE[1]

all ⇨ HOW MUCH/MANY

allow

1 allowing sb to do sth
2 not allowing sb to do sth
3 asking for permission
making sth possible ⇨ POSSIBLE[2]
see also REQUEST

1 allowing sb to do sth

– to tell sb that they can do sth: **let*** sb (do sth) (*cannot be used in the passive*), **allow** (sb **to** do) sth, **give*** sb **permission** (**to** do sth), (*formal*) **permit** (sb **to** do) sth; *noun* (U): **permission** ◦ *I want to go to France, but my parents won't let me.* ◦ *Did they allow you to visit?* ◦ *I'm sure she'll give you permission if you ask.* ◦ *You'll need your parents' permission.*
– to allow sth to happen: **agree** (**to** sth), **consent** (**to** sth); *nouns* (U): **agreement, consent** ◦ *Her parents won't agree to the marriage.* ◦ *to give your consent to sth*
– to accept sth and allow it to happen: **approve** sth; *noun* (U): **approval** ◦ *The plans still have to be approved.* ◦ *It will be essential to get the approval of the management.*

– if sb has given permission for sth, it is **allowed**, (*formal*) **permitted** ◦ *The school is very strict about dress: jeans and T-shirts are not allowed.* ◦ *Is photography permitted inside the church?*
– if you have been given permission to do sth, you are **allowed to do** sth, **free to do** sth ◦ *Are we allowed to smoke?* ◦ *You're free to come and go whenever you like.*
– if sth is allowed by the law, it is **legal**

– to allow sb to go into a place: **let*** sb **in**, **let*** sb **into** a place, (*formal*) **admit** sb (**to** a place); *nouns* (U): (*formal*) **admission, admittance** ◦ *Can't you persuade him to let us in?* ◦ *People under 18 are not admitted.* ◦ *a £3 admission fee* ◦ *No admittance!*
– to allow sb to go through/past a place: **let*** sb **through/past** (a place) ◦ *Let them through – it's an emergency!*
– to allow sb to leave a place: **let*** sb **out** ◦ *Let me out of here!*

■ official permission
– an official paper which shows that you are allowed to do sth: **permit, licence** (*AmE* **license**) ◦ *a work permit* ◦ *a driving licence*
– a piece of paper showing that you have the right to do sth: **authorization** (**to** do sth) (*noun* U) ◦ *Can I see your official authorization?*

2 not allowing sb to do sth

– to tell sb they cannot do sth: **forbid*** (sb **to** do) sth, **ban** (sb **from** doing) sth, (*formal*) **prohibit** (sb **from** doing) sth; an act of forbidding sth: (*formal*) **prohibition** (*noun* U) ◦ *The law forbids the sale of alcohol to anyone under 18.* ◦ *My father has banned me from going to any more parties.* ◦ *the prohibition of drugs*
– a law or rule that forbids sth: **ban, prohibition** ◦ *a ban on alcohol*
– to say no to sb who asks permission to do sth: **refuse** sb **permission** (**to** do sth), **refuse** sth ◦ *The plane was refused permission to land.* ◦ *Our request to leave was refused.*
– (especially in sports) not to allow or accept sth: **disallow** sth ◦ *The referee disallowed the goal.*

– if sth is not allowed, it is **forbidden, banned**, (*formal*) **prohibited** ◦ *Playing music after midnight is absolutely forbidden.* ◦ *Smoking is strictly prohibited.*
– if sth is not allowed by law, it is **illegal**
– if you want to say in a polite or weak way that sb is not allowed to do sth, you can say that they are **not supposed/meant to** do sth ◦ *You're not really supposed to smoke in here.*
– a place where you are not allowed to go is **out of bounds**

3 asking for permission

– to ask sb if they will let you do sth: **ask if** you **can** do sth, **ask** sb's **permission** (**to** do sth) ◦ *You'll have to ask their permission to camp in the field.*

– the word for making a request more polite: **please**

– to ask for permission to do sth, you can say **Can I . . .?** or **Could I** (**possibly**) **. . .?** or **May I . . .?** or **Is it all right if . . .?** ◦ *'Please could I take an extra day's leave this month?' 'No, I'm afraid you can't.'* ◦ *'Is it all right if I use the company car?' 'Yes, of course, go ahead.'*
– to ask for permission in a very polite way, you can say **Do you mind if . . .?** or **Would you mind if . . .?** ◦ *'Would you mind if my sister comes too?' 'Not at all. We'd love to meet her.'*

▷ more on saying yes or no to a request ⇨ YES/NO

almost

see also FAIRLY/VERY

– not far from doing sth or being sth: **almost, nearly** ◦ *I'll be with you in a minute – I've almost finished.* ◦ *She's been very ill – you know she nearly died.* ◦ *an almost perfect day*

Note: almost can be used with negative words like 'never', 'no one', 'nothing'; **nearly** cannot: ◦ *We almost never go to the cinema these days.*

– very near to being sth; almost completely: **practically, virtually, just about, as good as, to all intents and purposes** ◦ *These maths problems are practically/virtually impossible.* ◦ *She's got strong views on just about everything.* ◦ *It's not broken, but it's as good as useless in that condition.* ◦ *I haven't been promoted yet, but I'm already a manager to all intents and purposes.*

almost *contd.*

- nearly, but not completely (emphasizing a negative meaning): **not quite** ◦ *'Can I see your report?' 'Well, it's not quite finished, actually.'*

- almost not (emphasizing a negative meaning): **hardly**, **scarcely**, **barely** ◦ *There was hardly anybody there.* ◦ *You've hardly eaten anything.* ◦ *There was scarcely enough food for everyone* (= there almost wasn't enough food).
- almost not (emphasizing a positive meaning): **only just** ◦ *I only just caught the train* (= I nearly missed it).

- almost correct but not completely accurate: **rough** (*adverb* **roughly**), **approximate** (*adverb* **approximately**) ◦ *I don't know the exact increase; I think it's roughly three per cent.* ◦ *Could you give us an approximate figure for next year's sales, please?*

▷ absolutely or approximately correct ⇨ EXACT/APPROXIMATE

alone

see also TOGETHER

- without another person: **alone** ◦ *I don't like walking home alone after dark.*
  without another person or thing: (**all**) **on** your **own**, (**all**) **by** yourself, ◦ *'Did anyone help you?' 'No, I did it all by myself.'* ◦ *The house stands on its own outside the village.*
- the state of being alone: **solitude** (*noun* U); *adjective*: **solitary** ◦ *a life of solitude* ◦ *a solitary childhood*

- a long way away from other people or things: **isolated** (**from** sb/sth); *noun* (U): **isolation** ◦ *an isolated village*

■ wanting to be alone

- if you try not to meet other people, you **keep*** (yourself) **to** yourself ◦ *My neighbours keep themselves to themselves – I hardly see them.*
- when you do not touch or speak to sb, you **leave*** them **alone** ◦ *I wish you would leave me alone to make my own decisions.*

- the state of being alone or away from people who may disturb you: **privacy** (*noun* U) ◦ *to respect a person's privacy*
- if you do sth with no one else present, you do it **in private**, **privately** ◦ *Can I speak with you in private?*

▷ more on privacy ⇨ PRIVATE

■ not wanting to be alone

- if you are unhappy because you are not with other people, you are **lonely**; *noun* (U): **loneliness** ◦ *She had no friends and felt very lonely at her new school.* ◦ *the experience of loneliness in big cities*
- the feeling of being too much away from other people or things: **isolation** (*noun* U)

■ **MORE . . .**

- done by one person, without anyone else helping: **solo** (*adjective, adverb*), **single-handed** (*adjective, adverb*) ◦ *to fly solo for the first time* ◦ *to sail the Atlantic single-handed*

alphabet ⇨ LETTER[2]

also ⇨ AND/OR/BUT

always ⇨ HOW OFTEN

ambassador ⇨ GOVERNMENT

ambition

- wanting to succeed ⇨ SUCCEED/FAIL
- wanting sth a lot ⇨ WANT

amount ⇨ HOW MUCH/MANY

amusement

- enjoying yourself ⇨ ENJOY
- being entertained ⇨ ENTERTAINMENT

and/or/but

1 and/or
2 but
see also REASON, BEFORE/AFTER, CAUSE/EFFECT, SAY

1 and/or

- in addition: **too**, **as well** (**as** sb/sth), **also**, (in negative sentences) **either** ◦ *John would like to read it and I'd like to too.* ◦ *He teaches French as well as English.* ◦ *I want two pads of paper and I also need some pencils.* ◦ *I don't like meat and I'm not very keen on fish either.*
- one person or thing and another: **both . . . and**, **not only . . . but also** ◦ *We were influenced by both political and economic considerations.* ◦ *She not only sings but also plays the piano.*
- as two or more things that you can choose between: **either . . . or** ◦ *They say we can either have a pay rise or a shorter working week. Not both.*

■ first, second, etc

- as the first thing to be done or said: **first**(**ly**), **to begin/start with**, **in the first place**, **first of all** ◦ *To begin with, I'll remind you of what I said last time.* ◦ *There are several reasons for our decision. In the first place . . .*
- as the next thing to be said or done: **second**(**ly**), **third**(**ly**), etc, **in the second**, **third**, etc **place**, **next**
- as the last thing to be said or done: **finally**, **last**(**ly**), **to conclude**, **in conclusion** ◦ *And to conclude, I'd like to quote the words of Jonathan Swift . . .*
- last, but still important: **last but not least** ◦ *Last but not least, I would like to thank my children.*

- to say that there are other similar things or points, without saying what they are, you can say **and so on**, **et cetera** (*written abbreviation* **etc**) ◦ *The shop sells bread, cakes, sweets, fruit, vegetables etc, etc*

▷ more on being first, next, last ⇨ FIRST/NEXT/LAST

■ another thing

– as another thing to be said or done: **also**, **besides**, **anyway** ◦ *'Why did you leave early?' 'Well, it was beginning to rain and besides I was getting bored.'* ◦ *We don't need such a big car, and we can't afford it anyway.*
– as another thing to be said or done: (*more formal*) **furthermore**, (*more formal*) **moreover** ◦ *The school is achieving better examination results and, moreover, is sending more of its pupils on to university.*
– as a different thing that can be said or done: **alternatively** ◦ *You can catch the 8.30 direct to Oxford. Alternatively, you can take the 9.30 and change at Reading.*

– as another thing (and the one which is most important): **more than anything else**, **above all** ◦ *I wanted a meal and a drink and above all a good night's sleep.*
– as another thing (and one which is similar): **equally**, **likewise** ◦ *The government is anxious not to damage the beef industry. Equally, it is concerned about the threat to public health.*

– as another point or topic: **incidentally**, **by the way** ◦ *By the way, did you remember to write to your brother?*
– as a point that you have just remembered: **come to think of it**, **that reminds me** ◦ *I had a call from Alice – and that reminds me, have you got her camera?*

2 but

■ making a contrast within a sentence

– to show a contrast between two parts of a sentence, you can use **but**, **yet**, (*informal*) **only** ◦ *It's very fast but uses rather a lot of petrol.* ◦ *I know it's not really my fault, yet I still feel guilty.* ◦ *It's a lovely dress, only not quite my colour.*

– to introduce a statement that makes the main statement in a sentence more surprising, you can use **although**, (*more informal*) **though**, **even though** ◦ *Although he has a lot of money, he always wears old clothes.* ◦ *Okay, I'll do what you want, though I don't really like the idea.* ◦ *Even though she has a car, she always comes to work on her bicycle.*

■ making a contrast between sentences

– words which we can use in a sentence which expresses a contrast with another sentence: **however**, **even so**, **all the same**, (*formal*) **nevertheless**, (*informal*) **though** ◦ *Sweden is a cold country; however, the houses are very warm.* ◦ *I wasn't hungry. Nevertheless, I ate the food she gave me.* ◦ *He didn't work very hard. Even so, he passed his exam.* ◦ *She told me not to do it. All the same, I tried.* ◦ *It was very sad saying goodbye. I didn't cry, though.*

■ expressing different points of view

– to show two contrasting points of view, you can say (**on the one hand**,) **on the other hand** ◦ *On the one hand, I want to help, but on the other hand I don't want her to think I'm interfering.* ◦ *James spends all his money straight away. Alex, on the other hand, saves his.*

– when the opposite of sth is true, you can say **on the contrary** ◦ *I've never said I hate opera! On the contrary, I love it.*

angle

see also LINE, CIRCLE, SHAPE

– the space between two lines or surfaces that meet: **angle**
– angles are measured in **degrees** ◦ *There are 360 degrees in one complete turn.* ◦ *Line ab is at an angle of 45° to line bc.*

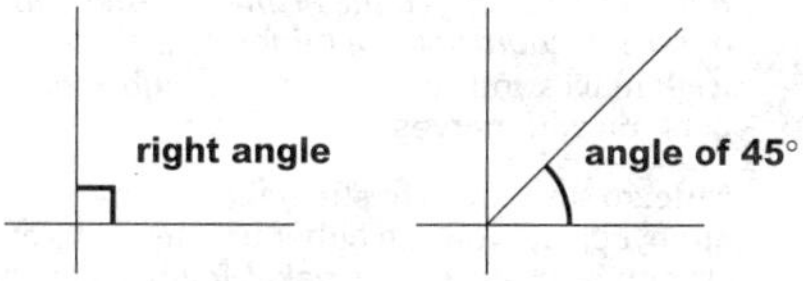

– an angle of 90°: **right angle**
– an angle of less than 90°: **acute angle**
– an angle between 90° and 180°: **obtuse angle**
– an angle of more than 180°: **reflex angle**
– if there is an angle of 90° between two lines or two things, one line or thing is **at right angles** (**to** the other), **at a right angle** (**to** the other), **perpendicular** (**to** the other) ◦ *The legs on a table are at right angles to the top of the table.*

– something which goes straight up from the ground or from a line at an angle of 90° is **vertical** ◦ *a vertical line* ◦ *a sweatshirt with vertical stripes*
– something which is not straight up is **at an angle** (**to** sth) ◦ *The nail was sticking out of the wood at an angle.*

– an instrument in the shape of a half circle used for drawing and measuring angles: **protractor**
– an instrument used for drawing straight lines and angles of 90°, 60°, 45° and 30°: **set square**

– the area of mathematics concerned with angles, lines, shapes, etc: **geometry** (*noun* U)
– the area of mathematics concerned with the angles and sides of triangles: **trigonometry** (*noun* U)

▷ more on mathematics ⇨ MATHEMATICS

angry

1 angry
2 what people do when they are angry
3 not angry
see also EMOTION

1 angry

– very unhappy because of sth that has happened which you do not like: **angry** (**with** sb) (**at**/**about** sth), **angry that …** (*adverb* **angrily**); *noun* (U):

angry *contd.*

anger ○ *I get so angry when I hear what is happening to the world's forests.* ○ *Why are you angry with me?* ○ *I could hear her speaking angrily on the phone.* ○ *a terrible feeling of anger and disappointment* ○ *to show your anger*
- to make sb angry: **anger** sb ○ *What angered me more than anything else was his dishonesty.*

■ rather angry
- rather angry: **annoyed**, **irritated**; *nouns* (U): **annoyance**, **irritation** ○ *His endless complaints were beginning to make me rather irritated.* ○ *I could easily understand her irritation.*
- to make sb rather angry: **annoy** sb, **irritate** sb; something that annoys you is **annoying**, **irritating**, an **annoyance**, an **irritation** ○ *Recent events have clearly annoyed the Prime Minister.* ○ *an annoying habit* ○ *a lot of minor irritations*
- if sth makes you very irritated, it (*informal*) **gets* on** your **nerves**

Note: to say that sb or sth makes sb angry, annoyed, etc, you can either use the verbs **anger** sb, **annoy** sb, etc or use **make*** followed by the adjectives **angry**, **annoyed**, etc; using **make** is more informal and more common: ○ *Why let him make you angry? Just ignore him!* ○ *It makes me so angry when I see all that food being wasted.*
- to repeatedly annoy sb, for example by asking them a lot of questions: **pester** sb; a person, especially a child, that does this is (*informal*) a **pest** ○ *Go away. Don't be such a pest!*
- to intentionally annoy sb in order to make them react: **provoke** sb; doing this is **provocation** (*noun* U); something that does this is a **provocation**; *adjective*: **provocative** (*adverb* **provocatively**) ○ *an act of provocation* ○ *a provocative remark*

■ unhappy, worried, etc
- if sb has made you sad and angry, you are **upset**, **offended**, you **take* offence** (*AmE* **offense**) (**at** sth) ○ *I got very upset about what she said about my father.*
- to hurt sb's feelings and make them feel annoyed: **upset*** sb, **offend** sb, **cause offence** (*AmE* **offense**) (**to** sb); a thing or person that does this is **offensive** (*adverb* **offensively**) ○ *The argument upset her terribly.* ○ *I'm sorry. I didn't mean to cause offence.* ○ *an offensive remark*
- if sb or sth makes you feel angry and unhappy because you think you are being treated unfairly, you **resent** them/it, you feel **resentment** (*noun* U); *adjective*: **resentful** ○ *He deeply resented the criticism.* ○ *She resented not winning the first prize again.* ○ *full of resentment* ○ *She wrote me a resentful letter.*
- angry and unhappy because of the way sb has treated you: **bitter** (*adverb* **bitterly**); *noun* (U): **bitterness** ○ *a deep feeling of bitterness towards her employer*

- unhappy and dissatisfied, because you cannot have or do what you want: **frustrated**; this feeling: **frustration** (*noun* U); something that causes this feeling: **frustration**

■ very angry
- very angry: **mad**, **furious** (*adverb* **furiously**) ○ *That sort of talk just makes me mad.* ○ *She was absolutely furious that she had to wait so long to see the doctor.* ○ *George furiously denied the accusation.*
- to make sb very angry: **infuriate** sb, (*informal*) **drive*** sb **mad**; something that makes you very angry is **maddening**, **infuriating** ○ *a maddening noise* ○ *Could you please switch off that infuriating radio!*

- if you are angry and unable to remain calm, you are **in a** (**bad/furious**) **temper** ○ *I wouldn't talk to him just now if I were you. He's in a furious temper.*
- to suddenly get angry: **lose*** your **temper** (**with** sb) ○ *I'm sorry I lost my temper with you last night.*
- to become angry, worried, etc: **get* worked up** ○ *Calm down – there's no need to get so worked up!*

■ people who get angry easily
- if you are easily made angry, you are **irritable**; *noun* (U): **irritability**
- if you easily become annoyed by people or things that seem slow, you are **impatient**; *noun* (U): **impatience**

- if you easily become angry and impatient, you have a **bad/short/quick temper**, you are **bad-tempered**, **short-tempered**, **quick-tempered** ○ *a bad-tempered old man*

2 what people do when they are angry
- to speak angrily to a person because they have done sth bad or wrong: **tell*** sb **off** (**for** doing sth); *noun*: **telling-off** ○ *The teacher told us off for talking.* ○ *I got a telling-off for arriving late.*
- to behave angrily towards a person because you are angry or upset about sth: **take* it out on** sb ○ *Don't take it out on me – it's not my fault that you didn't win.*

- to argue with a person angrily: **quarrel** (**with** sb) (**about/over** sth); *noun*: **quarrel**; to start a quarrel with a person deliberately: **pick a quarrel** (**with** sb) ○ *The children never stop quarrelling.*
- an angry quarrel: **row** ○ *He's had a row with his girlfriend.*

▷ arguing with sb ⇨ DISCUSS/ARGUE

- to make your eyebrows come together so that your face seems angry: **frown**, **scowl**; this kind of look: **frown**, **scowl** ○ *The frown on his face changed to a smile as soon as she apologized.*
- to stare at a person angrily: **glare** (**at** sb); this kind of look: **glare** ○ *They glared at each other for a few moments before he left.*
- to be quiet and unhelpful because you are angry with sb about sth: **sulk** ○ *What's he sulking about?*

■ things that people say when they are angry
- to use rude or bad language: **swear*** (**at** sb/sth), **curse** ○ *He was furiously angry, cursing and swearing and shaking his fist at the driver of the other car.*

- a word which is used in order to swear: **swear word**
- some words which show anger and impatience (but many people find these words offensive): **damn**, **blast**, **hell**, **shit** ◦ *Damn it! I've broken the screw!* ◦ *Oh hell! I've forgotten my keys.*

3 not angry

- to stay calm in an annoying situation: **keep*** your **temper**
- to try to relax and not get worried or upset: **take* it easy** ◦ *Take it easy – there's no point in getting so worked up.*
- to become quiet and calm: **calm down**

▷ being calm ➪ CALM

animal

1 different kinds of animal
2 parts of an animal
3 animal behaviour
4 animal sounds
5 keeping and looking after animals
6 killing animals

animals as food ➪ BIRD², FISH², FOOD, MEAT

see also BIRD¹, INSECT, FISH¹

1 different kinds of animal

- a living creature that is not a plant: **animal**
- an animal which feeds on milk from its mother's body when young: **mammal**
- an animal such as a snake or a crocodile that has a scaly skin and lays eggs: **reptile**
- an animal that can live both on land and in water: **amphibian**
- a large kind of animal which disappeared from the earth a long time ago: **dinosaur**

- an animal that has a body temperature that varies with the temperature of the surroundings is **cold-blooded**; *opposite*: **warm-blooded**

- all the animals in the world make up the **animal kingdom**
- a group of animals that are similar to each other: **species** (*plural* **species**) ◦ *an endangered species*
- a species of animal that no longer exists is **extinct**; *noun* (U): **extinction**

Note: animal is sometimes used to mean all living creatures that are not plants, sometimes to mean living creatures of this kind that are not humans, and sometimes to mean living creatures which have four legs (and therefore not including humans, birds, fish, insects or reptiles).

- animals living in natural surroundings are **wild** ◦ *wild rabbits*
- wild animals, birds and plants: **wildlife** (*noun* U)
- animals that are kept on farms or in people's homes and are not wild are **domestic** ◦ *domestic cats*
- animals that have become used to living near people and being controlled by them are **tame**, **domesticated**
- animals that live on farms: **farm animals**

▷ pictures of animals on p 16

▷ more on domestic animals ➪ CAT, COW, DOG, HORSE, PIG, SHEEP, FARM

▷ more on wild animals ➪ LION/LEOPARD/TIGER, SNAKE

2 parts of an animal

- the long thin part at the end of the body of an animal, bird or fish: **tail**
- one of the hard pointed things that cows, goats, etc have on their heads: **horn**

▷ picture on next page

- the foot of animals such as cats, dogs and bears: **paw**
- the foot of animals such as cows and horses: **hoof** (*plural* **hooves**)
- one of the sharp nails on the feet of some animals and birds: **claw**
- one of the front legs of an animal with four legs: **foreleg**; one of the back legs: **hind leg**

- the soft thick hair on the body of some animals (for example, cats): **fur** (*noun* U); *adjective*: **furry**
- the hair or fur covering an animal's body: **coat** ◦ *a dog with a smooth coat*
- the outer covering of many fish and reptiles: **scales** (*noun plural*); *adjective*: **scaly**

3 animal behaviour

- the natural home of an animal: **habitat** ◦ *the panda's natural habitat*
- the hidden home of some wild animals: **den** ◦ *a lion's den*
- a hole in the ground made by certain animals (for example, rabbits) in which they live: **burrow**
- an animal that lives naturally in an area is **native** (**to** a place), **indigenous** (**to** a place) ◦ *Lions are native to Africa.* ◦ *various native species of birds and animals*
- when animals hide away and spend the winter in a deep sleep, they **hibernate**

- a group of large animals (for example, cows, goats, sheep, elephants): **herd** ◦ *a large herd of wildebeest*

■ young animals

- young animals: **young** (*noun plural*) ◦ *Most animals will kill to protect their young.*
- a young animal: (*informal*) **baby** ◦ *a baby bird/elephant*
- when animals have sex and produce young, they **mate** ◦ *The penguins move away from the beach to make their nests and mate.*
- ready to mate: **on heat**
  to produce young animals: **breed*** ◦ *Some animals will not breed in zoos.*
- all the young animals that are born to one mother at the same time: **litter** ◦ *a litter of kittens/puppies*

animals

monkey

giraffe

zebra

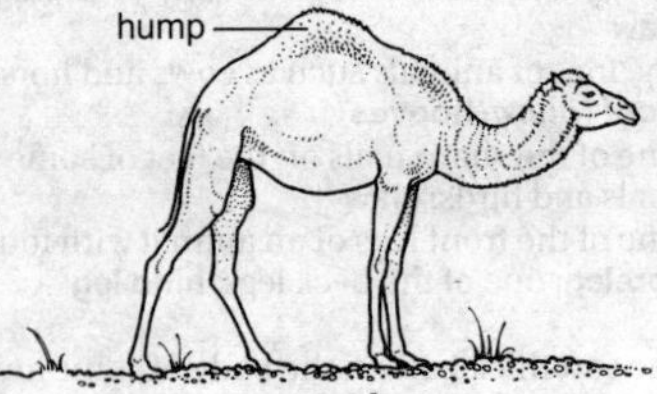

camel

kangaroo

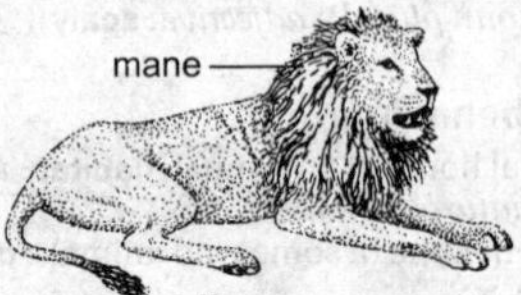

lion

leopard

tiger

crocodile

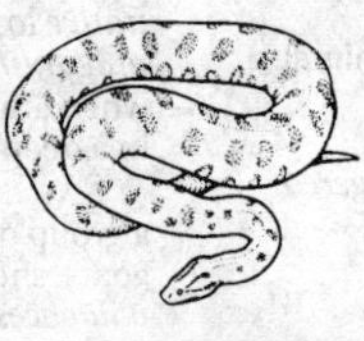

snake

hippo (*plural* **hippos**)

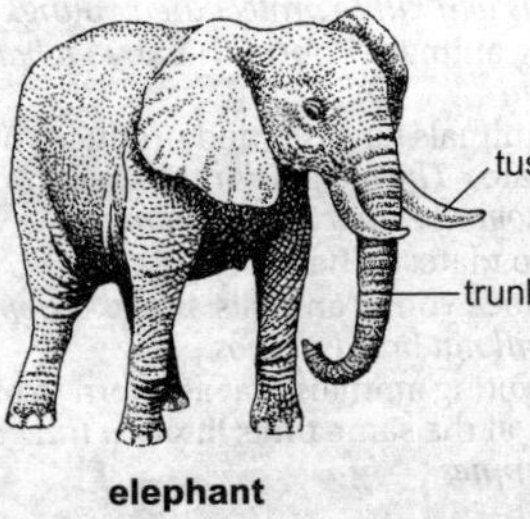

elephant

rhino (*plural* **rhinos**)

bat

mouse (*plural* **mice**)

hedgehog

squirrel

lizard

tortoise

rabbit

slug

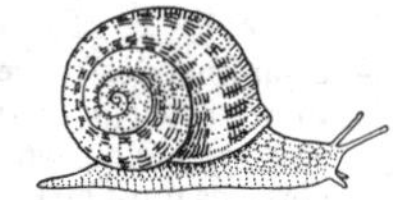
snail

worm

frog

bear

deer (*plural* **deer**)

fox

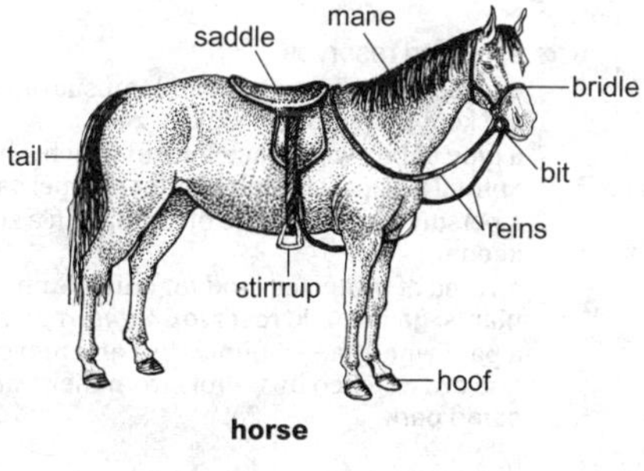

horse

cow

animal *contd.*

■ food and eating

- (used about animals) to eat: **feed*** (**on** sth) ◦ *Frogs feed mainly on insects.*
- an animal that eats only meat: **carnivore**; *adjective*: **carnivorous**
- an animal that eats only plants: **herbivore**; *adjective*: **herbivorous** ◦ *Cows are herbivorous animals but lions are carnivores.*

- (used about cows and sheep) to eat grass in a field: **graze** ◦ *Cows were grazing in the fields.*
- to bite sth (for example a bone) many times, as some animals do: **gnaw** (**at/on**) sth, **chew on** sth ◦ *The dog was chewing on a bone.*
- (used about a bird) to eat or bite sth with the beak: **peck** (**at**) sth ◦ *Look at that bird pecking at the berries in the tree.*
- when an animal uses its tongue to drink, it **laps** sth (**up**)

- (used about an animal or bird) to kill and eat other animals or birds: **prey on** sth ◦ *Lions prey on young antelopes and zebras.*
- an animal that kills and eats other animals: **predator**; an animal that is preyed on: **prey** (*noun* U)

- waste matter from the bodies of small animals and birds: **droppings** (*noun plural*)
- waste matter from the bodies of large animals: **dung** (*noun* U) ◦ *cow dung*

4 animal sounds

animal	sound
bees	**buzz**
bulls	**bellow**
birds	**chirp**
cats	**miaow, purr**
cocks	**crow**
cows	**moo**
dogs	**bark**
donkeys	**bray**
doves or pigeons	**coo**
ducks	**quack**
frogs	**croak**
hens	**cluck**
horses	**neigh**
lions	**roar**
owls	**hoot**
pigs	**grunt, squeal**
sheep	**bleat**
snakes	**hiss**
wolves	**howl**

- the sound an animal makes in the wild to attract attention: **call** ◦ *the mating call of the tree frog*
- the musical sound that a bird makes: **song**

Note: the words in the table can be used as verbs and nouns: ◦ *Frogs croak.* ◦ *a frog's croak*. Uncountable nouns can be made with '-ing': ◦ *the roaring of lions*.

5 keeping and looking after animals

- an animal that is kept at home for company or pleasure: **pet** ◦ *to keep a pet* ◦ *a pet parrot*
- a shop where small animals are sold: **pet shop**
- pets that are trained to behave well in the house and do not make it dirty are **house-trained** ◦ *Is your puppy house-trained?*
- to rub an animal gently with your hand: **stroke** sth

- to give an animal food: **feed*** sth ◦ *Did anybody remember to feed the cat?*
- food for cats, dogs, etc: **cat food** (*noun* U), **dog food** (*noun* U), etc
- cats, dogs, etc are given food in a **bowl**

▷ feeding animals on a farm ⇨ **FARM**

- to keep animals in order to produce young from them: **breed*** sth; a person who does this: **breeder** ◦ *to breed racehorses* ◦ *a dog breeder*
- a type of a particular animal: **breed** ◦ *a popular breed of cat*

- an animal doctor: **vet** ◦ *We took our cat to the vet to be treated for an injured leg.*
- a period of time when animals that may have diseases must be kept away from other animals: **quarantine** (*noun* U) ◦ *Our dogs have got to go into quarantine for six months.*

■ farms

- an area of land and buildings used for growing crops and keeping animals: **farm**
- a large area of farm land especially in America where cows and horses are kept: **ranch**
- a person who takes care of wild birds and deer on private land: **gamekeeper**

- to move animals forward together (in a herd): **herd** sth ◦ *I herded the sheep into the field and shut the gate.*
- to gather a group of animals in one place: **round** sth **up** ◦ *They rounded up the cows to take them into town.*

▷ more on farms ⇨ **FARM**

■ zoos and reserves

- a place where many wild and unusual animals are kept for people to look at: **zoo**
- a type of box with metal bars in which a bird or animal is kept so that it cannot escape: **cage**
- a person who takes care of animals in a zoo: **keeper**
- an area of protected land for animals and plants: **game park**, **reserve** ◦ *a nature reserve*
- a park where large animals live and move freely and are watched by visitors from their cars: **safari park**

- the protection of animals and the natural world: **conservation** (*noun* U); a person who does this: **conservationist**

6 killing animals

- to cause an animal to die: **kill** sth ◦ *I don't approve of animals being killed for sport.*
- to kill an animal because it is old, sick or dangerous: **put*** sth **down, destroy** sth ◦ *Following the accident, the horse had to be put down.* ◦ *The court ordered the dog to be destroyed.*
- to kill an animal for food: **slaughter** sth; *noun* (U): **slaughter** ◦ *They slaughtered a goat to celebrate his arrival.* ◦ *The sheep were sent for slaughter.*
- to kill a bird by twisting its neck: **wring*** the **neck** of sth
- a place where animals are killed for food: **slaughterhouse, abattoir**

- to look for and follow wild animals in order to catch or kill them either for food or for sport: **hunt** (sth); *noun* (U): **hunting**; a person who hunts: **hunter**
- to take or kill animals, birds or fish from sb's land without permission: **poach** sth; a person who does this: **poacher**

▷ more on hunting ⇨ HUNT

- a substance that is used for killing insects: **insecticide** (*noun* C/U) ◦ *to spray crops with insecticide*
- a substance that is used for killing animals and insects that eat food crops: **pesticide** (*noun* C/U) ◦ *the effect of pesticides on the environment*

■ **MORE ...**

- if an animal or insect destroys food and plants, it is a **pest**
- an animal, insect or plant that lives on another animal or plant and takes its food from it: **parasite**

- the study of animals: **zoology** (*noun* U); *adjective*: **zoological**; a person who studies animals: **zoologist**
- the study of all living things: **biology** (*noun* U); *adjective*: **biological**; a person who studies living things: **biologist**

- an imaginary animal that looks like a very large lizard: **dragon**
- an imaginary animal that looks like a horse and has a single horn: **unicorn**

---

annoy ⇨ ANGRY

---

answer

- to a letter ⇨ LETTER[1]
- to a question ⇨ QUESTION

---

anxious ⇨ WORRY

---

apologize ⇨ SORRY

---

appear

- arrive in a place ⇨ ARRIVE
- look as if ⇨ LOOK/SEEM
- be seen ⇨ SEE

---

approximate ⇨ ALMOST

---

architecture ⇨ BUILDING

---

area

- a piece of land ⇨ LAND
- the size of a place ⇨ SIZE

---

argue ⇨ DISCUSS/ARGUE

---

aristocracy ⇨ LORD/LADY

---

arm ⇨ HAND/ARM

---

army

1 people in an army
2 how an army is organized
3 things that soldiers use
4 working in the army

see also AIR FORCE, NAVY, WAR

1 people in an army

- the military forces of a country that are trained to fight on land: **army**
- a member of an army: **soldier**
- soldiers: **troops** (*noun plural*) ◦ *Thousands of troops have been stationed in the town.*
- a person who gives orders to others in the army, navy, air force, etc: **officer**

- a person who is not a member of an army, etc: **civilian** ◦ *Civilians as well as soldiers were killed in the fighting.*

■ joining and leaving an army

- when you become a member of the army, etc, you **join up** ◦ *Sergeant Andrews joined up five years ago.* ◦ *My grandfather joined up at the start of the war.*
- to get sb to join the army, etc: **recruit** sb; the process of getting people to join the army: **recruitment** (*noun* U) ◦ *The army is recruiting more women than before.* ◦ *an army recruitment centre*
- a person who has just joined the army: **recruit**
- a permanent member of the army: **regular (soldier)**

- a person who is forced to join the army: **conscript** (*AmE* **draftee**)
- if sb orders you to join the army, etc you are **called up**, (*formal*) **conscripted** (*AmE* **drafted**) (**into** sth); the system of making people join the army: **conscription** (*noun* U) (*AmE* **the draft**) ◦ *The government has called up all men between the ages of 18 and 35.*
- a person who joins the army without being forced to: **volunteer**

army *contd.*

- to leave the army without permission: **desert**; *noun* (C/U): **desertion** ◦ *He deserted after three years' service.* ◦ *to be shot for desertion*
- a person who leaves his/her duties in the army without permission: **deserter**
- a person who used to serve in the army, especially during a war: **veteran** ◦ *World War II veterans*

■ different kinds of soldiers
- the part of the army which fights on foot: the **infantry** (*noun* U, *with singular or plural verb*)
- the part of the army which fights in fast, heavily protected vehicles (in the past they fought on horseback): the **cavalry** (*noun* U, *with singular or plural verb*)
- the part of the army which fights using large guns: the **artillery** (*noun* U)
- soldiers who are trained to drop from aeroplanes by parachute: **paratroops** (*noun plural*); one of these soldiers: **paratrooper**
- a soldier who fights on land and at sea: **marine**
- one of a group of soldiers which is trained to make quick attacks in enemy areas: **commando** (*plural* **commandos**)
- a group of soldiers who protect sb/sth: **guard** ◦ *the presidential guard*
- a soldier who fights for any country or organization that will pay him/her: **mercenary**

■ ranks in the British army
- officers (starting with the highest rank) are: **Field Marshal, General, Brigadier, Colonel, Major, Captain, Lieutenant**
- other ranks are: **Sergeant, Corporal, Private**
- to give sb a higher rank: **promote** sb; *noun* (C/U): **promotion** ◦ *He was promoted from Lieutenant to Captain.* ◦ *I'm hoping for promotion soon.*
- to give sb a lower rank as a punishment: **demote** sb; *noun* (C/U): **demotion**

2 how an army is organized

- a group of soldiers, etc who are trained for a particular purpose: **force** ◦ *a United Nations peace-keeping force*
- armies are divided into smaller units; (starting with the largest) these include: **division, brigade, regiment, battalion, company, platoon**
- a small group of soldiers who work or are trained together: **squad**
- a group of soldiers who guard a town or building: **garrison** ◦ *The Romans had a garrison at Colchester.*

■ places where soldiers live and operate
- a building or group of buildings where soldiers live: **barracks** (*noun plural*) ◦ *The fighting stopped and the soldiers returned to barracks.*
- the room or building where soldiers eat together: **mess** (*AmE also* **mess hall**) ◦ *the officers' mess*
- a place where soldiers live and are trained: **camp**
- a military centre from where armed forces operate: **base**
- an administrative centre of an army, etc: **headquarters** (*noun plural*) (*abbreviation* **HQ**)

3 things that soldiers use

■ clothes and personal equipment
- a special set of clothes that soldiers, etc wear: **uniform** (*noun* C/U) ◦ *to wear a uniform* ◦ *Was he in uniform when you saw him?*
- a hat that soldiers, etc wear on their heads for protection in battle: **helmet**
- a small piece of metal or cloth with a design on it that is put on soldiers' uniforms to show their rank: **badge**
- a flat piece of metal with a design on it that is given to soldiers and others for bravery, long service, etc: **medal**
- all the clothes and other equipment that a soldier needs: **kit** (*noun* U)

■ army vehicles and weapons
- a container that is filled with material that will explode if it is thrown, dropped, etc: **bomb**
- a weapon that is used for shooting: **gun**

▷ more on bombs, guns and other weapons ⇨ **BOMB, GUN, WEAPON**

- a thick metal which covers army vehicles, warships etc to protect them from enemy bombs and bullets: **armour** (*AmE* **armor**) (*noun* U); a vehicle or ship that has armour is **armoured** (*AmE* **armored**) ◦ *an armoured car*
- a large heavy military vehicle covered in armour and armed with guns, that moves on special wheels: **tank**
- a small, strong, vehicle used for travelling over rough ground: **jeep**

4 working in the army

- to work for the army, etc as a soldier: **serve** (**in**/**with** sth); work done as a soldier: **service** (*noun* U) ◦ *During the war my uncle served in the Parachute Regiment.* ◦ *He saw active service in many different parts of the world.*
- a period of time that a young person must spend in his/her country's army, etc: **military service** (*noun* U), **national service** (*noun* U) ◦ *He's doing his military service.* ◦ *I'm about to be called up for national service.*
- to send a soldier, etc to work in a place: **post** sb **to** a place; a place where a soldier must stay when he/she is working: **post** ◦ *He's not sure where he's going to be posted next.* ◦ *Many of the soldiers had deserted their posts.*
- to control or be in charge of sb/sth: **command** sb/sth, **be in command** (**of** sb/sth) ◦ *a general commanding thirty thousand troops* ◦ *Who is in command of this platoon?*
- an officer who is in command of a group of soldiers: **commanding officer**
- an instruction to do sth: **order**; to give an order: **order** sb (**to** do sth) ◦ *The night before the battle they were given their orders.*

- to walk with regular steps: **march**; *noun*: **march** ◦ *The men were marching up and down the parade ground.* ◦ *It was a long march up the hill.*
- an occasion when soldiers march together for an inspection, a ceremony, etc: **parade**; taking part in a parade: **on parade**; to take part in a parade: **parade** ◦ *The returning soldiers paraded through the town.*
- a place where soldiers stand to be inspected, etc: **parade ground**

- when a soldier stands upright with his/her feet together, he/she **stands*/comes* to attention**
- when a soldier stands in a relaxed way, with his/her feet apart, he/she **stands* at ease**
- the command to stop marching: **Halt!**
- to show respect by raising your hand to your forehead: **salute** (sb); *noun*: **salute** ◦ *Always salute a superior officer!* ◦ *a smart salute*

arrange

- a plan ⇨ INTEND/PLAN
- the order of things ⇨ ORGANIZE

arrive

see also COME/GO, GREET, LEAVE, TRAVEL, VISIT

- (used about a person or thing that is travelling to a place) to come to a particular place: **arrive** (**at/in** a place), **reach** a place, **get*** to a place ◦ *We arrived two hours late.* ◦ *Has my letter arrived yet?* ◦ *to arrive at a hotel* ◦ *They should arrive in London just after six.* ◦ *The letter reached me in two days.* ◦ *When will we reach Paris?* ◦ *It will be dark by the time we get to Phoenix.*
- the act of arriving at a place: **arrival** (*noun* U) ◦ *Immediately on arrival, we went to the nearest police station.*

Note: you arrive **at** a building, **at** a point in the countryside such as a river, the top of a hill, a waterfall, etc, but **in** a town or a country. If a town or country is considered simply as a point on your journey where you stop briefly, you say that you arrive **at** it.

- the place where sb/sth is going or being sent: **destination** ◦ *I'm going to Delhi and Bangkok, but my final destination is Tokyo.*

- to arrive or come into sight: **appear** ◦ *Their car appeared round the corner as we were leaving the house.*
- to come near or nearer to the place that you are travelling to: **approach** a place ◦ *This is your captain speaking. We are now approaching Heathrow airport.*
- to manage, in spite of some difficulty, to reach a place, or to reach it on time: **make*** sth ◦ *Do you think we can make the meeting on time?* ◦ *With luck we'll make Cardiff by seven.*
- to arrive (especially when sb is expecting you): (*informal*) **show up, turn up** ◦ *I waited for two hours but he never showed up.* ◦ *What time did they turn up?*

- a person or thing that has arrived in a place: **arrival** ◦ *It didn't take long for the new arrivals to settle in.*
- a person who arrives late: **latecomer** ◦ *I had to get some extra chairs for the latecomers.*

arrow ⇨ WEAPON

art

see also LITERATURE, MUSIC, DESIGN

- the general word for paintings, drawings, sculptures, literature and music: **art** (*noun* U) ◦ *the history of art* ◦ *classical/romantic/impressionist art* ◦ *modern/abstract art* ◦ *a professor of Fine Art* ◦ *a work of art* (= one piece of art)
- activities such as painting, writing literature, making music: **the arts** (*noun plural*) ◦ *We depend on businesses to provide support for the arts.*

- a person who produces art, particularly painting: **artist**
- showing skill in art: **artistic** (*adverb* **artistically**) ◦ *an artistic child* ◦ *'Do you like this Christmas card I've designed?' 'Yes, it's very artistic.'*
- a way of painting, drawing, etc that is typical of a particular historical period, group of artists, etc: **style** ◦ *the impressionist style*
- a person whose job is to write about art, for example in a newspaper: (**art**) **critic** ◦ *The critics agreed that the exhibition was bad.*

- a place where artists learn: **art school, art college**
- a place where an artist works: **studio**

■ kinds of art
- to make a picture using paint: **paint** (sth); *noun* (U): **painting**
- to make a picture using a pen or pencil: **draw*** (sth); *noun* (U): **drawing**
- to make a picture using a camera: **photograph** sth; *noun* (U): **photography**
- the art of making shapes and objects from metal, wood, stone, etc: **sculpture** (*noun* U)

▷ more on painting, drawing, photography and sculpture ⇨ PAINT[1], DRAW, PHOTOGRAPH, SCULPTURE

- an activity that needs artistic ability as well as skill with the hands: **craft, handicraft**; the objects that are produced by this activity: **handicrafts** (*noun plural*) ◦ *Baskets and rugs and other local handicrafts were being sold in the market.*

■ where art can be seen
- a place where people can see works of art: **art gallery**
- a building where valuable and interesting objects are kept and shown to the public: **museum**
- a particular collection of works of art shown in a museum or art gallery: **exhibition**; one object in an exhibition: **exhibit**; to show something in an exhibition: **exhibit** sth ◦ *Have you seen the Turner exhibition yet?* ◦ *His paintings have been exhibited in the local art gallery.*

art *contd.*

– an organized group of events in art, literature, music, drama, etc: **festival** ◦ *the Edinburgh Festival* ◦ *a jazz festival*

■ **MORE ...**

– if a work of art looks real or genuine but is not, it is a **fake**; *adjective*: **fake** ◦ *Everyone knows it's a fake, but it's a very good one.* ◦ *a fake Picasso*

– to ask an artist to create a new work, often for a particular occasion: **commission** sth, **commission** sb **to** do sth ◦ *The picture of the house was commissioned by its owners just after it was built.* ◦ *She has been commissioned to do an official portrait of the Prime Minister.*

– to return a picture, sculpture, etc to its original condition: **restore** sth; a person who does this: **restorer**

– if something involves a person's sense of beauty, it can be called **aesthetic** (*adverb* **aesthetically**) ◦ *We have decided to change the design for purely aesthetic reasons.* ◦ *The effect is aesthetically pleasing.*

ashamed ⇨ SORRY

ask

– a question ⇨ QUESTION
– sb to do sth ⇨ REQUEST

asleep ⇨ SLEEP

astrology

see also STAR / PLANET / MOON

– the belief that the positions and movements of the stars and planets influence what people do and what happens to them: **astrology** (*noun* U); *adjective*: **astrological** ◦ *to believe in astrology*
– a person who studies the positions and movements of the stars and planets in order to find out how they are supposed to influence people's lives: **astrologer**

– a kind of map of the planets and stars in the sky which is divided into twelve equal parts: **the zodiac**
– the name of a group of stars which belong to one of the twelve parts of the zodiac: (**star**) **sign** ◦ *the signs of the zodiac* ◦ *'What's your star sign?'* ◦ *People born under the sign of Gemini are supposed to be intelligent and considerate.*
– a description of what is going to happen to you in the future, according to astrology: **horoscope**, (*informal*) **stars** ◦ *Have you read your stars today?*
– if you think that sth in your life has to happen or cannot be prevented, you say it is **in the stars** or **in** your **stars** ◦ *She's going to become famous – it's in her stars.*

■ the signs of the zodiac

Aries
21 March–
20 April

Taurus
21 April–
20 May

Gemini
21 May–
20 June

Cancer
21 June–
20 July

Leo
21 July–
19/22 August

Virgo
20/23 August–
22 September

Libra
23 September–
22 October

Scorpio
23 October–
21 November

Sagittarius
22 November–
20 December

Capricorn
21 December–
20 January

Aquarius
21 January–
19 February

Pisces
20 February–
20 March

◦ *I'm an Aries. What are you?* ◦ *Are you Gemini?* ◦ *a typical Leo*

astronaut ⇨ SPACE[2]

astronomy ⇨ STAR / PLANET / MOON

athletics

1 doing athletics
2 different kinds of athletics
see also SPORT

1 doing athletics

– the kinds of sport where people run, jump or throw things: **athletics** (*noun* U) ◦ *Is athletics popular in your school?*
– a person who does athletics: **athlete**
– a person who can do many different kinds of athletics (or other sports) is an **all-round athlete**, an **all-rounder** ◦ *He can swim, play tennis and run fast – in fact he's a pretty good all-rounder.*

– an organized event in which people try to win things: **competition**, **meeting** ◦ *an international athletics competition/ meeting*
– an athletics or sports competition: **games** (*noun plural*) ◦ *the Olympic Games*
– a person who takes part in a competition: **competitor**
– a person who helps an athlete to do well in their sport: **coach**, **trainer**

- the fastest, highest, longest, etc ever achieved in a certain type of competition: **record** ◦ *to set a new record* ◦ *to break a record*

▷ more on competitions, including results (winning and losing) and records ⇨ COMPETITION

- a large closed area for sports and games with seats for people to watch: **stadium** ◦ *an athletics stadium*
- part of a stadium with seats for people who are watching: **stand**
- a person who watches a competition: **spectator**; a large group of people who watch a competition: **crowd** ◦ *Only a small crowd was there to watch.*

- a special path, often in a circle, for racing: **track** ◦ *a running track*
- the area of land (especially inside the track) for athletic events which are not races: **field**

- a race or other competition in a sports meeting: **event** ◦ *He's in three different running events.* ◦ *the women's/men's event* ◦ *an indoor event*
- an event which is done on the track (= running a race): **track event**
- an event which is done on the field, for example jumping: **field event**

2 different kinds of athletics

■ running races

- a competition between people to see who can run the fastest: **race** ◦ *to be in a race* ◦ *to win/lose a race*

▷ more on running in a race ⇨ RACE[2]

- a race of a particular length: **the 100, 200**, etc **metres**
- a person who runs in a race: **runner** ◦ *a middle-distance runner*
- a race where people run over a short distance, often 100 metres: **sprint**; a person who sprints: **sprinter**; *verb*: **sprint** ◦ *a short sprint* ◦ *a fast sprinter*

- a race where people run and jump over small fences: **hurdles**; a person who hurdles: **hurdler**; *verb*: **hurdle** ◦ *He's in the 400 metres hurdles.*
- a race where a team of people run and pass each other a stick called a baton: **relay** (**race**)
- a race which is run over a distance of about 26 miles or 42 kilometres: **marathon**
- a race run across the country, over fields and through woods: **cross-country**
- a race across country or running on a track where runners have to jump over fences and holes full of water: **steeplechase**

■ jumping

- a competition where people try to jump as far as possible: **the long jump** (*AmE* **the broad jump**); a person who does this sport: **long-jumper** ◦ *to do the long jump*
- a long jump which is done with three jumps: **the triple jump**; a person who does this sport: **triple-jumper**
- a competition where people try to jump as high as possible: **the high jump**; a person who does this sport: **high-jumper**
- a competition where people use a long stick called a pole to jump as high as possible: **the pole vault**; a person who does this sport: **pole-vaulter**

■ throwing things

- a competition in which you throw a discus/hammer/shot/javelin as far as possible: **the discus/hammer/shot/javelin** ◦ *She's competing in the javelin and the shot.* ◦ *to throw the hammer/discus/javelin* ◦ *to put* (= throw) *the shot*

■ MORE ...

- an athletics competition where each person takes part in ten events: **decathlon**
- an athletics competition where each person takes part in five events: **pentathlon**

- an illegal drug that is taken by some athletes to make their bodies stronger: **steroid**
- a test to make sure that an athlete has not taken an illegal drug: **drug test**

atom ⇨ NUCLEAR

attach ⇨ JOIN

attack ⇨ FIGHT

attempt ⇨ TRY

attractive ⇨ BEAUTIFUL/ATTRACTIVE

audience

see also CINEMA, THEATRE

- a group of people who are watching and listening to a play, film or concert: **audience** (*with singular or plural verb*) ◦ *The audience was/were getting bored.* ◦ *a large and enthusiastic audience*
- the part of a theatre, cinema, etc where the audience sit: **auditorium**

audience *contd.*

- in a theatre, cinema, etc, each member of the audience has a **seat** ∘ *Did you manage to get a good seat?*

- a person who goes regularly to the theatre: **theatregoer** (*AmE* **theatergoer**)
- a person who goes regularly to the cinema: **cinema-goer** (*AmE* **movie-goer**)
- a person who goes regularly to concerts: **concert-goer**

- all the people who watch a television programme or listen to the radio: **audience** (*with singular or plural verb*) ∘ *He reached an audience of millions.* ∘ *Audience figures have been very high.*
- a person who listens to the radio: **listener**
- a person who watches the television: **viewer**

▷ more on television and radio ⇨ TELEVISION / RADIO

- a person who watches sport: **spectator**
- all the people who watch a sports event, for example a football match: **crowd** (*with singular or plural verb*) ∘ *There was a crowd of ten thousand at last night's match.*
- a large sports ground with rows of seats around it: **stadium**
- a part of the stadium where people sit and watch sport: **stand** ∘ *How much is a seat in the stands?*

▷ more on sport ⇨ SPORT

■ liking or not liking a performance
- to hit your hands together to show that you like sth: **clap** (sb/sth), **give*** (sb/sth) **a clap**, **applaud** (sb/sth) ∘ *They clapped politely when he had finished speaking.* ∘ *The players were applauded as they left the field.*
- the noise that people make when they clap: **clapping** (*noun* U), **applause** (*noun* U) ∘ *The applause went on for several minutes.*
- a period of clapping: **round of applause** ∘ *There was another round of applause.*
- when people shout during or after a performance to show that they like it, they **cheer** (sb/sth)
- the noise that people make when they cheer: **cheer**, **cheering** (*noun* U) ∘ *They gave her three cheers.*

- when people make a loud noise to show that they do not like a performance, they **boo** (**at**) (sb/sth) ∘ *The speaker was booed.*
- the noise that people make when they boo: **boo**, **booing** (*noun* U) ∘ *There were boos from the crowd when Barnes missed the goal.* ∘ *There was more booing than clapping at the end of the performance.*
- when people make a long 's' sound to show that they do not like a performance, they **hiss** (**at** sb/sth)
- the noise that people make when they hiss: **hiss**, **hissing** (*noun* U) ∘ *The audience greeted the performers with boos and hisses.*

■ **MORE ...**
- to shout a critical comment or question at a person who is speaking or performing in public: **heckle** (sb); a person who does this: **heckler** ∘ *When the audience started heckling him, he knew he had lost their sympathy.*

aunt ⇨ FAMILY

autumn ⇨ SEASON

average

1 numbers
2 things and people

1 numbers

- the number you get when you add two or more figures together and then divide the total by the number of figures you added: **average**; *adjective*: **average** ∘ *The average of 6, 7 and 8 is 7.* ∘ *the average age of people who buy cigarettes*
- to say that a number is an average of other numbers, you say **on average** ∘ *A tour guide earns about £5 an hour on average, depending on the weather and the number of tourists.*
- to do, get, etc a certain number as an average: **average** sth ∘ *My car averages 40 miles to the gallon.*
- (used about an amount) to result in an average: **average out** (**at** sth) ∘ *The bill should average out at about £6 each.*

2 things and people

- of a size or amount that is neither very large nor very small: **average**(**-sized**), **medium**(**-sized**) ∘ *an average-sized person* ∘ *'What were the crowds like?' 'About average for the time of year.'* ∘ *'Is she big or small?' 'I'd say medium.'*
- quite good but not very good: **fair**, **average** ∘ *Her work has been fair/average over the last year.*
- better/worse than the normal level: **above/below average** ∘ *His performance in the exams has been below average.*

- normal or typical; not special or unusual or different from others: **average**, **ordinary** ∘ *He's a fairly average kind of guy.* ∘ *to be of average intelligence/weight/height* ∘ *an average student.* ∘ *an ordinary person*

▷ being normal or typical ⇨ USUAL

avoid / prevent

1 keeping away from sb/sth
2 stopping sth
3 preventing movement
not allowing sth ⇨ ALLOW

1 keeping away from sb/sth

- to keep away from sb/sth: **avoid** sb/sth; *noun* (U): **avoidance** ∘ *We avoided the traffic by taking another route.* ∘ *I think he's trying to avoid me.* ∘ *Jane always avoids shopping on Saturday.*
- to manage to avoid sth: **escape** sth/doing sth ∘ *George was lucky to escape injury when his car skidded off the road.*

- not to take part in sth: **stay/keep* out of** sth ◦ *I'm just trying to keep out of trouble!*
- to make it unnecessary for sb to do sth: **save** sb (doing) sth ◦ *Thanks very much – you saved me having to go out to the shops.*

■ moving in order to avoid sth
- to move quickly in order to avoid sth: **dodge** (sth) ◦ *He managed to dodge the policeman and get into the building.*
- to change direction suddenly in order to avoid sth: **swerve** ◦ *The car swerved to avoid the children.*
- to move your head down quickly to avoid being seen or hit: **duck** ◦ *She ducked to avoid the flying ball.*

2 stopping sth
- to cause sb not to do sth: **stop** sb doing sth, (*more formal*) **prevent** sb (**from**) doing sth ◦ *Could you go and stop those children making such a noise?* ◦ *My sore throat prevented me from singing in the concert.*
- to cause sth not to happen: **prevent** sth, **prevent** sth (**from**) happening, **avoid** sth ◦ *His quick action prevented an accident.* ◦ *We were prevented from leaving by the police.* ◦ *I managed to avoid being caught.* ◦ *to try to avoid an argument*
- the act of preventing sth: **prevention** (*noun* U) ◦ *accident prevention* ◦ *the prevention of terrorism*
- a thing that you do in order to avoid danger or problems: **precaution** ◦ *to take precautions against disease*
- to limit the things that can happen or that people can do: **restrict** sb/sth (**to** sth) ◦ *The growth of the city is restricted by the surrounding mountains.* ◦ *We had almost nothing to live on and were restricted to one meal a day.*
- if you can prevent sth, it is **preventable, avoidable** ◦ *Most accidents in the home are preventable.* ◦ *avoidable problems*
- if sth cannot be prevented, it is **unavoidable, inevitable**, (*formal*) **inescapable** ◦ *an unavoidable delay* ◦ *It was inevitable that she would find out the truth in the end.* ◦ *The conclusion was inescapable: he had to return the money.*
- if you are unable to stop yourself from saying sth or doing sth, you **can't help** yourself, **can't help it, can't help** doing sth ◦ *'Can't you stop coughing?' 'I'm sorry – I can't help it!'* ◦ *I can't help crying when I watch these romantic films.*
- if you cannot prevent sth, but you decide to continue anyway, you say that it **can't be helped** ◦ *Paul can't play in the match? Oh well, it can't be helped, we'll just have to do our best without him.*

■ trying to prevent sth
- to make sb not want to do sth: **put* sb off** (sth/doing sth), **discourage** sb (**from** sth/doing sth) ◦ *Seeing that film's put me off the idea of a skiing holiday!*
- something which makes people not want to do sth: **deterrent** ◦ *the nuclear deterrent* ◦ *A small fine just isn't a big enough deterrent against dangerous driving.*
- to try to stop sth happening: **resist** (sth); *noun* (U): **resistance** ◦ *to resist change* ◦ *People have put up a lot of resistance against the new policy.*
- to try very hard to stop or prevent sth: **fight*** sth, **fight* against** sth ◦ *to fight a decision* ◦ *to fight against disease/unemployment/prejudice*
- to keep sb/sth safe from danger or attack: **protect** sb/sth (**from** sb/sth) ◦ *This cream should protect your skin from the sun.*

▷ more on protecting ⇨ PROTECT

■ stopping sb doing their work
- to prevent sb/sth from making progress: **hold*** sb/sth **back** ◦ *She's a really good student – unfortunately her poor spelling is holding her back.*
- to prevent sb from concentrating on their work: **distract** sb (**from** sth); *noun* (U): **distraction** ◦ *Some people like listening to music while they're working; others find it a distraction.*
- to prevent sth or slow down the progress that sb/sth makes: **interfere** (**with** sth) ◦ *These worries are starting to interfere with my work.*
- something which stops you from making progress: **obstacle, barrier** ◦ *One major obstacle to progress has been lack of funds.*

3 preventing movement
- to make it impossible for sb/sth to go into sth or along sth: **block** sth; not blocked: **clear** ◦ *We found that our way was blocked.* ◦ *The road is clear for miles ahead.*
- to stop sb/sth from moving: **obstruct** sb/sth; something which prevents sth moving: **obstruction** ◦ *Please move – you're obstructing the traffic.*
- to prevent sb/sth from entering a place: **shut*** sb/sth **out** (**of** a place) ◦ *The cat was bothering me so I shut it out of the room.*
- to prevent sb from leaving a place: **keep*** sb/sth **in** (a place) ◦ *I'm keeping Lucy in today – she seems to have a bad cold.*
- to prevent sb from going near a place: **keep*** sb **away** (**from** a place) ◦ *Can you keep him away while I make his birthday cake?*
- to prevent sb/sth from moving forward: **hold*** sb/sth **back** ◦ *The police were trying to hold back the demonstrators.*

---

baby

1 being a baby
2 looking after a baby
having a baby ⇨ BIRTH
see also CHILD, ANIMAL

1 being a baby
- a very young child: **baby** ◦ *a baby girl/boy* ◦ *baby clothes* ◦ *a cute baby girl*
- a baby or young child: (*rather formal*) **infant**; *noun* (U): **infancy** ◦ *'How many will be travelling?' 'Two adults and one infant.'*
- a small child who is starting to walk: **toddler**
- to move slowly with the body close to the ground or on the hands and knees: **crawl**

baby *contd.*

- to produce water from your eyes, and make a noise, because you are unhappy or have hurt yourself: **cry** ◦ *The baby cried all night.*
- to allow a liquid (saliva) to come out of the mouth: **dribble** ◦ *Oh no, she's dribbled all over me.*

▷ more on crying ⇨ **CRY**

2 looking after a baby

- to look after a baby: **take* care of** sb ◦ *When his wife left him, he had to give up his job and take care of the baby.*
- to comfort a crying child: **soothe** sb ◦ *She was crying but I managed to soothe her.*
- to hold sb closely in your arms as a sign of love: **cuddle** sb; *noun*: **cuddle** ◦ *She gave her baby a cuddle.*
- a rubber object that can be put in a baby's mouth to keep it quiet and happy: **dummy** (*AmE* **pacifier**)
- a small toy that a baby shakes to make a noise: **rattle**

■ going somewhere with a baby

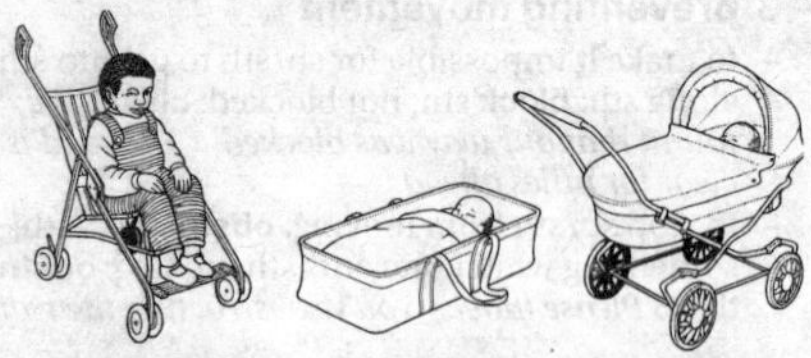

pushchair (*also* **buggy**) (*AmE* **stroller**) **carrycot** **pram** (*AmE* **baby carriage**)

■ getting a baby ready to sleep
- a bed for a baby or a young child, with high sides to prevent the child falling out: **cot** (*AmE* **crib**)
- to put a baby in its cot so that it will sleep: **put*** sb **to sleep** ◦ *You'll have to be quiet now – I've just put the baby to sleep.*

■ cleaning a baby
- to wash a baby: **bath** sb, **give*** sb **a bath**
- powder that you put on a baby to make it dry: **baby powder** (*noun* U)
- a liquid that you put on a baby to make its skin soft: **baby lotion** (*noun* U)
- a piece of soft thick cloth or paper that a baby or a very young child wears around its bottom and between its legs: **nappy** (*AmE* **diaper**) ◦ *disposable nappies*
- to remove a dirty nappy and put a clean nappy on a baby: **change** sb's **nappy, change** a baby ◦ *Does her nappy need changing?* ◦ *Is there somewhere I can change the baby?*
- to make sth wet by urinating: **wet** sth ◦ *I think he's just wet his nappy – he's crying.*
- a bowl that children sit on when they are too small to use a toilet: **potty**

■ giving food to a baby
- to give food to a baby: **feed*** sb; *noun*: **feed** ◦ *Is it time for his feed yet?*
- food which is specially prepared for babies: **baby food** (*noun* U)
- a piece of cloth or plastic that small children wear under their chin to protect their clothes while they are eating: **bib**
- a special high chair which babies sit in when they are eating: **high chair**
- the milk from a mother's breast: **breast milk** (*noun* U); to feed a baby with milk from the breast: **breastfeed*** (sb); a baby which is fed in this way is **breastfed** ◦ *Are you going to breastfeed?*
- a bottle which is used to give milk to a baby: (**feeding**) **bottle**
- to feed a baby with milk from a bottle: **bottle-feed*** (sb); a baby which is fed in this way is **bottle-fed**

▷ people who care for babies and children ⇨ **CHILD**

back

- going back ⇨ **COME/GO**
- position ⇨ **PLACE**[2]

bad

> **1** bad
> **2** worse
> **3** very bad; worst
> morally bad ⇨ **RIGHT/WRONG**[2]
> **see also GOOD**

1 bad

- not of a good quality or standard: **bad, poor** ◦ *Don't go to that restaurant – the service is really bad.* ◦ *poor quality paper*
- in a bad way: **badly** ◦ *a badly written book*
- not good or pleasant: **bad, nasty, horrible, unpleasant**; *nouns* (U): **nastiness, unpleasantness** ◦ *I've had a really bad day today.* ◦ *He made some really nasty comments about my work.* ◦ *I had a horrible feeling that something awful was going to happen.* ◦ *There's a rather unpleasant smell coming from the fridge.* ◦ *I don't like all this unpleasantness – let's be nice to each other.*
- not able to do sth well: **bad** (**at** sth), **no good** at sth, **hopeless** (at sth) ◦ *bad parents/drivers* ◦ *I'm sorry, I'm no good at making speeches.* ◦ *Alex is hopeless at writing letters.*

▷ not good at doing sth ⇨ **SKILL**

- if sth makes you ill, unhealthy or unhappy, it is **bad** (**for** you) ◦ *Eating too much fatty food is bad for you.*
- in bad health: **not well, ill**; *noun* (U): **illness**

▷ more on illness ⇨ **ILLNESS**

- if sth is not what is needed for a particular purpose, it is **wrong, unsuitable** (**for** sth) ◦ *That's the wrong way to put on your skis.* ◦ *I feel I chose the wrong university.* ◦ *That sort of paint is unsuitable for the outside of a building.*

▷ more on being suitable ➪ **USEFUL/SUITABLE**

- not good enough: **unsatisfactory** ◦ *Only two people came to the class yesterday – this is quite unsatisfactory.*
- below the usual or expected quality: **not up to standard, below standard, second rate** ◦ *I'm afraid your work isn't up to standard.* ◦ *That was rather a second-rate performance, wasn't it?*
- not good or bad: (*informal*) **so-so** ◦ *'How are you today?' 'Mm, so-so.'*

- to make sth useless or not as good as before: **damage** sth; the effect of damaging sth: **damage** (*noun* U) ◦ *The fire destroyed the library and damaged some nearby buildings.* ◦ *to damage sb's reputation* ◦ *The floods caused millions of pounds' worth of damage.*
- to damage sb's health, a situation, etc: **harm** sb/sth; *noun* (U): **harm**; causing harm: **harmful**
- to be careless or make a mistake, with the result that sth is no longer good: **spoil** sth, **ruin** sth ◦ *Don't put too much salt in the soup – you'll spoil it.* ◦ *I'm afraid I've ruined your jacket – I'll buy you a new one.*

▷ more on damage ➪ **DAMAGE**

2 worse

- the comparative form of 'bad'; of a lower quality, less suitable, etc: **worse** (**than** sb/sth) ◦ *This shop is even worse than the last one we went into.* ◦ *I was frightened of getting into worse difficulties.*
- the comparative of 'badly'; in a way that is less good: **worse** (**than** sb/sth) ◦ Good heavens! you sing even worse than I do!
- lower in quality: **inferior** ◦ *The clothes were cheaper but also of inferior quality.*

- to become worse than before: **get* worse, worsen, deteriorate**; *noun* (U): **deterioration** ◦ *The situation is getting worse by the day.* ◦ *Unfortunately her condition has worsened since the last time you visited.* ◦ *The standards in the school have deteriorated badly since the previous headmaster left.*

- (used about a situation that was already bad) to become worse: **go* from bad to worse** ◦ *Things seem to be going from bad to worse – what are we going to do now?*
- to make sth worse: **aggravate** sth ◦ *Don't laugh at him – you'll only aggravate the situation.*

3 very bad; worst

- worse than anything/anybody else: **worst** ◦ *It was the worst holiday I had ever had.* ◦ *What has been the worst experience in your life?*
- in a way that is worse than any other: (the) **worst** ◦ *A lot of us sang badly but I'm sure I sang the worst.*

- very bad: **awful, terrible, dreadful** ◦ *She failed her exams? How awful!* ◦ *He's a terrible driver – he's already had three accidents this year.*
- extremely bad: **atrocious** (*adverb* **atrociously**), **appalling** (*adverb* **appallingly**), **horrendous** (*adverb* **horrendously**) ◦ *I think she's behaved atrociously.* ◦ *How could he tell all those lies? It's quite appalling.* ◦ *Sorry we're late – the traffic on the motorway was horrendous.*
- very bad, and therefore disappointing: (*informal*) **lousy** ◦ *I had a lousy time at the party – I felt really ill all evening.*

Note: lousy cannot be used to talk about sth that is necessarily bad, such as an accident or failing exams, but only about sth that might be good, like a party.

- a bad problem, situation, etc is **serious**; *noun* (U): **seriousness** ◦ *a serious illness* ◦ *The pollution in this area is getting serious.* ◦ *I don't think any of us appreciated the seriousness of the situation.*
- too bad to bear: **unbearable** (*adverb* **unbearably**), **intolerable** (*adverb* **intolerably**) ◦ *unbearable pain* ◦ *intolerable suspense* ◦ *The journey seemed intolerably long.*

- frightening, evil: **sinister, horrible, horrific** ◦ *There's a rather sinister feeling in this house – I don't like it at all.* ◦ *The horrible face of the monster suddenly appeared at the window.* ◦ *I've just had a horrific dream.*

- extremely unpleasant; that can make you feel ill: **disgusting, foul, revolting** ◦ *The beds were uncomfortable and the food was disgusting.* ◦ *A foul/revolting smell was coming from the river.*

■ very bad events

- (used to talk about an event) having extremely bad results: **catastrophic, disastrous** (*adverb* **disastrously**); an event which has very bad effects: **catastrophe, disaster** ◦ *'How was your exam?' 'Catastrophic.'* ◦ *My interview went disastrously.* ◦ *There's been a terrible disaster – hundreds of people have been killed.*
- (used to talk about an event) causing death or great sadness: **tragic** (*adverb* **tragically**); an event which causes death or great sadness: **tragedy** ◦ *It's quite tragic, what happened to that young couple.* ◦ *It's a tragedy that so many young people have never had a job.*
- a bad surprise: **shock, blow** ◦ *I think it came as quite a blow for him when he lost his job.*

- bad consequences: **ill effects** ◦ *Despite eating the fish, I didn't suffer any ill effects.*

bag

see also CONTAINER

▷ see picture on next page

- a bag for carrying sports clothes and equipment: **sports bag**
- a small bag, worn on a belt around your waist, used for carrying money and other possessions: (*BrE, informal*) **bumbag**

■ using bags for travelling

- the bags, etc used for carrying your things on a journey: **luggage** (*noun* U), **baggage** (*noun* U) ◦ *'How much luggage are you taking with you?' 'Just one suitcase.'* ◦ *The security people were carefully checking everyone's baggage.*

bag *contd.*

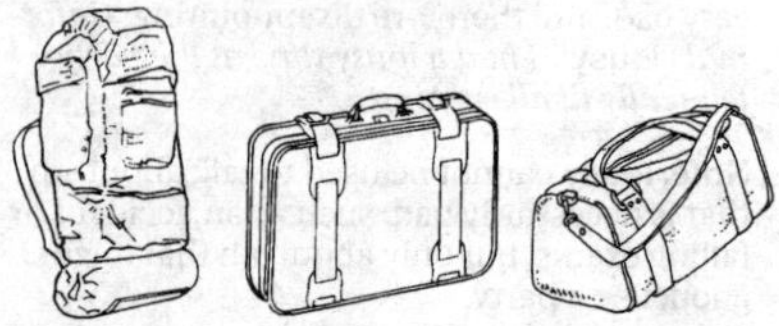

rucksack (*AmE* **backpack**) **suitcase** **holdall** (*AmE* **carry-all**)

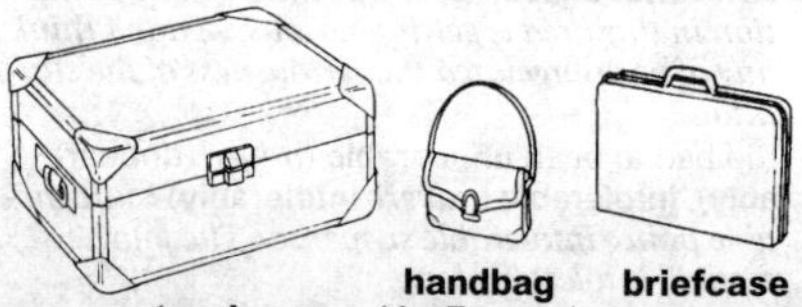

trunk **handbag** (*AmE* **purse**) **briefcase**

- luggage that weighs more than the limit set by an airline: **excess baggage** (*noun* U)
- bags, etc that you take with you to the seating area of an aeroplane: **hand luggage** (*AmE* **hand baggage**) (*noun* U) ◦ *Can I take my guitar as hand luggage?*
- a piece of paper with your name and address on that you tie to a bag: **label** ◦ *Have you put labels on all your bags?*

- to put your things into a suitcase, etc before you travel or go on holiday: **pack** (sth); *noun* (U): **packing** ◦ *Don't forget to pack your toothbrush!* ◦ *Have you packed yet?* ◦ *I haven't done my packing yet.*
- to take your things out of a suitcase, etc when you arrive somewhere: **unpack** (sth) ◦ *I'll meet you in the bar later. I want to unpack first.*

- a person whose job is to carry luggage at a station, airport, etc: **porter**
- a vehicle that you put your luggage on so that you can push it easily: (**luggage**) **trolley** (*AmE* **baggage cart**)

- the part of a car where you put luggage: **boot** (*AmE* **trunk**)
- a shelf above the seats on a train, bus, etc where you put hand-luggage: **luggage-rack**
- a place at a railway station, etc where you can leave your luggage for a short time: **left-luggage office** (*AmE* **baggage room**)

▷ more on travelling ⇨ TRAVEL

bake ⇨ COOK

ball

see also GAME

- the round thing that people use in games: **ball** ◦ *The children were playing with a ball in the street.* ◦ *a ball game* (= a game played with a ball)

- to make a ball move through the air with your hand(s): **throw*** sth; *noun*: **throw** ◦ *Throw me the ball.* ◦ *That was a good throw.*
- to make a ball move with your foot: **kick** sth; *noun*: **kick** ◦ *He kicked the ball into the net.* ◦ *Give it a good kick.*
- to hit a ball with your head: **head** sth; *noun*: **header** ◦ *He headed the ball into the goal.*
- to make a ball move with a bat, racket, etc: **hit*** sth; *noun*: **hit** ◦ *She hit the ball over the net.*

- when sb throws a ball and you manage to take hold of it in your hand, you **catch*** it; *noun*: **catch** ◦ *Catch!* (= catch the ball) ◦ *He made/took a brilliant catch.*
- to give the ball to another player in a game, either by throwing it or by kicking it: **pass** sth (**to** sb); *noun*: **pass** ◦ *Pass the ball over here!* ◦ *a long accurate pass*

- when a ball moves quickly up or away after it has hit a hard surface, it **bounces**; to make a ball do this: **bounce** sth ◦ *The ball bounced over the fence and disappeared into the grass.* ◦ *Tennis players bounce the ball a few times before they begin to play.*

bank

see also PAY[1], MONEY

- an organization which keeps money safely for its customers: **bank**
- a type of bank which specializes in lending money to people who want to buy a house: **building society**
- a local office of a bank: **branch** ◦ *Where's the nearest branch of the Bank of Scotland?*
- the type of business done by banks: **banking** (*noun* U) ◦ *the financial sector, including banking, insurance and investment services*

- the person who is in charge of a branch of a bank: (**bank**) **manager**
- a person who works in a bank: (**bank**) **clerk**
- the person that you pay money to or get money from: **cashier**
- a person who owns a bank or who has an important job in a bank: **banker**

- the long flat surface where customers are served: **counter**
- a machine outside a bank where you can get money: **cash dispenser, cash machine**

- to keep your money in a particular bank: **bank with** sth ◦ *I bank with Barclays.*
- the arrangement by which a bank looks after your money: (**bank**) **account**

■ keeping your money in a bank

- an account from which you can take out money at any time by using a cheque book or cheque card: **current account** (*AmE* **checking account**)
- an account where your money earns interest: **deposit account, savings account**
- an account which you share with sb else: **joint account**

- to start a new account with a bank: **open** an account
- to stop using an account: **close** an account

■ using a bank account
- to add money to your account: **pay*/put*** money **in** (**to** an account) ◦ *I paid £500 into my account.*
- a book used for putting money into or taking money out of some kinds of account: **passbook**

- to take money from your account: **take*/get*** money **out** (of an account), (*more formal*) **withdraw*** money (**from** an account) ◦ *I'd like to withdraw £200, please.*
- to get money from your account you write a **cheque** (*AmE* **check**) or use your **passbook**
- to get money from a cash machine you need a **bank card** and a secret number called a **PIN number**

▷ more on cheques ⇨ CHEQUE

- when a bank puts money into your account, it **credits** your account (**with** sth); when it takes money out, it **debits** your account (**with** sth) ◦ *They told me they had credited my account with £20.*
- an arrangement by which a bank pays a certain amount of money regularly, for example to pay a bill: **standing order**
- an arrangement by which money is automatically taken out of your account in order to pay a bill: **direct debit** (*noun* C/U) ◦ *I pay my electricity bill by direct debit.*

■ the amount of money in an account
- the amount of money in your account: (**bank**) **balance**
- a list showing how much you have paid into your account, how much you have taken out and how much you have left: **statement**
- if you still have some money in your account, you are **in credit**, (*informal*) **in the black**
- if you spend more money than you have in your account, you are **overdrawn**, (*informal*) **in the red**
- an amount of money that you spend that is more than the amount that you have in your account: **overdraft** ◦ *She wants to pay off her overdraft before she gets married.*

bar/pub

see also ALCOHOL, BEER, WINE, DRINK

- a place where people go to buy alcoholic drinks and meet their friends: **pub** (*AmE* **bar**), (*formal*) **public house** ◦ *We're off to the pub for a beer.*
- the pub you usually go to is your **local**
- a room (in a pub, hotel, restaurant, etc) where (especially alcoholic) drinks are served: **bar** ◦ *a hotel bar* ◦ *a cocktail bar* ◦ *a coffee bar* ◦ *a theatre bar*

- the long narrow high table or counter where drinks are served: **the bar** ◦ *'Where's Mary?' 'I think she's at the bar getting some drinks.'*
- a machine (often found in bars and pubs) which you can play games on: **fruit machine, slot machine**
- a machine which plays music: **jukebox** ◦ *Shall I put something on the jukebox?*
- some games which people sometimes play in bars and pubs: **pool, billiards, darts**

▷ more on pool, billiards and darts ⇨ GAME

■ people in a pub
- a man who serves you drinks from behind the bar: **barman** (*AmE* **bartender**); a woman who serves you drinks: **barmaid**
- the man/woman who owns or manages a pub: **landlord/landlady**
- a person who usually goes to one particular pub: **regular** ◦ *They know me well here. I'm a regular.*

■ drinking in a pub
- to choose a drink: **have** sth ◦ *What'll you have?* ◦ *I think I'll have a gin and tonic.*
- to fetch a drink (for example from a bar): **get*** sth ◦ *Could you get me another gin and tonic?*
- to get a drink for another person: **buy*** sb sth ◦ *I'll buy you a beer.*
- a number of drinks (one for each member of a group): **round** ◦ *Shall we have another round?* ◦ *It's my round!* (= It's my turn to buy the drinks.)

- the times that a pub is open: **opening hours**
- the time that a pub closes: **closing time** ◦ *We'd better finish our drinks – it's almost closing time.*
- the last ten or twenty minutes before closing time: **drinking-up time**

■ **MORE ...**
- to visit a lot of different pubs in an evening: **go* on a pub crawl** ◦ *'What are you doing tonight?' 'I'm going on a pub crawl with some friends.'*

basketball ⇨ SPORT

bathroom

see also TOILET, ROOM, HOUSE

- a room where there is a bath and a washbasin and sometimes a toilet: **bathroom**

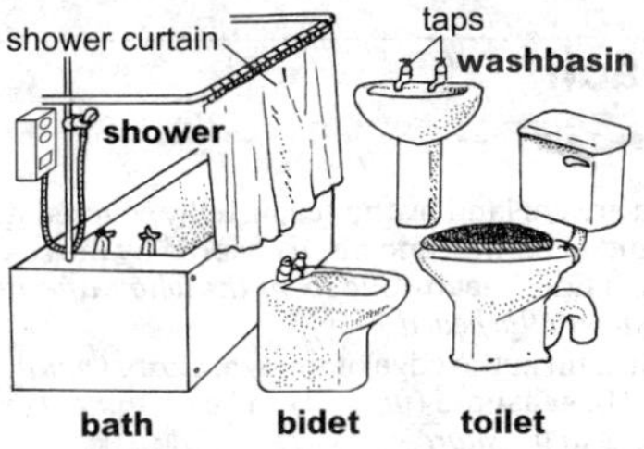

- a kind of handle that you turn to let water into a bath, basin, etc: **tap** ◦ *the hot/cold tap*
- to turn a tap to start or stop water coming out of it: **turn** sth **on/off** ◦ *Please don't forget to turn the hot water tap off.*
- to start water flowing into a bath: **run*** a bath ◦ *Shall I run your bath for you?*
- if the bath is so full that water pours over the edge, it **overflows** ◦ *Water came through the ceiling when the bath overflowed upstairs.*

bathroom *contd.*

- to allow water to go out of the bath, basin, etc: **let*** the water **out** ◦ *If the bath is too full, let some of the water out.*
- the hole where the water leaves a bath or basin: **plughole**
- a piece of rubber, metal or plastic which fits tightly into a plughole: **plug** ◦ *to put the plug in* ◦ *to pull the plug out*

- a small cloth that you use for washing your face: **flannel, facecloth** (*AmE* **wash-cloth**)
- a piece of cloth or paper that you use for drying yourself: **towel** ◦ *a hand towel* ◦ *a bath towel* ◦ *paper towels*
- a bar that you hang towels on: **towel rail**
- a mat that you stand on beside a bath: **bath mat**

- a substance which you use with water to wash yourself or to clean things: **soap** (*noun* U) ◦ *a bar of soap* ◦ *bath soap*
- a liquid that you use for washing your hair: **shampoo** (*noun* U)
- a liquid that you can add to the water in a bath to make a lot of bubbles and a pleasant smell: **bubble bath** (*noun* U), **bath oil** (*noun* U)

▷ having a bath or shower ⇨ WASH

- a kind of loose coat that you wear before or after a bath: **dressing gown, bathrobe** (*AmE also* **robe**)

■ **MORE . . .**
- a type of bath where you sit in a room which is very hot and full of steam: **sauna**; a room where you can have this kind of bath: **sauna** ◦ *to have/take a sauna*

- when a bathroom joins another room as part of a set, it is **en suite** ◦ *a bedroom with en suite bathroom*

beach

see also SEA

- an area of land by the sea, usually covered with sand or stones, and often covered by the sea at high tide: **beach** ◦ *She spent the whole afternoon lying on the beach.*
- the land at the edge of the sea: **shore** (*noun* C/U), **seashore** (*noun* U) ◦ *The swimmer kept close to the shore.*
- the type of ground found in deserts and on beaches, made of tiny pieces of stone: **sand** (*noun* U); having a lot of sand: **sandy** ◦ *children playing in the sand*
- a smooth, round stone that is found near the sea: **pebble** ◦ *a pebble beach* (= a beach with a lot of pebbles)
- the hard outer part of a small sea animal which you can find at the beach: **shell**

- a steep, rocky part of the coast: **cliff**
- a low hill of sand by the sea or in the desert: **dune, sand dune**

- a raised line of water which moves across the surface of the sea: **wave**
- the regular rising and falling of the level of the sea: **tide** ◦ *high/low tide*

▷ more on waves and tides ⇨ SEA

- an area on the coast where people go on holiday: **seaside** (*noun singular*) ◦ *a holiday by the seaside*
- a town with a lot of hotels by the sea: (**seaside**) **resort**
- the street which goes along the edge of the sea in a seaside town: **front, seafront**
- a large structure which is built out into the sea, and which has entertainments and amusements for people who are on holiday: **pier**

■ activities by the sea

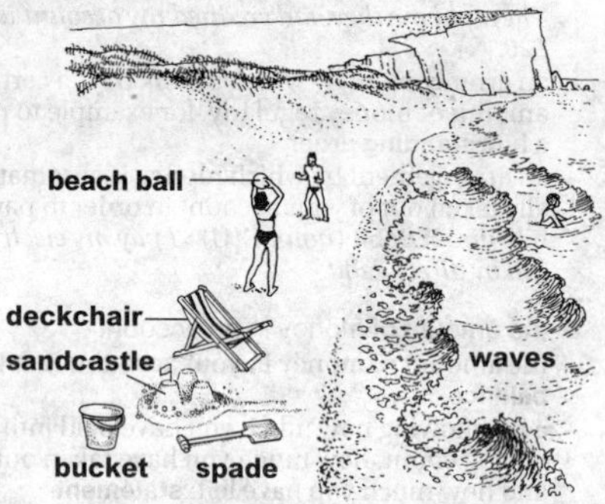

- to swim in the sea or in a lake or river: **bathe**; *noun* (U): **bathing** ◦ *a good beach for bathing*
- to walk in bare feet in shallow water, for example in the sea: **paddle** ◦ *We sat on the sand and watched the children paddling.*
- to take off most of your clothes and sit or lie in the sun to make your skin go brown: **sunbathe**
- to stand or lie on a special board (a **surfboard**) and ride on a wave towards the shore: **surf**; a person who surfs: **surfer** ◦ *We spent the day surfing and sunbathing.*
- to swim with a tube (a **snorkel**) which allows you to breathe underwater: **snorkel**

▷ swimming ⇨ SWIM

bean ⇨ VEGETABLE

beautiful/attractive

1 finding sb/sth attractive
2 people
3 things
4 places
5 not attractive
liking a person or thing ⇨ LIKE[2]

1 finding sb/sth attractive

- if you find sb/sth interesting or pleasing, you are **attracted** (**to** them/it); to cause sb to find sb/sth

interesting or pleasing: **attract** sb (**to** sb/sth) ∘ *We were attracted to one another from the moment we met.* ∘ *What attracted you to the job?*
- (used about things or ideas) to interest or please sb: **appeal** (**to** sb); *noun* (U): **appeal**; *adjective*: **appealing** ∘ *The idea of working abroad doesn't appeal to me at all.* ∘ *After I saw the accident, motor-racing lost its appeal for me.* ∘ *A day on the river? That sounds appealing.*
- the experience of being attracted to sb: **attraction** (**for/to** sb) (*noun* U/C) ∘ *sexual attraction* ∘ *I felt an immediate attraction to her.*

2 people
- a person's appearance in general: **looks** (*noun plural*) ∘ *He was known for his good looks rather than his talent.*
- a woman or girl who is pleasing to look at is **pretty**, **attractive**; very attractive: **beautiful** ∘ *Do you think she's attractive?*
- a man or boy who is pleasing to look at is **attractive**, **good-looking**, **handsome**
- (used mainly about children and babies) prettily attractive: **sweet**, (*especially AmE*) **cute** ∘ *a sweet little baby* ∘ *a child with a sweet face* ∘ *I think babies look cute in blue and pink.*

- excitingly attractive: **glamorous**; *noun* (U): **glamour** ∘ *She looks very glamorous in her expensive new clothes.*
- sexually attractive: **seductive**, (*informal*) **sexy** ∘ *She thought he looked very sexy in his black leather jacket.*

- to look as attractive as possible: **look** your **best**
- substances that you use to make yourself more attractive: **cosmetics** (*noun plural*)
- a place where people go for beauty treatments: **beauty salon**, **beauty parlour** (*AmE* **beauty parlor**); a person whose job is to try to make people look beautiful: **beautician**

▷ more on cosmetics ⇨ COSMETICS

3 things
- if sth is pleasing to look at, listen to, think about, etc, it is **attractive** (*adverb* **attractively**); *noun* (U): **attractiveness** ∘ *an attractive idea/personality* ∘ *The table was very attractively decorated.*
- something that people find attractive: **attraction** (**of** sth) ∘ *a tourist attraction* ∘ *the attractions of living in the country*

- very attractive or pleasing: **beautiful**, (*informal*) **lovely**; *noun* (U): **beauty** ∘ *beautiful eyes/music/weather* ∘ *What a lovely day!* ∘ *the beauty of the countryside*
- pleasant to look at: **pretty**; *noun* (U): **prettiness** ∘ *pretty wallpaper*

- attractive, making you want to do or try it: **tempting** ∘ *a tempting offer* ∘ *The food looked very tempting.*
- so interesting that you must do or try it: **irresistible** ∘ *an irresistible suggestion*

4 places
- a place which is famous for its attractive scenery: **beauty spot**
- pretty and interesting: **picturesque** ∘ *a picturesque little village in the hills*
- having beautiful scenery: **scenic** ∘ *We took the scenic route home, avoiding the motorway and the city.*
- very impressive and beautiful: **spectacular** ∘ *a spectacular view of the mountains*

5 not attractive
- not attractive: **unattractive**
- (used especially about a woman or girl) not attractive: **plain** ∘ *I find her rather plain compared to her sisters.*
- very unattractive: **ugly**; *noun* (U): **ugliness** ∘ *an ugly building/car*
- very ugly: **hideous** ∘ *a hideous orange and purple carpet*

- a very large and ugly building: **monstrosity**, **eyesore** ∘ *The tower block was a monstrosity which should never have been built.* ∘ *The new council building is a real eyesore.*

■ **MORE ...**
- to make sth appear more attractive than it really is: **glamorize** sth ∘ *Films often glamorize violence.*

---

because
- what makes sth happen ⇨ CAUSE/EFFECT
- giving the reason for sth ⇨ REASON

---

become ⇨ CHANGE

---

bed

1 beds
2 the things on a bed
3 bedrooms
4 going to bed and getting up
see also SLEEP, ROOM, FURNITURE

1 beds
- a piece of furniture that you lie on when you sleep: **bed**
- a bed for one person: **single bed**
- a bed for two people: **double bed**
- a pair of single beds: **twin beds**
- a pair of beds built one on top of the other: **bunk beds**
- a bed for a baby: **cot** (*AmE* **crib**)
- a bed that can be folded up: **camp bed** (*AmE* **cot**)
- a sofa that you can make into a bed: **sofa bed**

- the top end of a bed is its **head**
- the bottom end of a bed is its **foot** ∘ *He was standing at the foot of the bed.*
- the area that is next to a bed is the **bedside** ∘ *She sat at his bedside all night long.*

a train with beds: **sleeper**; a railway coach which has beds: **sleeping car** ∘ *the overnight sleeper from London to Inverness*
- a sleeping place on a train, ship, etc: **berth** ∘ *a cabin with four berths* ∘ *a top berth*

bed *contd.*

- a bed which is built into the wall, for example on a train or ship: **bunk**
- a bed made of canvas or strong net, which is hung up at both ends: **hammock**
- a large, soft bag that you use for sleeping in when you go camping, etc: **sleeping bag**

2 the things on a bed

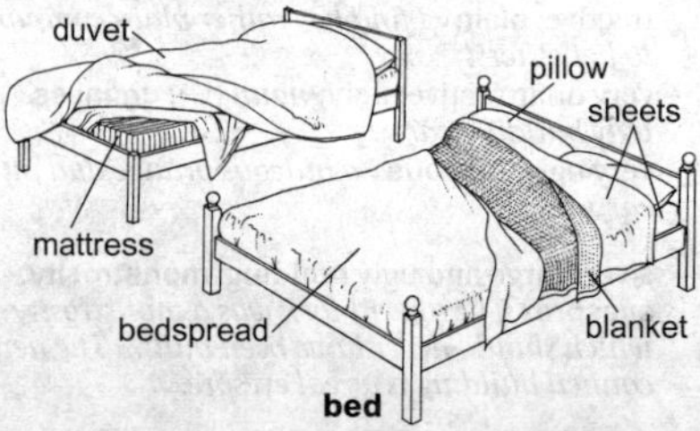

bed

- a cover for a pillow: **pillowcase**
- the sheet that goes on top of you: **top sheet**; the sheet that goes underneath you: **bottom sheet**

- a large piece of material (often made of wool) which keeps you warm in bed: **blanket**
- a thick cover that is filled with warm material, for example feathers: **duvet**, **quilt** (*AmE* **comforter**)
- a cover for a duvet or a quilt: **duvet/quilt cover**
- an attractive cover for a bed that you put on top of sheets and blankets: **bedspread**
- a general word for the sheets, blankets, etc on a bed: **bedclothes** (*noun plural*) ◦ *She pulled the bedclothes off him and said: 'Get up!'*

- a blanket which is heated by electricity: **electric blanket**
- a rubber container that is filled with hot water and put in a bed to warm it: **hot-water bottle**

■ making a bed
- when you tidy the bedclothes on a bed after sleeping in it, you **make*** the bed ◦ *The children all had to make their own beds.*
- if the bedclothes are untidy after a bed has been slept in, the bed is **unmade**
- when you replace bedclothes with clean ones, you **change** them or **change the bed** ◦ *The chambermaid in the hotel changes the sheets every day.* ◦ *We usually change the beds once a week.*

3 bedrooms

- a room which is used for sleeping in: **bedroom** ◦ *a double bedroom*
- a large bedroom with a number of beds in it, especially in a school, etc: **dormitory** ◦ *the girls' dormitory*
- a hospital room with beds in it: **ward** ◦ *the children's ward*

▷ bedrooms in hotels ⇨ HOTEL

■ the furniture in a bedroom

- a small table which is kept beside the bed: **bedside table**

4 going to bed and getting up

■ going to bed
- when you decide to rest in a bed, usually for the night, you **go* to bed** ◦ *Last night I went to bed early.*
- when you lie down on a bed, under the covers, you **get* into bed** ◦ *I fell asleep as soon as I got into bed.*
- when you are lying or sitting under the covers of a bed, you are **in bed** ◦ *The children are already in bed.*
- if you help a child to go to bed, you **put*** them **to bed** ◦ *I'll ring you after putting the children to bed.*

- to be in a flat position: **lie*** ◦ *I was lying in bed listening to the radio.*
- to get into a lying position: **lie* down**; to rest on a bed for a short time: **have a lie-down** ◦ *She lay down on the bed and fell asleep.*
- to get into a position under a cover that makes you feel safe, warm and comfortable: **snuggle down** ◦ *I snuggled down under the blanket to get warm.*

■ the time that you go to bed
- the time when you usually go to bed is (your) **bedtime** ◦ *I'm too tired to do any more, it's past my bedtime.*
- if you go to bed earlier/later than usual, you **have an early/late night** ◦ *I've had three late nights in a row and I' m worn out!*
- if you go to bed after your usual bedtime, you **stay up** ◦ *I stayed up to hear the election results.*
- if you do not go to bed because you are waiting for a person to come home, you **wait up** (**for** them) ◦ *Don't wait up – I'll be back very late.*
- if a person prevents you from going to bed, they **keep*** you **up** ◦ *I hope we're not keeping you up?*

■ what people wear in bed
- a soft loose shirt and trousers which men and women wear for sleeping: **pyjamas** (*AmE* **pajamas**) (*noun plural*); the top part of pyjamas: **pyjama top**; the bottom part: **pyjama trousers/bottoms** ◦ *a pair of pyjamas* ◦ *He's wearing green pyjama trousers and a red pyjama top from a different pair.*
- a loose dress which women wear for sleeping: **nightdress**, (*informal*) **nightie**
- a long shirt that a man or boy wears for sleeping in: **nightshirt**

■ getting up
- when you leave your bed after resting, you **get* up** ◦ *What time do you usually get up in the morning?*
- after you get up, you are **up (and about)** ◦ *He's usually up and about by 7.30.*
- to leave a bed (for any purpose): **get* out of bed** ◦ *I heard a noise and got out of bed to see what it was.*
- when you have been in bed, but are not now, you are **out of bed** ◦ *What are you doing out of bed – the doctor said you should stay there!*

- if you usually get up early, you are an **early riser**
- if you stay in bed later than usual, you **lie* in, have a lie-in**

bee

see also INSECT

- a black and yellow striped insect which makes honey: **bee** ◦ *a bee sting* ◦ *to be stung by a bee* ◦ *a swarm of bees* (= a group of bees moving together) ◦ *Bees were buzzing* (= making a noise) *in the flowers.*
- a very large bee that makes a loud noise when it flies: **bumble-bee**

- the sweet yellow sticky stuff produced by bees which people eat on bread: **honey** (*noun* U) ◦ *a pot of honey* ◦ *a slice of bread and honey*
- a structure made of wax in which bees make honey and keep their eggs: **honeycomb**

- a type of box that people use for keeping bees in: **hive, beehive**
- a person who keeps bees: **beekeeper**

beer

see also ALCOHOL

- a kind of alcoholic drink that is made from grain: **beer** (*noun* U/C) ◦ *In England beer is more popular than wine.* ◦ *'Anything to drink, sir?' 'Yes, I'll have a beer* (= a glass of beer) *please.'* ◦ *This is a really excellent beer* (= type of beer). *Where is it made?*

- light, yellow-coloured beer: **lager** (*noun* U/C)
- dark and bitter-tasting beer: **bitter** (*noun* U/C)
- strong black beer: **stout** (*noun* U/C)
- strong beer, light in colour, usually bottled: **pale/light/brown ale** (*noun* U/C)
- beer mixed with lemonade: **shandy** (*noun* U/C)

■ drinking beer
- beer which comes out of a tap in a pub or bar is called **draught** (*AmE* **draft**) beer ◦ *a pint of draught bitter*
- beer is also sold in **bottles** or **cans**; beer sold in a bottle: **bottled** beer; beer sold in a can: **canned** beer ◦ *They've only got it in cans, not on draught.* ◦ *bottled lager*
- a glass that you drink beer from: **beer glass**; a glass with beer, etc in it: **glass of** sth ◦ *Can you get me another glass of lager?*
- the amount of beer you buy in a pub or bar is usually a **pint** or a **half** (**pint**) ◦ *'Do you want a pint?' 'No thanks, just a half please.'*
- the white airy beer on top of a glass of beer: **froth** (*noun* U)

- a place where people go to buy and drink beer, etc: **bar, pub**
- a shop where beer and other alcoholic drinks can be bought: **off-licence** (*AmE* **package store**)

▷ more on bars and pubs ⇨ BAR/PUB

■ making beer
- beer is made in a factory called a **brewery**
- the grain which beer is made from: **barley** (*noun* U)
- flowers from the hop plant which are used for making beer: **hops** (*noun plural*)
- to make beer: **brew** sth ◦ *He brews all his own beer.*
- a person whose job is brewing beer: **brewer**
- beer may be delivered to a bar or pub in a large container called a **barrel** or a **keg**

before/after

see also FIRST/NEXT/LAST, EARLY/LATE

■ before
- earlier (than sb/sth): **before** (...), **earlier** (**on**) ◦ *Have you been there before?* ◦ *the day before my birthday* ◦ *She got there before us.* ◦ *I'll come and pick you up an hour before the film's due to start.* ◦ *I had a snack before going to bed.* ◦ *'Have you seen Sara?' 'Yes, I saw her earlier on.'*
- a particular length of time before now: **ago** ◦ *About four months ago I changed jobs.* ◦ *I last saw Mary about a year ago.*
- before a particular time or event: **in advance, beforehand** ◦ *Do we have to pay for the tickets in advance?* ◦ *Can you let me know beforehand how much the meal will cost?*
- coming before sth else that is more important: **preliminary** ◦ *They have to make some preliminary enquiries before they make any arrests.* ◦ *a preliminary exam*

- at an earlier time, but not now: **previously, formerly** ◦ *He was formerly managing director of the company.*
- belonging to an earlier time: **previous, former, old** ◦ *The previous owners did not take care of the place very well.* ◦ *Yesterday I met my former history teacher.* ◦ *I much prefer this house to their old one.*

- to exist or have a position before sb/sth: **be/come* before** sb/sth, **precede** sb/sth; *adjective*: **preceding** ◦ *A comes before B in the alphabet.* ◦ *Ignore the preceding comments.*

■ after
- later (than sb/sth): **after** (...), **afterwards** (*AmE* **afterward**), **later** (**on**) ◦ *The bus came soon after* ◦ *After a while, she decided to go.* ◦ *We arrived after them.* ◦ *After listening to his explanation, I realized he was speaking the truth.* ◦ *The postman usually comes after I leave the house in the*

before / after *contd.*

morning. ◦ *We can go for a drink afterwards if you like.* ◦ *I'll finish off the ironing later.*
– after a period of time: **in ...** ◦ *Can you come back in an hour?*
– at a later time: (*formal*) **subsequently** ◦ *She joined the company as a secretary and subsequently went on to become a director.*
– belonging to a later time or happening afterwards: **later**, (*formal*) **subsequent** ◦ *We can decide that at a later date/stage.* ◦ *I thought that was the end of the matter but subsequent events proved me wrong.*
– to exist or have a position after sb/sth: **be/come* after** sb/sth, **follow** sb/sth; *adjective*: **following** ◦ *April comes after March.* ◦ *Night follows day.*

■ people
– a person who used to be sth in the past can be called an **ex-...** ◦ *He bumped into his ex-wife in Seattle.* ◦ *the ex-president*
– a person who was previously in the job or position that sb is in now: **predecessor** ◦ *Who was Clinton's predecessor as president?*
– to have a job or important position after sb else: **succeed** sb (**as** sth) ◦ *Clinton succeeded Bush as President of the United States.*
– a person who succeeds sb: **successor to** sb (**as** sth) ◦ *a successor to the President* ◦ *her successor as chief executive*

begin

1 beginning
2 causing sth to begin
3 beginning again
see also END / FINISH

1 beginning

– to take place from a particular time: **start, begin*** ◦ *Does the show start at seven or seven thirty?* ◦ *What time does the class begin?*
– to take the first action in doing sth: **start** sth, **begin*** sth ◦ *I usually start work around half past eight.* ◦ *When did they start going out together?* ◦ *She stood up and began to tidy the room.*
– (used about an illness, pain, etc) to begin: **come* on** ◦ *I couldn't concentrate because I had a headache coming on.*

Note: begin and **start** can be followed by 'to' or the '-ing' form of a verb, but when **begin** and **start** are in the '-ing' form, they must be followed by 'to': ◦ *Oh no, it's starting to rain.* **Start** is more common than **begin** in spoken English.

– to begin to happen or exist in a particular place or at a particular time: (*formal*) **originate** (**in** sth), **originate** (**from/with** sb) ◦ *The custom originated in the nineteenth century.* ◦ *This style of architecture originated from the ancient Greeks.*

■ the time or place that sth starts
– the time that sth begins: **beginning, start** ◦ *I haven't seen you since the beginning of term.*
– the time when, place where or reason why sth starts: **origin** (*noun* C/U) ◦ *The revolutionary movement had its origins in the previous century.*
– a place or point where sth begins: **starting point** ◦ *That will be a good starting point for our discussion.*
– coming at the beginning: **first** (*adjective, adverb*) ◦ *The first month of the year is January.* ◦ *the first man on the moon* ◦ *This part was written first.*
▷ more on being or happening first ⇨ FIRST / NEXT / LAST
– at the beginning of a series of events: **at first, to begin with** ◦ *He didn't recognize anyone at first; then he spotted a familiar face.* ◦ *She didn't like David to begin with, but they get on fine now.*
– at/from the moment when sth starts: **at/from the beginning** (of sth), **at/from the start** (of sth) ◦ *at the beginning of May* ◦ *These negotiations have been difficult from the start.*
– at the beginning, before any changes or developments are made: **originally** ◦ *The roof was originally made of wood.*
– near the beginning of a period of time, a piece of work, etc: **early** (*adjective, adverb*) ◦ *in the early spring* ◦ *early in the morning* ◦ *He's in his early fifties.* ◦ *We arrived early.*

■ beginning a task, hobby, etc
– to begin a task: **set* about** sth/doing sth ◦ *Now we understand the problem, we can set about solving it.* ◦ *I have no idea how to set about this.*
– to start to concentrate on sth: **get* down to** sth/doing sth ◦ *I must get down to answering these letters.*
– to start doing sth regularly: **take*** sth **up** ◦ *I took up jogging last year and it's done me a lot of good.*
– a person who has just begun to learn to do sth: **beginner** ◦ *a class for beginners* ◦ *beginner's luck*
▷ beginning a journey ⇨ TRAVEL

■ the first part of sth
– to have sth as a first part: **begin* with** sth, **start with** sth, **open with** sth ◦ *What letter does your name begin with?* ◦ *The play starts with the hero's death.* ◦ *The service opened with a prayer.*
– that is done or said at the beginning of sth: **introductory, opening** ◦ *The chairman made some introductory remarks before the presentations began.* ◦ *the opening chapters of a book*
– the first part of sth: **beginning, start, opening** ◦ *I didn't like the beginning of the book.* ◦ *The start of the race was very exciting.* ◦ *The opening of the film was very dramatic.*
– the first part of a book, essay or talk, which explains what will follow: **introduction** ◦ *Make sure that your essay has a clear introduction and conclusion.*

2 causing sth to begin

– to cause sth to happen or exist: **start** sth ◦ *to start a fire* ◦ *I'm planning to start an import-export business.*

- to make sth ready to start operating: **open** sth ◦ *to open a bank account* ◦ *to open a discussion/debate/meeting* ◦ *to open a shop*
- to start a business: **set*** sth **up** ◦ *We set up our company twenty years ago.*

- to use sth for the first time: **introduce** sth (**into** sth); this action or process: **introduction** (*noun* U) ◦ *A new banking system has recently been introduced.* ◦ *The introduction of computerized checkouts has speeded up the process of shopping.*

- (used about a car, an engine, etc) to begin to work: **start** (**up**); to make a car, an engine, etc work: **start** sth (**up**) ◦ *The car won't start.* ◦ *I can't start the car.* ◦ *Pull the handle to start up the motor.*
- to do sth which causes sth else to begin: **set*** sth **off** ◦ *to set off a reaction* ◦ *I burnt the toast and set off the fire alarm.*

3 beginning again

- to start again after stopping: **start/begin* again** (*AmE* **start over**), **continue** ◦ *You've ruined my painting! I'll have to start all over again.* ◦ *The meeting continued after lunch.*
- to make sth start again: **start/begin*** sth **again**, **continue** sth, **renew** sth ◦ *The story will be continued next week.* ◦ *renewed outbreaks of violence* ◦ *to renew a friendship/relationship*
- to begin again after a failure: **make* a fresh start**
- to change your way of life for the better: **turn over a new leaf** ◦ *I'm going to turn over a new leaf and get to work on time in future.*

■ **MORE ...**
- the ability to begin to do things without suggestions or orders from anybody else: **initiative** (*noun* U) ◦ *The boss was out, so I used my initiative and solved the problem by myself.*

- to start an organization, institution, system, etc: **establish** sth, **found** sth; a person who establishes or founds sth: **founder** ◦ *Their system of social services was established over forty years ago.* ◦ *The school was founded in 1785.*

---

behaviour

> 1 the way that you behave
> 2 particular types of behaviour
> **see also PERSONALITY, ACTION**

1 the way that you behave

- to do things in a particular way: **behave**, **act** ◦ *I don't know what the matter is with him, but he was behaving very strangely.* ◦ *We all thought she had behaved very badly towards her employees.* ◦ *He was acting like a fool.* ◦ *to act suspiciously*
- the way that people or animals behave: **behaviour** (*AmE* **behavior**) (*noun* U) ◦ *Their behaviour in class was just terrible.* ◦ *sexual/social behaviour*

- to behave towards sb in a particular way: **treat** sb in a particular way; *noun* (U): **treatment** ◦ *The family he stayed with treated him very well.* ◦ *The treatment he received from the customs officials was quite shocking.*
- the way that sb behaves towards other people: **manner** ◦ *She's very nice but she's got a very strange manner.*

- something that sb does often: **habit** (*noun* C/U) ◦ *bad/good habits* ◦ *Out of habit, he set off towards the office before remembering that it was Sunday.*
- a way of behaving which a particular group or society has had for a long time: **custom** ◦ *an interesting local custom*
- the usual way that a person or a group of people live: **way of life** ◦ *When you live in a foreign country, it's important to respect other people's way of life.*
- the way that you live; the things that you do every day: **lifestyle** ◦ *to have a normal/unusual/extravagant lifestyle*

▷ more on habits and customs ⇨ HABIT

■ copying sb's behaviour
- to copy the behaviour of sb/sth: **imitate** sb/sth; *noun* (U): **imitation** ◦ *to learn through imitation*
- to copy the actions or way of speaking of sb/sth, often in order to be amusing: **imitate** sb/sth, **take*** sb **off**; *nouns*: **imitation**, **take-off** ◦ *He was brilliant at imitating his teachers.* ◦ *Have you seen her do her take-off of the Queen?*
- to try to copy sb or be like sb: **model** yourself **on/upon** sb

■ liking or not liking sb's behaviour
- to think that sb's behaviour is good or reasonable: **approve** (**of** sth); *noun* (U): **approval** ◦ *We all thoroughly approved of the way the celebrations had been organized.*
- to think that sb's behaviour is bad or foolish: **disapprove** (**of** sth); *noun* (U): **disapproval** ◦ *My parents always disapproved of the way I dressed.* ◦ *The elderly couple were looking at the youth with obvious disapproval.*
- having or showing disapproval: **disapproving** (*adverb* **disapprovingly**) ◦ *disapproving looks*

- to accept behaviour which you do not like: **tolerate** sth, **put* up with** sth ◦ *How can you put up with that sort of rudeness?*
- the ability to allow or accept sth that you do not like or agree with: **tolerance** (*noun* U); *opposite*: **intolerance** (*noun* U)
- having or showing tolerance: **tolerant** (*adverb* **tolerantly**); *opposite*: **intolerant** (*adverb* **intolerantly**)

- a person who does not allow people to break rules or behave badly is **strict** (*adverb* **strictly**) ◦ *I've got very strict parents – they only let me stay out until ten at night.*

2 particular types of behaviour

■ good and bad
- to act in the correct or proper way: **behave well**; behaving well: **well behaved** ◦ *The fans were generally well behaved.*
- to behave as well as possible on a particular occasion: **be on** your **best behaviour** ◦ *When we*

behaviour *contd.*

were young and we visited our grandparents, we were always told to be on our best behaviour.
- the ability to control your own behaviour: **self-control** (*noun* U) ◦ *to exercise self-control*

- not to act in the correct or proper way: **behave badly, misbehave**; behaving badly: **badly behaved**
- to behave in a silly way: **mess around/about, fool around/about** ◦ *Stop fooling about and listen to me.*
- to behave so badly that sb punishes you: **get* into trouble** ◦ *I was always getting into trouble when I was at school.*

▷ good and bad behaviour by children ⇨ CHILD

▷ punishment ⇨ PUNISH

- a person or thing that is good and that people should copy: **example** ◦ *Her behaviour was an example to us all.*
- to behave in a way that other people should copy: **set* an example** (**to** sb) ◦ *Teachers are supposed to set an example to their students.*
- to behave in a way that should/should not be copied: **set*** sb **a good/bad example, set* a good/bad example** (**to** sb) ◦ *We think you've set the others a very bad example.*

- if behaviour is good and is fair to other people, it is **right**; *opposite*: **wrong** ◦ *It isn't right to waste food when so many people don't have enough.* ◦ *Stealing is wrong.*
- having high standards of behaviour: **moral** (*adverb* **morally**); *opposite*: **immoral** (*adverb* **immorally**) ◦ *He's a very moral person and would never want to do anything wrong.* ◦ *I thought their behaviour was totally immoral.*
- a rule for good behaviour, based on what you believe is right: **principle** (*noun* C/U) ◦ *One of my principles is that I won't do anything that causes suffering to animals.* ◦ *I won't wear fur coats on principle* (= because of my moral beliefs).

▷ behaviour that is right or wrong ⇨ RIGHT/WRONG²

■ shocking
- an action or a situation or behaviour that shocks people: **scandal** ◦ *a political scandal*
- behaviour which is very shocking or wrong can be called **scandalous, disgraceful, disgusting** ◦ *It's scandalous that people can be allowed to do such things.* ◦ *a scandalous story* ◦ *disgraceful behaviour* ◦ *It's disgraceful!*

- the state of not being respected by other people, usually because you have behaved badly: **disgrace** (*noun* U) ◦ *to be in disgrace*
- to cause disgrace to sb/sth: **disgrace** sb/sth ◦ *She has disgraced the profession and should be sacked.*
- a person or thing that gives such a bad impression that other people feel ashamed: **a disgrace** (**to** sb) (*noun singular*) ◦ *He was a disgrace to his family.*

■ sensible or childish
- behaviour which is good and reasonable is **sensible** (*adverb* **sensibly**) ◦ *Phoning ahead was a very sensible thing to do.* ◦ *to behave sensibly*
- able to act in a sensible and adult way: **mature** (*adverb* **maturely**); *noun* (U): **maturity** ◦ *a mature person* ◦ *to behave with maturity*

- (used about teenagers or adults) behaving like a child: **childish, immature** ◦ *Don't be so childish – I'd really expect a boy of your age to be a little bit more sensible.*
- to be sensible enough not to do sth: **know* better** (**than …**) ◦ *You're old enough to know better.* ◦ *You should know better than to go out in the rain without a coat.*
- to become too old for certain types of behaviour: **grow* out of** sth ◦ *Teenagers can be very sulky, but they usually grow out of it.*

▷ being sensible ⇨ SENSIBLE

■ polite or rude
- if you act and speak in a way that is helpful and thoughtful towards other people, you are **polite** (*adverb* **politely**) ◦ *a polite person* ◦ *The bank wrote me a very polite letter.*
- not polite: **impolite** (*adverb* **impolitely**), **rude** (*adverb* **rudely**) ◦ *an impolite manner* ◦ *I'll continue with what I was saying before I was so rudely interrupted.*

■ embarrassing or tactful
- behaviour which makes you feel ashamed or uncomfortable is **embarrassing**; to behave in this way: **embarrass** sb; *noun* (U/C): **embarrassment** ◦ *an embarrassing mistake/remark* ◦ *I hope you didn't feel embarrassed by what I said.* ◦ *to be overcome with embarrassment*
- careful not to cause embarrassment or difficulty for sb: **tactful** (*adverb* **tactfully**); *noun* (U): **tact** ◦ *She tactfully avoided talking about their argument the day before.* ◦ *He's got absolutely no tact.*

▷ more on politeness and tact ⇨ POLITE

■ formal or casual
- the way you talk or behave on an official occasion or when you do not know the other people well is **formal** (*adverb* **formally**); *noun* (U): **formality** ◦ *a formal introduction* ◦ *He's always so formal – I wish he'd relax a bit.*
- not formal: **informal** (*adverb* **informally**); *noun* (U): **informality** ◦ *After the meeting, everyone sat around informally and chatted.* ◦ *I like the informality of the school.*
- very informal: **casual** ◦ *The party was a pleasant, casual affair.* ◦ *Most of us were in jeans and T-shirts or other casual clothes.*

- calm, serious behaviour which makes other people respect you: **dignity** (*noun* U) ◦ *She sat and waited with quiet dignity.*
- behaving with dignity: **dignified** ◦ *a dignified way of speaking/walking*

■ kind, friendly; unkind, cruel
- behaving to other people in a pleasant way: **friendly**; *noun* (U): **friendliness**; not friendly: **unfriendly** ◦ *a friendly act*

- giving help: **helpful** (*adverb* **helpfully**); *noun* (U): **helpfulness**; not helpful: **unhelpful**
- caring about how other people feel and doing things to help them: **kind** (*adverb* **kindly**); *noun* (U): **kindness**; not kind: **unkind** ◦ *They were very kind to us when we first arrived in the village.*
- not friendly, reasonable or helpful: **difficult** ◦ *He was being very difficult – when I asked him to do one thing, he did exactly the opposite.*
- behaviour that causes pain and suffering is **cruel** (*adverb* **cruelly**); *noun* (U): **cruelty**

- to behave badly or cruelly towards a person or animal: **mistreat** sb/sth; *noun* (U): **mistreatment** ◦ *mistreatment of animals*

▷ more on being kind or cruel ⇨ KIND/CRUEL

■ calm, gentle; violent, noisy
- quiet and not excited: **calm** (*adverb* **calmly**) ◦ *Everyone stay calm! Don't panic!*
- behaving in a careful way so that you do not hurt people or damage things: **gentle** (*adverb* **gently**); *noun* (U): **gentleness** ◦ *The nurse was very gentle and I didn't feel much pain.*

▷ more on being calm ⇨ CALM

- moving or behaving with too much force and not enough care; not gentle or calm: **rough** (*adverb* **roughly**); *noun* (U): **roughness** ◦ *to treat sb roughly*
- using physical strength, often in an uncontrolled way, to hurt sb or to damage sth: **violent** (*adverb* **violently**); *noun* (U): **violence** ◦ *There were violent disturbances around the city during the night.* ◦ *Is there too much violence on television?*
- causing a lot of damage: **destructive** ◦ *destructive behaviour*

- when sb argues and fights a lot, they and their behaviour are **aggressive** (*adverb* **aggressively**); *noun* (U): **aggressiveness** ◦ *Don't be so aggressive!* ◦ *an aggressive act* ◦ *to behave aggressively*
- to use your strength or power to frighten sb who is weaker: **bully** sb ◦ *Some of the older children bullied the little ones.*

- behaviour which is not quiet is **noisy** (*adverb* **noisily**); *noun* (C/U): **noise** ◦ *You're being a bit noisy – could you quieten down a bit.* ◦ *a noisy party* ◦ *The children were making a terrible noise.*
- noisy and uncontrolled: **rowdy** (*adverb* **rowdily**) ◦ *The group in the corner of the pub were being very rowdy.* ◦ *a rowdy party*

■ confident or shy
- feeling or showing that you are sure about your own abilities, opinions, etc: **confident** (*adverb* **confidently**); *noun* (U): **confidence** ◦ *a very confident performance* ◦ *behaving with confidence*
- to try to impress people by showing them how clever you are: **show* off** ◦ *She's always showing off in front of the class.*

- easily embarrassed; not relaxed with other people: **awkward** (*adverb* **awkwardly**); *noun* (U): **awkwardness** ◦ *He smiled awkwardly, trying to think of something to say.*
- too worried about what other people think of you: **self-conscious** (*adverb* **self-consciously**); *noun* (U): **self-consciousness** ◦ *I felt so self-conscious – everybody was wearing formal clothes and I turned up in my jeans!* ◦ *Teenagers often behave very self-consciously.*

■ **MORE ...**
- to try to improve your behaviour: (*informal*) **pull*** your **socks up**, **mend** your **ways** ◦ *If you don't pull your socks up you are not going to pass this exam.* ◦ *She was in prison for a while for stealing but I think she's mended her ways.*
- to get control of yourself and your feelings: **pull** yourself **together**, **get* a grip** (**on** yourself) ◦ *He really must pull himself together and try and go back to work again.*

- to do what you tell others to do: **practise what you preach** ◦ *You should practise what you preach and wear a helmet yourself!*

behind ⇨ PLACE[2]

believe

- what you think about sth ⇨ OPINION
- political beliefs ⇨ POLITICS
- religious beliefs ⇨ RELIGION
- believing that sth is true ⇨ TRUE

bell

see also SOUND

- a metal object that makes a sound in order to call, warn or wake people: **bell** ◦ *church bells* ◦ *the school bell* ◦ *a bicycle bell* ◦ *I think I heard the doorbell.* ◦ *Has the bell gone yet?* (= for the end of a lesson)
- (used about a bell) to make a sound: **ring***; to cause a bell to make a sound: **ring*** sth; *noun*: **ring** ◦ *We rang the doorbell.* ◦ *I'm sure there was a ring at the door.*
- to use a bell to call sb: **ring* for** sb ◦ *I'll ring for the nurse.*

- an object which is used like a bell and which makes a sound like a bee: **buzzer**; the sound that a buzzer makes: **buzz** ◦ *Press the buzzer if you know the answer to the question.*
- if you use a buzzer or an electric bell, you usually press a **button**

- when the bell on a clock rings to tell people what the time is, the clock **strikes*** ◦ *The clock struck three.*
- the sound that clocks or church bells make when they ring: **chime**; *verb*: **chime** ◦ *the chimes of Big Ben* ◦ *The town hall clock chimed eight.*
- the sound that church bells make when they play a tune: **peal**; *verb*: **peal** ◦ *the peal of wedding bells*
- the sound that a very small bell makes: **tinkle**; *verb*: **tinkle**

- a bell or other special sound that warns you of danger: **alarm** ◦ *a fire alarm* ◦ *a burglar alarm*

▷ more on alarm bells, etc ⇨ WARN

belong
– belonging to a group ⇨ **GROUP**
– possessing sth ⇨ **HAVE/POSSESS**

below ⇨ PLACE²

bend
– not standing upright ⇨ **STAND**
– being straight ⇨ **STRAIGHT**

beside
– near ⇨ **DISTANCE**
– position ⇨ **PLACE²**

bet

see also GAME, HORSE, CARDS

– to pay some money in the hope of winning sth: **bet* (on** sth), **have/place/put* a bet on** sth, **gamble (on/at** sth); *nouns* (U): **betting, gambling** ◦ *I never bet.* ◦ *George placed a small bet on the result of the general election.* ◦ *He lost all his money gambling at poker* (= a card game). ◦ *Betting is prohibited in this country.* ◦ *She's addicted to gambling.*
– an act of betting: **bet**; to offer sb a bet: **bet*** sb sth ◦ *to win/lose a bet* ◦ *I'll bet you £10 it rains tomorrow.*
– a person who gambles: **gambler** ◦ *She's become an incurable gambler.*

– to say that a particular horse, etc will win: **back** sth, **put*/lay* money on** sth ◦ *Which horse did you back?* ◦ *I always seem to back the loser.*
– the money that you bet on sth: **bet** ◦ *a £100 bet*
– the probability that a particular horse, etc will win: **odds** (*noun plural*) ◦ *She came in first at odds of ten to one* (= if you bet £1 on her, you win £10).

– a place where people go to place bets on horse races, etc: **betting shop**
– a person whose job is to take people's bets: **bookmaker**, (*informal*) **bookie**

– a game in which a small ball is dropped onto a moving wheel and people bet on which number it will land on: **roulette** (*noun* U)
– a place where people go to play card games, etc and gamble: **casino** (*plural* **casinos**)
– a type of betting in which people bet money on the results of football matches: **football pools** (*noun plural*), (*informal*) **the pools** (*noun plural*) ◦ *They won £2 million on the pools.*

– a way of raising money by selling tickets with numbers on them and giving prizes to people who have bought a winning ticket: **lottery**; the biggest prize in a lottery: **jackpot** ◦ *a lottery ticket* ◦ *to win the jackpot*

better/best ⇨ GOOD

between ⇨ PLACE²

Bible ⇨ CHRISTIAN, JEW

bicycle

see also MOTORCYCLE

– a bicycle with a strong light frame, wide wheels and many gears, for use on rough ground: **mountain bike**
– a light, fast bicycle with many gears: **racer, racing bike**
– a bicycle for two people: **tandem**
– a bicycle with three wheels: **tricycle**
– a person who rides a bicycle: **cyclist**

– to use a bicycle: **ride*** (sth) ◦ *When did you learn to ride a bicycle?*
– to travel somewhere using a bicycle: **cycle, go*** somewhere **by bicycle** ◦ *I cycled over to Ken's house yesterday.* ◦ *I always go to work by bike.*
– to use a bicycle for pleasure: **go* cycling** ◦ *Bill and Lucy are going cycling in the Highlands this weekend.*
– the sport of riding a bicycle: **cycling** (*noun* U)
– the sport of riding a mountain bike: **mountain biking** (*noun* U)

bicycle (*informal* **bike**)

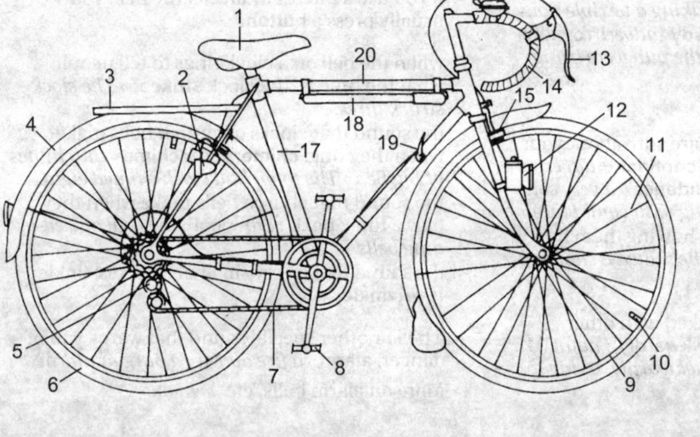

1 saddle (*AmE* seat)
2 rear light
3 rack
4 mudguard
5 gears
6 tyre (*AmE* tire)
7 chain
8 pedal
9 wheel
10 valve
11 spoke
12 front light
13 brake lever
14 handlebars
15 brake
16 bell
17 frame
18 pump
19 gear lever
20 crossbar

- to push the pedals round with your feet and move a bicycle forward: **pedal** (sth) ◦ *The hill was so steep I could hardly pedal up it.*
- to control the direction a bicycle is going in by turning the handlebars: **steer** (sth) ◦ *Chris steered his bike over to the side of the road.*
- to get into a different gear: **change gear**
- to climb onto a bicycle: **get* on**; *opposite*: **get* off**, (*formal*) **dismount**
- to fall off a bicycle in an accident, etc: **come* off** ◦ *Keith came off his bike as he was going round a sharp bend.*

- a type of lock that is used on a bicycle: **padlock**
- the rubber tube filled with air inside the tyre: **inner tube**

▷ more on wheels and tyres ⇨ WHEEL

■ **MORE ...**

- a part of a road that can only be used by bicycles: **cycle lane**

big / small

1 big and small
2 very big and very small
3 becoming bigger or smaller
see also IMPORTANT

1 big and small

- big in size: **big, large** ◦ *a big person/building/town/car* ◦ *a great big balloon* ◦ *These shoes are too big for me.* ◦ *a large store* ◦ *two large steaks* ◦ *a large area of land* ◦ *to get bigger*

  Note: big and **large** mean the same thing. **Large** is usually used more formally than **big**; it is not often used to describe people.

- not large in size or amount: **small, little** ◦ *a small person/building/project/improvement* ◦ *a small number of people* ◦ *a little girl* ◦ *to get smaller*

  Note: small is usually the opposite of **big** or **large**; we say **smaller** and **smallest** but not littler or littlest; **little** often follows other adjectives to express the way you feel about sth: ◦ *a horrid little boy* ◦ *a beautiful little house* ◦ *a tiny little place*

- how big or small sth is: **size** (*noun* C/U) ◦ *Have you got them in a smaller size?* ◦ *I was astonished at the size of the building.* ◦ *smaller in size*
- of a size that is neither very big nor very small: **medium(-sized), average(-sized)** ◦ *a medium-sized town* ◦ *'What sizes have you got?' 'Small, medium and large.'* ◦ *I wouldn't say she's particularly tall – just average, really.*

▷ more on size ⇨ SIZE

▷ the sizes of clothes ⇨ CLOTHES

▷ different ways of being big or small ⇨ FAT/THIN/THICK, HEIGHT, LONG/SHORT², WEIGHT, WIDE/NARROW

- having a lot of space: **roomy, spacious** ◦ *a spacious flat*
- taking up a lot of space; difficult to move or carry: **bulky** ◦ *They aren't heavy but they're difficult to carry because they're so bulky.*

2 very big and very small

- very large in size, amount or extent: **huge, massive, vast, enormous** ◦ *a huge elephant* ◦ *a massive earthquake* ◦ *a vast expanse of water* ◦ *an enormous building/person/field*
- big, tall and impressive: **imposing** ◦ *an imposing mountain/building*

- very small: **tiny, minute**, (*informal, especially in Scotland*) **wee**, (*formal*) **diminutive** ◦ *a tiny house/person/amount* ◦ *minute quantities of carbon monoxide* ◦ *a wee girl* ◦ *a diminutive figure*
- very small; so small that you cannot see it: **microscopic** ◦ *a microscopic animal*

3 becoming bigger or smaller

- to get bigger: **grow*, increase in size**; *noun* (U): **growth**; *adjective*: **growing** ◦ *The plant grew three centimetres in one week.* ◦ *The population has grown over the last ten years.* ◦ *The hole in the ozone layer is increasing in size every year.* ◦ *The doctors are worried about the growth of the tumour.* ◦ *a growing child*
- to become bigger or fuller: **swell*** (**up**); to make sth bigger or fuller: **swell*** sth; *adjective*: **swollen** ◦ *Your feet swell when they get hot.* ◦ *Two days of continuous rain had swollen the rivers.* ◦ *Her face was all swollen – it looked like somebody had hit her.*
- to get smaller: **shrink*, decrease in size**; to cause sth to get smaller: **shrink*** sth; *adjective*: **shrinking** ◦ *My jumper shrank in the wash.*

▷ more on the growth of people, animals or plants ⇨ GROW

- (used especially about metals and other materials; also used about commercial and other activities) to get bigger: **expand**; to cause sth to get bigger: **expand** sth; *noun* (U): **expansion**; *adjective*: **expanding** ◦ *Metals expand when they get hot.* ◦ *They're expanding the company over the next two years.*
- (used especially about metals and other materials; also used about commercial and other activities) to get smaller: **contract**; *noun* (U): **contraction** ◦ *Metals contract when they get cold.* ◦ *Further contraction of the steel industry is inevitable.*

- to make sth bigger in size (a photograph, for example): **enlarge** sth; an act of making sth larger: **enlargement**; a thing (usually a photograph) that has been made larger: **enlargement** ◦ *I need to enlarge this picture*
- to make sth look bigger than it is: **magnify** sth ◦ *We could see the cells magnified 6000 times under the microscope*

▷ becoming bigger/smaller in number or quantity ⇨ INCREASE/DECREASE

■ **MORE ...**

- small, neat and taking up little space: **compact** ◦ *These new computers are very compact – you can put them in a suitcase.*
- small enough to fit in your pocket: **pocket** (*only before a noun*) ◦ *a pocket calculator*

bill ⇨ PAY[1]

bird[1] kinds of bird and bird behaviour

1 birds
2 bird sounds
3 flying, walking, etc
4 eggs

birds that are kept for food ⇨ BIRD[2]

1 birds

– a creature with wings and feathers which can (usually) fly: **bird** ◦ *birds of prey* (= birds which kill and eat other animals and birds)
– a group of birds: **flock** ◦ *a flock of geese*
– an adult male bird: **cock** ◦ *a cock sparrow*
– a female bird: **hen** ◦ *The hen is usually smaller than the cock.*
– a young bird: **chick**

■ some large birds see picture below

■ some smaller birds
– a black bird with a yellow beak (the female is brown): **blackbird**
– a large black bird that makes a loud noise: **crow**
– a small brown bird with a bright red breast: **robin**
– a small brown bird that is very common: **sparrow**
– a fat grey bird that often lives in towns: **pigeon**
– a type of bird, similar to a pigeon, often used as a sign of peace: **dove**
– a white or grey seabird with a loud cry: **gull, seagull**
– a small yellow bird that sings and that people often keep in a cage as a pet: **canary**
– a small brightly-coloured bird that people often keep in a cage as a pet: **budgerigar**, (*informal*) **budgie**

2 bird sounds

– the musical sound that a bird makes: **song, birdsong**; *verb*: **sing*** ◦ *The birds were singing in the trees.*
– a short high sound that small birds make: **chirp**; *verb*: **chirp**
– a loud unpleasant sound that a bird makes: **squawk**; *verb*: **squawk**

3 flying, walking, etc

– to move through the air: **fly***
– to fly or move down suddenly: **swoop (down)** ◦ *The eagle swooped down on its prey.*
– (used about a bird) to sit or rest on a branch, etc after flying: **perch**
– (used about ducks and other birds that live near water) to walk along the ground with short steps, moving from one side to the other: **waddle**
– to travel from one part of the world to another when the seasons change: **migrate** ◦ *Swallows migrate at this time of year.*

4 eggs

– to build or use a nest: **nest** ◦ *The swallows are nesting under the roof.*
– to produce an egg: **lay*** (an egg) ◦ *The mother owl normally lays two eggs.*
– (used about a baby bird) to come out of an egg: **hatch**

■ **MORE . . .**
– a kind of box made of bars or wires in which a bird is kept so that it cannot escape: **cage, birdcage**
– a small table in a garden on which food is put to attract birds: **bird table**
– a mixture of small seeds that you give to birds that are kept in cages: **birdseed** (*noun* U) ◦ *Can you get some birdseed from the petshop?*
– if a bird eats or bites sth with its beak, it **pecks** (**at**) sth ◦ *The robin was pecking the ground for food.*

bird

- an area where birds are protected from hunters and animals: **bird sanctuary**
- a person who studies birds in their natural surroundings: **birdwatcher**; this activity: **bird-watching** (*noun* U)

bird² birds that are kept for food

see also FOOD, COOK, BIRD¹

- a female chicken: **hen**; a male chicken: **cock** (*AmE* **rooster**); a baby chicken: **chick**
- a male duck: **drake**; a young duck: **duckling**

- to produce an egg: **lay*** (an egg) ◦ *The hens are laying well at present.* (= they are producing a lot of eggs)
- the sound that a hen makes: **cluck**; *verb*: **cluck**
- (used about a male chicken) to make a loud noise, usually early in the morning: **crow**
- the sound that a duck makes: **quack**; *verb*: **quack**

■ cooking and eating chicken, etc
- the meat from a chicken, goose, duck, turkey: **chicken** (*noun* U), **goose** (*noun* U) **duck** (*noun* U) **turkey** (*noun* U) ◦ *We're having chicken stew for supper.* ◦ *chicken salad* ◦ *cold/fried/roast chicken* ◦ *Would you like some more duck?* ◦ *a turkey sandwich*
- the upper part of the leg of a chicken, etc (when you are eating it): **thigh**; the lower part of the leg: **drumstick** ◦ *Would you like a thigh or a drumstick?*
- the soft meat from the front of the chicken, etc: **breast** (*noun* U)

- a mixture of small bits of food put inside a chicken, etc, before cooking it: **stuffing** (*noun* U)

▷ ways of cooking chicken and other meat ⇨ MEAT

■ **MORE ...**

- the general word for any birds (turkeys, ducks, geese, etc) that are kept for their meat or eggs: **poultry** (*noun plural*); the meat from these birds: **poultry** (*noun* U) ◦ *to keep poultry* ◦ *I eat poultry but not red meat.*

- hens which are kept in very small cages: **battery hens**
- produced by hens that are allowed to move around freely: **free-range** ◦ *free-range eggs*
- to pull feathers out of a chicken, etc: **pluck** sth ◦ *to pluck a chicken*

birth

1 when a baby is born
2 before a baby is born
3 after a baby is born
actions that result in birth ⇨ SEX²
see also ANIMAL, BABY, CHILD, FAMILY

1 when a baby is born

- to come out of the mother's body at the beginning of life: **be born**, (*informal*) **arrive**; *nouns* (C/U): **birth**, (*informal*) **arrival** ◦ *I was born on the 21st of June.* ◦ *Has her baby arrived yet?* ◦ *the birth of her second child* ◦ *before/after birth*
- to produce a baby: **have a baby**, (*formal*) **give* birth** (**to ...**) ◦ *Has she had the baby yet?* ◦ *She gave birth to twins.*
- the act of giving birth to a baby: (*formal*) **childbirth** (*noun* U) ◦ *The mother died in childbirth.*
- connected with women giving birth: **maternity** (*only before a noun*) ◦ *a maternity hospital* ◦ *some maternity clothes*
- the last stage before the baby is born: **labour** (*noun* U) ◦ *She was in labour for more than eight hours.*
- a birth which involves cutting an opening in the mother's body: **Caesarean** ◦ *She had to have a Caesarean when her first child was born.*
- a person who has been trained to help a woman give birth: **midwife** (*plural* **midwives**)
- a baby which has just been born is **new-born** ◦ *the cry of a new-born baby*
- when a baby is born before the expected time, it is **premature** ◦ *The baby was eight weeks premature.* ◦ *a premature baby*
- to give birth before the baby is fully formed, with the result that the baby cannot live: **lose*** a baby, **miscarry**; the act of giving birth to a baby like this: **miscarriage** ◦ *She has lost the baby.* ◦ *She has had several miscarriages.*
- a baby which is dead when it is born is **stillborn** ◦ *a stillborn baby*

2 before a baby is born

- a woman who has a baby developing inside her is **pregnant**, (*less formal*) **expecting**; *noun* (U): **pregnancy** ◦ *Sue was five months pregnant.* ◦ *Did you know she's expecting a baby in June?* ◦ *She went for a pregnancy test.*
- the period of time when a woman is pregnant: **pregnancy** ◦ *a difficult/normal pregnancy*
- connected with the medical care of women before birth: **antenatal** ◦ *an antenatal clinic*

- to become pregnant: **conceive** (a baby); *noun* (U/C): **conception** ◦ *Their first child was conceived soon after they got married.* ◦ *Tests found that she was unable to conceive.* ◦ *the moment of conception*
- a baby (or young animal) at its earliest stage of development inside the mother: **embryo** (*plural* **embryos**)
- a baby (or young animal) that is developing inside the mother's body: **foetus** (*AmE* **fetus**)

birth *contd.*

- the ability to produce children: **fertility** (*noun* U) ◦ *Women can take drugs to increase their fertility.*
- ways of preventing a woman becoming pregnant: **contraception** (*noun* U)
- controlling the number of children in a family: **birth control** (*noun* U), **family planning** (*noun* U) ◦ *They need to decide on the best method of birth control.*

▷ methods of contraception ⇨ SEX²

- the act of ending a pregnancy intentionally: **abortion** (*noun* C/U) ◦ *Thousands of abortions are carried out every year.* ◦ *We argued about the rights and wrongs of abortion.*
- to have a pregnancy ended intentionally: **have an abortion** ◦ *She was reluctant to have an abortion.*

3 after a baby is born

- connected with the medical care of women after birth: **postnatal**
- an official piece of paper recording a person's birth: **birth certificate**
- the day of the year on which you were born: **birthday**
- the place where a person was born: **birthplace** ◦ *Shakespeare's birthplace is in Stratford upon Avon.*
- a person who was born in a particular place: **native**; connected with the place where a person was born: **native** ◦ *He is a native of Poland.* ◦ *She has never been back to her native land.*

■ **MORE . . .**

- the tube that connects a baby to its mother before it is born: **umbilical cord**
- equipment used in hospital for keeping alive babies that are not strong: **incubator**
- a baby that is artificially conceived outside the body: **test-tube baby**
- the number of babies born in a particular group of people during a particular period of time: **birth rate** ◦ *The birth rate has fallen to less than 1 in 1000.*

bit

- a small amount ⇨ HOW MUCH/MANY
- part of sth ⇨ PART/WHOLE

black ⇨ COLOUR

blame

see also CRITICISM, INSULT

- to say or think that sb/sth is responsible for sth bad: **blame** sb/sth (**for** sth), **blame** sth **on** sb/sth, **put*/lay* the blame** (**for** sth) **on** sb/sth ◦ *As usual, I got blamed for starting the fight.* ◦ *You can't blame everything on the government.* ◦ *The police put the blame for the accident on the weather.*
- to think that you are responsible for sth bad: **blame** yourself (**for** sth) ◦ *I blame myself for what happened.*
- responsibility for sth bad: **fault** (*noun* U) ◦ *'It's not my fault that they got lost.' 'Whose fault is it then?'* ◦ *It's nobody's fault.*
- when you have done sth wrong, you are **to blame** (**for** sth), **guilty** (**of** sth), **responsible** (**for** sth); *nouns* (U): **guilt**, **responsibility** ◦ *No one is to blame.* ◦ *Who's responsible for this mess?* ◦ *There's no doubt about his guilt.* ◦ *Responsibility must lie with the government.*
- to be blamed for sth: **take*/get* the blame** (**for** sth) ◦ *Why do I always have to take the blame?* ◦ *I shouldn't get the blame for something I didn't do.*
- the feeling you have when you know you have done sth wrong: **guilt** (*noun* U); *adjective*: **guilty** ◦ *a terrible sense of guilt* ◦ *a guilty feeling*

- when sb has not done anything wrong, they are **blameless**, **innocent** ◦ *I know she's entirely blameless.*

■ **MORE . . .**

- a person who is made to take all the blame for sth, while others are not punished: **scapegoat**, (*especially AmE* **fall guy**)
- when you are not sure if sb should be blamed and you prefer to believe that they may be innocent, you **give*** them **the benefit of the doubt**

blind ⇨ SEE

blood

1 blood in the body
2 losing blood
3 giving blood
see also HEART

1 blood in the body

- the red liquid that moves around your body: **blood** (*noun* U)
- the organ inside your chest that sends blood all round the body: **heart**
- one of the tubes that carry the blood from all parts of the body to the heart: **vein**
- one of the tubes that carry the blood from the heart to all parts of the body: **artery**
- the movement of the blood around the body: **circulation** (*noun* U) ◦ *Cold hands and feet are a sign of poor circulation.*

Note: the word **vein** is commonly used for both veins and arteries. Another word used to mean any of the tubes in the body which the blood passes through is **blood vessel**.

- the regular movement of the heart or the sound it makes: **heartbeat**
- the regular beating in your body as blood is pumped through it by the heart: **pulse**; to count how many times the heart beats in a minute: **take*/feel*** sb's **pulse** ◦ *The doctor took my pulse.*
- the force with which the blood moves around the body: **blood pressure** (*noun* U) ◦ *He's got high/low blood pressure.* ◦ *to have your blood pressure taken* (= measured)

2 losing blood

- (used about a person or a part of the body) to lose blood: **bleed*** ◦ *'Is it bleeding?' 'Not much; I think it's nearly stopped.'*
- blood flowing from a cut, etc: **bleeding** (*noun* U) ◦ *There was a lot of bleeding from the wound in his leg.*
- when blood comes out quickly and in large quantities, it **pours/streams** (**from, down**, etc sth) ◦ *Blood was pouring out of the wound.* ◦ *Blood was streaming down her arm.*
- when blood comes out with great force, it **spurts** ◦ *Blood was spurting from his nose.*

- covered in blood: **bloody** ◦ *a bloody finger*
- having marks of blood on it: **bloodstained** ◦ *bloodstained clothing*
- an area of blood on the ground: **pool of blood** ◦ *He was lying in a pool of blood.*

- a lump formed by blood as it dries: **clot**
- an area formed by dried blood on the skin: **scab**

3 giving blood

- to allow some of your blood to be taken so that it can be used to help cure other people: **give* blood, donate blood**; a person who does this: **blood donor** ◦ *After the accident people were asked to give blood.*
- one of several different types of human blood (O, A, B, or AB): **blood group, blood type** ◦ *Do you know your blood group?*
- an injection of blood into sb's body: **blood transfusion** ◦ *She had to have a blood transfusion.*
- a place where blood is stored until it is needed for transfusion: **blood bank**

- an examination of a small amount of sb's blood to check it for a medical condition: **blood test**
- the blood that is taken for a blood test: **blood sample**

■ **MORE ...**
- easily upset by the sight of blood: **squeamish** ◦ *I couldn't be a nurse. I'm far too squeamish.*
- full of violence and blood: **gory** ◦ *a gory film*
- involving bloody injuries: **gruesome** ◦ *The battlefield was a gruesome sight.*

---

blue ⇨ COLOUR

---

boat

1 different kinds of boat
2 parts of boats
3 people on boats
4 harbours and ports
5 travelling on a boat
6 the movement of boats
7 building boats

see also TRANSPORT, TRAVEL

1 different kinds of boat

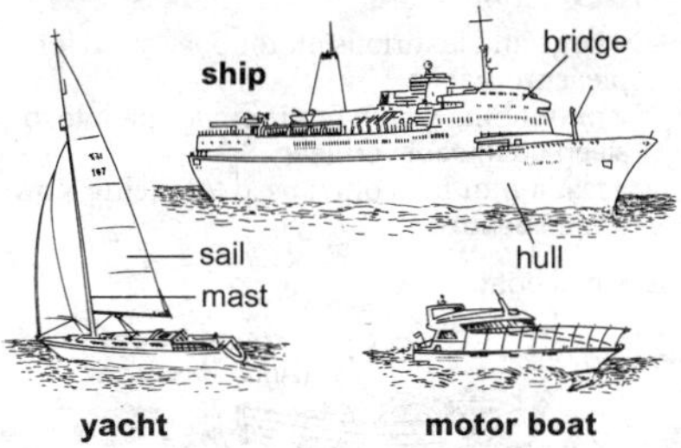

- a vehicle that is used for travelling across water: **boat**

■ working boats
- a large boat that is used for carrying passengers or goods by sea: **ship**, (*formal*) **vessel** ◦ *In which country was this vessel registered?*
- a ship that carries goods from one place to another: **freighter, cargo ship**
- a ship that is used for carrying large amounts of petrol, oil, etc: (**oil**) **tanker**
- a boat that is used for catching fish: **fishing boat**
- a type of fishing boat which pulls a long net through the sea to catch fish: **trawler**
- a long, narrow boat that is used for carrying goods along rivers and canals: **barge**

- a large ship that carries people long distances: **liner**
- a liner that is used for taking people on holiday tours: **cruise liner**
- a boat that carries people, cars, etc on short journeys: **ferry** ◦ *We took the car ferry from Dover to Calais.*
- a type of boat that moves over land or water on a cushion of air: **hovercraft**

- a small, strong boat which pulls larger boats into or out of a harbour: **tugboat**
- a special boat that is used to rescue people who are in danger at sea: **lifeboat**
- a small boat that is kept on a ship and is used by people to escape if the ship is going to sink: **lifeboat**

- a ship for use in war: **warship**

▷ more on warships ⇨ NAVY

■ sailing boats
- a boat or ship that has a sail on it which the wind can blow against and move the boat along: **sailing boat, sailing ship**
- a sailing boat used for pleasure: **yacht**

- to go somewhere in a sailing boat: **sail** (sth) ◦ *My brother's planning to sail (his yacht) to Bermuda.*
- using a sailing boat or yacht for sport or pleasure: **sailing** (*noun* U), **yachting** (*noun* U) ◦ *Would you like to go out sailing this afternoon?*
- a person who sails a yacht: **yachtsman**

■ motor boats
- a boat which is powered by an engine: **motor boat**

boat *contd.*

- a large and luxurious motor boat, used for pleasure: **yacht**
- a motor boat which has room for people to sleep on it: **cabin cruiser**
- a fast motor boat often used for racing: **power-boat**, **speedboat**

■ small boats

- a small, open boat, often used to take people to or from a larger boat: **dinghy**
- a simple, flat boat that you make by tying pieces of wood together: **raft**

- to make a rowing boat move you **row** (it) ◦ *We rowed to the other side of the lake.* ◦ *They rowed the boat back to shore.*
- using a rowing boat for sport or pleasure: **rowing** (*noun* U) ◦ *an Olympic rowing gold medallist*
- to make a canoe move you **paddle** (it) ◦ *Paddling a canoe is not easy!*
- using a canoe for sport or pleasure: **canoeing** (*noun* U) ◦ *We're going to go canoeing in Canada this summer.*

■ groups of boats

- a group of boats that sail and work together: **fleet** ◦ *a fishing fleet*
- a group of boats travelling together: **convoy** (*noun* C/U) ◦ *The boats travelled in convoy.*
- ships considered as a group or as traffic: **shipping** (*noun* U) ◦ *The English Channel has some of the busiest shipping lanes in the world.*

2 parts of boats

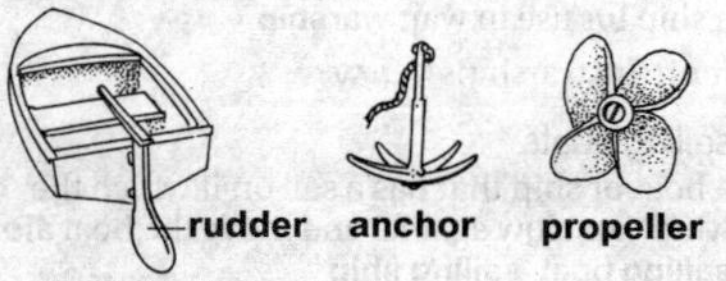

- one of the floors of a boat: **deck**; on a deck which is in the open air: **on deck** ◦ *Let's go and sit on deck.*
- a small room in a boat where sb can sleep: **cabin**; a kind of bed in a cabin: **bunk**, **berth** ◦ *a cabin with four berths*
- a round window on a boat: **porthole**

- the front part of a boat: **bow**
- the back part of a boat: **stern**
- the side of a boat that is on the left when you are facing the front: **port**
- the side of a boat that is on the right when you are facing the front: **starboard**

3 people on boats

- a person who works on a boat or ship: **sailor**
- the person who is in command of a boat or ship: **captain**
- all the people who work on a boat or ship: **crew** (*with singular or plural verb*) ◦ *This ship has a crew of 28.* ◦ *The crew were all swept overboard.*

▷ people who work in the navy ⇨ NAVY

- a person who is travelling on a ship but is not working on it: **passenger**
- the person on a ship who deals with money and with passengers' problems: **purser**
- a man/woman who looks after the passengers on a ship, etc: **steward/stewardess**

4 harbours and ports

- a sheltered area on the coast where boats are kept when they are not at sea: **harbour** (*AmE* **harbor**) (*noun* C/U) ◦ *a huge natural harbour* ◦ *They couldn't leave harbour because of the weather.*
- a harbour for pleasure boats: **marina**
- an area where ships load and unload goods and passengers: **port** (*noun* C/U) ◦ *a fishing port* ◦ *a ferry port* ◦ *The ship spent a week in port.*
- a town which has a port: **port** ◦ *Liverpool was once an important port.*

- an area of a port where the ships stop to be loaded, unloaded, repaired, etc: **dock** (*often plural*) ◦ *the London docks*
- a group of docks and buildings in a port: **the docks** (*noun plural*)
- a stone or metal platform in a port where boats are loaded and unloaded: **quay**
- a place where a ship can be tied up in a harbour: **berth**

- a platform built out into the sea, a river, etc as a landing place for boats: **jetty**
- a building in which boats are kept: **boathouse**

5 travelling on a boat

- to travel on water in a boat of any type: **sail** ◦ *We sailed to America in the QE2.*

- to get on a ship: **board** (sth), **go* on board**, (*formal*) **embark**; *noun* (U): (*formal*) **embarkation** ◦ *We boarded the ship at midday.* ◦ *Passengers can now board.*
- when you are on a ship you are **on board**, **aboard** ◦ *There were a thousand passengers on board.* ◦ *All aboard please!*
- to begin a journey by sea: **sail**, **set* sail** (**from/to/for** a place) ◦ *When does the ship sail?* ◦ *The Spanish fleet set sail for England in 1588.*
- when you are sailing on the sea in a ship, you are **at sea**
- to get off a ship: **go* ashore**, (*formal*) **disembark** ◦ *If you are not sailing with us on this trip, you should go ashore now.*

– illness caused by the rolling movement of a boat: **seasickness** (*noun* U); *adjective*: **seasick** ◦ *to suffer from seasickness* ◦ *I'm feeling rather seasick – I think I'll go and lie down.*

– a holiday where you travel by boat and visit a number of places: **cruise** ◦ *My parents went on a wonderful cruise up the river Nile this summer.*
– a long journey by sea: (*formal*) **voyage** ◦ *Captain Cook made his first voyage to the South Pacific in 1768.*

■ controlling a boat
– to move or guide a ship through a particular place: **navigate** (sth) ◦ *We managed to navigate the boat through the rocks.*
– to use a map, etc to find out which way a boat, etc should go: **navigate**; *noun* (U): **navigation**
– to act as the guide on a ship, for example when it is entering a harbour: **pilot** sth; a person who does this: **pilot**
– when a boat stops somewhere on the coast, it **puts* into** a place, **puts* in at** a place
– when a boat sails into a dock, it **docks**

■ accidents in boats
– when a boat goes down under the water because it cannot float, it **sinks***
– a ship which is destroyed by a storm or by moving onto rocks, etc is **wrecked**; a ship that has been sunk or badly damaged: **wreck**, **shipwreck**; a person or ship that has suffered an accident like this has been **shipwrecked**

– to fall from a boat into the sea: **fall* overboard**
– a person who is left in a place far from civilization after a shipwreck: **castaway** ◦ *Can you imagine being a castaway on a desert island?*
– a special signal to ask for help when you are in danger at sea, etc: **SOS** ◦ *They put out an SOS to say the ship was on fire.*

6 the movement of boats
– to stay on the surface of the water: **float**; a boat which is floating is **afloat** (*not before a noun*) ◦ *The yacht was badly damaged and could not remain afloat for much longer.*
– to be carried along by wind or water in no particular direction: **drift** ◦ *The boat drifted out to sea.*
– to move backwards and forwards: **pitch**; to move from side to side: **roll** ◦ *The trawler was pitching and rolling violently in the storm.*

7 building boats
– a person or company that builds ships: **shipbuilder**; the business of doing this: **shipbuilding** (*noun* U)
– a place where ships are built and repaired: **shipyard**
– to send a newly built ship into the water: **launch** (sth) ◦ *The Queen launched the Navy's latest nuclear submarine yesterday.*

body

1 the body and its parts
2 the shape of the body
3 functions of the body
4 looking after your body
5 body movements
animals' bodies ⇨ ANIMAL

1 the body and its parts

■ the body as a whole
– the whole physical form of a person or animal: **body** ◦ *the human body*
– related to the body: **physical** (*adverb* **physically**) ◦ *physical exercise* ◦ *in good physical condition* ◦ *physically exhausted*
– a dead body: **body, corpse**

– the part of you that is not physical: **spirit**
– the part of you that thinks and remembers: **mind**

▷ more on mind and spirit ⇨ MIND, SPIRIT

■ the outside of the body

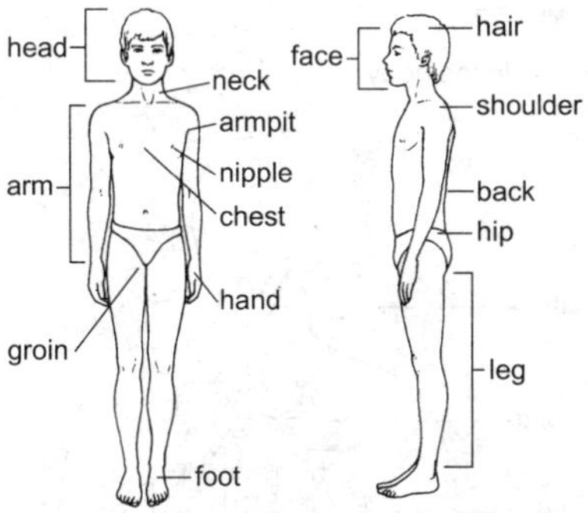

▷ head, hair and face ⇨ HEAD, HAIR, FACE
▷ hands and arms ⇨ HAND / ARM
▷ legs and feet ⇨ LEG / FOOT
▷ the sex organs ⇨ SEX²

– the main part of your body, not including the head, arms and legs: **body**, **trunk** ◦ *He had injuries to his head and body.*

– the part around the middle of your body: **waist**, (*informal*) **middle**
– the right or left part of your body: **side** ◦ *He is slightly paralysed on his left side.*
– the part of the side of your body above your legs and below your waist: **hip** ◦ *to stand with your hands on your hips* ◦ *She fell and broke a hip.*

– the back part of the body, from the neck to the bottom: **back**
– the part of your body on which you sit: **bottom**, (*informal*) **behind**, (*more formal*) **buttocks** (*noun plural*)

– the front part of your body, below your chest and above your legs: **stomach**, (*informal*)

body *contd.*

tummy, (*formal*) **abdomen**; connected with the abdomen: (*formal*) **abdominal**
- the small hollow in the middle of your stomach: **navel**, (*informal*) **tummy button**
- the upper part of the front of your body: **chest**
- one of two soft round parts of a woman's body that can produce milk: **breast**
- a woman's breasts (especially when giving measurements): **bust** ◦ *a 34-inch bust*

■ flesh and bones
- one of the hard parts inside the body of a person or an animal: **bone**
- all the bones in your body form your **skeleton**
- the natural outer covering of a human or animal body: **skin** (*noun* U)
- a piece of flesh inside the body which is used to produce movement: **muscle** (*noun* C/U); *adjective*: **muscular**
- the soft substance which is under the skin of animals and people: **fat** (*noun* U)
- the soft part under the skin, including muscle and fat: **flesh** (*noun* U)

▷ more on bones, skin and muscles ⇨ BONE, SKIN, MUSCLE

■ inside the body

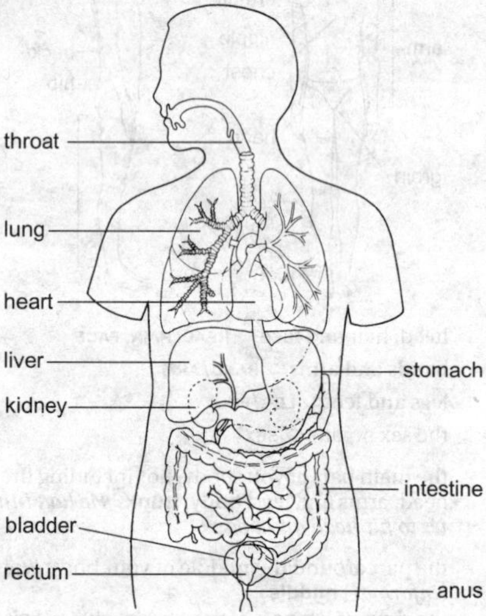

▷ teeth ⇨ TOOTH
▷ the heart ⇨ HEART
▷ the sex organs ⇨ SEX[2]

2 the shape of the body
- the size and shape of a person's body: **physique**, **build** ◦ *a strong muscular physique* ◦ *Police are looking for a young man of slim build.*
- the shape of a woman's body: **figure** ◦ *She's got a good figure.*
- the shape of the body around the waist: **waistline** ◦ *I have to watch my waistline* (= try not to get fat)*!*
- having too much flesh: **fat**
- not having much flesh: **thin**

▷ more on being fat or thin ⇨ FAT/THIN/THICK
- more than average height; not short: **tall**
- less than average height; not tall: **short**

▷ more on being tall or short ⇨ HEIGHT
- weighing a lot: **heavy**
- not weighing a lot: **light**

▷ more on how much a person weighs ⇨ WEIGHT
- having an unnatural shape: **deformed**; a deformed part of the body: **deformity** ◦ *children born with severe deformities*

3 functions of the body
- a part of the inside of your body that has a particular kind of work to do: **organ**
- an organ that makes chemical substances or that allows substances to be passed out of your body: **gland** ◦ *The doctor examined my neck for swollen glands.*
- a chemical produced in your body that controls growth and development: **hormone**; *adjective*: **hormonal**
- to change food in the stomach so that it can be used by the body: **digest** sth
- the process of digesting food: **digestion** (*noun* U)
- the parts of the body which work to digest the food you eat, for example your stomach, liver and kidneys: the **digestive system**

▷ eating ⇨ EAT
▷ the stomach ⇨ STOMACH
- to take air into your lungs and let it out again: **breathe**
- the parts of the body which are used for breathing: the **respiratory system**

▷ more on breathing ⇨ BREATHE
- one of the long thin threads in your body that carry feelings (for example, pain) to and from the brain: **nerve**
- your brain and all the nerves in your body: the **nervous system**

▷ feeling ⇨ FEEL
- the red liquid that moves round your body: **blood** (*noun* U)
- the movement of the blood around the body: **circulation**
- the regular movement of the heart or the sound it makes: **heartbeat**
- the regular beat that you can feel, for example in your wrist, as your blood moves through your body: **pulse** ◦ *The doctor took my pulse.*

▷ more on blood ⇨ BLOOD
- the liquid that comes out of your skin when you are hot, ill or afraid: **sweat** (*noun* U), (*formal*)

perspiration; *verbs*: **sweat**, (*formal*) **perspire** ◦ *Sweat was pouring off him.*

– the waste water that you pass out of your body when you go to the toilet: **urine** (*noun* U), (*informal*) **pee** (*noun* U); to pass waste water from the body: (*informal*) **pee**, (*informal*) **have a pee**, (*formal*) **urinate**
– the solid waste matter that is passed from the body through the anus: **faeces** (*noun* U), (*formal*) **excrement** (*noun* U)
– to get rid of waste material or water from the body: **go* to the toilet**, (*more informal*) **go* to the loo** ◦ *I need to go to the loo.*
– to send out wind (air that is formed in the stomach) from the anus: **break* wind**, (*informal*) **fart**

▷ using the toilet ⇨ TOILET

– the parts of the body which are used for producing babies or young animals: the **reproductive system**

▷ sex and reproduction ⇨ SEX²

4 looking after your body

– the condition of your body: **health** (*noun* U) ◦ *She's been in poor health ever since she had the baby.*
– in good physical health: **healthy**; *opposite*: **unhealthy** ◦ *an unhealthy lifestyle* (= a way of life which prevents you being healthy)
– physically strong and active: **fit**, **in good shape**; *opposite*: **unfit** ◦ *You need to be extremely fit to take part in competitive sport.*
– having a fit, strong and health body: **athletic** ◦ *She's very athletic.* ◦ *an athletic body/figure*
– the state of being physically fit: **fitness** (*noun* U) ◦ *Skiers need a high level of physical fitness.*

– things which are good to do to keep your body clean and healthy: **hygiene** (*noun* U); *adjective*: **hygienic** ◦ *personal hygiene*

▷ keeping the body clean ⇨ WASH

▷ not being in good health ⇨ ILLNESS

▷ being strong or weak ⇨ STRONG/WEAK

– using your body in a way that will make you more healthy: **exercise** (*noun* U); *verb*: **exercise** ◦ *You should take more exercise – why don't you walk to work?* ◦ *Eat sensibly and exercise regularly.*
– rubbing or pressing sb's body in order to reduce pain or stiffness: **massage** (*noun* C/U)

▷ taking exercise ⇨ EXERCISE

5 body movements

– to make short quick movements which you cannot control, because of being afraid, cold, etc: **shake**, **shiver**, **tremble**; a shaking movement: **shiver** ◦ *trembling with excitement* ◦ *shivering with cold*
– to make a sudden quick and uncontrollable movement: **twitch**; *noun*: **twitch** ◦ *The animal twitched and then lay still.*
– to make a sudden movement because of surprise, fear or excitement: **jump** ◦ *Oh, it's you – you made me jump!*

▷ the movements of muscles ⇨ MUSCLE

boil

– a way of cooking ⇨ COOK
– water ⇨ WATER

bomb

1 different kinds of bomb
2 using bombs
see also WEAPON, FIGHT, WAR

1 different kinds of bomb

– a container that is filled with material that will explode if it is thrown, dropped, etc: **bomb** ◦ *We were not far from the station when the bomb went off.* ◦ *The cathedral was hit by a bomb.*
– a small bomb that can be thrown by hand or fired from a special gun: **grenade** ◦ *a hand grenade*
– a bomb that explodes using the energy produced when an atom is split: **atomic bomb**, **atom bomb**, **nuclear bomb**

– a substance that can explode and that is used to destroy or damage sth: **explosive**; *adjective*: **explosive** ◦ *The suitcase was packed with explosives.* ◦ *an explosive device*

– a bomb that is hidden underground or underwater: **mine**; to put mines in a place: **mine** a place; an area of land or sea where mines have been hidden: **minefield**

– a bomb that is fired from a submarine or a ship and that can travel underwater: **torpedo** (*plural* **torpedoes**)
– a powerful exploding weapon that can be sent long distances through the air: **missile**; a missile that you can direct to a place while it is in the air: **guided missile**
– the part of a missile or torpedo that explodes when it hits sth: **warhead** ◦ *a nuclear warhead*

– a bomb that is connected to a clock: **time bomb**
– a bomb that is connected to a car: **car bomb**
– a bomb that is designed to start a fire: **fire bomb**, (*formal*) **incendiary device**
– a bomb that is made of a bottle filled with petrol: **petrol bomb**
– a bomb that is made to look like a letter or parcel: **letter bomb**, **parcel bomb**

2 using bombs

– when a bomb breaks open with a loud noise and causes a lot of damage, it **goes* off**, **explodes**, **bursts***; *noun*: **explosion** ◦ *The torpedo exploded as it hit the side of the ship.* ◦ *You could hear the sound of the explosion from three miles away.*

– to cause a bomb to explode: **set*** sth **off**, (*formal*) **detonate** sth; a device that causes a bomb to explode: **detonator**
– to be destroyed in an explosion: **blow* up**; to destroy sth in an explosion: **blow*** sth **up** ◦ *The car blew up when the door was opened.* ◦ *The terrorists tried to blow up the plane.*

bomb *contd.*

- to attack a place with bombs: **bomb** a place, **drop bombs on** a place ◦ *to bomb a city* ◦ *A lot of bombs were dropped but most did not go off.*
- a type of aeroplane that drops bombs: **bomber**
- the place where it is intended that a bomb should explode: **target** ◦ *to hit/miss the target*

- an attempt to hurt people and/or damage a place with bombs: **bomb attack** ◦ *There has been a terrorist bomb attack on a tourist bus this morning.*
- a warning that sb has left a bomb somewhere: **bomb threat**
- a person who throws bombs or leaves them to explode in a public place: **bomber** ◦ *The bombers left a one-thousand pound bomb in a car outside a police station.*

- to remove the part of a bomb that would cause it to explode: **defuse** a bomb
- removing or exploding bombs to make an area safe: **bomb disposal** (*noun* U)
- the section of the police that deals with bombs and bombers: **bomb squad**

bone

other parts of the body ⇨ BODY

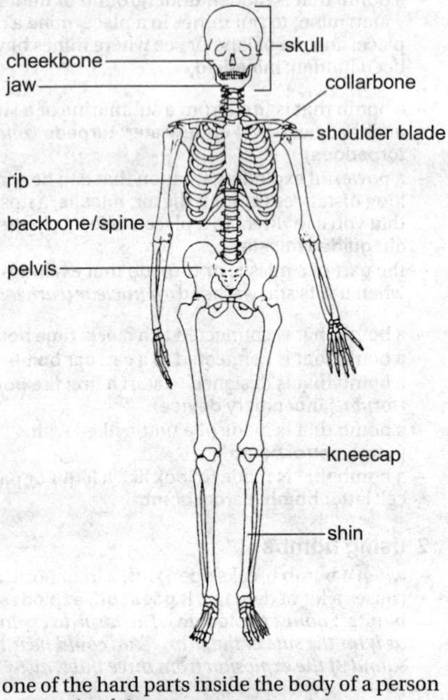

- one of the hard parts inside the body of a person or an animal: **bone**
- all the bones in your body form your **skeleton**
- a part of the body where two bones fit together: **joint**
- the joint in the middle of your arm: **elbow**
- the joint in the middle of your leg: **knee**
- the line of bones down your back: **backbone**, **spine**; *adjective*: **spinal** ◦ *spinal injuries*
- one of the small bones of the spine: **vertebra** (*plural* **vertebrae**) ◦ *He fell off a ladder and damaged several vertebrae in the lower part of his spine.*

- if your body (or part of it) is thin and the shape of the bones can be clearly seen, it is **bony** ◦ *bony fingers*

■ broken bones
- if sb does sth which causes a bone to separate into two or more pieces, they **break*** sth, (*more formal*) **fracture** sth ◦ *He fell and broke his leg.* ◦ *She fractured her ankle in a skating accident.*
- a bone or part of the body that is injured in this way is **broken**, **fractured**
- if sb does sth which causes a bone to come out of its proper position, they **dislocate** sth; *adjective*: **dislocated** ◦ *He dislocated his wrist.* ◦ *a dislocated arm*
- the white substance that becomes hard when it is dry and is put on in hospital to help broken bones to get better: **plaster** (*noun* U) ◦ *She has her leg in plaster.*
- a piece of wood or metal that is used to keep a broken bone in the right position: **splint**
- a piece of cloth that you use to support a broken arm: **sling** ◦ *He had his arm in a sling.*

- when a broken bone gets better, it **mends** ◦ *The broken bone in my foot had still not mended.*

book

1 physical parts of books
2 contents of books
3 different kinds of book
4 books to write in
5 writing and producing a book
6 buying, borrowing and keeping books
7 reading a book
see also WRITE

1 physical parts of books
- a number of pieces of paper, with words printed or written on them, joined together in a cover: **book** ◦ *At present I'm reading a book about space travel.* ◦ *This book has been a best-seller* (= bought by a lot of people) *for months.*
- one of the sheets of paper in a book: **page**; one side of a page: **page** ◦ *It was a very old book and some of the pages were missing.* ◦ *It's a long book – over five hundred pages.*
- the letters and words that are printed in a book: **print** (*noun* U) ◦ *This print is so small I can hardly read it.*

▷ more on pages ⇨ PAGE

- the outside part of a book or magazine: **cover**
- a book which has a hard cover: **hardback** ◦ *Until now, it's only been available in hardback.*
- a book which has a soft cover: **paperback** ◦ *Is there a paperback version?*

2 contents of books

- the name of a book: **title** ◦ *It's about a journey across Africa by train – but I can't remember the title.*
- (used about a book) named: **entitled** ◦ *The winner of this year's literature prize is a book entitled 'Tomorrow's Children'.*
- a short piece of writing at the beginning of a book which says sth about the book: **preface, foreword**

- one of the parts into which a book is divided: **chapter** ◦ *Chapter 12 is about pronouns.*
- the words at the beginning of a chapter or section, which tell you its name: **heading** ◦ *chapter headings* ◦ *a new section heading*
- a list of the main subjects in a book and the page numbers where you can find them: **contents** (*noun plural*) ◦ *the contents page*
- one of a set or series of books: **part, volume** ◦ *This encyclopedia comes in twelve volumes.*

- a list of names and subjects arranged in alphabetical order at the end of a book: **index** ◦ *Look it up in the index.*
- a list of the books and articles that a writer used when writing a book, or a list of books related to a particular subject: **bibliography** ◦ *There's a very useful bibliography at the end of this book.*
- a section at the end of a book which gives extra information: **appendix** (*plural* **appendices**)

- to say what the subject of a book is, you can say that it is **on/about** sb/sth, it **deals* with** sb/sth, it **covers** sth ◦ *Have you got a book about Venice?* ◦ *His first book dealt with vegetarian cookery.*
- when we want to talk about sth that is written in a book, we can say that the book **says*** sth ◦ *What does the encyclopedia say about Shakespeare's parents?*

3 different kinds of book

- a book which tells a story about people or events that are not real: **novel**
- a book which tells an exciting story, often about a crime: **thriller**
- a book which tells the story of sb's life: **biography**; a biography which sb writes about their own life: **autobiography**
- a book of stories for children: **story book**
- a book for children with pictures: **picture book**
- a book of songs: **song book**

- stories, novels, etc which describe events and people that do not really exist: **fiction** (*noun* U)
- books that are about real people and events: **non-fiction** (*noun* U)
- novels, poems and plays which are considered to be of high quality, and an important part of a country's culture: **literature** (*noun* U) ◦ *I'm studying 20th century German literature.*

▷ more on literature ⇨ LITERATURE

- a book which contains hymns: **hymn book**
- a book which contains prayers: **prayer book**
- the book which describes how the world was created according to the Christian and Jewish religions, and tells the story of the life of Jesus Christ: **the Bible**
- the holy book of the Muslims: **the Koran**
- the holy books of religion, such as the Bible: **scripture** (*noun* U), **the scriptures** (*noun plural*)

- a book which you use to find out information: **reference book**
- a small book with a soft cover which usually gives information or advice: **booklet**
- a book which consists of only a few pages giving some information: **pamphlet**

■ reference books

a book that ...	is called ...
gives lists of words and their meanings, etc	a **dictionary**
contains maps	an **atlas**
gives information about many subjects, arranged in alphabetical order	an **encyclopedia**
describes a town or country, and suggests interesting places to visit there	a **(travel) guide, guidebook**
explains how to do or operate sth, for example a computer	a **manual**
explains how to prepare food and cook it	a **recipe book, cookery book, cookbook**
you use to study and to help you understand a subject	a **textbook**
gives lists of people's names, addresses, telephone numbers, etc	a **directory**
has photos of things you can buy and details about prices, etc	**catalogue** (*AmE* **catalog**)

4 books to write in

- a book which consists of a number of blank pages which you can write in: **notebook**; a notebook that people use mainly at school: **exercise book**
- a small book that you keep the addresses of people you know in: **address book**
- a book in which you write down your appointments, etc; or a book in which you write down what happens to you each day: **diary**

- a book which has blank pages on which you can stick photos, stamps, etc: **album**
- a book which has large blank pages on which you can stick pictures, newspaper articles, etc: **scrapbook**

book *contd.*

5 writing and producing a book

- to put words about a particular subject on paper, creating a book: **write*** sth ◦ *My wife's writing a novel.*
- a person who writes books: **writer**
- a person who has written a particular book: **author** ◦ *Who's the author of this book?*
- the books, articles, etc written by a person or a group of people: **writings** (*noun plural*) ◦ *selected writings of 20th-century authors*
- the money which an author receives each time that a book that he/she has written is sold: **royalties** (*noun plural*)

▷ more on writing ⇨ WRITE

- to produce a book and make it available to the public: **publish** sth; a person or firm that publishes books: **publisher** ◦ *His book will be published in about six months' time.* ◦ *Her first novel was rejected by fifteen publishers.*
- to be published for the first time: **come* out**, **appear** ◦ *When this book first came out, it was considered to be very shocking.*

▷ more on publishing books ⇨ PUBLISH

- one book, of which many have been produced: **copy** ◦ *Is there a copy of 'Hamlet' in the library?*
- the form in which a book, newspaper, etc appears; or a number of copies of a book, newspaper, etc printed at the same time: **edition** *'Which edition have you got?' 'The second one – it's got two new chapters.'* ◦ *There were 6000 copies printed in this edition.*

6 buying, borrowing and keeping books

- a shop where you can buy books: **bookshop** (*AmE* **bookstore**)
- a small shop in the street, at a railway station, etc where you can buy newspapers, magazines and books: **bookstall** (*AmE* **news-stand**)
- a person who sells books: **bookseller**
- a small card with an amount of money written on it that you can use to buy a book: (*BrE*) **book token** ◦ *I bought him a £15 book token for his birthday.*
- not new when you buy it: **second-hand** ◦ *I got it second-hand.* ◦ *a second-hand bookshop*
- a place where you can go to read, study and borrow books: **library**

▷ more on libraries ⇨ LIBRARY

- a piece of furniture with shelves which you keep books in: **bookcase**
- a piece of wood attached to the wall which you can put books on: **shelf** (*plural* **shelves**)
- a heavy object used for holding books upright on a shelf: **bookend**

7 reading a book

- to turn back the cover of a book in order to look inside: **open** a book; *opposite*: **close** a book ◦ *She asked us to open our books at page 15.* ◦ *Now close your book and see how much you can remember.*
- to look at and understand written words: **read*** (sth) ◦ *'What are you doing?' 'I'm reading.' 'What are you reading?' 'A book about Henry VIII.'*

▷ more on reading ⇨ READ

- a piece of writing, usually in a newspaper or magazine, which gives sb's opinion of a book: **review** ◦ *Her first book got a really bad review in 'The Times'.*
- a person whose job it is to write reviews: **reviewer**, **critic**

■ **MORE...**

- the words that are sometimes written at the beginning of a book, where the author writes that the book is for a particular person: **dedication**; to write a dedication: **dedicate** sth **to** sb ◦ *There's a dedication to his wife at the beginning of his book.* ◦ *He dedicated it to his mother and father.*
- a short piece of writing at the beginning or end of a book in which the author thanks people who have helped him/her: **acknowledgements** (*noun plural*)

border ⇨ COUNTRY[1]

boring ⇨ INTERESTING

borrow/lend

see also GIVE

- to take or receive sth from sb/sth that you intend to give back: **borrow** (sth) (**from/off** sb/sth) ◦ *I've borrowed £10 from Arthur, but I've got to give it back by Friday.* ◦ *If we need more money, we'll have to borrow from the bank.*
- a person who borrows sth: **borrower**
- to allow sb to use sth which they must give back later: **lend*** sth (to **sb**), (*formal*) **loan** sth (**to** sb) ◦ *Arthur lent me £10 until Friday.* ◦ *The Queen loaned some paintings to the art exhibition.*
- if you borrow sth from sb, it is (*formal*) **on loan** ◦ *Several of the most valuable items are on loan from the British Museum.*
- a person or organization that lends you sth: (*formal*) **lender** ◦ *Banks and building societies are the main lenders of money in Britain.*

- when you give back sth which you have borrowed, you **return** it (**to** sb/sth), **take*/give*** it **back** (**to** sb/sth)

■ borrowing money

- money, etc that sb/sth lends you: **loan** ◦ *The bank have given me a £5000 loan.*
- money that you borrow in order to buy a house: **mortgage** ◦ *I've taken out an £80000 mortgage over 25 years.*
- the money that you pay to a bank, etc for borrowing an amount of money: **interest** (*noun* U)
- the percentage of interest that you pay for borrowing an amount of money: **interest rate** ◦ *The government has just brought interest rates down to 8%.*

bottle ⇨ CONTAINER

bottom ⇨ PLACE²

bowl ⇨ PLATE/BOWL/DISH

box ⇨ CONTAINER

boxing

other sports ⇨ **SPORT**

- the sport in which two people fight by hitting each other with their hands inside big gloves: **boxing** (*noun* U); *verb*: **box** ◦ *Shall we watch the boxing tonight?* ◦ *He learned to box at school.*

- a person who boxes: **boxer, fighter** ◦ *a professional boxer*
- a boxer who weighs very little: **lightweight** (*adjective, noun*) ◦ *He'll be fighting as a lightweight.*
- a boxer who weighs a lot: **heavyweight** (*adjective, noun*) ◦ *a heavyweight boxer*
- a boxer in between a lightweight and a heavyweight boxer: **middleweight** (*adjective, noun*)

- the place where boxers fight in a competition: (**boxing**) **ring**
- the ropes around the outside of the ring: **the ropes** ◦ *to have your opponent on the ropes*
- the corner of the ring where the boxers sit when they are not fighting: **corner** ◦ *The bell rang and the boxers went back to their corners.*

- a boxing competition between two people: (**boxing**) **match, fight** ◦ *He's been training hard for this match.* ◦ *Did you see the fight last night?*
- each part of a fight (which lasts two or three minutes): **round** ◦ *That's the end of the first round.* ◦ *Round Three!*
- an organized competition with a series of fights: **championship** ◦ *the 1993 World Boxing Championship*
- a boxer fighting in a competition: **contestant, competitor**
- the person whose job is to see that the rules are not broken, and who controls the match: **referee**
- the boxer who wins a championship: **champion** ◦ *the European heavyweight champion*

- the gloves worn by boxers: **boxing gloves**
- to hit sb with your fist: **punch** sb, **hit*** sb; *nouns*: **punch, hit** ◦ *to hit somebody below the belt* ◦ *a punch to the jaw*
- to hit sb hard so they fall down: **knock** sb **down**; to hit sb hard so that they cannot stand up: **knock** sb **out**; when sb has been knocked to the ground, they are **down** ◦ *He's down! – this could be the end of the fight.*

boy ⇨ CHILD

brain ⇨ MIND

brake ⇨ DRIVE

branch ⇨ TREE

brave

see also AFRAID, DANGEROUS

- not afraid of doing dangerous or difficult things: **brave** (*adverb* **bravely**), **courageous** (*adverb* **courageously**) ◦ *a brave soldier* ◦ *to fight bravely* ◦ *a courageous person*
- the ability to control your fear and to behave in a brave way: **bravery** (*noun* U), **courage** (*noun* U) ◦ *He showed great bravery.* ◦ *to face death with courage*
- courage and determination: (*informal*) **guts** ◦ *to have a lot of guts* ◦ *You need guts to disagree with your boss.*

- to be brave enough to do sth: **have the courage/nerve** (**to** do sth) ◦ *We didn't have the courage to admit what really happened.*
- to try hard to be brave enough to do sth: **pluck up** (**the**) **courage** (**to** do sth) ◦ *She finally plucked up the courage to ask him out.*

- a man/woman who has done sth brave and is admired for it: **hero/heroine** ◦ *a war hero*
- very brave behaviour: **heroism** (*noun* U); *adjective*: **heroic** (*adverb* **heroically**) ◦ *acts of heroism* ◦ *a heroic effort* ◦ *They died heroically, refusing to cooperate with the enemy.*
- courageous and willing to do dangerous things: **daring** ◦ *a daring fighter pilot* ◦ *a daring attack*
- a person who feels no fear is **fearless** (*adverb* **fearlessly**)
- a person who likes to try new things and have adventures is **adventurous**

- to persuade a person to do sth dangerous to show how brave they are: **dare** sb (**to** do sth) ◦ *They dared him to climb onto the school roof and jump off.* ◦ *Go on – do it! I dare you!*

- a badge that is given to a very brave person: **medal** ◦ *He was awarded a medal for bravery.*

■ not brave
- a person who has no courage and is afraid in unpleasant or dangerous situations: **coward** ◦ *Don't be such a coward! It won't hurt.*
- showing no courage: **cowardly**; *noun* (U): **cowardice** ◦ *cowardly behaviour* ◦ *a cowardly lie* ◦ *He was accused of cowardice.*

- if you do not have enough courage to do sth, you **daren't** do it, **don't dare** (**to**) do it, **don't have the nerve to** do it ◦ *We didn't dare go into the room without knocking.* ◦ *Nobody dared to speak until the door was closed.* ◦ *I didn't have the nerve to ask again.*
- if you suddenly lose your courage, you **lose* your nerve** ◦ *I was going to jump but I lost my nerve at the last minute.*

■ **MORE ...**
- a weak person who is not very brave: (*informal*) **wimp** ◦ *Don't be a wimp!*

brave *contd.*

- if sb is brave enough to do what they think is right, they **have the courage of** their **convictions** ◦ *Have the courage of your convictions and join the demonstration!*

bread

see also FOOD

- a kind of food which is made from flour and water: **bread** (*noun* U) ◦ *Can you cut me a slice of bread, please.* ◦ *She put some cheese on a bit/piece of bread.* ◦ *white/brown bread*
- bread that has been shaped and cooked in one large piece: **loaf** (**of bread**) (*plural* **loaves**)
- the outside of a loaf or slice of bread: **crust**
- very small pieces of bread, cake or biscuit: **crumbs** (*noun plural*) ◦ *breadcrumbs*

- a very small loaf of bread for one person: **roll** ◦ *rolls and butter for breakfast* ◦ *a ham roll* (= a roll filled with ham)
- a light roll with a curved shape: **croissant**
- bread that has been cut into slices: **sliced bread** (*noun* U), **sliced loaf**
- made from flour that contains all the grain: **wholemeal** ◦ *a wholemeal loaf*

- bread which has just been baked is **fresh** ◦ *They bake fresh bread daily.*
- old bread which is hard and dry is **stale** ◦ *The bread's gone stale.*

- a piece of wood used for cutting bread on: **breadboard**
- the knife used for cutting bread: **bread knife**
- a container for keeping bread in: **bread bin**

■ ways of eating bread

- two pieces of bread with sth in between: **sandwich** ◦ *a cheese sandwich* ◦ *Shall we make sandwiches for the journey?*
- bread which is made brown by heating: **toast** (*noun* U) ◦ *a slice of toast for breakfast*
- a machine which makes toast: **toaster**
- to put butter, jam, etc on bread: **spread*** A **on** B, **spread*** B **with** A ◦ *He spread jam on his bread.* ◦ *He spread his bread with jam.*

- some things that you can spread on bread: **butter** (*noun* U), **margarine** (*noun* U), **jam** (*noun* U) (= a sweet substance made from fruit), **marmalade** (*noun* U) (= jam made from oranges or lemons), **spread** (*noun* U) (= any soft food that you can spread onto bread), **honey** (*noun* U) (= the sweet substance made by bees) ◦ *bread and butter* ◦ *toast and marmalade* ◦ *chocolate spread*

▷ more on butter and margarine ⇨ BUTTER

■ making bread

- to prepare and cook bread: **bake** (sth); *noun* (U): **baking** ◦ *I'm going to do some baking this afternoon.*
- a person who bakes and sells bread and cakes: **baker**
- the place where a baker makes bread: **bakery**
- a place where bread, cakes, etc are sold: **baker's** (**shop**)

- the white or brown powder used to make bread: **flour** (*noun* U)
- the mixture of flour and water used to make bread: **dough** (*noun* U)
- the brown substance used to make bread rise: **yeast** (*noun* U)
- to move the dough around with your hands: **knead** sth ◦ *Knead the dough until smooth.*

▷ more on flour ⇨ FLOUR

break

1 breaking in two
2 breaking completely (into many pieces)
3 easy or difficult to break

machines which are broken and do not work ⇨ MACHINE

see also JOIN, REPAIR

1 breaking in two

- to separate into two or more pieces: **break***; to cause sth to do this: **break*** sth; *adjective*: **broken** ◦ *How did the teapot get broken?* ◦ *She broke her arm skiing.* ◦ *a broken window*
- to separate into two pieces: **break* in two/half** ◦ *It slipped from my fingers and broke in two on the kitchen floor.*

- to break in two suddenly, with a sharp noise: **snap**; the sound you hear when this happens: **snap** ◦ *I was bending the stick and it suddenly snapped.* ◦ *It broke in half with a snap.*
- to break into two or more parts from end to end: **split***; to cause this to happen: **split*** sth; the place where sth has split: **split** ◦ *The boots were old and the leather had split.* ◦ *He split the wood with an axe.* ◦ *There was a huge split in the trunk of the tree.*

- to separate from sth larger: **break*/come* off** (sth); to cause sth to do this: **break*** sth **off** (sth) ◦ *The handle has broken off my cup.* ◦ *One of the legs has come off this chair.* ◦ *Can you break a bit of chocolate off for me?*
- to remove sth from sth larger by using force: **pull** sth **off** (sth) ◦ *I accidentally pulled the handle off the door!*

- to break so that a line appears, but without breaking into pieces: **crack**; to cause this to happen: **crack** sth; a line made in this way: **crack** ◦ *The water was too hot and the glass cracked.* ◦ *There was a long crack down the middle of the mirror.*
- to break a small piece off the edge or the surface of sth made of glass or china: **chip** sth; a small piece that has broken off, or a place where a small piece has broken off: **chip** ◦ *Most of our cups and saucers are chipped.* ◦ *The plate had a chip in it.*

2 breaking completely (into many pieces)

- to separate into a lot of small pieces: **break* into pieces, fall* to pieces, disintegrate**; *noun* (U):

disintegration ◦ *The plant pot fell to pieces when I picked it up.*
- to cause sth to separate into a lot of small pieces: **break*** sth **into pieces/bits** ◦ *All the toys had been broken into pieces.*
- (used about sth that has different parts) to separate into pieces: **come*/fall* apart** ◦ *It was a very old book and it just came apart as I was reading it.*
- to break under force or pressure: **give* way**, **collapse**; *noun*: **collapse** ◦ *The platform gave way under the weight of all the people.* ◦ *The collapse of the stand led to the loss of many lives.*
- a boat or aeroplane that breaks into a lot of pieces **breaks* up** ◦ *The ship broke up on the rocks.*

- to break sth in such a way that it will never be repaired: **destroy** sth, **smash** sth (**up**)
- to press or break a hard object into very small pieces or into powder: **crush** sth ◦ *This machine crushes the rock into small pieces.*
- to break into long, thin, sharp pieces: **splinter**; a long, thin, sharp piece of wood, metal or glass that has broken off a larger piece: **splinter**
- to break into very small pieces: **shatter**; to break glass into very small pieces: **shatter** sth, **smash** sth ◦ *The glass fell and shattered on the floor.* ◦ *The force of the explosion shattered all the windows in the area.*

- if sth has broken or has been broken into many pieces, it is **in pieces**
- one of the small pieces into which sth breaks: **fragment** ◦ *The police found nothing but some fragments of bone.*
- the pieces from sth that has crashed to the ground or been destroyed: **debris** (*noun* U) ◦ *The debris from the plane crash was scattered over a wide area.*
- pieces of broken brick, stone, etc, especially from a damaged building: **rubble** (*noun* U)

- if sth is broken in any way, or is not in perfect order, it is **damaged**

▷ ways in which things can be damaged ⇨ **DAMAGE**

3 easy or difficult to break

- if sth can be broken easily, it is **fragile**; if it is not easily broken, it is **strong**, **tough**; if it cannot be broken, it is **unbreakable** ◦ *Be careful – that vase is very fragile.*
- to make sth stronger so that it will not break easily: **strengthen** sth, **toughen** sth ◦ *toughened glass*
- if sth is hard, but it is still easily broken, it is **brittle** ◦ *brittle bones*
- if sth bends easily without breaking, it is **flexible**

breakfast

see also MEAL

- a meal which you have when you get up in the morning: **breakfast** (*noun* C/U)
- the time that you eat breakfast: **breakfast time** ◦ *I'm not very hungry, I'm afraid – I had a huge breakfast this morning.* ◦ *Do you want some breakfast before you go?* ◦ *Hurry up, it's breakfast time!*

- food made from grain that you eat with milk: (**breakfast**) **cereal** (*noun* U) ◦ *a packet of cereal*
- a type of cereal made from corn (= maize) and eaten with milk: **cornflakes** (*noun plural*) ◦ *a bowl of cornflakes*
- oats (= a type of grain) cooked with water and milk that you eat hot: **porridge** (*noun* U) ◦ *Do you want cornflakes or porridge?*
- food made of grains, nuts, dried fruit, etc that you eat with milk for breakfast: **muesli** (*noun* U)

- cooked food which people sometimes eat for breakfast: **bacon and eggs** (= thin pieces of meat from the back or sides of a pig, with fried eggs), **boiled egg** (= an egg cooked in its shell in boiling water)

▷ more on eggs ⇨ **EGG**

- bread that you eat for breakfast: **bread** (*noun* U), **toast** (*noun* U) (= bread that has been heated to make it brown), **roll** (= a very small loaf of bread for one person), **croissant** (= a light roll with a curved shape) ◦ *a slice/piece of bread*
- things to put on bread: **butter** (*noun* U), **jam** (*noun* U) (a sweet substance made with fruit and sugar), **marmalade** (*noun* U) (= a bitter kind of jam usually made with oranges or lemons)

▷ more on bread and butter ⇨ **BREAD, BUTTER**

- drinks that people have for breakfast: **juice** (*noun* U) (= the liquid part of fruit), **tea** (*noun* U), **coffee** (*noun* U) ◦ *a glass of orange juice* ◦ *Another cup of coffee, please.* ◦ *a pot of tea for two*

▷ coffee and tea ⇨ **COFFEE/TEA**

▷ other drinks ⇨ **DRINK**

■ types of breakfast
- a breakfast with bacon, eggs, etc: **cooked breakfast**
- (in a hotel) a cooked breakfast served with cereal and toast and marmalade: **English breakfast**
- a breakfast with bread or croissant with butter, jam and coffee: **continental breakfast**

breathe

1 normal breathing
2 breathing with difficulty
3 being unable to breathe
see also AIR

1 normal breathing

- to take air into your body and let it out again: **breathe** ◦ *She's still breathing.* ◦ *The train was terribly crowded and I was finding it difficult to breathe.* ◦ *These substances are polluting the air we breathe.*

breathe *contd.*

– the action of breathing: (*formal*) **respiration** (*noun* U); connected with breathing: (*formal*) **respiratory** ◦ *respiratory illnesses*

– one of the two parts inside your chest that are used for breathing: **lung** ◦ *We filled our lungs with the wonderful sea air.*
– the tube that joins the throat to the lungs: **windpipe** ◦ *a blocked windpipe*

– to take air, etc into your lungs: **breathe** (sth) **in**, (*formal*) **inhale** (sth) ◦ *Breathe in slowly.* ◦ *Try not to breathe the smoke in.*
– to send air, etc out of your lungs: **breathe** (sth) **out**, (*formal*) **exhale** (sth)
– the air that you take in and let out: **breath** (*noun* U); an act of taking air into your lungs: **breath** ◦ *He's got bad breath* (= breath that smells unpleasant). ◦ *to take a deep breath*

– to breathe air in through the nose so that it makes a noise: **sniff**; *noun*: **sniff** ◦ *Stop sniffing and get a handkerchief!*
– to deliberately stop breathing for a short time: **hold*** your **breath** ◦ *We all held our breath and waited for the explosion.*
– to send air, etc out of your mouth: **blow*** (sth) ◦ *He blew a cloud of tobacco smoke across the room.*

2 breathing with difficulty

– breathing quickly after exercise: **out of breath** ◦ *These days she can't even go upstairs without getting out of breath.*
– breathing quickly or with difficulty: **breathless** ◦ *She sat breathless on the edge of the bed.* ◦ *He was breathless from running up the stairs.*
– to breathe quickly and noisily through your mouth: **gasp** (**for breath**) ◦ *She was coughing and gasping for breath.*
– to take short, quick breaths through your mouth: **pant** ◦ *She was panting heavily after the race.*

– to rest after exercise so that your breathing becomes normal again: **get*** your **breath back** ◦ *Give me time to get my breath back.*
– to breathe in deeply after an effort: **draw* breath** ◦ *She ran for a few metres and then stopped to draw breath.*

3 being unable to breathe

– to be unable to breathe because sth is blocking the air passage: **choke**; to cause sb to be unable to breathe: **choke** sb ◦ *A fish bone stuck in her throat and she choked to death.* ◦ *The smoke was choking us.*
– to die because of being unable to breathe: **suffocate**; to kill sb in this way: **suffocate** sb; *noun* (U): **suffocation** ◦ *She was suffocated by the smoke.* ◦ *to die of suffocation*
– to kill sb by squeezing their neck: **strangle** sb

– a sudden noise in your throat, often caused by eating too fast: **hiccup** (*often plural*) ◦ *You'll get hiccups if you eat so fast.*

– a chest disease which makes breathing difficult: **asthma** (*noun* U); *adjective:* **asthmatic** ◦ *an asthmatic child*

– the action of forcing air into a person's lungs when they have stopped breathing: **artificial respiration** (*noun* U) ◦ *We had to give her artificial respiration.*
– a type of artificial respiration in which you breathe into a person's mouth: **the kiss of life** ◦ *She dragged him out of the water and gave him the kiss of life.*

■ **MORE . . .**
– a device that a person suffering from asthma uses to help them breathe: **inhaler**
– a machine used in hospital to help a person with breathing problems: **ventilator** ◦ *She had to be put on a ventilator.*
– a device which you wear over your face and which provides oxygen for you to breathe: **oxygen mask**
– a short tube used by a swimmer which makes it possible to breathe underwater: **snorkel**

bridge

see also ROAD

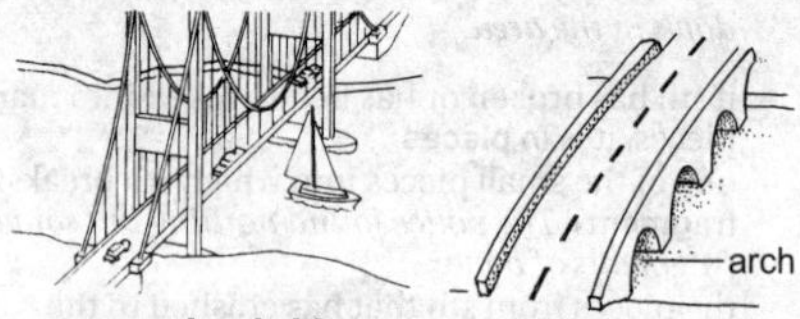

suspension bridge **bridge**

– a structure that carries a road, railway, etc across a river, valley, road, etc: **bridge** ◦ *They decided to build a new bridge over the river.* ◦ *a railway bridge*
– a bridge that is for people who are travelling on foot: **footbridge**
– a type of bridge that hangs from steel cables which are supported by towers at each end: **suspension bridge**
– a long, high bridge that carries a road or railway across a valley: **viaduct**
– a bridge that carries one road over another road: **flyover**

– a curved structure that is part of some bridges: **arch**

– to travel over a bridge from one side to the other: **cross** (sth), **cross over** (sth), **go*/drive*/walk across** (sth) ◦ *We drove across to the other side of the bridge.*

bring/take/carry

see also BAG, CONTAINER, TRANSPORT

■ bringing
– to come to a place carrying sth or together with sb/sth: **bring*** sb/sth ◦ *Diane's bringing some*

videos over to watch. ◦ *Is it all right if I bring the children?*
– to go to a place and bring sb/sth from there: **get***(sb) sb/sth, **fetch** sb/sth, **collect** sb/sth ◦ *I'll get you some bread from the baker's.*

▷ more on getting and fetching ⇨ GET/OBTAIN

■ taking
– to go to a place carrying sth or together with sb/sth: **take*** sb/sth ◦ *Could you take these books to the library for me?* ◦ *I've got to take him to the dentist this afternoon.*
– to take sth to the place requested: **deliver** sth ◦ *They told me that the carpet would be delivered on Tuesday.*
– to cause sth to be taken somewhere without going there yourself: **send*** sth (**to** sb/sth), **send*** (sb) sth ◦ *What is the quickest way to send this parcel to Hong Kong?* ◦ *Don't forget to send me a postcard.*

■ carrying
– to hold sb/sth in your hands or arms or on your back while you are moving from one place to another: **carry** sb/sth ◦ *Shall I carry your bags for you?* ◦ *She was carrying her baby in her arms.*
– to take hold of sb/sth and move them/it to a different position: **lift** sb/sth ◦ *They lifted the television onto the table.*
– to put sth heavy in sth or on sb/sth: **load** sth ◦ *We loaded all our suitcases into the car.*

– (used about a vehicle) to contain people or goods: **carry** sb/sth ◦ *The bus was carrying far more passengers than it should.*
– to have enough space to carry sb/sth: **take*** sb/sth ◦ *How many people can this bus take?*

▷ more on lifting things ⇨ LIFT

– something that can be carried is **portable** ◦ *a portable telephone* ◦ *a portable radio*
– the amount that you can carry in your arms: **armful** ◦ *I had an armful of papers.*
– something heavy that is carried or is going to be carried: **load** ◦ *The lorry had a full load of bricks.*

– a person whose job is to carry suitcases, etc at an airport, station, etc: **porter**
– a person whose job is to carry letters, important papers, etc, especially when they are urgent: **courier**

▷ carrying people who are injured ⇨ ACCIDENT

broad ⇨ WIDE/NARROW

brother ⇨ FAMILY

brown ⇨ COLOUR

brush

see also CLEAN/DIRTY

– one of the short, stiff hairs of a brush: **bristle** ◦ *a brush with stiff/soft bristles*

– to use a brush on sth: **brush** sth; *noun*: **brush** ◦ *to brush the floor/your hair* ◦ *I'll just give my hair a quick brush.*
– to clean a room, the floor, etc using a broom: **sweep*** sth; *noun*: **sweep** ◦ *The kitchen floor needs a sweep.*
– to rub sth hard to clean it, usually with a hard brush: **scrub** (sth); *noun*: **scrub** ◦ *The cleaners scrubbed the walls thoroughly to remove the mess.*

Buddhism ⇨ RELIGION

build

1 building sth
2 materials and equipment
3 people whose jobs are connected with building

different kinds of building ⇨ BUILDING

1 building sth

– to make sth (for example a house or a bridge) by putting different parts and materials together: **build*** sth, **put*** sth **up**, (*formal*) **construct** sth; *nouns* (U): **building, construction** ◦ *to build a house* ◦ *These blocks of flats were only put up five years ago, but they're already in bad condition.* ◦ *the construction industry* ◦ *The new shopping centre is already under construction* (= is already being built).

– a place like a house, church or school, that has a roof and walls: **building** ◦ *a historic building* ◦ *a tall/low building* ◦ *a row of buildings*
– something that has been built: **structure** ◦ *In front of the museum is a glass structure in the shape of a pyramid.*

– a diagram of a building, etc, showing exactly how it should be built: **plan** ◦ *The plans for the new shopping centre are on view at the City Architect's office.*
– an area of land where a building is being built: **building site**

– to build houses, shops, offices, etc on a piece of land: **build***, **develop** sth; *nouns* (U): **building, development** ◦ *They're planning to build on the*

build *contd.*

old football field. ◦ *There are plans to develop the area of waste land around the docks.*
– a person who develops land: **developer**
– an area where land is being developed: **development** ◦ *a housing development*

– to build sth again: **rebuild*** sth, **reconstruct** sth; *nouns* (U): **rebuilding**, **reconstruction** ◦ *The town was totally rebuilt after the war.* ◦ *Photographs and drawings were used to reconstruct the palace after the fire.* ◦ *Reconstruction work is likely to take several years.*

– to destroy a building: **pull** sth **down**, **demolish** sth, **knock** sth **down**; *noun* (U): **demolition** ◦ *They have pulled down many of the tower blocks that they built in the sixties.* ◦ *These buildings are going to be demolished to make way for the new road.*

2 materials and equipment

– one of the hard objects made of clay that is used for building the walls of houses: **brick** (*noun* C/U) ◦ *a lorryload of bricks* ◦ *Most of the houses here are built of brick.*
– a hard, solid substance that is found in the ground; it can be cut into shapes and used for building: **stone** (*noun* U) ◦ *a stone house* ◦ *built of stone*
– wood that is going to be used for building: **timber** (*noun* U) ◦ *a house with a timber frame*

▷ materials for covering roofs ⇨ ROOF

– a long iron or steel bar that is used in construction work: **girder** ◦ *The bridge is made from steel girders.*
– a long piece of metal or wood, etc that supports weight in a building, for example in a ceiling: **beam** ◦ *a low ceiling with old wooden beams*

– a grey powder which is mixed with water to stick bricks, etc together: **cement** (*noun* U); a machine for mixing cement: **cement mixer**
– a hard substance which is made from cement, sand, water and small stones: **concrete** (*noun* U) ◦ *a concrete floor*
– a substance that is put on walls and ceilings to make a smooth surface: **plaster** (*noun* U); to put plaster on a wall, ceiling, etc: **plaster** sth ◦ *The walls need to be plastered and then painted.*

– a large machine that is used for lifting heavy objects: **crane**
– a structure made of long metal tubes and wooden boards which is put up beside a building so that builders can stand on it to work: **scaffolding** (*noun* U)

3 people whose jobs are connected with building

– a person who builds houses and other buildings: **builder**; this work: **building** (*noun* U)
– a person who builds walls, etc with bricks: **bricklayer**; this work: **bricklaying** (*noun* U)
– a person who makes doors and window frames from wood: **joiner**; this work: **joinery** (*noun* U)
– a person who puts plaster on walls: **plasterer**; this work: **plastering** (*noun* U)
– a person who designs buildings: **architect**; this work: **architecture** (*noun* U)
– a person who designs roads and bridges, etc: a **civil engineer**; this work: **civil engineering** (*noun* U)

building

1 different kinds of building
2 the location of a building
3 parts of a building
4 looking at a building
5 the condition of a building

making a building ⇨ BUILD
see also HOUSE, FURNITURE

1 different kinds of building

– a place like a house, church or school, that has a roof and walls: **building** ◦ *There are a lot of new buildings in this street.* ◦ *Our company occupies the top two floors of the building.*
– a building that is made for people to live in: **house** ◦ *a house in the country* ◦ *a farmhouse*
– a large building which is divided into several parts: **block** ◦ *a block of flats* ◦ *an office block* ◦ *The school has a new sports block.*
– a very tall building: **skyscraper** ◦ *the skyscrapers of Manhattan*
– having many levels: **multi-storey** (*AmE* **multi-level**), **high-rise** ◦ *a multi-storey block of flats* ◦ *high-rise buildings*

▷ buildings which have particular uses ⇨ BANK, BAR / PUB, CASTLE, CHURCH, CINEMA, FACTORY, HOSPITAL, HOTEL, LIBRARY, PRISON, SCHOOL, SHOP, THEATRE, UNIVERSITY

▷ buildings connected with cars, trains and aeroplanes ⇨ CAR, TRAIN, PLANE

▷ buildings connected with sport ⇨ SPORT

▷ buildings where you can see paintings, etc ⇨ ART

▷ buildings connected with the police and the law ⇨ POLICE, LAW

– the style or design of a building or buildings: **architecture** (*noun* U); *adjective*: **architectural** ◦ *I'm studying classical architecture.* ◦ *a style of architecture* ◦ *This reminds me of the architecture of the early eighteenth century.* ◦ *This building has some unusual architectural features.*
– a person whose job is to design buildings: **architect**

2 the location of a building

– the place where a building is, in relation to the area around it: **situation**, **position**, **location** ◦ *The hotel is in a wonderful situation, overlooking the river.*
– to be in a particular place or position: **stand*** ..., **be located** ..., (*formal*) **be situated** ... ◦ *The church stands on the side of a hill.* ◦ *The house is situated in the heart of the city.*

- if the front of a building is opposite sth, it **faces** it ◦ *The school faces the fields.*
- if the back of a building is opposite sth, it **backs onto** it ◦ *The hospital backs onto the railway line.*
- if a building has a view over a particular area, it **overlooks** it ◦ *The house overlooks the river.*

- the place where a building was, is or will be situated: **site** ◦ *a building site* (= a place where a building is being built) ◦ *The new hospital is going to be built on the same site as the old one.*
- an area that has a lot of buildings is a **built-up** area ◦ *You should drive more slowly through a built-up area.*

3 parts of a building

- the part of a building that faces the street: **front**
- the part of a building that faces away from the street: **back**
- the part of a building that is not its front or back: **side** ◦ *We walked round to the side of the house.*

- the inside of a building: **inside**, **interior**; *adjectives*: **inside**, **interior** ◦ *The inside of the house has been beautifully renovated.* ◦ *an inside door*
- the outside of a building: **outside**, **exterior**; *adjectives*: **outside**, **exterior** ◦ *The satellite dishes are fixed to the outside of the building.* ◦ *The cathedral has a very fine exterior.* ◦ *The outside paintwork needs some attention.*

▷ more on being inside or outside ⇨ PLACE[2]

- the part of a building beneath the ground that forms its base: **foundations** (*noun plural*) ◦ *The men dug down to the foundations and finally found the leaking pipe.*
- the flat surface that you walk on inside a building: **floor**
- the part of a building that covers the top of it: **roof** ◦ *a flat roof* ◦ *we climbed onto the roof.*

- a part of a building that is separated from the rest by its own walls: **room**
- a solid, upright structure made of stone, brick, etc, that forms one of the sides of a building or room: **wall** ◦ *the wall of the house* ◦ *a picture on the wall*
- a thing that you open or close to get into or out of a building or room: **door** ◦ *the front/back door* ◦ *the main door* ◦ *an automatic door* ◦ *a revolving door*
- an opening in a wall, etc that you can see through and which lets light in: **window** ◦ *the upstairs/downstairs windows* ◦ *to clean the windows*

▷ more on floors, roofs, rooms, walls, doors and windows ⇨ FLOOR, ROOF, ROOM, WALL, DOOR, WINDOW

- the way into a public building: **entrance**; the way out: **exit**
- a long, narrow way with walls on both sides, that connects one place with another: **passage** ◦ *You can reach the kitchen along this passage.*
- the room or passage that is just inside the front entrance to a house: **hall** ◦ *I left my coat in the hall.*
- a long, narrow passage inside a building, with doors that open into rooms: **corridor** ◦ *to walk along a corridor*
- an area of ground without a roof, that has buildings or walls all around it: **courtyard** ◦ *There was a fountain in the middle of the courtyard.*

■ levels in a building

- a level in a building: **floor**, **storey** (*plural* **storeys**) (*AmE* **story**, *plural* **stories**) ◦ *My room's on the fourth floor.* ◦ *We walked up to the next floor.* ◦ *the top floor* ◦ *The hotel is fourteen storeys high.*
- the floor of a building at street level: **ground floor** (*AmE* **first floor**)
- the floor above the ground floor: **first floor** (*AmE* **second floor**)
- the floor of a building which is below ground level: **basement** ◦ *The staff have rooms in the basement.* ◦ *How do I get down to the basement?*

- the steps that join different levels inside a building: **stairs** (*noun plural*); a set of stairs with rails at the side that you can hold on to: **staircase** ◦ *to walk up/down the stairs* ◦ *Do these stairs go to the first floor?*
- a machine that is used for carrying things or people from one level of a building to another: **lift** (*AmE* **elevator**)
- a moving staircase, in a shop, etc: **escalator**
- a special staircase, usually on the outside of a building, which people can use to escape from a fire: **fire escape** ◦ *He managed to get out of the house down the fire escape.*

▷ more on stairs ⇨ STAIRS

4 looking at a building

- to take a person to see the different parts of a building, etc: **show*** sb **over/round/around** sth ◦ *I was shown all over the factory.* ◦ *They showed us round their new house.*
- to visit and look at the different parts of a building: **look round/around** (sth) ◦ *Having looked around, I decided that I liked the flat very much.*

- to examine a building carefully in order to find out if it is in good condition: **survey** sth; an act of surveying sth: **survey**; a person whose job is to do this: **surveyor** ◦ *to carry out a survey* ◦ *According to the survey, the house needs a lot of work.*

5 the condition of a building

- connected with the structure of a building: **structural** (*adverb* **structurally**) ◦ *The earthquake had caused a great deal of structural damage.* ◦ *Structurally, the building was in good condition.*
- strong (used about buildings): **solid** (*adverb* **solidly**) ◦ *The walls had been solidly built and remained standing for hundreds of years.*
- in good condition: **sound** ◦ *structurally sound*

- if a building is not in good condition because repair work has not been done, it is in **disrepair** (*noun* U) ◦ *The place has fallen into a state of disrepair.*
- no longer used and in bad condition: **derelict** ◦ *a derelict building*

building *contd.*

- to stop standing: **fall* down**, **collapse** ◦ *The building is badly damaged and likely to collapse.*
- the parts of a building that are left when it has been badly damaged or destroyed: **ruin**; badly damaged: **in ruins** ◦ *The house was now a ruin.* ◦ *After the war, the city was in ruins.*
- to mend an old or damaged building or part of a building: **repair** sth; this work: **repair** (*often plural*) ◦ *They're doing repairs on the church down the road.*
- to put a building back into its previous condition: **restore** sth; this work: **restoration** (*noun* U) ◦ *The ceiling has been restored to the way it looked before the fire.* ◦ *Restoration work has begun on the castle walls.*

■ **MORE ...**

- a tall, narrow building or part of a building: **tower** ◦ *a church tower*
- a tall vertical post that supports the roof of a building: **pillar**, **column**
- a structure made of two columns, joined over the top with a curve: **arch**
- a passage or entrance with an arch over it: **archway**
- a building and the land that surrounds it: (*formal*) **premises** (*noun plural*) ◦ *The police asked us all to leave the premises.*
- buildings, equipment, etc in a public place, which people can use for some purpose: **facilities** (*noun plural*) ◦ *This town needs better sports facilities.*
- (used about buildings and land when they are being bought or sold) a building and the land that surrounds it: (*rather formal*) **property** ◦ *The estate agent doesn't have any properties that would suit us just now.*

burn ⇨ FIRE

bury

- at a funeral ⇨ **FUNERAL**
- hiding sth ⇨ **HIDE**

bus

> **1** buses
> **2** travelling by bus
> **3** the people who work on a bus
>
> **see also** TRAVEL, TRANSPORT

1 buses

- a big public vehicle that takes passengers along a regular route from one place to another, making stops along the way: **bus** ◦ *I came on the bus.* ◦ *a double-decker bus* (= with two floors)
- a comfortable bus used for long journeys: **coach** ◦ *We're taking the coach to London.* ◦ *a coach journey*
- a vehicle like a bus that works by electricity and that runs on special rails in the road: **tram**
- a small bus, usually for no more than twelve people: **minibus**
- the part of a bus where the driver sits: **cab**
- the upstairs floor of a double-decker bus: **upper deck**, **upstairs**; the downstairs floor: **lower deck**, **downstairs**

2 travelling by bus

- a place where a bus stops so that you can get on or off: (**bus**) **stop** ◦ *This is my stop; I have to get off here.*
- a small building at a bus stop which gives protection from bad weather: (**bus**) **shelter** ◦ *Let's wait inside the bus shelter to keep out of this rain.*
- a building from which buses begin and end journeys: (**bus**) **station** ◦ *Excuse me, could you tell me where the main bus station is?*
- a line of people waiting for a bus: **queue** (*AmE* **line**) ◦ *Is this the queue for the number ten bus?* ◦ *She was standing in the queue for half an hour.*
- to form a queue: **queue** (**for** sth) (*AmE* **wait in line**)
- to use a bus: **take* a/the bus**, **go* by bus** ◦ *We couldn't get a taxi so we had to take the bus.* ◦ *I always go to work by bus.*
- to get on a bus: **catch*** a bus; to fail to catch a bus: **miss the bus** ◦ *Where can I catch a bus to the zoo?* ◦ *I missed the last bus and had to walk.*
- a person who travels on a bus: **passenger**
- the money that you pay for a journey: **fare** ◦ *What is the fare to Victoria Street?*
- a piece of paper that shows that you have paid for your journey: **ticket**
- a piece of paper that allows you to travel on a bus for a particular period of time: (**bus**) **pass**, **travel pass** ◦ *a weekly travel pass*
- a bus's regular journey: **route**; to travel on a route: **run*** ◦ *They've just changed the route of our local bus. It doesn't go to the town centre any more.* ◦ *This bus runs from the railway station to the airport.*
- the organization of buses and bus routes: (**bus**) **service** ◦ *The bus service here is very good on weekdays, but it's terrible on Sundays.*
- a written notice that gives the times when buses and coaches arrive and depart: **timetable** (*AmE* **schedule**)

3 the people who work on a bus

- a person who drives a bus: (**bus**) **driver**
- a person who collects the money for tickets on some buses: (**bus**) **conductor**; a female conductor can also be called a (**bus**) **conductress**
- a person who checks your ticket: (**ticket**) **inspector** ◦ *Keep your ticket in case the inspector comes to check it.*

business

> **1** business activity (buying and selling)
> **2** different kinds of businesses
> **3** running a business
>
> **see also** ECONOMY, INDUSTRY, BUY, SELL

1 business activity (buying and selling)

- things that are bought and sold: **goods** (*noun plural*)
- an organization that provides things that the public needs in everyday life: **service** ◦ *the telephone/train service*

- the activity of buying and selling goods and services: **business** (*noun* U), **trade** (*noun* U), **commerce** (*noun* U); *adjective*: **commercial** ◦ *the arms business* ◦ *foreign trade* ◦ *a company's commercial operations* ◦ *The decision was a purely commercial one; it was not in any way political.*
- a man/woman who buys and sells things to make money or who owns a business: **businessman/businesswoman** (*plural* **businessmen/businesswomen**)
- a person who owns or manages a large industrial company: **industrialist**

- to buy or sell particular goods and services: **trade** (**in** sth) (**with** sb), **deal* in** sth (**with** sb)
- a person who buys and sells particular goods and services: **dealer**, **trader** ◦ *an antiques dealer* ◦ *market traders* (= people who sell things in a market)

- to provide sb/sth with goods or services: **supply** sth (**to** sb), **supply** sb (**with** sth) ◦ *a contract to supply helicopters to Saudi Arabia* ◦ *Can you supply us with three thousand kilos of cement?*
- a person or a company that provides goods: **supplier** ◦ *the Queen's official suppliers of stationery*

▷ more on supplying sth ⇨ PROVIDE

- a person who buys things from a particular business: **customer** ◦ *Mrs Windsor is one of our most regular customers.*
- a person who receives a service from a professional person: **client** ◦ *to have lunch with a business client*
- a country, area or group of people who may want to buy sth: **market** ◦ *The Far Eastern market is expanding fast.*

- a business agreement or arrangement: **deal** ◦ *We're hoping to do a deal with a major Colombian coffee company.*
- if a deal is successful, it **goes* through**, you **pull** it **off**; if it is not successful, it **falls* through** ◦ *If everything goes to plan the deal should go through on Monday.* ◦ *We're still hoping to pull off the Saudi deal.*
- a written agreement that is signed after a deal is made, to make it legal: **contract**; to make a written agreement with sb for them to work for you: **contract** sb (**to** do sth) ◦ *We're signing the contract tomorrow.* ◦ *Our firm has been contracted to supply stationery to all government offices.*

- the amount of goods or services that a country, company, etc buys and sells: **business** (*noun* U) ◦ *Business is usually slow at this time of year.*
- the amount of goods or services that people want: **demand** (**for** sth) (*noun* U) ◦ *The demand for windscreens is so high that we'll have to take on more workers.*
- the level of demand that there is for a particular thing: **market** (**for** sth) ◦ *There's a growing market for used cars.*
- the amount of sth that is sold: **sales** (*noun plural*) ◦ *Sales are up 20%.*

■ business with other countries

- to send goods from one country to another: **export** sth; *noun* (U): **export** ◦ *the export of cars to Europe*
- to bring goods into one country from another country: **import** sth; *noun* (U): **import**
- goods which are exported: **exports** (*noun plural*); goods which are imported: **imports** (*noun plural*) ◦ *food exports*
- a person who brings things from another country to sell them in their own country: **importer**
- a person who sends things to another country to sell them: **exporter**

■ competition

- a situation where two or more companies are trying to sell the same thing to the same people: **competition** (*noun* U); *verb*: **compete** (**against/with** sb/sth) (**for** sth) ◦ *Increased competition from supermarkets has forced many small shops to close.* ◦ *My language school is in competition with ten others in this area.* ◦ *We can't compete with these foreign companies, as their labour costs are so low.*
- a situation in which one company controls a market or an industry: **monopoly** ◦ *They have a virtual monopoly on computers in our country.*

2 different kinds of businesses

- an organization that produces or sells goods or services: **company**, **firm** ◦ *to set up a new company* ◦ *an engineering firm*
- a firm, shop, factory, etc which produces or sells goods or provides a service: **business**

- owned by an individual or a group of people: **private**; owned by the government: **state-owned** ◦ *a private company/business*
- when a government takes control of a business, it **nationalizes** it; *noun* (U): **nationalization** ◦ *nationalized industries*
- when a government passes control of a state-owned business to a private company, it **privatizes** it; *noun* (U): **privatization** ◦ *British Airways was privatized during the 1980s.*

- a business that is owned and run by all the people who work in it: **cooperative**; *adjective*: **cooperative** ◦ *a manufacturing cooperative* ◦ *a cooperative farm*
- a large company that has offices, factories, etc in many countries: **multinational**; *adjective*: **multinational**
- (in Britain) a large company that sells shares in itself to the public: **public limited company** (*abbreviation* **plc**)

business *contd.*

3 running a business

- to start and organize a business: **go* into business**, **set*/start up** sth, **establish** sth; *noun* (U): **establishment** ◦ *They're planning to go into business together.* ◦ *I want to set up a record company.* ◦ *This company was established in 1894.*
- when one company buys or starts to control another company, it **takes*** it **over**; *noun*: **takeover** ◦ *The firm was taken over by a French company in 1994.*

- to cause a business to stop working: **shut*** sth **down**, **close** sth **down**; if a business stops working, it **shuts* down**, **closes down** ◦ *Many businesses have had to close down because of the poor state of the economy.*

■ investment
- to put money in the bank or into a business so as to make a profit: **invest** (sth) (**in** sth); *noun* (U): **investment** ◦ *He invested all his money in a property company.*
- an amount of money that has been put in a business: **investment**
- a person who puts money into a company because they hope to make a profit: **investor**

- one of the equal parts into which the money of a business company has been divided: **share** ◦ *I own three hundred shares in BP.*
- a person who owns shares in a company: **shareholder**
- a person whose job is to buy and sell shares in companies: **stockbroker**
- the part of a company's profits that is paid to the people who own shares in it: **dividend**
- a place where shares are bought and sold: **stock exchange**
- the business of buying and selling shares: **the stock market** ◦ *to make money on the stock market*

■ management
- to organize and control a business: **run*** sth, **manage** sth; *noun* (U): **management** ◦ *I run a small computer firm.* ◦ *We need to improve the management of this business.*
- one of the sections that a business is divided into: **department**; *adjective*: **departmental** ◦ *the sales department* ◦ *the personnel department* ◦ *a departmental meeting*
- a person who controls a company: **manager**; the group of people who manage a company: **management** (*with singular or plural verb*)

▷ more on managing sth ⇨ MANAGEMENT

- a person who gives advice to people about their business: **consultant** ◦ *a management consultant*
- a person who you know who may be able to help you in your business: **contact** ◦ *I have some useful contacts in Berlin.*

■ finances
- the money that a business has: **finances** (*noun plural*); *adjective*: **financial** ◦ *We can expect a significant improvement in our finances in the next financial year.* ◦ *We're in a terrible financial situation.*
- a person who provides money for big businesses and other organizations: **financier**
- a record of all the money that a person or business spends or receives: **accounts** (*noun plural*), **books** (*noun plural*); to write down the accounts: **do*/keep* the accounts**; this kind of work: **accountancy** (*noun* U), **bookkeeping** (*noun* U)
- a person who keeps accounts, advises on tax, etc: **accountant**

- the money that a business makes when it sells sth for more than it paid for it: **profit** (*noun* C/U); *opposite*: **loss** (*noun* C/U) ◦ *Profits are down on last year.* ◦ *pre-tax profit* (= the amount of profit you have before you pay tax on it) ◦ *They made a £7 million loss last year.*
- if a business makes a profit, it is **profitable**, **profit-making**, it **makes* money** ◦ *I hope we can make this business profitable by the end of the year.* ◦ *Does your business make much money?*
- the ability of a business to make a profit: **profitability** (*noun* U)

- the money that a person or company owes: **debt**
- if a company does not have enough money to pay all its debts, it is/goes **bankrupt**, (*informal*) **bust** ◦ *The firm went bust last July.*

▷ more on debt ⇨ DEBT

busy ⇨ WORK

but ⇨ AND/OR/BUT

butter

see also BREAD, COOK, FOOD

- the yellow fat made from milk which is put on bread, used for cooking, etc: **butter** (*noun* U) ◦ *a packet of butter*
- a yellow substance which looks like butter but is made from animal or vegetable fat: **margarine** (*noun* U) ◦ *a tub of margarine*
- a substance which has less fat than normal margarine: **low-fat spread** (*noun* U)

- to put butter on a piece of bread, etc: **butter** sth ◦ *Shall I help you to butter the sandwiches?* ◦ *buttered toast*
- to put butter, jam, etc, on bread: **spread*** A **on** B, **spread*** B **with** A ◦ *Spread margarine on it.* ◦ *Spread it with margarine.*
- butter which is easy to spread is **soft**; *opposite*: **hard** ◦ *It's too hard to spread.*
- to become soft or liquid: **melt**; to make sth soft or liquid: **melt** sth ◦ *Butter melts if you leave it in the sun.* ◦ *Melt the butter in a large pan.*

butterfly ⇨ INSECT

buy

1 different ways of buying things
2 people who buy things
3 paying for things
buying a house ⇨ **HOUSE**
see also SELL

1 different ways of buying things

- to obtain sth by paying money for it: **buy*** sth, **get*** sth, (*formal*) **purchase** sth ◦ *I need to buy some new shirts.* ◦ *Can you get some milk when you're at the shops?*
- to leave home or work in order to buy sth: **go* out for** sth, **go* out to get** sth ◦ *I'm going out to get some fish and chips.*

- a building or part of a building where things are bought and sold: **shop** (*AmE* **store**)
- to go out and buy different things in different shops: **go* shopping, shop** ◦ *We go shopping once a week.*
- the activity of buying things: **shopping** (*noun* U) ◦ *Her neighbour did her shopping while she was ill.*

▷ more on shops and going shopping ⇨ **SHOP**

- a system where you can buy sth by writing to a company and asking them to send it to you: **mail order** (*noun* U) ◦ *She buys her Christmas presents by mail order.*
- a book or magazine which lists and shows pictures of things that you can buy through the post: **(mail-order) catalogue**
- to write a letter, usually to a company, asking them to send you sth: **send* off for** sth ◦ *I'm sending off for some travel brochures.*
- to ask for sth to be made or supplied: **order** sth ◦ *We've ordered a new fridge and it's being delivered next week.*

- a public sale at which items are sold to the person who offers the most money: **auction** (*noun* C/U) ◦ *We bought our dining-room table in an auction.*
- (at an auction) to offer to buy sth at a particular price: **bid*** (sth) (**for** sth) ◦ *I bid £50 for the painting I wanted.*

- a machine from which you can buy things: **vending machine**

2 people who buy things

- a person in a shop who wants to buy sth: **customer**
- a person who buys sth expensive such as a house or a company: **buyer**, (*formal*) **purchaser** ◦ *I think we've found a buyer for our house.*
- anyone who buys goods or services: **consumer** ◦ *the protection of consumers' rights*
- a person who receives a service from a professional person, for example a lawyer: **client**

3 paying for things

- if you have enough money to buy sth, you can **afford** it ◦ *I'd love a new dress but I can't afford one just now.*
- to use your money to buy sth: **spend*** money (**on** sth) ◦ *I've just spent £60 on new shoes for the children.*

- to give sb money for sth that you want to buy: **pay*** (sb) (some money) (**for** sth) ◦ *How much did you pay for those earrings?*
- the piece of paper which shows that you have paid for sth: **receipt** ◦ *Please keep the receipt as goods cannot be exchanged without it.*

▷ different ways of paying ⇨ **PAY**[1]

- the amount of money you have to pay to buy sth: **price** (*noun* C/U) ◦ *Ask her the price of that necklace.* ◦ *It's gone up in price.*
- to say you are prepared to give a certain amount of money for sth: **offer** (sb) sth (**for** sth), **make*** sb **an offer** (**of** sth) **for** sth ◦ *I offered her £500 for her piano but she wouldn't accept it.*
- if sth is worth the money you paid for it, it is **a good buy** ◦ *This old car was a really good buy.*

■ tax on things you buy

- a tax (in Britain and Europe) which is paid on goods and services which are bought and sold: **VAT** (**value added tax**); in the United States, this tax is called **sales tax**
- tax paid on some things brought into the country: **duty** (*noun* U)
- if you do not pay this tax on sth, it is **duty-free** (*adjective, adverb*) ◦ *I bought some duty-free whisky at the airport.* ◦ *We got our car duty-free.*

▷ more on tax ⇨ **TAX**

■ **MORE ...**

- a written promise by a company that it will replace or repair sth that you buy if it goes wrong: **guarantee** ◦ *When my new watch stopped they gave me another one under the guarantee.*

- illegal ways of buying things or changing money: the **black market** ◦ *He buys his cigarettes at half the normal price on the black market.*

café ⇨ RESTAURANT

cake

see also FOOD

- a sweet food made with a mixture of flour, eggs, butter and sugar: **cake** (*noun* C/U) ◦ *We've got cakes for tea.* ◦ *a Christmas cake* ◦ *It's your birthday – you must cut the cake.* ◦ *a slice/piece of cake* ◦ *Would you like some more cake?*
- a small round sweet cake: **bun** ◦ *a currant bun* ◦ *a sticky bun*
- a type of small thin cake that is quite hard: **biscuit** (*AmE* **cookie**) ◦ *a packet of chocolate biscuits*
- very small pieces of bread, cake or biscuit: **crumbs** (*noun plural*)

- a very light cake: **sponge** (**cake**) (*noun* C/U) ◦ *I've made a sponge cake for tea.*

cake *contd.*

- a cake made with cream: **cream cake** (*noun* C/U)
- a cake made with lots of dried fruit: **fruit cake** (*noun* C/U)
- a cake made with cheese: **cheesecake** (*noun* C/U)
- cakes made with pastry: **pastries** (*noun plural*) ○ *They've got a large selection of cakes and pastries.*
- a small plain cake often served with butter, jam and cream: **scone**

■ making a cake

- to prepare and cook bread and cakes: **bake** (sth); *noun* (U): **baking** ○ *Bake the cake in a medium oven for twenty minutes.* ○ *freshly baked cakes* ○ *I'm going to do some baking this afternoon.*
- a container used for cooking cakes in the oven: **cake tin**
- the white powder used to make bread: **flour** (*noun* U)
- cakes are often made with dried fruit such as **raisins** and **currants**
- a sugary substance that is put on top of cakes: **icing** (*AmE* **frosting**); *verb*: **ice** (*AmE* **frost**) sth; with icing on it: **iced** (*AmE* **frosted**) ○ *Cover the cake with white icing.* ○ *Are you going to ice the cake?* ○ *an iced bun*

▷ more on flour ⇨ FLOUR

▷ cooking ⇨ COOK

- a person who bakes and sells bread and cakes: **baker**
- a place where bread, cakes, etc are sold: **baker's (shop)**

call/be called ⇨ NAME

calm

1 being calm
2 becoming calm
3 not being calm
see also QUIET

1 being calm

■ calm people

- if you are quiet and do not get excited, you are **calm** (*adverb* **calmly**) ○ *Try to keep calm – there's no need to panic.* ○ *The Prime Minister took the news of his defeat calmly.*
- if you are calm and you have your feelings under control, you are **composed, cool**; *nouns* (U): **composure, coolness** ○ *the ability to keep cool in a crisis* ○ *He showed great composure in a difficult situation.*
- if you stay calm in a difficult situation you **keep*** your **head, keep*** your **cool, stay cool** ○ *When the tyre burst, Ingrid kept her head and managed to steer to the side of the road.* ○ *Don't panic! Stay cool!*
- if you are not worried, you are **relaxed**, (*informal*) **laid-back** ○ *She's looking much more relaxed now after her holiday.* ○ *a laid-back attitude to life*

■ calm places and situations

- if there is no noise or unpleasant disturbance, a place is **calm, quiet, peaceful**; *nouns* (U): **calm, peacefulness** ○ *The city is calm again after last night's riots.* ○ *We camped in a peaceful spot beside the lake.* ○ *the calm of a summer evening*
- (used about the sea) with no big waves: **calm**
- (used about the weather) with no wind: **calm** ○ *a calm day*

2 becoming calm

- to become calm after a period of excitement, anger, etc: **calm (down), cool down, quieten (down)** ○ *When I explained what had actually happened she soon calmed down.* ○ *Cool down! What are you so angry about?* ○ *Quieten down, everyone!*
- to cause sb/sth to become calm: **calm** sb/sth **(down), quieten** sb/sth, **soothe** sb/sth, **pacify** sb/sth ○ *I tried to calm him down but he was furious.* ○ *to soothe a crying child*
- something which helps sb/sth to become calm is **calming, soothing** ○ *The ticking of the clock had a calming effect on the baby.* ○ *a soothing voice*
- a thing that gives a relaxed, peaceful feeling is **restful** ○ *quiet, restful music*
- to become less worried, frightened, etc: **relax**; to cause sb to become relaxed: **relax** sb ○ *I was so tense – I just couldn't relax.*
- to relax and not work too hard or worry: **take* it/things easy** ○ *After his heart attack Pete was told by his doctor to take things a bit easier.*
- to say or do sth to make sb/sth feel less frightened, worried or nervous: **reassure** sb/sth; *noun* (U): **reassurance**; *adjective*: **reassuring** ○ *I tried to reassure him that everything would be all right.* ○ *It was very reassuring to see the lights of home.*
- to calm sb down, you can say **Calm down** or **Relax** or (*informal*) **Cool it** ○ *Calm down and tell me what happened.* ○ *Relax – you're home now.*

3 not being calm

- if you are worried or not feeling comfortable you are **uneasy, nervous, tense, anxious** ○ *Hannah hated flying and was feeling a bit uneasy about her trip to Hong Kong.* ○ *Do you get nervous before exams?*
- a sudden feeling of fear that makes you do things without thinking carefully about them: **panic** (*noun* C/U); to experience panic: **panic**; *adjectives*: **panic-stricken**, (*informal*) **panicky** ○ *Keep calm! Don't panic! The police will be here in a minute.* ○ *Her voice sounded panicky.*
- if you are rather angry about sth, you are **irritated (about** sth) ○ *He gets irritated if you keep him waiting.*
- feeling very happy because you are looking forward to sth happening; not calm: **excited** ○ *The*

children are getting too excited – tell them to calm down.
- if you are unable to relax because you are bored, nervous or impatient you are **restless**; *noun* (U): **restlessness** ◦ *I spent a restless night worrying about my interview.*

▷ causing you not to be calm ➪ AFRAID, ANGRY, EXCITED, WORRY

■ **MORE . . .**
- a drug or medicine that makes you calm or sleepy: **sedative, tranquillizer**

camel ➪ ANIMAL

camera ➪ PHOTOGRAPH

camp

see also HOLIDAY

- a shelter made of nylon or canvas that you use to sleep in when you are camping: **tent**
- a large vehicle that can be pulled by a car and can be used for sleeping, cooking, etc while on holiday: **caravan** (*AmE* **camper**)

- to put up a tent and sleep in it: **camp** (**out**) ◦ *We camped in a field by a stream.* ◦ *We decided to camp out for the night.*
- sleeping or spending a holiday in a tent: **camping** (*noun* U) ◦ *They went on a camping holiday.*
- to spend a holiday living in a tent: **go* camping** ◦ *We're going camping in the South of France this summer.*
- a special place where people camp: **campsite** (*AmE* **campground**)
- a person who camps: **camper**

■ what you need when you camp
- a small electric light that you carry in your hand: **torch**
- gas that is kept in special bottles and used for heating and cooking: **butane** (**gas**) (*BrE also* **Calor gas**)
- a cooker which uses gas: **Calor gas stove, camping stove**
- a warm bag used for sleeping in: **sleeping bag**
- a small knife with one or more blades that fold down into the handle: **penknife, pocket knife**
- a fire which people sit around at night or use for cooking when they are camping: **campfire** ◦ *We all sang songs round the campfire.*

■ tents
- an extra cover over a tent which stops rain from getting inside the tent: **flysheet**
- a piece of material or part of the tent which lies on the ground and stops water from getting into the tent: **groundsheet**
- special material which keeps small insects out of the tent but lets air come in: **mosquito net**
- one of the metal things which hold up a tent: **tent pole**
- a piece of metal which you hammer into the ground to keep the ropes in place: **tent peg**
- ropes which are tied from the tent onto a peg in the ground: **guy ropes**

- to fit together the pieces of a tent so that you can sleep in it: **put* up** a tent, **pitch** a tent; *opposite*: **take* down** a tent
- to put up a tent and organize the things that you need: **set* up camp**
- to take down tents and leave the place where you were camping: **strike* camp** ◦ *We got up early and struck camp before dawn.*

can ➪ POSSIBLE[2]

cancer ➪ ILLNESS

candle ➪ LIGHT[3]

car

1 different kinds of car
2 the parts of a car
3 keeping and repairing a car
see also DRIVE, BUS, MOTORCYCLE, LORRY, TRAVEL, ROAD

1 different kinds of car
- a vehicle with an engine and four wheels that up to five people can travel in: **car, motor car** (*AmE* **automobile**) ◦ *a new/second-hand car* ◦ *Let's go for a drive in the car.* ◦ *We came by car.*
- a car with a fixed roof and a separate area for luggage: **saloon** (*AmE* **sedan**)
- a car with a door at the back and a large space for luggage behind the back seat: **estate** (**car**) (*AmE* **station wagon**)
- a car (usually small) with a large door at the back that opens upwards: **hatchback**

- a very large, expensive car: **limousine**, (*informal*) **limo**
- a low, fast car, usually with room for two people, often with a roof that can open: **sports car**
- a car with a roof that can open: **convertible**
- a strong car that is suitable for travelling over rough ground: **four-wheel drive** (**vehicle**)

- a car with a driver whose job it is to take you somewhere for money: **taxi**, (*especially AmE*) **cab** ◦ *You'll have to take a taxi from the airport to the hotel.*
- a vehicle like a car that is used for transporting things: **van**
- a large, black car used for carrying a dead body to a funeral: **hearse**

▷ more on taxis ➪ TAXI

car interior

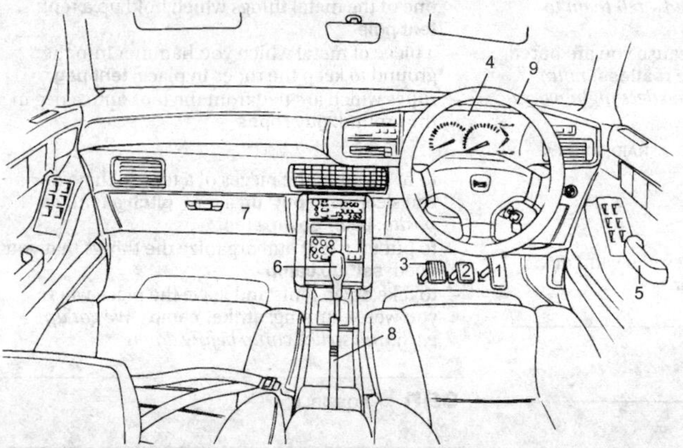

1 accelerator (*AmE* gas pedal)
2 brake (pedal)
3 clutch (pedal)
4 dashboard
5 door handle
6 gear lever (*AmE* gear shift)
7 glove compartment
8 handbrake
9 steering wheel

2 the parts of a car

■ car interior

- the electrical system that starts the engine of a car: **ignition**; the key that is used for starting the ignition: (**ignition**) **key** ◦ *I turned the key in the ignition but the engine didn't start.*
- an instrument for showing the speed of a car: **speedometer**
- an instrument for showing the distance a car has travelled: **milometer** (*AmE* **odometer**) (*informal* **clock**) ◦ *I bought this car with 20 000 miles on the clock.*
- a thing that gives a loud warning sound: **horn** ◦ *I sounded my horn.*
- a thing for heating the car: **heater** ◦ *Can you turn up the heater a bit? I'm rather cold.*
- where the driver sits: **driver's seat**; where a passenger sits: **passenger seat**
- a belt that you wear in a car, etc to protect yourself if there is an accident: **seat belt**, **safety belt**
- a special kind of bag in the front of a car that fills up with air to stop your head being injured if you crash: **air bag**

■ car exterior

▷ wheels and tyres ⇨ **WHEEL**

- the main outside part of a car: **bodywork** (*noun* U) ◦ *The engine's fine but the bodywork's starting to rust.*
- the metal frame of the car onto which the other parts fit: **chassis**
- a metal box which contains petrol: **petrol tank** (*AmE* **gas tank**)
- waste gas that comes out of a car, etc: **exhaust** (*noun* U); the pipe from which exhaust gases come out of the car's engine: **exhaust** (**pipe**)
- one of the windows at the side of the car: (**side**) **window**; to move a car window up or down by turning a handle: **wind*** sth **up**/**down** ◦ *Could you wind your window down to let a little air in?*

car exterior

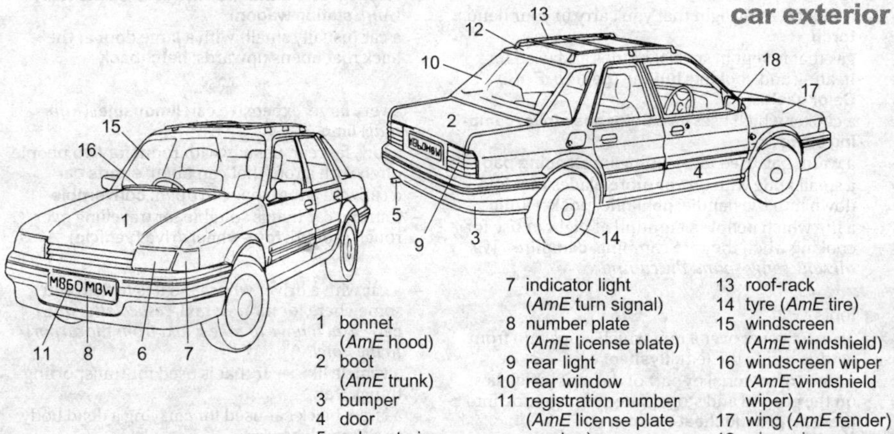

1 bonnet (*AmE* hood)
2 boot (*AmE* trunk)
3 bumper
4 door
5 exhaust-pipe
6 headlight
7 indicator light (*AmE* turn signal)
8 number plate (*AmE* license plate)
9 rear light
10 rear window
11 registration number (*AmE* license plate number)
12 roof
13 roof-rack
14 tyre (*AmE* tire)
15 windscreen (*AmE* windshield)
16 windscreen wiper (*AmE* windshield wiper)
17 wing (*AmE* fender)
18 wing mirror (*AmE* side mirror)

- a useful or attractive item that can be added to your car: **accessory** ◦ *My car has several accessories, including a CD player.*

■ the engine, etc

- a thing which provides electricity for starting a car: **battery**
- a set of wheels that pass power from the engine to the wheels of the car: **gears** (*noun plural*) ◦ *Most cars have five forward gears and a reverse.*
- a metal box containing the gears: **gearbox**
- if the gears of a car change automatically, the car is an **automatic** (**car**)
- a device containing water which helps to cool the engine: **radiator** ◦ *We'll have to stop at the next service station to put some more water in the radiator.*
- the thing which cools the engine by blowing air onto it: **fan**
- the belt that drives the fan: **fan belt**

▷ more on engines ⇨ MACHINE

3 keeping and repairing a car

- a building where cars are kept: **garage** ◦ *I put the car in the garage and went into the house.*
- a place where you can have your car repaired and which often sells petrol: **garage**
- a person whose job is to repair cars: (**car**) **mechanic, garage mechanic**
- to look at and repair a car, lorry, etc to make sure it is working properly: **service** sth; *noun*: **service** ◦ *My car is going to be serviced next week.* ◦ *When is the car due for its next service?*
- to take a car, etc to a garage to get a service: **take*** sth **in for a service, put*** sth **in for a service** ◦ *I've put my car in to the garage for its 10 000 mile service.*
- to put sth that is old or damaged back into good condition: **repair** sth, **fix** sth, **mend** sth ◦ *After the accident it took three weeks to repair the car.* ◦ *How long will it take you to fix the clutch?*
- a part for a car which you can use to replace an old part which is damaged or broken: **spare part, spare**
- a place, usually at a petrol station, where your car is washed automatically: **car wash**
- the amount of money that you spend to keep your car in good condition: **running costs** (*noun plural*) ◦ *My Metro has very low running costs.*

cards

other games ⇨ GAME

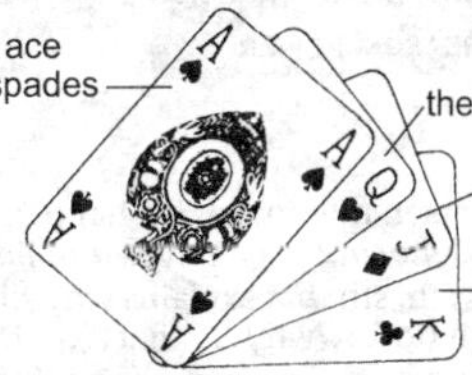

- one of a set of usually 52 small pieces of card with shapes or pictures on them that are used for playing games: (**playing**) **card**
- a set of these cards: **pack** (*AmE* **deck**) (**of cards**) ◦ *There are some cards missing from this pack.*
- one of the four sets of thirteen playing cards: **suit** ◦ *You need four cards of the same suit.*
- the names of the suits: **spades, clubs, hearts, diamonds**
- the names of the thirteen cards in a suit: **ace** (= the number one in a suit), **two, three, four, five, six, seven, eight, nine, ten, jack, queen, king** ◦ *I played a two.* ◦ *the king of spades*
- an extra card in a pack of cards, which can be used in some games instead of any card: **joker**
- a card which belongs to a suit which is chosen to have a higher value than all the others: **trump** ◦ *Hearts are trumps.*

■ playing a game of cards

- to play a game with cards: **play/have a game of cards, play cards** ◦ *We had a good game of cards last night.* ◦ *Let's play cards.*
- a particular kind of game that is played with cards: **card game** ◦ *Does anyone know any good card games?*
- to win or lose card games: **win*/lose* at cards** ◦ *I hate losing at cards.*
- a person who plays cards: **player** ◦ *This game needs four players.*

▷ more on winning and losing a game ⇨ WIN/LOSE

- to mix the cards: **shuffle** (sth) ◦ *Shuffle the cards well.*
- to give cards to each individual person who is playing the game: **deal*** (sth); the person who deals the cards is the **dealer** ◦ *Whose turn is it to deal?* ◦ *The person on the left of the dealer starts.*
- to divide the pack of cards into two or three parts: **cut*** (sth) ◦ *Cut the cards to see who starts.*
- a card which is on the table showing the picture side is **face up**; a card which is on the table so that you cannot see its picture side is **face down** ◦ *Place the cards face down on the table.*
- the cards that you have in your hand when you play cards: **hand** ◦ *I knew I'd win – I had a really good hand* (= I had good cards).
- the time in a game of cards when one person must play his/her cards: **turn, go** (*plural* **goes**) ◦ *Is it my turn?* ◦ *Whose go is it?*
- to remove a card from the pile of cards in the centre of the table: **take*** sth, **pick** sth **up** ◦ *It's your turn to pick up a card.*
- to put a card on the table for other players to see: **play** (sth) ◦ *Who played the ten?*

careful

1 avoiding accidents and mistakes
2 trying to do sth well
see also ACCIDENT, DANGEROUS, WARN

1 avoiding accidents and mistakes

- if you think about what you do so that you do not have an accident or make a mistake, you are **careful** (*adverb* **carefully**); *noun* (U): **care** ◦

careful *contd.*

Please be careful with that vase (= careful not to damage it). ◦ *Be very careful of the traffic on the main road* (= careful not to be hurt by it). ◦ *Be careful washing that blouse.* ◦ *Drive carefully!* ◦ *A great deal of care is needed in the transport of live animals.*
– if you are careful, you **take* care** (**to** do sth/**that...**) ◦ *Take care! Don't rush!* ◦ *Take care that you don't spill that coffee.*
– taking great care because of possible danger: **cautious** (*adverb* **cautiously**); *noun* (U): **caution** ◦ *I looked outside cautiously before leaving the house.* ◦ *Caution! Roadworks ahead!*

– if you behave in a careful way so that you do not hurt things or people, you are **gentle** (*adverb* **gently**); *noun* (U): **gentleness** ◦ *The doctor was very gentle with her.* ◦ *She touched the child with great gentleness.*

■ not being careful
– if you are not careful about what you are doing, you are **careless** (**about/with** sth) (*adverb* **carelessly**); *noun* (U): **carelessness** ◦ *a careless driver* ◦ *a careless mistake*
– if you are very careless and do not think about the possible danger or bad results of what you are doing, you are **reckless** (*adverb* **recklessly**); *noun* (U): **recklessness** ◦ *reckless disregard for the safety of other road users*

– if you are physically awkward and often drop or break things, you are **clumsy** (*adverb* **clumsily**); *noun* (U): **clumsiness**

2 trying to do sth well
– showing care and attention to details: **careful** (*adverb* **carefully**); *noun* (U): **care** ◦ *a careful piece of work* ◦ *Listen carefully!*
– if you show care and attention to details, you **take* care** (**over** sth/**that...**) ◦ *He takes great care over his reports.* ◦ *Take care that the figures add up correctly.*

– to do sth without hurrying: **take* your time** (**with/over** sth)
– to make a special effort to do sth carefully: **take*** (**great**) **pains** (**with** sth/**over** sth/**to** do sth); *adjective*: **painstaking** ◦ *We have taken great pains to find the truth.* ◦ *a painstaking process*
– to look at sth to make sure that it is correct or in good order: **check** (sth), **check** (**through**) sth ◦ *Check through your work before you hand it in.*

– careful and exact, without mistakes: **accurate** (*adverb* **accurately**) ◦ *an accurate description* ◦ *to copy something accurately*
– careful and complete: **thorough** (*adverb* **thoroughly**) ◦ *The police made a thorough search of the house.*
– if sth is done with great attention to details, it is **meticulous** ◦ *a meticulous investigation*

careless ⇨ CAREFUL

carry ⇨ BRING/TAKE/CARRY

castle

see also BUILDING

– a large building with high walls that was built in the past to live in and to defend people from attack: **castle** ◦ *a medieval castle* ◦ *a ruined castle* ◦ *Edinburgh Castle*
– a strong building like a small castle: **fort**

– a deep ditch that was dug around a castle and filled with water to prevent people crossing: **moat**
– a bridge across a moat that could be pulled up to prevent people crossing: **drawbridge**
– an underground prison (often in a castle): **dungeon**

cat

see also ANIMAL

– a small furry animal with four legs and a tail which is often kept as a pet: **cat**, (*informal*) **pussy**
– a young cat: **kitten**
– a male cat: **tom, tom-cat**
– a word used when you are speaking to or calling a cat: **puss** ◦ *Come here, puss!*
– a cat that has left its home and is lost: **stray cat**

– a cat's foot: **paw**
– the hair on a cat: **fur** (*noun* U)
– one of the long hairs that grow around a cat's mouth: **whisker** (*often plural*)

– a soft sound of pleasure made by a cat: **purr**; *verb*: **purr**
– a crying sound made by a cat: **miaow**; *verb*: **miaow**

– to give food to an animal: **feed*** sth; food that you buy to give to cats: **cat food** (*noun* U)

catch ⇨ HOLD/CATCH

Catholic ⇨ CHRISTIAN

cause/effect

1 causes
2 effects and results
3 causing and resulting
4 events which are connected
see also REASON, POWER

1 causes
– a thing or person that makes sth happen: **cause** ◦ *Pollution is the cause of many health problems.*
– the cause of sth; sth that explains why sth happens: **reason** (**for.../why.../that...**) ◦ *Do you know the reason for the delay?* ◦ *I can think of no good reason why he should go away so suddenly.*

- to be the real, possibly hidden, cause of sth: **lie* behind** sth ◦ *What do you think lies behind the increase in crime?*
- if sth is partly the cause of sth, it **contributes to** sth ◦ *His friendly personality contributes to his success as a teacher.*
- a person who causes sth to happen is **responsible for** it; *noun* (U): **responsibility** ◦ *Who was responsible for the accident?* ◦ *He refused to accept responsibility for what had happened.*

- a person or thing that changes sb/sth in a particular way: **influence** (**on** sb/sth) (*noun* C/U) ◦ *His influence on younger composers has been underestimated.*

2 effects and results

- something which happens because sth else causes it: **result**, **consequence** ◦ *The result of the accident was that he had to spend the night in hospital.* ◦ *The decision had unpleasant consequences for the people living in that area.* ◦ *a clear* (= certain or obvious) *consequence of her action*
- the final situation at the end of a process: **result**, **outcome** ◦ *What was the result of the election?* ◦ *The most likely outcome of our discussion is that we shall have to find a new secretary.*
- a change that is caused by sth: **effect** ◦ *You can't just ignore the possible effects of your own actions.* ◦ *a definite* (= certain) *effect*

- if you want to say how a result has happened, you can say that it **arises* from** sth, **comes* from** sth, **results from** sth ◦ *This sort of problem arises from an unhappy childhood.* ◦ *His bad health comes from smoking too much.* ◦ *His success results from a lot of hard work.*

- if a particular result is expected, it is **probable**, **likely**; *opposites*: **improbable**, **unlikely**

▷ more on being probable, likely, etc ⇨ POSSIBLE[1]
▷ more on knowing about the future ⇨ FUTURE

■ good effects
- a good effect: **benefit** ◦ *You should feel the benefit of the diet after two weeks.*
- if sth produces a good or useful effect, it is **beneficial**, **fruitful** ◦ *A week in a warm climate would have a beneficial effect on her.* ◦ *The discussions were particularly fruitful.*
- a useful effect of a process that had a different aim: **spin-off** ◦ *Military research sometimes has important commercial spin-offs.*

■ no effect
- if sth does not produce the effect or result that you want, it is **ineffective**, **useless** ◦ *I've stopped taking those tablets – they were completely ineffective.* ◦ *This skin cream is useless – look how burnt I've got.*
- if you try to do sth but do not succeed, you do it **in vain** ◦ *She tried in vain to make him change his mind.*
- if sb or sth is not changed by sth, they are **unaffected** by sth ◦ *Her work seems to be unaffected by all the problems she's having at home.*

3 causing and resulting

- to be the cause of sth: **cause** sth, **bring*** sth (**about**), **lead* to** sth ◦ *Overwork causes stress.* ◦ *The collapse of the economy has brought about many changes in the last year.* ◦ *Eating too many sweet foods can lead to health problems.*
- to do sth which starts a reaction: **set*** sth **off** ◦ *The photos set off more speculation about life on Mars.*

- to have sth as a result: **result in** sth, **end in** sth ◦ *The recent hot weather has resulted in a severe lack of water.* ◦ *Our discussion ended in a decision to close the factory.*
- to cause sb/sth to change in a particular way: **affect** sb/sth, **have an effect on** sb/sth ◦ *Exposure to the chemicals has seriously affected his health.* ◦ *His work has been affected by his problems at home.* ◦ *Those tablets have a very strange effect on me.*
- to begin to show the result that is required: **take* effect** ◦ *You need to wait quite a long time before the medicine takes effect.*
- to have an effect (especially on your feelings or attitude): **influence** sb/sth ◦ *Some people say that the weather influences the way they feel.*
- to have a good effect on sb/sth: **benefit** sb/sth, **make* a difference to** sb/sth ◦ *It will make a great difference to him if he can get away from the office for a few weeks.*

- (used about an effect) to become less strong: **wear* off** ◦ *The effect of those aspirins is wearing off – my headache's coming back.*

■ having an effect on a person
- to cause a reaction, usually physical, in sb: **give*** sb sth ◦ *Seafood gives me stomach-ache.*
- to cause a feeling in sb: **make*** sb (**feel**) sth ◦ *That film made me feel really sad.*
- to cause sb to decide to do sth: **prompt** sb **to** do sth ◦ *The letter prompted me to call my parents.*
- to cause sb to do sth when that person does not want to do it: **make* sb** do sth, **force** sb **to** do sth ◦ *I didn't like vegetables when I was a child, but my mother always made me eat them.*
- if an unpleasant situation causes sb to do sth extreme, it **drives*** them **to** do sth ◦ *The noise my neighbours made finally drove me to go to the police.*

■ expressing cause and result
- if you want to talk about the cause of sth, you can say **because of . . .**, **due to . . .**, **owing to . . .** ◦ *I couldn't sleep last night because of all the noise my neighbours were making.* ◦ *The increase in ice-cream sales was due to the unusually hot weather.* ◦ *Owing to the train strike, I was late for the meeting.*
- because of sb/sth (sometimes used in a negative way): **thanks to . . .** ◦ *Thanks to you, we're lost.*

- if you want to talk about the result of sth, you can say **so**, **therefore**, **as a result**, **consequently** ◦ *I was cold and tired and the heating was off, so I decided to go to bed.* ◦ *The sales staff travel all over the country. They are therefore well informed about local problems.*

cause / effect *contd.*

4 events which are connected

– if A is a possible cause of B, then there is a **connection** (*noun* C/U), **relationship** (*noun* C/U), **link** (*noun* C/U) between A and B ◦ *I can't see any relationship between violence on TV and the increase in crime.* ◦ *There is obviously a link between his poverty and his illness.*
– having a connection with sb/sth: **connected** (**to/with** sb/sth), **related** (**to** sb/sth), **linked** (**to/with** sb/sth) ◦ *Most people think that the two events are connected.* ◦ *The cost of vegetables is directly related to the size of the harvest.*
– to have a connection with sb/sth else: **be/have something, a lot**, etc **to do with** sb/sth ◦ *I think the poor attendance must have something to do with the weather.* ◦ *Is this letter anything to do with you?*

– to show that there is a connection between two or more things: **connect** sth **to/with** sth, **relate** sth **to/with** sth, **link** sth **to/with** sth ◦ *The fingerprints linked him with the scene of the crime.*
– to connect two or more things in your mind: **associate** sb/sth (**with** sb/sth); *noun*: **association** ◦ *Scientists see a clear association between diet and heart disease.*

– a number of connected events that happen one after the other: **sequence, chain** ◦ *the chain of events that led up to the disaster*

– having no connection with sth else: **unconnected** (**with** sth), **unrelated** (**to** sth) ◦ *She left for reasons that were quite unrelated with the row.* ◦ *Although these things happened at the same time, they were unrelated.*

CD ⇨ RECORD

centre ⇨ PLACE[2]

ceremony ⇨ RELIGION

certain ⇨ POSSIBLE[1]

chain ⇨ LOCK/CHAIN

chair

chairs for babies ⇨ BABY
see also FURNITURE, TABLE, SIT

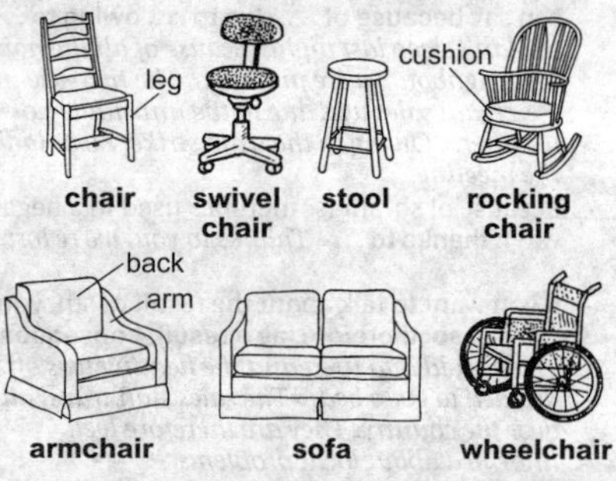

– a place to sit: **seat** ◦ *the back seat of a car* ◦ *to reserve a seat on a train* ◦ *Are there enough seats for everyone?*
– a seat with a back, for one person to sit on: **chair** ◦ *She sat down in her favourite chair.* ◦ *a comfortable chair* ◦ *The chair was very wobbly* (= it was not steady on the floor).

– a chair that you can adjust so that you can lie back in it: **reclining seat/chair** ◦ *There are reclining seats in the front of the car.*
– the part of a seat which supports your arm: **armrest**

– a piece of material that is on the outside of a chair: **cover**; to put a cover on a chair: **cover** sth; to put a new cover on a chair: **re-cover** sth ◦ *The sofa has a green cover.* ◦ *The chairs are all covered in blue silk.* ◦ *They're nice chairs, but they need re-covering.*

– if you keep a person in a chair by using a belt or strap, you **strap** them **in** ◦ *Don't forget to strap the baby into the high chair or he'll climb out and fall.*
– a belt in a car or on a plane for strapping yourself in: **seat belt** ◦ *Has everyone done up their seat belts?*

– a tidy pile of chairs: **stack** of chairs; to put chairs into a pile: **stack** sth (**up**) ◦ *Please stack the chairs (up) tidily before you leave the hall.*

change

1 changing, or causing sth to change
2 having, using or doing sth different
3 able, likely or willing to change

changing in size ⇨ BIG/SMALL
changing in quantity or amount ⇨ INCREASE/DECREASE
changing position ⇨ MOVE
the growth of people, plants, etc ⇨ GROW
political change ⇨ POLITICS

1 changing, or causing sth to change

– to become different: **change** (**from** ...) (**into** ...), **alter** ◦ *Everything's changed since you've been away.* ◦ *Since I was last there, it's changed from a sleepy village into a noisy town.* ◦ *The world has altered a lot since 1945.*
– to make sb/sth different: **change** sb/sth (**from** ...) (**into** ...), **make*** sb/sth **into** ..., **turn** sb/sth **into** ... ◦ *The operation has changed his life.* ◦ *They've made/turned that old shop into a restaurant.*
– not having changed: **unchanged** ◦ *The situation is still unchanged – there's no new information.*

– to change sth, often in order to make it better: **reform** sth; *noun* (C/U): **reform**; a person who tries to change society and make it better: **reformer** ◦ *another attempt to reform the social security system* ◦ *to introduce reforms*
– to change sb/sth completely: **transform** sb/sth; *noun* (C/U): **transformation**

– the process of becoming different or making sth different: **change** (*noun* C/U) ◦ *a slight change* *in temperature* ◦ *I've made a few changes to my report.* ◦ *You have to adapt to change.*

- a change from one state or form to another: **transition**; *adjective*: **transitional** ◦ *the transition from a socialist to a capitalist economy* ◦ *a transitional period*

- a big change can be called **major, significant, fundamental**; a small change can be called **minor, slight** ◦ *some major changes to the Health Service*
- a change which takes place slowly is **gradual** (*adverb* **gradually**); a change which takes place quickly is **sudden** (*adverb* **suddenly**) ◦ *Her work is gradually improving.* ◦ *a sudden change in the weather*

- to begin to be sth: **become*/get*/go*/turn** + adjective ◦ *It was becoming difficult to breathe.* ◦ *I soon got quite tired.* ◦ *She suddenly went pale and fell to the ground.* ◦ *Hasn't it turned cold in the last few days?*

- to become sth different: **turn into** sth ◦ *Some of the tadpoles have already turned into frogs.*
- to become sth gradually: **grow*** + adjective, **grow* into ...** ◦ *Soon it began to grow dark.* ◦ *He's growing into a bad-tempered old man.*
- to grow slowly or change into sth else: **develop** (**into ...**); *noun* (U): **development** ◦ *Over the years, our friendship has slowly developed into love.* ◦ *the rapid development of this city*

▷ more on development ⇨ **DEVELOP**

■ changing back
- to become the same as before: **change back** (**into/to ...**), **revert to ...** ◦ *He's changed back into the happy kind person we all knew before.* ◦ *The garden reverted to its natural state when the owners left.*
- to change sb/sth into what they were before: **change** sb/sth **back into ...**, **restore** sb/sth (**to ...**) ◦ *We changed our library back into a classroom.* ◦ *to restore a building to its former condition*
- to change sth so that it is the opposite of what it was: **reverse** sth; *noun*: **reversal** ◦ *They've reversed their decision to increase taxes.* ◦ *a major reversal in policy*

■ changing the form or use of sth
- to change from one form, system or use to another: **convert** (**from ...**) (**into/to ...**); to cause this to happen: **convert** sth (**from ...**) (**into/to ...**); *noun* (C/U): **conversion** ◦ *a sofa that converts into a double bed* ◦ *They're converting the house into four flats.*

- to make sth different in some way, but without changing it completely: **alter** sth; *noun* (C/U): **alteration** ◦ *The dress suits you, but I think you might need to alter the length.* ◦ *I've got to make some alterations to my essay.*
- to change sth slightly (especially a part of a machine): **adjust** sth; *noun* (C/U): **adjustment**; able to be adjusted: **adjustable** ◦ *He adjusted something in the engine and the car started first time.* ◦ *to make a few adjustments* ◦ *an adjustable chair*
- to change sth, so that you can use it in a different situation: **adapt** sth, **modify** sth; *nouns* (C/U): **adaptation, modification** ◦ *a specially adapted car for disabled drivers* ◦ *No further modifications to the system are being planned.*

- to organize sth in a new way so that it works better: **reorganize** sth; *noun* (C/U): **reorganization** ◦ *We're reorganizing the library to make it more useful to our students.*

▷ organizing things ⇨ **ORGANIZE**

■ changing what is written, planned, etc
- to make changes to sth in order to correct or improve it: **revise** sth; *noun* (C/U): **revision** ◦ *We're revising our plans.* ◦ *the revised edition of the Oxford English Dictionary*
- to change the words of sth: **rewrite*** sth ◦ *I've been told to rewrite my essay.*
- to change sth in order to make it easier to do or understand: **simplify** sth; *noun* (U/C): **simplification** ◦ *a simplified version of the Bible for children*

▷ plans ⇨ **INTEND/PLAN**

2 having, using or doing sth different
- to have or use sth instead of sth else: **change** sth, (*informal*) **switch** sth ◦ *I've decided to change my car for a new model.* ◦ *to change a light bulb* ◦ *I switched jobs last year.*
- to get off one train, bus, etc and onto another: **change** (sth) ◦ *You have to change (trains) at Gloucester.*
- to take off your clothes and put on different ones: **change** (**out of ...**) (**into ...**), **change** sth ◦ *I'm just going upstairs to change into something more comfortable.* ◦ *If your feet are hurting, why don't you change your shoes?*

- to change from being, working, etc in a particular place to being, working, etc in another place: **transfer**; to cause sb to do this: **transfer** sb; *noun* (C/U): **transfer** ◦ *I want to transfer to London so I can be nearer my family.* ◦ *to ask for a transfer to another department*
- to stop doing one thing and start doing sth else: **change over** (**from ...**) (**to ...**); *noun*: **changeover** ◦ *In Britain we're still changing over from feet and inches to metres and centimetres.* ◦ *The changeover has gone very smoothly.*
- if two things or events follow each other, regularly changing one after the other, they **alternate** ◦ *periods of exercise alternating with relaxation*

■ changing your religion
- to change to a new religion: **convert** (**from ...**) (**to ...**); to persuade sb to change to a new religion: **convert** sb (**from ...**) (**to ...**); *noun* (U/C): **conversion** (**to ...**) ◦ *to convert to Catholicism* ◦ *Her friends were surprised by her conversion to Islam.*

■ exchanging one thing for another
- to give sth in return for sth else: **change** sth (**for ...**), **exchange** sth (**for ...**), (*informal*) **swap** sth **for ...**; *nouns*: **exchange**, (*informal*) **swap** ◦ *Can I change this size 10 dress for a size 12 please?* ◦ *We exchanged addresses.* ◦ *We did a flat*

change *contd.*

exchange – they came to live in our flat, and we went to live in their flat in New York.
- to exchange sb/sth for sb/sth that is better or newer: **replace** sb/sth (**with** ...); *noun*: **replacement** ◦ *We're going to replace our old car with a beautiful new one.*

- to take the place or function of sb: **take*** sb's **place**, **replace** sb ◦ *I'm looking for somebody to take my place in this flat.* ◦ *Who will replace Stuart when he leaves?*
- to move into sb's place and to let them take your place: **change/swap places** (**with** sb) ◦ *Let's change places so you can see out of the window for a while.*

- able to be used in place of each other without making a difference: **interchangeable** ◦ *The words 'maybe' and 'perhaps' are often interchangeable.*

3 able, likely or willing to change

- changing often; showing a lot of difference: **variable**; *noun* (U): **variability** (**in/of** ...); *verb*: **vary** ◦ *'What's her work like?' 'Very variable – sometimes excellent, sometimes quite poor.'* ◦ *The prices vary according to size.*
- not changing: **invariable**
- likely to change, not reliable: **changeable** ◦ *changeable weather*

▷ differences between things ⇨ DIFFERENT

- a person or thing that can easily change or be changed to suit different conditions is **flexible**, **adaptable**; *nouns* (U): **flexibility**, **adaptability** ◦ *It's okay if we decide to stay a bit longer – they're very flexible here.* ◦ *Adaptability is essential to our survival.*
- a person or thing that cannot change, or cannot easily be changed to suit conditions, is **inflexible**; *noun* (U): **inflexibility**
- not to change your plan or opinion: **stick*** **to** sth ◦ *Decide what you want to do, and then stick to it – that's the best way to get what you want.*

- lasting for a long time; not likely to be changed: **permanent**; *noun* (U): **permanence** ◦ *I've had enough of travelling round – I'm looking for something more permanent now.*
- not permanent: **temporary** (*adverb* **temporarily**)
- not likely to change, move or end: **stable**; *opposite*: **unstable** ◦ *a stable relationship*
- the condition of being stable: **stability** (*noun* U); *opposite*: **instability** (*noun* U)
- arranged for the present time, but likely to be changed in the future: **provisional** (*adverb* **provisionally**) ◦ *We made a provisional arrangement to meet the following Wednesday.* ◦ *The meeting room is provisionally booked for the 21st.*

- a decision that can be changed is **reversible**; *opposite*: **irreversible** ◦ *I'm afraid the decision is irreversible.*

■ not wanting change
- not liking change: **conservative**; a person who does not like change: **conservative** ◦ *She's got quite conservative tastes – a dark colour would probably be best.*
- to try to stop change from taking place: **resist** sth; *adjective*: **resistant** (**to** sth); *noun* (U): **resistance** ◦ *The new teaching method met with a lot of resistance from the more conservative parents.*

■ **MORE ...**
- if you decide to do sth differently, just because you would like to change your routine, you can say that you are doing it **for a change** ◦ *Let's take a different route for a change.*
- if sth is more pleasant and enjoyable than the thing that usually happens, you can say that it **makes*** **a change** ◦ *We eat in the garden in fine weather – it makes a change.*

- a point in time when a big change happens: **turning point** ◦ *I think that my appearance on television was the turning point in my career.*

character ⇨ PERSONALITY

chase ⇨ HOLD/CATCH

cheap ⇨ PRICE

cheese

see also BUTTER, BREAD, FOOD, COOK

- a thick white substance or hard yellow substance made from milk: **cheese** (*noun* U/C) ◦ *bread and cheese* ◦ *cheese and biscuits* ◦ *cheese on toast* ◦ *They sell lots of different cheeses.*
- (used about cheese) with a strong flavour: **mature**; *opposite*: **mild** ◦ *mild cheddar cheese*
- the hard skin on some cheeses: **rind**

- soft white cheese in small lumps: **cottage cheese** (*noun* U)
- soft white cheese which looks like thick cream: **cream cheese** (*noun* U)
- a soft substance like cheese that you can spread on bread: **cheese spread** (*noun* U)

- a bit of cheese cut in any shape: **piece** (**of cheese**) ◦ *There's a piece of cheddar in the fridge.*
- a bit of cheese that has been cut thinly: **slice** (**of cheese**) ◦ *I was cutting slices of cheese for the sandwiches.*
- to rub cheese so that it breaks into small pieces, using a grater: **grate** sth; *adjective*: **grated** ◦ *Would you like some grated cheese on your pasta?*

▷ picture at COOK

cheque

see also PAY[1], BANK, MONEY

- a piece of paper, printed by a bank, that you can fill in, sign and use to pay for things: **cheque** (*AmE* **check**) ◦ *Do you take cheques?*

– a cheque that you can change into foreign money when you are travelling abroad: **traveller's cheque** (*AmE* **traveler's check**)
– a piece of paper like a cheque that you can buy from a post office and send to sb, and that they can exchange for money: **postal order**

– unused cheques are normally kept in a **chequebook** (*AmE* **checkbook**)
– a small plastic card that you often need when you pay by cheque: **cheque card**

– to use a cheque to pay for sth: **pay*** (**for** sth) **by cheque, write*** (sb) **a cheque, write* out a cheque** (**to** sb) ◦ *I don't have any cash on me. Is it all right if I pay by cheque?* ◦ *I wrote out a cheque for £350 for the new fridge.*
– to exchange a cheque for money: **cash** a cheque ◦ *Can I cash a cheque here, please?*

– to write the name of the person who will receive the money: **make*** a cheque **out to** sb, **make*** a cheque **payable to** sb ◦ *Who shall I make it out to?*
– to write your name on a cheque: **sign** (the cheque), **sign** (your name) (**on** the cheque) ◦ *Do I need to sign it again on the back?*

■ **MORE ...**
– if you write sb a cheque and then decide the money should not be paid, you can tell your bank to **stop** the cheque
– if your bank returns your cheque to you without making the payment, because there was not enough money in the account, the cheque **bounces**

– a cheque that has been signed, but that has an empty space so that the amount of money can be filled in later: **blank cheque**

chess

other games ➪ GAME

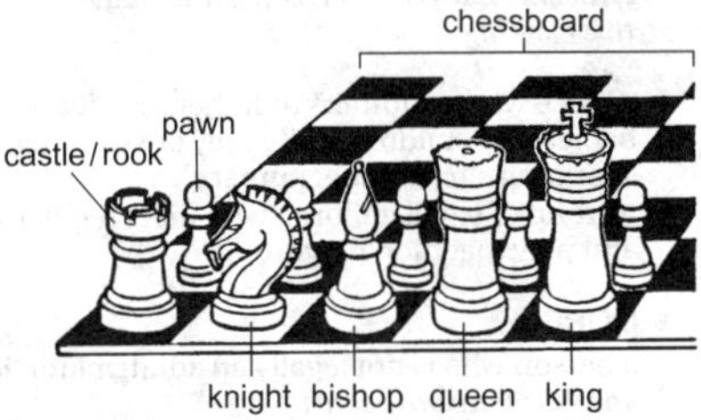

– a game for two people in which each player can move sixteen pieces around a board with black and white squares: **chess** (*noun* U) ◦ *Would you like a game of chess?* ◦ *Do you play chess?*
– a person who plays chess: **chess player**
– one of the small objects that you use when you are playing chess: (**chess**) **piece, man** (*plural* **men**), **chessman** (*plural* **chessmen**) ◦ *the black/white pieces*
– all the pieces and the board that you need to play chess: **chess set**

– to take a chess piece and move it to another place on the board: **move** (sth); *noun*: **move** ◦ *You can only move a king one space in any direction.* ◦ *'Have you moved?' 'Not yet.'* ◦ *a good/clever/stupid/careless move*
– the time in a game of chess when one person must move a piece: **move** ◦ *It's your move.*
– the first move in a game of chess: **opening move**
– to remove a chess piece of your opponent: **take*** sth ◦ *I took her queen and then she took my rook.*

– a stage in the game of chess when a person's king could be taken by the other person: **check** (*noun* U); when you are in this position, you are **in check**
– to cause sb to be in check: **put*** sb **in check**; to move a piece so you are no longer in check: **get* out of check** ◦ *You can get out of check by moving your queen in front of the king.*
– the end of a game of chess, when one player can not move their king out of check: **checkmate** (*noun* U)
– the end of a game of chess, when neither player can win: **stalemate** (*noun* U)
– when you put sb in check, you say **check** or (at the end of the game) **checkmate**

chicken ➪ BIRD[2]

child

1 being a child
2 looking after children
see also FAMILY

1 being a child

– a young person who is not fully grown: **child** (*plural* **children**), (*informal*) **kid**; the period of time when you are a child: **childhood** (*noun* U/C) ◦ *a small/little child* ◦ *a cute/sweet child* ◦ *She's got five small kids.* ◦ *Right kids, time for bed.* ◦ *childhood memories*
– a male child: **boy**; a female child: **girl**

– a child up to the age of about two: **baby**
– a young child who is learning to walk: **toddler**
– a young child: (*formal*) **infant** ◦ *an infant school*
– a child who goes to school: **schoolboy, schoolgirl, schoolchild** (*plural* **schoolchildren**)

▷ more on babies ➪ BABY

– the time when you are young, especially the time between being a child and being an adult: **youth** (*noun* U) ◦ *I was quite good at sport in my youth.*
– a young person who is growing from a child into an adult: **adolescent**; the period of time when a person is an adolescent: **adolescence** (*noun* U)
– a person between 13 and 19 years old: **teenager**; *adjective* (*only before a noun*): **teenage** ◦ *a book written for teenagers* ◦ *teenage magazines*

– to become bigger and taller: **grow*** ◦ *Haven't you grown!*

child *contd.*

– to grow from a child into an adult: **grow* up** ◦ *I grew up in the country.*

■ good and bad behaviour
– to behave properly: **behave**; a child who behaves well is **well-behaved** ◦ *I tell them to behave but they just don't seem to listen.* ◦ *I was a very well-behaved child at school.*
– to behave badly: **misbehave**; a child who behaves badly is **badly-behaved**, **naughty** ◦ *a naughty girl/boy*
– to do sth bad: (*informal*) **be/get* up to** sth ◦ *What have you been up to while I've been away?*
– a child who likes having fun, in a rather naughty way, is **mischievous**; *noun* (U): **mischief** ◦ *He's been up to his mischief again.*
– a child who behaves badly and makes people angry is a **nuisance**, **pest** ◦ *Go and play outside and don't make a nuisance of yourself.* ◦ *Why must you be such a pest!*

– to argue noisily about things which are not important: **squabble** ◦ *The kids were squabbling over who could have the last sweet.*
– to try and make sb angry or annoyed by saying unkind things: **tease** (sb) ◦ *They used to tease him about his long hair.*

■ hurting another child
– to frighten or hurt another smaller child: **bully** sb; *noun* (U): **bullying**; a person who does this: **bully** ◦ *He was bullied at school.*
– to squeeze a piece of sb's skin tightly between your thumb and forefinger: **pinch** sb/sth ◦ *He pinched me!*
– to hit sb with your fist: **punch** sb
– to pull hard on sb's hair: **pull** sb's **hair**

▷ what people are like and how they behave ⇨ **PERSONALITY, BEHAVIOUR**

■ playing and enjoyment
– a special thing that you give to children if they are good, or on a special occasion: **treat** ◦ *I've got a nice treat for you today – we're going to the zoo.*
– money given to children by their parents: **pocket money** (*noun* U)

– to do sth for enjoyment: **play** (**with** sb/sth) ◦ *Let's go out and play.* ◦ *to play games*
– an object for a child to play with: **toy** ◦ *to play with a toy*
– a public area of land where children can play: **playground**

▷ more on toys and playing ⇨ **TOY, PLAY²**

■ friends
– a friend that a child plays with: **playmate**
– the friend that a child likes best: **best friend**
– to spend time with sb: **go* round with** sb, **go* round together** ◦ *I used to go round with this girl at school but she moved away.*

▷ more on friends ⇨ **FRIEND**

2 looking after children

– to care for a child and make sure he/she is kept safe from injury, illness, etc: **take* care of** sb, **look after** sb ◦ *She wants to stay at home to look after her children.*
– to look after a child until he/she is an adult, and to teach him/her how to behave: **bring*** sb **up**, **raise** sb ◦ *They've brought up their children to be self-reliant and honest.*
– a person who has been brought up to behave correctly is **well brought up**
– the way sb is brought up: **upbringing** ◦ *to have a good upbringing*

– to do too much for a child, in a way which is bad for them: **spoil** sb; a child who has been treated in this way is **spoilt** ◦ *Don't spoil the children; they've got enough toys already.* ◦ *a spoilt child*

– to give a child less care and attention than he/she needs: **neglect** sb; *adjective*: **neglected** ◦ *He was neglected by his parents.* ◦ *a neglected child*
– a child who is not given enough of the things that everyone needs is **deprived**
– to treat a child in a very bad way, either physically or emotionally: **abuse** sb; *noun* (U) **abuse**; *adjective*: **abused** ◦ *She was abused as a child.* ◦ *sexual abuse* ◦ *an abused child*

■ people who look after children
– the mother and father of a child: **parents**
– a person, usually a woman, who lives with a family to help look after a young baby or child: **nanny**
– a person, usually a young woman, from another country who lives with a family to learn their language and helps with the housework and looking after the children: **au pair**
– a person who looks after a child while the parents are working: **childminder**; the work of a childminder: **childminding** (*noun* U); *verb*: **mind** sb ◦ *Can you mind my baby for a few hours?*
– a person who looks after a child for a short time when the parents are out of the house: **babysitter**; *verb*: **babysit*** ◦ *I'll come and babysit for you this evening.*

– a place where mothers or fathers can leave their babies and children while they are working, shopping, etc: **cr che, nursery**
– a group of small children who meet regularly and play together: **playgroup**

■ **MORE ...**
– a person who is not legally an adult: **minor, juvenile** ◦ *a juvenile court*

– a child who is unusually good at sth (for example mathematics or playing the violin): (**child**) **prodigy**
– (used about children, often in a rather critical way) behaving in a way that makes them seem older than they are: **precocious** ◦ *a precocious child* ◦ *precocious behaviour*
– a child who has difficulty learning things at school has **learning difficulties** ◦ *a school for children with learning difficulties*

- a doctor who is specially trained to treat children: **paediatrician**

chocolate ⇨ SWEETS

choose ⇨ DECIDE/CHOOSE

Christian

1 Christian beliefs
2 Christian practices
3 different kinds of Christian

other religions ⇨ JEW, MUSLIM, RELIGION
see also GOD, PRAY

1 Christian beliefs

- the religion which is based on the life and teachings of Jesus Christ: **Christianity, the Christian religion, the Christian Church**
- a person whose religion is Christianity: **Christian**
- the man who Christians believe is the son of God and who established the Christian religion: **Jesus Christ**
- the mother of Jesus: **the Virgin Mary**
- (in the Christian religion) the three forms of God: **the Trinity**; the three parts of the Trinity are **the Father, the Son** (Jesus Christ) and **the Holy Spirit/Ghost**
- in prayers, etc, God (or Jesus) is often called **Lord** ◦ *Let us give thanks to the Lord.*

- the object on which Jesus died: the **cross**; to kill sb on a cross: **crucify** sb; *noun*: **crucifixion** (*noun* C/U)
- the return to life of Jesus Christ after the crucifixion: **the Resurrection**

- the holy book of the Christian religion: **the Bible**; a copy of this book: **bible**
- the holy books of religion, such as the Bible: **scripture** (*noun* U), **the scriptures** (*noun plural*) ◦ *a quotation from scripture* ◦ *to read the scriptures*
- the first part of the Bible: **the Old Testament**; the second part: **the New Testament**
- connected with the Bible: **biblical** ◦ *biblical history*
- one of the four main parts of the New Testament: **Gospel** ◦ *St Matthew's/Mark's/Luke's/John's Gospel*
- one of the men chosen by Jesus to spread his teaching: **apostle** ◦ *the apostle Matthew*

2 Christian practices

- a building where Christians worship: **church**, (for some Protestant groups) **chapel**
- a person who attends church regularly: **churchgoer**

▷ more on churches and going to church ⇨ CHURCH

- a religious ceremony in a church: **service** ◦ *We normally go to evening service.*
- the ceremony using bread and wine as symbols of Christ's body and blood: **Communion** (*noun* U), **Holy Communion** (*noun* U), (especially in the Roman Catholic Church) **Mass** (*also* **mass**) (*noun* C/U) ◦ *I spoke to the priest after Mass.*
- a person who conducts services in a church: **priest, vicar, minister**

▷ more on priests, etc ⇨ PRIEST

- a ceremony using water to make sb a member of the Christian Church: **baptism** (*noun* C/U), **christening** (*noun* C/U)
- to perform the ceremony of baptism on a person; to give a child a name during the ceremony of baptism: **baptize** sb, **christen** sb ◦ *Have your children been baptized?* ◦ *He was christened Robert Louis.*
- the name given to a child at christening: **Christian name**
- (in the Roman Catholic Church) the act of telling a priest the bad things that you have done: **confession** (*noun* C/U)
- one of the important ceremonies like baptism and Communion in the Catholic and other churches: **sacrament**

- the time when Christians celebrate the birth of Christ: **Christmas** ◦ *Christmas Day*
- the day on which Christians remember the death of Christ: **Good Friday**
- the time when Christians celebrate the return to life of Christ: **Easter** ◦ *Easter Sunday*
- the day on which Christians remember Christ going to heaven: **Ascension Day**

- a model of a cross with a figure of Jesus: **crucifix**
- to use your hand to make a shape like a cross on your body: **make* the sign of the cross, cross** yourself

- a person who is recognized by the Church as having lived a very good or holy life: **saint** (*written abbreviation* **St**) ◦ *a painting of St Francis*
- a saint who is associated with a particular place or activity: **patron saint** ◦ *St Andrew is the patron saint of Scotland.*

3 different kinds of Christian

- a particular group of Christians: **Church**
- the worldwide Church which has its centre in Rome: **the (Roman) Catholic Church**; the beliefs and practices of this Church: **Catholicism** (*noun* U); a member of this Church: **Catholic**
- the head of the Roman Catholic Church: **the Pope**; *adjective*: **papal**
- one of the ancient churches of Eastern Europe and the Middle East: **Orthodox Church** ◦ *the Russian/Greek Orthodox Church*

- the movement for Church reform in the 16th century: **the Reformation**
- a reformed Church established after the Reformation is a **Protestant Church**; the beliefs and practices of Protestant Churches: **Protestantism** (*noun* U); a member of a Protestant Church: **Protestant**
- the established (= official) Church in England: **the Church of England, the Anglican Church**; the beliefs and practices of this Church: **Anglicanism** (*noun* U); a member of this Church: **Anglican**

Christian *contd.*

- the official Church in Scotland: **the Church of Scotland**
- a Protestant Church that was founded by John Wesley in the 18th century: **the Methodist Church**; the beliefs and practices of this Church: **Methodism** (*noun* U); a member of this Church: **Methodist**
- a Protestant Church that gives especial importance to baptism: **the Baptist Church**; a member of this Church: **Baptist**

Christmas

other Christian celebrations ⇨ **CHRISTIAN**

- December 25: **Christmas Day**
- the day before Christmas, December 24: **Christmas Eve**
- the day after Christmas, December 26: **Boxing Day**
- January 6: **Twelfth Night**
- the period of time during which people celebrate Christmas: **Christmas** (**time**) (*noun* U) ◦ *Are you looking forward to Christmas?* ◦ *the Christmas holidays* ◦ *The shops are always crowded at Christmas time.*

- what people say to each other at Christmas: **Happy Christmas!**
- a piece of card with a picture on the front and a message inside that people send to each other at Christmas time: **Christmas card** ◦ *Have you had a Christmas card from Ann yet?*
- inside the card you can write **Best wishes for Christmas and the New Year**
- an old man with a red coat and a long white beard who, children believe, brings presents at Christmas: **Father Christmas, Santa** (**Claus**) ◦ *What did Santa bring you?*

- something that is traditionally given to friends or family at Christmas: (**Christmas**) **present/gift** ◦ *When can we open our presents, Mummy?*
- a sock or sth similar which is filled with presents on Christmas morning: (**Christmas**) **stocking** ◦ *The children hung up their stockings.*
- coloured paper which is used to cover presents: **wrapping paper** (*noun* U); to cover a present with wrapping paper: **wrap** sth (**up**)

- a special tree that is put somewhere in the house at Christmas: **Christmas tree**
- lights that are put up at Christmas time in a town, or lights on a Christmas tree: (**Christmas**) **lights** ◦ *Have you been to see the lights in Oxford Street?*
- a small beautiful thing that people use to make their homes, etc look pretty: (**Christmas**) **decoration** ◦ *He made some Christmas decorations with silver paper.*
- strings covered with little pieces of shiny paper, used as a Christmas decoration: **tinsel** (*noun* U)
- to put decorations on a tree or in a room: **decorate** sth; (in a room) **put*** sth **up**, **hang*** sth **up** ◦ *to decorate the Christmas tree* ◦ *They've put Christmas decorations up for the staff party.*
- a plant with shiny dark green leaves and red berries that is used as a Christmas decoration: **holly** (*noun* U)
- a green plant with a small white fruit, which people hang up in their homes at Christmas: **mistletoe** (*noun* U) ◦ *It's traditional for people to kiss under a bunch of mistletoe.*

- a kind of song that people sing around Christmas time: (**Christmas**) **carol**
- a cardboard tube wrapped in coloured paper containing a small present; they are pulled apart by two people, each holding one end, at Christmas parties: (**Christmas**) **cracker** ◦ *to pull a cracker* ◦ *a box of crackers*

■ things that people eat at Christmas time

- the large main meal that people eat on Christmas Day: **Christmas dinner/lunch**
- the large bird which people eat on Christmas Day: **turkey** (*noun* C/U) ◦ *the Christmas turkey* ◦ *roast turkey*
- a special dark pudding made with dried fruit that people eat at Christmas dinner: **Christmas pudding** (*noun* C/U)
- a small pie made with dried fruit that people eat at Christmas time: **mince pie**
- a special dark rich fruit cake that people eat at Christmas time: **Christmas cake** (*noun* C/U)

church

1 the building
2 the activities in a church

buildings used by other religions ⇨ **JEW, MUSLIM, RELIGION**

1 the building

- a building where Christians go to pray: **church**, (for some Protestant groups) **chapel**
- a large church that is the most important one in a district: **cathedral** ◦ *St Paul's Cathedral*
- a building where monks or nuns live or used to live, now sometimes the name of an old church: **abbey** ◦ *Westminster Abbey*

- the table used in communion services: **altar**
- the raised place where a priest stands when he speaks to people in church: **pulpit**
- the place in a church where baptisms take place: **font**
- a part of a church with its own altar: **chapel**

- the space for people to pass between blocks of seats: **aisle**
- a long seat with a back, on which a number of people can sit: **pew**
- a large musical instrument consisting of pipes that is often found in churches: **organ**; a person who plays an organ: **organist**
- a window with pieces of coloured glass: **stained glass window**

- the tall part of a church: **tower**
- the part of a tower containing bells: **belfry**
- a tower with a pointed top: **steeple**

- the pointed top of a tower: **spire**
- a round roof: **dome** ◦ *the dome of St Peter's*

- the open space around a church: **churchyard**; when it is used as a place to bury the dead, it is also called a **graveyard**
- a stone which marks the place where sb is buried: **gravestone**

- the area which is served by one church: **parish** ◦ *the parish of St Cuthbert's* ◦ *the parish church* ◦ *the parish priest*
- a person who lives in a parish (and especially one who goes to church there): **parishioner**

2 the activities in a church

- a religious ceremony in a church: **service** ◦ *The vicar has to conduct three services on Sunday.*
- to go into a church in order to take part in a religious ceremony: **go* to church**, (*formal*) **attend** a church service ◦ *Many people never go to church.*
- if you are present during a church service, you are **in/at church**; being present: (*formal*) **attendance** (*noun* U) ◦ *I didn't see you in church last Sunday.*
- a person who attends church regularly: **churchgoer**
- the people who are in church for a particular service: **congregation** ◦ *It was a beautiful service and there was a large congregation.*

- a person who performs religious ceremonies: (especially in the Roman Catholic Church) **priest**, (in the Church of England) **vicar**, (in other Protestant Churches) **minister**

▷ more on ceremonies in church ⇨ CHRISTIAN

▷ more on priests ⇨ PRIEST

- to speak to God in order to give thanks or to ask for sth: **pray** ◦ *I went into the church and prayed.*

▷ more on praying ⇨ PRAY

- a religious talk in church: **sermon** ◦ *The bishop gave an inspiring sermon.*
- to give a religious talk in church: **preach** (**on/about** sth) ◦ *Who is preaching today?*

- a religious song: **hymn**
- a group of people who sing in church: **choir** ◦ *The choir sang three hymns.*

- money that is collected from people during some services in church: **collection** ◦ *There was a collection for the organ fund last Sunday.*

cigarette

see also HABIT

- a roll of tobacco in a thin tube of white paper that people smoke: **cigarette**
- a roll of tobacco leaves that people smoke: **cigar**
- a tube with a small bowl on the end for smoking tobacco: **pipe** ◦ *to smoke a pipe* ◦ *a pipe smoker* (= a person who smokes a pipe)
- a box of usually ten or twenty cigarettes: **packet** (*AmE* **pack**) (**of cigarettes**)
- the substance made from the dried leaves of the tobacco plant that fills cigarettes, etc: **tobacco** (*noun* U) ◦ *tobacco smoke* ◦ *the smell of tobacco*
- the drug that is contained in tobacco: **nicotine** (*noun* U)

■ the habit of smoking

- to have the habit of smoking cigarettes, etc: **smoke**; *noun* (U): **smoking** ◦ *I don't smoke.* ◦ *Smoking can seriously damage your health.*
- a person who smokes: **smoker**; a person who smokes a little/a lot: **light/heavy smoker**

■ smoking a cigarette

- to smoke a cigarette, etc: **have a cigarette**, **smoke** (sth); *noun*: **smoke** ◦ *How many cigarettes do you smoke a day?* ◦ *If you want to smoke please do so only in the permitted smoking areas.* ◦ *I'm going to pop outside for a quick smoke.*

- to make a cigarette, etc begin to burn: **light*** sth ◦ *He sat down and lit a cigar.*
- a short piece of wood that can be used to produce a flame: **match** ◦ *to strike a match* ◦ *a box of matches* ◦ *a matchbox*
- an object that produces a small flame for lighting cigarettes: (**cigarette**) **lighter**
- something that can be used to light a cigarette: **a light** ◦ *Have you got a light?*

- to stop a cigarette burning: **put*** sth **out** ◦ *Please put out your cigarette before you enter the building.*
- to put a cigarette out by pressing the end against a hard surface: **stub** sth **out** ◦ *to stub out a cigarette in an ashtray*

- the part of a cigarette that is left, after it has been smoked: (**cigarette**) **end**
- the grey powder that is left after a cigarette has burned: (**cigarette**) **ash** (*noun* U)
- a small dish for cigarette ash: **ashtray**

■ not smoking

- a place where it is forbidden to smoke is **non-smoking** ◦ *This is a non-smoking bar.* ◦ *a non-smoking carriage on a train*

- to stop smoking permanently: **give*** (sth) **up**, **stop**, (*AmE*) **quit** ◦ *I gave up smoking ten years ago.*
- to decide to smoke fewer cigarettes regularly: **cut* down** (**on** sth) ◦ *Please don't offer me a cigarette – I've been trying to cut down.*
- a person who does not smoke: **non-smoker** ◦ *Wanted: flatmate, non-smoker preferred.*

cinema

see also FILM, ENTERTAINMENT, THEATRE

- a building where people go to see a film: **cinema** (*AmE* **movie house**, **movie theater**)
- a kind of cinema, especially in America, where people can stay in their cars to watch a film: **drive-in**

- the part of the cinema where people sit to watch the film: **auditorium**
- the space between the rows of seats: **aisle**

cinema *contd.*

- the flat surface on which a film is shown: **screen**
- the machine that projects films on to the screen: **projector**

- if you go to see a film at the cinema, you **go* to the cinema, go* to the pictures** (*AmE* **go* to the movies**) ◦ *Let's go to the pictures tonight, shall we?*
- a film which is at a local cinema at the present time is **on** ◦ *What's on?* ◦ *This film is going to be on for another week.*
- to put on a film at a cinema: **show*** sth, **screen** sth ◦ *The Odeon is showing 'Gone With The Wind' again.*
- a short break between parts of a film when it is shown in a cinema: **interval** (*AmE* **intermission**) ◦ *We ate ice cream during the interval.*

- the group of people who are in a cinema to see a film: **audience**
- a man/woman who shows people to their seats: **usher/usherette**
- a person who often goes to the cinema: **cinema-goer** (*AmE* **movie-goer**)

▷ more on audiences ⇨ AUDIENCE

- when you pay to go into the cinema, you buy a **ticket** ◦ *Keep your ticket in case you need to get back in.*
- the cost of going into the cinema: **admission** ◦ *Admission: £4.50*
- the place where you buy a cinema ticket: **box office, ticket office**

▷ more on getting a ticket ⇨ TICKET

circle

1 describing or drawing a circle
2 moving in a circle or forming a circle
other shapes ⇨ SHAPE

1 describing or drawing a circle

- a line which curves round to form the shape of a ring. Every point on the line is the same distance from the centre: (used in mathematics) **circle**; (used generally) **circle, ring** ◦ *to draw a circle* ◦ *The children stood in a circle/ring and held hands.* ◦ *He arranged the candles in a circle on the cake.*
- to draw a circle round sth: **circle** sth, **ring** sth ◦ *The students had to circle the correct answer to each question.*

- a V-shaped instrument used for drawing circles: **compass, (pair of) compasses** (*noun plural*)

- a flat, round area, shaped like a circle: **circle**; *adjective*: **circular** ◦ *Cut out a circle of paper.* ◦ *the centre circle* (in a game of football for example) ◦ *a circular shape*
- a round object with a hole in the middle: **ring** ◦ *a wedding ring* ◦ *a keyring*
- a round flat object: **disc** (*AmE* **disk**) ◦ *an identity disc* (= a small disc like a coin which identifies a person or animal)
- any round object shaped like a ball (especially in mathematics): **sphere**; *adjective*: **spherical** ◦ *a spherical object*
- having the same shape as a circle or a sphere: **round** ◦ *a round window* ◦ *The earth is round.* ◦ *a round hole*

- the shape of half a circle: **semicircle**; *adjective*: **semicircular** ◦ *a semicircular stage*
- shaped like an egg: **oval** ◦ *an oval mirror*

▷ pictures of circle, sphere, oval and semicircle ⇨ SHAPE

■ the measurements of a circle

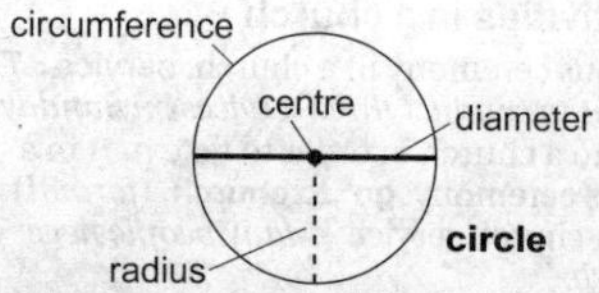

- the distance round a circle or sth circular: **circumference** ◦ *The circumference of the circle is 12 cm.* ◦ *The circle is 12 cm in circumference.*

2 moving in a circle or forming a circle

- to move approximately in a circle: **go*, walk, drive***, etc **round** sth, **circle** sth ◦ *to go round the world* ◦ *We had to drive round the roundabout a few times before we knew which road to take.* ◦ *The plane circled the city a few times before landing.*
- going round in a circle: **circular** ◦ *The bus follows a circular route.* ◦ *He made circular movements with his hand.*
- to move in a circle around a central point: **go* round** (sth), **revolve** (**round/around** sth) ◦ *The big hand of the clock goes round once an hour.* ◦ *The moon revolves around the earth.*
- in the same direction as a clock: **clockwise** (*adjective, adverb*); *opposite*: **anticlockwise** (*adjective, adverb*) ◦ *to go in a clockwise direction* ◦ *to turn anticlockwise*

▷ moving in a circle (like a wheel or ball) ⇨ TURN

- (used about a group of people) to form a circle around sb/sth: **gather round/around** sb/sth ◦ *The children gathered round the teacher to hear him tell a story.*
- to be or go all around sb/sth: **surround** sb/sth ◦ *The soldiers surrounded the city.* ◦ *a village surrounded by mountains*

city ⇨ TOWN

claim ⇨ HAVE/POSSESS

clap ⇨ AUDIENCE

class

- in school ⇨ SCHOOL
- social class ⇨ SOCIETY
- a category ⇨ TYPE

clean / dirty

1 clean
2 dirty
3 making sth clean
4 making yourself clean and tidy

1 clean

- free from dirt: **clean** ◦ *Your room looks very clean and tidy.* ◦ *Are your hands clean?*
- very clean: **spotless** (*adverb* **spotlessly**) ◦ *The kitchen looks absolutely spotless.* ◦ *spotlessly clean*
- changed and new (or washed) and therefore clean: **fresh** ◦ *I've put fresh towels in your room.*

■ clean and healthy
- keeping yourself and things around clean, so as to avoid the spread of disease: **hygiene** (*noun* U); *adjective*: **hygienic** ◦ *The restaurant has very high standards of hygiene.* ◦ *It is hygienic to wash your hands before you start cooking.*
- the state of being clean and hygienic: **cleanliness** (*noun* U)
- connected with the protection of health: **sanitary** ◦ *Sanitary conditions were not satisfactory.*
- a system for protecting public health, especially by removing waste: **sanitation** (*noun* U) ◦ *There is no sanitation in the poorer parts of the city.*

- completely clean and free from all dirt and bacteria: **sterile**; to make sth sterile: **sterilize** sth ◦ *sterile equipment* ◦ *Sterilize the needle before you use it.*
- to clean sth, for example a wound, with a substance that kills germs: **disinfect** sth ◦ *to disinfect a wound*
- a substance used for disinfecting things, for example a wound or a piece of medical equipment: **disinfectant** (*noun* U)

2 dirty

- a substance which is not clean: **dirt** (*noun* U), (*informal*) **muck** (*noun* U); disgusting dirt: **filth** (*noun* U) ◦ *There was dirt all over the carpet.* ◦ *We tried to get the dirt out of the cut.*
- covered with or containing dirt: **dirty**, (*informal*) **mucky** ◦ *dirty clothes* ◦ *My hands are a bit mucky – I've been cleaning my bike.*
- very dirty: **filthy** ◦ *We went for a walk across the fields and came back absolutely filthy.*

- a person or thing that is dirty or untidy: **a mess** ◦ *You look a mess – you'd better wash your hair and put some clean clothes on.*

- a fine dry powder that is made of very small pieces of earth or dirt: **dust** (*noun* U); covered with dust: **dusty** ◦ *Everything in the cupboard was covered in dust.* ◦ *dusty old books*
- soft, wet earth: **mud** (*noun* U); covered with mud: **muddy** ◦ *muddy water* ◦ *muddy shoes*
- a thick unpleasant sticky liquid: **slime** (*noun* U); covered with slime: **slimy**

■ marks and stains
- something on clothes, furniture, paper, etc, which spoils its appearance: **mark** ◦ *There were marks on the walls, where somebody had put their dirty hands.*
- a small round mark of a different colour on sth (clothes for example): **spot** (**of** sth) ◦ *There was a small spot of grease on his tie.*

- a mark on sth which is difficult to remove: **stain**; to make this kind of mark on sth: **stain** (sth) ◦ *There's a coffee stain on the carpet.* ◦ *Be careful, red wine stains.*
- to spread a sticky substance across sth: **smear** sth; a mark made in this way: **smear** ◦ *The child had smeared food all over her face.*
- to make a dirty or untidy mark by rubbing: **smudge** sth; a mark made in this way: **smudge** ◦ *The page was covered in ink smudges.*

■ dirty and unpleasant living conditions
- the state of being dirty or untidy: **mess** (*noun* C/U); *adjective*: **messy**; *opposite*: **tidy** ◦ *Who's going to tidy up this mess?* ◦ *a messy room/desk*
- to make sth messy: **mess** sth **up**, **make* a mess of** sth ◦ *I baked a cake and made a mess of the kitchen.*

▷ being tidy or untidy ⇨ TIDY

- very dirty, untidy and unpleasant: **squalid** ◦ *to live in squalid conditions* ◦ *a squalid house*
- the state of being very dirty and untidy: **squalor** (*noun* U) ◦ *to live in squalor*
- dirty-looking, without much light: **dingy** ◦ *a dark and dingy house*
- a room or house that is very dirty or untidy: (*informal*) **tip**, (*informal*) **pigsty** ◦ *His bedroom's a real tip/pigsty.*

■ dirty and harmful
- dirty conditions which are likely to cause disease are **insanitary**, **unhygienic** ◦ *insanitary conditions* ◦ *unhygienic habits*

- to add a substance that will make sth, particularly food or water, dirty, harmful or dangerous: **contaminate** sth; *noun* (U): **contamination** ◦ *contamination of the water supply*
- to make air and rivers dirty and dangerous: **pollute** sth; *noun* (U): **pollution**; *adjective*: **polluted** ◦ *beaches that are affected by pollution* ◦ *polluted rivers*

3 making sth clean

- to make sth clean: **clean** sth; an act of cleaning: **clean** ◦ *to clean the cooker/carpet/bedroom* ◦ *I'm going to give the car a clean.*
- to clean sth with water and often soap: **wash** sth; an act of washing: **wash** ◦ *to wash your clothes* ◦ *to wash the dishes* ◦ *This floor needs a wash.*

▷ more on washing ⇨ WASH

- a person whose job it is to clean things: **cleaner** ◦ *an office cleaner*
- a woman whose job it is to clean houses or offices: **cleaning lady**, **cleaning woman**

- something which is used for cleaning things: **cleaner** ◦ *Have you got any bathroom cleaner?* (= a substance to clean a bathroom with)
- a strong chemical substance used for cleaning things like toilets: **bleach** (*noun* U)

clean/dirty *contd.*

– to clean the inside of sth, getting rid of things you do not need: **clean** sth **out** ◦ *We had to clean out the flat when we left.* ◦ *to clean out a cupboard/drawer*
– to remove dirt and rubbish from a place: **clean** (sth) **up**; an act of cleaning around the house: **clean-up** ◦ *We'd better clean up this mess before they get back.* ◦ *This place needs a good clean-up.*

– if you remove dirt or a mark from a piece of clothing, a carpet, etc, you **get*** it **out** ◦ *I got the wine stain out with a special stain remover.*
– if dirt or a mark is removed by cleaning, it **comes* out** ◦ *Stains like this hardly ever come out.*

– a small piece of material used for cleaning things: **cloth**; a piece of old cloth that is used for cleaning things: **rag** ◦ *a damp/soft cloth*
– to clean a surface by rubbing it with a cloth, etc: **wipe** sth ◦ *Could you wipe the table?* ◦ *to wipe the floor* ◦ *to wipe your mouth*
– to remove sth by wiping: **wipe** sth **off** ◦ *She wiped the black mark off her face.*
– to use a cloth to remove some liquid, food, etc that has been spilt: **wipe** sth **up** ◦ *Could you wipe up that milk you've spilt, please.*
– to remove dirt, etc by moving a sharp edge across a surface: **scrape** sth **off** ◦ *Scrape the mud off your boots before you come in the house.*

– to make sth shine by rubbing it and often by putting a special cream or liquid on it: **polish** sth; an act of polishing: **polish**; *adjective*: **polished** ◦ *to polish a table/car/window* ◦ *to give sth a polish* ◦ *a polished floor*
– a cream, liquid, wax, etc, that you put on sth to clean it and make it shine: **polish** (*noun* U) ◦ *car/floor/shoe polish*

– to clean dust from a surface by wiping it with a dry cloth: **dust** sth ◦ *to dust furniture/shelves/books*
– a soft cloth that you use for dusting furniture: **duster**

– to remove dirt from the floor with a brush: **brush** sth, **sweep*** sth; an act of brushing sth: **brush**, **sweep** ◦ *to brush/sweep the floor* ◦ *to give sth a brush* ◦ *The floor needs a sweep.*
– an electric machine that cleans carpets by sucking up the dirt: **vacuum cleaner**, **hoover**
– to clean sth using a vacuum cleaner: **vacuum** (sth), **hoover** (sth) ◦ *to vacuum/hoover the carpet*
▷ more on brushes and brushing ⇨ BRUSH

– the work that is needed to keep a house clean and tidy: **cleaning** (*noun* U), **housework** (*noun* U) ◦ *Who does the cleaning in your house?* ◦ *to do the housework*
– to clean everything in a house thoroughly: **spring-clean** sth; an act of spring-cleaning: **spring-clean** ◦ *to give the house a spring-clean*

Note: with everyday actions such as cleaning, washing, dusting, etc, we use **do***: ◦ *to do the vacuuming/cleaning/washing-up/dusting* ◦ *I do the cleaning on Saturdays.*

– a large container for rubbish (usually kept outside the house): **dustbin** (*AmE* **garbage can**, **trashcan**)
– a small container that you keep inside your house for rubbish: **bin**, **waste-paper basket** (*AmE* **waste bin**, **wastebasket**)
▷ more on rubbish ⇨ RUBBISH

4 making yourself clean and tidy

– to use soap and water to make yourself clean: **wash** (sth/yourself), **have a wash** ◦ *to wash your face/hair/hands* ◦ *I'm just going to have a quick wash and then I'll be ready.*
– to make yourself look tidier and cleaner: **clean** (yourself) **up** ◦ *I'll just clean myself up a bit before I go.*
▷ more on washing yourself ⇨ WASH
▷ making your hair clean and attractive ⇨ HAIR

– a thin piece of soft paper that you use for wiping your nose, cleaning your skin, etc: **tissue** ◦ *a box of tissues* ◦ *I offered her a tissue to wipe away her tears.*
– soft, loose, cotton in a mass, used for cleaning the skin: **cotton wool** (*noun* U) ◦ *a piece of cotton wool*
– substances that you use to make yourself look more attractive: **cosmetics**
▷ more on cosmetics ⇨ COSMETICS

clear

– easy to see ⇨ SEE
– easy to understand ⇨ UNDERSTAND

clever

1 clever
2 not clever

1 clever

– good at learning and doing things: **clever** (*AmE* **smart**); *noun* (U): **cleverness** ◦ *to be clever at maths* ◦ *to be clever with your hands* ◦ *a clever child* ◦ *a clever opponent* ◦ *a smart student*
– good at thinking and solving problems: **intelligent**; *noun* (U): **intelligence** ◦ *an intelligent animal* ◦ *an intelligence test*
– (used especially about children) intelligent: **bright** ◦ *the brightest boy in the class*
– very intelligent: **brilliant**; *noun* (U): **brilliance** ◦ *She's brilliant at maths.*

Note: things, especially ideas, remarks, etc, can also be described in this way ◦ *a clever plan/invention* ◦ *an intelligent question* ◦ *a bright idea* ◦ *a brilliant suggestion*

– a person who is unusually intelligent: **genius**; this kind of intelligence: **genius** (*noun* U) ◦ *Ein-*

stein was a genius. ◦ *a writer of genius* ◦ *This work shows real genius.*
- quick at thinking and understanding: **sharp**, **quick-witted** ◦ *a sharp lawyer* ◦ *a quick-witted interviewer*
- using words in a clever and amusing way: **witty**; *noun* (U): **wit** ◦ *a witty speaker* ◦ *a witty remark* ◦ *She spoke with wit and wisdom.*

- the part of you which thinks: **brain**, **brains**, **mind** ◦ *Use your brains!* ◦ *I don't have the right kind of mind for this work.*
- if you are intelligent, you (*informal*) have **brains**, (*informal*) are **brainy** ◦ *He's the brainy one in the family.*

- using experience and knowledge to make good decisions: **wise**; *noun* (U): **wisdom** ◦ *a wise old person* ◦ *a wise choice*
- able to think or act in a reasonable way; showing good judgement: **sensible**; *noun* (U): **sense** ◦ *sensible parents* ◦ *a sensible suggestion* ◦ *There's a lot of sense in that suggestion.*

▷ more on being sensible ⇨ SENSIBLE

■ skill and talent
- able to do sth particularly well, especially through learning and practising: **skilful** (*AmE* **skillful**); *noun* (C/U): **skill** ◦ *a skilful football player* ◦ *to learn a new skill* ◦ *a game of skill and chance*
- having a natural ability to do sth particularly well: **talented**; *noun* (C/U): **talent** ◦ *a talented musician* ◦ *She has a talent for design.* ◦ *He shows great talent.*
- generally good at doing things: **able**; *noun* (U): **ability** ◦ *an able worker* ◦ *a player with great natural ability*
- (used about a person, an idea, etc) showing an ability to make things work: **practical** ◦ *a practical mind* ◦ *a very practical person*
- good at finding ways of doing things: **resourceful**; *noun* (U): **resourcefulness** ◦ *a resourceful teacher*
- showing an ability to find answers to problems or thinking of new things: **ingenious**; *noun* (U): **ingenuity** ◦ *an ingenious designer* ◦ *an ingenious solution to a problem* ◦ *He showed great ingenuity in solving his money problems.*

▷ more on skill ⇨ SKILL

■ doing well at school, etc
- if you do well in a school subject, a sport, etc, you are **good at** it
- if you are particularly good at a school subject, a sport, etc, you **shine*** (**at**/**in** it), (*formal*) **excel** (**at**/**in** it) ◦ *She always shone at languages and now she's a translator.* ◦ *He excelled at athletics.*

2 not clever
- not clever: **stupid**, (*informal, especially AmE*) **dumb**; *noun* (U): **stupidity** ◦ *Don't be so stupid!* ◦ *What a stupid thing to say!*
- a person who does not act in a reasonable or clever way: **fool**, **idiot**, (*informal*) **lunatic** ◦ *Don't believe him, you fool!* ◦ *What an idiot you are!* ◦ *The man's a lunatic!*
- a person who is unintelligent can be called (*informal*) **thick**, (*informal*) **dim** ◦ *She probably won't understand – she's a bit dim.*

- (used about a person, an action, an idea, etc) not sensible or reasonable: **stupid**, **foolish**, **silly**, (*informal*) **daft**; *nouns* (U): **stupidity**, **foolishness** ◦ *It would be foolish to believe everything you read in the newspapers.* ◦ *a silly mistake* ◦ *Don't be daft.*
- (used about a person, an action, an idea, etc) extremely foolish: **crazy**, **idiotic**, **mad**, **insane**; *nouns* (U): **craziness**, **idiocy** ◦ *a crazy idea* ◦ *You must be crazy!* ◦ *What an idiotic thing to do!* ◦ *The whole plan is insane!*
- an action or a thing which should be laughed at because it is foolish is **ridiculous**, **silly**, **absurd**; *nouns* (U): **absurdity**, **silliness** ◦ *a ridiculous suggestion* ◦ *I can't wear this – I'll look silly!* ◦ *an absurd hat* ◦ *to look ridiculous/absurd* ◦ *the absurdity of the idea*

- to behave in a foolish or stupid way: **fool about/around** ◦ *Please stop fooling about and answer my question seriously.*
- to make another person or yourself appear foolish or silly: **make* a fool of** sb/yourself ◦ *I think I made rather a fool of myself.*

■ **MORE...**
- the measure of people's intelligence: **IQ** (= Intelligence Quotient) ◦ *a high/low IQ* ◦ *A person of average intelligence has an IQ of 100.*

climb

see also HILL / MOUNTAIN

- to move towards the top of sth: **climb** (sth), **go* up** sth, (*formal*) **ascend** (sth); *nouns*: **climb**, (*formal*) **ascent** ◦ *to climb a tree/mountain* ◦ *There is a long and difficult climb before you get to the next village.* ◦ *the first ascent of Mount Everest*
- towards the top of a hill: **uphill** (*adjective, adverb*) ◦ *a steep uphill climb*

- to go or come down sth: **climb down** (sth), **go* down** sth, (*formal*) **descend** (sth); *noun*: **descent** ◦ *He had difficulty in climbing down the tree.* ◦ *She went down the stairs carefully.* ◦ *We began our descent from the summit at six o'clock.*
- towards the bottom of a hill: **downhill** (*adjective, adverb*) ◦ *to run downhill*

- to manage to go over to the other side of a wall, gate, etc: **climb over** sth ◦ *I climbed over the gate and ran across the field.*
- to climb with difficulty, using both your hands and feet: **clamber** ◦ *We clambered up to the top of the hill.*

■ climbing as a sport
- the sport of climbing hills or mountains: **climbing** (*noun* U); to do this sport: **go* climbing**; a person who climbs as a sport: **climber** ◦ *I went climbing in the Himalayas last summer.* ◦ *a rock-climber*

climb *contd.*

- the sport of climbing mountains: **mountaineering** (*noun* U); a person who climbs mountains: **mountaineer, mountain climber**
- the sport of climbing rocks and mountains with ropes, etc: **rock-climbing** (*noun* U)
- walking in the hills: **hillwalking** (*noun* U); a person who walks in hills: **hillwalker** ◦ *We're planning to go hillwalking this weekend.*

clock/watch

telling the time ⇨ TIME

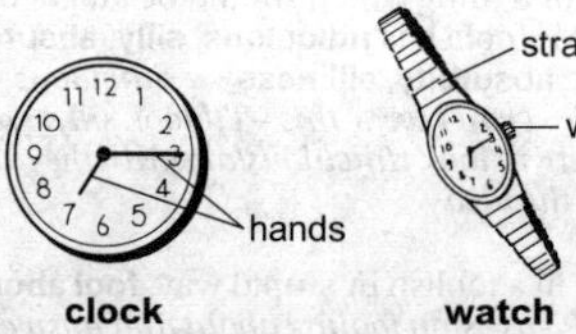

- a clock that you can set to wake you up: **alarm clock**
- a watch that is used to measure exactly how long sth takes: **stopwatch**

- a watch/clock that shows the time by numbers alone and does not have hands: **digital watch/clock**
- a device which provides electricity for a clock, watch, etc: **battery** ◦ *My watch has stopped – it probably needs a new battery.*
- a bar with a heavy weight on one end, used to operate some large clocks: **pendulum**

- the front part of a clock or watch: **face, dial**
- one of the pointers on the face of a clock or watch: **hand** ◦ *the hour/minute/second hand*

- the sound that a clock or watch makes: **tick**; to make this sound: **tick** ◦ *My alarm clock has a very loud tick.* ◦ *It hasn't stopped – I can hear it ticking.*
- when the clock rings a bell every quarter of an hour or every hour, it **strikes*** ◦ *I could hear the church clock striking in the distance.* ◦ *The clock struck three.*

- to make a clock or watch show the correct time: **set*** sth ◦ *Can you set the time on my new watch?*
- to make sth work by turning a key or a handle: **wind*** sth (**up**) ◦ *The clock's stopped. Can you wind it up please?*
- a handle or knob which you turn to make a clock or watch go: **winder**

- (used about a clock or a watch) giving the correct time: **right**; *opposite*: **wrong** ◦ *Is that the right time?* ◦ *I don't think my watch is right.* ◦ *I think that clock must be wrong.*
- when the time shown on a clock or watch is behind the correct time, the clock or watch is **slow**; *opposite*: **fast** ◦ *You're going to be late. Your watch is ten minutes slow.* ◦ *You'd better check the time. I think that clock's fast.*

- to set an alarm clock to wake you up: **set* the alarm** ◦ *I have to be up early tomorrow, so could you set the alarm for six?*
- when the alarm rings, it **goes* off** ◦ *I'm sorry I'm late. I didn't hear the alarm go off.*
- when you want to stop the alarm ringing, you **put*** it **off**, **switch** it **off**

■ **MORE . . .**

- in the same direction as the hands of a clock: **clockwise** (*adjective*, *adverb*); *opposite*: **anticlockwise** ◦ *in a clockwise direction* ◦ *Turn the handle clockwise.*

close

- shut ⇨ OPEN/SHUT
- not far ⇨ DISTANCE

cloth

1 kinds of cloth
2 designs on cloth
3 how cloth feels
other materials ⇨ MATERIAL

1 kinds of cloth

- any material made from cotton, wool, etc which you use for making clothes, curtains, etc: **cloth** (*noun* C/U), **material** (*noun* C/U) ◦ *How much cloth do you need to make the jacket?* ◦ *What kind of material do you think I should buy for the wedding dress?*
- (in industry) a material that is made by weaving or knitting: **textile** ◦ *They manufacture textiles.* ◦ *the textile industry*

- materials made from plants or the hair of animals are **natural** ◦ *natural fabrics like silk and wool*
- materials that are made by a chemical process are **man-made, synthetic** ◦ *Most man-made fibres are stronger than natural ones.*

■ cotton materials

- a natural cloth made from a tropical plant: **cotton** (*noun* U) ◦ *a cotton T-shirt* ◦ *This blouse is 70% cotton and 30% polyester.*
- thick strong cotton cloth, often blue, used for making jeans, etc: **denim** (*noun* U) ◦ *a blue denim jacket*
- thick soft cotton cloth, with raised lines: **corduroy** (*noun* U) ◦ *corduroy trousers*
- a strong cloth like cotton made from a plant: **linen** (*noun* U) ◦ *a linen handkerchief/suit*

■ wool materials

- cloth made from the hair of sheep, etc: **wool** (*noun* U) ◦ *'What's your coat made of?' 'It's pure wool.'* ◦ *a wool skirt*
- made from wool: **woollen** (*AmE* **woolen**) ◦ *a woollen jumper*
- made from wool or like wool: **woolly** (*AmE* **wooly**) ◦ *a warm woolly scarf*
- a type of thick woollen cloth: **tweed** (*noun* U) ◦ *a tweed jacket*
- a very soft, fine wool or material made from it: **cashmere** (*noun* U) ◦ *a cashmere sweater*

▷ more on wool ⇨ **WOOL**

■ man-made materials

- a strong man-made material that is used for making clothes, thread, etc: **nylon** (*noun* U) ◦ *nylon socks*
- a man-made material used in clothes, that is softer than nylon: **polyester** (*noun* U) ◦ *The sheets are 50% polyester, so they wash easily.*

■ fine or expensive cloths

- an expensive natural cloth made from threads produced by an insect: **silk** (*noun* U) ◦ *a silk blouse* ◦ *This tie is pure silk.*
- a smooth shiny material: **satin** (*noun* U) ◦ *a satin nightdress*
- a material made of cotton or silk, with a soft thick surface: **velvet** (*noun* U) ◦ *a black velvet dress*
- a cloth made of very fine threads in beautiful patterns: **lace** (*noun* U) ◦ *lace curtains* ◦ *a collar made of handmade lace*

2 designs on cloth

- an arrangement of lines, pictures, etc which make a regular design on cloth: **pattern**; having a pattern: **patterned** ◦ *The curtains have a pattern of birds and flowers.* ◦ *a blue patterned silk blouse*

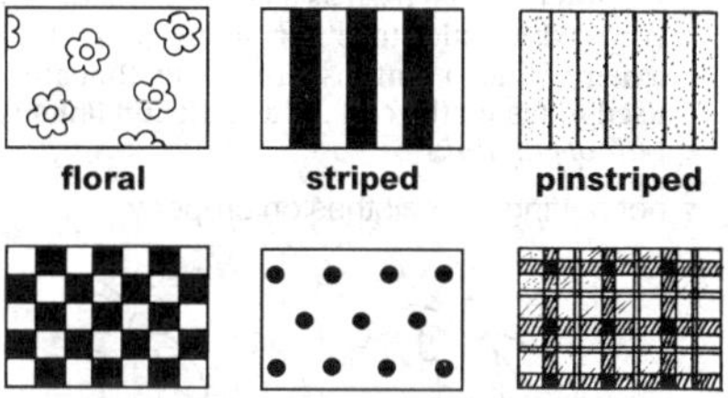

3 how cloth feels

- the way sth feels when you touch it: **texture**, **feel** ◦ *I like the colour of this material but I don't like the texture – it feels scratchy.*

- if sth is flat, without lumps or holes, so that your hand goes over it easily, it is **smooth**; *opposite*: **rough** ◦ *smooth as silk* ◦ *That jumper is too rough for me to wear.*
- smooth and soft: **silky** ◦ *The shirt feels really silky, but it's actually nylon.*

■ **MORE ...**

- material with rubber (or sth like rubber) in it to make it stretch: **elastic** (*noun* U)
- a very strong thick cotton cloth, used for sails, bags, etc: **canvas** (*noun* U) ◦ *canvas shoes*
- a piece of cloth with a design sewn in coloured thread: **tapestry** ◦ *tapestries hanging on the walls of a room*

- to make cloth by passing threads under and over a series of other threads which are attached to a frame: **weave*** (sth); something which is made in this way is **woven** ◦ *This coat is made from hand-woven Harris tweed.*
- a person who weaves cloth: **weaver**
- the frame used for weaving: **loom**

clothes

1 wearing clothes
2 kinds of clothes
3 parts of clothes
4 the size of clothes
5 buying clothes
6 how you look in clothes
7 taking care of your clothes

what clothes are made from ⇨ **CLOTH**

1 wearing clothes

- the general word for what you wear: **clothes** (*noun plural*), (*formal*) **clothing** (*noun* U) ◦ *She always wears such lovely clothes.* ◦ *a piece of clothing* ◦ *The police found several items of men's clothing in the room.*
- special clothes and other equipment that you need for a particular purpose: **kit** (*noun* U), **gear** (*noun* U) ◦ *sports kit* ◦ *Remember to bring your climbing gear.*

- to have clothes on your body: **wear*** sth, **have** sth **on**, **be dressed (in** sth) ◦ *I've got nothing to wear for the dance tomorrow.* ◦ *He was wearing a black jumper and blue jeans.* ◦ *She had her new dress on.* ◦ *It's half past nine! Aren't you dressed yet?* ◦ *Derek was dressed in his father's old suit.*

■ wearing nothing

- if you are wearing no clothes at all, you are **naked**, you have **nothing on**, you are **in the nude** ◦ *There were three naked men swimming in the lake.* ◦ *The children were running about in the garden with nothing on.* ◦ *They walk about the house in the nude.*
- completely naked: **stark naked**
- the state of having no clothes on: **nakedness** (*noun* U)
- a part of the body with no clothes on it is **bare** ◦ *It's too cold to go out with bare legs – put some tights on.*

■ choosing what to wear

- when you wear particular clothes for a particular purpose, you **dress for** sth ◦ *dressed for a day's work in the garden* ◦ *I can't go to the party – I'm not dressed for it.*
- a set of clothes that you wear together makes an **outfit** ◦ *I bought some shoes to go with my wedding outfit.*
- when you wear special clothes for a party or a formal occasion, you **dress up** ◦ *The whole family dresses up for Christmas dinner.*
- if you dress too smartly or too formally for an occasion, you are **overdressed** ◦ *I think you'll be overdressed if you wear that suit – everyone else will be wearing jeans.*

clothes *contd.*

■ wearing unusual clothes

– when you dress in unusual clothes for a party, play, etc, you **dress up** (**as** sb/sth) ◦ *The children love dressing up as ghosts.*
– the clothes that you wear when you dress up: **fancy dress** (*noun* U) ◦ *a fancy dress party*
– clothes, false hair, etc that you wear so that nobody recognizes you: **disguise** (*noun* C/U); to wear a disguise: **disguise** sb/yourself (**as** sb/sth) ◦ *Nobody noticed that they were escaping, because they were disguised as prison guards.*

■ putting clothes on and taking clothes off

– when you put your clothes on, you **get* dressed**; *opposite*: **get* undressed, undress** ◦ *Get dressed quickly or you'll miss the school bus!* ◦ *I got undressed and had a bath.* ◦ *He undressed so that the doctor could examine his chest.*
– to take all your clothes off: **strip** (**off**), **strip** your clothes **off** ◦ *It was so warm we all stripped off and dived into the river.*

– to put a piece of clothing on your body: **put*** sth **on**, (*informal*) **get*** sth **on**; *opposite*: **take*** sth **off** ◦ *Put your coat on if you're going out.* ◦ *Do I have to take my hat off in church?*
– to put some clothing on quickly and easily: **slip** sth **on, slip into** sth; *opposite*: **slip** sth **off, slip out of** sth ◦ *Wait for me – I'm just going to slip my boots on.* ◦ *She slipped out of her dressing gown and turned on the shower.*
– to put sth on or take sth off with force or in a hurry: **pull** sth **on/off** ◦ *He quickly pulled off his clothes and dived into the river.*
– to put sth on with difficulty: **get* into** sth ◦ *He's put on weight – he can't get into these jeans any more.*
– to put the bottom edge of a shirt or jumper inside the waist of your skirt or trousers: **tuck** sth **in, tuck** sth **into** sth ◦ *I usually wear my T-shirt tucked into my jeans.*
– if you decide not to take off a piece of clothing, you **keep*** it **on, leave*** it **on** ◦ *I'll keep my coat on – I'm not staying long.*

– if you change from one set of clothes into another, you **get* changed, change out of** sth, **change into** sth ◦ *Where do we get changed to go in the swimming-pool?* ◦ *You ought to change out of those wet clothes immediately.* ◦ *Why not change into something more comfortable?*
– if you then put on the first set of clothes again, you **change back** into them
– a room in a sports centre, etc where you get changed: **changing room** (*AmE* **locker room**)

– to put clothes on another person: **dress** sb, **get*** sb **dressed**; *opposite*: **undress** sb ◦ *We dressed the baby in warm clothes.*
– if you help sb to put sth on, you **help** sb **on with** sth ◦ *Let me help you on with your coat, Mrs Stokes.*
– to take all the clothes off sb: **strip** sb ◦ *They were stripped and searched.*

■ fastening clothes

– to fasten a piece of clothing: **do*** sth **up, fasten** sth; *opposite*: **undo*** sth ◦ *Do your coat up.* ◦ *Are the buttons at the back all fastened?* ◦ *Your shirt is undone.*
– (used about a piece of clothing) to be fastened: **do* up** ◦ *This skirt does up at the side.*
– (used about a piece of clothing) to become unfastened: **come* undone**

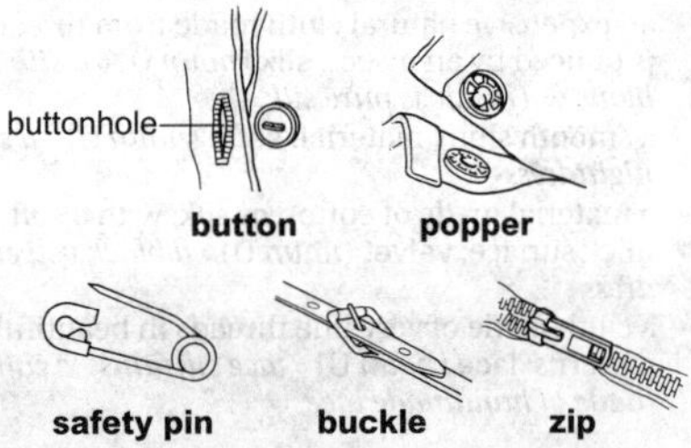

– to fasten sth with buttons: **button** sth (**up**); *opposite*: **unbutton** sth ◦ *You've buttoned your shirt up wrong.*
– to fasten sth with a zip: **zip** sth **up**; *opposite*: **unzip** sth ◦ *The zip's gone on my jeans, and I can't zip them up any more.*
– a nylon material used as a fastener, made of two strips which stick together: **velcro** (*noun* U)
– a pair of linked buttons, often gold, that are used to fasten the cuffs of a shirt: **cuff links** ◦ *a pair of cuff links*

■ not putting your clothes on properly

back to front / the wrong way round **inside out**

– if you put sth on wrong so that the front is at the back, it is **back to front, the wrong way round** ◦ *I think you've got that jumper on back to front.*
– if you put sth on wrong so that the inside is outside, it is **inside out** ◦ *Your T-shirt looks a bit funny – is it inside out?*
– if you put on two socks/shoes/gloves from two different pairs, you are wearing **odd** socks/shoes/gloves ◦ *Did you get dressed in the dark? You've got odd socks on.*

2 kinds of clothes

▷ clothes used in sport and swimming ⇨ SPORT, SWIM
▷ baby clothes ⇨ BABY

■ shirts and jumpers
- a piece of clothing, worn especially by men, that covers the arms and upper part of the body and usually has buttons down the front: **shirt** ○ *a silk/cotton shirt* ○ *a football shirt* ○ *a long-sleeved/short-sleeved shirt*
- a piece of clothing like a shirt, that women wear: **blouse**
- an informal shirt without collar or buttons, with short sleeves, made of soft cotton: **T-shirt**

- a warm piece of clothing, often made of wool, which you put over your head: **sweater**, **pull-over**, (*BrE*) **jumper**; if it has buttons down the front it is a **cardigan**
- a sweater with a round neck which comes up to your chin: **polo-neck** (*AmE* **turtleneck**) sweater
- a sweater with a neckline which goes down to a point, under your chin: **V-neck pullover**
- any piece of clothing that you wear on the top part of your body: **top** ○ *I'm looking for a top to go with this skirt.*
- a top made of thick cotton with long sleeves, which you sometimes wear for sport: **sweat-shirt**

■ jackets and trousers
- a short coat, with sleeves, that has buttons down the front: **jacket** ○ *the jacket of my grey suit* ○ *Even on hot days we had to wear our jackets in the office.*
- a jacket with two rows of buttons: **double-breasted** jacket; a jacket with one row of buttons: **single-breasted** jacket
- a short jacket with no sleeves, a V-neck, and buttons down the front: **waistcoat** (*AmE* **vest**)
- a piece of clothing that covers both legs, from waist to ankles: **trousers** (*AmE* **pants**) (*noun plural*)
- a jacket and trousers, or a jacket and skirt, made of the same material, usually rather formal: **suit**
- a set of clothes (top and trousers) made of thick cotton, which you wear for sport: **tracksuit**

▷ more on coats, jackets and trousers ⇨ **COAT, TROUSERS**

■ dresses and skirts
- a piece of clothing worn by girls or women, which covers the body from the waist down to the knees or below: **skirt** ○ *a pleated skirt* ○ *Skirts are shorter this year.*
- a skirt made of pleated wool, worn by men in Scotland: **kilt**
- a piece of clothing worn by a girl or a woman, that covers the body from the shoulders to the knees or below: **dress** ○ *a wedding dress*

■ formal clothes
- elegant clothes for formal dinners, etc: **evening dress** (*noun* U)
- a black or white jacket that men wear on formal occasions: **dinner jacket** (*AmE* **tuxedo**), (*informal*) **DJ**

■ other things that you wear or carry
- a thin piece of cloth or leather which you wear round your waist: **belt** ○ *The skirt looks good with a very wide belt.*
- a piece of clothing that covers your hand: **glove** ○ *a pair of gloves* ○ *leather gloves*
- a piece of clothing that you wear on your head: **hat**

▷ more on hats and other coverings for the head ⇨ **HAT, HEAD**

- an object which you carry to keep you dry when it is raining: **umbrella**
- glasses which you wear to protect your eyes from the sun: **sunglasses** (*noun plural*)
- a small bag in which a woman carries money, keys, etc: **handbag** (*AmE* **purse**)
- rings, necklaces, etc made of precious materials which you wear for decoration: **jewellery** (*AmE* **jewelry**) (*noun* U)

▷ more on glasses, bags and jewellery ⇨ **GLASSES, BAG, JEWELLERY**

■ shoes and socks
- a covering for your foot, usually made of leather or plastic: **shoe**
- a piece of clothing that you wear inside your shoes: **sock** ○ *a pair of cotton socks*

▷ more on shoes ⇨ **SHOE**

■ underwear
- the clothes that you wear next to your skin under other clothes: **underwear** (*noun* U), **underclothes** (*noun plural*) ○ *You'll need warm underwear if you go to Moscow in February.*
- a piece of underwear that you wear on the top part of your body: **vest** (*AmE* **undershirt**)

clothes *contd.*

- a small piece of underwear that you wear on the lower part of your body: **underpants** (*noun plural*), (*BrE*) **pants** (*noun plural*), **briefs** (*noun plural*) ◦ *a pair of underpants*
- pants for women are also called **knickers** (*noun plural*), (*informal*) **panties** (*noun plural*) ◦ *Are these your knickers?*
- loose pants for men: **boxer shorts** (*noun plural*)

- a piece of underwear that women wear to support the breasts: **bra**
- a piece of clothing with no sleeves that women wear under a dress or a skirt: **slip**, **petticoat**

- a thin nylon covering for a woman's legs and feet, that reaches to her waist: **tights** (*AmE* **pantyhose**) (*noun plural*) ◦ *Do you sell black tights?* ◦ *three pairs of tights*
- one of a pair of thin pieces of clothing that fit tightly over a woman's legs and feet: **stocking** ◦ *a pair of silk stockings*
- a short piece of elastic used to hold up a stocking by its top: **suspender** (*usually plural*)
- a hole in a pair of tights or stockings, which runs up the leg: **ladder** ◦ *You've got a ladder in the back of your tights.*

■ nightclothes

- a soft loose shirt and trousers which men and women wear for sleeping: **pyjamas** (*AmE* **pajamas**) (*noun plural*); the top part of pyjamas: **pyjama top**; the bottom part: **pyjama trousers/bottoms** ◦ *a pair of pyjamas* ◦ *He's wearing green pyjama trousers and a red pyjama top from a different pair.*
- a loose dress which women wear for sleeping: **nightdress**, (*informal*) **nightie**
- a piece of clothing like a loose coat which you wear indoors, after a bath or over nightclothes: **dressing gown**, **bathrobe** (*AmE* **robe**)
- a light soft shoe that is worn in the house, especially at bedtime: **slipper** ◦ *a pair of slippers*

■ clothes for work

- the clothes which some children wear at school, or which some people wear at work: **uniform** (*noun* C/U) ◦ *Our school uniform was all navy, with a blue and gold tie.* ◦ *a soldier in uniform*
- ordinary clothes worn by police officers instead of uniforms: **plain clothes** ◦ *Detectives in plain clothes mixed with the crowd.* ◦ *a plain-clothes policewoman*

- any clothes which you wear to protect yourself while you are working: **protective clothing** (*noun* U) ◦ *Everyone must wear protective clothing when we go down into the mine.*
- a piece of clothing which you wear in front of your normal clothes to keep them clean when you are doing housework or dirty work: **apron**
- a piece of clothing like a coat that you wear to protect your other clothes: **overall**
- a piece of clothing which goes over all your other clothes to keep them clean when you are working: **overalls** (*noun plural*)

3 parts of clothes

- the part which goes round your neck: **neck** ◦ *The neck of this jumper is too tight.*
- the part which fits round the neck of a shirt, coat, dress, etc and is usually made of double cloth: **collar** ◦ *a shirt/coat/jacket collar* ◦ *a stiff/soft collar*
- the part of a piece of clothing which goes round your middle is generally called the **waist**
- a small place inside your clothes that you can put things in: **pocket** ◦ *Don't walk with your hands in your pockets.* ◦ *It's in my trouser pocket/the pocket of my trousers.*

- a part of a piece of clothing which covers your arm: **sleeve**, **arm**; a piece of clothing without sleeves is **sleeveless** ◦ *I can't get my arm into the sleeve of the coat.*
- a double piece of cloth on the end of a sleeve: **cuff** ◦ *The sleeves are a bit long – you'll have to turn the cuffs back.*
- the part of a pair of trousers, etc that covers your leg: **leg** ◦ *The legs of these trousers are too wide.*
- the part of a trouser leg that covers the middle part of your leg: **knee** ◦ *My jeans have gone at the knees and there are two great holes in them.*

- the bottom edge of a skirt, dress or trousers, where the material is folded under and sewn: **hem** ◦ *There's a deep hem, so you can let it down and make the skirt longer if you want.*
- the smooth cloth sewn inside a coat, jacket, etc: **lining** ◦ *a silk lining*
- a fold in a piece of clothing, which is sewn down to make it permanent: **pleat**; a piece of clothing which has pleats is **pleated** ◦ *a pleated skirt*

4 the size of clothes

- if a piece of clothing is not too big for you and not too small, it is the **right size**, it **fits** you, it is a **good fit**; if it is too big or too small, it is the **wrong size**, it **doesn't fit** ◦ *The jacket is a really good fit – you ought to buy it.* ◦ *They're nice shoes, but they're the wrong size for me.* ◦ *Those jeans don't fit me any more.*
- one of a set of fixed measurements of clothes or shoes: **size** ◦ *Do you have the same skirt in a size twelve?* ◦ *I think you should try a larger size.*

- clothes which fit closely to your body are **tight**, **close-fitting**; if they fit very closely, they are **skintight** ◦ *tight jeans*
- clothes which don't fit closely are **loose**; if they fit very loosely on your body, they are **baggy** ◦ *a big loose coat* ◦ *a baggy jumper*

- (used about children) to become too big for your clothes: **grow* out of** sth, **outgrow*** sth; *opposite*: **grow* into** sth ◦ *When we grew out of our clothes, they were passed on to our younger brothers and sisters.* ◦ *The jumper's too big for the baby now, but he'll grow into it.*

- if a piece of clothing gets smaller, for example when you wash it in very hot water, it **shrinks*** ◦ *I put this jumper in the wash and it's shrunk almost to nothing.*

5 buying clothes

- a shop where you buy clothes: **clothes shop** (*AmE* **clothing store**)
- a shop where you buy shoes: **shoe shop** (*AmE* **shoe store**)
- if you have your clothes made specially for you, you go to a **tailor** or (for women's clothes) a **dressmaker** ◦ *'Where are you getting your wedding dress from?' 'I'm having it made. My mother knows a good dressmaker who can do it.'*
- clothes which are made specially for you are **made to measure**; clothes which you buy from a shop are **ready-made, off the peg**

- to put on a piece of clothing in a shop to see if it is the right size: **try** sth **on**
- the room where you try clothes on: **fitting room, changing room** ◦ *'Could I try these on, please?' 'Certainly. The fitting room is over there.'*

- to provide clothes for sb, especially children: **clothe** sb ◦ *I have to feed and clothe five children on my small salary.*

6 how you look in clothes

- the way you look in your clothes, etc is your **appearance** ◦ *Glasses really change your appearance – suddenly you look terribly serious.*
- if a piece of clothing looks good on you, it **suits** you ◦ *Red suits you – you look marvellous!* ◦ *It's a nice coat, but it doesn't really suit you.*

- if you dress in a careful, clean way, you look **tidy, neat**; *opposite*: **untidy** ◦ *a tidy appearance* ◦ *You need to look neat for work.*
- untidy and dirty: **scruffy** ◦ *to look scruffy*

▷ more on being tidy ⇨ TIDY

- if you usually wear clothes which make you look good/bad, you **dress well/badly**; *adjectives*: **well dressed/badly dressed**
- if the clothes you are wearing are suitable for a formal occasion, you are dressed **formally**; *opposite*: **casually**

- if you are clean, tidy and rather formally dressed, you, or your clothes, are **smart** (*adverb* **smartly**) ◦ *That's a very smart suit – are you going to a wedding?* ◦ *to look smart* ◦ *to dress smartly*
- everyday clothes (not particularly smart) are **casual** clothes
- to dress yourself more tidily: **smarten** yourself **up** ◦ *You'll have to smarten yourself up if you want to impress them at the interview.*

- someone who always dresses in very smart clothes and looks good in them is **elegant**; clothes which are very smart are **elegant** ◦ *Everyone in the wedding photos looks terribly elegant.*
- the way of dressing, etc that is most popular at any time: **fashion** (*noun* C/U); clothes which are popular in this way are **fashionable, in fashion**

▷ fashion ⇨ FASHION

■ clothes which are not in good condition

- (used about a piece of clothing) thin because you have had it for a long time: **worn** ◦ *The jacket is very worn, especially at the elbows.*
- old, worn and untidy: **shabby** ◦ *a shabby suit*

- to pull cloth, etc so that it comes apart or gets holes in it: **tear*** sth; a hole caused by tearing sth: **tear** ◦ *This is all torn – do you think it can be mended?* ◦ *Have you noticed there's a tear in your blouse?*
- to become torn: **tear*, get* torn** ◦ *How did your shorts get torn?*
- to make a long tear: **rip** sth; *noun*: **rip** ◦ *My jeans are ripped at the knee.* ◦ *a long rip in the material*

7 taking care of your clothes

▷ washing and ironing clothes ⇨ WASH, IRONING

- a soft brush that you use to clean dust or hairs off your clothes: **clothes brush**
- a metal, plastic or wooden object with a hook, which you use for hanging clothes in a wardrobe: **hanger, coat-hanger** ◦ *Keep the dress on a hanger.*
- to lay part of sth on top of the rest to make it smaller: **fold** sth (**up**) ◦ *When you finish ironing, fold all the clothes up and put them in your chest of drawers.*

- a cupboard for keeping clothes in: **wardrobe**
- a piece of furniture with drawers in, used for storing clothes, etc: **chest of drawers**

▷ pictures at BED

■ **MORE ...**

- if you disapprove of sb who is not wearing enough clothes, you say they are not **decent** ◦ *You can't wear that see-through blouse – it's not decent.*

- a person who takes his/her clothes off for money: **stripper**; the show he/she is in: **striptease (show), strip show**
- a woman with her breasts not covered is **topless** ◦ *a topless waitress* ◦ *She was sunbathing topless.*
- a person who likes to wear the clothes of sb of the opposite sex: **transvestite**
- a person who likes to be naked, often in groups with other people: **nudist, naturist** ◦ *a nudist beach*

- a statue or a painting of someone with no clothes on: **nude** ◦ *a seated female nude*

cloud ⇨ SKY

club

see also SPORT

- a group of people who meet to share an interest: **club, society**; the place where a club meets is also called a **club** ◦ *a rowing club* ◦ *a chess club* ◦ *a debating society*
- a club for young people, often run by a church or a local authority: **youth club**

club *contd.*

– a person who belongs to a club: **member**; a person who does not belong to the club: **non-member**
– all the members together are the **membership** (*noun* U) ○ *Club membership has been increasing this year.*
– to become a member of a club, etc: **join** sth ○ *I've decided to join the tennis club.*
– being a member of a club: **membership** (*noun* U) ○ *Annual membership costs £250.*
– to stop being a member of a club: **leave*** (sth), **resign** (**from** sth)
– a person that sb invites to their club: **guest**

– the most senior person who manages a club: **president**, **chairman**
– a person who types letters, answers phone calls, organizes meetings, etc in a club: **secretary** ○ *the secretary of the golf club*
– a person who looks after the money that belongs to a club: **treasurer**
– the group of people who have been chosen to manage a club: **committee**

coal

other fuels ⇨ FUEL, ELECTRICITY, GAS, OIL

– a hard, black substance, usually dug from under the ground, which is used as a fuel: **coal** (*noun* U) ○ *a bag of coal* ○ *a lump of coal* (= one piece of coal) ○ *a coal fire*
– a place where coal is dug from the ground: **mine**, **coal mine**
– a large area which has a lot of coal under the ground: **coalfield**
– a man who works in a mine: **miner**
– to use coal in a fire: **burn** sth ○ *Does your boiler burn oil or coal?*

coast ⇨ SEA

coat

other clothes ⇨ CLOTHES

– a piece of clothing that you wear outside, on top of your other clothes, to keep warm: **coat** ○ *Come in and take your coat off.* ○ *a fur coat*

▷ picture at CLOTHES

– a long thick coat, usually made of wool, that you wear in winter: **overcoat**
– a coat that you wear when it is raining: **raincoat**, (*informal*) **mac** ○ *Put your raincoat on – I'm sure it's going to rain.*
– a wool coat with a hood and special buttons (**toggles**): **duffel coat**
– a short warm coat with a fur-lined hood: **parka**
– a long loose flowing coat without sleeves or armholes: **cloak**

– able to keep out the rain: **waterproof**; able to keep out the wind: **windproof** ○ *a waterproof jacket*
– a short waterproof coat, usually with a hood: **anorak**
– a thin nylon waterproof coat for outdoor activities: **cagoule**

– a short coat, not always for wearing outside: **jacket** ○ *You'll need to wear a jacket and tie for the interview.* ○ *a leather jacket*

■ parts of a coat

– the part of a coat which fits around your neck: **collar** ○ *People were turning up the collars of their coats against the wind.*
– a long thin piece of cloth that goes around the waist of a coat: **belt** ○ *to fasten a belt* ○ *Why don't you do up your belt?*
– a small place in a coat or jacket for keeping things in: **pocket** ○ *He walks about with his hands in his pockets.*
– the part of a coat that you wear over your head in bad weather: **hood** ○ *Put your hood up, it's starting to snow.*

coffee/tea

1 coffee
2 tea
3 drinking coffee or tea
see also DRINK, CUP/GLASS

1 coffee

– the seeds of a tropical plant which are used for making coffee: **coffee** (*noun* U), **coffee beans** (*noun plural*) ○ *Coffee is one of Brazil's main exports.* ○ *roasted coffee beans* (= beans which have been cooked until they are brown)
– the drink that is made from coffee: **coffee** (*noun* U/C) ○ *Who'd like some coffee?* ○ *Anyone want a coffee* (= a cup of coffee)*?*

– strong coffee without milk, served in a small quantity: **espresso** (*plural* **espressos**)
– espresso coffee with hot milk added: **cappuccino** (*plural* **cappuccinos**)

■ making coffee

– fresh coffee that has been made into a powder: **ground coffee** (*noun* U)
– coffee which can be made quickly just by adding hot water: **instant** (**coffee**) ○ *I'm afraid we've only got instant.*

– to make coffee, you put some ground coffee in a **(coffee) pot** or some instant coffee in a **coffee cup** or **mug**
– you then **pour** hot water over the coffee
– (used with ground coffee) to separate the liquid from the solid you use a (**coffee**) **filter**
– special pots for making and serving coffee: **percolator**, **cafeti re**
– an electric machine which makes coffee for you: **coffee machine**

– a pot (usually electric) that is used for making water hot: **kettle** ○ *Have you put the kettle on?* ○ *Hasn't the kettle boiled yet?*

- to make coffee from beans, you must first **grind*** the beans into powder; to do this you use a **coffee grinder**

2 tea

- the dried leaves of a tropical plant which are used for making tea: **tea** (*noun* U) ◦ *Most tea is grown in India and China.* ◦ *a packet of tea*
- the drink that is made from tea: **tea** (*noun* U/C) ◦ *Would you like a cup of tea?* ◦ *'Tea or coffee?' 'I'll have tea, please.'* ◦ *A ham sandwich and a tea* (= a cup of tea), *please.* ◦ *Our supermarket sells lots of different teas* (= different kinds of tea).

■ making tea

- to make tea you need **tea leaves** (*noun plural*)
- a small paper bag with tea leaves in it: **tea bag**

- you put some tea leaves in a **teapot**, or you put a tea bag in a **teacup** or **mug**
- you then **pour** hot water over the tea

3 drinking coffee or tea

- coffee or tea without milk is **black**; coffee with milk is **white** ◦ *Two black coffees and one white, please.* ◦ *I'll have mine black.* ◦ *'How do you take your coffee?' 'Black with one sugar, please'* (= with one spoon of sugar).
- a small amount of sth, for example milk in coffee or tea: **a drop** (**of** sth) ◦ *'Do you want milk?' 'Just a drop, please.'*
- coffee or tea that is made with a lot of water is **weak**; *opposite*: **strong** ◦ *'How do you like your coffee?' 'Not too strong, please.'*
- if you normally have sugar in your coffee or tea, you **take*** sugar ◦ *Do you take sugar?*

- to put liquid into a cup, glass, etc from a jug, bottle, etc, to serve sb: **pour** sth (**for** sb), **pour** sb sth ◦ *He poured her a large mug of coffee.*
- to pour sth out of a container by accident: **spill** sth ◦ *Careful – you might spill it.*
- to move the coffee or tea round and round with a spoon: **stir** sth ◦ *She sat quietly, stirring her tea.*
- the small spoon that you use for adding sugar and stirring the tea or coffee: **teaspoon**, **coffee spoon**

- the time when people stop work for tea or coffee: **tea break**, **coffee break** ◦ *We have a tea break every two hours.*

■ MORE ...

- the substance in coffee which makes you stay awake: **caffeine** (*noun* U)
- with the caffeine taken out: **decaffeinated**; coffee with the caffeine taken out: **decaffeinated** (**coffee**) (*noun* U), (*informal*) **decaff** (*noun* U) ◦ *Do you have decaffeinated?*
- any drug which makes you feel awake, like coffee: **stimulant**

- tea that is made from special herbs or fruit: **herbal tea** (*noun* U)

coin ⇨ MONEY

cold

> **1** saying how cold sth is
> **2** when your body is cold
> **3** keeping cool when the weather is hot
> keeping food cold ⇨ FOOD
> **see also** HOT, WEATHER

1 saying how cold sth is

- not hot, having a low temperature: **cold**; *noun* (U): **cold** ◦ *Turn the heating up – I'm cold.* ◦ *a cold winter* ◦ *The water was extremely cold.* ◦ *Come inside – you shouldn't stay out in the cold so long.*
- a little cold: **cool**; *noun* (U): **cool** ◦ *a cool drink* ◦ *the cool of the evening*
- if sth is completely cold, it is **stone-cold** ◦ *I can't eat this soup – it's stone-cold!*
- to get colder: **cool down/off**; to make sb/sth get colder: **cool** sb/sth **down/off** ◦ *I'll eat it when it's cooled down a bit.*

- to become hard because of extreme cold: **freeze*** ◦ *The ground had frozen hard.*
- very cold: (*informal*) **freezing**, (*informal*) **freezing cold** ◦ *You've got no coat on – you must be freezing!* ◦ *I'd stay in today if I were you – it's freezing cold out there.*

▷ cold liquids ⇨ LIQUID, WATER, ICE

▷ measuring temperature ⇨ HOT

2 when your body is cold

- when your body shakes because of the cold, you **shiver**
- when your teeth knock together because you are shivering, they **chatter**
- the small points which appear on your skin when you are cold: **goose-flesh** (*noun* U), **goose pimples** (*AmE* **goose bumps**) (*noun plural*)
- a serious injury to the fingers, toes, etc caused by extreme cold: **frostbite** (*noun* U); *adjective*: **frostbitten**
- to die because of staying in extreme cold: **freeze* to death**, **die of cold**
- if you often feel cold (more than most people), you **feel* the cold** ◦ *Old people tend to feel the cold more than the young.*

3 keeping cool when the weather is hot

- a system for keeping buildings cool when the weather is hot: **air-conditioning** (*noun* U)
- a machine for air-conditioning: **air-conditioner**
- cooled by air-conditioning: **air-conditioned** ◦ *an air-conditioned office*
- an electrical machine with blades which turn around and keep the air moving in a room: **fan**
- to cool sb/sth by waving sth in the air: **fan** sb/sth/yourself ◦ *It was hot in the theatre and some of the audience started fanning themselves with their programmes.*

collect ⇨ GET/OBTAIN

college ⇨ UNIVERSITY

colour

1 colour
2 the different colours
3 making sth coloured
4 losing colour
5 different colours together

1 colour

- the quality that makes sth red, yellow, green, etc: **colour** (*noun* U) ∘ *Her paintings are wonderful – full of light and colour.*
- a particular colour: **colour** ∘ *What's your favourite colour?*
- having many colours: **colourful** ∘ *a colourful dress* ∘ *The garden is really colourful at this time of year.*
- having a particular colour: **coloured** ∘ *a pinkish-coloured flower* ∘ *coloured paper* ∘ *the parts of the map that are coloured green*

Note: the *AmE* spelling of **colour**, **coloured**, **colourful**, etc is **color**, **colored**, **colorful**, etc.

- photographs, television, etc can either be (**in**) **colour** or (**in**) **black and white** ∘ *a colour printer* ∘ *Are the photos in colour or black and white?* ∘ *a black and white TV*
- having no colour: **colourless** ∘ *Water is a colourless liquid.* ∘ *a colourless gas*
- not having much colour and therefore not attractive: **dull** ∘ *It's a nice dress but it's a very dull colour.* ∘ *a dull sky*
- a colour which is nearer to black than to white is **dark** ∘ *dark red curtains*
- a colour which is nearer to white than to black is **light**, **pale** ∘ *light brown* ∘ *a pale pink colour*
- a strong, easily noticeable colour is **bright** (*adverb* **brightly**), **strong** ∘ *bright red* ∘ *a brightly coloured shirt* ∘ *I like to wear strong colours like bright yellow and navy blue.*
- a colour which is dark and strong is **deep** ∘ *deep blue*
- very pale or light colours are called **pastel** colours ∘ *pastel blue/pink/green* ∘ *pastel shades*
- colours like reds, oranges and browns are **warm** colours ∘ *the warm colours of autumn*
- a type of a particular colour (lighter, darker, brighter, deeper, etc): **shade** ∘ *They had paint in lots of different shades of red.* ∘ *a lighter shade of green*
- a small amount of colour: **tint** ∘ *green, with a blue tint in it*
- the colour of a person's hair, skin, eyes: **colouring**

▷ the colour of people's skin ⇨ SKIN, FACE

2 the different colours

Note: to describe the shade that a colour is, you can use **dark**, **light**, **pale** or **bright** before the colour: ∘ *bright blue* ∘ *pale yellow* ∘ *dark brown*.
You can use a suitable noun before the colour to show what shade it is: ∘ *lemon yellow* ∘ *leaf green* ∘ *blood red*.
To say that a colour is quite similar to the colour that you are thinking of, you can use **-ish** with a colour: ∘ *a yellowish flower* ∘ *darkish brown hair*, or you can use **-y** at the end of a colour + **colour**: ∘ *a browny colour*.
You can use two colours together to describe colours which seem to be a mixture of two different colours: ∘ *brown-black* ∘ *browny-black* ∘ *bluish-green* ∘ *reddish-purple*.
To talk about a colour in general, use the noun without **a** or **the**: ∘ *I like bright red.* ∘ *My favourite colour is blue.* To talk about a particular colour or shade, use **a** with the noun for the **colour**: ∘ *It's a beautiful deep red.* ∘ *I've seen a shirt in a nice blue colour*. To talk about a particular colour that you can see, use **the**: ∘ *You should wear the pink with the blue*.

■ black & white

- the darkest colour possible: **black**
- very black: **jet black**, **pitch black** ∘ *jet black hair* ∘ *a pitch black night*

- the colour of snow or milk: **white** ∘ *as white as snow* ∘ *bright white*
- a slightly yellowy white; the colour of cream: **cream** ∘ *She wore a beautiful cream-coloured wedding dress.*
- almost white: **off-white**

- a colour which is black mixed with white: **grey** (*AmE* **gray**) ∘ *dark grey* ∘ *He's got grey hair.*
- a very dark grey: **charcoal** (**grey**)
- the colour of silver: **silver** ∘ *silver paint*

■ red & pink

- the colour of blood: **red** ∘ *dark/deep red* ∘ *rose red* ∘ *blood red*
- very dark red: **crimson**
- bright red: **scarlet**
- dark red-brown: **maroon**
- to become red: **redden** ∘ *His face reddened with anger.*
- a dark colour which is a mixture of red and blue: **purple**, **violet**

- a light red colour: **pink** ∘ *a pale pink rose*
- the pink colour of roses: **rose** (**pink**)

■ yellow & orange

- the colour of lemons or butter: **yellow** ∘ *light/pale yellow* ∘ *a bright yellow flower*
- the colour of gold: **gold**, **golden** ∘ *They had painted the roof gold.* ∘ *golden brown*
- the colour of oranges: **orange** ∘ *a bright orange scarf*

■ green

- the colour of grass: **green** ∘ *pale green eyes*
- a dark green-yellow colour: **olive green** ∘ *an olive green uniform*
- a green-brown colour which is used in the army: **khaki**
- a very bright green colour: **emerald** (**green**) ∘ *an emerald silk shirt*
- a bright yellow-green colour: **lime green**

■ blue
- the colour of the sky on a sunny day: **blue** ◦ *a light blue jumper* ◦ *a deep blue sky*
- the bright blue colour of the sky on a sunny day: **sky blue**
- a blue-green colour: **turquoise** (**blue**)
- bright, deep blue: **royal blue**
- dark blue: **navy** (**blue**)

■ brown
- having the colour of soil or wood: **brown**
- light brown: **beige, fawn**

3 making sth coloured
- to put colour on sth (by using paint, coloured pencils, etc): **colour** sth ◦ *to colour a picture* ◦ *to colour your hair* ◦ *Someone had coloured the ceiling black.*
- to put coloured paint on sth: **paint** sth ◦ *to paint a picture* ◦ *to paint a wall*
- to fill a shape, a picture, etc with colour using pencils, pens, etc: **colour** sth **in** ◦ *The little girl drew a picture and coloured it in.* ◦ *Draw lots of circles and then colour them in.*

▷ drawing and painting ⇨ DRAW, PAINT[1]

- a substance that you use to make clothes or hair a different colour: **dye** (*noun* C/U); *verb*: **dye** sth ◦ *blue dye* ◦ *hair dye* ◦ *You've dyed your jeans.* ◦ *You've had your hair dyed.*
- the dye which is already in the clothes when you buy them is usually called the **colour** ◦ *Don't wash it in very hot water – all the colour will come out.*
- a clear liquid chemical that you can use to make clothes white or lighter in colour: **bleach** (*noun* U); *verb*: **bleach** sth ◦ *bleached jeans*
- a special substance you use to make sth coloured (especially food): (**food**) **colouring** (*noun* C/U)

4 losing colour
- when the dye comes out of clothes in water, the colour **runs*** ◦ *Can I put this red shirt in with a white wash, or will it run?*
- colours that are not likely to come out of the clothes when you wash them are **fast** ◦ *fast colours* ◦ *Are your jeans colour fast?*
- if sth changes colour because of heat or sun, it **loses*** (**its**) **colour**, **discolours**; *adjective*: **discoloured** ◦ *When paper gets old it loses its colour.* ◦ *discoloured paper*
- to lose colour because of heat, sun or a lot of washing: **fade**; *adjective*: **faded** ◦ *If you leave them in the sun, they'll fade.* ◦ *faded jeans*

5 different colours together
- if two colours look nice together, they **go* together**, one of the colours **goes* with** the other ◦ *I think navy blue and red go well together.* ◦ *That blue doesn't really go with the orange.*
- if two bright colours look bad together, they **clash** ◦ *The bright purple and the orange clash a bit.*
- when a colour looks nice on you, it **suits** you ◦ *I'd prefer to wear blue – red doesn't really suit me.*
- the way in which colours are arranged, especially in a room: **colour scheme** ◦ *I thought the house was nice but I didn't like the colour scheme in the living room.*

■ MORE ...
- unable to see the difference between different colours: **colour-blind**
- the set of seven colours into which white light can be separated: **spectrum**
- the three colours (red, yellow and blue) which you can use to make any other colour: **primary colours**

comb ⇨ HAIR

come / go

1 coming and going
2 going to a place with or after sb/sth
3 going back to a place
see also TRAVEL

1 coming and going
- to move to or towards the person who is speaking or the place that sb is talking about: **come*** ◦ *Could you come here a minute, please?* ◦ *She asked me to come at once.*
- to move or travel from one place to another: **go*** ◦ *to go to the cinema/shops/bank* ◦ *to go somewhere by bus/train/boat/plane* ◦ *He's going abroad* (= to another country).

Note: if sb has gone to a place and has not yet returned, you say that they have **gone**. If sb has gone to a place and has returned, you say that they have **been**. ◦ *John has gone to London. He's expected back tomorrow.* ◦ *'Where have you been?' 'I've been to Paris. I got back this morning.'*

- to move near or nearer to sb/sth: **come*/go* up to** sb/sth, **approach** (sb/sth) ◦ *I went up to the policeman and asked him the way.* ◦ *The car was approaching us very fast.*
- not go near sb/sth: **stay away from** sb/sth ◦ *I suggest you stay away from that place – I don't like the look of the people who go in there.*
- (used about a person or thing that is travelling to a place) to come to a particular place: **arrive** (**at/in** a place), **reach** a place, **get*** to a place ◦ *What time are they expected to arrive?* ◦ *We should get there by midnight.*

▷ more on arriving at a place ⇨ ARRIVE

- to go from a place: **leave*** (a place), **go*** ◦ *We left the party early.* ◦ *I can't see Sarah anywhere. Did you see her go?*
- to go from a place: **go* away** (**from** a place), **leave*** (a place) ◦ *Kate has gone away for the weekend.* ◦ *I've been offered a job in Manchester but I don't want to leave London.*

come/go *contd.*

- to go away from your house, office, etc for a short time: **go* out** ◦ *I'm just going out to get some sandwiches.*
- to come or go somewhere quickly or briefly: (*informal*) **pop/nip across**, **out**, etc ◦ *I'm just nipping out for a few minutes.* ◦ *She said she'd pop over for a chat this evening.*

- to allow sb/sth to go away from a place: **let*** sb/sth **go**, **let*** sb/sth **out**, (*formal*) **release** sb/sth ◦ *Our teacher let us out early.*

▷ more on leaving a place ⇨ **LEAVE**

■ going or coming in a particular direction

- to go past sb/sth: **pass** (sb/sth), **go* by** (sb/sth) ◦ *You'll pass a bank and a post office and then you'll see the church on your right.* ◦ *I passed within a few feet of her but she didn't even notice me.* ◦ *The old man sat outside a cafe watching all the people go by.*
- to go in the direction mentioned: **pass over**, **by**, etc (sth) ◦ *The road then passes over the river Tweed.* ◦ *On your way to the cathedral you'll pass by the castle.*
- to go from one side of sth to the other side: **cross** (**over**) sth, **go*/come* across** (sth) ◦ *to cross the road* ◦ *to go across the border*

- to go in the direction of sb/sth: **move**, **come***, **go***, etc **towards** sb/sth; *opposite*: **move**, **come***, **go***, etc **away** (**from** sb/sth) ◦ *I managed to move towards the front of the crowd.* ◦ *Go away! I'm busy.*
- to change direction when you are moving: **turn** ◦ *Turn left after the shop.*

▷ more on the direction or way in which sb/sth is moving ⇨ **MOVE, TURN**

2 going to a place with or after sb/sth

- to come to a place carrying sth or together with sb/sth: **bring*** sb/sth ◦ *Can I bring a friend to the party?*
- to go to a place carrying sth or together with sb/sth: **take*** sb/sth ◦ *Please take me home.* ◦ *My dad's taking me to see the Liverpool-Chelsea match on Saturday.* ◦ *She takes her dog wherever she goes.*
- to go with sb to a place: (*formal*) **accompany** sb ◦ *The policeman asked the man to accompany him to the police station.*
- to help sb by going with them until they reach a particular place: **see*** sb to a place ◦ *Would you like me to see you home?*

▷ more on bringing and taking ⇨ **BRING/TAKE/CARRY**

- to come or go after sb/sth: **follow** (sb/sth) ◦ *You go now and I'll follow a bit later.* ◦ *I followed him into the supermarket.*

- to go in front of sb/sth to show them/it the way: **lead*** sb/sth ◦ *The guide led the tourists to their hotel rooms.* ◦ *Sarah led the horse into the stable.*
- to use your hand or finger to show sb that you want them to follow you or come closer to you: **beckon** (**to** sb), **beckon** sb (**to** do sth) ◦ *She beckoned me to follow her into the kitchen.*

3 going back to a place

- to move back to or from a place: **go* back** (**to** a place), **return** (**to/from** a place), **come***, **walk**, **run***, etc **back** (**to/from** a place) ◦ *We're going back to Milan tomorrow.* ◦ *When are you planning to return to Paris?* ◦ *She returned from her holiday full of energy to begin work again.* ◦ *Anna ran back to get her school bag.* ◦ *They flew back from Canada last week.*
- to return to your home or to your own country: **go*/come* home**
- to return to your house: **get* home**, **get* in** ◦ *What time did you get in last night?*
- an act of returning: **return** ◦ *On his return from New York, the Prime Minister went straight to the House of Commons.* ◦ *a return journey*

- to begin a journey back to a place: **start back** ◦ *We started back home at six o'clock.*
- to go back in the direction you came from, before you have reached the place that you were going to: **turn back** ◦ *The snow got so bad that we decided to turn back.*
- to arrive back at a place: **get* back**, **be back** ◦ *I'll see you when I get back from Italy.* ◦ *I'll be back tomorrow.*

comfortable

not worried or embarrassed ⇨ **WORRY**
the way you live ⇨ **LIVE[2]**, **RICH**, **POOR**

- when sth allows you to feel physically relaxed, it is **comfortable** (*adverb* **comfortably**), (*informal*) **comfy**; when you feel physically relaxed, you are **comfortable**; *noun* (U): **comfort** ◦ *a comfortable bed* ◦ *a pair of nice comfy sandals* ◦ *My grandmother likes to travel in comfort.*
- a thing that makes you feel comfortable: **comfort** ◦ *a hotel with all modern comforts*
- if sth is warm and comfortable it is **cosy** (*AmE* **cozy**) ◦ *The living room looked really cosy in the firelight.*
- great comfort and pleasure, often including the use of expensive and beautiful things: **luxury** (*noun* U); *adjective*: **luxurious** (*adverb* **luxuriously**) ◦ *a luxury hotel* ◦ *They are living in luxury in Hawaii.* ◦ *Their house is certainly not luxurious but it is comfortable.*

- to get into a comfortable position (sitting or lying): **make*** yourself **comfortable**, **settle down** ◦ *Sit down and make yourself comfortable.* ◦ *After dinner, my father settled down with the newspaper.*
- to get into a position that makes you feel safe, warm and comfortable: **snuggle up** (**to** sb), **snuggle down** ◦ *Diane snuggled up to her mother.* ◦ *We snuggled down in our sleeping bags to keep warm.*

■ not comfortable

- not comfortable: **uncomfortable** (*adverb* **uncomfortably**); *noun* (U): **discomfort** ◦ *an uncomfortable bed* ◦ *My toothache was causing me severe discomfort.*

- a thing that makes you feel uncomfortable: **discomfort** ○ *the discomforts of life on a farm*

■ **MORE ...**

- if you live without comfort, you **rough it** ○ *We spent three months in a tent roughing it in the Himalayas.*
- a thing or a place without pleasure or luxury is **austere, spartan**; *noun* (U): **austerity** ○ *The nuns led simple and austere lives.*

commerce ⇨ BUSINESS

committee ⇨ MEETING

common ⇨ USUAL

communication

see also CONVERSATION, SAY, SPEAK, WRITE

- to exchange information, thoughts, feelings, etc with sb, by speaking, writing letters, etc: **communicate** (**with** sb); *noun* (U): **communication** ○ *He's stopped communicating with his parents.* ○ *They communicate by sign language.* ○ *non-verbal communication* ○ *a breakdown in communication*

- if you communicate with sb, you are **in touch/contact** (**with** sb) ○ *Are you still in touch with Karen?* ○ *I'm trying to get in touch with Jim – do you have his new address?* ○ *Make sure you keep in touch!*
- to stop communicating with sb: **lose* touch/contact** (**with** sb) ○ *I lost touch with them years ago.*
- if you have stopped communicating with sb, you are **out of touch/contact** (**with** sb) ○ *We've been out of contact for years.*

- a way of communicating with sb: **means of communication** (*plural* **means of communication**) ○ *new means of communication such as the fax machine and e-mail*

▷ letters, faxes, e-mail, telegrams and telex ⇨ LETTER[1]

▷ the telephone ⇨ TELEPHONE

- television, radio, newspapers and other means of communication with large audiences: **the mass media** (*noun plural*)

▷ television and radio ⇨ TELEVISION/RADIO

▷ newspapers and magazines ⇨ NEWSPAPER/MAGAZINE

company ⇨ BUSINESS

compare/contrast

comparing quantities ⇨ HOW MUCH/MANY
comparing sizes ⇨ SIZE
see also DIFFERENT, SAME

- to see or show how sb/sth is similar to or different from sb/sth else: **compare** A and B, **compare** A **with/to** B; *noun* (C/U): **comparison** ○ *Think about the question for five minutes and then compare your ideas.* ○ *If you compare my writing with George's, you can see that his is much more elegant.* ○ *I'd like to make a comparison between the two methods.*
- comparing two or more things: **comparative** ○ *a comparative study*
- compared with what is usual or what you expect: **comparatively, relatively** ○ *You'll find that this exercise is comparatively easy.* ○ *We live in a relatively poor area of town.*

- when compared to sb/sth: **by/in comparison** (**with** sb/sth), **compared to/with** sb/sth, **unlike** sb/sth ○ *These people are so poor. I feel rich by comparison.* ○ *In comparison with the other children, she is very intelligent.* ○ *Compared to your mother, you're really quite tall.* ○ *Unlike many people, I have no desire to read endless stories about the Royal family in the newspapers.*

■ making a comparison

- the form of an adjective or adverb that expresses a greater amount, quantity, etc: **comparative** ○ *The comparative of 'fast' is 'faster'.*
- to compare people or things, you say **as ... as, not as ... as, not so ... as**, (after a comparative form) **than** ○ *Our car is just as fast as theirs.* ○ *The hotel wasn't as comfortable as we had expected.* ○ *This puzzle isn't so difficult as the last one.* ○ *She looks a lot happier than she used to.*
- to make a comparison stronger, you can use **even** before a comparative form ○ *She has even more/less money than he does.* ○ *It's even colder in here than it was outside.*

▷ being more or less in degree ⇨ FAIRLY/VERY

■ emphasizing differences

- to compare people or things in order to show the differences between them: **contrast** A **and/with** B ○ *Let's contrast the school systems in Japan and Britain.* ○ *The film contrasts his poor childhood with his later life as a millionaire.*
- a clear difference between people or things that is seen when they are compared: **contrast** (*noun* C/U) ○ *We noticed a striking contrast between the death rates in the two periods.*
- when compared to sb/sth (emphasizing the difference): **in/by contrast, in contrast to** sth, **as opposed to** sth ○ *The pianist played brilliantly. The orchestra, by contrast, was very dull.* ○ *Watching football, as opposed to playing it, is increasingly popular.*

▷ expressing contrasting ideas in speech or writing ⇨ AND/OR/BUT

■ **MORE ...**

- (especially in literature) a comparison between one thing and another (for example 'As busy as a bee'): **simile**

competition

1 different kinds of competition
2 the stages of a competition
3 being in a competition
4 the result of a competition
see also GAME, RACE[2], SPORT, TEAM

competition *contd.*

1 different kinds of competition

– an organized event in which people try to win sth: **competition, contest** ◦ *The competition is open to anybody over the age of twenty-one.* ◦ *an art competition* ◦ *a song contest*
– a competition or series of competitions to find who is best at sth: **championship** (*often plural*), **tournament** ◦ *the World Chess Championship*
– an organized game or sports event: **match** ◦ *a football/boxing/Scrabble match*
– something important which people go to (a sports competition, for example): **event** ◦ *The Olympics is usually a two-week event.* ◦ *an annual event* ◦ *a sporting event*

2 the stages of a competition

– one part of a competition: **round** ◦ *the first/final round* ◦ *She got through to the third round.*
– (especially used about races) one of the first parts of a competition: **heat** ◦ *If you come first or second in this heat you'll go through to the final.*
– the last part of a competition: **final** (*often plural*); a person who competes in a final: **finalist** ◦ *She was a finalist last year but isn't expected to do well this year.*
– the part before the final: **semi-final** (*often plural*) ◦ *He won the semi-final so he'll go through to the finals.*
– the part before the semi-final: **quarter-final** (*often plural*)

3 being in a competition

– to enter a competition: **go* in for** sth, **enter** (sth) ◦ *to go in for an art competition* ◦ *I've decided not to enter.*
– to put another person into a competition: **enter** sb **for** sth ◦ *My teacher entered me for the scholarship exam.*
– a person who enters a competition: **entrant** ◦ *There were over 200 entrants for the writing competition.*
– to decide not to be in a competition that you had entered for: **drop out** (**of** sth) ◦ *He had to drop out at the last minute.*
– to be in a competition: **compete** (**in** sth), **take* part** (**in** sth) ◦ *She's competing in the 100 metres and the long jump.* ◦ *He isn't taking part in the relay.*
– a person who competes in a sports or games competition: **competitor, contestant**
– (used about two people or teams in a sports competition) against: **versus** (*abbreviation* **v**, **vs**) ◦ *It's Canada versus Sweden in the final.* ◦ *Manchester United v Barcelona*
– a person that you compete against: **opponent** ◦ *His opponent was the 1994 champion.*
– having sb competing with you: **competition** (*noun* U) ◦ *He's got strong competition.*
– a thing (for example, a picture or a poem) that is entered for a competition: **entry** ◦ *His entry was definitely one of the best.* ◦ *All entries must be in by 1 May.*
– to officially forbid sb to do sth or win sth in a sport because he/she has broken a rule: **disqualify** sb (**from** sth) (**for** sth); *noun* (C/U): **disqualification** ◦ *She was disqualified from the race for pushing her opponent.*
– to officially forbid sb to take part in any sports for a period of time because they have broken a very important rule: **ban** sb (**from** sth) (**for** sth); *noun*: **ban** ◦ *They were banned from international athletics for taking drugs.* ◦ *to impose a ban on sb*

4 the result of a competition

– to decide who has won a competition: **judge** sth; a person who does this: **judge** ◦ *Who is judging the poetry competition?* ◦ *The decision of the judges was unanimous.*
– the position you are in during a competition or at the end of a competition: **place** ◦ *She was in third place at the end of round two.*
– to be first, second, third, ... last: **come* first, second, third, ... last**
– at the end of a competition, the person or team that comes first is the **winner**; the others are the **losers**; the person who comes second is the **runner-up**
– the winner of an important competition or a series of competitions: **champion** ◦ *the Olympic/world champion* ◦ *The Dutch are European champions.*

▷ more on winning and losing ⇨ WIN/LOSE

■ scores, times and distances
– the number of points that a team or competitor has: **score**; *verb*: **score** sth; the place where the score is shown: **scoreboard** ◦ *Is somebody keeping* (= writing down) *the score?* ◦ *How many points did you score?*
– a single mark that you get in a game or sport for doing well: **mark, point** ◦ *a high mark* ◦ *full marks* (= the highest possible number of marks) ◦ *Did he win that point?*
– the period of time that it takes sb to do sth in sport: **time**; to record the time that it takes for sb to do sth: **time** sb ◦ *She ran the race in a very fast time.* ◦ *They timed her and it was very fast.*
– a special watch or clock which records the time that it takes for sb to do sth: **stopwatch**
– how far sb jumps or throws sth: **distance** ◦ *a record distance of 70 metres*
– how high sb jumps: **height**
– the fastest, highest, longest, etc ever achieved in a certain type of competition: **record**
– to beat an existing record: **break* the record** ◦ *She has broken the world record in the 5 000 metres.*
– to make a new record: **set* a new record** ◦ *He's set a new world record.*
– a person who has broken a record: **record holder**

■ prizes
– something you get if you win a competition: **prize** ◦ *She won a prize for designing an anti-smoking poster.*

- a metal cup given as a prize: **cup** ◦ *We won the cup!*
- a prize for the person who does not win: **consolation prize**
- to give sb a prize in a competition: **award** sb sth ◦ *She was awarded first prize in a writing competition.*

- a large metal coin awarded as a prize, in the Olympics for example: **medal**
- in some international competitions there are three different coloured medals: (for third place) **bronze**; (for second place) **silver**; (for first place) **gold** ◦ *to win a gold medal* ◦ *Germany have won the gold.*
- a person who wins a medal: (**bronze/silver/gold**) **medallist** (*AmE* **medalist**)

■ **MORE ...**
- a person, team, horse, etc that most people think will win a competition: **favourite** (*AmE* **favorite**) ◦ *to be the favourite in a competition*
- a person who seems unlikely to win in a competition: **outsider**, **underdog**
- a person that you are competing with: **rival**
- to invite sb to take part in a competition: **challenge** sb (**to** sth) ◦ *My father has challenged me to a chess match this Sunday.*

- a person who tries very hard to win in a competition is **competitive** ◦ *a competitive player*
- a competition in which the standard is very high and people try very hard to win is **competitive** ◦ *It was a very competitive game.*

---

complain/protest

see also CRITICISM

- to say that you are not happy with sth: **complain** (**about** sth); *noun* (C/U): **complaint** ◦ *Why don't you complain to the waiter?* ◦ *a long list of complaints* ◦ *I wish to make a complaint!* ◦ *a letter of complaint*
- something that you think is unfair and that you want to complain or protest about: **grievance** ◦ *The meeting will give us all a chance to discuss our grievances.*

- in order to make a complaint, you **speak*/talk to** sb (**about** sth), **report** sth (**to** sb), **report** sb (**for** sth) ◦ *This is totally unacceptable. I'm going to speak to the head teacher about it.* ◦ *This should be reported to the director.* ◦ *I'll have to report you for being late.*

- to keep saying what is wrong about sth: **moan** (**about** sth), **grumble** (**about** sth), **have a moan/grumble** (**about** sth) ◦ *He never stops grumbling.* ◦ *They're having a good moan about the boss.*
- to complain about sth continuously in an annoying way: (*informal*) **nag** (sb) (**about** sth), (*informal*) **go* on** (**at** sb) (**about** sth) ◦ *Do stop nagging!* ◦ *There's no need to go on about it!*

- to say or show in a serious way that you think sth is not right or fair: **protest** (**about/against/at** sth), **speak* out** (**against** sth) ◦ *They're protesting about the cut in student grants.* ◦ *I felt I had to speak out against the decision.*
- an act of protesting: **protest** (*noun* C/U) ◦ *We've received hundreds of protests.* ◦ *a letter of protest* ◦ *He resigned from the Cabinet in protest against the decision to raise taxes.*
- an angry public protest against sth: **storm of protest**, **outcry** (**against/over** sth) ◦ *The decision has raised a storm of protest from local residents.* ◦ *a public outcry*

- to feel or say that you do not like or agree with sth: **object** (**to** sth); *noun* (C/U): **objection** ◦ *Most people object to the new tax.* ◦ *We have a number of objections to the plan.* ◦ *They went ahead in spite of our objections.*
- a person who objects to sth: **objector**

■ organized protests
- an organized public protest: **demonstration** ◦ *Thousands of people took part in demonstrations.*
- to take part in a demonstration: **demonstrate** (**against** sb/sth or **in favour of** sb/sth) ◦ *They're demonstrating against the government.*
- a person who takes part in a demonstration: **protester**, **demonstrator** ◦ *Several protesters were arrested when fighting broke out.*
- without fighting: **peaceful** ◦ *It started out as a peaceful demonstration, but soon developed into a full-scale riot* (= fighting).

- a public political meeting: **rally** ◦ *to organize a peace rally*
- an organized walk by a large group of people who are protesting: (**protest**) **march** ◦ *a peace march*
- to take part in a protest march: **march** ◦ *We're going to march to Downing Street and hand over a letter to the Prime Minister.*
- a person who takes part in a protest march: **marcher**

- to stop working as a protest: **strike***, **go* on strike**; *noun*: **strike** ◦ *They've decided to strike for better conditions.* ◦ *Teachers are staging a one-day strike.*

▷ more on strikes ⇨ EMPLOYMENT

■ **MORE ...**
- words often shouted by demonstrators to protest against sth: **down with** sb/sth, **no more** sth ◦ *Down with arms sales!* ◦ *No more war!*
- a large notice that is sometimes carried in a demonstration: **placard**

- refusing to obey certain laws or regulations as a means of protesting against sth: **civil disobedience** (*noun* U) ◦ *a campaign of civil disobedience*

---

complete ⇨ PART/WHOLE

---

completely ⇨ FAIRLY/VERY

compliment ⇨ PRAISE

computer

1 kinds of computers and their parts
2 using a computer

1 kinds of computers and their parts

– an electronic machine which can store and arrange information, make calculations and control other machinery: **computer** ◦ *a very powerful/fast computer*
– a small computer which is not part of a larger system: **personal computer**, **PC**
– a small computer which is used mainly for writing letters, reports, etc: **word processor**
– a small computer which you can carry with you and use outside the office: **laptop** (**computer**)

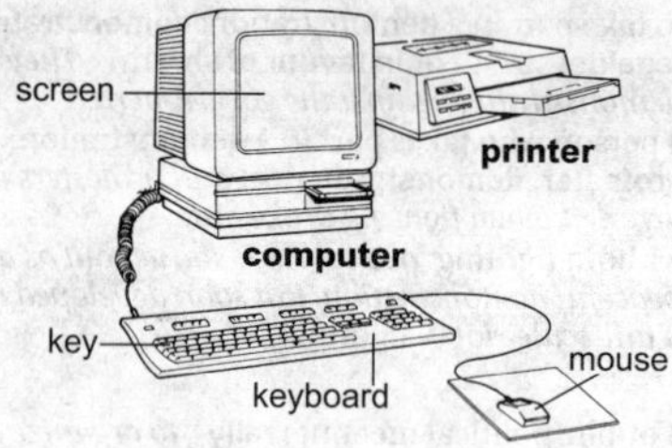

– a device inside a computer which stores large amounts of information: **hard disk**; a similar device that can be put into a computer and taken out again: (**floppy**) **disk**
– the part of a computer which passes information to and from a disk: **disk drive**
– the part of a computer where information is stored: **memory** ◦ *4 megabytes of memory*

2 using a computer

– the list on the screen of a computer which shows the things that you can do: **menu**
– a small sign on a computer screen which shows your position in a text, etc: **cursor**

– knowledge of how to use a computer: **computing** (*noun* U) ◦ *He knows a lot about computing.*
– knowledge of how to use a word processor: **word processing** (*noun* U) ◦ *The person appointed to this job will need good word-processing skills.*
– making books, magazines, etc using a computer: **desktop publishing** (*noun* U)
– a system for sending written messages by computer: **e-mail** (= electronic mail) (*noun* U)
– the system which makes it possible for people to communicate worldwide using computers: **the Internet**

▷ sending messages by e-mail ⇨ LETTER[1]

– if you use a computer to help you do sth, you can say that the task is **computer-assisted**, **computer-aided** ◦ *computer-assisted language learning* ◦ *computer-aided design*
– to introduce computers into a place or a system: **computerize** sth ◦ *The whole factory has been computerized.*

– a number of computers connected together in a larger system: **network**
– to start using a computer that is part of a larger system: **log in/on**, **log into/onto** sth ◦ *You have to have a password in order to log in.*
– to finish using a computer which is part of a system: **log out/off**, **log off** sth ◦ *Don't forget to log off.*

■ computer programs

– a set of instructions which make a computer perform certain tasks: (**computer**) **program**
– to produce a new program: **write*** a program, **program** a computer ◦ *I've written a program to calculate our annual salary bill.* ◦ *She programmed the computer to do her accounts for her.*
– a person whose job it is to program computers: **computer programmer**
– the programs written for a computer: **software** (*noun* U)

– if a computer or a computer program is easy to use, it is **user-friendly**

■ data

– information that you put into a computer: **data** (*noun* U)
– a large amount of information stored in a computer, which you can change and add to: **database**; a program which enables you to store and use this information: **database** (**program**) ◦ *We have a database with the names of all the doctors in Scotland.* ◦ *Which database program do you use?*
– information in the form of rows of numbers, used especially for doing accounts: **spreadsheet**; a program which enables you to store and use this information: **spreadsheet** (**program**)
– to put information into a computer: **input** sth, **key** sth **into** a computer, **key** sth **in** ◦ *Have you inputted that data yet?*
– a collection of information on a subject that is stored in a computer: **file**; stored in a computer file: **on file** ◦ *We have all your details on file.*
– to make a computer store information on a disk: **save** sth ◦ *Save your work regularly.*
– a copy of a computer file or a disk that you can use if the other one is damaged or lost: **backup** ◦ *Always make a backup copy.*

■ printing

– to transfer information from a computer onto paper: **print** sth **out** ◦ *When you are satisfied with what you have written, you can print it out.*
– information which has been transferred from the computer onto paper: **printout** (*noun* C/U), **hard copy** (*noun* U) ◦ *a printout of last month's sales figures* ◦ *The information's on a disk, but we need hard copy as well.*

▷ more on printing ⇨ PRINT

■ **MORE ...**
- instructions that are put into a computer in order to cause mistakes and destroy information: (**computer**) **virus**
- if a computer stops working suddenly, it **crashes** ○ *The system crashed, but fortunately we had backup copies of all our files.*

---

concert ⇨ MUSIC

condition ⇨ REPAIR

congratulate ⇨ PRAISE

connect ⇨ JOIN

connection ⇨ CAUSE/EFFECT

conquer ⇨ WIN/LOSE

conscious

see also ILLNESS

- if you are awake and are able to see, hear and feel things, you are **conscious**; the state of being conscious: **consciousness** (*noun* U) ○ *She was badly injured but still conscious.*
- not conscious, in a state like sleep because of illness or an accident: **unconscious**, **senseless**; *noun* (U): **unconsciousness** ○ *She remained unconscious for three days after the accident.* ○ *He lay senseless on the floor.*

- if you feel that you may become unconscious, you **feel* faint** ○ *I'm feeling a bit faint; I think I'll sit down for a minute.*
- to become unconscious: **lose* consciousness**
- to lose consciousness suddenly: **faint**, **pass out**, **black out** ○ *Several soldiers fainted in the heat.* ○ *I don't know what happened next – I must have passed out.*
- an occasion when sb loses consciousness: **faint**, **blackout** ○ *He fell down in a faint.* ○ *The accident was caused by the driver having a blackout.*
- a kind of deep unconsciousness which is the result of illness or injury: **coma** ○ *to be in a coma*
- to make a person unconscious by hitting them or by using a drug: **knock** sb **out** ○ *He knocked him out with a sudden punch to the jaw.* ○ *This drug can knock you out in seconds.*

- a drug that is used to make a person unconscious and stop them from feeling pain: (**general**) **anaesthetic** (*AmE* **anesthetic**) ○ *The anaesthetic took a long time to wear off.*
- to make a person unconscious before an operation in a hospital: **anaesthetize** (*AmE* **anesthetize**) sb

- to become conscious again after being unconscious for a time: **regain/recover consciousness**, **come* round** ○ *She began to come round when her mother started speaking to her.*
- to make a person become conscious again: **bring*** sb **round**, **revive** sb ○ *They brought me round by splashing cold water on my face.*

■ **knowing what is happening**
- if you have a full knowledge of what is happening, you are **aware of** sth; *opposite*: **unaware of** sth
- if you have a full knowledge of what you are doing, your action is a **conscious** one, you do it **consciously** ○ *a conscious decision*
- if you do sth without a full knowledge of what you are doing, your action is an **unconscious** one, you do it **unconsciously** or **subconsciously** ○ *an unconscious reaction*

■ **MORE ...**
- a state of unconsciousness that is like deep sleep, where a person's actions may be controlled by another person: **hypnosis** (*noun* U); using hypnosis: **hypnotism** (*noun* U); a person who uses hypnosis on other people: **hypnotist**; to use hypnosis on another person: **hypnotize** sb ○ *to be under hypnosis*
- something that produces hypnosis or a similar condition is **hypnotic** ○ *His voice had a hypnotic effect that made me feel very sleepy.*

Conservative ⇨ POLITICS

contact

- communicating with sb ⇨ COMMUNICATION
- touching sth ⇨ TOUCH

---

container

containers used for cooking ⇨ COOK
containers used for eating and drinking ⇨ PLATE/BOWL/DISH, CUP/GLASS
containers used for transporting goods ⇨ TRANSPORT
containers for rubbish ⇨ RUBBISH
containers for flowers ⇨ FLOWER

- an object which has sth inside it **contains** sth ○ *Each crate contains twelve bottles of beer.*
- something in which you put or keep things: **container** ○ *an airtight container*
- to be able to contain a certain amount of sth: **hold*** sth, **take*** sth ○ *This bag holds a lot more than you would imagine.* ○ *The tank can take 24 litres of petrol.*
- the empty area inside a large container: **space** (*noun* U), **room** (*noun* U) ○ *There's still a lot to pack. Is there any more space in that trunk?* ○ *Is there any room left in your suitcase?*
- the thing or things which are in a container: **contents** (*noun plural*) ○ *The customs officer asked to see the contents of my suitcase.*
- the greatest amount that a container or space can hold: **capacity** ○ *The petrol tank has a capacity of eight gallons.*

■ **some different kinds of container**
- a square or rectangular container that is used for holding solid objects: **box** ○ *a box of chocolates/matches* ○ *a cardboard box*
- a metal container with a lid: **tin** ○ *a biscuit tin* ○ *a tin of paint*
- a large box which is used for storing or transporting goods: **crate** ○ *a crate of beer*

container *contd.*

– a container which is used to cover or hold a particular thing, such as a camera or a violin: **case**

– a basket used for shopping: **shopping basket**
– a bag used for shopping: **shopping bag**
– a paper or plastic bag used for shopping, often given away free by shops: **carrier bag**
– a large bag for carrying or storing things: **sack** ◦ *a sack of potatoes/flour/rice*

▷ other kinds of bag ⇨ BAG

– a small, often round container made of plastic, with a lid, which is used for holding food: **tub** ◦ *a tub of margarine*
– a small round container made of metal, closed at both ends, which is used for keeping food for a long time: **can** (*BrE also* **tin**) ◦ *a can/tin of beans/peaches*
– a small round container made of metal, closed at both ends, which is used for holding drinks which are to be sold: **can** ◦ *a can of lemonade*
– something that you can buy in a can or tin is **canned/tinned**
– a round container that is used for cooking food or keeping food or drink in: **pot** ◦ *a yoghurt pot* ◦ *a clay pot* (= a pot made of clay)
–

– a container made of glass, with a lid, which is used for holding food: **jar** ◦ *a jar of jam* ◦ *a jam jar*
– a container with a handle, which is used for holding or pouring liquids: **jug** ◦ *a jug of water*
– a glass or plastic container with a narrow neck, for holding liquids: **bottle** ◦ *a bottle of orange squash* ◦ *a wine/milk bottle* ◦ *medicine bottles*
– a container like a bottle used for keeping things hot or cold: **flask, thermos** (**flask**) (*AmE* **Thermos bottle**)
– a bottle used for giving milk to a baby: **feeding bottle**

– to store sth in a bottle: **bottle** sth; something that you can buy in bottles is **bottled** ◦ *After three or four months the wine is bottled.* ◦ *bottled water/beer*

– a container made of plastic or cardboard, which is used for holding liquids which are to be sold: **carton** ◦ *a carton of fruit juice*
– a container made of cardboard in which food and other goods are sold: **packet** ◦ *a packet of cereal*
– a container made of paper or plastic that is closed at the top: **bag, packet** ◦ *a bag of crisps* ◦ *a packet of sweets*
– a long and thin container made of soft metal or plastic, which has a cap at one end and which is used for holding soft substances: **tube** ◦ *a tube of toothpaste/tomato purée*

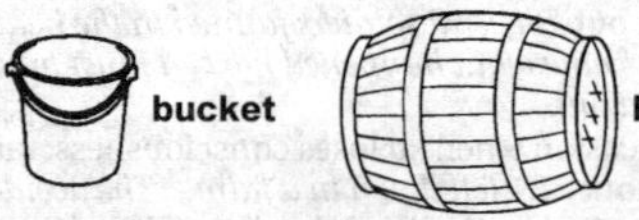

– a container made of plastic or metal, with a handle and an open top, which is used for carrying water and other liquids: **bucket** ◦ *a bucketful of water*
– a container made of wood or metal, which is closed at both ends and which is used for storing wine or beer: **barrel**
– a round container made of metal, which is closed at both ends and which is usually used for storing oil: (**oil**) **drum**
– a container made of metal or plastic, which is usually fixed in some place and which is used for storing water, oil, etc: **tank**

■ lids and tops
– a flat piece of plastic, or other material, which you can remove from the top of a container: **lid**
– a piece of metal or plastic which covers the opening of a bottle, jar, etc: (**bottle**) **top, cap**

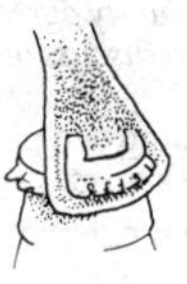

bottle-opener

corkscrew

tin-opener (*AmE* **can opener**)

- to remove the lid or top of a container: **open** sth, **take*/get*** sth **off** sth ○ *Could you open the wine for me?* ○ *I can't get the top off this jar.*
- to remove the top of a jar or bottle by turning it: **unscrew** sth, **screw** sth **off** ○ *to unscrew a lid*

- to put the lid or top on a container: **close** sth, **put*** sth **on** sth ○ *to put the lid on a jar*
- to put the top on a jar or bottle by turning it: **screw** sth **on** ○ *Screw the lid back on firmly after use.*

---

continue

1 actions and events
2 situations
see also BEGIN, END/FINISH, STOP

1 actions and events

- to go on happening or doing sth: **continue ..., go* on ..., carry on ...** ○ *He continues to make money, whatever he does.* ○ *I'll continue working until I die.* ○ *Do you want to continue with this arrangement?* ○ *How long has this been going on?* ○ *She carried on talking in spite of the noise from outside.* ○ *Please ignore me and carry on with your work.*

Note: all these words can be followed either by the '-ing' form of the verb or by 'with'. **Continue** can also be followed by 'to'.

- to continue without a break: **keep*** doing sth ○ *If it keeps raining, we'll have to cancel the match.* ○ *Keep smiling!*
- to continue for a period of time: **last** (**for ...**) ○ *How long does the play last?* ○ *The silence seemed to last for hours.* ○ *The course lasts a complete week.* ○ *What beautiful weather! I'm sure it won't last.*

- to continue to try to do sth, even when there are difficulties: **keep* at** sth, (*informal*) **stick* at** sth, **persevere** (**with** sth); *opposite*: **give*** (sth) **up** ○ *If you keep at it, I'm sure you'll find the answer in the end.* ○ *I find maths very difficult, but I'm going to persevere because it's such an important subject.* ○ *I've failed my driving test five times but I'm refusing to give up.*
- to continue to do sth in the same way as before: **keep*** sth **up** ○ *You're doing very well. Keep it up!*
- to continue doing sth even when people do not want you to: **persist** (**in** sth/doing sth); *adjective*: **persistent**; *noun* (U): **persistence** ○ *She persists in her belief that he is innocent.* ○ *persistent requests for more money*
- to continue moving: **continue, go* on, keep* going** ○ *We continued on that road for about another mile.* ○ *I can't go on – can we sit and rest for a moment?* ○ *Keep going along here until you come to the bus stop.*

- without a stop or a break: **on and on, non-stop**; *adjective*: **non-stop** ○ *He drove on and on until he saw the sun coming up.* ○ *She worked for eight hours non-stop to get it finished in time.* ○ *a non-stop flight*

■ stopping and starting again
- to cause sb/sth not to continue for a period of time: **interrupt** (sb/sth); *noun* (C/U): **interruption** ○ *Our lesson was interrupted by a visit from the headmaster.* ○ *Please excuse the interruption.*
- to begin again, after having stopped: **continue** (sth), **carry on**; *noun* (U): **continuation** ○ *She's going to continue her career after she's had her baby.* ○ *The speaker paused for a drink of water and then continued.*

■ doing sth repeatedly
- to do sth repeatedly: **keep*** (**on**) doing sth ○ *She keeps on making the same mistake.* ○ *Don't keep interrupting!*
- to complain repeatedly: **keep* on** (**at** sb) (**about** sth) ○ *The teacher keeps on at me about my awful handwriting.*

- done or happening many times: **repeated** (*adverb* **repeatedly**) ○ *There have been repeated attempts to change the law.* ○ *The police repeatedly warn people not to leave valuables in cars.*
- happening again and again for a long time: **continual** (*adverb* **continually**), **constant** (*adverb* **constantly**) ○ *They continually argue with each other.* ○ *This entrance is in constant use – please leave it open.*
- one after another, without a break: **running** (*used after a number and a noun*) ○ *You've been late for school for three days running.*

Note: continual is used to describe things which are done or happen repeatedly (see above); to describe a situation that goes on without stopping, we use **continuous** (see below).

2 situations

- to be in a particular situation or condition without changing: **continue, stay, remain** ○ *Will you continue as chairman for another year?* ○ *Food stays cold if you put it in the fridge.* ○ *The weather will remain cold and wet.*

- to continue to be in a particular place: **stay**, (*informal*) **stick* around**, (*more formal*) **remain** ○ *She stayed in bed all day on Saturday.* ○ *If you stick around after the show, you might meet some of the singers.*
- to remain in a place after other people have gone: **stay behind** ○ *I stayed behind at the end of the lesson to speak to the teacher.*
- to remain at a place of work or education in order to do or finish sth: **stay on** ○ *She has decided to stay on and take her exams again.*

- happening or existing without stopping: **continuous** (*adverb* **continuously**), **constant** (*adverb* **constantly**) ○ *a continuous process* ○ *He thinks of life as a continuous effort to make more*

continue *contd.*

money. ◦ *The constant rain prevented any outdoor sports.*
- the state of continuing smoothly, often from one thing to another, without interruption: **continuity** (*noun* U) ◦ *His books feature the same characters, providing a sense of continuity.*

- not changing, and lasting for a very long time or for ever: **permanent** (*adverb* **permanently**); *noun* (U): **permanence** ◦ *I don't want a temporary job – I'm looking for something permanent.* ◦ *She lives in London permanently now.*
- continuing for a long time: **lasting, long-lasting** ◦ *to have a lasting effect*
- not changing, and apparently lasting for ever: **perpetual** (*adverb* **perpetually**), **never-ending** ◦ *He lives in perpetual fear of being attacked.* ◦ *She felt perpetually tired.* ◦ *The day seemed never-ending.*

■ **MORE ...**
- to sit in your seat until the end of sth boring: **sit* through** sth ◦ *I had to sit through two hours of football with my boyfriend on Saturday.*
- to wait until the end of sth unpleasant: (*informal*) **stick* it**/sth **out** ◦ *We can't leave now – we'll just have to stick it out.*

- to keep sth at the same standard or level: **maintain** sth ◦ *We need to maintain these high standards if we want to keep making a profit.* ◦ *to maintain profitability*

contraception ⇨ SEX²

contrast ⇨ COMPARE/CONTRAST

control

- controlling a machine ⇨ MACHINE
- controlling people ⇨ POWER

conversation

see also SAY, SPEAK, TELEPHONE

- informal talk between two or more people: **conversation** (*noun* C/U) ◦ *to have a conversation* ◦ *I don't know how we're supposed to carry on a conversation with all that noise going on outside.* ◦ *When we arrived they were already deep in conversation.*
- words, expressions, etc that are used in conversation rather than in writing or in formal situations are **informal, colloquial**

- a conversation on a particular topic: **talk**; *verb*: **talk** (**to/with** sb) (**about** sth) ◦ *Your mother and I had a long talk with Mr Davis about your school report.* ◦ *They have been talking to the Americans about closer cooperation on arms reduction.*
- to have a short, often private, conversation with sb about a particular subject: **have a word** (**with** sb) ◦ *Can I have a quick word with you before you go home?*
- a serious conversation about a particular subject: **discussion** (**about** sth) (*noun* C/U); *verb*: **discuss** sth ◦ *We were having an interesting discussion about politics.* ◦ *They eventually agreed after much discussion.* ◦ *We need to discuss our holiday plans.*
- a formal discussion, for example between politicians: **talks** (*noun plural*) ◦ *peace talks*

▷ more on discussion ⇨ DISCUSS/ARGUE

- a friendly, informal conversation: **chat**; *verb*: **chat** (**to/with** sb) (**about** sth) ◦ *Why don't you come round for a chat?* ◦ *I think I need to have another chat with Jane about her application.* ◦ *We chatted for hours about all sorts of things.*
- to talk to sb in a friendly way because you are sexually attracted to them: (*informal*) **chat** sb **up** ◦ *He spent the whole evening trying to chat up my sister.*
- informal conversation, usually about other people's private affairs: **gossip** (*noun* U/C); *verb*: **gossip** ◦ *Don't trust him – he's always spreading gossip.* ◦ *They just sat in a corner gossiping the whole evening.* ◦ *Whenever they meet they always have a good gossip.*

- the thing that you are talking about: **subject, topic** (**of conversation**) ◦ *His favourite topic of conversation is football.*
- to start talking about sth different: **change the subject** ◦ *I could tell she was trying to change the subject.*

- to start talking when another person is already talking: **interrupt** (sb/sth), **butt in** (**on** sb/sth), **break* in** (**on** sth); *noun* (C/U): **interruption** ◦ *Please don't interrupt me when I'm trying to speak.* ◦ *It's rude to interrupt.* ◦ *I'm sorry to butt in on your conversation.* ◦ *There were so many interruptions he had to stop speaking.* ◦ *I hope we'll be able to talk without interruption.*

■ **MORE ...**
- a conversation, especially in a book or play, usually between two people: **dialogue** (*AmE* **dialog**) (*noun* C/U) ◦ *The whole of the first act is a dialogue between the two main characters.* ◦ *You'll find this easy to read because there's a lot of dialogue.*

- polite conversation about unimportant things: **small talk** (*noun* U) ◦ *I don't enjoy formal parties because I'm not very good at making small talk.*

- if you do not get a chance to say anything because the person you are talking to never stops talking, you **can't get a word in edgeways** ◦ *She talked non-stop – I couldn't get a word in edgeways.*
- a break in a conversation when people feel embarrassed because nobody is talking: **an awkward silence** ◦ *There was an awkward silence when Dave asked Kim if she was married.*

- to listen secretly to a private conversation: **eavesdrop** (**on** sb/sth) ◦ *Were you eavesdropping on our conversation?*
- a person who eavesdrops: **eavesdropper**

cook

1 cooking
2 preparing food for cooking
3 things that you add to food when you are cooking
4 heating food in order to cook it

cooking particular foods ⇨ **BREAD, CAKE, EGG, MEAT, FISH**

see also FOOD, KITCHEN

1 cooking

- to prepare and cook food: **cook**; *noun* (U): **cooking** ◦ *I'll cook if you wash up.* ◦ *I love cooking.* ◦ *I can't watch TV, I've got to do the cooking.*
- to prepare a particular food by heating it: **cook** sth, **do*** sth ◦ *If you cook the potatoes, I'll make the salad.* ◦ *How shall I do the chops?*
- to put different foods together to produce sth to eat: **make*** sth ◦ *Can you make the soup?* ◦ *I'm making spaghetti Bolognese for dinner.*
- to prepare a meal: **make*** sth, **get*** sth, **cook** sth ◦ *Who'll make the lunch?* ◦ *I'll get dinner tonight.* ◦ *I can't stay. I've got to go and cook the supper.*

- instructions on how to make sth to eat: **recipe** ◦ *Make sure you follow the recipe.*
- a book with recipes in it: **recipe book, cookery book, cookbook**
- a type of food prepared in a particular way: **dish** ◦ *There are some really nice dishes in that recipe book.* ◦ *a vegetarian dish*

- a person whose job is to cook: **cook**
- a person who works as the chief cook in a hotel or restaurant: **chef**
- if a person is good/bad at cooking, he/she is a **good/bad cook** ◦ *We had a great meal – he's a really good cook.*

- a person or business that provides food or drink, for example for a party or a public occasion: **caterer** ◦ *We can get caterers in for the wedding.*
- the activity or business of providing food or drink: **catering** (*noun* U) ◦ *She runs a successful catering company.*

2 preparing food for cooking

- the things you that need in order to make sth to eat: **ingredients** (*noun plural*) ◦ *Get all the ingredients ready before you start cooking.*
- to measure the amount of food you need by using kitchen scales: **weigh** sth
- the amount of sth that can be contained in a spoon: **spoonful** ◦ *a teaspoonful of salt*
- the amount of sth that can be contained in a cup: **cupful** ◦ *a cupful of flour*

▷ more on weighing things ⇨ **WEIGHT**

- to cut sth into pieces using a knife: **cut*** sth (**up**) ◦ *Cut the meat up into small pieces.*
- to cut sth (usually vegetables and fruit) into small pieces using a knife: **chop** sth (**up**) ◦ *Chop the onion finely.*

- to cut sth into small cubes: **dice** sth ◦ *Dice the potatoes and add to the soup.*
- to take the skin off a fruit or vegetable: **peel** sth ◦ *to peel an apple*

- to mix two or more types of food together: **mix** sth, **blend** sth ◦ *Mix the flour and sugar together in a bowl.*
- to mix sth quickly with a fork: **beat*** sth ◦ *Beat the flour and other ingredients together.*
- with a whisk (see picture) you **whisk** or **whip** eggs, cream, etc to make them light or stiff ◦ *whipped cream*
- with a sieve (see picture) you **sieve** food in order to separate solids from liquids or very small pieces of food from larger pieces ◦ *Sieve the flour before adding it to the mixture.*
- with a wooden spoon (see picture) you **stir** ingredients so as to mix them together slowly
- with a rolling pin (see picture) you **roll out** pastry (= a mixture of flour, water and fat that is used for making pies and cakes)
- with a grater (see picture) you **grate** food (for example cheese, carrots) into small pieces

- an electric machine which cuts up and mixes food: **food processor**
- an electric machine which mixes food, for example, to make a cake: (**food**) **mixer**
- an electric machine which makes food into liquid: **liquidizer, blender**; to make food into liquid: **liquidize** sth ◦ *Liquidize all the ingredients before adding to the soup.*

3 things that you add to food when you are cooking

- a substance, usually made from part of a plant, which is used to give flavour to food: **spice** (*noun* C/U); tasting of spices: **spicy**; some common spices are **pepper** (*noun* U), **ginger** (*noun* U), **cinnamon** (*noun* U) ◦ *mixed spices* ◦ *Indian food is hot and spicy.*
- the leaf of a plant used for giving food flavour: **herb**; some common herbs are **mint** (*noun* U), **parsley** (*noun* U), **basil** (*noun* U) ◦ *dried herbs* ◦ *a herb garden*

cook *contd.*

- a mixture of spices often used to make Indian food: **curry powder** (*noun* U)
- something that you add to food or drink to give it a particular taste: **flavouring** (*AmE* **flavoring**) (*noun* C/U); to add flavouring to food: **flavour** (*AmE* **flavor**) sth ◦ *strawberry flavouring*

- to add salt, pepper, spices, etc to food: **season** sth; *noun* (U): **seasoning** ◦ *Season with salt and pepper if desired.* ◦ *Add a little more seasoning.*
- a small amount of salt held between thumb and finger: **pinch of salt**

- a white or brown powder made from grain and used to make bread, cakes, biscuits, etc; it is sometimes used to make food thicker: **flour** (*noun* U); a special flour used to make food thicker: **cornflour** (*noun* U)
- a liquid made from meat or vegetables and added to soups, for example: **stock** (*noun* U) ◦ *vegetable stock* ◦ *a stock cube* (= a cube of dried stock)

▷ more on flour ⇨ **FLOUR**

4 heating food in order to cook it

- (used about food) to be prepared for eating by being heated: **cook**; to prepare food by heating it: **cook** sth ◦ *What can I smell cooking?* ◦ *Cook the chicken in a hot oven.*
- something which has finished cooking and is ready to eat is **cooked**, **done** ◦ *Is the rice done yet?*

- to make food that has already been cooked hot again: **heat** sth **up** ◦ *For lunch we could heat up what was left from yesterday.*
- to cook sth too much: **overcook** sth; *opposite*: **undercook** sth
- food which has been cooked too much is **overcooked**, **overdone**; food which has not been cooked enough is **undercooked**, **underdone** ◦ *overcooked vegetables* ◦ *I'm sorry, the fish is a bit underdone.*
- something which has not been cooked is **raw** ◦ *raw vegetables/meat*
- to cook sth too much so that it becomes black: **burn** sth ◦ *I've burned the cake.* ◦ *burnt toast*

- a metal container that is used for cooking: **pan**, **saucepan** ◦ *pots and pans* ◦ *a large saucepan* ◦ *a non-stick pan* (= with a special surface to stop food sticking to it)
- a shallow container for food; you can use it to cook sth in the oven or to serve food on the table: **dish** ◦ *a casserole dish*
- metal that is very thin like paper and is used for cooking: (**aluminium/kitchen**) **foil** (*noun* U) ◦ *Wrap the meat in aluminium foil before placing it in the oven.*

■ cookers

- a piece of equipment for heating food in order to cook it: **cooker** ◦ *a gas/electric cooker*
- the part of a cooker where the food is cooked by heat from above: **grill**
- the part of a cooker which has a door and which you put things inside in order to cook them: **oven** ◦ *Bake the pie in a hot/moderate/cool oven.*

- one of the parts on top of a cooker on which you put saucepans in order to heat food: (**gas/electric**) **ring**
- a ring when it is hot: **heat** ◦ *Take the saucepan off the heat.* ◦ *a high/medium/low heat*
- the fire on the ring or in the oven of a gas cooker: **gas** (*noun* U) ◦ *Put it on the gas.*
- to change the temperature of sth: **turn** sth **up/down** ◦ *Turn up the heat/gas.*
- one of the switches which control the amount of heat: **knob** ◦ *Push the knob in and turn it.*

- an electric machine which cooks food or makes it hot very quickly: **microwave** (**oven**)
- to cook food in a microwave: **microwave** sth ◦ *You can either microwave it or put it in the oven.*

■ cooking food in hot water

- (used about food) to be cooked in boiling (= very hot) water: **boil**; to cook food in this way: **boil** sth; cooked in this way: **boiled** ◦ *Are the potatoes boiling?* ◦ *Boil the potatoes for about twelve minutes.* ◦ *boiled eggs*
- to begin to boil: **come* to the boil**; to heat sth until it boils: **bring*** sth **to the boil** ◦ *When the water comes to the boil, add the pasta.*
- to boil too much so that liquid goes over the sides of the pan: **boil over** ◦ *Watch the milk – it's about to boil over.*

- to boil slowly and gently: **simmer**; to cook sth in this way: **simmer** sth ◦ *Let the liquid simmer gently for a few minutes.* ◦ *Simmer the sauce on a low heat for about ten minutes.*
- to cook sth in steam: **steam** sth; cooked in this way: **steamed** ◦ *steamed vegetables*

- to move a spoon round and round in a liquid: **stir** sth ◦ *Stir the mixture frequently to prevent it sticking to the bottom of the pan.*
- to remove all the water after cooking vegetables, pasta, etc: **strain** sth, **drain** sth ◦ *Drain the vegetables.*

■ cooking food in hot fat

- to cook sth (usually in a frying pan) in fat: **fry** sth; food cooked in this way is **fried** ◦ *fried eggs*
- liquid fat which comes from plants: **oil** (*noun* U) ◦ *cooking oil* ◦ *olive/sunflower oil*
- hard white fat from animals: **lard** (*noun* U)

■ cooking food in an oven

- (used about meat, etc) to be cooked in an oven: **roast**; to cook food in this way: **roast** sth; cooked in this way: **roast** (*only before a noun*) ◦ *The turkey is roasting in the oven.* ◦ *I'm going to roast*

a chicken. ◦ *We're having roast chicken for dinner.*
- (used especially about bread, cakes, etc) to be cooked in an oven: **bake**; to cook food in this way: **bake** sth; cooked in this way: **baked** ◦ *I could smell bread baking in the oven.* ◦ *to bake a cake* ◦ *baked fish*
- to cook meat and vegetables in liquid for a long time in an oven: **stew** sth, **casserole** sth; cooked in this way: **stewed** ◦ *Stew the meat for two hours.* ◦ *stewed beef/chicken*
- food that has been cooked by stewing: **stew** (*noun* C/U), **casserole** (*noun* C/U) ◦ *Would you like some more stew?* ◦ *a chicken casserole*

■ other ways of cooking
- to cook food under a grill: **grill** sth; cooked in this way: **grilled**; a pan used for grilling: **grill pan** ◦ *Shall I grill the fish or fry it?* ◦ *grilled steak*
- to cook meat, etc over an open fire outdoors: **barbecue** sth; cooked in this way: **barbecued**

cooperate ⇨ WORK

copy

copying the actions of other people ⇨ BEHAVIOUR

- something that is made to look exactly like sth else: **copy**, **duplicate**; *adjective* (*only before a noun*): **duplicate**; to make a copy: **copy** sth, **duplicate** sth ◦ *a copy of a report/picture/photograph* ◦ *a duplicate key*
- to write down sth exactly as it is written somewhere else: **copy** (sth **down/out**) ◦ *I copied down his address from the phone book.*
- a copy of sth that is usually smaller than the real thing: **model** ◦ *a model aeroplane*

- a machine that copies pieces of paper, books, etc: **photocopier**; a copy made with a photocopier: **photocopy**; to make a photocopy: **photocopy** sth
- thin paper with carbon on one side that you put between two pieces of paper to make a copy when you write: **carbon paper** (*noun* U)
- a copy of a letter, etc made with carbon paper: **carbon copy**
- when you write or make sth with two copies that are exactly the same, you do it **in duplicate**

- something that was made first, before any copies: **original**; *adjective*: **original** ◦ *Could you make a photocopy and give the original back to me?* ◦ *Is that an original painting?*
- a copy of a real thing: **imitation** ◦ *a poor imitation of the style of Picasso* ◦ *imitation leather*
- a copy of a painting, etc: **reproduction** ◦ *These vases are only reproductions, not originals.* ◦ *reproduction furniture*
- if sth is not an imitation or a reproduction, it is **genuine**, **real** ◦ *a genuine antique* ◦ *I think it's real silver.*

▷ more on being genuine or real ⇨ REAL/GENUINE

■ **MORE ...**
- to take and use sb else's words, ideas, etc as if they were your own: **plagiarize** sb/sth; *noun* (U/C): **plagiarism** ◦ *He was accused of plagiarism.*

- the legal right to be the only person or organization to be able to copy or print a book, perform a piece of music, etc: **copyright** (*noun* U/C)

corn ⇨ FARM

correct

- true ⇨ TRUE
- what is needed for sth ⇨ USEFUL/SUITABLE

cosmetics

looking attractive ⇨ BEAUTIFUL/ATTRACTIVE

- substances that you use to make yourself look more attractive: **cosmetics** ◦ *Have these cosmetics been tested on animals?* ◦ *the cosmetics industry*
- substances that you can put on your face (and body) to make yourself look more attractive or to change your appearance: **make-up** (*noun* U) ◦ *to wear a lot of make-up* ◦ *Actors use make-up.* ◦ *eye make-up* ◦ *She takes ages to put her make-up on in the morning.* ◦ *I was so tired that I forgot to take my make-up off last night.*
- to have make-up on your face: **wear*** sth ◦ *She wears bright red lipstick.*

■ some kinds of make-up

make-up that you put ...	is called ...
on your lips	**lipstick**
as a line around your eyes	**eyeliner**
around your eyes	**eyeshadow**
on your eyelashes	**mascara**
on your cheeks	**blusher**
on your nails	**nail varnish**, (*especially AmE*) **nail polish**

Note: words for cosmetics are normally uncountable; if you want to talk about a type of soap, perfume, etc, you can make them countable: ◦ *What a bright lipstick!* ◦ *Are you wearing a different perfume?* ◦ *a new range of cleansers and moisturizers*

- a dry, dusty substance that you can put on your face or body: **powder**; to put powder on: **powder** sth
- powder for the face: **face powder**
- powder for the rest of the body, often used after washing: **talcum powder**
- a substance that you can rub into your skin: **cream** ◦ *a small jar of face cream* ◦ *hand cream*
- a cream to stop your skin from becoming dry: **moisturizer**

cosmetics *contd.*

■ some things used for cleaning
- a substance that you use with water to help to wash yourself or to clean things: **soap**
- a cream or liquid that cleans your face: **cleanser**
- a liquid that removes eye make-up or nail varnish: **remover** ◦ *nail varnish remover*

▷ more on soap and washing ⇨ **WASH**

■ to make you smell good
- a substance that men or women use to prevent body smells: **deodorant**
- a liquid that women put on their bodies to make them smell attractive: **perfume, scent** ◦ *What perfume are you wearing?* ◦ *a bottle of perfume* ◦ *an expensive perfume* ◦ *a scent bottle*
- a liquid with a pleasant smell that men put on their faces after shaving: **aftershave** ◦ *a bottle of aftershave*

cost ⇨ PRICE

cough ⇨ ILLNESS

country[1] an area of land with its own people and government

1 being a country
2 the people of a country
3 parts of a country
4 relations between countries
5 moving from one country to another
6 having and showing feelings about your country

1 being a country
- an area of land with its own people, government, etc: **country**, (*formal*) **land** ◦ *Which country do you come from?* ◦ *Wales, the land of song*
- a country with its own government: **state**, (*more formal*) **nation** ◦ *member states of the European Union* ◦ *the nations of Western Europe*

- concerning all of a country: **national** ◦ *a national newspaper*
- over the whole of a country: **nationwide** (*adjective, adverb*) ◦ *a nationwide tour/campaign/survey*

- a country that is headed by a president: **republic**
- a country that is headed by a king or queen: **kingdom, monarchy**
- a country that is a union of states, in which each state retains control of some areas of government business: **federation**; *adjective*: **federal** ◦ *a federal law*

▷ more on government ⇨ **GOVERNMENT**

2 the people of a country
- a person who lives in a country: **inhabitant** ◦ *the inhabitants of India*
- a person who is legally a member of a country: **citizen, national**; *noun* (U): **citizenship** ◦ *a citizen of the United Kingdom* ◦ *French citizens/nationals* ◦ *American citizenship*
- being a citizen of a particular country: **nationality** (*noun* U/C) ◦ *What nationality are you?* ◦ *She has Greek nationality.*
- a person who is born in a particular place: **native** ◦ *She lives in England, but she is a native of Scotland.*
- belonging to the group of people who were the original inhabitants of a country: **indigenous, native** ◦ *The indigenous people of New Zealand are the Maoris.* ◦ *a native American*
- a man/woman from the same country as you is your **fellow countryman/countrywoman**

- all the citizens of a country: **the people** (*noun plural*), **country, nation** ◦ *the people of France* ◦ *The President made a speech to the nation.*
- the number of people who live in a particular place: **population** ◦ *The population of Wales is nearly 3 million.*
- if there are a lot of people living in a place, it is **densely/heavily populated**; if there are few people living in a place, it is **sparsely/thinly populated**
- if there are too many people living in a place, it is **overpopulated**; *noun* (U): **overpopulation**

▷ for a list of countries and adjectives ⇨ p518

3 parts of a country
- a part of a country or of the world: **region**; *adjective*: **regional**
- a part of a country: **area, district** ◦ *the Lake District*
- one of the main areas that a country is divided into: **province**; *adjective*: **provincial**
- an area in Britain, Ireland or America that has its own local government: **county**
- an official division of a country or a town: **district**
- a line that divides the regions or districts of a country: **boundary** ◦ *the county boundary*
- the town or city where the government of a country is: **capital**

4 relations between countries
- a line that divides two countries, and the land close to it: **border, frontier** ◦ *The refugees escaped across the border.* ◦ *the French border/frontier* ◦ *an international frontier*

- if sth belongs to or is connected with a country that is not your own, it is **foreign** ◦ *a foreign country* ◦ *a foreign language*
- a person who belongs to a foreign country: **foreigner**
- in or to a foreign country: **abroad, overseas** ◦ *My grandmother has never been abroad.* ◦ *to go abroad* ◦ *Our son lives overseas.*
- a person who lives outside his/her own country: **expatriate**

- if sth is concerned with what happens inside a country, it is **internal, domestic**; *opposite*: **external** ◦ *a country's internal political and economic affairs* ◦ *domestic flights* ◦ *The current economic problems are caused mainly by external factors.*
- involving two or more countries: **international** ◦ *an international trade agreement* ◦ *English as an international language*

- an agreement between two countries to support each other: **alliance** ◦ *a military alliance*
- if two or more countries have formed an alliance, they are **allied**; a country that you are allied with is your **ally** ◦ *Britain is allied with America.* ◦ *Britain's European allies*

- a country that is ruled or governed by another country: **colony**
- a group of countries that is governed by one country: **empire**
- if a country is not controlled by another country, it is **independent**; *noun* (U): **independence** ◦ *Slovenia became independent from Yugoslavia in 1991.*

- to send goods from one country to another: **export** sth; *noun* (U): **export** ◦ *goods manufactured for export*
- to bring goods into one country from another country: **import** sth; *noun* (U): **import** ◦ *the import of fine wines from abroad*
- goods which are exported: **exports** (*noun plural*); goods which are imported: **imports** (*noun plural*)

5 moving from one country to another

- an official document that you have to show when you leave or arrive in a country: **passport**
- an official mark in your passport that shows that you can leave or enter a country: **visa**

- to go away from your own country to live abroad permanently: **emigrate**; *noun* (U): **emigration**; a person who does this: **emigrant**
- to enter a country to live there permanently: **immigrate**; a person who does this: **immigrant**; the movement of immigrants into a country: **immigration** (*noun* U) ◦ *My grandfather was an immigrant to this country.* ◦ *The government is worried about the increase in immigration.*
- a person who goes to another country to look for work: **migrant**; *adjective*: **migrant** ◦ *a migrant worker*

■ being forced to leave a country

- to send a foreigner away from a country officially: **deport** sb; *noun* (C/U): **deportation**
- to force sb to live outside their own country for political reasons: **exile** sb; *noun* (U): **exile**; a person who lives outside their own country for political reasons: **exile** ◦ *Napoleon was exiled to St. Helena.* ◦ *to go into exile* ◦ *to live in exile* ◦ *Europe was flooded with exiles after the Russian Revolution.*
- a person who is forced to leave their country because it is difficult or dangerous for them to live there: **refugee** ◦ *political/economic refugees* ◦ *a refugee camp*
- protection that a government offers to people who have left their own country for political reasons: **political asylum** (*noun* U) ◦ *to ask for political asylum*
- if you are not a citizen of any country, you are **stateless**; *noun* (U): **statelessness**

6 having and showing feelings about your country

- the country where you were born, or where you feel that you belong: **homeland, home country**, (*formal*) **native land**

- the special song of a country: **national anthem**
- a flag that is used as a symbol of a country: **national flag**

▷ more on flags ⇨ FLAG

- the wish of a people to form an independent country: **nationalism** (*noun* U); *adjective*: **nationalistic**; a person who wishes this: **nationalist** ◦ *Welsh nationalism* ◦ *nationalistic feelings* ◦ *a Scottish nationalist*
- love of your country: **patriotism** (*noun* U); *adjective*: **patriotic**; *opposite*: **unpatriotic**
- a person who loves their country: **patriot**
- to harm or be disloyal to your country: **betray** sth; *noun* (C/U): **betrayal** ◦ *She betrayed her country by selling secrets to the enemy.*
- the crime of helping your country's enemies: **treason** (*noun* U); a person who betrays their country: **traitor** ◦ *to commit treason*

---

country² the countryside (compared to the town)

> different types of land ⇨ LAND
> the surface of the earth ⇨ GROUND
> **see also** FARM, TOWN

- land which is away from towns and cities, usually with fields, trees, etc: **country** (*often* **the country**) (*noun* U), **countryside** (*often* **the countryside**) (*noun* U) ◦ *miles and miles of open country* (= with very few buildings) ◦ *narrow country lanes* ◦ *We try to get out into the country every weekend.* ◦ *They used to live in Paris, so they're finding it hard to adjust to life in the country.* ◦ *the English countryside*
- the natural features that you see in an area of country: **landscape, scenery** (*noun* U) ◦ *the Scottish landscape* ◦ *superb mountain scenery*

Note: we use **the country** particularly when we want to make a contrast with towns and cities; we use **the countryside** when we want to emphasize the natural features of the country (fields, rivers, flowers, etc). **Landscape** and **scenery** both refer to the way the natural features of the countryside are arranged, but **scenery** is used if we want to emphasize the attractiveness of the landscape and our enjoyment of it.

- connected with the country, not the town: **rural** ◦ *rural life*
- connected with the town, not the country: **urban** ◦ *the urban environment*

■ wild and beautiful countryside

- a place which is a long way from the nearest town or main road is **remote, off the beaten track** ◦ *The area is popular with tourists, but our cottage was right off the beaten track.*
- country where people do not live, and there are no farms, etc is **wild**; *noun*: **wilderness** (*usually*

country[2] *contd.*

singular) ∘ *a wild uninhabited region* ∘ *lost in the wilderness*
- flowers and animals found in the countryside and which are not looked after by people are **wild** ∘ *wild strawberries* ∘ *wild horses*

- a place in the country which is attractive and interesting is **picturesque** ∘ *a picturesque village*
- a place which is famous for its beauty: **beauty spot**
- an area of beautiful country which is protected by the government: **national park**

■ rivers, woods, hills, etc
- water that flows down to the sea from higher ground: **river**; a small river: **stream**
- an area that is covered with trees: **wood** (*often plural*), **woodland** (*noun* U); *adjective*: **wooded** ∘ *a walk in the woods* ∘ *woodland flowers* ∘ *a wooded area*
- a large wood: **forest** (*noun* C/U)
- country with hills and mountains is **hilly**, **mountainous**; country without hills or mountains is **flat**
- a wild open area of high land that is covered with grass: **moor, moorland** (*noun* U/C) ∘ *a walk over the moor* ∘ *the Yorkshire moors*
- land that is covered with grass: **grassland** (*noun* U/C)

▷ more on rivers, hills and mountains ⇨ RIVER, HILL/MOUNTAIN

■ where people live in the country
- a group of houses in the country, often with a church, school, shops, etc but smaller than a town: **village** ∘ *a village pub* ∘ *village life*
- a small house in the country, often old and attractive: **cottage** ∘ *a country cottage*
- a large house in the country, often with a lot of land: **country house**

courage ⇨ BRAVE

court ⇨ TRIAL

cow

see also ANIMAL, FARM

- a large female animal that is kept on farms and produces milk: **cow**
- a young cow: **calf** (*plural* **calves**)
- an adult male of the cow family: **bull**
- a male of the cow family used for heavy farm work: **ox** (*plural* **oxen**)
- a group of cows: **herd** ∘ *a herd of cows in a field*
- the general word for cows on a farm: **cattle** (*noun plural*)

▷ picture at ANIMAL

- the sound that cows make: **moo**; *verb*: **moo**
- a loud sound that a bull makes: **bellow**; *verb*: **bellow**

- a farm that keeps cows to produce milk: **dairy farm**; a farmer who owns or runs this kind of farm: **dairy farmer**
- cows which are kept for their milk rather than their meat: **dairy cattle** (*noun* U)
- food that is made with milk, such as butter and cheese: **dairy products** (*noun plural*)
- a farm building where milk is kept to make butter and cheese: **dairy**
- to take milk from a cow: **milk** (a cow) ∘ *We start milking every morning at 6 o'clock.* ∘ *Have you ever milked a cow?*

- meat from a cow: **beef** (*noun* U)
- meat from a calf: **veal** (*noun* U)
- the skin of a cow (or other animal) that is made into leather: **hide** (*noun* C/U)

▷ more on meat ⇨ MEAT

crash ⇨ ACCIDENT

cricket ⇨ SPORT

crime

1 crime
2 different kinds of crime
3 preventing crime and catching criminals
4 trial and punishment
see also LAW

1 crime
- behaviour which is against the law: **crime** (*noun* U); *adjective*: **criminal** ∘ *Is crime on the increase?* ∘ *serious crime* ∘ *to fight crime* ∘ *crime prevention* ∘ *criminal behaviour*
- a criminal act: **crime**, (*formal*) **offence** (*AmE* **offense**)
- to do sth which is against the law: **break* the law, commit** sth ∘ *I didn't realize that I was breaking the law.* ∘ *to commit a crime* ∘ *to commit murder*
- a sudden increase in crime: **crime wave**

- a person who has committed a crime: **criminal**, (*formal*) **offender**
- an organized group of criminals: **gang**; a member of a gang: **gangster**
- a person who helps sb to commit a crime: **accomplice**
- a person who is harmed by a crime: **victim** ∘ *a victim of crime*

2 different kinds of crime
- to take sth that belongs to sb else secretly and without permission: **steal*** (sth) (**from** sb/sth); *noun* (C/U): **theft** ∘ *The safe was open but nothing had been stolen.* ∘ *car theft*
- a person who steals: **thief** (*plural* **thieves**)

▷ more on stealing ⇨ STEAL

- to kill sb on purpose: **murder** sb, **take*** sb's **life**; *noun* (C/U): **murder** ∘ *She was murdered by her gardener.* ∘ *an unsolved murder*
- a man/woman who commits a murder: **murderer/murderess**

▷ more on killing ⇨ KILL

- to make a sudden attack on sb: **assault** sb; *noun* (C/U): **assault** ◦ *to be assaulted in the street* ◦ *assaults on the police*
- to catch sb and keep them prisoner to get money, agreement to political demands, etc: **kidnap** sb, **take*** sb **hostage**
- a person who is caught in this way: **hostage** ◦ *The terrorists released three hostages after the government agreed to their demands.*
- a person who kidnaps sb: **kidnapper**
- to force sb to have sex: **rape** sb; *noun* (C/U): **rape**; a person who commits rape: **rapist**

- the crime of setting fire to a building on purpose: **arson** (*noun* U); a person who commits arson: **arsonist**
- the use of violent action (for example, bombing or shooting) for political reasons: **terrorism** (*noun* U); a person who takes part in terrorism: **terrorist**

- a person who sells illegal drugs: **drug dealer**, (*informal*) (**drug**) **pusher**; selling illegal drugs: **drug dealing** (*noun* U)
- to take things into or out of a country illegally: **smuggle** sth; *noun* (U): **smuggling**; a person who smuggles: **smuggler**

▷ the illegal use of drugs ⇨ DRUGS

- the crime of deceiving sb to get money: **fraud** (*noun* C/U)
- to make a copy of sth to deceive people: **forge** sth; *noun* (C/U): **forgery** ◦ *to forge sb's signature* ◦ *a forged ten-pound note* ◦ *The painting is an obvious forgery.*

- to force sb to give you money, etc to stop you telling a secret about them to other people: **blackmail** sb; *noun* (U): **blackmail**; a person who commits blackmail: **blackmailer**
- to say sth that is untrue about sb so that other people will have a bad opinion of them: **slander** sb; *noun* (U/C): **slander**; a person who commits slander: **slanderer**
- to write sth that is untrue about sb so that other people will have a bad opinion of them: **libel** sb; *noun* (U/C): **libel**

3 preventing crime and catching criminals

- the official organization whose job is to make sure that people obey the law and to prevent and solve crime: **the police** (*noun plural*) ◦ *The police were out in force to control the crowds.*
- a member of the police: **police officer**, **policeman**, **policewoman**, (*informal*) **cop**

▷ more on the police ⇨ POLICE

- a person who protects a building against robbers, etc: **security guard**; a security guard who works at night: **nightwatchman**
- a person (especially a police officer) who tries to find out about a crime, etc: **detective**
- a detective who is not a policeman: **private detective**, (*informal*) **private eye**

- to try to find out all the facts about sth: **investigate** sth; *noun* (C/U): **investigation** ◦ *Detectives are investigating the murder.* ◦ *The police have completed their investigations.*
- to believe that sb committed a crime: **suspect** sb (**of** sth/doing sth); *adjective*: **suspicious** ◦ *Do you suspect me of the murder?* ◦ *His strange behaviour made the police suspicious.*
- if the police believe that sb has done sth wrong, that person is **under suspicion** (**of** sth)
- if sth makes you feel that sb has done sth wrong, it is **suspicious** (*adverb* **suspiciously**) ◦ *He is under suspicion of murder.* ◦ *a suspicious-looking person* ◦ *to behave suspiciously*
- a person who the police think has committed a crime: **suspect**

- something that makes you believe sth: **evidence** (*noun* U) ◦ *There was no evidence that Tony had stolen the television.*
- a person who has seen a crime, etc and can tell others about it later: **witness**
- a mark made by the skin of your finger that is used for identifying you: **fingerprint**
- to give information to the police about sb who has done sth wrong: **inform against/on** sb
- a person who gives the police, etc information about sth that sb has done: **informer**

- (used about the police) to take sb prisoner in order to ask them about a crime: **arrest** sb; *noun* (C/U): **arrest** ◦ *A woman has been arrested in connection with the stolen handbag.* ◦ *The police have made ten arrests.* ◦ *You're under arrest!*
- to go to the police when they are trying to catch you: **give*** yourself **up** (**to** sb) ◦ *We told him he should give himself up.*
- while doing sth wrong: **in the act** (**of** doing sth) ◦ *He was in the act of stealing a car when I spotted him.*
- to find sb just as they are doing sth wrong: **catch*** sb **red-handed** ◦ *A policeman noticed the ladder against the wall and caught the burglars red-handed.*

- to ask sb questions about sth, to find out about a crime: **interrogate** sb; *noun* (C/U): **interrogation** ◦ *I was interrogated by two police officers.* ◦ *The interrogation lasted for five hours.*
- a person who asks sb questions in order to get information: **interrogator**

- to say that sb has broken the law or done sth wrong: **accuse** sb (**of** sth/doing sth); *noun*: **accusation** ◦ *He accused me of stealing apples from his orchard.* ◦ *to make a false accusation*
- to accuse sb officially of committing a crime: **charge** sb (**with** sth); *noun*: **charge** ◦ *He was charged with kidnapping the child.* ◦ *The police brought a charge of murder against him.*

- something you say or write formally: **statement** ◦ *We'd like you to come to the police station and make a statement.*
- to say that you have done sth bad or illegal: **confess** (**to** sth), **confess** (sth) (**to** sb); *noun*: **confession**

crime *contd.*

4 trial and punishment

- a process in which people decide if sb has broken a law: **trial** (*noun* U/C) ◦ *to put somebody on trial* ◦ *a murder trial*
- the person (in a trial) who is said to have broken a law: **the accused** (*plural* **the accused**)
- (in a trial) to decide that sb has broken a law: **find*** sb **guilty** (**of** sth), **convict** sb (**of** sth)
- to tell sb who has been found guilty of a crime what their punishment will be: **sentence** sb (**to** sth) ◦ *The judge sentenced her to prison for two years.*
- the punishment given: **sentence** ◦ *a four-year prison sentence*

▷ more on trials ⇨ TRIAL
▷ punishment ⇨ PUNISH

■ **MORE . . .**

- when criminals stop committing crimes, they (*informal*) **go* straight**
- a statement which says that sb was in a particular place at the time of a crime, so they could not have done it: **alibi** ◦ *John had a good alibi for the night of the murder.*
- a crime story where sb tries to find out who the criminal is: **detective story**
- a book, film, play, etc with a very exciting story, often about a crime: **thriller**

criticism

1 saying what is wrong with people and things
2 saying good and bad things about films, plays, books, etc
saying good things about sb/sth ⇨ PRAISE
see also BLAME, INSULT, COMPLAIN/PROTEST

1 saying what is wrong with people and things

- to say what you think is wrong with sb/sth: **criticize** sb/sth, **find* fault with** sb/sth; *noun* (C/U): **criticism** (**of** sb/sth) ◦ *Why do you always have to criticize everything I do?* ◦ *I have a few criticisms of your plan.* ◦ *He just can't take criticism.*
- a person, a written report, etc that makes criticisms of sb/sth is **critical** (**of** sb/sth) ◦ *The report was highly critical of the management.*
- a person who criticizes sb/sth: **critic** ◦ *one of the government's strongest critics*
- to criticize sb/sth very strongly: **attack** sb/sth, **condemn** sb/sth; *nouns* (C/U): **attack** (**on** sb/sth), **condemnation** (**of** sb/sth) ◦ *a speech condemning the government's policy* ◦ *He made a savage attack on his opponents.*
- to criticize sb continuously in an annoying way: (*informal*) **nag** (sb) (**about** sth), **get* at** sb (**about** sth), **go* on** (**at** sb) (**about** sth) ◦ *She's always nagging me about silly little things.* ◦ *He's always going on at me about my boyfriend.*
- criticism which says that sb/sth is very bad is **severe**, **strong**, **fierce**, **scathing**; *opposite*: **mild**, **gentle** ◦ *The report was scathing in its criticism of the hospital.*
- too critical: **overcritical**
- criticism which is made in order to be helpful is **constructive** ◦ *We welcome constructive criticism.*
- unkind or unfriendly statements about a person's appearance or character are called **personal remarks** ◦ *Let's have no more personal remarks!*
- when you say that a criticism you made earlier was wrong or unfair, you **take*** sth **back**, (*formal*) **withdraw*** sth ◦ *I'd like to take back what I said earlier – I realize now that I was being unfair.* ◦ *'How dare you accuse me of lying!' 'I'm sorry, I take it back.'*

2 saying good and bad things about films, plays, books, etc

- describing the good or bad points of a book, play, film, etc: **criticism** (*noun* U) ◦ *literary criticism*
- to give your opinion about a film, play, book, etc, in a newspaper article or on the television or radio: **review** sth
- a person whose job is to review films, plays, books, etc: **critic**, **reviewer** ◦ *a film/literary critic* ◦ *a film/book reviewer*
- a newspaper article written by a critic: **review** ◦ *a book review* ◦ *The film got good reviews.*

crop ⇨ FARM

crowd

groups of people ⇨ GROUP

- a large number of people in one place: **crowd** (*with singular or plural verb*) ◦ *A crowd was beginning to form outside the prison.* ◦ *The crowd were getting violent.*
- a very large number of people: **crowds** (*noun plural*) ◦ *Crowds of people gathered along the roadside.* ◦ *Large crowds are expected for the football match tomorrow.*
- a large crowd of people that may become violent and cause trouble: **mob** ◦ *There was an angry mob waiting outside as the prisoners left the court.*
- a place which is full of people is **crowded**, (*informal*) **packed** ◦ *It was so crowded in there that I could hardly breathe.* ◦ *The bar was packed so we decided to go somewhere else.*
- a place where there are too many people is **overcrowded**; a situation in which there are too many people: **overcrowding** (*noun* U) ◦ *an overcrowded train/prison/bar* ◦ *Overcrowding is a serious problem in some of the poorer areas of the city.*
- a large number of people in a small space: **crush**, **squash**, **squeeze** ◦ *There was a terrible crush in the lift.* ◦ *I know it's a bit of a squash but I'm sure you can fit in one more person.*
- to put a large number of people in a small place: **pack/squash/squeeze** sb **into, onto**, etc sth ◦

They tried to squash as many people as possible onto the bus.

■ how a crowd forms
- to come together as a group of people: **gather**, **mass** ◦ *A large crowd gathered near the place where the accident happened.* ◦ *Huge numbers of people massed in the central square.*
- to form a crowd around a person or thing: **crowd round** (sb/sth) ◦ *The children crowded round their teacher to hear the results of the competition.*

- when people from a crowd begin to move away in different directions, the crowd **disperses**

■ how a crowd moves
- a large crowd of moving people: **stream** of people ◦ *Streams of people were coming out of the tube station.*
- to go into a place and make it very full: **crowd into** sth ◦ *About fifty people crowded into the room to hear him speak.*
- when a large number of people come out of a place all at the same time, they **pour out** (**of** it) ◦ *The children poured out of the school gates at 3 o'clock.*

- to use force to move or try to move sb: **push** sb (**back**, **away**, etc), **push** (sb), **shove** (sb) ◦ *The police tried to push back the crowd.* ◦ *Fans in the queue were pushing and shoving as they waited to be let in.*
- to try to move through a crowd: **push** your **way through** (sth) ◦ *We'll have to try and push our way through to the front or we won't see anything.*
- to move people as if they were animals: **herd** sb **into**, **onto**, etc sth ◦ *The prisoners were herded into lorries and taken away.*

---

cruel ⇨ KIND/CRUEL

---

cry

see also PAIN, SAD

- to produce water from your eyes, and make a noise, because you are unhappy or have hurt yourself: **cry**, (*formal*) **weep*** ◦ *Don't cry! Everything's going to be all right.* ◦ *The baby was crying all night.*
- one of the drops of water that you produce when you cry: **tear** (*usually plural*) ◦ *She wiped away her tears.* ◦ *The tears started rolling down her cheeks.*
- if sb is crying, they are **in tears** ◦ *She was in tears over the death of her pet dog.*

- if sb is nearly crying, or crying just a little, they are **tearful** (*adverb* **tearfully**) ◦ *Poor little Johnny was rather tearful on his first day at school.*
- to start crying suddenly: **break*/burst* into tears, burst* out crying** ◦ *When I told her the bad news, she burst into tears.*

- if you have been trying not to cry for a long time, but you finally start crying, you **break* down** ◦ *When I said that, it all became too much for her and she finally broke down.*
- to cry very hard for a long time: **cry** your **eyes out**, **cry** your **heart out** ◦ *She's been crying her eyes out all day since she heard the dreadful news.*
- to cry until you fall asleep: **cry** yourself **to sleep** ◦ *I just can't forget him. I cry myself to sleep every night.*
- if you are nearly crying, but you are able to stop yourself, you **choke back the tears** ◦ *'Thank you, you've been so kind,' he said, choking back the tears.*

■ different ways of crying
- to cry while making a noise or while speaking: **sob**; *noun*: **sob** ◦ *'Why did this have to happen?' sobbed the woman.* ◦ *The child let out a loud sob.*
- to cry very loudly, like a baby: **bawl**
- to cry and sniff in an annoying way: **snivel** ◦ *Stop snivelling – you're not a child!*
- to cry with great pain or sadness, making a low noise: **moan**; *noun*: **moan** ◦ *The man was still alive – we could hear him moaning under the wreckage.*
- to cry very loudly and dramatically: **wail**
- to cry quietly, making a high noise: **whimper**; *noun*: **whimper** ◦ *The puppy whimpered with pain.*

■ **MORE ...**
- if a child cries a lot, other children sometimes call him/her a **cry-baby** ◦ *Don't be such a cry-baby!*
- if you cry, not because you are sad, but because your eyes are irritated, you say that your eyes **water** ◦ *These onions are making my eyes water!*

---

cup/glass

see also DRINK

- the general word for all cups, plates and dishes: **crockery** (*noun* U)

- the amount of liquid in a cup/mug/glass: **cup/mug/glass** (**of** sth) ◦ *All I've drunk today is one cup of tea.* ◦ *Another glass of wine?*
- the amount (of anything) that a cup/mug/glass can hold: **cupful/mugful/glassful** ◦ *Add a cupful of milk to the mixture and stir.* ◦ *two cupfuls of flour*

- to take liquid from a cup, glass, etc into your mouth: **drink*** (sth)
- to put liquid into a cup, glass, etc from a jug, bottle, etc, to serve sb: **pour** sth (**for** sb), **pour** sb sth ◦ *Shall I pour the tea?* ◦ *She poured him a glass of beer.*

cup/glass *contd.*

– to put liquid into a cup, glass, etc almost up to the top: **fill** sth (**up**) ∘ *Your glass is almost empty. Shall I fill it up?*
– if a cup, etc is filled right to the top edge, it is **full to the brim**
– to pour sth out of a container by accident: **spill** sth ∘ *I spilt coffee all over the carpet.*

– if a cup, glass, etc has a small piece broken off the rim, it is **chipped**
– if a cup, glass, etc is broken so that you can see a thin line, but it has not broken into pieces, it is **cracked**

cure ⇨ ILLNESS

curtain ⇨ WINDOW

custom

see also BEHAVIOUR, HABIT

– a way of behaving that a particular group has had for a long time: **custom** (*noun* C/U); *adjective*: **customary** ∘ *It's the custom in Britain to say 'Bless you!' to somebody when they sneeze.* ∘ *If you go to live in a place, you should try to accept local customs.* ∘ *According to custom, we give presents at Christmas.* ∘ *It's customary for the bride to wear white.*

– customs, beliefs, etc that have continued from the past to the present: **tradition** (*noun* C/U); *adjective*: **traditional** ∘ *We followed tradition and threw rice over the couple as they came out of the church.* ∘ *to break with tradition* (= not to do sth which is traditional) ∘ *It's traditional to eat turkey on Christmas day.*

– a social or religious custom that does not allow particular actions or words: **taboo** (*plural* **taboos**); *adjective*: **taboo** ∘ *strange customs and taboos* ∘ *taboo words* ∘ *Any swearing by men in the company of women was absolutely taboo.*

– the customs, ideas, religion, art, music, literature, etc of a particular group or society: **culture** (*noun* C/U) ∘ *people of many different cultures* ∘ *changes in language and culture*

cut

getting your hair cut ⇨ HAIR
cutting meat ⇨ MEAT
cutting other food ⇨ COOK
cutting grass ⇨ GRASS
cutting wood ⇨ WOOD

– to make an opening, wound or mark in sth using a sharp tool, for example a knife: **cut*** sth ∘ *Ouch! I've cut my finger!* ∘ *I cut myself shaving.*
– to remove sth from sth larger using a sharp tool such as a knife or scissors: **cut*** sth (**from** sth/**out of** sth/**off** sth), **cut*** sth **out**/**off** ∘ *She cut the dead flowers off the rose bush.* ∘ *He cut out the bad part of the apple.*

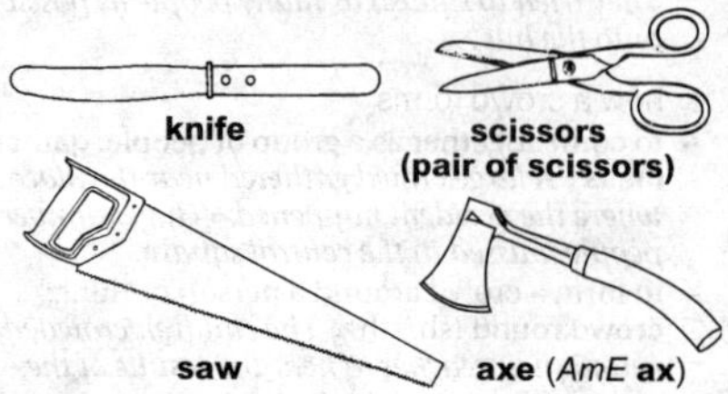

▷ more on knives and other tools ⇨ KNIFE/FORK/SPOON, TOOL

– to divide sth into pieces with a knife, etc: **cut*** sth (**in**/**into** . . .) ∘ *I'll cut the cake into eight.*
– to make a shape by removing material with a sharp tool, for example scissors: **cut*** sth **out** ∘ *The children cut out circles and stuck them onto pieces of card.*
– to be able to cut; to be able to be cut: **cut*** ∘ *This knife doesn't cut very well.* ∘ *This paper doesn't cut very easily.*
– something which cuts things well is **sharp**; *noun* (U): **sharpness**; something which cuts badly is **blunt**; *noun* (U): **bluntness** ∘ *a sharp/blunt knife* ∘ *test the sharpness of a carving knife*
– to make sth sharp: **sharpen** sth ∘ *to get scissors sharpened*

– to cut using scissors, with a short, quick action: **snip** sth; *noun*: **snip** ∘ *Could you just snip this piece of thread for me, please?*
– to cut a long narrow opening in sth: **slit*** sth; *noun*: **slit** ∘ *to slit open an envelope* ∘ *a skirt with a slit up the back*
– to cut sth like paper into small, thin pieces: **shred** sth ∘ *to shred paper*
– to cut sth (especially food) into flat pieces: **slice** sth (**up**) ∘ *Slice the mushrooms and add them to the sauce.*
– to cut sth (especially food or wood) into pieces: **chop** sth (**up**) ∘ *Now chop the onions and put them in the frying pan.* ∘ *to chop logs*

– to cut sth with long strokes: **slash** sth; *noun*: **slash** ∘ *Somebody had slashed our car tyres.*
– to cut sth, making a long, deep wound: **gash** sth; *noun*: **gash** ∘ *She had a horrible gash in her leg from the accident.*
– to cut sth using rough strokes with a tool such as a large knife or an axe: **hack** sth ∘ *The victim had been hacked to death with an axe.*
– to cut sth with the teeth: **bite*** (sth); *noun*: **bite** ∘ *Mind the dog – it sometimes bites.* ∘ *to bite into an apple* ∘ *Do you want a bite of this apple?*
– to cut sth by making a mark on a surface or by making a small wound on sb's skin, with sth sharp: **scratch** sth; an act of scratching or a place which has been scratched: **scratch** ∘ *Someone had scratched the paintwork on the car.* ∘ *'Ouch! I've cut myself!' 'Don't be silly – it's only a little scratch.'*

■ **MORE . . .**
– to cut off a person's arm or leg (or part of it) for medical reasons: **amputate** sth; *noun* (C/U): **amputation** ∘ *He had to have his leg amputated.*

- to cut up a dead body, plant, etc, in order to study its structure: **dissect** sth; *noun* (C/U): **dissection**

cycle ⇨ BICYCLE

damage

1 damage to things
2 damage to people, organizations, etc

1 damage to things

- to make sth useless or not as good as before: **damage** sth; the effect of damaging sth: **damage** (*noun* U) ◦ *Our roof was damaged in the storm.* ◦ *The fire caused £20 000 worth of damage.*
- to be careless or make a mistake, with the result that sth is no longer good: **spoil** sth ◦ *Don't put too much salt in the soup – you'll spoil it.*

- to intentionally damage sb else's property for no reason: **vandalize** sth; *noun* (U): **vandalism**; a person who vandalizes property is called a **vandal** ◦ *We couldn't ring because the phone box had been vandalized.*
- to cause damage intentionally and in secret, in order to stop an enemy or competitor from being successful: **sabotage** sth; *noun* (U): **sabotage**

▪ serious damage

- to damage sth so badly that it can no longer be used or so that it no longer exists: **destroy** sth, **ruin** sth, **wreck** sth ◦ *Several buildings were destroyed in the earthquake.* ◦ *Water got into the building and a lot of valuable paintings were ruined.* ◦ *The boat was wrecked by the storm.*
- the act of destroying sth or being destroyed: **destruction** (*noun* U) ◦ *the destruction of the city*
- causing serious damage: **destructive** ◦ *a highly destructive earthquake/wind/storm*

- a car, plane, boat, etc that has been destroyed as a result of an accident: **wreck**; the wreck of a ship: **shipwreck** ◦ *The wreck of a car was found at the bottom of the cliff.*
- the broken pieces of sth that has been wrecked: **wreckage** (*noun* U) ◦ *Rescue workers are searching for the wreckage of the plane.*

- to destroy sth by making it explode: **blow* sth up**, **blow* sth to bits/pieces** ◦ *The bomb blew the car to bits.*
- to completely destroy a building or buildings by fire: **burn** sth **down**, **burn** sth **to the ground**

▷ destroying a building on purpose ⇨ BUILD

- to break and fall into pieces: **fall* down**, **collapse**; *noun* (U/*singular*) **collapse** ◦ *Many buildings collapsed during the earthquake.*
- to fall to the ground because of the strength of the wind: **be blown down**, **blow* down** ◦ *A tree blew down in the storm.*

- the broken parts of a building which has collapsed: **ruins** (*noun plural*) ◦ *ancient Greek ruins*
- an old, broken-down building: **ruin** ◦ *The house is a ruin – no one lives there now.*
- (of a building) badly damaged or destroyed: **in ruins** ◦ *They came back to find their house in ruins.*

2 damage to people, organizations, etc

- to damage sb's health, a situation, etc: **harm** sb/sth; *noun* (U): **harm** ◦ *This kind of behaviour will harm the reputation of the school.* ◦ *It won't do you any harm to eat a little less.*
- to cause physical damage to sb/yourself, especially in an accident: **hurt*** sb/sth, **injure** sb/sth; *noun* (C/U): **injury** ◦ *I fell and hurt my arm.* ◦ *One person was seriously injured in the accident.*

▷ more on injury ⇨ INJURY

- if sb/sth is likely to hurt or kill sb/sth, it is **dangerous** (*adverb* **dangerously**)
- if sth is likely to harm you, it is **harmful** (**to** you/**to** your **health**), **bad for** you ◦ *Cigarettes are harmful to your health.* ◦ *Too much sugar is bad for you.*
- not dangerous: **safe** (*adverb* **safely**) ◦ *a safe journey* ◦ *Drive safely!*
- not likely to harm anybody: **harmless** (*adverb* **harmlessly**) ◦ *Don't worry – it's just harmless fun.*

▷ more on being dangerous or safe ⇨ DANGEROUS

▪ wanting to harm sb

- to want to harm sb else: **wish** sb **ill**, (*informal*) **have it in for** sb ◦ *I don't wish him ill, I'm just angry with him.*
- to harm sb because you are angry about sth that they did in the past: **take*** (your) **revenge on** sb

■ **MORE ...**

- weak, and easily harmed or damaged: **vulnerable** (**to** sth); *noun* (U): **vulnerability** ◦ *Be kind to him – he's feeling rather vulnerable at the moment.*

- money that you can claim from sb if they injure you or damage your property: **damages** (*noun plural*), **compensation** (*noun* U) ◦ *He broke his leg at work and received £1 000 in damages from his employer.*

dance

see also MUSIC

- to move around in time with music: **dance**; this kind of activity: **dancing** (*noun* U); an act of dancing: **dance** ◦ *People started dancing to the music.* ◦ *Let's dance!* ◦ *I'm going to take up dancing.* ◦ *Can I have the next dance with you?*
- a person who dances: **dancer**; if you dance with somebody else, that person is your **partner** ◦ *dancing partners* ◦ *to change partners*
- dancing as a form of art or entertainment: **dance** (*noun* U) ◦ *traditional/modern dance*

- a party where people dance together: **dance**, (*formal*) **ball** ◦ *an invitation to a dance* ◦ *to go to a ball*
- part of a room where people can dance: **dance floor**
- a large room that is used for traditional kinds of dancing: **ballroom**

dance *contd.*

- a place where people dance to popular music on records, etc: **disco** (*plural* **discos**), (*formal*) **discotheque** ∘ *to go to a disco* ∘ *disco dancing*
- a person whose job is to play and to introduce pop music in a disco or on the radio: **disc jockey, DJ**

▷ parties ⇨ PARTY

■ different kinds of dancing
- a particular way of dancing: **dance**
- one movement of a dance: **step** ∘ *I've forgotten the steps.*
- to do a particular dance: **dance** sth ∘ *to dance the waltz*

- a kind of dancing in which couples do formal dances together, usually holding each other: **ballroom dancing** (*noun* U)
- a kind of dancing in which couples are arranged in lines or circles and dance to traditional music: **country dancing** (*noun* U)
- a kind of dancing in which you tap different rhythms on the floor with special shoes: **tap-dancing** (*noun* U)
- a dance which has a three-beat rhythm: **waltz**; *verb*: **waltz**
- a dance which started in the 1940s in America, using jazz and rock and roll music: **jive**; *verb*: **jive**
- a dance which is traditional in a particular area: **folk dance**
- a story that is told with music and dancing but without words: **ballet**; works of this kind: **ballet** (*noun* U) ∘ *a performance of Tchaikovsky's ballet 'The Nutcracker'*
- a person who dances in ballets: **ballet dancer**; a female dancer can also be called a **ballerina**

■ **MORE ...**
- a person whose job is to plan the movements for a dance: **choreographer**; this work and the result of it: **choreography** (*noun* U) ∘ *the ballet 'Les Sylphides', with choreography by Mikhail Fokine*

dangerous

1 dangerous
2 not dangerous
3 doing sth dangerous
4 avoiding danger

1 dangerous
- if sb/sth is likely to hurt or kill sb/sth, it is **dangerous** ∘ *Boxing is a dangerous sport.* ∘ *a dangerous criminal* ∘ *a dangerous road*
- an activity that is dangerous is **risky** ∘ *It was a risky operation, but without it he would certainly have died.*
- the chance that sb/sth might be hurt or killed or that sth unpleasant might happen: **danger** (*noun* C/U), **risk** (*noun* C/U) ∘ *There was a real danger that the building would collapse.* ∘ *Journalists are used to facing danger.* ∘ *'Are there any risks involved in taking this medicine?' 'No, there's no risk at all.'*
- if sb/sth is so dangerous that it can kill you, it is **deadly, lethal** ∘ *a deadly poison* ∘ *a lethal weapon*

- if a problem or situation is important because it might be dangerous, it is **serious**; *noun* (U): **seriousness** ∘ *a serious illness* ∘ *the increase in serious crime* ∘ *I don't think you understand the seriousness of the situation.*
- a situation or an event that is dangerous and serious: **emergency**; *adjective*: **emergency** (*only before a noun*) ∘ *The doctor was called out on an emergency.* ∘ *The plane had to make an emergency landing.*

- a person or a thing that is dangerous: **danger** (**to** sb/sth), **threat** (**to** sb/sth), **risk** (**to** sb/sth) ∘ *the dangers of drugs* ∘ *a threat to national security* ∘ *Throughout the journey we were exposed to a lot of risks.*
- if sth dangerous may happen to you, you are **in danger** (**of** sth), **at risk** (**of** sth) ∘ *I was in danger of losing my job.* ∘ *at risk of catching cholera*

2 not dangerous
- not dangerous: **safe** (*adverb* **safely**); *noun* (U): **safety** ∘ *Don't sit on that chair. It isn't safe.* ∘ *You should put your wallet in a safe place when you are walking in the street.* ∘ *a safe driver* ∘ *Is it safe to drink the water here?* ∘ *Drive safely!*

- free from danger or from possible injury, damage, etc: **safe** (**from** sb/sth); *noun* (U): **safety** ∘ *I never feel safe walking home alone at night.* ∘ *Keep the papers where they will be safe from fire.* ∘ *She has been missing for several days and police now fear for her safety.* ∘ *road safety* ∘ *In the interests of safety, smoking is forbidden.*
- not hurt or damaged: **safe and sound** ∘ *The children were found safe and sound after spending a night in the forest.*
- not likely to be lost; safe: **secure**; *noun* (U): **security** ∘ *financial security*
- when a dangerous situation has ended, you are **out of danger**

3 doing sth dangerous
- to cause danger to sb/sth: **put*** sb/sth **at risk**, (*formal*) **endanger** sb/sth ∘ *Don't put your health at risk by overworking.* ∘ *to endanger sb's life*
- to do sth even though you know that sth dangerous or unpleasant may happen as a result: **risk** sth ∘ *If you give up your job now, you risk a long period of unemployment.*
- to do sth that you know might be dangerous: **take* a risk, take* risks, take* chances** ∘ *If you want to succeed in life you'll have to take risks.*
- to do sth for which you might be killed or punished: **risk** your **life, risk** your **neck** ∘ *The man risked his life to rescue the boy.*

- not afraid of doing dangerous or physically difficult things: **brave** (*adverb* **bravely**)
- to try to persuade sb to do sth dangerous or difficult to show that they are brave: **dare** sb (**to** do sth) ∘ *I dare you to run across the railway track when the train is coming.*

- an experience that is unusual, exciting or dangerous: **adventure** (*noun* C/U)

▷ more on being brave ⇨ **BRAVE**

4 avoiding danger

- to tell sb about sth bad which might happen, and to advise them to be careful: **warn** sb (**of/about** sth), **warn** sb **against** (doing) sth, **warn** sb **not to** do sth; *noun* (C/U): **warning** ◦ *They put up a red flag to warn you against swimming when it's dangerous.* ◦ *I warned you not to disturb the dog while it was asleep.*
- a machine which warns you about danger with a bell or other loud noise: **alarm** ◦ *I don't know why the car alarm went off.*

▷ more on warning ⇨ **WARN**

- to keep sb/sth safe from danger or attack: **protect** sb/sth (**against/from** sb/sth); *noun*: **protection** ◦ *vaccines to protect children from polio*
- to make or keep sb/sth safe from danger, death, loss, etc: **save** sb/sth (**from** sth) ◦ *You saved my life!*
- to save sb/sth from sth that is dangerous or unpleasant: **rescue** sb/sth (**from** sb/sth); *noun*: **rescue**; a person who does this: **rescuer** ◦ *The boys were rescued from the burning house.* ◦ *the mountain rescue services* ◦ *Rescuers arrived at the scene within the hour.*

- to cause sth not to happen: **prevent** sth, **prevent** sth (**from**) happening, **avoid** sth ◦ *How can we prevent war breaking out?* ◦ *We only just managed to avoid a serious crash.*
- a thing that you do in order to avoid danger or problems: **precaution** (*often plural*) ◦ *We took the precaution of taking out travel insurance before we went on holiday.*
- to be careful or pay special attention to sb/sth that is dangerous: **watch out** (**for** sb/sth), **look out** (**for** sb/sth) ◦ *Watch out! There's a hole in the pavement.* ◦ *Look out for the low beam at the top of the stairs.*

▷ more on protecting people and preventing danger ⇨ **PROTECT, AVOID/PREVENT**

- a written notice warning people to be careful of sb/sth may say **Beware** (**of** sb/sth) or **Danger!** ◦ *Beware of the dog!* ◦ *Danger – men at work!*

dare ⇨ BRAVE

dark ⇨ LIGHT[2]

date

see also **DAY, WEEK, YEAR**

- a particular day of the month or of the year: **date** ◦ *What date is it today?* ◦ *Today's date is 27th October 1996.* ◦ *What's your date of birth?*

- to write the date on a letter or document: **put* the date on** sth, **date** sth ◦ *Don't forget to put the date on the letter.* ◦ *The letter is dated 20th July.*
- to arrange a date to do something: **set*/fix a date** (**for** sth) ◦ *Let's have lunch sometime. Shall we fix a date for next week?* ◦ *They've set a date for the wedding at last.*
- to set a date in the past: **backdate** sth (**to** sth) ◦ *The pay award is backdated to April.* ◦ *a back-dated cheque*
- when sth belongs to a period in the past, it **dates back to** sth ◦ *It's a lovely old table – it dates back to the eighteenth century.*

- a time or date in the future when a task must be completed: **deadline** ◦ *The teacher set a deadline of two weeks for the essays to be handed in.*

- the end of the period when sth can be used: **expiry date**
- an expiry date on food: **sell-by date** ◦ *Don't eat the meat – it's past its sell-by date.*
- when sth will pass or has passed its expiry date it **expires** ◦ *You'd better check that your passport hasn't expired.*
- sth which has expired is **out of date** ◦ *You can throw out your library card now – it's out of date.*
- the date by which you must send in an entry or application for sth: **closing date**

daughter ⇨ FAMILY

day

1 today, tomorrow, etc
2 times of day
3 special days
see also WEEK, YEAR

1 today, tomorrow, etc

- a period of 24 hours: **day** ◦ *It took me three days to get to Adelaide.* ◦ *a ten-day holiday* ◦ *I'll be back in a day or two.*

▷ days of the week ⇨ **WEEK**

- this day: **today**
- the day before this day: **yesterday** ◦ *yesterday morning*
- the day after this day: **tomorrow** ◦ *tomorrow evening*
- two days ago: **the day before yesterday**
- two days after today: **the day after tomorrow**
- three, four, etc days after today: **in** three, four, etc **days' time**, three, four, etc **days from now**
- three, four, etc days before today: three, four, etc **days ago**
- a few days ago: **the other day** ◦ *I saw Mary in town the other day.*

- done or happening every day: **daily** (*adjective, adverb*) ◦ *a daily routine* ◦ *The equipment is checked daily.*
- to emphasize that sth is happening every day over a period of time, you can say **day by day** ◦ *She's getting stronger day by day.*

2 times of day

- the time when most people are awake: **day** ◦ *During the day, he worked as a bank clerk. At night, he painted.* ◦ *I like to begin my day with a good breakfast.* ◦ *Winter was approaching. The days were getting shorter.*
- the part of the day when it is light: **daytime** (*noun* U) ◦ *Come and see my new house in the*

day *contd.*

daytime so you can get a good look at the garden as well. ◦ *a daytime TV programme*
- the time when it is dark and people usually sleep: **night** (*noun* C/U)
- the part of the day when it is dark: **night-time** (*noun* U) ◦ *I don't like going out at night-time.*

▷ more on night ⇨ NIGHT

- the beginning of the day: **dawn** (*noun* C/U), **daybreak** (*noun* U), **sunrise** (*noun* U) ◦ *We got up at dawn.* ◦ *at the crack of dawn* (= very early in the morning) ◦ *It was not yet daybreak when the crowds started gathering outside the stadium.*
- the first part of the day until about 12 o'clock: **morning** ◦ *I'll see you in the morning.* ◦ *During the morning I write, but in the afternoon I like to go walking in the woods.*
- the middle part of the day, around 12 o'clock: **noon** (*noun* U), **midday** (*noun* U) ◦ *at noon* ◦ *after midday*
- the part of the day between noon and about 5 pm: **afternoon**
- the part of the day after 5 pm and before you go to bed: **evening** ◦ *I'll phone this evening.*
- the end of the day when the light begins to disappear: **dusk** (*noun* U), **sunset** (*noun* C/U)
- the middle of the night at 12 o'clock: **midnight** (*noun* U)

Note: you say **in/during the morning, afternoon, evening, daytime**; but **at dawn, noon, midnight, night-time**; you can say **in/during the night** or **at night**.

- to emphasize the whole day, you can say **the whole day long, the whole day through, all day long** ◦ *I've been studying for my exams all day long.*

3 special days
- the day in each year which has the same date as the day you were born: **birthday**
- 14th February: **St Valentine's Day**
- 25th December: **Christmas Day**
- the day to celebrate all mothers/fathers: **Mother's/Father's Day**
- the day before a special day or an important event: **eve** ◦ *Christmas Eve* ◦ *New Year's Eve* ◦ *on the eve of the election* (= just before the election)
- a day of rest from work or school: **holiday**

▷ more on holidays ⇨ HOLIDAY

dead ⇨ DIE

deaf ⇨ HEAR

debt

1 being in debt
2 paying debts
3 not paying debts

see also BORROW/LEND, BANK, PAY[1], MONEY

1 being in debt
- when you have to pay money to sb for sth they have done for you or given you, you **owe** them some money; money that is not yet paid is **owing** (*not before a noun*) ◦ *You owe me £5.* ◦ *How much is still owing to you?*

- an amount of money that you owe sb: **debt**
- when you owe an amount of money to sb, you are **in debt** (**to** sb); if the amount of money is large, you are **heavily** in debt
- after you have given back the money, you are **out of debt, no longer in debt**

- if you spend more money than you have in your bank account, you are **overdrawn**, (*informal*) **in the red**; an amount of money that you have spent that is more than the amount that you have in your bank account: **overdraft**
- if you still have some money in the bank, you are **in credit**, (*informal*) **in the black**

- a person who owes money: (*formal*) **debtor**
- a person who is owed money: (*formal*) **creditor**

- if you spend too much and do not pay the money you owe, you **get* into debt, run* up debts** ◦ *In just three weeks in London my daughter ran up debts of more than £1 000!*
- when sth has to be paid immediately, it is **due** ◦ *Your rent is due today.*

2 paying debts
- to pay the money you owe sb: **pay*** (**off**) a debt, **settle up** with sb ◦ *By Christmas, I hope to have paid off all my debts.* ◦ *I've just been paid, so I can settle up with you now.*

3 not paying debts
- a debt that has not yet been paid is **unpaid**, (*formal*) **outstanding**
- if you do not have enough money to pay your debts, you may become **bankrupt**; *noun* (U/C): **bankruptcy** ◦ *He couldn't pay his debts and became bankrupt.* ◦ *Her business career ended in bankruptcy.* ◦ *Economic difficulties are causing increasing numbers of bankruptcies.*
- to cause sb to become bankrupt: **bankrupt** sb ◦ *That house is much too expensive; the mortgage repayments will bankrupt us.*

- not paying a debt or a bill: (*formal*) **non-payment** (*noun* U) ◦ *The council prosecuted me for non-payment of my council tax.*
- to fail to pay money on time: **be/get* behind with** sth, **be in arrears with** sth ◦ *I'm three months behind with the rent.*

deceive

see also LIE[1], HONEST, TRUST

- to make sb think or believe sth that is not true: **deceive** sb (**into ...**), **trick** sb (**into ...**), **fool** sb (**into ...**) ◦ *He didn't deceive me for long.* ◦ *He fooled me into thinking it would be really easy.*
- to persuade sb to do sth by deceiving them: **deceive/fool** sb (**into** doing sth) ◦ *They were deceived into giving him all their money.*

– to persuade sb to believe sth or do sth by saying or promising sth that is false: **take* sb in** ◦ *Don't be taken in by his charming manner. He's a liar and a cheat.*

– the act of deceiving sb: **deceit** (*noun* U), **deception** (*noun* U) ◦ *He got the money out of me by deceit.*
– a thing that you do in order to deceive sb: **trick**, **hoax**, (*formal*) **deception** ◦ *The whole story of her disappearance turned out to be a hoax.* ◦ *a cruel deception*
– a person who carries out hoaxes: **hoaxer**

– to act dishonestly or unfairly in order to get sth, usually money, from sb or to win a game or competition: **cheat**; a person who cheats: **cheat** ◦ *He often cheats at cards, so watch him.* ◦ *My sister's a terrible cheat.*
– to take sth, usually money, from sb in a dishonest or unfair way: **cheat** sb **out of** sth ◦ *The company cheated its employees out of the pensions they had paid for.*
– to cheat sb by asking too much money for sth: (*informal*) **rip** sb **off** ◦ *You paid £100 for that watch? You've been ripped off!*

– to change sth, particularly a document or information, in order to deceive people: **falsify** sth ◦ *The police were accused of falsifying evidence.*
– the crime of deceiving sb in order to get money: **fraud** (*noun* C/U) ◦ *He was sent to prison for fraud.*

– a person or action that is dishonest and tries to deceive people is **deceitful** (*adverb* **deceitfully**) ◦ *It was such a deceitful thing to do – I shall never trust her again.*
– if sb is good or clever at deceiving people, they are **cunning** (*adverb* **cunningly**) ◦ *a cunning liar*

– if sth is likely to deceive sb or give a false impression, it is **deceptive** (*adverb* **deceptively**), **misleading** ◦ *Appearances can be deceptive.* ◦ *deceptively easy* (= not as easy as it looks) ◦ *I think the programme gave a rather misleading impression of what's actually happening.*

■ pretending to do sth or be sth
– to seem to do sth or to be sth in order to deceive sb: **pretend** (**to** do/be sth), **pretend** (**that**) ... ◦ *She's not really ill – she's only pretending!* ◦ *When he saw his boss coming, he pretended to be busy.* ◦ *We got into the pub by pretending we were over eighteen.*
– to pretend to be feeling sth: **put*** sth **on** ◦ *Don't worry about him being angry with you. He was just putting it on.*

– to pretend to be sb else: **pose as** sb/sth ◦ *He tried to get into the concert free by posing as a newspaper reporter.*
– a person who poses as sb else in order to deceive people: **impostor**
– to pretend to be another person by copying the way they act or speak: **impersonate** sb; *noun*: **impersonation** ◦ *He makes us laugh by impersonating famous people.*
▷ copying the behaviour of a person ⇨ BEHAVIOUR

– clothes, false hair, etc that you wear so that nobody recognizes you: **disguise** (*noun* C/U); to wear a disguise: **disguise** sb/yourself (**as** sb/sth) ◦ *I wonder if he would recognize us if we put on a disguise?* ◦ *She decided to go to the party in disguise so nobody would recognize her.* ◦ *The thief disguised himself as a security guard.*

■ **MORE ...**
– if sb can easily be deceived because they believe what other people tell them, they are **gullible**; *noun* (U): **gullibility** ◦ *You can be so gullible sometimes!*

– pretending to think or feel sth which in reality you do not: **hypocrisy** (*noun* U); *adjective*: **hypocritical** (*adverb* **hypocritically**) ◦ *He had the hypocrisy to say that people shouldn't behave like that!* ◦ *Politicians are so hypocritical, always saying one thing and doing another.*
– a person who is hypocritical: **hypocrite**

decide/choose

1 deciding
2 choosing
3 thinking before you decide or choose sth
4 changing or not changing a decision
5 good or bad at deciding
choosing sb in an election ⇨ ELECTION

1 deciding
– to think about two or more things and choose one of them: **decide** sth, **decide on/against** sb/sth, **decide to** do sth ◦ *Have you decided what you're going to do?* ◦ *The committee are taking a long time to decide on the matter.* ◦ *Eventually we decided against buying that particular house.* ◦ *I've decided not to take that job.*
– what you have decided: **decision** (**on** sth/**to** do sth) ◦ *I'm afraid our decision is final.* ◦ *I've made a decision to sell the house.*
– to decide sth (and be determined not to change your mind): **make* up** your **mind** (**to** do sth), **resolve to** do sth ◦ *I've made up my mind to work harder.*

– to decide on a date, price, etc: **set*** sth, **fix** sth ◦ *Linda and John have set a date for their wedding.* ◦ *'How much will it be?' 'I don't know; we haven't fixed a price yet.'*

– to come to a decision after a lot of discussion or thought: **arrive at a decision**, **reach a decision**, **come* to a decision** ◦ *We finally reached a decision about where to go on holiday.*
– a belief or an opinion that you reach after thinking about sth for a long time: **conclusion**
– to arrive at a particular conclusion: **come* to the conclusion that ...** ◦ *The conclusion we came to was that the school should be closed.*

2 choosing
– to decide what you want from a number of possible things: **choose*** (**between** A **and** B), **choose*** sb/sth (**as** sth); the act of choosing: **choice** ◦ *I had to choose between my family and my work.* ◦ *'Which film shall we go and see?' 'I*

decide / choose contd.

don't mind – you choose.' ◦ *John has been chosen as spokesman for the group.* ◦ *He faced a difficult choice.* ◦ *to make the right/wrong choice*
- to choose sb/sth from a group: **pick** sb/sth (**out**), (*formal*) **select** sb/sth (**as** sth); the act of selecting: **selection** (*noun* U) ◦ *I was surprised when they picked me for the job.* ◦ *The best candidates will be selected for interview.* ◦ *the selection of the football team*

- the right or chance to choose: **choice** (*noun* U), **option** (*noun* U) ◦ *We had to sell – we had no choice.* ◦ *'We're asking you to resign.' 'Do I have any option?'*
- if you can choose to do or not to do sth, it is **optional**; *opposite*: **obligatory** ◦ *The school offers some optional courses.*

- careful in choosing: (*informal*) **choosy** ◦ *She's very choosy about what she eats.*
- carefully chosen: **hand-picked** ◦ *These men have been hand-picked for the job.*
- chosen by chance: **random** (*adverb* **randomly**) ◦ *a random selection of songs* ◦ *randomly selected numbers*

■ different possibilities to choose between
- two or more things that you can choose from: **choice** ◦ *There's a good choice of food on the menu.*
- one of two things that you can choose between: **alternative**; *adjective*: **alternative** (*only before a noun*) (*adverb* **alternatively**) ◦ *If hotels are too expensive, youth hostels are a cheaper alternative.* ◦ *alternative arrangements* ◦ *Alternatively, you can go by bus.*
- a thing that you can choose: **option** ◦ *Helen looked carefully at all the options before deciding on a career.*

- if you like one person or thing more than another, you **prefer** sb/sth (**to** sb/sth) ◦ *I don't know which one I prefer – I can't choose!*
- to prefer to do sth: **choose* to** do sth ◦ *If you choose to ignore my advice, don't blame me if things turn out badly.*

▷ more on preferring sb/sth ⇨ PREFER

- a person or thing that has been chosen: **choice** ◦ *I admire your choice.*
- a number of people or things that have been chosen: **selection** ◦ *He sang a selection of his best-known songs.*

3 thinking before you decide or choose sth
- to think carefully about sth in order to make a decision: **consider** sth, **weigh** sth **up**
- to think carefully before deciding to do sth: **think*** sth **over**

- something that you need to decide about: **question, problem** ◦ *Tom's resignation raises the question of who will take over from him.* ◦ *The problem is urgent and we need to reach a decision soon.*
- the reasons for and against doing sth: **pros and cons** ◦ *You should consider all the pros and cons before you make a decision.*
- having considered all the facts and views: **on balance** ◦ *On balance, I think you've made a wise decision.*

▷ problems ⇨ PROBLEM

- to be willing to listen to or consider new ideas or suggestions: **have/keep* an open mind** ◦ *The police are keeping an open mind about the latest death.*
- not to be sure about what you should do: **have mixed feelings** (**about** sb/sth) ◦ *Julie had mixed feelings about leaving school.*

- if you want time to think about what sb has asked you before you give your answer, you say **I'll see** or **We'll see** ◦ *'Can we go to London for Easter, Daddy?' 'I'll see.'*
- if it is your responsibility to decide sth, it is **up to** you ◦ *It's up to you to decide what to do.*

- if you have not yet made a decision about sth, you are **undecided** ◦ *We are still undecided about where to go on holiday.*

4 changing or not changing a decision
- to change your decision: **change** your **mind** (**about** sb/sth) ◦ *Have you changed your mind about going to see him?*
- doubts about a decision you have made: **second thoughts** ◦ *I think he must be having second thoughts.*
- to decide not to do sth that you had promised to do: **back out** (**of** sth) ◦ *You can't back out of it now!*

- to continue to support a decision: **stand* by a decision, stick* to a decision** ◦ *He stood by his decision not to go.*
- if decisions are not changed, they **stand*** ◦ *Does your decision still stand?*

5 good or bad at deciding
- if you are good at making clear decisions quickly, you are **decisive** (*adverb* **decisively**); *opposite*: **indecisive** (*adverb* **indecisively**) ◦ *a decisive leader* ◦ *to act decisively* ◦ *His enemies accused him of being indecisive.*
- if you firmly decide to do sth, even if it is difficult or people are against you, you are **determined** (**to** do sth); *noun* (U): **determination** ◦ *She showed great determination to succeed in the job.*
- decisive and determined: **strong-willed** ◦ *You need to be strong-willed if you want to succeed in politics.*

■ **MORE ...**
- a situation in which you have to make a difficult choice between two or more things: **dilemma** ◦ *She was in a dilemma whether to report the matter or keep quiet.*
- to find it difficult to choose between two things: (*informal*) **be torn between** A **and** B ◦ *I'm torn between the blue dress and the green skirt.*

- to delay making a decision: **keep*/leave*** your **options open** ◦ *You should leave your options open until you have more information.*
- to delay making a decision until the following day: **sleep* on** sth ◦ *Okay, let's sleep on it and decide in the morning.*
- to be unwilling to decide between two things: **sit* on the fence** ◦ *You can't sit on the fence for ever – you'll have to make up your mind soon.*

- the standard that you use when you make a decision: **criterion** (*plural* **criteria**) ◦ *What are the criteria for deciding whether somebody should be promoted?*

decrease ⇨ INCREASE / DECREASE

deep

see also SIZE, HEIGHT

- the measurement of sth from top to bottom: **depth** (*noun* C/U) ◦ *the depth of a hole* ◦ *at a depth of 2000 metres*
- (used about things which are open at the front) the amount sth measures from the front to the back: **depth** (*noun* C/U) ◦ *The depth of the cupboard was 70 cm.*
- having a certain depth: **deep** ◦ *During last year's floods, the water in the High Street was nearly six feet deep.*

▷ picture at SIZE

- going a long way from the top to the bottom or from the front to the back: **deep** (*adjective, adverb*) ◦ *the deep end of a swimming pool* ◦ *a deep cut* ◦ *a deep hole* ◦ *The roots of this tree reach deep into the soil.* ◦ *to get deeper*
- not going a long way from the top to the bottom: **shallow** ◦ *a shallow river*

■ being in deep water
- if you are in water which reaches as far as your waist, the water is **knee-deep**, you are **knee-deep** in the water ◦ *She was standing knee-deep in the middle of the stream.*
- if you are in water which reaches as far as your waist, the water is **waist-deep**, you are **waist-deep** in the water
- if you go into water so that you can not put your feet down, you are **out of your depth** ◦ *Don't get out of your depth.*

defeat ⇨ WIN / LOSE

defend

- when fighting ⇨ FIGHT
- taking care of sb / sth ⇨ PROTECT

definite ⇨ POSSIBLE[1]

degree

- measure of an angle ⇨ ANGLE
- fairly, very, etc ⇨ FAIRLY / VERY
- measure of heat ⇨ HOT
- obtained at a university ⇨ UNIVERSITY

delay ⇨ EARLY / LATE

demand ⇨ REQUEST

democracy ⇨ GOVERNMENT

dentist

see also TOOTH

- a person whose job is to look after people's teeth: **dentist** ◦ *I went to the dentist for a check-up.*
- the work of a dentist: **dentistry** (*noun* U) ◦ *She studied dentistry at Dundee University.*
- the business of a dentist (or group of dentists): **practice** ◦ *Another dentist has joined the practice.*

- the place where a dentist works: **(dentist's) surgery**, (*informal*) **the dentist's** ◦ *to go to the dentist's*
- the person who arranges when you see a dentist: **receptionist**
- the time that you arrange to see a dentist: **appointment** ◦ *I'm sorry I'm late for my appointment.*
- the room in which you wait to see a dentist: **waiting room**

- the piece of furniture on which you sit or lie while the dentist treats you: **(dentist's) chair**
- if you go to the dentist's just to see if your teeth are healthy, you go for a **check-up**
- pain in your teeth: **toothache** (*noun* U/C) ◦ *Have you got toothache?*
- the substance that a dentist puts in a tooth that has a hole in it: **filling**; the dentist **fills** the tooth ◦ *I had three fillings last time I saw the dentist.*
- the tool which a dentist uses to make holes in teeth: **drill**; *verb*: **drill** (sth)
- to reduce the pain, a dentist may **give*** you an **injection**

▷ a note on toothache and other aches ⇨ PAIN

- if one of your teeth is removed, you **have** the tooth **out**; the dentist **takes*** the tooth **out**, (*formal*) **extracts** the tooth; *noun*: **extraction** ◦ *The tooth was so badly decayed that I had to have it out.*
- artificial teeth: **false teeth**, (*formal*) **dentures** ◦ *She went to have her new dentures fitted.*

depart ⇨ LEAVE

depend

- needing help ⇨ HELP
- needing sb / sth ⇨ NEED
- able to be trusted ⇨ TRUST

descend ⇨ CLIMB

describe

see also STORY, INFORM

- to say what sb/sth is like, or what has happened: **describe** sb/sth (**as** sth); *noun* (C/U): **description** ◦ *Can you describe to me what happened?* ◦

describe *contd.*

He was described as a young man in his early twenties. ◦ *The police need a description of the thief.*
- a description of sth that happened: **account** (**of** sth), **report** (**of/on** sth); *verb*: **report** (**on**) sth ◦ *We have asked for a full report on this incident.* ◦ *Give me an account of what happened.*
- providing a description: **descriptive** ◦ *a piece of descriptive writing*

- a small fact or piece of information: **detail**; the details of a description: **detail** (*noun* U) ◦ *Make sure you tell them all the details.* ◦ *an artist who pays great attention to detail*
- including all the details: **in detail** ◦ *I'd like you to describe the meeting in detail.*
- to describe sth in detail: **go* into detail(s)** ◦ *I'm afraid I haven't got time to go into detail(s) now.*

- an important or noticeable part of sth: **feature** ◦ *An unusual feature of this house is its pair of beautiful curved staircases.*
- a quality that is typical of sb/sth: **characteristic**; *adjective*: **characteristic** (*adverb* **characteristically**), **typical** (*adverb* **typically**) ◦ *It's a well-known characteristic of chameleons that they can change their colour.*

▷ typical ⇨ **TYPE**

- including a lot of detail: **detailed** ◦ *a detailed description of the house*
- containing a lot of facts: **factual** ◦ *a factual account of the event*
- containing a lot of ideas from the imagination of the speaker or writer: **imaginative** ◦ *imaginative writing*
- including a lot of interesting details: **colourful**, **vivid** ◦ *a colourful description of life in the army* ◦ *a vivid description of the scene*

- something that cannot easily be described is **beyond description**, **indescribable** (*adverb* **indescribably**) ◦ *beautiful beyond description* ◦ *living in indescribable conditions* ◦ *indescribably ugly*

desert ⇨ **LAND**

design

making things ⇨ **MAKE**
drawing pictures ⇨ **DRAW**

- the way in which sth is planned and made: **design** (*noun* U) ◦ *I'm not very impressed by the design of their new house.* ◦ *a design fault in the car engine* ◦ *interior design* (= the design of the insides of houses)
- the shape or arrangement in which it is planned to make sth: **design** ◦ *to produce a new design for a car, dress, kitchen*
- to plan, draw and develop sth for a particular purpose: **design** sth ◦ *She's been given the job of designing all the furniture for the new civic centre.*
- the art and skill of producing designs: **design** (*noun* U) ◦ *a student of garden design*
- a drawing which shows the design of sth: **design** ◦ *The architect showed me the designs for our new offices.*
- a quick, simple drawing of sth without much detail: **sketch**; to make a drawing of this type: **sketch** sth ◦ *Can you do me a quick sketch of the kind of design you have in mind?*
- a three-dimensional design of sth: **model** ◦ *If you go to the Town Hall, you can see a model of the new shopping centre.*
- the characteristics (materials, dimensions, etc) that the object being designed should have: **specifications** (*noun plural*) ◦ *They've changed the specifications and the cost will probably go up now.*
- if sth is designed for a specific purpose or person, it is **tailor-made** (**for** sb/sth) ◦ *holidays tailor-made for single people*

■ style and decoration
- the fashion, shape or design of sth: **style** ◦ *the latest styles in boots* ◦ *buildings designed in a classical style*
- a combination of colours in a design: **colour scheme**
- the way in which paint, wallpaper, etc are used to make a room look attractive: **decoration** (*noun* U)
- the furnishing and decoration of a room: **decor** ◦ a room with stylish and modern decor
- (used about a design) attractive to look at: **decorative**
- a regular arrangement of lines, shapes, colours, etc: **pattern**, **design**
- having a pattern: **patterned**

▷ picture of patterns ⇨ **CLOTH**

- without decoration: **simple** (*adverb* **simply**), **plain** (*adverb* **plainly**); *nouns* (U): **simplicity**, **plainness** ◦ *The basic design is very simple.* ◦ *You need a plain blouse with that patterned skirt.* ◦ *I like the simplicity of the decoration in this room.*
- not simple: **complicated**, **elaborate**
- very complicated: **intricate** (*adverb* **intricately**); *noun* (U): **intricacy** ◦ *an intricate pattern* ◦ *intricately carved chairs*

■ people who design things
- a person who designs things: **designer**
- a person who makes drawings, plans or sketches, especially of buildings or machines: **draughtsman** (*plural* **draughtsmen**) (*AmE* **draftsman**, *plural* **draftsmen**)
- a person who designs buildings: **architect**
- a person who designs clothes: **fashion designer**
- a person who designs and arranges furniture, objects, etc inside houses, offices, etc: **interior designer**

▷ more on buildings and clothes ⇨ **BUILDING, CLOTHES**

destroy ⇨ DAMAGE

develop

1 development
2 lack of development
see also CHANGE, GROW

1 development

- to grow slowly or change into sth else: **develop** (**from** sth) (**into** sth); *noun* (U): **development** ○ *We have developed from a small firm into a large multinational company.* ○ *the development of tourism*
- to develop naturally and gradually: (*formal*) **evolve**; *noun* (U): **evolution** ○ *His ideas on adult education evolved over a very long period.* ○ *the evolution of man*
- to become sth: **grow*** (**from** sth) (**into** sth); *noun* (U): **growth** ○ *to grow from a caterpillar into a butterfly*

- to develop and improve: **progress, come* along**; *noun* (U): **progress** ○ *'How's your work going?' 'It's progressing slowly.'* ○ *The project's coming along quite well now.* ○ *I've not been able to make much progress with my work today.* ○ *social progress*
- a change which speeds up the development of sth: **a step forward** ○ *a big step forward in the search for a cure for cancer*

- to cause sth to develop: **develop** sth; *adjective*: **developed** ○ *Start by stating your opinion, then develop your argument.* ○ *a fully developed plan*
- fully developed (either emotionally or physically): **mature**; *noun* (U): **maturity** ○ *She's very mature for her age.*
- highly developed: **advanced** ○ *advanced technology* ○ *an economically advanced country*

- to develop sth so that it becomes bigger in size, number or importance: **build* sth up** ○ *We're trying to build up our workforce.*
- to use sth as a base on which to develop ideas, etc: **build* on** sth ○ *Teachers should build on the knowledge that their students already have.*

■ stages in development

- the original idea, plan, etc from which sth develops: **basis** (*plural* **bases**) ○ *a good basis for further development*
- a period in the development of sth: **stage, step, phase** ○ *The first stage of development is when the child recognizes its mother's face.* ○ *an important step in the transition to a full market economy* ○ *We're now moving into the last phase of our plan.*
- an important development in sth: **breakthrough** ○ *a major breakthrough in cancer research*

2 lack of development

- not developed: **undeveloped** ○ *undeveloped ideas*
- below what is normal in development: **underdeveloped** ○ *The children were severely underdeveloped due to a lack of food.*
- very simple and not developed: **primitive** ○ *the history of primitive man* ○ *The facilities were very primitive – there were no showers or baths.*

- (used about countries and areas) poor and with little industry: **underdeveloped**; *opposite*: **developed** ○ *a shift of resources from developed to underdeveloped countries*
- the state of being underdeveloped: **underdevelopment** ○ *problems of undervelopment*
- trying to have more industry and a more advanced economic system: **developing** ○ *the developing nations*

- slow to learn or develop: **backward** ○ *a backward child who took a long time to learn to walk and talk*
- not yet fully developed (either emotionally or physically): **immature**; *noun* (U): **immaturity** ○ *He's too immature to get married – I think they should both wait until they're older.*

- to fail to develop or to make sth develop: **make* no progress, not get* anywhere** (**with** sth) ○ *We soon saw that we were making no progress so we decided to change our approach.* ○ *I'm getting absolutely nowhere in this job!*
- to stop sth from developing for a time: **set*** sb/sth **back**; *noun*: **setback** ○ *The computer failure has really set us back – we won't be finished until next week now.* ○ *Their plans suffered a setback.*

devil ⇨ SPIRIT

diamond ⇨ JEWELLERY

dictionary ⇨ WORD

die

1 dying and its causes
2 people who have died
3 after a person dies
4 existence after death
see also KILL

1 dying and its causes

- to stop living: **die**, (*formal*) **pass away**; *noun* (C/U): **death** ○ *She died peacefully.* ○ *She was told that her brother had passed away.* ○ *Most people are afraid of death.*
- to die suddenly: (*informal*) **drop dead** ○ *He dropped dead from overwork.*
- to be very ill and near to death: **be at death's door**

- a person or thing that will die is **mortal**; *opposite*: **immortal** ○ *All men are mortal.*

■ causes of death

- to die because of an illness or condition: **die** (**of/from** sth) ○ *She died of malaria.* ○ *He died from his wounds.* ○ *to die of natural causes* (= from old age or illness)
- to die because of an accident: **die in** sth ○ *How many people died in that plane crash?*
- to die in water (or other liquid) because it is impossible to breathe: **drown**

die *contd.*

- to die because you have no food: **starve to death**, **die of/from starvation**
- to die because there is no air to breathe: **suffocate**; *noun* (U): **suffocation**
- to die because it is very cold: **freeze* to death**

- something that can cause death is **deadly**, **lethal** ◦ *a deadly poison* ◦ *a lethal weapon*
- something that actually causes death is **fatal** ◦ *a fatal accident*
- to put your life in danger: **risk** your **life** ◦ *She risked her life to save her friend.*
- if sb does sth which results in their death, the action **costs*** them their **life** ◦ *His attempt to climb the mountain in bad weather cost him his life.*

▷ dangerous actions or situations ⇨ DANGEROUS

2 people who have died

- not being alive: **dead** ◦ *She had been dead for some hours.*
- people who have died: **the dead** (*noun plural*); *opposite*: **the living** ◦ *a church service in memory of the dead of two world wars* ◦ *Now we have to think of the living.*
- a person who has died is sometimes referred to as (*formal*) **the late ...** ◦ *the late Mr Hargreaves* ◦ *her late mother*

- a person who is killed or injured in a war or an accident: **casualty**; a person who is killed in this way: (*formal*) **fatality** ◦ *There were several fatalities in the crash.*
- the number of deaths in a certain period of time or in a certain place: **mortality** (*noun* U) ◦ *Infant mortality is high in some inner city areas.*

- the dead body of a person: **body**, **corpse** ◦ *The police have found a body in the canal.* ◦ *The corpse has been identified.*

3 after a person dies

- the place (in a hospital, etc) where dead bodies are kept before burial: **mortuary**, **morgue**
- medical examination of a dead body to find out how the person died: **post-mortem**, **autopsy**
- an official investigation to find out about an unexplained death: **inquest** ◦ *The inquest recorded a verdict of accidental death.*
- an official piece of paper that says that sb has died: **death certificate**
- an article about a person's life that is printed in a newspaper soon after their death: **obituary** ◦ *Have you read her obituary in 'The Times'?*
- something that is given to sb after they have died is **posthumous** (*adverb* **posthumously**) ◦ *His medal was awarded posthumously.*

▷ burying or burning a dead body ⇨ FUNERAL

- the legal document in which you write down who should have your money and property after you die: **will**; in this document you **leave*** sth **to** sb, (*formal*) **bequeath** sth **to** sb ◦ *His aunt left him some money in her will.*
- to receive money or property from a person who has died: **inherit** sth; the money or property that you receive: **inheritance**, **legacy** ◦ *She inherited a fortune from her father.*

- a woman whose husband has died and who has not married again: **widow**; a man whose wife has died and who has not married again: **widower**

■ thinking about people who have died

- the feeling of sadness caused by the death of sb you love: **grief** (*noun* U); to feel this sadness: **grieve** (**for** sb) ◦ *He is still grieving for his mother.*
- if you dress or behave in a special way because you are sad that sb has died, you are **in mourning** ◦ *They are still in mourning for their brother.*
- something which reminds people of sb who has died is **in memory of** sb ◦ *a monument in memory of soldiers killed in the war*

4 existence after death

- existence after death: **life after death** (*noun* U), **afterlife** ◦ *Do you believe in an afterlife?*
- the part of a person which some people think continues to exist after death: **soul**, **spirit** ◦ *the spirits of the dead*
- the place where some religions say good people will go when they die: **heaven**; the place where bad people will go: **hell**

different

1 A is not B
2 A is not exactly like B
3 A is completely different from B
see also CHANGE, SAME

1 A is not B

- different from the one or ones that have already been mentioned or understood: **other/another** ◦ *'Is she doing linguistics?' 'No, she's taking some other course, but I'm not sure what.'* ◦ *If you don't like it, get another one.*
- completely different: **separate** ◦ *It happened on three separate occasions.* ◦ *We sat at separate tables.*
- all the others: **the rest** ◦ *We'll have one chocolate each and keep the rest for later.*

Note: after words formed with 'any-', 'no-', or 'some-', and after question words, you can say that sb/sth is different by adding **else** ◦ *There's nothing on television. Let's find something else to do.* ◦ *Who else do you know here?*

2 A is not exactly like B

- not the same: **different** (**from/to** sb/sth) (*AmE also* **different than** sb/sth), **dissimilar** (**from/to** sb/sth) ◦ *My brother and I have very different characters.* ◦ *The street seemed very different from what I remembered.* ◦ *The survey showed quite dissimilar attitudes between the rich and the poor.*
- not the same as: **unlike** sb/sth ◦ *The soup tasted unlike anything I had ever eaten before.*
- different in size, amount, level, etc: **unequal** ◦ *It was an unequal contest because he was a better player than me.* ◦ *unequal sizes*

- to be different: **differ** (**from** sb/sth) ◦ *How does life in Britain differ from life in Italy?*
- the way in which, or the amount by which, people or things are not the same: **difference** (**in** sth), **difference** (**between** A and B) (*noun* C/U) ◦ *There's not much difference in price but there's a huge difference in quality.* ◦ *There are obvious differences between our lives and theirs.*

- clearly different: **distinct** (**from** sb/sth); a clear difference: **distinction** (**between** A and B). ◦ *Mozart's musical style is quite distinct from Beethoven's.* ◦ *There is a clear distinction between British English and American English.*
- clearly different and easy to recognize: **distinctive** ◦ *She wore a distinctive red hat and was easy to spot in the crowd.*
- a clear difference between people or things that is seen when they are compared: **contrast** (*noun* C/U); *adjective*: **contrasting** ◦ *I noticed a great contrast between the two writers.* ◦ *contrasting styles*
- to be clearly different: **contrast** (**with** sth) ◦ *Their attitudes to work contrast greatly. Jim loves his job, and John doesn't like work at all.*

- (used about a number of things) to be different from each other: **vary**; *noun* (C/U): **variation**; *adjective*: **various** ◦ *The size of the classes vary from ten to twenty students.* ◦ *There might be a slight variation in the price from shop to shop.* ◦ *We sell hats in various sizes and colours.*
- something that is only a little different from sth else is a **variation** (**on/of** sth) ◦ *It's not a new style, it's just a variation on an older one.*
- the quality of not being the same: **variety** (*noun* U) ◦ *There's not much variety in the houses around here.*

- a number of things which are different from each other: **variety** (**of** sth) (*noun singular*) ◦ *There's a large variety of wildlife in this area.* ◦ *It's a beautiful garden, with an amazing variety of unusual plants.*
- if several different types of people or things are together, they are **mixed**, **miscellaneous**; *noun*: **mixture** ◦ *mixed nuts* ◦ *a miscellaneous collection of photographs* ◦ *a mixture of nationalities*

■ showing or telling the difference

- to see how two or more people or things are different: **tell* the difference** (**between** A and B), **distinguish between** A and B, **distinguish** A **from** B ◦ *Can you tell the difference between butter and margarine?* ◦ *to distinguish right from wrong/between right and wrong*
- if you can tell the difference between two people or things, they are **distinguishable** ◦ *The male bird is distinguishable from the female by the colour of its beak.*
- to make sb/sth different from others: **distinguish** A (**from** B) ◦ *We distinguished the copies from the original by putting a red mark in the corner.*
- to show the difference between people or things: **draw*/make* a distinction between** A and B ◦ *Let's draw a distinction between writing for pleasure and writing for your living.*
- to see or show how sb/sth is similar to or different from sb/sth else: **compare** A and B, **compare** A **with/to** B; *noun* (C/U): **comparison** ◦ *If you compare them carefully, you'll see that this one is much better made.* ◦ *Let's make a comparison between the two methods.*
- to compare people or things in order to show the differences between them: **contrast** A **and/with** B ◦ *The film contrasts his poor childhood with his later life as a millionaire.*

▷ comparing and contrasting ⇨ COMPARE/CONTRAST

3 A is completely different from B

- as different as possible: **opposite**; a word or sth that is as different as possible from sth: **opposite** (**of** sth) ◦ *the opposite sex* ◦ *Ugly is the opposite of beautiful.* ◦ *Black and white are opposites.*
- the opposite of what you expect or what you have just said: **reverse** ◦ *I thought the job would be very relaxing, but it was just the reverse.*
- completely different from sth: **contrary to** sth ◦ *Contrary to what I had been told, the job turned out to be quite easy.*
- when the opposite of sth is true, you can say **on the contrary** ◦ *'You look terrible today. Are you ill?' 'On the contrary, I've never felt better.'*

■ **MORE ...**

- completely new and different: **revolutionary**; to make sth completely different: **revolutionize** sth ◦ *The Internet is a revolutionary way of communicating with people.* ◦ *This tool will revolutionize gardening.*

---

difficult ⇨ EASY/DIFFICULT

---

dig ⇨ GROUND

---

dinner ⇨ MEAL

---

direction

> **1** different directions
> **2** north, south, east, west
> **3** finding your way
> where sb/sth is ⇨ PLACE[1]
> parts and positions of things ⇨ PLACE[2]

1 different directions

- the line along which sb/sth is moving: **direction** ◦ I think we're going in the wrong direction. ◦ *Which direction is the wind coming from?*
- in a direction directly on the other side from sb/sth: **in the opposite direction** ◦ *'Where's Jackie?' 'Didn't you see her? She went off in the opposite direction.'*

- in the direction that is in front of you: **forwards**, **forward**; *adjective* (*only before a noun*): **forward** ◦ *I need to face forwards in trains, otherwise I feel ill.* ◦ *The car began to move forward.* ◦ *a sudden forward movement*
- in the direction that is behind you: **back**, **backwards**, **backward**; *adjective* (*only before a noun*): **backward** ◦ *The police made everybody*

direction *contd.*

move back. ◦ *He stepped backwards and fell into the river.* ◦ *a backward movement*
- the opposite way to what is usual: **backwards** ◦ *If you look at writing in the mirror, it reads backwards.* ◦ *to walk backwards*
- first in one direction, then the other: **backwards and forwards** ◦ *I've been going backwards and forwards between my flat and the office all day.*

- into sth or towards the centre of sth: **in, inwards, inward** ◦ *Could you all move in a little please?* ◦ *We stood in a circle and faced inwards.*
- out of sth or away from the centre of sth: **outwards** ◦ *The ripples on the pond spread outwards.* ◦ *This door opens outwards.*

- towards a higher place: **up, upwards, upward**; *adjective* (*only before a noun*): **upward** ◦ *We looked up, but we couldn't see anything.* ◦ *an upward movement*
- towards a lower place: **down, downwards, downward**; *adjective* (*only before a noun*): **downward** ◦ *Put the cards on the table facing downwards.*

- towards the side: **sideways** (*adjective, adverb*) ◦ *to make a sideways movement* ◦ *She jumped sideways to avoid the car.* ◦ *Can you turn your head sideways please?*
- in a direction towards the right/left side: **right/left** ◦ *to turn right* ◦ *to move to the left*

▷ right and left ⇨ RIGHT/LEFT

■ going in a particular direction
- the place towards which sb/sth is going: **destination** ◦ *We reached our final destination just before two o' clock in the morning.*

- to move in the direction of a place: **head for** sth, **make* for** sth ◦ *Let's head for that farm in the distance – they might be able to help us.*
- to take a direction which leads you away from the main path, road, etc: **branch off** ◦ *We have to branch off at the next road on the left.*

2 north, south, east, west

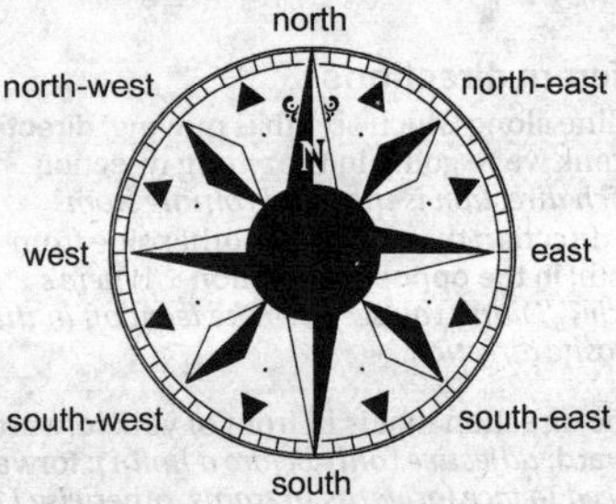

- in a direction towards the north/south/east/west: **north, northwards / south, southwards / east, eastwards / west, westwards** ◦ *We flew north for about an hour and then turned east.* ◦ *to drive westwards*

Note: a **north wind**, **south wind**, etc is a wind blowing from (not to) the north, south, etc.

- a railway, road, etc which goes towards the north/south/east/west is **northbound/southbound/eastbound/westbound** ◦ *You have to take the Victoria line southbound to get to the main railway station.* ◦ *There has been an accident on the northbound carriageway of the M1.*
- to a place usually north/south of where you are: **up/down** ◦ *I'm going up north for a job interview next week.* ◦ *Our cousins from Scotland are coming down to London.*

- in or facing the north/south/east/west: **north/south/east/west** ◦ *Her room is in the north wing of the hospital.* ◦ *the south-west coast of France*
- in or from the north/south/east/west of a place: **northern/southern/eastern/western** ◦ *He's got quite a strong northern accent.* ◦ *the southern states of the US*
- coming from or belonging to the East or Far East: **Oriental** ◦ *She's studying Oriental languages at university.*
- the part of the world which is furthest north/south, and where it is very cold: **North/South Pole**; of or near the North or South Pole: **polar** ◦ *These animals are mostly found in the polar regions of the world.*

- a person who comes from the north/south of a country: **northerner/southerner**

3 finding your way

- to find out where you are and in which direction you should be going: **find*** your **way** ◦ *It's hard to find your way in this place – all the roads look the same.*
- not to know where you are or in which direction you should be going: **be/get* lost, lose*** your **way** ◦ *Oh dear, I think we're lost.* ◦ *I'm surprised Henry hasn't arrived yet – I hope he hasn't lost his way.*

- to tell sb the best way to get to a place: **direct** sb, **give*** sb **directions** ◦ *I've given all the guests directions, so nobody should get lost.*
- to ask sb how to get to a place, you say **How do I get to ...** or **Can you tell me the way to ...** or **What's the best way to ...** ◦ *What's the best way to the station from here?*
- the ability to find your way easily: **sense of direction** ◦ *Don't ask me where we are – I've got no sense of direction.*

▷ going from one place to another ⇨ TRAVEL

dirt

- material which is not clean ⇨ CLEAN/DIRTY
- soil ⇨ GROUND

dirty ⇨ CLEAN/DIRTY

disagree

- in a discussion or argument ⇨ DISCUSS/ARGUE
- not having the same opinion as sb ⇨ OPINION

disappear

– no longer existing ⇨ **REAL/EXISTING**
– no longer seen ⇨ **SEE**

discover ⇨ FIND

discuss/argue

1 discussing
2 agreeing and disagreeing
3 arguing
4 topics of discussion or argument
5 opinions and reasons
6 ending an argument

see also CONVERSATION, MEETING, OPINION, SAY, SPEAK

1 discussing

– a serious conversation about a particular subject: **discussion** (*noun* C/U), **talk** (*noun* C/U) ◦ *We had a long discussion about politics.* ◦ *I think this needs further discussion.* ◦ *We'd better have a talk with Sarah about this.* ◦ *There's been plenty of talk but too little action.*
– to talk about sth seriously or formally: **discuss** sth (**with** sb), **talk about** sth (**with** sb), **talk** (**to** sb) (**about** sth), **talk** sth **over** (**with** sb) ◦ *When can we meet to discuss this?* ◦ *I'll talk to Peter about this and see what he says.* ◦ *I'll have to talk this over with my wife before I make a final decision.*
– to think about or discuss sth before deciding what to do: **debate** sth (**with** sb); *noun* (C/U): **debate** ◦ *They're debating what to do next.* ◦ *There's been a lot of debate about whether she should resign.*

– to discuss sth with sb before making a decision: **consult** (**with** sb) (**about** sth); *noun* (C/U): **consultation** ◦ *The President will consult with her advisers before making an announcement.* ◦ *private consultations* ◦ *The plan was introduced without proper consultation.*
– a formal discussion, for example between politicians: **talks** (*noun plural*) ◦ *Talks between the two leaders were held in Dublin yesterday.*

– to discuss sth in order to try to reach an agreement: **negotiate** (sth); *noun* (C/U): **negotiation** ◦ *The deal took nine months to negotiate.* ◦ *negotiations between trade unions and management* ◦ *There's no point in further negotiation.*
▷ more on negotiation ⇨ **AGREEMENT**

2 agreeing and disagreeing

– to think the same thing as another person: **agree** (**with** sb) (**on/about** sth), **agree with** sth; *noun* (U): **agreement** ◦ *I entirely agree with you on that.* ◦ *I agree with that idea absolutely.* ◦ *He said he was in total agreement with the Prime Minister on the subject of a single European currency.*
– if you agree with sb about sth, you are **with** sb (**on** sth), you **go* along with** sth ◦ *I'm with you on that.* ◦ *I don't go along with that idea.*
– if you agree only partly with sb/sth, you agree **up to a point** ◦ *I agree (with you) up to a point, but I don't think that's the real reason for his bad behaviour.*

– to have a different opinion from sb: **disagree** (**with** sb) (**on/about** sth), **disagree with** sth; *noun* (U): **disagreement** ◦ *They seem to disagree about almost everything.* ◦ *He's bound to disagree.* ◦ *There's been considerable disagreement on the subject.*
– to have a different opinion from sb: **differ** (**with** sb) ◦ *We differ on several important issues.*
– to say sth which means that what sb else has said is not true: **contradict** (sb/sth) ◦ *Why do you always contradict me?* ◦ *She contradicted everything he said.*

– if people accept that they have different opinions about sth and cannot agree, they **agree to differ**

■ saying that you agree

– to show that you agree with sb/sth, you can say: **Of course** or **Sure** or **I agree** (**with you**) or **You're quite right** (**about that**)
– to move your head up and down to show that you agree with sb/sth: **nod** (your **head**) ◦ *As I spoke, Charles was nodding his head in agreement.*
– if you agree with sth but you are not entirely happy about it, you can say **I suppose so** ◦ *'So do you accept what I'm saying?' 'I suppose so.'*

■ saying that you disagree

– to show that you do not agree with sb/sth, you can say: **I don't think so** or **I don't agree** (**with you**) or **I don't think that's right** or (*informal*) **No way!**
– to move your head from side to side to show that you do not agree with sb/sth: **shake*** (your **head**) ◦ *As I spoke, John was shaking his head in disagreement.*

3 arguing

– to talk (often angrily) about sth which you disagree with sb about: **argue** (**with** sb) (**about/over** sth); *noun* (C/U): **argument** ◦ *John could argue about politics all night.* ◦ *Stop arguing!* ◦ *I don't want to get into an argument with you about this.* ◦ *An argument blew up* (= started suddenly) *over who should chair the talks.* ◦ *a heated* (= angry) *argument*
– an argument or difference of opinion: **disagreement** ◦ *We had a disagreement with our neighbours over the noise they were making.*

– to argue angrily: **quarrel** (**with** sb) (**about/over** sth); an angry argument: **quarrel**, **row** ◦ *Pete's always quarrelling with his sister.* ◦ *She's had another row with her boyfriend.* ◦ *a row over money*
– a noisy argument, especially about sth which is not important: **squabble** (**with** sb); *verb*: **squabble** (**about/over** sth) ◦ *The children are squabbling over which TV channel to watch.*
– to argue with sb: (*informal*) **have it out** (**with** sb) ◦ *I went back to the shop and had it out with the manager.*
– a disagreement about sth, especially a legal matter or money: **dispute** (*noun* C/U), **conflict**

discuss/argue *contd.*

(*noun* C/U) ◦ *a pay dispute* ◦ *a bitter* (= angry) *dispute* ◦ *to avoid conflict between management and workers*

– to try to start an argument with sb: **pick a quarrel** (**with** sb) ◦ *Don't take any notice of him – he's just trying to pick a quarrel.*
– a person who argues a lot is **argumentative**, **quarrelsome** ◦ *He's become much more argumentative recently.* ◦ *a quarrelsome child*

4 topics of discussion or argument

– the thing that is being discussed: **subject**, **topic**, **issue** ◦ *Why do you keep trying to change the subject?* ◦ *I'm surprised nobody has raised the issue of unemployment.*
– if sth is not certain and could be discussed, it is **arguable**, **debatable** ◦ *A lot of what she said was highly arguable.* ◦ *a debatable point*
– something which you are discussing is **under discussion** ◦ *the topic under discussion*
– something which you are arguing about is **in dispute** ◦ *The cause of the accident is still in dispute.*
– a topic which a lot of people discuss: **talking point** ◦ *The future of the royal family has become quite a talking point in recent months.*

– public discussion and disagreement: **controversy** (*noun* C/U) ◦ *a new controversy over the death penalty* ◦ *His decision created a great deal of controversy.*
– something which causes controversy is **controversial** ◦ *a controversial statement*

5 opinions and reasons

– the different opinions held by two or more people are the different **sides** of an argument or discussion ◦ *It's important to see* (= understand) *both sides of the argument.*
– one set of opinions in an argument or discussion: **point of view** ◦ *Try to see my point of view.*
– to support one side of an argument against the other: **take* sides** ◦ *Both of them appealed to me for support but I refused to take sides.*
– if you do not get involved in an argument, you **stay out of** it ◦ *I'm glad I managed to stay out of it.*

– to give your opinion about sth and your reasons for what you think: **argue that . . .**, **argue for/against** sth; *noun* (C/U): **argument** ◦ *I've always argued that the business should expand.* ◦ *argue for the right to strike* ◦ *Sally argued against raising prices again so soon.* ◦ *an unconvincing argument*

– to agree with sb/sth and help that side: **support** sb/sth; *noun* (U): **support**; a person who supports sb/sth: **supporter** ◦ *Who supports that idea?* ◦ *I support Mary on this one.* ◦ *Can I rely on your support?*
– to disagree with sb/sth and help the other side: **oppose** sb/sth; *noun* (U): **opposition**; a person who opposes sth: **opponent** (**of** sth) ◦ *They're sure to oppose the plan.* ◦ *There's been a lot of opposition to the idea.* ◦ *a strong opponent of nuclear power*
– if you disagree with sth, you are **opposed to** it ◦ *I've always been opposed to experiments on animals.*
– to speak clearly and publicly against sth: **speak* out** (**against** sth) ◦ *She was the only one to speak out against the closure of the hospital.*

▷ more on supporting or not supporting sb/sth ⇨ **SUPPORT**

– the reasons for and against sth: **pros and cons** ◦ *We were discussing the pros and cons of having a national lottery.*
– a particular idea or opinion which is part of a discussion: **point** ◦ *I don't think you've quite understood my point.*
– a point that is connected to the discussion is **relevant**; *noun* (U) **relevance** ◦ *I'm afraid I don't see the relevance of that remark.*
– a point that is not connected to the discussion is **irrelevant**; *noun* (U) **irrelevance** ◦ *an irrelevant point/comment*
– to draw a person's attention to a point in an argument: **point** sth **out** ◦ *He pointed out that I had said exactly the same myself a little earlier.*
– to show by arguing that what you are saying is true: **prove** your **case/point** ◦ *I think I've proved my point.*

– a good argument which it is hard to disagree with is **persuasive**, **convincing**, **valid** ◦ *an extremely persuasive argument* ◦ *I don't think that argument is valid.*
– a poor argument which it is hard to agree with is **weak**, **feeble**, **unconvincing** ◦ *The arguments against us were very weak and we easily won the debate.*

– to make the final remark in a discussion or argument: **have the last word** ◦ *She always has to have the last word, even when she knows that she's wrong.*

6 ending an argument

– to be the person who is more successful in an argument: **win*** an argument; *opposite*: **lose*** an argument ◦ *I think you lost that argument!*
– to end an argument or disagreement: **come* to an agreement**, **reach** (**an**) **agreement**, **settle** sth ◦ *After weeks of argument, they've finally come to an agreement.* ◦ *It doesn't look as if they'll ever settle their differences.*

– when you become friendly with sb again after an argument, you **make* up**, **make* it up** (**with** sb), you are (*formal*) **reconciled** (**with** sb); *noun* (C/U): **reconciliation** ◦ *Why don't you two kiss and make up?* ◦ *Has she made it up with him yet?* ◦ *They were finally reconciled after months of disagreement.* ◦ *to bring about a reconciliation*
– to come between two people to try to make them stop arguing: **intervene** (**in** sth) ◦ *The headmaster decided it was time he intervened in the dispute.*

▷ agreeing about plans and arrangements ⇨ **AGREEMENT**

■ **MORE ...**

– a formal discussion or argument between two sides, for example in Parliament: **debate**; *verb*: **debate** (sth) ◦ *a debate in the House of Commons on Britain's future in Europe* ◦ *MPs debated the proposal till after midnight.*

– the topic of a formal debate: **motion** ◦ *Tonight's motion will be, 'This house believes that smoking should be banned in public places'.* ◦ *to speak for/against the motion*

– the people who speak against the motion in a formal debate: **the opposition** ◦ *speaking for the opposition*

disease ⇨ ILLNESS

dish ⇨ PLATE/BOWL/DISH

dishonest ⇨ HONEST

dislike

1 feeling that you do not like sb/sth
2 describing the person or thing that you do not like
3 showing or saying that you do not like sb/sth
see also LIKE[2]

1 feeling that you do not like sb/sth

– to think that sb/sth is unpleasant: **not like** sb/sth, **dislike** sb/sth, **not care for** sb/sth; *noun (singular)*: **dislike** (**of/for** sb/sth) ◦ *What is it about him that you dislike?* ◦ *I don't really care for football.* ◦ *She developed an intense dislike for her colleague.*

– to decide that you dislike sb/sth: **take* a dislike to** sb/sth ◦ *I don't know why, but he took a dislike to me from the start.*

– to dislike sb/sth very strongly: **hate** sb/sth, **loathe** sb/sth ◦ *I hate it when you go away.* ◦ *She loathes maths.*

– if you find sb/sth very unpleasant, you **can't stand** sb/sth, **can't bear** sb/sth ◦ *I can't stand violence.* ◦ *I couldn't bear it if you went away.*

– the feeling that you have if you dislike sb/sth very strongly: **hatred** (**of/for** sb/sth) (*noun* U/C), **hate** (*noun* U) ◦ *It's sad that there is so much hatred between people in the world.* ◦ *an intense hatred of injustice* ◦ *love and hate*

– a feeling of disliking sth so much that it makes you feel ill: **disgust** (**at** sth) (*noun* U); if you have this feeling, you are **disgusted** (**by** sth) ◦ *She felt a sense of disgust at so much cruelty.* ◦ *I was disgusted by the amount of waste.*

– a strong feeling of dislike towards sb/sth that is not based on reason or experience: **prejudice** (**against** sb/sth) (*noun* C/U); having or showing prejudice: **prejudiced** (**against** sb/sth) ◦ *racial prejudice* ◦ *He seems to be strongly prejudiced against modern teaching methods.*

– to think that sb/sth has no good qualities: **despise** sb/sth ◦ *I despise him for his laziness.*

– the feeling that you have if you despise sb: **contempt** (**for** sb) (*noun* U); *adjective*: **contemptuous** (*adverb* **contemptuously**) ◦ *I feel nothing but contempt for people who steal.* ◦ *She looked at me contemptuously. 'How could you do that?' she said.*

– to dislike sb/sth because you think that you are better than them: **look down on** sb ◦ *I have a feeling he looks down on me because I come from a poor family.*

– to dislike sth because you think it is not good enough for you: (*informal*) **turn your nose up at** sth ◦ *We shouldn't turn our noses up at their offer – it's better than nothing.*

– to feel that sb/sth is not acceptable or satisfactory: **disapprove** (**of** sb/sth); *noun* (U): **disapproval**; *adjective* **disapproving** (*adverb* **disapprovingly**) ◦ *My grandmother disapproves of women wearing short skirts.* ◦ *I saw the look of disapproval on her face.*

– to dislike or be against sb/sth: **object to** sb/sth; *noun*: **objection** ◦ *I strongly object to having to listen to that sort of bad language.* ◦ *Do you have any objections to the plan?*

– to feel annoyed, unhappy or uncomfortable because of sb/sth: **mind** sb/sth ◦ *Would you mind if I opened the window?* ◦ *I don't mind staying at home to look after the children.*

– to start disliking sb/sth, or to lose interest in sb/sth: **go* off** sb/sth ◦ *'I thought you were going to start learning Greek.' 'I was, but I've gone off the idea now.'* ◦ *I've gone off him since I heard what he did to Sophie.*

– to cause sb to dislike sth: **put*** sb **off** sth/doing sth ◦ *Falling off her horse has put her off riding.*

2 describing the person or thing that you do not like

– a person or thing that you dislike is **bad**, **nasty**, **unpleasant** ◦ *a bad day at the office* ◦ *a nasty remark/sight/taste* ◦ *an unpleasant experience*

– unpleasant to look at or listen to: **ugly**, **unattractive**; very ugly: **hideous** ◦ *an ugly building/town/person* ◦ *an unattractive child* ◦ *The view has been ruined by some hideous new buildings.*

▷ more on being bad or unpleasant ⇨ **BAD**

▷ attractive and unattractive ⇨ **BEAUTIFUL/ATTRACTIVE**

– liked by very few people: **unpopular**; *noun* (U): **unpopularity** ◦ *Your decision to change the timetable is unpopular with the students.* ◦ *an unpopular politician*

3 showing or saying that you do not like sb/sth

– to show or say that you do not like or agree with sth: **protest** (**about/against/at** sth); *noun* (C/U): **protest**; a person who makes a protest: **protester** ◦ *The students protested about the conditions in their classrooms.* ◦ *If they ask us to work extra hours again, we'll organize a protest.* ◦ *The miners went out on strike in protest against pit closures.*

– to state that you disagree with sth: **object** (**to** sth); *noun* (C/U): **objection**; a person who

dislike *contd.*

makes an objection: **objector** ◦ *I'd like to make an objection to the decision regarding the pay rise.* ◦ *My parents have no objection to my going abroad to study.*

▷ more on protesting ⇨ COMPLAIN/PROTEST

- to smile unpleasantly with one side of your mouth raised to show that you dislike sb/sth: **sneer**; *noun*: **sneer**; *adjective*: **sneering** ◦ 'You're not so clever now, are you?' he sneered. ◦ to make sneering remarks
- to make a sound (often when you are in a large group of people) that shows that you dislike sb/sth: **boo** (**at**) (sb/sth); the noise that people make when they boo: **boo, booing** (*noun* U) ◦ *The crowd booed as the Prime Minister got out of the car.* ◦ *We clapped the singers and booed the speakers.*
- when people who dislike sb/sth come together in a big group to express their feeling publicly, they sometimes shout **Down with** sb/sth ◦ *The protesters marched towards the city centre shouting 'Down with privatization!'*

disobey ⇨ OBEY

distance

1 measuring distances
2 long distances
3 short distances
see also LONG/SHORT[2]

1 measuring distances

- the amount of space between two places or points: **distance** (*noun* C/U) ◦ *a long/short distance apart* ◦ *a distance of twenty kilometres* ◦ *the distance between London and Birmingham*
- to ask what the distance is from one place to another, you say **how far** ◦ *How far is it to the petrol station?* ◦ *How far is it from Rome to Naples?*
- at a particular distance: **away, off** ◦ *The hotel is just half a mile away/off.*
- units used for measuring distances between places: **kilometre** (*abbreviation* **km**), **mile** (1 mile = 1.6 km) ◦ *a distance of three kilometres* ◦ *a ten-mile journey*

2 long distances

- at a long distance from sb/sth; not near: **a long way** (**away**), **far** (**away**); *adjective*: **distant** ◦ *The cinema's quite a long way from here.* ◦ *My boyfriend doesn't seem such a long way away now that I can phone him.* ◦ *'How far is it to Brighton?' 'Not far at all – about five miles.'* ◦ *It's too far to walk.* ◦ *We heard a distant cry for help.*
- not very near, but not too far away: (**at**) **some distance from** a place ◦ *The theatre is some distance from the station, but we can walk if it's a nice evening.*

  Note: far in this sense is normally used only in questions and in negative sentences. In affirmative sentences we say **a long way**.
- not at all near: (*informal*) **nowhere near** ◦ *Manchester's nowhere near London.*
- more distant: **further/farther** (**away**), **beyond . . ., past . . .** ◦ *How much further do we have to go?* ◦ *It's much further away than I expected.* ◦ *This bus doesn't go beyond/past the end of the road.*
- most distant: **furthest/farthest** ◦ *Which is furthest from London – Glasgow, Edinburgh or Stirling?*
- (used about one of two ends or sides) more distant: **far** (*adjective, only before a noun*) ◦ *at the far end of the street* ◦ *on the far bank of the river*
- a very long way (away): (*informal*) **miles** (**away**) ◦ *It'll take a long time to get there – it's miles away.* ◦ *I had to walk miles to get to the nearest phone box.*
- as far away as possible: **extreme, furthest** ◦ *He lives in the extreme north of Sweden.* ◦ *the furthest point from the sea*
- to continue over a long distance: **stretch . . ., extend . . .** ◦ *The road stretched for miles.*
- between places that are a long way from each other: **long-distance** ◦ *a long-distance phone call* ◦ *a long-distance foot path*
- a thing that can be seen, but is very far away, is **in the distance** ◦ *As we came over the hill we could see the town in the distance.*
- so far away that you cannot see it: **out of sight** ◦ *We waved goodbye until they were completely out of sight.*
- if sth is a long way from any other people or places, it is **remote** ◦ *a remote house/village*

3 short distances

- at a short distance from sb/sth: **near** (**. . .**), **close** (**to . . .**), **nearby, not far** (**away**) ◦ *Is there a bank near here?* ◦ *He stood very close to me, making me feel rather uncomfortable.* ◦ *Come a bit closer.* ◦ *Is there a school nearby?* ◦ *Not far away, children were playing.*
- in or near a place: **around** ◦ Are there any cinemas around here?

  Note: in the examples above, **near, close,** etc are prepositions and/or adverbs. **Near, close** and **nearby** can also be adjectives. As adjectives, **near, nearer, close** and **closer** can only be used *after* a noun. **Nearby** can only be used *before* a noun, and **nearest** and **closest** can be used *before or after* a noun. ◦ *We needn't take the car – it's quite near/close.* ◦ *Let's go to the Red Lion. It's a bit nearer.* ◦ *a nearby village* ◦ *Can you tell me where the nearest post office is?* ◦ *Let's go to whichever petrol station is closest.*

▷ coming or going nearer to sb/sth ⇨ COME/GO

- coming immediately after sth: **next** ◦ *The next building on your right is the Houses of Parliament.*
- at the side of sb/sth: **beside . . ., next to . . .** ◦ *She sat down next to me.*
- attached to sth or situated very close or next to sth: **adjacent, neighbouring** (*AmE* **neighboring**) ◦ *There are offices in the adjacent building.* ◦ *We*

walked to the neighbouring village five miles away.
- less distant (used about one of two ends or sides): **near** (*adjective, only before a noun*) ◦ *the near side of the road*

- in the nearest house or building to the one where you are: **next door**; *adjective*: **next-door** ◦ There are some really nice people living next door. ◦ *We went round to the next-door neighbours last night for a drink.*
- the area surrounding where you live, especially in a town: **neighbourhood** (*AmE* **neighborhood**) ◦ *They've moved to a new neighbourhood.*
- in the same area: **about, in the vicinity, locally**; *adjective*: **local** ◦ *Is Cathy anywhere about?* ◦ *There didn't seem to be any good schools in the vicinity.* ◦ *Do you live locally?* ◦ *You don't need to go to the supermarket for that – just go round the corner to the local shop.*

■ **MORE ...**
- the direct distance between two places without going along the roads: **as the crow flies** ◦ *It's three miles by road but two miles as the crow flies.*
- a very short distance from one place to another: **a stone's throw** ◦ *The place where I work is just a stone's throw from my house.*

- immediately in front of you: (**right**) **under** your **nose** ◦ *I've been looking for these keys all day, and all the time they've been right under my nose!*
- if sth is close enough to you to be touched or easily reached, it is **within reach** ◦ *Where we live is within easy reach of the countryside.*

district ⇨ COUNTRY[1]

dive ⇨ SWIM

divide

division of numbers ⇨ NUMBER
see also JOIN, PART/WHOLE

- to break or separate into parts: **divide** (**into** sth); to break or separate sth into parts: **divide** sth (**up**) (**into** sth); *noun* (U): **division** ◦ *When the path divides, take the left fork.* ◦ *They divided into two groups.* ◦ *We want to divide the house into flats.* ◦ *cell division in plants and animals* ◦ *The division of his property caused a lot of bad feeling among members of his family.*
- to divide into smaller parts: **subdivide**; to divide sth into smaller parts: **subdivide** sth; *noun* (U): **subdivision**

- to stop being together; to divide: **separate** (**from** sb/sth); to cause this to happen: **separate** sb/sth (**from** sb/sth); *noun* (U): **separation** ◦ *The wing had separated from the rest of the plane.* ◦ *The teacher separated the girls from the boys.*
- to divide people into groups: **split*** people (**up**) (**into** sth); to be divided into groups: **split*** (**up**) (**into** sth) ◦ *I'm going to split you into three groups.* ◦ *The students split up into several small groups.*

▷ being together or separated ⇨ TOGETHER

- to divide sth into two equal parts: **halve** sth
- to divide sth into parts with scissors or a knife: **cut*** sth **in/into ...** ◦ *He cut the apple in half.* ◦ *Cut the piece of paper into three.*
- to break sth into parts: **break*** sth **into ...** ◦ *He broke the bar of chocolate into two equal parts.*
- to divide sth (for example a country, a room) into two parts: **partition** sth; *noun* (U): **partition** ◦ *Germany was partitioned after the war.*
- a thing that is used to divide a room: **partition** ◦ *I'm thinking of putting up a partition between the kitchen and the dining area.*

▷ more on cutting and breaking ⇨ CUT, BREAK

- to divide sth and give some of it to other people: **share** sth (**out**), **share** sth (**with** sb); an amount that one person receives in this way: **share** ◦ *We shared out the remaining food.* ◦ *She always shares her sweets with her friends.* ◦ *What's my share?* ◦ *a bigger share of the profits*

divorce ⇨ MARRY

doctor

1 different kinds of doctors and their work
2 going to the doctor
see also DENTIST, HOSPITAL, ILLNESS, INJURY, MEDICINE, PAIN

1 different kinds of doctors and their work

- a trained person who helps people who are ill to get better: **doctor** (*abbreviation* **Dr**) ◦ *You should see a doctor.* ◦ *I've got an appointment with Dr Brown.*
- a doctor who treats all types of illnesses and does not work in a hospital: **GP** (= **general practitioner**), **family doctor** ◦ *See your GP if you need a vaccination.*
- a doctor with special knowledge of a particular area of medicine: **specialist** ◦ *a skin specialist* ◦ *a specialist in childhood diseases*
- a doctor who performs medical operations: **surgeon**; this kind of work is called **surgery** (*noun* U)
- a doctor who works in a hospital: **hospital doctor**
- a senior specialist doctor in a hospital: **consultant**

- a person who has some medical training but is not a doctor: **paramedic** ◦ *Firefighters and paramedics worked to save the accident victims.*

- to work as a doctor: **practise** ◦ *Although she qualified as a doctor, she has never practised.*
- the business of a doctor: **practice** ◦ *Dr Smith has a busy city centre practice.*
- the system in Britain that provides free or cheap medical care for everybody: **National Health Service** (*abbreviation* **NHS**)
- a doctor who is not working for the National Health Service is a **private** doctor

doctor *contd.*

2 going to the doctor

– you go to the doctor if you are **not feeling well**, if you are **ill**

■ where the doctor works

– the place where a doctor sees patients: **surgery**, **the doctor's** ◦ *Can you tell me where Dr Shaw's surgery is?* ◦ *I'll stop off at the doctor's to collect your medicine.*
– the surgery and offices where a group of doctors and nurses work together: **health centre**
– the room where patients wait to see a doctor: **waiting room** ◦ *I sat down in the waiting room.*

■ arranging to see the doctor

– an arrangement to see a doctor at a particular time: **appointment** ◦ *I'd like to make another appointment to see Dr Smith.* ◦ *I've got an appointment with Dr Lee.*
– if a doctor comes to your house to see you, he/she makes a **home visit**

– the person in the health centre or surgery who arranges when you can see a doctor: **receptionist** ◦ *The receptionist has given me an appointment for next Tuesday.*
– when you talk to a doctor about your health, you **see*** a doctor, (*formal*) **consult** a doctor ◦ *Which doctor do you usually see?* ◦ *I was told I should consult a doctor.*
– when the doctor meets and talks to patients, he/she **sees*** them ◦ *The doctor will see you now.*
– a person who is receiving medical treatment: **patient**

■ when you are with the doctor

– to look at sb/sth in order to find out what is wrong: **examine** sb/sth, **look at** sb/sth ◦ *The doctor examined his injured leg.* ◦ *Open your mouth wide; I want to look at your throat.*
– to find out what illness sb has: **diagnose** sth; an act of diagnosing sth: **diagnosis** (*plural* **diagnoses**) (*noun* C/U) ◦ *His illness was diagnosed as bronchitis.* ◦ *What was the doctor's diagnosis?*
– a change in your body that is a sign of illness: **symptom** ◦ *My daughter had malaria but the doctor didn't recognise the symptoms.* ◦ *flu symptoms*

– an examination of your body by a doctor to find out if you are healthy: **check-up**, **medical** ◦ *My father goes to see his doctor once a year for a check-up.* ◦ *She had to have a medical before she was given the job.*

– the instrument that a doctor uses for measuring the temperature of your body: **thermometer**
– the instrument that a doctor uses for listening to your breathing and heart: **stethoscope**
– to see whether your heart is working properly, the doctor may **take*** your **pulse** (by feeling your wrist), or **take*** your **blood pressure** (with an instrument attached to your arm)
– a small amount of blood, urine, etc that a doctor takes from you to help find out what is wrong: **sample**, **specimen** ◦ *They took a blood sample.* ◦ *a urine specimen*

– to give medical care to sb: **treat** sb (**for** sth); *noun*(U/C): **treatment** ◦ *The boy was treated for burns at the hospital.* ◦ *She received expert medical treatment.*
– the pills, liquids, etc that you take in order to treat an illness: **medicine** (*noun* C/U) ◦ *I was told to take the medicine four times a day after meals.*
– to say what medicine or treatment a patient should have: **prescribe** sth; the piece of paper on which a doctor writes down the medicine you have to take: **prescription** ◦ *The doctor prescribed antibiotics.* ◦ *I took the prescription to the chemist's.*

▷ more on medicine ⇨ MEDICINE

– to make sb healthy again: **cure** sb (**of** sth) ◦ *Thanks to the treatment he was given, he was completely cured.* ◦ *They managed to cure him of his drug addiction.*
– when you are healthy again, you **are/feel* better** ◦ *I'm feeling much better now.*

■ **MORE . . .**

a doctor who is an expert in . . .	**is called a . . .**
illnesses of the nervous system	**neurologist**
children's illnesses	**paediatrician** (*AmE* **pediatrician**)
the diseases of women (especially those affecting the reproductive system)	**gynaecologist** (*AmE* **gynecologist**)
looking after women who are pregnant	**obstetrician**
repairing damaged skin or improving the appearance of a person's face or body	**plastic surgeon**
treating people with mental illness	**psychiatrist**

– a doctor for animals: **vet**, (*formal*) **veterinary surgeon**

dog

1 different kinds of dog
2 parts of a dog
3 things that dogs do
4 looking after a dog
see also ANIMAL

1 different kinds of dog

– an animal, often kept as a pet or for working on a farm or hunting: **dog**

- a female dog: **bitch**; a male dog: **dog** ◦ *Is it a dog or a bitch?*
- a young dog: **puppy**, **pup**

- a dog that is kept for company or pleasure: **pet dog**
- a dog that is kept to work, for example on a farm: **working dog**
- a dog that is trained to help control sheep: **sheepdog**
- a dog that guards a house or a building: **guard dog**
- a dog that is trained to help a blind person: **guide dog**
- a dog that is trained to help the police: **police dog**

- a particular type of dog: **breed** ◦ *What breed is that dog?*
- a dog whose parents are not the same breed: **mongrel**
- if a dog is of pure breed, it is a **pedigree** dog ◦ *pure-bred pedigree pups*

2 parts of a dog

- a dog's foot: **paw**
- the mouth and nose of a dog: **muzzle**
- the hair on a dog: **coat** ◦ *a thick healthy coat*

3 things that dogs do

- the loud sound that a dog makes when it is excited: **bark**; *verb*: **bark** ◦ *The dog was barking at the postman.*
- a word to describe the sound of a dog's bark: **woof**
- a low sound that a dog makes to give a warning: **growl**; *verb*: **growl**
- a sound an angry dog makes while showing its teeth: **snarl**; *verb*: **snarl** ◦ *The dog snarled at the stranger.*
- the sound that a small dog makes when it is barking or excited: **yap**; *verb*: **yap**
- a crying sound that a dog makes, especially when it wants sth: **whine**; *verb*: **whine**
- a sound that a dog makes when it is frightened or in pain: **howl**; *verb*: **howl** ◦ *All over the town, dogs started howling.*

- when a dog moves its tail from side to side (because it is happy or excited), it **wags** its tail, its tail **wags**
- when a dog attacks sb/sth with its teeth, it **bites*** sb/sth
- when a dog tries to bite sb/sth, it **snaps at** sb/sth ◦ *The puppy snapped at the child's hand.*
- when a dog chews and bites a bone for a long time, it **gnaws** (**at**) a bone

4 looking after a dog

- to give food to an animal: **feed*** sth; food that you buy to give to a dog: **dog food** (*noun* U)
- to rub or touch a dog with your hand to show you are pleased with it: **pat** a dog
- to move your hand gently over sth: **stroke** a dog ◦ *She bent down to stroke the dog.*
- a dog that behaves well in the house and does not make it dirty is **house-trained**
- to go for a walk with a dog: **walk** a dog, **take*** a dog **for a walk**
- a band of leather, plastic, etc that is put around a dog's neck: **collar**
- a long piece of leather, plastic, etc attached to a dog's collar, to keep the dog under control: **lead** (*AmE* **leash**) ◦ *Please keep your dog on a lead.* ◦ *to let a dog off the lead*

- a small house for a dog: **kennel**
- a dog that has left its home and is lost: **stray dog**

- to keep animals in order to produce young from them: **breed*** sth ◦ *She breeds poodles.*

■ **MORE ...**
- connected with dogs or like a dog: **canine** ◦ *canine diseases*
- a disease that dogs get and pass to humans by biting them: **rabies** (*noun* U)

dollar ⇨ MONEY

door

going into a place ⇨ ENTER
see also HOUSE, BUILDING, ROOM

- a thing that you open or close to go in or out of a building or room, or to use a cupboard, etc: **door** ◦ *a car door* ◦ *the fridge door* ◦ *the kitchen door* ◦ *an open door* ◦ *The door was ajar* (= slightly open).
- the main door of a building: **front door**
- the door at the back of a building: **back door** ◦ *The back door leads into the garden.*
- a way into a building: **entrance** ◦ *There's another entrance round the back.*
- a way out of a building: **exit** ◦ *an emergency exit*

- a door that turns round: **revolving door**
- a door that opens both inwards and outwards: **swing door** (*often plural*)
- a door that can be opened by moving it to one side: **sliding door** ◦ *automatic sliding doors*
- a pair of glass doors that open onto a garden or balcony: **French windows** (*AmE* **French doors**) (*noun plural*)

- an opening in a floor or ceiling, for example on a boat: **hatch**
- a kind of door in a wall, fence, hedge, etc: **gate** ◦ *the garden gate*

▷ picture at WALL/FENCE/HEDGE

■ the area around a door
- an opening which a door fits into: **doorway** ◦ *He was standing in the doorway.*
- a single step outside the door of a building: **doorstep**
- a mat by a door which you can wipe your shoes on to clean them before going inside: **doormat**
- the room or passage that is just inside the front entrance to a house: **hall**

door *contd.*

– a covered area just outside the door of a building: **porch**

▷ picture at HOUSE

■ opening and closing a door

– if a door opens towards you, you must **pull** (it) ◦ *Pull the door hard to open it.*
– if a door opens away from you, you must **push** (it) ◦ *She pushed the door open and went in.*

– the part of a door that you hold in order to open it: **handle** ◦ *She turned the handle and opened the door.*
– a thing that is used to fasten a door so that you need a key to open it again: **lock**; to close a door with a key: **lock** sth; opposite: **unlock** sth ◦ *Please lock the door when you go out.*
– a bar of metal that you can slide along the inside of a door to fasten it: **bolt**; to shut sth with a bolt: **bolt** sth; *opposite*: **unbolt** sth ◦ *Lock and bolt the doors and windows.*
– a small piece of metal on which a door turns as it opens or closes: **hinge**

– to hit a door until it opens: **break*** sth **down** ◦ *The firefighters broke the door down to rescue her.*
– to break or damage a door by kicking it: **kick** sth **in** ◦ *They had to kick the door in to get into the building.*

▷ more on opening and closing doors, windows, etc ⇨ OPEN/CLOSE, LOCK

■ arriving at a door

– a bell on the outside of a house that you ring when you want to go in: **doorbell**
– to ring a doorbell: **ring*** (**at the door**) ◦ *I rang twice but nobody answered.*
– to make a noise by hitting a door: **knock** (**at the door**) ◦ *We knocked and went in.*
– to open a door because a person has knocked or rung the bell: **answer** (**the door**)

▷ bells ⇨ BELL

■ MORE ...

– a person whose job is to open and close the door for people in a hotel, etc: **doorman** (*plural* **doormen**)

doubt ⇨ POSSIBLE[1]

down ⇨ MOVE

draw

see also ART, PAINT[1], PICTURE

– to make a picture using a pen or pencil: **draw*** (sth); *noun* (U): **drawing**; a picture made in this way: **drawing**
– a drawing done quickly, without many details: **sketch**; to make a sketch: **sketch** (sth); *noun* (U): **sketching**

– a picture that is drawn or painted to make sth clear, for example a story or instructions: **illustration**; to make an illustration: **illustrate** sth; *noun* (U): **illustration**; a person who illustrates: **illustrator**
– a funny picture for a magazine or newspaper: **cartoon**; a person who draws cartoons: **cartoonist**

– a drawing done for scientific or industrial purposes: **technical drawing**; a person who does technical drawings: **draughtsman** (*AmE* **draftsman**)
– the production of drawings, diagrams, etc, often using a computer: **graphics** (*noun plural*); *adjective*: **graphic** ◦ *computer graphics* ◦ *graphic design*
– a drawing done to show how sth new should be made and what it should look like: **design**; to draw a design: **design** sth; *noun* (U): **design**; a person who designs: **designer**

▷ more on design ⇨ DESIGN

– a drawing done with untidy, meaningless lines or marks: **scribble**; to make a scribble: **scribble** (sth); *noun* (U): **scribbling**
– a drawing done while you are thinking about sth else: **doodle**; to draw in this way: **doodle**; *noun* (U): **doodling**

■ making a drawing

– a line that shows only the outside edge of an object in a picture: **outline**; something drawn in this way is drawn **in outline** ◦ *She quickly drew an outline of the house.*
– to fill an empty space in a picture with detail: **fill** sth **in**
– to draw sth, then make it darker with a pencil, etc: **shade** sth **in**

– the way of drawing objects in a picture so that they seem to be near or far away: **perspective** (*noun* U) ◦ *According to the rules of perspective, parallel lines should meet somewhere in the distance.*

– to add colour to a drawing: **colour** sth (**in**) ◦ *The area coloured yellow on the map is desert.* ◦ *The children were colouring in pictures of animals.*

■ things that are used for drawing

– people usually draw with a **pen** or a **pencil** ◦ *coloured pencils*
– to draw or write with coloured ink you can use a **felt-tip** (**pen**)
– a coloured stick, often made of wax: **crayon**
– sticks of black, burnt wood that can be used for drawing: **charcoal** (*noun* U)
– to draw or write on a blackboard, you use **chalk** (*noun* U/C) ◦ *a piece of chalk* ◦ *coloured chalks*

▷ more on pens and pencils ⇨ PEN/PENCIL

– a straight piece of wood or plastic which is used for measuring or drawing straight lines: **ruler**
– an instrument that you use to draw circles: **compass**, (**a pair of**) **compasses** (*noun plural*)

dream

– when you are asleep ⇨ SLEEP
– hoping or wishing ⇨ HOPE

dress ⇨ CLOTHES

drink

> **1** different kinds of drink
> **2** having a drink
> drinking in a bar or pub ⇨ **BAR / PUB**
> things we put drinks in ⇨ **CONTAINER**
> food and eating ⇨ **EAT, FOOD, MEAL, RESTAURANT**

1 different kinds of drink

- something to drink: **drink** ◦ *Can I have a drink please?* ◦ *food and drink*
- a cold drink that contains no alcohol: **soft drink**

▷ alcoholic drinks ⇨ **ALCOHOL, BEER, WINE**

- if a drink has air bubbles in it, it is **fizzy, carbonated, sparkling**; *opposite*: **still** ◦ *a fizzy drink* ◦ *carbonated water* ◦ *sparkling wine* ◦ *I prefer still orange to fizzy orange.*
- a drink which is no longer fizzy is **flat** ◦ *This lemonade's disgusting – it's completely flat.*
- to have a particular flavour: **taste** (**of** sth) ◦ *This tea tastes of lemon.* ◦ *to taste nice/awful/sweet/bitter/sour*

■ hot drinks

- some common hot drinks are: **coffee** (*noun* U/C), **tea** (*noun* U/C), **hot chocolate** (*noun* U/C) ◦ *I'm going to get another coffee.* ◦ *a mug of hot chocolate*

▷ more on coffee and tea ⇨ **COFFEE / TEA**

■ cold drinks

- water that you buy in a bottle: **mineral water** (*noun* U/C)
- slightly bitter water that is added to some alcoholic drinks: **tonic** (**water**) (*noun* U/C) ◦ *a gin and tonic*
- water with gas that is usually added to alcoholic drinks: **soda** (**water**) (*noun* U/C) ◦ *a whisky and soda*
- water from the tap: (**tap**) **water** (*noun* U) ◦ *Can I have some water, please?*

- a drink made from the juice of a fruit: (**fruit**) **juice** (*noun* U/C) ◦ *fresh orange juice*
- a fruit drink that you add water to: **squash** (*noun* U/C) ◦ *an orange squash*
- fruit-flavoured fizzy drinks: **lemonade** (*noun* U/C), **orangeade** (*noun* U/C), **fizzy orange/lemon** (*AmE* **soda pop**) (*noun* U/C)
- a drink made from milk, and sometimes ice cream, and flavoured with fruit: **milk shake** (*noun* C/U) ◦ *a strawberry milk shake*
- a fizzy drink that has no real sugar in it and will not make you fat: **diet** drink ◦ *diet lemonade*

2 having a drink

- to take liquid into your body through your mouth: **have** a drink, **drink*** (sth) ◦ *Can I have a cup of tea?* ◦ *They had a quick drink in the pub.* ◦ *I never drink water!*
- to fetch a drink from somewhere: **get*** a drink, **help** yourself (**to** a drink) ◦ *There's a beer in the fridge. Help yourself!*
- to finish drinking sth: **drink*** (sth) **up** ◦ *Drink up – we've got to go.*
- to drink sth quickly: **drink*** sth **down** ◦ *Come on, drink it down, it's not that bad.*
- to make food or drink, etc pass from your mouth down your throat: **swallow** (sth)

- to put liquid into a cup, glass, etc from a jug, bottle, etc, to serve sb: **pour** sth (**for** sb), **pour** sb sth ◦ *Pour yourself a drink.*
- to move a drink (for example coffee) round and round with a spoon: **stir** sth ◦ *The old man was stirring his coffee with a teaspoon.*
- to pour sth out of a container by accident: **spill** sth ◦ *I'm terribly sorry – I've spilt your beer.*

■ ways of drinking

- to take only a small amount of a drink into your mouth at one time: **sip** sth, **take* a sip** (**of** sth) ◦ *Sip it slowly – it's hot.* ◦ *She took a sip of her drink.*
- to take a large amount of a drink into your mouth: (*informal*) **swig** sth, **take* a swig** (**of** sth) ◦ *He took a swig of beer.*
- to take a liquid into your mouth by making your lips into a round shape and pulling your cheeks in: **suck** sth ◦ *The little boy was sucking his milk through a straw.*
- to eat or drink sth quickly: **gulp** sth (**down**) ◦ *He gulped his drink down and rushed out.*

■ wanting a drink

- to want a drink: **be/feel* thirsty**; *noun* (C/U): **thirst** ◦ *I'm really thirsty – can I have a drink?* ◦ *After all that work I've got a terrific thirst.* ◦ *I'm absolutely dying of thirst.*
- if you feel very thirsty, you can say you are (*informal*) **parched**
- to satisfy your thirst: **quench** your **thirst**

■ good wishes

- to express good wishes before they have an alcoholic drink, people sometimes say **Cheers!**
- to express good wishes to one particular person or thing with a drink: **drink* to** sb/sth, **drink* to** sb's **health** ◦ *Let's drink to the cook.*
- to express good wishes to one particular person or thing you can say: **Here's to** sb/sth ◦ *Here's to a happy New Year.*
- a formal way of offering to drink to sb's health: **propose a toast** ◦ *I want to propose a toast to our good friend Raymond, who is leaving us today.*

drive

> **1** using a car or other vehicle
> **2** controlling a vehicle
> **3** driving on the road
> **4** problems when driving
> **5** driving regulations
> **see also** **CAR, BUS, LORRY, MOTORCYCLE, TRAVEL, ROAD**

drive *contd.*

1 using a car or other vehicle

- to control a car or other vehicle: **drive*** (sth) ◦ *I want to learn to drive.* ◦ *to drive a lorry/bus/taxi*
- to go somewhere in a car: **drive***; a journey in a car or other vehicle: **drive** ◦ *They're planning to drive to Cardiff.* ◦ *The supermarket is only a five-minute drive from our house.* ◦ *Let's go for a drive this afternoon.*
- a person who is driving a car or other vehicle: **driver**; a person who drives a car: **motorist**
- a person whose work is to drive a car or other vehicle: **driver**, **chauffeur** ◦ *She's employed as a driver by a car delivery firm.* ◦ *a lorry driver*

■ passengers
- a person who travels in a car or other vehicle but does not drive it: **passenger** ◦ *Passengers should remain seated while the coach is moving.*
- to take sb somewhere in a car: **drive*** sb to a place
- to take sb in your car to a place where they want to go: **give*** sb **a lift** ◦ *Can you give me a lift to the station?*
- to collect sb in a car, etc: **pick** sb **up** ◦ *I'll pick you up outside the station at three o'clock.*
- to stop a car, etc and let sb get out: **drop** sb **off** ◦ *You can drop me off at the corner.*

- to wait at the side of a road and try to get a car to stop and take you somewhere: **hitchhike, thumb a lift**; sb who does this: **hitchhiker**

■ what a vehicle needs
- fuel for motor vehicles: **petrol** (*AmE* **gas, gasoline**, *nouns* U); petrol that does not contain lead is **unleaded**
- a heavy oil that is used in lorries, buses and some cars: **diesel** (*noun* U)
- a machine that provides petrol or diesel: **petrol pump**
- a liquid that makes car engines work smoothly: **oil** (*noun* U)
- a liquid that stops the water in a car radiator from freezing in cold weather: **antifreeze** (*noun* U)
- a machine that provides air to put in tyres: **air pump, air line**
- a place, usually at a petrol station, where your car is washed automatically: **car wash**

- a place where you can buy petrol and other things for your car: **petrol station, service station** (*AmE* **gas station**)
- a place where you get petrol, etc on a motorway: (**motorway**) **service area**
- a place where your car can be repaired: **garage**
- a person whose job is to serve you at a petrol station: (**petrol pump**) **attendant**

- to put fuel in a car, etc: **fill up, put* in some petrol**
- the measure of the amount of petrol that a car uses: **miles per gallon** (*abbreviation* **mpg**)

▷ more on fuel ⇨ FUEL

2 controlling a vehicle

- to make the engine of a vehicle start working: **start** a car, lorry, etc, **turn/switch on the ignition**
- to stop the engine: **turn/switch off the ignition**

- to control the direction in which a vehicle is going: **steer** (sth) ◦ *I'm still not very good at steering.*
- to signal that your car is going to turn: **indicate** ◦ *to indicate right/left*
- to sound the horn of a vehicle: **hoot** (the horn) ◦ *Why did he hoot at me? I wasn't doing anything wrong.*

■ brakes
- the part of a vehicle that slows it down or stops it: **brake** (*often plural*) ◦ *the footbrake* (= operated by your foot) ◦ *the handbrake* (= operated by your hand)
- the pedal that you push with your foot to make the footbrake work: **brake pedal**
- to prevent a vehicle from moving by using the handbrake: **put* on the handbrake**; *opposite*: **release the handbrake**
- to make a vehicle go slower or stop by using the footbrake: **brake, put* the brake(s) on, put*** your **foot on the brake** ◦ *Why did you brake so suddenly?* ◦ *She put her foot on the brake and managed to stop in time.*

■ changing gear
- a set of wheels in an engine which pass power from one part of the engine to another: **gears** (*noun plural*)
- to change from one gear to another while you are driving: **change gear** (*AmE* **shift gear**)
- to change gear, you need to press the **clutch** (**pedal**) with your foot and move the **gear lever, gear stick** (*AmE* **shift stick**) with your hand
- to put the engine into a higher/lower gear as you get faster or slower: **change up/down**
- to choose the gear which makes the vehicle go backwards: **change into reverse**, **put*** sth **into reverse**
- when the gears are being used, the engine is **in gear**; when the gears are not being used, the engine is **in neutral** (*noun* U)

3 driving on the road

- all the cars, lorries, buses, etc that are using the roads in a place: **traffic** (*noun* U) ◦ *light/heavy traffic* ◦ *The traffic was moving very slowly.*

- a sign which tells drivers where to go, what to do, what not to do, etc: **road sign, traffic sign**
- a sign with two or three coloured lights used for controlling traffic at road junctions: (**traffic**) **lights** (*noun plural*) (*AmE* **stoplight**) ◦ *The lights were red so we had to stop.*

▷ more on roads and road signs ⇨ ROAD

- the way that you decide to follow to get from one place to another: **route, way** ◦ *Which route did you take?* ◦ *Which way shall we go?*
- a map which shows all the roads in one area: **road map**

■ starting and stopping

- to drive a car, etc away from somewhere: **drive* off/away, move off** ◦ *He released the handbrake and we moved off.*
- to move away from the side of the road: **pull out** ◦ *I had to brake suddenly as a car pulled out in front of me.*
- to drive a car, etc off the road: **pull off** the road ◦ *They pulled off the motorway at a service station.*
- to stop at a place: **pull up** (**at** sth), **draw* up** (**at** sth) ◦ *Can you pull up at the next corner? I want to get out.* ◦ *A car drew up and three men got out.*

■ parking

- to stop and leave a car, lorry, etc somewhere for some time: **park** (sth); the action of doing this: **parking** (*noun* U) ◦ *Where shall we park?* ◦ *We can take the car if you want but parking may be a problem.*
- an area or building where you can leave your car: **car park** (*AmE* **parking lot**) ◦ *a multi-storey car park* (= a car park that has several levels)
- a metal post that you put coins in to pay for parking in the space beside it: **parking meter**
- a person whose job is to check if cars are parked in the wrong place: (*BrE*) **traffic warden**
- a piece of paper showing that you must pay a fine (= some money) for parking in the wrong place or for too long: **parking ticket**

■ turning

- to leave one road and go onto another: **turn off** (sth) ◦ *We turned off the A9 and headed for Aberdeen.*
- to move onto a different road: **turn onto** sth, **turn down** sth ◦ *We left the motorway and turned onto the road to Banbury.* ◦ *Could you turn down this road here?*
- to make a mistake when changing from one road to another: **take* a wrong turning**
- to turn the vehicle so as to go back where you came from: **turn round** ◦ *I think we've lost our way. We'll have to turn round.*
- to turn round and go back along the same road: **do*/make* a U-turn**

- to move a car backwards: **reverse** (sth), **back** (sth) (**into** sth) ◦ *He reversed the car out of the drive.* ◦ *Can you back the car into this space?*
- to change direction suddenly: **swerve** ◦ *She had to swerve to avoid the dog.*

■ passing

- to pass a vehicle because you are moving faster: **overtake*** (sth), **pull ahead** (**of** sb/sth)
- to allow another vehicle to go before you: **give* way** (**to** sb/sth) ◦ *You must give way to traffic coming from the right.*
- cars, etc that are coming towards you: **oncoming** traffic

■ driving fast or slow

- the measure of a car's speed: **mph** (**miles per hour**), **km/h** (**kilometres per hour**) ◦ *a 50 km/h speed limit*
- to travel at a certain speed: **go* at . . ., do* . . .** ◦ *I think I was going at about 50 mph at the time.* ◦ *He must have been doing over a hundred!*
- to make a car go more slowly: **slow down, brake** ◦ *We slowed down as we came to a junction.* ◦ *I braked too hard and the car skidded.*
- to make a car go faster: **speed up, accelerate** ◦ *You'll have to speed up a bit or we'll be late.*

- to drive very fast: **speed*** ◦ *We sped through the town.*
- to make a car go very fast by pressing down on the accelerator pedal: **put*** your **foot down**
- at the fastest possible speed: **at full speed, at top speed** ◦ *He drove at top speed all the way.*

- to drive very slowly because there is a lot of traffic: **crawl** ◦ *Traffic was crawling through the town centre because of the roadworks.*

■ dangerous driving

- if you drive without thinking about how dangerously you are driving, you are being **careless, reckless** ◦ *guilty of careless driving* ◦ *a reckless driver*
- to drive quickly across a set of traffic lights when they are red: (*informal*) **jump the lights** (*AmE* **run* a red light**)

4 problems when driving

- an unpleasant event that happens when you are driving: **accident** ◦ *They're very late. I hope they haven't had an accident.*
- to hit sb with a car: **run*** sb **over**, **knock** sb **down** ◦ *I was nearly run over by a bus.*
- an accident when a car, etc hits sth and is damaged: **crash**
- if you put on the brake too hard, the vehicle may get out of control and **skid** ◦ *The car skidded into a tree.*

▷ more on crashes and other accidents ⇨ ACCIDENT

- when a car stops suddenly because the engine fails, it **stalls**; when sb causes this to happen, they **stall** sth ◦ *I jammed on the brakes and the engine stalled.* ◦ *I stalled the engine when I was waiting at the junction.*
- if a car stops working when it is being driven, it **breaks* down**
- to pull a car along by using a chain or a rope: **tow** sth; a car that is being towed is **on tow**
- when a tyre gets a hole in it and the air comes out, you have a **puncture** (*AmE* **flat**)

▷ more on punctures ⇨ WHEEL

- a long line of cars, etc that cannot move or that can only move slowly: (**traffic**) **jam** ◦ *Sorry I'm so late home, I got stuck in a traffic jam.*
- if the roads are full of cars, etc which are moving slowly, there is (**traffic**) **congestion** (*noun* U) ◦ *a scheme to reduce traffic congestion*

- to be unable to find your way to a place: **get* lost, lose*** your **way** ◦ *We got lost and had to stop and ask the way.*

- illness caused by travelling in a car: **carsickness** (*noun* U), **travel-sickness** (*AmE* **motion sickness**) (*noun* U); *adjectives*: **carsick, travel-sick** ◦ *I used to get carsick when I was little.*

drive *contd.*

5 driving regulations

- an official piece of paper that says you are allowed to drive a car: **driving licence** (*AmE* **driver's license**)
- an examination to measure your driving skill and knowledge of the rules of driving: **driving test** ◦ *Mick's so happy; he's just passed his driving test.*
- an organization which teaches people to drive: **driving school**
- a sign with a large red letter L on it that you fix to a car, etc when you are learning to drive: (*BrE*) **L-plate**

- a round, official piece of paper that you put on your vehicle's windscreen to show that you have paid the necessary tax: **tax disc**

- the book of rules that say how you should drive on public roads: **highway code**
- the right to continue moving while other cars, etc must stop: **right of way** (*noun* U), **priority** (*noun* U) ◦ *Keep going. You have right of way here.* ◦ *Who has priority on a roundabout?*

- the highest speed at which you are allowed to drive on a particular piece of road: **speed limit** ◦ *I didn't think I was exceeding the speed limit.*
- driving faster than you are allowed to: **speeding** (*noun* U) ◦ *The police stopped the woman for speeding.*

- when you should not drive because you have drunk more than the legal amount of alcohol, you are **over the limit** ◦ *You mustn't drive – you're well over the limit.*
- driving when you have drunk too much alcohol: **drink-driving** (*noun* U)
- a person who drives after drinking too much: **drink-driver**
- a test given by the police to check the amount of alcohol in sb's body: **breath test**; the machine they use to do this: **breathalyser**; to use a breathalyser: **breathalyse** sb ◦ *Did the police breathalyse you?*

- if a judge decides that you should not be allowed to continue driving because you have broken the law, you **lose* your licence**, you are **banned from driving** ◦ *Simon was banned from driving for a year after he was found guilty of drink-driving.*

drop ⇨ FALL

drug

- for an illness ⇨ **MEDICINE**
- illegal drugs ⇨ **DRUGS**

drugs

> drugs used for medicine ⇨ **MEDICINE**
> **see also** CRIME

- a substance that people use to give themselves exciting or pleasant feelings: **drug** ◦ *Do you think he takes drugs?*
- a drug that is strong and dangerous: **hard drug**
- a drug that some people think is not so dangerous: **soft drug**
- a drug that makes you feel happy or full of energy: **stimulant**
- a drug that makes you relax your mind and body: **depressant**

- a drug that is made from the dried leaves or flowers of the hemp plant, and which is smoked in a cigarette or a pipe: **cannabis** (*noun* U), **marijuana** (*noun* U), (*informal*) **dope** (*noun* U)
- a cigarette that contains marijuana: (*informal*) **joint**
- a drug made from the seeds of the poppy flower: **opium** (*noun* U)
- a drug that is used by doctors to relieve pain and that some people use for pleasure: **heroin** (*noun* U)
- a white powder used as a stimulant that is usually breathed in through the nose: **cocaine** (*noun* U), (*informal*) **coke** (*noun* U); a variety of cocaine: **crack** (*noun* U)
- a powerful drug that causes you to see, hear, feel, etc things that are not real: **LSD** (*noun* U), (*informal*) **acid** (*noun* U)

- a person who takes illegal drugs: **drug user**
- not able to stop taking drugs: **addicted** (**to** sth), (*informal*) **hooked** (**on** sth); the state of being addicted: **addiction** (**to** sth) (*noun* U/C), (*formal*) **dependence** (**on** sth) (*noun* U) ◦ *He's addicted to heroin.* ◦ *receive treatment for drug dependence*
- drugs that you can easily become addicted to are **addictive**
- a person who cannot stop taking drugs: (**drug**) **addict**, (*informal*) **junkie**

- to put a drug into sb/yourself with a needle (= **syringe**): **inject** sth (**into** sb/sth), **inject** sb/yourself **with** sth
- feeling in a pleasant and excited state after taking drugs: **high** (**on** sth) ◦ *The police think that our attackers were probably high on drugs.*
- an amount of drugs that is too large: **overdose** ◦ *She died of a heroin overdose.*

- a person who sells illegal drugs: **drug dealer**, (*informal*) (**drug**) **pusher**; selling illegal drugs: **drug dealing** (*noun* U)
- a person who buys and sells illegal drugs: **drug trafficker**
- to take sth into or out of a country illegally: **smuggle** sth ◦ *He was caught trying to smuggle cannabis through Heathrow airport.*

drum ⇨ MUSIC

drunk ⇨ ALCOHOL

dry ⇨ WET/DRY

duck ⇨ BIRD[2]

during ⇨ TIME

duty

things that must happen or be done ⇨ MUST
duties at work ⇨ WORK

- something that you must do because people expect you to do it, or because you think it is right: **duty** (*noun* C/U), (*formal*) **obligation** (*noun* C/U) ◦ *I felt I had a duty to speak out.* ◦ *a sense of duty* ◦ *to do your duty* ◦ *We all have an obligation to protect the environment.*
- the duty of a particular person: **responsibility** (*noun* C/U); a person who has a particular responsibility is **responsible** (**for** sth/doing sth) ◦ *It's my responsibility to make sure that the lights are turned out.* ◦ *We all have responsibilities towards our families.* ◦ *Don't ask him to do it – he hates responsibility.* ◦ *Who is responsible for cleaning this office?*

- if it is sb's duty to do sth, or if it is right for them to do it, they **should** do it, **ought to** do it, **are supposed to** do it ◦ *The government should do something about it.* ◦ *You ought to report this to the police.* ◦ *She's supposed to check all the rooms before she locks the building at night.*

- to have confidence that a person will actually do what they are supposed to do: **trust** sb (**to** do sth) ◦ *I trusted her to finish the job properly.*

▷ trusting sb ⇨ TRUST

ear

other parts of the head ⇨ HEAD
see also HEAR

- one of the two parts of the body that are used for hearing: **ear** ◦ *He pulled his hat down over his ears.* ◦ *She spoke softly in his ear.*
- the soft rounded part of your ear that hangs down below the rest: (**ear**) **lobe**
- if sb's ears stand out from the rest of their head, they **stick* out**

- the thin piece of skin inside your ear that is tightly stretched and allows you to hear sounds: **eardrum**
- the yellow substance that is found in your ears: **wax** (*noun* U)
- a pain inside your ear: **earache** (*noun* U/C) ◦ *I've got earache.*

▷ a note on earache and other aches ⇨ PAIN

- a piece of jewellery that is worn on the ear: **earring** ◦ *What pretty earrings!*

early / late

1 early
2 on time
3 late
see also TIME, BEFORE/AFTER, WAIT

1 early

- before the usual or expected time: **early** (*adjective, adverb*) ◦ *Early arrivals should be shown into the reception room.* ◦ *Am I early?* ◦ *I don't want to get there too early.*
- coming or happening before the proper time; too early: **premature** ◦ *The decision was a bit premature – we probably should have waited a few more weeks.* ◦ *a premature baby*
- near the beginning of a period of time: **early** (*adjective, adverb*) ◦ *I would guess that she's in her early seventies.* ◦ *early in 1973*

- at an earlier time: **earlier** (**on**) ◦ *It's colder than it was earlier on.*
- no earlier than: **at the earliest** ◦ *'What time should we come?' 'Six o'clock at the earliest.'*
- earlier than sb/sth: **before** sb/sth ◦ *We both left at the same time but our friends arrived before us.*

2 on time

- not late or early: **on time**, **punctual** (*adverb* **punctually**) ◦ *The train got in on time.* ◦ *Try to be punctual for meetings.* ◦ *We started punctually.*
- at the right time or a little bit early: **in good time** ◦ *Make sure you leave the house in good time – sometimes the bus goes a little bit early.*
- exactly at the right time; with no time to spare: **just in time** ◦ *We got there just in time – the train was about to leave.*

3 late

- after the usual or expected time: **late** (*adjective, adverb*) ◦ *Hurry up, we're going to be late.* ◦ *It's too late to change your mind now.* ◦ *half an hour late*
- near the end of a period of time: **late** (*adjective, adverb*) ◦ *In late 1988 I left my job and moved to a near area.* ◦ *We arrived late at night.*
- at the last possible moment; only just in time: **at the last minute**, **at the eleventh hour** ◦ *They managed to clear the area at the eleventh hour – two minutes later the bomb exploded.*

- at a later time: **later** (**on**) ◦ *See you later.* ◦ *Later on that evening, they met up with some friends and went to a club.*
- no later than: **at the latest** ◦ *I want the work done by tomorrow at the very latest.*
- later than sb/sth: **after ...** ◦ *They got there after we did.*

- late or slow in doing sth: **behind** (**with** sth), **behind schedule** ◦ *I'm sorry, I'll have to go – I'm a bit behind with my work.*
- to continue later than the expected time: **overrun***, **run* late** ◦ *The show overran by half an hour.* ◦ *I'm afraid you'll have to wait a few minutes for your appointment, we're running a bit late.*
- late in arriving, happening, being paid, returned, etc: **overdue** ◦ *I must take back this library book – it's a week overdue.*

■ delay

- to make sb/sth slow or late: **delay** sb/sth, **hold*** sb/sth **up**; an occasion when this has happened:

early / late *contd.*

delay, **hold-up** ◦ *The plane was delayed by an hour.* ◦ *I'm sorry I'm late – I was held up at work.* ◦ *They apologized for the delay.* ◦ *a traffic hold-up*
– to make sb late when they have to go somewhere: **keep*** sb ◦ *What can be keeping her? She said she'd be here by eleven.*

– to decide not to do sth until a later time: **delay** sth/doing sth, **put*** sth **off**, **put* off** doing sth; this lack of action: **delay** (*noun* U) ◦ *They delayed the start of the match until the rain stopped.* ◦ *She always puts off doing her homework until the last minute.* ◦ *We need the money without delay.*
– to arrange for sth to happen at a later time than planned: **postpone** sth, **put*** sth **back**; *noun* (C/U): **postponement** ◦ *The meeting has been postponed until next week.* ◦ *My appointment has been put back an hour to 4 o'clock.*

■ without delay
– without delay or hesitation: **straight ...** ◦ *You should go straight home after school.*
– without waiting for any time to pass: **immediately, at once, right away, straight away** ◦ *She came home and immediately went to bed.* ◦ *I made an excuse, but he knew at once that I was lying.* ◦ *Write it down straight away before you forget it.*
– happening or done without delay: **immediate** ◦ *I asked for an immediate reply to my letter.*
– immediate and rather surprising: **instant** (*adverb* **instantly**) ◦ *The show was an instant success.*

■ **MORE ...**
– (used about things) coming too late: **belated** ◦ *a belated birthday card*
– a person who arrives late: **latecomer** ◦ *Latecomers are not allowed into the theatre once the play has started.*
– late, but not too seriously late: **better late than never** ◦ *It won't be finished until next week, but better late than never I suppose.*

earn ⇨ PAY²

earth

– the whole world ⇨ WORLD
– the ground that you walk on ⇨ GROUND
– the land, not the sea ⇨ LAND

east ⇨ DIRECTION

Easter

– holiday ⇨ HOLIDAY
– Christian belief ⇨ CHRISTIAN

easy / difficult

1 easy/difficult
2 simple/complicated
3 convenient/awkward
4 dealing with difficulties

1 easy/difficult

– not difficult to do, understand, etc: **easy** (*adverb* **easily**); *noun* (U): **ease** ◦ *It won't take long to learn – it's really easy.* ◦ *I can easily run a mile without stopping.* ◦ *She passed the exam with ease.*
– if sth is extremely easy, you can say that **there's nothing to it** ◦ *There's nothing to it – watch, and copy me.*

– not easy to do, understand, etc: **difficult**, **hard** ◦ *I found Chinese a very difficult language to learn.* ◦ *Her accent is quite hard to understand.* ◦ *I was surprised at the difficulty of some of the questions.*
– the work or effort caused by sth which is difficult: **difficulty** (**in** sth/doing sth) (*noun* U), **trouble** (doing sth) (*noun* U) ◦ *You might have difficulty (in) reading my writing.* ◦ *to do sth with difficulty* ◦ *I'm sorry I'm late – I had a bit of trouble finding the way.*
– something that is very difficult and needs a lot of effort to do is **tough** ◦ *I was asked a lot of tough questions at the interview.*

– if sth is difficult for you to understand, it **puzzles** you, it is **puzzling** ◦ *I found his behaviour puzzling.*
– if sth is impossible for you to understand, it is **beyond** you, (*informal*) it **beats*** you ◦ *All that astrophysics stuff is beyond me!* ◦ *It beats me why she's suddenly started behaving like that.*

■ particular kinds of difficulty
– something that is difficult to do or understand: **difficulty** (*often plural*) ◦ *They've had a lot of difficulties over the past year, but things seem to be going quite well for them now.*
– a situation that is difficult to understand or deal with: **problem** ◦ *If you have any problems, please don't hesitate to contact me.* ◦ *Problems started to arise as soon as the plan was put into action.*
▷ different kinds of problem ⇨ PROBLEM

– something that makes a situation difficult: **complication**; *verb*: **complicate** sth ◦ *There's been a small complication, so the work won't be ready until tomorrow.* ◦ *The situation had been complicated by the sudden arrival of her parents.*
– something that is not good or that causes problems: **disadvantage**, **drawback** ◦ *One disadvantage of working from home is that you don't get to meet many people.*

– something that is interesting and difficult in a way that forces you to make a lot of effort in order to get good results: **challenge**; *adjective*: **challenging** ◦ *I feel that I need a challenge.* ◦ *We've begun working on a very challenging project.*
– something that requires great effort: **struggle** ◦ *It was a great struggle for him to pass his exams.*
– a very unpleasant and difficult experience: **ordeal** ◦ *a terrible ordeal*
– a time of great danger or difficulty: **crisis** (*plural* **crises**) ◦ *Events reached a crisis in 1939.*

2 simple/complicated

- without great detail; easy to understand, do or use: **simple** (*adverb* **simply**), **straightforward**; the quality of being simple: **simplicity** (*noun* U) ○ It's quite simple really – just follow the instructions. ○ *The book is written very simply so that learners can follow it.* ○ *This computer software is very straightforward – it's designed for beginners.* ○ *Learners will appreciate the simplicity of this grammar book.*

- easy to see, hear or understand: **plain** ○ *in plain English*
- very simple to understand: **elementary**, **basic** ○ *elementary mathematics* ○ *a basic course in French*
- (used about machines, systems, books, etc) easy to use: **user-friendly** ○ *These new computers are much more user-friendly than the old ones.*

- having a lot of detail; difficult to understand, do, etc: **complicated**, **complex**; *noun* (U/C): **complexity** ○ *a complicated piece to play on the piano* ○ *The problem is rather complex – it might take some time to explain it to you.* ○ *I don't think you fully understand the complexity of the problem.* ○ *She tried to explain the complexities of the plan.*

■ making sth simple
- to make sth simpler: **simplify** sth ○ *to simplify a complex problem* ○ *a simplified dictionary for children*
- to try to make sth more simple than it really is: **oversimplify** sth ○ *You won't achieve anything by oversimplifying the situation.*

3 convenient/awkward

- easy to find, reach, use, etc: **convenient** (*adverb* **conveniently**) ○ *The hotel is conveniently situated 2 km from the airport.*

- not easy to find, reach, use, etc: **inconvenient** (*adverb* **inconveniently**)
- having hidden or unexpected difficulties: **tricky** ○ *some tricky problems*
- not convenient, causing difficulties or embarrassment: **awkward** ○ *She put me in a very awkward situation by telling everybody my plans.*

4 dealing with difficulties

- to experience a difficulty or a problem: **run* into** sth, **run* up against** sth ○ *We were doing very well at first, but then we ran into difficulties.* ○ *I've run up against a problem and I can't see how to solve it.*
- if you have difficulties doing sth, you can say that you have **a job** doing it/**to** do it ○ *I had a dreadful job getting the tyre off the wheel.* ○ *We'll have a hard job to keep up with them.*

- to continue to try to do or understand sth, although you are finding it difficult: **persevere** (**with** sth); *noun* (U): **perseverance** ○ *I'm so glad I persevered with that job – it was really worth it now that I've been promoted.*

- to try very hard to do sth which is difficult: **struggle** (**with** sth) ○ *You've been struggling with that exercise for ages – can I help you with it?*

■ **MORE ...**
- to choose to do sth that is easy, instead of doing sth which would be more difficult but more satisfying or challenging: **take* the easy way out, take* the easy option** ○ *Instead of apologizing to us personally, he took the easy way out and asked somebody else to do it for him.*

- more difficult than you would imagine: **easier said than done** ○ *'Why don't you move house if you don't like it there?' 'That's easier said than done!'*

---

eat

1 the food you eat
2 wanting to eat
3 eating
4 after eating

see also FOOD, DRINK, KNIFE/FORK/SPOON, PLATE/BOWL/DISH

1 the food you eat

- the general word for things that people usually eat: **food** (*noun* U) ○ *There's not much food in the fridge!* ○ *food and drink* ○ *baby food*
- food that you have or want to have on a particular occasion: **something to eat** ○ *Would you like something to eat?*

- the flavour of a particular food or drink: **taste** ○ *I don't know what you put in it but it's got a really strange taste.*
- anything which a person can eat is **edible**; *opposite*: **inedible**

▷ more on taste ⇨ TASTE

- food which is eaten at a particular time of the day: **meal**
- a small meal, for example a sandwich, that you can eat between main meals: **snack**
- light food and drinks served in public places: (*rather formal*) **refreshments** ○ *Light refreshments will be available.*

▷ more on meals ⇨ MEAL

- the food that a person usually eats: **diet** (*noun* C/U) ○ *People who live on the East coast of Africa have a diet mainly of fish and rice.* ○ *A healthy diet is important for a long life.* ○ *a balanced diet* (= having a healthy variety of different kinds of food) ○ *illnesses caused by poor diet*
- when you eat only certain foods, for example because you want to lose weight or for medical reasons, you follow a special **diet** ○ *a high-fibre diet* ○ *a low-calorie diet*

- to have sth as your only food: **live on** sth ○ *They live on fish and chips!*
- to eat or drink less of sth: **cut* down on** sth ○ *I'm cutting down on sugar.*

eat *contd.*

- to avoid eating or drinking sth: **keep* off** sth ◦ *He's going to try and keep off fatty foods for a while.*
- food that you need to stay healthy: **nourishment** (*noun* U); to give sb nourishment: **nourish** sb; food which is good and healthy is **nourishing**, **nutritious** ◦ *You can't just eat sweets and crisps – you need to get some proper nourishment.* ◦ *a nutritious meal*
- the food that you eat and the way it affects your health: **nutrition** (*noun* U) ◦ *I'm studying food and nutrition at college.*

■ eating a lot

- to eat too much: **overeat***
- a person who eats too much is **greedy**; *nouns* (U): **greed, greediness** ◦ *You're only allowed one biscuit, not three – don't be so greedy.* ◦ *I've never seen such greediness – she ate the whole cake herself!*
- a person who eats too much: **glutton**, (*informal*) **pig** ◦ *Greedy pig!*
- to eat a lot, in a greedy way: **gorge** yourself (**on** sth), (*informal*) **make* a pig of** yourself ◦ *There was so much to eat – I ended up making a real pig of myself.*

■ not eating enough

- a person who has not been given enough food is **underfed**
- to have nothing or very little to eat: **starve**; *noun* (U): **starvation**; *adjective*: **starving**, **(half-) starved** ◦ *There are people starving all over the world.* ◦ *a famine* (= a period when there is not enough food) *leading to mass starvation* ◦ *a starving child* ◦ *Those poor animals – they look half-starved.*
- the illness that people can have from not eating enough food: **malnutrition** (*noun* U) ◦ *to suffer from malnutrition*
- a person who is suffering from malnutrition is **malnourished**

■ choosing to eat a little

- to choose not to eat very much because you want to lose weight: **diet, go*/be on a diet** ◦ *I want to lose weight so I'm going on a diet.*
- to choose not to eat, for religious reasons for example: **fast**; *noun*: **fast** ◦ *Muslims fast during Ramadan.*

2 wanting to eat

- when you need or want to eat sth, you are **hungry**; the feeling that you want or need to eat: **hunger** (*noun* U) ◦ *I'm hungry – what time's dinner?* ◦ *suffering from hunger*
- a bit hungry: **peckish** ◦ *to feel a bit peckish*
- very hungry: **famished, ravenous, starving** ◦ *I'm absolutely famished.*
- the desire or need for food: **appetite** (*noun* C/U) ◦ *Jack's got a huge appetite – you'd better make enough for four.* ◦ *I don't think she's well – she's got no appetite.*
- to become hungry because of working: **work up an appetite**

3 eating

- to take food into your body through your mouth: **eat*** (sth) ◦ *I'm hungry. I really must have something to eat.* ◦ *Are you ready to eat now?*
- to take liquid into your body through your mouth: **drink*** (sth)
- to eat and/or drink: (*formal*) **consume** sth; *noun* (U): **consumption** ◦ *Only food bought here may be consumed on the premises.*
- to cut food with your teeth: **bite*** (**into** sth); *noun*: **bite** ◦ *She bit into her sandwich.* ◦ *Can I have a bite of your apple?*
- the amount of food you put in your mouth at one time; a small amount of food: **mouthful** ◦ *I'm not really hungry, I'll just have a mouthful.*
- to break up food in your mouth with your teeth: **chew** (sth)
- to make food or drink pass into your body from your mouth: **swallow** (sth)
- to send food or liquid out of your mouth: **spit*** sth **out**
- the wet substance in your mouth which helps you to chew and swallow the food: **saliva** (*noun* U)
- to pull a liquid into your mouth by making your lips into a round shape and pulling your cheeks in: **suck** (sth) ◦ *You should suck cough sweets slowly, not chew them.*
- to move your tongue across sth: **lick** sth ◦ *to lick an ice cream*
- to eat food very quickly: **bolt** sth (**down**), **gobble** sth (**up**) ◦ *Don't bolt your food – you'll get indigestion.*
- to eat or drink sth very quickly: **gulp** sth (**down**) ◦ *I woke up really late, gulped down my tea and ate my toast on the bus.*
- to eat sth by taking small bites: **nibble** (**at/on**) sth ◦ *She nibbled a piece of cheese.*
- to give food to sb/sth: **feed*** sb/sth

▷ feeding a baby ⇨ BABY

▷ feeding an animal; the way animals eat ⇨ ANIMAL

4 after eating

- when you have had enough to eat you are (*informal*) **full** (**up**) ◦ *'Would you like some more?' 'No thanks, it was lovely but I'm full.'*
- if you cannot eat any more, then you **can't manage** sth ◦ *That was a lovely meal but I'm afraid I can't manage any more.*
- to change food in the stomach so that it can be used by the body: **digest** sth; *noun* (U): **digestion**; the system in your body which causes food to be digested: **digestive system** ◦ *Small babies cannot digest solid food.*
- when your stomach hurts because it cannot digest the food, you have **indigestion** (*noun* U) ◦ *Onions give me indigestion.*
- air that you swallow when you are eating or drinking; the gas in your stomach: **wind** (*noun* U)

– to bring the gas up through your mouth: **belch**, (*informal*) **burp**
– the sound that you make when you bring gas up through your mouth: **belch**, (*informal*) **burp** ◦ *to give a burp*

– to bring food up through the mouth when you are ill: **be sick** (**especially** *AmE*) **throw* up**, (*formal*) **vomit**; to avoid vomiting: **keep*** sth **down** ◦ *He can't keep anything down – he was sick three times during the night and then he threw up again this morning.*

■ **MORE ...**
– if you see sth nice to eat and the smell makes you feel hungry, it **makes*** your **mouth water** ◦ *Mm, that smells delicious, it's really making my mouth water.*

– to give people only a small amount of sth (not as much as they may want): **ration** sth; *noun* (U): **rationing** ◦ *During the war, food, clothes and petrol were all rationed.* ◦ *Rationing did not end until the 1950s.*
– the amount given to sb when there is not enough to go round, for example in a war: **ration**

---

economy

1 different economic systems

– the operation of a country's money supply, trade and industry: **economy**; connected with the economy of a country: **economic** ◦ *an improvement in the economy* ◦ *a successful economic policy* ◦ *economic problems*
– the study of the way in which economies work: **economics** (*noun* U) ◦ *She studied economics at university.*
– an expert in economics: **economist**

– the economic system in which individuals own and control businesses: **capitalism** (*noun* U); *adjective*: **capitalist**; a person who supports capitalism: **capitalist** ◦ *the capitalist system*
– the economic system in which the state controls the economy of a country: **socialism** (*noun* U); *adjective*: **socialist**; a person who supports socialism: **socialist**
– an economic system in which some businesses are owned and controlled by the state, and other businesses are owned and run by individuals: **mixed economy**

– the operation of trade and business without government control: **free enterprise** (*noun* U), **private enterprise** (*noun* U)
– an economy where the government does not fix prices: **free-market economy**

▷ political ideas ⇨ **POLITICS**

2 money

– the means of paying for sth or buying sth: **money** (*noun* U)
– the system or kind of money that a country uses: **currency** ◦ *a strong currency* ◦ *plans for a single European currency*
– connected with money, especially currencies: **monetary** ◦ *the Government's monetary policy*

– money that you use to start a business or that you put in a bank, etc to make more money: **capital** (*noun* U)
– the management of money: **finance** (*noun* U); *adjective*: **financial** ◦ *to be in financial difficulties*

– to reduce the value of the money of one country in relation to the value of money in another country: **devalue** sth; *noun* (C/U): **devaluation** ◦ *The pound has been devalued by 3% against the franc.*

▷ more on money ⇨ **MONEY**

– the money that you have to pay to the government so that it can provide public services: **tax** (*noun* C/U) ◦ *to increase taxes*
– the system by which a government takes money from people so that it can pay for services: **taxation** (*noun* U)
– to raise money through taxation: **tax** sb/sth
– a statement by the Government saying how much money it intends to spend and how it is going to collect the money: **budget**
– the government department that controls taxation and government spending: **the Treasury**

▷ more on taxation ⇨ **TAX**

3 trade and industry

– the amount of goods or services that people want: **demand** (**for** sth) (*noun* U)
– the amount of sth that businesses produce: **supply** (*noun* U)
– the level of demand that there is for a particular thing: **market** ◦ *There's not much of a market for wooden toys these days.* ◦ *The used car market has been declining for some years.*

– the activity of buying and selling goods and services: **business** (*noun* U), **commerce** (*noun* U); *adjective*: **commercial**
– the work done in factories and large organizations: **industry** (*noun* C/U); *adjective*: **industrial** ◦ *the steel industry* ◦ *manufacturing industry* ◦ *industrial expansion*

▷ more on business and industry ⇨ **BUSINESS, INDUSTRY**

4 economic conditions

– the total value of the goods and services bought and sold in an economy each year: **gross national product** (*abbreviation* **GNP**) (*noun singular*)

– a period in which an economy or a business grows or develops quickly: **boom**; *verb*: **boom** ◦ *There was a boom in the economy during the mid-1980s.* ◦ *Business is booming!*
– to be financially successful: **prosper**; *noun* (U): **prosperity**; *adjective*: **prosperous** ◦ *The country*

economy *contd.*

is going through a period of prosperity. ○ *a prosperous company*

– a failure in the business world: **crash** ○ *the Wall Street crash of 1929*
– a sudden fall in trade or the value of sth: **slump**; *verb*: **slump** ○ *a slump in house prices* ○ *The pound slumped against the German Mark.*
– a period when a country's economy is not successful: **recession** (*noun* C/U); a very serious recession: **depression** (*noun* C/U) ○ *The economy is moving out of recession.* ○ *We're facing another depression.*

– the general rise in prices in an economy: **inflation** (*noun* U); *adjective*: **inflationary** ○ *Inflation is now under 2% per year.* ○ *A reduction in interest rates could be highly inflationary.*

edit

– producing a book ⇨ **PUBLISH**
– making a film or video ⇨ **FILM, VIDEO**

education

see also TEACH, LEARN, SCHOOL, UNIVERSITY

– the teaching or training of people, especially in schools, colleges, etc to improve their knowledge and develop their skills: **education** (*noun* U/*singular*); *adjective*: **educational** ○ *The British education system* ○ *adult education* ○ *sex education* ○ *I hated my school but I have to admit that it gave me an excellent education.* ○ *educational materials*
– to teach or train sb, especially in a school, university, etc: **educate** sb ○ *I was educated in France.*

– education of very young children, before they go to school (usually from the age of 3 to 5): **pre-school education**
– the first stage of education (from about the age of 5): **primary education**
– the second stage of education (from about the age of 11 or 12): **secondary education**
– education in a university or college: **tertiary education**
– education at a university: **higher education**
– education for people who have left school, but not at a university: **further education**
– education that is connected with the skills you need to do a particular job: **vocational education**

– an area of knowledge that is studied at school, college, etc: **subject** ○ *My favourite subject at school was French.*
– a complete series of lessons or classes related to a particular subject: **course** (**in/on** sth) ○ *an advanced English course* ○ *She wants to do a course in social work.*
– to spend time learning about sth: **study** sth ○ *I spent a year studying Russian.*

– a class in the evening where people go to learn sth: **evening class** ○ *I'm attending evening classes to improve my Italian.*

– a written, spoken or practical test of what you know or can do: **exam**, (*formal*) **examination** ○ *I've passed my history exam.*
– an examination that you have passed or a course of study that you have successfully completed: **qualification** ○ *a teaching qualification* ○ *These days, people need more and more qualifications to get a job.*
– to pass an examination which is necessary to do a particular job: **qualify** (**as** sth) ○ *He qualified as a teacher about three years ago.*
– if you have passed an examination or completed a course of study, you are **qualified**; *opposite*: **unqualified** ○ *She's a qualified physiotherapist.* ○ *They said I was unqualified to do that job.*

▷ more on studying and examinations ⇨ **STUDY, EXAM**

– somebody who has had a good education is **well educated**; not well educated: **uneducated**

■ **MORE ...**
– connected with the educational activities of schools, colleges and universities: **academic** (*adverb* **academically**) ○ *the beginning of the academic year* ○ *The school has improved academically in the past year.*

effect ⇨ CAUSE/EFFECT

effort

– hard work ⇨ **WORK**
– trying to do sth ⇨ **TRY**

egg

see also BIRD, FOOD, COOK

– an oval object with a hard shell that comes from a bird: **egg** ○ *Most birds lay their eggs in a nest.*
– an egg from a hen used as food: **egg** (*noun* C/U) ○ *a dozen eggs* ○ *eggs and bacon* ○ *I can't eat anything with egg in it.*
– the hard outside part of an egg: **shell**
– the white part of an egg: (**egg**) **white**
– the yellow part of an egg: **yolk**

■ cooking with eggs
– to break an egg open: **crack** sth ○ *Crack the eggs into a bowl.*
– to cook an egg in its shell in boiling water: **boil** an egg; *adjective*: **boiled** ○ *boiled eggs for breakfast*
– a boiled egg which has a soft yellow part is **soft-boiled**; *opposite*: **hard-boiled** ○ *a hard-boiled egg*
– a small cup for holding a boiled egg: **eggcup**
– to cook an egg without its shell in boiling water: **poach** an egg; *adjective*: **poached**
– to cook an egg in hot oil: **fry** an egg; *adjective*: **fried** ○ *fried eggs*
– eggs that have been mixed and beaten and fried, sometimes with vegetables or cheese: **omelette**
– eggs that are mixed together with milk and then cooked in a saucepan: **scrambled egg** (*noun* U), **scrambled eggs** (*noun plural*)

election

> **1** different kinds of election
> **2** people who want to be elected
> **3** the process of electing sb
> **4** the result of an election
>
> **see also** POLITICS, GOVERNMENT, PARLIAMENT

1 different kinds of election

- choosing a member of parliament, a president, etc by voting; the time when this happens: **election** (*noun* C/U); *adjective*: **electoral** ◦ *to call an election* ◦ *Elections will be held in March.* ◦ *parliamentary/presidential elections* ◦ *election results* ◦ *to stand for election* ◦ *electoral reform*
- an election in which the voters in a country choose their national parliament: **general election**
- an election in which the voters in a district choose their local council: **local election**
- a special election to choose a new Member of Parliament; it is held when the previous member has resigned or died: **by-election**

- an election in which all the voters of a country vote on whether to do sth or not: **referendum** ◦ *to hold a referendum on abortion*

2 people who want to be elected

- a person who wants to be elected to a particular position: **candidate** ◦ *the Labour Party candidate*
- to be a candidate in an election: **stand*** (**for** sth), (*especially AmE*) **run*** (**for** sth) ◦ *She's decided to stand for the European Parliament.* ◦ *He's running for president.*

- a plan to do a number of things to win an election, persuade people to accept a change, etc: **campaign**; to take part in a campaign: **campaign** (**for/against** sb/sth); a person who takes part in a plan to make sth happen or to prevent sth: **campaigner**
- a written statement by a party that explains what it would do if it became the government: **manifesto** (*plural* **manifestos**)
- information or ideas used by the government in order to influence or persuade people about sth: **propaganda** (*noun* U) ◦ *anti-European propaganda*
- a short phrase that is used in election campaigns, etc and that is easy to remember: **slogan**

3 the process of electing sb

- to show your choice in an election by raising your hand or writing on a piece of paper: **vote** (**for/against** sb/sth) ◦ *Have you been to vote yet?* ◦ *I'm not going to tell you who I voted for.*
- the choice you make in an election: **vote** ◦ *There were more votes against the motion than in favour.*

- a person who votes or who has the right to vote in a political election: **voter**
- all the people in a country who have the right to vote in an election: **the electorate** (*with singular or plural verb*)

- a district that has its own Member of Parliament: **constituency**
- a person who lives in a constituency: **constituent**

■ going to vote in a political election
- a place where you go to vote in an election: **polling station**
- a piece of paper on which you write your choice: **ballot paper**
- after making your choice, you put your ballot paper into a **ballot box**

- the day when people vote in an election: **polling-day**
- voting in an election: **polling** (*noun* U) ◦ *In Britain, polling always takes place on a Thursday.*

4 the result of an election

- after people have finished voting, officials **count** the votes
- if the result of the election is very close, the official in charge may order a **re-count** ◦ *It's very close. There'll probably have to be a re-count.*

- the total number of votes given at an election: **vote** ◦ *She got less than 10% of the vote.*
- to receive a certain number of votes at an election: **poll** sth ◦ *He polled 12987 votes.*
- the difference in the number of votes for the person/party who came first and the person/party who came second: **majority** ◦ *to get an overall majority* (= a majority over all the other people/parties together)

- to choose sb by voting: **elect** sb (**to** sth) (**as** sth); to elect sb again: **re-elect** sb ◦ *She was elected to the Italian parliament in 1987.* ◦ *He was elected as MP for Bath.*
- to be elected to a political position: **get* in, get* into** sth ◦ *The Tories got in at the last election.* ◦ *His ambition is to get into Parliament.*
- a person who is successful in an election **wins*** (the election)

- a place in a parliament or council that sb wins in an election: **seat** ◦ *Labour has a majority of 10 seats on the council.*
- elected for a position, but not yet in office: **elect** (*adjective, after the noun*) ◦ *the President elect*

▷ people who are elected to parliament or to a town council ⇨ PARLIAMENT, TOWN

■ **MORE ...**
- a type of electoral system where the candidate with the most votes will become the representative for a particular district: **first-past-the-post system**
- a type of electoral system where the final result depends on the percentage of the vote that each party received in an election: **proportional representation** (*noun* U)

electricity

1 producing electricity
2 using electricity
other fuels ⇨ **FUEL, COAL, GAS, NUCLEAR, OIL**

1 producing electricity

– a type of energy that provides heat, light, and power to work machines: **electricity** (*noun* U) ◦ *It's a very powerful motor and uses a lot of electricity.* ◦ *Don't waste electricity!*
– connected with electricity: **electrical** ◦ *an electrical engineer*

– a place where electricity is produced: **power station**
– a machine that uses fuel or other kinds of energy to produce electricity: **generator**
– to produce electricity: **generate** sth ◦ *This new power station will generate enough electricity to meet the needs of much of the south-east of Scotland.*

– a unit for measuring the power of electricity: **watt** (*abbreviation* **W**) ◦ *a 40-watt light bulb*
– a unit for measuring the force of electricity: **volt** (*abbreviation* **V**); the number of volts that sth produces or uses: **voltage** (*noun* U) ◦ *a 9-volt battery*
– the flow of electricity through a wire: **current**; a unit for measuring this: **amp** ◦ *an electric current* ◦ *a 13-amp fuse*

■ batteries
– a device that provides electricity for a radio, torch, car, etc: **battery** ◦ *I need a new battery for my watch* ◦ *a car/radio/torch battery*
– a car battery that has no more power is **flat**; a battery for a radio, etc that has no more power is **dead** ◦ *I couldn't start the car this morning, because the battery was flat.*
– a battery which is losing power is **running down** ◦ *'What's wrong with this torch?' 'I think the batteries are running down.'*

– a battery that you can use again is **rechargeable**
– when a rechargeable battery stops working, you have to **recharge** it
– a thing you use to recharge a battery: (**battery**) **charger**

2 using electricity

– using electricity: **electric** ◦ *an electric light/heater/blanket/cooker*
– using electricity or connected with electricity: **electrical**

Note: we use **electric** for specific machines that use electricity ◦ *an electric shaver/motor*; we use **electrical** in a more general sense ◦ *electrical equipment* ◦ *electrical goods.*

– a device that allows you to turn an appliance on or off: **switch**
– if you want to use sth which is electrical, you **put* it on, turn** it **on, switch** it **on** ◦ *It's dark in here, can you put the light on, please?* ◦ *Turn on the radio.*
– if you want to stop using sth, you **turn** it **off, switch** it **off** ◦ *Can you switch off the cooker for me, please?* ◦ *Turn the telly off before you go to bed.*
– to put off a light: **turn** sth **out**, **put*** sth **out** ◦ *She turned out the light/turned the light out.*

– a hole in a wall where you can connect sth to the electricity supply: **socket**, **power point**
– a plastic or rubber object with two or three metal pins, that is put into a socket to allow electricity to pass into an appliance: **plug**
– to put sth into a socket: **plug** sth **in**; to take sth out of the socket: **unplug** sth, **take* the plug out** ◦ *It's obvious why it's not working; it's not plugged in!* ◦ *Please unplug the computer when you've finished with it.*
– a device that allows you to put more than one plug into the same socket or to use different kinds of plug: **adaptor**
– if you have to use equipment far away from a socket, you need an **extension lead**

– wire covered with plastic that carries electricity: **wire** (*noun* C/U)
– a wire that connects an appliance to its plug: **flex**
– the plastic tube that protects the wire: **insulation** (*noun* U)
– to connect the flex to a plug: **wire** a plug
– the system of wires in a building: **wiring** (*noun* U)

– a thin wire or a part of a plug that protects electrical equipment from a voltage that is too high: **fuse**
– when a piece of equipment stops working because a fuse has melted, it **fuses**, **blows* a fuse**; to cause a piece of equipment to do this: **fuse** sth ◦ *All of a sudden the lights fused and we were plunged into darkness.* ◦ *I think I must have fused the lights.*

– the quantity of electricity that you use is measured with a **meter**
– a person who comes to check how much electricity you have used: **meter reader**
– a piece of paper that tells you how much electricity you have used and how much it costs: **electricity bill**
– a company that supplies electricity: **electricity company**
– when the electricity company decides to stop the supply of electricity, they **cut* off** the electricity

– when your house receives no electricity for a short time, there is a **power cut**, the electricity **goes* off**
– when the electricity returns, it **comes* back on** ◦ *'The light's gone off!' 'I expect there's been a power cut. It'll probably come back on in a little while.'*

– a person who puts the wiring or electrical appliances into a building or does repairs: **electrician**

■ **MORE ...**
- a large metal structure that holds the power line: (**electricity**) **pylon**
- electricity generated by water: **hydroelectricity** (*noun* U); *adjective*: **hydroelectric** ◦ *hydro-electric power*
- a generator which uses the energy of the sun: **solar panel**

- a wire that carries electricity is **live** ◦ *Be careful not to touch the live wire!*
- a wire that makes an appliance safer by connecting it to the ground: **earth** (*AmE* **ground**)

- the effect on your body when some electricity goes through it: (**electric**) **shock** ◦ *Don't touch that wire – you'll get a shock.*
- to be killed by electricity: be **electrocuted**

elephant ⇨ ANIMAL

embarrassed

- sorry for what you have done ⇨ SORRY
- worried or anxious ⇨ WORRY

emotion

1 emotions
2 feeling emotions
3 showing emotions
4 not showing emotions

1 emotions

- something that you feel in your mind: **feeling**, **emotion** ◦ *a feeling of hopelessness/relief* ◦ *He felt a mixture of emotions: hate, jealousy and fear.*
- a person's emotions: **feelings** ◦ *to hurt a person's feelings* (= to make sb unhappy) ◦ *I find it very difficult to hide my feelings.*
- connected with a person's emotions: **emotional** (*adverb* **emotionally**) ◦ *emotional problems* ◦ *emotionally disturbed children*
- strength of feeling: **emotion** (*noun* U), **feeling** (*noun* U) ◦ *a voice full of emotion* ◦ *She spoke with considerable feeling.*

Note: feeling, but not **emotion**, can also be used to talk about what you feel in your body: ◦ *a feeling of hunger* ◦ *I've lost the feeling in my legs.*

▷ particular emotions ⇨ AFRAID, ANGRY, DISLIKE, EXCITED, HAPPY, LOVE, PROUD, SAD, SORRY, SURPRISE, SYMPATHY, WORRY

2 feeling emotions

- the way that you feel at a particular time is your **mood**; if you are feeling happy, you are **in a good mood**; if you are feeling angry or unhappy, you are **in a bad mood, in a** (**bad**) **temper** ◦ *What sort of a mood was she in?*

- to experience an emotion: **feel*** happy, sad, etc ◦ *She began to feel worried.* ◦ *He didn't feel sorry at all.*
- something that causes you to feel an emotion, especially sadness, sympathy, gratitude, etc, is **moving**, **touching**; if you have this feeling, you are **moved** (**by** sth), **touched** (**by** sth) ◦ *a touching scene* ◦ *a moving account of the tragedy* ◦ *I was moved to tears by the music.* ◦ *We were touched by your kind words.*
- to make sb feel sad or angry: **affect** sb ◦ *The whole town was affected by the disaster.*

- the place where a person feels emotions: **heart** ◦ *She's got a kind heart.* ◦ *I felt in my heart that it would be better to leave her.*
- to be strongly affected by an action, criticism, etc: **take*** sth **to heart** ◦ *Don't take it to heart – it was just a bad joke.*

■ a person's emotional character
- a person's personality, especially as it affects the way they behave and feel: **temperament** ◦ *She has a very calm temperament.*
- easily made to feel unhappy or annoyed: **sensitive** (**about** sth); too sensitive: **over-sensitive** ◦ *She's very sensitive about her height.*
- having quick and strong emotional reactions: **emotional** ◦ *Charles is much more emotional than he appears.*

- not knowing or caring how another person feels and whether you have hurt them: **insensitive**; *noun* (U): **insensitivity** ◦ *I was really shocked at the questions they asked that poor woman – I don't know how people can be so insensitive.*
- not easily worried or annoyed by what people say about you: (*informal*) **thick-skinned** ◦ *I don't think George will mind the criticisms – he's pretty thick-skinned, you know.*

3 showing emotions

- to show a feeling: **express** sth ◦ *He finds it difficult to express his feelings.* ◦ *We would like to express our thanks for all you have done for us.*
- the look on a person's face: **expression**; showing a lot of feeling: **expressive** (*adverb* **expressively**) ◦ *She had a serious expression on her face.* ◦ *He was wearing a sad expression.* ◦ *an expressive face*

- to produce water from your eyes, and make a noise, because you are unhappy or have hurt yourself: **cry**; the water produced from your eyes when you cry: **tears** (*noun plural*) ◦ *I was crying with happiness.* ◦ *tears of joy*
- an expression on your face when the corners of your mouth turn up because you are happy: **smile**; when you make this expression, you **smile** (**at** sb/sth)
- to become red in the face: **blush**; *noun*: **blush** ◦ *to blush with embarrassment* ◦ *to blush at the thought of something*
- to make short quick movements because you are nervous, frightened, excited, etc: **shake***, **tremble** ◦ *My hand shook as I signed the cheque.* ◦ *I could see he was trembling with fear.*

▷ more on crying ⇨ CRY

4 not showing emotions

- to avoid showing your feelings: **hide*** sth, **hold*** sth **back/in** ◦ *I was trying to hide my anxiety.* ◦ *A good cry will do you good – don't hold it back.*

emotion *contd.*

- the ability to control your feelings and not show strong emotion: **self-control** (*noun* U) ◦ *to lose your self-control*
- to hide your amusement by not laughing or smiling: **keep* a straight face**
- a person who does not show any pleasant feelings is **distant**, **cold**; this quality: **coldness** (*noun* U)

empire ⇨ GOVERNMENT

employment

1 being employed
2 giving up your job
3 being made to give up your job
4 not having a job
5 looking for a job
6 giving sb a job
see also WORK, PAY²

1 being employed

- to give work to sb and pay them for doing it: **employ** sb ◦ *She was employed as a secretary for a couple of months.* ◦ *How many people does your firm employ at present?*
- the state of being employed, or the act of employing sb: **employment** (*noun* U) ◦ *to look for employment*
- to be employed: **work** ◦ *She works for a large pharmaceutical company.*
- a person's employment: **job**, **work** (*noun* U), (*formal*) **occupation** ◦ *It's not easy to find a job at the moment.* ◦ *My work involves using computers a lot of the time.*

■ different ways of being employed

- working for only part of the day, or for only a few days a week: **part-time** (*adjective, adverb*) ◦ *to take a part-time job* ◦ *I only work part-time.*
- working all day, five or six days a week: **full-time** (*adjective, adverb*)
- work which is not regular, and which is usually paid hourly is **casual** ◦ *casual office staff* ◦ *to do casual work*
- a job which is only for a limited period is **temporary**; *opposite*: **permanent** ◦ *She's got a temporary job working in a newspaper office.*

■ people at work

- a person who employs other people: **employer**
- a person who is in charge of a company or other organization: **manager**
- a person whose job is to give orders to other people at work: (*informal*) **boss**
- the group of managers who are in charge of a company: **management** (*with singular or plural verb*) ◦ *The management has/have decided to introduce a new shift system.*

▷ the work of managers ⇨ MANAGEMENT

- a person who is employed: **employee** ◦ *This factory has 200 employees.*
- an employee, especially one who does physical work: **worker**
- the group of people who work in an office, a shop, a bank, etc: **staff** (*often with a plural verb*) ◦ *Their staff are so polite and friendly. I really like eating there.* ◦ *The manager decided to advertise for extra staff to help with the Christmas sales.*
- a person who is responsible for the employees in a company: **personnel manager**

■ changes in your employment

- to give sb a better or more important job: **promote** sb ◦ *They promoted her to office manager two months ago.* ◦ *I've been promoted!*
- the act of being promoted or of promoting sb: **promotion** (*noun* C/U) ◦ *They've given her another promotion!* ◦ *I was expecting promotion, but unfortunately didn't get it this time.*
- to say that sb would be suitable for a job, position, etc: **recommend** sb **for/as** sth ◦ *My boss recommended me for the new post in the marketing department.*

■ not at work

- a period of time in which you do not go to work: **time off** (*noun* U) ◦ *Could I have some time off next week?* ◦ *The doctor advised me to take time off.*
- a single day on which you do not go to work: **day off** ◦ *I had to take a day off to go to the funeral.*
- the time when you are not at work because you have taken time off: **absence** (*noun* C/U) ◦ *His absence created a lot of problems for the office.*
- when you are not present at work, you are **absent** ◦ *I wonder what's wrong with him. He's been absent for a couple of days.*

- the permission you need to be absent from work: **leave** (*noun* U) ◦ *I'd like to take a couple of weeks' leave.*
- away from work with permission: **on leave** ◦ *He's away on leave at the moment. Can I help you?*
- leave taken because you are not well: **sick leave** (*noun* U)
- leave taken by a woman because she is expecting a baby: **maternity leave** (*noun* U)

▷ more on holidays ⇨ HOLIDAY

■ trade unions and strikes

- a group of people whose job is to protect the rights of employees: (**trade**) **union**
- a person who is an active member of a union, and often has an official position in one: **trade unionist**

- (used about workers) to refuse to work in order to try to get more pay, better working conditions, etc: **strike***, **go* on strike**; refusing to work: **on strike**; an occasion of striking: **strike**, **stoppage** ◦ *to go on strike for higher pay* ◦ *Do you know why the bus drivers are striking?* ◦ *How long have they been on strike?* ◦ *a one-day strike*
- a person who is on strike: **striker**
- strikes or other ways of trying to get more pay, better conditions, etc: **industrial action** (*noun* U) ◦ *The nurses are threatening to take industrial action.*
- the relations between the management and the workers: **industrial relations** (*noun plural*)

2 giving up your job

- to stop working (usually because you have reached the maximum working age): **retire** (**from** sth); *adjective*: **retired** ◦ *George has retired from the bank and gone to live in the country.* ◦ *a retired sea captain* ◦ *Now I'm retired I want to see the world.*
- the act of retiring, or the situation where you have retired and do not work any more: **retirement** (*noun* U) ◦ *He took early retirement at 55.*

- a person who has retired because they have reached retirement age: **pensioner** ◦ *an old-age pensioner*
- the money that a pensioner gets from the government or from the employer they worked for: **pension**

- to voluntarily leave a job: **give* up** your **job**, **resign** (**from** sth), (*informal*) **quit*** ◦ *She decided to give up her job.* ◦ *I'm going to resign.* ◦ *If your job is so badly paid, why don't you quit?*
- the act of resigning: **resignation** ◦ *to give in/hand in your resignation*

3 being made to give up your job

- to order an employee to leave his/her job: **sack** sb, **fire** sb, (*informal*) **give*** sb **the sack**, (*formal*) **dismiss** sb; the act of dismissing sb: **dismissal** ◦ *He was sacked because he was always late for work.* ◦ *If you're not careful they'll give you the sack.* ◦ *a case of unfair dismissal*
- if sb tells you to leave your job, you (*informal*) **get* the sack**
- to order an employee to stop working for a period of time: **suspend** sb; *noun* (U/C): **suspension** ◦ *He was suspended on full pay while the investigation was carried out.*
- to dismiss sb from work for economic reasons: **make*** sb **redundant**; the act of making sb redundant or being made redundant: **redundancy** ◦ *I've been made redundant.* ◦ *Another 30 redundancies have just been announced.*
- not to dismiss sb: **keep*** sb **on** ◦ *I was lucky to be kept on. Quite a few people lost their jobs.*

4 not having a job

- without a paid job: **unemployed**, **out of work** ◦ *I'm unemployed at the moment.* ◦ *a decrease in the number out of work*
- people without a paid job: **the unemployed**
- the situation of not having a job: **unemployment** (*noun* U) ◦ *to have a period of unemployment*
- the number of people who are unemployed: **unemployment** (*noun* U) ◦ *Unemployment is still rising despite the economic recovery.*

5 looking for a job

- to write to an employer to say you are interested a paid job in a cin a particular job, usually one that has been advertised: **apply for** sth, **put* in for** sth ◦ *I've decided to apply for that job I told you about.* ◦ *Why don't you put in for that job?*
- a person who applies for a job: **applicant**
- the process of applying for a job: **application** ◦ *There were over 200 applications for the job.* ◦ *Have you filled in the application form?*
- a piece of paper that states your qualifications, work experience, etc: **CV**, **curriculum vitae**
- a statement, usually in the form of a letter written by the current or former employer, that describes your character, ability and experience: **reference** ◦ *They require two references, including one from my present employer.*
- the person who writes a reference: **referee** ◦ *Would you be willing to act as my referee?*

- a meeting at which sb is asked questions to see if they are suitable for a job: **interview** ◦ *My interview didn't really go very well – I was so nervous.*
- to ask a candidate questions about their experience, etc during an interview: **interview** sb

6 giving sb a job

- a paid job in a company or office: **position**, **post** ◦ *to apply for the position of assistant sales manager*
- a job or a post that is not occupied: **vacancy**; *adjective*: **vacant** ◦ *At present we don't have any vacancies.* ◦ *The post has been vacant for some time.*

- to ask sb to take a job: **offer** sth **to** sb, **offer** sb sth ◦ *They offered me the job.*
- to agree to an offer: **take*** sth, **accept** sth ◦ *If they offer you the job, will you take it?*
- to refuse an offer: **turn** sth **down** ◦ *He was offered the job, but he turned it down.*

- to give sb a job: **employ** sb (**as** sth), **take*** sb **on**, **recruit** sb ◦ *He's been employed as a chef.* ◦ *She was taken on as part of the government training scheme.* ◦ *The company recruits about 30 new members of staff each year.*
- to give sb a job for a short time: **hire** sb ◦ *We hire extra staff during the busy summer season.*
- to choose sb for a particular post or job: **appoint** sb (**to** sth); the new post or job: **appointment** ◦ *A new person has been appointed to the post of Sales Director.* ◦ *His appointment will take effect from April 1st.*

- to become part of a company, office, etc as an employee: **join** sth ◦ *She joined the firm a month after leaving school.*

■ MORE . . .

- if sb does work for different employers and is paid separately for each piece of work, their work is **freelance** (*adverb* **freelance**) ◦ *a freelance journalist/photographer* ◦ *to do freelance work* ◦ *She works freelance from home.*
- working for yourself and not for another person or company: **self-employed** ◦ *a self-employed window cleaner*

- a job or profession for which you are trained and which you do for a long time: **career** ◦ *a career in medicine/teaching*

- the money that the government pays to unemployed people: **unemployment benefit** (*noun* U), (*BrE, informal*) **dole** (*noun singular*)
- to register officially as sb who is unemployed: **sign on**, (*informal*) **go* on the dole** ◦ *When did*

employment *contd.*

you sign on? ◦ *If you lose your job, you'll have to go on the dole.*
– to be officially unemployed: (*informal*) **be on the dole** ◦ *I've been on the dole for nearly a year.*

empty ⇨ FULL

encourage

see also ADVISE/SUGGGEST, PERSUADE

– to give sb hope and support to do sth: **encourage** sb (**to** do sth); *noun* (C/U): **encouragement** ◦ *I was ready to leave my job, but my wife encouraged me to stay.* ◦ *Her parents gave her every encouragement.*
– if sth encourages you, it is **encouraging**, you feel **encouraged** ◦ *The latest unemployment figures are most encouraging.* ◦ *I felt really encouraged by what they said.*
– something which encourages you to do sth: **incentive** ◦ *The annual bonus is a real incentive to work harder.*

– to encourage sb's interest in sth: **motivate** sb (**to** do sth) ◦ *A good teacher knows how to motivate her students.*
– a feeling of interest in doing sth: **motivation** (**to** do sth) (*noun* C/U) ◦ *She doesn't seem to have the motivation to work hard at school.*
– if sth motivates you, it is **motivating**, you feel **motivated** ◦ *I find it a very stimulating subject.* ◦ *a highly motivated student*
– to greatly encourage sb to do sth special: **inspire** sb (**to** do sth), **stimulate** sb **to** do sth; *nouns* (C/U): **inspiration, stimulation** ◦ *What was it that inspired you to write?* ◦ *a source of inspiration*

– if you want to give sb encouragement, you can say **Good luck!** or (*informal*) **Go for it!**
– to shout words of encouragement at sb: **cheer** sb **on** ◦ *The players were cheered on by the crowd.*

■ not encouraging
– to make sb lose hope and confidence: **discourage** sb; *noun* (C/U): **discouragement** ◦ *Don't let this problem discourage you.*
– if sth discourages you, it is **discouraging**, you feel **discouraged** ◦ *The results are very discouraging.* ◦ *I felt pretty discouraged when I got my essay back.*
– to make sb decide not to do sth: **put*** sb **off** (**doing** sth), (*formal*) **deter** sb (**from** doing sth) ◦ *Don't be put off by what they say.* ◦ *Nothing would deter me from going.*

end/finish

1 periods of time
2 situations, processes, actions, etc
3 objects and places
4 supplies, resources, etc
stopping doing sth ⇨ STOP
see also BEGIN, CONTINUE

1 periods of time

– the last point of a period of time: **end** (**of** sth) ◦ *the end of the month/year* ◦ *Please reply by the end of April.*
– to come to the end of a period of time: **end, come* to an end** ◦ *My last year at university is about to come to an end.*
– when a period of time has ended, it is **up** ◦ *Stop writing now, please. Your time is up.* ◦ *You must return the car before the week is up.*

2 situations, processes, actions, etc

– the final point or moment of sth: **end** ◦ *See me at the end of the lesson.* ◦ *He left before the end of the party.*
– the end of a race, competition, etc: **finish** ◦ *It was a close finish.* ◦ *from start to finish*
– coming at the end: **last** (*adjective, adverb*) ◦ *The last month of the year is December.* ◦ *This is the last cigarette I shall ever smoke.* ◦ *He didn't win the race – he came last!.*

▷ more on being or happening last ⇨ FIRST/NEXT/LAST

– to reach its end: **finish, end, come* to an end** ◦ *What time does the show finish?* ◦ *The course ended with a party for all the students.*
– to come to the end of sth: **finish** sth/doing sth, **end** sth ◦ *She finished her drink and left.* ◦ *We should finish painting this wall today.* ◦ *They have decided to end their relationship.*
– finished: **over** ◦ *When the film was over, there was a discussion.*

▷ ending a relationship ⇨ RELATIONSHIP

– to finish making sth that has taken time or effort: **complete** sth ◦ *The new building should be completed by July.* ◦ *Have you completed your research yet?*
– to continue with an activity until it is successfully completed: **see*** sth **through** ◦ *I'll see this project through and then I'm going to leave the company.*

■ the end of a book, film, conversation, story, etc
– the last part of a story, film, etc: **end, conclusion** ◦ *That is the end of the story.* ◦ *a surprising conclusion to the story*
– the way in which a story, etc comes to an end: **ending**; to reach the end: **end** ◦ *a happy/sad ending* ◦ *The story ends with the prince marrying the princess.*
– when a conversation, meeting, etc ends, it **comes* to a close, draws* to a close**; to start to end sth: **bring*** sth **to a close** ◦ *As the play drew to a close, it was obvious who was the murderer.* ◦ *The priest brought the service to a close with a prayer.*
– coming to an end: **closing, concluding** ◦ *the closing moments in a film*

– at the end of a series of events: **in the end, finally, eventually** ◦ *In the end he lost his job and had to sell his house.*
– at the end of a list: **lastly, last of all** ◦ *Lastly, I should like to thank you all for listening to me.*

■ not ending

– without an end: **endless** (*adverb* **endlessly**) ○ *They quarrelled endlessly, but never considered divorce.*

3 objects and places

– the last part of sth: **end** ○ *the end of a pencil* ○ *the end of the street* ○ *a cigarette end* ○ *You hold that end and we'll lift this together.*

– the place where sth, especially a surface, ends: **edge** ○ *The paper was going brown around the edges.* ○ *She drove the car over the edge of the cliff.*

– the thin or pointed end of sth: **tip** ○ *the tips of your fingers*

4 supplies, resources, etc

– to use sth until no more is left: **use** sth **up**, (*more formal*) **exhaust** sth (*usually passive*) ○ *I used up all my coins in the parking meter.* ○ *Our food supplies will be exhausted in a few days.*

– when a supply of sth comes to an end, it **runs* out** ○ *The milk has run out – shall I get some more?*

– to have no more of sth: **run* out** (**of** sth), **be out of** sth ○ *I'm afraid we've run out of time.* ○ *We're out of coffee. Would you like tea instead?*

■ **MORE ...**

– to gradually bring sth to an end: **phase** sth **out** ○ *This system of payment is being phased out.*

– to end sth: (*formal*) **terminate** sth; an act of ending sth: (*formal*) **termination** ○ *to terminate a contract* ○ *to terminate a pregnancy* ○ *the termination of your contract*

– time or space that has no end: **infinity** (*noun* U) ○ *the infinity of space*

enemy

see also FRIEND

– a person who hates and tries to harm sb/sth: **enemy** ○ *Being a politician, he makes many enemies.* ○ *Andrew used to be a good friend of mine, but now we're bitter enemies.*

– to dislike sb strongly: **hate** sb; *nouns* (U): **hatred**, **hate** ○ *Religious hatred was tearing the country apart.* ○ *The victim's parents felt nothing but hate for the murderer.* ○ *love and hate*

– unfriendly feelings towards sb/sth: **ill feeling** (*noun* U), **hostility** (*noun* U); *adjective*: **hostile** ○ There's a lot of ill feeling about the decision to close the factory. ○ *She was full of hostility towards me.* ○ *a hostile attitude/look/intention*

– to cause sb to become sb's enemy: **turn** sb **against** sb ○ *That woman is turning him against us.*

– to make sb angry so that they become your enemy: **antagonize** sb ○ *Don't antagonize your boss – you may regret it!*

■ in a war

– (in a war) the army or country that your country is fighting against: (**the**) **enemy** (*with singular or plural verb*) ○ *The enemy was/were advancing on all fronts.* ○ *under attack from enemy aircraft*

– either of two groups of people who fight against each other: **side** ○ *Don't shoot him; he's on our side!*

▷ fighting and war ⇨ FIGHT, WAR

■ helping the enemy

– to give secret information to your enemy to help them defeat your country, army, etc: **betray** sb/sth; *noun* (U): **betrayal** ○ *You have betrayed your country.* ○ *an act of betrayal*

– the act of causing harm to sb/sth that trusts you: **treachery** (*noun* U); *adjective*: **treacherous** ○ *an act of treachery* ○ *treacherous behaviour*

– an act of causing harm to your country by helping its enemies: **treason** (*noun* U) ○ *an act of treason* ○ *to commit treason*

– a person who behaves in a treacherous way or who commits treason: **traitor** ○ *He is a traitor to his country.*

engine ⇨ MACHINE

enjoy

see also ENTERTAINMENT, LIKE², HAPPY

– to get pleasure from sth: **enjoy** sth/doing sth, **like** sth/doing sth; to enjoy sth very much: **love** sth ○ *Did you enjoy the party last night?* ○ *I've really enjoyed meeting you.* ○ *I love sailing.*

– an activity or person that gives you enjoyment and pleasure: **fun** (*noun* U); if you do sth for enjoyment and pleasure, you do it (**just**) **for fun** ○ *We had a lot of fun on holiday.* ○ *It's not much fun being in hospital.* ○ *My uncle is good fun.* ○ *The party was great fun.* ○ *I'm learning Spanish, just for fun.*

– to be happy doing sth: **enjoy** yourself, **have a good time**, **have fun** ○ *We really enjoyed ourselves last night – thank you very much.* ○ *Just relax and have fun.*

– the feeling of being happy: **pleasure** (*noun* U) ○ *I think I get more pleasure out of doing my garden than anything else.* ○ *It gives me great pleasure to be here with you today.*

– the feeling you have when you enjoy sth: **enjoyment** (*noun* U) ○ *I get a great deal of enjoyment from my work with children.*

– something that you enjoy is **enjoyable** ○ *an enjoyable holiday*

– the feeling of pleasure that you get when you have done or got what you wanted: **satisfaction** (*noun* U); something that gives you this feeling is **satisfying** ○ *I'm not getting much satisfaction from my work at present.* ○ *That was a really satisfying meal.*

– to give sb satisfaction: **satisfy** sb

– something that makes you smile or laugh or enjoy yourself is **amusing**, **entertaining** ○ *His speech was very amusing – I didn't know he had such a good sense of humour.* ○ *an entertaining evening*

– to make time pass pleasantly for sb: **amuse** sb, **entertain** sb ○ *Could you keep the guests amused while I finish the cooking?*

enjoy *contd.*

- to think about sth that you know you will enjoy: **look forward to** sth ◦ *I'm really looking forward to seeing you all again.*
- if you are looking forward to sth and you feel very impatient about it, you can say that you (*informal*) **can't wait** ◦ *'Is Lucy looking forward to Christmas?' 'Oh yes, she can't wait.'*
- something very special or enjoyable which you give sb: **treat** ◦ *The children were allowed to go to bed an hour later than usual as a special treat.*

■ **MORE ...**
- to allow yourself to enjoy sth freely, without worrying about what other people think: (*informal*) **let*** your **hair down** ◦ *Come on! Let your hair down for once! Enjoy yourself!*
- to enjoy sth very much: (*informal*) **have the time of** your **life** ◦ *'Did you enjoy Disneyland?' 'Yes, we had the time of our lives.'*

- a person who does not want other people to enjoy themselves: **spoilsport** ◦ *Come on! Don't be a spoilsport!*

enough

1 enough
2 more than enough
2 not enough
see also HOW MUCH/MANY

1 enough
- as much or as many as is necessary: **enough (of) ...**, (*formal*) **adequate**, (*formal*) **sufficient** ◦ *Have we got enough people?* ◦ *I'm afraid that not enough of the children are really interested.* ◦ *Will that be enough or do you need some more?* ◦ *an adequate amount of food* ◦ *sufficient resources*
- to the necessary degree: **enough**, (*formal*) **sufficiently** ◦ *The rope isn't strong enough.* ◦ *You can't do it because you haven't practised enough.* ◦ *I hope they're sufficiently well-equipped to do this.*
- to be enough for sb/sth: **satisfy** sb/sth ◦ *We haven't got enough goods to satisfy demand.*
- to be enough for everyone to have some: **go* round** ◦ *Is there enough food to go round?*

- not very much, but enough: **reasonable** ◦ *It's a reasonable salary but I was expecting to get more.* ◦ *a reasonable amount of room to work in*
- only just enough; minimum or basic: **bare** ◦ *We just took the bare essentials so we didn't have too much to carry.* ◦ *the bare minimum*

■ having enough money
- to have enough and no more to live: **get* by (on** sth) ◦ *I don't earn very much but we get by.* ◦ *I can't get by on £30 a week* (= £30 a week is not enough money for me to live).
- if you have enough money for sth, you can **afford** sth/**to** do sth ◦ *I wish I could afford a holiday in Bermuda!* ◦ *We can't afford to buy her a piano.*

2 more than enough
- enough or more than enough: **plenty (of ...)**, **ample**, (*formal*) **abundant** ◦ *We've got plenty of time before the train goes.* ◦ *Another three chairs should be plenty.* ◦ *'How much will I need?' '£50 should be ample.'* ◦ *an abundant supply of food*

- more than you need; more than is reasonable: **too much/many**, **excessive** ◦ *You eat too much.* ◦ *We have too many dentists and not enough doctors.* ◦ *He drinks excessive amounts of alcohol.*
- an amount of sth that is more than you need: **surplus** (*noun* C/U), **excess** (*noun singular*) ◦ *a surplus of coffee on the world market* ◦ *a wine surplus*

3 not enough
- not enough: (*formal*) **inadequate** (*adverb* **inadequately**), (*formal*) **insufficient** (*adverb* **insufficiently**) ◦ *inadequate pay* ◦ *The amount of food was completely inadequate for a growing child.* ◦ *We were given insufficient time to discuss the matter.*

- if you do not have enough of sth, you are **short (of** sth), **lacking in** sth ◦ *We're a bit short of milk, you'd better get some on the way home.* ◦ *He's a nice person but he's rather lacking in conversation.*
- if you have too little of sth, you **lack** sth; *noun*: **lack** ◦ *It's quite a good essay but it lacks detail.* ◦ *a lack of enthusiasm*

- sth which does not exist in large enough quantities or which is difficult to find is **scarce**
- a situation in which sth is scarce: **scarcity** (*noun* C/U), **shortage** ◦ *Food was scarce during the war.* ◦ *a scarcity of clean water* ◦ *a petrol shortage*

- if sb/sth does not have enough of sth that should be there (particularly for their health), they are **deficient (in** sth); *noun* (C/U): **deficiency** ◦ *Their diet is deficient in calcium and iron.* ◦ *a vitamin deficiency*

enter

see also COME/GO, ARRIVE, LEAVE

- to come or go into a place: (*formal*) **enter** (sth), **come*/go* in/inside, come*/go* into** sth ◦ *Knock before entering.* ◦ *The students all stood up when the teacher entered the room.* ◦ *I knocked on the door and went in.* ◦ *'Come in!'* ◦ *She came quietly into the room and sat down by the fire.*
- to enter a place, usually with some difficulty: **get* in/inside, get* into** sth ◦ *How on earth did you manage to get in?* ◦ *They got into the building through a side door.*
- an act of coming or going into a place: **entrance** ◦ *His entrance was greeted by applause.*

- to enter a place secretly or quietly: **sneak/slip in, sneak/slip into** sth ◦ *I slipped into the lecture room and took a seat at the back.*

■ entering with force
- to enter a building by force, usually to steal sth: **break* in, break* into** sth ◦ *The thieves broke in through the back door.*

– to make or force a way into sth or through sth: **penetrate** sth; *noun* (U): **penetration** ◦ *The bullet had penetrated his heart.*
– to go or move into a place where there is not much space: **squeeze into** sth ◦ *We all squeezed into the lift*.

■ allowing sb into a place
– to allow sb/sth to enter a place: **let*** sb/sth **in**, **let*** sb/sth **into** sth, (*formal*) **admit** sb/sth (**into/to** sth) ◦ *Please let me in. I'm a friend of the owner.* ◦ *Why don't you open the curtains and let some light into the room?*
– the right to enter a place: **entrance** (*noun* U), **entry** (*noun* U), **admittance** (*noun* U) ◦ *an entrance fee* ◦ *The sign says 'No entry'.* ◦ *No admittance without a ticket.*

– not to allow sb/sth to enter a place: **keep*** sb/sth **out** (**of** a place) ◦ *Keep the dog out of the house.*
– to forbid sb officially to enter or go through a place: **bar** sb (**from** sth) ◦ *They were barred from the club for bad behaviour.*
– to lock a door so that sb cannot get into or out of a place: **lock** sb **out/in** ◦ *Oh no. I've left my house keys at the office and locked myself out.*

■ ways into a place
– a thing that you open or close to go in or out of a building or room, or to use a cupboard, etc: **door** ◦ *to open/shut/close the door* ◦ *an open door* ◦ *the front door*
– a thing like a door that closes an opening in a wall, hedge, fence, etc: **gate** ◦ *a gate into a field*
– a gate that goes round and allows one person at a time to pass through it (for example at a sports ground): **turnstile**

▷ more on doors ⇨ DOOR

– a door, gate or opening where you go into a place: **entrance** ◦ *I'll meet you at the entrance to the cinema.*
– a door, gate or opening where you go out of a place: **exit** ◦ *This plane has two exits at the front and two at the rear*.
– a way of entering or reaching a place: **access** (**to** sth) (*noun* U) ◦ *No access* ◦ *wheelchair access*

entertainment

1 entertaining and being entertained
2 shows
3 music and dance
4 the circus
5 outside entertainments
6 relaxing and enjoying yourself

see also GAME, SPORT, TELEVISION/RADIO, CINEMA, FILM, THEATRE, PLAY[1]

1 entertaining and being entertained

– things to do that interest and amuse people: **entertainment** (*noun* C/U) ◦ *outdoor entertainments* ◦ *There isn't much entertainment for young people in this town.* ◦ *the entertainment industry*
– something that offers entertainment: **amusement** ◦ *an amusement arcade*

– to interest and amuse sb: **entertain** sb; *adjective*: **entertaining** ◦ *Can you entertain the children while I go out for a minute?* ◦ *a very entertaining film*
– a person who entertains as a job: **entertainer** ◦ *a children's entertainer*

– the part of the entertainment industry that makes and puts on films, plays, shows, etc: **show business** (*noun* U)

– to take part in a play or to sing, dance, etc in front of an audience: **perform** (sth) ◦ *She is currently performing at the Royal Opera House.*
– something that you perform in front of an audience: **performance** ◦ *There will be two performances daily.* ◦ *They put on a brilliant performance.*
– a person who performs: **performer**

– a series of performances of music, plays, etc often held regularly in one place: **festival** ◦ *a film festival* ◦ *an annual festival of the arts* ◦ *the Edinburgh Festival*

– to get pleasure from doing sth: **enjoy** yourself, **enjoy** sth/doing sth, **have a good**, **great**, etc **time** (doing sth), **have fun** (doing sth) ◦ *I enjoy going to the theatre.* ◦ *I had a great time last night – I really enjoyed myself.* ◦ *How was the party? Did you have fun?*
– to keep yourself entertained: **amuse** yourself ◦ *I had to amuse myself for a few hours while I waited for her to arrive.*

▷ more on enjoying sth ⇨ ENJOY

– a group of people who are watching or listening to a play, film, concert, etc: **audience** (*with singular or plural verb*)

▷ more on audiences ⇨ AUDIENCE

2 shows

– a form of entertainment at the theatre or on television: **show** ◦ *There are lots of shows on in London.* ◦ *a Christmas show* ◦ *a television/radio show* ◦ *a game show*

– a particular activity that is organized for people to watch: **display** ◦ *a display of folk dances from around the world*
– a particular collection of works of art shown in a museum or art gallery: **exhibition** ◦ *an exhibition of Victorian photographs*
– a public display or exhibition for people to visit (to show new products, for example): **show** ◦ *a motor show* ◦ *a flower show* ◦ *a fashion show*
– something important that happens which people go to (a sports competition, for example): **event** ◦ *a horse-racing event*

– a traditional show at Christmas to entertain children: **pantomime**
– a show that is meant to make people laugh: **comedy show**
– a person who stands up in front of people and tells them funny stories to make them laugh: (**stand-up**) **comic/comedian**
– something said or done to make you laugh, especially a funny story: **joke**

▷ jokes and other things that are funny ⇨ FUNNY

entertainment *contd.*

- a model of a person or animal that you can move by pulling strings or by putting your hand inside it and moving your fingers: **puppet**
- a show where people with puppets perform a small play: **puppet show**
- a theatre for puppet shows: **puppet theatre**

▷ picture at TOY

- a way of entertaining people by making things happen that look impossible: **magic** (*noun* U)
- a person who does this kind of entertaining: **magician**, **conjurer**
- an act of using magic in this way: **trick**, **conjuring trick** ◦ *to do/perform a conjuring trick*
- a show where a magician does tricks: **magic show**

3 music and dance

- a performance of music: **concert** ◦ *a classical concert*
- a play in which the actors sing the words to music: **opera**
- a story which is told with music and dancing but without words: **ballet**
- a performance with pop or rock music: **pop concert**, **rock concert**
- a play or film which has music and dancing in it: **musical**
- an entertainment with singing, dancing, etc in a restaurant or night-club: **cabaret** (*noun* C/U)

▷ more on music and dancing ⇨ MUSIC, DANCE

4 the circus

- a show performed in a large tent by a group of people and (sometimes) animals: **circus**
- a person in a circus who wears funny clothes and makes people laugh: **clown**
- a person who performs difficult or unusual physical acts: **acrobat**
- a bar hanging from two ropes high above the ground, used as a swing by acrobats: **trapeze**; a person who performs on a trapeze: **trapeze artist**
- a rope stretched high above the ground on which acrobats and trapeze artists walk in a circus: **tightrope**

- a person who throws and catches more than two objects at one time: **juggler**; *verb*: **juggle** (sth) ◦ *Can you juggle?* ◦ *We saw him juggling five balls.*
- a person who puts fire in his/her mouth: **fire-eater**

5 outside entertainments

- a public entertainment that is held outside and moves around from town to town, where you can ride on machines or play games and try to win prizes: **fair**, **funfair**; the place where a fair is held: **fairground**
- a machine you can ride on at a fair: **ride** ◦ *Which rides did you go on?*
- a permanent place of public entertainment where you can ride on different machines: **amusement park**
- a park where all the amusements are based on one idea or topic: **theme park**
- a type of railway at fairs and amusement parks which goes up and down and has sharp bends: **rollercoaster**

- entertainment that people watch in the street: **street entertainment** (*noun* U)
- to sing or play music in a public place so that people will give you money: **busk**; a person who does this: **busker**

- a small container with chemicals in it that burns or explodes with coloured lights or bangs: **firework** (*usually plural*) ◦ *We went to the park to see the fireworks.* ◦ *a firework display*

- a day or time when people celebrate sth (especially a religious event): **festival** ◦ *Christmas is an important festival for Christians.*
- a public festival that takes place outdoors, during which there is a procession in the street and music and dancing: **carnival** ◦ *the annual Notting Hill Carnival in London*

6 relaxing and enjoying yourself

- if you want to have a drink and meet and talk to people, you can go to a **pub** or **bar**
- if you want to dance and meet people, you can go to a **disco** (*plural* **discos**) or (**night**)**club**
- if you want to meet people, especially your friends, and eat, drink, dance and enjoy yourself, you can have a **party** or go to a **party**
- entertainment at night, like pubs, clubs and discos: **nightlife** (*noun* U) ◦ *What's the nightlife like in this town?*
- to go out at night to pubs, clubs and discos: **go*/be out on the town** ◦ *We're exhausted – we were out on the town last night.*

▷ more on pubs and bars ⇨ BAR/PUB

▷ more on parties ⇨ PARTY

enthusiasm ⇨ INTERESTING

entrance

- a door ⇨ DOOR
- any kind of way into a place ⇨ ENTER

envelope ⇨ LETTER[1]

environment

> **1** the world we live in
> **2** damaging the environment
> **3** protecting the environment
>
> the conditions in which you live, work, etc ⇨ SITUATION
>
> **see also** NATURE

1 the world we live in

- the natural surroundings where plants, animals and people live: **the environment** (*noun singular*) ◦ *to protect/damage the environment*

- connected with the environment: **environmental** ◦ *People need to be educated on environmental issues.*

- the air that surrounds the earth: **the atmosphere** (*usually singular*)
- the layer of gas high in the atmosphere that helps to protect the earth from radiation from the sun: **ozone layer** ◦ *Scientists have discovered a hole in the ozone layer.*
- the normal weather conditions of a particular country: **climate** ◦ *a wet/dry/hot/cold climate* ◦ *a tropical/temperate climate*

▷ weather and climate ⇨ WEATHER

- things like oil, coal, etc which are found naturally in certain places and that people can use: **natural resources** (*noun plural*) ◦ *It's frightening when you think how quickly we're using up the world's natural resources.*

2 damaging the environment

- to cause damage to the environment, for example with the smoke or other waste from factories, making it dirty and dangerous: **pollute** sth; *noun* (U): **pollution** ◦ *Most of the rivers in the area are badly polluted.* ◦ *The government has introduced strict laws to try to control pollution.*
- something which pollutes the environment: **pollutant**
- rain that contains dangerous substances from factories, etc that damage the environment: **acid rain** (*noun* U)
- bad air (a mixture of smoke and fog) experienced in some polluted industrial cities: **smog** (*noun* U)

- cutting down trees over a large area so that forests are lost: **deforestation** (*noun* U)
- the warming of the earth which causes changes in the climate: **global warming** (*noun* U)
- the effect of carbon dioxide being trapped in the earth's atmosphere, which causes global warming: the **greenhouse effect** (*noun singular*)

3 protecting the environment

- to protect sth (for example animals or plants): **conserve** sth; *noun* (U): **conservation**
- a person who studies the environment and works to protect it: **environmentalist**, **conservationist**
- the scientific study of the relationship between living things and their natural surroundings: **ecology** (*noun* U); a person who studies these things: **ecologist**
- a political party which works to protect the environment: the **Green Party**, (*informal*) the **Greens**

- to process used objects and materials (paper, bottles, etc) so that they can be used again: **recycle** (sth); *noun* (U) **recycling**; if materials can be used in this way, they are **recyclable** ◦ *recycled paper/glass* ◦ *We take our empty jars and bottles to the bottle bank for recycling.* ◦ *recyclable packaging*
- a place where people leave used bottles to be recycled: **bottle bank**

- something that will not damage the environment is **environmentally friendly**, **green** ◦ *green products*
- something that will decay naturally and so will not damage the environment is **biodegradable** ◦ *biodegradable packaging*
- something which does not contain chemicals which could damage the ozone layer is **ozone-friendly** ◦ *ozone-friendly aerosols*
- petrol which does not contain lead is **unleaded**, **lead-free**

- different types of energy (from the sun, the wind, etc) which do not damage the environment as much as traditional types (oil, coal, etc): **alternative energy** (*noun* U) ◦ *We need to develop new alternative energy sources.*
- energy from the heat of the sun: **solar energy** (*noun* U), **solar power** (*noun* U)
- energy from the wind: **wind power** (*noun* U)
- energy from the water in rivers: **hydroelectric power** (*noun* U)

---

envy ⇨ WANT

---

equal ⇨ SAME

---

error ⇨ MISTAKE

---

escape

see also HOLD/CATCH, PRISON

- to leave a place or a situation that you do not want to be in: **escape** (**from** sth), **get* away** (**from** sth), **run* away** (**from** sth) ◦ *He grabbed me by the hair but I managed to escape.* ◦ *Once she starts talking you can't get away from her.* ◦ *When I was thirteen, I ran away from home.*
- an act of escaping: **escape** ◦ *The escape took place in the middle of the night.* ◦ *They had a narrow escape* (= they only just managed to escape).

- to watch over sb in order to prevent them from escaping: **guard** sb ◦ *He is being guarded night and day.*

- to get out of a place where you are being held, for example a prison: **break* out** (**of** sth), **get* out** (**of** sth); *noun*: **breakout** ◦ *During the fire, several prisoners broke out.* ◦ *The rabbit got out of its cage in the night – somebody must have left the door open.*
- to escape suddenly from sb who is holding you: **break* free/away** (**from** sb/sth), **break* loose** ◦ *She hit him with her handbag and managed to break free.*

- to escape with something that you have stolen: **get* away with** sth, **make* off with** sth ◦ *The thieves got away with £1 000 in cash.*
- an escape after a crime: **getaway**; a car, etc that criminals use to escape from a crime: **getaway**

escape *contd.*

car, etc ◦ *to make a quick getaway* ◦ *Police have found the getaway car.*
- to escape from a place or person by running as fast as possible: **run* for** your **life, run* for it** ◦ *I grabbed the money and ran for my life.*
- to move from place to place, so that people cannot find you: be **on the run** ◦ *Most of the gang are still on the run.*

- once you have escaped, you are **free** (**from** sb/sth)
- a place where sb who has run away from sb/sth can hide: **refuge**
- protection from danger: **refuge** (*noun* U) ◦ *He took refuge in the Spanish embassy.*

essential

- very important ⇨ IMPORTANT
- something that you must have ⇨ NEED
- something that you must do ⇨ MUST

even

- a number ⇨ NUMBER
- making a comparison ⇨ COMPARE
- expressing surprise ⇨ SURPRISE

event ⇨ HAPPEN

everybody ⇨ HOW MUCH/MANY

evil ⇨ RIGHT/WRONG[2]

exact/approximate

see also ALMOST, TRUE

- absolutely correct: **exact** (*adverb* **exactly**), **precise** (*adverb* **precisely**), (*informal*) **just** ◦ *Have you got the exact time?* ◦ *an exact description/copy* ◦ *to copy/describe sth exactly* ◦ *That's precisely what she said.* ◦ *That's just what I've always wanted!*
- the quality of being clear or exact: **precision** (*noun* U) ◦ *The plans were drawn with great precision.*
- if sb takes care to be correct in what they say, they are **precise** (**about** sth) ◦ *He was quite precise about it – there was no possibility of misunderstanding.*
- careful and without mistakes: **accurate** (*adverb* **accurately**); *noun* (U): **accuracy** ◦ *Is your watch accurate?*

▷ being careful ⇨ CAREFUL

- having an exact meaning: **strict** ◦ *in the strict sense of the word* ◦ *a strict interpretation of the law*
- exact and full of details: **detailed, specific** ◦ *a detailed drawing* ◦ *He gave us a very specific description of the man.*
- exactly right or suitable: **perfect** (*adverb* **perfectly**) ◦ *That's the perfect gift for him!* ◦ *She recited the poem perfectly.*
- (used about a place) exactly: **right** ◦ *We are now standing right on the spot where the body was found.*
- (used about the time) exactly: **on the dot, sharp, precisely** ◦ *I want you to be here at twelve on the dot.* ◦ *We set off at 12 o'clock sharp.*

■ not exact
- not exact: **vague, inexact** ◦ *I only had a vague idea of what was going to happen.*
- not accurate: **inaccurate**; *noun* (C/U): **inaccuracy** ◦ *There are a few inaccuracies in your essay which need to be put right before you hand it in.*
- if you use a word which almost describes what you want to say, but is not the exact term, you can say **sort of, kind of** before the word itself ◦ *a kind of pink colour*

- not detailed: **broad** ◦ *a broad interpretation*
- almost correct, but not completely accurate: **rough** (*adverb* **roughly**), **approximate** (*adverb* **approximately**) ◦ *a rough calculation/estimate* ◦ *It'll be roughly £100.* ◦ *an approximate description*
- approximately: **about, around, in the region of** ◦ *'How much did you get?' 'About 10 kilos.'* ◦ *I'm not quite sure how big his farm is but I guess it's somewhere in the region of 100 hectares.*

- to calculate approximately the quantity or size of sth: **estimate** sth; *noun*: **estimate**
- to think that the quantity or size of sth is bigger than it really is: **overestimate** sth; *opposite*: **underestimate** sth ◦ *There's rather a lot of paint – I'm afraid I rather overestimated the amount we'd need.*

exam

1 different kinds of exam
2 doing an exam
3 giving an exam

1 different kinds of exam

- a written, spoken or practical test of what you know or can do: **exam**, (*formal*) **examination** ◦ *a maths exam* ◦ *I've got three exams tomorrow.* ◦ *an oral* (= spoken, not written) *exam*
- a kind of exam that is usually fairly short and not very formal: **test** ◦ *a spelling test*

- an exam which you take in order to enter a school, university, etc: **entrance exam/examination**
- an exam that you have passed or a course of study that you have successfully completed: **qualification** ◦ *a postgraduate qualification in accounting* ◦ *They're looking for somebody with the right qualifications.*

▷ more on qualifications ⇨ EDUCATION

▷ university exams and qualifications ⇨ UNIVERSITY

2 doing an exam

- to do an exam: **take*** an exam ◦ *How many A Levels* (= advanced exams in British schools) *are you taking this year?*

- to put your name on a list for an exam: **enter for** sth; to do this for sb else: **enter** sb **for** sth ◦ *My teacher entered me for GCSE Maths.*
- a person who is taking an exam: **candidate** ◦ *All candidates should remember that there must be no talking during the exam.*

- to read and study sth that you have learnt before, especially when preparing for an exam: **revise** (sth); *noun* (U): **revision** ◦ *I can't come out – I'm revising for my exams.* ◦ *We've got three weeks for revision.*

- a set of exam questions on a particular subject: **paper** ◦ *The physics paper was very difficult.* ◦ *Have you got a copy of last year's paper?*
- something that is asked in an exam: **question** ◦ *an exam question* ◦ *How many questions did you answer?*
- what you write or say in a test or exam: **answer**; *verb*: **answer** sth ◦ *Write the answers on the paper provided.* ◦ *Only answer three questions.*

■ the result of an exam
- to achieve a successful result in an exam: **pass** (sth); *noun*: **pass** ◦ *I've passed!* ◦ *to get a good pass*
- not to achieve a successful result in an exam: **fail** (sth); *noun*: **fail** ◦ *to fail an exam* ◦ *She passed history and maths but failed German.*

- the final mark given in an exam: **result** ◦ *What were your results like?* ◦ *He got a good result.*
- (used about exam marks) to be announced: **come* out** ◦ *When do the results come out?*
- an official piece of paper that says that you have passed an exam: **certificate**

- to be in a particular position (among a group of people) depending on the number of marks you get for an exam: **come*** first, second, etc ◦ *George came second in the chemistry exam.*
- to have the highest number of marks in a class or group of people sitting the same exam: **come* top**; *opposite*: **come* bottom** ◦ *Alice came top in English.*
- the highest mark in a class or a group of people sitting the same exam: **top mark**
- the highest possible marks: **top marks**, **full marks** ◦ *She got top marks in her physics exam.*

3 giving an exam
- to test what sb knows or can do: **examine** sb **in/on** sth, **test** sb **on** sth ◦ *You will be examined on this at the end of the year.* ◦ *We were tested on our spelling.*
- to prepare questions for an exam: **set* an exam/examination**
- a person who tests sb in an exam: **examiner**
- to look at an exam answer, show where there are mistakes and give it a number or a letter to show how good it is: **mark** sth ◦ *to mark an exam paper* ◦ *to mark sth right/wrong*
- a number or letter given for exams to show how good it is: **mark**, **grade** ◦ *What mark did you get?* ◦ *a high mark* ◦ *He got a Grade A in maths.*
- the mark that you have to get in order to pass an exam: **pass-mark** ◦ *The pass-mark is 55 per cent.*
- (used about an examiner, etc) to decide that sb has passed an exam: **pass** sb; *opposite*: **fail** sb ◦ *The examiners passed most of the candidates.* ◦ *I think we'll have to fail her.*

---

example

helping sb to understand sth ⇨ **UNDERSTAND**

- something that we use to help sb understand an explanation or to support an argument: **example** ◦ *This dictionary has plenty of examples to show how words are used.*
- a person, thing, etc that we use to show what others of the same kind are like: **example** ◦ *This is a typical example of this artist's work.*
- an event or situation that we use as an example: **instance** ◦ *I have given just one instance of the hard work Mrs Woods has done for us recently.*
- a situation of a particular type (often used about illnesses): **case** ◦ *This is a typical case of pre-exam stress.*

- a small amount of sth that you can use in order to decide if you like it or not: **sample** ◦ *a free sample of shampoo*
- a small amount of sth that shows what the rest is like: **sample**, **specimen** ◦ *to take a blood sample/urine specimen*

■ making use of examples
- to say sth as an example: **give*** (sb) **an example (of** sth): ◦ *You still don't understand? Let me give you an example.*
- to explain sth by using an example: **illustrate** sth; an example you use to illustrate sth: **illustration** ◦ *That illustrates my point exactly.* ◦ *She showed us some photos as an illustration of the bad conditions in the houses.*

- when you give an example, you can say **for example**, **for instance**; the short form is **eg** ◦ *There were lots of different kinds of fruit in the market, for example, apples, bananas, oranges and strawberries.* ◦ *The people there are very kind. For instance, somebody carried my bags all the way to the station.*

- if an example is used to show sth which is the same as other things in a larger group, you can say that it **represents** that group, or that it is **typical**, **representative** of it ◦ *My ideas represent the general feeling of most of the students in the class.* ◦ *Is this piece of work representative of the work you've done this year?*

■ examples which people copy
- a person, thing or act that we think it is good to copy: **example** ◦ *This brave child is an example to us all.*
- a good example to copy: **model** ◦ *Use this letter as a model to help you write your own business letters.*
- to copy what sb else has done: **follow** sb's **example** ◦ *I followed her example and went on a diet.*

▷ more on copying the behaviour of others ⇨ **BEHAVIOUR**

example *contd.*

- an act that people see as an example which they can follow in the future: **precedent**
- if you do sth that other people may later copy, you **set* a precedent** ◦ *If you don't make him pay, you'll set a precedent, and nobody will want to pay.*

exchange ⇨ CHANGE

excited

other emotions ⇨ **EMOTION**
dangerous situations ⇨ **DANGEROUS**

- a feeling of pleasure and interest in sth that is happening or expected to happen: **excitement** (*noun* U); an event or experience that causes this kind of feeling is **exciting**; *opposite*: **unexciting** ◦ *scenes of wild excitement* ◦ *an exciting adventure* ◦ *It wasn't a very exciting party.*
- a person who feels excitement is **excited** (*adverb* **excitedly**) ◦ *to get excited* ◦ *The children were running excitedly round the garden.*
- to make a person feel excited: **excite** sb ◦ *Don't excite the children too much just before bed time.*

- a sudden feeling of pleasure and excitement: **thrill**; having this feeling: **thrilled** (*not before a noun*); causing this feeling: **thrilling** ◦ *What a thrill to meet your hero face to face!* ◦ *All of us were absolutely thrilled by what we had just seen.* ◦ *a thrilling experience*
- a feeling of great excitement among a group of people: **sensation**; something that causes this feeling: **sensation**; *adjective*: **sensational** (*adverb* **sensationally**) ◦ *The news of their marriage caused a sensation.* ◦ *a sensational story*

- the excitement that you feel when you wait for sth good, bad or exciting to happen: **suspense** (*noun* U) ◦ *Please just tell us the result – I can't stand the suspense!*
- nervous, worried excitement: **tension** (*noun* C/U); a situation, etc that causes this, or a person who feels this, is **tense** ◦ *a lot of tensions and difficulties* ◦ *political tension* ◦ *a tense moment/situation*
- the most important and exciting part of a story, event, etc: **climax** ◦ *to reach a climax*

- so excited that you do not appear to be in full control of your behaviour: **mad** (*adverb* **madly**), **wild** (*adverb* **wildly**), **crazy** (*adverb* **crazily**); to start to behave like this: **go* mad/wild/crazy** ◦ *wildly excited* ◦ *The crowd went mad when we scored the winning goal.*

- a person who easily gets excited is **excitable**

- not excited: **calm** ◦ *feeling quite calm* ◦ *a calm moment*
- to become less excited: **calm down** ◦ *The teacher told the class to calm down and get on with their work.*

▷ being calm ⇨ CALM

excuse ⇨ FORGIVE

exercise

see also ATHLETICS, SPORT, LEARN

- use of the body in a way that will keep you healthy: **exercise** (*noun* U); *verb*: **exercise** ◦ *His doctor advised him to take more exercise.* ◦ *strenuous/vigorous exercise* (= exercise that uses a lot of energy) ◦ *It's important to exercise regularly.*
- a movement or activity that you do in order to keep fit or to train for a sport: **exercise** (*often plural*) ◦ *He does keep-fit exercises every morning.*
- exercise in schools is often called **PE** (= physical education) ◦ *a PE teacher*

- having a strong healthy body: **fit, in good shape**; *opposite*: **unfit**; the state of being physically fit: **fitness** (*noun* U) ◦ *You should really try to get more fit.* ◦ *The doctor said I was overweight and unfit.*
- to become healthy by exercising: **get* into shape**
- to stay healthy by exercising: **keep* fit** ◦ *He keeps fit by playing tennis twice a week.*
- to lose weight by exercising: **work** sth **off** ◦ *He worked off several pounds in the gym.*

- to do exercise to make yourself strong and fit: **work out**; *noun*: **workout** ◦ *She works out at the City Gymnasium.* ◦ *an energetic workout*
- to do exercise so as to be in good condition to do a sport: **train** (**for** sth), **be in training** ◦ *I'm training for the marathon* ◦ *Top athletes have to be in training all the time.*
- to do some exercises before you start doing a sport: **warm up**; *noun*: **warm-up** ◦ *The 100-metre finalists are warming up beside the track.* ◦ *Let's start with a warm-up.*

- a large room with equipment for doing different kinds of exercises: **gymnasium** (*plural* **gymnasia** or **gymnasiums**), **gym**

■ kinds of exercise

- energetic physical exercises (often done to music) that increase the amount of oxygen in your blood: **aerobics** (*noun* U) ◦ *to go to aerobics classes*
- a type of exercise in which you lie face down on the floor and push your body up with your hands: **press-up** (*AmE* **push-up**)
- to jump over a rope that you or two others hold and turn so that it goes over your head and under your feet: **skip** (*AmE* **jump rope**); the rope is called a **skipping rope** (*AmE* **jump rope**)
- to make a movement in which you roll forward with your feet going over your head: **somersault**
- a system of exercises for the mind as well as the body: **yoga** (*noun* U) ◦ *a yoga class*

exist ⇨ REAL/EXISTING

expect

- thinking that sth will happen ⇨ FUTURE

- wanting sth to happen ⇨ **HOPE**
- thinking that sth is likely to happen ⇨ **POSSIBLE**[1]

expensive ⇨ PRICE

experience

- things that you have done ⇨ **ACTION**
- a way of learning ⇨ **LEARN**
- work that you have done ⇨ **WORK**

experiment

- science and research ⇨ **SCIENCE, STUDY**
- trying sth ⇨ **TRY**

explain ⇨ UNDERSTAND

explore ⇨ TRAVEL

export ⇨ BUSINESS

extremely ⇨ FAIRLY / VERY

eye

other parts of the head ⇨ **HEAD**
see also SEE

- one of the two parts of the body that you use to see with: **eye** ◦ *She opened/closed her eyes.* ◦ *I've got brown eyes.*

▷ picture at **FACE**
- the whole of the eye, including the part which is hidden inside your head: **eyeball**
- the coloured part of the eye: **iris**
- the round black hole in the middle of the eye: **pupil**
- the piece of skin that can move to cover the eye: **eyelid**
- one of the hairs that grow on your eyelids: **eyelash**
- the part at the back of the eyeball that is sensitive to light: **retina**

- the colour of a person's eyes can be **blue**, **green**, **brown**, **grey**, **hazel** (= light brown) ◦ *a girl with blue eyes* ◦ *green-eyed*

- unable to see: **blind**; *noun* (U): **blindness** ◦ *He is blind in one eye.*
- if your eyes do not move together properly, you have a **squint**
- the thing that people wear to help them see more clearly: **glasses** (*AmE* **eyeglasses**) (*noun plural*) ◦ *to wear glasses* ◦ *a new pair of glasses*

▷ other problems in seeing ⇨ **SEE**

▷ more on glasses ⇨ **GLASSES**

- to shut your eyes and open them again very quickly: **blink** ◦ *She blinked as he took the photograph.*
- to close and open one eye quickly, usually as a signal to sb: **wink (at** sb); an act of winking: **wink** ◦ *My friend winked at me across the room.* ◦ *He gave her a big wink.*
- to look at sth with your eyes almost closed: **squint (at** sb/sth) ◦ *to squint in bright sunlight*
- a drop of water that comes from your eyes when you are crying: **tear** ◦ *She had tears in her eyes.*
- if your eyes fill with liquid, they **water** ◦ *Peeling onions makes my eyes water.*
- if you feel a sudden sharp pain in your eyes, they **sting*** ◦ *Soap makes your eyes sting.*

■ **MORE ...**
- if sb hits you on the eye, you may get a **black eye** (= a dark mark around the eye)

- a piece of material that you wear over one eye: **patch** ◦ *He had a patch over his eye.*
- to cover a person's eyes with a piece of cloth, etc, so that they cannot see: **blindfold** sb; the piece of cloth is called a **blindfold** ◦ *The prisoner was blindfolded.*

face

1 parts of the face
2 the appearance of the face
3 facial expressions
other parts of the head ⇨ **HEAD**
see also BEAUTIFUL / ATTRACTIVE, COSMETICS

1 parts of the face

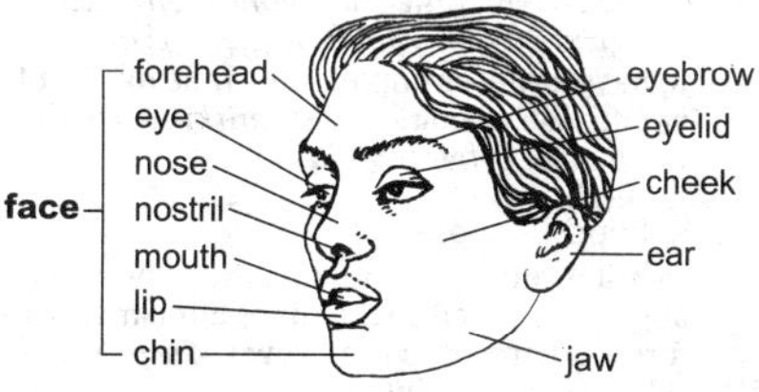

▷ more on eyes ⇨ **EYE**

▷ more on noses ⇨ **NOSE**

▷ more on mouths ⇨ **MOUTH**

▷ more on ears ⇨ **EAR**

- the front part of your head: **face**; *adjective*: **facial**
- a part of the face, for example the mouth or the nose: **feature** ◦ *strong/handsome features*
- a small round hollow on your chin, cheek, etc that is often only seen when you smile: **dimple** ◦ *She has a very attractive dimple on her left cheek.*

2 the appearance of the face

- a person's appearance in general: **looks** (*noun plural*) ◦ *He has good looks and intelligence.*
- the natural colour and quality of the skin on your face: **complexion** ◦ *a healthy complexion*

▷ the appearance of the skin ⇨ **SKIN**

- the hair which grows on a man's cheeks and chin: **beard**
- if a man does not have any hair on his face, he is **clean-shaven**

▷ beards and other hair on the face ⇨ **HAIR**

face *contd.*

3 facial expressions

- the expression on a person's face: **look, face** ◦ *She had a look of surprise on her face.* ◦ *the children's happy faces*
- if your face shows no feeling, understanding or interest, it is **blank** or you look **blank** (*adverb* **blankly**) ◦ *She looked at me blankly.*
- to make expressions with your face in order to annoy sb or show your feelings: **make*/pull a face** (**at** sb) ◦ *The children made faces behind the teacher's back.*

- to become red in the face: **flush**; *adjective*: **flushed** ◦ *The wine made him flush.* ◦ *Are you all right? You look flushed.*
- to become red in the face because of strong feeling: **redden** ◦ *He reddened in anger.*
- to become red in the face because of a feeling of shame or embarrassment: **blush** ◦ *She blushed when she heard her name.*

■ happy expressions
- to turn up the corners of your mouth to show happiness or pleasure: **smile**; *noun*: **smile** ◦ *She turned and smiled at me.* ◦ *He has a wonderful smile.*
- to have a big smile on your face: **beam, grin**; *nouns*: **beam, grin** ◦ *He beamed with delight.* ◦ *She grinned at his joke.* ◦ *to give a grin*
- to have a silly or unpleasant smile on your face: **smirk**; *noun*: **smirk** ◦ *Stop smirking. Your work wasn't any better than hers.*

■ unhappy expressions
- to bring your eyebrows together when you are angry or worried so that lines appear on your forehead: **frown**; *noun*: **frown** ◦ *He frowned when he saw the bill.*
- a look that shows you are angry or in a bad mood: **scowl**; *verb*: **scowl** ◦ *The little girl scowled at her mother.*

■ **MORE ...**
- a person's face seen from the side: **profile**
- a medical operation to make your face look younger: **facelift**

- a covering for the face (or part of it), worn to protect the face or to make it look different: **mask** ◦ *a surgeon's mask* ◦ *The robbers wore masks.*

fact

- something that is true ⇨ TRUE
- something that is known ⇨ INFORMATION

factory

1 kinds of factory
2 making things in a factory
3 places and things in a factory
4 people who work in a factory
see also INDUSTRY, PROVIDE, MAKE, MACHINE

1 kinds of factory

- a building or a group of buildings where goods are produced or put together in large quantities: **factory** ◦ *This factory supplies most of the chips that are needed by the computer industry.*
- a factory which produces certain materials used in industry: **works** ◦ *a steelworks* ◦ *a brickworks*
- a large factory, producing electricity, cars, etc: **plant** ◦ *There's a huge car plant just outside the town.*
- a factory that produces certain materials (for example paper and textiles): **mill** ◦ *a paper/cotton mill*

- the activity of making things in a factory or in other large organizations: **industry** (*noun* C/U) ◦ *the steel/car industry*
- connected with industry: **industrial** ◦ *industrial processes*
- an area where there are a lot of factories: **industrial estate**

▷ more on industry ⇨ INDUSTRY

2 making things in a factory

- to make sth in a factory: **make*** sth, **manufacture** sth; a person or company that does this: **manufacturer** ◦ *Do you know what that factory makes?* ◦ *a car manufacturer*
- the process of making things in a factory: **production** (*noun* U), **manufacture** (*noun* U) ◦ *We specialize in the manufacture of picture frames.*
- a thing that is made in a factory: **product** ◦ *a range of products* ◦ *the quality of our products*
- the amount of sth that is made in a factory: **production** (*noun* U) ◦ *With this new machine, we can now step up* (= increase) *production by 50%.* ◦ *We have to cut back on* (= reduce) *production of tyres, due to shortage of rubber.*

- the making of large quantities of things which are all the same: **mass production** (*noun* U)
- to produce sth in large quantities: **mass-produce** sth; *adjective*: **mass-produced**

- a basic natural material that is used for making things in factories, etc: **raw material** (*noun* C/U) ◦ *a shortage of raw materials*

■ the working day in a factory
- a period of time during which one group of workers works in a factory: **shift** ◦ *I'm doing an eight-hour shift tomorrow.* ◦ *the day/night shift*
- a pause to relax during a shift: **tea break**
- to record the time that you arrive at work, by putting a card into a small machine with a clock: **clock in/on**; to record the time that you leave work: **clock out/off**

3 places and things in a factory

- the area of a factory where things are made: **shop floor**
- a series of machines which are placed in a factory so that a product is progressively put together: **assembly line, production line** ◦ *to work on an assembly line*
- a belt which moves all the time, transporting articles and materials to different parts of the factory: **conveyor belt**

– a machine that can move, and that can be made to do some of the work that people do: **robot**

– a restaurant for the people who work in a factory, usually located inside the factory buildings: **canteen**

4 people who work in a factory

– a person who does manual work in a factory: (**factory**) **worker**
– an experienced worker who is in charge of other workers: **foreman** (*plural* **foremen**)
– a person who controls a factory or a business: **manager**
– the group of people who control a factory or business: **management** (*with singular or plural verb*) ◦ *talks between management and workers*
– the total number of workers who work in a factory: **workforce** (*with singular or plural verb*) ◦ *We have a workforce of 300.* ◦ *a skilled workforce*

▷ more on management ⇨ MANAGEMENT

fail ⇨ SUCCEED/FAIL

fair ⇨ GOOD

fairly/very

1 to some degree
2 to a great degree
3 to a greater or lesser degree
4 as much as possible
5 too much

1 to some degree

– to a small degree: **a little**, (*more informal*) **a** (**little**) **bit** ◦ *I thought it was a little odd that no one else at the party had come in fancy dress.* ◦ *We'll have to walk a bit faster.* ◦ *'How are you?' 'A bit better, thanks.'* ◦ *She's a little bit too cautious to be a really successful manager.*

Note: a (**little**) **bit** can also be used with **of** plus a noun: ◦ *I have to admit that not getting that job is a bit of a disappointment.*

– to some extent; more than a little, but not very: **fairly**, **quite**, **rather**, (*more informal*) **pretty** ◦ *He told me my essay was fairly good but needed more examples.* ◦ *'Do you like my new dress?' 'Well it's quite nice, but I think green would suit you better.'* ◦ *'I have to say I was rather disappointed by the play.' 'Yes it was pretty awful, wasn't it?'*
– to a certain degree, compared with sth else: **relatively** ◦ *The crossword in the Telegraph is relatively easy.*

Note: fairly and **quite** are weaker than **rather** and **pretty**; **fairly** often has a more positive meaning than **rather**: ◦ *I'm fairly happy with your progress.* ◦ *I thought the lecture today was rather boring.* If you use **rather** with a positive word, it sounds as if you are surprised or pleased: *He's rather good actually, isn't he?* **Quite** and **rather** can be used with a verb: ◦ *I rather/quite like George, but I can't stand his wife.*
Quite a and **rather a** can be used with a noun: ◦ *She's quite a kind person really.* ◦ *The lecture was rather a bore, but the party afterwards was fun.* **Rather** (but not **fairly**, **quite** or **pretty**) can be used with comparatives: ◦ *rather warmer* **Quite** has two meanings: (1) rather (see above); (2) completely (see below).

– to the necessary degree: **enough**, (*formal*) **sufficiently** ◦ *strong/hard/long enough for this purpose* ◦ *I don't like it enough to want to buy it.* ◦ *It's sufficiently powerful to pull two trailers.*

2 to a great degree

– (used to make an adjective or adverb stronger) to a great degree: **very**, (*more informal*) **really** ◦ *I'm very pleased with your work – you've improved a lot.* ◦ *a really enjoyable holiday* ◦ *a really beautifully painted ceiling*
– (used to make a comparative adjective stronger): **much**, **very much**, **far**, **a lot** ◦ *He's much better now.* ◦ *This book is far easier to understand than the last one I read.* ◦ *a lot more interesting*
– (used to make a superlative adjective stronger): **very** ◦ *the very highest quality*
– (used to make a verb stronger): **very much**, **a lot**, **really** ◦ *I think they liked your speech very much.* ◦ *He has suffered a lot.* ◦ *I really admire your parents.*

– to emphasize 'very' you can add **indeed** ◦ *The traffic was moving very slowly indeed.*

■ stronger than very
– to a very great degree: **extremely**, **terribly**, (*informal*) **awfully** ◦ *an extremely foolish action* ◦ *It's all gone terribly wrong.* ◦ *That's awfully kind of you.*
– to such a great extent that it is difficult to believe: **incredibly**, **unbelievably**, **amazingly** ◦ *The exam was incredibly difficult.* ◦ *She looks amazingly well.*

Note: these adverbs have corresponding adjectives (**extreme**, **terrible**, **great**, **awful**; **incredible**, **unbelievable**, **amazing**) which you can use to express similar meanings: ◦ *extreme foolishness* ◦ *a terrible mistake* ◦ *incredible difficulty*

3 to a greater or lesser degree

– to a greater degree: **more** ◦ *a far more interesting film* ◦ *I want that house more than anything else in the world.*
– to the greatest degree: **most** ◦ *Which book did you enjoy most?*

– to a greater degree than others: **particularly**, **especially** ◦ *I found this book particularly interesting.* ◦ *The other route is especially beautiful.*

– to a smaller degree: **less** ◦ *a less well known artist* ◦ *I now respect her even less than I used to.*
– to the smallest degree: **least** ◦ *He's probably my least favourite person.*

4 as much as possible

– to the greatest possible degree: **completely**, **totally**, **quite**, **absolutely** ◦ *I'm completely exhausted.* ◦ *She's totally committed to the com-*

fairly / very *contd.*

pany. ∘ *There are two quite different courses.* ∘ *I'm absolutely certain I gave it to you.*

– to the greatest possible degree (especially when you are talking about sth bad): **utterly** ∘ *That's utterly ridiculous!*

Note: completely, **totally** and **absolutely** have corresponding adjectives (**complete, total, absolute**) which you can use to express similar meanings: ∘ *complete exhaustion* ∘ *total commitment* ∘ *absolute certainty*

▷ not completely ⇨ ALMOST

– completely and only: **simply**, **perfectly**, **purely** ∘ *It simply didn't occur to him to ask.* ∘ *a perfectly wonderful evening* ∘ *for purely selfish reasons*

– (used to make negative forms stronger) absolutely not: **not at all, not a bit, not in the least** ∘ *He's not at all as I imagined.* ∘ *I'm not a bit tired.* ∘ *Surprisingly, she didn't seem in the least worried about it.*

5 too much

– to a greater extent than is good, allowed or possible: **too, over-** ∘ *I was told I was too old to apply for the job.* ∘ *I always eat too much at Christmas.* ∘ *over-enthusiastic* ∘ *over-excited* ∘ *to overwork* ∘ *to overspend*

– to a greater extent than is necessary: **excessively, unduly** ∘ *excessively high wages* ∘ *I'm not unduly worried about him – he's often late.*

fall

1 falling
2 causing people and things to fall
3 not falling
see also STAND

1 falling

– to come or go down towards the ground: **fall***, **drop**; an act of falling: **fall** ∘ *He fell off a ladder.* ∘ *We collected some of the peaches that had dropped from the tree.* ∘ *George has had another bad fall while climbing in the Alps.*

– the amount of sth that falls or the distance that sth falls: **fall** ∘ *a heavy fall of snow* ∘ *a fall of three thousand feet*

■ ways that people fall

– to suddenly stop standing: **fall*** (**down/over**) ∘ *The boy slipped and fell over on the ice.*

– to fall suddenly in a heavy way, without control: **tumble, have a tumble** ∘ *She had a nasty tumble from her horse.*

– to hit your foot against sth when you are walking, and fall or nearly fall: **trip over/on** sth, **trip over**, **stumble** (**over** sth) ∘ *I tripped over someone's bag that was on the floor.* ∘ *A hole in the ground made the horse stumble.*

– to fall down and perhaps become unconscious: **collapse** ∘ *The winner collapsed at the end of the race.*

– to fall from sth: **fall* off** (sth), **come* off** (sth) ∘ *What happened? Did you fall off?* ∘ *Mary came off her bike and broke her leg.*

– to fall from an enclosed place: **fall* out** (**of** sth) ∘ *Diane leaned too far out of the window and nearly fell out.*

– to fall over the side of a ship: **fall* overboard**

– to fall, dive, jump, etc suddenly and with force into sth: **plunge** (**into** sth) ∘ *A woman plunged to her death from the cliffs at Beachy Head yesterday.*

– with your head before the rest of your body: **headlong** (*adjective, adverb*) ∘ *He fell headlong into the crowd below.*

– to slide accidentally, lose your balance and fall or nearly fall: **slip** ∘ *Jerry slipped on the rocks and fell into the sea.*

■ ways that things fall

– (used about rain, snow, etc) to fall from the sky: **fall***, **come* down** ∘ *The rain was coming down in torrents.*

– (used about a liquid) to fall in small drops: **drip**; the sound of water dripping: **drip** ∘ *Water was dripping through the roof.* ∘ *the steady drip of water from the tap*

– a small amount of water that drips: **drip** ∘ *Drips of water fell from the leaves of the trees.*

– to drop from an upright position: **fall* over** ∘ *There were too many books on the bookcase; not surprisingly, it fell over.*

– to fall down or inwards suddenly: **fall* down, collapse, come* down**; *noun*: **collapse** ∘ *The fence collapsed when Harry sat on it.* ∘ *The bridge came down in the floods.* ∘ *The collapse of the stand caused many casualties.*

– to fall inwards: **cave in** ∘ *The roof of the tunnel had caved in and we could go no further.*

– to slide out of the correct position or out of sb's hand: **slip** ∘ *The top book slipped off the pile and fell on the floor.*

2 causing people and things to fall

– to make or let sb/sth fall: **drop** sb/sth ∘ *The planes dropped food and medicine.* ∘ *That vase is very expensive. Whatever you do, don't drop it!*

– to cause sb to fall or nearly fall over: **trip** sb **up** ∘ *Bill stuck his foot out and tripped David up.*

– to cause sb/sth to fall over by pushing them/it: **push** sb/sth **over** ∘ *He pushed her over and ran towards the door.*

– to cause sb/sth to fall over: **knock** sb/sth **over** ∘ *Be careful not to knock the drinks over.*

– to cause sb to fall to the ground: **knock** sb **down** ∘ *She was knocked down by a cyclist.*

– to cause sth to fall or turn over: **tip** sth (**over/up**) ∘ *The baby leaned out of his pushchair and tipped it over.*

– (in sport) to cause an opposing player to fall down: **bring*** sb **down** ∘ *Waddle was brought down in the penalty area.*

– when the wind makes sb/sth fall, it **blows*** sb/sth **down/off/over**; sth that falls because of the wind **blows* down/off/over** ∘ *The wind blew my hat off.* ∘ *The fence blew down in the storm.*

– to cause sth to fall by cutting it: **cut*** sth **down**, **chop** sth **down** ◦ *We cut the tree down/cut down the tree.*

▷ destroying a building ⇨ BUILD

– the natural force that causes things to fall to the ground: **gravity** (*noun* U) ◦ *the force of gravity*

3 not falling

– a thing that does not fall down **stays up** ◦ *Those shelves won't stay up long if you don't use big enough screws.*
– something is not likely to fall if it is **firm**, **steady**; *opposite*: **unsteady** ◦ *It seems quite steady – I don't think it will fall.*

– to make yourself or sth steady: **steady** yourself/sth ◦ *I thought I was going to fall, so I steadied myself by putting my hand out.*
– to remain steady and upright when you might expect to fall: **keep*** your **balance**; *opposite*: **lose*** your **balance** ◦ *The bridge wobbled dangerously but Henry managed to keep his balance and he didn't fall.*
– to fall over or nearly fall over because you cannot stand steadily: **overbalance** ◦ *Peter leaned forward too far and overbalanced.*

– to prevent sth from falling: **hold*/keep*** sth **up** ◦ *You'll need a belt to hold your trousers up.*
– to put an object under or behind sth to give it support so that it will not fall: **prop** sth **up**; an object that you use to prop sth up: **prop** ◦ *Can you prop the table up with something? It's very unsteady.* ◦ *What can we use as a prop to hold the bookcase up?*

■ **MORE ...**
– having the feeling that everything is going round and that you are going to fall: **dizzy**; a dizzy feeling: **dizziness** (*noun* U) ◦ *I often feel dizzy if I stand up too quickly.*

false ⇨ TRUE

family

1 being a family
2 taking care of a family
3 parents and children
4 brothers, sisters and cousins
5 husbands and wives

1 being a family

– parents and their children: **family** (*with singular or plural verb*) ◦ *He would like to spend more time with his family.* ◦ *Where do your family live?* ◦ *the Jones family* ◦ *a friend of the family* ◦ *a family holiday* ◦ *the family car*
– a family where the children live with only one parent: **one-parent family**, **single-parent family**
– the group of children in a family: **family** ◦ *My son and his wife are coming for Christmas and they're going to bring the family.*
– a name given to all the members of a family: **surname**, **family name** ◦ *'What's your surname?' 'Jones.'*
– the way a family lives: **family life** (*noun* U) ◦ *How are you enjoying family life?*
– all the people who live in one house: **household** ◦ *a large household*
– anything connected with the private family home is **domestic** ◦ *domestic life* ◦ *domestic violence*

– the group of people who are related to one another: **family** (*noun* C/U) ◦ *My family came to Canada in the 19th century.* ◦ *members of my family* ◦ *She lives on her own – she hasn't got any family.* ◦ *We're having a family get-together on Saturday.*

■ being related
– a member of your family: **relation**, **relative**; *adjective*: **related** (**to** you); the way you are connected: **relationship** ◦ *We've got the relations coming over for the day.* ◦ *We've got the same name but we're not related.* ◦ *'Is he related to you?' 'Yes he's my brother.'* ◦ *'What's the relationship between Sue and Lucy?' 'They're cousins.'*
– a person who is not a member of your family is **unrelated**, **not related**
– near in a family relationship (for example a cousin): **close**; *opposite*: **distant** ◦ *a close/distant relative of mine*

■ similarities between family members
– to look like or be like a parent or older member of your family: **take* after** sb ◦ *You really take after your mother.*

– something such as an illness or a quality which is passed from parents to children is **hereditary** ◦ *All the men in that family are bald – I suppose it's hereditary.*
– something which is passed on from a parent to all their children and their children's children **runs* in the family** ◦ *All her children are very artistic – it must run in the family.*

2 taking care of a family

– to look after children in a family until they are adults and to teach them how to behave: **bring*** sb **up**, **raise** sb ◦ *Bringing up children is never easy.* ◦ *to raise a family*
– the way sb is brought up: **upbringing** ◦ *to give a child a good upbringing*

– a person who earns all or most of the money in a family: **breadwinner** ◦ *My father recently lost his job so my mother's the main breadwinner now.*
– to have enough money to be able to look after a family: **support** a family ◦ *I need a job so I can support my family.*

3 parents and children

– a mother or father: **parent** (*usually plural*); *adjective*: **parental** ◦ *I'm going to meet her parents.* ◦ *parental love*
– the state of being a mother or a father: **parenthood** (*noun* U)
– a parent who brings up a child on their own: **single parent**
– names for a father: **dad**, **daddy**, (*formal*) **father**

family *contd.*

- the state of being a father: **fatherhood** (*noun* U), (*formal*) **paternity** (*noun* U)
- behaving like a father: **fatherly**, **paternal** ◦ *fatherly concern* ◦ *paternal duties*

- names for a mother: **mum** (*AmE* **mom**), **mummy**, (*formal*) **mother** ◦ *Where does your mum work?*
- the state of being a mother: **motherhood** (*noun* U) ◦ *Motherhood really suits her.*
- connected with women who are going to have or have just had a baby: **maternity** ◦ *a maternity dress* ◦ *maternity leave* (= time off from work in order to have and care for a baby)
- behaving like a mother: **motherly**, **maternal** ◦ *She's a motherly sort of person.* ◦ *maternal instincts*
- a woman who is expecting a baby: **expectant mother**

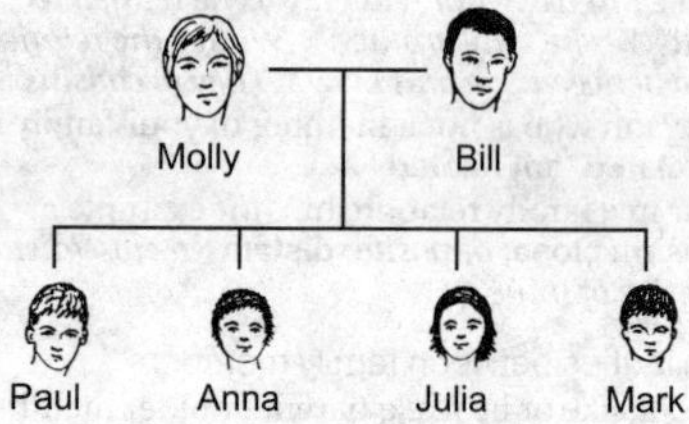

- Molly and Bill have four **children**
- Anna and Julia are their **daughters**, (*informal*) **girls** ◦ *The girls are cooking the supper tonight.*
- Paul and Mark are their **sons**, (*informal*) **boys** ◦ *He's extremely proud of his boys.*

- Paul is older than Mark: Paul is Molly and Bill's **older/elder son**; Mark is their **younger son**
- Anna is older than Julia: Anna is Molly and Bill's **older/elder daughter**; Julia is their **younger daughter**
- Paul is older than Anna, Julia and Mark: he is Molly and Bill's **oldest/eldest** (child)
- Mark is younger than Anna, Julia and Paul: he is their **youngest** (child)

Note: elder and **eldest** can only be used before the noun; they cannot be used with 'than'.

- to take a child into your home and make him/her your son/daughter by law: **adopt** (sb); *noun* (C/U): **adoption**; the child is **adopted**
- to take a child who needs a home into your family and to care for him/her without becoming the legal parents: **foster** (sb)
- the people who foster a child are called **foster parents**, **foster mother**, **foster father**
- a child who has been fostered is a **foster child** (*plural* **foster children**)

- if your father/mother marries again, your new parent is a **stepmother/stepfather**; you are their **stepson/stepdaughter**, **stepchild** (*plural* **stepchildren**)

- the parents of your parents: **grandparents**; female: **grandmother**, (*informal*) **granny** or **grandma**; male: **grandfather**, (*informal*) **grandad** or **grandpa**
- the children of your children: **grandchildren**; female: **granddaughter**; male: **grandson**
- the parents of your grandparents: **great-grandparents**; female: **great-grandmother**; male: **great-grandfather**

4 brothers, sisters and cousins

- Anna (see above) is Paul's **sister**; Paul is Anna's **brother**
- Anna and Julia are **sisters**; Paul and Ken are **brothers**
- Paul is older than Anna: Paul is Anna's **big brother**, **older/elder brother**; Anna is Paul's **little sister**, **younger sister**

- a brother/sister with whom you share one parent: **half-brother/half-sister**
- if your mother or father marries again and your new parent has a child by a previous marriage, this child is your **stepsister**, **stepbrother** ◦ *This is Steve, my stepbrother.*

- either of two children who have the same parents and are born at the same time: **twin** ◦ *They're twins.* ◦ *my twin sister*
- twins who look exactly the same are **identical twins**
- three children who have the same parents and are born at the same time: **triplets**
- four children who have the same parents and are born at the same time: **quads**

- the brother of your father or mother: **uncle**
- the sister of your father or mother: **aunt**, (*informal*) **auntie**
- a child of your uncle or aunt: **cousin**

- the son of your brother or sister: **nephew**
- the daughter of your brother or sister: **niece**

Note: the husband of your aunt is also called your **uncle**. The wife of your uncle is also called your **aunt**.

5 husbands and wives

- the person that a woman is married to: **husband**
- the person that a man is married to: **wife** (*plural* **wives**)

▷ being married ⇨ MARRY

- the father/mother of your husband or wife is your **father-in-law/mother-in-law** (*plural* **fathers-in-law/mothers-in-law**)
- the parents of your husband or wife: **parents-in-law**, (*informal*) **in-laws** ◦ *She doesn't get on very well with her in-laws.*

- the wife of your son is your **daughter-in-law**; the husband of your daughter is your **son-in-law**
- the husband of your sister, or the brother of your husband or wife, is your **brother-in-law**; the wife of your brother, or the sister of your husband or wife, is your **sister-in-law**

■ **MORE ...**

- a person in your family who lived a long time before you, from whom you are descended: **ancestor**; all of a person's ancestors when you

think of them as a group: **ancestry** (*noun* U); *adjective*: **ancestral** ◦ *My ancestors came from Scotland.* ◦ *They were very proud of their ancestry.*
- a person who is related to sb who lived a long time ago is that person's **descendant**
- a single stage in a family history: **generation** ◦ *The photograph shows three generations in our family – my grandparents, my parents, and me.*

- the family consisting just of parents and their children: (*formal*) **nuclear family**
- the family including grandparents, aunts, uncles, cousins, etc: (*formal*) **extended family**
- your closest relative, who should be told if you are injured or killed: **next of kin**

- a person who takes responsibility for a child in a church ceremony (a christening/baptism) and promises to bring them up as a Christian: **godfather/godmother**, **godparent**; the child is their **godson/goddaughter**, **godchild** (*plural* **godchildren**)

- a special Sunday in the year when children give their mother a small present: **Mother's Day**, **Mothering Sunday**
- a day when children give their father a small present: **Father's Day**

famous

see also KNOW, OPINION

- a person, place or thing that is known by a lot of people is **famous** (**for** sth), **well-known** (**for** sth), (*formal*) **noted** (**for** sth); being well-known: **fame** (*noun* U) ◦ *a famous author* ◦ *Oxford is famous for its colleges.* ◦ *She is well-known for her interest in helping children from deprived backgrounds.* ◦ *The city is noted for its architecture.* ◦ *Fame has not changed him.*

- not well-known: **unknown**, **obscure** ◦ *an almost unknown 19th-century artist* ◦ *an obscure German composer*

- well-known; often seen or heard: **familiar** (**to** sb); *opposite*: **unfamiliar** ◦ *The President's face is familiar to people all over the world.* ◦ *The audience couldn't understand the music because the style was unfamiliar to them.*

- the opinion that people in general have about what a person or thing is like: **reputation**, **name** ◦ *He has a reputation for being difficult to work for.* ◦ *That company has a name for good quality products.* ◦ *We don't want to lose our good name.*
- to become well-known and respected: **make* a name for** yourself, **make*** your **name** ◦ *She's made a name for herself as a consultant.* ◦ *He made his name in the theatre.*

- to get a bad reputation: **get* a bad name**; to cause another person, group, etc to get a bad reputation: **give*** sb/sth **a bad name** ◦ *It gives the school a bad name when people see our pupils fighting in the street.*

■ reasons for being famous
- famous for being bad: **notorious** ◦ *a notorious liar*
- famous for being a particular kind of person or for a particular quality: **known** (**as** sth), (*more formal*) **famed for** sth ◦ *She's known mainly as a singer, but she plays the piano too.* ◦ *He's known as an art lover.* ◦ *She's famed for her generosity.*
- famous for achievements in a particular field: **distinguished**, (*formal*) **eminent** ◦ *a distinguished politician* ◦ *an eminent surgeon*

■ famous people
- a famous person (especially in entertainment): **celebrity**, **personality**, **star**; this kind of fame: **stardom** (*noun* U) ◦ *We watched the celebrities arriving for the opening night of the play.* ◦ *a well-known television personality* ◦ *a film star* ◦ *a football star* ◦ *to shoot to stardom* (= to become famous suddenly)
- a very important person: (*informal*) **VIP** ◦ *These seats are reserved for VIPs.*

far ⇨ DISTANCE

farm

1 buildings and land
2 the work of a farm
3 animals
4 crops
the countryside ⇨ COUNTRY[2]
see also ANIMAL, FOOD

1 buildings and land

- an area of land and buildings used for growing crops and keeping animals: **farm**
- the house on a farm where the farmer lives: **farmhouse**
- an outside area near a farmhouse that is surrounded by buildings and walls: **farmyard**
- a large building on a farm in which crops or animals are kept: **barn**
- a building on a farm used for animals: **shed** ◦ *a cowshed* ◦ *the milking sheds*
- a building where milk is kept and butter and cheese are made: **dairy**

- land that is used for growing crops or keeping animals: **farmland** (*noun* U)
- an area of land on a farm, used for growing crops or keeping animals: **field**
- a field or an area of land on a farm where grass is grown to feed cows: **pasture** (*noun* C/U)
- a large area of land, usually in a tropical country, where a crop like tea, cotton or tobacco is grown: **plantation** ◦ *a coffee/cotton/banana plantation*

▷ more on fields ⇨ FIELD

2 the work of a farm

- to use land for growing crops or keeping animals: **farm** (sth) ◦ *Who farms the land around the village?*
- the work or business of keeping or managing a farm: **farming** (*noun* U), (*formal*) **agriculture**

farm *contd.*

(*noun* U); *adjective*: **agricultural** ◦ *the farming industry* ◦ *mixed farming* (= producing both animals and crops) ◦ *the Ministry of Agriculture* ◦ *agricultural land*

- a person who owns or manages a farm: **farmer**
- a person who works on a farm: **farm worker, farm labourer**

- crops, animals and dairy products produced on a farm: **produce** (*noun* U) ◦ *agricultural produce*

3 animals

- a farm which keeps cows and produces mainly milk and milk products: **dairy farm**; the work or business of keeping or managing a dairy farm: **dairy farming** (*noun* U)
- a large area of farm land, especially in America, where cows and horses are kept: **ranch**; the work or business of keeping or managing a ranch: **ranching** (*noun* U) ◦ *a cattle ranch*
- a farm where pigs are kept: **pig farm**
- a farm where sheep are kept: **sheep farm**
- a person who looks after sheep: **shepherd**
- animals on a farm: **livestock** (*noun* U)

- to give an animal food: **feed*** sth (**on** sth) ◦ *We're having to feed our pigs on apples and cabbages!*
- food that is given to farm animals: **feed** (*noun* U) ◦ *cattle feed*
- a long narrow container from which farm animals eat and drink: **trough**
- grass which has been cut and dried and is used for feeding animals: **hay** (*noun* U)

- dried stems of wheat plants which are used for animals to sleep on: **straw** (*noun* U)

▷ farm animals ⇨ BIRD², COW, HORSE, PIG, SHEEP

4 crops

- plants that are grown on a farm for food: **crop** (*usually plural*) ◦ *The main crops are oats and barley.*
- a farm where crops are grown: **arable farm**; the work or business of keeping or managing an arable farm: **arable farming** (*noun* U)

- to prepare land to grow crops: **cultivate** sth ◦ *to cultivate the soil*
- to put seeds, etc in the ground to grow crops: **sow*** sth ◦ *to sow a field with wheat* ◦ *Have they sown the potatoes yet?*
- to supply land and crops with water through pipes, channels, etc: **irrigate** sth; *noun* (U): **irrigation**
- to put natural or artificial substances on land to make it more fertile: **fertilize** sth; a substance used for fertilizing: **fertilizer** (*noun* U)

- to cut or pick crops when they are ready: **harvest** (sth); the work of harvesting, or the time when this is done: **harvest**
- the crops that have been gathered in: **harvest** ◦ *a good/bad harvest*

- a large vehicle that is used for heavy work on farms: **tractor**
- a machine which is pulled along by a tractor to break up and turn over the soil: **plough** (*AmE* **plow**)
- to break up and turn over the soil before planting crops: **plough** (*AmE* **plow**) (sth)
- a machine that cuts corn and separates seeds from the stem: **combine, combine harvester**

- a crop which is grown to produce seeds which are made into flour, etc: **cereal crop**
- some common cereal crops: **wheat** (*noun* U), **barley** (*noun* U), **maize** (*noun* U), **rice** (*noun* U)
- a general word for crops such as wheat: **corn** (*noun* U)
- seeds obtained from corn: **grain** (*noun* U) ◦ *an increase in exports of grain*

- a single seed of corn: **grain** ◦ *a grain of wheat*
- the top part of a plant that produces grains: **ear** ◦ *an ear of corn*
- the hard part at the top of a maize plant, on which the grains grow: **(corn) cob, cob**

■ **MORE ...**

- keeping farm animals in such a way as to make them produce as much as possible: **factory farming** (*noun* U)
- methods of farming which use chemicals, etc in order to produce as much as possible: **intensive farming** (*noun* U)
- methods of farming which do not use artificial chemicals: **organic farming** (*noun* U)

fashion

1 in fashion
2 not in fashion
see also CLOTHES, BEAUTIFUL / ATTRACTIVE

1 in fashion

- the way of dressing, etc that is most popular at any time: **fashion** (*noun* C/U) ◦ *a new fashion for smart well-tailored suits* ◦ *It was the fashion for men to have long hair.* ◦ *the latest fashion news from Paris* ◦ *sixties fashion* (= the fashion of the 1960s)
- a particular way of dressing: **style** ◦ *She's always dressed in the very latest style.*

- a general movement of fashion: **trend** ◦ *There is a trend for people to buy smaller cars these days.*
- a short-lived fashion: **craze, fad** ◦ *a sudden craze for Batman T-shirts*
- a person or thing that is a fashion among a particular group of people: **cult** ◦ *a cult movie*

- something which is popular is **in fashion, fashionable**, (*informal*) **trendy**, (*informal*) **in** ◦ *It's rather fashionable at the moment to go to Vietnam for holidays.* ◦ *a trendy restaurant* ◦ *Short skirts are in again.*
- when a new fashion starts, it **catches* on, comes* in, comes* into fashion** ◦ *I don't think skirts for men will ever catch on.* ◦ *Military-style coats are coming in.*

- something which is made in recent times is **new** ◦ *This is the newest washing machine on the market.*
- something which is made in a recent style is **modern** ◦ *modern architecture*
- a thing which is of the present time is **contemporary** ◦ *contemporary music* ◦ *contemporary styles*
- a thing which is of lasting value, always in fashion, is **classic** ◦ *You can't go wrong with a classic navy coat and a good pair of shoes.*

▷ more on being modern ⇨ **MODERN**

- a person who follows fashion, dressing or behaving in a fashionable way, is **fashionable** (*adverb* **fashionably**), **trendy** (*adverb* **trendily**) ◦ *a fashionably dressed woman* ◦ *She's very trendy, always wearing the latest styles.*
- a person or thing that is fashionable and attractive is **stylish** (*adverb* **stylishly**), has **style** (*noun* U)

■ making fashion
- a person who makes drawings to show how to make clothes, etc: **designer** ◦ *a fashion designer* ◦ *designer clothes* (= made by a fashion designer)
- a person who is paid to wear clothes for fashion shows or for magazines: **model** ◦ *a fashion model* ◦ *a supermodel* (= very famous and very well paid)
- an event at which models wear clothes made by a designer so that people can see them: **fashion show**

2 not in fashion
- to become less fashionable: **go* out** (**of fashion**), **be on the way out** ◦ *Those short jackets everyone had last year have gone out altogether now.* ◦ *'Shall I buy those boots?' 'Well, I think that style's on the way out.'*
- a thing which was recently in fashion but now is not, is **out of fashion, out** ◦ *Platform shoes are completely out.*
- a person or thing which is not in fashion is **unfashionable** ◦ *unfashionable ideas*

- something which was out of fashion and then returns to fashion **comes* back, is back in fashion** ◦ *Hippy fashions came back in the early nineties.*

fast/slow

> **1** speed
> **2** doing sth quickly or slowly
> **3** moving fast or slowly
> **4** changing to a faster or slower speed
> controlling the speed of a car, etc ⇨ **DRIVE**
> **see also MOVE**

1 speed
- a person or thing that can move or act at great speed is **fast** (*adjective, adverb*) ◦ *a fast car* ◦ *She's a fast worker.* ◦ *She works fast.*
- done or happening at speed or in a short time: **quick** (*adverb* **quickly**), **rapid** (*adverb* **rapidly**); *nouns* (U): **speed**, (*formal*) **rapidity** ◦ *a quick meal* ◦ *quick reactions* ◦ *quick thinking* ◦ *The crash happened so rapidly I can hardly remember it.* ◦ *speed of movement*
- done or happening quickly, or when you do not expect it: **sudden** (*adverb* **suddenly**) ◦ *a sudden movement*
- suddenly, unexpectedly: **all of a sudden** ◦ *All of a sudden there was a loud explosion.*

- moving, doing sth or happening without much speed: **slow** (*adverbs*: **slow, slowly**); *noun* (U): **slowness** ◦ *Haven't you finished yet? You're being terribly slow!* ◦ *a slow train* ◦ *'How's your son?' 'Getting better slowly.'* ◦ *Could you walk a bit slower, please?* ◦ *slow-moving traffic*

- how fast or slowly sth moves or happens: **speed** (*noun* C/U), **pace** (*noun singular*) ◦ *to travel at a higher/lower speed* ◦ *the speed of light/sound* ◦ *the increasing pace of industrialization in developing countries*

2 doing sth quickly or slowly
- to move or act very quickly: **rush** ◦ *Don't rush – take your time.*
- to do sth quickly, without enough thought: **rush** (**into** sth/doing sth); to make sb do sth in a hurry: **rush** sb (**into** sth/doing sth) ◦ *Do you think she's rushing into this marriage?* ◦ *Don't rush them – let them take their time to decide.*

- if you do sth too quickly or without enough thought, you or your actions are **hasty** (*adverb* **hastily**); *noun* (U): **haste** ◦ *Don't be too hasty. This is an important decision.* ◦ *In her haste to leave, she forgot her handbag.*
- if you do sth quickly in order to finish it soon, you do it **in a hurry, in a rush** ◦ *I can't stop now; I'm in a terrific hurry.* ◦ *I'm afraid it was written in rather a rush and it's not very good.*

- to move or do sth quickly: **hurry** ◦ *We hurried over to help.*
- to move or do sth more quickly: (*informal*) **hurry up, get* a move on** ◦ *Hurry up or you'll be late for work.* ◦ *Get a move on. Our guests will be here soon.*

- very soon or very quickly: **in a minute/moment, right away, in no time** (**at all**) ◦ *I'll have your car running again in no time at all.*
- happening at once, without delay: **immediate** (*adverb* **immediately**), (*formal*) **instantaneous** (*adverb* **instantaneously**) ◦ *an immediate reply* ◦ *an instantaneous decision*

▷ more on sth happening soon ⇨ **SOON**

- to do sth without hurrying: **take*** your **time** (**over** sth) ◦ *Take your time over your dinner and enjoy it.*
- something you do without hurrying is **leisurely** ◦ *a leisurely walk*

- to make sb/sth slow or late: **delay** sb/sth, **hold*** sb/sth **up** ◦ *Sorry I'm late. I was delayed by the fog.*
- a situation where you have to wait for sth: **delay, hold-up** ◦ *Delays are likely on the roads because of the heavy traffic.*

fast/slow *contd.*

- to do sth slowly or waste time: **dawdle** ◦ *Don't dawdle or you'll be late for school.*

- something which happens slowly or over a long period of time happens **gradually**, **little by little**, **bit by bit**; *adjective*: **gradual** ◦ *Pedro's English gradually improved during the term.* ◦ *Little by little the shop became successful.* ◦ *a gradual improvement*

3 moving fast or slowly

- as fast as possible: **at full speed**, **at top speed**, **flat out** ◦ *They drove flat out to get to the station in time.*
- going or sent quickly: **express** (*adverb* **express**) ◦ *an express letter* ◦ *to send a letter express*

- to go or move very quickly: **speed***, **fly***, **race** ◦ *The Orient Express sped through the night.* ◦ *The cyclists raced by.*
- to run very quickly or suddenly: **dash**; a sudden run: **dash** ◦ *He dashed to the window.* ◦ *When it started to rain, we made a dash for the bus shelter.*
- to take sb to a place very quickly: **rush** sb somewhere ◦ *They rushed her to hospital.*

- to move forward slowly or change very slowly: **creep*** ◦ *Our profits are creeping up each month.*
- very slowly: **at a snail's pace** ◦ *The traffic in town was moving at a snail's pace.*

▷ driving fast or slow ⇨ **DRIVE**
▷ walking slowly ⇨ **WALK**

4 changing to a faster or slower speed

- to go faster or do sth faster: **accelerate**, **quicken**, **speed up**; to make sth go faster: **accelerate** sth, **quicken** sth, **speed** sth **up**; *noun* (U): **acceleration** ◦ *I accelerated into the fast lane.* ◦ *If you don't speed up, you'll never finish.* ◦ *He quickened his pace.*
- to cause sb/sth to do sth more quickly: **hurry** sb/sth ◦ *The teacher hurried her students for an answer.*
- a sudden increase in speed or effort: **spurt** ◦ *He put on a spurt towards the end of the race.*

- to move or happen more slowly: **slow** (**down**/**up**) ◦ *Can't you slow down a bit?* ◦ *The rate of change has slowed down recently.*
- to make sth move or happen more slowly: **slow** sth (**down**/**up**) ◦ *a campaign to slow down the traffic in the town centre*
- to make a car, etc move more slowly: **reduce speed**

fat/thin/thick

1 people and animals
2 things
see also **BIG/SMALL, HEIGHT, SIZE, WEIGHT**

1 people and animals

■ fat

- having too much flesh: **fat**, (*more polite*) **overweight** ◦ *a fat person* ◦ *The doctor thinks I'm a bit overweight.*
- (used about a part of the body) covered in too much flesh: **fat**, **thick**, **heavy** ◦ *a fat stomach* ◦ *thick arms* ◦ *heavy thighs*

- rather fat, but looking nice: **plump** ◦ *a plump baby*
- round and rather fat: **chubby** ◦ *chubby cheeks*
- with a lot of loose flesh: **flabby** ◦ *flabby arms*
- rather fat and strong: **stout** ◦ *He was slim and athletic as a young man but now is getting rather stout.*

- to become fatter: **get* fat**, (*more polite*) **put* on weight** ◦ *I think she's put on a bit of weight during the summer.*
- to make a person (or an animal) fatter by giving them a lot of food: **fatten** sb/sth **up**
- food which makes you fat is **fattening** ◦ *Are potatoes fattening?*

■ thin

- not having much flesh on your body: **thin**
- thin in an attractive way: **slim**, **slender**
- thin and healthy: **lean** ◦ *a lean and athletic body*
- thin in an unattractive way: **skinny**
- tall and thin with long arms and legs: **lanky** ◦ *a lanky youth* ◦ *long, lanky legs*

- to become thinner: **get* thin**, **lose* weight** ◦ *You seem to have lost some weight – have you been ill?*
- to try to become thinner, especially by eating less: **try to lose weight**, **slim**, **diet** ◦ *I can't eat that chocolate pudding – I'm slimming.*
- the plan that you have in order not to put on weight: **diet** ◦ *to be on a diet* ◦ *a strict diet* ◦ *'Would you like some dessert?' 'I won't thanks, I'm on a diet.'*
- to be careful about what you eat so that you do not get fat: **watch** your **weight**, **watch** your **figure**

2 things

- something which is thick or full is **fat**, **thick**; *nouns* (U): **fatness**, **thickness** ◦ *a fat wallet* (= one with a lot of money in it) ◦ *a thick file* (= a file with a lot of papers in it) ◦ *a thick piece of wood*

- small in size from one side to the other: **thin**; *noun* (U): **thinness** ◦ *a thin line* ◦ *The house had very thin walls – you could hear everything from the next room.*

- a liquid that is not thick and that flows easily is **thin** ◦ *thin soup* ◦ *a thin sauce*
- to make a liquid less thick: **thin** sth (**down**) ◦ *You can thin the paint down by adding some water.*

■ **MORE ...**

- a disease which makes people become very thin because they do not want to eat: **anorexia** (*noun* U); a person who has this disease is (an) **anorexic**

father ⇨ FAMILY

fault

- saying that sth is sb's fault ⇨ **BLAME**
- a mistake ⇨ **MISTAKE**

favourite ⇨ LIKE[2]

fear ⇨ AFRAID

feel

> **1** feeling sth through your skin or fingers
> **2** feelings in your body
> other senses ⇨ **HEAR, SEE, SMELL, TASTE**
> emotions ⇨ **EMOTION**
> thinking and having opinions ⇨ **THINK, OPINION**

1 feeling sth through your skin or fingers

- to be aware of sth through your skin or fingers: **feel*** sth ◦ *Tell me if you can feel this.* ◦ *He felt something dripping on his head.*
- the ability to feel things through your skin and fingers: (**sense of**) **touch** ◦ *Blind people rely heavily on their sense of touch.*

- to put a part of your body, usually your fingers, on sth: **touch** (sth); an act of doing this: **touch** ◦ *Don't touch! It's hot.* ◦ *I touched her skin and could feel how hot and feverish she was.* ◦ *He could feel the touch of the cold metal on his skin.*
- to learn about sth by touching it with your hands: **feel*** sth ◦ *The doctor felt my stomach and took my temperature.*
- to find the correct way to go somewhere in the dark by feeling things: **feel*** your **way** ◦ *I felt my way along the corridor until I reached the window.*

- to have a particular physical quality when touched: **feel*** + adjective, **feel* like** sth; this quality: **feel**, **texture** ◦ *to feel hard/soft/smooth/rough* ◦ *It was a very old piece of wood and felt just like stone.* ◦ *I don't like the feel of this jacket – it irritates my skin.* ◦ *the texture of dried mud*
- giving pleasure through the senses: **sensuous** ◦ *the sensuous pleasure of silk sheets*

▷ more on touching ⇨ **TOUCH**

2 feelings in your body

- to be aware of your physical condition: **feel*** + adjective, **feel*** sth; what you feel: **feeling**, **sensation** ◦ *I feel sick.* ◦ *As I reached the top of the stairs, I began to feel dizzy.* ◦ *to feel comfortable/uncomfortable* ◦ *She could feel her skin burning.* ◦ *I felt a pain in my toe.* ◦ *a feeling of hunger* ◦ *a pleasant feeling* ◦ *I woke up after experiencing a strange flying sensation.*
- if you have the impression of sth happening, you **feel* as if/as though . . .**, or **it feels*** (**to** you) **as if/as though . . .** ◦ *I felt as though I'd been walking for hours.*
- the ability to feel in your body: **feeling** (*noun* U) ◦ *After the injection, you'll have no feeling in your toe for about an hour.*

▷ feeling pain ⇨ **PAIN**
▷ feeling ill ⇨ **ILLNESS**
▷ feelings on the skin ⇨ **SKIN**

female ⇨ SEX[1]

fetch ⇨ GET/OBTAIN

few ⇨ HOW MUCH/MANY

field

> boundaries that are put around a field ⇨ **WALL/FENCE/HEDGE**
> **see also FARM**

- an area of land on a farm, used for growing crops or keeping animals: **field** ◦ *a field of barley* ◦ *Shall we go for a walk in the fields?* ◦ *a ten-acre field*
- a field of grass for animals to eat: **meadow**
- a field or an area of land on a farm where grass is grown to feed cows: **pasture** (*noun* C/U)
- a field where horses are kept: **paddock**
- a field in which fruit trees grow: **orchard** ◦ *an apple orchard*
- a field where rice is grown in water: **paddy field**, **rice field**

- a model of a man dressed up in old clothes and put in a field to frighten birds away: **scarecrow**

fight

> **1** fighting
> **2** starting a fight; attacking
> **3** hitting and hurting
> **4** defending
> **5** ending a fight; winning and losing
> kinds of fighting which are sports ⇨ **SPORT, BOXING**
> **see also WEAPON, WAR, ARMY**

1 fighting

- to use physical strength, guns, knives, etc against sb/sth: **fight*** (**with/against** sb/sth) (**about/over** sth); *noun* (U): **fighting** ◦ *My great-grandfather fought in the First World War.* ◦ *Demonstrators fought with the police for several hours.* ◦ *The two boys were fighting over whose turn it was to use the computer game.* ◦ *The fighting continued for five days.*
- an act of fighting: **fight**, **struggle**, (*more formal*) **conflict** (*noun* C/U) ◦ *Don't get into any fights at school, will you?* ◦ *an armed conflict/struggle*

- a person who fights: **fighter**
- a person who fights against you: **opponent** ◦ *My opponent was six inches taller than me and almost double my weight.*
- (in a war) the army or country that your country is fighting against: (**the**) **enemy** (*with singular or*

fight *contd.*

plural verb) ◦ *The enemy was hiding in the woods ahead of us*.

▷ more on enemies ⇨ **ENEMY**

– if you are ready or likely to fight you are **aggressive** ◦ *a very aggressive child*
– angry and aggressive: **fierce**, **ferocious**; *noun* (U): **ferocity** ◦ *a fierce dog* ◦ *a ferocious look*
– if you use your physical strength to hurt or kill sb, you are **violent**; *noun* (U): **violence** ◦ *a violent attack* ◦ *violence against women*

■ fighting in the street or other public places
– a noisy fight among a group of people, usually in a public place: **brawl**, (*informal*) **punch-up**; to fight in this way: **brawl** ◦ *Two men were involved in a punch-up outside the Red Lion pub.* ◦ *Some football fans were arrested for brawling in the street.*
– a person who gets involved in this kind of fight can be called a **hooligan**
– fighting and noisy violent behaviour by a crowd of people: **riot**, **rioting** (*noun* U); to behave in this way: **riot**; a person involved in a riot: **rioter** ◦ *Police used tear gas to stop the riots.* ◦ *Rioting continued throughout the night.* ◦ *Rioters smashed up shops and set fire to cars.*

2 starting a fight; attacking

– to start a fight with sb on purpose: **pick a fight** (**with** sb) ◦ *Don't go picking fights with Gordon; you won't stand a chance.*
– to invite sb to fight against you: **challenge** sb (**to** a fight); *noun*: **challenge** ◦ *He challenged me to a fight in the playground at lunchtime.* ◦ *to accept a challenge to a fight*

– physical strength: **force** (*noun* U) ◦ *The police used force to break up the demonstration.*
– to try to hurt or defeat sb/sth by using force: **attack** (sb/sth) ◦ *She attacked him from behind.*
– an act of attacking: **attack** (*noun* C/U) ◦ *a prolonged and vicious attack* ◦ *to launch an attack* (= to begin attacking sb/sth) ◦ *under attack* (= being attacked)
– a violent attack: **assault**; to make an assault: **assault** sb/sth ◦ *We began the assault on the town at 3 a.m.* ◦ *I was assaulted by three men.*
– an attack that is not caused by an earlier action is **unprovoked**

– to begin an attack on sb: **come* at**/**for** sb, **go* for** sb ◦ *He came at me with a gun.* ◦ *The dog went for me when I tried to pat its head.*

– to attack sb by running directly at them: **charge** (sb); *noun*: **charge** ◦ *Mounted police charged the demonstrators.* ◦ *a sudden charge*
– to attack sb/sth suddenly from a hidden place: **ambush** sb/sth; *noun*: **ambush** ◦ *We were ambushed as we were travelling along a valley.*
– to hide and wait for sb in order to attack them unexpectedly: **lie* in wait for** sb/sth

3 hitting and hurting

– to harm or hurt sb or part of their body: **injure** sb/sth; *noun* (C/U): **injury** ◦ *Shaun was badly injured during the boxing match.* ◦ *He had a serious injury to his head.*
– to injure sb with a weapon: **wound** sb; this kind of injury: **wound** ◦ *He was wounded in the leg.* ◦ *The doctor treated his wounds.*

– to hurt sb badly in a fight: **beat*** sb **up** ◦ *He had been badly beaten up by a member of a rival gang.*
– to hit sb so that they become unconscious and cannot get up again for a while: **knock** sb **out** ◦ *Tyson was knocked out in the eighth round of the match.*
– to make sb/sth die: **kill** sb/sth ◦ *I only meant to hurt him – I didn't want to kill him!*

▷ more on injury and killing ⇨ **INJURY, KILL**

■ ways of hitting
– to touch sb/sth with a lot of force: **hit*** sb/sth, (*formal*) **strike*** sb/sth ◦ *I hit him so hard that he fell over.*
– to hit sb/sth with your fist (= your hand with the fingers held together tightly): **punch** sb/sth; *noun*: **punch** ◦ *I punched him in the stomach as hard as I could.* ◦ *to give sb a punch in the face*
– a hard knock from your hand that is intended to hit sb/sth: **blow** ◦ *She aimed a blow at his face.*
– to use your foot to hit sb/sth: **kick** sb/sth; *noun*: **kick** ◦ *I was knocked to the ground and kicked in the stomach.* ◦ *a vicious kick to the head*
– to aim strong blows or attacks at sb/sth: **hit* out** (**at** sb/sth), **strike* out** (**at** sb/sth) ◦ *He struck out wildly at the guards as they tried to take him into the police station.*

▷ more on hitting ⇨ **HIT**

4 defending

– to fight to protect yourself, another person, a place, etc: **defend** yourself/sb/sth (**against** sb/sth); *noun* (U): **defence** (*AmE* **defense**); defending yourself: **self-defence** (*AmE* **self-defense**) (*noun* U) ◦ *Would you be able to defend yourself if someone attacked you in the street?* ◦ *I go to self-defence classes every week.*

– to hit sb who hits you: **hit* back** (**at** sb) ◦ *He didn't expect the smaller boy to hit back at him.*
– to fight against sb/sth that has attacked you: **fight* back** (**against** sb/sth), **put* up a fight**/**struggle** (**against** sb/sth), (*more formal*) **resist** (sb/sth); *noun* (U): **resistance** (**to** sb/sth) ◦ *I was attacked by a mugger, but I fought back and he ran off.* ◦ *They put up a brave fight against a much stronger enemy.* ◦ *armed resistance*

– to continue to defend yourself: **hold* out** (**against** sb/sth) ◦ *They held out for four hours before being forced to surrender.*
– to fight sb/sth that has been attacking you and push them/it away: **fight*** sb/sth **off**, **beat*** sb/sth **off** ◦ *I beat off my attacker and ran after him.*

5 ending a fight; winning and losing

– to be the best or strongest in a fight: **win*** (sth) ◦ *to win a war/fight/battle*
– a person who wins a fight: **winner**

- to win a fight against sb/sth: **beat*** sb/sth, **defeat** sb/sth; *noun* (C/U): **defeat** ○ *We were beaten by superior forces.* ○ *Bruno was defeated for the third time in a row.*

- not to win a fight: **lose*** (a fight), **be beaten/defeated** (**by** sb)
- a person who loses a fight: **loser**

▷ more on winning and losing ⇨ **WIN/LOSE**

- an agreement to stop fighting: **ceasefire** ○ *The rebels have broken the ceasefire and fighting has begun again.*
- an agreement to stop fighting for a time: **truce** ○ *A truce was called while the sides exchanged prisoners.*
- to stop fighting and admit that you have lost: **give* in** (**to** sb), **surrender** (**to** sb); *noun* (C/U): **surrender** ○ *Whatever they do, we shall never give in.* ○ *The soldiers put their hands up and surrendered.* ○ *unconditional surrender*

---

film

1 different kinds of film
2 what you see and hear in a film
3 making a film
4 seeing a film

see also **VIDEO, PHOTOGRAPH**

1 different kinds of film

- a story, play, etc which is told in moving pictures: **film**, (*especially AmE*) **movie** ○ *Let's go out and see a film.* ○ *an entertaining/exciting/enjoyable film* ○ *a boring film* ○ *a film critic* (= a person who tells the public what is good or bad about a film)

a film that ...	is called a ...
gives facts and information about something	documentary
uses drawings which appear to move	cartoon
has no spoken words	silent film/movie
people make themselves for fun	home movie
is very exciting	thriller
makes people afraid	horror film
is about cowboys in the west of the USA	western
is amusing and has a happy ending	comedy
includes singing and dancing	musical

- a film which continues the story of a previous one: **sequel** (**to** sth)
- a film of a story which has been filmed before: **remake** (**of** sth)
- a short film which advertises a longer film: **trailer** (**for** sth)

2 what you see and hear in a film

- the words and actions of an actor in a film: **part**, **role** ○ *His ambition is to play the part of King Lear.* ○ *Sean Connery, in the role of James Bond*
- the events of a story in a film, play, etc: **plot** ○ *a simple/complicated plot* ○ *I couldn't follow the plot.*
- one part of a film in which a particular event happens, or in which the events happen in a particular place: **scene** ○ *the fight scenes* ○ *the bedroom scene*
- the way a story ends: **ending** ○ *a happy/sad ending*

- the techniques that are used to make things look or sound real: **special effects** ○ *They won a prize for the special effects – the dinosaurs were really frightening.*

- a song or music that is often repeated in a film and becomes associated with it: **theme song**, **theme music** (*noun* U)

- the words of a film, usually translated from another language, that you see at the bottom of the screen: **subtitles** (*noun plural*) ○ *The film had English subtitles.*
- to change a film so that the words are said in a different language: **dub** sth ○ *I don't like films that are dubbed into English. I prefer subtitles.*

- the list of the names of the people who made a film, which is shown at the beginning or the end of the film: the **credits** (*noun plural*) ○ *Everyone left as soon as the credits came up.*

3 making a film

- the industry that makes films for showing in the cinema, or films considered as an art form: **the cinema** (*noun singular*), (*especially AmE*) **the movies** (*noun plural*) ○ *She moved to Hollywood because she wanted to work in the movies.*

- a man/woman who plays a part in a film: **actor**; a female actor can also be called an **actress**
- a very well-known film actor or actress: (**film**) **star**; to take an important part in a film: **star** (**in** sth); to have a particular actor or actress in the main part in a film: **star** sb ○ *The film stars Sylvester Stallone.*
- with many famous actors: **all-star** (*adjective, only before a noun*) ○ *an all-star cast*
- one of two or more stars in a film: **co-star**; to be a co-star with sb else: **co-star** (**with** sb); to have two or more people as co-stars: **co-star** sb ○ *He co-starred with Marlon Brando.* ○ *The film co-stars Hugh Grant and Andi McDowell.*

- a person who has a very small part in a film: **extra** ○ *They used hundreds of extras for the crowd scenes.*
- a man who does dangerous or difficult things in a film in the place of another actor: **stuntman** (*plural* **stuntmen**); a woman who does this: **stuntwoman** (*plural* **stuntwomen**)
- all the actors in a film: the **cast** (*with singular or plural verb*)
- to choose the people who will act the different parts in a particular film: **cast** (a film), **cast** sb

film *contd.*

(**as** sb/sth) ◦ *They haven't finished casting yet.* ◦ *He was cast as a Roman soldier in 'Ben Hur'.*

– the way that sb acts in a play or film: **performance** ◦ *She gave a brilliant/terrible/inspired performance.*

▷ more on actors and acting ⇨ ACT[2]

– the person who tells the actors, etc what to do: (**film/movie**) **director**; his/her job is to **direct** the film ◦ *Stephen Spielberg is one of the world's most famous directors.* ◦ *He directed the film as well as acting in it.*
– the person who organizes the business side of making a film: **producer**; his/her job is to **produce** the film
– a person who writes for films, television or radio, etc: **scriptwriter**; his/her job is to write the **script**, **screenplay**
– the person who cuts and arranges parts of a film in a particular order: **editor**; his/her job is to **edit** the film

– the piece of equipment that is used to make a film: **camera**
– a man who operates a film camera: **cameraman** (*plural* **cameramen**); a woman who does this: **camerawoman** (*plural* **camerawomen**)

– to make a film: **film** (sb/sth), **shoot*** (sb/sth) ◦ *Filming lasted six months.* ◦ *They shot the whole film in six months.*

– the building where a film is made: **studio** (*plural* **studios**)
– the specially built rooms, buildings or scenery where the events of a film take place: **set**

4 seeing a film

– when you watch a film, you **see*** it ◦ *Have you seen 'Jurassic Park'?*
– a building where people go to see a film: **cinema** (*AmE* **movie house, movie theater**)

▷ more on cinemas ⇨ CINEMA

■ **MORE ...**
– the first time that a film is shown to the public: **premiere**
– an event when different films are shown in a short period of time: **festival** ◦ *the Cannes Film Festival*

– the technique of making drawings appear to move in a film: **animation** (*noun* U); made using this technique: **animated** ◦ *Donald Duck is one of Walt Disney's most famous animated characters.*
– when the action in a film is made to seem much slower than it really is, it is **in slow motion**

– an official who removes parts of a film that might offend people, and decides whether or not everyone should be allowed to see it: **censor**; to do this job: **censor** sth; the process of doing this: **censorship** (*noun* U) ◦ *I don't really approve of censorship but I think there is too much sex and violence in some films.*

final(ly) ⇨ FIRST/NEXT/LAST

find

see also LOOK FOR

■ finding what you have lost
– to get back sth that you have lost: **find*** sth ◦ *I've looked everywhere for that key but I can't find it anywhere.*
– to notice sth that you have been looking for: **see*** sth ◦ *I'd been looking for my glasses for ages when I finally saw them under the sofa.*
– to be found: **turn up** ◦ *'I can't find that book anywhere!' 'Don't worry, I'm sure it will turn up somewhere soon.'*

■ difficult to find
– to put sth in a place where you think people will not be able to find it: **hide*** sth ◦ *I've hidden the children's Christmas presents under the bed.*
– to go to a place where you think people will not be able to find you: **hide*** ◦ *She hid behind the door and listened to their conversation.*

▷ more on hiding ⇨ HIDE

■ finding sth that you need
– to get sth that you want, especially after making an effort to look for it: **find*** sth ◦ *Guess what! I've found a job!* ◦ *Did you manage to find a good hotel?*
– to find sth that will be useful: **get* hold of** sth ◦ *If you can get hold of a ladder, you'll make things much easier for yourself.*

■ finding sth by chance
– to find sth by chance: **find*** sth, **come* across** sth, **discover** sth; *noun* (C/U): **discovery** ◦ *I came across these old photos when I was cleaning yesterday.* ◦ *Look what I discovered when I was clearing out the attic!* ◦ *A little while later we made another exciting discovery.*
– to discover sb as they are doing sth bad: **catch*** sb (doing sth), **catch*** sb **red-handed** ◦ *I caught her stealing money from my purse.*

■ finding information
– to get some information by asking or studying: **find*** (sth) **out** ◦ *'Do you know that man's name?' 'No, but I can find out for you.'* ◦ *I'm trying to find out how much it costs.*
– to find or learn sth which nobody knew or had found before, or which you did not know before: **discover** sth; *noun* (C/U): **discovery** ◦ *Archaeologists have discovered the remains of an ancient civilization.* ◦ *They think they may have discovered a new cure for cancer.* ◦ *to make a discovery* ◦ *the discovery of America*
– a person who discovers sth: **discoverer** ◦ *the discoverer of penicillin*

▷ studying to find things out ⇨ STUDY

– to travel round a place in order to find out about it: **explore** (a place); *noun* (C/U): **exploration** ◦ *a rocket that is exploring space* ◦ *Let's go out and explore.* ◦ *We decided to make another exploration of the house.* ◦ *a journey of exploration*

- a person who explores places: **explorer**
- a long journey that you make in order to discover sth: **expedition**

finger ⇨ HAND/ARM

finish ⇨ END/FINISH

fire

1 fire
2 smoke
3 starting a fire
4 using fire for heat, etc
5 stopping a fire
6 protecting people against fire

1 fire

- the heat and light produced by sth which is burning: **fire** (*noun* C/U) ◦ *Make sure you know what to do if there's a fire.* ◦ *a forest fire* ◦ *The school was destroyed by fire.*
- a large or dangerous fire: **blaze** ◦ *Two children died in the blaze.*
- an area of heat and light which rises from sth which is burning: **flame** ◦ *the flame of a candle*

- if there is a fire, sth is **burning**, **on fire**, **alight** (*adjective, not before a noun*) ◦ *a burning oil well* ◦ *The house is on fire!* ◦ *Most of the building was already alight.*
- burning strongly: **ablaze** (*adjective, not before a noun*), **in flames**
- to be on fire; to be able to be on fire: **burn** ◦ *The fire is burning well.* ◦ *This kind of material doesn't burn very easily.*
- if sth is able to burn easily, it is **flammable**, **inflammable**; *opposite*: **non-flammable** ◦ *Caution: flammable.*

- to begin to burn, often accidentally: **catch* fire** ◦ *Be careful – your skirt might catch fire.*
- to begin to burn suddenly and strongly: **burst* into flames**, **go* up** (**in flames**) ◦ *The car crashed and immediately burst into flames.* ◦ *Everything we owned went up in flames.*

- to burn unsteadily: **flicker** ◦ *a flickering flame*
- when a fire gets bigger and moves over a larger area, it **spreads*** ◦ *By now the fire had spread to other parts of the town.*
- a small piece of burning wood, etc which can fly out of a fire: **spark** ◦ *Watch out for the sparks.*

- when a fire finishes, it **goes* out**; when it has finished, it is **out** ◦ *Try not to let the fire go out.*
- the grey dust which is left after sth has burnt: **ash** (*noun* U)
- when the last part of a fire continues to burn slowly without a flame, it **smoulders** (*AmE* **smolder**) ◦ *Don't touch it – it's still smouldering.*
- small pieces of coal or wood which are still smouldering: **embers** (*noun plural*)
- the black dust which can be found in places where there has been a fire: **soot** (*noun* U); *adjective*: **sooty**

■ damage caused by fires

- to hurt sb by fire: **burn** sb; a red mark on the skin where it has been burnt: **burn** ◦ *His back was horribly burnt.* ◦ *She had severe burns on her arms.*
- to destroy or damage sth by fire: **burn** sth; to be destroyed or damaged by fire: **burn**, **get* burnt** ◦ *He asked me to take the papers outside and burn them.* ◦ *The toast has got burnt!*
- to burn sth so that it is slightly damaged: **scorch** sth ◦ *I'm afraid I scorched your dress while I was ironing it.*

- to completely destroy sth by fire: **burn** sth **down**, **burn** sth **to the ground**, **burn** sth **out** (*usually passive*) ◦ *It's not the first time they've tried to burn down the school.* ◦ *The hotel was burnt to the ground.* ◦ *The car was completely burnt out.*
- (used about buildings) to be completely destroyed by fire: **burn down**, **burn to the ground**

2 smoke

- the cloud of gas which you can see in the air when sth is burning: **smoke** (*noun* U) ◦ *The first thing we noticed was the smell of smoke.* ◦ *thick/dense smoke*
- to give out smoke: **smoke** ◦ *smoking factory chimneys*
- having a lot of smoke; smelling or tasting of smoke: **smoky** ◦ *a room with a smoky atmosphere* ◦ *a smoky flavour*

- an amount of smoke in the air: **cloud** (of smoke) ◦ *a cloud of dense black smoke*
- a small amount of smoke: **puff** (of smoke) ◦ *little puffs of smoke*
- an unpleasant and dangerous mixture of smoke and gases: **fumes** (*noun plural*) ◦ *the smell of exhaust fumes*

- the passage by which smoke leaves a building, for example from the fireplace to a hole in the roof: **chimney**

3 starting a fire

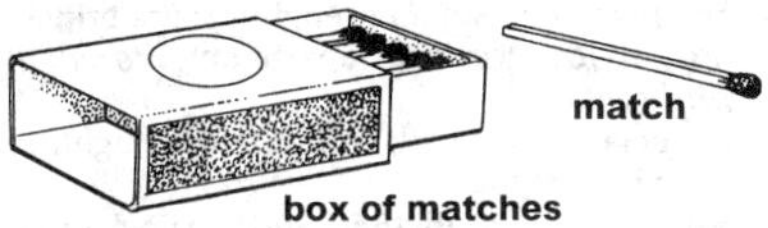

- the thin wooden part of a match: **matchstick**
- a small box for matches: **matchbox**
- an object which produces a small flame for lighting cigarettes, etc: (**cigarette**) **lighter**
- to make a match burn: **light*** a **match**, **strike*** a **match**

- to start a fire, especially in a house to keep warm: **light*** (a fire); to begin to burn: **light*** ◦ *to light a fire* ◦ *I can't get this fire to light.*
- to start a fire, especially to cause damage: **set*** sth **on fire**, **set* fire to** sth ◦ *They killed most of the villagers and set their houses on fire.*

fire *contd.*

- something which you can use to start a fire (for example a match or lighter): **light** ◦ *Have you got a light?*

4 using fire for heat, etc

- a fire which is used to heat a room: **fire** ◦ *I spent the whole evening reading by the fire.* ◦ *We lit a fire to keep warm.*
- the light from a fire: **firelight** (*noun* U) ◦ *sitting around chatting in the firelight*
- the place in a room where a fire is lit: **fireplace**
- a shelf on top of a fireplace: **mantelpiece**

▷ picture at ROOM

- a substance which can be burnt in order to produce heat: **fuel** (*noun* U)
- a type of solid black fuel which is found under the ground: **coal** (*noun* U)
- wood which is burnt as a fuel: **firewood** (*noun* U); a piece of firewood: **log** ◦ *a roaring log fire*
- a fuel which does not produce smoke when it burns is **smokeless**

▷ more on coal, wood and fuel ⇨ COAL, WOOD, FUEL

▷ other ways of heating a house or room ⇨ HOT

5 stopping a fire

- to stop a fire: **put* sth out**, (*formal*) **extinguish sth** ◦ *It took them several hours to put out the blaze.*
- to put out a small fire (for example a candle) by blowing on it: **blow* sth out** ◦ *See if you can blow out all the candles in one breath.*
- to put out a fire by beating it: **beat* sth out** ◦ *She managed to beat the flames out before they spread too far.*
- to try to put out a fire: **fight*** a fire

- a metal container containing a substance which is used to put out fires: **(fire) extinguisher**

- a person whose job is to fight fires: **firefighter**, **fireman**
- an organized team of firefighters: **fire brigade**, **fire service** (*AmE* **fire department**) ◦ *to call the fire brigade*
- a special vehicle with equipment for fighting fires: **fire engine**
- a place where firefighters and fire engines are based: **fire station**
- if you need to call the fire service on the phone, you **dial 999** (in the UK), **dial 911** (in the US)

6 protecting people against fire

- a machine which makes a loud noise to warn people that there is a fire: **fire alarm**, **alarm** ◦ *If you hear the fire alarm, you must leave the building as quickly as possible.*
- an alarm which sounds automatically when there is smoke in a room: **smoke alarm**

- a way of leaving a building when there is a fire: **fire exit**
- a special outside staircase for leaving a building when there is a fire: **fire escape**
- something which cannot be destroyed by fire is **fireproof**

■ **MORE ...**

- a large fire which people build in the garden in order to burn rubbish: **bonfire**
- a small object, often fired into the air like a rocket, which burns with coloured lights and loud noises, and which is used after dark on special occasions: **firework**

- a large machine like an oven, in which fire is used to melt metal, burn rubbish, etc: **furnace**

- the crime of starting a fire on purpose: **arson** (*noun* U) ◦ *He's suspected of committing several acts of arson.*

first/next/last

1 order
2 first
3 next
4 last
first, second, third, etc ⇨ NUMBER
see also BEFORE/AFTER

1 order

- the way in which people or things are arranged in relation to each other: **order** (*noun* C/U) ◦ *Somebody had put the names on the list in a different order.* ◦ *in order of importance*
- the order in which things happen: **sequence** (*noun* C/U) ◦ *What was the sequence of events?*
- happening one after the other: **consecutive** (*adverb* **consecutively**)
- arranged in the order in which the events happened: **chronological** ◦ *a chronological account of the war*

- first one then the next: **one after another**, **one after the other** ◦ *They came onto the stage one after the other and bowed to the audience.*
- a number of people or things that follow one after another: **succession** ◦ *He's suffered from a succession of defeats in the last year.*
- coming one after the other: **running** (*used after a number and a noun*), **in succession**, **successive**, **consecutive** ◦ *three years running* ◦ *The champion had had five successive wins at Wimbledon.*

2 first

- coming before all others in time, order or importance: **first** (*adjective, adverb*) ◦ *It's the first house on the right.* ◦ *our first child* ◦ *The First World War* ◦ *Do you remember the first time we met?* ◦ *When John first met Laura, he didn't like her very much.*
- the first person or thing: **the first** (*plural* **the first**) ◦ *We were the first to arrive.* ◦ *The mining industry was one of the first to be nationalized.* ◦ *That's the first I've heard about it.*

- coming at the beginning of sth: **initial** ◦ *In the initial stages, it seemed possible that the plan could fail.*
- at the beginning: **at first, initially** ◦ *At first, I thought he was lying, then I realized he was telling the truth.*
- first, before changes or developments: **original** (*adverb* **originally**) ◦ *We changed our original plans and decided to go earlier.* ◦ *He's from London originally, but now he lives in Paris.*
- the first part of sth (for example a film or a book): **beginning, start** ◦ *an exciting beginning* ◦ *That was the start of our adventure.*

▷ more on beginning ⇨ BEGIN

- when first seen or examined: **at first sight, at first glance** ◦ *At first glance, I thought he was carrying a gun, then I realized it was just an umbrella.*
- as the first or most important thing: **first of all** ◦ *First of all, we visited the museums; then in the afternoon we went shopping.*
- as the first point in a list: **firstly, first, in the first place** ◦ *There are two reasons for the success of this scheme: firstly ...*

■ first in importance
- to be more important than anything else: **come* first** ◦ *My children come first, before anything else.*
- something that is most important or that you must do before anything else: **priority** (*noun* C/U) ◦ *His work takes priority over everything else.*
- the first or most important position: **top, head** ◦ *Her name was at the top of the list.* ◦ *He was at the head of the queue.*

▷ being important ⇨ IMPORTANT

■ competitions
- to be the best, the first or the most successful in sth: **win*** (sth); to win in a race or competition: **come* first** ◦ *Obviously I had hoped to win, but I'm still pleased that I came second.* ◦ *She came first in the swimming competition.*
- the first place or position: **the lead** ◦ *'Who's in the lead?' 'Italy are at the moment.'*

▷ winning and losing ⇨ WIN / LOSE

■ the first of its kind
- a picture, book, etc as it was produced by the person who made it: **original** ◦ *This is only a copy of the painting – the original's kept locked away.*
- the first model or design of sth from which other forms will be copied or developed: **prototype** ◦ *a prototype computer terminal*
- to be one of the first people to do sth or develop sth: **pioneer** sth; a person who does this: **pioneer** ◦ *Our company has pioneered the use of seat belts in buses.* ◦ *a pioneer of modern medicine*

3 next
- coming immediately after sb/sth in space or time: **next** (*adjective, adverb*) ◦ *The next bus comes at six o'clock.* ◦ *We'll go to the zoo next time you're in London.* ◦ *Who's next?* ◦ *the next on the list* ◦ *What did you do next?*
- immediately after sth in space or time: **then** ◦ *First you'll see the garage on your left, and then the turning into our street.*
- planned to come next in order: **to follow** ◦ *There's apple pie next and then some cheese to follow.*

Note: when we are talking about the day of the week, the week, the month or the year that follows the present one, we do not use **the**; in other uses, we do use **the**: ◦ *I'll be in Paris next week.* ◦ *The next week was not a very enjoyable one.*

4 last
- coming after all others in time, order or importance: **last** (*adjective, adverb*) ◦ *the last one* ◦ *That's the last time I take those children out for the day – they didn't even say thank you.* ◦ *to come last in a race*
- the last person or thing: **the last** (*plural* **the last**) ◦ *the last in the queue* ◦ *We were the last to get to the party.* ◦ *That was the last I ever heard of her.*
- the one before the last: **last but one** ◦ *It's the last house but one on the right.*

- last in a series: **last, final** ◦ *the last chapter in a book* ◦ *I answered the final question in the last half-hour of the exam.* ◦ *I'll give you five pounds for it, and that's my final offer.* ◦ *The final report will be published by the Government next year.*
- as the last of a series: **lastly, finally** ◦ *First, I telephoned; then I sent a letter; lastly, I went round and saw him myself.*
- last and most important: **ultimate** ◦ *Our ultimate goal is to visit all the countries in Africa.*

- only remaining: **last**; the only remaining person or thing: **the last** (*plural* **the last**) ◦ *Who wants the last piece of cake?* ◦ *Will the last person out please lock the door.* ◦ *You'd better take this appointment – it's the last one.* ◦ *The last of the guests have left.*

- nearest to the present; most recent: **last**; on the occasion nearest to the present: **last** ◦ *She arrived last week/Tuesday.* ◦ *I can't remember the last time we went to see them.* ◦ *When did you last see her?*
- (used about a book, film, record, etc) the one most recently produced: (*informal*) **latest** ◦ *Have you heard their latest record?*

- the place or time when sth stops: **end** ◦ *the end of the road* ◦ *at the end of July*
- the last part of sth: **end, ending** ◦ *The film was good but I didn't really like the ending.*

▷ more on ending ⇨ END / FINISH

---

fish[1] living fish

fish as food ⇨ FISH[2]
other animals that live in the sea ⇨ ANIMAL

- an animal that lives and swims in water: **fish** (*plural* **fish** or, if you mean kinds of fish, **fishes**) ◦ *We caught a lot of fish.* ◦ *There are a great many different fishes* (= different kinds of fish) *in the rivers around here* ◦ *a fish farm* (= a place where fish are bred before they are sold)

fish[1] *contd.*

- a type of animal that lives in water and has a shell: **shellfish** (*plural* **shellfish**)

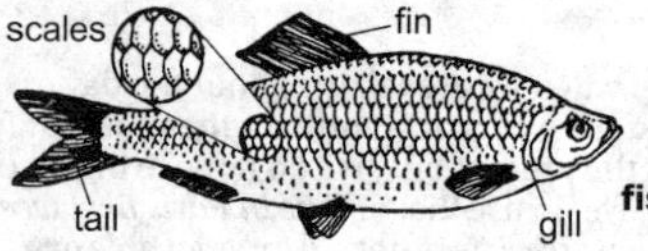

- an opening on the side of a fish's head through which it breathes: **gill**
- the outer covering of many fish and reptiles: **scales** (*noun plural*); *adjective*: **scaly**
- a small golden-coloured fish that some people keep in a glass bowl or in a garden pond: **goldfish** (*plural* **goldfish**)
- a long fish that looks like a snake: **eel**
- a large dangerous sea fish with sharp teeth: **shark**

■ catching fish

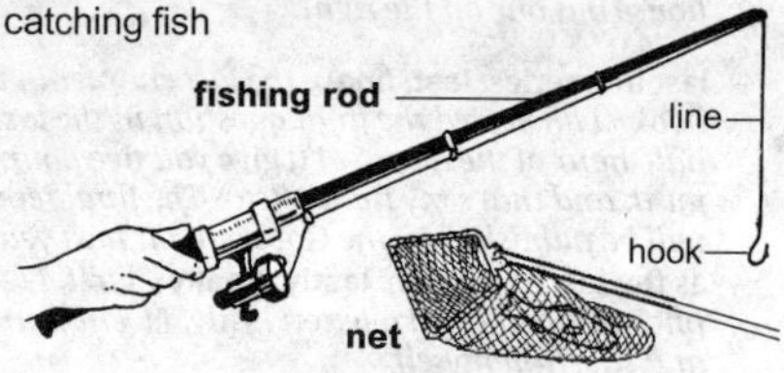

- to try to catch fish using rods or nets: **fish** (**for** sth) ◦ *They're fishing for trout.* ◦ *to go fishing*
- catching fish as a job, or for sport or pleasure: **fishing** (*noun* U) ◦ *a fishing trip* ◦ *the fishing industry*
- food that is put onto a hook to try to catch fish: **bait** (*noun* U)
- to take a fish out of water using a rod or a net: **catch*** sth

- a person whose work is to catch fish: **fisherman** (*plural* **fishermen**)
- a boat used for catching fish: **fishing boat**
- a big boat used to catch large numbers of fish at sea: **trawler**
- a number of fish that have been caught: **catch**, **haul** ◦ *a catch of herring*

■ **MORE ...**

- a person who goes fishing as a sport: **angler**; the name of the sport: **angling** (*noun* U) ◦ *an angling competition*

- a large tank for fish, or a building in a zoo for tropical fish: **aquarium**

fish[2] fish as food

catching fish ⇨ FISH[1]
see also FOOD, COOK

- an animal that lives and swims in water: **fish** (*plural* **fish** or, if you mean kinds of fish, **fishes**)
- the meat that comes from a fish: **fish** (*noun* U) ◦ *Shall we have fish for dinner?*
- a type of animal that lives in water and has a shell: **shellfish** (*plural* **shellfish**)
- the general word for animals from the sea that are eaten: **seafood** (*noun* U) ◦ *a seafood restaurant*

- some types of fish that people often eat: **cod** (*plural* **cod**), **herring**, **plaice** (*plural* **plaice**), **salmon** (*plural* **salmon**), **sardine**, **trout** (*plural* **trout**), **tuna** (*plural* **tuna**) ◦ *smoked salmon* ◦ *a tin of sardines* ◦ *whole fresh trout*

■ some shellfish and other sea animals

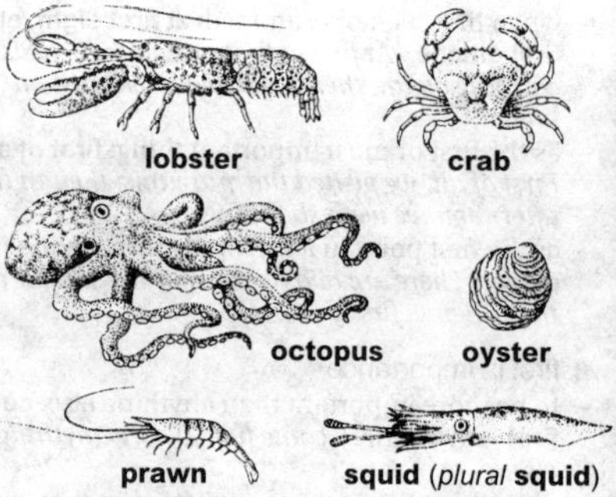

■ ways of cooking fish

- you can **fry** fish (= cook it in hot oil), **grill** fish (= cook it under a grill), **steam** fish (= cook it in steam), **poach** fish (= cook it in a saucepan in a small amount of liquid), **bake** fish (= cook it in the oven) ◦ *Shall we fry the fish or grill it?*

- small pieces of fish made into the shape of a small cake: **fishcake**
- fish which is fried and served with fried potatoes: **fish and chips**

■ buying fish

- a shop where you buy fish: **fishmonger's**; a person who sells fish: **fishmonger**
- a shop which sells cooked fish, often with chips: **fish and chip shop**

■ **MORE ...**

- one of the hard parts in a fish: **bone**; fish which has a lot of bones in it is **bony**
- to remove the bones from a fish: **fillet** sth; a piece of fish with the bones removed: **fillet**; *adjective*: **filleted** ◦ *I'd like three cod fillets please.* ◦ *It shouldn't have any bones in it – I asked the fishmonger to fillet it.*
- a thick flat piece of fish: **steak** ◦ *a salmon steak*

flag

see also COUNTRY[1]

- a flag that is used as a symbol of a country: **national flag**
- the national flag of the United Kingdom: **the Union Jack**

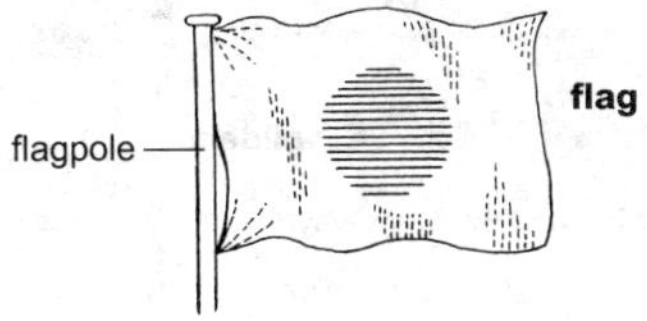

- the national flag of the USA: **the Stars and Stripes**

- to lift a flag up to a high position: **raise** sth; *opposite*: **lower** sth ◦ *The flag was raised as the Queen entered the castle.*
- if a flag is placed half way down a flagpole (usually because sb has died), it is flying **at half-mast**

- to move a flag backwards and forwards: **wave** sth ◦ *The crowds were in the street, cheering and waving flags.*

flat

- a kind of house ⇨ HOUSE
- with a level surface ⇨ SURFACE

floor

other parts of houses or other buildings ⇨ HOUSE, BUILDING
cleaning a floor ⇨ CLEAN / DIRTY

- the flat surface that you walk on inside a building: **floor** ◦ *a wooden/stone/concrete floor* ◦ *to sit on the floor*
- a long piece of wood which fits together with others to make a floor: **floorboard**

- a level in a building: **floor** ◦ *the ground/first/top floor*
- one of the floors in a ship or a bus: **deck** ◦ *the top deck* ◦ *on a lower deck*

■ different kinds of floor covering
- a thick piece of material made from wool or sth similar, which is used to cover floors and stairs: **carpet** ◦ *to lay a carpet* (= to put a new one on a floor)
- to put carpets in a building: **carpet** sth ◦ *The house is carpeted throughout.*
- a carpet which covers the whole area of the floor: **fitted carpet**
- a small carpet: **rug, mat** ◦ *There was a Chinese rug in front of the fire.* ◦ *a straw mat* ◦ *a bath mat*

- strong smooth materials that are used for covering floors: **vinyl** (*noun* U), **linoleum** (*noun* U), (*informal*) **lino** (*noun* U)
- a flat, square object which fits together with others in rows to cover a floor, wall, etc: **tile**; if you put these on a floor or wall, you **tile** sth ◦ *floor tiles* ◦ *We're going to tile the bathroom floor.*

flour

cooking with flour ⇨ BREAD, CAKE, COOK

- a white or brown powder made from grain and used to make bread, cakes, biscuits, etc: **flour** (*noun* U)
- flour with an added substance which makes cakes rise when they are cooked: **self-raising flour** (*noun* U); flour without this substance: **plain flour** (*noun* U)
- flour which has the whole of the grain in it: **wholemeal flour** (*noun* U)
- flour that is usually used to make liquids thick: **cornflour** (*noun* U)

- a mixture of flour and water that is used for making bread: **dough** (*noun* U)
- a mixture of flour, water and fat that is used for making pies and cakes: **pastry** (*noun* U)
- a type of food made from a mixture of flour, eggs and water: **pasta** (*noun* U) ◦ *spaghetti, lasagne and other kinds of pasta*

- to remove lumps from flour, etc: **sieve** sth; the instrument used for this: **sieve** ◦ *Sieve the flour into a bowl.*

▷ picture at COOK

- to make grain (for example, wheat) into flour: **grind*** sth
- a place where flour is produced: **mill**

flower

see also PLANT, GARDEN

- the part of a plant or tree from which the seeds or fruit grow: **flower** ◦ *This flower has a lovely scent.*
- a flower or a mass of flowers on a fruit tree: **blossom** (*noun* C/U) ◦ *Look at the cherry/apple blossom.*
- the smell of a flower: **scent** ◦ *What a beautiful scent those roses have!*

- a plant that is grown or picked for its flowers: **flower** ◦ *a flower garden*
- flowers that grow in fields and wild places: **wild flowers** ◦ *Some wild flowers common around here are primroses, dandelions and daisies.*

■ flowers which people often grow or buy

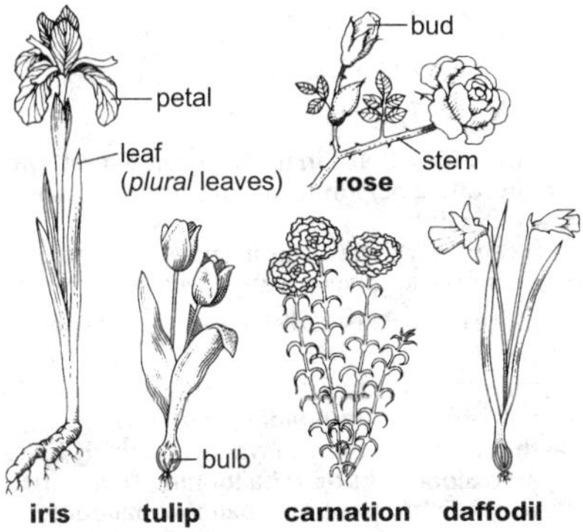

flower *contd.*

■ parts of flowers

- the round root of certain plants: **bulb** ◦ *I planted some tulip bulbs over there.*
- one of the parts of a plant or flower from which a new plant grows: **seed**
- fine yellow dust which makes other flowers produce seeds when it is carried to them by the wind or by insects: **pollen** (*noun* U)

■ flowers which are growing

- a piece of ground in a garden or a park where flowers are grown: **flower bed**
- a box full of soil in which flowers can be grown outside a window: **window box**
- a pot in which a plant can be grown: **flowerpot**
- a flowering plant which is grown in a pot: **pot plant**

- (used about trees or plants) to produce flowers: **flower** ◦ *This tree flowers in early spring.*
- when a flower opens, it **comes* out** ◦ *The tulips haven't come out yet.*
- when a flower has opened, it is **out** ◦ *The daffodils should be out in March.*

■ using flowers

- to take flowers from where they are growing: **pick** sth ◦ *We went for a walk in the wood and picked some bluebells.*
- a number of flowers which have been picked and put or fastened together: **bunch** ◦ *a bunch of daffodils*
- a bunch of flowers which are given or carried on a special occasion: **bouquet** ◦ *The bride carried a bouquet of white roses.*
- a flower which sb wears in their jacket to a wedding, dance, etc: **buttonhole**
- a shop which sells flowers: **florist's**, **flower shop**

- a display of flowers: **arrangement**; to make an arrangement of flowers: **arrange** sth
- a pot in which cut flowers are put: **vase** ◦ *She arranged the flowers in a vase.*

fly[1]

- type of insect ⇨ INSECT

fly[2] move through the air

see also PLANE, BIRD

- any vehicle that can fly in the air: **aircraft** (*plural* **aircraft**); a person who controls or flies an aircraft: **pilot**
- a vehicle which travels in space: **spacecraft**; a person who travels in a spacecraft: **astronaut**

▷ more on rockets and space travel ⇨ SPACE[1]

- the sport or activity in which a person flies in a hang-glider: **hang-gliding** (*noun* U)
- the sport or activity in which people fly in hot-air balloons: (**hot-air**) **ballooning** (*noun* U); a person who travels in a balloon: **balloonist**

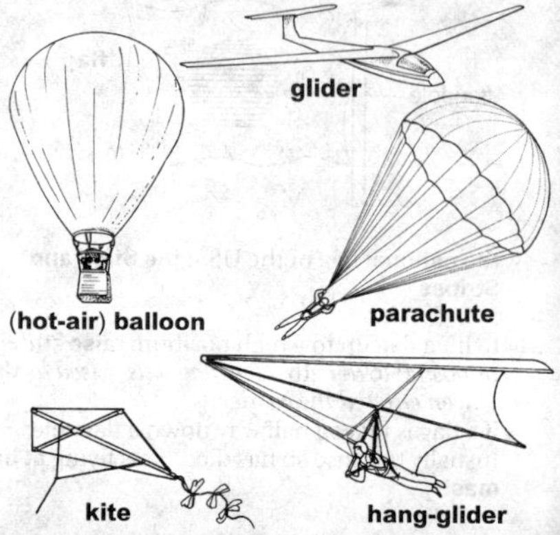

- the sport or activity in which a person jumps from an aeroplane in a parachute: **parachuting** (*noun* U); a person who uses a parachute as a sport: **parachutist**
- the sport or activity in which a person flies in a glider: **gliding** (*noun* U); a person who flies in a glider: **glider pilot**

- to move through the air: **fly***; *noun* (U): **flight** ◦ *A bird flew into the garden.* ◦ *It's unusual to see swans in flight* (= flying).
- to move wings up and down in order to fly forward: **flap** sth ◦ *The bird flapped its wings and took off into the blue sky.*
- if a bird flies without moving its wings, or if an aeroplane flies without using an engine, it **glides**
- to move slowly through the air: **float** ◦ *The balloon floated over the sea.*
- (used about birds and helicopters) to stay in the air in one place while flying: **hover**
- to move quickly over a surface, near it but hardly touching it: **skim** ◦ *I watched the gulls skimming across the water.*

- to begin to fly: **take* off** ◦ *We took off into a cloudless sky.*
- to come down to earth after flying: **land** ◦ *The stork landed on its nest.*

- a bird or plane that is a long way from the ground is **high**; *opposite*: **low** ◦ *flying high in the sky*
- to go higher in the sky while flying: **go* up**, **climb**, (*formal*) **ascend** ◦ *The balloon went up higher and higher until we could no longer see it.* ◦ *The plane climbed to a height of ten thousand feet.*
- to go lower in the air while flying: **go*/come* down**, (*formal*) **descend**

■ **MORE . . .**

- if a bird cannot fly, it is **flightless** ◦ *Penguins are flightless birds.*

- the scientific study of the way that things move through the air: **aerodynamics** (*noun* U); something that moves through the air quickly and easily is **aerodynamic**

follow ⇨ COME/GO

food

1 different kinds of food
2 food and your health
3 keeping food
shops which sell food ⇨ SHOP
containers for food ⇨ CONTAINER
see also COOK, DRINK, EAT, MEAL, TASTE

1 different kinds of food

- the general word for things that people usually eat: **food** (*noun* U/C) ◦ *food and drink* ◦ *food shopping* ◦ *baby food* ◦ *a food store* ◦ *frozen foods*
- a type of food prepared in a particular way: **dish** ◦ *There are some really nice dishes in that recipe book.* ◦ *She served up a delicious dish of beef and dumplings.*

▷ food that comes from animals ⇨ BIRD², EGG, FISH², MEAT

▷ food that is made from milk ⇨ BUTTER, CHEESE, MILK

▷ food that comes from plants ⇨ FRUIT, NUT, POTATO, RICE, VEGETABLE

▷ plants that are produced for food on farms ⇨ FARM

▷ food that is made from flour ⇨ BREAD, CAKE, FLOUR

▷ food that is eaten at breakfast ⇨ BREAKFAST

■ some kinds of cooked food (with meat and vegetables)

- meat and vegetables in liquid, cooked slowly in the oven: **casserole** (*noun* C/U), **stew** (*noun* C/U) ◦ *a chicken casserole* ◦ *beef stew*
- meat or vegetables cooked in strong spices: **curry** (*noun* C/U) ◦ *vegetable/chicken curry*
- meat or vegetables cooked in pastry or with a layer of potato on top: **pie** ◦ *chicken pie* ◦ *shepherd's pie* (= minced meat with potato on top)
- a dish of vegetables and/or meat cut into pieces and fried quickly in hot oil: **stir-fry**

- a type of food made from a mixture of flour, eggs and water: **pasta** (*noun* U)
- a round flat piece of dough (like bread) that is covered with tomatoes, cheese, onions, etc and is cooked in an oven: **pizza** (*noun* C/U)

■ some kinds of sweet food

- sweet food often served at the end of a meal: **sweet** (*noun* C/U), **pudding** (*noun* C/U), (*more formal or AmE*) **dessert** (*noun* C/U)
- a frozen sweet food made from cream (or other types of fat): **ice cream** (*noun* C/U) ◦ *Four chocolate ice creams, please.* ◦ *a dish of vanilla ice cream*
- a mixture of chopped fruit, usually in a sweet juice: **fruit salad** (*noun* C/U) ◦ *Would you like fruit salad for dessert?*
- a transparent dessert which is made of fruit-flavoured water: **jelly** (*AmE* **jello**) (*noun* C/U) ◦ *ice cream and jelly*
- a dessert made from cake with fruit and jelly covered with custard and cream: **trifle** (*noun* C/U)

- a dessert made of fruit inside a case of pastry or cake: **pie** (a pie usually has pastry on the top as well as the bottom), **tart**, **flan** ◦ *apple pie* ◦ *jam tart* ◦ *fruit flan*
- a sweet yellow sauce made from milk, sugar and flour: **custard** (*noun* U) ◦ *Would you like some custard with your pie?*
- a type of very thin round cake that is made by frying a mixture of flour, milk and eggs: **pancake**

■ things which can be added to food to make it taste good

▷ salt and pepper ⇨ SALT/PEPPER

▷ other things (for example herbs and spices) which are added to food while it is being cooked ⇨ COOK

- a yellow mixture made from the seeds of the mustard plant; it has a strong taste and is eaten in small amounts, usually with meat: **mustard** (*noun* U)
- a thick red liquid made from tomatoes and spices and eaten cold with hot or cold food: (**tomato**) **ketchup** (*noun* U)
- a sour liquid usually made from wine, sometimes put on potato chips or salad: **vinegar** (*noun* U)
- a hot-tasting food that is made from fruit or vegetables with sugar and spices; you eat it with cheese or meat: **chutney** (*noun* U)

- a mixture of oil and vinegar and herbs which is put on salad: (**salad**) **dressing** (*noun* U/C) ◦ *I'll make a nice dressing for the salad.*
- a thick yellow or white liquid made of eggs and oil and put on salad: **mayonnaise** (*noun* U)

- a thick liquid that you eat with other food: **sauce** (*noun* U/C) ◦ *The chicken was served with a delicious sauce.* ◦ *cheese sauce*
- a sauce made of meat juices and eaten hot with cooked meat: **gravy** (*noun* U)

- a white or brown substance added to food and drinks to make them sweet: **sugar** (*noun* U)
- the thick fatty part of milk which is sometimes added to sweet foods: **cream** (*noun* U) ◦ *strawberries and cream*

2 food and your health

- if food helps to make you healthy, it is **good for you**; *opposite*: **bad for you** ◦ *Come on, eat up your vegetables – they're good for you.*
- food which contains a lot of fat, oil, cream, sugar, etc is **rich** ◦ *a rich chocolate cake*
- natural food that some people think is especially good for your health because it has been produced without using chemicals: **health food** (*noun* C/U)
- food which does not contain healthy ingredients: **junk food** (*noun* U) ◦ *crisps and hamburgers and other junk food*

- food which is too old to be sold and eaten is **past its sell-by date**

food *contd.*

- the substance found in meat, fish and beans that is important for helping people and animals to grow and be healthy: **protein** (*noun* U/C) ◦ *Eggs are a good source of protein.*
- the substances in food, for example sugar, that give your body energy: **carbohydrates** (*noun plural*) ◦ *Most vegetables and fruit are very low in carbohydrates.*
- the oily substance under the skins of animals: **fat** (*noun* U) ◦ *I don't like meat with too much fat on it.*
- the parts of plants used as food that your body does not digest, but that are thought to be good for you: **fibre** (*AmE* **fiber**) (*noun* U) ◦ *The doctor told me I should have more fibre in my diet.*

- one of several substances in food that are important for good health: **vitamin** ◦ *There's lots of vitamin C in oranges.*
- a unit for measuring the amount of energy that a certain amount of food will produce: **calorie** ◦ *Chocolate is very high in calories.*

- the food that a person or animal usually eats: **diet** (*noun* C/U) ◦ *a healthy/unhealthy diet*

▷ eating food in order to be healthy ⇨ EAT

3 keeping food

- if food remains fresh (= in good condition so that it can be eaten), it **keeps*** ◦ *Will the chicken keep, or shall I throw it away?* ◦ *How long does cream cheese keep for?*
- if food is/becomes no longer in a good condition to eat, it is/goes **bad**, **off** (*not before a noun*) ◦ *I left the fridge open all night and all the food's gone off.*

- a soft blue or green substance found on some food (especially bread or cheese) which is bad: **mould** (*AmE* **mold**) (*noun* U); with mould on it: **mouldy** (*AmE* **moldy**) ◦ *mouldy bread*
- (used about bread, cake, etc) old and bad: **stale** ◦ *We'd better finish this cake or it'll go stale.* ◦ *stale bread*
- (used about fruit, vegetables or meat) old and bad: **rotten** ◦ *a nasty smell of rotten tomatoes*
- (used about milk, cream, etc) no longer fresh; tasting bad: **sour** ◦ *The milk's gone sour, so don't drink it.*

- a small room or cupboard in a kitchen where food is kept: **larder**
- a metal box like a cupboard where food is kept cold (but not frozen): **fridge** (*AmE* **icebox**), (*formal*) **refrigerator**
- a metal box where food is kept frozen (below 0°): **freezer**, **deep-freeze**
- if you put food in a freezer, you **freeze*** it; food which is kept in a freezer is **frozen** ◦ *frozen vegetables* ◦ *frozen chicken*
- to leave frozen food in a warm place so that it can be eaten or cooked: **defrost** sth ◦ *Defrost the cake for two hours before serving.*
- a fridge and freezer put together in one box: **fridge-freezer**
- a thin, transparent material used for covering food to keep it fresh: **cling film** (*noun* U) ◦ *Wrap the food in cling film and put it in the fridge.*

■ **MORE . . .**

- a substance that is added to food to give it colour or flavour: **additive** ◦ *no artificial additives*
- a substance that is added to food to help it to stay fresh for longer: **preservative** ◦ *Junk food usually contains lots of additives and preservatives.*

foolish ⇨ STUPID

foot ⇨ LEG/FOOT

football

1 different kinds of football
2 where football is played
3 people in football
4 playing a game of football

see also GAME, SPORT

1 different kinds of football

- a game played by two teams of eleven players who try to kick a ball into a goal: **football** (*noun* U), **soccer** (*noun* U)

Note: the word **soccer** is used in newspapers and on television in Britain. In the US, **soccer** is the word commonly used for this game since **football** is used for **American football**.

- a kind of football played in the US: (**American**) **football** (*noun* U)

Note: American football is played with an oval ball by two teams of 11 players. Points can be won by scoring a **field goal** (this is done by kicking the ball over the bar of the goalposts) or by scoring a **touchdown** (this is done by carrying the ball over the opposing team's goal line and putting it on the ground).

- a kind of football that is played by two teams of 13 or 15 players with an oval ball that can be carried or kicked: **rugby** (*noun* U), **rugger** (*noun* U)

Note: in rugby, points can be won by scoring a **goal** (this is done by kicking the ball over the bar of the H-shaped goalposts) or by scoring a **try** (this is done by carrying the ball over the opposing team's goal line and putting it on the ground).

2 where football is played

- the whole piece of land used for a football match: **football ground**
- the area of land which is marked with lines where the game is played: (**football**) **pitch**
- a large sports ground with rows of seats around it: **stadium** ◦ *a football stadium*
- a part of a stadium where people sit and watch sport: **stand** ◦ *We got a seat in the main stand.*

3 people in football

- a person who plays football: **football player**, **footballer**

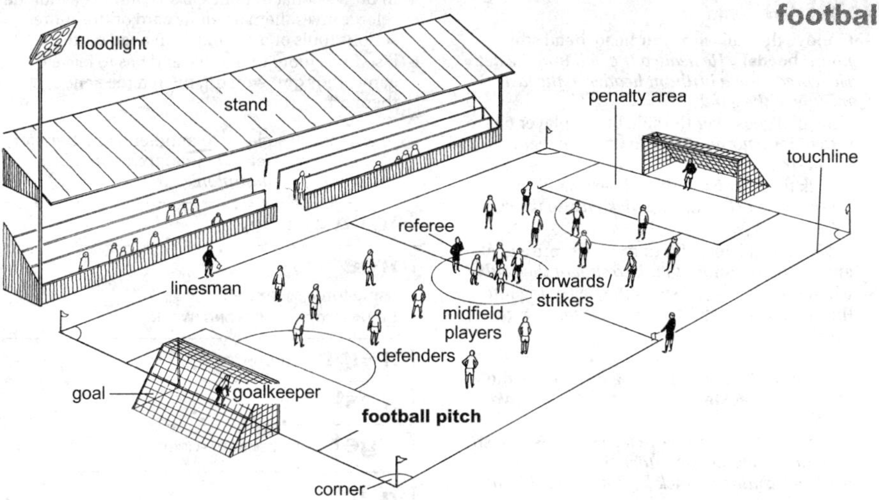

- a group of players who play together in a football match against another group: (**football**) **team**

▷ more on teams ⇨ TEAM

- a person who manages a football team: **manager** ◦ *the Liverpool/Scotland manager*
- a person who trains a football team: (**football**) **coach**
- the player who is the leader in a football team: **captain**
- an organization which manages a particular football team: **football club**
- the person who controls a football match: **referee**, (*informal*) **ref**; *verb*: **referee** (sth) ◦ *The referee blew the whistle.* ◦ *Who's refereeing this afternoon's match?*
- an official who watches to see that the rules are not broken and to see when the ball goes over the line: **linesman** (*plural* **linesmen**)

- a large group of people watching a football match: **crowd**
- people who support a particular team and go to watch their matches: (**football**) **supporters**, (**football**) **fans** ◦ *She belongs to the Rangers Supporters Club.*
- a football fan who is very violent: (**football**) **hooligan**; violent behaviour by fans: **hooliganism** (*noun* U)

4 playing a game of football

- an occasion of playing football: **game** (**of football**); a game of football in a competition: (**football**) **match** ◦ *Who'll be in goal in the game on Saturday?* ◦ *Have you heard the result of the Scotland-England match?*

- the clothes that each person in a football team wears when they are playing a match: (**football**) **strip**
- footballers usually wear a **football shirt**, **football shorts**, **football boots** and (to protect their legs) **shin-pads**

- when a football team play a match on their own football ground, they play **at home**; it is a **home match/game**
- when a football team go to another team's ground to play a match, they play **away**; it is an **away match/game**

- the beginning of a game of football when the first person kicks the ball: **kick-off**; *verb*: **kick off** ◦ *Kick-off is at two o'clock.*
- the decision about which team is going to kick off is usually made by tossing (= throwing) a coin; this is called the **toss** ◦ *Our team won the toss and we kicked off.*
- the time when the game stops halfway through the match: **half-time**; each part of the match is called a **half** ◦ *The score was two all at half-time.* ◦ *the first/second half*

■ scoring a goal

- the aim of the game is for each team to try and get the ball into the other team's goal; when they do this, they **score** (**a goal**) ◦ *And it's a goal! – Johnson has just scored a great goal.*
- the person who scores: **scorer**

- the total number of goals scored: **the score** ◦ *'What's the score?' 'One-nil.'* (= 1:0)
- to make the same number of goals as the other team: **equalize**; the goal that makes the score equal: **equalizer** ◦ *The equalizer came in the second half.*
- the final number of goals in a match: **result** ◦ *the result of the England-Ireland match* ◦ *to read the football results*

■ using the ball

- to move the ball with your foot: **kick** sth; *noun*: **kick** ◦ *He kicked the ball hard at the goal.* ◦ *to give the ball a kick*

football *contd.*

- to move the ball with your head: **head** sth; *noun*: **header** ◦ *He headed the ball into the net.* ◦ *He scored with a brilliant header in the last minute of the game.*
- if the ball goes over the side line, a player has to **throw* it in**; *noun*: **throw-in** ◦ *to take the throw-in*
- to kick the ball to another player: **pass** sth; *noun*: **pass** ◦ *He made a quick pass to the centre.*

- to kick the ball in order to try and score a goal: **shoot***; *noun*: **shot** ◦ *to take a shot at the goal*
- when the goalkeeper stops the ball going into the goal, this is called a **save** ◦ *He made a great save!*

- to try and take the ball from a member of the other team: **tackle** sb; *noun*: **tackle** ◦ *to make a tackle*
- when a team tries to score a goal, it **attacks** (sb/sth); *noun*: **attack** ◦ *to attack the other team's goal* ◦ *a sustained attack leading to a brilliant goal*
- when a team tries to prevent a goal being scored, it **defends**; *noun* (C/U): **defence**; a player whose main work is to defend is a **defender** ◦ *They lost because they had a very poor defence.* ◦ *He plays in defence.*

■ breaking the rules

- doing sth wrong in football is called a **foul** ◦ *It was a deliberate foul – he tripped me from behind!* ◦ *to commit a foul*
- if one team commits a foul, the other team may be given a **free kick** ◦ *Scotland have been awarded a free kick.*
- if one team commits a foul in the penalty area, the other team may be given a **penalty** (**kick**); the place where the penalty is taken from: **penalty spot** ◦ *It's Jackson to take the penalty.*

- a player who goes into a part of the football pitch where he is not allowed is **offside**; *opposite*: **onside**

■ **MORE ...**

- the period of time in the year when football is played: **season** ◦ *The football season is starting soon.*
- a group of football teams who play against each other: **league** ◦ *to come top of the league*

- in some matches, if the score at the end of the second half is equal, the teams play **extra time** (*noun* U) ◦ *They're into extra time now.*
- the time added at the end of a match because sb was hurt: **injury time** (*noun* U)

- an extra member of a team who plays if sb is ill or hurt: **reserve**, **substitute**, (*informal*) **sub**: *verb*: **substitute** (sb) (**for** sb); an occasion when a player is substituted: **substitution** ◦ *Smith is being substituted – Jones is coming on instead.* ◦ *It looks as if United want to make another substitution.*

- in professional matches, if sb commits a foul the referee gives them a **yellow card** or (for more serious fouls or a second foul) a **red card**
- if sb fouls more than once and has to leave the game, they **get* sent off**, the referee **sends*** them **off**

- to give or sell a player to another team: **transfer** sb; *noun*: **transfer** ◦ *They've given him a free transfer to Southampton.*

forbid ⇨ ALLOW

force

- using force ⇨ POWER
- being strong ⇨ STRONG/WEAK

foreign ⇨ COUNTRY[1]

forest ⇨ TREE

forget ⇨ REMEMBER/FORGET

forgive

see also ANGRY, PUNISH, SORRY

- to stop being angry with sb or about sth: **forgive*** (sb) (sth), **forgive** sb **for** sth/**for** doing sth; the act of forgiving sb or being forgiven: **forgiveness** (*noun* U) ◦ *Please forgive the delay.* ◦ *I forgive you.* ◦ *Can you forgive me for what I did?* ◦ *She couldn't forgive him for walking out on her and the children.* ◦ *to ask for forgiveness*
- to forgive sb for behaving badly: **excuse** sb (**for** sth/**for** doing sth), **excuse** sth ◦ *Excuse me for bothering you.* ◦ *Nothing could excuse such rudeness.*

- if an action is too bad to be forgiven, it is **unforgivable** ◦ *unforgivable behaviour*
- a person who is happy to forgive is **forgiving**; *opposite*: **unforgiving**
- if you decide to take no action about sth that a person has done wrong, you **overlook** it ◦ *We'll overlook this mistake, but in future you will have to do better.*
- kindness or forgiveness that is shown to a person who is going to be punished: **mercy** (*noun* U) ◦ *to show (no) mercy* ◦ *to beg for mercy*

fork ⇨ KNIFE/FORK/SPOON

formal ⇨ BEHAVIOUR, POLITE

fortunate ⇨ LUCK

forward ⇨ MOVE

four ⇨ NUMBER

fox ⇨ ANIMAL

free

1 free to move where you want
2 free to do and say what you want

1 free to move where you want

- if you are not in prison or under the control of sb else, you are **free**; *noun* (U): **freedom** ◦ *After ten years in prison, he was now a free man.* ◦ *He was given back his freedom after thirty years in jail.*
- to cause a person or animal to be free: **free** sb/sth, **set*** sb/sth **free**, **let*** sb/sth **go**, **release** sb ◦ *He's hoping he'll be freed from jail next month.* ◦ *They held the hostages for more than a year before letting them go.*
- to get away from a place where you do not want to be: **escape** (**from** a place), **break* out of** a place ◦ *The monkey had escaped from the zoo.* ◦ *Three men broke out of prison last night.*

▷ more on escaping ⇨ ESCAPE

■ not free

- a person who is kept in a place by sb else and who is not free to go where they want: **prisoner**, **captive**
- a building where prisoners are kept as a punishment: **prison**
- if you are not free, you are **captive**; *noun* (U): **captivity**
- to catch sb/sth and make them a prisoner: **capture** sb/sth, **take*** sb **prisoner**; *noun* (U): **capture** ◦ *Several of the tourists were taken prisoner by the terrorists.* ◦ *We have only just been given news of his capture.*

▷ more on prison ⇨ PRISON

2 free to do and say what you want

- if you are not controlled by rules, the government, etc, you are **free** (**to** do sth); *nouns* (U): **freedom**, **liberty** ◦ *a free country* ◦ *free time* ◦ *You're free to go where you want.* ◦ *the freedom of the press* ◦ *restrictions on individual liberty*
- to cause sb/sth to be free: **liberate** sb/sth (**from** sth); *noun* (U): **liberation** ◦ *the country's liberation from colonial rule*
- a person's legal right to freedom and equality in their own country, no matter what their sex, race or religion: **civil rights** (*noun plural*), **civil liberties** (*noun plural*)
- the right to say what you think about anything in public: **free speech** (*noun* U), **freedom of speech** (*noun* U)
- not controlled by another person, country, etc: **independent**; *noun* (U): **independence** ◦ *an independent country* ◦ *He's grown up now and he wants his independence.*

freeze

- water becoming ice ⇨ ICE
- frozen food ⇨ FOOD

frequent ⇨ HOW OFTEN

friend

see also ENEMY, RELATIONSHIP

- a person who you know and like (not a member of your family): **friend**, (*informal*) **mate** ◦ *a good/loyal friend* ◦ *one of my best friends* ◦ *an old friend of mine* (= a person who has been a friend for a long time) ◦ *close friends* (= friends who like and trust each other a lot) ◦ *me and my mates*
- a girl or woman's female friend: (*especially AmE*) **girlfriend**
- a person that you become friendly with by writing letters: **penfriend**, (*informal*) **penpal**
- a person that you know but who is not a close friend: **acquaintance**

▷ boyfriends and girlfriends ⇨ LOVE

■ becoming friends and stopping being friends

- to become a friend of sb: **make* friends** (**with** sb) ◦ *I find it quite easy to make friends.*
- to choose to be a friend to sb: (*formal*) **befriend** sb ◦ *She befriended an elderly woman in the village.*
- when a friendship comes to an end, you **fall* out** (**with** sb), **stop being friends** (**with** sb) ◦ *They fell out over money – he borrowed quite a lot from her and never gave it back.*
- to be friends again after falling out: **make* up** (**with** sb) ◦ *I'm sorry for what happened; couldn't we make up now and be friends again?*

■ friendly behaviour

- when you are sb's friend, you are **friends** (**with** sb), **friendly** with **sb**; *noun* (C/U): **friendship** ◦ *We've been friends for years.* ◦ *Are you still friends with Julie?* ◦ *You're quite friendly with Sam these days – why don't you ask him over?* ◦ *Our friendship has survived many difficult times.*
- if you have a friendly relationship with sb you are **on good terms with** sb ◦ *I'm not on good terms with my employer at present.*
- when you behave in a kind and pleasant way, you are **friendly** (**to/towards** sb); *opposite*: **unfriendly** ◦ *She seems quite friendly.* ◦ *You could try and be a bit more friendly towards her – she's really very nice.*
- the quality of being friendly: **friendliness** (*noun* U) ◦ *The friendliness of the people in the village was wonderful.*
- to give help to a friend in times of difficulty: **stick* by** sb, **stand* by** sb, **support** sb; *adjective*: **supportive** ◦ *It was a difficult time for me but my friends stood by me.* ◦ *When he was depressed, his friends were very supportive.*

friendly ⇨ BEHAVIOUR

frightened ⇨ AFRAID

frightening ⇨ AFRAID

from

- from a place ⇨ MOVE
- from a time ⇨ TIME

front ⇨ PLACE²

fruit

1 different kinds of fruit
2 parts of a fruit
3 buying and eating fruit
4 growing fruit

see also FOOD, COOK, VEGETABLE

1 different kinds of fruit

- the part of a plant or tree that contains seeds and that is used for food: **fruit** (*noun* U/C) ◦ *Would anybody like some fruit?* ◦ *Oranges, lemons and limes are all citrus fruits.*
- a small soft fruit with seeds: **berry** ◦ *poisonous berries*
- a hard dry fruit with a shell: **nut**

▷ more on nuts ⇨ NUT
▷ picture of different kinds of fruit below

- a soft round fruit with a large stone in its centre: **peach**
- a yellow-green fruit that tastes like a lemon: **lime**
- a fruit like a small sweet orange with a skin that is easy to take off: **tangerine**

■ dried fruit

- fruit which has had all its water removed: **dried fruit** (*noun* U) ◦ *dried apricots/figs/dates*
- a dried plum: **prune**
- different kinds of dried grape (often used in making cakes): **raisin**, **sultana**, **currant**

2 parts of a fruit

- the outer covering of a fruit: **skin**; the skin of a lemon or orange: **peel** (*noun* U) ◦ *a banana skin* ◦ *Do you like this cake? It's flavoured with lemon peel.*
- to remove the skin from a fruit: **peel** sth
- a small seed in an apple, orange, lemon, etc: **pip**
- the hard centre of apples, pears, etc: **core**
- the large seed in certain fruits, for example plums and peaches: **stone** ◦ *cherry stones*
- the solid part of a fruit that we eat: **flesh** (*noun* U)
- the liquid part of a fruit: **juice** (*noun* U) ◦ *fruit juice*

3 buying and eating fruit

- fruit which is ready to be picked and eaten is **ripe**; *noun* (U): **ripeness**; to become ripe: **ripen** ◦ *If it isn't ripe, it won't taste very nice.* ◦ *They won't ripen if you put them in the fridge.*
- fruit which is not ready to be eaten is **unripe**
- if a fruit has ripened too much, it is **overripe** ◦ *Make sure they're not overripe when you buy them.*
- fruit which tastes as if it has a lot of sugar is **sweet**; *opposite*: **sour** ◦ *These gooseberries are rather sour – you'd better add some sugar.*
- fruit with a lot of juice is **juicy** ◦ *some delicious juicy pears*
- fruit which is not cooked or frozen or from a tin is **fresh** ◦ *fresh fruit and vegetables*
- when fresh fruit is easily available, it is **in season**; not easily available: **out of season** ◦ *Apples are expensive at present – I suppose they're out of season.*
- a person who sells fruit and vegetables: **greengrocer**; a shop that sells fruit and vegetables: **greengrocer's (shop)**
- you can buy fruit in a **bag**, **packet**, **tin** (*especially AmE* **can**) or **jar** ◦ *a bag of apples* ◦ *a half-kilo packet of frozen raspberries* ◦ *a tin/can of peaches* ◦ *a large jar of olives*

▷ pictures at CONTAINER

■ making juice

- to press out the juice from fruit: **squeeze** sth; *adjective*: **squeezed** ◦ *freshly squeezed orange juice*
- an instrument for squeezing lemons or oranges: **lemon-squeezer**
- a machine for pressing juice from fruit: **juice extractor**

fruit

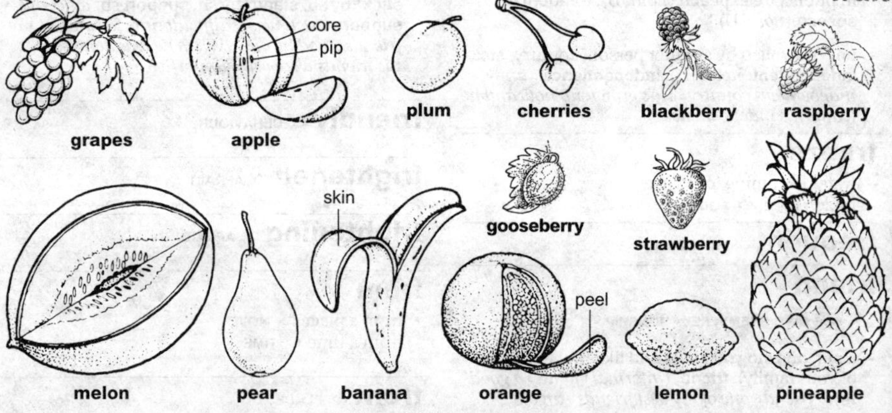

■ food made with fruit
- fruit which is cut up and mixed together, usually in a sweet juice: **fruit salad** (*noun* C/U) ◦ *I think I'll have fruit salad for dessert.*
- to cook fruit with a small amount of sugar and water: **stew** sth; *adjective*: **stewed** ◦ *stewed plums/apples/rhubarb*
- different kinds of food made with fruit and pastry (= a mixture of flour, fat and water): **pie, tart** ◦ *apple pie and custard* ◦ *strawberry tarts with cream*

- a transparent soft food made with fruit and water, that shakes when it is moved: **jelly** (*AmE* **jello**) (*noun* U/C) ◦ *raspberry jelly and ice cream*
- a sweet substance made with fruit and sugar, which is eaten on bread: **jam** ◦ *plum jam*

4 growing fruit
- different kinds of fruit grow on a **bush**, a **tree** or a small **plant** ◦ *a gooseberry bush* ◦ *pear trees* ◦ *strawberry plants*
- a piece of land where fruit trees are grown: **orchard** ◦ *an apple orchard*
- grapes grow on a **vine**; the place where grapes are grown: **vineyard**
- a number of fruits growing together: **bunch** ◦ *a bunch of grapes/bananas*

- to take fruit from its plant: **pick** sth ◦ *Don't pick them – they're not ripe yet.* ◦ *Let's go blackberry picking.*

fuel

see also ELECTRICITY

- material that is burned to give heat or power: **fuel** (*noun* C/U) ◦ *a shortage of fuel* ◦ *smokeless fuel*
- a thick liquid that comes from under the ground and is used as a fuel or to make machines work smoothly: **oil** (*noun* U), **petroleum** (*noun* U)

■ fuel for cars, etc
- fuel for motor vehicles such as cars: **petrol** (*AmE* **gasoline, gas**) (*noun* U); petrol that does not contain lead is **unleaded**
- a heavy oil that is used in lorries, buses and some cars: **diesel** (*noun* U)

▷ getting fuel for a car ⇨ DRIVE

■ fuel for heating and cooking
- a black mineral dug from the ground, that is burned to give heat or energy: **coal** (*noun* U)
- fuel that is a gas or mixture of gases and is used for cooking, heating, etc: **gas** (*noun* U)
- a fuel from petroleum that is used in heaters, lamps, etc: **paraffin** (*AmE* **kerosene**) (*noun* U)
- a fuel made by burning wood in an oven with very little air: **charcoal** (*noun* U)

▷ more on coal, gas and oil ⇨ COAL, GAS, OIL

■ using fuel
- (used about a vehicle) to use a particular fuel: **run* on** sth ◦ *My car runs on unleaded petrol.*
- to use fuel: **burn** sth, **consume** sth; *noun* (U): **consumption** ◦ *We burned nearly all our fuel supplies over the winter.* ◦ *higher/lower fuel consumption*
- a measurement of the amount of petrol, etc a vehicle uses: **miles per gallon** (*abbreviation* **mpg**)
- to provide a plane, etc with more fuel: **refuel** (sth) ◦ *We landed at Nairobi for refuelling.*

full / empty

1 full
2 empty

see also CONTAINER, LIQUID

1 full
- holding or containing as much or as many of sth as possible: **full** (**of** sth) ◦ *a full bottle of milk* ◦ *The fridge is full of food.* ◦ *I feel too full* (= of food) *to move.*
- completely full: **full up** (*not before a noun*) ◦ *The car's full up – there's really no room for anyone else.*

- to make sth full: **fill** sth (**up**) ◦ *Fill it to the top.* ◦ *Fill up your plates.* ◦ *Don't forget to fill up your car with petrol before you leave.* ◦ *She has filled her house with beautiful things.*
- to fill sth with liquid right to the top: **fill** sth **to the brim**
- completely full of a liquid: **full to the brim**
- if a container already has some liquid in and you then fill it right to the top, you **top** it **up**; *noun*: **top-up** ◦ *Can you top up my glass, please?* ◦ *I'd like a top-up* (= give me some more drink).

- to make sth full again: **refill** sth; a container that holds a substance which refills sth else: **refill** ◦ *Please refill the tank before you return the car.* ◦ *My biro's running out of ink – I wonder if it's possible to buy a refill.*

- full of people: **crowded** ◦ *a crowded bus/train/bar*
- full of a lot of people or things: **packed/crammed** (**with** sb/sth), **packed/crammed full** (**of** sb/sth) ◦ *It was so packed, we could hardly move.* ◦ *The box was packed full of clothes.*
- when all the places or seats in a restaurant, theatre, train, etc are used, it is **booked up, fully booked** ◦ *'I'd like to book a table for four for tonight, please.' 'I'm sorry, we're fully booked.'*

▷ more on crowds ⇨ CROWD

2 empty
- the opposite of full: **empty** ◦ *an empty bottle/suitcase/house/stomach*
- to make sth empty: **empty** sth (**out**) ◦ *Can you empty the rubbish bin?* ◦ *She emptied out all the contents of my bag onto the table and checked them.*
- empty; without its usual contents: **bare** ◦ *The room was bare – all the furniture had gone.* ◦ *a bare cupboard*
- empty because all the people have left: **deserted** ◦ *The streets were deserted.*

full / empty *contd.*

- not completely empty and not completely full: **half full**, **half empty** ◦ *The sweet jar was only half full.* ◦ *a half-empty bottle*

fun

- enjoying yourself ⇨ ENJOY
- being entertained ⇨ ENTERTAINMENT

funeral

see also DIE

- to put a dead body in the ground: **bury** sb; *noun* (C/U): **burial** ◦ *The body was taken back to his home town for burial.*
- to burn a dead body: **cremate** sb; *noun* (C/U): **cremation** ◦ *Would you rather be buried or cremated?*
- a ceremony (usually in a church) for burying or burning a dead person: **funeral** ◦ *Are you going to the funeral?* ◦ *It was a very moving funeral service.*
- a box in which a dead body is placed: **coffin** (*AmE* **casket**)
- a car (or other vehicle) in which a dead body is carried to the funeral: **hearse**

- an area in which dead bodies are buried: **cemetery**
- a cemetery near a church: **graveyard, burial ground**
- the place in which a dead body is buried: **grave** ◦ *to dig a grave* ◦ *We put flowers on the grave.*
- a large, elaborate grave, often with a carved stone above it: **tomb**
- a stone above a grave that shows the name of the person buried there: **gravestone, tombstone**

- a building in which dead bodies are burned: **crematorium** (*plural* **crematoria** or **crematoriums**)
- a container in which the ashes of a dead person are placed: **urn**

- a person whose business is to organize funerals: **undertaker, funeral director** (*AmE also* **mortician**)
- a person who goes to a funeral as a relative or friend of the person who has died: **mourner**

■ **MORE ...**

- words about a dead person, especially those written on a tombstone: **epitaph**

funny

1 different ways in which things or people are funny
2 being funny in order to annoy or attack people
3 funny people

see also ENJOY, ENTERTAINMENT

1 different ways in which things or people are funny

- making you laugh or smile: **funny, amusing**; *verb*: **amuse** sb ◦ *He's very funny.* ◦ *a funny play* ◦ *an amusing incident* ◦ *Did you find the book amusing?* ◦ *What's amusing you?* ◦ *I was very amused by your speech.*
- funny and slightly ridiculous: **comic, comical** ◦ *They looked really comical in their funny hats.*
- very funny: **hilarious** ◦ *He told us a hilarious story.* ◦ *We had a hilarious afternoon.*
- perhaps funny, but also stupid: **ridiculous, absurd** ◦ *What a ridiculous hat!* ◦ *It was an absurd situation.*
- using words in a clever and amusing way: **witty** (*adverb* **wittily**) ◦ *a witty speaker* ◦ *a witty remark*
- if a thing is not funny, but important, it is **serious** (*adverb* **seriously**) ◦ *Please don't laugh – I'm being serious.* ◦ *Did you seriously mean that?*

- to make sounds to show that you are happy or amused: **laugh** (**at** sb/sth); *noun* (U): **laughter** ◦ *to laugh out loud* ◦ *She laughed at what I told her.* ◦ *the sound of laughter* ◦ *We could hear laughter in the next room.*
- the feeling that you experience when sth funny makes you laugh: **amusement** (*noun* U) ◦ *I could see the amusement on his face.* ◦ *The mistake caused much amusement.*

▷ laughing ⇨ LAUGH

- the amusing quality of a thing, person, situation, etc: **humour** (*AmE* **humor**) (*noun* U) ◦ *He was so angry that he couldn't see the humour of the situation.*
- if you are able to see when sth is funny and to laugh at things, you have a **sense of humour** ◦ *Ian's got a great sense of humour.*

■ jokes

- something that is said or done to make you laugh: **joke** ◦ *to tell a joke* ◦ *a dirty joke* (= about sex) ◦ *Have you heard the joke about the elephant at the North Pole?* ◦ *It was only a joke.*
- to say sth that is not meant to be serious: **joke, say* sth in fun**, (*informal*) **kid** ◦ *Did she say that? You must be joking!* ◦ *She just said it in fun – she didn't really mean it.* ◦ *I'm not kidding - it's really true!*
- to understand what is funny about a joke: **get* it, get*/see* the joke** ◦ *Everyone else laughed, but I just didn't get it at all.* ◦ *She obviously couldn't see the joke and felt very embarrassed.*
- the last part of a joke, which makes people laugh: **punchline** ◦ *When the punchline came, everyone laughed, except me!*

■ funny plays and drawings

- an amusing play, film, etc: **comedy** ◦ *There's a comedy on TV at eight o'clock.*
- a short comedy scene which is part of a show: **sketch** ◦ *They did a sketch about a doctor's waiting room.*
- a funny drawing, especially in a newspaper: **cartoon**

2 being funny in order to annoy or attack people

- to laugh at a person, often in an unkind way, or make other people do this: **make* fun of** sb, **poke fun at** sb ◦ *They made fun of our accents.*
- to try to make sb angry by saying unkind things: **tease** (sb) ◦ *The other children teased her – I suppose because she was fat.*
- to make fun of sb by making them believe sth that is not true: (*informal*) **pull** sb's **leg** ◦ *He says that I need to put on a bit of weight, but he's just pulling my leg.*
- to copy the way a person speaks or behaves, in an amusing way: **do* an impression of** sb ◦ *Can you do an impression of the Prime Minister?*

- something that you do to annoy sb or to make them look silly, which makes other people laugh: **practical joke**
- to trick a person in order to amuse yourself or other people: **play a joke/trick on** sb ◦ *Every April 1st the children play a practical joke on their teacher and she pretends to be surprised.*
- to accept jokes about yourself without getting angry: **take* a joke** ◦ *Can't you take a joke?*

- meaning the opposite of what you say: **irony** (*noun* U); said or written in this way: **ironic, ironical** (*adverb* **ironically**) ◦ *Irony is an important element of British humour.* ◦ *an ironic comment* ◦ *'Very funny,' he said ironically.*
- attacking bad or foolish people or behaviour by making fun of them: **satire** (*noun* C/U); containing or using satire: **satirical** ◦ *a work of bitter satire* ◦ *a political satire* ◦ *a satire on 19th-century society* ◦ *a satirical play*

3 funny people

- a person who makes people laugh: **comedian**; a person who tells jokes: **comic** ◦ *My favourite comedian is still Charlie Chaplin.* ◦ *a TV comic* ◦ *a stand-up comic* (= one who tells jokes to an audience)
- a person who makes people laugh, especially in a circus: **clown**
- a person who likes to make jokes or play tricks: **joker** ◦ *He's a bit of a joker, so don't believe everything he says.*

---

furniture

> furniture used in a bedroom ⇨ BED
> **see also** ROOM

- articles like chairs and tables that are used in rooms, houses, offices, etc: **furniture** (*noun* U) ◦ *a piece of furniture* ◦ *We haven't got much furniture.* ◦ *bedroom/office furniture* ◦ *a furniture shop* ◦ *She likes to buy antique* (= old and valuable) *furniture.*
- the furniture and the carpets and curtains, etc in a room or house: **furnishings** (*noun plural*)
- to put furniture in a room or house: **furnish** sth ◦ *We can't afford to furnish our new house!*
- when a room or house has furniture in it, it is **furnished**; *opposite*: **unfurnished** ◦ *We're renting an unfurnished flat.*

▷ chairs and tables ⇨ CHAIR, TABLE

■ some kinds of furniture

- a long flat piece of wood, glass, etc, used for standing things, that is fixed to a wall or inside a piece of furniture: **shelf** (*plural* **shelves**) ◦ *a bookshelf*
- a container which forms part of a piece of furniture such as a desk, that you can pull out to put things in or take things out: **drawer**

- a piece of furniture, usually with shelves inside and a door or doors at the front, used for storing food, clothes, etc: **cupboard** ◦ *a kitchen cupboard*
- a kind of low cupboard that is used for storing plates, etc in a dining room: **sideboard**
- a piece of furniture with cupboards at the bottom and shelves at the top, used for holding dishes, cups, etc: **dresser**
- a piece of furniture with shelves which you keep books in: **bookcase**

- a piece of furniture that has been made to fit a particular space and has been fixed there is **fitted, built-in** ◦ *fitted cupboards* ◦ *a built-in wardrobe*
- a room in which (some of) the furniture has been fitted and permanently fixed is **fitted** ◦ *a fully fitted kitchen/bedroom*

■ the condition of furniture

- clean, not broken or damaged: **in good condition** ◦ *The sofa is still in good condition. Why do we need a new one?*
- old and in bad condition because it has been used too much: **shabby** ◦ *a shabby armchair*
- if a piece of furniture (for example a table or a chair) moves from side to side because all its legs do not touch the floor or because it is not very strong, it **wobbles**; *adjective*: **wobbly** ◦ *a wobbly table*
- wooden furniture that has been made shiny is **polished**; in order to make wooden furniture shiny, you **polish** it or **give*** it a **polish**; the cream or liquid that you use to do this is **polish** (*noun* U) ◦ *a polished table top* ◦ *furniture polish*

■ moving your furniture

- moving the furniture of one house or building, etc to another: **removal** (*noun* C/U) ◦ *The company is going to pay all our removal expenses.*
- a lorry which is used to move furniture from one building to another: **removal van**

---

future

> 1 the future
> 2 thinking about what will happen in the future
> 3 knowing or saying what will happen in the future
> wanting sth to happen ⇨ HOPE
> **see also** PAST[2], PRESENT[2], TIME

1 the future

- the time that will come after the present: **the future** ◦ *We need to make plans for the future.* ◦ *in the near future* (= soon) ◦ *in the distant future*

future *contd.*

- what will happen to sb/sth in the time after the present: **future** ◦ *The company's future is looking very good at the moment.* ◦ *They invested a lot of money in their children's futures.* ◦ *She has a very bright future* (= likely to be successful). ◦ *a secure future* (= free from worry or doubt)

- happening or belonging to the time after the present: **future** (*only before a noun*) ◦ *Have you met her future husband?* ◦ *the future tense* (= the tense of a verb that expresses what will happen after the present)
- in the future: **to come**, **ahead** ◦ *Don't eat too much – there's still dessert to come.* ◦ *In years to come people will look back on what happened today.* ◦ *There may be trouble ahead.*

■ a period of time in the future
- from now into the future: **in future**, **from now on**, **from this moment on**, (*formal*) **henceforth** ◦ *In future, we shall all have to spend less.* ◦ *From now on, I'm going to concentrate on my acting career.*
- for the present and the immediate future (but likely to change after a while): **for now**, **for the time being** ◦ *I'm going to stay in this job for now, but there is a chance of another position in the new year.*
- for all time in the future: **forever** (*BrE also* **for ever**), **for good** ◦ *I'm stopping smoking – and this time not for a day but forever.* ◦ *We're leaving England for good.*
- over a short/long period of time in the future: **in the short/long term**; *adjective*: **short-term/long-term** ◦ *They could see the benefits in the short term, but nobody had thought about the long-term effects.*

■ a point of time in the future
- at some time in the future: **one day**, **some day**, **in time** ◦ *Some day, you'll be able to tell your grandchildren.* ◦ *You'll know the results in time – you'll just have to wait.*
- not long after the present time or the time mentioned: **soon** ◦ *See you soon!* ◦ *We'll be home very soon.* ◦ *I'll write as soon as I can.*

▷ happening soon ➪ **SOON**

2 thinking about what will happen in the future

- to think that sth will happen: **expect** sth, **expect** (**that**) ..., **think*** (**that**) ...; the belief that sth will happen: **expectation** ◦ *I am expecting a letter from the bank.* ◦ *She failed her exams, but she never did any work so what did she expect?* ◦ *'Are you going to the party?' 'I expect so.'* ◦ *I never thought she'd do that.* ◦ *My expectation is that the strike will be over by Tuesday.*
- to know or guess that sth is going to happen in the future: **foresee*** sth, **see* into the future** ◦ *We could not have foreseen that this would happen.* ◦ *How do I know what will happen? I can't see into the future.*
- the ability to see what will probably happen in the future: **foresight** (*noun* U) ◦ *to show foresight*
- something that is not expected is **unexpected** (*adverb* **unexpectedly**) ◦ *an unexpected result*

- to wait with pleasure for sth which you expect to happen: **look forward to** sth ◦ *I'm really looking forward to seeing her when she comes.*
- hope for the future: **expectations** (*noun plural*) ◦ *They had great expectations for their children.*

- to plan sth well before it happens: **plan ahead** ◦ *The birth of their baby was not due for a few months but they wanted to plan ahead.*
- to think about sth in the future and prepare for it: **look ahead** (**to** sth), **think* ahead** (**to** sth) ◦ *We're looking ahead to the future and thinking of buying a house.* ◦ *You have to think ahead in this job, so that you're always ready for the next thing.*
- to expect sth to happen and to prepare for it: **anticipate** sth ◦ *The police didn't anticipate any trouble, so they weren't prepared when it finally came.*
- careful thought and preparation for the future: **forethought** (*noun* U) ◦ *You can avoid the problem with a bit of forethought.*

▷ making plans ➪ **INTEND/PLAN**

3 knowing or saying what will happen in the future

- to say that sth will happen (often because you have special knowledge): **predict** sth, **prophesy** sth; *nouns*: **prediction**, **prophecy** ◦ *They correctly predicted that their profits would rise in the following year.* ◦ *to prophesy disaster* ◦ *to make a prediction about sth*
- something that was or is expected is **predictable** (*adverb* **predictably**) ◦ *a predictable situation*
- to use reliable information to say what will probably happen in the future: **forecast*** sth; *noun*: **forecast** ◦ *They forecast a good year for the company.* ◦ *The weather forecast is good for the next few days.* ◦ *a confident forecast of increasing profits*

- a statement about what is going to happen to a person in the future, based on the position of the stars and planets when he/she was born: **horoscope**

▷ more on horoscopes ➪ **ASTROLOGY**

■ **MORE ...**
- the power that some people believe controls everything that happens to you: **fortune** (*noun* U), **fate** (*noun* U)
- to tell a person what is going to happen in their future: **tell*** sb's **fortune**
- a person who tells people's fortunes: **fortune-teller**
- a person who tells or claims to tell what will happen in the future: **prophet**
- a way of thinking which supposes that things will always go right: **optimism** (*noun* U); *adjective*: **optimistic** ◦ *facing the future with optimism* ◦ *an optimistic view of life*
- a person who is optimistic: **optimist**

- a way of thinking which supposes that things will always go wrong: **pessimism** (*noun* U); *adjective*: **pessimistic** ○ *I feel a bit pessimistic about this plan.*
- a person who is pessimistic: **pessimist**

gallon ⇨ LIQUID

game

1 different kinds of game
2 playing games

1 different kinds of game

- a form of play or sport with rules: **game**
- a game which needs a lot of physical effort: **sport** ○ *My favourite sports are football, cricket and tennis.*
- a game played with a ball: **ball game**
- a game that you play on a computer: **computer game**
- one of a number of different games that are played with cards: **card game**

▷ more on card games ⇨ CARDS

▷ sports ⇨ SPORT

■ board games

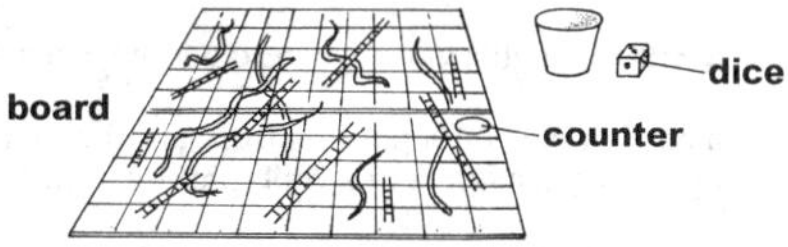

- a game played on a flat hard piece of wood or cardboard: **board game** ○ *Scrabble, Monopoly and Trivial Pursuit are popular board games.*
- a small cube with a different number of spots on each side, used in certain games: **dice** (*plural* **dice**)
- a small object that is used in some games to show where the player is on the board: **counter**

- a game for two people in which each player can move sixteen pieces around a board with black and white squares: **chess** (*noun* U)
- a game which is played on a chessboard using round black and white pieces: **draughts** (*AmE* **checkers**) (*noun* U)

▷ more on chess ⇨ CHESS

■ puzzles and quizzes

crossword

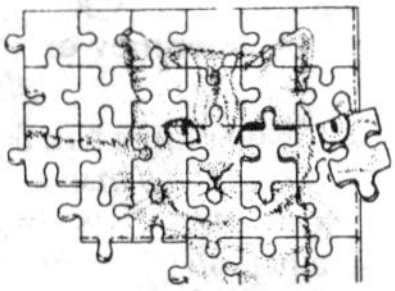

jigsaw

- a game that tests your knowledge or intelligence: **puzzle** ○ *to do a puzzle* ○ *a mathematical puzzle*
- a word game with black and white squares where you write the words in the white squares: **crossword** (**puzzle**); to find the right word you have to solve a **clue** ○ *I can't do this crossword; the clues are too difficult.* ○ *to solve a crossword puzzle*
- a picture on cardboard or wood that is cut into small pieces; you have to join the pieces together to make the picture: **jigsaw** (**puzzle**)
- a game where people have to answer questions about sth: **quiz** ○ *a general knowledge quiz* ○ *a pub quiz* (= a quiz played in a pub)

■ other indoor games

- a game in which you roll a ball towards a group of wooden objects and try to knock down as many of them as you can: **bowling** (*noun* U); a place where people play this game: **bowling alley** ○ *ten-pin bowling*
- games in which two players try to **pot** (= hit) different coloured balls into pockets at the edges of a table using a long stick (**cue**): **snooker** (*noun* U), **billiards** (*noun* U), **pool** (*noun* U)
- a game in which you throw an object like an arrow (**dart**) at a round board with numbers on it (**dartboard**): **darts** (*noun* U)

■ games played for money

- a building or room with a lot of different machines which you can put money in and try and win more money: **amusement arcade**
- the highest amount of money that you can win in a game: **jackpot** ○ *You've hit* (= you've won) *the jackpot.*
- to risk some money on the result of sth: **bet*** (**on** sth), **gamble** (**on**/**at** sth)

▷ more on betting ⇨ BET

2 playing games

- the equipment needed to play a game: **game** ○ *We went to the toyshop to buy a game for the family at Christmas.*
- to play a game: **play** sth; a time when you play a game: **game** ○ *Do you play tennis?* ○ *Let's play another game of draughts.*
- to play a game to try and beat another person or team: **play** (**against**) sb ○ *England are playing Scotland in the final.*
- an organized event in which people try to win sth: **competition**
- a game played in a competition: **match** ○ *a cricket match* ○ *a snooker match*

- a person who is playing a game: **player** ○ *a football/chess/darts player*
- the person or team you play against: **opponent** ○ *a tough opponent* (= difficult to beat)
- a group of people who play a game or sport together against another group: **team**

- a group of people who meet to share an interest (for example in a game or sport): **club**; the place where a club meets is also called a **club** ○ *a tennis/golf/cricket/athletics club*

▷ more on competitions, teams and clubs ⇨ COMPETITION, TEAM, CLUB

game *contd.*

– an official statement that tells you what you can or cannot do in a game: **rule**; something which is not allowed in a game is **against the rules** ◦ *to break a rule*
– to play a game in a dishonest or unfair way: **cheat**; *noun* (U): **cheating**; a person who cheats: **cheat** ◦ *You can't do that – it's cheating.* ◦ *He's such a cheat.*
– the kind of action done by sb when they cheat or break the rules in a game (for example in football): **foul** ◦ *to commit a foul*

– the person who controls a game and makes sure that the players obey the rules: (in football, rugby, etc) **referee**, (in cricket, tennis, etc) **umpire**
– an instrument that produces a high sound, that referees use to make signals: **whistle** ◦ *The referee had already blown his whistle.*

– to take a piece (for example in chess) or a counter (for example in Monopoly) and move it to another place on the board: **move** (sth); *noun*: **move** ◦ *You can only move your counter one square in any direction.* ◦ *a clever move*
– the time in a game when one person must do sth (for example, move their piece): **move, turn, go** (*plural* **goes**) ◦ *It's your move/turn/go.* ◦ *You've had your go already.*

– a single mark that you get in a game or sport for doing well: **point**
– (in football, rugby, etc) a point that is scored when the ball goes into the goal: **goal**
– the number of points that a team or competitor has: **score**; *verb*: **score** sth

– to be the person with the most points in a competition; **win***, **come* first**
– if you do not win, you **lose***
▷ more on winning and losing ⇨ WIN/LOSE

garage ⇨ CAR

garden

1 different kinds of garden
2 parts of a garden
3 working in a garden
see also FLOWER, PLANT, TREE, VEGETABLE

1 different kinds of garden

– a piece of land where flowers and vegetables are grown: **garden** (*AmE* **yard**) ◦ *Let's go out in the garden.* ◦ *a well-kept* (= tidy) *garden* ◦ *The garden has become rather overgrown* (= with plants which have grown big and untidy).
– a public garden with grass, trees and open spaces: **park**
– a garden where plants are grown for scientific study: **botanical gardens** (*noun plural*)

– the land which belongs to and surrounds a large building is its **grounds** (*noun plural*) ◦ *The grounds are open to the public.*
– a concrete or stone area behind a house, which has a wall or fence around it: **backyard**
– a small piece of public land that can be rented for growing vegetables on: **allotment** ◦ *We grow all our vegetables on our allotment.*

2 parts of a garden

– a garden at the front of a house: **front garden**
– a garden at the back of a house: **back garden**
– an area next to a house where people can sit, eat, etc: **patio** (*plural* **patios**)
– the end of a garden that is furthest from the house: the **bottom** of the garden ◦ *There's a river at the bottom of the garden.*

– a piece of ground in a garden where flowers, vegetables, etc are grown: (**flower**) **bed** ◦ *a rose bed*
– a small piece of land where you grow vegetables: **vegetable plot**
– an area of grass that is regularly cut: **lawn** ◦ *I'm going to mow the lawn* (= cut the grass).
▷ more on grass and lawns ⇨ GRASS

– a small wooden building for keeping garden tools: **garden shed**
– a building made of glass in which plants are grown: **greenhouse**

– a way through a garden where people can walk: **path**
– a garden may be separated from another garden by a **hedge**, a **fence** or a **wall** (picture at WALL)

3 working in a garden

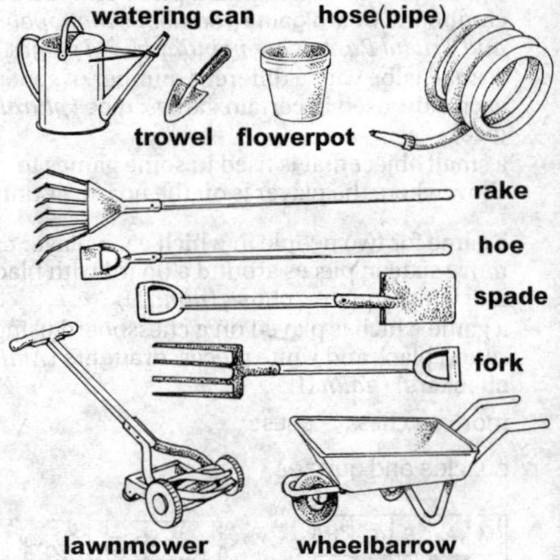

– the work that you do in a garden: **gardening** (*noun* U) ◦ *I'm going to do some gardening.* ◦ *gardening gloves* (= gloves used for gardening)
– a person who works in a garden: **gardener** ◦ *She's a keen gardener.* ◦ *Do you have a gardener?*

– to move earth, make a hole to plant sth in, etc: **dig*** (sth) ◦ *to dig the flower beds*
– to remove a plant, etc from the earth by digging: **dig*** sth **up** ◦ *to dig up a shrub*

- to put plants, seeds, etc in the ground to grow: **plant** sth ◦ *We've been buying flowers and shrubs to plant in the front garden.*
- to fill a garden, area of land, etc with plants: **plant** sth (**with** sth) ◦ *a bed planted with tulips and daffodils*

▷ more on growing plants ⇨ PLANT

- to remove weeds (= wild plants that are not wanted in a garden): **weed** (sth), **do* the weeding** ◦ *I spent the afternoon weeding the strawberry bed.* ◦ *I wish I had a proper hoe to do the weeding with.*
- to smooth the soil, collect up leaves, stones, etc: **rake** sth (**up**) ◦ *to rake up the grass cuttings*

■ **MORE ...**
- a place where plants, seeds, gardening equipment, etc are sold: **garden centre**
- if you are good at growing plants, you have (*informal*) **green fingers**

---

gas

1 some common kinds of gas
2 gas for heating your house and cooking
other fuels ⇨ FUEL, COAL, ELECTRICITY, OIL

1 some common kinds of gas
- a substance that is like air (not solid or liquid): **gas** (*noun* C/U)
- a gas which is part of the atmosphere and which you breathe out: **carbon dioxide** (**CO_2**) (*noun* U)
- a gas which is essential for plant and animal life: **oxygen** (**O_2**) (*noun* U)
- a gas which combines with oxygen to make water: **hydrogen** (**H_2**) (*noun* U)
- a poisonous gas which is produced when certain things are burned, for example when a car burns petrol: **carbon monoxide** (**CO**) (*noun* U)
- a gas that forms most of the atmosphere: **nitrogen** (**N_2**) (*noun* U)

2 gas for heating your house and cooking
- a gas or a mixture of gases that is used for heating, cooking, etc: **gas** (*noun* U) ◦ *a gas cooker/fire* ◦ *gas central heating*
- gas that comes from under the ground or under the sea: **natural gas** (*noun* U)

- if you want to use the gas for cooking, you **turn on** the gas ◦ *I turned on the gas to make some coffee.*
- when you finish using the gas you **turn off** the gas ◦ *Turn off the gas/turn the gas off before you go out.*

- the object which measures how much gas you have used: **gas meter**
- a person who comes to check how much gas you have used: **meter reader**
- the piece of paper which tells you how much money you have to pay for the gas you have used: **gas bill**
- a company which supplies gas: **gas company**
- when the gas company decides to stop the supply of gas, they **cut* off** the gas ◦ *If you don't pay your gas bill, the gas company will cut off your gas supply.*
- a place where gas is made or processed: **gasworks** (*plural* **gasworks**)
- a tube which carries gas into or through your house: **gas pipe**
- a small container for gas which you keep inside the home, for cooking: **gas cylinder**
- if gas escapes into the air, there is a **gas leak**

---

general ⇨ USUAL

---

generous

see also GIVE, KIND / CRUEL

- if a you are happy to give people money, help, etc, and you do this more than is necessary, you are **generous** (*adverb* **generously**); *noun* (U): **generosity** ◦ *a generous gift* ◦ *a generous employer* ◦ *They're very generous with their money.* ◦ *Please give generously.* ◦ *She was surprised by his generosity.*
- if you are happy to give a lot of help, money, etc, you are **free with** it ◦ *They were very free with the wine.*

■ not generous
- the opposite of generous is **mean**, (*informal*) **stingy**; *nouns* (U): **meanness**, (*informal*) **stinginess** ◦ *Was it mean of us to let them pay for everything?* ◦ *He hoped she didn't think he was mean.* ◦ *Don't be so stingy – buy me one too!*
- a person who likes to have a lot of money but does not like spending it: **miser**

---

gentle
- being kind to sb ⇨ KIND / CRUEL
- being careful with sth ⇨ CAREFUL

---

genuine ⇨ REAL / GENUINE

---

get / obtain

1 receiving and obtaining sth
2 looking for and finding sb/sth
3 going to get sb/sth
4 bringing things together (collecting things)
see also HAVE / POSSESS

1 receiving and obtaining sth
- to become the owner or the user of sth by your own effort: **get*** sth, (*formal*) **obtain** sth, (*formal*) **acquire** sth ◦ *I'm saving up to get a new car.* ◦ *It takes several weeks to obtain a visa.*
- to become the owner or the user of sth that sb sends you or gives you: **get*** sth, (*formal*) **receive** sth; *noun* (U): (*formal*) **receipt** ◦ *What did you get for Christmas?* ◦ *Did you receive the application form we sent you?* ◦ *We will pay you on receipt of the goods.*

- to get sth with your hand: **take*** sth ◦ *Here! Can you take this screwdriver a minute?*

get/obtain *contd.*

- to get sth from a high place: **take*** sth **down** ○ *Can you take down that picture?*
- to take sth roughly or suddenly: **snatch** sth, **grab** sth ○ *Julia snatched the ball off Hamish.* ○ *He grabbed my handbag and ran off.*
- if you can touch sth and get it for sb, you can **reach** it ○ *Can you reach the newspaper?*
- to get sth by hard work, great effort, etc: **gain** sth ○ *to gain a degree*

■ being able to get sth

- if you can get sth, it is **obtainable**; *opposite*: **unobtainable** ○ *The shop told me that the computer I want to buy is unobtainable at the moment.*
- if you can buy or use sth, it is **available**; *opposite*: **unavailable**; *noun* (U): **availability** ○ *Did you find the hotel? Were there any rooms available?*

2 looking for and finding sb/sth

- to get sth that you want after looking for it or by chance: **find*** sth ○ *I found this dress in a shop in the High Street.*
- to find sth that will be useful: **get* hold of** sth ○ *Do you know where I could get hold of a book on rabbits?*
- to find sb or make contact with sb: **get*** (**hold of**) sb ○ *Where have you been? I've been trying to get hold of you all day!*
- to get back sth you have lost or that sb took from you: **find*** sth, (*formal*) **recover** sth ○ *I found my comb under the sink.* ○ *The police recovered my wallet after five days.*
- to get sth back from somewhere: (*formal*) **retrieve** sth (**from** sth) ○ *My computer broke down, but luckily I managed to retrieve most of my data.*

▷ more on finding things ⇨ FIND

3 going to get sb/sth

- to go and bring sb/sth from a place: **get*** sb/sth (**for** sb), **fetch** sb/sth (**for** sb), **collect** sb/sth (**for** sb); if you are talking about a thing (not a person), you can also say **get*** (sb) sth, **fetch** (sb) sth ○ *I've got to get some parcels from the post office.* ○ *She very kindly offered to fetch the children for me.* ○ *Mrs Bartlett collects the children from school every day.* ○ *When you're in town, can you get me my trousers from the cleaners?*
- an act of collecting sth: **collection** ○ *Rubbish collection is on Tuesdays and Fridays.*
- to tell sb to go and get sb/sth: **send*** (sb) (**for** sb/sth) ○ *I've sent Damian for some potatoes.*

4 bringing things together (collecting things)

- to bring a number of things together in a place: **collect** sth, **gather** sth (**together**) ○ *Could you collect all the old newspapers and put them in the rubbish, please?* ○ *I gathered my papers together and went off to work.*
- to bring together a number of objects of a particular type over a period of time because they interest you: **collect** sth; a person who does this: **collector**; the things which are collected: **collection** ○ *I collect old coins.* ○ *a stamp collector* ○ *a collection of miniature teapots*

ghost ⇨ SPIRIT

gift ⇨ GIVE

girl ⇨ CHILD

give

1 giving things to people who need them or want to use them
2 giving things to people in order to please them
3 giving things to people who have done good work, etc
4 giving so as to help other people
giving things when you die ⇨ DIE
see also BORROW/LEND

1 giving things to people who need them or want to use them

- to let sb have sth so that they can look at it, use it or keep it for a time: **give*** sb sth, **give*** sth **to** sb ○ *She refused to give me my passport back.*
- to give sth to sb so that they take it in their hand: **hand** sb sth, **hand** sth **to** sb ○ *Can you hand me the screwdriver please?*
- to pick sth up and give it to sb: **pass** sb sth, **pass** sth (**to** sb) ○ *Can you pass the ketchup, please?*
- to give sth, often sth that you no longer want, without asking for or receiving money in return: **give*** sth **away** ○ *When she retired, she gave away all her books.*
- to give sth which is needed for some purpose: **provide** sth ○ *As it is a weekend course, accommodation will be provided.*
- to give a person what they need in order to live: **provide for** sb ○ *He finds it difficult to provide for a large family on a small salary.*
- to be able to give sth to sb: **spare** sth ○ *Can you spare ten pence for a cup of tea?*

▷ more on providing people with things ⇨ PROVIDE

■ giving sth back

- if sb has sth which you own and then they give it to you, they **give*** it **back**, **hand** it **back**, **return** it **to** you ○ *The chairman handed the papers back to the secretary.* ○ *When must I return these books to the library?*
- to be given sth back: **get*** sth **back**
- to give back money to sb who has lent it to you: **repay*** sth ○ *I managed to repay the loan after two months.*

■ giving things to a number of people

- to separate sth into parts and give them to each of a number of people: **share** sth (**out**) (**among/between** people), **divide** sth (**out/up**) (**among/between** people) ○ *We shared out the food between the three of us.*
- what each person gets when sth is shared: **share**

▷ more on sharing things ⇨ DIVIDE

- to give things to a number of people: **hand** sth **out**, **distribute** sth; the act of doing this: **distribution** (*noun* C/U) ◦ *Please hand these papers out to the rest of the class.* ◦ *I saw somebody distributing leaflets in the street.*

■ giving something and getting something else

- to give or receive sth in return for sth else: **swap** A (**for** B) (**with** sb), (*more formal*) **exchange** A (**for** B) (**with** sb) ◦ *Some people swap houses for a holiday.* ◦ *Can I exchange this sweater if it's the wrong size?*

- to give sb (such as an official in the government) money or a gift to persuade them to do sth to help you: **bribe** sb (**to** do sth); the money given: **bribe**; the act of bribing: **bribery** (*noun* U) ◦ *Gordon tried to bribe the traffic warden not to give him a parking ticket.* ◦ *to offer a bribe to sb* ◦ *to take/accept bribes*

2 giving things to people in order to please them

- a thing that you give to sb in order to please them: **present**, **gift** ◦ *to give sb a present* ◦ *a Christmas/birthday/wedding present* ◦ *There was a free gift in the cornflakes packet.*
- to be given sth as a present: **get*** sth ◦ *What did you get for Christmas?*

- to ask if sb would like to be given sth: **offer** sb sth, **offer** sth **to** sb ◦ *He offered me a cigarette.*
- to give sb sth that is very special or enjoyable: **treat** sb **to** sth; *noun*: **treat** ◦ *Go on, treat yourself to a new dress.* ◦ *As a special treat I've arranged a trip to the theatre.*

▷ more on offering ⇨ **OFFER**

- a person who likes to give a lot of presents, money, help, etc is **generous** (*adverb* **generously**); *opposite*: **mean** ◦ *Please give generously.* ◦ *It was mean of him not to offer to pay for your taxi.*
- to give too much to sb or do too much for sb, especially a child, so that you have a bad effect on their character: **spoil** sb ◦ *a spoilt child*

3 giving things to people who have done good work, etc

- money given in return for helping the police, finding sth that was lost, etc: **reward**; to give a reward: **reward** sb (**for** sth) ◦ *We were given a day's holiday as a reward for working so hard.*

- something that is given to sb who is successful in a competition, etc: **prize** ◦ *I won first prize in the competition.*
- to give sth officially to sb as a prize, payment, etc: **award** sth (**to** sb); something that is given in this way: **award** ◦ *The Nobel prizes are awarded every year in Stockholm.* ◦ *The policewomen received awards for bravery.*
- to give sth to sb formally or publicly: **present** sb **with** sth, **present** sth **to** sb ◦ *The dancers were presented with flowers at the end of the show.*
- a formal ceremony at which a prize, etc is given: **presentation**

4 giving so as to help other people

- to give money or other things to a particular cause: **give*** sth (**to** sth), **contribute** sth (**to** sth), (*more formal*) **donate** sth (**to** sth) ◦ *to give money to a good cause*
- the money, etc that is given: **contribution**, **donation** ◦ *to make a donation*
- a person who gives (some of) the money, etc that is needed for sth: **contributor**, **donor**
- an organization that collects money, etc to help the poor, the sick, etc: **charity**; the help given in this way: **charity** (*noun* U) ◦ *OXFAM and Save the Children are well known charities in Britain.* ◦ *We're going on a walk to raise money for charity.*

---

glad ⇨ HAPPY

---

glass¹

- for drinking out of ⇨ **CUP/GLASS**

---

glass² material for making things

broken glass ⇨ **BREAK**
other materials ⇨ **MATERIAL**

- a hard material which you can usually see through, and which is used to make windows, bottles, etc: **glass** (*noun* U) ◦ *a large sheet of glass* ◦ *a piece of clear/coloured glass*

- a piece of glass in a window: **pane** (of glass), **window pane**
- a special kind of glass that you can see yourself in: **mirror** ◦ *to look at yourself in the mirror*
- an object made from glass which you use to drink from: **glass**
- a building with glass walls and roof which is used for growing plants: **greenhouse**, **glasshouse**

▷ more on windows, mirrors and glasses ⇨ **WINDOW, MIRROR, CUP/GLASS**

---

glasses

see also EYE, SEE

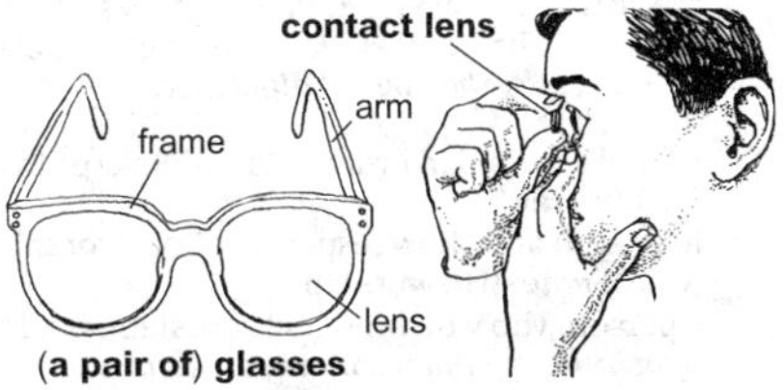

- the thing that people wear to help them see more clearly: **glasses** (*AmE* **eyeglasses**) (*noun plural*), (*formal*) **spectacles** (*noun plural*), (*informal*) **specs** (*noun plural*) ◦ *a pair of glasses* ◦ *Does anyone know where my glasses are?* ◦ *He can't see a thing without his specs.*

- a small piece of plastic that fits into your eye to help you see better: **contact lens** ◦ *a pair of contact lenses*

glasses *contd.*

- glasses that you wear in order to protect your eyes from the sun: **sunglasses** (*noun plural*), **dark glasses** (*noun plural*)
- special glasses that you wear to protect your eyes from water, dust, wind, etc: **goggles** (*noun plural*)
- a small container for keeping your glasses in: (**glasses**) **case**

- to use glasses: **wear* glasses** ◦ *Does she wear glasses?* ◦ *I need to wear glasses for reading.*
- to place a pair of glasses on yourself: **put*** your glasses **on**; *opposite*: **take*** your glasses **off** ◦ *I'll need to put my glasses on to see that small print.* ◦ *He took off his glasses and looked at the audience.*

- a person whose job is to test eyes and sell glasses: **optician**
- a shop where you can buy glasses and have your eyes tested: **optician's** ◦ *I've got an appointment at the optician's this afternoon.*

god

see also CHRISTIAN, JEW, MUSLIM, RELIGION

- a being who is worshipped by a group of people: **god**; a female god: **goddess** ◦ *Mars was the Roman god of war and Venus the goddess of love.*
- the creator and ruler of all things (according to Christians, Jews and Muslims): **God** ◦ *to believe in God*
- the name for God that Muslims use: **Allah**
- the name for God that Christians often use in prayers: **Lord** ◦ *Have mercy on us, O Lord.*

- connected with God or a god: **divine** ◦ *divine protection*
- connected with God or with religion: **holy, sacred** ◦ *a holy book* ◦ *holy water* ◦ *sacred music*

- the belief in a god or gods who made the world and can control what happens in it: **religion** (*noun* U) ◦ *I like discussing religion with him.*
- the study of what God is like: **theology** (*noun* U); *adjective*: **theological** ◦ *He's reading theology at St Andrews.* ◦ *theological differences*

- to speak to God in order to give thanks or to ask for sth: **pray**
- to pray to and show respect for God: **worship** (God); *noun* (U): **worship**
- a person who worships God: **worshipper** ◦ *The worshippers gathered outside the shrine.*
- an image that people worship as a god: **idol** ◦ *a huge wooden idol*

▷ more on praying ⇨ PRAY

- a person who does not believe that God exists: **atheist**; the belief that God does not exist: **atheism** (*noun* U); *adjective*: **atheistic** ◦ *a convinced atheist* ◦ *an atheistic society*
- a person who believes that you cannot know whether God exists or not: **agnostic**; what an agnostic believes: **agnosticism** (*noun* U)
- writing or speaking about God in a way that does not show respect: **blasphemy** (*noun* U) ◦ *to accuse sb of blasphemy*

gold / silver

other metals ⇨ METAL
gold and silver in jewellery ⇨ JEWELLERY

- a precious yellow metal which is used for making coins, jewellery, etc: **gold** (*noun* U) ◦ *to be made of gold* ◦ *Do you like my new ring? It's real gold.* ◦ *to be decorated with gold*
- made of gold, or the colour of gold: **gold** ◦ *a gold watch/ring* ◦ *gold shoes*
- a beautiful thing which is made of gold or which looks like gold can be called **golden** ◦ *golden hair* ◦ *golden sands*

- a valuable grey-white metal which is used for making coins, jewellery, etc: **silver** (*noun* U)
- made of silver, or the colour of silver: **silver** ◦ *silver earrings* ◦ *a silver spoon*

- containing no other metals: **pure, solid** ◦ *pure gold* ◦ *a solid silver brooch*
- having a thin covering of gold/silver: **gold-/silver-plated** ◦ *a gold-plated necklace* ◦ *a silver-plated teapot*

- a place where people get gold/silver from the ground: **gold/silver mine**
- a collection of very valuable objects made of gold, silver, etc: **treasure** (*noun* U)

■ **MORE ...**
- a unit of measurement used for describing how pure gold is: **carat** (*AmE* **karat**) ◦ *an eighteen carat gold ring*

golf ⇨ SPORT

good

1 good
2 better
3 very good; best
4 perfect

morally good ⇨ RIGHT / WRONG[2]

see also BAD

1 good

- of a high quality or standard: **good** ◦ *It isn't new but it's in very good condition.* ◦ *What a good idea!*
- in a good way: **well** ◦ *I thought they organized the party very well.* ◦ *a very well-written letter*

- how good or bad sth is: **quality** (*noun* U) ◦ *good quality clothes* ◦ *an improvement in quality*

- able to do sth well: **good** (**at** sth/doing sth), (*formal*) **competent** ◦ *He's a very good driver.* ◦ *I've never been very good at mathematics.* ◦ *Are you good at remembering people's names?* ◦ *an extremely competent accountant*
- the ability to do sth well: **skill** (*noun* C/U)

▷ more on skill ⇨ SKILL

- if you like sth, it is **good, nice, lovely** ◦ *a good day at the seaside* ◦ *a nice hot cup of tea* ◦ *such lovely countryside*
- something that gives you pleasure is **enjoyable** ◦ *an enjoyable outing to the seaside*
- if sth is useful or satisfying enough to be worth the cost or effort, it is **worthwhile, worth** your/sb's **while**, (*informal*) **worth it** (*not before a noun*) ◦ *I had a lovely time – I'd say the journey was really worth it.*

- if sth makes sb/sth well, healthy or happy, it is **good** (**for** them/it) ◦ *Drink more milk – it's good for you!* ◦ *All this bad publicity is not good for the school.*
- in good health: **well** ◦ *'How are you?' 'Very well, thank you.'*

- if sth is what is needed for a particular purpose, it is **right** (**for** sth), **suitable** (**for** sth), **good** (**for** sth) ◦ *Do you think this is the right sort of dress for a dinner party?* ◦ *a beach suitable for swimming* ◦ *These potatoes are good for boiling.*

- a good thing that you get as a result of sth else: **benefit** (*noun* C/U), **advantage**(*noun* U/C) ◦ *'What are the benefits of working for this company?' 'You get six weeks' paid holiday and a company car.'* ◦ *There's no obvious advantage in booking in advance.*
- a good thing that you get in addition to what you expect: **bonus** ◦ *It's a beautiful house, and the fact that it's in a good area is a bonus.*

■ good, but not very good
- good, but not very good: **fairly/quite good, not bad, OK** (*also written* **okay**), **all right, reasonable** ◦ *The local cheese is fairly good.* ◦ *'Do you think this suit is smart enough for my interview?' 'Well, it's not perfect, but it's OK.'* ◦ *'Did you enjoy the party?' 'It was all right.'* ◦ *The hotel was not bad and the weather was reasonable.*

- good enough for some purpose: **adequate** (*adverb* **adequately**), (*more formal*) **satisfactory** (*adverb* **satisfactorily**) ◦ *'How's your new flat?' 'It's adequate, but we're looking for something a bit bigger.'* ◦ *He said my work was satisfactory, but that's not enough for me – I shall have to work harder.*
- to be good enough, but not very good: **do*** ◦ *'Is this OK?' 'Well, it'll do, I suppose, but I'm not very happy with it.'*

2 better
- the comparative form of 'good'; of a higher quality, more suitable, etc: **better** (**than** sb/sth), (*formal*) **superior** (**to** sb/sth) ◦ *The food in that restaurant is much better than in this one.* ◦ *Would it be better if I waited outside?* ◦ *The new machine is far superior to the old model.*
- the comparative of 'well'; in a superior way; to a higher degree: **better** ◦ *She speaks French much better than I do/much better than me.* ◦ *I'd like him better if he was less arrogant.*

- to be much better than others: **stand* out** ◦ *Most of the entries in the competition were very good, but Richard's painting really stood out.*

- to achieve or produce sth that is better than what came before: **improve on** sth, **be an improvement on** sth ◦ *If you can improve on my score, I'll buy you a drink.* ◦ *That performance was a considerable improvement on your last one.*

■ getting better
- to become better than before: **get* better, improve**; *noun* (C/U): **improvement** (**on/in** sth) ◦ *The situation is beginning to get better.* ◦ *Your German has really improved since you went to Germany.* ◦ *Her work is showing considerable improvement.*
- to start to become better than before: **pick up, look up** ◦ *After a difficult period last year, business is beginning to pick up.* ◦ *Things seem to be looking up now.*

- to become well again after you have been ill: **get* better, recover, make* a good recovery**

▷ getting better after an illness ⇨ ILLNESS

■ making sth better
- to make sth better: **improve** sth ◦ *If I can improve my typing speed, I might be able to get a job as a secretary.*
- to contribute to making sth better: **help** (sth) ◦ *Try this medicine – it should help your cough.*
- something which makes an unpleasant or inconvenient situation better: **remedy** ◦ *The best remedy for this sort of problem is for you to take a holiday.*

3 very good; best
- better than anything/anybody else: **best** ◦ *That's the best film I've ever seen.* ◦ *I'd like you to meet Peter – he's my best friend.* ◦ *It's best to ask before you go in there.* ◦ *My teachers are very demanding – they refuse to accept second-best* (= not quite the best).
- in the best way; to the greatest degree: **best** ◦ *I work best at night.* ◦ *Which do you like best – the green dress or the red one?* ◦ *Lucy sang best of all.*

- to look as beautiful or attractive as possible: **look** your **best** ◦ *Try to look your best for the interview – first impressions are very important.*
- to do sth as well as you can: **do*/try** your **best, do*** sth **to the best of** your **ability** ◦ *Don't worry if you don't succeed – the important thing is that you try your best.* ◦ *Just do it to the best of your ability – I'll understand if it's not perfect.*

- very good: **excellent, outstanding** ◦ *What an excellent performance!* ◦ *James Page won the prize for outstanding achievement.*
- in a very good way: **extremely well, excellently** ◦ *The buildings in the old town have been extremely well restored.* ◦ *I thought she spoke excellently.*
- the quality of being excellent: **excellence** (*noun* U) ◦ *The school's main aim is academic excellence.*

- of the best quality: **first-class, first-rate** ◦ *a first-class restaurant* ◦ *a first-rate production of Hamlet*

good *contd.*

– most popular, important, etc: **top** ◦ *They played all the top songs from the 1960s.* ◦ *Three top musicians played at the concert.*
– a high standard: **quality** (*noun* U) ◦ *If you're looking for quality you'll have to be prepared to spend more than that.*

– (used about sth that you like very much) very good or enjoyable: **wonderful, marvellous** (*AmE* **marvelous**), **fantastic**, (*informal*) **great**, (*informal*) **super**, (*informal*) **lovely** ◦ *'Jim and I are getting married.' 'That's absolutely wonderful!'* ◦ *We had a marvellous time in Spain last year.* ◦ *The scenery was fantastic.* ◦ *'Did you enjoy the party?' 'Yes thanks, it was great.'* ◦ *We had a really lovely time.*
– in a very good or enjoyable way, which you like very much: **wonderfully, marvellously** (*AmE* **marvelously**), **fantastically** ◦ *The new system worked wonderfully at first.*

– to do sth better than anybody else: **be best at** sth ◦ *Who's best at maths in your family?*
– to be very good at doing sth: **excel** (**in**/**at**/**as** sth) ◦ *This school is specially for children who excel in music.* ◦ *She really excels at her subject.* ◦ *He excels as a leader.*
– having a natural ability to do a particular task, and doing it very well: **born** (*only before a noun*) ◦ *She's a born organizer.*

– a person or thing that is the best and cannot be defeated is **unbeatable** ◦ *He is unbeatable in the 100 metres.* ◦ *an unbeatable record*
– (used about a performance, especially in sport) the best that has been done: **record** (*noun, adjective*) ◦ *He broke the world high-jump record.* ◦ *The Chinese woman ran the 5000 metres in record time.*

4 perfect

– having nothing wrong; as good as can be: **perfect** (*adverb* **perfectly**) ◦ *Nobody's perfect!* ◦ *You have to type two pages perfectly to pass the exam.*
– the state of being perfect: **perfection** (*noun* U)
– the best possible; the best that can be imagined: **ideal** (*adverb* **ideally**) ◦ *In an ideal world there would be no poverty.* ◦ *They are ideally suited to each other.*

■ not perfect
– not perfect: **imperfect** (*adverb* **imperfectly**) ◦ *It was a good plan but it was imperfectly carried out.*
– something that is wrong with sth: **fault, defect** ◦ *There's a fault in the system and we can't use any of the computers.* ◦ *There's a defect in the design of this equipment.*
– not working properly: **faulty, defective** ◦ *a faulty TV/switch/motor*

■ wanting things to be perfect
– an idea or thing which seems perfect to you and which you want to achieve: **ideal** ◦ *When we were young we were full of great ideals.*
– imagining that things, especially people and world affairs, can be perfect: **idealistic** ◦ *Some of your opinions are a bit idealistic – you should maybe try to be more practical.*
– the belief that things can be perfect: **idealism** (*noun* U); a person who holds such a belief: **idealist** ◦ *A bit of idealism is not a bad thing.*
– a person who cannot leave a task until he/she considers it to be perfect: **perfectionist**

■ **MORE ...**
– the person or thing that is best or in first place: **leader** ◦ *Our company is the leader in the computer software market.*
– of the highest quality: **second to none** ◦ *The food here is second to none in the whole country.*

– if sb/sth allows you to show your best qualities, it **brings* out the best in** you ◦ *Sylvia's new boyfriend seems to bring out the best in her.*

government

1 different kinds of government
2 the top people in government
3 parts of government and people who work in government
4 local government
5 doing the work of government
6 changing one government for another

the ability to control people ⇨ **POWER**

1 different kinds of government

– the group of people who govern a country: **government, the Government** (*with singular or plural verb*), (*especially AmE*) **administration, the Administration** (*with singular or plural verb*) ◦ *They're trying to form a new government.* ◦ *He has resigned from the Government.* ◦ *The British Government is opposed to this proposal.* ◦ *the Clinton Administration*
– a method or system of government: **regime** ◦ *a military regime*

– a country or part of a country with its own government: **state** ◦ *India has been an independent state since 1947.* ◦ *California is one of the biggest states in the US.*
– the government of a country: **the state** (*noun* U) ◦ *the power of the state* ◦ *the relationship between the church and the state*
– the laws of a country saying how it is to be governed: **constitution**; *adjective*: **constitutional** ◦ *Britain has an unwritten constitution.* ◦ *constitutional changes*

– government of a country: **central government**
– government of a town or district: **local government**

– a country which governs itself and is not controlled by another country is **independent**; *noun* (U): **independence**
– the right of an independent country to govern itself: **sovereignty** (*noun* U) ◦ *national sovereignty*

– a system in which the government of a country is elected by all of the people: **democracy** (*noun*

U); *adjective*: **democratic**; a country which has this system: **democracy**
– a government which is headed by a president: **republic**; *adjective*: **republican**
– a system in which the government is headed by a king or queen: **monarchy**; *adjective*: **monarchical**; a country which has a king or queen: **monarchy**, **kingdom**
– a system in which the government has total power and is not freely elected: **dictatorship** (*noun* U); *adjective*: **dictatorial**; a country that is governed in this way: **dictatorship**

– a situation in which there is no effective government in a country: **anarchy** (*noun* U); *adjective*: **anarchic** ○ *During the civil war, there was complete anarchy in the country.*

■ groups of countries
– the organization formed to encourage peace in the world and to deal with problems between nations: **the United Nations**, **the UN**
– a group of countries that used to form the British Empire and that now try to work and trade together in a friendly way: **the Commonwealth**
– an economic and political association of certain European countries: **the European Union**, **the EU**

– a group of countries that is governed by another country: **empire**; *adjective*: **imperial** ○ *the Roman Empire*
– a country or area that is ruled by another country: **colony**; *adjective*: **colonial**
– to take control of a place as a colony: **colonize** sth; *noun* (U): **colonization**; keeping countries as colonies: **colonialism** (*noun* U)

– a union of states which each retain control of some areas of government business: **federation**; *adjective*: **federal**

2 the top people in government

– the leader of a country: **head of state** ○ *a meeting of all the heads of state of the Commonwealth*
– the head of state in a republic: **president**; the position of being president: **the presidency**; connected with the president: **presidential** ○ *to be elected president* ○ *President Chirac* ○ *to be nominated for the presidency* ○ *presidential duties*
– the head of state in a monarchy: **king / queen**
– a person who has total power in a country: **dictator**

▷ kings and queens ⇨ **KING / QUEEN**

– the leader of the government in Britain and in some other countries: **prime minister** (*abbreviation* **PM**)
– the leader of the government in the United States and in other countries that do not have a prime minister: **president**
– the leader of the government in Germany: **chancellor**

– a person who controls the public affairs of a colony, or of a province or state: **governor** ○ *the Governor of California*

3 parts of government and people who work in government

– the part of government that makes important decisions for the country: **the executive** (*noun* U); *adjective*: **executive** ○ *executive power*
– the part of a government that makes laws: **the legislature** (*noun* U); *adjective*: **legislative**
– the part of a government that administers the law: **the judiciary** (*noun* U); *adjective*: **judicial**

– work and ideas that are connected with governing a country, a town, etc: **politics** (*with singular or plural verb*)
– a person whose job is in politics, especially a member of parliament: **politician**

▷ more on politicians and politics ⇨ **POLITICS**

■ parliament
– a group of people who discuss and make the laws of a country, or the place where they meet: **parliament**; *adjective*: **parliamentary**
– a group of people with the same political opinions who try to win election to parliament: **party** ○ *the French Socialist Party*
– political actions carried out by or for political parties: **party politics**
– the politicians who are in parliament, but who do not support the government: **the Opposition**

▷ more on parliaments ⇨ **PARLIAMENT**

■ government departments
– a part of the government responsible for a particular area of government activity: **ministry**, **department**; connected with a government ministry or minister: **ministerial** ○ *the Ministry of Health/Transport/Education* ○ *the Department of the Environment* ○ *ministerial duties*
– all the government departments and the people who work in them: **the Civil Service**

– a member of the government, often the head of a government department or part of one: **minister** (*AmE* **secretary**)
– (in Britain) the head of a major government department: **secretary**, **Secretary of State**
– the group of important ministers who have regular meetings with the Prime Minister: **the Cabinet** (*with singular or plural verb*); a minister who is a member of the Cabinet: **cabinet minister** ○ *a cabinet meeting*

– a person who works for a government department: **civil servant**, (often used in a negative way) **bureaucrat** ○ *a senior civil servant in the Home Office* ○ *the uncontrolled power of the bureaucrats*
– a person who has a position of authority in a country: **official** ○ *a government official*

– the department that deals with political and economic relations with other countries: **Ministry of / for Foreign Affairs** (*in the US* **the State Department**); the person in charge: **Foreign Minister**, **Minister of / for Foreign Affairs** (*in Britain* **Foreign Secretary**) (*in the US* **Secretary of State**)
– the department that is responsible for internal affairs, for example the police and the prisons: **Ministry of / for Home Affairs** (*in Britain* **the**

government *contd.*

Home Office); the person in charge: **Interior Minister, Minister of/for Home Affairs** (*in Britain* **Home Secretary**)
- the department that controls public money: **Treasury**; the person in charge: **Minister of Finance** (*in Britain* **Chancellor of the Exchequer**) (*in the US* **Treasury Secretary**)
- the department that collects taxes: **Inland Revenue** (*in the US* **Internal Revenue**)
- the department that is responsible for defence: **Ministry of Defence** (*in the US* **the Pentagon**); the person in charge: **Minister of Defence, Defence Secretary**
- the department that is responsible for finding out secret information about other countries: **the secret service, the intelligence service**

■ representing your country in another country
- the part of government which represents a country in other countries: **the diplomatic service**
- one of the officials who represent their country abroad: **diplomat**
- the most senior person who represents his or her country in a foreign country: **ambassador** ◦ *The Spanish Ambassador*
- the ambassador of one Commonwealth country in another: **High Commissioner** ◦ *the Kenyan High Commissioner in London*
- the office of an ambassador and his/her staff: **embassy**
- an official who works in a foreign country helping people from his/her country who are living or visiting there: **consul**; *adjective*: **consular** ◦ *the British Consul* ◦ *the Consular Service*
- the office of a consul: **consulate**

4 local government
- elected officials who are in charge of a town, city, county, etc: **council** (*with singular or plural verb*) ◦ *local council elections* ◦ *our town/city/county council*
- paid officials who carry out the decisions of the local government: **local authority** (*with singular or plural verb*)
- a large building that contains the local government offices for a town or city: **town hall, city hall**
- an area in Britain, Ireland or the USA that has its own government: **county, district**
- one of the main areas that some countries are divided into for the purpose of government: **province, region**; *adjectives*: **provincial, regional** ◦ *provincial government* ◦ *the regional assembly*

▷ government of towns ⇨ **TOWN**

5 doing the work of government
- to control the public affairs of a country, city, etc: **govern** (sth), **rule** (**over**) sth ◦ *This party is not fit to govern.* ◦ *Napoleon ruled over most of Europe.* ◦ *The Communist Party ruled the Soviet Union for 74 years before it was overthrown.*
- an act or method of governing: **government** (*noun* U) ◦ *We need a period of strong government.*
- the control and management of the business of government: **administration** (*noun* U); *adjective*: **administrative** ◦ *the administration of the tax laws* ◦ *efficient administration* ◦ *administrative efficiency*
- a plan of action or statement of aims and ideas: **policy** (**on** sth) ◦ *Labour's policy on taxation* ◦ *the government's education policy* ◦ *a policy review*
- to make a new a policy, law, etc: **bring*** sth **in**, **introduce** sth ◦ *The new drinking laws will be brought in by the end of the year.*
- something which is accepted and approved by the government is **official**; not official: **unofficial** ◦ *official unemployment figures* ◦ *an official report*
- concerning all the people in a country or area: **public** ◦ *public health*

6 changing one government for another

■ becoming a government
- to make or organize a government: **form a government** ◦ *The party that wins the election will form the next government.*
- to be elected to power: **come* in, come* to power** ◦ *The law was in place before the present government came in.* ◦ *The government came to power in 1987.*
- the party that is ruling a country is **in power, in government, in office** ◦ *This party has been in government for more than ten years.*
- the joining of two or more political parties for a temporary period, usually to form a government: **coalition** ◦ *A government was formed out of a coalition between the Socialists and the Communists.*
- to become the government (often by force): **take* control** (**of** sth) ◦ *The military has just taken control of the country.*
- running or governing a place: **in control** (**of** sth) ◦ *The military is in control now.*
- the period that an elected government is in power: **term** ◦ *Bush ran unsuccessfully for a second term.*
- a person who has a job or important position after sb else: **successor** ◦ *John Major was Margaret Thatcher's successor.*

■ losing power
- to lose power or be defeated: **fall*** ◦ *The Labour government fell and the Conservatives took office.*
- to leave your job or position: **resign** (**from** sth), **resign** sth, (*informal*) **quit*** (sth); the act of resigning: **resignation** ◦ *The minister resigned his post over a sex scandal.* ◦ *a resignation speech*

■ using violent action to change the government
- changing or trying to change the political system by violent action: **revolution** (*noun* C/U); *adjective*: **revolutionary** ◦ *If the government carries on like this there'll be a revolution.* ◦ *to*

achieve power through revolution ○ *revolutionary ideas*

- to remove a leader or a government from power by using force: **overthrow*** sb/sth; *noun*: **overthrow** ○ *The president was overthrown after a three day battle.* ○ *the overthrow of the Nationalist government*
- a sudden and violent change of government organized by a small group of people: **coup** ○ *It is now clear that senior army officers were involved in yesterday's attempted coup.*

■ **MORE . . .**

- a system of government by a large number of officials: **bureaucracy** (*noun* C/U)
- connected with bureaucracy, especially when it is too complicated and follows rules too closely: **bureaucratic**
- official rules that seem unnecessary and often cause delay and difficulty in achieving sth: **red tape** (*noun* U) ○ *There's too much red tape in local government.*

- dishonest or illegal behaviour by people in official positions: **corruption** (*noun* U); not honest, moral or legal: **corrupt** ○ *The minister was accused of corruption.*

---

grammar

1 rules and structures
2 grammar in words
3 nouns and pronouns
4 verbs
5 sentences and clauses
see also LANGUAGE, WORD, MEANING

1 rules and structures

- the way in which words, sentences, etc are formed and used in a language: **grammar** (*noun* U); *adjective*: **grammatical** ○ *to study English grammar* ○ *I made a few grammatical errors in this essay.*
- a description of what is usual or correct in the grammar of a language: **rule** ○ *learning the rules of a language* ○ *to break a rule*
- if sth in the grammar of a language follows a clear rule, we say that it is **regular**; *opposite*: **irregular** ○ *'Work' is a regular verb. 'Write' is irregular.*

- a book written about the grammar of a language: **grammar** ○ *You'll need to buy a good dictionary and a basic grammar.*

- a group of words which is used to make a statement, ask a question, give an order, etc, and which, in the written language, begins with a capital letter and usually ends with a full stop: **sentence** ○ *I've nearly finished my letter – just a couple more sentences to write.* ○ *a correct sentence*
- a group of words which contains a verb and forms a sentence or part of a sentence: **clause**
- a group of words (smaller than a clause): **phrase** ○ *a noun/verb/preposition phrase* (= a phrase in which the most important word is a noun/verb/preposition)
- a way in which words or groups of words are combined: **structure** ○ *the structure of English sentences*
- relating to structure: **structural** ○ *I still make a lot of structural mistakes.*
- the system of rules for the structure of sentences: **syntax**; *adjective*: **syntactic** ○ *English syntax* ○ *syntactic structures*

- if sth you say or write follows the rules of a language correctly, it is **grammatical**; *opposite*: **ungrammatical** ○ *Is this sentence grammatical?* ○ *You can't say that – it's ungrammatical.*

2 grammar in words

■ word classes

- a word that is the name of a person, place, thing or idea, such as 'friend', 'America', 'coat', 'cheese', 'warmth': **noun**
- a word that is used in place of a noun or a phrase containing a noun, such as 'I', 'she', 'yours', 'anyone': **pronoun**
- a word that is used before a noun or pronoun to show time, place, direction, etc, such as 'at', 'on', 'over', 'towards', 'with' ': **preposition**
- a word that is used with a noun and tells you more about the noun, such as 'old', 'lazy', 'tired': **adjective**
- a word that is used to indicate an action or state, such as 'leave', 'think', 'remain', 'be': **verb**
- a word that is used with a verb, adjective, etc and tells you more about it, such as 'carefully', 'lazily', 'well': **adverb**
- a word that is used for joining together words, phrases or sentences, such as 'and', 'but', 'because', 'if': **conjunction**

- one of the grammatical categories noun, verb, adjective, etc: **part of speech**
- a word seen from a grammatical point of view: **form** ○ *'Went' is the past form of the verb 'to go'.*

- (used about a noun, verb, etc) showing that we are speaking about one person or thing: **singular** (*adjective, noun*); more than one person or thing: **plural** (*adjective, noun*) ○ *a singular noun/verb* ○ *a noun/verb in the singular* ○ *'Feet' is the plural of 'foot'.*

- (used about an adjective or adverb) making a comparison: **comparative** (*adjective, noun*) ○ *The comparative of 'good' is 'better'.*
- (used about an adjective or adverb) saying that sth is of the highest degree or quality: **superlative** (*adjective, noun*) ○ *'Best', 'oldest' and 'most importantly' are all superlatives.*

3 nouns and pronouns

- a noun (such as 'table', 'tree', 'computer') which you can use in the singular or plural: **countable noun, count noun**
- a noun (such as 'furniture', 'water', 'anger') which you cannot use in the plural: **uncountable noun, mass noun**

grammar *contd.*

- the way in which nouns in some languages are grouped into different classes: **gender** ◦ *In German there are three genders; in French there are two.*
- the three genders commonly found in European languages: **masculine**, **feminine**, **neuter** ◦ *a masculine noun* ◦ *If the noun is feminine, the adjective must be feminine too.*

- a word (such as 'these', 'some', 'the', 'each') that comes before a noun to show how it is being used: **determiner**
- the determiners 'a' (or 'an') and 'the' are called the **articles**
- 'a' (or 'an'): **indefinite article**
- 'the': **definite article**

- a word such as 'I', 'you', 'she', 'it', 'him', 'we', 'they', 'them' that refers to a person or thing: **personal pronoun**
- a word such as 'my', 'yours', 'his', 'their', 'theirs' that refers to a person, place, thing, etc that sth belongs to or is connected with: **possessive pronoun**
- a word such as 'myself', 'yourself', 'themselves' that refers to the subject of the sentence: **reflexive pronoun**
- a word such as 'who', 'which', 'whose', 'that' that refers to the noun or sentence which comes immediately before the pronoun: **relative pronoun**

4 verbs

- the verb that is the most important verb in a verb phrase: **main verb**
- a verb such as 'be', 'do', 'have' that combines with another verb in order to form questions or to change the tense, etc: **auxiliary verb**
- a verb such as 'must', 'may', 'can', 'will', 'ought' that expresses possibility, obligation, ability, etc: **modal verb**
- a verb such as 'to cut yourself' that describes actions in which the subject and the object of the verb are the same: **reflexive verb**
- a verb such as 'blow up', 'put sth off' that includes an adverb or preposition: **phrasal verb**

- the most basic form of the verb (for example 'be', 'come'), in English usually preceded by 'to': **infinitive**
- a form of the verb which is used as an adjective or to help form some tenses: **participle** ◦ *the past/present participle*

- a form of the verb which shows if sth happens in the past, present or future: **tense** (*noun* C/U) ◦ *the present/past/future tense*

- a form of the verb (such as 'was writing') that tells you that an action, state, etc is/was/will be continuing: **continuous** (**tense**), **progressive** (**tense**) ◦ *the present/past/future progressive*
- a form of the verb (such as 'have finished') that describes actions, states, etc which happened in the past and have some present effect, or which are seen from the point of view of the present: **perfect** (**tense**) ◦ *the present/past/future perfect*
- a form of the verb that expresses doubt, uncertainty, wishes, etc: **subjunctive**

- if the subject of a sentence performs the action (for example 'The dog chased the rabbit.'), the verb/sentence is **active** (*noun, adjective*) ◦ *The verb is in the active.* ◦ *an active sentence*
- if the subject of a sentence does not perform the action but is affected by it (for example 'The rabbit was chased by the dog.'), the verb/sentence is **passive** (*noun, adjective*)

5 sentences and clauses

■ types of sentence
- a sentence that has the form of a statement, such as 'You should read this book.' is **declarative**
- a sentence that has the form of a question, such as 'Should I read this book?' is **interrogative**
- a sentence that has the form of an order, such as 'Read this book.' is **imperative**
- a sentence that states that sth is the case, such as 'Grammar is difficult.' is **affirmative**
- a sentence that states that sth is not the case, such as 'Grammar isn't difficult.' is **negative**

- a way of telling people what sb said by repeating their exact words (for example, 'He said, "I'll be down soon."'): **direct speech** (*noun* U)
- a way of telling people what sb said, not using the actual words (for example, 'He said he would be down soon.'): **indirect speech** (*noun* U)

■ types of clause
- a clause that can stand alone: **main clause**
- a clause that cannot stand alone as it is dependent on the main clause: **subordinate clause**
- a subordinate clause that begins with 'who', 'which', 'that', etc: **relative clause**
- a clause that is joined to another clause by 'and', 'but', or 'or': **coordinate clause**

■ parts of a clause
- the word or words that describe an action, state or habit: **verb**
- the word or words that say who or what does the action: **subject**
- the word or words that say who or what is affected by the action: the **object**
- the word or words that come after a linking verb such as 'be': **complement**
- the word or words that give extra information about the time, place, reason, etc of an action, state or habit: **adverbial**

grape

- the fruit ⇨ FRUIT
- made into wine ⇨ WINE

grass

see also PLANT, GARDEN

- a short green plant with thin leaves which grows in parks, gardens and fields: **grass** (*noun* U) ◦ *Don't walk on the grass.* ◦ *a field of long grass*
- a single piece of grass: **blade of grass**

- a flat area of grass, usually next to a house, which is cut regularly: **lawn** ◦ *They were playing on the lawn.*
- short, thick grass and the layer of soil underneath it: **turf** (*noun* U)
- covered with lots of growing grass: **grassy** ◦ *a grassy plain*

- a field of grass for animals to eat: **meadow**
- an area of land where farmers grow grass to feed animals: **pasture** (*noun* C/U)
- grass which is cut and dried and used as food for animals: **hay** (*noun* U); a large pile of hay: **haystack**

- land covered with grass: **grassland** (*noun* U), **grasslands** (*noun plural*)
- a wild open area of high land that is covered with grass: **moor** (*often plural*), **moorland** (*noun* U/C)
- a very large area of flat grassy land with few trees, especially in North America: **prairie**

■ cutting grass
- to cut an area of grass with a machine: **cut* the grass, mow* the lawn** ◦ *When are you going to mow the lawn?*
- a machine for cutting grass: **mower, lawnmower** ◦ *an electric lawnmower*

▷ picture at GARDEN

green ⇨ COLOUR

greet

see also MEET, LEAVE

- to speak to sb when you meet them: **say* hello** (**to** sb), **greet** sb; *noun*: **greeting** ◦ *She walked straight past without even saying hello.* ◦ *We were greeted at the door by the manager.* ◦ *a friendly greeting*
- to say hello to sb who is arriving somewhere, for example at your house: **welcome** sb; an act of welcoming sb: **welcome**, (*formal*) **reception** ◦ *I'm sorry I wasn't here to welcome you.* ◦ *They gave us a warm/friendly welcome.* ◦ *The Prime Minister was given a warm reception.*

■ spoken greetings

situation	greeting
any situation of greeting sb	**Hello!**
greeting sb you have not met before (*formal*)	**How do you do?**
greeting a friend (*informal*)	**Hi!** or **Hiya!**
	table contd.

situation	greeting
in the morning	**Good morning!**
in the afternoon	**Good afternoon!**
in the evening	**Good evening!**

Note: when somebody says one of these greetings to you, you can answer with the same words: *'I'm Norman Miller. How do you do?' 'How do you do?'* When somebody asks you '*How are you?*' you can say '*Very well, thank you.*' or '*Fine, thanks. How are you?*'

■ greetings which are not spoken
- to take sb's hand and move it up and down as a greeting or when you say goodbye: **shake*** sb's **hand, shake* hands** (**with** sb); *noun*: **handshake** ◦ *We shook hands and he asked me to come in.* ◦ *an enthusiastic handshake*

- to touch sb with your lips to show love or affection, or as a greeting: **kiss** (sb); *noun*: **kiss** ◦ *They said goodbye and kissed each other on both cheeks.* ◦ *Give grandma a kiss before she leaves.*
- to say goodbye/goodnight to sb by kissing them: **kiss** sb **goodbye/goodnight** ◦ *He kissed me goodbye on the platform.*

- to move your hand from side to side as a greeting, when sb is leaving, etc: **wave** (**at/to** sb); *noun*: **wave** ◦ *Who are you waving at?* ◦ *He greeted us with a wave.*

■ greetings on special days
- a card which you send sb on a special occasion: (**greetings**) **card** ◦ *a Christmas card* ◦ *a birthday card*
- a greeting which you would say or write to sb on their birthday: **Happy birthday!**; at Christmas: **Happy Christmas!**; at New Year: **Happy New Year!**

■ written greetings
- when you send sb a greeting (for example in a letter or a postcard), you send them your **greetings, wishes,** (*formal*) **regards** ◦ *Greetings from Edinburgh!* ◦ *With best wishes from Michael.* ◦ *Please give my regards to your parents.*

ground

1 the surface of the earth
2 holes in the ground
3 the movement of the ground
4 digging the ground
the countryside ⇨ COUNTRY[2]
large areas of ground ⇨ LAND

1 the surface of the earth
- the solid surface of the earth: **ground** (*noun* U), **earth** (*noun* U) ◦ *to sit/stand/lie on the ground* ◦ *above/below ground* ◦ *at ground level* ◦ *The earth/ground shook.* ◦ *The satellite fell to earth.*
- the solid surface of the earth (in contrast with the sea): **land** (*noun* U) ◦ *After three days at sea she was glad to reach dry land.* ◦ *Penguins can't move very fast on land.*

ground *contd.*

- below the surface of the earth: **underground** (*adjective, adverb*) ∘ *an underground car park* ∘ *They spent several days underground.*

Note: the **ground** is the solid surface under your feet when you are outside; when you are inside a building, the surface under your feet is the **floor**; we talk about sitting, standing, lying, etc on the ground or floor.
The earth is the name of the planet on which we live; **earth** can also be used to talk about the world in contrast to the sky; if we describe something falling from a great height, we are more likely to use **earth**.
Land is the surface of the earth which is not sea; it is also a large area which you buy, live on or grow food on.

- the type of ground which trees and plants grow in: **soil** (*noun* U), **earth** (*noun* U) ∘ *Is the soil in your garden good for roses?* ∘ *wet/heavy soil* (= with a lot of water in it) ∘ *dry/light soil* (= without a lot of water in it) ∘ *a lump of earth* ∘ *We filled in the hole with earth.*
- when land is good for farming and growing plants, etc, it is **rich**, **fertile**; *opposites*: **poor**, **infertile**

- very wet earth: **mud** (*noun* U); *adjective*: **muddy** ∘ *a muddy field*
- an area of soft, wet ground: **bog**, **marsh**, **swamp**; *adjectives*: **boggy**, **marshy**, **swampy** ∘ *a boggy area* ∘ *marshy ground*
- heavy earth which is used to make pots, etc: **clay** (*noun* U)

- dry earth: **dirt** (*noun* U) ∘ *a dirt track*
- tiny pieces of very dry earth which rise into the air like a cloud: **dust** (*noun* U); *adjective*: **dusty** ∘ *a dusty track*

- the very hard, stony part of the earth: **rock** (*noun* U) ∘ *Beneath the soil was a layer of rock.*
- having many stones or rocks: **stony**, **rocky** ∘ *stony ground*
- the type of ground found in deserts and on beaches, made of tiny pieces of stone: **sand** (*noun* U); *adjective*: **sandy** ∘ *sandy soil*

▷ more on stone ⇨ **STONE**

- when the ground has no parts higher or lower than others, it is **level**, **flat** ∘ *We looked for a level/flat piece of ground to make a football pitch.*
- when it is not level, it is **uneven**
- an area of lower ground: **dip** ∘ *The cottage lay in a dip in the ground.*
- a deep track that a wheel makes in soft ground: **rut**

2 holes in the ground

- a hole in the side of a hill or mountain or under the ground: **cave**; a large cave: **cavern**
- a deep hole in the ground which can lead to underground caves: **pothole**
- a large hole that is made in the ground in order to dig out stone, etc: **pit** ∘ *a gravel pit*

3 the movement of the ground

- a sudden violent movement of the earth's surface: **earthquake**; a small earthquake: **tremor** ∘ *There was a violent earthquake followed by several small tremors.*
- a sudden fall of earth, rocks, etc down the side of a hill or mountain: **landslide**
- a movement like a landslide, when a huge mass of snow moves downward: **avalanche**
- damage to the ground due to heavy rain, floods, removal of trees, etc: **erosion** (*noun* U); to cause erosion: **erode** sth (*usually passive*) ∘ *soil erosion* ∘ *The cliffs are being gradually eroded by the sea.*

4 digging the ground

- to make a hole in the ground by moving earth with a spade, your hands, etc: **dig*** (sth) ∘ *I could see some men digging a hole in the road.* ∘ *He was digging in the garden.*
- to get sb/sth out of a place by digging: **dig*** sb/sth **out** (**of** sth) ∘ *a gold coin that had been dug out of a field*
- to look for sth by digging: **dig* for** sth ∘ *The police were out digging for evidence.*
- to remove sth from the ground by digging: **dig*** sth **up** ∘ *I want to dig up those plants and put them in the back garden.*
- to make a hole or take soil away by digging: **dig*** sth **up** ∘ *They're digging up the road outside.*
- to put sth into a hole in the ground: **bury** sth ∘ *buried treasure*

▷ more on holes ⇨ **HOLE**

- to dig deep into the ground: **excavate** sth; *noun* (U/C): **excavation** ∘ *They're excavating here to make the foundations of the new museum.*
- to dig in the ground for coal, gold, etc: **mine** (**for** sth) ∘ *to mine for silver*
- a hole or system of holes and passages that people dig under the ground in order to obtain coal, gold, or other minerals: **mine** ∘ *a diamond mine*
- a person who mines: **miner**

▷ coal mines ⇨ **COAL**

- a machine that is used for digging: **digger**
- to make sth flat: **level** sth ∘ *The ground needs levelling.*
- a machine like a large tractor which is used for levelling the ground: **bulldozer**
- to level sth with a bulldozer: **bulldoze** sth

group

> **1** groups of people
> **2** being in a group
> **3** the head of a group
>
> groups of animals ⇨ ANIMAL
> groups of things ⇨ TOGETHER
>
> **see also** SOCIETY

1 groups of people

- a number of people who are together, or who have sth in common: **group** (*with singular or plural verb*) ◦ *Groups of schoolchildren were hanging around near the school gates.* ◦ *A group of local farmers has/have made a protest.*
- a large number of people in one place: **crowd** (*with singular or plural verb*)
- a group of (young) friends: (*informal*) **crowd** (*with singular or plural verb*), (*informal*) **gang** (*with singular or plural verb*) ◦ *I don't know why you go around with that crowd; they're all mad.*
- a group of people, especially rich people, who spend a lot of time together or who have similar interests: **set** ◦ *the golfing set* ◦ *the jet set* (= rich and fashionable people)
- a group of criminals: **gang**

▷ more on crowds ⇨ CROWD

- two people together: **pair** ◦ *a pair of young lovers*
- two people who are married, living together, etc: **couple**

▷ people in twos ⇨ TWO

■ organized groups

- an organized group of people who do sth together: **organization** ◦ *We want to start a new organization for overseas students.* ◦ *a housing association* ◦ *the Football Association*
- a group of people who meet to share an interest: **club**, **society** ◦ *a working men's club* ◦ *a cricket club* ◦ *a drama society*
- a group of people who play a game or sport together against another group: **team**

▷ more on clubs ⇨ CLUB

▷ teams ⇨ TEAM

2 being in a group

- a person who is part of a group: **member** ◦ *I wouldn't want to be a member of that club.*
- the state of being a member of sth: **membership** (*noun* U) ◦ *If you want to renew your membership of the Association, you should apply before the end of the year.*
- the number of people who are members of sth: **membership** (*noun* U) ◦ *Church membership has been decreasing steadily.*
- to be a member of a group: **belong to** sth ◦ *She belongs to the local tennis club.*
- to become a member of a group: **join** sth ◦ *I'd like to join a health club.*

- to make sb part of a group: **include** sb (**in** sth); *noun* (U): **inclusion** ◦ *She was overjoyed to be included in the British Olympic team.* ◦ *His inclusion in the team was quite unexpected.*
- to prevent sb from being part of a group: **exclude** sb (**from** sth); *noun* (U): **exclusion** ◦ *People over 30 are excluded from membership of the club.*

- to make a group: **form** sth ◦ *The school hockey team was formed in 1987.*
- to organize people into a group or groups: **group** people ◦ *The basketball teacher grouped the boys according to their height.*
- to come together in a group: **gather**, **assemble** ◦ *A crowd quickly gathered at the scene of the accident.* ◦ *The staff assembled to hear what the chairman had to say.*
- to join together and act in agreement: **unite**; *adjective*: **united** ◦ *Several groups of health workers have decided to unite to form a larger association.* ◦ *It was because we were absolutely united that we managed to achieve our objectives.*

- (used about a group) to stop being together: **separate**, **break* up**, **split* up**; to cause a group to stop being together: **separate** sth, **break*** sth **up**, **split*** sth **up** ◦ *We set off on our walk as a group, but we soon separated.* ◦ *The police broke up the crowd after some people started throwing bottles.*

3 the head of a group

- a person who controls an organization or part of an organization: **head** ◦ *the head of the English department*
- a person whose job is to give orders to other people at work: (*informal*) **boss**
- the second most important person in an organization or a part of an organization: **deputy**; *adjective*: **deputy** ◦ *This is my deputy, Mr Williams.* ◦ *the deputy head*

- a person who is the head of sth or in charge of sth: **leader** ◦ *a strong/weak leader* ◦ *a trade union leader*
- to be the leader of sth or to be in charge of sth: **lead*** sb/sth ◦ *He has successfully led the country through several difficult years.*
- the state of being a leader: **leadership** (*noun* U) ◦ *a leadership contest* ◦ *We were not very satisfied with his leadership.*

- the leader of a team in sport: **captain** ◦ *the captain of a football team*
- to be the captain of a group or a team: **captain** sb/sth ◦ *We don't yet know who will be captaining the side next season.*

- to choose sb to be a leader by voting for them: **elect** sb; *noun* (C/U): **election**

▷ more on elections ⇨ ELECTION

grow

> becoming larger in number or amount ⇨ INCREASE / DECREASE
> **see also** BIG / SMALL

- to increase in size: **grow***; *noun* (U): **growth** ◦ *Hasn't Ben grown!*

grow *contd.*

- to develop into an adult form: **grow*** (**from** sth) (**into** sth) ○ *The grass will never grow if we don't have some rain soon.*
- to grow very quickly: (*informal*) **shoot* up** ○ *Andrew's shooting up – he's already taller than his father!*
- to begin to be sth: **become*** sth ○ *to become an adult*
- to gradually become sth: **grow* into** sth; **turn into** sth ○ *This small seed will grow into a tall tree.* ○ *Your son is turning into a very handsome young man.*
- to grow slowly, or change into sth else: **develop**; *noun* (U): **development** ○ *to develop from a child into an adult* ○ *the development of the human embryo*

- (used about people) to become an adult: **grow* up** ○ *I grew up in India.*
- when sb has become an adult, both physically and mentally, they are **grown up**, **mature** ○ *They're not grown up enough to get married yet.*
- a person who has grown up: **adult**, (*informal*) **grown-up**

- if a plant or animal has grown to a point where it will not grow any more, it is **fully developed**, **fully-grown**, **mature** ○ *a fully-grown elephant* ○ *a mature tree*

▷ more on the way things develop ⇨ DEVELOP

- to grow big enough to fit your clothes: **grow* into** sth ○ *It's a bit big for you now, but you'll soon grow into it.*
- to grow to be too big to fit your clothes or too old for sth: **grow* out of** sth, **outgrow*** sth ○ *Henry's already grown out of his shoes.* ○ *When is he going to grow out of this childish behaviour?*

■ making things grow
- to plant sth and look after it: **grow*** sth (**from** sth) ○ *'Did you buy that plant?' 'No, I grew it from seed.'*
- to grow sth in large quantities in order to sell it: **produce** sth ○ *We produce mainly cereal crops on our farm.*

▷ more on growing plants ⇨ PLANT, FARM

guess ⇨ POSSIBLE[1]

guilty ⇨ TRIAL

guitar ⇨ MUSIC

gun

1 different kinds of guns and parts of guns
2 using a gun
see also WEAPON, FIGHT, WAR

1 different kinds of guns and parts of guns

- a weapon that is used for shooting: **gun**
- a gun that you can carry: **firearm**
- a small gun that you can hold in one hand: **pistol**, **hand gun**
- a number of large guns on wheels: **artillery** (*noun* U)

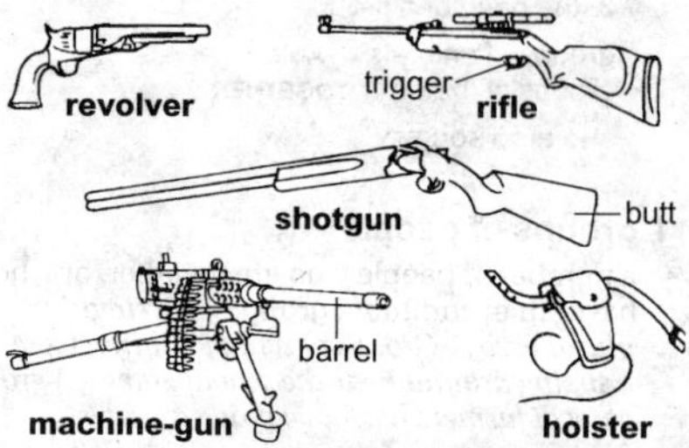

- a small rounded piece of metal that is fired from a gun: **bullet**
- a metal container filled with explosives that is fired by a large gun: **shell** ○ *Shells were landing in the city centre every few minutes.*
- the supply of bullets for a gun: **ammunition** (*noun* U)

2 using a gun

- to use a gun: **fire** (sth) (**at** sb/sth), **fire** (sth) **into** sth, **shoot*** (**at** sb/sth) ○ *to fire at the enemy* ○ *He fired the gun into the air.* ○ *Don't shoot! I'm unarmed.*
- an act of firing a gun, or the noise that it makes: **shot** ○ *How many shots were fired?* ○ *We heard a shot.*
- the sound that a gun makes: **bang**
- shooting from guns: **fire** (*noun* U), **gunfire** (*noun* U) ○ *We were under fire from all sides.* ○ *I heard the sound of gunfire in the distance.*
- to injure or kill sb with a gun: **shoot*** sb/sth (**dead**) ○ *He was shot dead by enemy soldiers.*

- to put a bullet or number of bullets into a gun: **load** (sth); *opposite*: **unload** (sth) ○ *He loaded his gun and waited by the door.* ○ *The sergeant ordered his men to unload their weapons.*
- to take a gun out of sth suddenly: **pull** sth **out**, **draw*** sth ○ *She walked into a bank and pulled out a gun.*
- to point a gun at sb/sth before you try to hit them/it with it: **aim** (sth) (**at** sb/sth), **take* aim** (**at** sb) (**with** sth) ○ *I aimed the gun at the deer and pulled the trigger.* ○ *Ready! Take aim! Fire!*
- something that you aim at: **target**
- the distance that it is possible to shoot a gun: **range** ○ *long-range artillery*
- from a very close position: **point-blank** ○ *He shot him at point-blank range.*

- to point a gun at sb and say that you will shoot them if they do not obey you: **hold*** sb **at gunpoint**
- a person who uses a gun to rob or kill people: **gunman**

- to prepare to fight by picking up and carrying a weapon, or by giving a weapon to another person: **arm** yourself/sb; *opposite*: **disarm** sb ○ *He*

armed himself with a pistol. ◦ *The policeman pushed the woman against the wall before disarming her.*
– if you are carrying a gun or another weapon, you are **armed**; *opposite*: **unarmed** ◦ *If you see this man, do not go near him. He is armed and dangerous.*

– the sport of shooting at targets or killing birds: **shooting** (*noun* U) ◦ *I've won several prizes for shooting.* ◦ *pigeon shooting*
– a person who can shoot very accurately: **marksman** (*plural* **marksmen**)
– if you are good at shooting, you are a **good shot**

– a group of soldiers who have been ordered to shoot and kill a prisoner: **firing squad**

habit

things that usually happen ⇨ USUAL
see also BEHAVIOUR

– something that sb does often: **habit** ◦ *My sister has an annoying habit of always leaving the light on when she goes to bed.*
– if you do sth without thinking about it, just because it is what you usually do, you do it **out of habit** ◦ *I still get up early out of habit.*
– doing sth very often: **habitual** ◦ *a habitual smoker/drinker*
– done very often: **habitual** ◦ *After I've showered, I have my habitual early morning cup of tea.*

– if you do sth regularly, you are **in the habit of** doing sth, you **like to** do sth ◦ *Her husband was in the habit of leaving his clothes lying on the floor.* ◦ *I like to have my bath in the evening.*
– if you start to do sth regularly, you **get* into the habit of** doing sth, you **make* a habit of** doing sth ◦ *I'm trying to get into the habit of going to bed a bit earlier.* ◦ *I don't mind you coming late once or twice but try not to make a habit of it.*
– if you stop doing sth regularly, you **get* out of the habit of** doing sth ◦ *I've got out of the habit of going to parties.*

– to talk about sth that happened often or regularly in the past, you can say that sb **used to** do sth, or that they **would** do sth ◦ *When we were young we used to spend hours playing in the garden.* ◦ *In those days, I would run five miles before breakfast and another five miles after supper.*
– to talk about sth annoying that sb does very often, you can say that they **always** do it, or that they **will** do it ◦ *She's always leaving the door open, it's really annoying.* ◦ *She will leave the door open – I wish she'd remember to shut it.*

– a fixed and usual way of doing things: **routine** ◦ *Regular exercise should be part of our daily routine.*
– a way of behaving which a particular group has had for a long time: **custom** ◦ *an unusual custom* ◦ *It was their custom to exchange presents on Christmas Eve.*
– according to custom: **customary**
– the usual way that a person or a group of people live: **way of life**

Note: habit is used to talk about sth done by one person; **custom** is usually used to talk about sth that is done by a group of people (for example a community or nation).

▷ more on customs ⇨ CUSTOM

■ bad habits
– a habit which annoys other people: **bad habit** ◦ *I didn't enjoy sharing a flat with him – he's got some really bad habits.* ◦ *One of my worst habits is biting my nails.*
– to start doing sth regularly which is not good: **get* into bad habits**

– to stop a bad habit: **give*** sth **up**, **break* the habit**, (*informal*) **kick the habit** ◦ *I'm trying to give up smoking at the moment.* ◦ *I've smoked for years and just can't kick the habit.*
– to stop doing sth as you grow older: **grow* out of** sth
– to smoke, drink, eat, etc less: **cut* down** (**on** sth) ◦ *Doctors say that it's important to cut down on fats and sugar in your diet.*

– if sb is unable to stop taking sth harmful, they are **addicted** (**to** it); *noun* (C/U): **addiction** ◦ *to be addicted to alcohol/coffee/cigarettes* ◦ *to suffer from drug addiction*
– a substance that people can get addicted to is **addictive**
– a person who cannot stop taking or doing sth harmful: **addict** ◦ *a heroin addict*

■ **MORE . . .**
– to have or start having a way of life which is boring and difficult to change: **be in a rut**, **get* into a rut** ◦ *All you do is get up in the morning, go to work, come home, watch telly or go to the pub; it's not surprising you feel you're getting into a rut!*

hair

1 hair on the head, face, etc
2 different kinds of hair
3 looking after your hair
hair on animals ⇨ ANIMAL
see also HEAD, FACE

1 hair on the head, face, etc
– one of the long thin things that grow on the skin of people and animals: **hair** ◦ *The dog left hairs all over the furniture.*
– the hairs that grow in a mass on top of your head: **hair** (*noun* U) ◦ *She's got lovely hair.*
– having a lot of hair: **hairy**

– the hair which grows on a man's cheeks and chin: **beard**; *adjective*: **bearded** (*only before a noun*) ◦ *Has your father got a beard?* ◦ *He's growing a beard.* ◦ *a tall, bearded man in a hat*
– the hair which grows on a man's top lip between the mouth and the nose: **moustache** (*AmE* **mustache**) ◦ *He's growing a moustache.*

hair *contd.*

- the hair that grows on a man's face in front of his ears: **sideboards** (*noun plural*) (*AmE* **side-burns**)
- if a man does not have any hair on his face, he is **clean-shaven**
- hair that grows on the body: **body hair** (*noun* U)
- hair that grows around the sex organs: **pubic hair** (*noun* U)

2 different kinds of hair

- light-coloured hair is **fair**; *opposite*: **dark**; a person with fair hair is **fair-haired**; *opposite*: **dark-haired**
- fair or yellowish hair is **blond**; a woman who has this colour of hair: **blonde**; *adjective*: **blonde** ◦ *The picture showed a blonde woman wearing dark glasses.*
- a white woman who has dark brown hair: **brunette** ◦ *She's a brunette.*
- dull brown hair is **mousy**
- light orange hair is **ginger**
- reddish brown hair is **red, auburn, chestnut**
- a person (especially a woman) who has red hair: **redhead**; *adjective*: **redheaded**

straight **wavy** **curly**

- a piece of hair that curves round: **curl**; *verb*: **curl** ◦ *Does your hair curl naturally?*
- your hair can be **long, short** or **medium length** ◦ *short curly hair*
- hair that is smooth and nice to touch is **soft**
- hair that grows thickly is **bushy** ◦ *He had very bushy eyebrows.*

3 looking after your hair

■ things you use

- a piece of metal or plastic with a row of narrow pointed parts (**teeth**) for making your hair tidy: **comb**; *verb*: **comb** sth ◦ *I must go and comb my hair.*
- a tool with stiff pointed parts for making your hair tidy: **hairbrush, brush**
- to make hair tidy using a brush: **brush** sth; *noun*: **brush** ◦ *She brushed the children's hair.* ◦ *to give your hair a good brush*
- a tool for cutting hair (and other things): **scissors** (*noun plural*)
- a small tool that you can use for pulling out single hairs: **tweezers** (*noun plural*)
- a sharp instrument for cutting hair off the skin: **razor**
- a thin sharp piece of metal that you put in a razor: **razor blade**
- to remove hair with a razor: **shave** sth (**off**), (used about a man shaving his face) **shave, have a shave** ◦ *I decided to shave my beard off.* ◦ *He looks as if he hasn't shaved for a week.* ◦ *I had a wash and a shave and felt much better.*
- a soft brush that is used to put soap on the skin before shaving: **shaving-brush**
- a kind of soap that you often buy in an aerosol can, and that you use for shaving: **shaving foam** (*noun* U), **shaving-cream** (*noun* U)
- an electric tool that is used for shaving: **shaver**
- a liquid that you use for washing your hair: **shampoo** (*noun* U); when you use this, you **shampoo** your hair ◦ *a bottle of shampoo*
- a liquid that keeps your hair in good condition: **conditioner** (*noun* U)
- a liquid in a special container that is sprayed on hair to keep it in place: **hairspray** (*noun* U)
- a machine that you use for drying hair: **dryer, hairdryer**

■ going to the hairdresser

- a person whose job is to cut, wash and arrange people's hair: **hairdresser**, (especially in women's hairdressing) **stylist**; the work of a hairdresser: **hairdressing** (*noun* U)
- a shop where a hairdresser works: **hairdresser's**
- a man who cuts men's hair: **barber**; his shop is called a **barber's**
- to make hair short by using scissors, etc: **cut*** sth ◦ *I'm going to get my hair cut.*
- when sb cuts your hair, you have a **haircut** ◦ *Do you think I need a haircut?*
- to cut hair a little in order to make it neat and tidy: **trim** sth; *noun*: **trim** ◦ *Just give it a trim, please.*
- to arrange sb's hair while it is wet so that it becomes curly or wavy: **set*** sb's **hair** ◦ *She went to the hairdresser's to have her hair set.*
- the treatment of hair with special chemicals in order to make it curly or wavy: **perm**; *verb*: **perm** sth ◦ *to have your hair permed*
- to work on a person's hair (to cut it, brush it, etc): **do*** sb's hair ◦ *Can you do my hair today?* ◦ *I must get my hair done.*
- to change the colour of your hair: **dye** sth ◦ *I'm sure she dyes her hair.* ◦ *I'm going to dye my hair red.*
- to change the colour of your hair a little bit: **tint** sth ◦ *She had her hair tinted.*

■ styles of hair

- the way in which your hair has been cut or arranged: **hairstyle, style** ◦ *A short hairstyle doesn't suit him.*
- the way in which your hair has been cut: **cut, haircut**
- an arrangement of your hair in a particular way by a hairdresser: (*informal*) **hairdo** (*plural* **hairdos**) ◦ *I've just had a new hairdo.*
- to cut or arrange sb's hair in a particular way: **style** sth ◦ *I can see you've had your hair styled.*
- to let your hair become longer: **grow*** your **hair, let*** your **hair grow**

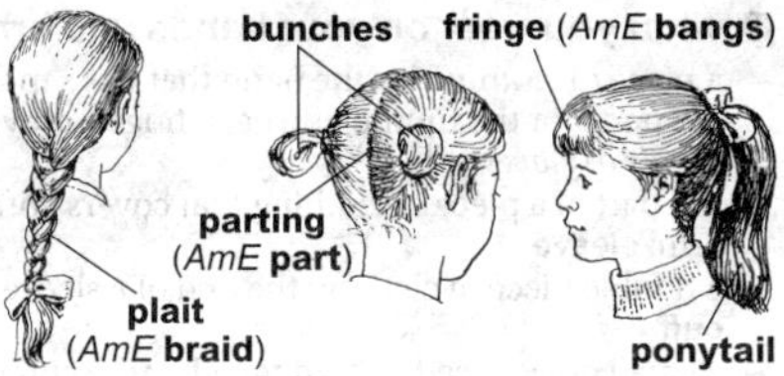

- to fasten your hair in position: **tie** sth ◦ *Her hair was tied in a bow.*
- a long thin piece of material that is used for tying or decorating the hair: **ribbon**
- to make plaits: **plait** (*AmE* **braid**) sth

■ problems with hair
- a person who has lost all or most of the hair on top of their head is **bald**; *noun* (U): **baldness** ◦ *My dad's starting to go bald.*
- a covering of false hair that you wear on your head to hide your own hair or because you are bald: **wig, hairpiece**

- small pieces of dead skin in the hair that look like white dust: **dandruff** (*noun* U) ◦ *anti-dandruff shampoo*

half ⇨ NUMBER

hammer ⇨ TOOL

hand/arm

1 parts of the hand and arm
2 doing things with your hands and arms
3 what you wear on your hands and arms
other parts of the body ⇨ BODY
breaking a bone in your arm ⇨ BONE

1 parts of the hand and arm

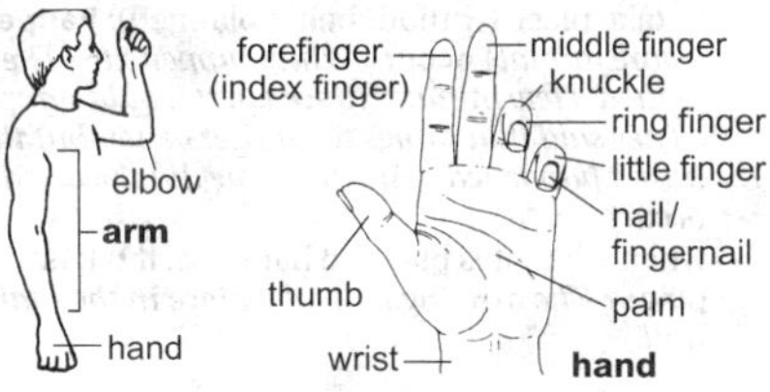

- the upper part of the arm from the shoulder to the elbow: **upper arm**
- the lower part of the arm from the elbow to the wrist: **forearm**
- the muscle in the front of the top of the arm: **biceps** (*plural* **biceps**)

- the hand when the fingers are tightly closed together: **fist**
- the top part of a finger: **fingertip**
- the bones at the joints in your fingers: **knuckles** (*usually plural*)

2 doing things with your hands and arms

- a person who uses his/her right hand more easily than the left is **right-handed**; *opposite*: **left-handed**
- work which you do with your hands is **manual** (*adverb* **manually**) ◦ *manual work* ◦ *They had to do it manually when the machine broke down.*

- to cross your arms in front of your chest: **fold** your **arms**, **cross** your **arms** ◦ *She sat down and folded her arms.*
- to move your arms backwards and forwards or from side to side: **swing*** your **arms**

■ touching and hitting
- to put a part of your body, usually your fingers, on sth: **touch** sb/sth ◦ *Don't touch the painting!*
- to push sth firmly: **press** sth ◦ *Press this button for attention.*
- to move your hand backwards and forwards on the surface of sth while pressing firmly: **rub** sth, **give*** sth **a rub** ◦ *She rubbed her eyes sleepily.*
- to move your hand gently over sb/sth: **stroke** sb/sth ◦ *She stroked the cat.*

- to touch or feel sth with your fingers: **finger** sth ◦ *She fingered the gold chain round her neck.*
- to push sth with your finger or other sharp object: **poke** sth, **prod** sth, **give*** sth **a poke/prod** ◦ *She accidentally poked him in the eye.* ◦ *She gave her husband a prod to wake him.*
- to move sth with a quick movement of the finger: **flick** sth ◦ *He flicked the insect off his shirt.*

- to hit sb/sth hard with your fist (= closed hand): **punch** sb/sth; *noun*: **punch** ◦ *Steve punched George in the face.* ◦ *a vicious punch to the jaw*
- to hit sb/sth with the inside of your hand: **slap** sb, **give*** sb **a slap** ◦ *She slapped my face.*
- to slap a child: **smack** sb, **give*** sb **a smack**

▷ more on touching and hitting ⇨ TOUCH, HIT

■ catching and holding
- to keep sth in your hand, or to keep sth in a certain position: **hold*** sth ◦ *Could you hold this glass a minute while I get some food?*
- to put your hand round sth and hold it (and move it towards you): **take*** sth ◦ *He held out three cards and asked me to take one.* ◦ *to take sb's hand*

- to take hold of sth that is moving, usually with your hands: **catch*** sth
- to move your hand so that you can get hold of sth: **stretch out** your **arm**, **reach** (**out**) (**for** sth) ◦ *He stretched out his arm to pick up the phone.* ◦ *I reached for the book on the top shelf.* ◦ *He reached out for the ice cream.*
- to use your hand like a spoon to lift sth: **scoop** sth **out/up** ◦ *The small girl scooped out a hole in the sand.*
- to put your hands together in the shape of a cup: **cup** your **hands**; to hold sth in this way: **cup** sth **in** your **hand** ◦ *She cupped her hands to collect water from the spring.* ◦ *He cupped his chin in his hand.*
- an amount of sth that you can hold in one arm/hand: **armful/handful** ◦ *She was carrying an armful of books.* ◦ *a handful of sand*

hand / arm *contd.*

- to hold sth in your hand and press it hard: **squeeze** sth; *noun*: **squeeze** ◦ *He squeezed her arm.* ◦ *a gentle squeeze*
- to squeeze sth between two of your fingers: **pinch** sth; *noun*: **pinch** ◦ *Ouch! You're pinching me!* ◦ *She gave the other girl a nasty pinch.*

▷ more on catching and holding ⇨ CATCH / HOLD

■ holding another person

- (used about two people) to hold each other's hands: **hold* hands**; holding hands: **hand in hand** ◦ *The newly engaged couple sat holding hands.*
- (of more than two people) to join together by holding each other's hands: **join hands** ◦ *Then we all joined hands and sang Auld Lang Syne.*
- with your arm linked together with sb else's arm: **arm in arm** ◦ *Jim and Mary were walking arm in arm.*

▷ holding sb in a friendly or loving way ⇨ LOVE

arm in arm **arms folded / arms crossed**

■ communicating a meaning

- a movement of the hand, head, etc that expresses some meaning: **gesture** ◦ *She made a gesture of annoyance.* ◦ *a welcoming gesture*
- to show sb (often with a movement of your finger or hand) that you want him/her to come closer: **beckon** (**to**) sb (**to** do sth) ◦ *She beckoned to me to come up onto the stage.*
- to show respect by raising your hand to your forehead: **salute** (sb); *noun*: **salute** ◦ *The soldiers looked to the right and saluted.*
- to hit your hands together to show that you like sth: **clap** (sb/sth), **give** sb/sth **a clap**; the noise that people make when they clap: **clapping** (*noun* U) ◦ *The audience clapped enthusiastically.* ◦ *Let's give him a clap!* ◦ *There was a lot of noisy clapping at the back of the theatre.*

- to raise your hand, especially in a classroom: **put*** your **hand up** ◦ *Please put your hand up if you have a question.*
- to move your hand so that it can be seen: **stick*** your **hand out** ◦ *The driver stuck his hand out to show that he was turning left.*
- to show where sth is or draw attention to sth by using your finger: **point** (**at/to** sb/sth) ◦ *The guide pointed to the historic painting.*

▷ using your hand to say hello or goodbye ⇨ GREET

3 what you wear on your hands and arms

- a piece of clothing for the hand that has separate parts for the thumb and each finger: **glove** ◦ *a pair of gloves*
- the part of a piece of clothing that covers your arm: **sleeve**
- a double piece of cloth on the end of a sleeve: **cuff**
- a small object used to hold together the cuff on a shirt: **cuff link** (*usually plural*)

▷ more on clothes ⇨ CLOTHES

- a round piece of jewellery that you wear on your finger: **ring** ◦ *She was wearing a wedding ring.*
- a piece of jewellery that you wear round your wrist or on your arm: **bracelet**

▷ more on rings, bracelets, etc ⇨ JEWELLERY

■ **MORE . . .**

- treatment for your hands and fingernails to make them healthy and beautiful: **manicure** ◦ *to have a manicure*
- small scissors that you use for cutting your nails: **nail scissors** (*noun plural*)

- a pair of metal rings joined by a chain for putting round the wrists of prisoners: **handcuffs** (*noun plural*) ◦ *They caught the thief and put him in handcuffs.*

happen

1 something happening
2 different kinds of event
3 happening at the same time
4 expecting sth to happen
happening always, often, usually ⇨ HOW OFTEN, USUAL
causing sth to happen ⇨ CAUSE / EFFECT
see also ACTION

1 something happening

- to take place (without being planned): **happen**, (*more formal*) **occur** ◦ *What happened?* ◦ *They waited a few minutes to see what would happen.* ◦ *They said that things would get better, but that hasn't happened.* ◦ *At what time did the accident occur?*
- when sth that is planned happens, it **takes* place** ◦ *The meeting will take place in the main hall.*

- to begin to exist or happen: **come* about**, (*more formal*) **arise*** ◦ *How did this situation come about?* ◦ *More and more problems began to arise.*
- to happen over a period of time: **go* on** ◦ *How long has this been going on for?*
- something that is happening now is **in progress, going on** ◦ *I'm afraid you can't go in – there's a meeting in progress.* ◦ *Can you tell me what's going on in there?*

- to be about to happen: **come* up** ◦ *There's an interesting conference coming up next year.*
- to happen unexpectedly: **come* up, crop up** ◦ *I'm afraid I won't be able to come tonight – something has come up.*

- if sb experiences sth or something is done to sth, it **happens to** sb/sth ◦ *Some terrible things happened to people who were put in this prison.* ◦ *What happened to the money that I left on the table?* (= where is the money?) ◦ *'I wonder what happened to Susan Baxter?' 'I think she went to live in Canada.'*

■ where sth happens
- a place where sth happens: **scene** ◦ *He was the first to arrive at the scene of the accident.*
- the situation in which sth happens or that caused sth to happen: **context, setting** ◦ *It's easier to understand the book when you put it in its historical context.*

2 different kinds of event
- something that happens, especially sth important: **event** ◦ *Christmas is an important event in our family.* ◦ *At the trial, witnesses were asked about the events leading up to the murder.* ◦ *an annual event*
- an unimportant event: **incident** ◦ *an amusing little incident*
- any kind of event or incident or happening: (*formal*) **occurrence** ◦ *a common/frequent/regular occurrence*
- full of interesting and important events: **eventful** ◦ *a very interesting and eventful day.*

- a special event or celebration: **occasion** ◦ *An eighteenth birthday is a very special occasion.*
- a social event: **affair** ◦ *The wedding was a very enjoyable affair.*
- something that is grand, interesting or unusual to look at: **spectacle** ◦ *The street party was an amazing spectacle – there were dancers, actors, musicians all wearing beautiful costumes.*
- events that happen at a formal meeting or ceremony: **proceedings** (*noun plural*) ◦ *The newspapers gave an account of the day's proceedings.*

- the things that are happening in a particular place or at a particular time: **situation** ◦ *I'm in a very difficult situation at the moment.* ◦ *I don't know how to get out of this situation.*

▷ more on situations ⇨ SITUATION

- something that has happened to you: **experience** ◦ *an unpleasant/exciting/unusual experience*
- one separate event in your life, in a novel, etc: **episode** ◦ *It was the most embarrassing episode in my entire life.*
- the most important and exciting part of an event: **climax** ◦ *The evening reached its climax at midnight when everybody was singing and dancing on the tables.*
- a new or recent event: **development** ◦ *We're not expecting any further developments today.*
- an experience or event which is unusual, exciting or dangerous: **adventure** ◦ *We had lots of adventures while we were on holiday.*

- a number of things that happen or that come one after another: **sequence of events**
- a series of events that are connected: **chain of events** ◦ *a chain of events that led to the closing of the business early this year*

■ bad events
- an event that causes a lot of harm or damage: **disaster, catastrophe**; *adjectives*: **disastrous, catastrophic** ◦ *a major oil disaster in the North Sea.* ◦ *The war had a catastrophic effect on the whole country.*
- a serious event that needs immediate action: **emergency** ◦ *In an emergency, press the red button for help.*
- an unpleasant event that happens unexpectedly and causes damage, injury or death: **accident** ◦ *to be in a car accident*
- an event (especially one that involves violence or danger): **incident** ◦ *There were a number of violent incidents after the football match.*

▷ more on accidents ⇨ ACCIDENT

3 happening at the same time
- to happen at the same time as sth else: **coincide** (**with** sth), **clash** (**with** sth) ◦ *The meeting coincided with my doctor's appointment.* ◦ *I'm pretty sure that the programmes clash.*
- happening at the same time: **simultaneous** (*adverb* **simultaneously**) ◦ *The two events were simultaneous.* ◦ *They happened simultaneously.*
- when two or more similar things happen at the same time by chance, it is (a) **coincidence** (*noun* C/U); *adjective*: **coincidental** ◦ *What a coincidence!* ◦ *It was pure coincidence that we ended up working in the same office together.*

4 expecting sth to happen
- to think or believe that sth will happen: **expect** sth (**to** happen) ◦ *We're not expecting anything new to happen in the next few days.* ◦ *I don't expect things to change immediately.*
- something which people expect to happen is **expected**; not expected: **unexpected** (*adverb* **unexpectedly**) ◦ *an expected reaction* ◦ *an unexpected rise in the number of new students* ◦ *He arrived quite unexpectedly.*

▷ more on things happening in the future ⇨ FUTURE

- the way in which things happen that you did not expect: **chance** (*noun* U)
- without being planned: **accidentally, by accident, by chance** ◦ *I accidentally pressed the off button.* ◦ *We met by chance on the train.* ◦ *I came across the letter by chance while I was looking for something else.*

- the feeling that you have when sth happens that you do not expect: **surprise** ◦ *I got quite a surprise when I arrived home to find a huge bouquet of flowers on my front doorstep.*
- to happen or do sth when sb is not expecting it: **take*** sb **by surprise** ◦ *The news of their wedding took me quite by surprise.*

▷ more on surprising events and feelings of surprise ⇨ SURPRISE

happy

not happy ⇨ SAD
other emotions ⇨ EMOTION
see also ENJOY, LAUGH

happy *contd.*

- feeling, showing or giving pleasure or satisfaction: **happy** ◦ *a film with a happy ending* ◦ *Today has been the happiest day of my life.* ◦ *I'm so happy to hear that your mother is feeling better.* ◦ *I'm not happy about the changes, but what can I do?* ◦ *Aren't you happy with my work?*
- very happy: **delighted**; *noun* (U): **delight** ◦ *They are delighted at the news.*

- happy and wanting to show it: **cheerful** (*adverb* **cheerfully**); *noun* (U): **cheerfulness** ◦ *George remained cheerful all through his illness.* ◦ *She waved cheerfully at me across the street.*
- if you feel generally happy at a particular time, you are **in a good mood** ◦ *I'm afraid I'm never in a good mood first thing in the morning.*

- happy about a particular thing: **pleased, glad**; something that makes you pleased is **pleasing**, a **pleasure**; a state or feeling of being happy: **pleasure** (*noun* U) ◦ *I'm glad you could come.* ◦ *a pleasing result* ◦ *It is a pleasure to meet you.* ◦ *Knowing you are happy gives me more pleasure than anything else.*
- pleased because you have got or done what you want: **satisfied**; *noun* (U): **satisfaction**; something that causes this feeling is **satisfying**, it **satisfies** you ◦ *a satisfied customer* ◦ *the satisfaction of knowing you are right* ◦ *I wasn't satisfied by his explanation.*
- happy and satisfied: **contented** (*adverb* **contentedly**); *noun* (U): **contentment** ◦ *a contented smile* ◦ *He sat contentedly in front of the fire and read a book.* ◦ *She sighed with contentment.*
- generally satisfied with your life: **content** ◦ *For the first time in my working life, I felt completely content.*

- to feel happier than before: **cheer up** ◦ *Cheer up! It's not the end of the world!*
- to make sb more cheerful than before: **cheer** sb **up** ◦ *I thought these flowers might cheer you up.*

■ showing you are happy
- the expression on your face when you are happy: **smile**; when you turn up the corners of your mouth to make this expression, you **smile** (**at** sb/sth) ◦ *a charming smile* ◦ *She gave me a welcoming smile.* ◦ *Who were you smiling at?*
- to smile with great pleasure: **beam** ◦ *Beaming with pride, he showed us the baby.*

harbour ⇨ BOAT

hard ⇨ EASY/DIFFICULT

hard/soft

> see also SURFACE, MATERIAL

■ hard
- not easy to bend or break; able to stay in the same shape when pressed: **hard**; *noun* (U): **hardness** ◦ *hard wood/cheese/nuts* ◦ *a hard bed/chair/sweet* ◦ *The frozen ground was as hard as iron.* ◦ *Digging was difficult because of the hardness of the ground.*
- extremely hard: **rock hard** ◦ *I threw the bread away – it was rock hard.*
- to become hard: **harden** ◦ *Butter hardens when you put it in the fridge.*

- able to stay the same shape when pressed; quite hard: **firm**; *noun* (U): **firmness** ◦ *a firm cushion/bed*
- not easily folded, bent, or moved: **stiff**; *noun* (U): **stiffness** ◦ *You can make a box out of stiff paper or cardboard.*
- to become stiff: **stiffen**; to cause sth to become stiff: **stiffen** sth ◦ *material used to stiffen a belt/collar*

- hard but easily broken: **brittle** ◦ *Old people often have brittle bones.*
- very stiff; not possible to bend; very strong: **rigid**; *noun* (U): **rigidity** ◦ *Make sure the tent poles are rigid.*
- able to bend easily without breaking: **flexible** ◦ *flexible plastic tubing*

■ solid
- hard or firm; not in the form of liquid or gas: **solid**; to become solid: **solidify** ◦ *The pond was frozen solid.* ◦ *Melted butter will solidify if you remove it from the heat.*
- to change from solid to liquid by means of heat: **melt**; to cause sth to do this: **melt** sth ◦ *The ice cream is melting!* ◦ *You can melt butter by heating it.*

■ soft
- not hard or firm; changing shape easily when pressed: **soft**; *noun* (U): **softness** ◦ *a soft bed/pillow* ◦ *soft cheese* ◦ *a chocolate with a soft centre*
- to become soft: **soften**; to make sth soft: **soften** sth ◦ *Soften the butter by warming it a little.* ◦ *You can soften your skin by putting cream on it.*
- weak and soft; not stiff: **limp** ◦ *Those flowers have gone all limp.*
- soft, loose and hanging downwards: **floppy** ◦ *a puppy with floppy ears*

■ smooth
- smooth and nice to touch; not rough on the surface: **soft**; *noun* (U): **softness** ◦ *soft leather* ◦ *the softness of a baby's skin*
- smooth and soft to touch; like silk: **silky** ◦ *silky hair* ◦ *silky material*

▷ smooth and rough ⇨ SURFACE

harm

- hurting your body ⇨ INJURY
- damaging sth ⇨ DAMAGE

hat

> other things that you wear on your head ⇨ HEAD
> other clothes ⇨ CLOTHES

- a piece of clothing that you wear on your head: **hat** ◦ *Put your hat on before you go out in the rain.* ◦ *He took his hat off.*

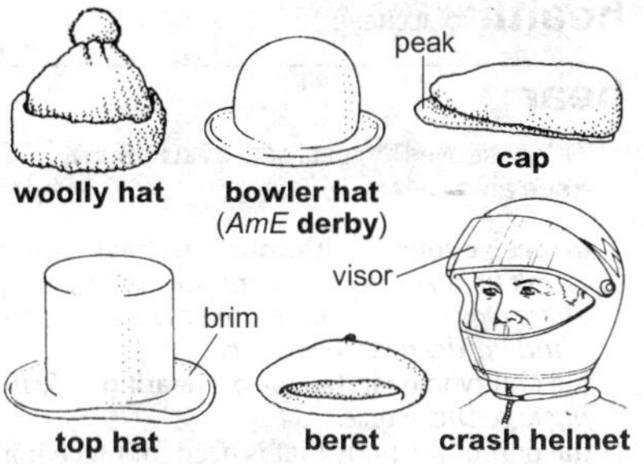

- a hat that protects you from the sun: **sunhat**
- a hat that you wear for some sports: **cap** ◦ *a baseball cap* ◦ *a swimming cap*

- the flat edge around a hat, which keeps the sun or the rain out of your face: **brim**
- the pointed front part of a hat that is above your eyes: **peak**; a cap with a peak: **peaked cap**

- a hard hat which you wear to protect your head: **helmet**
- a hard hat that is worn by motorcyclists, racing drivers, etc: **crash helmet**

hate ⇨ DISLIKE

have/possess

1 having
2 getting, keeping, losing
see also GIVE, BORROW/LEND

1 having

- to have sth as your property: **have (got)** sth, (*more formal*) **possess** sth; *noun* (U): **possession** ◦ *We lost everything in the war. When it ended, we had nothing.* ◦ *Has she got a flat?* ◦ *She's quite well off and possesses some beautiful things.* ◦ *The farm is no longer in my possession.*
- if sth is legally your property, you **own** it, it **belongs to** you, it is **yours**, it is **your own**; *noun* (U): **ownership** ◦ *'Do you own your house?' 'No, it's rented.'* ◦ *I can't lend it to you; it doesn't belong to me.* ◦ *Who does this coat belong to?* ◦ *At last – a room of my own!* ◦ *The ownership of the land is in dispute.*

- the person who owns sth: **owner** ◦ *Are you the owner of this vehicle?* ◦ *a landowner* ◦ *a car-owner*
- a person who owns a hotel, newspaper, business, etc: (*formal*) **proprietor**; a woman who is a proprietor can also be called a **proprietress**

- if sth belongs to a particular person or group, it is **private**, **privately owned** ◦ *a private house* ◦ *private property*
- if sth belongs to a particular person or is for their use only, it is **personal** ◦ *This car is for your personal use.*
- if sth is for everyone to use and does not belong to a particular person, it is **public** ◦ *a public library* ◦ *a public telephone*
- an industry, business or company that is owned by the nation is **publicly owned**; the state of being publicly owned: **public ownership** (*noun* U)

- if you own sth and do not like to share it with anybody else, you are **mean**, **possessive** ◦ *Don't be so mean – let him have it if you don't need it!* ◦ *Tony is really possessive about his car – he never lets anyone else drive it.*

■ the things that you own
- what you own: **possessions** (*noun plural*), **belongings** (*noun plural*), **property** (*noun* U) ◦ *He has few personal possessions.* ◦ *I've left all my belongings back at the hotel.* ◦ *The police found stolen property in the warehouse.*
- things that you own or have with you: (*informal*) your **stuff** (*noun* U), your **things** (*noun plural*) ◦ *Can I put my stuff over here?* ◦ *We'll just leave our things in the car.*
- the small things that you own that are worth a lot of money: **valuables** (*noun plural*) ◦ *Please put your valuables in the hotel safe.*

2 getting, keeping, losing

- to become the owner or user of sth: **get*** sth, (*more formal*) **obtain** sth, (*formal*) **acquire** sth ◦ *I've just got myself a new computer.* ◦ *This book can be obtained in paperback.* ◦ *The zoo has just acquired a female panda.*
- the act of acquiring sth: **acquisition** (*noun* U); something that you have acquired: **acquisition** ◦ *My wife collects china and is very pleased with her latest acquisition.*

▷ more on getting ⇨ GET

- to continue to have sth: **keep*** sth, (*informal*) **hold* onto** sth, (*informal*) **hang* onto** sth ◦ *How long can I keep your book?* ◦ *I'm going to hold on to this stamp – it might be worth a lot of money some day.*
- to no longer have or own sth: **lose*** sth; *noun* (C/U): **loss** ◦ *Many people lost their homes in the earthquake.* ◦ *My business has failed. I've lost everything.* ◦ *serious losses during the war* ◦ *They announced 200 job losses.*
- to cause sb to lose sth: **cost*** sb sth ◦ *His rudeness to the customer cost him his job.*

▷ more on keeping and losing things ⇨ KEEP, LOSE[2]

- to ask for sth because you think you should have it or that it belongs to you: **claim** sth ◦ *If nobody claims the wallet after one month you can keep it.*
- if sb has sth that you own and then they give it to you, they **give*** it **back**, **hand** it **back**, **return** it **to** you ◦ *The police handed me back my wallet.*
- to be given sth back: **get*** sth **back** ◦ *I lost my keys but fortunately soon got them back.*

■ **MORE . . .**
- things of value that a person or company owns: **assets** (*noun plural*) ◦ *The company is having to sell its assets in order to survive.*
- all the money and property that a person owns when they die: **estate** (*noun* U) ◦ *His estate was valued at more than a million pounds.*

head

other parts of the body ⇨ **BODY**

- the top part of your body above the neck: **head**
- the bones of the head: **skull**
- the hairs that grow in a mass on top of your head: **hair** (*noun* U)
- the skin on the top of your head that is under the hair: **scalp**
- the part of your body inside your head that controls your thoughts, feelings and movements: **brain**
- the front part of your head: **face**

▷ more on hair ⇨ **HAIR**

▷ parts of the face ⇨ **FACE, EAR, EYE, MOUTH, NOSE**

■ movements
- to move your head down and then up again quickly as a way of saying 'yes' or as a greeting or a sign: **nod** (your **head**); *noun*: **nod** ∘ *She nodded in agreement.* ∘ *He gave a nod of approval.*
- to move your head from side to side as a way of saying 'no': **shake*** your **head** ∘ *She shook her head sadly.*
- to push your head further out than sth else: **stick*** your **head out** ∘ *Don't stick your head out of the window.*

■ pain and injury
- a pain in your head: **headache**
- a very bad headache that makes you feel ill: **migraine** (*noun* C/U) ∘ *to suffer from migraine*
- an injury to the brain caused by sth hitting the head: **concussion** (*noun* U); *verb*: **concuss** sb ∘ *He was rushed to hospital suffering from concussion.* ∘ *The fall left her badly concussed.*

▷ note on headaches and other aches ⇨ **PAIN**

■ coverings for the head
- something that you wear on your head, usually when you are outside: **hat** ∘ *Put your hat on.*
- a hard hat which you wear to protect your head: **helmet** ∘ *a policeman's helmet*
- a type of helmet worn by motor cyclists, racing drivers, etc: **crash helmet**

▷ more on hats ⇨ **HAT**

- a square of cotton or silk material, with designs on it, that you wear round your neck or on your head: **headscarf**, **scarf**
- a large piece of cloth, made of wool, etc that is worn over the head and shoulders by women: **shawl**
- a piece of thin material that women wear to cover their head or face: **veil**
- a covering for the head, made by wrapping a long strip of cloth around the head: **turban**
- a type of head covering that is worn for decoration, especially as part of a national costume: **headdress**

- if you are not wearing a hat or other head covering, you are **bareheaded**

health ⇨ ILLNESS

hear

other senses ⇨ **FEEL, SEE, SMELL, TASTE**
see also SPEAK

- to receive sounds with your ears: **hear*** (sb/sth) ∘ *I can't hear very well.* ∘ *What can you hear?* ∘ *There was so much noise from the audience we could hardly hear the music.*
- the ability to hear: (**sense of**) **hearing** ∘ *My hearing is getting worse.*
- the part of the body that is used for receiving sounds: **ear**

▷ the ear ⇨ **EAR**

- to pay attention in order to hear sth: **listen** (**to** sb/sth) ∘ *Listen – can you hear the bells?* ∘ *to listen to music*
- to manage to hear sth: **hear*** sth, **catch*** sth, **get*** sth ∘ *I'm sorry, I didn't quite hear what you said. Could you repeat it please?* ∘ *Did you catch her name?* ∘ *He told me the address but I didn't quite get the number.*
- to hear other people's conversation by accident: **overhear*** sth ∘ *I'm sorry, I couldn't help overhearing your question – can I help you?* ∘ *I overheard them talking about me.*
- if you do sth where sb else can hear it, you do it **within/in** their **hearing**; when sb is near enough to hear sb/sth, they are **within earshot**; *opposite*: **out of earshot** ∘ *You shouldn't say things like that in the children's hearing.* ∘ *Now he's out of earshot you can say what you like about him.*

- if you did not hear what sb said, you can say **Sorry?** or (*formal*) **I beg your pardon?** ∘ *Sorry? What were you saying?* ∘ *I beg your pardon? Did you say something?*
- to use a louder voice: **speak* up** ∘ *Could you speak up a bit please – I can't hear you properly.*

▷ more on listening ⇨ **LISTEN**

■ sounds
- anything that a person or animal can hear: **sound** (*noun* C/U) ∘ *I heard the sound of a blackbird singing.*
- a sound, especially if it is loud, unpleasant or unwanted: **noise** (*noun* C/U) ∘ *I thought I could hear a noise downstairs.*
- a sound that can be heard is **audible**; *opposite*: **inaudible** ∘ *an audible sigh* ∘ *an almost inaudible whisper*
- easy to hear: **clear** (*adverbs* **clearly**, **loud and clear**) ∘ *a very clear voice* ∘ *We can hear you loud and clear.*
- if a noise is so loud that you cannot hear anything else, you are **deafened** (**by** it); very loud: **deafening** ∘ *Standing beside the road, we were deafened by the noise of the traffic.* ∘ *The music was deafening. I couldn't hear myself speak.*

▷ more on sounds ⇨ **SOUND**

■ unable to hear well
- unable to hear anything or to hear well: **deaf**; *noun* (U): **deafness** ∘ *a deaf old man* ∘ *My*

mother is very deaf. ○ *His deafness can cause problems on the telephone.*
- completely unable to hear: (*informal*) **stone-deaf**, (*formal*) **profoundly deaf**
- to become less able to hear well: **go* deaf** ○ *I think I must be going deaf.*
- deaf people: **the deaf** ○ *a school for the deaf*

- a device that helps deaf people to hear: **hearing aid** ○ *to wear a hearing aid*
- to understand what a person is saying by looking at the movements of their lips: **lip-read***; *noun* (U): **lip-reading** ○ *He lip-reads perfectly.* ○ *I'm not much good at lip-reading.*
- a way of communicating with hand movements: **sign language** (*noun* C/U); to communicate using signs: **sign** ○ *The teacher speaks and signs at the same time.*
- the words at the bottom of a cinema or television screen, showing the words that are being spoken: **subtitles** ○ *She can't hear what they say but she can read the subtitles.*

---

heart

the red liquid that moves through your body ⇨ BLOOD
other parts of the body ⇨ BODY

- the organ inside your chest that sends blood round the body: **heart**
- the regular movement of the heart: **heartbeat**; *verb*: **beat*** ○ *a regular heartbeat* ○ *Her heart beat faster as she ran towards him.*
- if your heart beats strongly, it **thumps, throbs** ○ *His heart was thumping with excitement.*

- if your heart is not strong and does not work well, it is **weak** ○ *She has a weak heart and can't do very much.*
- illness of the heart: **heart disease** (*noun* C/U), **heart condition**
- a sudden illness when the heart stops working correctly: **heart attack** ○ *He died of a heart attack.*

- an operation in which the heart is taken from one person's body and put into another's: **heart transplant**

---

heat ⇨ HOT

---

heaven ⇨ RELIGION

---

heavy ⇨ WEIGHT

---

height

1 people
2 things
3 places and positions
see also SIZE, DEEP

1 people
- a person who is of more than average height is **tall**; *opposite*: **short** ○ *She is very tall for her age.* ○ *He is shorter than most of his friends.*

- how tall or short sb is: **height** (*noun* C/U) ○ *He was of medium height.*
- having a particular height: **tall** ○ *'How tall are you?' 'About one and a half metres.'* ○ *When I was fifteen, I was already six feet tall.*

- (in children's stories) a person of human shape who is very big and tall: **giant**

2 things
- measuring a lot from bottom to top: **high, tall**; *opposite*: **low** ○ *a high mountain* ○ *a tall/low building* ○ *a forest of tall eucalyptus trees*

Note: tall means almost the same as **high**; it is normally used to describe people, trees, and buildings.

- the measurement of sth from the bottom to the top: **height** (*noun* C/U) ○ *The architects were told to reduce the height of the building.* ○ *These trees can reach a height of over 30 metres.*
- having a particular height: **high, tall** ○ *This mountain is 4000 metres high.* ○ *The statue will be ten feet tall.*

3 places and positions
- a long way above the ground: **high** (*adjective, adverb*); *opposite*: **low** (*adjective, adverb*) ○ *a room with a high ceiling* ○ *Put medicines on a high shelf so that children can't reach them.* ○ *I think that picture is rather low down.* ○ *low-flying aircraft*
- the distance that sth is from the ground: **height** (*noun* C/U) ○ *We are flying at a height of 3000 metres.*

- the height or position of sth in relation to sth else: **level** ○ *What's the level of the water at high tide?* ○ *at ground level*
- the scientific name for the height of sth from the ground or sea level: **altitude** ○ *We will be flying at an altitude of 12000 metres.*

- the highest level or part of sth: **top** ○ *We climbed to the top of the mountain.* ○ *the top of a building*

▷ being in a higher position ⇨ PLACE[2]

■ changing the height or position of something
- if a movement is from a high level or position to a lower level or position, it is **down, downwards**; *adjective*: **downward** ○ *The lift is on its way down.* ○ *a downward movement*
- to bring sth from a high position to a lower position: **lower** sth, **put*/bring*/move** sth **down** ○ *We lowered the shelves because they were too high.* ○ *Try moving that picture down a bit.*

- if a movement is from a low level or position to a higher level or position, it is **up, upwards**; *adjective*: **upward** ○ *The path goes up to the castle.* ○ *an upward movement*
- to bring sth from a low position to a higher position: **raise** sth, **put*/bring*/move** sth **up** ○ *to raise a flag* ○ *Put up your hand if you need some help.*

helicopter ⇨ PLANE

help

1 giving help
2 ways of helping people
3 needing help

1 giving help

– to do sth for sb in order to make their work or their life easier: **help** (sb) (do sth/**to** do sth), (*informal*) **give*/lend*** sb **a hand** (**with** sth), (*formal*) **assist** (sb) (**in/with** sth); *nouns* (U): **help, assistance** ◦ *Can I help?* ◦ *I helped her off the train/across the road/out of the car.* ◦ *Can you give me a hand with my homework?* ◦ *The man is assisting the police with their enquiries.* ◦ *Do you need any help?* ◦ *The policeman thanked him for his assistance.*

– giving help: **helpful, useful, a help** (**to** sb) ◦ *helpful information* ◦ *useful advice* ◦ *You've been a great help.*
– not giving much help: **unhelpful, not much help, not a lot of help** ◦ *an unhelpful suggestion* ◦ *The map you gave me wasn't much help – I got lost three times.*
– not giving any help at all: **useless** ◦ *A blunt knife is useless.* ◦ *useless advice*

– something that helps sb or is useful to sb **does*** them **good** ◦ *Please take this medicine; it'll do you good.* ◦ *It'll do you good to get out into the country for a bit.*
– if you do sth or give sth to sb to help them, you do it **for** their **good** ◦ *I know you don't want to go into hospital, but it's for your own good.* ◦ *The Prime Minister said he resigned for the good of the country.*

– a person who helps: **helper** ◦ *We need some extra helpers if we're going to get all these sandwiches made in time for lunch!*
– a person who helps people in their job: **assistant**; *adjective* (*only before a noun*): **assistant** ◦ *Let me introduce my assistant, David.* ◦ *an assistant manager*

– a person who is willing to help is **helpful, cooperative**; *opposites*: **unhelpful, uncooperative** ◦ *The staff are very helpful.* ◦ *The police were completely unhelpful.* ◦ *His secretary was uncooperative, and she refused to let me see him.*
– a person who thinks about what sb needs or wants is **thoughtful**; *opposite*: **thoughtless** ◦ *I'm sorry. It was very thoughtless of me.*
– if you say or show that you will help sb/sth, you **offer** sth/**to** do sth; *noun*: **offer** ◦ *to offer assistance* ◦ *Nigel offered to give me a lift to the station.* ◦ *Helen accepted his offer of help.*

– to make a special effort to help sb: **go* out of** your **way** (**to** do sth), (*informal*) **bend* over backwards** (**to** do sth) ◦ *The hotel staff bent over backwards to make our stay as comfortable as possible.*
– to do sth for sb, even though it causes you a lot of work or trouble: **take* the trouble to** do sth ◦ *She took the trouble to write letters to everyone to thank them.*
– to do sth helpful for sb: **do*** sth **for** sb, **do*** sb **a favour, do*** sb **a good turn** ◦ *John, can you do me a favour? I need to borrow some money.*
– if you do sth to help sb, you do it **for** sb's **sake** ◦ *We moved to the country for my son's sake.*
– when you give sth to sb who has helped you, you **repay*** sb (**for** sth) ◦ *How can we ever repay you for your kindness?*

2 ways of helping people

■ helping sb to do sth
– to work with sb else to do sth: **cooperate with** sb, **collaborate with** sb; *nouns* (U): **cooperation, collaboration** ◦ *Couldn't we cooperate on this project to save time and money?* ◦ *to work in collaboration with sb*

– to help sb to know the right way to do sth: **show** sb sth ◦ *Can you show me how to wire this plug?*
– to show sb the way to a place: **lead*** sb, **guide** sb, **lead* the way** ◦ *She led them through a maze of narrow streets.* ◦ *He guided us to our seats.* ◦ *Sam led the way and the rest of us followed.*
– to explain to sb how to get to a place: **direct** sb, **give*** sb **directions** ◦ *Could you direct me to the bus station, please?*
– to tell sb what you think they should do: **advise** sb (**to** do sth); *noun* (U): **advice** ◦ *Her doctor advised her to give up smoking.* ◦ *legal advice*

■ helping sb when they are poor, ill, weak, etc
– to give sb help, money, friendship, etc when they need it: **support** sb; *noun* (U): **support**; giving sb support: **supportive** ◦ *I'll always be there to support you.* ◦ *I don't know what I would have done if you hadn't been there to give me support.*
– to give sb hope and support to do sth: **encourage** sb (**to** do sth); *noun* (C/U): **encouragement** ◦ *He gave me encouragement to apply for the job.*
– to help sb who is in a difficult position: **help** (sb) **out**

▷ more on support and encouragement ⇨ SUPPORT, ENCOURAGE

– to help and watch over sb who is ill or weak: **take* care of** sb, **look after** sb ◦ *John's being taken good care of in hospital.* ◦ *Kevin had to look after the children while his wife was in hospital.*
– to try to make sb feel less sad or less worried about sth: **comfort** sb; a person or a thing that comforts: **comfort** ◦ *Her father was always there to comfort her.* ◦ *The good news was a great comfort to him.*

– an organization that sends money, food, clothes, etc to a country or people to help them: **charity**
– money, food, etc that is sent to a country or people in order to help them: **aid** (*noun* U), **relief** (*noun* U) ◦ *medical aid* ◦ *disaster relief for the flood victims*

▷ helping sb when they are in danger ⇨ DANGER
▷ helping to make sb/sth safe ⇨ SAFE

3 needing help

- to ask sb to help you: **ask** sb **for help, ask** sb **a favour, ask a favour of** sb ◦ *Can I ask you a favour?*
- to go to sb to ask them for help, advice, etc: **go*** **to** sb (**for** sth), **turn to** sb (**for** sth) ◦ *Frank went to the police for help.* ◦ *She had nobody to turn to when her husband left her.*

- if you are in a very bad situation and need help from sb else, you are **helpless**; *noun* (U): **helplessness** ◦ *We were helpless against the enemy attack.* ◦ *a helpless baby*
- if you need sb/sth to support or help you, you **depend on** sb/sth, you are **dependent** (**on** sb/sth); *noun* (U): **dependence** (**on** sb/sth) ◦ *He's blind and completely dependent on his dog to guide him round town.*
- if you are not supported very well, you are **insecure**; *noun* (U): **insecurity** ◦ *The future of the company looks very insecure.* ◦ *feelings of insecurity*

■ not needing help
- if you can do things yourself and do not want or need help, you are **independent, self-reliant**; *nouns* (U): **independence, self-reliance** ◦ *Mary wanted to be independent, so she left home and went to live in London.*
- to take care of yourself without help: **stand* on** your **own** (**two**) **feet** ◦ *You're always asking for money from your parents: it's about time you learned to stand on your own two feet!*
- if you do sth without any other person to help you, you do it **on** your **own,** (**all**) **by** yourself ◦ *She decorated the house on her own.* ◦ *My nephew painted this picture all by himself.*
- if you decide to do sth without help from another person, you (*informal*) **go* it alone** ◦ *After all his friends refused to help him, Hanif decided to go it alone.*

hen ⇨ BIRD²

herb ⇨ COOK

hide

hiding information, your feelings, etc ⇨ SECRET
see also FIND, LOOK FOR

- to put sth in a place where nobody else can find or see it: **hide*** sth ◦ *What are you hiding behind your back?* ◦ *I can't remember where I hid my keys!*
- to put sth into the ground and cover it up with earth so that nobody can see or find it: **bury** sth ◦ *The dog buried a bone in the garden.*
- a place which is suitable for hiding sth or yourself: **hiding place**

- to put sth on or in front of sth in order to hide it: **cover** sth (**up/over**) (**with** sth) ◦ *He covered the child over with a blanket.* ◦ *to cover yourself up with a towel*
- something that you wear to cover your face or part of your face: **mask**; to hide your face with a mask: **mask** sth ◦ *a masked gunman*
- clothes, false hair, etc that you wear so that nobody recognizes you: **disguise** (*noun* C/U); to change the appearance, sound, etc of sb/sth so that people cannot recognize them/it: **disguise** sb/sth (**as** sb/sth) ◦ *to wear a disguise* ◦ *to be in disguise* ◦ *I tried to disguise my voice.* ◦ *She was disguised as a policewoman.*

- to allow sth to be seen that was previously hidden: **reveal** sth (**to** sb) ◦ *She opened the curtains to reveal a beautifully sunny day.*

■ hiding yourself
- to put yourself in a place where you think people will not find you: **hide*** ◦ *Quick! Hide under the bed!*
- to be in a place or go to a place where you think you will not be found for a long period of time: **be in hiding, go* into hiding** ◦ *Some of those who refused to fight went into hiding in the forests.*

- to wait where you cannot be seen by sb who you intend to attack: **lie* in wait** (**for** sb)
- a surprise attack from a hidden position: **ambush**; to carry out an ambush on sb/sth: **ambush** sb/sth
- to wait where you cannot be seen, especially when you are intending to do sth bad: **lurk** ◦ *I thought I saw somebody lurking in the doorway.*
- to go somewhere very quietly, so that no one will see or hear you: **sneak** ◦ *We managed to sneak into the theatre unseen.*

■ to stop hiding yourself
- to stop hiding: **come* out** (**of/from** a place), **come* out of hiding** ◦ *'Here I am,' she said, and came out from behind a tree.* ◦ *When the fighting was over, the villagers came out of hiding.*

■ **MORE ...**
- a way of disguising soldiers or their equipment so that they are difficult to see: **camouflage** (*noun* U); verb: **camouflage** sb/sth ◦ *The soldiers camouflaged their truck with earth and leaves.*

- to move sb/sth from one place to another in secret: **smuggle** sb/sth (**into/out of** a place) ◦ *to smuggle drugs into a country*

high ⇨ HEIGHT

hill/mountain

1 hills and mountains
2 volcanoes
3 groups of hills and mountains
see also CLIMB, COUNTRY², LAND

1 hills and mountains
- an area of high land that is not as high as a mountain (often with grass or trees growing on the sides and top): **hill**
- an area where there are a lot of hills is **hilly**
- hilly areas in general: **the hills** (*noun plural*) ◦ *We like to spend our weekends walking in the hills.*
- the side of a hill: **hillside** ◦ *a thickly wooded hillside*

hill / mountain *contd.*

- the top of a hill: **top, hilltop** ◦ *It took us an hour to get to the top.* ◦ *a hilltop restaurant*
- the bottom of a hill or mountain: **bottom** ◦ *We picnicked near the bottom of the hill.*

- a very high hill (usually rocky, often with snow on the top): **mountain**
- an area where there are lots of mountains is **mountainous**
- mountainous areas in general: **the mountains** (*noun plural*) ◦ *Do you prefer the mountains or the sea?*
- a very high point on a mountain: **peak** ◦ *We couldn't see the peak because it was hidden in cloud.*
- the highest point on a mountain: **top, mountain top, summit**
- the steep side of a mountain: **mountainside**

Note: the names of some mountains can have **Mount** (*abbreviation* **Mt**) before them. You can say *Everest* or *Mount Everest*.

■ height and steepness
- a very big hill or mountain is **high, tall;** *noun* (C/U): **height** ◦ *What is the height of Mt Kilimanjaro?*
- the height of hills and mountains is measured in **metres** or (especially in Britain and America) **feet** ◦ *There are no mountains over 5000 feet in Britain.*

- a piece of land that goes up or down: **slope** ◦ *a grassy slope*
- a slope which goes up fast is **steep** (*adverb* **steeply**) ◦ *The path rises steeply through the forest.*
- a very steep slope on the side of a mountain: **precipice**
- a slope that is not steep is **gentle** (*adverb* **gently**) ◦ *a gentle slope*
- to go up or down (steeply or gently): **slope** ◦ *The garden slopes down the side of the hill.*
- the measurement of how steep a slope is: **steepness** (*noun* U), (*formal*) **gradient** ◦ *a gradient of 1 in 5 (= 20%)*

2 volcanoes
- a mountain with a hole in the top through which fire sometimes comes out: **volcano** (*plural* **volcanoes**); *adjective*: **volcanic**
- the hole in the top of a volcano: **crater**
- when a volcano explodes and throws out burning rocks, etc, it **erupts;** *noun*: **eruption** ◦ *It hasn't erupted for hundreds of years.* ◦ *The eruption caused widespread damage and sent a black cloud of ash high into the atmosphere.*
- the burning rocks, etc that come out of a volcano when it erupts: **lava** (*noun* U)

- a volcano that sometimes erupts is **active**
- a volcano that has not erupted for a long time is **dormant**
- a volcano that never erupts is **extinct**

3 groups of hills and mountains
- a group of hills or mountains in one area: **range** ◦ *a range of hills* ◦ *a mountain range*
- a space between hills or mountains, often with a river running down it: **valley** ◦ *We walked a little further up the valley.*

- an area of hills and high land: **highlands** (*noun plural*); *adjective*: **highland** ◦ *highland streams*
- an area of low country with no large hills: **lowlands** (*noun plural*); *adjective*: **lowland** ◦ *lowland farms*
- the hills that are found near a range of high mountains: **foothills** (*noun plural*) ◦ *We went walking in the foothills of the Himalayas.*

■ MORE ...
- a space between two mountains where people can go through on a road or path: **pass** ◦ *a high mountain pass*
- the narrow edge along the top of a hill or mountain: **ridge** ◦ *The path follows the ridge for half a mile.*

- a river of ice that moves slowly down a valley between high mountains: **glacier**
- a large amount of snow and rock that slides suddenly down the side of a mountain: **avalanche**

- a machine that carries people up and down a mountain in a carriage hanging from a moving cable: **cable car**

Hindu ⇨ RELIGION

hire ⇨ RENT

history

1 belonging to the past
2 the study of the past
3 periods and dates in history

the past ⇨ PAST[2]
old things ⇨ NEW / OLD

1 belonging to the past
- events of the past when you are thinking of them as a whole: **history** (*noun* U); *adjective*: **historical** (*adverb* **historically**) ◦ *Scottish history* ◦ *the history of England* ◦ *a museum of local history* ◦ *the historical facts* ◦ *a place which is of great importance historically*

- the time before history was written down: **prehistory** (*noun* U); *adjective*: **prehistoric** ◦ *European prehistory* ◦ *a prehistoric painting/animal*

2 the study of the past
- the study of past events and social, political and economic developments: **history** (*noun* U) ◦ *I studied history at university.* ◦ *a history professor*
- a person who studies history: **historian**
- a book written about a historical topic: **history** ◦ *a history of the French Revolution*

- the study of ancient civilizations based on objects or parts of buildings that are found in the ground: **archaeology** (*AmE* **archeology**); connected with archaeology: **archaeological** (*AmE* **archeological**) ◦ *an archaeological dig*
- an expert in archaeology: **archaeologist** (*AmE* **archeologist**)

3 periods and dates in history

- the time before the present; the things that happened in that time: **the past**
- a portion of time in the life of a person or nation: **period** ◦ *the Tudor period* ◦ *the early period of Soviet rule in Russia*
- a period in the past (often connected with sb or sth): **time, day** ◦ *In Shakespeare's time, all the actors were men.* ◦ *In my grandmother's day, women wore long dresses.*
- a particular period of history: **age** ◦ *the ice age* ◦ *Stone Age man* ◦ *We live in the modern age.*
- a period of time in history that is special for some reason: **era** ◦ *the postwar era*

- belonging to times long past: **ancient** ◦ *ancient history* ◦ *the ancient world*
- belonging to the Middle Ages in European history (= between about 1100 and 1500): **medieval** ◦ *medieval art* ◦ *during the medieval period*
- of the present or recent period: **modern** ◦ *modern history*

- a particular period of 100 years that is used for giving dates: **century** ◦ *during the thirteenth century* (= from 1200 to 1299) ◦ *We are living in the twentieth century.*
- the period before Christ: **BC**; the period after Christ: **AD** ◦ *The Buddha is thought to have died in 483 BC.*

- to have existed since a particular time: **date back to ..., date from ...** ◦ *This vase dates back to the Roman period.*
- to discover how old sth is: **date** sth ◦ *They are trying to date the fossils that they have just found.*

■ **MORE ...**

- the traditions, qualities and cultural achievements of a country that have existed for a long time and have great importance for the country: **heritage** (*noun* U) ◦ *We should preserve our national heritage.* ◦ *Old buildings are part of our cultural heritage.*

- a collection of historical documents which record the history of a place or an organization: **archives** (*noun plural*), **archive** ◦ *He carried out his research in the library's archives.* ◦ *archive material*

---

hit

1 hitting on purpose
2 hitting by accident
see also PUNISH

1 hitting on purpose

- to touch sb/sth with a lot of force: **hit*** sb/sth, (*formal*) **strike*** sb/sth ◦ *I hit him on the arm with my umbrella and he ran away.* ◦ *to hit a ball with a bat* ◦ *Tell the court how often you saw him strike the child.*
- an act of hitting sb with your hand, a weapon, etc: **blow** ◦ *to aim a blow at sb* ◦ *He was killed by a blow to the head.*
- an act of hitting sb/sth, especially in sport: **hit** ◦ *What a hit!* (= in cricket, baseball, etc)

■ hitting with your hand

- to hit sb/sth hard with your fist (= your closed hand): **punch** sb/sth; an act of punching: **punch** ◦ *to give sb a punch on the nose*
- to hit sb (usually with your fist) so that they become unconscious and cannot get up again for a while: **knock** sb **out**
- to hit sb with the inside of your hand: **slap** sb, **give*** sb **a slap** ◦ *She slapped his face/gave him a slap on the face.*
- to slap a child: **smack** sb, **give*** sb **a smack** ◦ *Were you ever smacked as a child?*

■ hitting with your foot

- to hit sb/sth with your foot: **kick** sb/sth; an act of kicking: **kick** ◦ *to kick a ball* ◦ *He got a kick on the shin.*
- to kick sb/sth very hard: **boot** sb/sth ◦ *The goalkeeper booted the ball back down the field.*

■ hitting with your head

- to hit the ball with your head in football: **head** the ball ◦ *He headed the ball into the back of the net.*
- to hit sb/sth with the head: **butt** sb/sth ◦ *The goat tried to butt me in the stomach.*

■ hitting repeatedly

- to hit sb/sth many times, usually very hard: **beat*** sb/sth ◦ *to beat a drum* ◦ *to beat sb to death*
- to hit sb/sth with your fist (= your closed hand) or a heavy object: **thump** sb/sth; the noise or action of thumping: **thump**
- to attack sb by repeatedly hitting or kicking them: **beat*** sb **up** ◦ *He was beaten up by members of a rival gang.*
- to hit sb/sth hard many times: **batter** sb/sth ◦ *They are accused of battering their baby daughter.*
- to touch or hit sb/sth quickly and gently: **tap** sb/sth, **tap** (**on/at** sth); an act of tapping: **tap** ◦ *Somebody was tapping on the window.* ◦ *I felt a light tap on my shoulder.*
- to touch or hit sth quickly and gently with your fingers or feet: **tap** your fingers or feet (**on** sth) ◦ *You could see she was nervous by the way she was tapping her fingers on the table.* ◦ *We were all tapping our feet to the music.*

■ hitting and making a noise

- to make a loud noise by hitting sth hard: **bang** (sth); a sound of sth being banged: **bang** ◦ *to bang a drum* ◦ *I was woken up by someone banging on the door.* ◦ *The balloon burst with a bang.*
- to make a noise by hitting sth: **knock**; the noise or action of knocking: **knock** ◦ *Knock before you enter.* ◦ *I heard a knock at the door.*

hit *contd.*

2 hitting by accident

- to touch sb/sth quite hard by accident: **hit*** sb/sth ◦ *She was hit on the head by a falling branch.* ◦ *The car only just managed to avoid hitting a lorry.*
- to hit sb/sth by accident (especially when moving in a careless manner): **bump into/against** sb/sth, **knock into/against** sb/sth, **collide** (**with** sb/sth) ◦ *She wasn't looking where she was going and bumped into a lamp post.* ◦ *I ran round the corner and collided with Frances who was coming in the opposite direction.*
- to bump into/against sth and make a loud noise: **bang** (**into/against** sth), **crash into/against** sth; the act or sound of banging or crashing: **bang, crash** ◦ *He banged into the table in the dark.*

- when part of your body touches sth by accident, you **hit*/bump/knock/bang** it (**on/against** sth) ◦ *The ceiling's very low, so please be careful not to knock your head against it when you get up.*
- a lump on the body caused by bumping into sth: **bump** ◦ *a bump on the head*

- to hit sth against or on sth by accident when you are moving it: **bump** sth (**against/on** sth) ◦ *When you move the tables, please be careful not to bump them against the walls.*
- to hit sb/sth when you are walking, running or driving and cause them to fall over: **knock** sb/sth **over** ◦ *Why don't you watch where you are going? You nearly knocked me over!*

- an accident when a car or other vehicle hits sth and is damaged: **crash, collision**; *verb*: **crash** (**into** sb/sth), **collide** (**with** sb/sth) ◦ *a car/plane/train crash* ◦ *I knew we were going to crash.* ◦ *The bus collided with a lorry.*

▷ more on crashes ⇨ ACCIDENT

hold/catch

1 holding
2 taking hold
3 letting go
holding sb in a friendly or loving way ⇨ LOVE

1 holding

- to keep sth in your hand, or to keep sth in a certain position: **hold*** sth; the act of holding sth: **hold** ◦ *He was holding a gun in his hand.* ◦ *Hold the camera very still.* ◦ *Her hair was held in place by a hair slide.*
- to continue to hold sth: **hold* on** (**to** sth) ◦ *I can't hold on much longer!* ◦ *Hold on to the rope very tightly – don't let go.*
- to hold sth and move with it: **carry** sth ◦ *Shall I carry your bags for you?*

▷ more on carrying sth ⇨ BRING/TAKE/CARRY

- to hold sb on the ground: **hold*** sb **down** ◦ *They held him down until the police arrived.*
- to hold sth above your head: **hold*** sth **up** ◦ *Can you hold the picture up so that everyone can see it?*
- to hold sth so that it does not fall down: **hold*** sth **up** ◦ *He used a piece of string to hold his trousers up.*
- to hold sb/sth in order to stop them/it from falling or breaking: **support** sb/sth ◦ *The bridge is supported by two main towers.*

- to hold sth very tightly with your hand: **clasp** sth ◦ *She clasped the child's hand.*
- to hold sth tightly, especially because you are afraid or excited: **clutch** sth ◦ *She ran towards me, clutching her new doll.*
- to hold sth very firmly: **grip** sth, **cling* on** (**to**) sth, **hang* on to** sth; a firm hold: **grip** ◦ *He gripped my arm.* ◦ *He held her in a tight grip, so that she could not run away.*
- to hold on to a person or thing so that you do not fall: **cling*** (**on**) **to** sb/sth, **hang* on to** sb/sth ◦ *The terrified child clung on to his mother's arm.* ◦ *The rescue workers found the man still clinging to the rock face.*

- to hold sth in your hand and press it hard: **squeeze** sth; *noun*: **squeeze** ◦ *to squeeze water out of a cloth* ◦ *She gave my hand a squeeze.*
- to hold things together very tightly, especially using a special tool: **clamp** sth; a tool for doing this: **clamp**

▷ picture at TOOL

2 taking hold

- to put your hand round sth and hold it (and move it towards you): **take*** sth ◦ *He took the money and put it in his pocket.* ◦ *Can you take this bag for a moment?*
- to stretch out your arm to try and get sth: **reach** (**out**) **for** sth ◦ *He reached for another chocolate, but the box was empty!*
- to take sth (from sb) in an aggressive way: **grab** (sth), **snatch** (sth) ◦ *Don't grab! Just wait your turn.* ◦ *The little girl snatched the toy from her brother.*
- to take sb/sth in your hands: **take* hold of** sb/sth

- to take hold of sth that is moving, usually with your hands: **catch*** sth; an act of catching sth, usually a ball: **catch** ◦ *She threw the ball and I caught it.* ◦ *to make a catch*
- to fail to catch sth: **miss** sth; *noun*: **miss** ◦ *He tried to catch the ball, but missed.* ◦ *After three misses, I finally managed to catch the ball.*

■ catching a person

- to get hold of sb/sth that you have been looking for: **catch*** sb/sth ◦ *The police have caught the man they were looking for.*
- to catch sb and keep him/her so that they cannot escape: **capture** sb; *noun* (U): **capture** ◦ *The escaped prisoners were soon captured.*
- a person who has been captured: **prisoner**
- a place where prisoners are kept: **prison**

▷ more on prisoners and prison ⇨ PRISON

■ catching an animal
- to get hold of an animal, fish, bird, etc: **catch*** sth ◦ *to catch a bird in a net* ◦ *I caught a rabbit.*
- to look for and follow wild animals in order to catch or kill them either for food or for sport: **hunt** (sth); *noun* (U): **hunting**; a person who hunts animals: **hunter**

▷ more on hunting ⇨ **HUNT**

▷ catching fish ⇨ **FISH**[1]

■ trying to catch sb/sth
- to try to move faster than a person or thing that is in front of you in order to catch them/it: **chase** (**after**) sb/sth, **go*/come*/run* after** sb/sth, (*formal*) **pursue** sb/sth ◦ *That dog was chasing our cat.* ◦ *She threw a piece of wood into the sea and the dog went after it.* ◦ *Quick! They're coming after us!* ◦ *I ran after her, but she disappeared into the crowd.*
- to be chasing sb/sth: **be after** sb/sth ◦ *They're after you! Run!*
- the act of chasing sb/sth: **chase** ◦ *a car chase* ◦ *a police chase*
- a person who chases sb/sth: **pursuer**

- to get nearer to a person or thing that you are chasing: **gain on** sb/sth ◦ *Drive faster, they're gaining on us.*
- to reach a person or thing that is in front of you: **catch* up** (**with** sb/sth), **catch*** sb/sth **up** ◦ *I eventually managed to catch up with the rest of the group.*

3 letting go
- to stop holding sb/sth: **let*** sb/sth **go**, **let* go** (**of** sb/sth), (*formal*) **release** sb/sth ◦ *You can let go of the rope now.* ◦ *Hundreds of balloons were released and floated up to the ceiling.* ◦ *Don't let go, whatever you do!*
- to allow sth to fall: **drop** sth ◦ *Drop everything and run!*
- to hold sth less tightly: **relax** your **hold**

- to leave a place or a situation that you do not want to be in: **escape** (**from** sth), **get* away** (**from** sth) ◦ *How did the prisoners escape?*

▷ more on escaping ⇨ **ESCAPE**

hole

1 an empty space in sth solid
2 an opening through sth

1 an empty space in sth solid
- an empty space in sth solid: **hole** ◦ *Rabbits live in holes.* ◦ *a hole in the ground/road* ◦ *a deep hole* ◦ *to put sth in/down a hole*
- a large hole that is made in the ground: **pit** ◦ *They dug a big pit to bury the rubbish.*
- a rough hole in a road: **pothole**

- to make a hole in the ground: **dig*** sth ◦ *to dig a hole in the ground* ◦ *to dig a tunnel*
- to put the earth back inside a hole: **fill** sth (**up**/**in**) ◦ *to fill a hole with earth* ◦ *We filled in the hole in the wall with stones and cement.*
- to put sth in a hole in the ground to cover it up: **bury** sth ◦ *The dog buried its bone in the back garden.*

- if sth has an empty space (like a hole) inside, it is **hollow**; *opposite*: **solid** ◦ *a hollow tree/wall/bone*
- to take the inside part of sth out in order to make sth else: **hollow** sth **out** ◦ *to hollow out a tree to make a boat*

- a hollow place on a hard surface: **dent** ◦ *There's a dent in the car door where the other car hit it.*
- to make a dent in sth: **dent** sth

2 an opening through sth
- an opening through sth: **hole** ◦ *a hole in the fence* ◦ *a hole in a jumper/pocket/bucket* ◦ *Push the wire through the hole.* ◦ *a bullet hole* ◦ *a buttonhole* ◦ *a keyhole* ◦ *There was a gaping hole* (= a very big hole) *in the roof where the bomb had fallen.*

- an empty space in sth or between two things: **gap** ◦ *She looked through a gap in the curtains.* ◦ *a ten-inch gap*
- a very narrow opening: **crack** ◦ *He could just see them through a crack in the wall.* ◦ *The door was open just a crack.*

- a small hole or crack through which liquid or gas can escape: **leak** ◦ *There's water dripping out of the bucket – there must be a leak somewhere.*
- (used about liquid or gas) to be released in this way: **leak** ◦ *Water was leaking through a hole in the roof.*

- a small hole in a bicycle or car tyre: **puncture** ◦ *I can't ride my bike, it's got a puncture.* ◦ *to mend a puncture*
- to make a small hole in sth with air inside: **puncture** sth ◦ *to puncture a tyre/balloon/football*
- to make a hole in sth with a sharp point: **pierce** sth ◦ *Pierce the top of the tin.*

- a tool used for making small holes (for example in a wall or a piece of wood): **drill**
- to make a small hole in sth, using a drill: **drill** sth ◦ *They drilled some holes in the wall to put up the shelves.*

▷ picture at **TOOL**

- to fill a hole with sth: **plug/block** sth (**up**), **stop** sth **up**; *opposites*: **unplug** sth, **unblock** sth ◦ *The holes were securely plugged so that the water could not escape.*

■ **MORE ...**
- a small opening in a wall, rock, etc: **cranny** ◦ *He hid something in a small cranny in the wall.*
- a very small narrow opening: **chink**

holiday

1 time when people do not work
2 special days and times which are holidays
3 going away on holiday
see also TRAVEL

holiday *contd.*

1 time when people do not work

- a period of time when people do not work, and when they may go away, rest, have fun, etc: **holiday** (*often plural*), (*especially AmE*) **vacation** (*noun* C/U), (*formal*) **leave** (*noun* U) ◦ *the school holidays* ◦ *Are you taking any holiday this summer?* ◦ *Jim's in the army but he'll be home on leave soon.*
- a day of rest from school or work: **holiday, day off** ◦ *I'm not going to work today – it's my day off.*
- a short period of time when you do not work: **break**, time **off** ◦ *I'm taking a short break and going to my sister's for a few days.* ◦ *You look exhausted – you should take a few days off and relax.*

- when you are not working, you are **on holiday, off** ◦ *I can't come I'm afraid – I'm on holiday that week.* ◦ *I'm off next Friday.*

2 special days and times which are holidays

- Saturday and Sunday: **weekend**
- a weekend with a Monday or a Friday or both as a holiday: **long weekend** ◦ *We're having a long weekend at the seaside.*

- a day which is a holiday for most people in a country: **public holiday**
- (in Britain) a day when the banks close and which is usually a holiday for most people in the country: **bank holiday** ◦ *Bank Holiday Monday* ◦ *the August Bank Holiday*

- January 1: **New Year's Day**
- May 1: **May Day** (celebrated in Britain on the first Monday in May)
- July 4 (in the United States): **Independence Day**
- the fourth Tuesday in November (in the United States) or the second Monday in October (in Canada): **Thanksgiving**
- December 25: **Christmas Day**

- the period when people celebrate Christmas: **Christmas holiday(s)**
- the period when people celebrate Easter: **Easter holiday(s)**
- the period over the summer when people are on holiday: **summer holiday(s)** ◦ *We usually go away during the summer holidays.*
- a short holiday that some schools have, in the middle of a term: (*BrE*) **half-term (holiday)**

3 going away on holiday

- a time when you travel away from home to relax: **holiday** (*often plural*) (*AmE* **vacation**) ◦ *Have a nice holiday!* ◦ *Where are you spending your holidays?*
- to leave your home and go somewhere else for a holiday: **go* (away) on holiday, go* away** ◦ *They're going on holiday to Greece this year.* ◦ *We're only going away for a few days.*
- a holiday for two people who have just got married: **honeymoon** ◦ *They're on their honeymoon.*

- the place or shop where you can choose and book a holiday: **travel agent's, travel agency**
- a magazine that advertises holidays which you can buy: **(holiday) brochure**
- to reserve and pay for a holiday before you go: **book** sth ◦ *We've booked two weeks in Austria in July.*

- a book that tells you everything you need to know about going on holiday somewhere: **travel guide, guide book**
- a book that tells you how to say things in another language: **phrase book**

- a place where a lot of people go on holiday: **resort** ◦ *a skiing/seaside resort*
- a place where you pay to stay and sometimes have your meals: **hotel**
- a place that provides accommodation and entertainment for people on holiday: **holiday camp**

▷ more on staying in hotels ⇨ **HOTEL**

■ ways of taking your holiday

- a special holiday where you pay for your travel, hotel and some or all of your meals before you leave: **package holiday**
- a holiday on a large ship: **cruise** ◦ *to go on a round-the-world cruise*
- a holiday in Africa, looking at wild animals: **safari** ◦ *to go on safari*
- a journey when you visit a place and return: **trip** ◦ *a trip to the seaside*

- to travel around on holiday carrying your luggage in a bag on your back: **go* backpacking** ◦ *They went backpacking round Europe last summer.*
- to go on a holiday with a tent: **go* camping**
- a holiday that you spend doing sports or other outdoor activities: **adventure/activity holiday**
- a holiday that you spend walking or cycling: **walking/cycling holiday**
- a holiday that you spend travelling round a place, for example in a car or a bus: **touring holiday**
- a holiday when you do some work: **working holiday**

▷ more on camping ⇨ **CAMP**

■ **MORE ...**

- the time of year which is the most popular with tourists: **high season**; the time of year which is the least popular with tourists: **low season**

- something that you buy on holiday to remind you of a place: **souvenir** ◦ *Did you bring back any souvenirs?* ◦ *a souvenir of Rome*

holy ⇨ GOD, RELIGION

home ⇨ HOUSE

honest

good and bad behaviour ⇨ RIGHT/WRONG[2]

- if you say things that are true and you do not deceive people or steal, you are **honest**; *noun*

(U): **honesty** ◦ *an honest worker* ◦ *a reputation for honesty*
- what an honest person shows or does is **honest** ◦ *an honest face* ◦ *an honest opinion*

- if the things you say are true, you **tell* the truth**, you are **truthful** (*adverb* **truthfully**) ◦ *I'm telling you the truth, you must believe me.* ◦ *a truthful account of what happened*
- if you really mean or believe what you say, you are **sincere**; *noun* (U): **sincerity** ◦ *my sincere apologies* ◦ *to speak with complete sincerity*
- in a way which is true, not pretended: **really**, **truly**, **genuinely** ◦ *I think he genuinely felt sorry.*

- when sb wants a truthful opinion, they say **be honest**, **tell me honestly** ◦ *Be honest – do you really like this dress?*
- when sb gives a truthful opinion, they say **to be honest**, **in all honesty** ◦ *To be perfectly honest, I have never liked children.*
- when sb wants to emphasize a statement, they say **honestly** ◦ *Honestly, it really did happen like that!* ◦ *I honestly don't know where she is.*

- if you tell the truth about sth that you have been keeping secret, you **own up** (**to** sth), (*informal*) **come* clean** (**with** sb) (**about** sth) ◦ *Why not just own up? They're bound to find out sooner or later anyway.* ◦ *She eventually came clean with me about her police record.*

- willing to speak honestly: **open** (*adverb* **openly**), **straightforward**; *noun* (U): **openness** ◦ *She was quite open about her past.* ◦ *His manner was pleasant and straightforward.*
- saying exactly what you mean (even if it is unpleasant): **frank** (*adverb* **frankly**); *noun* (U): **frankness** ◦ *To be perfectly frank, I don't like that dress.* ◦ *a frank discussion*
- saying what you think, without embarrassment: **outspoken**
- saying exactly what you think (not very politely): **blunt** (*adverb* **bluntly**); *noun* (U): **bluntness** ◦ *He can be very blunt at times.*

▷ more on saying what is true ⇨ TRUE

- if you believe that a person is honest and reliable, you **trust** them; a person who can be trusted is **trustworthy** ◦ *I don't trust him - he lied to me before.*
- the quality that a person has if they are honest and live according to strict moral ideas: **integrity** (*noun* U) ◦ *a person of integrity*

▷ more on trusting people ⇨ TRUST

■ not honest
- the opposite of honest is **dishonest**; dishonest behaviour: **dishonesty** (*noun* U) ◦ *a dishonest salesman* ◦ *dishonest earnings*
- not meaning or believing what you say: **insincere**
- a person who does not tell the truth is **untruthful**, is a **liar**, **tells* lies** ◦ *a reputation for being untruthful* ◦ *a habitual liar*
- something that is not true is **untruthful**; if it is not completely untrue but gives a wrong idea, it is **misleading** ◦ *a misleading advertisement*

▷ more on telling lies ⇨ LIE[1]

- to make sb believe sth that is not true: **deceive** sb
- if sb deceives other people or is generally dishonest, they are **deceitful** ◦ *a deceitful child*
- behaviour that is intended to deceive sb is **deceitful** (*adverb* **deceitfully**) ◦ *He has acted very deceitfully.*

▷ more on deceiving sb ⇨ DECEIVE

- not honest, moral or legal: **corrupt**; this kind of behaviour, especially by people in official positions: **corruption** (*noun* U) ◦ *corrupt business practices* ◦ *corrupt officials who accept bribes* ◦ *police corruption*

---

hope

1 hope
2 things that you hope for
3 no hope

thinking about the future ⇨ FUTURE, INTEND / PLAN

see also SUCCEED / FAIL, WANT

1 hope

- to want sth to happen or be true: **hope for** sth, **hope to** do sth, **hope** (**that**) **. . .** ◦ *We are hoping for good weather.* ◦ *I hope to finish the work by tomorrow.* ◦ *I hope she didn't think I was rude.*
- the feeling of wanting sth to happen and thinking that it will: **hope** (*noun* U) ◦ *Don't lose hope!* ◦ *full of hope* ◦ *hope of success* ◦ *hopes for peace* ◦ *Is there any hope of finding a solution?* ◦ *There isn't much hope that they will be found alive.*
- if you think that sth you want to happen will happen, you are **hopeful** (*adverb* **hopefully**) ◦ *The doctors are very hopeful that she will recover.* ◦ *She waited hopefully for her exam results.*
- to hope that sb will do or give you what you want: **expect** sth (**from** sb), **expect** sb **to** do sth ◦ *I'm expecting a big effort from the whole team.* ◦ *Does he expect us to finish everything this morning?*

Note: hope expresses what you *want* to happen; **expect** mainly expresses what you *think will* happen. ◦ *I hope it's sunny at the weekend.* ◦ *The doctors do not expect the baby to live.*

- because you want sth to happen: **in the hope of** sth, **in the hope that . . .** ◦ *A lot of people turned up in the hope of seeing the film.* ◦ *I came in the hope that we could find a solution.*
- with the hope that sth might happen, although not very likely: **on the off chance** (**of** sth) ◦ *All these people have come on the off chance of seeing the band performing live.*
- to give people reason to hope that sth will happen: **hold* out . . . hope** (**of** sth) ◦ *The rescue team still held out some hope of finding survivors.* ◦ *The doctors don't hold out much hope of recovery.*

- making you think that sth good will happen: **hopeful** ◦ *a hopeful sign*
- if things happen as planned: **hopefully** ◦ *Hopefully, they'll come round to our point of view.*

hope *contd.*

■ wishes
- to say that you hope sb will have sth: **wish** sb sth ◦ *I wish you a pleasant journey.* ◦ *She rang me up to wish me a happy birthday.*
- to express a wish that sb will be successful, you say **good luck** ◦ *Good luck with your new job!*

2 things that you hope for
- a person or thing that gives you hope: **hope** ◦ *She is our best hope of winning a gold medal.*
- an event or situation that you want to happen but which is not likely: **dream** ◦ *His dream was to give up his job and live in the country.*
- hope for the future success of sb/sth: **hopes** (*noun plural*), **expectations** (*noun plural*) ◦ *They had great expectations for their eldest daughter, but she failed to live up to them.*
- signs that sb will do well in an activity: **promise** (*noun* U); *adjective*: **promising** ◦ *a singer of great promise* ◦ *a promising young lawyer*
- if the things that you hope for really happen, they **come* true** ◦ *My dream has come true!*
- if you are sad that sth was not as good as you had hoped, you are **disappointed** ◦ *We were disappointed with our hotel; it was very noisy.*
- something that is not as good as you had hoped is **disappointing** (*adverb* **disappointingly**), a **disappointment** ◦ *The response to our advert was disappointing.* ◦ *a disappointingly poor performance* ◦ *His new book is a big disappointment.*

3 no hope
- without hope: **hopeless** (*adverb* **hopelessly**); *noun* (U): **hopelessness** ◦ *The situation looked hopeless.* ◦ *a hopeless situation* ◦ *He wandered hopelessly round the house.* ◦ *a feeling of hopelessness*
- to stop being hopeful: **give* up hope** ◦ *You mustn't give up hope.*
- to lose all hope: **despair** (**of** sb/sth) ◦ *He despaired of ever finding a solution to their problems.*
- the state of having lost all hope: **despair** (*noun* U); in this state: **in despair**
- filled with despair and ready to do anything to change the situation: **desperate** (*adverb* **desperately**); *noun* (U): **desperation** ◦ *I took the money because I was desperate.* ◦ *desperately unhappy* ◦ *In desperation he went to a psychiatrist for help.*

■ **MORE . . .**
- to hope that sb/sth will be successful: **keep*** your **fingers crossed** ◦ *I'll keep my fingers crossed for you!*
- to express the hope that sb will be more successful in the future (after sb has failed in sth), you can say **better luck next time**

horse

1 different kinds of horse
2 parts of a horse and equipment for a horse
3 things that horses do
4 looking after a horse
5 riding a horse

see also ANIMAL

1 different kinds of horse
- a large animal that is used for riding on: **horse**
- a male horse: **stallion**
- a female horse: **mare**
- a young horse: **foal**
- a type of small horse: **pony**
- a horse used for racing: **racehorse**
- an animal like a small horse, with long ears: **donkey**
- an animal that has a donkey and a horse as parents: **mule**

2 parts of a horse and equipment for a horse
▷ picture at ANIMAL
- a set of leather straps which is used to fasten a horse to a cart or carriage: **harness**; to fasten a horse in this way: **harness** a horse (**to** sth)

3 things that horses do
- to move fairly quickly lifting the feet off the ground: **trot**; *noun*: **trot**
- to run at a steady speed: **canter**; *noun*: **canter** ◦ *to go for a quick canter round the field*
- to run at a fast speed: **gallop**; *noun*: **gallop** ◦ *He rode off at a gallop.*
- to run away very suddenly: **bolt** ◦ *The noise of the shotgun made the horses bolt.*
- to jump into the air with all four feet off the ground: **buck** ◦ *The horse bucked and I fell off.*

Note: trot, **canter** and **gallop** can be used about the rider as well as the horse: ◦ *Mary trotted to the end of the field.* ◦ *The horse began to gallop.*

- the long high sound that a horse makes: **neigh**; *verb*: **neigh**

4 looking after a horse
- a building where horses are kept: **stable**
- a field where a horse is kept: **paddock**
- a person whose job is to brush, clean and look after horses: **groom**; to do this work: **groom** a horse
- a U-shaped piece of metal that is put on a horse's hoof: **horseshoe**
- a person who puts shoes on horses' hooves: **blacksmith**

5 riding a horse
- to travel along, sitting on and controlling a horse: **ride*** (sth); a person who rides a horse: **rider**
- the sport or hobby of riding a horse: **riding** (*AmE* **horseback riding**)

- to ride a horse for pleasure or sport: **go* riding** (*AmE* **go* horseback riding**)
- on a horse: **on horseback** ◦ *Police on horseback were controlling the crowd.*
- to ride on a horse without a saddle: **ride* bareback**
- to get onto a horse: **mount** (a horse); *opposite*: **dismount**

■ sports with horses
- a sport where horses race and people try to win money by choosing the winner: **horse racing** (*noun* U)
- a race between horses: **horse race**
- a person who rides racehorses: **jockey**
- an event where several horse races are held: **race meeting**
- a place where horse races take place: **racecourse** (*AmE* **racetrack**)

- to pay some money in the hope of winning sth: **bet*** (**on** sth); an act of betting: **bet** ◦ *to lose money betting on horses* ◦ *to put a bet on a horse*
- the horse that has the best chance of winning a particular race: **favourite** (*AmE* **favorite**)

▷ more on betting ⇨ BET

- a sport where people ride horses over a series of fences: **showjumping** (*noun* U); a person who does this sport: **showjumper**
- a game played between two teams on horseback: **polo** (*noun* U)
- riding on horseback in the countryside for pleasure or on holiday: **pony-trekking** (*noun* U) ◦ *We went pony-trekking in the Lake District.*

hospital

1 different kinds of hospital
2 parts of a hospital
3 people in a hospital
4 going into hospital
5 treatment in hospital

see also DOCTOR, ILLNESS, MEDICINE

1 different kinds of hospital

- a place where ill or injured people are looked after: **hospital** ◦ *My sister works in a local hospital.* ◦ *a private hospital* ◦ *an NHS* (= National Health Service) *hospital* ◦ *I've got to go into hospital.*
- a small hospital or a part of a larger hospital where you go for special treatment: **clinic** ◦ *He's being treated in a private clinic.* ◦ *the family planning clinic*
- a hospital where women have babies: **maternity hospital**
- a hospital for people with illnesses of the mind: **mental hospital**, **psychiatric hospital**
- a small private hospital, especially for old people: **nursing home**
- a special hospital where people who are dying are cared for: **hospice**

Note: there is no **the** before **hospital** when you are talking about a person going there or being there because they are ill: ◦ *He's very ill in hospital.*; **the** is used before **hospital** when you are talking about going there as a visitor or when you talk about sb who works in a hospital: ◦ *'Is Mary home yet?' 'No. In fact I'm going to the hospital this afternoon to see her.'* ◦ *My brother works at/in the hospital.*

2 parts of a hospital

- a separate part or room in a hospital: **ward** ◦ *the children's ward* ◦ *Where's Ward 7, please?*
- the part of a hospital where people who have been injured in accidents are taken for immediate treatment: **casualty** (**department**), **accident and emergency** (**department**) (*abbreviation* **A and E**) ◦ *The casualty department is always very busy on Saturday nights.* ◦ *He was taken to casualty after the accident.*
- the place where operations are done: (**operating**) **theatre**
- the place where patients who are very seriously ill or injured receive special care: **intensive care** (*noun* U) ◦ *He was in intensive care for five days after the accident.*

- the place where dead bodies are kept before they are buried or burned: **mortuary, morgue**

3 people in a hospital

- a person who is receiving medical treatment: **patient** ◦ *Has the patient been examined by a doctor?*
- a person who goes to see a doctor in a hospital but does not stay overnight: **out-patient** ◦ *the out-patients' department*

- a doctor with special or deep knowledge of a particular area of medicine: **specialist** ◦ *My doctor says I need to see a specialist.* ◦ *a heart specialist* (= a specialist in illnesses of the heart)
- a senior specialist doctor in a hospital: **consultant** ◦ *a consultant gynaecologist*
- a doctor who performs medical operations: **surgeon**

- a person who looks after sick or injured people: **nurse**
- the work done by nurses: **nursing** (*noun* U) ◦ *a career in nursing*
- a female nurse who is in charge of a ward in a hospital: **sister**

4 going into hospital

- when you have to be treated in hospital and spend more than a day there, you **go* into** hospital ◦ *She's going into hospital for an operation.*
- a special vehicle for taking ill or injured people to and from hospital: **ambulance** ◦ *I called an ambulance to take her to hospital.*
- to take sb into hospital as a patient: **admit** sb, (*informal*) **have** sb **in** ◦ *He was admitted at 11.30.* ◦ *The doctor told me they would have to have me in for a few days to try to find out what was wrong.*
- to spend more than one day in hospital: **stay** ◦ *She stayed in hospital for six weeks.*
- to allow sb to leave hospital and go home: **discharge** sb ◦ *I'm hoping to be discharged tomorrow.*

hospital *contd.*

5 treatment in hospital

- what is done to make sb get better: **treatment** (*noun* C/U) ◦ *a new treatment for lung cancer* ◦ *free treatment on the NHS*
- to give medical treatment to sb who is ill: **look after** sb
- to make sb healthy again: **cure** sb (**of** sth) ◦ *The treatment cured her of cancer.*

- a kind of photograph that shows the bones and organs of a person or animal: **X-ray**; to take this kind of photograph: **X-ray** sb/sth, **take*** an **X-ray** (**of** sb/sth) ◦ *We're going to X-ray your hand to check that no bones are broken.*
- the place where X-rays are done: **X-ray department**

- medical treatment in which your body is cut open so that part of it can be removed or repaired: **operation**, **surgery** (*noun* U); *verb*: **operate** (**on** sb/sth) ◦ *The operation on his knee was a success.* ◦ *She needed immediate surgery.* ◦ *He was operated on for cancer.*

▷ more on operations ⇨ OPERATION

hot

1 saying how hot sth is
2 when your body is hot
2 keeping warm when the weather is cold

hot weather ⇨ WEATHER
making food hot; cooking ⇨ COOK

see also COLD

1 saying how hot sth is

- not cold, having a high temperature: **hot**; *noun* (U): **heat** ◦ *a hot day* ◦ *the heat of the sun* ◦ *extreme/fierce/scorching heat*
- to get hotter: **heat up**; to make sth get hotter: **heat** sth (**up**) ◦ *Wait for the oven to heat up before you put the cake in.* ◦ *This huge house is impossible to heat.*
- a little hot: **warm**; *noun* (U): **warmth** ◦ *warm clothes* ◦ *Are you warm enough?* ◦ *the warmth of the sun*
- to get warmer: **warm up**; to make sb/sth get warmer: **warm** sb/sth (**up**) ◦ *We jumped up and down to try and warm up.* ◦ *Come and warm yourself by the fire.*
- a little warm: **lukewarm** ◦ *lukewarm water*
- (used about liquids) only slightly warm: **tepid**

- very hot: (*informal*) **boiling**, (*informal*) **boiling hot** ◦ *Can I have a drink? I'm absolutely boiling.* ◦ *a boiling hot day*
- so hot that you cannot touch it: **red-hot**
- (used about a very hot liquid) to burn sb/sth: **scald** sb/sth; very hot liquid is **scalding, scalding hot**

▷ more on hot liquids ⇨ LIQUID, WATER

■ measuring temperature

- the measurement of how hot or cold sth is: **temperature** ◦ *The temperature in Cairo was over 40°C.* ◦ *a high/low/average temperature*
- an instrument for measuring temperature: **thermometer**
- the unit that we use for measuring temperature: **degree**
- two systems of measuring temperature: **Celsius** (sometimes called **Centigrade**) (**C**) and **Fahrenheit** (**F**)
- when sth gets hotter, its temperature **rises***; when it gets cooler, its temperature **falls***

2 when your body is hot

- the salty water which comes from your skin when you are hot: **sweat** (*noun* U); *verb*: **sweat**; covered with sweat: **sweaty** ◦ *I felt really hot and sweaty.*

▷ being hot because you are ill ⇨ ILLNESS

3 keeping warm when the weather is cold

- a piece of equipment that is used to heat a room: (**gas/electric**) **fire**, (**gas/electric**) **heater** ◦ *I lit the gas fire.* ◦ *I turned on the electric heater.*
- a fire that burns inside a house to keep it warm: **fire** ◦ *a wood/coal fire*
- a system for keeping houses warm in cold weather: (**central**) **heating** (*noun* U)
- a type of heater made of metal and filled with water (usually part of a central heating system): **radiator**

▷ more on fires ⇨ FIRE

- a rubber container that is filled with hot water and put inside a bed to warm it: **hot-water bottle**
- a special blanket heated by electricity which is used to warm a bed: **electric blanket**

▷ clothes that keep you warm ⇨ CLOTHES

hotel

1 different kinds of hotel
2 parts of hotels
3 staying in a hotel
4 people who work in hotels

see also TRAVEL, HOLIDAY

1 different kinds of hotel

- a place where you stay when you are travelling or on holiday: **hotel** ◦ *a first-class hotel* ◦ *We stayed in a small country hotel.*
- a hotel where you can park your car near your room: **motel**
- a small hotel sometimes in a private house: **guest house**
- a private house where you can spend the night and have breakfast in the morning: **bed and breakfast** (*abbreviation* **B&B**)
- a place (like a cheap hotel) where people can stay when they are living away from home: **hostel** ◦ *a youth hostel* (= a hostel for people who are walking, cycling, etc in the countryside)

2 parts of hotels

- the entrance hall in a hotel: **lobby, foyer**
- the place in a hotel where you go to say you have arrived, to make enquiries, etc: **reception** ◦ *Please leave your key at reception when you go out.* ◦ *the reception desk*
- a machine in a hotel, etc that is used to carry people from one floor to another: **lift** (*AmE* **elevator**)

- a place in a hotel, etc where you can buy and drink alcoholic and other drinks: **bar**; a smart, comfortable bar in a hotel: **lounge bar**
- a room in a hotel, etc where you eat meals: **dining-room, restaurant**

3 staying in a hotel

- a person who is staying at a hotel: **guest**, (*formal*) **resident**
- a person who is not staying in a hotel, but may be visiting or using the hotel: **non-resident** ◦ *The bar is open to non-residents.*

- to stop at a hotel and remain for a night or more: **stay** (**at/in** a hotel)
- to arrange to stay at a hotel, etc at a particular time: **book** (a room), **make* a reservation** ◦ *If we don't book in advance, we may not get a room for the night.*
- to arrange for sb to stay in a hotel, etc: **book** sb **in** ◦ *Could you book us in for the sixteenth and seventeenth of March.*
- if a room in a hotel is not being used by a guest, it is **vacant**; *noun*: **vacancy** ◦ *The sign outside the hotel said "No Vacancies".*
- a hotel that has no vacant rooms is **fully booked, booked up**

- when you arrive at a hotel (and sign your name on a list), you **book in, check in** ◦ *We checked in as soon as we arrived.*
- when you pay your bill and leave a hotel, you **check out** ◦ *Mr. Stevens has already checked out.*

■ rooms

- a hotel room for one person to stay in: **single (room)**
- a hotel room for two people to stay in: **double (room)** ◦ *We need one single and two doubles, please.*
- a hotel room where two people can stay in separate beds: **twin-bedded room, twin**
- a set of rooms in a hotel with bedroom, bathroom and sitting-room: **suite** ◦ *a penthouse suite* (= on the top floor of a hotel) ◦ *the bridal suite* (= for a newly married couple)
- a room that is joined to another to form one unit is **en suite** ◦ *All the rooms have a bathroom en suite/an en suite bathroom.*

■ meals

- hotel accommodation with all meals included: **full board** (*noun* U)
- hotel accommodation with breakfast and evening meal included: **half board** (*noun* U)
- hotel accommodation with breakfast included: **bed and breakfast**

4 people who work in hotels

- the man/woman who controls a hotel: **manager/manageress**
- the person who owns a hotel: **proprietor**; a female proprietor can also be called a **proprietress**
- the person in a hotel who answers the phone, greets new guests and arranges for them to have a room, etc: **receptionist**
- a woman who cleans and tidies hotel bedrooms: **chambermaid**
- a man/woman who brings food and drink to customers in a hotel dining-room, etc: **waiter/waitress**
- a person who is in charge of the entrance of a hotel, etc: **porter** (*AmE* **doorman, door-keeper**)

---

hour ⇨ TIME

---

house

1 the house you live in
2 different kinds of house
3 outside a house
4 inside a house
5 looking after a house
6 buying, selling and renting a house
7 leaving and returning to your house

other buildings ⇨ BUILDING
building a house ⇨ BUILD

1 the house you live in

- a building that is made for people to live in: **house**
- buildings for people to live in: **housing** (*noun* U) ◦ *We need more housing for old people.*

- the place where you sleep and keep your possessions is where you **live** ◦ *He lives at number 10.* ◦ *At present we're looking for somewhere to live.*
- the place where you live or where you feel that you belong is your **home** (*noun* C/U) ◦ *We have a beautiful home and two lovely children.* ◦ *I'm looking forward to going home.* ◦ *to run away from home*
- the town that you come from is your **home town**

- if you go and live in another house, you **move, move house**; the change that you make is a **move** ◦ *She's moving house next week and has asked me to help her with the move.*
- a person who has no home is **homeless**

▷ more on changing where you live or not having anywhere to live ⇨ LIVE²

- all the people who live together in a house and the things that are needed to look after them: **household** ◦ *a large household* ◦ *household expenses* ◦ *household equipment*
- a person who rents or owns and occupies a house: **householder**
- connected with the home or family: **domestic** ◦ *domestic life* ◦ *domestic jobs*

house *contd.*

■ the location of a house

– the area surrounding a house: **neighbourhood** (*AmE* **neighborhood**) ◦ *a residential neighbourhood*
– a person who lives near you: **neighbour** (*AmE* **neighbor**) ◦ *Too much noise will wake the neighbours.*
– the next house, room or building is **next door**; *adjective*: **next-door** ◦ *the people (who live) next door* ◦ *to go next door* ◦ *our next-door neighbours*

▷ more on the location of buildings ⇨ **BUILDING**

– a line of similar houses that are all joined together: **terrace**
– an area where a large number of houses are planned and built as a group: (**housing**) **estate**; an estate that is built by a local government council: **council estate**; a house that is built and owned by a local government council: **council house**
– an area where people live that is outside the main part of a city or town: **suburb, the suburbs** (*noun plural*); *adjective*: **suburban** ◦ *to commute from the suburbs* ◦ *suburban houses/gardens/streets*

2 different kinds of house

a house that is . . .	is called a . . .
not joined to any other house	**detached** house
joined to another house on one side	**semi-detached** house (*AmE* **duplex**)
one of a row of similar houses that are all joined together	**terraced** house (*AmE* **row house**)
all on ground level	**bungalow**
small, usually old and in the country	**cottage**
where a farmer lives	**farmhouse**
large and in the country	**country house**
very large	**mansion**
the home of a king or queen	**palace**
small, with only one room, often made of wood	**hut**
made of snow	**igloo**

■ flats

– a set of rooms on one floor (= level) of a larger building: **flat** (*AmE* **apartment**) ◦ *a first-floor flat* ◦ *a self-contained flat* (= with its own private entrance, kitchen and bathroom) ◦ *an unfurnished flat to let*
– a large flat at the top of a tall building: **penthouse**
– a building that contains individual flats on different floors: **block of flats** (*AmE* **apartment block**)
– a very tall block of flats: **tower block** (*AmE* **high-rise apartment building**)

■ the size and condition of a house

– a house or room that has plenty of space is **roomy, spacious** ◦ *a spacious living-room*
– a house or room which has very little space is **tiny, cramped** ◦ *a tiny flat in Kensington* ◦ *They lived in rather cramped conditions.*

– a house that is suitable to be lived in is **habitable**; *opposite*: **uninhabitable** ◦ *The house was uninhabitable because of the damp.*
– a house that has been well looked after is **in good condition, well maintained**
– an area of a city where living conditions are extremely bad and the buildings are in bad condition: **slum** ◦ *inner-city slums* ◦ *slum dwellings*

3 outside a house

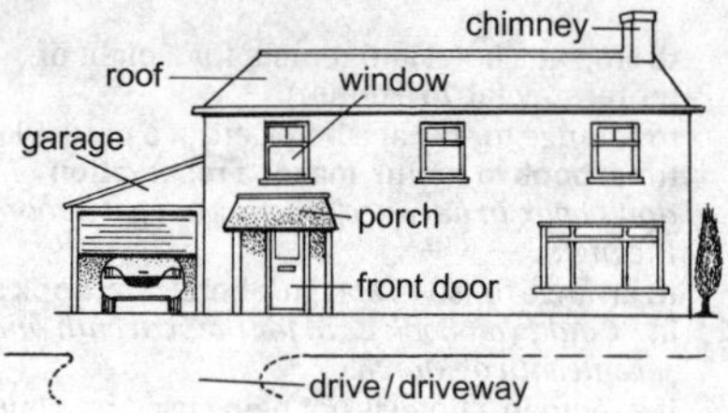

▷ more on doors, roofs and windows ⇨ **DOOR, ROOF, WINDOW**

– the outside of a building: **outside, exterior**; *adjectives*: **outside, exterior** ◦ *to paint the outside of the house* ◦ *an outside toilet* ◦ *exterior doors/walls*
– when you are outside a building, you are **outside, out of doors**; *adjectives*: **outside, outdoor, exterior** ◦ *to go outdoors/outside* ◦ *Let's have lunch out of doors.* ◦ *outdoor games*

– a piece of land where flowers and vegetables are grown: **garden** (*AmE* **yard**) ◦ *the back/front garden*
– a concrete or stone area behind a house, that has a wall or fence around it: **backyard**
– the land or gardens that surround a large building are its **grounds** (*noun plural*) ◦ *a ticket to visit the house and grounds*
– an area next to a house where people can sit, eat, etc: **patio** (*plural* **patios**)

▷ more on gardens ⇨ **GARDEN**

4 inside a house

– a part of a house that is separated from the rest by its own walls, floor and ceiling: **room**
– the tables, chairs, beds etc which are in rooms: **furniture** (*noun* U)

▷ the rooms in a house ⇨ **BATHROOM, BED, KITCHEN, TOILET, ROOM**

▷ furniture ⇨ CHAIR, TABLE, FURNITURE

- the area of a house that is just inside the front entrance: **hall** ◦ *Hang your coat in the hall.*
- a long, narrow passage with doors that open into rooms: **corridor**

- a series of steps that lead from one level to another: **stairs** (*noun plural*), **staircase** ◦ *at the top/bottom of the stairs* ◦ *to run up the stairs* ◦ *a wooden staircase*
- the floor (= level) of a building which is above you is **upstairs** (*adverb, adjective*) ◦ *to go upstairs* ◦ *The bedrooms are upstairs.* ◦ *the upstairs rooms*
- the level below you in a building is **downstairs** (*adverb, adjective*) ◦ *to go downstairs* ◦ *It's warmer downstairs.* ◦ *the downstairs toilet*

▷ more on stairs ⇨ STAIRS

- the space inside the roof of a house: **attic, loft** ◦ *We have converted our loft into a games room.*
- an underground room that is used for storing things: **cellar**
- an extra part built on to a house: **extension** ◦ *They've had an extension built on at the back of their bungalow.*

- the inside of a building: **inside, interior**; *adjectives*: **inside, interior** ◦ *an interior decorator*
- when you are inside a house, you are **indoors, inside**; *adjective*: **indoor** ◦ *Let's go indoors/inside.* ◦ *an indoor swimming pool*

5 looking after a house

- the work that is needed to keep a house clean and tidy: **housework** (*noun* U) ◦ *to do the housework.*
- a woman who spends her working time doing housework, cooking and looking after her family: **housewife** (*plural* **housewives**)

- a person who is paid to work in another person's house: **servant** ◦ *Most people don't have servants these days.*
- a person who is paid to look after the organization of another person's house and housework: **housekeeper**; this person's job is to **keep* house** (**for** sb)
- the most important male servant in a big house: **butler**

▷ cleaning a house ⇨ CLEAN / DIRTY

▷ people who look after other people's children ⇨ CHILD

- to put paint and/or wallpaper onto walls, ceilings and doors in a house or room: **decorate** (sth) ◦ *This room needs decorating.*
- to mend an old or damaged building or part of a building: **repair** sth; this work: **repair** (*often plural*) ◦ *The roof needs to be repaired.* ◦ *the repairs that need to be done*
- to repair and decorate a house, room or building, etc: **do*** sth **up** ◦ *Now the old house has been done up, you can hardly recognize it.*
- to build or fit sth new into a room or building, etc: **put*** sth **in** ◦ *He's just put in a new central heating system.* ◦ *They're having a sauna put in.*
- the activity of making or repairing things yourself: (*BrE*) **DIY, do-it-yourself** ◦ *a DIY expert* ◦ *He's very keen on DIY.*
- the cost or process of keeping a house in good condition: **upkeep** (*noun* U), **maintenance** (*noun* U) ◦ *We'd like to buy the house, but the upkeep would be too expensive for us.* ◦ *regular maintenance*

▷ more on painting a house ⇨ PAINT²

a person who ...	is called ...
paints a room, puts up wallpaper, etc	a **painter**, a **decorator**
mends a pipe, puts in a new bath, etc	a **plumber**
repairs or puts in sth electrical	an **electrician**
mends or puts in a gas fire, gas cooker, etc	a **gas fitter**
repairs a roof, removes a wall, etc	a **builder**
repairs a telephone	a **telephone engineer**

6 buying, selling and renting a house

- if a house is available for buying, it is **for sale, on the market**; when you make a house available like this, you **put*** it **up** for sale, **put** it **on the market** ◦ *That house has been for sale for over a year.*
- if you take a person to look at the rooms, etc in a house, you **show** them **round** (it), **show** them **over** it ◦ *Would you like me to show you round?*

- a person whose job is to buy and sell houses and land for other people: **estate agent** (*AmE* **real estate agent, realtor**)
- an organization like a bank, that lends money to people who want to buy a home: **building society**
- money that you borrow from a bank or a building society in order to buy a house: **mortgage** ◦ *to have/take out a mortgage* ◦ *mortgage repayments*

■ renting a house
- if you pay money for the use of a room, house, flat, etc, you **rent** it; the money you pay: **rent** (*noun* C/U) ◦ *They pay £100 per week in rent.*

▷ more on renting a house ⇨ RENT

7 leaving and returning to your house

- when you are in your house, you are **at home, in** ◦ *Is Tom in?*
- if you are not in your house, you are **not at home, out** ◦ *Whenever I call, he's out.*
- when you leave your home for a short time, you **go* out** ◦ *She went out about five minutes ago.*
- if you do not go out, you **stay in** ◦ *I'm staying in to watch television tonight.*
- when you go back to your house, you go **home** ◦ *What time did you get home?* ◦ *He's not home yet.*

house *contd.*

- if you do not go home, you **stay out** ◦ *I don't want to stay out very late.*
- if you take sb to their home to make sure that they get there safely, you **see* sb home** ◦ *Shall I see you home?*
- in the direction of your home: **homeward** (*adjective, adverb*) ◦ *the homeward journey*
- if you are not in the town or place where your home is, you are **away (from** it) ◦ *working away from home* ◦ *away on holiday*
- if you are sad because you are away from home, you are **homesick**; being homesick: **homesickness** (*noun* U)

■ **MORE ...**

- a pleasant house with a garden, usually in a warm place: **villa** ◦ *a villa in the south of France*
- a house made of wood and found in mountain areas or on holiday camps: **chalet** ◦ *a Swiss chalet*
- the study of managing a house and housework: **home economics** (*noun* U), **domestic science** (*noun* U)

how likely ⇨ POSSIBLE[1]

how much/many

1 how much/many?
2 some
3 a few/a little
4 a lot
5 all, most or none
6 more or less

as much or as many as necessary ⇨ ENOUGH
being exact or approximate about quantities ⇨ EXACT/APPROXIMATE

see also INCREASE/DECREASE, NUMBER, SIZE, WEIGHT

1 how much/many?

- how much/many there is or are of sth: **quantity**, (used with uncountable nouns) **amount**, (used with countable nouns) **number** ◦ *small quantities of rice/nails* ◦ *The school has bought a large amount of furniture/a large number of chairs and tables.* ◦ *a considerable number of people/animals/books*
- to ask about amount or quantity, you say **how much/many** ◦ *Ask him how much money he's got.* ◦ *How many biscuits have you had?*

2 some

- a quantity: **some**, (in negative sentences and some questions) **any** ◦ *We need some biscuits/cheese from the shop.* ◦ *'Can you lend me some tea?' 'I don't think I've got any.'* ◦ *Do you have any of those English apples you had last week?*
- more than two but not very many: **several** ◦ *We'll need several more tins of paint.*

3 a few/a little

- a small quantity: (used with uncountable nouns) **a little**, (*informal*) **a bit (of** sth), (used with countable nouns) **a few**, (*informal*) **one or two**, (*informal*) **a couple (of ...)** ◦ *Add a little milk.* ◦ *'More sugar?' 'Just a little.'* ◦ *All I wanted was a bit of peace.* ◦ *'Is there any cheese?' 'There might be a bit in the fridge.'* ◦ *There are a few books on the shelf.* ◦ *'Are there any cakes left?' 'Yes, a few.'* ◦ *I need to ask you one or two questions.* ◦ *Were there any phone calls while I was out?' 'Just one or two.'* ◦ *Have you got a couple of minutes to spare?* ◦ *These pens were reduced, so I bought a couple.*
- a small number (especially of people): **a handful (of ...)** ◦ *A handful of people were left at the end.* ◦ *A lot of people went to the lecture, but only a handful stayed for the discussion afterwards.*
- (used about a liquid) a very small amount: **a drop** ◦ *There's a tiny drop of lemonade left if you want it.*
- a very small amount of sth (usually not wanted): **scrap** ◦ *a scrap of tartan cloth* ◦ *a few scraps of food*
- almost none: **hardly/scarcely any**, (used with uncountable nouns) **little, not much**, (used with countable nouns) **few, not many** ◦ *There are hardly any apples on the tree this year.* ◦ *Be careful with the milk – there's hardly any left.* ◦ *I had no food and little money.* ◦ *We need a lot of rain because there has been very little all summer.* ◦ *There's not much traffic about this morning.* ◦ *'Is there anything good on television?' 'Not much.'* ◦ *Few students passed their exams.* ◦ *They expected a lot of applications, but in fact there were very few.* ◦ *Not many people watch this programme.* ◦ *A lot of tourists arrive by plane, but not many drive.*

Note: the difference between **little/few** and **a little/a few**. If we say 'There's little time left', we sound negative, so it could mean 'There's little time left so hurry up'. If we say 'There's a little time left', we sound more positive, so we could mean 'There's a little time left so don't worry'.

- the smallest possible amount of sth: **minimum** (*noun, adjective*) ◦ *£10 is the minimum I'll accept for it.* ◦ *the minimum qualifications required*

4 a lot

- a large quantity: (used with uncountable nouns) **much, a good/great deal**, (used with countable nouns) **many, quite a few** ◦ *too much crime* ◦ *It took so much time.* ◦ *You were making a great deal of noise last night.* ◦ *There weren't many people there.* ◦ *There were quite a few students at the party but almost no teachers.*
- much or many: **a lot (of ...)**, (*informal*) **lots (of ...)** ◦ *There were a lot of people there last night.* ◦ *a lot of money/food/problems* ◦ *'How many people were there?' 'A lot.'* ◦ *'Did you see any lions?' 'Yes, lots.'*

Note: in affirmative statements, it is more common to use **a lot of, lots of**, etc than **much. Much** is normally used only in questions and negative sentences or with **too, so**, or comparatives: ◦ *So much damage was done.* ◦ *There was much more food than I could eat.*

- other informal expressions for much or many: **loads** (**of . . .**), **masses** (**of . . .**), **lots and lots** (**of . . .**), **heaps** (**of . . .**), **piles** (**of . . .**) ◦ *I can't stop and talk – I've got heaps of work to do.*
- other expressions for a large number: **dozens** (**of . . .**), **hundreds** (**of . . .**), **thousands** (**of . . .**), **millions** (**of . . .**), **countless** ◦ *dozens of people* ◦ *I've got hundreds of things to do.* ◦ *countless people*
- large numbers of people: **masses/crowds/hordes** (**of . . .**) ◦ *hordes of people*

- the largest possible amount of sth: **maximum** (*noun, adjective*) ◦ *the maximum that we can hope to achieve* ◦ *The maximum number of people we can take is sixteen.*

5 all, most or none

- all the people or things in a group of three or more: **all** (*with a plural noun*), **every** (*with a singular noun*), (*informal*) **the lot** ◦ *Almost all the flowers have died.* ◦ *Did you remember to bring them all?* ◦ *All new students should assemble in the hall.* ◦ *Every student was given a dictionary.* ◦ *I had to examine every part very carefully.* ◦ *Every single one of the trees had been cut down.* ◦ *They'd cut down the lot.*

- the two; the one as well as the other: **both** (**of**) . . . ◦ *Both her parents are dead.* ◦ *Both of the twins are good at maths.* ◦ *I like them both.*
- one or the other of two; it does not matter which: **either** (**of**) . . . ◦ *I don't want either of them* (= I don't want one or the other).

- every person: **everyone**, **everybody** ◦ *Everyone is invited.* ◦ *Everyone's entitled to their own opinion.* ◦ *She seems to know everybody.*
- all of the things: **everything** ◦ *Everything was taken – even the fridge.* ◦ *Tell me everything you know.*
- every one in a group of people or things when you think about them individually: **each** (*with a singular noun*) ◦ *You get one mark for each correct answer.*

- the complete number or amount of people or things in a group: **total**; *adjective*: **total** ◦ *Count them up and put the total at the bottom.* ◦ *The total number of missing children was smaller than had been feared.*
- as a total: **altogether** ◦ *You owe me ten pounds altogether.*
- the whole amount of a possible total: **a hundred per cent** ◦ *We had a hundred per cent pass rate* (= everybody passed).

■ more than half
- more than half, or nearly all, of a group of people or things: **most, the/a majority** (**of . . .**) ◦ *I eat most kinds of food except for red meat.* ◦ *The majority of people in the class come from Spain.*
- to form the largest or greatest part of sth: **be in the/a majority**

■ less than half
- less than half, or not very many, of a group of people or things: **the/a minority** (**of . . .**) ◦ *Only a small minority of people in the town are in favour of the new bypass.*
- to form the smallest part of sth: **be in the/a minority** ◦ *The people who wanted to go to the theatre were in a minority so we went to the cinema instead.*

■ none
- no thing: **nothing, not . . . anything** ◦ *'What do you want?' 'Nothing.'* ◦ *There was nothing left after we'd eaten.* ◦ *Nothing really interests me at the moment.* ◦ *I've got nothing to do.* ◦ *I haven't got anything to do.*
- no person: **nobody, no one, not . . . anybody, not . . . anyone** ◦ *I met nobody/no one.* ◦ *No one was there.* ◦ *I didn't meet anybody/anyone.*

- (used about more than two people or things) not one; not any: **no, none, not . . . any** ◦ *I've got almost no money left.* ◦ *No dogs are allowed in here.* ◦ *'Do they have any children?' 'No, none.'* ◦ *They have no children/haven't any children.*
- (used about two people or things) not one and not the other: **neither, not . . . either** ◦ *In my view, neither team was really any good.* ◦ *I asked John and then I asked Mary, but neither wanted to help me.* ◦ *We didn't like either of the two houses we were offered.* ◦ *They offered me both, but I didn't take either.*

Note: to talk about a particular group or part of a larger number or amount, we can use an expression with 'of': ◦ *Some of the furniture was rather old.* ◦ *Several of her friends came to see her.* ◦ *Could I have a little of that cheese?* ◦ *He read a bit of the book aloud to us.* ◦ *A couple of these articles are quite interesting.* ◦ *Jane has sold a few of her pictures.* ◦ *Hardly any of my plants flowered.* ◦ *Not many of our employees speak Japanese.* ◦ *Each of the winners received a cup.* ◦ *None of the houses had central heating.*

6 more or less

■ more
- a larger number or amount: **more** ◦ *We were expecting many more guests.* ◦ *There weren't many people yesterday. I hope there'll be more today.* ◦ *You eat a lot more than I do.*
- the largest number or amount: **the most** ◦ *Who has read the most books this year?* ◦ *I may eat more than you but Caroline eats the most.*

- to be greater than sth: **exceed** sth ◦ *The number of people entering must not exceed the number of places available.*
- to be more in number than sb/sth else: **outnumber** sb/sth ◦ *The women were outnumbered by the men by three to one* (= There were three times more men than women).

- more than a particular number or amount: **above . . ., over . . .,** (*formal*) **in excess of . . .** ◦ *children aged eleven and above* ◦ *Over a million people were in the square.* ◦ *sales in excess of 100 000 units a year*
- not less than a certain number and probably more: **at least . . .** ◦ *At least a hundred have died.*

- two times the quantity of sth else: **twice the . . ., double the . . .** ◦ *We're getting double the usual number of applications this year.*
- three times the quantity of sth else: **treble the . . .**

how much / many *contd.*

– the same amount again; double: **as many / much again** ◦ *We paid £200 for the hotel, and as much again (= another £200) for the food.*

■ less

– a smaller quantity: (used with uncountable nouns) **less**, (used with countable nouns) **fewer** ◦ *I'm trying to spend less money on clothes.* ◦ *He weighed less than two kilos when he was born.* ◦ *I didn't have a lot of money then, but now I've got even less.* ◦ *There seem to be fewer policemen on the streets than there used to be.* ◦ *There weren't many students last year, but there are even fewer this year.*

– the smallest quantity: (used with uncountable nouns) **least**, (used with countable nouns) **fewest** ◦ *She did the least work.* ◦ *I seem to be the one with fewest problems.*

Note: many people use **less** with plural nouns, particularly when speaking: ◦ *three people or less* ◦ *There are less cars on the roads than there used to be*. However **fewer** is the form that is still considered to be correct, particularly in writing: ◦ *three people or fewer* ◦ *fewer cars on the roads.* We use **less** with time, distances and other measures: ◦ *less than five seconds* ◦ *less than ten miles* ◦ *less than three kilos*.

– less than a particular number or amount: **lower than . . ., under . . .** ◦ *The numbers are lower than last year's.* ◦ *'How many came to your lecture?' 'Under fifty.'*

– not more than a certain number or amount and probably less: **not more than . . ., . . . at the most** ◦ *'How much do you need?' 'Not more than a litre.'* ◦ *We only saw a dozen elephants at the most.*

■ no difference

– if there is no difference between two quantities, they are **the same**, **equal**; *opposites*: **different**, **unequal** ◦ *the same number/an equal number* ◦ *You need different amounts of butter and flour in these two recipes.*

– approximately the same: **equivalent** (**to . . .**) ◦ *roughly equivalent quantities of gold and silver*

▷ more on being the same or different ⇨ **SAME, DIFFERENT**

■ proportion

– the relationship in size or quantity of one thing to another thing: **proportion** (**of** sth **to** sth) ◦ *What is the proportion of fat to flour in this cake?* ◦ *The oil and flour have to be mixed in the correct proportions.*

– related in amount or number to sth else: **proportional** (**to** sth), **in proportion** (**to** sth) ◦ *The cost will be directly proportional to the amount used.* ◦ *Salaries have not risen in proportion to the cost of living.*

– the relation between two amounts calculated by the number of times one is bigger than the other: **ratio** ◦ *The ratio of men to women in the company is three to one* (written 3:1).

▷ more on comparing things ⇨ **COMPARE / CONTRAST**

how often

see also TIME

– to ask how many times sth happens in a certain period, you say **how often**, **how many times** ◦ *How often do you have your hair cut?* ◦ *How many times a year do you go to the cinema?*

– the number of times that sth happens in a certain period: **frequency** (*noun* U), (*formal*) **incidence** (*noun* U) ◦ *The frequency of violent attacks is increasing.* ◦ *This area has a high incidence of disease.*

■ always

– at all times; regularly: **always** ◦ *The bus is always late in the morning.* ◦ *We always spent our summers in the South of France.* ◦ *I'll always remember that day.* ◦ *I have always admired her work*.

– on every occasion: **whenever**, **every time** ◦ *Whenever I see her she's with her mother.*

■ often

– many times: **often**, **frequently**, **a lot**; *adjective*: **frequent**; *noun* (U): **frequency** (**of** sth) ◦ *She often has visitors.* ◦ *She is frequently asked out.* ◦ *We don't go to the cinema a lot these days.* ◦ *Violent attacks are becoming more frequent.* ◦ *the alarming frequency of cancer among workers at the plant*

– very often: **all the time** ◦ *Can't we go somewhere different for a change? We go there all the time.*

– repeated many times: **again and again**, **over and over again** ◦ *I say this over and over again, but do you ever listen?*

– again and again (in an annoying way): **always**, **forever**, **constantly**; *adjective*: **constant** ◦ *He's always banging the front door – it really annoys me.* ◦ *constant interruptions*

– happening every day: **daily** (*adjective, adverb*) ◦ *a daily coach service to Cambridge*

– happening every hour: **hourly** (*adjective, adverb*) ◦ *The buses run hourly from the centre of town.*

■ fairly often

– fairly often: **usually**, **mostly**, (*informal*) **more often than not** ◦ *We usually have lunch at one o'clock.* ◦ *I sometimes walk to work, but more often than not I take the bus.*

– on some occasions: **sometimes**, (**every**) **now and again**, (**every**) **now and then** ◦ *I sometimes take the bus to work.* ◦ *Every now and then I like to change my hairstyle.*

– sometimes but not very often: **occasionally**, **on occasion(s)**, **from time to time**; *adjective*: **occasional** ◦ *We occasionally go out to a restaurant, but we're quite often invited to somebody's house.* ◦ *I have the occasional glass of wine but I usually don't drink.*

▷ more on things happening usually ⇨ **USUAL**

■ not often

– few times: **not very often**, **seldom**, **infrequently**; *adjective*; **infrequent** ◦ *I don't see them very often.* ◦ *She seldom went to bed before 11 o'clock.*

- almost never: **hardly ever, rarely,** (*informal*) **once in a blue moon** ◦ *We hardly ever go to the theatre any more – it's too expensive.* ◦ *She rarely appears in public these days.* ◦ *We only ever see them once in a blue moon.*

■ never
- at no time: **never, not . . . ever** ◦ *'Have you ever been to America?' 'No, never.'* ◦ *I never go to bed before midnight.* ◦ *Don't you ever miss your old schoolfriends?*

■ happening more often or less often
- to become more frequent: **increase, grow***; *noun*: **increase** ◦ *The divorce rate is increasing.* ◦ *There has been an increase in the number of students taking the Cambridge exam.*
- happening more frequently: **increasing** (*adverb* **increasingly**), **growing** ◦ *A growing number of students are taking the Cambridge exam.*
- something which is increasing over a period of time is **on the increase** ◦ *Drugs-related crime is definitely on the increase.*

- to become less frequent: **decrease**; *noun*: **decrease**
- happening less frequently: **decreasing**

▷ more on things increasing or decreasing ➪ INCREASE / DECREASE

human ➪ PERSON

humour ➪ LAUGH

hundred

other numbers ➪ ONE, TWO, NUMBER

- the number 100: **hundred**
- 100th: **hundredth** ◦ *her hundredth birthday*
- one part in a hundred ($\frac{1}{100}$): **hundredth** ◦ *He won by one hundredth of a second.*

- one part in every hundred (%): **per cent** (*AmE* **percent**); *noun*: **percentage** ◦ *Eighty per cent of people said they were less happy now than they were five years ago.* ◦ *a 50% increase* ◦ *Prices have risen by over 29% in the last six months.* ◦ *an increasing percentage of people who own their own homes*

- a particular period of 100 years that is used for giving dates: **century** ◦ *the twentieth century* (= the dates from 1900 to 1999)
- any period of 100 years: **century** ◦ *My family have lived here for centuries.*

- the year that comes exactly one hundred years after an important event or the beginning of sth: **centenary** ◦ *The university will celebrate its centenary next year.* ◦ *an exhibition to mark the centenary of sb's birth*

hungry ➪ EAT

hunt

see also ANIMAL

- (used about people or animals) to look for and follow wild animals in order to catch or kill them: **hunt** (sth); *noun* (U): **hunting** ◦ *Owls hunt by night.* ◦ *to hunt deer* ◦ *I don't like the idea of hunting wild animals.*

- to spend time hunting: **go* hunting**
- an event in which people go out to hunt for certain animals: **hunt** ◦ *a fox hunt*
- a person who hunts: **hunter**
- animals which hunters hunt: **game** (*noun* U); large animals like elephants and lions: **big game** ◦ *a big game hunter*
- a kind of dog which is used in hunting: **hound** ◦ *a foxhound*
- sports in which people hunt and kill animals: **field sports, blood sports**

- a series of marks in a long line that a person or animal leaves behind: **trail, tracks** (*noun plural*) ◦ *to follow a person's tracks* ◦ *a trail of footprints*
- to get hold of an animal, fish, bird, etc: **catch*** sth
- a piece of equipment for catching animals, birds, etc: **trap**; to catch an animal in a trap: **trap** sth ◦ *to be caught in a trap*

Note: killing birds and small animals (such as rabbits) for food or sport is not usually called hunting. If small animals or birds are killed with a gun, this is called **shooting**. If they are caught in a net, box, hole, etc, this is called **trapping**. Fish are not hunted. The word for catching and killing fish is **fishing**.

▷ more on shooting and fishing ➪ GUN, FISH[1]

- (used about an animal or bird) to kill and eat other animals or birds: **prey on** sth
- an animal that kills and eats other animals: **predator**; an animal that is preyed on: **prey** (*noun* U)
- a bird that kills and eats other birds and small animals: **bird of prey**

hurry ➪ FAST

hurt

- damaging sth ➪ DAMAGE
- hurting your feelings ➪ EMOTION
- hurting your body ➪ INJURE
- causing pain ➪ PAIN

husband ➪ MARRY

ice

cold temperatures ➪ COLD
cold weather ➪ WEATHER, SNOW

- water that is very cold and has become solid: **ice** (*noun* U) ◦ *There's ice all over the roads.* ◦ *The ice on the pond was about four centimetres thick.* ◦ *thin/thick ice* ◦ *snow and ice* ◦ *Can I have some ice in my juice?*
- covered with ice, or as cold as ice: **icy** ◦ *The roads are very icy.* ◦ *an icy wind*
- a very thin layer of small thin pieces of ice on the ground, the trees, etc: **frost** (*noun* U) ◦ *The fields were covered in frost.*

- a large piece of ice: **block of ice**

ice *contd.*

- a thin area of ice: **sheet of ice** ◦ *The lake was covered with a thin sheet of ice.*
- a pointed piece of ice that is formed when very cold water falls or runs down from sth: **icicle**
- a very large block of ice that is floating in the sea: **iceberg**
- a mass of ice, formed by snow moving slowly down a hill or mountain into a valley: **glacier**

- rain that falls in small hard balls of ice: **hail** (*noun* U); *verb* **hail** ◦ *Look – it's hailing!*
- a small hard ball of hail: **hailstone**
- a storm of hailstones: **hailstorm**

- a small block of ice that you put in a drink to make it cold: **ice cube**
- a drink with ice in it is **iced** ◦ *iced tea*

- to change from water into ice: **freeze***; *adjective*: **frozen** ◦ *to prevent water in pipes freezing* ◦ *The pond was frozen but the ice wasn't thick enough to walk on.*
- water freezes and becomes ice when the temperature falls **below zero, below freezing**
- the temperature at which water freezes: **freezing-point** (= 0°C)
- to become covered with ice: **ice over/up** ◦ *The freezer completely iced up so I couldn't open the door.*

- to become liquid again after being frozen: **melt** ◦ *The ice on the pond is melting at last.*

▷ frozen food ⇨ FOOD

■ moving on ice
- to move along a smooth surface: **slide*** ◦ *Cars were sliding around on the icy road.* ◦ *to slide down a hill*
- to slide accidentally, lose your balance and fall or nearly fall: **slip (over)** ◦ *I slipped over on the ice and hurt my head.*
- (used about a surface) difficult to move over because of frost or ice: **slippery** ◦ *a slippery road/path*

- boots with thick metal blades on the bottom, that you wear to move around on ice: **ice skates**
- to move over ice wearing ice skates: **skate**
- a sharp metal tool used (especially by mountain climbers) to cut ice: **ice-axe**

▷ more on skating ⇨ SPORT

idea

- something that you think ⇨ THINK
- what you think about sb / sth ⇨ OPINION
- an intention or plan ⇨ INTEND / PLAN
- a suggestion ⇨ ADVISE / SUGGEST

if

see also CAUSE / EFFECT

- a word used to show that one thing depends on another: **if** ◦ *If it rains tomorrow, I'll take the umbrella.* ◦ *If I had enough money, I'd go on holiday.* ◦ *I'd have been a lot more careful if I'd known how dangerous it was.* ◦ *If you don't like it, don't drink it!*
- something that must happen so that sth else can happen or be possible: **condition** ◦ *One of the conditions of the job is that you agree to work on Sundays.*
- when we want to say that sth can only happen if a particular situation exists, we can use these expressions: **only if . . ., providing/provided (that) . . ., as/so long as . . ., on condition (that) . . .** ◦ *You can borrow my car but only if you put some petrol in it.* ◦ *She agreed to stay in the job, provided that they gave her more money.* ◦ *You can work here, as long as you don't make a noise.* ◦ *You can go to the disco on condition that you come home before midnight.*

- when you think that sth will happen, and you talk about the result, you can say: **assuming (that) . . .** ◦ *Assuming that Tom comes to the party, we can get a lift home with him.*
- to talk about sth that you will do because sth else might happen, you can say **in case** ◦ *Leave me your address in case there are any letters for you.* ◦ *I don't think it'll rain, but I'll take my umbrella just in case.*

■ if not
- a word that you use to say that one thing depends on something else happening or not happening: **unless** ◦ *Unless you stop talking* (= if you don't stop talking), *I shall have to ask you to leave the library.* ◦ *We can eat in the garden this evening, unless the weather changes* (= if the weather doesn't change).
- words that you use to say that sth will happen if sth else does not happen: **otherwise, or else, if not** ◦ *You must get to the station before 3 o'clock, otherwise you'll miss the train.* ◦ *You'd better write the phone number down or else you'll forget it.*

■ imagining and wishing
- when you imagine a situation, you can say **supposing . . ., what if . . .** ◦ *Supposing we stayed at home this evening? Then we could watch that film on television.* ◦ *What if they find out? We must be very careful.*
- when you wish sth, you can say **if only** ◦ If only I had more money! ◦ *If only I had tried harder!*

▷ more on wishing ⇨ WANT

ill ⇨ ILLNESS

illegal

- the law ⇨ LAW
- against the law ⇨ CRIME

illness

1 being ill
2 becoming ill
3 signs of illness
4 different kinds of illness
5 becoming better after illness
6 being well
mental illness ⇨ **MIND**
see also DOCTOR, HOSPITAL, MEDICINE, OPERATION, PAIN

1 being ill

- not in good health: **not well** (*not before a noun*), **ill** (*not before a noun*), **unwell** (*not before a noun*), **sick** ◦ *She's not looking very well.* ◦ *He was feeling ill.* ◦ *She has been unwell for several years.* ◦ *a sick child*
- not having or showing good health: **unhealthy** ◦ *He looked pale and unhealthy.*
- (used about a part of the body) affected by illness: **diseased** ◦ *The surgeon removed the diseased kidney.*

Note: in British English **to be sick** means to bring up food from the stomach. In *AmE* it means the same as **to be ill**. In both *BrE* and *AmE* **sick** is used before a noun to mean **ill**.

- the state of being ill: **illness** (*noun* U), **sickness** (*noun* U) ◦ *mental illness* ◦ *unable to work due to hunger and sickness*
- a type or period of ill health: **illness** ◦ *Tuberculosis is a serious illness but it can be treated quite easily.* ◦ *His illness had kept him in bed for more than a week.*
- illness of the body in humans, animals or plants: **disease** (*noun* C/U) ◦ *attempts to prevent the spread of disease*
- the state of being unable to use part of your body properly: **disability** (*noun* C/U) ◦ *She copes very well with her disabilities.* ◦ *physical/mental disability*

Note: illness is a more common word than **disease** and often refers to the experience of being ill. **Disease** is used especially to refer to a particular illness which has a name.

■ serious illness

- a short period when you suffer badly from a disease: **attack** (**of** sth) ◦ *He suffered an asthma attack/an attack of asthma.*
- very ill: **seriously ill**; how badly ill sb is: **seriousness** (*noun* U) ◦ *He's not seriously ill.* ◦ *The doctor doubted the seriousness of his condition.*
- a very bad illness: **serious illness**
- more ill: **worse**; *verb*: **worsen** ◦ *I'm afraid she's worse today.* ◦ *His condition worsened during the night.*
- dangerously ill: **critically ill** ◦ *She's critically ill in hospital.*
- an illness that causes or ends in death is **fatal** ◦ *This disease is usually fatal.*
- an illness that is likely to end in death is **terminal** (*adverb* **terminally**) ◦ *terminally ill*

■ people who are ill

- to have an illness: **have** (**got**) sth, **suffer from** sth ◦ *They think he's got cancer.* ◦ *He's been suffering from asthma most of his life.*
- a person who is receiving medical treatment: **patient**
- a person who has been very ill for a long time and needs to be looked after by sb else: **invalid** ◦ *He's been an invalid since the accident.*
- a person who is unable to use part of his/her body properly is **disabled** ◦ *disabled people*
- people who are ill: **the sick** ◦ *The sick were being treated in a temporary hospital.*
- often ill: **sickly** ◦ *a sickly child*
- an example of sb who is ill with a disease: **case** ◦ *Cases of cholera are rare in Britain.*

2 becoming ill

- to start being ill: **be taken ill**, **fall* ill** ◦ *He was taken ill on his way home.*
- to start being ill with a particular illness: **catch*** sth, **come* down with** sth, **get*** sth, (*formal*) **contract** sth ◦ *I've caught a cold.* ◦ *He came down with malaria.* ◦ *She's got hay fever again.* ◦ *Several of the tourists had contracted dysentery.*
- to be in the first stages of an illness: **sicken for** sth ◦ *You seem to be sickening for something – perhaps it's flu.*

■ causes of illness

- a disease that can easily move from one person to another is **infectious**, (*informal*) **catching** ◦ *Flu is very infectious.* ◦ *Is she very ill? I hope it's not catching.*
- if you have a disease that can easily move to another person, you are **infectious**
- a disease that you can get by touching sb or sth is **contagious** ◦ *Measles is a contagious disease.*
- if you have a disease that others can get by touching you, you are **contagious** ◦ *Is he still contagious?*
- to cause sb or sth to have a disease: **infect** sb/sth; the process or result of becoming infected: **infection** (*noun* U) ◦ *I must have got infected by drinking that water.* ◦ *A dirty water supply can be a source of infection.*
- a very small living thing that causes disease: **virus**; small living things that exist in the air, soil, people's bodies etc and which sometimes cause disease: **bacteria** (*noun plural*); a general word for viruses and bacteria: **germ** ◦ *The virus that causes Aids is called HIV.* ◦ *Germs spread in dirty places.*
- dirty and likely to cause disease: **insanitary**, **unhygienic** ◦ *living in very unhygienic conditions*

- when a disease moves from one person to another, it **spreads***; *noun*: **spread** ◦ *They're trying desperately to prevent the spread of the disease.*
- a time when many people in one area suddenly get a disease: **epidemic**, **outbreak** ◦ *a flu epidemic* ◦ *an outbreak of cholera*

- if you become ill when you eat, touch or breathe sth that does not normally make other people ill, you have an **allergy** (**to** sth), you are **allergic**

illness *contd.*

(**to** sth) ◦ *an allergy to cats/shellfish/pollen* ◦ *I'm allergic to goat's milk.*

■ **preventing disease**

– keeping yourself and things around clean, so as to avoid the spread of disease: **hygiene** (*noun* U); *adjective*: **hygienic**; *opposite*: **unhygienic** ◦ *You need high standards of hygiene when you are preparing food.* ◦ *It's more hygienic to use paper tissues.*

– if you are protected from a disease, you are **immune** (**to** it); *noun* (U): **immunity** (**to** sth) ◦ *You should be immune to measles if you've had it already.*
– to destroy a disease: **wipe** sth **out**, (*formal*) **eradicate** sth ◦ *Smallpox has been completely wiped out.*

▷ medicines which prevent disease ⇨ MEDICINE

3 signs of illness

– a change in your body that is a sign of illness: **symptom** (**of** sth) ◦ *Spots are one of the symptoms of measles.*

– to have a very hot body: **have/run* a temperature**, (*especially AmE*) **have a fever**; *adjective*: **feverish** ◦ *I think I've got a temperature.* ◦ *She was running a temperature.* ◦ *He looked feverish.*
– to measure a person's temperature: **take*** sb's **temperature** ◦ *The nurse took her temperature; it was 40°.*
– an instrument for measuring sb's temperature: **thermometer**

– if you feel ill in your stomach, you **feel* sick**
– to bring food up from the stomach and out of the mouth: **be sick**, **throw* up**, (*formal*) **vomit** ◦ *The children were all sick in the back of the car.*
– a pain in your stomach: **stomach-ache** (*noun* C/U), (*informal*) **tummy-ache** (*noun* C/U) ◦ *I've got a tummy-ache.*
– waste matter from the bowels coming out very often, partly in liquid form: **diarrhoea** (*AmE* **diarrhea**) (*noun* U)

▷ illness in the stomach ⇨ STOMACH

▷ aches in other parts of the body ⇨ PAIN

– to send air out of your mouth and throat with a sudden loud noise: **cough**; *verb*: **cough**
– to breathe noisily and with difficulty: **wheeze**

– a small red mark on your skin: **spot**
– a group of spots that cover an area of skin: **rash**
– a place on the body that is bigger or fatter than usual: **swelling**

– a diseased lump that grows in or on a person's body: **growth**, (*formal*) **tumour** (*AmE* **tumor**); one that can lead to death is **malignant**
– a sore area on the inside or outside of the body which is very painful and can bleed: **ulcer** ◦ *stomach ulcers* ◦ *a mouth ulcer*

– if you feel that you are about to become unconscious, you feel **faint**; to become unconscious suddenly: **faint**, (*informal*) **pass out** ◦ *I feel faint; I must sit down.* ◦ *He used to faint at the sight of blood.* ◦ *She passed out when she heard the news*
– the feeling that everything is going round and that you are going to fall: **dizziness** (*noun* U); *adjective*: **dizzy**
– a sudden attack of certain diseases, in which you become unconscious: **fit** ◦ *an epileptic fit*
– a condition of extreme weakness caused by damage to the body: **shock** (*noun* U) ◦ *to be in shock*
– being unable to move the body or part of it: **paralysis** (*noun* U); to cause paralysis: **paralyse** sb/sth ◦ *complete paralysis from the neck down* ◦ *The stroke paralysed his left arm.*

– a medical test that shows that a disease is present in sb is **positive**; *opposite*: **negative** ◦ *All the tests were negative.* ◦ *The results of the test were positive.*

4 different kinds of illness

– a disease caused by germs: **infection** ◦ *a viral infection* ◦ *a throat infection*
– one of many diseases in which the body becomes very hot: **fever** (*noun* U) ◦ *yellow fever* ◦ *rheumatic fever*
– a very serious disease in which lumps grow in the body in an uncontrolled way: **cancer** (*noun* U) ◦ *cancer of the lung* ◦ *breast cancer*

– an illness that quickly reaches its worst stage and does not usually last long is an **acute** illness ◦ *acute appendicitis*
– an illness that continues for a long time is **chronic** ◦ *chronic bronchitis*
– a disease that can be cured is **curable**; *opposite*: **incurable**

▷ types of illnesses, see table on page 229

■ **some other illnesses**

– an illness that is passed from person to person by sexual contact: **sexually transmitted disease** (*abbreviation* **STD**) (*noun* C/U), **venereal disease** (*abbreviation* **VD**) (*noun* U)
– an illness that destroys the body's ability to fight infection: **Aids** (*noun* U)

– an illness that gives a person very severe headaches: **migraine** (*noun* C/U)
– a disease that makes people become very thin because they do not want to eat: **anorexia** (*noun* U); a person who has this disease is (an) **anorexic**
– an illness that causes a person to fall down unconscious: **epilepsy** (*noun* U); *adjective*: **epileptic**
– an illness which affects the skin, nerves and flesh, causing deformity: **leprosy** (*noun* U)

▷ sickness caused by movement in a car, boat, etc ⇨ TRAVEL

5 becoming better after illness

– to become better after illness: **be/get* better**, **get* well**, **recover** (**from** sth), **get* over** sth; *noun*: **recovery** ◦ *I'm much better now.* ◦ *He soon got better.* ◦ *She recovered slowly.* ◦ *It took him a long time to get over his hepatitis.* ◦ *to make a good/rapid recovery*

an illness connected with ...	which:	is called...
colds and coughs	makes you sneeze makes you cough a lot is the result of being in a cold or damp place is like a cold but more serious; you have a temperature and your arms and legs ache	a **cold** a **cough** a **chill** **flu** (*noun* U), (*formal*) **influenza** (*noun* U)
breathing	causes difficulty in breathing makes you sneeze a lot affects part of the lungs and gives you a cough affects the lungs badly and makes breathing difficult gradually destroys the lungs	**asthma** (*noun* U); *adjective*: **asthmatic** **hay fever** (*noun* U) **bronchitis** (*noun* U) **pneumonia** (*noun* U) **tuberculosis** (*noun* U), (*abbreviation* **TB**); *adjective*: **tubercular**
the heart and blood vessels	suddenly makes the heart not work properly suddenly attacks the brain and can leave a person paralysed	a **heart attack**, a **coronary**; *adjective*: **coronary** a **stroke**
bones and muscles	causes pain in the muscles and joints causes pain and swelling in the joints attacks the backbone and can cause paralysis	**rheumatism** (*noun* U); *adjective*: **rheumatic** **arthritis** (*noun* U); *adjective*: **arthritic** **polio** (*noun* U)
stomach and liver	makes your appendix very painful so that it usually has to be removed makes your liver become inflamed makes your skin become yellow	**appendicitis** (*noun* U) **hepatitis** (*noun* U) **jaundice** (*noun* U)
bites or cuts caused by animals or insects	causes a fever after you have been bitten by a mosquito causes madness and death after you are bitten by an infected animal makes your muscles, especially on the face, become stiff after you get an infected cut	**malaria** (*noun* U); *adjective*: **malarial** **rabies** (*noun* U); *adjective*: **rabid** **tetanus** (*noun* U)
children	gives you a temperature and red spots on the skin that itch a lot gives you a temperature and small red spots causes the neck and lower face to swell gives you a bad cough with a loud noise when you breathe in after coughing	**chicken-pox** (*noun* U) **measles** (*noun* U) or **German Measles** (*noun* U) **mumps** (*noun* U) **whooping cough** (*noun* U)
unhygienic conditions	spreads quickly and kills many people causes diarrhoea and vomiting and can lead to death is caused by eating bad or unclean food causes a severe form of diarrhoea	**plague** (*noun* U) **cholera** (*noun* U) **food poisoning** (*noun* U) **dysentery** (*noun* U)
sunshine	is caused by spending too much time in strong sunlight or other heat is caused by too much sun on the skin	**sunstroke** (*noun* U), **heatstroke** (*noun* U) **skin cancer** (*noun* U)

– a return to good health: **cure** ◦ *The new drug brought about a miraculous cure.*

– to wish sb a recovery from illness you can say (or write) **Get well** (**soon**)

– to rest and recover from an illness over a period of time: **recuperate**, (*formal*) **convalesce**; the period of recovery: **recuperation** (*noun* U), (*formal*) **convalescence** (*noun singular*/U) ◦ *He was convalescing in the country.*

– to know that you are healthy enough to do sth: **feel* up to** sth ◦ *I don't feel up to going back to work yet.*

– to be improving in health: **make* good progress**, (*informal*) **be on the mend** ◦ *The patients are making good progress.* ◦ *Yes, I'm definitely on the mend at last!*

illness *contd.*

– no longer seriously ill: **out of danger** ◦ *It was good to hear that she's out of danger now.*
– to be affected by a form of treatment: **respond to** sth ◦ *He responded well to the new treatment.*

6 being well

– the condition of your body: **health** (*noun* U) ◦ *He has always enjoyed the best of health.* ◦ *She's in good health.*
– in good health: **well, all right, fine** ◦ *Is she well enough to travel now?* ◦ *Are you all right?* ◦ *I'm feeling fine now, thanks.*
– not often ill; strong and well; showing good health: **healthy** ◦ *a healthy baby* ◦ *healthy skin and hair*
– the state of being physically fit: **fitness** (*noun* U); *adjective*: **fit** ◦ *to try and improve your physical fitness* ◦ *fit and well*

Note: fine is not used in questions or in negative statements.

▷ looking after your body ⇨ **BODY**

– to ask about sb's health, you say **How are you?**

■ **MORE ...**

– some other (*informal*) expressions for saying that sb is not well: **under the weather, not looking yourself, in a bad way** ◦ *I really feel under the weather today.* ◦ *She's really not looking herself.* ◦ *He was in a bad way when I saw him.*

– a period of time spent away from work because of illness: **sick leave** (*noun* U) ◦ *He was given a month's sick leave.*
– a government payment to a person who is away from work because of illness: **sickness benefit** (*noun* U) ◦ *She wasn't entitled to sickness benefit.*
– a period of time when a person or animal that has (or may have) an infectious disease must be kept away from other people or animals: **quarantine** (*noun* U) ◦ *All dogs brought into Britain must be kept in quarantine for six months.*

– a person who is an expert in the study of diseases, especially one who tries to find out how sb has died: **pathologist**

– a person who is always worried about their health even when there is nothing wrong with them: **hypochondriac**

imagination

1 having imagination
2 using your imagination
3 dreams and fantasies

see also THINK

1 having imagination

– the ability to form pictures in your mind or to create new ideas: **imagination** (*noun* C/U) ◦ *to have a vivid/fertile imagination* ◦ *I think her paintings show a lot of imagination.* ◦ *You need to use your imagination.*
– having or showing imagination: **imaginative**; *opposite*: **unimaginative** ◦ *The council have come up with a very imaginative plan for improving the city centre.* ◦ *an imaginative child*
– the ability to imagine the future: **vision** (*noun* U) ◦ *The company needs people with vision to plan for the 21st century.*

2 using your imagination

– to form a picture or idea of sth in your mind: **imagine** sth, **think* of** sth ◦ *He imagined what it would be like to stand on the top of Mount Everest.* ◦ *Think of what you'd feel if you were in the winning team in the World Cup.*
– to use your imagination to develop an idea: **think*** sth **up**; to do this especially with sth unusual or not very sensible: **dream** sth **up** ◦ *I'll try to think up a better way of celebrating his birthday.* ◦ *What kind of fashion design has she dreamt up this time?*
– to have a picture in your mind of sb/sth: **visualize** sb/sth ◦ *It's hard to visualize what this place looked like before the war.*

3 dreams and fantasies

– to imagine sth that you would like to happen: **dream (about/of** sb/sth), **dream (that) ...** ◦ *He's always dreaming about retiring to a tropical island.* ◦ *I never dreamt that I would be so lucky!*
– a pleasant situation that you like thinking about but which is not likely to happen: **dream** ◦ *She has a dream of setting up her own business.*
– to imagine pleasant scenes that are not connected with what you are doing: **daydream**; *noun*: **daydream** ◦ *She sits at the window and daydreams.*

– a pleasant situation that you like thinking about but which is very unlikely to happen: **fantasy** ◦ *He has fantasies of being President.*
– thinking about pleasant things that are not likely to happen: **fantasy** (*noun* U) ◦ *He lives in a world of fantasy.* ◦ *a fantasy world*
– not real: **imaginary** ◦ *imaginary fears* ◦ *an imaginary friend*

▷ real, not imaginary ⇨ **REAL/EXISTING**

imitate

– copying sb's behaviour ⇨ **BEHAVIOUR**
– making a copy of sth ⇨ **COPY**

immediately ⇨ SOON

important

1 important
2 very important
3 saying that sth is important
4 unimportant

1 important

– having value or interest; necessary: **important**; *noun* (U): **importance** ◦ *an important meeting/decision/idea* ◦ *It's important not to make any mistakes here.* ◦ *It's very important that you arrive on time.* ◦ *I don't think she properly understood the importance of the occasion.* ◦ *This problem is of secondary importance* (= less important than sth else).

- interesting or important; deserving to be noticed: **significant**; *noun* (U): **significance** ◦ *It's significant that this has already happened three times before.* ◦ *The fact that both crimes were committed at night is significant.*
- famous or important in history: **historic** ◦ *a historic event*

- important because of having a high position or rank: **senior** ◦ *a senior official*
- important because of having power: **influential** ◦ *an influential person in the art world*
- important because of being famous: **prominent** ◦ *prominent politicians*
- important because of being successful in your job: **leading** ◦ *a leading cancer specialist*

- needing to be treated as important: **serious** (*adverb* **seriously**); *noun* (U): **seriousness** ◦ *This is a very serious problem.* ◦ *Don't laugh – this is serious.* ◦ *Why can't you ever take anything seriously?*
- treating sth as important; not joking: **serious** ◦ *Are you serious about going to Paris?*

- to be important: **matter** ◦ *You're happy now and that's all that really matters.* ◦ *'I'm so sorry I missed the meeting.' 'It doesn't matter.'*
- if sth is important to you, it **concerns** you, **means*** sth **to** you, **matters to** you, (*formal*) is **of concern to** you ◦ *I'm not bothered – her problems don't concern me at all.* ◦ *It doesn't matter to me what she decides to do.* ◦ *I don't know what I'd do without my children – they mean everything to me.*

2 very important

- very important: **big**, **major**, **considerable** ◦ *a big contract/opportunity* ◦ *major investments*
- absolutely necessary: **essential**, **crucial** (*adverb* **crucially**), **vital** (*adverb* **vitally**) ◦ *These days a degree is essential if you want to work for this company.* ◦ *It's crucial that you get there on time – otherwise you'll miss the whole concert.* ◦ *It's vitally important that you see a doctor.*
- important and needing to be done immediately: **urgent** (*adverb* **urgently**); *noun* (U): **urgency** ◦ *Sorry, can I use your phone? I've got an urgent call to make.* ◦ *We are urgently reconsidering the matter.*

▷ more on being necessary ⇨ NEED

■ most important

- something that is very important and that you must do before anything else: **priority** ◦ *Finding a place to live is a priority at the moment.*

- most important: **main**, **principal**, **chief** ◦ *My main problem is that I haven't got any money.* ◦ *The principal aim of this meeting is to solve staffing problems.* ◦ *His chief reason for leaving was ill-health.*
- mostly: **mainly**, **principally**, **chiefly** ◦ *I was mainly responsible for writing our publicity material.*

- first and most important: **primary** (*adverb* **primarily**), **basic** (*adverb* **basically**), **fundamental** (*adverb* **fundamentally**) ◦ *The primary cause of this problem is lack of money.* ◦ *The basic ingredients are flour, eggs and milk.* ◦ *Fundamentally, this is an environmental issue.*

- the most important quality of sth: **essence** (**of** sth) (*noun* U) ◦ *The essence of her argument was that we should be putting more money into education.*
- the starting point from which sth can develop: **basis** ◦ *The article on page 22 will form the basis of our discussion.*
- basic facts or principles: **fundamentals** (*noun plural*) ◦ *You need to understand the fundamentals of a subject like maths before you can study it at a higher level.*
- the most important things: **essentials** (*noun plural*) ◦ *Just bring the essentials – a toothbrush and a change of clothes.*

- to be more important than sb/sth: **come* before** sb/sth ◦ *My children come before everything.*

3 saying that sth is important

- to show by what you say or do that sth is important: **emphasize** sth, **stress** sth; *nouns*: **emphasis**, **stress** ◦ *I must emphasize that we will not tolerate lateness.* ◦ *I would like to stress three points in my talk today.* ◦ *They put a lot of emphasis on spoken English in that school.*
- to tell or show sb that you think sth is very important: **impress** sth **on** sb ◦ *I tried to impress on them the fact that we expect very high standards here.*

- to give emphasis to sth, you can say **particularly**, **especially**, **in particular**, **more/most importantly**, **notably** ◦ *My children, in particular the eldest one, are all good swimmers.* ◦ *How are we going to be able to afford the rent? And, more importantly, how will we feed the children?* ◦ *Some Prime Ministers, notably John Major, were reluctant to sign the agreement.*
- to a much greater degree than all the others: **most of all**, **above all** (**else**) ◦ *I want you to work hard, but most of all, I want you to have fun.* ◦ *It's my family that matters above all.*
- if you want people to know that sth you mention is just as important as the things mentioned before, you can say **last but not least** ◦ *Jane, Jackie, Susan, John, and last but not least, Bob.*

- if you have been laughing and you want to explain that what you are going to say next is not a joke but is serious, you can begin with **in all seriousness ...** or **joking apart ...** ◦ *In all seriousness, you're not going out in that old dress, surely?* ◦ *Joking apart, do you really think that?*
- a subject or incident that you should not joke about because it is serious is **no laughing matter**, **no joke** ◦ *This is no joke, you know!*
- when sth needs to be treated more seriously, it is **beyond a joke** ◦ *This situation has got beyond a joke.*

4 unimportant

- not having any importance: **unimportant** ◦ *an unimportant person/event*

important *contd.*

- very unimportant: **insignificant, trivial** ◦ *Don't bother with such insignificant details.* ◦ *a trivial mistake*
- small, not having much importance: **minor, negligible** ◦ *That's just a minor problem.* ◦ *The damage done was negligible.*
- if you want to say that sth is not very important, you can use the words **mere** (*only before a noun*) (*adverb* **merely**), **simple** (*only before a noun*) (*adverb* **simply**), **just, only** ◦ *A mere 2% of the population is unemployed in that country.* ◦ *a simple mistake* ◦ *It's just a minor error – don't worry about it.* ◦ *Sorry, I was only asking.*
- to become less important: **decline**; *noun* (U): decline ◦ *the declining influence of the Conservative Party* ◦ *the decline of the coal industry*

impossible ⇨ POSSIBLE[2]

in/out ⇨ PLACE[2]

include ⇨ PART/WHOLE

income ⇨ PAY[2]

increase/decrease

1 becoming more
2 becoming less

quantities ⇨ HOW MUCH/MANY
getting bigger/smaller in size ⇨ BIG/SMALL
changes in the price of sth ⇨ PRICE

1 becoming more

- to become more in quantity, importance, etc: **go* up, increase, rise*, grow***, (*informal*) **be on the increase** ◦ *The number of students has gone up/increased over the last year.* ◦ *Her work has increased in importance.* ◦ *Prices have risen again.* ◦ *The number of people with jobs has grown over the last two months.* ◦ *The power of the tabloid press continues to grow.* ◦ *Crime is on the increase.*
- to cause sth to become more: **increase** sth, **raise** sth ◦ *ways to increase food production* ◦ *They have promised not to raise taxes this year.*
- a situation in which sth increases: **increase (in** sth) (*noun* C/U), **rise (in** sth), **growth (in** sth) (*noun* C/U) ◦ *a pay increase* ◦ *a sudden/sharp increase in the number of burglaries in this area* ◦ *a pay rise* ◦ *a steady rise in the number of cases of stomach cancer* ◦ *economic growth*
- becoming more: **increasing, rising, growing** ◦ *An increasing number of people are buying their own homes.* ◦ *rising taxes* ◦ *growing prosperity*
- more (and continuing to become more): **more and more** ◦ *More and more people are cycling to work.*
- (used about the range or degree of sth) to become more and continue to become more: **become*/get* more and more** ◦ *People are becoming more and more aware of environmental issues.*
- to become two/three times as much or as many **double/treble**; to make sth two/three times as much or as many: **double/treble** sth ◦ *Those plants seem to have doubled in size since I last saw them.* ◦ *They've doubled the number of jobs over the past year.*
- to make sth the largest possible amount: **maximize** sth ◦ *We've maximized our profits this year.*

■ increasing slowly

- to gradually become more: **build* up, pile up, mount up**; *noun*: **build-up (of** sth) ◦ *These problems have been gradually building up over the last few years.* ◦ *My work has been piling up over the last few weeks.* ◦ *We don't spend very much but it all mounts up.* ◦ *a gradual build-up of tension*
- to cause sth to gradually become more: **build*** sth **up** ◦ *I'm gradually building up my collection of books.*

■ increasing quickly

- to increase very quickly: **shoot* up, leap* up, jump**; *noun*: **jump (in** sth) ◦ *University enrolments have shot up in the last ten years.* ◦ *a huge jump in the number of tourists*
- a sudden increase in (mainly economic) value or activity: **boom** ◦ *a boom in sales* ◦ *the property boom of the 1980s*

■ adding sth

- to put sth together with sth else so that you increase the quantity, value, etc: **add** sth (**to** sth) ◦ *Can you add this to my bill?*
- a thing which is added: **extra, addition**; *adjectives*: **extra, additional** ◦ *I bought all the food on the list, plus a few extras just in case.* ◦ *This dress will make a nice addition to my wardrobe.* ◦ *additional costs*
- to add sth to sth to make it more or complete: **supplement** sth (**by/with** sth); a thing that is added to sth to make it complete: **supplement**; *adjective*: **supplementary** ◦ *I have to supplement my income by working extra hours.* ◦ *vitamin supplements to improve your diet* ◦ *a supplementary charge*

2 becoming less

- to become less in quantity, importance, etc: **go* down, decrease, shrink***, (*formal*) **decline** ◦ *Air pollution has decreased/gone down by 10%.* ◦ *The number of workers in the steel industry is decreasing.* ◦ *Their share in the market has shrunk recently.* ◦ *His influence in public affairs has declined.*
- to cause sth to become less: **reduce** sth, **decrease** sth ◦ *Exercise reduces the risk of heart disease.* ◦ *to reduce/decrease sth in size*
- to slowly become less strong, less important, etc: **lessen** ◦ *The floods have not lessened; they've got worse.*
- to have less of sth: **lose*** sth; *noun*: **loss** ◦ *She seems to have lost interest in food recently.* ◦ *to lose business/sales* ◦ *Have you lost weight?* ◦ *The company made huge losses last year.*
- to use less of sth: **cut* down on** sth ◦ *I'm cutting down on cigarettes.*

- to reduce sth by half: **halve** sth ◦ *to halve the price of sth*
- to make sth the smallest or lowest amount possible: **minimize** sth ◦ *an attempt to minimize costs*

- a situation in which sth decreases: **decrease (in** sth) (*noun* C/U), **reduction (in** sth) (*noun* C/U), (*formal*) **decline (in** sth) (*noun* C/U) ◦ *a decrease in size* ◦ *a small reduction in price* ◦ *There has been a decline in the number of young people starting to smoke.* ◦ *a sharp/gradual decline in sales*

- becoming less: **decreasing, declining** ◦ *the decreasing number of people who smoke* ◦ *the rapidly declining birth rate* ◦ *declining standards*
- less (and continuing to become less): (with uncountable nouns) **less and less**, (with countable nouns) **fewer and fewer** ◦ *We're finding less and less gold each year.* ◦ *Each year, fewer and fewer people are going to classical concerts.*
- (used about the range and degree of sth) to become less and continue to become less: **become*/get* less and less** ◦ *Smoking is becoming less and less acceptable.*

■ decreasing quickly
- (used about prices, trade, etc) to decrease quickly: **slump, collapse**; *nouns*: **slump, collapse** ◦ *Share prices have collapsed.* ◦ *a slump in the housing market*

■ decreasing slowly
- to decrease slowly over a period of time: **drop off** ◦ *The number of people leaving school at sixteen has dropped off over the past year.*
- (used especially about pain, noise, activity, etc) to decrease slowly: **die down, ease (off)** ◦ *The traffic dies down once the rush hour is over.* ◦ *The work gradually eased off towards the end of the day.* ◦ *The pain is easing off a bit.*

independent

- countries ⇨ COUNTRY[1]
- people ⇨ HELP

industry

> making things ⇨ MAKE, FACTORY
> **see also** BUSINESS, ECONOMY, EMPLOYMENT, MANAGEMENT

- the work done in factories and large organizations: **industry** (*noun* C/U) ◦ *the growth of the car industry* ◦ *to develop the tourist industry* ◦ *The Government was planning to privatize the steel industry.*
- connected with industry: **industrial** ◦ *industrial development*
- industry that is involved in making things: **manufacturing industry** (*noun* C/U)
- industry that makes things like steel or large, heavy objects: **heavy industry** (*noun* C/U)
- industry that makes small goods: **light industry** (*noun* C/U)
- industry involved in helping people to do sth: **service industry** (*noun* C/U) ◦ *Service industries such as tourism and catering play an important part in the national economy.*
- industry that can be done at home: **cottage industry** (*noun* C/U) ◦ *Pottery, weaving, and knitting are important cottage industries in the north of Scotland.*

- if a country, area, town, etc has a lot of factories, etc, it is **industrial** ◦ *an industrial area*
- to develop industries in a country: **industrialize** (sth); *noun* (U): **industrialization** ◦ *Britain became industrialized at the beginning of the nineteenth century.* ◦ *the industrialized countries of the West*

- a person who owns or manages a large industrial company: **industrialist**

inferior

- of poor quality ⇨ BAD
- of lower rank ⇨ RANK

influence ⇨ POWER

inform

> facts that are heard, told or discovered about sth ⇨ INFORMATION
> what you say and how you say it ⇨ SAY

- to give sb a piece of information: **tell*** sb (sth), **let*** sb **know** (sth), **inform** sb (**about/of** sth), **inform** sb **that...** ◦ *You never told me you were getting married.* ◦ *Can you tell us about your childhood?* ◦ *Let me know what happens.* ◦ *You'd better inform the police of the accident.* ◦ *He finally informed his boss that he was going to resign.*
- a person who gives sb information: (*formal*) **informant** ◦ *He refused to name his informant.*

- to make sth known publicly, in an official way: **announce** sth ◦ *I am very pleased to announce a record increase in half-yearly profits.*
- a statement that tells people about sth: **announcement** ◦ *to make an announcement*
- a written statement giving information or news that is put where everybody can read it: **notice**; a board on a wall for putting notices on: **noticeboard** (*AmE* **bulletin board**), **board** ◦ *There's a notice on the board about tomorrow's meeting.*

- to give sb information about what has happened, or what you have seen, heard, read, etc: **report** sth (**to** sb) ◦ *We'd better report this to the police.* ◦ *The accident wasn't even reported in the newspapers.*
- to give sb information which they need: **brief** sb (**on** sth), **fill** sb **in** (**on** sth) ◦ *The minister was fully briefed before the meeting.* ◦ *Can you fill me in on the latest situation?*

- something which is reported, or a written or spoken description of an event or a situation: **report** ◦ *We've had a report of renewed fighting in the south of the country.* ◦ *an official report on the state of the economy*

inform *contd.*

- a report or description of sth which has happened: **account** ◦ *He gave us a detailed account of the trial.*

▷ news reports ⇨ **NEWS, NEWSPAPER**

- to give sb information about how to get to a certain place: **direct** sb, **give*** (sb) **directions** ◦ *Can you direct me to the station?*

- to give information (for example to the police) about sb who has done sth wrong: **inform on/against** sb, (*informal*) **tell* on** sb ◦ *She would never inform on her own son.* ◦ *You won't tell on me, will you?*
- a person who gives information to the police, etc: **informer** ◦ *a police informer*

- to give sb wrong information about sth: **mislead*** sb, **misinform** sb ◦ *We were misled into thinking it was a good investment.* ◦ *I'm afraid you've been misinformed.*
- information which gives you the wrong idea is **misleading** ◦ *a misleading advertisement*

▷ giving wrong information deliberately ⇨ **DECEIVE**

information

1 different kinds of information
2 collecting information
3 storing information
giving information ⇨ **INFORM**
see also KNOW, NEWS

1 different kinds of information

- facts that are heard, told or discovered about sth: **information** (**about/on** sb/sth) (*noun* U) ◦ *For further information on classes, please contact the secretary.* ◦ *The guidebook has a lot of useful information about Paris.* ◦ *reliable information* (= information that you can be sure is true) ◦ *false information* (= information that is not true) ◦ *a valuable piece of information*

- if you have a lot of information about sth, you are **well informed** ◦ *He's extremely well informed on the subject.*

- a piece of information that you know is true: **fact** ◦ *a scientific fact* ◦ *Stick to the relevant facts.* ◦ *The fact that he has a criminal record is not important in this case.*
- a small piece of particular information about sth: **detail** (*often plural*) ◦ *Just tell me the basic facts – don't worry about all the details.*
- detailed information: **facts and figures** (*noun plural*), (*formal*) **particulars** (*noun plural*) ◦ *Can you give us the particulars of all the items that were stolen?*
- something that you do not want anybody else to know: **secret**; *adjective*: **secret** ◦ *I can't tell you; it's a secret.* ◦ *They tried to keep their relationship secret.*

▷ more on secrets ⇨ **SECRET**

- a short description of the main points of sth, for example a report: **summary, outline** ◦ *a news summary* ◦ *I'll just give you an outline of what happened.*
- to make a summary of sth: **summarize** sth ◦ *Can you summarize the main points for us?*

- information about how to get to a certain place: **directions** (*noun plural*) ◦ *We'd better stop and ask for directions.*
- information about how to use sth or how to do sth: **instructions** (*noun plural*) ◦ *instructions on how to operate the photocopier*

- a collection of facts or information about sth: **data** (*noun* U) ◦ *Very little data is available on the subject.* ◦ *to gather/collect data*
- numbers which have been collected to provide information about sth: **statistics** (*noun plural*); *adjective*: **statistical** (*adverb* **statistically**) ◦ *unemployment statistics* ◦ *statistical evidence* ◦ *It's been statistically proved.*

- something that gives you a lot of useful information is **informative**; *opposite*: **uninformative** ◦ *Your letter was very informative.* ◦ *an informative guided tour*

2 collecting information

- to get information about sth: **find*** sth **out** (**about** sth) ◦ *What did you manage to find out about his family?*
- a place where you get information from (for example a person or a book): **source** (of information) ◦ *I heard it from a very reliable source.*

- to get information: **collect** sth ◦ *I've collected my data – now I have to start analysing it.*
- to collect information and arrange it in a list, book, etc: **compile** sth ◦ *He's compiling a dictionary of Indian English.*

- careful study of sth in order to find out information about it: **research** (**into** sth) (*noun* U) ◦ *carry out research into tropical diseases* ◦ *medical/scientific research*
- a list of questions that a researcher asks people in order to collect information about sth: **questionnaire** ◦ *answer/complete a questionnaire*
- a report which is the result of research into people's behaviour, opinions, etc: **survey** ◦ *conduct a survey to find out about people's eating habits*

▷ more on research ⇨ **STUDY**

- to collect information about sb/sth in a secret way: **spy** (**on** sb/sth) ◦ *spying on the enemy* ◦ *She's been accused of spying.*
- a person who spies on another person, country or organization: **spy**

3 storing information

- a collection of papers containing information on a particular subject: **file** ◦ *We keep files on all our students.*
- information which is stored in a file is **on file** ◦ *We should still have all the information on file.*

- a list of names, etc: **register** ◦ *the class register*
- a list of things, for example the things you can buy from a company, the books in a library, or

the paintings in an exhibition: **catalogue** (*AmE* **catalog**)
- a list of facts, numbers, etc arranged in a series of rows and columns: **table**
- a book that contains information, for example a dictionary: **reference book**
- a book that contains information about a school, university, business, etc: **prospectus**

▷ reference books ⇨ BOOK

- a machine that can store and arrange information: **computer**
- a collection of data stored in a computer: **database**

▷ more on storing and using information in computers ⇨ COMPUTER

■ **MORE ...**
- a piece of information that is useful to the police in helping to solve a crime: **clue, lead** ◦ *They spent the whole morning searching the house for clues.* ◦ *We're following up a number of useful leads.*
- detailed information about sth: **the ins and outs** (**of** sth) ◦ *He didn't take long to understand all the ins and outs of the problem.*
- to have information available whenever you need it: **have** sth **at** your **fingertips** ◦ *She has all the facts at her fingertips.*

injury

1 being injured
- to cause physical damage to your body, especially in an accident: **hurt*** sb/sth, **injure** sb/sth; *noun* (C/U): **injury** ◦ *I fell and hurt my arm.* ◦ *Several people were injured when the bus crashed.* ◦ *Luckily, his injuries weren't serious.* ◦ *internal injuries* (= to the inside of your body) ◦ *She was lucky to escape injury.*
- the bad effect of an accident, illness, etc: **harm** (*noun* U); *verb*: **harm** sb/sth ◦ *He fell off his bike but fortunately did not come to any serious harm.*
- something that can cause injury or illness is **dangerous, harmful**; *opposite*: **harmless** ◦ *dangerous sports* ◦ *harmless activities*

▷ dangerous situations ⇨ DANGEROUS

Note: hurt and **injure** are similar in meaning, but **hurt** can be used in less serious situations. **Harm** is not used for describing a physical injury but for any kind of bad effect.

- an injury (caused by a knife, a gun, etc), often received in fighting: **wound**; to cause a wound: **wound** sb (*usually passive*) ◦ *a bullet wound* ◦ *He died of his wounds.* ◦ *Many soldiers were wounded in the battle.*
- if you injure yourself or part of your body, you are **injured, hurt** (*not before a noun*); *opposite*: **unhurt** (*not before a noun*) ◦ *The injured passengers were taken to hospital.* ◦ *The doctor treated his injured leg.* ◦ *No one was seriously injured.* ◦ *Was anyone hurt?* ◦ *I was frightened but unhurt.*
- if the effects of an injury last for some time, the part can be called **bad** ◦ *He's had a bad leg ever since that fall last year.*
- an injury that causes death is **fatal** (*adverb* **fatally**) ◦ *fatally injured*

■ people who have been injured
- a person who has been injured in an accident or war: **casualty, victim** ◦ *There were numerous casualties.* ◦ *the victims of road accidents*
- people who have been hurt: **the injured** (*noun plural*); in a war: **the wounded** (*noun plural*) *The injured were taken to hospital.*

2 different kinds of injury

■ cuts
- an injury caused by sth sharp like a knife: **cut**; *verb*: **cut*** sb/sth ◦ *I cut my finger with a vegetable knife.* ◦ *a deep/serious cut* ◦ *a slight/superficial cut*
- a small cut: **scratch**; *verb*: **scratch** sb/sth ◦ *They survived the accident without even a scratch.* ◦ *If you tease the cat it'll scratch you.*
- a light cut caused by sth rough moving over the skin: **graze**; *verb*: **graze** sb/sth *She fell over and grazed her knee.*
- to damage sb's body badly, often by cutting off parts of it: **mutilate** sb/sth; *noun* (U): **mutilation** ◦ *badly mutilated bodies*
- to lose blood: **bleed*** ◦ *My finger's still bleeding. I need a bandage.*
- an area of dried blood that forms where there has been a cut: **scab**
- a mark that is left on your skin after a cut or wound has healed: **scar**; *adjective*: **scarred** ◦ *The accident left him scarred for life.*

■ bites
- a painful place on the skin caused by the teeth of an animal, insect, etc: **bite**; *verb*: **bite*** sb/sth ◦ *She had several nasty bites on her leg.*
- a sudden pain that is the result of an insect or plant pushing sth sharp into the skin: **sting**; *verb*: **sting*** sb/sth ◦ *I was stung by a wasp.*

■ burns
- an injury caused by fire or heat: **burn**; *verb*: **burn** sb/sth ◦ *He'd got a nasty burn on his leg.* ◦ *She was badly burned in the fire.*
- an injury caused by very hot liquid: **scald**; *verb*: **scald** sb/sth

■ being hit
- a dark mark on the skin caused by knocking sth, being hit, etc: **bruise**; *verb*: **bruise** sb/sth ◦ *He had several cuts and bruises on his face.* ◦ *I fell over and bruised my arm.*
- badly bruised: **black and blue** ◦ *to be beaten black and blue*
- a person who has been badly beaten is **battered** ◦ *a refuge for battered wives*
- a hard raised place on the skin caused by a blow: **bump** ◦ *a bump on the head*

injury *contd.*

– an injury to the brain caused by a blow to the head: **concussion** (*noun* U); *verb* (*usually passive*): **concuss** sb ◦ *He was rushed to hospital suffering from concussion.* ◦ *She was badly concussed.*

■ injuries to bones and muscles

– to damage a bone so that it breaks or cracks: **break*** sth, (*formal*) **fracture** sth; *noun*: **fracture** ◦ *He fell and broke his collar-bone.* ◦ *a hip fracture*
– to injure part of your body by bending or turning it suddenly: **sprain** sth; *noun*: **sprain** ◦ *She tripped and sprained her ankle.* ◦ *a sprained wrist*
– to injure part of your body by using it too much: **strain** sth ◦ *I've strained my back carrying that box.*
– to damage a muscle by using too much force: **pull a muscle** ◦ *He pulled a muscle playing football.*

■ injuries that stop your body working well

– an injury that makes you unable to use part of your body properly: **disability** (*noun* C/U); having a disability: **disabled** ◦ *He's unable to work because of his disability.* ◦ *a disabled soldier*
– to cause an injury that makes you unable to walk: **cripple** sb ◦ *She was crippled in a road accident.*
– to walk in an uneven way because of injury: **limp**; *noun* (*singular*): **limp** ◦ *to walk with a limp*
– (mainly used about animals) unable to walk properly: **lame**; *noun* (U): **lameness** *a lame horse*
– to make a person unable to see: **blind** sb ◦ *He was blinded in a fire at the factory.*
– to make a person unable to hear: **deafen** sb ◦ *We were deafened by the explosion.*

3 dealing with injuries

– medical help that you give to an injured person before a doctor arrives: **first aid** (*noun* U) ◦ *to give sb first aid*
– a small piece of sticky material that is used to cover a cut: (**sticking**) **plaster** (*noun* C/U) ◦ *You need to put a plaster on that cut.*
– a long piece of soft white material that is wrapped round a wound or injury: **bandage**, (*more formal*) **dressing**; *verb*: **bandage** sth ◦ *The nurse bandaged my arm.*
– to clean a wound and put a bandage, etc on it: **dress** sth
– when a wound or cut gets better, it **heals**
– one of the small pieces of thread that a doctor uses to sew your skin together if you cut yourself very badly: **stitch**; *verb*: **stitch** sth ◦ *His arm was so badly cut that he needed several stitches.*

▷ dealing with broken bones ⇨ BONE
▷ taking an injured person to hospital ⇨ ACCIDENT
▷ treatment in hospital ⇨ HOSPITAL

■ **MORE ...**

– to ask for money from sb because they have injured you (usually through a court): **claim damages/compensation**
– to pay sb money because you have injured them: **compensate** (sb) (**for** sth)

innocent ⇨ TRIAL

insect

1 different kinds of insect
2 things that insects do
3 avoiding or killing insects
see also SPIDER

1 different kinds of insect

– a small animal with six legs and usually one or two pairs of wings: **insect**
– a small insect, especially one that causes damage or is found in dirty places: **bug**

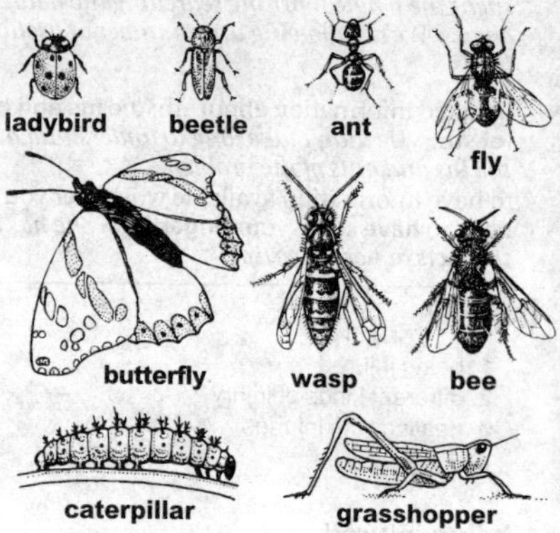

▷ bees ⇨ BEE

– an insect like a butterfly that normally flies at night: **moth**
– a flying insect that often destroys vegetation and crops: **locust**
– an insect that makes a loud noise by rubbing its wings together: **cricket**
– a small flying insect that bites people and animals and sucks their blood: **mosquito** (*plural* **mosquitoes**)
– a small insect like a mosquito that bites: **gnat**, **midge**
– a very small jumping insect that lives on cats, dogs, etc: **flea** ◦ *Their dog's got fleas!*
– a small insect that lives on the skin and in the hair of people and animals: **louse** (*plural* **lice**)
– a small insect that lives in the skin of an animal and sucks its blood: **tick** ◦ *sheep ticks*
– an animal like an insect that lives in hot countries and has a long tail that produces a poisonous sting: **scorpion**
– a large brown or black insect, often found in dirty places: **cockroach**
– a long thin crawling animal with many pairs of legs: **centipede, millipede**

- an insect like an ant, that eats and destroys wood: **termite**
- an insect that grows from the eggs of flies that have been laid in meat, cheese, etc: **maggot**

2 things that insects do

- the sound that an insect makes when flying: **buzz**; *verb*: **buzz**
- when an insect such as a mosquito or an ant pricks your skin and sucks your blood, it **bites*** you; *noun*: **bite** ◦ *I've got mosquito bites all down my arm!*
- when a bee or wasp pricks your skin, it **stings*** you; *noun*: **sting** ◦ *a bee sting* ◦ *Ow! I've been stung by a wasp.*

- a large group of insects flying together: **swarm** ◦ *a swarm of midges/bees/wasps*
- to move slowly with the body close to the ground or some other surface: **crawl** ◦ *Some kind of insect just crawled under your chair.*
- completely covered with insects: **crawling with** sth ◦ *The kitchen was crawling with cockroaches.*

- the fine yellow powder that bees and other insects collect from flowers and carry to other flowers: **pollen** (*noun* U)

3 avoiding or killing insects

- to hit an insect with sth flat or with your hand: **swat** sth ◦ *to swat a fly*
- a chemical used to kill insects that destroy plants: **insecticide** (*noun* C/U)
- a chemical used to keep insects away: **repellent** (*noun* C/U) ◦ *mosquito repellent*
- liquid in a special container (an aerosol) that is used for killing flies or other insects in the house: **fly spray** (*noun* U)

- a fine cotton net which covers a bed to prevent mosquitoes biting you during the night: **mosquito net**

inside ⇨ PLACE[2]

instrument

- a kind of tool ⇨ TOOL
- for making music ⇨ MUSIC

insult

see also BLAME, CRITICISM

- not polite: **rude**; *noun* (U): **rudeness** ◦ *He was so rude to me!*
- to speak to sb in a rude way: **insult** sb ◦ *I've never been so insulted in all my life.*
- a rude thing that sb says: **insult**, **abuse** (*noun* U); *adjectives*: **insulting**, **abusive** ◦ *And then they started shouting insults at each other.* ◦ *a term of abuse* ◦ *insulting behaviour* ◦ *an abusive remark*

- to insult sb using bad language: **swear* at** sb ◦ *He just started swearing at me for no apparent reason.*
- to insult sb by laughing in a rude way: **laugh at** sb/sth, **make* fun of** sb/sth ◦ *You're laughing at me!* ◦ *Don't make fun of her – she can't help it.*
- to use insulting words about sb (such as 'liar', 'coward'): (*informal*) **call** sb **names**
- saying the opposite of what you really mean, either as a joke or to insult sb: **sarcasm** (*noun* U); *adjective*: **sarcastic** ◦ *I'm fed up with your sarcastic comments.*

- to make sb feel bad by speaking or acting rudely: **hurt** sb's **feelings**, **offend** sb, **cause/give* offence** (*AmE* **offense**) (**to** sb) ◦ *Be careful what you say – she's easily offended.* ◦ *I hope I didn't cause any offence.*
- causing sb to feel offended: **offensive**; *opposite*: **inoffensive** ◦ *offensive behaviour/remarks*
- to be offended by sth: **take* offence** (*AmE* **offense**) (**at** sth) ◦ *You didn't need to take offence.*
- to offend sb, for example by not looking at them or not talking to them: **snub** sb; *noun*: **snub** ◦ *I'm sure it was a deliberate snub.*

■ **MORE ...**
- people who are not sensitive and do not get hurt when they are insulted are **thick-skinned**

insurance

events causing damage, injury, loss, etc ⇨ ACCIDENT

- a kind of contract (= written agreement) in which, in return for a regular payment, a company agrees to pay you a sum of money if you lose sth, become ill, etc: **insurance** (**against** sth) (*noun* U) ◦ *insurance against accidental injury*

- insurance in case you die suddenly: **life insurance**
- insurance in case you become ill: **health insurance**, **medical insurance**
- insurance in case you have an accident or you lose sth when you are travelling: **travel insurance**
- insurance in case your house is damaged or sth is stolen from it: **household insurance**

- insurance in case your car is damaged or stolen: **motor insurance**, **car insurance**
- the most basic motor insurance: **third party insurance**; a fuller and more expensive motor insurance: **comprehensive insurance**

■ arranging insurance
- a company that specializes in insurance: **insurance company**
- a person who sells insurance: **insurance salesman/woman** (*plurals* **salesmen/women**), **insurance broker**

- if you need insurance, you can **take* out** insurance (**against** sth), **insure** sb/sth (**against** sth) ◦ *I've taken out health insurance.* ◦ *It is sensible to insure the contents of your house against theft.*
- to have insurance against sth: **be covered** (**against** sth) ◦ *Are you covered against fire damage?*

insurance *contd.*

- the agreement that you make with an insurance company, or the document that shows this: (**insurance**) **policy** ◦ *a life insurance policy*
- the amount of money that you pay regularly to an insurance company: **premium** ◦ *to pay monthly premiums of £30*

■ getting money from an insurance company
- to ask for money from an insurance company after you have been injured, etc: **claim** (sth), **claim** (**on** sth) ◦ *Can't you claim on your insurance for the camera you lost?*
- when an insurance company gives money to sb who makes a claim, it **pays*** (sb) (sth), **pays* out** sth (**to** sb) ◦ *Insurance companies had to pay out millions of pounds after storms devastated southern England.*

intelligent ⇨ CLEVER

intend/plan

1 intentions
2 plans
3 making a plan
4 using a plan
see also DECIDE/CHOOSE, PROMISE, READY, WANT

1 intentions
- the reason for doing or making sth: **purpose**, **object**, **point** ◦ *the purpose of their visit* ◦ *the object of the inquiry* ◦ *What's the point of working so hard?*
- a result that you want to cause to happen: **aim**, **objective** ◦ *Our aim is to improve language teaching in schools.* ◦ *You need to be clear about your objectives.*

▷ more on reasons for doing sth ⇨ REASON

- to have a particular purpose in mind: **mean* to** do sth, **intend to** do sth, **plan to** do sth/**on** doing sth ◦ *I meant to be here two hours ago, but the traffic was really heavy.* ◦ *We had intended to drive to London, but in the end we decided to go by train.* ◦ *I'm planning to go to France for my summer holiday.* ◦ *Are you planning on working late tonight?*
- to have an idea of sth that you might possibly do: **think* of** doing sth ◦ *Kate's thinking of studying geography at university.*
- to plan sth or make sth for a particular person or purpose: **intend** sth **for** sb/sth, **intend** sb **to** do sth, **mean*** sb **to** do sth ◦ *You shouldn't have read that letter – it wasn't intended for you.* ◦ *These classes are intended for beginners.* ◦ *I didn't intend/mean you to do all the work.*

- what you intend or mean to do: **intention** (**to** do sth/**of** doing sth) (*noun* C/U) ◦ *Our intention is to leave early in the morning.* ◦ *I had no intention of hurting his feelings.*
- a thing that is intended is **deliberate** (*adverb* **deliberately**), **intentional** (*adverb* **intentionally**), it is done **on purpose** ◦ *That was no accident; it was deliberate!* ◦ *Did you go that way intentionally or did you lose your way?*
- if sth happens without being intended, it is **accidental**, **unintentional**, it happens **accidentally**, **by accident**, **by chance** ◦ *This new drug was discovered completely by accident.*

- if you want to say that you intend to do sth, you can use **will**, **shall** or **going to** ◦ *I'll send this letter off first.* ◦ *Don't worry. I'll be there!* ◦ *I'm going to carry on until I finish.*
- with the intention of doing sth: **to** do sth, **so as to** do sth, **in order to** do sth ◦ *I slowed down so as to give the others a chance to catch up.* ◦ *We left early in order to avoid the traffic.*

2 plans
- an idea or arrangement for doing sth in the future: **plan** ◦ *a peace plan* ◦ *a plan for reducing traffic in the city centre* ◦ *I have no plans to stay in Britain.*
- before sth becomes a proper plan, it is an **idea** ◦ *I've had an idea. Why don't we hire a car and go by road?*

- plans or preparations for things to be done in the future: **arrangements** (*noun plural*) ◦ *Jack and Sally are busy making arrangements for their wedding.*
- a plan for some work: **project** ◦ *a building project* ◦ *Who's organizing this project?*
- an official plan for organizing sth: **scheme** ◦ *What do you think of Tom's new scheme for recycling waste paper in the office?*

■ plans on paper
- a list, drawing or diagram that shows how sth is to be organized: **plan** ◦ *You can see the plans for the new shopping centre at the Town Hall.*
- a plan of things to do: **programme** (*AmE* **program**) ◦ *a programme of events*
- a list that shows the times that things are planned to happen: **timetable**, **schedule** (*noun* C/U) ◦ *a school/train timetable* ◦ *I've got a busy schedule for the next few days.* ◦ *The project is behind schedule* (= they have done less than was planned).
- a drawing that shows how sth should be made or how the parts of sth are arranged: **design** ◦ *a design for a house*

▷ more on designing things ⇨ DESIGN

3 making a plan
- to make preparations for sth in the future: **arrange** sth, **arrange** (**for** sb/sth) (**to** do sth), **organize** sth ◦ *We're arranging a leaving party for Pablo.* ◦ *Who organized the conference?*
- the way in which sth has been organized: **organization** (*noun* U) ◦ *I didn't think much of the organization of the sports day!*
- a person who organizes events, activities, etc: **organizer** ◦ *the organizers of the conference*

- to decide, organize or prepare for sth: **plan** (sth), **make* plans**; the process of making a plan: **planning** (*noun* U) ◦ *Have you planned what you're going to do this summer?* ◦ *Paul is making*

plans for his retirement. ◦ *A lot of planning has gone into this project.*
- to think about or prepare for what you will do in the future: **plan/think* ahead** ◦ *You have to think ahead in this job.*
- to arrange for sth to happen at a certain time in the future: **timetable** sth, **schedule** sth ◦ *I've scheduled your next meeting for ten o'clock.*

- to think up a plan to do sth: **make* a plan, draw* up a plan** ◦ *Before you start writing your essay, it's a good idea to make a brief plan.* ◦ *The council has drawn up a plan to recycle its rubbish.*
- to secretly plan to do sth bad or illegal: **plot** (**to** do sth); this kind of plan: **plot, conspiracy**; a person who takes part in a plot: **conspirator** ◦ *They were plotting to overthrow the government.* ◦ *a conspiracy to kidnap the Prime Minister*

- to suggest a possible plan: **propose** sth/doing sth, **put*** sth **forward**; *noun*: **proposal** ◦ *I propose that we all have lunch together.* ◦ *The minister put forward a new plan to help the homeless.* ◦ *What did she think of your proposal to recruit more staff?*
- to give the most important ideas or parts of a plan: **outline** sth, **sketch** sth **out**; *noun*: **outline** ◦ *He outlined the main points of the plan.* ◦ *Tony sketched out next year's business plans to his bank manager.* ◦ *Here is a brief outline of what we want to do over the coming year.*

- to arrange with sb that you or they will do sth: **agree** (**with** sb) (**on/about** sth), **agree to** do sth; *noun* (U): **agreement** ◦ *We need to agree on a date for our next meeting.* ◦ *We arrived at the agreed time.* ◦ *We found that we were in complete agreement about the children's education.*

■ not planned
- if sth is not planned but happens naturally, it is **spontaneous** (*adverb* **spontaneously**) ◦ *spontaneous applause* ◦ *I don't think his speech was planned – it seemed quite spontaneous.*
- not intended: **involuntary** (*adverb* **involuntarily**) ◦ *She gave an involuntary gasp of pain when the doctor inserted the needle.*

- without having much time to plan sth: **at short notice** ◦ *I can't teach the lesson at such short notice. I need time to prepare.*
- not thinking about what will probably happen in the future: **short-sighted** ◦ *The Government's education policy is extremely short-sighted.*

4 using a plan
- to start using a plan: **carry** sth **out**, (*formal*) **implement** sth ◦ *Although he did not agree with the plan, Jenkins was ordered to carry it out.* ◦ *Many teachers are finding it hard to implement the Government's educational reforms.*
- to do what a plan tells you to do: **follow** sth, **keep* to** sth
- when a plan is being used, it is **in operation**

- to manage to do what you have planned: **succeed** (**in** sth/doing sth); *noun*: **success**; *adjective*: **successful**; *opposite*: **unsuccessful**
- if a plan does not succeed, it **fails, falls* through, goes* wrong**; *noun* (U/C): **failure**
- if sth happens without difficulty or as you planned it, it **goes* according to plan, goes* smoothly, works out** ◦ *All our holiday plans fell through when I lost my job.* ◦ *So far the building work is going according to plan.*

---

interested ⇨ INTERESTING

---

interesting

1 interesting
2 not interesting
3 being interested
4 not interested
see also LIKE², ENJOY

1 interesting
- a thing that you enjoy doing, thinking or learning about is **interesting** ◦ *an interesting book/subject/job/hobby* ◦ *I thought his lecture was very interesting.*
- a person who you enjoy listening to is **interesting** ◦ *an interesting speaker*

- very interesting: **fascinating** ◦ *a fascinating story/woman*
- interesting and enjoyable: **amusing, entertaining** ◦ *an amusing film* ◦ *an entertaining evening/speaker*

- to make sb want to learn or hear more about sth or to get involved in sth: **interest** sb (**in** sth) ◦ *I enjoyed the class very much as the subject interests me a great deal.* ◦ *Can I interest you in coming to the exhibition?*
- to interest sb very much: **fascinate** sb ◦ *Archaeology has always fascinated me.* ◦ *I was fascinated to hear about her trip to South America.*

- to get the interest of other people: **attract** sb, **attract** sb's **attention** ◦ *The film attracted a lot of publicity.* ◦ *What attracted my attention was the title of the book.*
- a thing that is interesting and attracts people's attention: **attraction** ◦ *The Eiffel Tower is a major tourist attraction.*

■ interesting events
- things that interest and amuse people: **entertainment** (*noun* U) ◦ *There were singing, dancing and comedy shows for our entertainment.*
- to interest and amuse: **entertain** sb; a person who does this: **entertainer** ◦ *We entertained the children with games and tricks.*
- full of interesting events: **eventful** ◦ *an eventful day*
- full of variety, interest and excitement: **lively, colourful** (*AmE* **colorful**) ◦ *a lively party* ◦ *a colourful show*
- to make sth more interesting and exciting: **liven** sth **up** ◦ *This party needs livening up – let's have some dancing!*

▷ more on entertainment ⇨ ENTERTAINMENT

interesting *contd.*

2 not interesting

- not interesting: **boring, uninteresting, dull** ○ *a boring programme/book* ○ *an uninteresting job* ○ *a dull conversation* ○ *My life is too busy to be dull.*
- to make a person tired and uninterested: **bore** sb; a person or activity that does this: **bore** ○ *Am I boring you?* ○ *Football bores me to death – I'd much rather watch tennis.* ○ *Don't invite Edward – he's a terrible bore.* ○ *Have you got to copy all of that? What a bore!*
- boring and lasting for a long time: **tedious** ○ *What a tedious film – it just went on and on!*
- dull and without variety: **monotonous**; *noun* (U): **monotony** ○ *monotonous work* ○ *The monotony of this work is driving me mad.*

3 being interested

- wanting to know or hear more about sth: **interested** (**in** sth/doing sth); *noun* (U/*singular*): **interest** (**in** sth/doing sth) ○ *What sort of music are you interested in?* ○ *She was interested to hear all our news.* ○ *He's never shown much interest in going to university.* ○ *I've lost interest in this book.* ○ *I wish you took more interest in what I say.*
- the quality that makes sth interesting: **interest** (*noun* U) ○ *Is this book of interest to you?* ○ *a matter of great interest to many people* ○ *His meeting with Picasso helped to stimulate his interest in painting.*

- a thing that you enjoy doing or learning about: **interest** ○ *One of my interests is modern jazz.* ○ *Tell me about your interests.*
- something that you do regularly for pleasure in your spare time: **hobby** ○ *'What hobbies do you have?' 'Tap dancing, rock climbing and stamp collecting.'*
- to take an active interest in sth: **follow** sth ○ *Have you been following the football?*
- to be or become interested in sth: **be/get* into** sth ○ *He's heavily into modern jazz.* ○ *When did you get into local politics?*
- to start doing sth regularly: **take*** sth **up** ○ *I took up jogging last year and it's done me a lot of good.* ○ *Winter is a good time to take up a new hobby.*

- to be interested in or worried about sb/sth: **care** (**about** sb/sth) ○ *Do you really care about me?*

■ being very interested

- a feeling of pleasure and interest in sth that is happening or expected to happen: **excitement** (*noun* U); a person who feels excitement is **excited**

▷ more on being excited ⇨ EXCITED

- to be very interested in sth and like it very much: **love** sth/doing sth; *noun* (C/U): **love** ○ *I've always loved animals.* ○ *He loves fishing.* ○ *a love of food/music/sport*
- strong and eager interest: **enthusiasm** (**for/about** sth) (*noun* U); full of enthusiasm: **enthusiastic** (**about** sth), **keen** (**to** do sth), **keen on** sth ○ *He didn't show much enthusiasm for the idea.* ○ *She's very enthusiastic about her new job.* ○ *a keen gardener* ○ *We're keen to see as many of the sights as possible.* ○ *She's very keen on sport.*
- a person who is very interested in an activity or subject: **fan, enthusiast** ○ *a football fan* ○ *an opera enthusiast*

- extremely interested: (*informal*) **mad** (**keen**) **about/on** sth ○ *The kids are mad about this new American pop group.* ○ *My son is mad keen on spaceships at the moment.*
- to be so excited about sth that you forget what you are doing: **be/get* carried away** ○ *We got so carried away with the music that we didn't notice when everybody else stopped dancing.*

4 not interested

- not interested: **uninterested**; to become uninterested: **lose*** (**all**) **interest** (**in** sth) ○ *I used to like photography but I lost interest in it when I broke my camera.*
- to become impatient with or annoyed by sb/sth: **be/get* tired of** sb/sth/doing sth ○ *We're tired of watching the same old programmes repeated again and again on television.*
- feeling uninterested and tired because sth is not exciting or because you do not have anything to do: **bored** (**with** sth); very bored: **bored stiff**, **bored to tears**; *noun* (U): **boredom** ○ *I'm bored with this – can we do something else now?* ○ *I was bored stiff but everyone else seemed to find the talk interesting.*

- bored or unhappy: (*informal*) **fed up** (**with** sb/sth/doing sth) ○ *I'm fed up with having to wait for you all the time.* ○ *What's the matter? You look fed up.*
- without interest or wanting to do anything: **apathetic**; *noun* (U): **apathy** ○ *'Why do so few local people turn up to meetings?' 'I think it's just apathy.'*
- if you are not interested in sb/sth, you (*informal*) **don't* care** (**about** sb/sth) ○ *I don't care who wins the election.*
- if you are completely uninterested in sth and do not want to do it or be troubled by it, you **couldn't care less** ○ *'You could lose a lot of money if you don't take this job.' 'I really couldn't care less.'*
- not enthusiastic: **unenthusiastic**
- if you are not interested enough in sth to want to do it, you (*informal*) **can't be bothered** ○ *I really couldn't be bothered to go to the party.*

international ⇨ COUNTRY[1]

introduce ⇨ MEET

invent

see also DESIGN, MAKE

- to think of sth or make sth for the first time: **invent** sth ○ *Who invented the bicycle?*
- the act or process of making or designing sth for the first time: **invention** (*noun* U) ○ *Before the invention of the washing machine, clothes had to be washed by hand.*

- a thing that has been made or designed for the first time: **invention** ◦ *What would you say is the most useful invention of the 20th century?*
- a person who invents sth: **inventor**

- a person who has clever and original ideas is **inventive, original** ◦ *an original thinker*
- ideas or people that deal with things in a new way are **innovative** ◦ *an innovative approach to small car design*
- a person who introduces changes: **innovator**
- a new idea or way of doing sth: **innovation**

- an official licence from the government that gives a person or company the right to make or sell a certain product and stops other people from copying it: **patent**
- to obtain a patent for sth: **patent** sth ◦ *What a brilliant invention! Do you think it's been patented?*

investigate

- trying to find out a fact ⇨ LOOK FOR
- studying sth ⇨ STUDY

invite

see also MEAL, PARTY

- to ask sb to come to sth (for example a party or a meal or to your house): **invite** sb (**to/for** sth), **ask** sb (**to** sth); *noun* (U): **invitation** ◦ *She invited me to go for a drink with her.* ◦ *They've invited us for dinner on Saturday.* ◦ *They forgot to ask Bob to the wedding.* ◦ *a letter of invitation*
- to ask sb to do sth with you: **invite** sb **to** do sth ◦ *We've been invited to join them for a game of tennis.*
- a written or spoken request to come to a party, etc: **invitation**, (*informal*) **invite** ◦ *a wedding invitation* ◦ *Haven't you sent out the invitations yet?* ◦ *I've got an invite to the party.*

- to ask sb to come to your house: **ask** sb **over/round, invite** sb **over/round** ◦ *Why don't we ask them over?*
- to have sb as a guest at your house: **have** sb **over/round** ◦ *I had them round for a meal at the weekend.*
- to ask sb to come back to your house (after going somewhere else with them): **ask** sb **back, invite** sb **back** ◦ *Shall we invite them back for a coffee after the film?*
- to ask sb to come into your house: **ask** sb **in, invite** sb **in** ◦ *Aren't you going to invite me in?*

- to ask sb to come with you somewhere: **ask** sb **along, invite** sb **along** ◦ *I hope you don't mind if I invite Max along.*
- to take sb with you to a place: **bring*** sb **along** ◦ *Why don't you bring him along?*
- to ask sb to go out with you as your guest: **ask** sb **out, invite** sb **out** ◦ *He's so shy, I thought he'd never ask her out.*
- to take sb somewhere as your guest: **take*** sb **out** ◦ *Let me take you out for a meal.*

- a person who has been invited to a house, party, etc: **guest**
- a man/woman who has invited people to his/her house: **host/hostess** ◦ *I still haven't met the host.*

■ not invited
- a person who has not been invited is **uninvited** ◦ *an uninvited guest*

▷ going to a party when you are not invited ⇨ PARTY

■ different ways of inviting people
- to invite sb to sth, you can say **Can you come (...)?** or **Would you like to come (...)?** ◦ *'Can you come round for a meal some time this week?' 'Yes, I'd love to – thanks.'* ◦ *'Would you like to come to dinner next Saturday?' 'I'm very sorry but I'm afraid I can't. I'm going to the theatre that evening.'*
- in a formal written invitation, you can write: (your name) **requests the pleasure of** sb's **company** (**at...**) ◦ *Mr and Mrs Johnson request the pleasure of your company at their daughter's wedding.*

■ replying to an invitation
- to give an answer to an invitation: **reply** (**to** sth); *noun*: **reply** ◦ *Have you replied to the invitation?* ◦ *So far we've only had six replies.*
- (written on invitations) please reply: **RSVP**
- to say yes to an invitation: **accept** sth; *noun* (U): **acceptance** ◦ *I'd be pleased to accept your kind invitation.*
- to say no to an invitation: **turn** sth **down, refuse** sth, (*formal*) **decline** (sth); *noun*: **refusal** ◦ *I can't believe she turned down my invitation!* ◦ *We've had five acceptances and only one refusal.*

iron ⇨ METAL

ironing

see also CLOTHES, WASH

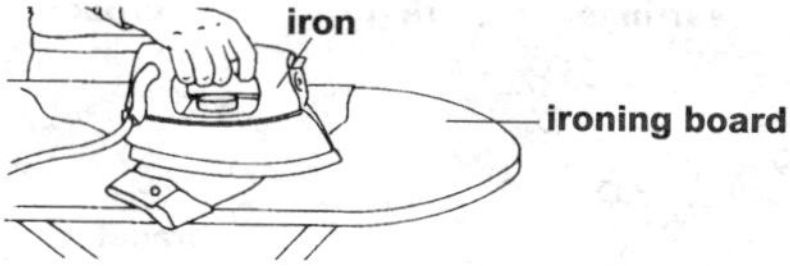

- to use an iron to make clothes flat and smart after you have washed and dried them: **iron** (sth), **press** sth; an act of ironing: **press** ◦ *Your shirt needs ironing.* ◦ *Could you iron my trousers for me?* ◦ *Those trousers could do with a press.*

- clothes which are to be ironed: **ironing** (*noun* U) ◦ *a large pile of ironing*
- to iron the things that need to be ironed: **do* the ironing** ◦ *I can't chat for long – I've got to do the ironing.*

- before you iron sth and make it flat and smooth, it is **creased**, full of **creases** ◦ *Pack it carefully so that it doesn't get creased.* ◦ *to iron the creases out of sth*
- a neat line that you make deliberately when you iron sth: **crease** ◦ *trousers with a sharp crease*

ironing *contd.*

- if the iron is too hot and you burn the cloth a little, you **scorch** it; the mark you make: **scorch mark**
- if sth does not need ironing (because it is made of polyester, etc), it is **drip-dry** ◦ *a drip-dry shirt*

Islam ⇨ MUSLIM

island ⇨ LAND

jam ⇨ BREAD

jealous

- because you love sb ⇨ LOVE
- because of wanting sth ⇨ WANT

Jew

other religions ⇨ RELIGION

- the religion of the Jewish people: **Judaism** (*noun* U)
- a person whose religion is Judaism: **Jew**
- connected with Judaism and Jews: **Jewish**

- the holy book of Judaism: **the Bible**
- a building in which Jews pray: **synagogue**
- a Jewish religious leader and teacher of Jewish law: **rabbi**
- food which is acceptable according to Jewish belief: **kosher** food

jewellery

see also CLOTHES

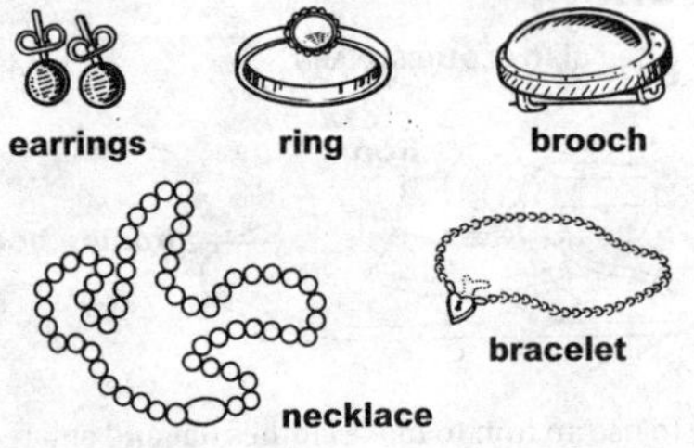

- rings, necklaces, etc made of precious materials, that you wear for decoration: **jewellery** (*AmE* **jewelry**) (*noun* U) ◦ *She always wears the most beautiful jewellery!* ◦ *a piece of jewellery*

- a band of metal that you wear on your finger: **ring** ◦ *a diamond ring*
- a ring that a woman wears to show that she has promised to marry sb: **engagement ring**
- a gold ring that women or men wear when they are married: **wedding ring**
- the third finger, usually of your left hand: **ring finger**

- a piece of jewellery that you wear around your neck: **necklace**
- a necklace made of tiny rings of metal linked together: **chain** ◦ *a thin gold chain*
- a necklace made of beads (= small balls of glass, wood, plastic, etc): **beads** (*noun plural*), **string of beads**
- an ornament that you wear on a chain round your neck: **pendant**

- a piece of jewellery that you wear in your ears: **earring** ◦ *a pair of earrings*
- to make a hole in sth with a sharp point: **pierce** sth ◦ *earrings for pierced ears*

- a piece of jewellery that you wear round your wrist or arm: **bracelet**
- a bracelet which is a ring of solid metal, plastic, wood etc: **bangle**

- a piece of jewellery with a pin on the back, that women wear on a dress, blouse or jacket: **brooch**
- a piece of jewellery with a pin which men wear on their ties: **tiepin**

■ what jewellery is made of

- any valuable stone used in jewellery: **jewel, precious stone**

a precious stone that is ...	**is ...**
very hard and white	a **diamond**
bright green	an **emerald**
bright red	a **ruby**
deep blue	a **sapphire**
white and round and found in the shell of an oyster (= a kind of shellfish)	a **pearl**

- a valuable metal used in jewellery: **precious metal**
- a valuable yellow metal: **gold** (*noun* U) ◦ *Is that necklace real gold?*
- valuable white-grey metals: **silver** (*noun* U), **platinum** (*noun* U) ◦ *a silver bracelet* ◦ *a platinum ring*

▷ gold and silver ⇨ GOLD/SILVER

■ people who make and sell jewellery

- a person who makes or sells jewellery: **jeweller** (*AmE* **jeweler**)
- a shop where jewellery is sold: **jeweller's** (**shop**), **jewellery shop**
- someone who makes jewellery, etc out of precious metals: **goldsmith**, **silversmith**

■ **MORE ...**

- if you put a jewel in a bright light so that it gives out many little flashes of light, it **glitters, sparkles** ◦ *glittering diamonds*

- a collection of valuable things – gold, jewels, money, etc: **treasure** (*noun* U) ◦ *a treasure hunter* (= a person who goes looking for treasure)

job

- having employment ⇨ EMPLOYMENT

– some work that needs to be done ⇨ WORK

join

1 joining
2 mixing
3 uniting
4 materials used for joining things together

people and things together ⇨ TOGETHER
people meeting ⇨ MEET
fastening clothes ⇨ CLOTHES

1 joining

– when two or more things come together in the same place, they **join** (**up**), **meet*** (**up**), or one of them **joins/meets*** (**up with**) the other ◦ *The two rivers meet just to the south of the city.* ◦ *Where does this road join the motorway?*
– when things which form part of a machine or a system come together, they are **connected**, they **connect** (**up**), or one of them **connects** (**up**) **with** the other ◦ *All the computers in this office are connected.* ◦ *The tunnels connect up several metres further on.*

– to put together two or more things: **join/connect** things (**together/up**), **join** A **to/onto** B, **connect** A **to/with** B ◦ *You'll need to join the two parts together if they're going to work properly.* ◦ *Carefully join the top of the model to the bottom.* ◦ *to connect a computer to a network*

– to join sth to sth else: **attach** sth (**to** sth), **fix** sth (**on/to** sth), **fasten** sth (**on/to** sth); *opposite*: **detach** sth (**from** sth) ◦ *A note was attached to the top of the letter with a paper clip.* ◦ *to fix a shelf to a wall*

– a place where two or more things are fastened or connected: **joint** ◦ *If you don't make the joint stronger I think the whole thing will fall apart.*
– a line where two parts of an object have been joined: **join** ◦ *It had been so well mended that you couldn't see the join.*
– a place where two wires, pipes, etc join together: **connection** ◦ *I tried to mend the radio but there was a loose connection somewhere.*

– to separate things which were joined: **disconnect** things, **disconnect** A **from** B ◦ *Someone had disconnected the video from the television.*

– something, often a house, which is not joined to sth else is **detached** ◦ *a detached cottage*
– something which can be detached is **detachable** ◦ *a coat with a detachable lining*

2 mixing

– to join together to form a separate substance: **mix** ◦ *Oil and water don't mix.*

– to put two or more things together to make another thing: **mix** sth **with** sth, **mix** things (**together**) ◦ *Mix the flour with the sugar and the butter.* ◦ *If you mix red and white together, you get pink.*

– to make sth by putting things together: **mix** sth ◦ *to mix cement*
– a machine that is used for mixing things: **mixer** ◦ *a cement mixer* ◦ *a food mixer*
– something that has been made by mixing things: **mixture** (*noun* C/U) ◦ *a cake mixture*
– if sth is not mixed with anything else, it is **pure** ◦ *pure water* ◦ *pure gold*

– to put sth together with sth else so that you increase the size, number, etc: **add** sth (**to** sth) ◦ *She added some carrots to the soup.*
– when things come together so that they are mixed, they **combine**; *noun* (C/U): **combination** ◦ *The two companies have combined to form a new organization.* ◦ *The combination of the water and the flour produces a sticky paste.*
– to join or mix two or more things together: **combine** sth (**with** sth) ◦ *The two colleges have been combined.* ◦ *The art college was combined with the technical college to form a new university.*

3 uniting

– (used about people) to come together for a particular purpose: **unite** (**with** sb/sth), **join forces** (**with** sb/sth) ◦ *The two parties have united to form a coalition government.* ◦ *Teachers and parents have joined forces to try to save the school.*
– to join separate parts together to make one unit: **unify** sth; *noun* (U): **unification**; *adjective*: **unified** ◦ *the unification of Germany* ◦ *a unified legal system*

– the act of joining or the situation of being joined: **union** (*noun* U/*singular*) ◦ *the union of several colleges into a single university*

4 materials used for joining things together

■ joining pieces of paper, plastic, etc
– a thick sticky liquid that is used for joining things together: **glue** (*noun* U), (*more formal*) **adhesive** (*noun* U) ◦ *I need some strong glue to stick the handle back on this cup.*
– to join one or more things together with glue: **glue** sth (**on/to** sth) ◦ *Glue these two pieces together.*
– to attach sth to sth else by using glue, etc: **stick*** sth (**on/to** sth) ◦ *to stick a stamp on an envelope* ◦ *Try sticking it on with this glue.*

– a strip of paper, plastic, etc which has adhesive on one or both sides, and is used for fastening, sticking, etc: **sellotape** (*noun* U), (**adhesive**) **tape** (*noun* U)
– to fasten sth with adhesive tape: **sellotape** sth, **tape** sth ◦ *I sellotaped the poster to the wall.*

▷ more on joining pieces of paper together ⇨ PAPER

■ joining things with rope or string
– to fasten sth or fix sth in position with rope or string: **tie** sth (**up**); *opposite*: **untie** sth ◦ *I need some string to tie these sticks together.* ◦ *You can untie the dog now.*

join *contd.*

▷ more on joining things with string or rope ⇨ STRING / ROPE

■ joining pieces of wood, metal, etc
- a small thin piece of metal with a point at one end which you hit into things with a hammer to join them together: **nail**
- a small piece of metal with a sharp end and a round head, which you turn round using a special tool (= **screwdriver**) to join two things together: **screw** ◦ *He screwed the leg back onto the chair.*

▷ more on nails and screws ⇨ TOOL

joke ⇨ FUNNY

journalism ⇨ NEWSPAPER / MAGAZINE

journey ⇨ TRAVEL

judge ⇨ TRIAL

juice
- in a fruit ⇨ FRUIT
- as a drink ⇨ DRINK

jump

see also ATHLETICS

- to move quickly off the ground by pushing yourself up with your legs and feet: **jump**; *noun*: **jump**; to make a big jump: **leap***; *noun*: **leap** ◦ *A frog jumped out of the water and onto a lily leaf.* ◦ *When she heard the news, she leapt into the air and shrieked with excitement.*
- to jump or move quickly: **spring** ◦ *When he heard the alarm, Ray sprang out of bed.*

- to jump on one leg: **hop**; *noun*: **hop**
- to move along quickly and lightly with little jumps and steps: **skip**; *noun*: **skip**
- to jump up and down: **bounce** ◦ *Stop bouncing on the bed.*
- to roll right over with your feet going over your head: **somersault**; *noun*: **somersault** ◦ *to do a forward/backward somersault*

- to get over sth by jumping: **jump (over)** sth, **leap* over** sth ◦ *The horse jumped the gate and ran off down the lane.*
- to jump over or onto sth in one movement, using your hands or a pole to help you: **vault (over)** sth ◦ *to vault over a wall*

- to jump over a rope that you or two other people hold at each end, turning it round and round over your head and under your feet: **skip**; *noun* (U): **skipping**
- the rope used in skipping: **skipping rope**
- a piece of equipment for jumping up and down on, made of a piece of strong material attached to a metal frame by springs: **trampoline**; the sport of using a trampoline: **trampolining** (*noun* U)
- the sport of jumping off a high place with a long rope (which can stretch) tied around you: **bungee jumping** (*noun* U)
- to jump into water with your head first: **dive**

- a piece of strong cloth that is tied to sb and that lets them fall slowly to the ground when they jump from an aeroplane: **parachute**; to use a parachute: **parachute** ◦ *Pull this cord to make the parachute open.* ◦ *The pilot parachuted to safety.*

keep

keeping money ⇨ MONEY
places where we keep clothes, food, books, cars ⇨ CLOTHES, FOOD, BOOK, CAR

- to continue to have sth: **keep*** sth, (*informal*) **hang* onto** sth, (*formal*) **retain** sth ◦ *You can keep that book; I don't need it any more.* ◦ *I 'd like to hang on to this video for another week, if that's all right.* ◦ *Please retain your ticket while you are on the train.*

- to bring together a number of objects of a particular type over a period of time because they interest you: **collect** sth; a person who does this: **collector**; the things which are collected: **collection** ◦ *a collector of fossils* ◦ *a stamp collection*

■ not keeping sth
- to be unable to find sth: **lose*** sth ◦ *She's lost the car keys!*
- to give sth, often sth that you no longer want, without asking for or receiving money in return: **give*** sth **away** ◦ *We don't need these clothes any more. Why don't we give them away?*
- to remove sth that you do not want: **get* rid of** sth; to do this by, for example, putting sth in a dustbin: **throw*** sth **away / out** ◦ *I can't find Sunday's paper. Do you think I threw it out with the rubbish?*

▷ more on losing and giving ⇨ LOSE, GIVE

■ keeping things for use in the future
- if you do not want to give sth or sell sth to sb, you **hold* on to** it ◦ *Whatever our money problems we must try to hold on to the house.*
- if you do not throw sth away or if you do not use all of it, you **save** sth (**for** sb/sth), **save** sb sth ◦ *Save that box – it might come in useful.* ◦ *I'll be home late so please save me some dinner.*

- to keep sth to use in the future: **store** sth ◦ *Store the biscuits in a cool dry place.*
- an amount of sth that you keep to use in the future: **store** ◦ *a store of potatoes for the winter*
- something you keep for a special reason or to use later: **reserve** ◦ *coal/oil/gold reserves* ◦ *a reserve water supply*

▷ saving money ⇨ MONEY

■ keeping things safe or in a good condition
- to keep sth, such as a house or a machine, in a good condition: **maintain** sth; *noun* (U): **maintenance** ◦ *to maintain your house* ◦ *routine maintenance of the gas boiler*
- to keep sth safe or in a good condition: **preserve** sth; *noun* (U): **preservation** ◦ *They've managed*

to preserve most of the wall paintings in the caves.
- the work of protecting wild animals and the countryside: **conservation** (*noun* U)
- an area of land where the plants, animals, etc, are protected by law: **reserve** ◦ *a nature reserve* ◦ *a game reserve*

■ **MORE ...**
- to keep money or sth valuable or useful until a later time when you may really need it: **save** (sth) **for a rainy day**

key ⇨ LOCK

kick ⇨ HIT

kill

1 killing people
2 different ways of killing
killing animals ⇨ ANIMAL
see also DIE

1 killing people
- to cause sb to die: **kill** (sb) ◦ *She was killed instantly in the crash.* ◦ *Smoking kills.*
- a person who kills: **killer**
- something that can cause death is **deadly**, **lethal** ◦ *a lethal mixture of drugs*
- something that actually causes death is **fatal** ◦ *The illness is not usually fatal.*

- to kill sb illegally and on purpose: **murder** sb; *noun* (C/U): **murder** ◦ *This man had committed three murders.* ◦ *It was a case of murder.*
- a man/woman who commits a murder: **murderer/murderess** ◦ *a convicted murderer*
- to kill a particular person for political reasons: **assassinate** sb; *noun* (C/U): **assassination**
- a person who assassinates sb: **assassin**

- the crime of killing without intending to do so: (*formal*) **manslaughter** (*noun* U) ◦ *to commit manslaughter*
- any kind of killing of one person by another: (*formal*) **homicide** (*noun* U) ◦ *a homicide investigation*

- the act of killing yourself: **suicide** (*noun* C/U); to kill yourself: **commit suicide**, **take*** your **own life** ◦ *She committed suicide by taking an overdose.* ◦ *The police think that he took his own life.*

- involving a lot of killing: **bloody** ◦ *a bloody battle*
- the killing or wounding of people: **bloodshed** (*noun* U) ◦ *Our aim is to avoid further bloodshed.*
- the killing of a large number of people: **massacre**; *verb*: **massacre** people
- the killing of a large number of people in a cruel way: **slaughter** (*noun* U); *verb*: **slaughter** people ◦ *the slaughter of innocent civilians*
- killing (and other violent acts) for political purposes: **terrorism** (*noun* U) ◦ *an act of terrorism*
- a person who kills (or does other violent acts) for political purposes: **terrorist**
- punishment by being killed: **capital punishment** (*noun* U), **the death penalty** ◦ *He received the death penalty.*

▷ different kinds of punishment ⇨ PUNISH

2 different ways of killing
- to kill by squeezing the neck or throat with hands, rope etc: **strangle** sb/sth; *noun* (U): **strangulation**; a person who strangles sb: **strangler**
- to kill by stopping a person breathing: **suffocate** sb; *noun* (U): **suffocation**
- to kill by keeping sb/sth under water: **drown** sb/sth
- to kill by electricity: **electrocute** sb/sth; *noun* (U): **electrocution**
- to kill with a gun: **shoot*** sb/sth

▷ using a gun ⇨ GUN

- something that causes death or illness if you eat, drink or touch it is **poisonous**, (*formal*) **toxic** ◦ *poisonous fruit* ◦ *a snake's poisonous bite* ◦ *The factory was giving off toxic smoke.*
- to kill by using poison: **poison** sb/sth; a person who poisons sb: **poisoner**

■ **MORE ...**
- painless killing of people who are suffering: **euthanasia** (*noun* U)
- the killing of a race or group of people: **genocide** (*noun* U)

- sb who is killed because of their beliefs: **martyr**; the killing of sb because of their beliefs: **martyrdom** (*noun* U) ◦ *a Christian martyr* ◦ *to suffer martyrdom*

kilo ⇨ WEIGHT

kilometre ⇨ DISTANCE

kind ⇨ TYPE

kind/cruel

1 kind
2 unkind
3 cruel

1 kind
- if you care about how other people feel and you do things to help them, you are **kind** (*adverb* **kindly**), **kind-hearted**; *noun* (U): **kindness** ◦ *It was kind of you to visit me.* ◦ *a kind-hearted person* ◦ *He very kindly walked with me all the way to the station.*
- if you think about how other people feel before you do or say things, you are **considerate**, **thoughtful**; *noun* (U): **thoughtfulness** ◦ *How thoughtful of you to come round and see me.*
- very kind and thoughtful: **good**, (*informal*) **sweet** ◦ *It was so good of you to come.* ◦ *How sweet of you to remember my birthday!*
- if you show that you understand other people's feelings and problems, you are **sympathetic** (*adverb* **sympathetically**) ◦ *a sympathetic smile/response*

kind / cruel *contd.*

– if you are happy to help people, you are **helpful**; *noun* (U): **helpfulness** ◦ *a helpful shop assistant*
– if you are happy to give money and help freely, you are **generous** ◦ *a generous donation to charity*
▷ being sympathetic, helpful or generous ⇨ **SYMPATHY, HELP, GENEROUS**

– if you behave in a careful way so that you do not hurt things or people, you are **gentle** (*adverb* **gently**); *noun* (U): **gentleness**
– a person who is always gentle and loving is **tender-hearted**; things that they do or say are **tender**; *noun* (U): **tenderness** ◦ *tender words* ◦ *a tender kiss* ◦ *to speak with tenderness*

– to help a person who is suffering to feel better: **comfort** sb; this kind of help: **comfort** (*noun* U) ◦ *to comfort a crying child* ◦ *to offer some comfort* ◦ *words of comfort*
– to give sb extra attention and kindness: **make* a fuss of** sb ◦ *Everybody made a big fuss of her on her birthday.*

– if you behave in a kind and pleasant way, you are **friendly**; the quality of being friendly: **friendliness** (*noun* U) ◦ *People around here seem very friendly.*
– if you are friendly and helpful to the people who live near you, you are **neighbourly** (*AmE* **neighborly**) the quality of being neighbourly: **neighbourliness** (*AmE* **neighborliness**) (*noun* U) ◦ *a neighbourly thing to do*
– if you are friendly and welcoming to visitors, you are **hospitable** ◦ *a really hospitable couple*

– kind and understanding behaviour: **humanity** (*noun* U); *adjective*: **humane** ◦ *The guards tried to show some humanity to their prisoners.* ◦ *humane conditions*

2 unkind

– not kind: **unkind** (*adverb* **unkindly**); *noun* (U): **unkindness** ◦ *an unkind thought/remark* ◦ *to treat sb unkindly*
– if you do not think about how other people feel, you are **inconsiderate, thoughtless, insensitive**; *nouns* (U): **thoughtlessness, insensitivity** ◦ *a thoughtless action* ◦ *I was astonished at the insensitivity of her remarks.*
– if you do not behave in a kind and pleasant way, you are **unfriendly**; *noun* (U): **unfriendliness**
– if you are not friendly and welcoming to visitors, you are **inhospitable**

■ very unkind
– a person or thing that is unpleasant and unkind is **nasty, mean** ◦ *Children can be very nasty to each other.* ◦ *That was a nasty thing to do!* ◦ *a mean trick*
– if you want to hurt other people, you are **malicious, spiteful**; a wish to do this is **malice** (*noun* U), **spite** (*noun* U) ◦ *a malicious remark* ◦ *a spiteful thing to do* ◦ *I don't feel any malice towards her.* ◦ *He did it out of spite.*

3 cruel

– deliberately causing physical or mental pain to sb: **cruel** (*adverb* **cruelly**); *noun* (U): **cruelty** ◦ *Don't be so cruel – can't you see she's been crying?* ◦ *a cruel punishment* ◦ *to treat a person cruelly* ◦ *to prevent cruelty to animals*

– to behave badly or cruelly towards a person or animal: **ill-treat** sb/sth, **mistreat** sb/sth; **abuse** sb/sth; *nouns* (U): **ill-treatment, mistreatment, abuse** ◦ *to mistreat an animal* ◦ *She was badly abused as a child.* ◦ *ill-treatment of prisoners*
– the act of causing very great pain to a person as a punishment or to get information out of them: **torture** (*noun* C/U); *verb*: **torture** sb; a person who does this: **torturer** ◦ *He died under torture.* ◦ *methods of torture*
– severe and cruel treatment is **harsh** ◦ *harsh punishment/criticism* ◦ *harsh words*

– a thing or person that shows great cruelty with violence is **brutal** (*adverb* **brutally**), **vicious** (*adverb* **viciously**); *noun* (U): **brutality** ◦ *He was brutally attacked on the way home.*
– cruel and fierce: **savage** ◦ *a savage attack*
– enjoying violence and killing: **bloodthirsty**
– having or showing no pity: **cold-blooded** ◦ *a cold-blooded murderer*
– extremely cruel: **barbaric, barbarous** ◦ *barbaric weapons* ◦ *a barbarous act*
– an extremely cruel act, especially in a war: **atrocity** ◦ *The soldiers were accused of committing atrocities.*
– the cruel killing of a large number of people or animals: **slaughter** (*noun* U), **massacre** ◦ *the slaughter of innocent civilians* ◦ *There were reports of a massacre.*

– very cruel behaviour: **inhumanity** (*noun* U); *adjectives*: **inhumane, inhuman** ◦ *the inhumanity of war* ◦ *inhumane treatment* ◦ *The men were kept in inhuman conditions.*
– getting pleasure from being cruel: **sadism** (*noun* U); *adjective*: **sadistic**; a person who gets pleasure from being cruel: **sadist** ◦ *sadistic pleasure*

■ **MORE ...**
– if sb wants to be kind or helpful, but does not succeed, they are **well-meaning, well-intentioned**; this person's actions are **well-meant** ◦ *Well-meaning friends gave her plenty of advice.* ◦ *Their offers of help were well-meant, but I just wanted them all to go away.*

– to cause a person or group to suffer because of their beliefs, opinions or culture: **persecute** sb; *noun* (U/C): **persecution**; a person who does this: **persecutor** ◦ *the persecution of minorities* ◦ *to suffer persecution*
– government which is cruel and unjust is **oppressive**; *noun* (U): **oppression** ◦ *oppressive laws*

king / queen

see also GOVERNMENT

– a man who rules a country (usually the son of the previous ruler): **king**

- a woman who rules a country (usually the daughter of the previous ruler); the wife of a king: **queen** ◦ *Queen Victoria*
- another name for a king or queen: **monarch**
- a man who rules an empire (a group of countries that is governed by one country): **emperor**
- a woman who rules an empire; the wife of an emperor: **empress**
- a man who rules a small country; the son of a king or queen: **prince**
- a daughter of a king or queen; the wife of a prince: **princess**

- a series of rulers who are from the same family: **dynasty, the House of . . .** ◦ *the Ming dynasty* ◦ *the House of Windsor*
- concerned with a king, a queen or a member of their family: **royal** ◦ *the royal family* ◦ *a royal visit*
- members of the family of the king or queen: **royalty** (*noun* U) ◦ *I don't think people these days are much impressed by royalty.*

- the title that you use when you talk about or to a king or queen: **Majesty** ◦ *The Mayor was presented to Her Majesty the Queen.*
- the title that you use when you talk about or to a member of a royal family: **Highness** ◦ *His Royal Highness the Prince of Wales*
- the position of being king or queen: **the throne** ◦ *The Queen came to the throne in 1952.*

- a large house that is or was the home of a king or queen: **palace** ◦ *Buckingham Palace*
- the official home of a king or queen: **the Court** (*noun* U) ◦ *the Court of Queen Anne*

- the ring of gold and jewels that a king or queen wears on their head: **crown**
- to put a crown on the head of a new king or queen in an official ceremony: **crown** sb ◦ *The queen was crowned in Westminster Abbey.*
- the ceremony in which a king or queen is crowned: **coronation**
- a special chair that a king, queen, etc sits on during ceremonies: **throne**

■ government with a king or queen
- a country that is ruled by a king or queen: **kingdom** ◦ *the United Kingdom*
- a country that is ruled by a prince: **principality** ◦ *the Principality of Monaco*
- the system of government by a king or queen: **monarchy** (*noun* U)
- a country that is ruled by a king or queen: **monarchy** ◦ *How many monarchies are left in Europe?*
- the state as represented by a king or queen: **the Crown** ◦ *This land belongs to the Crown.*
- a person who supports a monarchical system of government: **monarchist, royalist**

- to rule a country as a king or queen: **reign** (**over** sb/sth) ◦ *Queen Victoria reigned for more than sixty years.*
- a period of time that sb reigns: **reign** ◦ *during the reign of George V*
- the right to become king, etc after sb else: **succession** (*noun* U) ◦ *Prince William is second in succession to the throne.*
- to become king, etc after sb else: **succeed** (sb) ◦ *Who will succeed the present Queen?*
- to give up being a king or queen: **abdicate**; *noun*: **abdication** ◦ *Edward VIII abdicated in favour of his brother.*
- to remove a ruler from power: **depose** sb ◦ *The king was deposed after the revolution.*

kiss

- as a way of greeting sb ⇨ GREET
- when you love sb ⇨ LOVE

kitchen

see also HOUSE, COOK, WASH

- a room where food is kept and cooked: **kitchen** ◦ *He's in the kitchen cooking the children's supper.* ◦ *a kitchen cupboard*

- a table used for preparing food, eating meals, etc: **kitchen table**
- a flat surface in a kitchen that you use for preparing food on: **worktop, work surface** (*AmE* **counter**)
- a small room or cupboard in a kitchen where food is kept: **larder** ◦ *There is plenty of food in the larder.*

- a piece of equipment that you use to cook food: **cooker**
- a piece of equipment that cooks and heats food very quickly: **microwave** (**oven**)
- a cupboard that keeps food and drink cold: **fridge**, (*formal*) **refrigerator**
- a cupboard that keeps food frozen: **freezer**
- a machine that washes plates, cups, knives and forks, etc: **dishwasher**
- the place where you wash dishes by hand in a kitchen: **sink** ◦ *the kitchen sink*
- the place beside a sink where you put plates, cups, knives, etc to dry: **draining board**

▷ more on cookers ⇨ COOK

▷ more on fridges ⇨ FOOD

- a container that you put kitchen rubbish in: **bin** ◦ *Throw the rubbish in the bin.*

knee ⇨ LEG

knife/fork/spoon

see also COOK, EAT

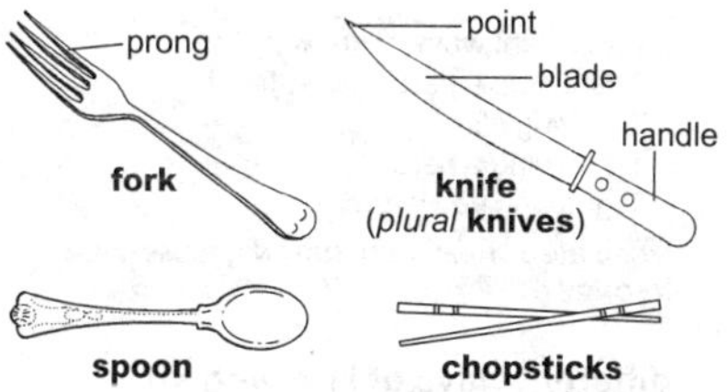

- the general name for all knives, forks and spoons used for eating: **cutlery** (*noun* U) ◦ *stainless steel cutlery*

knife/fork/spoon *contd.*

■ knives
- a knife used for preparing food in a kitchen: **kitchen knife**
- a knife used for cutting bread: **bread knife**
- a large knife used for cutting pieces of cooked meat: **carving knife**
- a small knife used for cutting and chopping vegetables: **vegetable knife**

- a knife that cuts very easily is **sharp**; *opposite*: **blunt** ◦ *Slice the ham with a sharp knife.*
- to make sth sharp: **sharpen** sth ◦ *The carving knife needs sharpening.*
- if a knife is a good one, it **cuts*** (**well**) ◦ *This knife doesn't cut very well. Have you got a sharper one?*
- to divide sth by using a knife: **cut*** sth (**up**) ◦ *Cut the chicken up into small pieces.*
- to remove sth by using a knife: **cut*** sth (**out**) ◦ *Make sure you cut the bad bits out of the potatoes.*

■ spoons
- the amount one spoon can hold: **spoon**, **spoonful** ◦ *a spoon of sugar* ◦ *two spoonfuls of medicine*
- to serve sth using a spoon: **spoon** (sth) (**out**) ◦ *Spoon the sauce over the fish.*
- to move sth round and round with the spoon: **stir** sth ◦ *Stir the porridge to prevent it sticking.*
- a small spoon used for stirring tea: **teaspoon**
- a medium-sized spoon used for eating sweet things: **dessertspoon**
- a spoon used for eating soup: **soup spoon**
- a large spoon used for measuring or serving food: **tablespoon** ◦ *Add two tablespoons of flour.*
- a large spoon used for serving food: **serving spoon**
- a large spoon with a long handle used for serving soup: **ladle**
- a spoon made of wood used for cooking: **wooden spoon** ◦ *She stirred the soup with a wooden spoon.*

■ **MORE ...**
- a small knife that you can carry in your pocket, with one or more blades that fold down into the handle: **penknife**, **pocket knife**

knit ⇨ WOOL

know

1 different ways of knowing sth
2 knowing a particular subject
3 having a skill
4 knowing a person
5 getting knowledge

see also THINK, UNDERSTAND, REMEMBER/FORGET

1 different ways of knowing sth

- to have information, facts, etc in your mind: **know*** (sth), **know*** (**that**) ... ◦ *Do you know her address?* ◦ *'It's getting late.' 'I know. I won't be long.'* ◦ *I had been there before so I knew what to expect.* ◦ *They didn't know that I had given him some money.*
- to have information about sth: **know* about** sth ◦ *The police know all about his involvement in the crime.* ◦ *She knows a lot about modern jazz.*
- to have heard of sb/sth: **know* of** sb/sth ◦ *I know of one student who attended all the courses.*

■ recognizing and identifying
- to know again sb or sth that you have seen or heard before: **recognize** sb/sth ◦ *She'd lost so much weight that I nearly didn't recognize her.*
- able to be recognized: **recognizable**; *opposite*: **unrecognizable** *an easily recognizable tune/voice* ◦ *Those glasses make you almost unrecognizable.*
- to say who or what sb/sth is: **identify** sb/sth ◦ *They asked him to identify the body.* ◦ *Can you identify this song?*
- to know the difference between two things: **tell*** (sb/sth **from** sb/sth), **tell*** sb/sth **apart** ◦ *It's almost impossible to tell the twins apart.*

■ realizing
- to know and understand that sth is true: **realize** (**that**) ..., **be**, **become**, etc **aware/conscious** (**of** sth/**that** ...) ◦ *Do you realize that we've missed the last bus?* ◦ *He was aware of all the dangers before he started the journey.* ◦ *Were you aware that you were breaking the law?* ◦ *I became conscious of the policeman looking at me.*
- not aware: **unaware** ◦ *She seemed unaware of all the trouble she had caused.*

- the knowledge that people have about certain problems or topics of general interest: **awareness** (*noun* U) ◦ *He's trying to raise people's awareness of the dangers of passive smoking.*

■ knowing sth quite well
- if you have a good knowledge of sth, you are **familiar with** it, it is **familiar** (**to** you); being familiar with sth: **familiarity** (**with** sth) (*noun* U) ◦ *I'm not familiar with all her novels.* ◦ *His face looks familiar.* ◦ *Is this name familiar to you?* ◦ *He was able to escape from the fire because of his familiarity with the building.*
- when you have become familiar with sth, you are **used to** it ◦ *I shall never get used to this new timetable.*

- if you do not have a good knowledge of sth, you are **unfamiliar with** it, it is **unfamiliar** (**to** you); not being familiar with sth: **unfamiliarity** (**with** sth) (*noun* U) ◦ *She seemed quite unfamiliar with the procedure for getting a visa.* ◦ *an unfamiliar part of the town*
- if you have not become familiar with sth, you are **new to** it ◦ *You should try to help him – he's still new to the job.*
- not seen, met, visited, etc before: **strange** ◦ *I rang my friend's number, but a strange voice answered the telephone.* ◦ *Don't talk to strange people in the street.*

■ being well-known
- a person, place, etc that is known by a lot of people is **well-known**, **famous**; being well-known: **fame** (*noun* U) ◦ *a well-known politician* ◦ *famous works of art*

- known by many people: **public** ◦ *The news was not made public until yesterday.*
- if sth is known by many people, it is **public/common knowledge** (*noun* U)

▷ more on being famous ⇨ FAMOUS

■ knowing about the future
- to know or guess that sth is going to happen in the future: **foresee*** sth; the ability to foresee sth: **foresight** (*noun* U) ◦ *Nobody could have foreseen that disaster.* ◦ *With a bit of foresight, they could have avoided that problem.*

▷ more on the future ⇨ FUTURE

2 knowing a particular subject
- information about a topic: **knowledge** (*noun* U/*singular*) ◦ *How's your knowledge of Greek history?* ◦ *to have a good knowledge of a subject*
- if you have a lot of knowledge about a subject, you are **knowledgeable** (**about** sth), **well-informed** (**about** sth) ◦ *She seems very knowledgeable about animals.* ◦ *a well-informed group of visitors*
- if you have little or no knowledge about sth, you are **ignorant** (**of/about** sth); *noun* (U): **ignorance** (**of** sth) ◦ *I'm completely ignorant about computers.* ◦ *His ignorance of the rules is astonishing.*
- a person who has special knowledge of a topic: **expert** (**on/in** sth) ◦ *an expert on international terrorism* ◦ *a computer expert*
- a subject that you know a lot about is your **speciality**, **specialism** ◦ *His speciality is modern American literature.*

- knowledge of many things which you get from ordinary life rather than special study: **general knowledge** (*noun* U) ◦ *Here's a test of your general knowledge!*

3 having a skill
- an ability that you need in order to do a job or perform an activity: **skill** (*often plural*) ◦ *She has excellent interpersonal skills.*
- the ability to do sth well: **skill** (**in/at** sth/doing sth) (*noun* U); having skill: **skilled** (**in/at** sth) ◦ *You need a lot of skill to do this well.* ◦ *a skilled gardener*
- knowledge or skill that you get from seeing or doing sth: **experience** (**in/of** sth) (*noun* U) ◦ *to learn by experience* ◦ *to know sth from experience* ◦ *How many years' experience of teaching do you have?*
- if you have knowledge of sth or skill in sth because you have done it often before, you are **experienced** (**in/at** sth) ◦ *an experienced teacher/counsellor* ◦ *Are you experienced at looking after children?*
- special knowledge or skill: **expertise** (*noun* U), (*informal*) **know-how** (*noun* U) ◦ *I don't have much expertise in dealing with computers.* ◦ *They have the know-how to produce nuclear weapons.*

▷ more on skill ⇨ SKILL

▷ knowing a language ⇨ LANGUAGE

4 knowing a person
- to have met or seen sb before: **know*** sb ◦ *'Do you know Bob?' 'No, I don't think we've met.'*
- to know sb, but not very well: (*formal*) **be acquainted** (**with** sb) ◦ *Are you two acquainted?* ◦ *He is acquainted with several government ministers.*
- to have seen sb before but not to have talked to them: **know*** sb **by sight** ◦ *I only know the director by sight.*
- to have heard about sb but not to have met them: **know*** sb **by name** ◦ *I've never been to the Institute though I know some of the staff by name.*
- a person you have known for a long time is an **old** friend or acquaintance
- a person that you do not know: **stranger**

5 getting knowledge
- to get knowledge or skill: **learn** (sth), **learn** (**how**) **to** do sth, **learn about** sth ◦ *We learnt very little science at school.* ◦ *I'm learning to play the piano.*
- to come to know sth, especially for the first time: **find*** sth **out**, **find* out about** sth, **discover** sth; what you discover: **discovery** ◦ *I've found out where the party's going to be.* ◦ *We didn't find out about the burglary until we got back from holiday.* ◦ *He discovered the truth about his parents' marriage.* ◦ *I made a shocking discovery.*
- to know sth by doing or seeing it: **experience** sth, **see*** sth ◦ *They experienced rock-climbing for the first time.* ◦ *We saw the effects of prompt treatment of the disease.*

▷ more on learning ⇨ LEARN

■ wanting to get knowledge
- if you want to know or learn as much as possible about sth, you are **interested** (**in** sth), **curious** (**about** sth); the quality of being interested: **interest** (*noun* U/*singular*), **curiosity** (*noun* U) ◦ *She's very interested in the new project.* ◦ *I was full of curiosity about what was in the letter.*

- asking a lot of questions, especially about what other people are doing: **inquisitive**; *noun* (U): **inquisitiveness** ◦ *Don't be so inquisitive – it's got nothing to do with you.* ◦ *an inquisitive child*
- too interested in finding out other people's affairs: (*informal*) **nosy** ◦ *I hope you don't think I'm being nosy asking you all these questions.*

▷ more on being interested in sth ⇨ INTERESTING

■ **MORE ...**
- to know nothing about sth: (*informal*) **not have a clue** ◦ *I'm afraid I don't have a clue what you're talking about!*
- if you do not know about sth that other people know about, you are (*informal*) **in the dark** ◦ *Don't keep me in the dark – are you getting married or not?*

- as far as I know about sth (although I may be wrong): **to the best of my belief/knowledge** ◦ *To the best of my knowledge, she has never been to China.*
- from my own (limited) information: **for all I know** ◦ *For all I know, he may be an alien from Mars!*

know *contd.*

– I don't know: (*informal*) **search me!**

– the feeling or understanding that makes you believe or know sth without any reason or proof: **intuition** (*noun* C/U); *adjective*: **intuitive** (*adverb* **intuitively**) ◦ *to have an intuition about sth* ◦ *to know sth by intuition* ◦ *an intuitive understanding of the needs of young children*

lack ⇨ HAVE/POSSESS

ladder

see also CLIMB

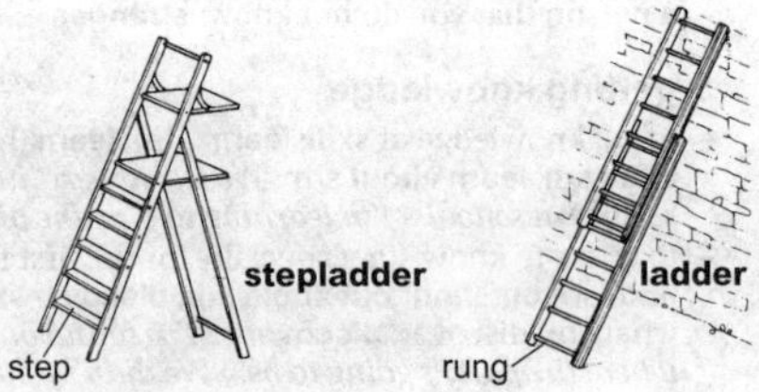

– a piece of equipment that is used for climbing up sth: **ladder** ◦ *The fireman climbed up the ladder and managed to reach the cat.* ◦ *I was standing on the ladder picking cherries when my friends arrived.* ◦ *My foot slipped on the rung and I fell off the ladder.*

– a ladder made of rope: **rope ladder**

lady ⇨ LORD/LADY

land

1 areas of land
2 high and low land
3 what grows on the land
4 owning land and building on land

different parts of the world ⇨ WORLD
the surface of the land ⇨ GROUND
using land for farming ⇨ FARM

1 areas of land

– the surface of the earth, where it is not covered with water: **land** (*noun* U) ◦ *Is it quicker by sea or by land?* ◦ *The land is very fertile around here.* ◦ *a piece of land*

– a piece of land: **area** (of land); a large area of land: **expanse** (of land) ◦ *a wide area of unspoilt countryside* ◦ *a vast expanse of open grassland*

– an area that has a particular feature or is of a particular type: **district**; an area larger than a district: **region** ◦ *a rural district* ◦ *a mountainous region*

– an area of land with its own people, government, etc: **country**, (*formal*) **land** ◦ *We come from different countries.* ◦ *my native land*

– an area that belongs to a particular country or ruler: **territory** ◦ *enemy territory*

▷ more on countries ⇨ COUNTRY[1]

– one of the main areas of land in the world (Europe, Asia, Africa, etc): **continent**; *adjective*: **continental**

– a piece of land with water all around it: **island**

– the main part of a country or continent, not including the islands around it: **mainland** (*noun singular*); *adjective* (*only before a noun*): **mainland** ◦ *We managed to catch the last boat back to the mainland.* ◦ *mainland Britain*

– a piece of land that is almost surrounded by water: **peninsula** ◦ *the Iberian peninsula* (= Spain and Portugal)

– a piece of land that sticks out into the sea: **cape** ◦ *sail round Cape Horn*

– the land beside or near the sea: **coast**; *adjective*: **coastal**; the shape of the coast: **coastline** ◦ *It's a small town on the east coast.* ◦ *a rocky coastline*

– away from the coast: **inland** ◦ *a few miles inland*

▷ more on land near the sea ⇨ SEA

– land that is away from towns and cities, usually with fields, trees, etc: **country** (*often* **the country**) (*noun* U), **countryside** (*often* **the countryside**) (*noun* U) ◦ *How do you like living in the country?* ◦ *enjoying the peace and quiet of the countryside*

▷ more on the countryside ⇨ COUNTRY[2]

– the size of a piece of land: **area** ◦ *What's the total area of Scotland?*

– units for measuring the area of a piece of land: **hectare, acre**; units for measuring very large areas: **square kilometre, square mile** ◦ *a ten-hectare farm* ◦ *The total area of Scotland is just over 30 000 square miles.*

▷ more on measuring area ⇨ SIZE

2 high and low land

– an area of land where there are a lot of hills is **hilly**

– an area where there are a lot of mountains is **mountainous**

– a space between hills or mountains, often with a river running down it: **valley**

▷ more on hills and mountains ⇨ HILL/MOUNTAIN

– land which is not hilly is **flat**

– a large area of flat land: **plain** ◦ *the great plains of the American Midwest*

– an area of high, flat land: **plateau**

– the measurement of the height of a piece of land above the level of the sea: **altitude** ◦ *Our farm was at an altitude of over 6 000 feet.*

– the average level of the sea, used to measure altitude: **sea level** ◦ *a thousand metres above sea level*

– a line on a map which joins together places with the same altitude: **contour** ◦ *study the contour lines on a map to see how steep the hill is*

3 what grows on the land

– when land is good for farming and growing plants, etc, it is **rich, fertile**; *opposites*: **poor, infertile**

- all the plants, trees, etc which are found in a particular place: **vegetation** (*noun* U) ◦ *dense tropical vegetation*
- the bushes and plants which grow around and under trees: **undergrowth** (*noun* U)

- an area that is covered with trees: **wood** (*often plural*), **woodland** (*noun* U); *adjective*: **wooded** ◦ *a walk in the woods* ◦ *a wooded area*
- a large wood: **forest** (*noun* C/U)
- an area of thick forest in a hot tropical country: **jungle** (*noun* C/U)

- a large area of wild uncultivated land: **bush** (*often* **the bush**) (*noun* U)
- a large area of land which is covered with grass: **grassland** (*noun* U), **grasslands** (*noun plural*)
- a wild open area of high land that is covered with grass: **moor** (*often plural*), **moorland** (*noun* U/C)
- a large area of flat, open grassland (especially in North America): **prairie**
- an area of land (especially in a town) which is not used for anything: **wasteland** (*noun* U/C)

- a large area of land, usually covered with sand, with very little water and very few plants: **desert** (*noun* C/U)
- a green area in a desert where there is water and plants can grow: **oasis**

4 owning land and building on land

- an area of land that belongs to a particular person, company, etc: **land** (*noun* U) ◦ *The house is being sold with 30 acres of land.* ◦ *We're looking for a piece of land to build on.*
- a large area of land that belongs to one person or family: **estate**
- a person who owns an area of land: **landowner**

- a person who buys and sells land for other people: **estate agent**
- a small area of land to be bought or sold: **plot** ◦ *We've just bought a small plot of land for our new house.*
- the place where a building, town, etc was, is or will be situated: **site** ◦ *the site of the new museum*
- an area of land which has buildings on it is **built-up** ◦ *a built-up area*

▷ building on land ⇨ **BUILD**

■ **MORE ...**

- to go onto sb's land without permission: **trespass** (**on** sth)
- a person who trespasses: **trespasser** ◦ *The notice says 'Trespassers will be prosecuted'* (= brought to a court of law).

language

1 varieties of language
2 systems of language
3 using and studying languages

communicating your meaning in language ⇨ **SAY**
spoken language ⇨ **SPEAK, CONVERSATION**
written language ⇨ **WRITE**

1 varieties of language

- the system of spoken or written signs that enables people to communicate: **language** (*noun* U) ◦ *What distinguishes human language from animal communication systems?* ◦ *the spoken/written language*
- a particular system of spoken or written signs understood by a group of people: **language** ◦ *How many languages do you speak?* ◦ *to learn a language*
- connected with language: **linguistic**; the study of language: **linguistics** (*noun* U) ◦ *linguistic abilities/skills* ◦ *linguistic minorities*

- a form of a language that is spoken by people from a particular region: **dialect** (*noun* C/U) ◦ *the Yorkshire dialect* ◦ *a poem written in dialect*
- a variety of a language that people generally accept as normal and correct: **standard language** (*noun* C/U)
- the language that you learn to speak first: **mother tongue, first language**
- a language that belongs to a country that is not your own: **foreign language**
- a language that is used in your country but is not your first language: **second language**
- a language that is used by deaf people, and consists of movements of the body, especially the hand: **sign language** (*noun* C/U)

- the way in which people from a particular region pronounce the words in their language: **accent** ◦ *He has such a strong accent; I can hardly understand what he's saying!* ◦ *to speak with an American accent*

- a way of using language which is suitable to a particular situation or purpose: **style** (*noun* C/U); relating to style: **stylistic** (*adverb* **stylistically**) ◦ *a book written in a comic style* ◦ *a poetic style of language*
- used in writing and in serious situations: **formal** ◦ *Your letter to the bank manager needs to be more formal than that.*
- used in speaking and in ordinary everyday situations: **informal, colloquial** ◦ *a colloquial expression*
- used in poetry and similar written language: **literary**
- used to speak or write in an expert way about how things work or are made: **technical** ◦ *the technical language used in a computer magazine*

language *contd.*

- very informal words, often used by a particular group: **slang** (*noun* U) ◦ *'The nick' is slang for police station.* ◦ *a slang expression*

- language that is rude and unpleasant: **bad language** (*noun* U) ◦ *to use bad language*
- to use rude and unpleasant language: **swear** ◦ *Don't swear in front of your grandmother!*
- a rude and unpleasant word: **swear word**
- a rude word which refers to sex: **four-letter word**, **obscenity** ◦ *When I arrived he was standing in the middle of the road shouting obscenities at the other driver.*

2 systems of language

- the way in which sounds are made in a language: **pronunciation** (*noun* C/U) ◦ *I can write French quite well, but I find the pronunciation difficult.*
- the way that your voice rises and falls when you speak: **intonation** (*noun* U)

▷ more on pronunciation ⇨ SPEAK

- a written or printed sign that represents a sound and which forms a word or part of a word: **letter**
- to say or write the letters of a word: **spell** (sth)

▷ the sounds and spelling of words ⇨ WORD, LETTER[2]

- the way in which words, sentences, etc are formed and used in a language: **grammar** (*noun* U); *adjective*: **grammatical** ◦ *English grammar* ◦ *a grammar book* ◦ *grammatical mistakes*

▷ more on grammar ⇨ GRAMMAR

- the marks that you use to divide up sentences and show meaning in writing: **punctuation** (*noun* U)
- one of the signs which you use to divide up sentences or to show meaning in writing: **punctuation mark**

▷ more on punctuation ⇨ PUNCTUATION

- a sound or letter, or a group of sounds or letters, with a particular meaning: **word**
- a number of words that go together to express a particular meaning (for example 'as a matter of fact', 'with all due respect', 'blue with cold'): **expression**

- an expression with a meaning that you cannot guess from the meanings of the individual words: **idiom** ◦ *The idiom 'to go up the wall' means to become extremely angry.*
- a phrase that people say in order to give advice: **saying** ◦ *'Don't put all your eggs in one basket' is a saying which means 'Don't depend too much on one thing, because if you lose it, you'll lose everything'.*
- a phrase or idea which has been used so often that it has lost its meaning or interest: **clich** ◦ *Do you believe the old cliché that travel broadens the mind?*

▷ more on words and expressions ⇨ WORD

- the relationship between a word, phrase, sentence, etc and the thing or idea it represents: **meaning** (*noun* C/U)
- the words that come before or after a word, sentence, etc and that help you to understand its meaning; the situation in which a word is used: **context** (*noun* C/U) ◦ *This sentence doesn't make sense unless you look at the context.* ◦ *Some words have different meanings depending on the context.*

▷ more on meaning ⇨ MEANING

3 using and studying languages

- to be able to use a particular language: **speak*** a language ◦ *Does she speak German?*
- able to speak two languages equally well: **bilingual** ◦ *a bilingual secretary*
- able to speak or write a language well: **fluent** (**in** sth) (*adverb* **fluently**) ◦ *She's fluent in Italian.* ◦ *He speaks Russian fluently.*
- to use a particular language on a certain occasion: **talk/speak*** (**in**) a language ◦ *They were talking in Chinese so I didn't understand them.* ◦ *Let's speak French.*

- to change what sb has said or written into another language: **translate** (sth) (**from** sth) (**into** sth); *noun* (C/U): **translation** ◦ *Could you help me translate this letter into Italian please?* ◦ *I've got to do this translation for my class on Thursday.*
- a person who translates: **translator**
- a person who translates what sb says into another language: **interpreter**

- a book that contains lists of words and their meanings or words with the same or similar meaning in another language: **dictionary** ◦ *I'll look it up in the dictionary.*
- a book of useful expressions that you may need to use when you go to a foreign country, with translations into another language and help with pronunciation: **phrase book**
- a book written about the grammar of a language: **grammar**

- a person who studies languages or who is able to speak several languages: **linguist**
- the study of the science of languages: **linguistics** (*noun* U)

large ⇨ BIG/SMALL

last

- continuing ⇨ CONTINUE, TIME
- in sequence ⇨ FIRST/NEXT/LAST

late ⇨ EARLY/LATE

laugh

see also FUNNY, HAPPY

- to make sounds which show that you are happy or think sth is funny: **laugh** (**at** sb/sth); *noun*: **laugh** ◦ *Tell me that joke again – it always makes me laugh.* ◦ *You'll laugh at this story.* ◦ *She gave a loud laugh. 'That's so funny,' she said.*

- the sound of people laughing: **laughter** (*noun* U) ○ *I could hear laughter coming from the next classroom.*
- when we write down the sound that people make when they laugh, we write **ha! ha!**

- to laugh openly and noisily: **laugh out loud** ○ *This book will make you laugh out loud.*
- to suddenly start laughing loudly: **burst* out laughing** ○ *When she understood the joke she suddenly burst out laughing.*
- to laugh very long and loudly: **have a good laugh**, **roar with laughter**, **laugh your head off** ○ *We had a really good laugh about my mistake.* ○ *Everyone roared with laughter when I fell off my bicycle.* ○ *I laughed my head off when I heard what he'd done.*

- to manage not to smile, even when you think sth is very funny: **keep* a straight face** ○ *When I saw what she was wearing I couldn't keep a straight face.*

■ different ways of laughing
- to laugh in a childish way: **giggle**; *noun*: **giggle**; if you cannot stop giggling, You **get*/have** (**a fit of**) **the giggles** ○ *Stop giggling! You're not a child any more!* ○ *She opened her mouth to speak, and then burst into giggles.* ○ *I got the giggles when I saw him and had to leave the room.*
- to laugh quietly, often when you remember sth: **chuckle**; *noun*: **chuckle** ○ *Why were you chuckling to yourself just now?*
- to laugh quietly or in secret, in an annoying way: **titter**, **snigger** (*AmE* **snicker**) ○ *The girls sat at the back of the classroom tittering.* ○ *The children sniggered when their teacher arrived wearing one blue sock and one red one.*
- to laugh with a very high, long sound: **squeal with laughter**; *noun*: **squeal of laughter** ○ *The behaviour of the monkeys made the children squeal with laughter.*

■ **MORE ...**
- when a lot of people laugh loudly together, we hear **peals of laughter** ○ *I could hear peals of laughter coming from the next room.*
- when a lot of people laugh quietly at sth, we hear a **ripple of laughter** ○ *There was a ripple of laughter in the audience.*

- if you are laughing so much that you cannot stop, you are **doubled up**, **in stitches** ○ *Dan told us some really funny stories last night – we were doubled up.* ○ *The sketch had me in stitches.*
- if you laugh so much that you cry, you can say that the **tears roll down** your **cheeks** ○ *We laughed until the tears rolled down our cheeks.*

- to touch sb lightly with your fingers to make them laugh: **tickle** sb; *noun*: **tickle** ○ *Please! Don't tickle me!*
- if sb laughs very easily when you tickle them, they are **ticklish**

lavatory ⇨ TOILET

law

1 different kinds of law
2 making laws
3 allowed or not allowed by law
4 working in the law
5 obeying the law
6 not obeying the law

see also TRIAL

1 different kinds of law

- what a country says that a person may or may not do: **law**; all the laws of a country: **the law** (*noun* U) ○ *Is there a law against begging?* ○ *Stealing is against the law.*
- connected with the law: **legal** ○ *the legal profession* ○ *She decided to take legal advice.*
- a group of laws: **legislation** (*noun* U) ○ *We're looking for an expert on European maritime legislation.*
- the law and the way it is used: **justice** (*noun* U) ○ *the criminal justice system* ○ *the administration of justice*

- a law that is fair is **just**; *opposite*: **unjust**

- a law made by a government: **act** ○ *an act of parliament* ○ *the Sex Discrimination Act*
- a law passed by parliament and written down formally: **statute**; *adjective*: **statutory** ○ *the statute book* (= a collection of all the laws made by government) ○ *a statutory right*
- the laws in England based on decisions made by judges, not laws made by parliament: **common law** (*noun* U)
- an official order given by a government or ruler: **decree**; to make a decree: **decree** sth/**that ...**, **issue a decree** (**that ...**) ○ *The President decreed that all shops would close on national holidays.*

- the set of principles and laws of a country that describe the powers of the government and the duties of the people: **constitution**; *adjective*: **constitutional** (*adverb* **constitutionally**); not allowed by the constitution: **unconstitutional** ○ *the constitution of the United States*

- an official statement that tells you what you can or cannot do, say, etc, in an institution, a sport, etc: **rule** ○ *Smoking in the rooms is against the school rules.* ○ *the rules of football*
- a law or rule that controls how sth is done: **regulation** ○ *fire/safety regulations*
- a law or regulation made by local government: **by-law**

▷ more on rules and regulations ⇨ RULE

2 making laws

- the act of making laws: **legislation** (*noun* U); *adjective*: **legislative** ○ *In this session of Parliament the Government has a heavy programme of legislation.* ○ *the legislative process* (= the process of making laws)

law *contd.*

- when a new law is agreed and approved by parliament, it **is passed** ◦ *The new law was passed by fifteen votes.*
- when a law begins to be used or comes into operation it **takes* effect, comes* into effect** ◦ *The new law on driving tests comes into effect from January 1st.*
- a law that is being used is **in force** ◦ *The new seat-belt law is now in force.*

3 allowed or not allowed by law

- allowed or recognized by the law: **legal** (*adverb* **legally**), **lawful** (*adverb* **lawfully**); something that is allowed or recognized by the law: **right** (**to** do sth) ◦ *Is it legal for children to enter pubs?* ◦ *I am the lawful owner of this house.* ◦ *In Britain you have the right to vote at 18.*
- the state of being legal: **legality** (*noun* U) ◦ *Are you certain of the legality of what you are suggesting?*
- to make sth legal: **legalize** sth ◦ *a campaign to legalize cannabis*
- not allowed or recognized by law: **against the law, illegal** (*adverb* **illegally**), **unlawful** (*adverb* **unlawfully**) ◦ *It is illegal to drive a car without a driving licence.* ◦ *an illegal rock festival* ◦ *unlawful entry into a house*
- the state of being illegal: **illegality** (*noun* U)
- to make sth illegal: **ban** sth, **prohibit** sth; *nouns*: **ban** (**on** sth), **prohibition** (**of** sth) ◦ *Pornographic magazines should be banned.* ◦ *Many people support the ban on corporal punishment in schools.*
- to say that it is illegal for sb to do sth: **ban** sb **from** doing sth, **prohibit** sb **from** doing sth ◦ *He was banned from driving for a year.*

4 working in the law

- a person who has studied law and whose job is to give advice about the law: **lawyer** (*AmE also* **attorney**)
- a lawyer (in Britain) who gives legal advice, prepares documents and usually speaks in less serious court cases: **solicitor**
- a lawyer (in Britain) who usually speaks in more serious court cases: **barrister**
- to work as a lawyer: **practise** (**as** sth), **practise law** ◦ *He's been practising as a solicitor for twenty years.*
- to act or speak for sb else in court: **represent** sb; *noun*: **representation** ◦ *The man asked for proper legal representation after he was arrested.*
- a person who receives a service from a lawyer or other professional person: **client**
- the money that you pay to a lawyer for his/her services: **fee** (*often plural*) ◦ *Her fees are very high, but she is the best barrister in London.*
- a person whose job is to apply the law and decide what punishment to give to sb who breaks the law: **judge**
- the law as a subject of study or as a profession: **law** (*noun* U) ◦ *Elizabeth is studying law at university.*

5 obeying the law

- to behave legally: **obey the law**
- to obey a law, etc: (*formal*) **observe** sth ◦ *to observe the speed limit*
- a person who normally obeys the law is **law-abiding** ◦ *a law-abiding citizen*
- a situation in which the law is obeyed by most people most of the time: **law and order** (*noun* U) ◦ *a general breakdown in law and order*
- to make sure that people obey a law: **enforce** sth; *noun* (U) : **enforcement** ◦ *It's the job of the police to enforce the law.*

6 not obeying the law

- to do sth that is against the law: **break* the law, disobey the law**
- something which is illegal and which people are punished for: **crime** (*noun* C/U), (*more formal*) **offence** (*AmE* **offense**); *adjective*: **criminal** ◦ *to commit a crime* ◦ *Serious crime is on the increase.* ◦ *a driving offence* ◦ *criminal behaviour* ◦ *It is a criminal offence to take money from the till.*
- a person who breaks the law: **criminal**, (*more formal*) **offender**
- the official organization whose job is to make sure people obey the law and to prevent crimes, etc: **the police** (*with plural verb*)

▷ more on crime and the police ⇨ **CRIME, POLICE**

■ MORE ...

- a paragraph in a legal document: **clause** ◦ *Clause three specifically states that only the insured person may drive the car.*
- the conditions of an agreement: **terms** (*noun plural*) ◦ *The contract set out the terms for the sale of the house.*
- the state of being legally responsible for sth: **liability** (*noun* U); *adjective*: **liable** (**for** sth) ◦ *The hotel cannot accept liability for theft of items not left in the hotel safe.* ◦ *They are liable for any damage they may cause.*

lazy

see also WORK

- a person who does not want to work hard is **lazy, idle**; *nouns* (U): **laziness, idleness** ◦ *Sunshine makes me feel lazy.* ◦ *Get out of bed, you lazy thing!*
- the opposite of lazy is **hard-working** ◦ *a hard-working team*
- when you are lazy and relaxing, doing nothing in particular, you **laze around/about, lounge around/about** ◦ *We lazed around in the garden while the others went for a walk.* ◦ *I hate the kind of holiday where you just lounge about on a beach.*
- if you spend your time sitting and not doing anything else, you **sit* around/about** ◦ *She sat around at home all day, waiting for him to call.* ◦ *In the evenings we just sat about and had a laugh.*

- a lazy person who avoids work: (*informal*) **lay-about**
- a lazy, rude or untidy person: (*informal*) **slob**

leader ⇨ GROUP

leaf ⇨ PLANT

learn

see also TEACH, SCHOOL, UNIVERSITY, EDUCATION

- to get knowledge or skill: **learn** (sth), **learn** (**how**) **to** do sth, **learn about** sth ◦ *I love the job, but I've still got a lot to learn.* ◦ *The staff were learning how to use the new computer system.* ◦ *Young children learn to walk when they are about 18 months old.* ◦ *The students were learning about Britain.*
- the process of learning: **learning** (*noun* U) ◦ *to have learning difficulties*

- a person who is learning sth: **learner** ◦ *a language learner*
- a person who has just begun to learn sth: **beginner** ◦ *I'm just a beginner, so don't talk too quickly.* ◦ *He's in the beginners' class.*
- at a high level: **advanced** ◦ *an advanced level class* ◦ *an advanced student*

- something that you have not learned before is **new** (**to** you) ◦ *The job is all very new to me at the moment, but I'll soon learn.*
- if you can learn sth without difficulty, it is **easy**; *opposite*: **hard**, **difficult** ◦ *You can learn how to use the machine very quickly – it's easy.* ◦ *a hard problem* ◦ *a difficult subject*
- if you learn things easily, you are a **quick** learner, you learn **quickly**; if you do not learn things easily, you are a **slow** learner, you learn **slowly** ◦ *He doesn't learn very quickly I'm afraid – he's a bit slow.*

- if you want to know or learn as much as possible about sth, you are **interested** (**in** sth), **curious** (**about** sth); the quality of being interested: **interest** (*noun* U/*singular*), **curiosity** (*noun* U) ◦ *to show interest* ◦ *She has had a lifelong interest in astronomy.* ◦ *She was full of curiosity.*
- the natural force that causes a person to know how to do sth without thinking or learning about it: **instinct** (*noun* U/C); *adjective*: **instinctive** (*adverb* **instinctively**) ◦ *a natural instinct* ◦ *Ants cooperate with each other entirely by instinct.* ◦ *I didn't have to learn to do it – it was instinctive.* ◦ *He instinctively knew what to do.*

■ different ways of learning

- to spend time learning about sth: **study** (sth) ◦ *I want to go to university and study French.* ◦ *He studied hard for his exams.*
- a person who studies: **student**

▷ more on studying ⇨ STUDY

- to learn how to do a job: **train to** do sth, **train** (**as** sth) ◦ *I'm training to be a teacher.* ◦ *I trained as a lawyer, but I'm now a computer operator.*
- a person who is being trained: **trainee** ◦ *a trainee teacher*
- to do sth many times so that you become good at it: **practise** (*AmE* **practice**) (sth); *noun* (U): **practice** ◦ *If you want to improve, you have to practise.* ◦ *I'm going to do my piano practice.*
- a piece of work that is intended to help you learn sth: **exercise**, **task** ◦ *a grammar exercise* ◦ *The teacher set us an interesting task.*

- to learn sth by practising (not by deliberately studying it): **pick** sth **up** ◦ *'Where did you learn to speak English?' 'I just picked it up while I was living in the States.'*
- to get some information by studying, searching or asking for it: **find*** sth (**out**) ◦ *Can you find the answer to the first question?* ◦ *Where did you find out about this?*
- to know how or why sth happens (as a result of learning sth new): **understand*** (sth), **see*** (sth) ◦ *'Do you understand what I mean?' 'Oh yes, I see now.'*
- to find an answer to sth, or to understand sth by thinking about it: **work** sth **out**, **figure** sth **out** ◦ *He's very clever – he figured it out all on his own.*

- to read and study sth that you have learnt before, especially when preparing for an exam: **revise** (sth); *noun* (U): **revision** ◦ *to revise for an exam* ◦ *to do some revision*
- to learn sth so that you can remember it exactly: **learn** sth **by heart**, **memorize** sth ◦ *I don't need the book – I've learned the poem by heart.* ◦ *I want you to memorize this phone number.*

■ MORE . . .

- to become familiar with sth so that you are able to do it properly: **get* the hang of** sth ◦ *I was just starting to get the hang of skiing when I broke my leg.*
- to study or practise sth in order to get back a skill that you have lost: **brush up** (**on**) sth ◦ *I need to brush up on my French before we go to Paris.*

least

- the smallest quantity ⇨ HOW MUCH/MANY
- to the smallest degree ⇨ FAIRLY/VERY

leave

1 leaving a place
2 leaving sb and saying goodbye
3 leaving sb/sth somewhere
going to live in another country ⇨ COUNTRY[1]
leaving a person (ending a relationship) ⇨ RELATIONSHIP
leaving your job ⇨ EMPLOYMENT
see also ARRIVE, COME/GO, TRAVEL

1 leaving a place

- to go from a place: **leave*** (a place), **go*** ◦ *I can't find Phil. Do you think he's left already?* ◦ *I usually leave the office at six.* ◦ *I have to go now.*
- to go away from your house, office, etc for a short time: **go* out** ◦ *Chris has gone out to the pub for a couple of hours.*
- to leave a place suddenly or quickly and go somewhere for a short time: **pop out**, **nip out** ◦ *I'm just popping out to the shop. Do you want anything?*

leave *contd.*

– to leave a place because it is time: **go***, **be off**, **get* off** ◦ *We'd better go, or we'll miss the train.* ◦ *It's late; I must be off.* ◦ *I'll get off now. I'll be back tomorrow at seven.*

– to leave a place for a long time (at least several days) or for ever: **go* away** (**from** a place), **leave*** (a place) ◦ *They've gone away. They don't live here any more.* ◦ *Michael and Paula have left Colchester and gone to live in Wales.*
– to go away from your parents' home for ever: **leave* home**
– to leave a place and go somewhere where you cannot be found: **disappear** (**to/from** a place); *noun* (C/U): **disappearance** ◦ *Mr Gates disappeared last year and hasn't been heard from since.*

– to stop living in or using a room or building: (*formal*) **vacate** sth ◦ *Guests should vacate their rooms by ten o'clock on the day of departure.*

■ leaving to travel
– to begin a journey: **leave***, **set* off/out**, **start** (**out**), (*formal*) **depart** ◦ *I'm leaving for Phoenix in the morning.* ◦ *We're setting off at dawn.* ◦ *to start out on a journey* ◦ *Your train departs in five minutes.*
– an act of leaving a place and starting on a journey: **departure** ◦ *The departure of this flight will be delayed by approximately thirty minutes.* ◦ *arrivals and departures*

– to start a journey by car: **drive* off/away** ◦ *He started the engine and drove off.*
– to start a journey by aeroplane: **take* off** ◦ *Our plane takes off at six fifty-five.*
– to pay your bill and leave a hotel, etc: **check out** (**of** sth)
– to go with sb to an airport, station, etc to say goodbye to them: **see*** sb **off** ◦ *I'll come and see you off.*

■ leaving a place where you do not want to be
– to find a way of leaving a place where you do not want to be: **escape** (**from** sth); *noun* (C/U): **escape** ◦ *A prisoner has escaped.* ◦ *Escape was impossible.*
– to succeed in leaving or escaping from sb or a place: **get* away** (**from ...**) ◦ *The fox managed to get away from the dogs that were chasing it.*
– to leave without permission (especially in the army, etc): **desert** (sth); *noun* (C/U): **desertion**

▷ more on escaping ⇨ ESCAPE

■ making sb leave a place
– to tell sb that they have to go to a different place: **send*** sb **away** ◦ *My parents sent me away to boarding school when I was eight.*
– to tell a sports player to leave a game and not return after he/she has broken a rule, etc: **send*** (sb) **off** ◦ *The Arsenal striker was sent off for hitting the referee.*

– to move towards sb/sth to try to make them go away: **chase** sb/sth ◦ *The farmer chased the boys off his land.*
– to tell sb in a strong way to leave a place: **order** sb **out**
– to force sb to leave a place: (*informal*) **throw*** sb **out** ◦ *He was thrown out of the country for not having a work permit.*
– to make sb leave a school, university, etc, as a punishment: **expel** sb (**from** sth)

– to move people from a dangerous area to another place: **evacuate** sb/sth; *noun* (C/U): **evacuation** ◦ *Thousands of people were evacuated to escape the floods.* ◦ *The city was evacuated one hour before the earthquake.*
– a person who is evacuated: **evacuee**

– to tell sb to go away from a place, you can say (*informal*) **Go away!** or **Clear off !** or **Push off!** ◦ *Go away and leave me alone!* ◦ *This is my land so clear off before I call the police!*
– to a child you can say: **Run along!** ◦ *Run along now will you Jimmy!*
– to make sb or sth go away by saying 'shoo!' and waving your arms: **shoo** sb/sth **away**, **off**, **out**, etc ◦ *The farmer was trying to shoo the cows away from the gate.*

2 leaving sb and saying goodbye
– to go away from sb: **leave*** sb, **part** (**from** sb) ◦ *Is it all right if I leave you here?* ◦ *They parted at the station.*

– when you leave sb, you can say **Bye**, **Bye-bye**, **See you**, **See you later**, **See you soon**, (*more formal*) **Goodbye**
– if you leave sb at night, you can say **Good night**

3 leaving sb/sth somewhere
– to forget to bring sb/sth with you, or to decide not to take them/it with you: **leave*** sb/sth (**behind**) ◦ *Unfortunately, I've left your essay in my car.* ◦ *We'll have to go back – we've left George behind!* ◦ *I think I'll leave this coat. I can get a new one in London if I need one.*
– to leave sb/sth that you are responsible for: **abandon** sb/sth ◦ *an abandoned baby*

left ⇨ RIGHT/LEFT

leg/foot

1 parts of the leg and foot
2 movements of the legs and feet
3 what you wear on your legs and feet
animals' bodies ⇨ ANIMAL
see also BODY, BONE

1 parts of the leg and foot

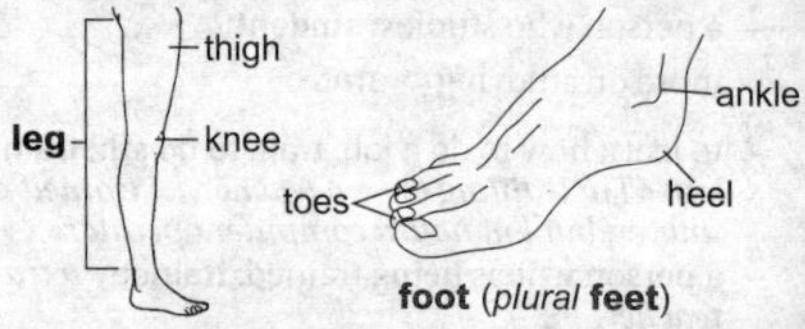

- the back of your leg below the knee: **calf** (*plural* **calves**)
- the front of your leg below the knee: **shin**
- the flat part of your foot on which you walk: **sole**

- the part of your body between your stomach and the front of your thighs: **groin**
- the flat area that is formed by the top parts of your legs when you sit down: **lap** ◦ *She was sitting on her mother's lap.*

2 movements of the legs and feet

- to be on your feet, upright: **stand***; to move into this position: **stand*** (**up**), **get* up** ◦ *He stood up and walked to the door.*
- to put your body into a sitting position: **sit*** (**down**)
- to put one leg over the other: **cross** your **legs** ◦ *She sat back and crossed her legs.*
- to be on your knees: **kneel***; to move into this position: **kneel*** (**down**) ◦ *He was kneeling on the floor.*

▷ sitting and standing ⇨ SIT, STAND

- to move along on foot at a fairly slow speed: **walk** ◦ *'Did you come by bus?' 'No, I walked.'*
- to move on your legs, going faster than when you walk: **run*** ◦ *I ran to catch the bus.*
- to walk with difficulty because, for example, you have hurt your leg: **limp**; *noun*: **limp** ◦ *I limped over to the ambulance and waited to be taken to the hospital.* ◦ *She has walked with a limp ever since the accident.*
- if you walk or run somewhere, you **go* on foot**

- to put your foot down on sth: **tread* on** sth ◦ *I'm terribly sorry – did I tread on your toe?*
- to put your foot down very heavily on the ground or sth else: **stamp** (**on** sth) ◦ *She stamped her feet to keep warm.*
- a mark left on the ground by sb's foot or shoe: **footprint** ◦ *footprints in the sand*
- a line of marks left by an animal's feet: **track** (*usually plural*) ◦ *We followed the elephant's tracks.*

▷ more on walking and running ⇨ WALK, RUN

- to hit or move sb/sth with your foot: **kick** sb/sth; *noun*: **kick** ◦ *to kick a ball* ◦ *He gave me a kick on the ankle.*

- the part of a bicycle or other machine that you push with your foot: **pedal**; to push the pedals of a bicycle with your feet in order to ride it: **pedal** (sth) ◦ *He had to pedal hard to get up the hill.*

▷ using a bicycle ⇨ BICYCLE

3 what you wear on your legs and feet

- a piece of clothing that covers both legs and reaches from your waist to your ankles: **trousers** (*AmE* **pants**) (*noun plural*); short trousers that end above the knee: **shorts** (*noun plural*)
- a thin nylon covering for a woman's legs and feet, that reaches to her waist: **tights** (*AmE* **pantyhose**) (*noun plural*) ◦ *I'd like some black tights.* ◦ *a pair of tights*
- one of a pair of thin pieces of clothing that fit tightly over a woman's legs and feet: **stocking** ◦ *a pair of stockings*

▷ more on trousers ⇨ TROUSERS

- one of two pieces of clothing that cover the feet: **sock** ◦ *a pair of yellow socks*
- a covering for the foot, usually made of leather or plastic: **shoe** ◦ *a pair of shoes*
- having no covering on your feet: **barefoot** (*adjective, adverb*) ◦ *All of us were barefoot.* ◦ *She was walking barefoot.*

▷ more on shoes ⇨ SHOE

■ **MORE ...**

- a person who specializes in treating foot problems: **chiropodist**
- a small painful area of hard skin on a toe: **corn**

legal

- the law ⇨ LAW
- against the law ⇨ CRIME

lemon ⇨ FRUIT

lend ⇨ BORROW/LEND

less

- a smaller amount ⇨ HOW MUCH/MANY
- to a smaller degree ⇨ FAIRLY/VERY

lesson ⇨ TEACH

let ⇨ ALLOW

letter[1] written message

1 letters and other kinds of written message
2 writing a letter
3 sending and receiving letters
see also WRITE

1 letters and other kinds of written message

- a written message which you send to sb: **letter** ◦ *I got a letter from my sister yesterday.* ◦ *a business letter* ◦ *a love letter*
- a short letter: **note**
- a note which is sent from one person to another within a company or organization: **memo** (*plural* **memos**), (*formal*) **memorandum** (*plural* **memoranda**)
- a card that you write a message on and send to sb: **postcard** ◦ *'Have a lovely holiday!' 'Thanks. I'll send you a postcard.'*

- a written message which you send by telephone lines, using a special machine: **fax**; to send a fax: **fax** (sb) (sth), **fax** (sth) (**to** sb); the machine used for sending a fax: **fax** (**machine**) ◦ *Why not send a fax?* ◦ *I'll fax you my new address.*

- a system for sending written messages by computer: **e-mail** (= electronic mail) (*noun* U); *verb*: **e-mail** sb (**with** sth), **e-mail** sth (**to** sb); a message sent in this way: **e-mail** ◦ *an e-mail message* ◦ *I'll get in touch by e-mail.* ◦ *Could you e-mail me*

letter[1] *contd.*

once you know the results? ◦ *Please send me a fax or an e-mail by tomorrow.*

- a message which you can send very quickly, and which is delivered on a printed form: **telegram**
- a message which you type on a special machine; it is sent by telephone and is immediately printed by another machine in the receiver's office: **telex**; to send a telex: **telex** (sb) (sth) ◦ *I've telexed her about the contract.*

2 writing a letter

- to put a written message on paper: **write*** (**to** sb), **write*** (sb) a **letter**, (*informal*) **drop** sb **a line** ◦ *Why don't you ever write?* ◦ *I've got to write to the bank this afternoon.* ◦ *I spent most of the afternoon writing letters.* ◦ *I must drop Mary a line to let her know I've had the baby.*
- to write a letter using a machine: **type** a letter ◦ *Was the letter hand-written or typed?*
- paper used for writing letters: **writing paper** (*noun* U), **notepaper** (*noun* U)
- to say the words of a letter so that a secretary can write them down: **dictate** a letter

- to write a letter as an answer to a letter you have received: **reply** (**to** sb/sth), **answer** (sth), **write* back**; *nouns*: **reply**, **answer** ◦ *I wrote to her ages ago but she never replied.* ◦ *I still haven't answered Aunt Elsie's letter.* ◦ *I wrote back straight away, telling them that I'd already paid.* ◦ *Did you get a reply to your letter?*

- to write to an organization to order sth or to ask them to send you sth: **write* off/away for** sth, **send* off/away for** sth ◦ *I'm going to write off for those free train tickets.*
- to write a letter to an organization, for example a radio station, in order to give an opinion, make a complaint, etc: **write* in** (**to** sb/sth) ◦ *A lot of listeners wrote in to complain about the presenter's bad language.*

■ the beginning and end of a letter

- at the beginning of a letter you write **Dear . . .** ◦ *Dear Mrs Kirkpatrick*
- if you are writing a formal letter to sb whose name you do not know, you write **Dear Sir** for a man, **Dear Madam** for a woman, or **Dear Sir/Madam** if you do not know whether the receiver is a man or a woman
- if you want the reader to know that you are writing about a particular subject which he/she already knows about, you write (*formal*) **with reference to**, followed by the subject of the letter ◦ *With reference to your advertisement in today's Guardian . . .*

- at the end of a formal letter, you write **Yours sincerely** if you know the name of the receiver, or **Yours faithfully** if you do not know his/her name
- at the end of a fairly formal but friendly letter, you can write (**Kind**) **Regards, Best Wishes**
- at the end of an informal letter, you can write (**Lots of**) **love, All the best**
- your name, written by hand in a special way so that nobody else can copy it: **signature**
- to put your signature on sth: **sign** (sth)
- if you have already signed an informal letter, and you would like to write sth more, you can write **PS** (= postscript) and then the message ◦ *PS Paula sends her love.*

- the number of your house or flat, the name of your street and the name of your town which you write on a letter: **address**
- a paper cover for a letter: **envelope**
- to write the name and address of the receiver on an envelope: **address** the envelope

- to put some other material in an envelope with a letter: **enclose** sth ◦ *She enclosed a map with the invitation, so that the guests would be able to find her house.*

3 sending and receiving letters

- the act of writing and sending letters; the letters you write and receive: (*formal*) **correspondence** (*noun* U) ◦ *My secretary deals with all my correspondence.*
- to communicate with sb by letter: (*formal*) **correspond** (**with** sb) ◦ *We've been corresponding now for two years and we still haven't met!*
- a person who you correspond with: (*formal*) **correspondent**
- a person who you become friendly with by exchanging letters: **penfriend** (*especially AmE* **pen pal**) ◦ *Robert has penfriends all over the world.*

■ sending letters

- to send a letter, etc: **send*** sth, **post** (*AmE* **mail**) sth ◦ *I sent it yesterday, so it should arrive today.* ◦ *Could you post this letter for me on your way to the shops please?*

▷ more on posting letters ⇨ POST

■ receiving letters

- a general term for letters, parcels, etc that you receive: **post** (*noun* U), (*especially AmE*) **mail** (*noun* U) ◦ *Did any post come this morning?*
- a covered hole in the door of a house, flat, etc, through which the postman puts letters: **letter box**
- to receive a letter, etc from sb: **have/get*** sth (**from** sb), **hear* from** sb ◦ *Did you get my letter?* ◦ *I heard from Julie this morning – she's getting married!*
- to take a letter out of its envelope: **open** a letter

letter[2] written signs

see also WRITE, WORD

- a written or printed sign which represents a sound and which forms a word or part of a word: **letter** ◦ *The last letter of the alphabet is 'Z'.*
- a mark written above a letter which shows that it has to be pronounced in a certain way: **accent** ◦ *The 'e' in café has an acute accent.*
- an ordered list of the letters which are used in a language: **alphabet** ◦ *There are 26 letters in the English alphabet.*

- if a list is arranged with the first letter of each word following the order of the letters in the alphabet, the list is **in alphabetical order**, arranged **alphabetically** ○ *Information in this encyclopaedia is arranged alphabetically.*

- a larger letter which is used for the first letter of names and sentences: **capital letter**, **capital** ○ *a capital H* ○ *Write your surname in capitals, please.*
- the first letter of a name: **initial** ○ *The case had the initials 'J.D.' on it.*
- letters which are not capitals: **small letters** ○ *Should I use capital letters or small letters for the title?*
- the terms used for small letters/capital letters in printing: **lower/upper case** ○ *If you press this key, all the letters will be in upper case.*
- the sort of letters which slope forwards: **italics** (*noun plural*) ○ *All the examples in this book are in italics.*

- to write or say the letters of a word in the correct way: **spell** (sth) ○ *'Your name, please.' 'Gray.' 'Do you spell that with an a or an e?' 'With an a.'*

▷ more on spelling ⇨ WORD

level ⇨ SURFACE

library

see also BOOK

- a place where you can go to read, study and borrow books: **library** ○ *You don't need to buy that book – it's in the library.* ○ *a school/university library*
- a library which is open to everyone: **public library**
- a library where you can work and read, but you cannot borrow books: **reference library**

- a book which belongs to a library: **library book**
- a list, either on cards or on a computer, of all the books which you can find in the library: **catalogue** (*AmE* **catalog**) ○ *'Excuse me, do you have this book?' 'I'm not sure – have a look in the catalogue.'*
- a person who works in a library: **librarian**

- a card which you have to show to the librarian when you want to borrow a book: **library card/ticket**
- to take a book away from a library for a limited period of time: **borrow** a book, **take*** a book **out** ○ *I think I'll take these three out.*
- to bring back a book that you have borrowed from a library: **return** a book, **take*** a book **back**
- the date by which you must return a book is the date that it is **due back** ○ *This book's due back tomorrow.*
- a sum of money that you have to pay if you do not return a book on time: **fine**

lie[1] telling a lie

see also HONEST, TRUE

- to say sth which you know is not true: **lie** (**to** sb) (**about** sth), **tell*** (sb) **a lie**, **tell*** (sb) **lies** ○ *He must be lying.* ○ *She lied about her age.* ○ *Did you lie to me?*
- an untrue thing that sb says: **lie** ○ *You mustn't tell lies!* ○ *How could you possibly believe such a blatant* (= obvious) *lie?* ○ *The whole book is just a pack of lies* (= all lies).
- a small lie, especially one told by a child: **fib**; *verb*: **fib**
- a person who tells lies: **liar**, **fibber**
- a person who tells lies is **dishonest**; *noun* (U): **dishonesty** ○ *I was shocked by her dishonesty.*

- to think of sth which is not true: **make*** sth **up**, **think*** sth **up** ○ *He made up a story about being a famous actor.* ○ *You'll have to think up a good excuse.*

- to give sb wrong information about sth: **mislead*** sb, **misinform** sb
- information which gives you the wrong idea is **misleading** ○ *to make a misleading statement*
- to cheat or trick sb by lying to them: **deceive** sb ○ *He tried to deceive us into paying double the normal price.*

▷ more on deceiving ⇨ DECEIVE

- to make sb believe sth which is not true: **take*** sb **in** ○ *I was completely taken in by her story.*
- if you get tricked into believing sth which is not true, you **fall* for** sth ○ *I play the same trick on her every year, and she falls for it every time.*
- a person who easily believes lies is **gullible** ○ *He's so gullible he'll fall for anything.*

■ **MORE ...**

- a lie which you believe is harmless, and which you tell sb in order to avoid hurting them: **white lie**

- the crime of telling a lie in court: **perjury** (*noun* U)
- the crime of saying untrue things about sb in public: **slander** (*noun* U); *verb*: **slander** sb
- an untrue thing that a person says about sb in public: **slander** ○ *I've never heard such a vicious slander.*
- the crime of writing untrue things about sb: **libel** (*noun* U); *verb*: **libel** sb ○ *The magazine is being sued for libel.* ○ *He claims to have been libelled in a newspaper article.*
- an untrue thing that a person writes about sb: **libel**

- an instrument used by the police, etc, in order to know if sb is lying: **lie detector**

lie[2] not standing or sitting

see also SIT, STAND

- to be, or put yourself, in a horizontal position (so that you are not standing or sitting): **lie*** (**down**) ○ *'Where's Mary?' 'I think you'll find her lying down in her room.'* ○ *She lay flat on her back in the sunshine.*
- to lie down so as to rest: (*informal*) **have a lie-down** ○ *I'm not feeling very well. I think I'll go and have a lie-down.*

lie[2] *contd.*

- to put sb carefully in a lying position: **lay*** sb **down** ◦ *Francesca laid her baby down in his cot.*
- to lie down to be in a more comfortable position: **lie* back**, (*more formal*) **recline** ◦ *The picture showed a woman reclining on a sofa.*

▷ lying in bed ⇨ BED

- to move from a lying or sitting position to a standing position: **get* up**, **stand* up**, (*more formal*) **rise*** ◦ *Don't try to get up. Just lie there quietly until the doctor comes.* ◦ *He rose and addressed the audience.*
- to move from a lying position to a sitting position: **sit* up** ◦ *Sit up and try to drink this.*

- the way that sb/sth is lying, standing or sitting: **position** ◦ *Which position do you prefer sleeping in – on your back, your front or your side?*
- to relax by lying down with all your body flat: **stretch** (yourself) **out** ◦ *He stretched himself out on the settee.*
- to sit or lie with your arms and legs spread out in an untidy way: **sprawl** ◦ *Dave was sprawled on the sofa watching TV.*

life

1 life as a whole
2 the early part of life
3 the middle part of life
4 the later part of life

being alive (not dead) ⇨ LIVE[1]
where people live and how they live ⇨ LIVE[2]

see also YOUNG/OLD

1 life as a whole

- the period of time when you are alive: **life** ◦ *I've had a wonderful life.* ◦ *He spent his life working for others.*
- the time that your life lasts: **lifetime** ◦ *You must have seen many changes in your lifetime.*
- lasting your whole life: **lifelong** (*only before a noun*) ◦ *a lifelong ambition* ◦ *a lifelong friend*

- all the things you do and the way that you do them: **life** (*noun* C/U) ◦ *to lead a busy life* ◦ *my professional/private life* ◦ *life in the country*
- the manner in which you live: **way of life**, **lifestyle** ◦ *I need to change my way of life – I'm not getting enough exercise.* ◦ *We have completely different lifestyles.*
- to spend the time that you are alive in a particular way: **live** ◦ *to live quietly/happily*
- to survive an unpleasant experience: **live through** sth ◦ *My grandmother lived through two world wars.*

- your life before now: **past** ◦ *in my past* ◦ *a man with an unhappy past*
- your life after now: **future** ◦ *a bright future*

■ writing about sb's life
- the story of a person's life written by that person: **autobiography**; *adjective*: **autobiographical** ◦ *Her novel is full of autobiographical details.*
- the story of a person's life written by somebody else: **biography**; *adjective*: **biographical**; the author of a biography: **biographer** ◦ *Several biographies have been written of him, but this is the first official one.*

2 the early part of life

- to come into the world: **be born**; the time when you are born: **birth** (*noun* C/U) ◦ *When were you born?* ◦ *before I was born*
- a very young boy or girl: **baby**; this period of life: **infancy** (*noun* U)

▷ more on babies ⇨ BIRTH, BABY

- a young person who is not fully grown: **child** (*plural* **children**); this period of life: **childhood** (*noun* C/U) ◦ *an unhappy childhood*
- a young person who is growing from a child into an adult: **adolescent**; this period of life: **adolescence** (*noun* U)
- a person between 13 and 19 years old: **teenager**; *adjective* (*only before a noun*): **teenage**; during this time, you are **in** your **teens**
- to grow from a child into an adult: **grow* up**
- a young adult: **young person**; this period of life: **youth** (*noun* U) ◦ *the young people of today* ◦ *a youth club*

▷ more on children ⇨ CHILD

3 the middle part of life

- a person who is fully grown: **adult**, (*informal*) **grown-up**; *adjectives*: **adult**, **grown-up**
- when sb has become an adult, both physically and mentally, they are **mature**; this period of life: **maturity** (*noun* U)

- what you do regularly to earn money: **job**, **work** (*noun* U); to do a job to earn money: **work** ◦ *to get a job* ◦ *to have a job* ◦ *to lose your job* ◦ *to find work* ◦ *to be out of work* ◦ *to work for a living* ◦ *Who do you work for?*
- your working life: **career** ◦ *Her career is more important to her than her family.*

▷ work ⇨ WORK, EMPLOYMENT

- to take sb as your husband or wife: **marry** sb, **get* married** ◦ *They got married in 1988.*
- to begin to lead a responsible life as an adult, especially by staying in the same place, getting married, etc: **settle down** ◦ *I would like to get married and settle down soon.*
- to have your first child: **start a family**
- to look after a child until he/she is an adult and to teach him/her how to behave: **bring*** sb **up**, **raise** sb

▷ more on marriage and families ⇨ MARRY, FAMILY

- an adult who is not particularly young or old (between about 40 and 60) is **middle-aged**; this period of life: **middle age** (*noun* U) ◦ *in late/early middle age*

4 the later part of life

- a person over 60 or 70 is **old**, (*more formal and polite*) **elderly**; this period of life: **old age** (*noun* C/U) ◦ *an elderly aunt* ◦ *approaching old age*

- to stop living: **die** ◦ *He died at the age of 74.* ◦ *to die of heart disease*
- to live longer than another person: **outlive** sb ◦ *She outlived her husband by nearly ten years.*

▷ more on dying ⇨ DIE

- a person who has stopped work permanently, usually because of reaching a certain age, is **retired**; to become retired: **retire**; the time when you retire or the period of life when you are retired: **retirement** ◦ *a retired teacher* ◦ *My father has just retired.* ◦ *I'm looking forward to a long retirement.*
- money that is paid regularly to sb who has stopped working because of old age: **pension** ◦ *They live on a small pension.*
- an old person who no longer works: (**old-age**) **pensioner**, **senior citizen**

- a special home where old people live together: (**old people's**) **home**
- a special home where old and sick people can be cared for: **nursing home**

■ **MORE...**
- not old enough to do sth; not yet adult: **under age** ◦ *You can't go into pubs – you're under age.*
- to reach the age when you are legally an adult: **come* of age** ◦ *When you come of age, you can leave home and get married without your parents' consent.*

lift

see also BRING/TAKE/CARRY

- to move sth to a higher position: **lift** sth (**up**), **raise** sth ◦ *The baby lifted up her head to look at her mother.* ◦ *to raise a flag* ◦ *to raise your hand*
- to take hold of sth and lift it up: **pick** sth **up** ◦ *I picked up my bag and rushed out to the bus stop.* ◦ *Could you children pick your clothes up, please.*

- to take hold of sb/sth and move them/it to a different position: **lift** sb/sth ◦ *It needed three men to lift the new fridge up the stairs.* ◦ *Can you lift my bag down from the luggage rack, please?*
- to hold sb/sth in your hands or arms or on your back while you are moving from one place to another: **carry** sb/sth ◦ *We had to carry our suitcases up five flights of stairs.*

■ some machines which lift things
- a large machine with a long metal arm that is used for moving or lifting heavy objects: **crane**
- a piece of equipment used for lifting a car, etc off the ground so that you can change a wheel, repair the car, etc: **jack**; to lift a car by using a jack: **jack** sth **up**
- a bar or tool that is used to lift or open sth when you put pressure on one end: **lever**

- a machine in a large building that is used for carrying people or things from one floor to another: **lift** (*AmE* **elevator**)
- a device for pulling or carrying skiers up a slope, etc: **ski lift**

light[1]

- not heavy ⇨ WEIGHT

light[2] light/dark

1 light
2 dark
3 shade

light and dark colours ⇨ COLOUR
things that produce light ⇨ LIGHT[3]

1 light

- the brightness that allows you to see things: **light** (*noun* U) ◦ *the light from the sun* ◦ *artificial light* ◦ *There's not much light in this room.*
- the brightness that makes it light during the day: **daylight** (*noun* U)
- when there is daylight, it is **light** ◦ *Even though it was nearly midnight, it was still light.*
- to become lighter: **lighten** ◦ *The sky gradually lightened.*

- powerful, intense light is **strong**, **bright** ◦ *Where are my sunglasses? The light's too strong for me.* ◦ *bright sunshine*
- having a lot of light: **light**, **bright** (*adverb* **brightly**); *noun* (U): **brightness** ◦ *a lovely light room* ◦ *brightly lit houses* ◦ *I was dazzled by the brightness of the lights.*
- very bright: **brilliant** (*adverb* **brilliantly**); *noun* (U): **brilliance** ◦ *We came out of the tunnel into the brilliant sunshine*
- so bright that it makes it difficult to see other things: **blinding** ◦ *There was a blinding flash of light and then a strange object descended from the sky.*

- not bright but pleasant and relaxing: **soft** (*adverb* **softly**) ◦ *soft lighting and romantic music*

- to produce light: **shine*** ◦ *The sun was shining brightly.*
- reflecting light: **shiny** ◦ *shiny black shoes*
- to shine in a way that annoys you: **glare**; *noun* (U): **glare** ◦ *I can't stand the glare – it's hurting my eyes.*

- to give a warm light without smoke or flames: **glow**; *noun*: **glow**; *adjective*: **glowing** ◦ *a warm glow* ◦ *We sat round the glowing remains of the fire and sang songs.*
- to burn or shine in an unsteady way: **flicker**; *noun*: **flicker** ◦ *The torch flickered and then went out, leaving us in darkness.*
- to give many little flashes of light: **glitter**; *adjective*: **glittering** ◦ *glittering jewels*
- to shine from a wet surface: **glisten**; *adjective*: **glistening** ◦ *Her eyes glistened with tears.*
- to shine with many small points of light: **sparkle**; *adjective*: **sparkling** ◦ *The lake sparkled in the moonlight.* ◦ *sparkling eyes*

- a sudden bright light: **flash**; *adjective*: **flashing** ◦ *There was a flash of lightning and then the rain started to come down.* ◦ *'Do you like discos?' 'Well, I love dancing but I don't like the flashing lights.'*

light[2] *contd.*

- a small flash of light created by electricity: **spark**

■ light from the sun, moon and stars
- the light which comes from the sun, moon, stars: **sunlight** (*noun* U), **moonlight** (*noun* U), **starlight** (*noun* U)
- if a place is lit by the sun, moon, stars, it is **sunlit**, **moonlit**, **starlit** ◦ *a sunlit garden* ◦ *a moonlit/starlit night*
- the light and heat which come from the sun when there are no clouds in the sky: **sunshine** (*noun* U)

▷ more on the sun, moon and stars ⇨ SUN, STAR/PLANET/MOON

2 dark

- with no light: **dark** ◦ *It's too dark to see anything now – we'll have to wait until the morning.*
- the absence of light: **the dark** (*noun singular*); the situation or quality of being dark: **darkness** (*noun* U) ◦ *What are you doing sitting there in the dark?* ◦ *She groped around in the darkness looking for a candle* (= she used her hands to find the way).
- the period before/after it becomes dark: **before/after dark** ◦ *We should aim to arrive before dark.*
- completely dark: **pitch-dark** ◦ *a pitch-dark night*
- to become dark: **get* dark**, **go* dark**, **darken** ◦ *It's getting dark early these days.* ◦ *The sky suddenly darkened, and we heard a clap of thunder in the distance.*
- to make sth dark: **darken** sth ◦ *She was lying in a darkened room.*
- not bright: **dull**; *noun* (U): **dullness** ◦ *It's been such a dull day today.*
- dark and depressing: **gloomy** ◦ *We need to paint this room with some bright colours – it's so gloomy like this.*
- (usually used to talk about the light inside a building) quite dark, but not completely dark: **dim** (*adverb* **dimly**); *noun* (U): **dimness** ◦ *a dim light* ◦ *a dimly lit room*
- to become dim: **dim**; to cause sth to become dim: **dim** sth ◦ *The lights dimmed and the film started.* ◦ *to dim the lights*
- the time when it is dark and people usually sleep: **night** (*noun* C/U)
- the time when it is dark: **night-time** (*noun* U)
- the period of time in the evening when it is starting to get dark: **dusk** (*noun* U), **twilight** (*noun* U) ◦ *We arrived home as dusk was falling.*

▷ more on night ⇨ NIGHT

3 shade

- an area that is out of direct sunlight, and that is darker and cooler than other areas: **shade** (*noun* U) ◦ *Let's sit in the shade – it's too hot in the sun.*
- protected from the light of the sun: **shady** ◦ *We looked for a shady spot in the garden.*
- a dark shape on a surface which is produced by sth that is between light and that surface: **shadow** (*noun* C/U); a place which has a lot of shadows is **shadowy** ◦ *The shadows on the lawn were lengthening.* ◦ *Her face was in shadow.*
- to protect sb/sth from direct light: **shade** sb/sth (**from** sth) ◦ *to shade your eyes with your hand*

■ **MORE . . .**
- (used about a material) that allows light to pass through it, so that you can see through it: **transparent** ◦ *transparent plastic*
- not transparent: **opaque** ◦ *opaque glass*

light[3] things that produce light

lights used on cars, lorries, etc ⇨ CAR
light used in taking photographs ⇨ PHOTOGRAPH
light and dark ⇨ LIGHT[2]

- something that is made in order to produce light: **light** ◦ *an electric light*
- the lights used in a room, building, etc: **lighting** (*noun* U)
- a glass ball with a thin piece of wire inside it, which produces light when placed in an electric lamp: (**light**) **bulb** ◦ *to change a light bulb* ◦ *You need a 60 watt bulb for that light.*
- a kind of hard white light: **fluorescent** light ◦ *fluorescent lighting*
- a type of light created by a special gas, used for making bright lights and signs: **neon** light ◦ *a neon sign*
- a piece of equipment that uses electricity or oil to produce light: **lamp** ◦ *a bedside lamp* ◦ *a reading-lamp* ◦ *an oil lamp*
- a cover for a lamp that makes it more attractive and makes the light softer: (**lamp**)**shade**
- a light which uses a special kind of oil to make it work: **paraffin lamp**
- a small electric light that you carry in your hand: **torch** (*AmE* **flashlight**)
- a light in a street: **street light**
- a tall pole in a public place with a street light on the top: **lamp-post**
- a light that gives a strong, broad beam and is often used in sports stadiums: **floodlight**; if a place is lit by floodlights, it is **floodlit**
- a strong light that is used for looking for people or things over a large area of ground: **searchlight** ◦ *The helicopter's searchlights scanned the ground below.*
- a light which is used in the theatre to make the actors and the stage very bright: **spotlight**
- a tall building in or by the sea, which has a strong flashing light on top to warn ships of dangerous rocks in the area: **lighthouse**

■ candles
- a round piece of wax with a string (= **wick**) through the middle, which you can burn to give light: **candle** ◦ *She lit the candles and we all sang Happy Birthday.* ◦ *to blow out the candles* (= to stop them burning)
- the light that a candle produces: **candlelight** (*noun* U) ◦ *a romantic dinner by candlelight*
- a holder for one or several candles: **candlestick**

■ using lights

- when a light is working, it is **on**; *opposite*: **off** ◦ *There must be somebody in – the lights are all on.* ◦ *That's strange – all the lights are off.*
- (used about a light) to start working: **come* on**; *opposite*: **go* out/off** ◦ *What time do the street lights come on?* ◦ *All of a sudden the lights went out.*
- to make an electric light start working: **turn** sth **on**, **switch** sth **on**, **put*** sth **on** ◦ *Could somebody switch the lights on please?*
- to make a light stop working: **turn** sth **off/out**, **switch** sth **off**, **put*** sth **off/out** ◦ *Please switch the light off! I'm trying to get to sleep!*
- a small button or sth similar that you press up or down in order to switch a light on or off: **switch**
- not to turn sth off: **leave*** sth **on** ◦ *Leave the lights on – it might deter burglars.*

- to use a flame to make a gas or oil lamp, a candle, etc start burning: **light*** sth ◦ *Have you got a match? I want to light this lamp.*
- to cause a gas or oil lamp, a candle, etc to stop burning: **put*** sth **out** ◦ *Don't forget to put the lamp out before you go to bed.*

- to reduce the amount of light coming from an electric or gas light: **turn** sth **down**
- (used about lights) to become less light: **go* down**, **dim** ◦ *The lights in the auditorium went down and the play began.*

■ **MORE ...**

- to give light to sth or to decorate sth with lights: **illuminate** sth ◦ *The castle is illuminated at night.*
- bright lights that are used to decorate a street, town, etc: **illuminations** (*noun plural*) ◦ *Have you seen the illuminations in Oxford Street at Christmas?*

lightning ⇨ STORM

like¹

- similar ⇨ SAME

like² liking a person or thing

> **1** feeling that you like sb/sth
> **2** describing the person or thing that you like
> **3** showing or saying that you like sb/sth
> **see also** DISLIKE

1 feeling that you like sb/sth

- to think that sb/sth is pleasant: **like** sb/sth/doing sth, **be fond of** sb/sth/doing sth; a feeling of liking sb/sth: **fondness** (*noun* U/*singular*) ◦ *I've never liked playing party games.* ◦ *I'm very fond of her apple pies.* ◦ *a fondness for country and western music*
- to like one person or thing more than another: **prefer** sb/sth/doing sth (**to** sb/sth/doing sth) ◦ *I prefer him to her.* ◦ *Do you prefer red wine or white?* ◦ *Do you prefer reading or watching the television?*

▷ more on preferring sb/sth ⇨ PREFER

- to feel that sb/sth is acceptable or satisfactory: **approve of** sb/sth; *noun* (U): **approval** ◦ *Joanna doesn't approve of her sister's boyfriend.*
- if you are pleased because you or a person close to you has done sth good, you are **proud of** sb/sth; *noun* (U): **pride** ◦ *Their daughter's success made them very proud.* ◦ *We're proud of this beautiful new building.* ◦ *to take pride in your success*

▷ more on being proud ⇨ PROUD

■ liking something

- to think it is a good thing to do sth: **like to** do sth, **prefer to** do sth ◦ *I prefer to eat organic food if possible.*

- to like sth: **be keen on** sth/doing sth, **have a liking for** sth ◦ *'Do you like classical music?' 'Not really – but I'm quite keen on jazz.'* ◦ *She has a liking for Australian beer.*
- to like sth very much: **love** sth/doing sth ◦ *'Are you enjoying your new job?' 'Yes, I love it.'* ◦ *I love getting up late at the weekend.*

- to get pleasure from sth: **enjoy** sth/doing sth; *noun* (U): **enjoyment** ◦ *There's nothing I enjoy more than a quiet evening at home with a good book.* ◦ *Do you enjoy working there?* ◦ *We all got a lot of enjoyment out of making that video.*
- to like the idea of having sth or doing sth: **fancy** sth/doing sth ◦ *Do you fancy going to the cinema tonight?* ◦ *I think I fancy one of those cream cakes with my tea.*
- to be satisfied with sth: **be happy/content with** sth ◦ *We don't have much money, but we're happy with what we've got.*
- if you like sth (especially sth which you have just bought, been given, etc), you are **pleased with** it ◦ *I'm very pleased with my new camera.*

▷ more on enjoying things ⇨ ENJOY

- having a strong interest in sth: **keen on** sth, **enthusiastic** (**about** sth) (*adverb* **enthusiastically**); *noun* (U): **enthusiasm** (**for/about** sth) ◦ *keen on football/playing the piano* ◦ *enthusiastic about a new job* ◦ *always energetic and full of enthusiasm*
- if you are very enthusiastic about sth, for example Mozart's music, you can say that you are a **lover of** Mozart, a Mozart-**lover**, a Mozart **enthusiast/fan**, (*informal*) **mad/crazy about** Mozart ◦ *She's an opera-lover* ◦ *My brother's mad about football at the moment.*

■ liking somebody

- to find sb pleasant: **like** sb, **care for** sb, **be fond of** sb ◦ *I care for him a lot but I don't want to marry him.* ◦ *We've become quite fond of our teacher.*
- a feeling of liking sb: **affection** (*noun* U) ◦ *She has a lot of genuine affection for her sister's three children.*
- to have a strong feeling of affection for sb: **love** sb; *noun* (U): **love** ◦ *I love you.* ◦ *to be in love*

▷ more on love ⇨ LOVE

- to have a very high opinion of sb: **admire** sb, **think* highly of** sb, **look up to** sb; *noun* (U): **admiration** ◦ *She told me she thinks very highly of*

like² *contd.*

you. ◦ *His students really look up to him – he knows so much about his subject.* ◦ *We were filled with admiration at his courage and determination.*

– a person who admires and is very enthusiastic about a rock star, footballer, etc: **fan** ◦ *Millions of fans were waiting outside as the group left the building.* ◦ *a fan club* (= a group of fans of a particular person) ◦ *fan mail* (= letters that famous people receive from their fans)

2 describing the person or thing that you like

– a person or thing that you like is **nice**, **lovely** ◦ *You'll like him – he's really nice.* ◦ *'My sister and her children are coming to stay next week.' 'That's nice.'* ◦ *What a lovely dress!* ◦ *'Would you like a cup of tea?' 'Oh yes please, that'd be lovely.'*
– something that gives you pleasure is **enjoyable** ◦ *an enjoyable party/film/picnic*
– nice, enjoyable: **pleasant** ◦ *We had a very pleasant time.*
– (used about people) friendly: **pleasant**, **likeable** ◦ *pleasant people to spend the evening with* ◦ *a very likeable man*
– pleasant to look at: **beautiful**, **attractive**
▷ more on being pleasant or good ⇨ GOOD
▷ attractive and unattractive ⇨ BEAUTIFUL / ATTRACTIVE
– (used about an experience) making you feel good: **satisfying** ◦ *It's very satisfying to sit down with a good book after a long day's work.*
– very exciting and enjoyable: **great**, **terrific**, **wonderful**, **marvellous** (*AmE* **marvelous**) ◦ *You're going to America? That's terrific!* ◦ *What a wonderful concert!* ◦ *a marvellous result*
– causing you to have a high opinion of sb / sth: **impressive**; something which is impressive **impresses** you, **makes* a good impression on** you ◦ *That was a very impressive performance.* ◦ *His refusal to get angry made a very good impression on all of us.*
– the one you like most: **favourite** (*AmE* **favorite**) (*noun, adjective*) ◦ *Which member of the group is your favourite?* ◦ *Which is your favourite fruit?*
– your favourite friend: **best friend** ◦ *I'd like you to meet Joe – he's my best friend.*
– a person or thing that is liked or wanted by many people is **popular**; *noun* (U): **popularity** ◦ *These cars are very popular at the moment.* ◦ *This method has gained popularity over the last few years.*
– to make a large number of people like sb / sth: **popularize** sb / sth ◦ *This magazine was responsible for popularizing the miniskirt.*

3 showing or saying that you like sb/sth

– to tell sb that you like sth that they have done: **praise** sb (**for** sth) ◦ *Her teacher praised her for her performance.*
– to praise sb too much because you want to please them or because you want to get an advantage for yourself: **flatter** sb; *noun* (U): **flattery**
– to shout in a way that shows that you like a person or have enjoyed a performance: **cheer** sb / sth; the noise that people make when they cheer: **cheer**, **cheering** (*noun* U) ◦ *The crowd gave a loud cheer when their team scored a goal.*

■ **MORE ...**
– if sb is good at judging what is attractive, suitable or of good quality, we say that they have **good taste** ◦ *He's got good taste in clothes.*
– if you are not sure whether you like sb / sth or not, you can say that you **have mixed feelings** (**about** them / it) ◦ *I should have known this would happen – I had very mixed feelings about him from the start.*
– if sth seems to become nicer as time passes, it **grows* on** you
– the things that you like and the things that you do not like: **likes and dislikes** ◦ *Please write a list of your likes and dislikes so that we can find a suitable partner for you.*

line

1 marks on a surface
2 people and things in lines

1 marks on a surface

– a long thin mark on the surface of sth: **line** ◦ *to draw a line* ◦ *a dotted line*
– something which is marked with lines is **lined** ◦ *lined paper* ◦ *His face was heavily lined.*
– a straight piece of wood or plastic used for measuring or drawing straight lines: **ruler**
– to draw a line under a word: **underline** sth ◦ *Underline the most important words.*
▷ drawing ⇨ DRAW

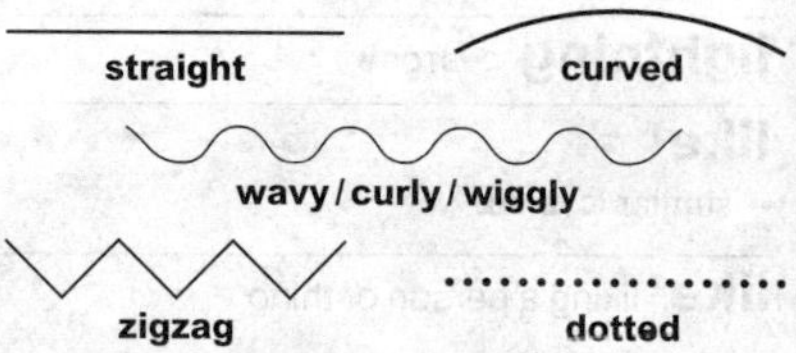

◦ *a straight line* ◦ *Please sign on the dotted line.*
▷ things that are straight ⇨ STRAIGHT

■ lines which go round something
– the distance round the edge of a shape; the outside edge of sth, for example the boundary of a piece of land: **perimeter** ◦ *the perimeter of a rectangle* ◦ *a perimeter fence*
– a line that shows the shape or outside edge of sth: **outline** ◦ *She drew the outline of a horse and then coloured her picture in.*
▷ the distance round a circle ⇨ CIRCLE

■ the position of lines
– the space between two lines or surfaces that meet, measured in degrees: **angle** ◦ *an angle of 45 degrees (45°)* ◦ *a right angle* (= an angle of 90°)

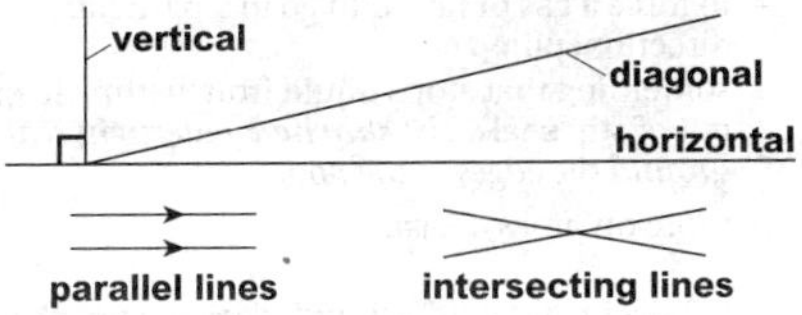

▷ more on angles ⇨ ANGLE

2 people and things in lines

- a single row of writing on a page: **line** ◦ *to start a new line* ◦ *a line of a poem*

- people waiting for sth, one behind the other: **queue**, (*especially AmE*) **line** ◦ *a bus queue* ◦ *There was a long line of people waiting for the exhibition.*
- people or things arranged in a line: **line**, **row** ◦ *children standing in a line* ◦ *a long line/row of houses* ◦ *a row of books/desks/seats*
- to stand in a row with other people: **line up**; to put things in a line: **line** sth **up** ◦ *The children lined up behind their teacher.*
- when people move in a line, one behind the other, they walk **in single file**

lion / leopard / tiger

see also ANIMAL

- a large animal of the cat family that lives in Africa and parts of southern Asia: **lion**
- a large animal of the cat family with yellow fur and dark spots: **leopard**
- a large animal of the cat family with yellow fur and black stripes: **tiger** (picture at ANIMAL)
- a female lion: **lioness**
- a young lion, leopard or tiger: **cub**
- a group of lions living together: **pride** ◦ *a pride of lions*
- the hidden home of some wild animals like lions: **den**

- the loud noise made by a lion or tiger: **roar**; *verb*: **roar**

lip ⇨ MOUTH

liquid

1 describing liquids
2 measuring liquids
3 solids in liquids
4 movement of liquids

see also WATER, CONTAINER

1 describing liquids

- a substance like water that is not a solid or gas: **liquid** (*noun* C/U), (*more formal and technical*) **fluid** (*noun* C/U) ◦ *Water is a colourless liquid.* ◦ *Drink plenty of fluids, but do not eat anything.* ◦ *body fluids* ◦ *cleaning fluid*
- in the form of a liquid: **liquid** ◦ *liquid soap* ◦ *liquid foods*
- a substance or object that is hard, not liquid: **solid**; to change from a liquid to a solid: **solidify** ◦ *Butter is a solid, but when it melts it becomes liquid.*
- to change from solid to liquid by means of heat: **melt**; to cause sth to do this: **melt** sth ◦ *If you leave the butter in the sun, it will melt.* ◦ *Melt the butter in a pan.*

- a liquid which contains very little water is **thick**; *opposite*: **thin** ◦ *Heat the sauce until it turns thick.* ◦ *thin soup*
- the degree of thickness or firmness that a liquid has: **consistency** ◦ *Add water until the mixture has a smooth consistency.*

- to make a liquid weaker by adding water or another liquid: **dilute** sth; *adjective*: **diluted** ◦ *Dilute the mixture with water.*
- a liquid which has been made stronger by the removal of some liquid is **concentrated** ◦ *concentrated orange juice*

- the top part of an area of liquid: **surface** ◦ *We could see something floating on the surface of the water.*
- the thin solid surface that can form on liquids: **skin** ◦ *When hot milk cools, a skin forms on the top.*
- a liquid (for example a mixture used in cooking sth) which has no lumps is **smooth**; *opposite*: **lumpy**

- a hollow ball containing air or gas, in liquid or floating in the air: **bubble**; full of bubbles: **bubbly**
- to produce bubbles or to rise with bubbles: **bubble** ◦ *When the liquid starts to bubble very quickly, turn down the heat.*

■ hot and cold liquids

- to reach a high temperature at which bubbles rise to the surface and the liquid changes to gas: **boil** ◦ *Heat the liquid until it boils.*
- to become hard (and often change to ice) because of exteme cold: **freeze***

- a liquid that is very cold is **icy**, (*informal*) **freezing (cold)** ◦ *I had a freezing cold shower.*
- fairly cold: **cool**
- slightly warm: **tepid**
- very hot **scalding (hot)**, (*informal*) **boiling (hot)**

▷ more on boiling and freezing ⇨ WATER, ICE

■ different kinds of liquid

- (in chemistry) a liquid substance which can dissolve metal and may burn your skin: **acid** (*noun* C/U); containing acid: **acid**, **acidic**; the quality of being acid: **acidity** (*noun* U) ◦ *sulphuric acid* ◦ *a slightly acidic substance* ◦ *a high acidity level*
- the opposite of acidic: **alkaline**; a substance which is alkaline: **alkali** (*noun* C/U) ◦ *an alkaline solution*

▷ liquids that we drink ⇨ DRINK

▷ liquids in food and cooking ⇨ FOOD, COOK

▷ liquids used in body care ⇨ COSMETICS

▷ oil and petrol ⇨ OIL

liquid *contd.*

2 measuring liquids

■ metric measurements
- the basic unit for measuring amounts of liquid: **litre** (*abbreviation* **l**) ◦ *a litre of wine*
- one thousandth of a litre (used for measuring small amounts): **millilitre** (*abbreviation* **ml**)

■ non-metric measurements
- the basic unit for measuring amounts of liquid: **pint** (*abbreviation* **pt**) ◦ *a pint of milk/beer*
- two pints: 1 **quart**
- eight pints: 1 **gallon** ◦ *a gallon of petrol*
- one twentieth of a UK pint (one sixteenth of a US pint): 1 **fluid ounce** (*abbreviation* **fl oz**)

■ comparing the metric and non-metric measurements
- 1 UK pint = 0.568 litre
- 1 US pint = 0.473 litre
- 1 UK quart = 1.136 litres
- 1 US quart = 0.946 litre
- 1 UK gallon = 4.546 litres
- 1 US gallon = 3.785 litres

3 solids in liquids

- (used about sth which is solid) to mix with a liquid so that the solid itself becomes liquid: **dissolve** (**in** sth) ◦ *Wait until the sugar dissolves in the water.*
- to make sth dissolve: **dissolve** sth (**in** sth) ◦ *Dissolve the powder in water.*
- something that can be dissolved is **soluble** ◦ *Glucose is soluble in water.*
- a liquid (usually water) in which sth solid has been dissolved: **solution**

- to remove a liquid from a mixture of solids and liquids by pouring them through a special container (a **strainer**): **strain** sth ◦ *Strain the vegetables and serve.*
- to separate food from water by pouring them both through a special container: **drain** sth ◦ *Drain the pasta.*
- an apparatus for holding back solid substances from a liquid that passes through it: **filter** ◦ *a coffee filter*
- to pass a liquid through a filter: **filter** sth

4 movement of liquids

- to move in a continuous way: **flow, run*** ◦ *The river flows through the centre of the town.* ◦ *Is the tap running?*
- to flow away: **drain** (**away**); to make a liquid flow away: **drain** sth (**away/off/from**) ◦ *Any excess liquid will drain away through this pipe.* ◦ *The doctor drained some fluid from the wound.*

- a long, hollow tube or cylinder made of plastic or metal that carries gas or liquid: **pipe**; to carry gas or liquid in pipes: **pipe** sth ◦ *a water pipe* ◦ *Water is piped to people's homes.*
- a machine which is used for forcing a gas or a liquid in a particular direction: **pump** ◦ *a petrol pump*
- to force a gas or liquid to go in a particular direction: **pump** sth
- something that stops liquid from getting in or out of sth: **seal** ◦ *The ship had watertight seals around the edges of the doors.*

▷ more on pipes ⇨ PIPE

- to take in and hold a liquid: **soak** sth **up**, **absorb** sth ◦ *This cloth should soak up most of the water.* ◦ *Within a short time, the liquid had been entirely absorbed.*
- a material which absorbs liquids easily is **absorbent** ◦ *Cotton is a very absorbent material.*
- a material which allows liquid to pass through slowly is **porous** ◦ *porous rocks*

- to transfer liquid from one container or place to another: **pour** sth ◦ *I'll pour you a beer.* ◦ *He poured another can of oil into the engine.*
- to move a liquid round and round using a spoon, etc: **stir** sth; an act of stirring: **stir** ◦ *You must stir the sauce or it will stick to the bottom of the pan.* ◦ *Give the mixture a quick stir.*
- to move a liquid from side to side or up and down with short quick movements: **shake*** sth ◦ *Shake the bottle before you open it.*

■ spilling and leaking
- (used about a liquid) to come out of a container by accident: **spill**; to cause a liquid to do this: **spill** sth ◦ *The milk spilled all over the floor.* ◦ *He spilled the milk all over the floor.*
- to knock sth over (usually containing liquid): **upset*** sth ◦ *She upset her coffee when she tried to reach for the sugar.*
- to be so full of liquid that the liquid pours over the edge: **overflow** ◦ *Don't leave the tap on or the bath will overflow.*
- to escape through a hole or gap: **leak** ◦ *Oil was leaking from the tank.*
- a hole which a liquid can get through; or the liquid which escapes: **leak** ◦ *I think there's a leak in the water tank.*

- to remove liquid or dirt with a cloth: **wipe** sth **up** ◦ *Will somebody please wipe up the mess?*

■ moving quickly or with force
- to flow out of or into sth quickly or in large amounts: **pour**, **stream** ◦ *Water was pouring all over the floor.*
- a constant movement of a liquid: **stream** ◦ *a stream of blood*
- a strong fast stream of sth, especially water: **torrent** ◦ *A torrent of flood water swept through the valley.*

- to flow out suddenly and in great quantities: **gush** ◦ *Water came gushing through the dam gates.*
- to come out with great force: **spurt** (**out**) (**of** sth) ◦ *When I opened the container, the juice spurted out all over me.*
- to be forced out of sth in a thin fast stream: **squirt**; to make a liquid move in this way: **squirt** sth (**at** sb/sth), **squirt** sb/sth (**with** sth) ◦ *Squirt a bit of washing-up liquid into the sink.* ◦ *They*

were squirting each other with water from plastic bottles.

- to press sth hard so that some liquid comes out, or to force liquid out of sth by pressing: **squeeze** sth (**out**) ○ *Squeeze some lemon juice over the salad.*

- to come out in very small drops and with great force: **spray**; to send a liquid out in this way: **spray** sth **on/onto/over** sb/sth, **spray** sb/sth **with** sth ○ *The farmers were spraying their crops with special chemicals.*
- liquid in very small drops which is blown through the air: **spray** (*noun* U) ○ *We went for a walk along the beach and got wet through with sea spray.*
- liquid in a special container which is forced out under pressure when you push a button: **spray** ○ *a perfume spray*

- to fly about in drops and make sb/sth wet: **splash** (**on/over/onto**) sb/sth; to cause a liquid to do this: **splash** sth **on/over/onto** sb/sth, **splash** sb/sth (**with** sth); an act or sound of splashing: **splash** ○ *The rainwater splashed onto her trousers as the car drove quickly past.* ○ *Stop it – you're splashing me!* ○ *The dog jumped into the river with a great splash.*
- a mark or spot that was made by sth splashing: **splash** ○ *There were small splashes of rain on the window.*

■ moving slowly or in small amounts

- a small rounded mass of liquid: **drop** ○ *a drop of blood/oil/water*
- to fall in drops: **drip** ○ *Sweat was dripping from his face.*

- to flow in a thin stream: **trickle**; *noun*: **trickle** ○ *Sweat was beginning to trickle down his face.* ○ *In dry weather, this stream reduces to a mere trickle.*
- to flow slowly out of sth: **ooze** (**from** sth)

listen

see also HEAR, SOUND

- to receive sounds with your ears: **hear*** (sb/sth) ○ *Can you hear that knocking noise?* ○ *I can't hear you very well – can you speak up a bit?*
- to pay attention in order to hear: **listen** (**to** sb/sth) ○ *Listen to that noise! I've never heard anything like it!* ○ *to listen carefully* ○ *to listen to the radio*
- a person who listens, especially to the radio: **listener** ○ *In this programme, listeners phone in to tell us their opinions.* ○ *She's a good listener* (= she pays attention to you when you are speaking).

- care that you take in listening, watching or thinking about sth: **attention** (*noun* U); *adjective*: **attentive** (*adverb* **attentively**) ○ *May I have your attention, please?* ○ *My attention wandered after an hour and I didn't hear the end of his speech.* ○ *a very attentive audience* ○ *to listen attentively*
- to listen, watch, etc with care and concentration: **pay* attention** (**to** sb/sth) ○ *Could you please pay attention to what I'm saying?*
- to listen secretly to other people's conversation: **eavesdrop** (**on** sb/sth), **listen in** (**on/to** sth); a person who does this: **eavesdropper** ○ *to eavesdrop on sb's phone calls* ○ *I love to listen in to the children's conversation when they are playing.*

■ not listening

- to pay no attention to sb/sth: **ignore** sb/sth, **take* no notice** (**of** sb/sth) ○ *We ignored the fire alarm because we thought it was a test.* ○ *Take no notice of John – he doesn't mean to be rude.*
- to decide to stop paying attention: (*informal*) **switch off** ○ *I didn't hear what he said next because I had already switched off.*

■ **MORE ...**

- to listen to sth particularly carefully: **prick up** your **ears** ○ *He pricked up his ears when he heard the word 'money'.*
- if you listen to sth but you then ignore it or quickly forget it, it (*informal*) **goes* in one ear and out the other** ○ *It's a waste of time telling Dad what to buy – it'll just go in one ear and out the other.*

- to use a tiny, hidden microphone to listen to what other people say: **bug** sth; this kind of microphone: **bug** ○ *Don't say anything – this room is bugged!* ○ *to plant a bug* (= to put one in a place)

literature

see also BOOK

- novels, poems and plays, which are considered to be of high quality and an important part of a country's culture: **literature** (*noun* U); *adjective*: **literary** ○ *I'm studying 20th century English literature at university.* ○ *We have to study all the important literary works of the last hundred years.*

- a book which tells a story about people and events which are not real: **novel**; a person who writes novels: **novelist** ○ *'What are you reading?' 'It's a novel by Thomas Hardy.'* ○ *a historical novel* (= which tells a story related to a particular point in history)

- stories, novels, etc which describe events and people that do not really exist: **fiction** (*noun* U)
- books that are about real people and events: **non-fiction** (*noun* U)

- a story which is written for actors to perform in the theatre, on television or on radio: **play**; a person who writes plays: **playwright**, **dramatist**; the writing and performance of plays: **drama** (*noun* U) ○ *We're going to see a play by Beckett.* ○ *Sheila says she's going to start drama classes.*
- a piece of writing usually in short lines, which sometimes rhyme: **poem**; a person who writes poems: **poet** ○ *She recited a poem by Tennyson.*
- poems, seen as a type of literature: **poetry** (*noun* U) ○ *a book on modern poetry*

literature *contd.*

- a short piece of writing on one subject: **essay** ◦ *Have you ever read any of Montaigne's essays?*

▷ for more on plays and poems ⇨ PLAY[1], POEM

- the way that sb usually writes; a recognized way of writing: **style** ◦ *the inimitable style of Oscar Wilde* ◦ *in the style of a 19th century romantic novel*

- describing the good or bad points of a book, play, film, etc: **criticism** (*noun* C/U) ◦ *I have to do a criticism of this poem before my class on Monday.* ◦ *an expert in literary criticism*
- a person who writes criticism: **critic**

litre ⇨ LIQUID

little

- a small size ⇨ BIG/SMALL
- a small quantity ⇨ HOW MUCH/MANY

live[1] to be alive; to have life

living in a place; earning your living ⇨ LIVE[2]

- the quality that people, animals and plants have when they are not dead: **life** (*noun* U); to have life: **live** ◦ *What do you think is the purpose of life?* ◦ *Animals can't live without oxygen.*
- a person or animal that has life is **alive** (*not before a noun*), (used about people) **living**, (used about animals) **live** ◦ *Are her parents still alive?* ◦ *Does she have any living relatives?* ◦ *the transport of live animals.*

- to come out of the mother's body at the beginning of life: **be born**; *noun* (C/U): **birth**
- to stop being alive: **die**; *noun* (C/U): **death**

▷ birth and death ⇨ BIRTH, DIE

- the length of time that sb normally lives: **life expectancy** (*noun* U) ◦ *a country where life expectancy is less than 50 years*
- to live longer than sb else: **outlive** sb ◦ *He outlived all his children.*
- to continue to live after a difficult or dangerous situation: **survive** (sth); a person who survives: **survivor** ◦ *Only five passengers survived the crash.* ◦ *None of the victims of the earthquake survived.* ◦ *the survivors of the accident*

■ living things
- living things in general: **life** (*noun* U) ◦ *Do you think there is life on any other planet?*
- the smallest living part of an animal or plant: **cell**
- a living thing, especially a very small one that you can only see with a microscope: **organism**

▷ different kinds of living thing ⇨ ANIMAL, PLANT

■ human life
- the existence of an individual person: **life** ◦ *Many lives were lost in the fire.*
- the state of being alive as human beings: **life** (*noun* U) ◦ *a great loss of life in the war*
- the period of time when you are alive: **life** ◦ *I've lived in Africa all my life.*

▷ the period between your birth and death ⇨ LIFE

- to manage to live: **exist**, **survive** ◦ *How can you exist on so little food?*
- to continue to live after an illness or accident: **live** ◦ *Will she live, doctor?*

live[2] where people live and how they live

1 living in a place
2 changing where you live
3 the cost of living
4 different standards of living

being alive ⇨ LIVE[1]
the stages of a person's life ⇨ LIFE

see also HOUSE, HOTEL, TOWN

1 living in a place

- the place where you sleep and keep your possessions is where you **live** ◦ *How long have you lived here?*
- the house where you normally live or where you feel that you belong is your **home** ◦ *a home in the country* ◦ *to leave home*
- when you first begin to live independently in a house, you **set* up house** ◦ *We left home and set up house together in another part of town.*

- the number or name of the house and the name of the street and town where you live: **address** ◦ *a change of address*

- to live somewhere for a short time as a visitor or guest: **stay**; a period of time that you stay somewhere: **stay** ◦ *I'm staying at a hotel.* ◦ *to go to stay with friends* ◦ *Why don't you stay the night?* ◦ *Did you enjoy your stay?*
- somewhere to live or stay: **accommodation** (*noun* U) ◦ *The first thing you must do is to find some accommodation.* ◦ *The price of the holiday includes flights and accommodation.*

■ the people who live in a place
- a person who lives in a country, town, etc: **inhabitant**; *verb*: **inhabit** a place ◦ *The town has 20 000 inhabitants.* ◦ *Is the island inhabited?*
- if your home is in a particular country, town, house, etc, you are a **resident** (**of** that place); *adjective*: **resident** (**in** a place) ◦ *a residents' association* ◦ *Are you resident in the UK?*
- a person who uses a particular room, house, etc: (*formal*) **occupant**; *verb*: **occupy** sth ◦ *The occupant of Room 101 doesn't want to be disturbed.* ◦ *The new flats are not occupied yet.*

- a person who lives near you: **neighbour** (*AmE* **neighbor**)
- the neighbour in the house nearest to yours: **next-door neighbour** (*AmE* **next-door neighbor**) ◦ *Have you met your next-door neighbours yet?*
- a particular part of a town and the people who live there: **neighbourhood** (*AmE* **neighborhood**) ◦ *a very friendly neighbourhood* ◦ *Is there a post office in the neighbourhood?*

- a person who was born in a particular place: **native** ◦ *Are you a native of Aberdeen?*

- a person who lives in a particular place: **local** ◦ *If you get lost, ask one of the locals.*
- a group of people who live in a particular place, area or country: **community** ◦ *to work in the community* ◦ *the local business community*
- a person who lives in a city: **citizen** ◦ *the citizens of London*

■ living with other people
- to live in the same house, etc as another person: **live together**, **live with** sb ◦ *I used to live with an elderly aunt.*
- if two or more people live in a house, flat, or room and each person pays part of the rent, etc, they **share** the house, flat, or room
- a person who shares a room in a flat, etc: **roommate**
- a person who shares a flat: **flatmate**
- to start living with sb: **move in with** sb

▷ living in a rented house or room ⇨ RENT

- to live in the same house and have a sexual relationship with sb, without being married to them: **live together**, **live with** sb ◦ *They've been living together for ten years.* ◦ *He lives with his girlfriend.*
- if married people decide to live in separate homes, they **separate**; then they **live apart** (**from** each other)

■ having no permanent house of your own
- a person who has nowhere to live is **homeless**; all the people who have no homes are **the homeless** (*noun plural*); the condition of being homeless: **homelessness** (*noun* U) ◦ *Homelessness is a growing problem in inner-city areas.*
- a person who lives in an empty building without the permission of the owner: **squatter**; *verb*: **squat**; a place where squatters are living: **squat** ◦ *He ran away from home and lived in a squat in the city.*
- if you sleep outside because you have no home, you **sleep* rough**, **live rough** ◦ *people sleeping rough in cardboard boxes*

- to give sb a place to live: **house** sb ◦ *The council has a responsibility to house homeless families.*
- to force a person to leave the building or land where they live: **evict** sb (**from** sth); *noun* (C/U): **eviction** ◦ *The families were evicted for not paying the rent.*

2 changing where you live
- if you go and live in another house, you **move**, **move house**; the change that you make is a **move** ◦ *She's moving house next week and has asked me to help her with the move.*
- when you stop living in a house and take your belongings away, you **move out** (**of** sth), (*formal*) **vacate** sth ◦ *When are you moving out?* ◦ *The lawyers say we must vacate the flat by the end of the month.*
- when you bring your belongings to a new house and begin to live in it, you **move into** it, **move in** ◦ *Have you met the people who have moved in next door?*
- a party that people give after they move into a new house: **house-warming** (**party**) ◦ *When are you having your house-warming party?*
- when you start to feel comfortable in a new home, you **settle into** it, **settle in** ◦ *Are you settling in all right?*

- to go and live permanently in a new country, area or town, etc: **settle** in a place; a person who does this: **settler** ◦ *They got married and settled in a town where nobody knew them.* ◦ *American settlers who moved out west*
- a person who lives outside their own country: **expatriate** ◦ *American expatriates in London*

▷ moving from one country to another ⇨ COUNTRY[1]

3 the cost of living
- to have a certain amount of money that you can spend in order to live: **live on** sth ◦ *We lived on £50 a month in those days.*
- a way of earning money to buy the things that you need: **living**; if you earn enough money for this, you **make* a**/your **living** ◦ *What do you do for a living?* (= what is your job?) ◦ *He made his living as an insurance salesman.*
- the price of all the things that you need in order to live a normal life: **the cost of living** ◦ *The cost of living has risen sharply in the last year.*

- to have enough money for your needs: **make*** (**both**) **ends meet** ◦ *We both need to work to make ends meet.*
- to have just enough to live on: **manage** ◦ *It's difficult to manage on £150 a week.* ◦ *We couldn't manage without help from the Social Services.*
- to get what you need to live from sb/sth: **live off** sb/sth ◦ *He lived off his parents until he found a job.* ◦ *to live off the state*
- to make a habit of getting money, food, etc from sb when you do not really intend to give it back or do anything else in return: (*informal*) **sponge off** sb ◦ *Mike is always sponging off his friends.*

4 different standards of living
- the level of money and comfort that people have in their everyday lives: **standard of living** ◦ *a high/low standard of living* ◦ *We have got used to a better standard of living.*

- difficulty or problems, often because of not having enough money: **hardship** (*noun* C/U) ◦ *During the depression many people suffered real hardship.*
- if you live in unpleasant or unhappy conditions, you have a **hard life**
- to have sth as your only food: **live on** sth ◦ *to live on bread and water*
- with no money, no home and no job: **down and out**; a person who is in this situation: **down and out**

- wealth, comfort and pleasure: **luxury** (*noun* U); *adjective*: **luxurious** ◦ *He inherited a large amount of money and is now living a life of luxury.* ◦ *a luxurious existence*

live² *contd.*

– to have plenty of money and live very comfortably: **live well** ◦ *We lived well while the money lasted.*

▷ rich and poor people ⇨ RICH, POOR

lock/chain

see also OPEN/SHUT

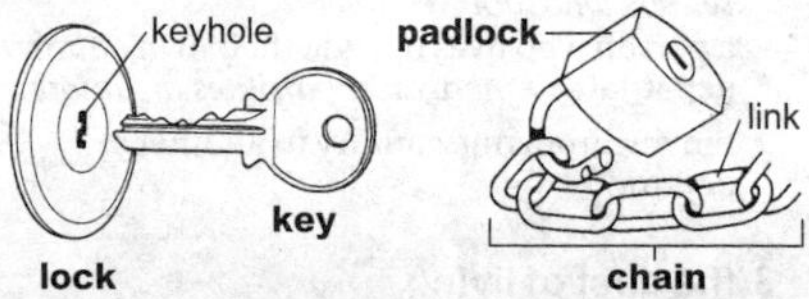

– to close or fasten sth with a lock: **lock** sth; *opposite*: **unlock** sth ◦ *Please make sure you lock the door before you leave.*
– to close sth or make sth safe with a padlock: **padlock** sth
– to fasten sb/sth to sth else using a chain: **chain** sb/sth (**to** sth), **chain** sb/sth (**up**) ◦ *The gate was locked and chained.* ◦ *Don't worry, the bikes are all chained up, so they're quite safe.*

– to keep sb/sth in a room, a building, a cupboard, etc by locking the door: **lock** sb/sth **in** (sth) ◦ *Can you help me? I've locked my keys in the car.*
– to keep sb out of a room or a building by locking the doors: **lock** sb **out** (of sth) ◦ *I had somehow managed to lock myself out of my house!*
– to put sth away by locking it somewhere: **lock** sth **away/up**

– to open sth which is locked: **open** sth **up** ◦ *The manager opens the shop up at nine o'clock every morning.*
– to lock all the doors and windows of a building: **lock up** ◦ *Don't forget to lock up before you leave.*

– a metal ring which you put through your keys to keep them all together: **keyring**
– several keys together on a keyring: **bunch of keys**

long/short¹ time

1 how long?
2 a short period of time
3 a long period of time
see also TIME

1 how long?

– to continue for a period of time: **last** (**for**) ..., **go* on** (**for**) ... ◦ *The play lasts for three hours.* ◦ *It went on all night.*
– lasting a certain length of time: **long** ◦ *How long did the party go on for?* ◦ *I don't know how long they've been here.* ◦ *It's a very short sonata – only five minutes long.*
– how long sth lasts: **length** (*noun* U), **duration** (*noun* U) ◦ *a play two hours in length* ◦ *a flight of one hour's duration*
– how long sb does sth for: **length of time** ◦ *There is a limit on the length of time a driver can go without a break.*

– to make sth last for a shorter time: **cut*** sth **short**, **shorten** sth ◦ *We've had to cut short our holiday.* ◦ *an illness which shortens the lives of millions of people*
– to make sth last for a longer time: **extend** sth, **prolong** sth, **lengthen** sth ◦ *We're extending our stay by a few extra days.* ◦ *to prolong sb's life*

2 a short period of time

– not lasting long: **short**, **brief** (*adverb* **briefly**) ◦ *a short conversation* ◦ *a short time ago* ◦ *a brief phone call* ◦ *I spoke to him briefly this morning.*
– for a short or indefinite period of time: **for a** (**short**) **while**, **for a** (**short**) **time**, (*informal*) **for a bit** ◦ *Let's stop for a while.* ◦ *We lived in Italy for a short time.* ◦ *We'll stay for a bit and then we'll go.*
– a very short period of time: **moment**, **second**, **minute** ◦ *Can you wait just a second, please?* ◦ *They'll be back in a couple of minutes.*
– lasting for only a short time; not permanent: **temporary** (*adverb* **temporarily**) ◦ *a temporary job* ◦ *I'm afraid you can't speak to her at the moment; she's temporarily engaged.*

– happening a short time ago: **recent** (*adverb* **recently**) ◦ *a recent decision* ◦ *She died quite recently.*
– after a short time in the future: **soon**, **shortly** ◦ *See you soon!* ◦ *We're leaving shortly.*
– over a short period of time in the future: **in the short term**; *adjective*: **short-term** ◦ *They're only short-term solutions.*

▷ happening soon ⇨ SOON

3 a long period of time

– a period of time which is not short is **long** (*adjective, adverb*) ◦ *to last a very long time* ◦ *It was a very long performance.* ◦ *a long journey* ◦ *Have you lived here long?*
– a fairly long period of time: **quite a while**, (**quite**) **some time** ◦ *We've been waiting quite a while.* ◦ *It will take quite some time to set up this project.*
– a long period of time: **hours**, **days**, **months**, **years**, **ages** ◦ *It was so boring – he went on for hours and hours.* ◦ *He's been doing the same job for years.* ◦ *We've got ages yet – the train won't be here for another half an hour.*
– (used about meetings, conversations, reports, etc) for a long time: **at length**; *adjective*: **lengthy** ◦ *She spoke at length about the problems in her country.* ◦ *a lengthy discussion*

Note: long (on its own, without **time**) is used in questions and negative sentences, but not in affirmative sentences except in expressions with **too** and **ago**; **a long time** can be used without these restrictions: ◦ *Have you known her long?* ◦ *We hadn't been waiting long.* ◦ *It lasted too long.* ◦ *It lasted a long time.*
– In negative sentences, **long** and **for a long time** can have different meanings: ◦ *I haven't been ill for a long time* (= It is a long time since I was

last ill). ○ *I haven't been ill long* (= my illness has not lasted a long time).

- lasting longer than necessary or wanted: **long-drawn-out, protracted** ○ *The trial was a very long-drawn-out affair.* ○ *after three years of protracted negotiations*
- over a long period of time in the future: **in the long term**; *adjective*: **long-term** ○ *In the long term, it's much better to put money into housing and education.*

- that can or does last a long time: **long-lasting** ○ *a long-lasting effect*
- strong and able to last a long time: **durable** ○ *a tough and durable surface*
- (used about arrangements and relationships) that has lasted for a long period of time: **long-standing** ○ *a long-standing friendship between two countries*
- (used about food and other products) specially prepared to last a long time: **long-life** ○ *long-life milk* ○ *a long-life battery*
- (used about plays, films, etc) having many performances over a long period of time: **long-running** ○ *a long-running show*
- (used about an illness or anything which is bad) lasting for a long time: **chronic** ○ *chronic diarrhoea* ○ *a chronic shortage of water*

- for all time in the future: **forever** (*BrE also* **for ever**), **for good, permanently** ○ *She's not going away forever.* ○ *We're leaving England for good.* ○ *We're going to move away from the city permanently.*
- lasting for a long time or forever: **permanent** ○ *a permanent job* ○ *a permanent solution to a problem*

---

long / short² size

see also SIZE, WIDE / NARROW

- large in size from one end to the other: **long**; *opposite*: **short** ○ *a long river* ○ *long hair* ○ *I'm going to grow my hair long.* ○ *short legs*

- the measurement of sth from one end to the other: **length** (*noun* C/U) ○ *We measured the length of the room with a tape-measure.* ○ *It's two metres in length.* ○ *The two sticks are the same length.*
- having a certain length: **long** ○ *How long is your living room?* ○ *I'm looking for a piece of wire about three centimetres long.*
- a measurement which is equal to the length of sth: **length** ○ *How many lengths of the swimming pool can you swim?* ○ *a length of dress material*

- the length of a journey; the amount of space between two points or places: **distance** (*noun* C/U) ○ *the distance from Paris to London* ○ *the distance between two points*

▷ more on distance ⇨ DISTANCE

■ changing the length of something
- to become longer: **lengthen**; to make sth longer/shorter: **lengthen/shorten** sth ○ *to lengthen/shorten a skirt*
- to make sth longer or larger: **extend** sth; *noun*: **extension** ○ *They're planning to extend the motorway.* ○ *the extension of the shopping centre*
- to pull sth so that it becomes wider or longer: **stretch** sth; to become wider or longer in this way: **stretch** ○ *We stretched the material over the frame.* ○ *My jumper stretched when I washed it.*
- (used mainly about clothes): to become shorter or smaller: **shrink***; to make sth shorter or smaller: **shrink*** sth ○ *My trousers have shrunk.*
- to reduce the length of sth: **cut*** sth **down** ○ *This essay is too long – you'll have to cut it down.*

---

look

1 looking in different directions
2 looking quickly, carefully, secretly, etc
3 looking at sth happening
see also SEE, LOOK FOR, FIND

1 looking in different directions

- to turn your eyes in a particular direction in order to see sb/sth: **look (at** sb/sth), **take*/have a look (at** sb/sth) ○ *Pay attention everyone! Look at this!* ○ *Look over there and tell me what you can see.* ○ *Don't look!* ○ *Why are you looking at me like that?* ○ *Look both ways carefully before you cross the road.* ○ *Take a look at this!* ○ *That's unusual – can I have a look?*

- to look outside when you are in a room, etc: **look out (of** sth) ○ *to look out of a window*
- to turn your head in order to look at sb/sth: **look round** ○ *She heard footsteps behind her but did not look round.*
- to look behind you: **look back** ○ *We looked back several times, but couldn't see anyone following us.*
- to lower your eyes to look at sth: **look down** ○ *Keep climbing and don't look down!*
- to raise your eyes to look at sth: **look up** ○ *He looked up as I came into the room.*

- to look in a particular direction: **look towards** sb/sth ○ *She was looking towards me across the crowded room.*
- to stop looking at sb/sth: **look away (from** sb/sth) ○ *You might miss something if you look away, even for a moment.*
- to look inside sth: **look into** sth ○ *He looked into the box and saw something move.*
- to look at a mirror, a person's eyes, etc: **look into** sth ○ *If you look into the lake, you'll see your own face.* ○ *She looked into his eyes and knew that he was lying.*
- to look at all the different parts, rooms, etc of a building: **look round** sth ○ *Would you like to look round the house by yourselves?*

2 looking quickly, carefully, secretly, etc

■ looking for a long time
- to look at a thing or person continuously for a long time: **stare (at** sb/sth) ○ *It's rude to stare.* ○ *She stared at him in surprise.*
- to stare angrily: **glare (at** sb/sth) ○ *She glared at me and I realized my mistake.*

look *contd.*

- to look steadily at sb/sth for a long time: **gaze** (**at** sb/sth) ◦ *She sat and gazed into the distance for a while.*

■ looking quickly
- to take a quick look: **glance** (**at** sb/sth); *noun*: **glance** ◦ *She glanced in the mirror as she walked past.* ◦ *I only had time for a quick glance at your essay.*
- to look at sth quickly to get a general idea of what it is like: **look** sth **over** ◦ *Have you looked over my report yet?* ◦ *The boss wants to look the accounts over next week.*

■ looking carefully
- to look carefully at sb/sth: **look hard** (**at** sb/sth) ◦ *She looked at him hard and wondered if she could trust him.*
- to look at every detail of sth: **scrutinize** sth; *noun*: **scrutiny** ◦ *The guard scrutinized our passports.*
- to look at sth, usually a text, a picture or sb's face, very carefully: **study** sth ◦ *Study the instructions carefully before you begin to work.*
- to look carefully at sb/sth in order to find sth out: **examine** sb/sth, **inspect** sth ◦ *The police are examining security videos to try to identify the criminal.* ◦ *You should inspect the engine before you buy a car.*
- to look closely at sb/sth because you cannot see them/it very well: **peer** (**at** sb/sth) ◦ *He peered at the photograph until he found his father's face.*

■ looking secretly
- to look at sth quickly and secretly: **peep** (**at** sth), **have/take*** a **peep** (at sth), (*informal*) **sneak a look** (**at** sth) ◦ *She couldn't resist peeping inside the box.* ◦ *I sneaked a look at the letter as it lay open on the breakfast table.*
- to look around secretly and without permission in order to find out information: **snoop around** ◦ *The police caught him snooping around the back door of the bank.*

■ looking in order to check that sth is all right
- to look at sth in order to check that what you think or have been told about it is true: **see*** (sth) **for** yourself, **check** (**up**) (**on** sth) ◦ *If you don't believe me, then come and see for yourself.* ◦ *I looked into the bedroom to check on what the children were doing.*

3 looking at sth happening
- to look at a person doing sth or at sth happening: **watch** sb/sth ◦ *Watch me!* ◦ *She watched how to do it.* ◦ *I watched him cross the street.*
- to look at programmes on television: **watch television**
- to look at or watch a film, play, etc: **see*** sth ◦ *Have you seen 'Gone with the Wind'?* ◦ *Did you see the game between Arsenal and Juventus?*
- to watch sb/sth carefully: **observe** sb/sth; the act of observing: **observation** (*noun* U) ◦ *to observe an animal in its natural surroundings* ◦ *The police have had him under observation for some time.*
- a person who watches sth: **observer** ◦ *an observer of animal behaviour*
- the people who watch a play, a concert, a speech or the television, etc: **audience** ◦ *The audience clapped and cheered.*
- a person who watches a sport: **spectator** ◦ *The spectators were asked to stand well back from the road.*
- a person who watches sth happening near them without taking part in it: **onlooker**; to do this: **look on** ◦ *The crowd of onlookers were horrified by what had happened.* ◦ *People stood around looking on as the prisoners were put in the van.*
- a person who watches out for danger: **lookout**; to do this: **look out**, **keep* a lookout** (**for** sb/sth) ◦ *He had to look out for anyone coming along the street, while the others emptied the shop window.*

▷ more on audiences ⇨ AUDIENCE

look after

- looking after a child ⇨ CHILD
- protecting sb / sth ⇨ PROTECT

look for

see also FIND

- to try to find sb/sth that is lost, or sth which you need to know or have: **look for** sb/sth, **search for** sb/sth; an act of searching for sth: **search** ◦ *I'm looking for some information on CD players.* ◦ *The police are searching for two prisoners who escaped last night.* ◦ *The search is continuing for the missing boy.*
- to look for sth very thoroughly and in a lot of places: **hunt for** sth ◦ *I've been hunting for this book all day.*
- to look for sth in the dark by feeling with your hands: **grope** (**around**) (**for** sth) ◦ *'I can't see a thing!' she said, groping around for some matches.*
- to try to get sth that you want or need: (*formal*) **seek*** sth ◦ *You should seek professional advice on this matter.*
- to examine sb/sth carefully because you are looking for sb/sth: **search** sb/sth (**for** sb/sth) ◦ *Were you searched when you crossed the border?* ◦ *They searched the house for drugs, but found nothing.*
- to look at a number of things in order to find what you are looking for: **look/search through** sth (**for** sth), **go* through** sth ◦ *I must look through all these old clothes and decide which ones I want to keep.* ◦ *I'm sure somebody's been through my things while I was away – everything's been moved.*
- to pay attention in order to find or see sb/sth: **look out for** sb/sth, **keep* an eye open/out for** sb/sth ◦ *I'll look out for you at the concert tonight.*

■ looking for sth which may be wrong
- to examine sth in order to make sure that there are no mistakes or that there is nothing wrong: **check** sth ◦ *Check your work for mistakes before you hand it in.*

– to try to find out what sb is doing: **check** (**up**) **on** sb/sth

■ looking for information
– to try to find out the facts about sth: **look into** sth, **inquire into** sth, **investigate** sth; *nouns*: **inquiry**, **investigation** ○ *They wouldn't give me an immediate answer but they promised they'd look into it.* ○ *to investigate a complaint* ○ *to set up an inquiry into an accident*
– a person who looks for information: **investigator**
– to look for information in a book: **look** sth **up** (**in** sth) ○ *If you don't believe me, look it up in the dictionary.*
– to look for information by studying sth carefully and in detail: **research** (**into**) sth; *noun* (U): **research**; a person who does research: **researcher**

▷ more on research ⇨ STUDY

look/seem

looking like sb/sth else ⇨ SAME
see also OPINION

– to have an idea or feeling that sth may be the case: **feel* that . . .**; *noun*: **feeling** ○ *I felt that the others might have disapproved of what I had said.* ○ *She began to have the feeling that everyone was staring at her.*
– the effect that a person or thing produces on you: **impression** ○ *I got the impression that my visit was not really welcome.* ○ *I was under the impression that she was not employed at present.* ○ *He sometimes gives the impression of being rather fed up with life.*

– to give the impression of being or doing sth: **seem** (**to** sb) (**to** be) **. . ., seem like . . ., seem as if . . .** ○ *Mike seems rather worried.* ○ *We seemed to be falling.* ○ *It seems to me that you were right all along.* ○ *It seemed like a dream.*
– to seem (from what you can see or have been told): **appear**, **look (like) . . .** (**to** sb), **look** (**to** sb) **as if/though . . .** ○ *They appear to be happy – do you think they really are?* ○ *He looks ill – I hope he isn't.* ○ *That looks like the right place.* ○ *She looks (to me) as though she needs a good night's sleep.*
– to seem (from what you can hear or have been told): **sound like . . ., sound as if . . .** ○ *That sounded like gunfire.* ○ *It's beginning to sound rather as if the holiday will have to be cancelled.*

– according to what people say (but which may not be true): **apparently** ○ *Apparently, the strike has been called off.*
– as it seems: **by the look of it**, **by the sound of it** ○ *That's the end of the sunshine for this afternoon, by the look of it.* ○ *By the sound of it, he's having a great time in Germany.*

– the way that a person or thing looks: **appearance** (*noun* U) ○ *You could change your appearance by growing a beard.*

lord/lady

see also KING/QUEEN

– a word that shows a person's profession or rank: **title** ○ *to be given a title* ○ *a hereditary title* (= one that you can pass on to your son or daughter)

– a person who belongs (by birth) to a high social class, often with a special title: **aristocrat**; the people who are aristocrats: **the aristocracy** (*with singular or plural verb*); belonging to or connected with the aristocracy: **aristocratic** ○ *The British aristocracy nowadays hold little political power.*
– (in Britain) an aristocrat with a title or a man who has been chosen by the government to sit in the House of Lords: **peer**, **lord**; a woman peer: **peeress** ○ *He was hoping to be made a peer.*
– (in Britain) a man who is a peer is called **Lord . . .**; a woman who is a peer or who is the wife of a peer is called **Lady . . .** ○ *Lord and Lady Callaghan*

– (in Britain) the rank of a peer: **peerage** ○ *She was given a peerage by the Queen.*
– (in Britain) if your peerage cannot be passed on to your son or daughter, it is a **life** peerage ○ *Mrs Thatcher was made a life peer after being prime minister for 11 years.*

– some ranks of men/women in the British peerage (most senior first): **duke/duchess**, **earl/countess**, **baron/baroness** ○ *He was born the son of a duke.* ○ *the Earl of Essex* ○ *Baroness Blenkinsop*
– a man who has been given a rank of honour and who can use 'Sir' in front of his name: **knight**; the rank that a knight has: **knighthood**

lorry

see also DRIVE, TRANSPORT

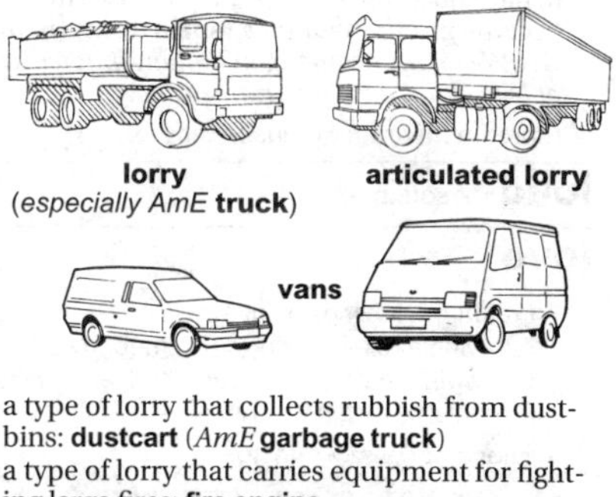

– a type of lorry that collects rubbish from dustbins: **dustcart** (*AmE* **garbage truck**)
– a type of lorry that carries equipment for fighting large fires: **fire engine**
– a type of lorry with a big round tank for carrying large amounts of liquids: **tanker** (*AmE* **tank truck**) ○ *a petrol tanker* ○ *a milk tanker*

– a vehicle with no engine, that is pulled behind a lorry: **trailer**

– a person who drivers a lorry: **lorry driver**, **truck driver** (*AmE informal* **trucker**)
– the part of a lorry where the driver sits: **cab**

– to put things onto a lorry: **load** sth (**with** sth); *opposite*: **unload** (sth); the goods that a lorry

lorry *contd.*

carries: **load** ◦ *a lorry loaded with medical supplies* ◦ *The lorry was carrying a load of cement.*

lose[1]

– not to win ⇨ **WIN/LOSE**

lose[2] unable to find sth

see also FIND

– to be unable to find sth: **lose*** sth ◦ *John has lost his coat. Has anybody seen it?*
– if you have lost sth and cannot see where it is, you **can't find** it ◦ *Help, I can't find my glasses!*
– difficult or impossible to find: **lost** ◦ *In the confusion, Peter got lost.*
– to become lost: **disappear, be missing, go*** ◦ *'Where's Alice?' 'I don't know; she's completely disappeared.'* ◦ *That's odd – there's a bottle of wine missing.* ◦ *'What have you lost?' 'My passport, my tickets, my credit cards – everything's gone!'*
– to notice that you have lost sth: **miss** sth ◦ *When did you first miss your wallet?*

– if you lose sth you may **look for** it, **search for** it, **try to find** it ◦ *'What are you looking for?' 'The keys I lost yesterday.'* ◦ *I can't find my ring – I've searched everywhere.*
– to get back sth that has been lost or stolen: **find*** sth, **recover** sth (**from** sb/sth) ◦ *I've found my glasses!* ◦ *My car was stolen last night but fortunately the police have already recovered it.*

▷ more on looking for sb/sth ⇨ **LOOK FOR**

– a kind of contract (= written agreement) in which you pay money to a company that agrees to pay you a sum of money if you lose sth, become ill, etc: **insurance** (**against** sth) (*noun* U) ◦ *We lost our camera on holiday, but we were able to claim for it on the insurance.*

▷ more on insurance ⇨ **INSURANCE**

loud ⇨ SOUND

love

1 different feelings of love
2 having a relationship with somebody
3 showing that you love somebody
4 problems in relationships
other emotions ⇨ **EMOTION**
see also LIKE[2], DISLIKE, FRIEND, MARRY

1 different feelings of love

– strong, warm feelings of liking, attraction, etc for sb: **love** (*noun* U); *verb*: **love** sb ◦ *a mother's love for her children* ◦ *I love her dearly.*

– a loving feeling towards sb: **affection** (*noun* U/C), **fondness** (*noun* U); having this feeling: **affectionate** (**towards** sb) (*adverb* **affectionately**), **fond** (**of** sb) (*adverb* **fondly**) ◦ *an affectionate child* ◦ *He is very fond of his granddaughter.* ◦ *He spoke fondly of his family and friends.*

– to love and admire sb very much: **adore** sb, **be devoted to** sb; *nouns* (U): **adoration, devotion** ◦ *He adores his mother – he'd do anything for her.*
– to love and admire sb a lot or too much: **idolize** sb, **worship** sb

■ romantic and sexual love

– very strong feelings of affection for and sexual attraction to sb: **love** (*noun* U) ◦ *your love life* (= the part of your life concerned with love) ◦ *a love story/letter/song*
– to experience this love for sb: **love** sb, **be in love** (**with** sb) ◦ *I love you with all my heart.* ◦ *They were deeply/passionately/madly in love (with each other).*
– to begin to have feelings of love for sb: **fall* in love** (**with** sb)
– love which you feel the first time you see sb: **love at first sight** ◦ *When he saw her it was love at first sight.*

– a situation of being in love or falling in love: **romance** (*noun* U); *adjective*: **romantic** ◦ *It was a beautiful night; there was romance in the air.* ◦ *a romantic candle-lit dinner* ◦ *He isn't very romantic; he never says he loves me.*

– to have the beginnings of romantic or sexual feelings for a person: **be attracted to** sb, **be interested** (**in** sb), (*informal*) **fancy** sb ◦ *I'm definitely attracted to her, but I don't think she's interested in me.* ◦ *I think Bob fancies you!*

– to have very strong feelings of romantic love for sb: (*informal*) be **mad/crazy/nuts about** sb, be **head over heels** (**in love with** sb) ◦ *I'm absolutely crazy about her; I can't stop thinking about her.*

2 having a relationship with somebody

– a romantic and/or sexual relationship between two people which is usually quite serious: **relationship** ◦ *to have a relationship with sb* ◦ *My girlfriend left me recently so I'm not in a relationship at the moment.* ◦ *They've had their problems but it's a very strong relationship.*
– having a relationship: **together** ◦ *We've been together for three years now.*
– a relationship (usually sexual) between two people who are not married and are not permanent partners: **romance**, (**love**) **affair** ◦ *It was just a short romance – it didn't last long.* ◦ *She had a passionate affair with a barman in Corfu.*
– a man/woman with whom sb is having a romantic or sexual relationship: **boyfriend/girlfriend**
– a man or woman who is having a sexual relationship with sb who is married to sb else: **lover**; a woman who is having a sexual relationship with a married man: **mistress**

– to spend time with sb at the beginning of a relationship: **go* out with** sb, **see*** sb ◦ *Tim's been going out with Kate for a few months now.* ◦ *How long have they been seeing each other?*
– a meeting between two people who like each other in a sexual and/or romantic way: **date** ◦ *I've got a date with Jake tonight.*

- to ask sb for a meeting like this: **ask** sb **out**, **ask** sb **for a date**

3 showing that you love somebody

- to touch sb with your lips to show love or affection or as a greeting: **kiss** (sb); *noun*: **kiss** ○ *She kissed him gently on the lips.* ○ *a long passionate kiss*
- (used about a couple) to keep kissing each other for a long time: (*BrE informal*) **snog** ○ *I saw them snogging in the back of the car.*
- (used about a couple) to kiss and touch in a sexual way: **pet**
- to hold sb close to you in an affectionate way: **hug** (sb), (*formal*) **embrace** (sb); *nouns*: **hug**, **embrace** ○ *hugs and kisses* ○ *Give your father a big hug.* ○ *We hugged and then said goodbye.* ○ *a warm/passionate embrace*
- to stroke sb in a gentle and loving way: **caress** (sb); *noun*: **caress** ○ *She caressed him gently on the face.* ○ *a soft caress*
- to hold sb closely in your arms as a sign of love: **cuddle** (sb); *noun*: **cuddle** ○ *He cuddled her until she stopped crying and fell asleep.* ○ *Give me a cuddle!*
- (used about two people) to hold each other's hands: **hold* hands** ○ *They walked beside the loch, holding hands.*

▷ holding sb's hand or arm ⇨ HAND / ARM

■ speaking to the person you love

- when you speak to sb you know very well and like or love (for example, a child), you can say: (**my**) **love**, (**my**) **dear**, (*especially AmE*) **honey** ○ *Come on, love – we'll go and find your mummy.* ○ *How are you, my dear?* ○ *You look gorgeous, honey.*
- When you speak to a person that you love very much, you can say: (**my**) **darling**, (**my**) **dearest**, (**my**) **sweetheart**

■ making love

- to take part in a sexual act with another person: **have sex** (**with** sb), **go* to bed with** sb, **sleep* with** sb; a more polite (and loving) way of saying this: **make* love** (**to** sb) ○ *Do you think they've slept together?* ○ *After making love, they fell asleep.*

▷ sexual behaviour and making love ⇨ SEX[2]

4 problems in relationships

- to cause sb to feel emotional pain in a relationship: **hurt*** sb, **break*** sb's **heart** ○ *I've been badly hurt in several relationships.* ○ *She broke his heart by going off with another man.*
- the feeling you get when you think sb loves another person more than you: **jealousy** (*noun* U); *adjective*: **jealous** ○ *a jealous lover* ○ *He gets jealous whenever she talks to another man.*

▷ problems in a marriage ⇨ MARRY

- to gradually stop loving or liking sb over time: **grow* apart** (**from** sb) ○ *It had to end – our lives were so different and we just grew apart.*

- to decide to be lovers again after breaking up: **make*** (**it**) **up with** sb, **get* back together** (**with** sb) ○ *to kiss and make up* ○ *They finally got back together again after three years apart.*

▷ the end of a relationship ⇨ RELATIONSHIP

■ **MORE ...**

- the day (February 14) for lovers: **Valentine's day**; the card that some people send on this day: **valentine** (**card**)

---

low ⇨ HEIGHT

---

luck

see also HAPPEN

- the way in which things happen that you did not expect: **chance** (*noun* U) ○ *It was just chance that we met.* ○ *I came across the letter by chance while I was looking for something else.*
- the way in which good or bad things happen by chance: **luck** (*noun* U), (*more formal*) **fortune** (*noun* U) ○ *I've had a lot of good/bad luck recently.* ○ *Things had been going very badly, but a few months ago his luck changed.* ○ *There's no skill in it – it's just a matter of luck.* ○ *When we won the first prize, we just couldn't believe our luck.* ○ *a change of fortune*

- the power that some people believe controls everything that happens to you: **fate** (*noun* U) ○ *I can't make a decision about this – I'll just leave it to fate.*
- a belief that cannot be explained by reason or science: **superstition** (*noun* C/U); a person who believes in superstitions is **superstitious** ○ *He's very superstitious – he never walks under ladders because he believes it's bad luck.*
- when two or more things happen at the same time by chance, it is (a) **coincidence** (*noun* C/U) ○ *What a coincidence that you both caught the same train!*

■ having good luck

- success or good things that happen by chance: (**good**) **luck** (*noun* U), (*more formal*) **good fortune** ○ *I hope you have some luck this time – you deserve it.* ○ *beginner's luck* (= luck that you have when you do sth for the first time) ○ *I had the good fortune to be standing right next to the person who I most wanted to meet.*
- to wish sb success: **wish** sb (**good**) **luck**; if you want to wish sb good luck, you can say **Good luck!** ○ *I've got my driving test this afternoon so wish me good luck!* ○ *Good luck with your exams!*

- a person who has luck is **lucky**, (*more formal*) **fortunate** ○ *They were lucky to survive.* ○ *You've been very fortunate.*
- to be lucky on a particular occasion: **be in luck** ○ *You're in luck; this is the last one in the shop.*
- a thing that brings success or good luck is **lucky** ○ *What's your lucky number?*
- a situation or event that has a good result is **lucky** (*adverb* **luckily**), **fortunate** (*adverb* **fortunately**) ○ *They had a lucky escape.* ○ *Fortunately, they managed to get out of the boat before it sank.*

luck *contd.*

– something good that happens unexpectedly: **stroke of luck** ◦ *By a stroke of luck, the bus arrived just as it started to rain.*
– a lucky thing that happens by accident, not because of skill: **fluke** ◦ *It wasn't a fluke – I could do it again.*

■ having bad luck
– failure or bad things that happen by chance: **bad luck** (*noun* U), (*more formal*) **misfortune** (*noun* U) ◦ *He's had a lot of bad luck recently.*
– something bad that happens unexpectedly: **misfortune, bit of bad luck** ◦ *to suffer a misfortune* ◦ *She's had a bit of bad luck – her car's been stolen.*
– not lucky: **unlucky, unfortunate** (*adverb* **unfortunately**) ◦ *an unlucky person* ◦ *an unfortunate situation* ◦ *Unfortunately, the train had already left.*
– to be unlucky on a particular occasion: **be out of luck** ◦ *I'm afraid you're out of luck; we sold the last one yesterday.*
– to be unfortunate for sb: **be bad/hard luck (on** sb) ◦ *It was very hard luck on her that she failed her driving test for a third time.*
– to show sympathy when sb has had bad luck, you can say **Bad luck** ◦ *Bad luck, but never mind – you can always try again.*

■ **MORE . . .**
– to wish for success or good luck: (*informal*) **keep*** your **fingers crossed** ◦ *'I've got a job interview this afternoon.' 'I'll keep my fingers crossed for you.'*
– something that you say while touching sth made of wood in the superstitious hope of avoiding bad luck: **touch wood** ◦ *I've never had anything stolen from me in my life – touch wood.*
– something which seems unlucky but turns out to be a good thing: **a blessing in disguise** ◦ *Losing my job turned out to be a blessing in disguise – I've now been offered a much better one.*

luggage ⇨ BAG

lunch ⇨ MEAL

machine

1 different kinds of machine
2 parts of a machine
3 power for a machine
4 using a machine
5 working or not working well
6 knowing about machines

machines used in building ⇨ BUILD
machines used on farms ⇨ FARM

see also TOOL

1 different kinds of machine

– a piece of equipment with several moving parts, which performs a particular activity: **machine** ◦ *a washing machine* ◦ *Can you work this machine?*
– machines in general: **machinery** (*noun* U) ◦ *farm machinery*
– worked by, connected with, or produced by machines: **mechanical** (*adverb* **mechanically**) ◦ *a mechanical device*
– operated by hand and not by machine: **manual** (*adverb* **manually**) ◦ *This car has a manual gearbox.* ◦ *If you press this button here, you can then operate the machine manually.*
– a machine that can work by itself without direct human control is **automatic** (*adverb* **automatically**) ◦ *an automatic gearbox* ◦ *The doors open automatically.*
– a machine that provides the power needed for sth to work or move: **motor, engine** ◦ *an electric motor* ◦ *a petrol/diesel/steam/jet engine*

Note: normally we use **engine** for vehicles and **motor** for small machines that we use in the house, office, workshop, etc.

2 parts of a machine

– one of the pieces that make up a machine: **part** ◦ *a simple machine with only a few moving parts*
– the moving parts of a machine: **machinery** (*noun* U)
– the parts of a machine that are used for operating it: **controls** (*noun plural*) ◦ *the controls of an aeroplane*
– something that is used for measuring speed, fuel levels, etc in a machine: **instrument** ◦ *the instrument panel of a plane*
– a handle that you pull or push in order to make a machine, etc work: **lever** ◦ *To increase the speed, pull this lever.*
– a small device that you press up or down in order to start or stop a machine: **switch**
– a type of small switch on a machine that you press in order to operate sth: **button**
– a kind of switch on a piece of equipment that you turn with your hand in order to change the level of sth: **dial**

■ parts of engines (mainly petrol engines)
– a device you use to start an engine: **starter**
– the electrical system that starts the engine of a car: **ignition**
– a device that controls the power of an engine by increasing or decreasing the amount of fuel it can use: **throttle**
– a device which makes the fuel richer in an engine when it is cold: **choke**
– a device that mixes petrol and air in an engine: **carburettor** (*AmE* **carburetor**)
– a thing that produces sparks (= small amounts of light and heat from electricity) in an engine: **spark plug** (*BrE also* **sparking plug**)
– a piece of metal that fits tightly inside a tube and, by moving up and down in the tube, causes other parts of an engine to move: **piston**; the tube that a piston moves in: **cylinder** ◦ *a six-cylinder engine*
– a mechanical device that controls the flow of air, water or gas in a pipe or tube: **valve**
– a system that uses air, water, etc to stop an engine from becoming too hot: **cooling system**

– a device that is used for keeping an engine cool: **radiator**

3 power for a machine

– what is needed to make machines work: **power** (*noun* U), **energy** (*noun* U) ◦ *electrical power* ◦ *nuclear energy*
– an engine or machine that uses a certain kind of fuel **runs* on** it, (used about large machines) is **powered** by it ◦ *My car runs on unleaded petrol.* ◦ *a nuclear-powered submarine*
– (used about an engine or machine) having great power: **powerful, high-powered** ◦ *a high-powered sports car*
– a measure of the power of an engine: **horse-power** (*abbreviation* **hp**) (*plural* **horsepower**) ◦ *a 20 horsepower engine*
– the size of petrol engines is measured in **litres** or **cubic centimetres** (*abbreviation* **cc**) ◦ *a 2.0 litre engine*

▷ more on the power used by machines ⇨ ELECTRICITY, FUEL

4 using a machine

– to make a machine work: **work** sth, **operate** sth ◦ *How do you work this thing?* ◦ *You can operate the television with the remote control.*

– (used about a machine) to be in use: **run***; to make a machine run: **run*** sth ◦ *The engine had been running for several minutes when it suddenly stopped.* ◦ *He ran the engine for a few minutes to warm it up.*

– (used about a machine) to begin to work: **start** (**up**); to make an engine begin to work: **start** sth (**up**) ◦ *She pressed the button and the motor started up immediately.* ◦ *You start it by pressing this button.*
– (used about a machine) to stop working: **turn** (itself) **off**, **switch** (itself) **off**; to make a machine stop working: **turn** sth **off**, **switch** sth **off** ◦ *It switches off automatically if it gets too hot.* ◦ *As soon as they saw that something was wrong, they turned off the machine.* ◦ *How do you switch this thing off?*

5 working or not working well

– when a machine does what you want it to do, it **works** ◦ *'Has the lawnmower been fixed?' 'Yes, it's working well now.'*
– if a machine is working properly, it is **in order, in** (**good**) **working order** ◦ *It is an old fridge, but it is in perfect working order.*

– to stop working properly: **break* down**; a situation when a machine has stopped working properly: **failure** ◦ *We lost three days' production because one small piece of machinery broke down.* ◦ *an engine failure*
– to start not working properly; to develop a problem: **go* wrong** ◦ *If it goes wrong within three months, we'll give you a complete refund.*
– a machine that does not work properly is **faulty, broken, out of order** ◦ *The remote control seems to be faulty – it's not changing channels properly.* ◦ *The coffee machine is out of order.*
– (used mainly about small machines and machines in the house) to cause a machine not to work properly: **break*** sth ◦ *I think I've broken your calculator/dishwasher/bicycle.*

■ making a machine work well

– to adjust an engine or other machine so that it runs smoothly and efficiently: **tune** sth
– to put oil on or into sth to make it work smoothly: **oil** sth, **lubricate** sth

▷ more on oil ⇨ OIL
▷ repairing a machine ⇨ REPAIR

6 knowing about machines

– a person whose work involves practical skills, especially in industry or science: **technician** ◦ *a laboratory technician*
– a person whose job is to design, build or repair engines and other large machines: **engineer**
– the work which is done by an engineer: **engineering** (*noun* U) ◦ *electrical engineering* ◦ *mechanical engineering*
– a person whose job is to work a particular machine or piece of equipment: **operator** ◦ *a computer operator*
– a person whose job is to repair and work with machines and tools: **mechanic** ◦ *a car mechanic*

– the scientific knowledge that is needed to invent machines and to make them work: **technology** (*noun* U); *adjective*: **technological**; a person who is an expert in technology: **technologist** ◦ *computer technology*
– involving detailed knowledge of the machines, materials, systems, etc that are used in industry or science: **technical** (*adverb* **technically**)

■ **MORE ...**

– to put a machine or piece of equipment in place, so that it is ready to work: **install** sth ◦ *We are waiting to have our new cooker installed.* ◦ *How much will it cost to install the equipment?*

– the use of machines, instead of people, to do work: **automation** (*noun* U); a process that is done or is controlled by machines, without needing people, is **automated** ◦ *Automation in the printing industry has led to the loss of a lot of jobs.* ◦ *The whole manufacturing process is now completely automated.*
– a machine that can move and that can be made to do some of the work that a person does: **robot**
– to alter a process, etc so that machines do the work instead of people: **mechanize** sth ◦ *to mechanize agricultural production*

mad ⇨ MIND

magazine ⇨ NEWSPAPER / MAGAZINE

magic

see also ENTERTAINMENT

– the power that seems to make extraordinary or impossible things happen: **magic** (*noun* U); *adjectives*: **magic, magical** ◦ *a story full of magic and mystery* ◦ *The book disappeared as if by magic.* ◦ *black magic* (= a type of magic that is

magic *contd.*

used to do bad things) ◦ *a magic spell* ◦ *magical powers*
- a state or condition caused by magic; the words used to cause this: **spell** ◦ *The princess was put under a spell and couldn't speak.* ◦ *a book of spells* ◦ *to cast a spell on sb*
- the use of magic to do bad things: **witchcraft** (*noun* U)

- a man with magical powers: **magician, wizard** ◦ *Merlin was a famous magician.* ◦ *the wicked wizard*
- a woman with magical powers: **witch**
- a small creature in stories with magical powers: **fairy** ◦ *a fairy story*

- if you think that magic, ghosts etc are real you are **superstitious**; a particular belief of this sort: **superstition**; the tendency to be superstitious: **superstition** (*noun* U) ◦ *She'll never walk under a ladder – she's very superstitious.* ◦ *The people here have a lot of very unusual superstitions.*

magnet ⇨ METAL

mail ⇨ POST

main ⇨ IMPORTANT

major ⇨ IMPORTANT

make

1 making things
2 parts and materials
3 the process of making sth

making clothes ⇨ CLOTHES, SEW
making works of art ⇨ ART, PAINT[1], SCULPTURE

see also BUILD, TOOL

1 making things

- to put things together, or change sth, so that sth new exists: **make*** sth (**from** sth), **make*** sth (**out**) **of** sth ◦ *to make a cake/pullover/car* ◦ *They have succeeded in making fuel from sugar cane.* ◦ *I have no idea what it is made of.*
- to cause sth new to exist or happen: **create** sth; *noun* (U): **creation** ◦ *the creation of the world*
- something which has been created: **creation**

- to make sth (for example in a factory) or grow sth (for example on a farm): **produce** sth; *noun* (U): **production** ◦ *The country produces about 100 000 tons of wheat a year.* ◦ *production difficulties*
- to make sth in large quantities using machines, usually in a factory: **manufacture** sth
- a thing that is produced in a factory: **product** ◦ *a wide range of products*
- food that is produced on a farm: **produce**
- the amount of sth that is produced: **production** ◦ *Production is increasing to 5000 units a week.* ◦ *a decline in sugar production*

▷ more on factories and farms ⇨ FACTORY, FARM

2 parts and materials

- any kind of substance that can be used for making sth: **material** (*noun* C/U) ◦ *a revolutionary new material for making contact lenses* ◦ *a store of building material*
- the basic natural materials that are used for making things in factories, etc: **raw materials**
- one of the parts that together form sth, especially a machine: **part**, (*formal*) **component** ◦ *the various parts of a computer* ◦ *car components*

▷ more on materials ⇨ MATERIAL

3 the process of making sth

- to think of sth, or make sth, for the first time: **invent** sth; the act of inventing sth: **invention** (*noun* U) ◦ *the invention of the personal computer*
- something which has been invented: **invention**; a person who invents things: **inventor**
- to plan, draw and develop sth for a particular purpose: **design** sth; a person who designs things: **designer** ◦ *She helped to design the Severn Bridge.* ◦ *a fashion designer*
- the shape or arrangement in which it is planned to make sth: **design** ◦ *We are working on a new design for a cooker.*

▷ more on invention and design ⇨ INVENT, DESIGN

- to put a number of parts together in order to make sth: **assemble** sth, **put*** sth **together**
- to change raw materials with chemicals: **process** sth ◦ *a food processing factory*
- a series of actions that you need to do to make a particular product: **process** ◦ *Producing an electric light bulb is a complicated process.* ◦ *a production process*

- to complete the last details of sth: **finish** sth **off** ◦ *There's only a little left to do; I'll finish it off tomorrow.*
- the last small details needed to complete sth: **finishing touches** (*noun plural*) ◦ *to put the finishing touches to sth*

- a man/woman who makes things skilfully, especially with their hands: **craftsman/woman** (*plural* **craftsmen/women**); the skill of making things in this way: **craftsmanship** (*noun* U)
- a place where things are made or repaired: **workshop**

■ ways of making things
- if a person, not a machine, makes sth, they make it **by hand**; made by hand: **handmade**; made by a machine: **machine-made** ◦ *handmade paper*
- made at home: **home-made** ◦ *home-made cakes*
- something which is like sth natural but is made by people is **artificial, synthetic, man-made**

- clothes, etc which are made in a standard style and which you can buy or use immediately are **ready-made**
- things which are made or built for a particular purpose or a particular person are **tailor-made**, **custom-built**

- to produce an exact copy of sth: **reproduce** sth

– a copy of sth: **reproduction** ◦ *It's a reproduction of a painting by Leonardo da Vinci.*

▷ more on making copies of things ⇨ COPY

male ⇨ SEX[1]

man

see also CHILD, WOMAN, FAMILY, SEX[1]

– an adult male person: **man** (*plural* **men**), (*informal*) **guy**, (*informal*) **fellow,** (*BrE informal*) **bloke**, (*BrE informal*) **chap** ◦ *He's a nice guy.* ◦ *This evening I met a bloke in the pub who said he knew your sister.*
– a young adult male: **young man**, (often used to express a bad opinion of sb) **youth** ◦ *Three youths were arrested by the police after the fight.*
– what you call a man when you talk to him: (*formal*) **sir**

– a person who has the physical characteristics of a man or boy is **male**; *noun*: **male** ◦ *the male sex* ◦ *Males tend to die younger than females.*
– a person who is like a man is expected to be, either physically or in his behaviour, is **masculine**, **manly**; *nouns* (U): **masculinity**, **manliness**; very masculine in an aggressive way: **macho** ◦ *masculine behaviour* ◦ *a manly physique*
– a man whose behaviour is typically like a woman's is **effeminate**

■ titles before a man's name
– used as a title before a man's name: **Mr** ◦ *Mr R C Bright* ◦ *Can I see you for a minute, Mr Smith?*
– the title for sb who is a doctor: **Dr** (*short for* Doctor) ◦ *Let me introduce you to Dr Clark.*
– the title for sb who has been given a high British honour: **Sir** ◦ *Sir John Gielgud*
– the title for sb who is a lord: **Lord** ◦ *Lord Olivier*

■ men in relationships
– the person that a woman is married to: **husband**
– the person that sb lives with, as if they were married: **partner**
– a man who has formally promised to marry a woman is her **fianc**
– a man with whom sb has a romantic and/or sexual relationship: **boyfriend**
– a man or woman who is having a sexual relationship with sb, outside marriage: **lover** ◦ *She has had numerous lovers.*

– not married: **single, unmarried**
– a man who is not married is sometimes called a **bachelor**
– a man whose wife has died: **widower**

– a man who is sexually attracted to other men: **gay, homosexual**; *adjectives*: **gay, homosexual** ◦ *a campaign to stop discrimination against homosexuals* ◦ *gay men*

▷ love, sex and marriage ⇨ LOVE, SEX[2], MARRY

management

see also BUSINESS, EMPLOYMENT, OFFICE

– to be in charge of a company or other organization: **run*** sth, **manage** sth; *noun* (U): **management**; *adjective*: **managerial** ◦ *I manage a small engineering firm.* ◦ *Sheila's learning new management skills at the local college.* ◦ *John has got good managerial experience.*

– to manage some public or business activity (or some part of it): **administer** sth; *noun* (U): **administration**; *adjective*: **administrative** ◦ *Who is administering the examination?* ◦ *the administration of justice* ◦ *Unfortunately, I have to spend more and more of my time on administration.* ◦ *heavy administrative duties*

– the group of people who control a business or other organization: **management** (*with singular or plural verb*) ◦ *The management bears no responsibility for cars left in this car park.*

■ people in management
– a person who manages sth: **manager**, **director** ◦ *our personnel manager* ◦ *our director of finance*
– a person who controls a whole business or company: **managing director**, **chief executive** (*AmE* **president**)
– a woman who manages a shop or a restaurant: **manageress**
– a person whose work is in administration: **administrator** ◦ *We have too many administrators and not enough doctors!*
– one of a group of people who are responsible for controlling the policy and major decisions of a company: (**company**) **director** ◦ *She's on the board* (= group) *of directors.*
– a person who has an important position in an organization: **executive** ◦ *one of their sales executives*

– the most important person in an organization or part of an organization: **head** ◦ *The head of the Bank of England is the Governor.* ◦ *my head of department*
– a person whose job is to give orders to other people at work: (*informal*) **boss**
– a person who is the head of sth or in charge of sth: **leader** ◦ *She's proved to be an excellent leader of this organization.*

– the second most important person in an organization or a part of an organization: **deputy**; *adjective*: **deputy** ◦ *the deputy director/governor*
– a person who helps another person: **assistant**; *adjective*: **assistant** ◦ *the assistant manager*

– to make sure that work is done properly, or that people are doing their work properly: **supervise** sb/sth, **oversee*** sb/sth; *noun* (U): **supervision** ◦ *Jim supervises the work of trainees.*
– a person who supervises sb/sth: **supervisor** ◦ *Jim works as a supervisor in a factory.*

– a person whose job it is to keep a record of all the money that a business spends and receives: **accountant**

■ committees
– a group of people who have been chosen to discuss and/or to decide certain things: **committee** (*with singular or plural verb*) ◦ *A committee has been set up to plan the new city centre.* ◦ *She has been elected chairwoman/chair* (= the person in charge) *of the finance committee.*

management *contd.*

– a small committee that is made up of members of a larger committee: **subcommittee** (*with singular or plural verb*)

▷ committee meetings ⇨ **MEETING**

■ **MORE ...**

– the relationship in a company between management and employees: **industrial relations** (*noun plural*) ◦ *Our company has very good industrial relations.*

– the room where senior managers have important meetings: **boardroom**

manner

– a way of behaving ⇨ **BEHAVIOUR**
– method of doing sth ⇨ **METHOD/MANNER**

many ⇨ HOW MUCH/MANY

map

see also TRAVEL, WORLD

– a drawing of a place, for example a town or country, showing the hills, rivers, roads, towns, etc: **map** ◦ *They opened out the map and spread it on the ground.* ◦ *a map of the world*
– a map showing the roads in a town or city: **road map, street map, street plan**
– a book of maps: **atlas** ◦ *an atlas of the British Isles*
– a map of the world in the shape of a ball, showing the continents and seas: **globe**

– the relationship between the number of centimetres/inches on the map and the number of kilometres/miles on the land: **scale** ◦ *The scale of this map is one inch to the mile.* ◦ *a scale of 1:500 000*
– a map which covers a large piece of land, only showing the most important things: **small-scale** map ◦ *This is a small-scale map – our road won't be on it.*
– a map which covers a small piece of land in great detail: **large-scale** map ◦ *We need a large-scale map to see where all the footpaths are.*

– if you need to know where a place is, you can **look for** it **on the map**, **find*** it **on the map** ◦ *I've been looking for your village on the map but I just can't find it.*
– the line on a map which you follow in order to get from one place to another: **route** ◦ *the quickest route from London to Bath*
– to follow a route on a map: **read*** a **map** ◦ *Can you read the map while I drive?*
– to make a map for sb in order to help them find a place: **draw*** sb **a map** ◦ *I'll draw you a map of how to get to my house.*

– the mountains, rivers and other natural things which we find on a map: **physical features**
– the lines which show how high and how steep a hill or mountain is: **contour lines** (*noun plural*)
– a small round object with a needle which always points north, used for finding directions: **compass** ◦ *Do you know how to find your way with just a map and compass?*

market ⇨ SELL, BUSINESS

marry

1 being married
2 getting married
3 problems in a marriage
see also FAMILY

1 being married

– the person that a woman is married to: **husband**
– the person that a man is married to: **wife** (*plural* **wives**)
– the person that sb is married to (man or woman): (*formal*) **spouse**
– two people who are married: (**married**) **couple**
– to live with a person as if you were married: **live with** sb ◦ *She's not married but she's living with somebody.*
– the person that sb lives with, as if they were married: **partner**

– if you have a husband or a wife, you are **married** (**to** sb) ◦ *She's married to a farmer.*
– the state of being husband and wife: **marriage** (*noun* C/U), (*formal*) **matrimony** (*noun* U)
– connected with being married: **marital** ◦ *They're having marital problems.* ◦ *pre-marital sex* ◦ *an extra-marital affair*
– the state of being married; the time people spend together as a married couple: **married life** (*noun* U) ◦ *Married life seems to suit you!* ◦ *I spent most of my married life in India.*

– the members of your husband's or wife's family are (*informal*) your **in-laws** ◦ *She doesn't get on very well with her in-laws.*

▷ in-laws ⇨ **FAMILY**

– a woman whose husband has died: **widow**
– a man whose wife has died: **widower**

– if you are not married, you are **unmarried**, **single**
– a man who is not married is sometimes called a **bachelor**

2 getting married

– to take sb as your husband or wife: **get* married**, **marry** (sb) ◦ *We've decided to get married next year.* ◦ *Will you marry me?* ◦ *I don't think he'll ever marry.*

■ before you get married
– to ask sb to marry you: **propose** (**to** sb); *noun*: **proposal** ◦ *He proposed to her and she accepted.* ◦ *a proposal of marriage*
– when people have agreed to get married, they are **engaged** ◦ *We're engaged to be married.* ◦ *Mike and Jill are getting engaged.*
– a man who is engaged to be married to sb is her **fianc** ; a woman who is engaged to be married to sb is his **fianc e** ◦ *I'd like you to meet my fiancée.*

- when two people officially tell people that they are getting engaged, they **announce** their **engagement**
- a ring which a man gives to a woman when they get engaged: **engagement ring**

■ when you get married
- the ceremony at which a man and a woman become husband and wife: **wedding**
- the woman who gets married at a wedding: **bride**
- the man who gets married at a wedding: **groom**, **bridegroom**
- to join two people together as husband and wife: **marry** sb ◦ *We asked the vicar to marry us in the local church.* ◦ *They were married the next day.*
- the ring worn by a married person: **wedding ring**

▷ more on weddings ⇨ WEDDING

3 problems in a marriage
- when a husband and wife decide not to live together because they have problems in their relationship, they **break* up**, **split* up**, (*formal*) **separate**; *noun*: **separation**; a husband and wife in this situation are **separated** ◦ *They aren't happy together so they've decided to separate.*
- if a husband and wife do not live together, they **live apart** ◦ *We've been living apart for a few years now.*

- to leave your husband or wife because you do not want to continue your relationship: **leave*** sb, (*informal*) **walk out** (**on** sb) ◦ *I've had enough – I'm leaving you.* ◦ *After years of ill-treatment she walked out on her husband.*
- to leave a husband or wife to be with another person: **leave*** sb **for** sb ◦ *She left her husband for another man.*

- a sexual relationship between a married person and sb who is not their wife or husband: **affair**; sexual behaviour of this sort: (*formal*) **adultery** (*noun* U), (*formal*) **infidelity** (*noun* U) ◦ *She doesn't know it but her husband's having an affair.* ◦ *to commit adultery*
- the person who has an affair is **unfaithful** (**to** sb); *opposite*: **faithful** (**to** sb) ◦ *She was never unfaithful to him.*

■ marriages which end by law
- the end of a marriage by law: **divorce** (*noun* C/U) ◦ *I want a divorce.* ◦ *the high rate of divorce in some countries*
- to go through the process of divorce: **get* a divorce**, **get* divorced**, **divorce** (sb) ◦ *We've been separated for four years so we've decided to get a divorce.* ◦ *Do you think they'll divorce?*
- a person who has divorced is **divorced**, (usually used about a woman) a **divorcee** ◦ *I think she's divorced.* ◦ *to marry a divorcee*
- after a divorce, the woman who was a man's wife is his **ex-wife**, (*informal*) **ex**; he is her **ex-husband**, (*informal*) **ex**

- to be able to keep your children after a divorce: **get* custody** (**of** sb) ◦ *Mothers get custody of their children more often than fathers.*
- the money a person must pay by law to an ex-husband or ex-wife after they are divorced: **alimony** (*noun* U), **maintenance** (*noun* U)
- to marry again: **remarry**

■ MORE . . .
- the surname that a woman has before she is married and takes her husband's name: **maiden name**

- the system of marriage in which it is possible for a person to have more than one wife: **polygamy** (*noun* U)
- the system of marriage in which each person has only one husband or wife: **monogamy** (*noun* U)

- a marriage to sb chosen by the bride's and groom's parents: **arranged marriage**
- (in some countries) the money or property given or received by a woman's family when she marries: **dowry**

match ⇨ FIRE

material

see also GLASS, GOLD/SILVER, METAL, STONE, WOOD

- a substance that can be used for making or doing sth: **material** (*noun* C/U) ◦ *building/cleaning/painting materials* ◦ *dress material* ◦ *strong/tough/coarse/delicate material* ◦ *solid material* ◦ *material in liquid form*
- material which is made from natural animal or vegetable substances is **natural**; material which is made by a chemical process is **synthetic**, **man-made**, **artificial**
- material in its natural state is **raw** ◦ *If raw materials continue to become more expensive, the cost of manufactured goods is bound to rise too.*

- any material made from cotton, wool, etc which you use for making clothes, curtains, etc: **cloth** (*noun* U), **fabric** (*noun* C/U)

▷ more on cloth and wool ⇨ CLOTH, WOOL

- material made from the skin of animals, especially cows: **leather** (*noun* U)
- a kind of leather which has a soft and smooth surface: **suede** (*noun* U)
- a tough, waterproof, elastic material made from the juice of a particular kind of tree, or made artificially: **rubber** (*noun* U) ◦ *a pair of rubber boots* ◦ *rubber gloves*

■ synthetic materials
- a light, artificial material which does not break easily and is used for making many different sorts of objects: **plastic** (*noun* U) ◦ *made of plastic* ◦ *plastic toys* ◦ *plastic bags*
- a synthetic material, often used for clothes, stockings, etc: **nylon** (*noun* U) ◦ *nylon rope*
- a tough, light kind of artificial material often used to make bags for food: **polythene** (*AmE* **polyethylene**) (*noun* U) ◦ *a polythene bag*

mathematics

see also NUMBER

- the science or study of numbers: **maths** (*AmE* **math**) (*noun* U), (*formal*) **mathematics** (*noun* U) ◦ *He's very good at maths.* ◦ *a maths exam* ◦ *There is a shortage of mathematics and science graduates.*
- connected with mathematics: **mathematical** (*adverb* **mathematically**)
- a person who is an expert in mathematics: **mathematician**

- the part of mathematics which involves counting with numbers: **arithmetic** (*noun* U)
- the part of mathematics in which letters and symbols are used to represent numbers: **algebra** (*noun* U)
- the part of mathematics which studies lines, angles, shapes, curves, etc: **geometry** (*noun* U)
- numbers that have been collected in order to provide information about sth: **statistics** (*noun plural*); the science of collecting and analysing these numbers: **statistics** (*noun* U); *adjective*: **statistical** (*adverb* **statistically**)
- a person who is an expert in statistics: **statistician**

- a question that you must find the answer to in mathematics: **problem**
- to find the answer to sth by adding numbers, taking numbers away, etc: **work** sth **out**, **calculate** sth ◦ *I'm trying to work out how much I owe you.* ◦ *I've calculated the cost of going on holiday this year.*
- something calculated by using numbers in this way: **sum**, **calculation** ◦ *a difficult sum* ◦ *a complicated calculation*
- a small electronic machine that calculates sums: **calculator**
- a statement that two quantities are equal (for example, 2a + 5b = 60): **equation**
- to find an answer to a mathematical problem: **solve** sth ◦ *It was rather a difficult problem to solve.* ◦ *to solve an equation*
- the result you get when you solve a mathematical problem: **answer**, **solution** ◦ *Did you manage to find the answer?*

- a long thin mark on the surface of sth: **line**
- the space between two lines or surfaces that meet: **angle**
- the physical outline or outer form of sth: **shape**
- a line which curves round to form the shape of a ring so that every point on it is the same distance from the centre: **circle**
- an object that has length, width and height; not a flat object: **solid**; *adjective*: **solid**

▷ more on lines, angles, circles and other shapes ⇨ LINE, ANGLE, CIRCLE, SHAPE

- a mathematical diagram in which a line or curve shows the relationship between two quantities: **graph**
- a fixed line used for marking measurements on a graph: **axis**
- the axis going from top to bottom: **vertical axis**, **y axis**
- the axis going from left to right: **horizontal axis**, **x axis**

■ **MORE ...**

- a basic understanding of numbers and mathematics: **numeracy** (*noun* U); a person who has this kind of understanding is **numerate**

maximum ⇨ HOW MUCH/MANY

may

- may possibly happen ⇨ POSSIBLE[1]
- is permitted ⇨ ALLOW

maybe ⇨ POSSIBLE[1]

meal

1 different kinds of meal
2 having a meal
see also COOK, FOOD, PARTY, RESTAURANT

1 different kinds of meal

- food which is eaten at a particular time of the day: **meal**; the time when you eat the meal: **mealtime** ◦ *The pub round the corner serves hot and cold meals.* ◦ *I don't like a heavy meal* (= with a lot of food) *in the middle of the day.* ◦ *to have regular mealtimes*

■ the main meals of the day

- the meal that you eat when you get up: **breakfast** (*noun* C/U) ◦ *a cooked breakfast* ◦ *I haven't had any breakfast.*
- the meal taken in the middle of the day: **lunch** (*noun* C/U), **dinner** (*noun* C/U) ◦ *a cold lunch* ◦ *Let's stop now – it's time for lunch.*
- the small meal taken in the afternoon: **tea** (*noun* C/U)
- the evening meal: **tea** (*noun* C/U), **supper** (*noun* C/U), **dinner** (*noun* C/U) ◦ *Do you want some dinner tonight or will you be eating out?*
- the time when you have breakfast, lunch, tea, dinner: **breakfast time** (*noun* U), **lunchtime** (*noun* U), **teatime** (*noun* U), **dinner time** (*noun* U) ◦ *Is it teatime yet?*

▷ more on breakfast ⇨ BREAKFAST

Note: people in Britain use different words for the midday and evening meals depending on where they live, etc. **Lunch** is more commonly used than **dinner** for the midday meal. If the evening meal is called **tea**, it is likely to be eaten in the early evening. **Supper** is eaten later. **Dinner** is often used to refer to more formal evening meals.

- lunch while you are working: **working lunch** ◦ *I'll be having a working lunch with some colleagues today.*
- lunch with people for business reasons: **business lunch**
- sandwiches or sth that you have brought from home for lunch: **packed lunch**

- a meal outdoors in the country: **picnic** ◦ *It's a lovely day – let's go for a picnic.*
- a small meal or one with very light food such as salad: **light meal**
- a very small meal: **snack** ◦ *I'm not having a proper lunch today – just a quick snack.*
- a formal dinner for a large number of people: **banquet**

2 having a meal

- to eat a meal: **have** a meal ◦ *Make sure you have a good meal before you leave – it's a long journey.* ◦ *Shall we have supper at seven tonight?*
- to miss a meal: **skip** a meal ◦ *I'm skipping lunch today – I'm on a diet.*
- to go out to a restaurant, etc for a meal: **eat* out**, **go* out for a meal**, (*formal*) **dine out** ◦ *We normally eat out about once a week.*

Note: Note: we use 'a' in **have a meal, have a cooked breakfast**, **have a picnic lunch**, etc; but we say **have breakfast**, **have lunch**, **have tea**, **have dinner**, without 'a'.

- a room where food is cooked and which is often used for eating meals: **kitchen** ◦ *Let's eat in the kitchen.* ◦ *to eat at the kitchen table*
- a separate room which is only used for eating meals: **dining room**; the table in a dining room: **dining table**, **dining-room table**

▷ more on kitchens ⇨ KITCHEN

■ things we use when eating a meal

- a piece of cloth that you put over the table when you are having a meal: **tablecloth**
- a small piece of material that you put under a hot dish, plate, etc: **mat** ◦ *a table mat*
- a piece of cloth or paper that you use when you are eating to protect your clothes or to wipe your hands or mouth: **napkin**, **serviette**

▷ other things we use when eating a meal ⇨ PLATE/BOWL/DISH, CUP/GLASS, KNIFE/FORK/SPOON

■ before the meal

- to cook food and/or put different foods together to make a meal: **make*** sth, **get*** sth, **cook** sth ◦ *Who'll make the lunch?* ◦ *I'll get dinner tonight.* ◦ *I can't stay. I've got to go and cook the supper.*
- to put the plates, etc on the table ready for eating: **lay* the table**

■ during the meal

- to take food from a large bowl or plate and put it onto individual plates: **serve** (sth) (**up**/**out**), (*informal*) **dish** (sth) **up** ◦ *Shall I serve out the fruit salad?*
- if you want people to serve themselves during a meal, you say: **help yourself**, **serve yourself** ◦ *Help yourselves – there's plenty more in the oven.*
- when you want people to start eating, you say: **please start**, (*informal*) **tuck in** ◦ *Come on, tuck in!*
- the amount of food for one person: **helping**, (especially in a restaurant) **portion** ◦ *Who would like a second helping?* ◦ *They're very small portions, aren't they?*
- the amount of food on a plate: **plate**, **plateful** ◦ *He was eating a large plate of chips.*

▷ eating and drinking ⇨ EAT, DRINK

■ the parts of a meal

- one part of a meal: **course** ◦ *a three-course dinner*
- a small amount of food (for example soup) that you eat before the main part of the meal: **starter**
- the main part of a meal: **main course**
- the sweet part of a meal: **sweet**, **pudding**, (*more formal or AmE*) **dessert**
- a type of food prepared in a particular way: **dish** ◦ *What a delicious dish! You must give me the recipe.* ◦ *an Indian dish*

■ after the meal

- the food that is left at the end of a meal: **leftovers** (*noun plural*) ◦ *Put the leftovers in the fridge and we'll have them for dinner tomorrow.*
- to take the plates, etc away after a meal: **clear the table**, **clear** (sth) **away** ◦ *I'll clear away the plates and make some coffee.*
- to wash the plates, etc after a meal: **wash** (sth) **up**, **do* the washing-up**, **do* the dishes** ◦ *Shall I wash up?* ◦ *I hate doing the washing-up.* ◦ *Let's do the dishes first and then we can relax.*
- to dry the plates, etc after they have been washed up: **dry** (sth) **up**, **do* the drying-up**

▷ more on washing dishes ⇨ WASH

meaning

1 having meaning
2 different kinds of meaning
see also UNDERSTAND, SAY, LANGUAGE, WORD,

1 having meaning

- the relationship between a word, phrase, sentence, etc and the thing or idea it represents: **meaning** (*noun* U/C) ◦ *What is the difference in meaning between 'sour' and 'bitter'?* ◦ *I couldn't understand the meaning of the poem.* ◦ *to have a different meaning.*
- a meaning or possible meaning of a word, phrase, sentence, etc: **sense** ◦ *The word 'funny' has two senses: strange and amusing.* ◦ *I think you're using that word in a rather unusual sense.*
- the meaning or intention of sth: **significance** ◦ *What is the significance of the rings on the Olympic flag?*
- the general meaning of sth (without all the details): **the gist** ◦ *Although I don't speak German, I got the gist of what they were saying.*
- a shape or mark, or a movement of the body which has a particular meaning: **sign** ◦ *a dollar sign* ◦ *to give sb a sign to do sth*
- a picture, object, etc which represents an idea: **symbol** ◦ *Mathematics uses a lot of symbols which I don't understand.* ◦ *The dove is a symbol of peace.*
- a movement of the body which has a particular meaning: **gesture** ◦ *She made a gesture of annoyance.*

▷ more on signs, symbols, gestures, etc ⇨ SIGN

- to have a meaning: **mean*** sth ◦ *'What does 'forecast' mean?' 'It means saying what will probably happen in the future.'*

meaning *contd.*

- to have a meaning which sb can understand: **make* sense** ◦ *This sentence doesn't make sense to me.*
- (used about a look, expression, etc) trying to express a certain feeling or idea: **meaningful** (*adverb* **meaningfully**), **significant** ◦ *I tried to say something meaningful, but I could only think of clichés.* ◦ *to glance meaningfully at somebody*

■ similar and different meanings

- a word which has the same meaning as another word, or a very similar meaning: **synonym**; *adjective*: **synonymous** (**with** sth) ◦ *'Wide' and 'broad' are synonyms.* ◦ *I'm trying to find a word which is synonymous with 'slow'.*
- a word or expression which can be used in the same way as another one is an **equivalent** (**of** sth); *adjective*: **equivalent** (**to** sth) ◦ *What's the Spanish equivalent of 'a week on Tuesday'?*
- a word which has a completely different meaning from another word: **opposite** ◦ *The opposite of 'easy' is 'difficult'.*

■ having no meaning

- something which has no (clear) meaning: **nonsense** (*noun* U), **rubbish** (*noun* U) ◦ *What nonsense!* ◦ *That's a load of rubbish!*
- a form of talk which has no meaning: **gibberish** (*noun* U)

2 different kinds of meaning

- if the meaning of sth is easy to understand, it is **clear**; *opposite*: **unclear**
- if sth has two or more possible meanings, it is **ambiguous** (*adverb* **ambiguously**) ◦ *I'm not sure if she liked it or not – her comments were rather ambiguous.*
- something which could be understood in different ways, or the quality of having two or more different meanings: **ambiguity** (*noun* C/U) ◦ *Can you see the ambiguity in the sentence 'I feel like a well-cooked steak'?*

- the most basic meaning of a word or expression: **literal** meaning ◦ *The literal meaning of 'cool' is 'fairly cold' but it is also used to mean 'unfriendly'.*
- an imaginative meaning of a word or expression: **figurative** meaning ◦ *'We died laughing' is a figurative use of the verb 'die'.*
- a way of describing sth by comparing it to sth else which has similar qualities: **metaphor**; *adjective*: **metaphorical** (*adverb* **metaphorically**) ◦ *Saying that a person 'is a ray of sunshine' is a metaphor meaning that they are bright and happy.*

- a way of expressing yourself by saying the opposite of what you really mean: **irony** (*noun* U); *adjectives*: **ironic, ironical** ◦ *'That's just great,' he said, with heavy irony.*
- irony which is used to criticize sb or to be unkind to them: **sarcasm** (*noun* U); *adjective*: **sarcastic** ◦ *a sarcastic remark*

- the words that come before or after a word, sentence, etc and that help you to understand its meaning; the situation in which a word is used: **context** (*noun* C/U) ◦ *If you don't know the meaning of a word, try to guess it from the context.* ◦ *The Prime Minister said that his words had been taken out of context and deliberately misunderstood.*

measure ⇨ SIZE, WEIGHT

meat

1 different kinds of meat
2 cooking, eating and buying meat
live animals ⇨ ANIMAL
see also FOOD, COOK, BIRD[2]

1 different kinds of meat

- the flesh of animals or birds that people eat: **meat** (*noun* U) ◦ *I don't eat meat but I like fish.*

meat from this kind of animal ...	**is called ... (*noun* U)**
a cow	**beef**
a young cow	**veal**
an adult sheep	**mutton**
a young sheep	**lamb**
a pig	**pork**
a chicken	**chicken**
birds like chickens and turkeys	**poultry**
a deer	**venison**

- beef, lamb and mutton are sometimes called **red meat** (*noun* U); chicken, turkey, pork and veal are called **white meat** (*noun* U) ◦ *People are eating less red meat than they used to.*
- meat from wild animals: **game** (*noun* U)
- the greasy substance under the skins of animals: **fat** (*noun* U); meat with a lot of fat is **fatty**; *opposite*: **lean**
- meat which is soft and easy to cut or bite is **tender**; *opposite*: **tough**

■ parts of animals used for meat

- a thick flat piece of meat (usually beef): **steak** (*noun* U/C) ◦ *We can't afford to eat steak.* ◦ *a piece of steak* ◦ *a large steak*
- a small thick piece of meat, often with a bone in it: **chop, cutlet** ◦ *pork chops* ◦ *a lamb cutlet*
- a large piece of meat that you cook in the oven: **joint** ◦ *a joint of beef*
- some types of meat from the inside parts of an animal: **kidney** (*noun* C/U), **liver** (*noun* U), **tongue** (*noun* U)

■ meat which has been prepared for cooking and eating

- meat which has been cut into very small pieces with a special machine: **mince, minced meat** (*noun* U) (*AmE* **ground beef**) ◦ *half a kilo of mince*
- thin pieces of salted or smoked meat from the back or sides of a pig, usually eaten hot: **bacon** (*noun* U)
- meat from a pig's back leg that has been smoked, etc, to keep it fresh: **ham** (*noun* U) ◦ *a ham sandwich*
- a mixture of chopped meat, spices, etc, made into a long thin shape: **sausage** (*noun* C/U) ◦ *pork sausages* ◦ *sausage and chips*

2 cooking, eating and buying meat

- you can **fry** meat (= cook it in hot fat), **grill** it (= cook it under a grill), **roast** it (= cook it in an oven, not using water), **casserole** or **stew** it (= cut it up and cook it with vegetables and water), **barbecue** it (= cook it over an open fire) ◦ *grilled steak* ◦ *roast pork* ◦ *barbecued chicken*
- a dish made by stewing meat: **casserole** *noun* C/U), **stew** (*noun* C/U) ◦ *chicken stew*

- meat which is not cooked at all is **raw**

- minced meat that has been formed into a flat round shape and then fried or grilled: **hamburger, burger**
- small pieces of meat, vegetables, etc, that are cooked and served on a stick: **kebab**
- minced meat cooked in the shape of a ball: **meatball**
- a hot sausage that is eaten in a hot bread roll: **hot dog**
- a thin sauce that is made from the juices that come out of meat while it is cooking: **gravy** (*noun* U)

- a shop where you buy meat: **butcher's (shop)**; a person who sells meat: **butcher**

■ **MORE . . .**

- (used about steak) not cooked for very long and still pink inside: **rare**; moderately cooked: **medium-rare**; cooked completely: **well-done** ◦ *'How would you like your steak, madam?' 'I'll have it medium-rare, please.'*

- to cut a large piece of cooked meat into slices: **carve** sth ◦ *Shall I carve the joint?*

- a person who does not eat meat: **vegetarian**; without meat: **vegetarian** ◦ *vegetarian food*
- a person who does not eat any food which comes from animals, including milk and eggs: **vegan**
- an animal that only eats meat: **carnivore**; *adjective*: **carnivorous**

medicine

1 medicines and what they do
2 different kinds of medicine and how they are taken
3 getting the medicine that you need

see also DOCTOR, HOSPITAL, ILLNESS, INJURY, OPERATION

1 medicines and what they do

- a substance that you use when you are ill or injured in order to get better: **medicine** (*noun* C/U) ◦ *You won't get better if you don't take your medicine.* ◦ *cough medicine*
- a chemical that is used as a medicine: **drug** ◦ *a powerful new drug* ◦ *different drugs for treating malaria* ◦ *the drug manufacturers*

- to use medicine or medical care to try to make sb who is ill or injured well again: **treat** sb/sth; *noun* (C/U): **treatment** ◦ *a new drug to treat cancer* ◦ *He was treated for shock.* ◦ *She's undergoing treatment for malaria.*
- to make sb healthy again: **cure** sb (**of** sth); *noun*: **cure** ◦ *The treatment cured him of tuberculosis.* ◦ *The new drug brought about a miraculous cure.*
- to make an illness or injury end or disappear: **cure** sth ◦ *This medicine should cure your indigestion.*
- a medicine or treatment that can cure an illness: **cure** ◦ *a cure for Aids*
- sth that makes you better when you are ill or in pain: **remedy** ◦ *Hot lemon with honey is said to be a good remedy for colds.*

- when the effects of taking a medicine disappear slowly, they **wear* off**

2 different kinds of medicine and how they are taken

- to make sb take some medicine: **give*** sb sth, (*formal*) **administer** sth (**to** sb) ◦ *The nurse gave him an injection.* ◦ *The doctor administered a pain-killing drug.*
- the amount of medicine that you take at one time: **dose** ◦ *You can reduce the daily dose.*
- the amount of medicine that you should take over a period of time: **dosage** ◦ *The dosage is two tablets three times a day.*
- a particular medicine taken regularly over a period of time: **course** (**of** sth) ◦ *The doctor prescribed a course of antibiotics.*

■ medicine that you put in your mouth

- a small round piece of medicine that you swallow: **pill, tablet**
- a very small container with medicine inside that you swallow whole: **capsule**
- medicine that you suck like a sweet (for coughs or sore throats): **lozenge**
- liquid medicine that you take for a cough: **cough mixture** (*noun* U)
- to swallow some medicine: **take*** sth ◦ *Take two tablets three times a day.*

medicine *contd.*

■ medicine that you put on your body

– a smooth thick substance that you put on your skin: **ointment** (*noun* U), **cream** (*noun* U)
– a liquid that you put on your skin: **lotion** (*noun* U)
– to put medicine on to your body: **apply** sth **to** sth; to put it on by rubbing: **rub** sth **into** sth, **rub** sth **in** ◦ *Rub the ointment gently into the affected part.*
– to clean and cover a wound: **dress** sth; the covering (which may include medicine such as an ointment): **dressing**

■ medicine that you put directly into the body

– medicine that is put into the body with a needle: **injection**, (*informal*) **jab** (*AmE* **shot**) ◦ *The doctor gave me a penicillin injection.* ◦ *Have you had your jabs?* (= injections needed before you can travel to another country)
– to give an injection: **inject** sb **with** sth ◦ *They injected him with morphine.*
– the instrument that is used for giving an injection: **syringe**; the sharp part of a syringe: **needle**

■ medicines for particular illnesses

– a medicine that is used for reducing or stopping pain: **painkiller**; a common type of medicine that reduces pain or fever: **aspirin** (*noun* C/U) ◦ *to take an aspirin*
– a medicine that prevents a cut, etc from becoming infected: **antiseptic** (*noun* C/U)
– a medicine that is used for treating an illness by killing the bacteria that cause it: **antibiotic**; a common type of antibiotic: **penicillin** (*noun* U) ◦ *They're treating the infection with antibiotics.*

– a medicine that makes you calm: **sedative, tranquillizer**
– a medicine that helps you to sleep: **sleeping pill**

– to protect sb from a disease by giving them an injection: **vaccinate** sb (**against** sth), **immunize** sb (**against** sth); an injection of this kind: **vaccination** (*noun* C/U), **immunization** (*noun* U/C) ◦ *They'll have to be vaccinated against cholera before they can travel.*
– a medicine that is used to prevent a poison from having an effect: **antidote**

■ problems in taking medicine

– if you react to a medicine by becoming more ill or developing red spots on your body, you are **allergic** (**to** it) ◦ *Are you allergic to penicillin?*
– an amount of medicine that is too large and is therefore dangerous: **overdose** ◦ *She died from an overdose of aspirin.*

3 getting the medicine that you need

– (used about doctors) to say what medicine or treatment a patient should have: **prescribe** sth; the piece of paper on which a doctor writes down the medicine you have to take: **prescription** (*noun* C/U) ◦ *What did the doctor prescribe for your cough?* ◦ *Antibiotics are only available on prescription.*

– a person who prepares and sells medicines: **chemist, pharmacist** (*AmE* **druggist**)
– a shop which sells medicines: **chemist's, pharmacy** ◦ *You can get these tablets at the chemist's.*

■ **MORE . . .**

– medicines or treatments which are different from those that most doctors are trained to give: **alternative medicine** (*noun* U)
– a plant whose leaves or seeds are used as a medicine: **herb**; *adjective*: **herbal**
– a person who sells or prescribes herbs for medical use: **herbalist**
– a way of treating illness or stopping pain by putting thin needles into parts of the body: **acupuncture** (*noun* U)

meet

see also VISIT

– to come together by chance or because you have arranged it: **meet*** (sb) ◦ *Where shall we meet for lunch?*
– an act or occasion of meeting sb: **meeting** ◦ *an unexpected meeting* ◦ *an uncomfortable meeting*

▷ more on meetings ⇨ MEETING

– the first words you say (for example 'Hello' or 'Hi') when you meet sb: **greeting** ◦ *to give sb a friendly greeting*

▷ more on greetings ⇨ GREET

– to visit or meet a person often: **see* a lot of** sb; *opposite*: **not see* much of** sb ◦ *We used to see a lot of them when we lived in Glasgow.* ◦ *We don't see much of Mark these days.*
– to visit or meet a person more/less often: **see* (a lot) less/more** of sb

■ meeting sb for the first time

– to see and talk to sb for the first time: **meet*** (sb) ◦ *I first met my future husband at a horse race.* ◦ *Where did you two first meet?*
– to tell two or more people who have not met before what each other's names are: **introduce** sb (**to** sb); *noun*: **introduction** ◦ *Have you two been introduced?* ◦ *Pauline – I'd like to introduce you to Andrew from the graphics department.* ◦ *Shall I make the introductions?*
– to get to know sb (especially by being introduced): (*formal*) **make*** sb's **acquaintance**
– the greeting which you use when you are formally introduced to sb: **How do you do?** (usually the reply is the same: **How do you do?**)

■ meeting sb by arrangement

– to plan to meet sb at a particular time and place: **meet*** (sb), **see*** sb, **join** sb (**for** sth) ◦ *We arranged to meet outside the cinema.* ◦ *I promised to meet the children at the station at half past eight.* ◦ *I'll see you later in the cafeteria.* ◦ *Would you like to join us for dinner this evening?*
– to meet socially or in order to discuss or do sth: **get* together** (**with** sb); a social meeting of family or friends: **get-together** ◦ *Let's get together one evening and plan the holidays.* ◦ *to have a family get-together*

– to meet sb after first separating and doing different things: **meet* up** (**with** sb) ◦ *If you go to the* *bank, then I'll park the car and we can meet up in the shopping centre in half an hour.*

– a place where people meet: **meeting place**, (*formal*) **rendezvous** ○ *I went to our usual meeting place, but she wasn't there.* ○ *Our rendezvous will be the hotel foyer.*
– a formal arrangement to meet sb at a particular time: **appointment** (**with** sb) ○ *I've got an appointment with the dentist at half past three.* ○ *to make/cancel an appointment*

– an appointment to meet sb (especially a girlfriend or boyfriend): **date** ○ *I've got a date with Kevin tonight.*

■ meeting sb by chance

– to come together with sb by chance: **run* across/into** sb, **meet*** (sb) (**by chance**), (*informal*) **bump into** sb ○ *I ran into Paul at the bus stop.* ○ *We met again quite by chance at the England–France rugby international.* ○ *I bumped into an old friend today.*
– to meet sb unexpectedly, coming close to them and looking at them: **come* face to face** (**with** sb) ○ *I ran indoors and came face to face with a burglar.*
– to meet sb unexpectedly: **come* across** sb, (*formal*) **encounter** sb ○ *Coming out of the Underground station, I encountered a tramp.*
– an unexpected (and often unpleasant) meeting: **encounter** ○ *I had an awkward encounter with my boss today.*

---

meeting

1 different kinds of meeting
2 organizing and controlling a meeting
3 taking part in a meeting
see also MEET, SPEAK

1 different kinds of meeting

– an occasion where people come together at a particular time and place to talk about something: **meeting**; *verb*: **meet*** ○ *What time is the staff meeting today?* ○ *We're meeting at ten o'clock in Room 8.*
– a large formal meeting where people discuss political or professional subjects: **conference** ○ *an international conference on the environment*

– a small group of people who have regular meetings to discuss the problems of the organization, club, etc which they belong to: **committee**; a meeting of this kind of group: **committee meeting**
– a meeting to ask sb questions: **interview** ○ *a job interview*

■ a meeting with a doctor, lawyer, etc

– a meeting, usually between two people, where one person gives professional help to the other: **consultation** ○ *The specialist gives consultations between 9am and 12am.*
– a particular time for a meeting with a doctor, lawyer, etc: **appointment** ○ *I've got an appointment with Mr Green at eleven o'clock this morning.* ○ *I must make an appointment to see the doctor today.*

– if you do not go to the meeting that you have arranged, you **break*** the **appointment**
– if you go to the meeting that you have arranged, you **keep*** the **appointment**

2 organizing and controlling a meeting

– if people come together for a meeting, they **have** a meeting, **hold*** a meeting ○ *Are we having a meeting on Monday?* ○ *The conference will be held in June.*
– to plan and prepare for a meeting: **arrange** sth, **organize** sth ○ *It's my job to arrange the meetings.* ○ *a well-organized conference*
– to formally ask people to come to a meeting: **call** a meeting ○ *We have a lot of problems to discuss. I shall have to call a meeting.*
– to tell people not to come to a meeting that you have arranged: **cancel** sth
– to ask people to change the date of a meeting you have arranged, and to come later: **postpone** sth

– the person who is in charge of a committee or a meeting: **chairman, chairwoman, chairperson, chair**
– to be in charge of a meeting: **chair** sth, **be in the chair, take* the chair** ○ *I'm chairing next week's committee meeting.* ○ *Mrs Black was in the chair at the last meeting.*

Note: you use **chairperson** or **chair** if you do not want to indicate whether the person is a man or a woman.

– when a meeting begins, sb **opens** it, it **opens**
– when a meeting ends, sb **closes** it, it **closes**
– if a meeting closes, but will start again later, it **is adjourned**, it **adjourns** ○ *This meeting is adjourned. We will continue the discussion tomorrow.* ○ *The meeting adjourned at five o'clock.*

3 taking part in a meeting

– to go to a meeting: **attend** (sth); *noun* (U): **attendance** ○ *I'm afraid I can't attend the meeting next week.* ○ *It wasn't a good meeting; very few people attended.* ○ *Attendance at Friday's meeting is not compulsory.*
– the number of people present at a meeting: **attendance** (*noun* C/U) ○ *There was a good attendance at the meeting.*

– a person who goes to a meeting to speak for other people: **delegate**
– a group of people who go to a meeting to speak for others: **delegation**

– the list of subjects which people discuss at a meeting: **agenda**; if you have officially decided to talk about a subject at a meeting, it is **on the agenda**; one of the subjects on an agenda: **item** ○ *We come to the next item on the agenda.*
– the written record of what people said at a meeting: **minutes** (*noun plural*); to write down an official record of what people said at a meeting: **take* the minutes**

■ speaking at a meeting

– to speak for a specific period of time about a particular subject: **speak*, make* a speech**; the

meeting *contd.*

person who speaks at a formal meeting: **speaker** ◦ *I'm speaking at the European languages conference next week.* ◦ *He's always very nervous before making a speech.*
- to speak about a new subject at a meeting: **bring* sth up**, **raise** sth ◦ *The meeting was quite friendly until their side brought up the subject of a pay rise.*
- if sth is mentioned in a discussion, it **comes* up** ◦ *Did the subject of pay increases come up?*
- to speak formally to the people at a meeting: **address** sb/sth

■ **MORE ...**
- a term used for important meetings in certain organizations: **Assembly** ◦ *the UN General Assembly*
- a large formal meeting where politicians, professional people, or people who share the same interests come together: **congress**, **convention** ◦ *There will be a congress in Athens this year to discuss European industry.* ◦ *the Democratic National Convention*
- a large political meeting: **rally** ◦ *an election rally*
- a meeting or a series of meetings of a court or a parliament: **session**

- an official meeting which takes place every year, for an organization to discuss the activities of the last year and to look at its financial situation: **annual general meeting**, **AGM**

- an idea which people discuss and vote on at a formal meeting: **motion**
- if the idea is accepted, the motion is **carried**; if it is not accepted, the motion is **defeated**

memory ⇨ REMEMBER/FORGET

mend ⇨ REPAIR

menu ⇨ RESTAURANT

metal

1 different kinds of metal
2 making things from metal

1 different kinds of metal
- a type of solid mineral substance: **metal** (*noun* C/U) ◦ *Iron is a metal.* ◦ *precious metals* (= valuable metals used in making jewellery, etc) ◦ *a lump of metal* ◦ *to make sth in metal* ◦ *to be made of metal* ◦ *a metal chair* ◦ *a shiny metal surface*
- looking like metal or making a noise like one piece of metal hitting another: **metallic** ◦ *a metallic colour* ◦ *a metallic sound*

- a valuable yellow metal which is used for making coins, jewellery, etc: **gold** (*noun* U)
- a valuable grey-white metal which is used for making coins, jewellery, etc: **silver** (*noun* U)
- a valuable greyish-white metal, often used for making jewellery: **platinum** (*noun* U)

▷ more on gold and silver ⇨ GOLD/SILVER

- a common reddish-brown metal that is used for pipes: **copper** (*noun* U)
- a brown coloured metal that is made from copper and tin: **bronze** (*noun* U)
- a yellow metal which is a mixture of copper and zinc: **brass** (*noun* U)

- a common hard grey metal: **iron** (*noun* U)
- a very strong metal that is made from mixing iron with carbon and used for making knives, tools, machines, cars, etc: **steel** (*noun* U)
- steel that does not stain or rust: **stainless steel** (*noun* U)
- a soft, heavy grey metal used in pipes and roofs: **lead** (*noun* U)
- a soft whitish metal that is often mixed with other metals: **tin** (*noun* U)
- a light silver-coloured metal that is used for making cooking pots, etc: **aluminium** (*AmE* **aluminum**) (*noun* U)

- a heavy silver-coloured metal that is usually in liquid form: **mercury** (*noun* U)
- a radioactive metal which can be used to produce nuclear energy: **uranium** (*noun* U)

- a metal (for example, steel, brass) formed as a mixture of metals: **alloy**
- rock or earth from which metal can be obtained: **ore** (*noun* C/U) ◦ *iron ore*

- a piece of iron that can attract and pick up iron and steel: **magnet**
- having the ability to attract iron and steel: **magnetic**
- the power of magnets to attract: **magnetism** (*noun* U)

2 making things from metal
- a workshop where metals are heated and shaped: **forge**
- a person who works in a forge making and repairing things made of metal, especially horseshoes: **blacksmith**

- a place where steel is made: **steelworks** (*plural* **steelworks**)
- to heat metal until it becomes soft: **melt** sth **down**; *adjective*: **molten** ◦ *molten iron*
- old metal which can be melted down and used again: **scrap** (**metal**) (*noun* U) ◦ *They're selling the car for scrap.*
- a large enclosed fire which is used for heating water or melting metal: **furnace** ◦ *to heat sth in a furnace*
- a place where metal or glass is melted and shaped into objects: **foundry**

- to join pieces of metal by heating them and pressing them together: **weld** sth (**to**/**onto** sth) ◦ *They welded the roof onto the car.* ◦ *to weld two things together*
- a person who does the work of welding things: **welder**
- a soft mixture of metals used for joining harder metals or wires together: **solder** (*noun* U)
- to join or mend sth (usually sth small) with solder: **solder** sth (**onto** sth) ◦ *If the wire breaks you can solder it back together.*

■ some things made of metal
- a block of metal: **bar** ◦ *a gold bar*
- a thin straight piece of metal: **rod**
- a long, thin piece of metal, like string or rope, which is used for carrying electricity, making fences, etc: **wire** (*noun* C/U) ◦ *a piece of wire* ◦ *a wire fence*
- a line of metal rings that are joined together: **chain**

▷ more on wire ⇨ WIRE

▷ more on chains ⇨ LOCK/CHAIN

- rings, necklaces, etc made of precious materials, which you wear for decoration: **jewellery** (*AmE* **jewelry**) (*noun* U)

▷ more on jewellery ⇨ JEWELLERY

■ **MORE ...**
- (used about a metal) to become less bright: **tarnish**
- the reddish brown substance which forms on the surface of iron, etc, and is caused by the action of air and water: **rust** (*noun* U); *adjective*: **rusty** ◦ *Check the car for rust before you buy it.* ◦ *If you leave your bike outside in the rain, it'll get rusty.*

- (used about a metal) to become weak or to be destroyed by chemical action: **corrode**; to cause a metal to do this: **corrode** sth; a substance which can corrode sth is **corrosive** ◦ *The tank was corroded by acid leaking from a broken pipe.*

- an instrument that is used for detecting metals that are under the ground: **metal detector**

---

method/manner

see also ACTION, BEHAVIOUR

- how sth is done or can be done: **way** ◦ *That hasn't worked. We'll have to think of a better way of doing it.* ◦ *Is there any way in which I can help?*
- a way of doing a particular kind of thing: **method**, **means** (*plural* **means**) ◦ *Which method of payment will you be using?* ◦ *The government employ various methods for calculating the number of unemployed workers.* ◦ *A bicycle is my only means of transport.*
- a particular way of doing sth scientific, artistic or professional: **technique** ◦ *He uses some very interesting photographic techniques.* ◦ *a teaching technique*

- the way that you choose to do sth or the way that sth happens: **manner**, **style** ◦ *It was not so much what they did but the manner in which it was done that annoyed people.* ◦ *He's nice but he's got a very strange manner.* ◦ *a new management style*

- a number of things that are done in a certain order for a particular purpose: **process** ◦ *I'm studying the process of manufacturing light bulbs.*
- the actions that you must take in order to do sth in the correct or usual way: **procedure** ◦ *This is the normal procedure for getting a visa.* ◦ *You must follow the correct procedure.*

- a general way of dealing with people or doing things: **approach** (**to** sb/sth); *verb*: **approach** sb/sth ◦ *Other countries have adopted a slightly different approach.* ◦ *There are various ways of approaching the problem.*

- a thing that you want to achieve by using a particular method: **aim**, **objective**, **goal** ◦ *aims and methods* ◦ *My main objective is to make sure that my children get a good education.*
- an idea or arrangement for doing, making or achieving sth in the future: **plan**
- an official plan for organizing sth: **scheme** ◦ *The government has developed a new scheme to help the long-term unemployed.*

▷ more on making plans ⇨ INTEND/PLAN

- to ask sb in what way they do sth, you say **how**, or, to show surprise, **however** ◦ *How do you spell your name?* ◦ *However did you manage to find me here?*
- the way in which: **how** ◦ *I don't know how to use a computer.* ◦ *I don't know how we're going to manage.*
- in any way you like: **however** ◦ *You can wrap up the parcel however you want.*
- in a way that is not known or certain: **somehow**, (*informal*) **somehow or other** ◦ *Somehow I managed to get away without anyone noticing.*
- in the same way: **similarly** ◦ *They're identical twins and they not only look the same but they behave similarly too.*

■ **MORE ...**
- a general plan that you use in order to do or achieve sth: **strategy**; *adjective*: **strategic** ◦ *the Government's strategy to beat inflation* ◦ *strategic planning*
- a particular way of achieving some part of a plan: **tactic** (*usually plural*); *adjective*: **tactical** ◦ *We had a meeting to discuss tactics for marketing our new product.* ◦ *military tactics* ◦ *a tactical decision/error*

- the science or study of methods: **methodology** (*noun* U) ◦ *research methodology* ◦ *teaching methodology*

---

metre ⇨ SIZE

---

middle ⇨ PLACE²

---

might ⇨ POSSIBLE¹

---

mile ⇨ DISTANCE

---

milk

see also DRINK

- the white liquid taken from cows or other animals, which people drink and which is used for cooking: **milk** (*noun* U) ◦ *a glass of milk* ◦ *goat's milk* ◦ *Two pints of skimmed milk, please.*
- the thick yellow-white substance which is the fat part of milk: **cream** (*noun* U) ◦ *strawberries and cream*
- a thick layer on top of milk that has been heated and then left to cool: **skin** (*noun* C/U)

milk *contd.*

- milk which has been heated so that it is safe to drink is **pasteurized**
- milk which has all the cream removed: **skimmed milk**; milk which has half of the cream removed: **semi-skimmed milk**
- milk which has been made recently is **fresh**
- if milk tastes bad because it is no longer fresh, it is **sour**, **off** (*not before a noun*) ◦ *sour milk* ◦ *Don't use that milk – I think it's gone off.*
- containers for milk: **bottle**, **carton**, **jug** ◦ *a bottle of milk* (= with milk in it) ◦ *a milk bottle* (= the empty container) ◦ *a half-litre carton of milk*

▷ pictures at CONTAINER

■ things made with milk
- coffee with milk is **white**; without milk: **black** ◦ *Can I have a white coffee, please?*
- if something is made with a lot of milk, it is **milky** ◦ *milky tea*
- if something is made with a lot of cream, it is **creamy** ◦ *a creamy sauce*
- the yellow fat made from milk which is put on bread, used for cooking, etc: **butter** (*noun* U)
- a thick white substance or hard yellow substance made from milk: **cheese** (*noun* U/C)
- a slightly sour thick liquid food made from milk: **yoghurt** (*noun* U/C)
- food made with milk, such as butter, cheese and yoghurt: **dairy products** (*noun plural*)

▷ more on butter and cheese ⇨ BUTTER, CHEESE

- a drink made with milk, flavouring and sometimes ice cream: **milk shake** ◦ *a strawberry milk shake*
- a thick sweet yellow substance made from milk and eggs: **custard** (*noun* U) ◦ *apple pie and custard*

■ producing milk
- a farm which produces milk, butter, cheese, etc: **dairy farm**
- a place on a farm where milk is kept and butter, cheese, etc are made: **dairy**
- a person who delivers milk to your door: **milkman** (*plural* **milkmen**)

mind

1 the brain and the mind
2 mental health and mental illness
see also THINK

1 the brain and the mind

- the part of your body inside your head that controls your thoughts, feelings and movements: **brain**
- a person's thoughts and feelings: **mind** (*noun* C/U) ◦ *There's no doubt in my mind about his innocence.* ◦ *to be fit in mind and body*
- the part of your mind of which you are not aware: **the subconscious (mind)**, **the unconscious (mind)**
- the part of you that is not physical; your thoughts and feelings, not your body: **spirit** (*noun singular*); *adjective*: **spiritual** ◦ *the life of the spirit* ◦ *spiritual needs*
- connected with the mind: **mental** (*adverb* **mentally**), **psychological** (*adverb* **psychologically**) ◦ *mental abilities* ◦ *psychological problems* ◦ *She was very strong both physically and psychologically.*
- a type of mind or way of thinking: **mentality** ◦ *I can't understand his mentality.*
- the ability to remember things: **memory** (*noun* C/U) ◦ *a good memory for dates* ◦ *loss of memory*
- the ability to learn or understand: **intelligence** (*noun* U) ◦ *She shows signs of exceptional intelligence.*
- the ability to think clearly; intelligence: **mind**, **brain** ◦ *She has a brilliant mind.* ◦ *Use your brain!* ◦ *to have a good brain*
- the power of the mind to choose what actions to take: **will** (*noun* C/U) ◦ *a strong will* ◦ *to exercise free will*

▷ more on memory ⇨ REMEMBER/FORGET

▷ more on intelligence ⇨ CLEVER

- the study of the mind and the way people behave: **psychology** (*noun* U); connected with psychology: **psychological**
- a person who is trained in psychology: **psychologist**

2 mental health and mental illness

- the condition of people's minds: **mental health** (*noun* U)
- in good mental health: **sane**; a state of good mental health: **sanity** (*noun* U) ◦ *Her advice kept me sane.* ◦ *The change of scene restored my sanity.*
- a state of mind which is not normal: **mental illness** (*noun* C/U), (*informal*) **madness** (*noun* U), (*formal*) **insanity** (*noun* C/U)
- connected with mental illness: **mental** (*adverb* **mentally**) ◦ *a mental hospital* ◦ *a mental patient* ◦ *mentally disturbed*
- a person whose mind does not work in a normal way is **mentally ill**, (*especially AmE*) **crazy**

Note: a person with a mental illness used to be called a **madman/madwoman** or **lunatic**, but these words and the adjectives **mad** and **insane** are not usually used nowadays.

- a feeling of worry caused by difficulties in your life: **stress** (*noun* U) ◦ *work-related stress* ◦ *to experience a lot of stress*
- a type of mental illness in which you feel extremely unhappy: **depression** (*noun* C/U); a person in this condition is **depressed** ◦ *After his divorce, he went into a deep depression.* ◦ *She's had several bouts of depression this year.*
- if you become so depressed that you cannot work, you have a **nervous breakdown**, (*informal*) you **crack up** ◦ *You'll crack up completely unless you take a holiday.*
- a mental illness that causes strong feelings of fear and worry: **neurosis** (*plural* **neuroses**); *adjective*: **neurotic** (*adverb* **neurotically**)

- a belief that is completely wrong: **delusion** ◦ *to suffer from delusions*
- a type of mental illness that makes sb believe that other people want to hurt them: **paranoia** (*noun* U); *adjective*: **paranoid**
- a serious mental illness in which a person confuses the real world with the world of the imagination and behaves in strange ways: **schizophrenia** (*noun* U); a person who has this illness: **schizophrenic**; *adjective*: **schizophrenic**

- the study and treatment of mental illness: **psychiatry** (*noun* U); *adjective*: **psychiatric**; a person who is trained in psychiatry: **psychiatrist**
- a way of treating mental illness by asking questions about a person's past life or dreams: **psychoanalysis** (*noun* U); *adjective*: **psychoanalytic(al)**; a person who is trained in psychoanalysis: **psychoanalyst, analyst**
- a way of treating mental illness without drugs: **psychotherapy** (*noun* U); a person who is trained in psychotherapy: **psychotherapist**
- a person who is trained to talk and listen to people with personal and psychological problems: **counsellor** (*AmE* **counselor**); a series of meetings with a counsellor: **counselling** (*AmE* **counseling**) (*noun* U) ◦ *He's been having counselling to help him get over the shock.*

- a place where mentally ill people are treated: **mental hospital**

mine

- coal mines ⇨ COAL
- digging for minerals ⇨ GROUND

minimum ⇨ HOW MUCH/MANY

minor ⇨ IMPORTANT

minute ⇨ TIME

mirror

see also GLASS, SEE

- a special kind of glass that you can see yourself in: **mirror** ◦ *a bathroom/bedroom/shaving mirror* ◦ *to look at yourself in a mirror* ◦ *I glanced in the mirror as I walked out.* ◦ *She could see his expression in the mirror.*
- a mirror which shows a person from head to foot: **full-length mirror**

- a mirror inside a car, lorry, etc, that you use to see what is behind you: **rear-view mirror**
- a mirror on the side of a car, lorry, etc: **wing mirror**

- what you see in a mirror: **reflection**; to make a reflection: **reflect** sth ◦ *He studied his reflection thoughtfully.* ◦ *She caught sight of her reflection in the shop window.* ◦ *He could see himself reflected in the surface of the water.*
- when a mirror becomes covered in steam, it **steams up** ◦ *It was difficult to shave because the mirror had steamed up.*

mistake

1 making a mistake
2 saying that sb has made a mistake
3 avoiding or correcting mistakes

1 making a mistake

- something that you do or say that is wrong: **mistake*** (*noun* C/U), (*more formal*) **error** (*noun* C/U) ◦ *She told him that there was a mistake in the bill.* ◦ *I made the mistake of asking for a pay rise.* ◦ *a small/bad/costly/fatal mistake* ◦ *A computer error resulted in many people not being paid on time.* ◦ *a serious error of judgement* ◦ *The plane crashed as a result of human error.*

- to do sth which is a mistake: **make* a mistake**, (*more formal*) **make* an error** ◦ *I've made a lot of spelling mistakes in this – I think I'll have to do it again.*
- as a result of a mistake or carelessness: **by mistake**, (*more formal*) **in error** ◦ *I'm sorry. I broke it by mistake.* ◦ *It was sent to him in error – it should have been sent to me.*
- to be wrong or confused about sb or sth: **mistake*** sb/sth ◦ *He mistook her for her sister since they looked so like each other.* ◦ *I mistook what he said. I thought he said the film was on tonight.*

- if you have made a mistake, you are **wrong** (**about** sb/sth), **wrong** (**to** do sth/**in** doing sth) (*adverb* **wrongly**), (*more formal*) **mistaken** (**about** sth) (*adverb* **mistakenly**) ◦ *It's true I was wrong about the date of the battle of Hastings.* ◦ *I was wrong in thinking that I could manage on my own.* ◦ *You are very much mistaken if you think I'm going to buy you another one.* ◦ *They thought mistakenly that he was going to come too.*
- to make a mistake or a series of mistakes: **go* wrong** ◦ *We tried to be good parents but both our children have ended up in prison. Were did we go wrong?*
- if you are not wrong, you are **right, correct** ◦ *You were right about the film. I really enjoyed it.* ◦ *She felt she had done the right thing.* ◦ *That's not the correct answer.*

- if sth contains mistakes, it is **wrong, incorrect**; *opposites*: **right, correct**
- if sth is not careful and exact and it contains mistakes, it is **inaccurate** (*adverb* **inaccurately**); *opposite*: **accurate** (*adverb* **accurately**) ◦ *We lost our way because the map was inaccurate.* ◦ *He described the man so accurately that the police were able to identify him.*

- a mistake in the planning or organization of sth: **mix-up, muddle, confusion** ◦ *They told me there had been a bit of a muddle in the travel arrangements and so we got the wrong tickets.* ◦ *Sorry. There seems to be a slight confusion here – I asked for a single room, not a double.*
- a mistake caused by thinking that sb/sth is sb/sth else: **confusion** (*noun* C/U), **muddle**; to make this kind of mistake: **confuse** A **and/with** B, **muddle** A (**up**) **with** B, **muddle** A **and** B ◦ *To*

mistake *contd.*

avoid confusion, the wires have been colour-coded. ◦ *I made the awful mistake of confusing her with her daughter.* ◦ *I think you've muddled me up with a colleague who has a similar name.*

– a mistake which happens because you didn't do sth or notice sth: **oversight** ◦ *Because of an oversight, I didn't receive your cheque in time.*

2 saying that sb has made a mistake

– responsibility for a mistake: **fault** (*noun* U) ◦ *It's not my fault!*
– to say that sb is responsible for a mistake: **blame** sb (**for** sth), **put* the blame on** sb (**for** sth) ◦ *I wasn't even there, so don't blame me.*
– to say that sb has made a mistake or that they have done sth wrong: **accuse** sb (**of** sth); *noun*: **accusation** ◦ *It wasn't my mistake so I don't see why they accused me of harming the company.* ◦ *The main accusation was that we had not checked the figures carefully enough.*

– to agree that you made a mistake: **take*/accept the blame** (**for** sth) ◦ *It wasn't my mistake, so I'm not going to take the blame.*
– to agree, often without wanting to, that you have done sth wrong: **admit** (**to**) sth, **admit** doing sth/(**that**) . . .; *noun*: **admission** ◦ *I was wrong. I admit it.* ◦ *I admit I broke it, but it was an accident.* ◦ *They accepted his admission that he had made a terrible mistake.*

▷ more on blaming sb for sth ⇨ BLAME

– to say that sb has done sth badly: **criticize** sb (**for** sth); an act of criticizing: **criticism** (*noun* C/U) ◦ *The government was criticized for not taking action earlier.* ◦ *Constructive criticism is always useful.* ◦ *He got a lot of criticism for the way he behaved at the meeting.* ◦ *My main criticism is that it is very difficult to read.*
– making criticisms: **critical** ◦ *He was very critical of the way they had done the work.* ◦ *to make a critical remark/comment*

▷ more on criticizing sb ⇨ CRITICISM

3 avoiding or correcting mistakes

– to look at sth to make sure that it is correct or in good order: **check** (**up**), **check** (**through**) sth ◦ *Just to be sure, I decided to check up.* ◦ *I've checked it and it seems to be working OK.*
– to do sth with no mistakes: **get*** sth **right** ◦ *I just can't get this paragraph right.*

– to make a mistake right: **put*** sth **right**, **correct** sth ◦ *Could you put this right for me, please?* ◦ *I prefer teachers to correct my English.* ◦ *He wrote to the newspaper asking them to correct some errors in an article they had published.*
– an act of making sth right: **correction** (*noun* C/U) ◦ *Do your corrections before you start on the next exercise.* ◦ *The essay was in need of correction.*

■ **MORE . . .**
– to do sth very badly and make a lot of mistakes: (*informal*) **mess** sth **up**, (*informal*) **make* a mess of** sth ◦ *I've really messed up my chances of getting that job.* ◦ *They've made a mess of the repair to my car.*

mix

– different things together ⇨ DIFFERENT, TOGETHER
– putting things together ⇨ JOIN

modern

see also NEW/OLD, PRESENT[2], FUTURE, FASHION

– the period we live in: **the present day**, **today** ◦ *People have farmed like this from the eighteenth century right up to the present day.* ◦ *We're doing a programme on the problems of young people today.*
– of the present or recent period: **modern**, **present-day**, **contemporary** ◦ *modern history/technology* ◦ *modern languages* ◦ *the modern world* ◦ *contemporary design/art/music*

Note: present-day and **contemporary** are used to talk about the present time and recent times including the last few years; **modern** is used to talk about ideas, art, literature, and lifestyles which have existed over a longer period (for example, 'modern art' means art during this century).

– with all the newest methods, technology, etc: **modern**, **up-to-date**, **up-to-the-minute**, **new** ◦ *a modern kitchen* ◦ *a modern cooker* ◦ *up-to-the-minute computer technology* ◦ *a totally new way of thinking about the work environment*
– very modern: **ultra-modern** ◦ *an ultra-modern kitchen/hotel*
– very modern and using modern technology: **high-tech** ◦ *high-tech equipment*
– not modern: **old-fashioned**, **outdated**, **out-of-date** ◦ *an old-fashioned typewriter* ◦ *outdated industrial practices*

– to make sth modern and up-to-date: **modernize** sth, **update** sth, **bring*** sth **up to date**; *noun*: **modernization**; *adjective*: **modernized** ◦ *We're going to modernize our kitchen.* ◦ *to update a computer system* ◦ *It's high time somebody brought this company up to date.* ◦ *the modernization of the steel industry* ◦ *an entirely modernized flat*

– having ideas that are a long way ahead of those of the period in which you live: **ahead of** your **time**; *opposite*: **behind the times** ◦ *He was brilliant but too much ahead of his time.* ◦ *Her ideas are a bit behind the times.*

money

1 money
2 looking after your money
3 getting and having money
4 spending money
5 making your money increase
6 giving or providing money

money paid as a punishment ⇨ PUNISH

see also BUY, SELL, BORROW/LEND, BET, TAX, ECONOMY

1 money

- the means of paying for sth or buying sth: **money** (*noun* U)
- connected with money: **financial** (*adverb* **financially**) ◦ *financial difficulties/considerations*

- money which you can carry in your hand: **cash** (*noun* U)
- a piece of money made of metal: **coin**; a piece of money made of paper: **note** (*AmE* **bill**) ◦ *a £20 note* ◦ *a dollar bill*
- coins of low value: **change** (*noun* U) ◦ *Do you have any change for the phone?*

- the money of a particular country: **currency** (*noun* C/U) ◦ *a single European currency* ◦ *foreign currency*

■ British money
- British money: one **penny** (**p**) x 100 = one **pound** (**£**)
- the system of money used in Britain: **sterling** (*noun* U) ◦ *the pound sterling*

amount		coin / note
1p	**a penny** (*informal* **one p**)	**a penny** (*informal* **a one-p piece**)
2p	**two pence** (*informal* **two p**)	**a two-pence piece** (*informal* **a two-p piece**)
£1	**a pound** (*informal* **a quid**)	**a pound**
£5	**five pounds** (*informal* **five quid**)	**a five-pound note** (*informal* **a fiver**)
£10	**ten pounds** (*informal* **ten quid**)	**a ten-pound note** (*informal* **a tenner**)
£2.55	**two pounds fifty-five pence / p** (*informal* **two fifty-five**)	

■ American money
- US money: one **cent** (**c**) x 100 = one **dollar** (**$**)

amount		coin / note
1c	**one cent**	**a penny**
5c	**five cents**	**a nickel**
10c	**ten cents**	**a dime**
25c	**twenty-five cents**	**a quarter**
$1.00	**one dollar** (*informal* **a buck**)	**a dollar bill**
$10.00	**ten dollars** (*informal* **ten bucks**)	**a ten-dollar bill**

2 looking after your money

- people often carry their money in a **purse** or (normally for banknotes and credit cards) a **wallet** (*AmE* **billfold, pocket book**)
- a strong box or small room in which money is kept so that it will not be stolen: **safe**
- an organization which keeps money safely for its customers: **bank**
- the arrangement by which a bank looks after your money: (**bank**) **account**

▷ more on banks ⇨ BANK

- a record of all the money that a person or business spends or receives: **accounts** (*noun plural*) ◦ *I spent all this morning doing my accounts.* ◦ *to check the accounts*
- a person who keeps accounts, advises on tax, etc: **accountant**
- a person who looks after the money in a club, organization, etc: **treasurer**
- a person who looks after the money in a college, university, etc: **bursar**

3 getting and having money

- money that you get regularly for work you have done: **pay** (*noun* U)
- the amount that you are paid in a week/month/year: **income** (*noun* U), (*formal*) **earnings** (*noun plural*)
- to get money by working: **earn** sth, **make* money** ◦ *She earns about £30 000 a year.* ◦ *We don't make a lot of money in this business.*
- money that is spent for a particular purpose, especially while doing your job: **expenses** (*noun plural*) ◦ *travel/medical expenses* ◦ *I'll be able to claim expenses.*

▷ more on money that you get for the work you do ⇨ PAY[2]

- the amount of money sb has to live or to do sth: **means** (*noun plural*) ◦ *a man of limited means*
- having very little money and a low standard of living: **poor**; (*noun* U): **poverty**
- having a lot of money or property; not poor: **rich, wealthy**; *noun* (U): **wealth**

▷ more on being rich and poor ⇨ RICH, POOR

- a strong desire for more money, possessions, etc than you really need: **greed** (*noun* U); *adjective*: **greedy**

4 spending money

- to use your money to buy sth: **spend*** (money) (**on** sth) ◦ *How much do you spend on food each week?* ◦ *If you go on spending like that, you'll soon have nothing left.*
- the act of spending or using money; the amount that is spent: (*formal*) **expenditure** (*noun* U/*singular*) ◦ *reduced expenditure on school text books* ◦ *an expenditure of over £100*
- money that is spent in a particular way: **spending** (*noun* U) ◦ *We plan to increase spending on roads.* ◦ *consumer spending*

- the amount of money you have to pay to buy sth: **price** (*noun* C/U)
- the amount of money you have to pay for services such as electricity: **cost** (*noun* U)
- how great the cost of sth is: **expense** (*noun* C/U) ◦ *Running a car is a great expense.* ◦ *at great/little/no expense*

money *contd.*

– more on prices ⇨ **PRICE**

– to give sb money for sth you want to buy: **pay*** (sb) (some money) (**for** sth); the act of paying for sth: **payment** (*noun* U); the amount that you pay for sth: **payment** ◦ *to pay for sth by cheque/credit card/postal order* ◦ *When do you want me to pay you for the flowers you bought?* ◦ *payment in cash*
– the money that you get back if you pay more than the amount sth costs: **change** (*noun* U)

▷ more on paying ⇨ **PAY**[1]

– an amount of money that you owe sb: **debt**

▷ more on debts ⇨ **DEBT**

■ having enough money
– if you have enough money to be able to buy or do sth, you can **afford** sth
– if you manage not to spend more money than you can afford, you **make* ends meet** ◦ *However careful I am, I just can't make ends meet.*
– if you always spend more than you can afford, you **live beyond** your **means**

■ spending a lot of money
– spending too much money: **extravagance** (*noun* U); a person who likes spending a lot of money on things they do not really need is **extravagant** ◦ *If you carry on with such extravagance, you'll be broke in no time.*
– to spend too much money: (*informal*) **throw*** your **money about/around**, (*informal*) **spend* money like water**

– to spend a lot of money on sth that you do not really need: (*informal*) **splash out** (**on** sth), **blow*** sth **on** sth ◦ *She's blown all her week's wages on a new pair of shoes.*

■ spending money with care
– to avoid spending money, so that it can be used for sth later: **save** (sth) ◦ *He's trying to save £10 a week.*
– to save for a particular purpose: **save up** (**for** sth), **put*** sth **aside/by** (**for** sth) ◦ *We're saving up for a new car.* ◦ *Her grandparents had put some money by for her wedding.*
– money that you have saved for future use: **savings** (*noun plural*)
– to use as little money as possible: **economize** (**on** sth) ◦ *Try to economize on fuel.*
– to use less money than usual: **cut* back** (**on** sth) ◦ *Money is tight – we're having to cut back.*

– to plan carefully how much money to spend on sth: **budget** (sth) **for** sth; a plan of how you will spend money: **budget** ◦ *Don't forget to budget for possible increased costs.* ◦ *'How much will you spend on new furniture?' 'We've budgeted £1500.'* ◦ *Our total budget for the new sports ground is £100000.*

5 making your money increase
– to put money in the bank or into a business so as to make a profit: **invest** (sth) (**in** sth); *noun* (U): **investment** ◦ *Huge sums of money have been invested in the Channel Tunnel project.*
– an amount of money that has been put in a business: **investment** ◦ *to make an investment in sth*

– the money that you earn from investments or that you pay for borrowing money: **interest** (**on** sth) (*noun* U) ◦ *Money in this account will earn 6% interest.* ◦ *high interest rates*

▷ more on investment ⇨ **BUSINESS**

6 giving or providing money
– money given in church: **collection** ◦ *She put a pound in the collection.*
– money given to children by their parents: **pocket money** (*noun* U)
– money given to a former husband or wife after a divorce: **alimony** (*noun* U)
– money given to support a child or former wife or husband: **maintenance** (*noun* U)
– money given to help pay for a student at college: **scholarship**, **grant**
– money given in return for helping the police, finding sth that was lost, etc: **reward**

– a person who dislikes giving or spending money is **mean**, **stingy**; the quality of being mean: **meanness** (*noun* U)
– a person who is willing to give more money, help, etc than is usual or necessary is **generous**; the quality of being generous: **generosity** (*noun* U)

▷ giving money or other things to people so as to please them or help them ⇨ **GIVE**

– to provide money for a particular purpose: **fund** sth, **finance** sth ◦ *The government is refusing to fund the new bridge.*
– a sum of money that is collected or available for a particular purpose: **fund** ◦ *I agreed to contribute to the fund for cancer relief.*
– to obtain money for a particular purpose: **raise** money (**for** sth)

■ MORE ...
– the side of a coin with the head of a person on it: **heads** (*noun plural*); the other side: **tails** (*noun plural*)
– to throw a coin in the air to see which side it lands on: **toss** (**up**) (**for** sth), **spin* a coin** ◦ *Let's toss for it: heads or tails?*

– when a child saves money, he/she might put it in a **piggy bank** or **money box**

month ⇨ YEAR

moon ⇨ STAR/PLANET/MOON

moral ⇨ RIGHT/WRONG[2]

more¹
- a larger quantity ⇨ **HOW MUCH / MANY**
- to a greater degree ⇨ **FAIRLY / VERY**

more² additional

a bigger quantity ⇨ **HOW MUCH / MANY**

- an additional number or amount: **more** ◦ *Are there any more questions?* ◦ *I give him a lot but he always wants more.* ◦ *I could spend £10, but I can't afford much more.* ◦ *Do you want some more?* ◦ *This is really exciting – tell me more.*
- an additional amount of sth: (*formal*) **further** (*adjective, adverb*) ◦ *We'll need further information.* ◦ *Can I have time to consider the matter further?*

- in addition to the one(s) that sb has already mentioned: **other, another, additional** ◦ *Any other questions?* ◦ *Would you like another biscuit?* ◦ *There will be an additional charge of £5.*
- (used after words formed with 'any-', 'no-' and 'some-' and question words) additional: **else** ◦ *Do you need anything else?* ◦ *Who else shall we ask?*

- in addition to sth: **as well (as . . .), plus . . ., in addition (to . . .)** ◦ *As well as a new dress I want to buy her some shoes, plus a few little extras like some earrings and a scarf.* ◦ *In addition to the problems we had last year, we are now expecting a huge rise in prices and unemployment.*
- to emphasize that sth is in addition to sth, you can say **on top of . . ., over and above . . .** ◦ *On top of everything else, I've now got to look after his goldfish!* ◦ *This is over and above the basic rate for the job.*

- more than is usual: **extra** ◦ *We need an extra person to make up numbers.* ◦ *It'll cost you an extra £5 if you want it delivered.*
- a thing which is added: **extra, addition** ◦ *This computer program has several optional extras, including a spell checker.* ◦ *The heating system is a later addition to the house.*

most
- the largest quantity ⇨ **HOW MUCH / MANY**
- to the greatest degree ⇨ **FAIRLY / VERY**

mother ⇨ FAMILY

motor ⇨ MACHINE

motorcycle

driving cars and other vehicles ⇨ **DRIVE**
wheels and tyres ⇨ **WHEEL**
see also BICYCLE

- a seat for a passenger behind the driver: **pillion**
- a hard hat worn by a motorcyclist to protect his/her head: **(crash) helmet**
- the part of a helmet that you can pull down to protect your face: **visor**

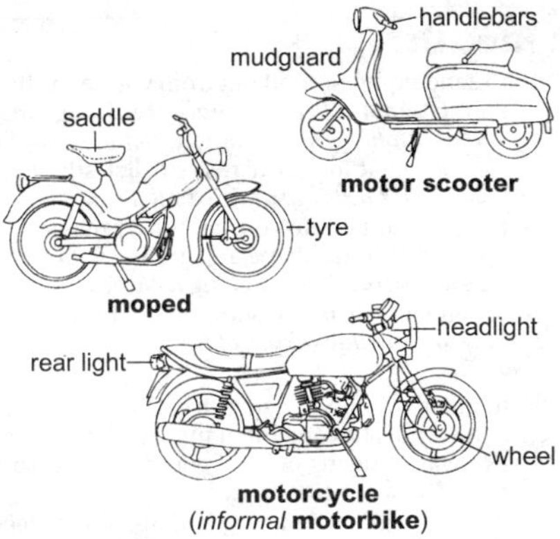

- to go on a motorcycle: **ride*** (sth); *noun*: **ride** ◦ *Have you ever ridden a 1 000 cc motorbike?* ◦ *Shall we ride over to see Peter this afternoon?* ◦ *I've just got my new motorbike; would you like me to take you for a ride?*
- a person who rides a motorcycle: **motorcyclist**

- to climb onto a motorcycle: **get* on** (sth), (*formal*) **mount** (sth); *opposite*: **get* off** (sth), (*formal*) **dismount** (sth)
- to fall off a motorcycle in an accident: **come* off** ◦ *She skidded on a corner and nearly came off.*

mountain ⇨ HILL / MOUNTAIN

mouth

see also FACE

- the part of your face that you use for eating and speaking: **mouth**
- concerning or using the mouth: **oral** (*adverb* **orally**) ◦ *oral hygiene* ◦ *medicine to be taken orally*

- one of the two soft red or brown parts above and below your mouth: **lip** ◦ *the upper/lower lip* ◦ *to kiss somebody on the lips*
- the soft part inside your mouth that you can move: **tongue**
- one of the hard white parts inside your mouth that you use for eating: **tooth** (*plural* **teeth**)
- either of the bones in your head that contain your teeth: **jaw**
- the back part of your mouth and the passage down your neck through which air and food pass: **throat**

▷ teeth ⇨ **TOOTH**

■ actions involving the mouth

▷ eating and drinking ⇨ **EAT, DRINK**

- the liquid that is produced in the mouth: **saliva** (*noun* U), (*informal*) **spit** (*noun* U); to produce saliva: (*formal*) **salivate** ◦ *to salivate at the sight of food*
- to have liquid coming out of your mouth: **dribble** ◦ *Babies can't help dribbling.*

mouth *contd.*

- to send liquid or food out from your mouth: **spit*** (sth **out**) ◦ *People usually think it is rude to spit in public.* ◦ *He spat out the wine.*
- to move your tongue across sth: **lick** sth; *noun*: **lick** ◦ *to lick a stamp* ◦ *to give sth a lick*
- to take a liquid into your mouth by making your lips into a round shape and pulling your cheeks in: **suck** sth ◦ *a baby sucking a bottle*
- to send air, etc out of your mouth: **blow*** sth ◦ *I had to blow into a kind of tube.*

- to press your lips against sb else's lips or cheek, as a way of showing them that you love them, or as a way of saying hello or goodbye: **kiss** (sb); *noun*: **kiss** ◦ *to give sb a kiss*
- to open your mouth wide and breathe in deeply, especially when you are tired or bored: **yawn**; *noun*: **yawn** ◦ *I kept yawning all through the lecture.*

■ **MORE ...**
- a piece of cloth, etc that is put over a person's mouth to stop them talking: **gag**; to put this over sb's mouth: **gag** sb ◦ *The robbers tied him up and gagged him before starting to search the house.*

move

1 moving and not moving
2 causing sth to move
3 directions of movement
4 ways of moving

ways of moving ⇨ JUMP, RUN, SWIM, TURN, WALK
coming and going ⇨ COME/GO
travel ⇨ TRAVEL, DRIVE, FLY²
the movement of water and other liquids ⇨ WATER, LIQUID

1 moving and not moving

■ moving
- to change position: **move**; *noun* (C/U): **movement** ◦ *Don't move – there's a bee on your arm.* ◦ *I think I saw something move behind the trees.* ◦ *The dancer's movements were smooth and beautifully controlled.* ◦ *During the night there was very little movement on the streets.*
- a change of place or position: **move** ◦ *The children stood quietly, watching every move the gorilla made.*
- the way that sth moves, or the fact that it is moving: **motion** (*noun* U) ◦ *The motion of the car sent the baby to sleep.*

■ not moving
- not moving: **motionless**, **still**, (used about cars, etc) **stationary** ◦ *to lie motionless* ◦ *Stand still!* ◦ *a stationary vehicle*

■ able to move
- something, especially a structure or part of a structure, that can be moved is **movable** ◦ *a movable screen*
- designed so that it can be moved or carried easily: **mobile**, **portable** ◦ *a mobile phone* ◦ *a mobile home* ◦ *a portable television*
- when sth is not firmly fixed and therefore is able to move, it is **loose** ◦ *a loose tooth* ◦ *The ropes on the lorry weren't tied properly and they came loose on the motorway.*

■ not likely to move or able to move
- a thing which is well fixed and not likely to move is **secure**, **stable** ◦ *Those new shelves don't look very secure to me.* ◦ *The ladder was not stable and the builder fell off.*
- not moving or shaking: **steady** ◦ *You need a steady hand to take good photographs.*
- to make sth steady: **steady** sth ◦ *He knocked the vase and it started to fall over, but he managed to steady it just in time.*

- not moving or not able to move: **immobile:** to make it impossible for sth to move: **immobilize** sth ◦ *For several seconds the lioness stood immobile, sniffing the air.* ◦ *The thieves immobilized the car by stealing its wheels.*
- to stop suddenly and not be able to move: **freeze*** ◦ *She heard steps coming up the stairs and froze.*

- unable to move your body or part of it because of an accident or illness: **paralysed** (*AmE* **paralyzed**); *noun* (U): **paralysis** ◦ *She broke her back in the crash and became paralysed from the waist down.*

- if sth becomes fixed in a particular position so that it cannot be moved, it **sticks***, **gets* stuck**, **jams**, **gets* jammed** ◦ *This door keeps sticking and I have to use all my strength to open it.* ◦ *The car got stuck in the mud.* ◦ *The key turned half-way and then it jammed.*
- (used mainly about clothes) to get stuck in sth: **catch*** ◦ *My coat caught in the car door.*
- unable to move because you are in a difficult or dangerous situation: **trapped** ◦ *The climbers were trapped at the top of the mountain after the fog came down.*

2 causing sth to move

- to change the position of sth: **move** sth, **shift** sth ◦ *Can you help me to move this table?* ◦ *I spent the afternoon shifting the furniture in my bedroom around.*
- to start sth moving: **put*/set*** sth **in motion** ◦ *Jill pressed the button to set the machine in motion.*

- to move sb/sth to a particular position: **put*** sb/sth somewhere, **place** sth somewhere ◦ *Could you put the boxes over there, please.*
- to hold sb/sth in your hands, in your arms or on your back while you are moving from one place to another: **carry** sb/sth
- to move or try to move sb/sth towards you: **pull** sb/sth
- to move or try to move sb/sth away from you: **push** sb/sth
- to make sth move with a quick, sudden movement: **flick** sth; *noun*: **flick** ◦ *He flicked some ash off the end of his cigarette.* ◦ *The frog caught the fly with a flick of the tongue.*

▷ more on putting, carrying, pulling and pushing
⇨ **PUT, BRING/TAKE/CARRY, PULL/PUSH**

3 directions of movement

- nearer to sb/sth: **to, towards ...** ◦ *You move first to the left, then to the right.* ◦ *Okay, now walk towards me.*
- away, showing the place where sth starts or started: **from ...** ◦ *When do the children come home from school?* ◦ *A strange noise came from the next room.*
- to a different place or in a different direction: **away** (**from ...**) ◦ *Did you ever run away from home when you were a child?* ◦ *Go away!*
- from one place to another and then back again: **back and forth, to and fro** ◦ *Every week I go back and forth between Cardiff and London.* ◦ *I spend all my time going to and fro between work and home.*

- to a position in or inside sth: **into ..., in** (...) ◦ *Everyone cheered when she walked into the room.* ◦ *Do you want a lift? Get in!*
- away from, or no longer in, a particular place: **out** (**of ...**) ◦ *She refused to come out of her bedroom.* ◦ *I'll put the cat out.*

- from one end or side of sth to another: **through** (...) ◦ *I usually go through the park on my way home.* ◦ *The train's going through a tunnel.*
- from one end of sth to or towards the other end: **along** (...) ◦ *I love walking along the river in the early morning.*
- from one side of sth to another: **across** (...), **over** (...) ◦ *We had to find a way of getting across the river.* ◦ *He climbed over the wall and ran away.*

- from the top towards the bottom of sth: **down** (...) ◦ *The boy came running down the hill.* ◦ *She stood at the bedroom window, looking down into the garden.*
- from the bottom towards the top of sth: **up** (...) ◦ *I walked up the stairs behind him.* ◦ *There's a good view from here. Why don't you climb up too?*

- in front or to the side of sb/sth: **by** (...), **past** (...) ◦ *He drove straight by without stopping!* ◦ *They walked past the post office and went into the baker's.*
- in a circle: **round/around** (...) ◦ *Can you run round the block without stopping?*

- to move further in a particular direction in order to make space for sb/sth else: **move across/along/down/over/up** ◦ *Could you move up please? We're all a bit squashed here.*

- to move forward: (*formal*) **advance**, (*formal*) **progress**; *noun* (U): **progress** ◦ *The demonstrators began to advance towards the line of police.* ◦ *The heavy traffic meant we made very little progress.*
- to move away from sth: (*formal*) **retreat**; *noun*: **retreat** ◦ *The burglar started to enter the house, but he retreated immediately when he heard a dog barking.*
- to move back or away from sb/sth: **draw* back/away** (**from ...**), **back away** (**from ...**) ◦ *The crowd drew back to let the police through.*

4 ways of moving

■ quickly or easily

- to move somewhere quickly: **speed*, fly*, rush** ◦ *We sped round the corner.* ◦ *When I saw the time, I flew downstairs and jumped in a taxi.* ◦ *After work I rushed home to pick up my sports gear.*
- to move very quickly and with a loud noise (usually used about a car, motor bike, plane, etc): **zoom** ◦ *The plane zoomed low overhead.*
- to move suddenly and quickly in a certain direction: **dart, shoot*** ◦ *She darted into the office.* ◦ *Somebody shot past me. I couldn't see who it was.* ◦ *The pain shot down her arm.*

- to move over a smooth surface: **slide***; to make sth move in this way: **slide*** sth ◦ *She came sliding across the ice.* ◦ *The barman slid the bottle along the bar.* ◦ *a sliding door*
- to move smoothly on wheels, or as if on wheels: **roll** ◦ *The car began to roll backwards down the hill.*

- to move smoothly without noise or effort: **glide** ◦ *The skaters glided across the ice on the pond.*
- able to move in a smooth and attractive way: **graceful** (*adverb* **gracefully**); *noun* (U): **grace** ◦ *a graceful dancer* ◦ *to walk gracefully*
- able to move quickly and easily: **agile**; *noun* (U): **agility** ◦ *as agile as a cat*

■ slowly or with difficulty

- to move forward very slowly: **crawl, creep*** ◦ *The traffic was crawling along the road.* ◦ *We crept along at five miles an hour.*
- to move forward, with difficulty, by pushing: **push** ◦ *Frank pushed his way through the crowd to get to the front.* ◦ *to push past sb*

- to change direction suddenly, especially in a car: **swerve** ◦ *He swerved to avoid a lorry and ended up in a field.*
- (used about a vehicle) to be out of control and move sideways across the road: **skid**; *noun*: **skid** ◦ *The car skidded on a patch of ice.*

- to move suddenly in a particular direction, especially when out of control: **lurch** ◦ *The taxi driver let out the clutch and the car lurched forward.*
- to move in an uneven way, for example when going over rough ground: **bump** ◦ *We bumped along the track to the cottage.*
- to move forward with a sudden pull, push or other movement: **jerk, jolt**; *adjective*: **jerky** (*adverb* **jerkily**) ◦ *The lorry jolted down the bumpy road.* ◦ *jerky movements*
- to make sb/sth move suddenly: **jolt** sb/sth; *noun*: **jolt** ◦ *The crash jolted all the passengers forward.* ◦ *The train stopped with a jolt.*

■ up and down

- to move upwards: **go* up, rise*** (**up**) ◦ *We watched the balloon rise up into the clouds.*

move *contd.*

– to move downwards: **go* down**, (*formal*) **descend** ◦ *The sun went down.* ◦ *Our plane descended through the clouds.*
– to move downwards through water: **sink*** ◦ *The ship hit an iceberg and sank.*

– to move up and down continuously (like a ball): **bounce**; to make sth move in this way: **bounce** sth ◦ *The ball bounced twice and then he kicked it.* ◦ *I love bouncing on the trampoline.*
– to move in a lively way, usually up and down: **dance** ◦ *Emma was dancing up and down with excitement.*

■ from side to side or backwards and forwards
– (used about aeroplanes and ships) to move up and down or from side to side: **pitch** ◦ *The ship pitched and rolled in the rough sea.*
– to move gently up and down or from side to side: **wave**; to make sth move in this way: **wave** sth ◦ *The long grass waved in the breeze.* ◦ *The children waved their flags and cheered.*
– to move backwards and forwards or from side to side: **rock**; to make sb/sth move in this way: **rock** sth ◦ *She rocked her baby to sleep in its cradle.*
– to move continuously and very quickly from side to side: **vibrate** ◦ *The sound is produced when the strings of the instrument vibrate.*
– to move from side to side or up and down with short, quick movements: **shake***; to make sb/sth move in this way: **shake*** sb/sth ◦ *The baby rabbits were shaking with fear.* ◦ *Sheila shook her mother to wake her up.* ◦ *Shake the bottle before drinking.*
– a slight shaking or trembling movement: **tremor**

– to move about with short, quick movements, especially from side to side: **wriggle**; to move a part of your body in this way: **wriggle** sth; a wriggling movement: **wriggle** ◦ *Shaun wriggled out of his sleeping bag.* ◦ *She wriggled her toes.*
– to move from side to side in an unsteady way: **wobble**; *adjective*: **wobbly** ◦ *Put something under the table leg. It's wobbling.* ◦ *wobbly jelly*

– to move backwards and forwards or from side to side, while hanging from sth: **swing** ◦ *The monkey was swinging from branch to branch.*
– to move or swing slowly from side to side: **sway**, **roll** ◦ *The dancers were swaying in time to the music.* ◦ *The ship was rolling in the storm.*

■ round and round
– to move round in a circle, especially in the air: **circle** (sb/sth) ◦ *The birds were circling overhead.* ◦ *We circled the town centre three times before we found a place to park.*
– (used about liquids, the air, etc) to move round and round continuously: **circulate** ◦ *Blood circulates round the body.* ◦ *Leave a gap between the heater and the wall to allow the air to circulate freely.*
– to move round very quickly: **whirl**; to make sth move in this way: **whirl** sth ◦ *The people whirled round and round on the merry-go-round.*
– to move round and round: **swirl**; to make sth move in this way: **swirl** sth ◦ *Her long skirt swirled around her ankles as she danced.*

– to move by turning over and over: **roll**; to make sth move in this way: **roll** sth ◦ *He dropped the ball and it rolled into the road.* ◦ *They were trying to roll the log up the path.*

■ nervously
– to move about or keep moving sth in a restless way: **fidget** (**about**) (**with** sth) ◦ *Stop fidgeting and sit still.*
– to shake because you are cold, frightened, etc: **tremble**, **shiver** ◦ *He was trembling with fear.* ◦ *Her hand was trembling as she picked up the pen to sign.* ◦ *You're shivering. Shall I shut the window?*

■ caused by wind or water
– when the wind moves, it **blows***; when it causes sth to move, it **blows*** sth ◦ *The wind was blowing gently through the trees.* ◦ *The yacht was blown far out to sea.*
– to move up and down or from side to side quickly and lightly: **flutter**; to make sth do this: **flutter** sth ◦ *A leaf fluttered to the ground.* ◦ *The bird fluttered its wings and tried to fly.*
– to be moved or carried along by wind or water: **drift** ◦ *The boat drifted out to sea.*

much

– a large quantity ⇨ HOW MUCH/MANY
– to a great degree ⇨ FAIRLY/VERY

murder ⇨ KILL

muscle

see also BODY

– a piece of flesh inside the body which is used to produce movement: **muscle** (*noun* C/U); *adjective*: **muscular** ◦ *This exercise will help to strengthen the muscles in your stomach.* ◦ *muscular pain*
– a part that joins a muscle to a bone: **tendon**

– when a muscle becomes smaller and tighter, it **contracts**, **tightens** (**up**); to cause this to happen: **contract** sth, **tighten** sth; *noun* (U): **contraction**
– when a muscle becomes very stiff and tight, because for example you are frightened or about to run fast, it **tenses**; to cause this to happen: **tense** sth ◦ *Tense your neck muscles.*
– when you cause a muscle to become less tight, you **relax** it; the muscle **relaxes**; *noun* (U): **relaxation**
– when you bend or move a muscle, you **flex** it ◦ *He took off his T-shirt and flexed his muscles.*

– to damage a muscle by using too much force: **pull** sth, **strain** sth ◦ *I tried to move the cupboard by myself and pulled a muscle in my back.*
– a sudden pain in a muscle that makes it difficult to move: **cramp** (*noun* U) ◦ *The sea was very cold and I got cramp in my foot.*
– a sudden tightening of a muscle that you cannot control: **spasm**

– a sudden, violent and uncontrollable movement of the muscles: **convulsion** (*often plural*) ◦ *to have convulsions*

– a person or a part of the body that has strong muscles is **muscular** ◦ *a muscular body*
– muscles which are solid and hard are **firm**; *opposite*: **flabby** ◦ *firm stomach muscles*
– a programme of exercises to make your muscles bigger and stronger: **body-building** (*noun* U); a person who does this: **bodybuilder**

▷ taking exercise ⇨ EXERCISE

music

1 different kinds of music
2 making music
3 musical instruments and their players
4 listening to music
5 describing musical sounds

see also SING, DANCE

1 different kinds of music

– an arrangement of sounds that are played on instruments or sung: **music** (*noun* U); *adjective*: **musical** ◦ *What sort of music do you like?* ◦ *a music lover* ◦ *a music lesson* ◦ *a musical instrument*

music that ...	is called ...
is modern and popular among young people	**pop (music)**
is a type of pop music with a very strong beat	**rock (music)**
is a type of popular music that comes from the south and west of the United States	**country and western music**
has strong rhythms and was originally played by African-Americans	**jazz**
is traditional in a particular country	**folk music**
is serious and traditional in style	**classical music**
is serious and modern in style	**modern music**
is a kind of classical music, written for small groups of instruments	**chamber music**

▷ more on pop and rock music ⇨ POP/ROCK

– a complete musical work: **piece (of music)** ◦ *I love that piece. Can you play it again?*
– one of the main parts of a long piece of classical music: **movement** ◦ *the opening/last movement*

– a piece of music which has words which you sing: **song**
– a piece of music which is played for people to dance to: **dance**
– a piece of music which is played for soldiers to march to: **march**

– a classical piece for one solo instrument and an orchestra: **concerto** (*plural* **concertos**)
– a long classical piece which is written for an orchestra: **symphony**

– a piece of music which is for one person to play or sing: **solo** (*plural* **solos**)
– a piece of music which is for two, three, four, five people to play or sing: **duet**, **trio** (*plural* **trios**), **quartet**, **quintet** ◦ *a piano trio written in 1956*

– a play in which the actors sing the words to music: **opera**; works of this kind: **opera** (*noun* U) ◦ *an opera by Puccini* ◦ *When did you last go to the opera?* ◦ *I love opera.*
– a story which is told with music and dancing but without words: **ballet**; works of this kind: **ballet** (*noun* U) ◦ *I prefer ballet to opera.*
– a play or film which has music and dancing in it: **musical**

2 making music

– a person who plays or writes music: **musician** ◦ *a professional musician*

– to use a musical instrument to make music: **play** an instrument, **play** some music ◦ *Can you play the piano?* ◦ *to play a tune*
– a person who plays music is a **player** of a particular instrument ◦ *a trumpet player*
– to understand a piece of music when it is written on paper: **read* music**
– to play a piece of music without ever seeing it written down: **play** (sth) **by ear** ◦ *I can't read music – I only play by ear.*

– to make musical sounds with your voice: **sing*** (sth); a person who sings: **singer** ◦ *to sing a song* ◦ *I sing in our local church choir.* ◦ *a pop singer*
– to sing a tune with your lips closed: **hum** (sth) ◦ *Just hum the tune if you don't know the words.* ◦ *She was humming quietly as she worked.*
– to make a musical sound by blowing air through your lips: **whistle** (sth) ◦ *to whistle a tune*

– a large group of musicians who play different musical instruments together: **orchestra** ◦ *a symphony orchestra*
– a small group of people who play jazz or pop music, or a group that play the same kind of instruments: **band** ◦ *a jazz band* ◦ *a brass band*
– a person who plays or sings a piece of music alone: **soloist**
– a group of three, four or five people who play music together: **trio** (*plural* **trios**), **quartet**, **quintet** ◦ *a concert given by the Modern Jazz Quartet*

▷ more on orchestras ⇨ ORCHESTRA

■ writing music
– to invent music: **compose** (sth), **write*** sth; the work of composing sth: **composition** (*noun* U) ◦ *Do you know who composed that last piece we heard?* ◦ *He has been asked to write a piece spe-*

music *contd.*

cially for the occasion. ◦ *She's studying musical composition.*

– a person who composes music: **composer**
– a piece of music which has been written by a composer: **composition** ◦ *At present he's working on a new composition for the cello.*

– the signs on paper that represent musical sounds: **music** (*noun* U) ◦ *Can you read music?*
– a sign on paper that represents a single sound: **note**
– a short unit into which a line of music is divided: **bar** ◦ *We sang a few bars.*

3 musical instruments and their players

– something that is used for playing music: (**musical**) **instrument**

– a large musical instrument which is played by pressing down black and white bars (= **keys**) : **piano** (*plural* **pianos**) ◦ *a grand piano* (= a full-size piano usually used for concerts) ◦ *learning to play the piano* ◦ *a piano stool* (= a chair for sitting on when you play the piano)
– a person who plays the piano: **pianist**, **piano player** ◦ *a concert pianist*

– a small electronic piano: **keyboard**
– an electronic instrument that can produce many different kinds of sounds: **synthesizer**
– a large musical instrument with pipes through which air is forced; it has keys like a piano: **organ** ◦ *the organ in our local church*
– a person who plays the organ: **organist**

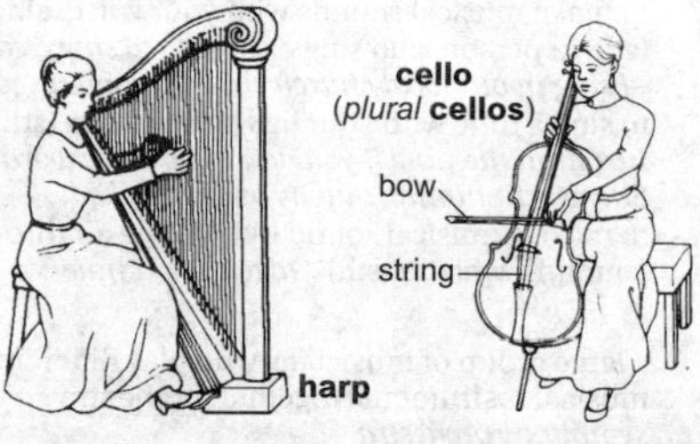

– a person who plays a violin: **violinist**
– a person who plays a cello: **cellist**
– a person who plays a harp: **harpist**
– a person who plays a guitar: **guitarist**

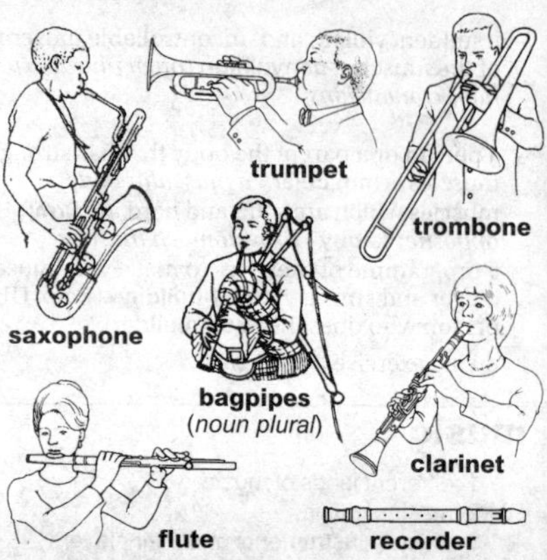

– a person who plays a flute: **flautist** (*AmE* **flutist**)
– a person who plays a clarinet: **clarinettist**
– a person who plays a trumpet: **trumpeter**
– a person who plays a trombone: **trombonist**
– a person who plays a saxophone: **saxophonist**
– a person who plays the bagpipes: **piper**

– a person who plays a drum: **drummer**

4 listening to music

– music that you hear as it is happening is **live** ◦ *a live concert*
– music that you hear on a record, etc is **recorded**
▷ recorded music ⇨ RECORD

– a performance of music for a particular audience: **concert** ◦ *a pop concert* ◦ *to go to a concert* ◦ *a concert programme* (= a piece of paper or leaflet with information about the concert)
– a building where people go to hear concerts: **concert hall**
– a building where operas are performed: **opera house**
– an extra performance of a piece of music, that an audience might ask for at the end of a successful concert: **encore**

– a person who enjoys music very much: **music lover**
– a person whose job is to criticize and discuss music: **music critic**

5 describing musical sounds

– a single musical sound made by a voice or an instrument: **note** ◦ *a high/low note*

- a series of notes that go up or down in a fixed order: **scale**
- a series of notes arranged in a pleasant pattern: **tune, melody** ◦ *The children played us a tune on their recorders.*
- a set of notes that is based on one particular note: **key** ◦ *the key of G minor* ◦ *a change of key* ◦ *What key is this piece in?*

- how high or low a note or voice is: **pitch** ◦ *I can't sing at that pitch.*
- if an instrument or a voice is at the correct pitch, it is **in tune**; if not, it is **out of tune** ◦ *He always sings out of tune.*
- to adjust a musical instrument so that it plays at the correct pitch: **tune** sth ◦ *This piano needs tuning again.*
- a note that is slightly higher than the correct one is **sharp** (*adverb* **sharp**); *opposite*: **flat** (*adverb* **flat**) ◦ *It sounds sharp to me.* ◦ *to sing flat*

- two or more musical notes that are played at the same time: **chord** ◦ *a major/minor chord*
- when different notes are played or sung together in a pleasing way, the result is **harmony** (*noun* U) ◦ *to sing/play in harmony*

- when music is not played or sung loudly, it is **soft** (*adverb* **softly**) ◦ *low lights and soft music*
- a change from a soft sound to a louder sound: **crescendo** (*plural* **crescendos**) ◦ *The piece ends with a huge crescendo.*

- a regular repeated pattern of sound in music: **rhythm**; *adjective*: **rhythmic, rhythmical** (*adverb* **rhythmically**) ◦ *Latin American rhythms* ◦ *You seem to have a natural sense of rhythm.*
- a strong rhythm: **beat** ◦ *We could feel the beat of the music.*
- the rhythmical pattern of a piece of music: **time** (*noun* U) ◦ *to keep time with the music*

■ **MORE ...**
- if you are good at recognizing and appreciating musical sounds, you **have an ear** for music, you **have a good ear** for music
- if you are not able to hear or sing the difference between notes in music, you are **tone-deaf**

- to change a piece of music so that it sounds different, for example using other instruments or another style: **arrange** sth; music that has been arranged: **arrangement** ◦ *a new arrangement of an old song*
- to invent a musical performance as it is happening: **improvise** (sth); *noun* (C/U): **improvisation** ◦ *He just sat down at the piano and improvised.*

Muslim

see also RELIGION

- the religion which is based on the teachings of the prophet Mohammed: **Islam** (*noun* U); connected with Islam: **Islamic, Muslim** ◦ *Islamic law* ◦ *Muslim countries*
- a person whose religion is Islam: **Muslim**
- the name of God in Islam: **Allah**
- the founder of Islam: **Mohammed, the Prophet**
- the holy book of Islam: **the Koran**
- a building in which Muslims pray: **mosque**
- the month in which Muslims do not eat or drink during the daytime: **Ramadan**

must

1 ways of expressing what must be done
2 things that must be done
3 making sb do sth
things that you need to have ⇨ NEED
see also POSSIBLE[1]

1 ways of expressing what must be done

■ necessary to do sth
- if you think that it is necessary that sb does sth, you can say that they **must** (do sth), **have to** (do sth), **have got to** (do sth), **need to** (do sth) ◦ *You must try to be on time in future!* ◦ *Must she go away?* ◦ *Do I have to show my passport?* ◦ *Sorry, I've got to go.* ◦ *Have we got to listen to another speech?* ◦ *I need to get up at half past six if I'm going to catch the 8.15 train.*

- to say that sth was necessary in the past, you can say that sb **had to** (do sth), **needed to** (do sth) ◦ *I'm sorry I'm late. I had to go to the bank.* ◦ *'Why did you come back?' 'I needed to see you.'*

Note: must often suggests that sth is necessary because the speaker wants it to be done; **have to** often suggests that sth is necessary because of the situation or because of a law or a rule; **have got to** is a little more informal than **have to**; **need to** often suggests that sth is necessary if sth else is to be possible.

■ necessary not to do sth
- if you think that it is necessary that sb does not do sth, you can say that they **must not** (do sth) ◦ *You must not say that! They won't like it at all!* ◦ *I mustn't forget to put the chicken in the oven before we go out.*
- if you want to say that it is necessary not to do sth because it is not permitted, you can say that sb is **not allowed to** (do sth) or **can't** (do sth) ◦ *We weren't allowed to smoke at my school.* ◦ *We can't wear jeans in my office.*

▷ more on being allowed to do sth ⇨ ALLOW

■ not necessary to do sth
- if you think that it is not necessary that sb does sth, you can say that they **don't have to** (do sth), **haven't got to** (do sth), **don't need to** (do sth), **needn't** (do sth) ◦ *You don't have to wear a tie, but you can if you want.* ◦ *I'm so glad I haven't got to go into hospital.* ◦ *George doesn't need to go to the dentist again, does he?* ◦ *'Have I really got to do my homework now?' 'No, you needn't do it now, but you'll have to after supper.'*

- to say that sth was not necessary in the past, you can say that sb **didn't have to** (do sth), **didn't need to** (do sth), **needn't have** (done sth) ◦ *Are you telling me now that I didn't have to re-type those letters?* ◦ *It was kind of you to help, but you really didn't need to, you know.* ◦ *I now realize that I needn't have done all that cleaning.*

must *contd.*

■ right or desirable (but not necessary)

– if you think that it is right or a good idea that sb does sth, you can say that they **should** (do sth), **ought to** (do sth) ◦ *Shouldn't I show you my essay again before I hand it in?* ◦ *You should try the chicken chasseur – it's extremely good.* ◦ *There ought to be more lights along this road – it's dangerous.* ◦ *Oughtn't you to go to the doctor with that cough?*

– to give advice, you can also say that sb **must** (do sth) ◦ *You must try and see that film – it's brilliant.*

– to say that sth was right or a good idea in the past, you can say that sb **should have** (done sth), **ought to have** (done sth) ◦ *You should have thought about that before you sold the house!* ◦ *We ought to have foreseen this.*

2 things that must be done

– something that has to be done, because sb has said that you must do it or because you have promised to do it: **obligation** (*noun* C/U) ◦ *to have family obligations* ◦ *You're under no obligation to buy.*

– if you officially have to do sth, it is **compulsory**, **obligatory** ◦ *It's obligatory to carry some form of identification with you.*

– not obligatory: **optional** ◦ *an optional course*

– something that you have to do because the situation requires it: **necessity**; *adjective*: **necessary** ◦ *Wearing a cycle helmet is a real necessity in town.* ◦ *Don't spend all the money unless it's absolutely necessary.*

– absolutely necessary: **essential**, **vital** ◦ *A good diet is essential to a healthy life.* ◦ *It's vital that everyone is here on time.*

– something that has to be done, either because it is your job or because you are morally obliged to do it: **duty** ◦ *I feel I have a duty to help him.*

– to tell sb that they are free from a duty, responsibility, etc: **excuse** sb (**from** sth) ◦ *I was excused from games because of my bad leg.*

– free from having to do sth or pay sth: **exempt** (**from** sth) (*not before a noun*); *noun* (C/U): **exemption** ◦ *exempt from military service*

– to make sb exempt from sth: **exempt** sb (**from** sth)

▷ more on duty ⇨ DUTY

3 making sb do sth

– to make sb do sth: **force** sb **to** do sth, **compel** sb **to** do sth (*usually passive*), **oblige** (*AmE* **obligate**) sb **to** do sth (*usually passive*) ◦ *I felt compelled to tell them what I thought of the plan.*

– to say to sb that they must do sth: **tell*** sb **to** do sth, **order** sb **to** do sth; *noun*: **order** ◦ *The policeman told the driver to get out of the car.* ◦ *to give sb an order*

– to ask for sth in a way that shows that you expect to get it: **demand** sth/**to** do sth ◦ *I went into the shop and demanded to see the manager.*

– to say that you must have sth, or that sth must happen: **insist** (**on** sth), **insist that . . .**; *noun* (U): **insistence** ◦ *We insist on punctuality.* ◦ *I insisted that she tell me the truth.*

▷ more on giving orders ⇨ ORDER²

name

1 names and titles
2 giving names
3 using names
see also WORD

1 names and titles

– the word you use to refer to a person, animal, place or thing: **name** ◦ *'What's your name?' 'Peter.'*

– to have a name: **be called** sth ◦ *What a lovely dog! What's he called?*

– your personal name, which your friends and family use when they speak to you: **first name** (*AmE* **given name**), **Christian name**, (*formal*) **forename**

– the name that you share with your family: **surname**, **family name**, **last name**

– a name that some people have between their first name and their family name: **middle name**

– your first name, middle name(s) and surname: **full name** ◦ *Please write your full name on the form.*

– the first letters of your names: **initials**

– the surname that a woman has before she gets married and takes her husband's name: **maiden name**

– a name that some people give to their friends: **nickname** ◦ *His nickname was 'Smiley', because he was always happy.*

– if sb's name is Elizabeth, for example, but everybody calls her Liz, we say that the name 'Liz' is **short for** 'Elizabeth' or that Elizabeth is called Liz **for short**

– a funny or friendly name that some people give to sb they like a lot: **pet name**

– a word or short form that you use before sb's name: **title**

▷ titles used before men's names ⇨ MAN

▷ titles used before women's names ⇨ WOMAN

2 giving names

– to give sb/sth a name: **call** sb/sth sth, **name** sb/sth sth ◦ *What are they going to call their new baby?* ◦ *They named their son Francis and their daughter Anne.*

– to give sb/sth a nickname: **nickname** sb/sth sth ◦ *They nicknamed him 'Lofty' because he was so tall.*

– to give sth a new name: **rename** sth (sth) ◦ *Leningrad was renamed St Petersburg.*

– to give a child the same name as another person in the family, a good friend or a famous person: **name/call** sb **after** sb (*AmE* **name** sb **for** sb) ◦

They named her after her grandmother. ◦ *He's called Elvis, after Elvis Presley.*
- to officially give a child a name at a church ceremony: **christen** sb (sth), **baptize** sb (sth); *nouns*: **christening, baptism** ◦ *Jamie's going to be baptized next week.* ◦ *We're going to Rosie's christening.*

3 using names
- to use a particular name for sb: **call** sb sth; to use sb's first name, nickname, etc: **call** sb **by** their first name, nickname, etc ◦ *Please call me Bob.* ◦ *Everyone uses his nickname, no one ever calls him by his real name.*
- to tell sb another person's name, so that the two people can meet, for example at a party: **introduce** sb (**to** sb) ◦ *She introduced me to some really interesting people at the party.*

▷ introducing sb ⇨ MEET

- to write your name, often in a particular way, so that other people cannot copy it, on a letter, form, etc: **sign** your **name**, **sign** (sth); your name written in this way: **signature** ◦ *Where do I sign?* ◦ *to sign a letter/contract* ◦ *Do you need my signature?*

- a piece of paper, for example a driving licence or passport, that says who you are: **identification**, (*especially AmE*) **ID** ◦ *Do you have any identification/ID on you?*
- a means of identification used in some countries: **identity card**
- to be able to give sb's name by looking at a photograph, for example: **identify** sb ◦ *The police showed me a photograph of a man, and asked me if I could identify him.*
- a card that has a person's name, company address and telephone number written on it: **business card**
- a list of names with addresses and telephone numbers: **phone book**, (**telephone**) **directory**

- a piece of paper or material that has a name written on it: **label**
- to put a label on sth: **label** sth ◦ *You should label your luggage before you go on holiday.* ◦ *a luggage label*

■ **MORE ...**
- if sb writes a letter, a book, a poem, etc and does not write his/her name on it, it is **anonymous** (*adverb* **anonymously**)
- a name that a writer uses, that is not his/her real name: **pseudonym, pen-name** ◦ *Eric Blair wrote under the pseudonym of George Orwell.*
- a false name which a criminal uses: **alias**

- if a famous person gives you their signature, it is called an **autograph** ◦ *I saw Pavarotti in a restaurant and he gave me his autograph!*

---

narrow ⇨ WIDE/NARROW

---

nation ⇨ COUNTRY[1]

---

natural
- connected with nature ⇨ NATURE
- normal ⇨ USUAL

---

nature

see also ENVIRONMENT, ANIMAL, PLANT

- everything in the world that was not made by people (the land, the sea, the plants, animals, etc): **nature** (*noun* U) ◦ *the wonders of nature* ◦ *If we destroy too many forests, we will destroy the balance of nature.*
- connected with things that were not made by people: **natural**; *opposites*: **artificial, man-made** ◦ *the natural world* ◦ *the exploitation of the world's natural resources* ◦ *I don't like zoos – animals should be allowed to live in their natural surroundings.* ◦ *artificial flowers* ◦ *man-made materials such as polyester*

- the natural surroundings where plants, animals and people live: **the environment** (*noun singular*) ◦ *Nowadays people are more aware of the need to protect the environment.*
- the natural place where a particular type of animal or plant lives: **habitat** ◦ *to study animals in their natural habitat.*
- the relationship between living things and their natural surroundings: **ecology** (*noun* U); *adjective*: **ecological** ◦ *an ecological disaster caused by an oil spill*

- when an animal or plant lives in its natural surroundings, it is **wild** ◦ *wild animals*
- wild animals, birds, etc: **wildlife** (*noun* U) ◦ *Did you see that wildlife programme on TV last night?*
- any place that is far from towns and cities, and where animals, birds, etc live in their natural surroundings: **the wild** (*noun singular*) ◦ *There are very few tigers still living in the wild.*
- the natural force that makes a person or animal do sth without having to learn to do it: **instinct** (*noun* U/C); *adjective*: **instinctive** ◦ *Migrating birds know where to fly by instinct.* ◦ *an instinct to run away from danger* ◦ *instinctive behaviour*

- the slow development of animals and plants over millions of years: **evolution** (*noun* U); *verb*: **evolve**; *adjective*: **evolutionary** ◦ *the theory of evolution* ◦ *Plants and animals evolved over millions of years.* ◦ *evolutionary processes*
- when a type of animal or plant dies out and does not exist any more, it becomes **extinct**; *noun* (U): **extinction** *Dinosaurs are extinct.* ◦ *Many species of animals are in danger of extinction.*
- a type of animal or plant that is in danger of becoming extinct is an **endangered species**

■ studying nature
- the study of plants and animals: **natural history** (*noun* U) ◦ *the Natural History Museum*
- a person who studies animals and plants: **naturalist**
- the study of the relationship between living things and their surroundings: **ecology** (*noun* U)
- a person who studies ecology: **ecologist**

▷ the scientific study of living things ⇨ SCIENCE

navy

see also ARMY, AIR FORCE, BOAT, WAR

– the part of a country's armed forces that uses ships for fighting wars: **navy**; *adjective*: **naval** ◦ *The Royal Navy* (= the British navy) ◦ *a naval officer*

– a person who gives orders to others in the navy, army, air force, etc: **officer**
– an officer of high rank in the navy: **admiral**
– the officer who is in charge of a ship: **captain**
– a soldier who is trained to fight on land or at sea: **marine**
– all the people who work on a ship: **crew** (*with singular or plural verb*)
– a member of the crew of a ship: **sailor**

– a ship for use in war: **warship**
– a group of warships: **fleet**
– a centre from where the navy operates: **naval base**

– large types of warship: **battleship, cruiser**
– smaller types of warship: **frigate, destroyer**
– a ship that carries military aircraft: **aircraft carrier**

– a type of boat that can travel under water and on the surface: **submarine**
– a device on a submarine through which you can see the area above: **periscope**
– a bomb shaped like a tube that is fired from a submarine and can travel underwater: **torpedo** (*plural* **torpedoes**)
– (used about submarines) to go down under the water: **dive, submerge**
– to come to the surface of the water: **surface** ◦ *The submarine surfaced after thirty days underwater.*

near ⇨ DISTANCE

nearly ⇨ ALMOST

necessary

– something that you must have ⇨ NEED
– something that you must do ⇨ MUST

need

needing to do sth ⇨ MUST

– when sb must have sth, they **need** it, **are in need of** it, (*informal*) **could do with** it ◦ *We need some more milk – there's none in the fridge.* ◦ *I'm in need of a holiday.* ◦ *That child could do with a bath and some clean clothes.*
– a situation in which sth is needed: **need** ◦ *There is a growing need for specialist nurses.*
– something that you need: **necessity, need** ◦ *Just bring the necessities – a change of clothes, food and water.* ◦ *Love and security are basic human needs.*

– needed by sb or sth: **necessary** ◦ *Are all these clothes really necessary?* ◦ *to take necessary precautions against illness or injury*
– absolutely necessary: **essential, vital** ◦ *For this job, a knowledge of French is essential.*
– necessary because of some official or technical reason: **required** ◦ *At least three people are required to operate the machine.* ◦ *No special qualifications are required.*

– if sb has a very strong need for sth, they are **desperate for** sth, they **badly need/want** sth ◦ *I'm desperate for a glass of water.* ◦ *She badly needs help.*

– to need sb/sth and feel that you could not live or work properly without them/it: **depend on** sb/sth (**for** sth), **rely on** sb/sth (**for** sth); *noun* (U): **dependence** (**on** sb/sth); *adjective*: **dependent** (**on** sb/sth) ◦ *She relies on other people to look after her.* ◦ *to be dependent on drugs*

■ not needing sth
– not necessary: **unnecessary** (*adverb* **unnecessarily**) ◦ *Why did you have to say that? It was quite unnecessary!* ◦ *These executives earn unnecessarily large salaries.*
– an amount that is more than you need: **surplus**; *adjective*: **surplus** ◦ *food surpluses*

– if you do not need sth, you **can do without** it ◦ *Don't worry – I think I can do without the dictionary.*
– not needing help or support from anybody: **independent**; *noun* (U): **independence** ◦ *She's a very independent child.*

▷ needing or not needing help ⇨ HELP

needle ⇨ SEW

negative ⇨ YES/NO

nervous

– frightened ⇨ AFRAID
– anxious ⇨ WORRY

never ⇨ HOW OFTEN

new/old

1 new
2 old

young and old people ⇨ YOUNG/OLD

1 new

■ not existing or done before
– seen, made, introduced or invented for the first time; not existing before: **new** ◦ *a new computer game* ◦ *We're going round this afternoon to see their new baby.* ◦ *a new method of treating cancer patients*
– done or experienced for the first time: **new** ◦ *I've decided to learn a new language.* ◦ *'Have you used a computer before?' 'No it's all very new to me.'*

– to cause sth new to happen or exist: **create** sth; *noun* (U): **creation** ◦ *We're trying to create an entirely new kind of environment for children to grow up in.* ◦ *The creation of new jobs will bring more wealth to the area.*

– to think of sth or make sth for the first time: **invent** sth; *noun* (U): **invention** ◦ *The invention of the computer has led to huge changes in the way we live.*
– a thing that has been made or designed by sb: **invention** ◦ *The mobile phone is a very useful invention.*

▷ more on inventions ⇨ INVENT

– of the present or recent period: **modern, contemporary** ◦ *a modern building* ◦ *contemporary art*

▷ more on being modern ⇨ MODERN

■ just beginning; recent
– just beginning: **new** ◦ *a new day*
– a person who has just arrived in a place: **newcomer** ◦ *a newcomer to an area/a school*

▷ beginning ⇨ BEGIN

– recently bought: **new** ◦ *Do you like my new shoes?*
– recently bought and never used before: **brand new** ◦ *He got a brand new bike for Christmas.*

■ changed or different
– changed or different: **new** ◦ *We're moving to a new house.* ◦ *My brother's got a new job.*
– new or different: **fresh** ◦ *fresh ideas* ◦ *a fresh approach to the problem*

– new or interesting; different from others of its type: **original, novel** ◦ *an original piece of music* ◦ *a novel idea*
– the quality of being new and interesting: **originality** (*noun* U) ◦ *It's the originality of his ideas that makes his work so interesting.*

■ making sth like new again
– to exchange sth for sth that is better or newer: **replace** sth; a thing that takes the place of sth that is old or broken: **replacement** ◦ *If anything goes wrong with your TV set, we'll replace it with a new one.* ◦ *a replacement for a broken cup*
– to put sth old or damaged back into good condition: **repair** sth, **mend** sth, (*informal*) **fix** sth ◦ *I'm taking the camera to be repaired.*
– to put a building, painting, etc back into a previous condition: **restore** sth ◦ *The roof of the church was restored after the fire.*
– to improve a building or a room by repairing it, painting it, etc: **do* sth up**
– not new but looking new or hardly used: **as good as new** ◦ *All it needs is a bit of cleaning and then it'll be as good as new.*

▷ more on repairing things ⇨ REPAIR

2 old

– having existed for a long time: **old** ◦ *an old friend* (= one you have had for a long time) ◦ *the old part of the city*

– very old and therefore unusual or valuable: **antique** ◦ *an antique clock*
– an old and valuable object, for example a piece of furniture: **antique** ◦ *All the chairs are antiques.*
– a shop where you can buy antiques: **antique shop**
– belonging to times long past: **ancient** ◦ *ancient civilizations* ◦ *We now know a lot about how people used to live in ancient times.*
– ancient times, especially those of the Egyptians, Greeks and Romans: **antiquity** (*noun* U) ◦ *myths and legends from antiquity*
– buildings, works of art, coins, etc that remain from ancient times: **antiquities** (*noun plural*) ◦ *a museum with many Roman antiquities*
– not new or modern: **old-fashioned, outdated, out of date** ◦ *old-fashioned clothes* ◦ *outdated computer software*
– no longer used because it is out of date: **obsolete** ◦ *an obsolete piece of machinery*
– very old-fashioned; no longer in common use: **archaic** ◦ *an archaic word* ◦ *archaic laws*

■ much used
– having been used a lot; not new: **old** ◦ *old shoes/furniture* ◦ *We've got quite an old car, but it still works.*
– already used or owned by sb else: **second-hand, used** ◦ *second-hand clothes* ◦ *a used car*
– something that is old and damaged because it has been used a lot is **worn (out)** ◦ *The carpet is looking a bit worn.* ◦ *This coat is worn out – I'll have to get a new one.*
– something that is completely worn out and is not useful any more (*informal*) **is past it**, (*informal*) **has had it** ◦ *These shoes have had it – I'm going to throw them out.*

news

see also NEWSPAPER / MAGAZINE, TELEVISION / RADIO

– information about things that have happened recently: **news** (*noun* U) ◦ *a piece of news* ◦ *Have you heard the news?* ◦ *I've got some good/bad news for you.* ◦ *an interesting item of news in today's paper*
– a description of a news event: **story** ◦ *The plane crash was the front-page story in all the newspapers.* ◦ *The official story is that he resigned because he wants to spend more time with his family.*
– a written or spoken description of what a person has seen, heard or done: **report** ◦ *a report from one of our foreign correspondents* ◦ *an official report*

– a printed report about a club or organization that is sent out regularly to keep people informed of its news: **newsletter, bulletin** ◦ *a monthly newsletter*

■ people who report the news
– a person whose job is to collect, write or publish news: **journalist**; the work of a journalist: **journalism** (*noun* U)
– a person who writes about the news in a newspaper or reports it on the television or radio: **reporter**
– a reporter who writes about particular subjects or sends reports from a particular place: **cor-**

news *contd.*

respondent ∘ *our political/medical/New York correspondent*

■ hearing and talking about the news

- when news becomes known, it **breaks*** ∘ *The news of the Prime Minister's resignation broke on Tuesday morning.*
- when news which was secret becomes known, it **gets* out**, **gets* about**; when it is known, it is **out** ∘ *Don't let it get about!* ∘ *The news was already out.*
- if you are the first to tell a person about sth important and usually unpleasant that has happened, you **break* the news** (**to** them) ∘ *Be sure to break the news to her gently!*

- to discuss other people and their personal affairs: **talk**; what people say when they do this: **talk** (*noun* U) ∘ *The neighbours have been talking.* ∘ *There's talk that his business is going badly.*
- news or information that people are talking about but that may not be true: **rumour** (*noun* C/U) ∘ *There's a rumour going round that she's leaving.*

- if you are told about sth, you **hear* about** it ∘ *Did you hear about my accident?*
- if you find out some news, for example from a newspaper, you **see*** it ∘ *I see that house prices are going up.*
- if you learn sth from the television or radio news, you **see*** or **hear*** it **on the news** ∘ *I heard on the news that there's been a terrible plane crash.*
- if you find out information or news after other people, you **catch* up** (on it) ∘ *Come over for a chat so we can catch up on each other's news.*

- the way you receive a piece of news is the way you **take*** it ∘ *How did she take it when you told her the news?* ∘ *She took it very well.*
- the sudden and very strong feeling of surprise that is caused by sth unpleasant (for example bad news): **shock** (*noun* C/U); *verb*: **shock** sb; *adjective*: **shocking** ∘ *Her husband's death came as a terrible shock to her.* ∘ *I was deeply shocked.* ∘ *shocking news*
- something that causes great excitement, surprise or interest: a **sensation**; *adjective*: **sensational** ∘ *to cause a sensation* ∘ *a sensational story*

■ **MORE ...**

- information that you learn from a person who learnt it from somebody else is **second-hand** (*adjective, adverb*) ∘ *second-hand news*
- to tell people sth that was officially a secret: **leak** sth; *noun*: **leak** ∘ *The story was leaked to the press.* ∘ *a series of leaks from a government department*

newspaper/magazine

1 different kinds of newspaper and magazine
2 the work of producing newspapers
3 what is in newspapers and magazines
4 buying and selling newspapers

see also NEWS, RADIO/TELEVISION

1 different kinds of newspaper and magazine

- large, printed pieces of paper containing news, advertisements and articles on various subjects: **newspaper**, **paper** ∘ *a morning/evening newspaper* ∘ *a daily/Sunday paper* ∘ *a popular/serious paper* ∘ *a national/local paper* ∘ *She opened the paper and turned to the sports page.*
- a newspaper that has small pages, a lot of pictures and short simple articles: **tabloid** (**paper**); a newspaper that has large pages and contains serious reports and articles: **broadsheet** (**paper**)

- a kind of book with a paper cover which is published every week, month, etc: **magazine** ∘ *a weekly/monthly magazine* ∘ *women's magazines* ∘ *a gardening/computer/football magazine* ∘ *glossy magazines* (= magazines printed on good quality paper and having a lot of colour photographs)
- a magazine that is serious and is about a specialized subject: **journal**, **periodical** *a medical journal* ∘ *the periodicals section in the university library*
- a magazine that you may get free with a newspaper, particularly at the weekend: **supplement** ∘ *the Sunday colour supplements*
- a magazine for children which tells stories through pictures: **comic**

- newspapers, television, and radio are called the (**mass**) **media** (*noun plural*) ∘ *He tried to keep the story out of the media.* ∘ *the political power of the mass media*
- newspapers and the journalists who work for them: **the press** (*noun singular, with singular or plural verb*) ∘ *the local/national press* ∘ *the popular press*

2 the work of producing newspapers

- an organization which produces a particular newspaper: **paper**, **newspaper** ∘ *Which paper does she work for?*
- the person or company that publishes a newspaper, magazine, etc: **publisher**
- the person or company that owns a newspaper, magazine, etc: **proprietor**

- one of many newspapers or magazines that have been produced on a particular day: **copy** ∘ *Do you have a copy of yesterday's paper?*
- the copies of a particular newspaper that are printed at the same time: **edition** ∘ *the early evening edition* ∘ *a special edition*
- all the copies of a magazine that are produced on a particular date: **issue** ∘ *last month's issue* ∘ *six issues a year*

- when papers, magazines, etc appear for sale in the shops, they **come* out** ◦ *When does the next issue come out?*

- to write articles that appear in newspapers or magazines: **write*** (**for** sth) ◦ *He writes for the 'Daily Mail'.*
- a person whose job is to collect, write or publish news: **journalist**; the work of a journalist: **journalism** (*noun* U); *adjective*: **journalistic** ◦ *a journalist on the 'Daily Telegraph'* ◦ *a journalistic style of writing*
- a person who writes about the news in a newspaper or magazine or speaks about it on the television or radio: **reporter**; the work of a reporter is to **report** the news
- a reporter who writes about particular subjects or sends reports from a particular place, especially abroad: **correspondent** ◦ *our Middle East correspondent* ◦ *the sports correspondent for 'The Guardian'*
- a person who takes photographs for newspapers: **press photographer**

- the person who is in charge of planning a newspaper: **editor**; the editor's job is to **edit** the newspaper; connected with the work of an editor: **editorial** ◦ *the editor of the 'Sunday Times'* ◦ *He edits the sports page.* ◦ *editorial policy*

3 what is in newspapers and magazines

- the first page of a newspaper: **the front page**; the last page: **the back page**
- the outside of a magazine: **cover**

- a title of a report in a newspaper, printed in large letters: **headline**
- one of the long, narrow printed sections of a newspaper page: **column**

- information about things that have happened recently: **news** (*noun* U) ◦ *I heard an interesting piece of news.* ◦ *Is there any more news about the accident?*
- a piece of writing in a newspaper or magazine: **article**
- an article which describes a news event: **report, story** ◦ *All the newspapers ran the story.*

- an article which gives the opinion of the editor on an important subject: **editorial, leading article**
- an article that is part of a regular series, or is written by the same writer: **column**; a journalist who writes regular articles in a newspaper or magazine: **columnist** ◦ *a gardening column* ◦ *a political columnist*
- an article that is based on the answers that a particular person gave to a set of questions: **interview**
- an article that is written about a person's life, soon after they have died: **obituary**
- an article that describes and gives an opinion about a new book, film or play, etc: **review**; a person who writes reviews: **reviewer, critic** ◦ *She writes the film reviews in 'The Observer'.* ◦ *a book reviewer* ◦ *book reviews* ◦ *a film review* ◦ *a film/theatre critic*

- if a member of the public wants to express an opinion in a newspaper or magazine, they write a **letter to the editor**
- the section where you can read or place personal messages in a paper: the **personal column**
- the section where you can place short advertisements: **classified advertisements**, (*informal*) **classified ads**

▷ more on advertisements ⇨ ADVERTISEMENT

- a funny drawing that makes a joke about a current event: **cartoon**; a person who draws cartoons: **cartoonist**
- a series of drawings that tell a story: **comic strip, strip cartoon**

4 buying and selling newspapers

- to buy a newspaper or magazine regularly: **take*** sth ◦ *Which paper do you take?*
- a person who reads a magazine: **reader** ◦ *letters from our readers*
- all the people who read a particular magazine, newspaper, etc: **readership** (*noun singular*) *a paper with a readership of over four million*
- the number of copies of a newspaper, magazine, etc that are sold each time it is produced: **circulation**
- a person who receives a particular magazine regularly: **subscriber**
- to pay for a magazine or newspaper to be sent to you regularly: **subscribe** (**to** sth) ◦ *Do you subscribe to 'Private Eye'?*
- the money you pay to subscribe to sth: **subscription**

- a person or shop that sells newspapers, magazines, etc: **newsagent**
- a place on the street where you can buy a newspaper: **news-stand**
- a boy or girl who delivers newspapers to people's houses: **paperboy/girl**

■ **MORE ...**

- a meeting when a famous or important person answers questions from journalists: **press conference** ◦ *to hold/call a press conference*
- an official announcement or account of sth that is given to the press by a government department, an organization, etc: **press release** ◦ *The minister issued a press release, denying all knowledge of the matter.*

- a piece that has been cut out of a newspaper: **cutting**, (especially *AmE*) **clipping** ◦ *a press cutting*

---

next ⇨ FIRST/NEXT/LAST

---

nice ⇨ GOOD, LIKE²

---

night

see also DAY

- the time when it is dark and people usually sleep: **night** (*noun* C/U) ◦ *in the middle of the night* ◦ *He died on the night before his ninetieth birthday.* ◦ *I prefer to work at night.* ◦ *Night falls* (= begins) *quickly in tropical countries.*

night *contd.*

- the time when it is dark: **night-time** (*noun* U)
- the end of the day when the light begins to disappear: **dusk** (*noun* U), **sunset** (*noun* C/U)
- the time when the night begins: **nightfall** (*noun* U) ◦ *at nightfall*
- the time when the night ends and a new day begins: **dawn** (*noun* C/U)
- the middle of the night at 12 o'clock: **midnight** (*noun* U)
- the hours between midnight and the morning: **the small hours** ◦ *I sat up until the small hours, writing letters to people who I thought might give me a job.*

- this night: **tonight**
- the night before this one: **last night**
- the night after this one: **tomorrow night**
- two nights ago: **the night before last**

Note: when sth happens in the night, you can say **at night**, **during the night**, **in the night**; when you give the name of a day, you use **on**: ◦ *on Saturday night*. You say **by night** when you contrast night with the day: ◦ *Owls sleep during the day and hunt by night.*

- done or happening every night: **nightly** (*adjective, adverb*) ◦ *The film will be shown nightly, except on Sundays.*
- when the night begins you can say **it gets* dark** ◦ *Make sure you're home before it gets dark.*
- to emphasize that sth happens during the whole period of the night, you can say **all night long** ◦ *The baby cried all night long.*

▷ going to bed ⇨ BED

no ⇨ YES/NO

noise ⇨ SOUND

normal ⇨ USUAL

north ⇨ DIRECTION

nose

see also FACE

- the part of the face that is used for breathing and smelling: **nose**
- one of the two openings at the end of the nose: **nostril**
- a nose with a sharp point is a **pointed nose**; one which is not pointed and is rather wide at the end can be called a **flat nose**
- a nose which curves upwards is a **turned-up nose**
- a short, turned-up nose is a **snub nose**; *adjective*: **snub-nosed**

- connected with the nose: **nasal** *the nasal passages* (= nostrils)

- to notice or identify sth by using your nose: **smell** sth ◦ *Can you smell gas?*
- the ability to smell: **smell** (*noun* U) ◦ *Dogs have a good sense of smell.*
- to take air into your body and let it out again: **breathe**

▷ more on breathing and using the sense of smell ⇨ BREATHE, SMELL

■ when you have a cold, etc

- to clear your nose by blowing strongly through it into a piece of cloth or paper: **blow*** your **nose**
- a square piece of cloth or soft paper that you use for blowing your nose: **handkerchief**, (*informal*) **hanky**; a paper handkerchief is often called a **tissue**
- to clear your nose using your fingers: **pick** your **nose** ◦ *Stop picking your nose!*
- the liquid produced by the nose: (*formal*) **mucus** (*noun* U), (*informal*) **snot** (*noun* U)
- if liquid flows from the nose, the nose **runs***; *adjective*: **runny** ◦ *This medicine should stop your nose running.* ◦ *She's got a runny nose.*

- to breathe air in through the nose in a way that makes a noise, especially when you have a cold or you have been crying: **sniff** ◦ *Stop sniffing and blow your nose.*
- to sniff continuously: **sniffle**
- a sudden burst of air coming out through the nose and mouth, especially when you have a cold: **sneeze**; *verb*: **sneeze** ◦ *a loud sneeze* ◦ *I wonder what's making me sneeze.*
- what you say to a person who has just sneezed: **Bless you!**
- what you say when you have just sneezed: **Excuse me.**

■ animals' noses

- the nose and mouth of a bird: **beak**
- the nose of an elephant: **trunk**
- the long nose of certain animals, especially a pig: **snout**

nothing ⇨ HOW MUCH/MANY

noun ⇨ GRAMMAR

now ⇨ PRESENT[2]

nuclear

see also WEAPON, WAR

- the smallest part of an element that can be part of a chemical reaction: **atom**; *adjective*: **atomic** ◦ *atomic particles*
- a very small unit of a substance consisting of one or more atoms: **molecule**; *adjective*: **molecular** ◦ *the molecular structure of a chemical* ◦ *molecular biology*

- the central part of an atom: **nucleus** (*plural* **nuclei**); *adjective*: **nuclear** ◦ *nuclear physics*

■ nuclear power

- very powerful energy that is produced when the nucleus of an atom or atoms is split. It can be used to produce electricity: **nuclear power/energy** (*noun* U), **atomic power/energy** (*noun* U)

- connected with the energy that is produced when the nucleus of an atom is split: **nuclear**; *opposite*: **non-nuclear** ◦ *a nuclear explosion* ◦ *a nuclear disaster* ◦ *non-nuclear sources of energy*

- a building where electricity is generated using nuclear energy: **nuclear power station**
- a large machine that produces nuclear energy: **nuclear reactor**
- a material that produces nuclear energy: **nuclear fuel** (*noun* U)
- metals that can be used to produce nuclear energy: **uranium** (*noun* U), **plutonium** (*noun* U)

▷ other ways of generating electricity ⇨ ELECTRICITY

- sending out powerful and very dangerous rays of nuclear energy: **radioactive**; the state of being radioactive: **radioactivity** (*noun* U)
- the rays that are sent out by radioactive substances: **radiation** (*noun* U) ◦ *the level of radiation near the power station*
- dangerous waste material produced from nuclear reactors: **nuclear waste** (*noun* U), **radioactive waste** (*noun* U)
- radioactive waste matter that is carried in the air after a nuclear explosion: **fallout** (*noun* U)

- an area not having or allowing any nuclear weapons or materials is **nuclear-free** ◦ *a nuclear-free zone*

---

number

1 whole numbers
2 numbers that show position in a sequence
3 fractions
4 exact and inexact numbers
5 doing things with numbers

quantities ⇨ HOW MUCH / MANY
measurements ⇨ SIZE, WEIGHT
the study and use of numbers ⇨ MATHEMATICS
see also ONE, TWO, HUNDRED

1 whole numbers

- a word or symbol that indicates a quantity: **number**; *adjective*: **numerical** ◦ *a number between 10 and 20* ◦ *The answers were given in numerical order.*
- letters that represent numbers (I, II, III, IV, etc): **Roman numerals**
- a written sign for a number (0 to 9): **figure** ◦ *Write the number in figures as well as words.* ◦ *a six-figure number* (= between 100 000 and 999 999)

- a number that is used to identify sth: **number** ◦ *What's your telephone number?*
- used before a number to show its position in a sequence: **number** (*written abbreviation* **no**) ◦ *I live at number 16.* ◦ *I'm staying at the Grand Hotel in room no 134.* ◦ *What's the answer to question number one?* ◦ *What number are you on?* (= how far have you got in a list of things to do or questions to answer)
- to give a number to sth: **number** sth; *adjective*: **numbered** ◦ *Number each page in order from 1 to 20.* ◦ *I couldn't put the pages in order because they weren't numbered.*
- a number that can be divided by two (2, 4, 6, 8, etc) is an **even** number
- a number that cannot be divided by two (1, 3, 5, 7, etc) is an **odd** number
- the number 0: **zero**, **nought**, **nil** ◦ *Three, two, one, zero and lift off!* ◦ *I got nought out of ten in the test.* ◦ *To write a million you put a one followed by six noughts.* ◦ *The final score was two nil.*
- a number which is less than zero is a **negative** number; (used about a number) below zero: **minus** ◦ *–2 (minus two) is a negative number.*
- a number which is greater than zero is a **positive** number; (used about a number) above zero: **plus** ◦ *a temperature of plus three degrees*

Note: in British English **nought** is normally used when talking about the figure 0 in numbers; **zero** is more common in scientific and technical uses; **nil** is used mainly in talking about scores in sport; **O** (pronounced oh) is often used in giving telephone numbers.

- the names of the numbers: (1) **one**, (2) **two**, (3) **three**, (4) **four**, (5) **five**, (6) **six**, (7) **seven**, (8) **eight**, (9) **nine**, (10) **ten**, (11) **eleven**, (12) **twelve**, (13) **thirteen**, (14) **fourteen**, (15) **fifteen**, (16) **sixteen**, (17) **seventeen**, (18) **eighteen**, (19) **nineteen**, (20) **twenty**, (21) **twenty-one**, (22) **twenty-two**, etc; (30) **thirty**, (40) **forty**, (50) **fifty**, (60) **sixty**, (70) **seventy**, (80) **eighty**, (90) **ninety**, (100) **a hundred**, (1 000) **a thousand**, (1 000 000) **a million**, (1 000 000 000) **a billion**
- a group of twelve: **dozen** (*plural* **dozen**); six or a group of six: **half a dozen** ◦ *a dozen eggs* ◦ *three dozen bottles of wine*

Note: in numbers greater than a hundred, we say **and** before the last part of the number: ◦ *sixty-two* ◦ *three hundred and two* ◦ *two thousand three hundred and two* ◦ *two million six hundred thousand five hundred and ninety-five*. We usually use **a** rather than **one** for numbers between a hundred (100) and a hundred and ninety-nine (199) or for a thousand, a million or a billion: ◦ *There are a hundred and fifty people in the school* ◦ *'How many have you got left?' 'About a thousand.'* If the number needs to be emphasized, we use **one**: ◦ *There are exactly one hundred tickets left.* ◦ *'Did you say five hundred?' 'No, one hundred.'*; but we usually use **one** with numbers greater than a thousand, a million or a billion: ◦ *one thousand, three hundred and sixty* (1 360).
Numbers between 1 100 and 1 999 can be spoken as hundreds, especially in informal usage: ◦ *eleven hundred* (1 100). Dates are always written in numbers. When we say dates between 1 001 and 1 999, we usually omit **hundred**: ◦ *in 1066 (ten sixty-six)* ◦ *1789 (seventeen eighty-nine)*.

2 numbers that show position in a sequence

- a number that shows the position of sth in a sequence: **ordinal** (**number**)

number *contd.*

- the names of the ordinals: **first** (**1st**), **second** (**2nd**), **third** (**3rd**), **fourth** (**4th**), etc; **twenty-first, twenty-second, twenty-third, twenty-fourth**, etc; **hundredth; thousandth; millionth; billionth**

- introducing the first point on a list: **first, firstly**
- introducing the second, third, fourth, etc point on a list: **second** (or **secondly**), **third** (or **thirdly**), **fourth**, etc ◦ *I'll tell you why I'm leaving – firstly, I've got a new job; and secondly, I 'm going to get married.*

3 fractions

- a number that is not a whole number (for example, ⅚): **fraction**
- a fraction expressed in tenths (for example, 0.75): **decimal**
- the dot used in a decimal: **decimal point**

fraction		decimal	
½	**a half** (*plural* **halves**)	0.5	**(nought) point five**
¼	**a quarter**	0.25	**(nought) point two five**
¾	**three quarters**	0.75	**(nought) point seven five**
⅓	**a third**	0.33	**(nought) point three three**
⅔	**two thirds**	0.66	**(nought) point six six**
1½	**one and a half**	1.5	**one point five**
1¾	**one and three quarters**	1.75	**one point seven five**

- to divide sth in half: **halve** sth
- to divide sth into quarters: **quarter** sth

4 exact and inexact numbers

- a particular quantity of sth: **number** (*followed by a plural verb*) ◦ *There was a large number of people waiting for the gates to open.* ◦ *People came in large numbers.* ◦ *A small number of cars were parked in the middle of the road.* ◦ *A number of people were there.*
- to say how many people or things there are, you can say that they **number** a certain amount ◦ *They numbered about 30* (= there were about 30 people in total).
- to be more in number than sb/sth else: **outnumber** sb/sth ◦ *Women medical students now outnumber the men in many places.*

- correct or accurate: **exact** (*adverb* **exactly**) ◦ *We need to know the exact number of people you are expecting.* ◦ *Can you be a bit more exact please?*
- almost correct but not quite: **rough** (*adverb* **roughly**) ◦ *I don't need to know exactly, but can you give me a rough estimate?* ◦ *There is roughly five pounds left.*
- in 10s, 100s or 1000s; not being very accurate: **in round figures/numbers** ◦ *He gave the answer in round figures.*

- a number greater than nine: **double figures** ◦ *I started off by earning seven pounds an hour but now I'm into double figures.*

▷ more on being exact ⇨ EXACT/APPROXIMATE

- a small number of people or things: **a few, one or two**, (*informal*) **a couple** ◦ *Only a few (people) came to the party.* ◦ *I only saw one or two pictures I liked.* ◦ *A couple of people recognized me.*
- to emphasize that a quantity is big, you can say **dozens (of …), hundreds (of …), thousands (of …), millions (of …)** ◦ *Hundreds of people went to the concert.* ◦ *They spend millions of pounds on computer games.*

- to calculate the approximate number of sth: **estimate** sth; the number you get if you estimate sth: **estimate** ◦ *Can you estimate the length of the room?* ◦ *It's probably about ten metres long, but that's just an estimate.*
- to decrease a number to the nearest whole number: **round** sth **down**; to increase a number to the nearest whole number: **round** sth **up** ◦ *If it comes out at a decimal, round it up to the nearest whole number.*

5 doing things with numbers

- to find the answer to sth by adding numbers, taking numbers away, etc: **work** sth **out, calculate** sth ◦ *I'm trying to work out who owes who what.* ◦ *I've calculated the cost of going on holiday this year.*
- something calculated by using numbers in this way: **sum, calculation** ◦ *to do a sum in your head* ◦ *to get your sums right* ◦ *a difficult calculation*
- the four types of mathematical calculation: **addition** (*verb*: **add**; *symbol:* +), **subtraction** (*verbs*: **subtract, take away**; *symbol:* –), **multiplication** (*verb*: **multiply**; *symbol:* ×), **division** (*verb*: **divide**: *symbol:* ÷)

Note: these calculations can be said as follows:
2 + 3 two plus three *or* two and three
9 – 6 nine minus six *or* nine take away six
4 × 2 four multiplied by two *or* four times two
8 ÷ 2 eight divided by two

The answer to a sum is shown by writing the symbol = (called an **equals sign**) or by saying **equals** or **is** ◦ *Two and/plus two is/equals four.*

- a small electronic machine used for calculating numbers: **calculator**

- to multiply sth by two: **double** sth; a number or amount that is two times as big as another one is **twice …, double …** ◦ *Think of a number and then double it.* ◦ *I work twice the hours he does.*
- to multiply sth by three: **treble** sth; a number or amount that is three times as big as another one is **three times …, treble …**

- a number that contains another number an exact number of times: **multiple** ◦ *90 is a multiple of 10.*
- the number you get when you multiply another number by itself: **square**; to multiply a number by itself: **square** sth ◦ *100 is the square of 10.* ◦ *10 squared is 100.*

- a number that produces another number when multiplied by itself: **square root** ◦ *The square root of 49 is 7.*

- the number you get when you add two or more figures together and then divide the total by the number of figures you added: **average**; *adjective*: **average** ◦ *The average of two, three and four is three.*
- the relation between two amounts, calculated by the number of times one is bigger than the other: **ratio** ◦ *The ratio of men to women in the company is three to one.* (written 3:1)

▷ more on averages ⇨ AVERAGE

- to say numbers in their proper order one after the other: **count** ◦ *I learnt to count when I was five.*
- to say numbers one after another until you get to a particular number: **count up to** sth ◦ *Can you count up to 100 in Japanese?*

- to calculate the total number of sth by starting with one and counting upwards: **count** sth ◦ *The teacher counted the children as they got on the bus.*
- the amount that you get when you add two or more numbers together: **total**
- to find a total: **total** sth (**up**), **count** sth **up** ◦ *Count them up and put the total at the bottom.*
- to know/not know how many there are of sth when you are counting: **keep*/lose* count** (**of** sth) ◦ *I can't keep count when there are people asking me questions all the time.* ◦ *I'll have to start again, I've lost count.*
- to count sth again: **re-count** sth: *noun*: **re-count** ◦ *I'm sure there should be more than that – I'd better do a re-count.*

nurse ⇨ HOSPITAL

nut

see also FRUIT, FOOD

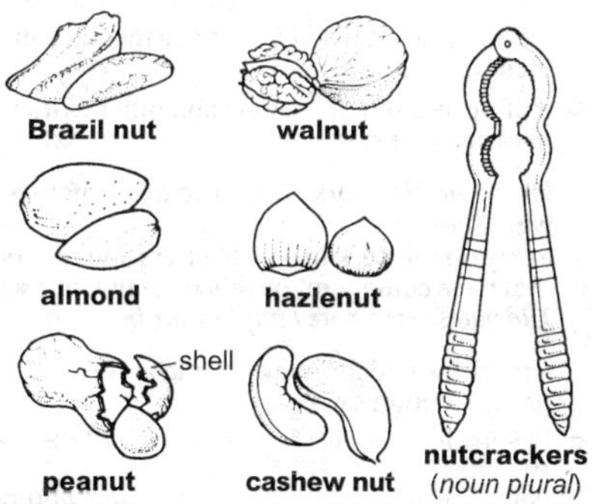

- the hard outside part of a nut: **shell**
- to break open the shell of a nut: **crack** a nut
- containing nuts or tasting of nuts: **nutty** ◦ *a nutty flavour*
- covered with salt: **salted** ◦ *salted peanuts*
- cooked in the oven: **roasted** ◦ *dry-roasted peanuts*
- cut up to be used in cooking: **chopped** ◦ *chopped walnuts*
- made into a powder: **ground** ◦ *ground almonds*

obey

see also ORDER², LAW

- to do what sb tells you to do: **obey** (sb/sth), **do* as** you are **told**; *noun* (U): **obedience**; *adjective*: **obedient** ◦ *to obey an order* ◦ *For once she did as she was told.* ◦ *Our headmaster insisted on absolute obedience.* ◦ *an obedient child*
- to obey a law or a rule: **observe** sth, (*formal*) **comply** (**with** sth); if you obey the law, you are **law-abiding** ◦ *a careless driver who doesn't observe the speed limit* ◦ *All office buildings must comply with fire and safety regulations.* ◦ *a very law-abiding person*

■ not obeying
- to refuse to do what you are told to do: **disobey** (sb/sth); *noun* (U): **disobedience**; *adjective*: **disobedient** ◦ *to disobey an order* ◦ *an act of disobedience* ◦ *a disobedient child*
- to openly refuse to obey sb that you should obey: **defy** sb/sth; *noun* (U): **defiance**; *adjective*: **defiant** (*adverb* **defiantly**) ◦ *Rita defied her parents and stayed out until two o'clock in the morning.* ◦ *They continued to smoke in defiance of the regulations.* ◦ *He turned the music up in an act of defiance.*

- to fight against a law, the government, authority, etc: **rebel** (**against** sb/sth); *noun* (U/C): **rebellion** ◦ *Children sometimes rebel against their parents.* ◦ *an act of rebellion*
- refusing to accept or obey authority: **rebellious** ◦ *rebellious children*
- refusal to obey certain laws in order to protest about sth: **civil disobedience** (*noun* U) ◦ *a campaign of civil disobedience*

obstinate ⇨ WILLING

obtain ⇨ GET/OBTAIN

obvious ⇨ TRUE

odd ⇨ NUMBER

off

- going somewhere ⇨ COME/GO
- at a distance ⇨ DISTANCE
- position ⇨ PLACE²

offer

see also GIVE, INVITE

- to ask sb if they would like sth, or if they would like you to do sth for them: **offer** sb sth, **offer** sth (**to** sb), **offer to** do sth (**for** sb); *noun*: **offer** ◦ *I've been offered a job in Cardiff.* ◦ *a job offer* ◦ *He offered to paint the house for me.* ◦ *Thanks for the offer.*

offer *contd.*

- to offer sb an amount of money for sth: **offer** (sb) sth, **make*** (sb) **an offer** ∘ *How much are they offering for the car?* ∘ *They've made an offer for the house.*

- to say yes to an offer: **accept** sth, **take*** sth **up**, **take*** sb **up on** sth; *noun* (U): **acceptance** ∘ *He immediately accepted my offer.* ∘ *They said they would take up the offer.* ∘ *I think I'll take you up on your offer.*
- to say no to an offer: **turn** sth **down**, **refuse** sth, **reject** sth; *nouns*: **refusal**, **rejection** ∘ *I'm afraid I'll have to turn down your offer/turn your offer down.* ∘ *They made me an offer I couldn't refuse.* ∘ *I can't believe she rejected your offer.* ∘ *Please confirm your acceptance of this offer.*

- if you make an offer to sb and then you decide you do not want to make the offer, you **take*** sth **back**, (*formal*) **withdraw*** sth ∘ *I'm afraid I'll have to take back my offer.* ∘ *If you speak to him like that, he'll just withdraw his offer.*

■ ways of offering sth
- to make an offer, you can say **Would you like ...?** or **Can I ...?** or **Shall I ...?** ∘ *'Would you like me to give you a hand?' 'Thanks for the offer, but I think I'll be all right.'* ∘ *'Can I get you a drink?' 'Yes please – I'd love a beer.'* ∘ *'Shall I carry your bag for you?' 'No thanks, I can manage.'*
- if you are offering food, drink, etc, or if you want to give sth to sb, you can say **Have ...** or **Help yourself ...** ∘ *'Have some more rice.' 'No thank you, I'm full.'* ∘ *I really like this photo.' 'Have it. I'd like to give it to you.'* ∘ *'Help yourself to the cake.' 'Thank you, it looks delicious.'*

Note: we do not use 'please' in English when we are offering sth to sb.

office

see also BUSINESS, MANAGEMENT, WORK

- a room or building used as a place where written work is done, especially connected with business and administration: **office**
- a large building which contains just offices: **office block**

- work that is done in an office is **office work** (*noun* U), **clerical work** (*noun* U)
- the hours during which business is normally done in an office: **office hours** (*noun plural*) ∘ *I usually phone her during/outside office hours.*

■ people in offices
- a person who works in an office: **office worker**, **clerical worker**
- the group of people who work in an office: **office staff** (*noun* U)
- a person who is in charge of an office and tells the other people what to do: **boss**, **office manager**
- a person in an office who makes appointments, answers the telephone, writes letters, etc: **secretary**; *adjective*: **secretarial** ∘ *secretarial staff* ∘ *secretarial skills*
- a secretary who works especially for a senior person in an office, helping to organize their work: **personal assistant**
- a person whose job it is to keep records, accounts, etc in a bank, shop, etc: **clerk** ∘ *a bank clerk*
- a person whose job is to receive clients and to direct them to the right room, office, etc: **receptionist**
- a person whose job is to connect people through the telephone: **telephonist**, **switchboard operator**

▷ more on using the telephone ⇨ TELEPHONE

■ writing letters, etc and doing paper work
- a kind of table used for writing letters, etc and for doing other office work: **desk**
- a machine used for writing letters, etc: **typewriter**
- an electronic machine that can store and arrange information, make calculations and control other machinery: **computer**
- a kind of small computer used for writing: **word processor**
- a person in an office who writes letters, etc using a machine: **typist**
- a person who enters information into a computer: **keyboarder**
- to write sth using a typewriter or word processor: **type** (sth) ∘ *Could you type this letter for me, please?*
- letters, etc that have to be typed: **typing** (*noun* U) ∘ *My boss came in and said he had a lot of typing for me.*
- to say or read aloud a letter, a message, etc, while sb else writes it down: **dictate** sth ∘ *to dictate a letter to a secretary*

▷ more on writing ⇨ WRITE

▷ computers ⇨ COMPUTER

- an informal written message to sb in another office or department of the same company or organization: **memo**, (*formal*) **memorandum**
- a written description of sth that has been done: **report** ∘ *I'm typing a report on last week's meeting.*
- A description of what is said at a meeting: **minutes** (*noun plural*)

▷ writing and sending letters and other written messages ⇨ LETTER[1]

- all the written work done in an office: **paperwork** (*noun* U)
- a tray on the desk in which letters, memos, etc that have come into the office are put: **in-tray** ∘ *Did you see the note I put in your in-tray?*

- a machine which you use to make copies of papers: **photocopier**
- to copy papers with a photocopier: **photocopy** sth
- papers which have to be photocopied: **photocopying** (*noun* U) ∘ *Do you have a lot of photocopying to do?*
- a copy of a paper made with a photocopier: **photocopy** ∘ *Could I have two photocopies of this, please?*

▷ more on copying papers ⇨ COPY
▷ more on looking after papers ⇨ PAPER

official ⇨ GOVERNMENT

often ⇨ HOW OFTEN

oil

1 producing oil
2 different oil products
oil used for cooking ⇨ COOK
see also FUEL, COAL, ELECTRICITY, GAS

1 producing oil

- a thick liquid that comes from under the ground and is used as a fuel or to make machines work smoothly: **oil** (*noun* U), **petroleum** (*noun* U) ◦ *North Sea oil* ◦ *petroleum products like petrol and diesel*
- a hole that is made deep in the ground or under the sea in order to obtain oil: **oil well**
- a structure with equipment to obtain oil from under the sea: **oil rig**, **oil platform**
- a large area where you oil is found: **oilfield**
- to take oil out of the ground: **extract** sth ◦ *Most oil in Northern Europe is extracted from under the sea.*
- to make a hole in the ground to look for oil: **drill for** oil

- an organization that extracts and sells oil: **oil company**
- a place in which oil is stored on land: **oil terminal**
- a long tube that carries oil from an oilfield to an oil terminal: (**oil**) **pipeline**
- a place where oil is made into different products: (**oil**) **refinery**
- a very large boat which is specially designed to carry a lot of oil: (**oil**) **tanker**

- when an oil tanker loses its cargo of oil, there is an **oil spill**
- an area of oil on the surface of the sea, which is the result of a large oil spill: **oil slick**

2 different oil products

- oil that is not refined: **crude oil** (*noun* U)
- refined oil used as a fuel in cars, etc: **petrol** (*AmE* **gasoline**, **gas**) (*noun* U)
- a heavy oil that is used in lorries, buses and some cars: **diesel** (*noun* U)
- a type of fuel made from oil, used for heaters or special engines: **paraffin** (*AmE* **kerosene**) (*noun* U)

- oil that is used to make engines or other machines work smoothly: (**lubricating**) **oil** ◦ *I have to change the oil in the car.*
- to put oil on sth to make an engine or other machine work more smoothly: **oil** sth, **lubricate** sth ◦ *Oil the moving parts of your bicycle carefully.*
- covered with oil or like oil: **oily** ◦ *an oily rag*
- a container for lubricating oil: **oil can**
- a thick oily substance that is used to make parts of machines work more smoothly: **grease** (*noun* U)
- to put grease on sb: **grease** sth
- covered in grease or containing a lot of grease: **greasy**

▷ getting oil and petrol for your car ⇨ DRIVE

old

- not recently made or bought ⇨ NEW/OLD
- not young ⇨ YOUNG/OLD

on ⇨ PLACE[2]

one

see also TWO, HUNDRED, NUMBER

- the number 1: **one** ◦ *One and one are two.* ◦ *I can't lend you my pen – I've only got one and I need it.*
- not done before; before any others: **first** ◦ *This is the first time I've been here.* ◦ *I came first in the swimming competition* (= I won).

▷ being first ⇨ FIRST/NEXT/LAST

- one person: **individual**; of or for one person: **individual** ◦ *the rights of the individual* ◦ *to treat a person as an individual* ◦ *It is difficult for a teacher to give individual attention to children in a large class.*

- only one: **single** (*only before a noun*) ◦ *a single red rose* ◦ *There's not a single person here that I know.*
- as an individual thing: **singly**, **individually** ◦ *You can buy the cassettes singly or in packs of three.*
- containing only one of sth: **single-** ◦ *a single-storey building*
- a bed/room that is for the use of only one person: **single bed/room**

- with no others existing or present: **only**, **the one**, **sole** (*only before a noun*) (*adverb* **solely**) ◦ *She was the only one to understand what I meant.* ◦ *Shellfish are the one thing I can't eat.* ◦ *He was the sole survivor of the disaster.* ◦ *I was solely responsible for the accident.*
- if you do sth with no other person present or helping you, you are **alone**, **on** your **own**, **by yourself** ◦ *Are you alone?* ◦ *She brought up four children entirely on her own.* ◦ *I can do it by myself, thank you very much.*

▷ being alone or doing things on your own ⇨ ALONE

▷ not alone; together ⇨ TOGETHER

■ one time only

- one time only; on one occasion: **once** ◦ *I go swimming once a week.* ◦ *I've only been here once before.*
- one more time: **once more** ◦ *I'll just try ringing her once more.*
- something unusual, happening only once: (*informal*) **one-off** ◦ *She got a very high mark in her exam but it was just a one-off.*

only ⇨ HOW MUCH/MANY

open/shut

1 being open or shut
2 making sth open or shut
3 shops, offices, etc being open or shut

opening or closing bottles and other containers ⇨ CONTAINER

1 being open or shut

– a door, window, etc that allows people or things to move in, out, through, etc is **open** ◦ *an open door/window/gate*
– completely open: **wide open** ◦ *She left the window wide open.* ◦ *a wide-open door*
– (used about a door) slightly open: **ajar** (*not before a noun*) ◦ *The door was ajar so I could hear what they were saying.*

– a door, window, etc that does not allow people or things to move in, out, through, etc is **shut** (*not before a noun*), **closed** ◦ *Is the window shut? It's very cold in here.* ◦ *a closed door/window/drawer*

– to become open: **open** ◦ *The door opened and in walked Charles.*
– to become closed: **shut***, **close** ◦ *The window won't shut.* ◦ *I got out of the lift and I heard the door closing behind me.*

2 making sth open or shut

– to make sth open: **open** sth ◦ *to open a letter/window/door/gate/book* ◦ *We all watched with growing excitement as he opened the box.*
– to make sth open by breaking it, smashing it, splitting it, slitting it, tearing it, etc: **break*/smash/split*/slit*/tear*** sth **open** ◦ *He used a large axe to break open the metal box.* ◦ *She tore open the parcel and pulled out a beautiful doll.*

– to make sth closed: **shut*** sth, **close** sth ◦ *Please shut the door.* ◦ *Close your eyes and go to sleep.* ◦ *to close a door/window/gate/book*
– to shut sth very loudly and with great force: **slam** sth, **bang/slam** sth **shut**; (used about a door, etc) to shut with a loud noise: **slam (shut)**, **bang shut** ◦ *She got up angrily and left the room, slamming the door behind her.* ◦ *I heard the door bang shut in the wind.*

– something that is used for fastening a door, lid, etc so that you need a key to open it: **lock**
– to close sth using a lock: **lock** sth; to open sth using a lock: **unlock** sth ◦ *to lock/unlock a door/car/suitcase*

– to keep sb/sth out of a place by keeping it closed: **shut*** sb/sth **out** (**of** a place) ◦ *They shut the dog out of the house during the day.* ◦ *They closed the window to shut out the noise.*
– to keep sb/sth in a place by keeping it closed: **shut*** sb/sth (**up**) **in** sth, **lock** sb/sth (**up**) **in** sth ◦ *They took her prisoner and shut her up in small dark room.*

▷ locks ⇨ LOCK/CHAIN

– to fix, join or shut and lock sth firmly: **fasten** sth ◦ *fasten your shoe laces* ◦ *fasten your seat belts*
– to fasten a piece of clothing: **do*** sth **up** ◦ *Do up your shoe laces.*

– to open or close curtains: **draw* the curtains** ◦ *It was getting dark so I drew the curtains and switched on the lights.*
– to open the door after sb has knocked or rung the bell: **answer the door** ◦ *Can somebody answer the door please?*

3 shops, offices, etc being open or shut

– when a shop, office, etc is open for business, it is **open**; when it starts business for the day, it **opens** ◦ *Are the shops open today?* ◦ *What time do the shops open?*
– when a shop, office, etc is not open, it is **closed**, **shut** (*not before a noun*); when it finishes business for the day, it **shuts*** ◦ *They shut during the lunch hour.*
– the time when a shop, office, etc is normally open: **opening hours** (*noun plural*), **business hours** (*noun plural*)

opera ⇨ MUSIC

operation

see also DOCTOR, HOSPITAL, ILLNESS, MEDICINE

– a form of medical treatment in which your body is cut open so that part of it can be removed or treated: **operation**, **surgery** (*noun* U); *adjective*: **surgical** ◦ *The operation on his shoulder was a success.* ◦ *an operation for appendicitis* ◦ *She needs emergency surgery.* ◦ *surgical instruments*
– to do an operation: **operate** (**on** sb), **perform an operation** (**on** sb) ◦ *They decided to operate immediately.* ◦ *perform a kidney operation*
– to go to hospital for an operation: **have an operation** ◦ *When is she going to have her hip replacement operation?*
– to have an operation in which sth will be removed: **have** sth **out** ◦ *I've got to have my appendix out.*

– a big operation is a **major** operation; *opposite*: **minor**
– when you get better after an operation you **recover** (**from** the operation), **make* a good/complete recovery**

– a doctor who performs operations: **surgeon** ◦ *a brain/heart surgeon*
– the room in a hospital where operations are done: **operating-theatre**, **theatre** (*AmE* **theater**) ◦ *He's just been taken into theatre.*
– the table on which a patient lies during an operation: **operating-table**

– the place where patients who are very seriously ill or injured receive special care: **intensive care** (*noun* U) ◦ *She's still in intensive care.*

– a substance that stops you feeling pain when a doctor is performing an operation on you: **anaesthetic** (*AmE* **anesthetic**); one that only affects part of the body and does not make you unconscious: **local anaesthetic**; one that makes you unconscious: **general anaesthetic**

- a person who gives anaesthetics to patients: **anaesthetist** (*AmE* **anesthetist**)
- to give sb an anaesthetic: **anaesthetize** (*AmE* **anesthetize**) sb
- putting one person's blood into another person's body: (**blood**) **transfusion** ∘ *He was given several transfusions during the operation.*

- to cut off a person's arm or leg, or part of it: **amputate** sth; *noun* (C/U): **amputation** ∘ *The doctors decided to amputate his leg below the knee.* ∘ *They're hoping that amputation won't be necessary.*
- an operation in which a part of one person's body is taken out and put into another person's body: **transplant**; *verb*: **transplant** sth ∘ *a heart transplant*
- a medical condition in the body that cannot be treated by an operation is **inoperable** ∘ *He was suffering from an inoperable cancer.*

---

opinion

1 having opinions
2 forming and changing opinions
3 saying what you think

see also KNOW, THINK

1 having opinions

- what you think about sb/sth: **opinion** (*noun* C/u), **idea**, **thought**, **view** ∘ *What's your opinion of the new chairman?* ∘ *a wide range of opinions* ∘ *She has her own ideas about how to deal with violence against women.* ∘ *Can you give us your thoughts on the subject?* ∘ *I've never made any secret of my views on the matter.*
- what people in general think: **opinion** (*noun* U) ∘ *Public opinion is against the new legislation.*

- to have an opinion about sth: **think*/feel*** sth (**about** sb/sth), **think*/feel*** (**that**), (*formal*) **be of the opinion that . . .** ∘ *What do you think about the idea?* ∘ *I felt that he made the wrong decision.* ∘ *Most people are of the opinion that he should resign.*
- to have an opinion about sth (because of your own experience): **find* . . .** ∘ *I find him rather rude.* ∘ *She finds his films rather boring.*

- a strong opinion: **belief**; to hold a strong belief: **believe** (**that**) **. . .** ∘ *a strong belief in private enterprise*

▷ more on belief ⇨ TRUE

- the way you think and feel about sb/sth: **attitude** (**to/towards** sb/sth) ∘*He has a rather careless attitude towards his schoolwork.*
- the way that sb looks at a particular situation: **point of view**, **position** ∘ *He's always supported that point of view.* ∘ *The Prime Minister made his position very clear.*
- a person's way of looking at life, etc: **outlook** (**on** sth) ∘ *an optimistic outlook on life*

- an opinion that you cannot explain exactly: **feeling**, **impression** ∘ *The general feeling was that we should not go.* ∘ *I had the impression that he didn't want to take the test.*
- an opinion which may not be based on real evidence: **theory** ∘ *She had a theory that television sets caused harmful radiation.*

▷ more on feelings and impressions ⇨ LOOK/SEEM

- to have the same opinion as sb else: **agree** (**with** sb) (**on/about** sth); to have a different opinion from sb else: **disagree** (**with** sb) ∘ *For once we agree about something!* ∘ *I disagree with you.*
- a subject which people disagree about: **a matter of opinion** ∘ *Of course it's a matter of opinion whether the government is doing a good job.*

▷ agreeing and disagreeing in a discussion ⇨ DISCUSS/ARGUE

■ good and bad opinions

- to think that sb/sth is good or acceptable: **approve** (**of** sb/sth); *opposite*: **disapprove** (**of** sb/sth) ∘ *Her mother doesn't approve of her new boyfriend.*
- to think that sb/sth is good: **have a good/high opinion of** sb/sth, **think* highly of** sb/sth ∘ *I've always thought highly of Jane.*
- to think that sb/sth is bad: **have a bad/low opinion of** sb/sth

- if your opinion of sth is good, you can say that you **like the sound of** it, it **sounds like a good idea**, it is **a good thing** ∘ *I don't like the sound of the new proposals.* ∘ *It would be a good thing if you apologized.*

- the opinion that people in general have about sb/sth: **reputation** ∘ *That restaurant's got a very good reputation.*
- to have a high opinion of sb/sth: **respect** sb/sth
- the feeling that you have when you have a very high opinion of sb/sth: **respect** (**for** sb/sth)
- showing respect for sb: **respectful** ∘ *respectful behaviour*

2 forming and changing opinions

- to form an opinion: **make* up** your **mind** (**about** sth) ∘ *Should children learn foreign languages in primary school? I can't make up my mind about that.*

- to reach a belief or opinion as a result of thinking about sth or studying sth: **conclude that . . .**; *noun*: **conclusion** ∘ *The jury concluded that he was not involved in the robbery.* ∘ *We discussed the matter at length, but unfortunately we couldn't reach a conclusion.*

- having considered everything: **all in all, altogether, all things considered** ∘ *All in all, he seems to have done a good job.* ∘ *All things considered, it was a good choice.*
- when first seen or considered: **at first sight** ∘ *At first sight it seemed like a good idea.*

- to change your opinion: **change** your **mind** (**about** sb/sth) ∘ *I hope he changes his mind about the visit.*

opinion *contd.*

3 saying what you think

- if you give your opinions and do not try to hide them, you are **open** about them, you speak **openly** ◦ *I wish you would be more open with me about what you think of her.*
- to say openly what your opinions are: **speak*** your **mind** ◦ *He's never afraid to speak his mind in public.*

- to give different opinions: **argue** (**with** sb) (**about** sth); *noun* (C/U): **argument** ◦ *They're always arguing about what to do.* ◦ *Let's not have an argument!*

▷ more on arguing ⇨ DISCUSS/ARGUE

- to introduce sth that is your opinion, you can say **I think** (**that**) . . ., **I feel** (**that**) . . ., **in my opinion** ◦ *I think we should go ahead with the plan.* ◦ *I feel that we should give him another chance.* ◦ *In my opinion, we should never have come.*
- if you want to emphasize that you are giving your own opinion, you can say **personally** ◦ *Personally, I think he should have resigned.*

- to show that you are giving your opinion openly and honestly, you can say **frankly, to be honest, to be frank** ◦ *Frankly, you're taking a terrible risk.* ◦ *To be perfectly honest, I don't think she has any chance at all.*

■ **MORE . . .**

- if you are willing to listen to and accept other people's opinions, you are **broad-minded**, you **have/keep* an open mind** ◦ *We should keep an open mind about the matter.*
- to allow other people to have different opinions from you: **tolerate** sth ◦ *He's prepared to tolerate a wide range of views on the issue.*

- a feeling of liking or disliking of sb/sth, which is not based on reason or experience: **prejudice** (*noun* C/U); *adjective*: **prejudiced** ◦ *He has a prejudice against women drivers.*
- having very strong and unreasonable opinions: **bigoted** ◦ *There's no point in arguing with such bigoted people.*

opposite ⇨ DIFFERENT

or ⇨ AND/OR/BUT

orchestra

see also MUSIC

- a large group of musicians who play different musical instruments together: **orchestra**; connected with an orchestra: **orchestral** ◦ *a symphony orchestra* ◦ *a chamber orchestra orchestral music*
- the area in front of the stage in a theatre where an orchestra may sit for a play or an opera: **orchestra pit**

- to stand in front of an orchestra and direct it: **conduct** (sth) ◦ *Who will be conducting this evening?* ◦ *a recording of Beethoven's Fifth Symphony conducted by Klemperer*
- a person who conducts an orchestra: **conductor** ◦ *the conductor of the London Symphony Orchestra* ◦ *a guest conductor*
- a stick that the conductor of an orchestra uses: **baton**

■ sections of the orchestra

- something that is used for playing music: (**musical**) **instrument** ◦ *orchestral instruments*

- all the orchestral instruments that have strings: **the strings** (*noun plural*); *adjective*: **stringed** ◦ *a serenade for strings* ◦ *stringed instruments*

- a musical instrument that you blow to produce a sound: **wind instrument** ◦ *The trumpet and the clarinet are both wind instruments.*
- the group of wind instruments that are made of wood: **the woodwind** (*with singular or plural verb*); *adjective*: **woodwind**
- the group of wind instruments that are made of brass: **the brass** (*with singular or plural verb*); *adjective*: **brass** ◦ *The brass was far too loud.* ◦ *the brass section* ◦ *brass instruments*

- the section of an orchestra that consists of instruments that you play by hitting them: **the percussion** (*with singular or plural verb*); *adjective*: **percussion** ◦ *percussion instruments*
- a person who plays percussion instruments: **percussionist**

▷ more on musical instruments and their players ⇨ MUSIC

order[1]

- how sth is arranged ⇨ ORGANIZE
- sequence ⇨ FIRST/NEXT/LAST

order[2] saying that sb must do sth

see also OBEY, REQUEST

- to say to sb that they must do sth: **tell*** sb **to** do sth, **order** sb **to** do sth ◦ *He told me to get my hair cut.* ◦ *You'll be all right if you do as you're told.* ◦ *We were ordered to get out of the car.*
- an act of saying that sb must do sth: **order**; in the army, police force, etc an order is sometimes called a **command** ◦ *to carry out an order* ◦ *He refused to obey my orders.* ◦ *He gave the command to open fire.*

- to tell sb officially that they should do sth: **direct** sb **to** do sth, **instruct** sb **to** do sth; *noun*: **instruction** ◦ *They were directed to close down the factory.* ◦ *I've been instructed to show you around.* ◦ *I want you to make sure he carries out my instructions.*
- to say very strongly that sb must do sth: **insist that . . .**; *noun* (U): **insistence**; *adjective*: **insistent** ◦ *They refused to get married in spite of their parents' insistence.* ◦ *She was most insistent that we should come.*

- to keep telling sb to do things in an unpleasant way: **order** sb **about/around**, (*informal*) **boss** sb (**about/around**), (*informal*) **push** sb **about/around** ◦ *He loves ordering people about.* ◦ *Stop*

bossing me around! ◦ *She lets herself get pushed around by the boss.*
- a person who likes ordering other people around is (*informal*) **bossy** ◦ *He's one of the bossiest people I've ever met.*

■ ordering sb not to do sth
- to tell sb they cannot do sth: **forbid*** (sb **to** do) sth, **ban** (sb **from** doing) sth, (*formal*) **prohibit** (sb **from** doing) sth; an act of forbidding sth: (*formal*) **prohibition** (*noun* U) ◦ *They've been forbidden to go back into the school.* ◦ *He's been banned from driving for a year.* ◦ *Smoking is strictly prohibited.*
- a law or rule that forbids sth: **ban, prohibition** ◦ *a ban on tobacco advertising*

ordinary ⇨ USUAL

organize

organizing an event ⇨ INTEND/PLAN
managing a company ⇨ MANAGEMENT

- to put things in the particular way that you want them to be: **organize** sth, **arrange** sth ◦ *a well organized office* ◦ *The book has 20 chapters organized into four sections.* ◦ *We have arranged the room in the most practical way possible.* ◦ *She's very good at arranging flowers.*
- a particular way of organizing or arranging sth: **organization, arrangement** ◦ *We were particularly impressed by the organization of the warehouse.* ◦ *Do you like the new arrangement in here?*
- to change the way sth is arranged: **reorganize** (sth), **rearrange** sth; *noun* (U): **reorganization** ◦ *I'm going to reorganize the timetable for next week.* ◦ *Do we need to rearrange the furniture?*
- a list, drawing or diagram that shows how sth is to be organized: **plan** ◦ *This is the plan for our new kitchen.*

- when everything is in its right place, it is **in order, tidy**; to make sth tidy: **tidy** sth, (*informal*) **sort** sth **out** ◦ *It took me three hours to put all my papers in order.* ◦ *a tidy desk/bedroom* ◦ *We need to tidy the house before the guests arrive.* ◦ *I spent the afternoon sorting out the mess in the children's room.*

▷ more on making things tidy ⇨ TIDY

- the way in which people or things have been arranged in relation to each other: **order** (*noun* U) ◦ *alphabetical order* ◦ *in order of size* ◦ *a list of dates in chronological order* (= the order in which things happened)
- to put things into groups: **sort** sth (**into** sth) ◦ *Please sort these papers into the correct files.*

- a set of rules or ideas for organizing sth: **system**; a thing that is done using a system is **systematic** ◦ *The Council have established a new system for recycling rubbish.* ◦ *We have a very complicated filing system in our office.* ◦ *a systematic approach to training*
- the way that the parts of sth are put together or organized: **structure**; to give sth a particular structure: **structure** sth ◦ *the political structure of a country* ◦ *The course has been carefully structured to meet the students' needs.*
- if you are good at organizing things and you can work well without making mistakes or wasting time or energy, you are **efficient**; *noun* (U): **efficiency** ◦ *a very efficient manager* ◦ *Our boss wants to improve the company's efficiency.*

■ not tidy or well organized
- the state of being untidy: **mess, muddle** ◦ *This room is in a mess.* ◦ *What a muddle! I can't find anything!*
- a lack of order or organization: **disorder** (*noun* U), **confusion** (*noun* U) ◦ *His financial affairs are in complete disorder.*
- not in good order: **out of order** ◦ *The book had fallen apart and all the pages were out of order.*
- not in its proper place: **out of place** ◦ *She doesn't like anything to be out of place.*

- something that is not well organized is **disorganized, confused, untidy**; if sth has no order or organized plan, it is **haphazard** ◦ *His filing system seems to be completely haphazard.*
- a state of great disorder: **chaos** (*noun* U); in a state of chaos: **chaotic** ◦ *The accident has caused chaos on the motorway.* ◦ *a chaotic situation*

other

- something different ⇨ DIFFERENT
- something added ⇨ MORE[2]

ought ⇨ MUST

out/outside ⇨ PLACE[2]

over ⇨ PLACE[2]

owe ⇨ DEBT

own ⇨ HAVE/POSSESS

packet ⇨ CONTAINER

page

see also BOOK, PAPER

- a piece of paper which forms part of a book, magazine, etc: **page** ◦ *Somebody's torn out the first page of this book.*
- one of the two surfaces of a piece of paper: **side**; one side of a piece of paper (especially in a book, etc, or when you are writing sth) **page** ◦ *Write on both sides of the paper.* ◦ *Just write one page, explaining your reasons for wanting the job.* ◦ *The picture is on page 4.* ◦ *a blank page* (= with nothing written on it)
- the first/last page of a newspaper: **front/back page**

- the empty space at the side of a page: **margin** ◦ *Leave a margin on the left.*
- the lower part of a page: **foot, bottom** ◦ *The details are at the foot of the page.*
- the upper part of a page: **top** ◦ *Write your name at the top of the page.*
- the number which is written on a page in a book, etc: **page number**

page *contd.*

– when we want to write a page number, we can use the short form: **p** (*plural* **pp**) ◦ *p23* ◦ *pp34-38*
– to look at the next page: **turn** (**over**) the page; to look at a previous page: **turn back** ◦ *If you turn the page you will see a photo of the writer.* ◦ *Turn back to page 20.*
– if you want the reader to turn the page because there is some important information on the other side, you can write **PTO** at the foot of the page; this stands for 'please turn over'

pain

1 feeling pain
2 showing pain
3 reducing pain
4 wanting to cause pain
see also ILLNESS, SUFFER

1 feeling pain

– the unpleasant feeling that you have when part of your body has been hurt or when you are ill: **pain** (*noun* C/U) ◦ *I've got a dreadful pain in my back.* ◦ *Is she in pain?*
– to cause pain: **hurt*** (sb/sth) ◦ *My toe hurts.* ◦ *Stop it. You're hurting me!* ◦ *It hurts a lot just above the knee.*
– to cause a sharp pain: **sting*** (sth) ◦ *Soap stings your eyes.* ◦ *This ointment will sting a bit.*
– a pain which is not sharp but which lasts a long time: **ache**; *verb*: **ache** ◦ *the aches and pains of old age* ◦ *My leg has been aching all day.*
– a pain which lasts a short time only: **attack** ◦ *a sudden attack of toothache*

– something which causes pain is **painful**; *opposite*: **painless** ◦ *a painful illness* ◦ *a painless operation*
– to experience pain: **suffer** (**from** sth); *noun* (U): **suffering** ◦ *Jane suffers from severe headaches.* ◦ *The famine caused great hardship and suffering.*
– to live with pain: **put* up with** sth, **bear*** sth, (*formal*) **endure** sth ◦ *He had to put up with a great deal of pain.* ◦ *The pain was almost more than he could bear.*

– a part of your body which feels painful is **sore**; *noun* (U): **soreness** ◦ *I've got a sore throat.* ◦ *My finger still feels sore.*
– a part of your body which is painful when you touch it is **tender** ◦ *Don't touch my arm. It's still tender from the injection.*

– pain which is not very bad: **discomfort** ◦ *She felt a mild discomfort in her stomach.*
– to cause slight pain or soreness: **irritate** sb/sth, **bother** sb ◦ *Very bright sunlight irritates her eyes.* ◦ *'Does your tooth still hurt?' 'A bit, but it's not bothering me as much as it did.'*
– very bad pain: **agony** (*noun* U) ◦ *After breaking my arm, I was in absolute agony.*
– a pain that is very strong is **acute**, **agonizing**, **bad**
– a very strong and sudden pain is **sharp**; *opposite*: **dull** ◦ *a sharp pain* ◦ *a dull ache*

■ pain in different parts of the body
– in the head: **headache** ◦ *I've got a terrible headache.*
– in the throat: **sore throat** ◦ *Have you got a sore throat?*
– in the ear: **earache** (*noun* U) ◦ *I've got earache.*
– in a tooth: **toothache** (*noun* C/U)
– in the back: **backache** (*noun* C/U), **back pain** (*noun* C/U)
– in the stomach: **stomach-ache** (*noun* C/U), (*more informal*) **tummy-ache**

– a very bad headache that makes you feel ill: **migraine** (*noun* C/U) ◦ *to have a bad migraine* ◦ *to suffer from migraine*
– a sudden pain that you get in the side of your body, for example after running: **stitch**
– a sudden pain that is the result of an insect or plant pushing sth sharp into the skin: **sting**

Note: in British English we always say **a** headache, but the other aches are normally used without an article: ◦ *I've got toothache.* In American English, **a** or **an** is usually used with aches: ◦ *I have a toothache.*

2 showing pain

■ movements
– if your body is bent as a result of bad pain, you are **doubled up in/with pain**
– to make a sudden quick movement of your face as a result of pain: **wince** ◦ *He winced when the nurse gave him the injection.*

■ sounds
– to shout or make a loud noise: **cry** (**out**); *noun*: **cry** ◦ *She cried out in pain.* ◦ *a terrible cry of pain*
– a loud and sharp cry: **yell**, **shriek**; *verbs*: **yell**, **shriek** ◦ *a yell of pain* ◦ *He gave a sudden shriek.*
– a loud long cry: **howl**; *verb*: **howl** ◦ *He let out a long howl of pain.* ◦ *One of the victims was howling with pain.*
– a loud high cry: **scream**; *verb*: **scream** ◦ *She started screaming even before the dentist had touched her!*
– a deep cry: **groan**; *verb*: **groan** ◦ *He gave an awful groan.*
– a low sad cry: **moan**; *verb*: **moan** ◦ *The child was moaning quietly to herself.*

– to express a sudden sharp pain, you can say **ow!** or **ouch!** ◦ *Ow! I've pricked my finger.*

3 reducing pain

– to stop or reduce pain: **relieve** sth; *noun* (U): **relief** ◦ *I couldn't get any relief from the pain in my back.*
– to make pain less severe: **soothe** sth ◦ *a lotion which soothes sunburn*

– a medicine that is used for reducing or stopping pain: **painkiller** ◦ *to take a couple of painkillers*
– a substance that stops you feeling pain when a doctor is performing an operation on you: **anaesthetic** (*AmE* **anesthetic**) (*noun* C/U)

4 wanting to cause pain

– to cause pain to sb/sth badly or repeatedly: **torment** sb/sth ◦ *Stop tormenting that poor dog!*

- deliberately causing physical or mental pain to sb: **cruel** (*adverb* **cruelly**); *noun* (U): **cruelty**
- the act of causing very great pain to a person as a punishment or to get information out of them: **torture** (*noun* C/U); *verb*: **torture** sb

▷ being cruel ⇨ KIND/CRUEL

paint[1] painting pictures

painting a room ⇨ PAINT[2]
see also ART, PICTURE, DRAW

- to create pictures with paint: **paint** (sth); *noun* (U): **painting** ◦ *to paint a picture of a person/place* ◦ *Painting is my favourite hobby.*
- a person who paints pictures: **painter** ◦ *a portrait/landscape painter*
- a person who produces art, especially paintings and drawings: **artist**
- a picture that is painted: **painting**

■ things which are used for painting

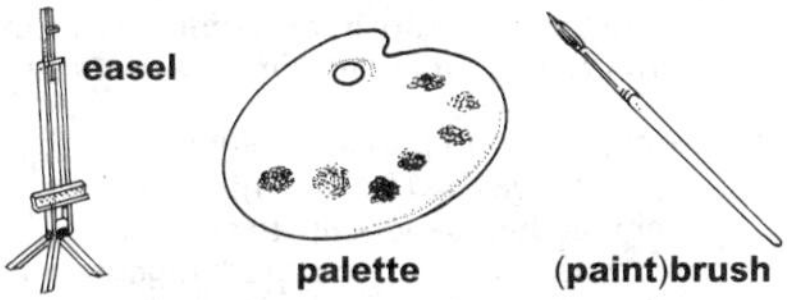

- coloured liquid used for painting: **paint** (*noun* U)
- a collection of tubes, blocks, etc of paint that an artist uses: **paints** (*noun plural*) ◦ *I'll bring my paints tomorrow.*
- a box of paints: **paintbox**
- paints that are mixed with oil: **oil paints** (*noun plural*), **oils** (*noun plural*); a painting done with oil paints: **oil painting** ◦ *He prefers working in oils.*
- paints that are mixed with water: **watercolours** (*noun plural*); a painting done with watercolours: **watercolour**

- strong cloth for painting on with oil paints: **canvas** (*noun* C/U); a finished painting on this material: **canvas**

paint[2] painting a house, a room, etc

looking after a house ⇨ REPAIR
painting a picture ⇨ PAINT[1]

- to put paint onto a surface: **paint** (sth) ◦ *John's busy painting.* ◦ *to paint the bathroom/ceiling/front door*
- when you use paint, you **put*** it **on**, (*formal*) **apply** it
- a layer of paint: **coat** (of paint); the first coat you put on: **undercoat**; the last coat you put on: **topcoat** ◦ *Will one litre of paint be enough for two coats?*

- after paint has been put onto a surface, it takes some time to **dry**; during this time, it is **wet** ◦ *Careful! It's still wet.*

- to put paint, wallpaper, etc onto walls, ceilings and doors in a room or building: **decorate** (sth), **do* the decorating**; the way a house, etc is decorated: **decoration** (*noun* U) ◦ *We decorated the living room ourselves.* ◦ *Who does the decorating in your household?* ◦ *I like the house, but not the decoration.*
- a person who paints the inside or outside of buildings: **painter, decorator**

■ things that are used for painting
- coloured liquid used for painting: **paint** (*noun* U)
- you can spread paint with a **roller** (= a cylinder covered in material) or a **paintbrush** (picture at BRUSH).
- paint that is used for painting doors, etc and which looks shiny when it is dry: **gloss** (**paint**) (*noun* U)
- paint that is not shiny: **matt** (**paint**) (*noun* U)
- paint that is often used for walls and ceilings: **emulsion** (**paint**) (*noun* U)
- a kind of colourless paint that is used to protect wood and metal, especially furniture: **varnish** (*noun* U); to put varnish on sth: **varnish** (sth)
- a kind of white paint that is often used for walls: **whitewash** (*noun* U); to put whitewash on sth: **whitewash** (sth) ◦ *All the houses in the village were whitewashed.*
- paint which is used directly from an aerosol can: **spray paint** (*noun* U)

■ removing paint
- to remove paint from a surface with the sharp edge of a tool: **scrape** (the paint) **off** (sth); the tool that is used: **scraper** ◦ *It took hours to scrape the paint off all the doors.*
- to remove old paint with heat or a flame: **burn** (the paint) **off**
- to make a surface smooth before you paint it: **rub** (sth) **down, sandpaper** sth ◦ *Rub the door down thoroughly.*
- liquid that removes old paint from surfaces: **paint stripper** (*noun* U)

paper

1 paper
2 for wrapping
3 for cleaning
4 for writing and office work
5 unwanted paper
see also OFFICE

1 paper
- a material that you use for wrapping things in, writing on and drawing on: **paper** (*noun* U) ◦ *The printer is out of paper.* ◦ *a paper bag* ◦ *a piece of paper*
- a piece of paper for writing or printing on, usually in a standard size: **sheet** (of paper)
- without writing or printing on it: **blank, clean** ◦ *He gave us a blank sheet of paper and told us to draw a picture.* ◦ *Take a clean sheet of paper and start again.*
- one of the two surfaces of a piece of paper: **side** ◦ *Write on both sides of the paper.*

paper *contd.*

- a piece of paper which forms part of a book, magazine, etc: **page**

▷ more on pages in books ⇨ PAGE

- a small piece of paper: **scrap** ◦ *a scrap of paper*
- a long, thin piece of paper: **strip**
- strong paper which does not bend easily: **card** (*noun* U)
- strong card used for making boxes, etc: **cardboard** (*noun* U)

■ folding, tearing, etc

- to turn a piece of paper onto itself: **fold** sth; *opposite*: **unfold** sth ◦ *Fold the map carefully.* ◦ *Take a sheet of paper and fold it in two.*
- to pull a piece of paper so that it comes apart: **tear*** sth ◦ *He tore the page out of the book and put it in his pocket.*
- to become torn: **tear*** ◦ *Be careful! If you pull it, it'll tear.*
- to pull sth made of paper into pieces: **tear*** sth **up** ◦ *She tore up his photo.*
- to tear sth suddenly and violently into small pieces: **rip** sth **up** ◦ *I was so angry, I ripped the letter up and threw it in the bin.*

2 for wrapping

- shiny paper that is used to cover chocolates, etc: **silver paper** (*noun* U)
- paper that is used for wrapping sth up in order to send it: **brown paper** (*noun* U)
- thin soft paper that is used for handkerchiefs, for wrapping things so that they will not break, etc: **tissue** (**paper**) (*noun* U)
- paper that is used to cover a present before you give it to sb: **wrapping paper** (*noun* U)
- a piece of paper which covers sth when you buy it: **wrapper** ◦ *a sweet wrapper*
- to cover sth in paper in order to send it or to give it as a present: **wrap** sth (**up**) (**in** sth) ◦ *The present was wrapped in beautiful red shiny paper.*
- to take the paper off sth: **unwrap** sth, **undo*** sth, **open** sth ◦ *Unwrap it carefully.* ◦ *'Can I open my present now?' 'No, you have to wait until your birthday.'*

3 for cleaning

- a soft thin piece of paper which you use as a handkerchief, then throw away: **tissue** ◦ *a box of tissues*
- tissue paper that you use to clean yourself in a toilet: **toilet paper** (*noun* U); a roll of toilet paper: **toilet roll**
- tissue paper that is used in a kitchen: **kitchen paper** (*noun* U); a roll of kitchen paper: **kitchen roll**

4 for writing and office work

- paper that is used for writing letters: **writing paper** (*noun* U), **notepaper** (*noun* U)
- a number of pieces of paper that are fastened together at one end: **pad** ◦ *a note pad* ◦ *a pad of writing paper*
- a piece of paper containing important information: **paper** (*usually plural*), **document** ◦ *There's a big pile of papers on his desk.* ◦ *an important document*
- work consisting of reading papers or writing information on paper: **paperwork** (*noun* U) ◦ *I have to do more and more paperwork these days.*
- a set of papers relating to a person or subject: **file**
- to put a paper or papers in their correct place in a file: **file** sth **away** ◦ *I filed it away and forgot about it.*
- the job of putting documents in files: **filing** (*noun* U) ◦ *I spent all afternoon doing the filing.*
- an envelope or cover used for keeping papers together: **folder**, **file**
- a metal box with drawers used for keeping files in an office: **filing cabinet**
- a piece of paper on which you give information for official reasons: **form** ◦ *an application form for a driving-licence*
- to write the necessary information on a form: **fill** sth **in** ◦ *How do I fill in the form/fill the form in?*

■ holding pieces of paper together

- a piece of wire used for attaching pieces of paper together: **paper-clip**; to attach pieces of paper with a paper-clip: **clip** sth **together** ◦ *I'll clip these together so we don't lose them.*
- a small piece of wire that you push through pieces of paper with a special tool to hold them together: **staple**; to attach pieces of paper with a staple: **staple** sth (**together**) ◦ *Staple the pages of your essay together before you hand it in.*
- the tool used for attaching pieces of paper with staples: **stapler**
- a very short piece of pointed metal with a round head, used for attaching paper to the wall or to a notice board: **drawing pin** (*AmE* **thumbtack**)
- a general term for paper, pens, pencils, etc: **stationery** (*noun* U)
- a person who sells paper and other writing materials: **stationer**
- a shop where you can buy stationery: **stationer's**

5 unwanted paper

- paper that is not wanted but that can be used again: **scrap paper** (*noun* U) ◦ *Have you got some scrap paper I could use to write a shopping list?*
- paper that is not wanted and is to be thrown away: **waste paper** (*noun* U)
- to process waste paper so that it can be used again: **recycle** sth; *adjective*: **recycled** ◦ *This card is printed on recycled paper.*
- a container in which you put paper, etc that you want to throw away: (**rubbish**) **bin**, **waste-paper basket** (*AmE* **waste-basket**, **waste-bin**) ◦ *'Do you want this letter?' 'No, put it in the bin please.'*
- a bin which you find in the street: **litter bin**
- pieces of paper, etc which people have thrown away in a bin or on the street: **litter** (*noun* U)

parcel

see also POST

- something which is covered with paper and sent through the post: **parcel** (*AmE also* **package**) ◦ *I've got to go and collect a parcel from the Post Office.* ◦ *a parcel of books*
- a parcel that is delivered by hand or that has an unusual shape: **package**
- paper that is used for wrapping sth up in order to send it: **brown paper** (*noun* U)
- paper which is used to cover a present before you give it to sb: **wrapping paper** (*noun* U)

▷ using paper to wrap a parcel, etc ⇨ PAPER

- thin cord that is used for tying round a parcel: **string** ◦ *We tied the parcel up with string.*
- sticky paper that is used for holding a package together: **tape** (*noun* U), **sellotape** (*noun* U); to put sellotape on sth: **sellotape** sth
- a piece of paper or card on which you write the name and address of the person you are sending a parcel to: **label**

parent ⇨ FAMILY, CHILD

parliament

1 parliaments and their members
2 working in parliament
see also GOVERNMENT, POLITICS

1 parliaments and their members

- a group of people who discuss and make the laws of a country; the place where they meet: **parliament**; *adjective*: **parliamentary** ◦ *parliamentary democracy*
- in different countries this institution is called **Parliament** (*noun singular*), **Congress** (*noun singular*), the **National Assembly** ◦ *Parliament* (= the UK Parliament) *has agreed to send aid to the area.*
- connected with Congress: **congressional** ◦ *a congressional committee*
- many parliaments consist of two parts: a **lower house** and an **upper house**
- in the British Parliament, the lower house is the **House of Commons, the Commons**; the upper house is the **House of Lords, the Lords**
- in the United States Congress, the lower house is the **House of Representatives**; the upper house is the **Senate**
- a person who has been elected to Parliament, Congress, etc: **member** (**of** sth)
- a member of the House of Commons: **Member of Parliament** (**MP**)
- a member of the European Parliament: **MEP** (Member of the European Parliament)
- a member of the House of Lords: **peer**; a male peer is called **Lord ...**; a female peer is called **Lady ...** ◦ *Lord Owen* ◦ *Lady Thatcher*
- a member of the US House of Representatives: **Congressman/woman** (*plural* **Congressmen/women**) ◦ *Congressman Jones*
- a member of the US Senate: **Senator** ◦ *Senator Smith*
- a district that has its own member of parliament: **constituency**; a person who lives in a constituency: **constituent**
- a place in parliament that sb wins in an election: **seat**

▷ more on elections ⇨ ELECTION

- the building in which the United Kingdom parliament works: **the Houses of Parliament**
- the building in which the United States Congress works: **the Capitol**
- the person who controls business in the House of Commons or the US Congress: **the Speaker**
- a member of the UK Parliament who does not have an important position in a political party: **backbencher, backbench MP**

2 working in parliament

- a meeting of parliament: **sitting;** a series of meetings of parliament: **session** ◦ *an all-night sitting* ◦ *the 1993/4 session of parliament*
- when parliament is meeting, it is **in session**
- to have a meeting or a series of meetings: **sit*** ◦ *Parliament was still sitting at 3 am*
- formal discussion or argument of a topic in parliament, etc: **debate**; *verb*: **debate** (sth) ◦ *a debate on capital punishment.* ◦ *The Lords are still debating the Government's proposals.*
- to make a law or laws: **legislate** (**for/against** sth); the act of making laws; the laws that are made: **legislation** (*noun* U) ◦ *The government is seeking to legislate against racial discrimination.* ◦ *to introduce new legislation on obscenity*
- to introduce a new law, etc: **bring*** sth **in, introduce** sth ◦ *The government want to bring in a law to ban cruelty to animals.*
- a plan for a possible new law: **bill** ◦ *Parliament is debating a bill that would reduce income tax by 5%.*
- a law made by a government: **act** ◦ *the 1983 Mental Health Act*

part/whole

1 part
2 whole
all or some of a group ⇨ HOW MUCH/MANY

1 part

- some, but not all, of a thing or number of things: **part** ◦ *This part of the house was built over four hundred years ago.* ◦ *a part of the body* ◦ *What part of town are you from?*
- the other part; the part that is left: **the rest** ◦ *This part of the town is quite nice; the rest is awful.*
- to break or split into parts: **divide** (**into** sth); to break or split sth into parts: **divide** sth (**up**) (**into** sth); *noun* (U): **division** ◦ *The house was divided into flats.* ◦ *the division of the property between the three brothers*

part / whole *contd.*

- one of the parts into which sth has been or can be divided: **section** ◦ *the financial section of the newspaper* ◦ *the string section of an orchestra*

- to divide sth and give some of it to other people: **share** sth (**out**) ◦ *We shared the pizza between the four of us.*
- a part or amount of sth that has been divided between several people: **share** ◦ *We each pay a share of the bills.*
- a part or share: **portion** ◦ *What portion of your salary goes on tax?* ◦ *a small portion of chips*

▷ dividing things into parts ⇨ **DIVIDE**

- a small part or amount of sth: **bit, piece** ◦ *There is a bit of food at the corner of your mouth.* ◦ *a piece of cake*
- a small piece that has broken off sth bigger: **fragment** ◦ *I found a fragment of glass on the carpet.*
- a large or thick part or piece of sth: **chunk** ◦ *a chunk of stone that had fallen from the house*

- a part of a town, a country or the world: **area**
- a part of a town or a country: **district** ◦ *railway services in rural districts* ◦ *postal districts*
- a part of a country (which may not have any fixed boundaries): **region** ◦ *the coal-mining region of south Wales*

- a single thing that is complete in itself, but which can be part of a bigger thing: **unit** ◦ *The course is divided into ten units.*
- an office, shop, etc that is part of another larger organization: **branch** ◦ *your local branch of Barclays Bank*
- one of the parts that makes up a whole thing, especially a machine: **part, component** ◦ *spare parts for a car* ◦ *the electronic components of a computer*

- one important part of a plan, system, etc: **element** ◦ *Strategy is an important element of the game.*
- one part in the progress or development of sth: **stage** ◦ *the early stages of the match* ◦ *At this stage I can't tell whether we will win the match or not.*
- what is left behind after other parts have been used or taken away: **remains** (*noun plural*) ◦ *I gave the remains of the dinner to the dog.*

- an exact part of a number: **fraction**
- one of two equal parts of sth: **half** (*plural* **halves**)
- one of three equal parts of sth: **third**
- one of four equal parts of sth: **quarter**
- one of five, six, etc equal parts of sth: **fifth, sixth,** etc
- a number which is not a fraction: **whole number**

▷ numbers and fractions ⇨ **NUMBER**

2 whole

- all that there is of sth: **all** (**of**) **. . ., the whole** (**of**) **. . .,** (*informal*) **the** (**whole**) **lot** (**of . . .**) ◦ *They've taken all my money.* ◦ *It's all gone.* ◦ *They've taken all of it.* ◦ *Have you eaten it all?* ◦ *I've spent the whole of my life looking after other people.* ◦ *He drank the whole lot in one go.*
- without anything left or missing: **whole** (*adjective, only before a noun*), **full** (*adjective, only before a noun*), **entire** (*adjective, only before a noun*) ◦ *I've just hoovered the whole house.* ◦ *a full tube of toothpaste* ◦ *to eat an entire box of chocolates*
- completely: **in full** ◦ *Write your name in full.* ◦ *The fees must be paid in full.*

- to have as its parts or members: **comprise** sth ◦ *a tool kit comprising a screwdriver, two spanners and a hammer*
- to have as one part: **include** sth ◦ *The price of the meal included a salad and a cup of coffee.*
- if sth has all its parts, it is **complete** ◦ *a complete set of cards/plates/pictures* ◦ *I don't think this chess set is complete.*
- if sth is not complete, one or more parts is **missing** ◦ *One of the teaspoons is missing.*

- to put the parts of sth together to make the complete object: **assemble** sth; *noun* (U): **assembly**
- to separate sth into the different parts that it is made of: **take*** sth **apart, take*** sth **to bits/pieces, dismantle** sth ◦ *James took the radio apart to see if he could mend it.* ◦ *I think Dad's taking the car to pieces.* ◦ *He dismantled the shelves and packed them into a box.*

party

1 different kinds of party
2 having a party
see also ENTERTAINMENT, DANCE

1 different kinds of party

- a social occasion where people are invited to eat, drink and enjoy themselves: **party** ◦ *Did you enjoy the party?* ◦ *party games* ◦ *a birthday/Christmas party*
- a party or social event: (*informal*) **do** ◦ *We're having a little do in the office on Friday to say goodbye to George.*
- to come together as a group of people at sb's house, in a pub, etc: **get* together**; *noun*: **get-together** ◦ *We should get together some time before you go.* ◦ *We're having a little get-together at my house on Saturday.*
- to do sth special and enjoyable on a special day or because of a special event: **celebrate** sth; *noun*: **celebration** ◦ *I'm planning a party to celebrate my parents' wedding anniversary.* ◦ *Christmas celebrations*

- a party to celebrate moving into a new house: **house-warming party**
- a party to say good-bye to sb: **farewell party**
- a party for the people who work in an office or a group of workers: **office party**

- a party at sb's house to eat dinner: **dinner party**
- a formal party to celebrate sth or to welcome important guests: **reception**
- a formal party to celebrate a wedding: **wedding reception**
- a formal party where people drink alcoholic drinks and make polite conversation: **cocktail party**
- a large formal party where people dance: **ball**
- a party where people eat food cooked on a fire outside: **barbecue**
- a party at which people wear unusual or funny clothes: **fancy dress party**

2 having a party

- to organize a party: **have/give*/hold*/throw* a party** (**for** sb) ◦ *I'm having a party next week – do you want to come?* ◦ *She gave a party for all her friends.* ◦ *We're throwing a party for Jack – he's leaving next week.*
- to organize sth (for example food or entertainment) for a party: **lay*** sth **on** ◦ *It was a terrific party – they laid on lots of fantastic food.*

- to tell sb that you would like them to come to a party: **ask** sb (**to** sth), **invite** sb (**to** sth) ◦ *How many people have you invited?*
- a written or spoken request to come to a party, etc: **invitation** ◦ *'Are you going to their party?' 'No, I haven't had an invitation.'*
- when you invite sb to a party, you can say **Can you come to my party?** or **Would you like to come to my party?**

▷ more on inviting sb to sth ⇨ INVITE

- a man/woman who gives a party: **host/hostess**
- a person who comes to a party: **guest** ◦ *The guests are arriving – can somebody answer the door?*
- a list of all the people coming to a party: **guest list**
- a person who comes to a party who is not invited is **uninvited** ◦ *an uninvited guest*
- to go to a party when you have not been invited: **gatecrash** (sth); a person who gatecrashes a party: **gatecrasher** ◦ *We gatecrashed Andrew's party.* ◦ *I've never seen him before – he must be a gatecrasher.*

- at the end of a party when people go home, the party **breaks* up**

■ **MORE ...**
- a party for women only, usually held for a woman who is getting married: **hen-party**, **hen-night**
- a party for men only, usually held for a man who is getting married: **stag-party**, **stag night**

pass

- moving to a place ⇨ MOVE
- passing an exam ⇨ EXAM

past¹

- on the other side of sth ⇨ PLACE²

past² time

1 belonging to the past
2 thinking back to times in the past
see also PRESENT², FUTURE, TIME

1 belonging to the past

- the time before the present; the things that happened in that time: **the past** ◦ *She enjoys talking about the past.* ◦ *All that's in the past now: we should think about the future.* ◦ *in the distant past*
- already gone; belonging to the past: **past** ◦ *past events* ◦ *a past relationship* ◦ *the past tense* (= the tense of a verb that expresses what happened in the past)

- past events or experiences connected with an object, person or place: **history** ◦ *The city has a very interesting history.*
- a person's life before now: **past** ◦ *We spent a long time getting to know each other and talking about our pasts.*

■ a short time in the past
- a particular length of time before now: **ago** ◦ *three weeks ago*
- a very short time ago: **just now**, **(just) a moment/minute ago** ◦ *He was here just now.* ◦ *She phoned just a moment ago.*
- two or more days ago: **the other day** ◦ *Did you see that programme the other day about Turkey?*
- at a point in time a few weeks or months ago: **recently**, **not long ago** ◦ *I met her quite recently.* ◦ *She had a baby not long ago.*
- during a period between not long ago and now: **recently**, **lately** ◦ *Recently, our company profits have begun to improve.*
- that happened not long ago: **recent** ◦ *recent history* ◦ *a recent decision of the European Court*
- nearest to the present; most recent: **last** ◦ *Last year I decided to concentrate on my musical interests.*
- just finished; last: **past** (*adjective, only before a noun*) ◦ *this past week* ◦ *She's been working very hard for the past few weeks.*
- at an earlier time: **before** ◦ *I hope it's all right – I've never cooked it before.*

▷ happening before or after sth else ⇨ BEFORE/AFTER

■ a long time in the past
- during a period a long time in the past: **in the past**, **long ago**, **at one time**, **once** ◦ *At one time, lots of people lived in the city centre, but most now live in the suburbs.* ◦ *Stone age people used to live here long ago.*
- at a point a long time in the past: **a long time ago**, **long ago**, **once** ◦ *I knew a man who had once met Gandhi.*
- at a particular period in the past: **in those days** ◦ *In those days, people didn't have to worry about locking their doors at night.*

- events of the past when you are thinking of them as a whole: **history** (*noun* U); *adjective*:

past² *contd.*

historical ◦ *a period in European history* ◦ *the history of East Africa* ◦ *historical events*
– having existed for a long time: **old** ◦ *the old part of a city*

▷ more on history and things that are old ⇨ **HISTORY, NEW/OLD**

2 thinking back to times in the past

– to think about sth in your/sb's past: **look back** (**on** sth), **think* back** (**to/on** sth) ◦ *This book looks back on the last 20 years of film.* ◦ *I was just thinking back to the time when I was a student.*
– to cause sb's thoughts to return to a past time: **take*** sb **back** (**to** sth) ◦ *This song really takes me back* (= reminds me of times past).
– a feeling of affection or sadness for things that are in the past: **nostalgia** (**for** sth) (*noun* U/C); *adjective*: **nostalgic** (*adverb* **nostalgically**) ◦ *to experience feelings of nostalgia* ◦ *He felt a nostalgia for his school days.* ◦ *Listening to my old records made me feel very nostalgic.*

– thinking about sth that happened in the past (often seeing it differently from the way that you saw it then): **in retrospect, with hindsight** ◦ *In retrospect, I can see why we were wrong.* ◦ *With hindsight, I would do things again very differently.*

path ⇨ ROAD

pay¹ paying money to buy sth

1 paying for sth
2 paying a bill
3 methods of payment
4 things that are paid for
see also BUY, MONEY, PRICE, SHOP, RESTAURANT

1 paying for sth

– to give sb money for sth you want to buy: **pay*** (sb) (some money) (**for** sth); the act of paying for sth: **payment** (*noun* U); the amount that you pay for sth: **payment** ◦ *How much did you pay for that picture?* ◦ *Payment must be made before goods are delivered.* ◦ *I have to make one more payment of £50.*
– a piece of paper showing that sth has been paid: **receipt** ◦ *Could you give me a receipt?*

– to pay all the money that you owe: **pay*** sth **off** ◦ *I'm determined to pay off all my debts.*
– to pay for sth before you receive it: **pay*** (**for** sth) **in advance**
– failure to pay sth: (*formal*) **non-payment** (*noun* U)

■ paying gradually
– the system of buying goods or services and not paying for them until later: **credit** (*noun* U); to buy sth in this way: **buy*** sth **on credit** ◦ *a credit account* (= an arrangement with a shop to buy things on credit)
– the first payment that you have to make when you buy on credit: **deposit**
– a regular payment that you make when you buy sth on credit: **instalment** (*AmE* **installment**) ◦ *to pay in monthly instalments*
– the money that you pay for borrowing money: **interest** (**on** sth) (*noun* U) ◦ *How much interest will I have to pay if I pay for the car over twelve months?*

▷ owing money ⇨ **DEBT**

■ giving money back
– to give back money that you owe: **repay*** sb (**for** sth), **repay*** sth (**to** sb); *noun*: **repayment** ◦ *When are you going to repay the money I lent you?*
– to give back money that has been paid for sth (for example in a shop): **refund** (sb) sth, **refund** sth (**to** sb); *noun*: **refund** ◦ *If the cruise is cancelled, they'll have to refund all the passengers the cost of their tickets.* ◦ *I'm going straight back to the shop to demand a refund.*

2 paying a bill

– a piece of paper that shows how much you must pay for things you have bought or for a service provided, for example in a restaurant: **bill** (*AmE* **check**) ◦ *Could you bring me the bill?*
– to pay what you owe when you are given a bill: **pay*** the **bill**, **settle** the **bill**
– to share the payment of a bill, for example in a restaurant, with sb else: **go* halves** (**with** sb) ◦ *Let's go halves, shall we?*

– an official piece of paper that lists goods or services that you have bought and which says how much you must pay for them: **invoice**
– to send a bill to sb: **invoice** sb (**for** sth) ◦ *Do I need to pay now or will you invoice me?*
– when it is time for a bill to be paid it is **due for payment**, (*formal*) **payable**
– if payment is made in good time, it is **prompt** (*adverb* **promptly**) ◦ *They will expect prompt payment.*
– a bill that has not been paid is **unpaid**

– if you agree that you (not another person) pay for sth, you **pay***, **foot the bill** ◦ *It's okay, I'll pay.* ◦ *John footed the entire bill.*

3 methods of payment

– money (coins and notes) that you can carry in your hand: **cash** (*noun* U); to pay using cash: **pay* in cash** ◦ *'How do you want to pay?' 'I'll pay in cash.'*
– the money you get back if you pay more than the amount sth costs: **change** (*noun* U) ◦ *I don't think this is the right change – I'm sure I gave you a ten-pound note.*

– a piece of paper, printed by a bank, that you can fill in, sign and use to pay for things: **cheque** (*AmE* **check**); to pay using a cheque: **pay* by cheque** (*AmE* **check**), **give*** sb **a cheque** ◦ *Can I give you a cheque?*
– a cheque that you can change into foreign money when you are travelling abroad: **traveller's cheque** (*AmE* **traveler's check**)
– a piece of paper like a cheque that you can buy from a post office and send to sb, and that they

can exchange for money: **postal order** ◦ *I'll send you a postal order.*

- a small plastic card that allows you to get goods and services without using money (you usually receive a bill once a month for what you have bought): **credit card**
- a small plastic card that you can use to pay for goods and services; money is deducted directly from your bank account: **debit card**, **Switch card**
- to pay using a plastic card: **pay* by credit card**, **debit card**, etc

- an arrangement by which a bank pays a certain amount of money regularly from your account to sb, for example to pay a bill: **standing order**
- an arrangement by which money is automatically taken out of your bank account in order to pay a bill: **direct debit** (*noun* U/C) ◦ *I agreed to pay by direct debit.*

▷ more on paying by cheque or using a bank ⇨ CHEQUE, BANK

- a piece of paper that you can exchange for certain goods and services: **voucher** ◦ *a gift voucher* (= a voucher given to sb as a gift)

4 things that are paid for

- money that you pay for the use of a house, land, etc: **rent** (*noun* U) ◦ *to pay the rent*
- money that you pay for driving on some roads and bridges: **toll** (**charge**)
- money that you pay to receive a magazine regularly or to be a member of a club: **subscription**; to get sth by paying a subscription **subscribe** (**to** sth) ◦ *Members must pay their subscriptions before the end of December.*

- money that is paid to sb for helping the police, finding a lost dog, etc: **reward**
- money that you pay to sb because you have injured them or lost or damaged their property: **compensation** (*noun* U), **damages** (*noun plural*); *verb*: **compensate** sb (**for** sth)

- money that is paid to free sb who has been captured by criminals: **ransom** (*noun* C/U)

▷ money that you pay to people who work for you ⇨ PAY[2]

---

pay[2] money for the work that you do

1 regular pay for the work you do

- money that you get regularly for work you have done: **pay** (*noun* U) ◦ *I'm going to ask for a pay rise.*
- the amount you are paid in a week/month/year: **income** (*noun* U), **earnings** (*noun plural*) ◦ *Average incomes have fallen by 2% this year.*
- to get money by working: **earn** sth, **make* money** ◦ *She earns £200 a week as a hairdresser.* ◦ *He earns his living as an artist.* ◦ *He writes, but doesn't make a lot of money out of it.*

- money which is paid monthly into your bank account: **salary**; money which is paid daily or weekly in cash: **wages** (*noun plural*)
- money for work that is done only once, or which is not done regularly: **payment** (*noun* U/C) ◦ *She received no payment for the extra work she had done.*
- money that is received for professional work, for example by a lawyer or doctor: **fee**

2 other kinds of pay

- money that is given to a person who is no longer working because of old age or sickness: **pension**
- money that is given to a person who is unemployed: **unemployment benefit** (*noun* U)
- money that is given to a person who is poor, old or sick: **social security** (*noun* U) (*AmE* **welfare**)
- money that is given to a person who is ill and unable to work: **sick pay** (*noun* U)
- money that is given to a student, to support him/her while studying: (**student**) **grant**

- money that you receive regularly to help you pay for sth that you need: **allowance** ◦ *a clothes/travel allowance*
- money that is paid to sb for selling sth: **commission** (*noun* U) ◦ *to be on commission* (= to be paid according to how much you sell)
- extra money that you pay to a taxi-driver, hairdresser, etc to thank them for their work: **tip**; to give sb a tip: **tip** (sb) (some money) ◦ *I forgot to tip the taxi driver.*

3 how much you are paid

- if you are paid a lot of money, you are **well-paid**, you **have a high income**, you **earn a lot**
- if you are paid very little money, you are **poorly paid**, **badly paid**, you **don't earn much**
- if you receive too much pay, you are **overpaid**; *opposite*: **underpaid**

- when workers ask for more money, they make a **pay claim**
- if your pay goes up, you get a **pay/salary/wage increase**, **pay/wage rise**; if your pay goes down, you get a **pay cut**, a **reduction in pay**

4 getting paid

- to give sb money for sth: **pay*** sb (sth), **pay*** sth **to** sb ◦ *I haven't been paid yet this month.*
- the day of the week/month when you receive your pay: **pay-day**
- the piece of paper which shows how much you are being paid: **payslip**
- the envelope containing a person's wages: **pay packet**

- money taken away from your pay, for example for tax: **deduction**; the amount of money you have left after tax, etc has been taken away: **take-home pay** ◦ *I take home £150 after deductions.*
- your total income, before tax, etc is taken away: **gross income**; *opposite*: **net income**

pay² *contd.*

▷ paying tax ⇨ TAX

– money paid to sb before the time that it is usually paid: **advance**; money paid to sb after the time that it is usually paid: **arrears** (*noun plural*), **back pay** (*noun* U)

pea ⇨ VEGETABLE

peace

– not noisy ⇨ CALM
– not war ⇨ WAR

pen/pencil

see also WRITE, DRAW, PAPER

■ pens

– a long thin instrument that contains ink and is used for writing or drawing: **pen**
– a pen that has a very small ball at the end which rolls the ink onto the paper: **biro** (*plural* **biros**), **ballpoint (pen)**
– a pen that you fill with ink: **fountain pen**
– a pen that has a soft end; these pens are available in many different colours: **felt-tip pen**, **felt tip**
– a pen that has a soft end and produces thick lines: **marker (pen)**
– a thick coloured pen used to mark important parts of a text: **highlighter**
– the black or coloured liquid inside a pen: **ink** (*noun* U)
– a small tube containing ink, which you put inside some pens: **(ink) cartridge**
– the metal point of a pen where the ink comes out: **nib**
– paper used to dry ink on a page: **blotting paper** (*noun* U)

■ pencils

– a long thin instrument, made of wood, with a black or coloured substance in the middle, used for writing or drawing: **pencil** ◦ *a pencil case* (a small bag in which you keep pens, pencils, etc)
– a coloured pencil used for drawing or writing, especially by children: **crayon**

Note: if you are talking about the method of writing or drawing, you can use **pen**, **pencil**, etc as uncountable nouns: ◦ *In this school the children are expected to write in pen* (= using a pen).

– the black substance inside a pencil: **lead** (*noun* C/U) ◦ *a pencil lead*
– the end part of the pencil which you write with: **point**
– if a pencil has a fine point, it is **sharp**; *opposite*: **blunt**
– an instrument which is used to make a pencil sharp: **(pencil) sharpener**
– to use a sharpener: **sharpen** sth ◦ *Have you got something I can sharpen this pencil with?*
– a small object used to remove pencil marks from paper: **rubber** (*especially AmE* **eraser**)
– to remove pencil marks from paper: **rub** sth **out** (*especially AmE* **erase** sth) ◦ *Rub it out and start again.*

people

people together ⇨ GROUP
people as individuals ⇨ PERSON, PERSONALITY
see also MAN, WOMAN, CHILD, FAMILY, SOCIETY

– a man, woman or child: **person** (*plural* **people**) ◦ *I want a job in which I can meet all sorts of different people.*
– all people: **the human race** (*noun singular*), **humanity** (*noun* U), **man** (*noun singular, without 'the' or 'a'*), **mankind** (*noun* U) ◦ *the future of the human race* ◦ *Humanity is facing an ecological crisis.* ◦ *the difference between man and the animals*
– a member of the human race: **human**, **human being**; *adjective*: **human** ◦ *Humans are unique in their capacity for language.* ◦ *I could not understand how one of my fellow human beings could treat an animal in such a way.* ◦ *the human body*

Note: when talking about people in general, some people do not like to use the words **man** and **mankind** because they seem to exclude women. They prefer to say **people** or **human beings**.

– feelings, behaviour, etc that are common to all people: **human nature** (*noun* U) ◦ *It's only human nature to want to do the best for your children.*
– (used especially about people in public places or doing public things) people in general: **the public** ◦ *Buckingham palace was opened to the public in 1993.* ◦ *a member of the public*
– all the people of a country: **the people** ◦ *the people of France* ◦ *the French people*
– the number of people who live in a particular place: **population** ◦ *What's the population of Manchester?*
– a place that has lost a large part of its population is **depopulated** ◦ *depopulated villages*
▷ the people of a country ⇨ COUNTRY¹

■ races and ethnic groups

– one of the groups into which people can be divided according to their skin colour, hair type, etc: **race** (*noun* C/U); *adjective* **racial** (*adverb* **racially**) ◦ *the different races of Australia* ◦ *a child of mixed race* ◦ *racial identity* ◦ *a racially motivated attack*
– (used about a group of people) having the same language, customs, history, etc: **ethnic** ◦ *an ethnic group* ◦ *ethnic minorities*
– a group of people that speak the same language, have the same customs and live in a traditional way, often led by a chief: **tribe**; *adjective*: **tribal** ◦ *nomadic tribes in the Sahara* ◦ *tribal customs*
– if sb has dark-coloured skin and is of African or Caribbean origin, they are often called **black** ◦ *a black person* ◦ *black people in Britain* ◦ *black Americans*

- if sb has light-coloured skin and is of European origin, they are often called **white** ◦ *Police are looking for a white male aged about 20.*

- one of the original people of Australia: **Aborigine**
- a person who comes from Africa: **African**
- a black person who comes from America: **African-American**, **Afro-American**
- a black person who comes from the Caribbean: **Afro-Caribbean**
- a person who comes from an Arab country: **Arab**
- a person who comes from Asia: **Asian**
- a person who comes from Europe: **European**
- a person who comes from Mexico, Central America or South America: **Latin American**
- a person whose first language is Spanish, especially one from a Latin American country: **Hispanic**
- one of the original people of America: **Native American**

pepper ⇨ SALT / PEPPER

perfect ⇨ GOOD

perhaps ⇨ POSSIBLE[1]

permanent ⇨ CONTINUE

permit ⇨ ALLOW

person

racial and other social groups that a person belongs to ⇨ **GROUP, PEOPLE**
what a person looks like ⇨ **BEAUTIFUL / ATTRACTIVE, BODY, FACE, HAIR**
what makes one person different from another person ⇨ **PERSONALITY**

- a man, woman or child: **person** (*plural* **people**) ◦ *That's terrible – what kind of a person would do a thing like that?* ◦ *a mature and confident person* ◦ *all kinds of people*
- more formal or more scientific words for a person: **human, human being**; *adjective*: **human** ◦ *Human beings have larger brains than other animals.* ◦ *human behaviour* ◦ *the human race* (= all human beings)

- one single person: **individual**; for, from or belonging to a single person: **individual** ◦ *Each individual must take responsibility for his or her own safety.* ◦ *the needs of an individual person* ◦ *individual opinions*
- a person's inner nature, including the mind and the spirit: (*formal*) **self** (*noun* U) ◦ *self-knowledge*

- belonging to or connected with a particular person: **personal** ◦ *I'm not interested in your personal views on the matter.* ◦ *personal belongings* (= the things that a person owns) ◦ *personal qualities* (= the good or bad things about a person) ◦ *These children are your personal responsibility.* ◦ *personal relationships*
- as an individual person: **personally** ◦ *We're holding you personally responsible.* ◦ *Do you have any idea what it meant to him personally?*

personality

1 what makes you different from somebody else
2 particular differences
see also PERSON, BEHAVIOUR

1 what makes you different from somebody else

- the qualities of a person: **personality**, **character**, **nature** ◦ *to have an attractive/interesting/complex personality* ◦ *Even though they're twins, they have very different characters.* ◦ *It's in her nature to be kind to people.*
- a person's personality, especially as it affects the way they behave and feel: **temperament** ◦ *an excitable/artistic temperament*
- a particular quality that is typical of sb: **characteristic** ◦ *Bossiness is one of his less appealing characteristics.*

- to have a particular characteristic because your mother, father or other member of your family has it: **get*** sth **from** sb ◦ *He's very open and friendly – he gets it from his father.*
- (used about a characteristic or talent) particular to a family: **in the family** ◦ *They're all very musical – it's in the family.*

- to ask about sb's personality, you can say **What is he/she like?** or **What sort of a person is he/she?**

- to appear to be a particular type of person (even if you are not): **come* across** (**as** sth) ◦ *She came across as quite a shy person when we met her, but apparently she's not like that at all.*
- the effect that a person produces on sb else: **impression** ◦ *He made a bad impression on everyone.*

2 particular differences

■ nice or unpleasant

- pleasant and good: **nice**, **sweet**; *opposites*: **nasty**, **unpleasant** ◦ *I like her – she's a really nice person.* ◦ *a sweet child* ◦ *a thoroughly nasty individual*
- easily liked by other people: **charming** ◦ *You'll find him absolutely charming.*
- kind and pleasant: **friendly**; *opposite*: **unfriendly** ◦ *friendly neighbours/colleagues*
- generally happy: **cheerful**; cheerful or friendly: **good-natured**

■ kind or unkind

- caring about how other people feel and doing things to help them: **kind**, **kind-hearted**; *opposite*: **unkind**
- happy to help people: **helpful**
- understanding other people's feelings and problems: **sympathetic**
- happy to give money and help freely: **generous**; *opposite*: **mean**

personality *contd.*

– thinking only about your own needs or wishes and not about other people's needs and wishes: **selfish**, **self-centred**; *opposites*: **unselfish**, **selfless** ◦ *Think about other people for a change and don't be so selfish.* ◦ *an unselfish act*
– a person who thinks about himself/herself too much: **egotist**

▷ more on being kind, helpful, sympathetic and generous ⇨ KIND/CRUEL, HELP, SYMPATHY, GENEROUS

– having skill in dealing with people; careful not to cause embarrassment: **tactful**; *opposite*: **tactless**

▷ more on being tactful ⇨ POLITE

■ gentle or aggressive

– behaving in a careful way so that you do not hurt things or people: **gentle**
– ready or likely to fight or argue: **aggressive**
– a person who uses his or her greater strength or power to hurt or frighten sb who is weaker: **bully** ◦ *Leave her alone! Don't be such a bully.*
– liking to give orders to other people, often in an annoying way: **bossy**

■ tolerant or intolerant

– able or willing to accept things that you do not like or agree with: **broad-minded**, **tolerant**; *opposites*: **narrow-minded**, **intolerant** ◦ *I like to think I'm fairly broad-minded but this sort of behaviour is quite unacceptable.*
– tolerant; not easily worried or annoyed: **easy-going** ◦ *You can ask her anything – she's very easygoing.*

▷ attitudes to particular groups in society ⇨ SOCIETY

– not willing to change your mind or say that you are wrong: **stubborn**, **obstinate** ◦ *He's stubborn – he won't do anything he doesn't want to.*
– not willing to consider other people: **unreasonable**
– not allowing people to break rules and behave badly: **strict**
– treating each person or side equally: **fair** ◦ *He's quite strict with people but very fair.*

– not easily made angry: **calm**, **relaxed**
– easily made angry: **irritable** ◦ *She's getting rather irritable in her old age.*
– not easily annoyed by people or things that seem slow: **patient**; *opposite*: **impatient**
– if you easily become angry and impatient, you have a **bad/short/quick temper**

▷ more on being calm or angry ⇨ CALM, ANGRY

■ sociable or shy

– enjoying the company of other people: **sociable**; *opposite*: **anti-social** ◦ *He's a bit anti-social – he doesn't really go out very often.*
– friendly and talkative; likes meeting new people: **outgoing**; *opposites*: **shy**, **reserved** ◦ *She's the outgoing type – she gets invited to lots of parties and makes friends very easily.* ◦ *I've always been shy.*
– liked by many people: **popular**; *opposite*: **unpopular** ◦ *She's popular with both staff and students.*

– fond of talking (in a friendly way): **chatty**; *opposite*: **quiet** ◦ *I liked him – he was really friendly and chatty.* ◦ *Tim is very quiet, but don't think he's not interested.*
– a person who talks too much is **talkative**, (*informal*) a **chatterbox** ◦ *He's such a chatterbox!*

– full of life and energy; very active: **lively**
– a person who is cheerful and lively and enjoys being with other people: **extrovert**; *opposite*: **introvert** ◦ *Ann's a complete extrovert and loves parties, but Jim's a bit of an introvert and prefers a quiet evening at home.*
– able to express your feelings freely or naturally: **uninhibited** ◦ *She's quite uninhibited – you never know what she's going to do next.*

■ fun or boring

– able to make other people laugh or have a good time: **funny**, **amusing**, (*informal*) **a good laugh**, (*informal*) (**good/great**) **fun**; *opposite*: **serious** ◦ *Such a funny man!* ◦ *'What's she like?' 'You'll like her. She's a really good laugh.'* ◦ *'I'm going to stay with the Hendersons.' 'Oh, you'll have a wonderful time – they're great fun.'* ◦ *I suppose he's quite nice but I found him a bit serious.*

– if you see what is funny in life, can make jokes, etc, you have **a** (**good**) **sense of humour**; *opposite*: **no sense of humour**
– enjoyable to be with; having interesting things to say: **interesting**; *opposites*: **dull**, **boring**
– the quality of having a strong, interesting and attractive character: **personality** (*noun* C/U) ◦ *I think you'll like her – she's quite a personality!* ◦ *rather dull and with little personality*

▷ more on being funny or interesting ⇨ FUNNY, INTERESTING

■ honest or dishonest

– telling the truth; not stealing or deceiving people: **honest**; *opposite*: **dishonest** ◦ *an honest and loyal friend*
– if you can be sure that sb will do what they ought to do or what they have said they will do, they are **reliable**, **dependable**, **trustworthy**; *opposite*: **unreliable**, **untrustworthy** ◦ *I wouldn't lend her money; she's not very trustworthy.* ◦ *He'll probably be late – he's hopelessly unreliable.*
– not changing in your friendship or beliefs; faithful: **loyal**; *opposite*: **disloyal** ◦ *a loyal friend*

▷ more on being honest or trustworthy ⇨ HONEST, TRUST

■ sensible or irresponsible

– able to think or act in a reasonable way; show-

ing good judgement: **sensible** ◦ *She's a sensible girl and I'm sure she wouldn't do anything stupid.*
- that you can trust to behave well and sensibly: **responsible**; *opposite*: **irresponsible** ◦ *'Shall we send Robert?' 'Yes, he's very responsible. He won't let us down.'*
- careful to do sth correctly and well: **conscientious**; *opposite*: **careless**
- able to act in a sensible and adult way: **mature**; *opposite*: **immature** ◦ *You can trust him – he's very mature for his age.*

▷ more on being sensible ⇨ SENSIBLE

- able to plan and carry out work well: **organized**; *opposite*: **disorganized**
- making sensible decisions and good at dealing with problems: **practical** ◦ *He's clever, but not very practical.*
- liking to keep things in good order: **tidy**, **neat**; *opposite*: **untidy**

▷ more on being tidy ⇨ TIDY

■ hardworking or lazy
- having a lot of energy to do things: **active**, **energetic** ◦ *She's very active – always running around, seeing people, doing lots of sport.*
- working with effort and energy: **hard-working**
- not wanting to work: **lazy**

▷ more on being hard-working or lazy ⇨ WORK, LAZY

■ brave or cowardly
- a person's inner strength: **character** (*noun* U) ◦ *to have strength of character*
- not wanting or needing to take help from other people: **independent**

- ready to do things that are dangerous or difficult without showing fear: **brave**; *opposite*: **cowardly**; a person who is cowardly: **coward**
- liking to try new things or have adventures: **adventurous**

▷ more on being brave ⇨ BRAVE

■ ambitious and confident
- having a strong desire to be successful, to have power, etc: **ambitious** ◦ *She'll probably go far, she's a very ambitious woman.*
- feeling or showing that you are sure about your own abilities, opinions, etc: **confident**, **self-confident** ◦ *He's got no confidence in his own ability.*
- expressing your opinions clearly and confidently so that people listen and take notice of you: **assertive** ◦ *If you were a bit more assertive, you would find it easier to say no.*

- somebody who usually believes that the future will be good: **optimist**; *opposite*: **pessimist**

▷ more on being successful ⇨ SUCCEED/FAIL

■ clever and talented
- good at learning and doing things: **clever** ◦ *She's clever at maths.* ◦ *He's actually a lot cleverer than he looks.*
- having a number of different skills and abilities: **talented** ◦ *a talented child/musician*
- good at studying or thinking: **intelligent**, (*informal*) **brainy**
- interested in or good at sports: (*informal*) **sporty**
- good at running and other athletic sports; physically strong: **athletic**
- interested in or good at music: **musical**
- interested in or good at drawing, painting, etc: **artistic**

▷ more on being clever ⇨ CLEVER

■ proud or modest
- too proud of yourself, your abilities, etc: **conceited**, (*informal*) **big-headed**
- thinking that you are better and more important than other people, and not caring about their feelings: **arrogant**

- not having or expressing a high opinion of your own qualities or abilities: **modest** ◦ *That's not true, he's just being modest – he's actually very intelligent.*

▷ more on being proud ⇨ PROUD

persuade

see also ADVERTISEMENT, ADVISE/SUGGEST, ENCOURAGE

- to make sb do sth by talking to them and giving them good reasons: **persuade** sb (**to** do sth), (*informal*) **get*** sb to do sth; *noun* (U): **persuasion** ◦ *Did you manage to persuade them to stay?* ◦ *We got them to leave after a lot of persuasion.*
- to succeed in making sb believe sth: **convince** sb (**of** sth/**that**...) ◦ *The policeman convinced us that it would be dangerous to drive any further.*
- if sth succeds in persuading you, it is **convincing** (*adverb* **convincingly**), **persuasive** (*adverb* **persuasively**), you are **convinced** ◦ *a convincing argument* ◦ *a persuasive speech* ◦ *She argued her case very persuasively.* ◦ *I'm now quite convinced that I should stay in my job.*

- to persuade sb to do sth that they do not want to do: **talk** sb **into** sth/doing sth, **push** sb **into** sth/doing sth ◦ *They talked us into joining them on their holiday.* ◦ *My parents tried to push me into studying medicine.*
- to persuade sb to do sth wrong: (*informal*) **put*** sb **up to** sth ◦ *He's never stolen anything before – he must have been put up to it by his friends.*

- to try very strongly to persuade sb to do sth: **urge** sb (**to** do sth) ◦ *She urged us to go before it was too late.*

persuade *contd.*

– to try to persuade sb, for example not to do sth stupid: **reason with** sb ◦ *The police are trying to reason with the hijackers.*

– to persuade sb gently: **coax** sb (**into** sth/doing sth); *noun* (U): **coaxing** ◦ *We had a tough time coaxing him into taking the medicine.* ◦ *She finally agreed to come to the party, after a lot of coaxing.*
– to try to persuade sb to do sth (especially sth which they should not do) by offering them sth in return: **tempt** sb (**to** do sth), **tempt** sb **into** sth/doing sth; *noun* (C/U): **temptation** ◦ *They tried to tempt me to stay.* ◦ *Advertisements are designed to tempt people into spending more money than they need to.* ◦ *The offer of a company car was a big temptation.* ◦ *We managed to resist the temptation to go.*
– something which tempts you to do sth is **tempting** ◦ *a tempting offer*

– an amount of money or some other gift which you give sb in order to persuade them to do sth for you: **bribe** ◦ *to offer/accept/reject a bribe*
– to persuade sb to do sth for you by giving them a bribe: **bribe** sb (**to** do sth) ◦ *We tried to bribe the guard with a bottle of whisky.*
– the crime of giving bribes: **bribery** (*noun* U)

■ persuading sb not to do sth
– to persuade sb not to do sth: **dissuade** sb (**from** sth/doing sth), **talk** sb **out of** sth/doing sth ◦ *I tried to dissuade them from selling their house.* ◦ *Did you manage to talk them out of coming with us?*

– to try to persuade sb not to do sth: **discourage** sb (**from** sth/doing sth), **discourage** sth; *noun* (U): **discouragement** ◦ *Parents should discourage their children from smoking.* ◦ *Smoking should be discouraged.*

■ **MORE ...**
– to be able to persuade sb to do anything you want them to do: (*informal*) **twist** sb **round** your **little finger** ◦ *She knows how to twist her parents round her little finger.*

– information, often untrue, which is made public by a government or large organization in order to persuade people to believe sth: **propaganda** (*noun* U)

photograph

1 different kinds of photograph
2 taking a photograph
3 how pictures are produced from a film
4 how photographs are shown
films shown in a cinema ⇨ FILM
see also PICTURE

1 different kinds of photograph
– a picture which is taken with a camera: **photograph**, (*informal*) **photo** (*plural* **photos**) ◦ *Do you have a photograph of yourself?* ◦ *They have family photos all over the wall.*
– a photograph that is taken quickly and informally: **snap, snapshot** ◦ *Have I shown you my holiday snaps?*
– one of a series of photographs: **shot** ◦ *Here's another shot of us.* ◦ *Just one more shot!*
– a photograph which is in colour: **colour photograph**
– a photograph which is not in colour: **black and white photograph**
– a photograph in a small frame that you shine a bright light through in order to see it: **slide, transparency** ◦ *He showed slides to illustrate his talk.*
– a picture of a person or thing that is taken from a very short distance away: **close-up** ◦ *Here's a close-up of our daughter.*

2 taking a photograph
– a person who takes photographs: **photographer** ◦ *a press photographer* (= a person who takes photographs for a newspaper) ◦ *a fashion photographer* (= a person who takes photographs of people wearing new and fashionable clothes)

– the process of taking photographs: **photography** (*noun* U); connected with photography: **photographic** ◦ *photographic equipment*
– to make a photograph of sb/sth: **take*** a **photo** (**graph**) (**of** sb/sth), **take*** a **picture** (**of** sb/sth), **photograph** sb/sth ◦ *Hang on a minute – I want to take a photo!* ◦ *We took hundreds of pictures on our trip.* ◦ *Her hobby is photographing landscapes.*

■ the camera

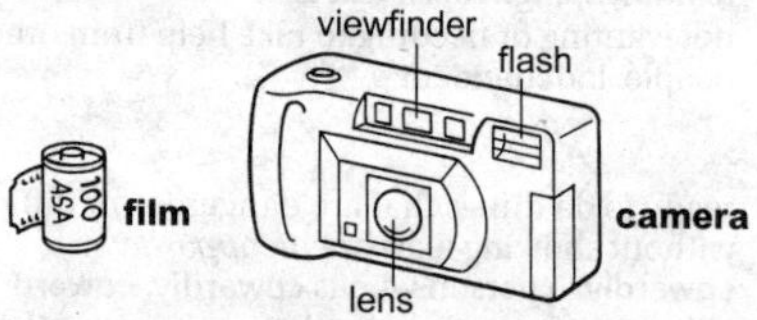

– a camera which is quick and easy to use: **automatic** (**camera**); a camera which is not automatic is **manual**
– a camera which produces a completed picture in a few seconds: **Polaroid** (**camera**)

– the part at the front of a camera that opens for a very short time to let light in: **shutter**
– a piece of glass that can be added to a lens to change the light that enters the camera: **filter** ◦ *an ultraviolet filter*
– a stand with three legs that is used to support a camera: **tripod**

■ the film
– a roll of thin plastic that you use in a camera to take photographs: **film**
– a single photograph on a film: **exposure** ◦ *I only have two exposures left.*
– how sensitive a film is to light: **film speed** ◦ *a film speed of 200 ASA*

- when you put the film in, you **load** your camera
- to move the film forward for the next picture, you **wind*** it **on**
- to move the film back when it is finished, you **rewind*** it

■ setting the camera
- if you change a control on your camera, you **set*** the control (**at/to** sth) ◦ *Set the shutter speed to 1 second.*
- one particular position of a control: **setting** ◦ *the film speed setting*
- the size of the opening through which light enters a camera: **aperture** ◦ *an aperture setting of f8*
- the length of time that light is allowed into the camera: **exposure** ◦ *a long/short exposure*

- to make sure that your picture will be clear, you **change/adjust the focus**
- if you want to make a particular object clear, you **focus** on it
- if the lines of an object in a picture are clear, the picture is **in focus**
- if a photograph is not clear, it is **out of focus**, **blurred**
- if you want to make one particular object or detail in a picture appear much bigger, you **zoom in** (**on** it)

3 how pictures are produced from a film
- when you have finished a film, sb will **develop** it; a piece of developed film which can be made into a photograph: **negative**
- to make a photograph from a negative: **print** sth; a photograph made from a negative: **print** ◦ *I want to have another print made from this negative.* ◦ *a colour print*
- if you make a photograph larger, you **enlarge** it, **blow*** it **up** ◦ *That will look really good if you blow it up.*
- a photograph that has been made larger: **enlargement**

- if a photograph is produced successfully, it **comes* out** (**well**) ◦ *Only one of our photos came out.*

4 how photographs are shown
- a border of wood, metal, etc, that supports a photograph on a wall or other surface: **frame**; if you place a photograph in a frame, you **frame** it
- a book in which you keep photographs: (**photograph**) **album**

- to shine light through a slide or a transparency to make a picture on a wall or screen: **project** sth (**on/onto** sth) ◦ *project the pictures onto the living-room wall*
- the apparatus for doing this is a (**slide**) **projector**

■ **MORE . . .**
- a person who looks good in photographs is **photogenic**

piano ⇨ MUSIC

picture

1 different kinds of picture
2 describing pictures
3 books, etc that have pictures
4 showing pictures
pictures in your mind ⇨ IMAGINATION
see also ART, DESIGN, DRAW, PAINT[1], PHOTOGRAPH

1 different kinds of picture
- a painting, drawing or photograph: **picture** ◦ *to paint/draw a picture* ◦ *to look at a picture*
- a picture that you have in your mind, perhaps after reading or seeing sth: **image** ◦ *The exotic names conjured up images of faraway places.*
- like a picture or using pictures: **pictorial** ◦ *a pictorial history*

- a picture that is drawn or painted to make sth clear, for example a story or instructions: **illustration**; to make an illustration: **illustrate** sth; *noun* (U): **illustration**; a person who illustrates: **illustrator**

- a simple picture that is used to explain what sth looks like or how sth works: **diagram**
- a mathematical diagram which uses lines or curves to represent quantities or measurements: **graph**
- a drawing which shows information in the form of a diagram: **chart**
- the production of drawings, diagrams, etc, using a computer or other professional techniques: **graphics** (*noun plural*); *adjective*: **graphic**
- a drawing of a place, for example a town or country, showing the hills, rivers, roads, towns, etc: **map**

▷ more on maps ⇨ MAP

- pictures or writing on a wall, etc in a public place that are rude, funny or political: **graffiti** (*noun plural*)

2 describing pictures
- the main thing, person or idea that is in a picture: **subject** ◦ *Horses are always difficult subjects.*
- a picture that shows things in a true way is **realistic**
- a picture which gives a general effect without specific detail is **impressionistic**

- a picture that shows a view of the land or countryside: **landscape** ◦ *a landscape painter*
- a place, event, etc that is painted: **scene** ◦ *He loved to paint scenes of country life.* ◦ *a battle scene*
- a picture that shows an object, flowers, fruit, etc: **still life**

■ pictures of people
- a picture that shows a particular person: **portrait**; the art of making portraits: **portrait painting** (*noun* U), **portraiture** (*noun* U); a person

picture *contd.*

who paints portraits: **portrait painter** ◦ *to paint somebody's portrait* ◦ *a portrait of the artist as an old man*
- a picture that is made by an artist of him/herself: **self-portrait**
- a person who is being painted or drawn: **model**
- to stand, sit, etc in a particular position so that sb can paint a picture of you: **pose**; the position that you sit in for this purpose: **pose** ◦ *How do you want me to pose?*
- if you sit so that an artist can copy you for a picture, you **sit* for** sb
- a person in a picture: **figure** ◦ *a landscape painting with three figures in the foreground*
- a person's face or head seen from the side, not the front: **profile**; a person who is shown this way is **in profile** ◦ *Stamps always show the Queen's left profile.* ◦ *I prefer to draw people in profile.*

■ parts of a picture
- the part of a picture that is behind the main people or objects: the **background** ◦ *There were mountains and white clouds in the background.*
- the part of a picture that appears closest to the person who is looking at it: the **foreground** ◦ *Notice the details in the foreground.*
- the darker parts of a picture, where there is less light: **shade** (*noun* U) ◦ *There's not enough contrast between the light and shade.*

3 books, etc that have pictures
- a magazine for children that tells stories through pictures: **comic** (**book**)
- a book that contains mainly pictures (especially one for children): **picture-book**
- a large book with blank pages where you can stick pictures, etc: **scrapbook**
- the words that are written above or below a picture (in a book, newspaper, etc) to explain what it is about: **caption** ◦ *The cartoon is only funny when you've read the caption.*
- a card that usually has a picture on one side, that you can send by post: **postcard** ◦ *Did you get my postcard?*
- a picture which has been cut into shapes that can be fitted together again as a game: **jigsaw** (**puzzle**) ◦ *Do you like doing jigsaws?*

4 showing pictures
- to put a picture on a wall: **put*** sth **up**, **hang*** sth; to be on a wall (especially in an art gallery): **hang*** ◦ *I like this poster – I think I'll put it up in my room.* ◦ *Where should we hang this?*
- places where people can look at pictures: **art gallery**
- a collection of pictures which are arranged for people to look at: **exhibition**; to show a picture in an exhibition: **exhibit** sth ◦ *an exhibition of watercolours*
- a border of metal, wood, etc which supports a picture on a wall: **frame**; to put a frame around a picture: **frame** sth ◦ *to have a picture framed*

■ MORE...
- a picture that is reproduced on paper by printing: **print**
- a picture that is printed from a cut, metal plate: **engraving**; to make an engraving: **engrave** (sth); *noun* (U): **engraving**; a person who makes engravings: **engraver**
- a picture made of many pieces of coloured stone, glass, etc: **mosaic**
- a picture that is made from an arrangement of other pictures, photographs, etc: **collage**
- a picture that is made on a person's body by pricking the skin with a needle and filling the holes with coloured inks: **tattoo**

piece ⇨ PART/WHOLE

pig

see also ANIMAL, FARM

- a fat animal with short legs and a curly tail which is kept on farms for its meat: **pig**
- a male pig: **boar** (*AmE* **hog**)
- a female pig: **sow**
- a baby pig: **piglet**
- a short low noise that pigs make: **grunt**; *verb*: **grunt**
- a high noise that pigs make when they are excited or frightened: **squeal**; *verb*: **squeal**
- a farm where pigs are kept for their meat: **pig farm**
- a small farm building where pigs are kept: **pigsty**, **sty** (*AmE* **pigpen**)
- meat from a pig: **pork** (*noun* U)
- salted or smoked meat from a pig, usually eaten hot: **bacon** (*noun* U)
- meat from the upper part of a pig's leg: **ham** (*noun* U)

▷ more on meat ⇨ MEAT

- leather that is made from the skin of a pig: **pigskin** (*noun* U) ◦ *pigskin gloves*

pint ⇨ LIQUID

pipe

see also WATER, GAS

- a long, hollow tube or cylinder made of plastic or metal that carries gas or liquid: **pipe** ◦ *a gas pipe* ◦ *the hot-water pipe* to carry liquid or gas in pipes: **pipe** sth ◦ *The oil is piped to the coast for export.*
- a long hollow pipe made of glass, rubber, etc: **tube** ◦ *The patient was connected by tubes to a kidney machine.* ◦ *a bicycle inner tube*
- a long rubber or plastic pipe that is used for getting water from a tap to another place: **hosepipe**, **hose** ◦ *a garden hose* ◦ *a fire hose* (= a pipe used for carrying water to a fire)
- a line of connected pipes that are used for carrying liquid or gas: **pipeline** ◦ *The oil pipeline stretches from Iraq to the Turkish coast.*

■ pipes in buildings
- a large pipe that carries water or gas to a building: **main** (*often plural*) ◦ *We'll have to turn off the water at the mains.*
- all the pipes and water tanks, etc in a building: the **plumbing** (*noun* U) ◦ *The plumbing in this house is very old and noisy.*
- if you fit new pipes, etc into a room, building, etc, you **put*** them **in**, **install** them ◦ *He's just put in a new central heating system.* ◦ *They're having a shower put in.*
- a person whose job is to put in and repair water pipes, etc: **plumber**

■ pipes that carry water, etc away
- a pipe or hole that dirty water, etc goes down to be carried away: **drain**
- (used about a liquid) to flow away: **drain** (**away**); to cause a liquid to drain away: **drain** sth ◦ *Dirty water drains away through this pipe under the sink.* ◦ *He drained the water from the heating system.*
- the whole system that is used to remove water from a place: **drainage** (*noun* U)

▷ toilets ⇨ TOILET

- the long metal or plastic pipe that is fixed under the edge of a roof to carry away rainwater: **gutter**
- a pipe which goes down the side of a building, especially one that carries water from the roof into a drain: **drainpipe**

■ problems with pipes
- to make it difficult or impossible for anything to pass through a pipe, gutter, etc: **block** (sth) (**up**), **clog** (sth) (**up**) (**with** sth) ◦ *The water won't go down the sink – it's completely blocked up.* ◦ *There's something clogging up the gutter.*
- something that is blocking a pipe, etc: **blockage**; to remove a blockage: **unblock** sth ◦ *a blockage in the drainpipe* ◦ *I can't unblock the sink.*
- to break open suddenly and violently: **burst*** ◦ *a burst pipe*
- a small hole or crack that liquid or gas can get through: **leak**; to get out through a hole or crack: **leak** ◦ *a leak in a pipe* ◦ *The pipes are leaking.* ◦ *Water is leaking through the ceiling from the bathroom pipes.*

---

pity ⇨ SAD, SYMPATHY

---

place[1] where sb/sth is

1 places
2 where?
3 being or not being in a place
see also PLACE[2], DIRECTION, MOVE, PUT, DISTANCE

1 places
- a particular position or area: **place**, **spot** ◦ We always go to the same place for our holidays. ◦ *We found a nice little spot to put up our tent.*
- the area near or around sth: **surroundings** (*noun plural*) ◦ *The school is set in beautiful surroundings.*
- an area which is different in some way from those around it: **zone** ◦ *a war zone*
- the place where sth happens: **scene** ◦ *the scene of the accident*

▷ parts of a country or town ⇨ COUNTRY[1], TOWN
▷ parts of the world ⇨ WORLD

■ space
- an area which is empty or available for use: **space** (*noun* C/U); having a lot of space: **spacious** ◦ *a parking space* ◦ *We need a lot of space to work in.* ◦ *There wasn't enough space on the shelf for all the books.* ◦ *a spacious flat*
- enough space: **room** (*noun* U) ◦ *I couldn't get on the bus – there was no room.* ◦ *Is there any room left in the cupboard or is it full?*
- to create more space or room for sb/sth: **make* room/space for** sb/sth ◦ *Can you make room for one more person?*

2 where?
- at, in or to a place: **where ...** ◦ *This is where she was born.* ◦ *Where are you going?*
- (used when you ask a question and want to show surprise) where: **wherever ...** ◦ *Wherever did you buy that dress?*

- at, in, or to the place where you are or live: **here** ◦ *Come here.* ◦ *The people here don't seem very friendly.*
- not at, in, or to the place where you are or live: **there** ◦ *She's over there somewhere.* ◦ *'Do you like Rome?' 'I've never been there.'*

- the place where sb/sth is or should be: **position**, **location** ◦ *The pilot confirmed his position to the air-traffic controllers.* ◦ *The location of the flat is ideal.*
- to be in a particular place: **be located ...**, (*formal*) **be situated ...** ◦ *The hotel is located just outside the city.*
- (used about towns, areas of countryside, etc) to be in a particular place: **lie* ...** ◦ *The village lies six miles south of Bath.*
- the place where sb/sth can be found: (*formal*) **whereabouts** (*with singular or plural verb*) ◦ *I need to know the exact whereabouts of the people on this list.*

▷ more on the location of buildings ⇨ BUILDING

■ not being definite about a place
- at, in, or to a place that you do not know or name exactly: **somewhere** (*AmE also* **someplace**) ◦ *She's going to study somewhere in the States – I can't remember where exactly.*
- at, in, or to another place: **somewhere else** (*AmE also* **someplace else**), (*formal*) **elsewhere** ◦ *We always go to the same restaurant. Let's go somewhere else for a change.* ◦ *If customers aren't happy with the service, they'll go elsewhere.*

- at, in, or to any place: **anywhere** (*AmE also* **anyplace**) (*usually used in questions and negative statements*) ◦ *Do you know anywhere where I can get a map of the city?* ◦ *I can't find my keys anywhere.*

place[1] *contd.*

- in any place, it does not matter where: **anywhere** ◦ *'Where shall I put your book?' 'Oh anywhere will do.'*
- at, in, or to any other place: **anywhere else** (*usually used in questions or negative statements*) ◦ *I only know London – I've never lived anywhere else.*
- at, in or to any place: **wherever** ◦ *You can sit wherever you like.*

- at, in, or to all places: **everywhere**, (*informal*) **all over the place** ◦ *I've tried everywhere, but I can't find a pair of shoes to fit me.* ◦ *We've been all over the place looking for you.*
- in every part of sth: **all over** (sth), **throughout** sth ◦ *He was famous all over the world.* ◦ *The disease had spread throughout the city.*

- not in any (particular) place: **nowhere** ◦ *'Where have you been?' 'Nowhere, I've been waiting for you.'*

■ not knowing where you are
- to be in a situation where you do not know where you are or which direction you should be going in: **be lost** ◦ *Oh dear – I think we're lost.*
- to become lost: **get* lost**, **lose*** your **way** ◦ *You'd better take a map – you don't want to lose your way.*

▷ finding your way ⇨ DIRECTION

3 being or not being in a place

- being in a place: **presence** (*noun* U); *adjective*: **present** ◦ *I could feel the presence of somebody else in the room.* ◦ *Who was present at the meeting?*
- not being in a place: **absence** (*noun* U); *adjective*: **absent** ◦ *He finally returned to work after a long period of absence.* ◦ *A lot of people were absent from work today – they've all got flu.*
- at the place where sth happened: **on the spot** ◦ *Ask Peter about the accident – he was on the spot when it happened.*

■ **MORE ...**
- a place which is easy to reach is **accessible**; *noun* (U): **accessibility** ◦ *We need to go somewhere which is accessible by car.*
- a place which is very difficult to reach is **inaccessible**; *noun* (U): **inaccessibility** ◦ *The island is inaccessible except by private boat.*

place[2] parts and positions

1 sides and surfaces
2 in front or behind
3 at the side
4 above or below
5 in or out
6 in the middle

where sb/sth is ⇨ PLACE[1]

see also DISTANCE, DIRECTION, MOVE, PUT

1 sides and surfaces

- the outside part of sth: **surface** ◦ *the surface of the earth*
- any of the flat outer surfaces of an object: **side** ◦ *A cube has six sides.*
- the place where a surface ends on the side of an object; the area near this: **edge**, **side** ◦ *Don't put your cup on the edge of the table – it might get knocked off.* ◦ *Move the books to the side of the table so that I can put the tray in the middle.*

▷ more on surfaces ⇨ SURFACE

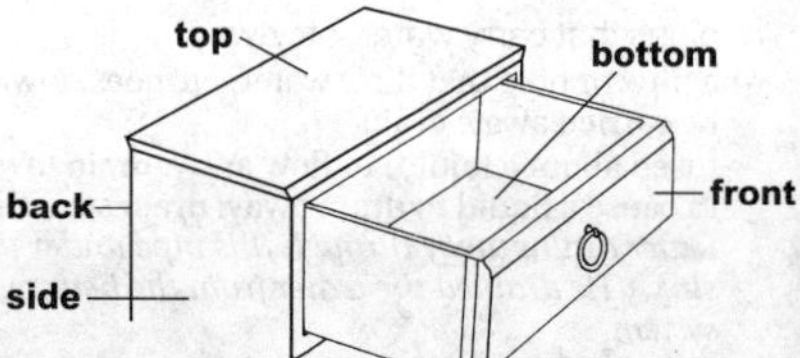

■ top and bottom
- the highest level or part of sth: **top** ◦ *There was an incredible view from the top of the tower.* ◦ *They climbed to the top of the hill.*
- on the highest part or surface of sth: **on top** (**of ...**) ◦ *I've put the medicine on top of the cupboard so that the children can't reach it.* ◦ *They've got a beautiful Christmas tree with a star on top.*
- the lowest part of sth: **bottom** ◦ *The body was discovered at the bottom of the river.* ◦ *What's that in the bottom of your cup?*

- with the top side or part where the bottom should be: **upside down** ◦ *My little sister was hanging upside down from the branch of the tree.*

■ front and back
- the side or surface of sth that faces forward and is seen: **front**; *adjective*: **front** ◦ *The front of the house needs painting.* ◦ *She stood at the front door and rang the bell.* ◦ *the front seat of a car*
- on the front surface of sth: **on the front** (**of ...**) ◦ *Write your name and subject on the front of the book.*
- the side or surface of sth that is furthest from the front: **back**; *adjective*: **back** ◦ *Turn round, I don't want to look at the back of your head.* ◦ *We arrived late so we had to sit in the back row.* ◦ *Come round to the back door when you arrive – we'll be in the garden.*
- the back part of sth, especially of a car: **rear**; *adjective*: **rear** ◦ *the rear of the building* ◦ *I saw him from the rear.* ◦ *I can't see anything out of the rear window.* ◦ *Look in the rear view mirror before you overtake.*
- on the back surface of sth: **on the back** (**of ...**) ◦ *The price is on the back of the book.*

- if the back part of sth, for example a pullover, is where the front should be, we say that it is **back to front** (*AmE* **backwards**) ◦ *Did you know you're wearing that pullover back to front?*

■ side and middle
- any of the surfaces of sth except the top or bottom: **side** ◦ *the four sides of a box*
- any of the surfaces of sth except the top, bottom, front or back: **side** ◦ *The door was on the side of the house.*
- either of the two flat surfaces of sth thin like paper: **side** ◦ *The pattern was printed on both sides of the material.*
- either of the two parts of a place or object: **side** ◦ *the other side of the room/road/river*
- the part of sth that is about the same distance from the ends or sides of sth: **middle, centre** (*AmE* **center**) ◦ *the middle of the road/room* ◦ *the centre of a circle*

▷ the right or left side of sth ⇨ RIGHT/LEFT

■ inside and outside
- the inner part or surface of sth: **inside**; *adjective*: **inside** ◦ *the inside of the box* ◦ *Put your wallet in your inside pocket – it's safer.*
- the inner part of sth, especially of a building, car, etc: **interior**; *adjective*: **interior** ◦ *They're having the interior completely redecorated.* ◦ *interior walls*
- the outer part or surface of sth, not the inside: **outside, exterior**; *adjectives*: **outside, exterior** ◦ *The outside of the car looked all right but the engine was worn out.* ◦ *The exterior of the church needs cleaning.*
- connected with the inside part: **inner**; connected with the outside part: **outer** ◦ *the inner ear* ◦ *Take off the outer packaging and put the dish in the oven.*

- if the inside of sth, for example a piece of clothing, is on the outside, it is **inside out** ◦ *Did you know you've got your jumper on inside out?*

▷ picture at CLOTHES

2 in front or behind
- further forward than sb/sth: **in front** (**of ...**) ◦ *The children ran on in front.* ◦ *Would you like to stand in front of me since you're smaller?*
- at or to the back of sb/sth: **behind** (**...**) ◦ *If you stand behind me, they might not see you.* ◦ *Our dog always runs behind the sofa when people come to visit.* ◦ *Look behind before you pull out of the parking space.*

- in the part that is nearest the front: **at/in the front** (**of ...**) ◦ *a room at the front of the house* ◦ *She sat in the front (of the car).*
- in the part that is furthest from the front: **at/in the back of** (**...**) ◦ *a garden at the back of the house* ◦ *The children can sit in the back of the car.*

- to have the front part towards sb/sth: **face** sb/sth ◦ *The Town Hall faces the river.*
- in a position directly facing sb/sth: **opposite** (**...**) ◦ *If you sit opposite me I'll be able to see you better.*

- in the direction that is in front of you: **forwards, forward** ◦ *Could everybody please move forward?* ◦ *Face forwards so you can see what I'm doing.*
- at a certain distance in front, in the direction that you are going or looking: **ahead** (**of ...**) (*adjective, adverb*) ◦ *The road ahead looked narrow and steep.* ◦ *We could now see their car about 50 metres ahead of us.* ◦ *Look, I'll go ahead and see if I can find help.*
- in the direction that is behind you: **back, backwards, backward**; *adjective*: **backward** ◦ *Could everyone take a step back please?* ◦ *She went away without even giving a backward glance.*

3 at the side
- along or at the side of sb/sth: **next to ..., by ..., beside ..., at the side** (**of ...**) ◦ *Next to the bank is the post office.* ◦ *Come and sit by me.* ◦ *Stay close beside me and don't get lost.* ◦ *I sat at the side of his bed.* ◦ *He was waiting at the side of the road.*

- on the other side of a place: **across ..., over ...** ◦ *The children's school is just across/over the road from our house.*
- on the other side of or further than a place: **past ...** ◦ *You'll see the pub just past the church.*
- on the other side of a curved path or area: **around ..., round ...** ◦ *There's a phone box just round the corner.*

4 above or below
- in a higher position than sb/sth else: **above** (**...**), **over ...** ◦ *I hung the picture on the wall above/over my desk.* ◦ *The people who live above us make a lot of noise.* ◦ *We looked up at the sky above.*

Note: when sth moves from one side of sth to another, you can only use **over**: ◦ *Sometimes the planes fly directly over the house.*

- above your head: **overhead** (*adjective, adverb*) ◦ *overhead cables/wires.* ◦ *A flock of birds flew overhead.* ◦ *The storm's directly overhead now.*
- in a higher position than sth else: **upper** ◦ *the upper floors of a building*

- supported by a surface: **on ...** ◦ *'Where's my dictionary?' 'It's on the desk over there.'* ◦ *Put the book on the table please.*
- on sth, and partly or completely covering it: **over ...** ◦ *If it starts raining, we'll have to put a cover over all these things.*

- in a lower position than sb/sth else inside the same building, on the same part of the body, etc: **below** (**...**) ◦ *He looked over the bridge at the river rushing past below.* ◦ *Your skirt should come to just below the knee.*
- in or to a lower position than sth else or covered by sth else: **under ..., underneath** (**...**), (*more formal*) **beneath ...** ◦ *'Where's my pen?' 'It's under your notebook.'* ◦ *The cat was asleep under the table.* ◦ *We finally found the letter underneath a pile of books.* ◦ *The boat disappeared beneath the waves.*

Note: when sth moves from one side of sth to another, you can only use **under**: ◦ *We had to crawl under the fence to get into the garden.*

place² *contd.*

– under the surface of the ground: **underground** (*adjective, adverb*) ◦ *There's an underground river running through the town.* ◦ *The cables all run underground.*

5 in or out

– at or to the inner part of sth: **in …, inside …** (*AmE also* **inside of …**) ◦ *Could you pack the books in these boxes?* ◦ *Hello! Come in – how are you?* ◦ *Kingston is in Jamaica.* ◦ *Inside the church, it was cool and quiet.* ◦ *We opened the door and went inside.*
– at or to a place that is not inside sth: **outside** (**…**) (*AmE also* **outside of …**) ◦ *I had to wait outside the room while they made their decision.*

Note: at is used to describe a particular position or point and with buildings when we are thinking of their use or who lives there: ◦ *at the top of a hill* ◦ *at the bottom of the page* ◦ *Who's at the door?* ◦ *at home/school/church* ◦ *I spent the night at Jo's (house).*

– in the direction of sth or moving to a position inside sth: **into …** ◦ *I looked down into the hole, but I couldn't see anything.* ◦ *Thousands of people poured into the city centre.*
– away from a place or no longer in a place: **out** (**of …**) ◦ *I didn't feel like getting out of bed.* ◦ *Have you taken the chicken out of the oven?* ◦ *He opened the window and put his head out.* ◦ *John was out of the room when the news was announced.*

– towards the inside or centre of sth: **in, inwards, inward** ◦ *Could everybody move in a bit please?* ◦ *We had to stand in a circle facing inwards.*
– towards the outside: **outwards, outward** ◦ *The door opens outwards.*

– in or into a house, building, etc: **inside, indoors**; *adjectives*: **inside, indoor** ◦ *'Where's John?' 'He's inside.'* ◦ *It's getting a bit cold – shall we go indoors?* ◦ *We'll have to have the party indoors if it starts raining.* ◦ *It's a wonderful house – they've even got an indoor swimming pool.*
– not in a house, building, etc: **outside, outdoors**; *adjectives*: **outside, outdoor, open-air** ◦ *It looks really cold and wet outside. Let's stay in this evening.* ◦ *Look! The sun's shining. Shall we go outside?* ◦ *We sat outdoors before dinner.* ◦ *They had organized outdoor activities for the children.* ◦ *It was warm enough to swim in the open-air swimming pool.*

– on the inside of sth, especially of the human body or of an institution, country, etc: **internal** (*adverb* **internally**); on the outside: **external** (*adverb* **externally**) ◦ *the internal organs* ◦ *a country's internal affairs* ◦ *The doctor examined her internally, but could find nothing wrong.* ◦ *The external signs appear very late – you would never know that she was so ill.*

Note: we use **in** with countries: ◦ *in Canada* ◦ *in the United States* and with large islands: ◦ *We spent our holidays in Corsica.* With small islands, we use **on**: ◦ *She lives on the Isle of Wight.*

6 in the middle

– near the centre of sth: **in the middle** (**of …**) ◦ *in the middle of the room*
– in the middle: **middle** (*only before a noun*) ◦ *I usually wear this ring on my middle finger.* ◦ *'Which button should I push?' 'The middle one.'*
– in the centre (especially of a town): **central** ◦ *This flat is quite expensive but it's very central.*
– in the space that separates two things: **between** A **and** B ◦ *a stream running between the gardens and the field*
– surrounded by people or things; in the middle of a group of people or things: **among …** ◦ *They live in a little house among the trees – it's quite hard to see it from the road.*
– at a position that is the same distance from two points: **halfway/midway** (**between** A **and** B) ◦ *the halfway point of the walk* ◦ *We live midway between London and Brighton.*

plan ⇨ INTEND/PLAN

plane

1 aircraft and their parts
2 travelling by plane
3 flying a plane
see also FLY², TRAVEL, TRANSPORT

1 aircraft and their parts

– any vehicle that can fly in the air: **aircraft** (*plural* **aircraft**) ◦ *a jet aircraft* (= powered by a jet engine)
– a vehicle with wings and one or more engines that can fly through the air: **plane, aeroplane** (*AmE* **airplane**) ◦ *to travel by plane* ◦ *a plane ticket* ◦ *a plane crash* ◦ *a supersonic plane* (= a plane that can fly faster than the speed of sound)

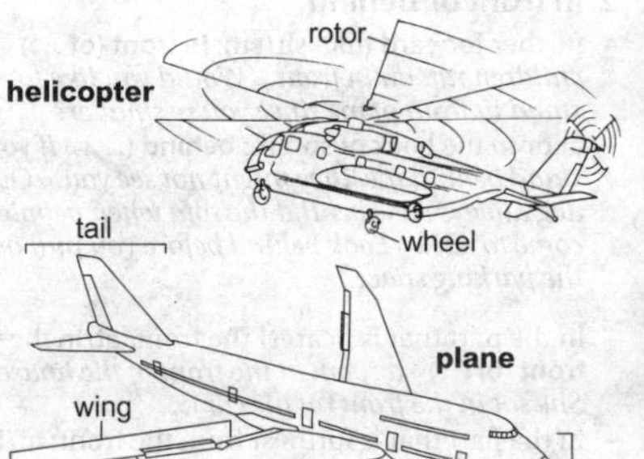

– a large plane that carries passengers: **airliner**; a very large jet plane that carries passengers: **jumbo (jet)**
– a plane that carries goods: **cargo plane**
– a plane that takes off and lands on the sea: **seaplane**
– a small plane: **light aircraft** (*plural* **light aircraft**); a small plane with two/four/eight, etc seats: **two-seater, four-seater, eight-seater**, etc

- a type of very small and very light aircraft: **microlight**

▷ small aircraft that do not have engines ⇨ **FLY**[2]

▷ aircraft that are used in war ⇨ **AIR FORCE**

2 travelling by plane

- to travel by plane: **fly***; a journey on a plane: **flight** ◦ *Is it cheaper to fly to London or go by train?* ◦ *Our flight to Australia was very long and tiring.*
- a company that provides regular flights for people and goods: **airline** ◦ *Which airline would you prefer to fly with?*
- a flight made regularly according to a timetable: **scheduled flight**
- a flight in a plane hired for a particular purpose or a particular group of people: **charter flight** ◦ *I'm going to take a charter flight; it's much cheaper.*
- a plane that travels frequently between two places: **shuttle** ◦ *I'm catching the shuttle up to Edinburgh.*

- the amount of money you pay to travel by plane: (**air**) **fare**
- a ticket to travel by air: **air ticket** ◦ *a one-way ticket* ◦ *a return ticket* ◦ *a first-class ticket*
- a place where air tickets can be bought and where you can arrange your journey: **travel agent's, travel agency**

- a place where planes can land and take off, and that has buildings for passengers to wait in: **airport** ◦ *Heathrow airport*
- an airport building where journeys begin and end: **terminal** ◦ *European flights leave from Terminal 3.*

- to go to an airline desk at an airport and say that you have arrived: **check in** (**at** sth); the place where you do this: **check-in** (**desk**) ◦ *Where's the check-in for flights to Johannesburg, please?*
- bags, etc that you take with you onto a plane: **hand luggage** (*AmE* **hand baggage**) (*noun* U) ◦ *Can I take my guitar as hand luggage?*
- money that you have to pay for bags, etc that are heavier than the weight limit: **excess baggage** (**charge**) ◦ *Will I have to pay excess baggage?*

- a place in an airport where you wait before getting on your plane: **departure lounge**
- a shop in an airport where you can buy goods which have no tax on them: **duty-free shop**
- an exit from the terminal building to the plane: **gate** ◦ *Passengers for flight ZX123 to Nairobi should proceed to gate 17.*
- (used about a plane) to be ready for passengers to get on: **board** ◦ *Flight SA999 to Rio de Janeiro is now boarding.*
- to get on a plane: **board** ◦ *How much longer before we board?*
- a ticket that you need in order to board a plane: **boarding card, boarding pass**

- a person who is travelling on a plane, etc but is not working on it or controlling it: **passenger**
- the person who is in charge of a plane: **captain** ◦ *This is your captain speaking.*
- all the people who look after the passengers on a plane: **cabin crew** (*with singular or plural verb*)
- a person who looks after the passengers on a plane: **flight attendant**; a man who does this is also called a **steward**; a woman who does this is also called a **stewardess**

- the part of a plane where the passengers sit: **cabin**
- the part of an airliner with the cheapest passenger seats: **economy class** (*noun* U); parts with more expensive seats: **first class** (*noun* U), **business class** (*noun* U), **club class** (*noun* U) ◦ *I usually fly economy.* ◦ *a business-class seat*
- happening or provided during a journey on a plane: **in-flight** ◦ *in-flight movies*

- to get off a plane: **disembark**
- to stop for a short time on a plane journey: **stop over**; *noun*: **stopover** ◦ *We're planning to stop over in London.* ◦ *We had a two-hour stopover in Delhi on our way to Sydney.*
- a plane that leaves soon after another arrives and that takes you on the next part of your journey: **connection** ◦ *If this plane is late, I'll miss my connection in Dallas.*
- to change to a different plane during a journey: **transfer** ◦ *At Heathrow we transferred to a domestic airline.*

- a feeling of tiredness caused by travelling to a place where the local time is very different: **jet lag** (*noun* U); sb who suffers from this is **jet-lagged**

3 flying a plane

- to control a plane and make it fly: **fly** (sth) ◦ *I've always wanted to learn to fly.* ◦ *Flying an airliner is a highly skilled and responsible job.*
- a person who flies a plane, etc: **pilot**; a person who sits next to the pilot and helps to fly the plane: **co-pilot**
- a person who uses maps, etc to find out which way a plane should go: **navigator**
- all the people who work on a plane: **crew** (*with singular or plural verb*) ◦ *The plane has a crew of seven.*
- the part of a plane where the pilots sit: **cockpit**

- to leave the ground and start flying: **take* off**; *noun*: **take-off** ◦ *We took off at three-thirty.* ◦ *Take-off has been delayed for thirty minutes.*
- to come back to the ground: **land, touch down**; *noun*: **landing** ◦ *We should be landing in just a few minutes.* ◦ *The plane had just touched down when there was a bomb alert.* ◦ *It was a rather bumpy landing!*
- to move slowly along the ground before take-off or after landing: **taxi** ◦ *The plane taxied up to the terminal building.*

- a place where passenger planes take off and land: **airport**
- an area of land, smaller than an airport, where planes can take off or land: **airfield**
- a piece of land that is cleared for planes to land and take off: **airstrip, landing strip**

plane *contd.*

- a long piece of ground with a hard surface where aircraft take off and land at an airport, etc: **runway**
- a place where helicopters take off and land: (**helicopter**) **pad**
- a tall airport building from where planes are controlled: **control tower**
- a person at an airport who gives radio instructions to pilots from the control tower: **air traffic controller**
- a system for finding out the position of aircraft, etc by using radio waves: **radar** (*noun* U) ∘ *a radar screen*

- to go higher in the sky: **go* up, climb** ∘ *Is the plane still going up?* ∘ *We climbed to a height of ten thousand feet.*
- to go lower or come down: **go* down,** (*formal*) **descend**
- to fly downwards very quickly: **dive*** ∘ *The fighter dived down to attack the enemy bomber.*
- if an aircraft flies without using an engine, it **glides**
- the height of an aircraft above sea level: **altitude**

■ accidents in planes

- an accident in a plane, etc: (**plane**) **crash**; *verb*: **crash** (sth)
- to land an aircraft causing damage to it: **crash-land** (sth); the pilot or the aircraft **crash-lands**; *noun*: **crash landing** ∘ *He was forced to crash-land in a field.* ∘ *The plane ran out of fuel and had to make a crash-landing in the desert.*
- if a plane falls from the sky or lands in a place outside an airport, it **comes* down** ∘ *The plane came down in the middle of a field.*
- broken pieces of a plane, etc that has been badly damaged: **wreckage** (*noun* U) ∘ *The rescuers managed to pull three survivors from the wreckage.*

- a plastic or rubber jacket filled with air that keeps sb floating in water: **life jacket**
- a thing that you put over your face to be able to breathe in an emergency in a plane: **oxygen mask**
- a piece of strong cloth that is tied to sb and that lets them fall slowly to the ground when they jump from a plane: **parachute; to use a parachute: parachute** ∘ *He parachuted safely to the ground.*

▷ picture at FLY²

■ **MORE ...**

- a special route in the air which planes fly through: **flight path**: ∘ *Our flight path takes us over the South of France and the Mediterranean*
- violent or uneven movement of air, making flight uncomfortable: **turbulence** (*noun* U)

- the business of flying (building aircraft, flying them, running airlines, etc): **aviation** (*noun* U) ∘ *the aviation industry*
- done from an aircraft: **aerial** (*adjective, only before a noun*) ∘ *an aerial attack/photograph*
- an occasion when people can look at planes and watch them flying: **air show**

planet ⇨ STAR/PLANET/MOON

plant

1 different kinds of plant
2 parts of a plant
3 growing and taking care of plants
see also TREE

1 different kinds of plant

- a living thing that grows in the ground: **plant**
- a plant like a small thick tree with many branches: **bush**
- a small bush: **shrub**
- a plant that grows up trees and walls or along the ground: **creeper**
- a plant that is grown or picked for its flowers: **flower**
- a plant that is eaten as food: **vegetable**
- a plant whose leaves, seeds, etc are used in medicines and to give food more flavour: **herb**

▷ more on flowers and vegetables ⇨ FLOWER, VEGETABLE

- a wild plant that is not wanted in a garden: **weed**
- plants that grow in the sea: **seaweed** (*noun* U)

toadstool **mushrooms** **cactus** (*plural* **cactuses** *or* **cacti**)

- a plant (such as a mushroom or toadstool) which is not green and does not have leaves or flowers: **fungus** (*plural* **fungi** *or* **funguses**) (*noun* C/U) ∘ *edible fungi* ∘ *fungus growing on the bark of a tree*

- a small green plant, with no flowers, that grows in a flat mass in damp places, especially on rocks or trees: **moss** (*noun* U)
- a green plant with a lot of long thin leaves but no flowers: **fern**
- a short green plant with thin leaves that covers the ground in parks, gardens and fields: **grass** (*noun* U)
- a tall plant like grass, that grows in or near water: **reed**
- a tall tropical plant of the grass family: **bamboo** (*noun* C/U)

▷ more on grass ⇨ GRASS

2 parts of a plant

▷ illustration of a plant ⇨ FLOWER

- the long thin part of a plant which the leaves and flowers grow on: **stalk, stem**
- one of the parts of a plant that grows under the ground: **root**
- the round root of certain plants: **bulb** ∘ *Tulips and daffodils grow from bulbs.*

- one of the small hard parts of a plant from which a new plant can grow: **seed** ◦ *a packet of flower seeds*

- the flat green part of a plant: **leaf** (*plural* **leaves**)
- the part of a plant from which the seeds or fruit grow: **flower**
- a young tightly closed leaf or flower before it opens: **bud**
- the part of a plant which contains seeds and is eaten: **fruit**
- a hard sharp point growing on the stem of some plants: **thorn**; *adjective*: **thorny**
- a small thorn: **prickle**; *adjective*: **prickly**

▷ more on fruit ⇨ FRUIT

3 growing and taking care of plants

- (used about a plant) to live in a place: **grow*** ◦ *Rice doesn't grow in cold places.*
- to put plants, seeds, etc in the ground to grow: **plant** sth ◦ *Plant the bulbs in October or November.*
- to plant sth and look after it: **grow*** sth ◦ *We grow a lot of our own vegetables.*
- to plant seeds in the ground: **sow*** sth ◦ *to sow grass seed*
- the earth that plants grow in: **soil** (*noun* U) ◦ *sandy soil* ◦ *poor/rich soil*

- when plants first show above the ground they **come* up** ◦ *The lettuces are starting to come up.*
- a very young plant which has grown from a seed: **seedling**
- to pull a plant out of the ground: **pull** sth **up**, **uproot** sth
- to move a plant from one place to grow it in another place: **transplant** sth
- to cut off part of a plant in order to help it to grow: **prune** sth *The roses need pruning.*
- to take away wild plants from a garden: **weed** (sth) ◦ *Can I help you to weed the garden?*

- to give water to plants: **water** sth ◦ *Don't forget to water the plants when I'm on holiday.*

- substances which you can add to the soil to help plants grow: **fertilizer** (*noun* U) (= any natural or chemical substance which helps plants grow), **compost** (*noun* U) (= a mixture of old waste vegetable and plant material), **manure** (*noun* U) (= waste material from animals) ◦ *a compost heap* (= a place where you keep compost)

- a pot in which a plant can be grown: **flowerpot**
- a plant which is grown and kept indoors: **pot plant, house plant**
- a building made of glass in which plants are grown: **greenhouse**

- a piece of land (usually near a house) where flowers and vegetables are grown: **garden** (*AmE* **yard**)

▷ more on gardens ⇨ GARDEN

■ **MORE ...**

- the study of plants: **botany** (*noun* U); a person who studies plants: **botanist**
- the study of how to grow flowers, fruit and vegetables, or the business of growing these plants: **horticulture** (*noun* U)
- a vegetable or fruit that is grown naturally without artificial chemicals is **organic** ◦ *organic vegetables*

---

plastic ⇨ MATERIAL

---

plate/bowl/dish

see also MEAL, COOK, CUP/GLASS

- a flat, usually round dish that is used for eating or serving food: **plate** ◦ *a dinner plate* ◦ *a side plate* (= a small plate used at the side of a bigger plate)
- a small round plate that you put under a cup: **saucer**
- the amount of food on a plate: **plate, plateful** ◦ *a plate of sandwiches* ◦ *huge platefuls of spaghetti*

- a shallow container used for cooking or serving food: **dish** *Put the vegetables in the serving dishes.*
- a deep round container without a lid used for serving food or for eating food such as soup, breakfast cereal, ice cream: **bowl** ◦ *a soup bowl* (= a bowl for eating soup) ◦ *Would you like a bowl of soup* (= a bowl with soup in it)*?*

- the general word for all cups, plates and dishes: **crockery** (*noun* U) ◦ *Where do you keep the crockery?*
- plates, cups and saucers that are made of a high quality white clay: **china** (*noun* U) ◦ *a china teapot*

- if a plate, bowl, etc has a small piece broken off it, it is **chipped**; if it is broken so that you can see a thin line, but it is not broken into pieces, it is **cracked**

---

play[1] a story acted in a theatre

1 kinds of play
2 the action and people in a play
3 producing a play
4 seeing a play

see also FILM, TELEVISION/RADIO

1 kinds of play

- a story which is written to be performed by actors in the theatre, on television, or on radio: **play** ◦ *to see a play* ◦ *to go to a play* ◦ *a radio play*
- plays in general (as a form of writing and performance): **drama** (*noun* U); connected with plays or the theatre: **dramatic** ◦ *20th century drama* ◦ *a drama student* ◦ *an amateur dramatic society*

play[1] *contd.*

- a play which is serious, with a sad ending: **tragedy**; serious plays in general: **tragedy** (*noun* U); something that has a sad ending in the style of tragedy is **tragic** ∘ *Shakespeare's tragedies* ∘ *Greek tragedy*
- a play which is amusing, with a happy ending: **comedy**; amusing plays in general: **comedy** (*noun* U); sth that makes you laugh is **comic** ∘ *He's just written a new comedy.* ∘ *a comic character*
- a play which is funny and full of ridiculous situations: **farce**; such plays in general: **farce** (*noun* U)
- a play which is short and funny, often as part of comedy television programme: **sketch** ∘ *a television programme with some amusing sketches*
- a play which has singing and dancing: **musical**
- a play which is based on traditional stories, with singing, dancing and jokes, and is usually performed around Christmas: **pantomime**, (*informal*) **panto** (*plural* **pantos**)

2 the action and people in a play

- the events of a story in a play, film, etc: **plot** ∘ *Could you understand the plot?*
- the words and actions of an actor in a play, film, etc: **part**, **role** ∘ *Who played the part of the old man?* ∘ *a difficult role for an inexperienced actor*
- a person who is part of the story of a play: **character** ∘ *the two main characters in this play*
- to perform a part (= pretend to be a different person) in a play or film: **act**; *noun* (U): **acting**
- a man/woman who acts in a play or film: **actor**; a female actor can also be called an **actress**

▷ more on actors and acting ⇨ ACT

- one of the main parts a play is divided into: **act**
- one part of an act in a play: **scene** ∘ *Act 1, Scene 2 of 'Macbeth'* ∘ *the ghost scene in 'Hamlet'*
- a place represented on the stage of a theatre: **scene** ∘ *a street scene* ∘ *a scene change*
- the furniture, painted cloth, etc that are used on the stage: **scenery** (*noun* U)
- objects that are on the stage and are used by the actors in a play: **props** (*noun plural*)

3 producing a play

- to do sth in front of an audience: **perform** (sth) ∘ *to perform a play*
- an occasion when sth is performed: **performance** ∘ *We saw a performance of 'Macbeth' at the National Theatre.* ∘ *There are two performances, at 2pm and 8pm.*
- to practise for a play or film: **rehearse** (sth); the time when this happens: **rehearsal** (*noun* C/U); the last rehearsal, when all the actors wear their costumes: **dress rehearsal** ∘ *We need to rehearse that scene again.* ∘ *We'll have to have another rehearsal tomorrow.* ∘ *It went very well in rehearsal.*
- to arrange the performance of a play: **produce** sth, **put* sth on** ∘ *He's producing 'Twelfth Night' in Stratford.* ∘ *The National Theatre is putting on a new season of Ibsen plays.*
- the complete preparation and performance of a play, opera, etc: **production** ∘ *a new production of 'Pygmalion'*
- to tell the actors what to do in a play: **direct** (sb/sth); the person who does this: **director**
- a person who organizes the business side of presenting a play in the theatre: **producer**
- to choose the people who will act in a play: **cast*** a play, **cast*** sb (**as** sb/sth); all the actors and actresses in a particular play: **cast** (*with singular or plural verb*) ∘ *He always seems to be cast as a villain.* ∘ *an all-star cast*
- writing and performing plays as art and entertainment: **theatre** (*AmE* **theater**) (*noun* U) ∘ *a study of 20th century theatre*
- a person who writes plays: **playwright**, **dramatist**
- a person whose job is to give an opinion about plays, films, etc: **critic** ∘ *a drama/ theatre critic*

4 seeing a play

- a building where you go to see plays, shows, etc: **theatre** (*AmE* **theater**)
- if you go to see a play, you **go* to the theatre** ∘ *We usually go to the theatre once a month.*
- the group of people who go to see a particular performance of a play: **audience** (*with singular or plural verb*)

▷ more on theatres and audiences ⇨ THEATRE, AUDIENCE

■ MORE...

- a successful play that the public likes: a **success**, a **hit**
- a play, film, book, etc that is a total failure: a **flop**; *verb*: **flop**

play[2] having fun; enjoying yourself

see also GAME, SPORT

- to do sth that gives you pleasure and enjoyment: **play** (**with** sb/sth); *noun* (U): **play** ∘ *Let's go out and play.* ∘ *Play is an important part of a child's education.*
- an object for a child to play with: **toy** ∘ *The children were playing with their toys.*
- a form of play or sport with rules: **game** ∘ *party games* ∘ *a ball game a game of football*
- to play a game: **play** sth ∘ *to play games* ∘ *Let's play hide-and-seek* (= a game in which one child hides and other children look for him/her).

▷ more on toys ⇨ TOY

- pleasure and enjoyment: **fun** (*noun* U), (*more formal*) **amusement** (*noun* U) ∘ *We had great fun with the kids yesterday.* ∘ *The children enjoyed themselves, but there wasn't much amusement for the grown-ups.*
- to behave in a silly way: **play/fool/mess** (**about/around**) (**with** sb/sth) ∘ *Stop messing about – you'll break something.* ∘ *There's no need to be so serious – we're only fooling around.*

▷ more on fun and enjoyment ⇨ ENJOY

- a public place where there are things for children to play with: **playground**
- a place where very young children go to learn and play: **playgroup, playschool**
- a room in a house used for children to play in: **playroom**

- to jump over a rope that you, or two other people, hold at each end, turning it round and round under the feet and over the head: **skip**
- to walk in a shallow pool or in the sea: **paddle**

- to use sth in order to play on it or play with it: **go* on** sth, **have a go on/with** sth ◦ *I want to go on the see-saw, mummy.* ◦ *Would you like to have a go on the swing?* ◦ *Why can't I have a go with your skipping rope?*
- when people do sth or play with sth one after the other, they **take* turns** (**to** do sth/**at** doing sth); one person after another has a **turn** ◦ *The children took turns to go on the swing.* ◦ *It's my turn!*

pleasure

- enjoying sth ⇨ ENJOY
- being happy ⇨ HAPPY

poem

see also LITERATURE

- a piece of writing usually in short lines, which sometimes rhyme: **poem** ◦ *a poem by Burns about a mouse* ◦ *a book of poems* ◦ *a love poem*
- poems, seen as a type of literature: **poetry** (*noun* U) ◦ *I enjoy reading poetry.*
- relating to poetry or having the qualities of poetry: **poetic** ◦ *a poetic description of a country scene*
- a collection of poems, often by different authors: **anthology** ◦ *an anthology of 20th century Scottish poetry*
- writing which is not poetry: **prose**

- a short and often amusing poem: **rhyme**
- a short poem for children, like a song: **nursery rhyme**
- a long song or poem which tells a story: **ballad**
- a very long poem which tells the story of a hero and his adventures: **epic**

- a person who writes poems: **poet**
- to say a poem from memory: **recite** sth ◦ *At the party, Jenny sang a song and John recited a poem.*
- a performance when sb reads poems to an audience: **poetry reading**

- one row of words in a poem: **line** ◦ *A sonnet is a type of poem with fourteen lines.*
- a group of lines which form part of a poem: **verse** ◦ *I can't remember the second verse. How does it go?*

- a regular repeated pattern of sound used in songs, poems, etc: **rhythm** (*noun* C/U)
- the technique of using words which have the same sound as each other, especially at the ends of lines: **rhyme** (*noun* U); a word which has the same sound as another word: **rhyme**; if words have the same sound, they **rhyme** ◦ *an interesting use of rhyme* ◦ *In this type of poetry, the last two lines usually rhyme.*
- writing that is arranged in lines which have a definite rhythm and which often rhyme at the end: **verse** (*noun* U) ◦ *Molière wrote his plays in verse.*
- poetry which does not rhyme: **blank verse**

police

see also CRIME, LAW

- the official organization whose job is to make sure that people obey the law and to prevent and solve crime: **the police** (*noun plural*) ◦ *Quick – there's been a burglary. Call the police!*
- a member of the police: **police officer, policeman** (*plural* **policemen**), **policewoman** (*plural* **policewomen**), (*informal*) **cop**
- all the police officers in a country or area: **police force**
- a number of police officers: **police** (*noun plural*) ◦ *How many police were on duty that night?*

- the person who controls a police force: **chief of police**
- (in Britain) the head of a police force in a particular area: **Chief Constable**
- other ranks of police in Britain (beginning with the most senior): **superintendent, inspector, sergeant,** (**police**) **constable** (*abbreviation* **PC**)
- a police officer whose job is to find out about crime: **detective**
- (in Britain) the police department that tries to find out about crimes: **Criminal Investigation Department** (*abbreviation* **CID**)
- a section of the police force that deals with a particular kind of crime: **squad** (*with singular or plural verb*) ◦ *the drugs/bomb/fraud squad*

- the building where the police work: (**police**) **station**
- a room in a police station where prisoners are locked up: **cell**
- the central office of a police force or other organization: **police headquarters** (*with singular or plural verb*)

- the special clothes that police officers wear when they are working: **uniform**

police *contd.*

- when a police officer who is working does not wear a uniform, he/she is **in plain clothes**; a police officer who does not wear a uniform is a **plain-clothes** police officer

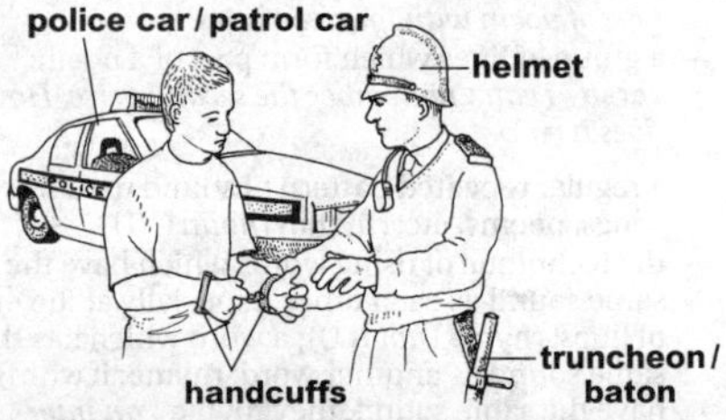

■ the work that the police do

- to keep control in a place by using the police or a similar official group: **police** sth ◦ *The country needs more officers to police the streets of Britain effectively.*
- to try to stop people committing crimes: **fight* crime, enforce the law**

- when a police officer is working, he/she is **on duty**
- to go around a town, building, etc to make sure nothing is wrong: **patrol** (sth); doing this: **on patrol** ◦ *PC Skinner was patrolling the area as usual when he heard a shot.* ◦ *to be out on patrol*
- a group of police who go around the streets to make sure that there is no trouble: **patrol**
- to go with sb to protect them or prevent them from escaping: **escort** sb; the person who is being escorted is **under escort** ◦ *The prisoner arrived at the court under escort.*
- a person or group of people who escort sb: **escort** ◦ *a police escort*

- if you want to call the police by telephone, you **dial 999** (in the UK), **dial 911** (in the US)
- to ask or tell the police, firemen, etc to go somewhere: **call** sb **out** ◦ *PC Jones has just been called out to a bank robbery.*

polite

> **1** being polite
> **2** not being polite
> **see also** BEHAVIOUR

1 being polite

- if you act and speak in a way that is helpful and thoughtful towards other people, you are **polite** (*adverb* **politely**), (*formal*) **courteous** (*adverb* **courteously**); *nouns* (U): **politeness, courtesy** ◦ *It's polite to say 'please' and 'thank you'.* ◦ *a very polite child* ◦ *'How very kind of you,' he replied courteously.* ◦ *She didn't even have the courtesy to say she was sorry.*

- to treat sb in a polite way: **show respect to** sb/sth ◦ *You should show more respect to your grandmother.*

- the way in which a person acts or behaves: **behaviour** (*AmE* **behavior**); the way of behaving that is thought to be polite in a particular society or culture: **manners** (*noun plural*) ◦ *His behaviour is dreadful.* ◦ *good/bad manners* ◦ *It's bad manners to stare at people.*
- a person who has good manners and behaves in a polite way is **well-behaved**, (*rather formal*) **well-mannered** ◦ *well-behaved children*

- the way you talk or behave on an official occasion or when you do not know the other people well is **formal** ◦ *a formal speech* ◦ *a formal letter of complaint*
- the skill of saying and doing the right thing so that people are not offended or upset: **tact** (*noun* U), **diplomacy** (*noun* U) ◦ *Being a social worker requires a lot of tact.*
- if you behave with tact, you are **tactful** (*adverb* **tactfully**), **diplomatic** (*adverb* **diplomatically**) ◦ *You'll have to break the news to her very tactfully.* ◦ *I tried to be diplomatic, but in the end I couldn't help losing my temper.*

- the word for making a request or order more polite: **please** ◦ *Please could you tell me the way to the station?* ◦ *Pass the jam, please.*

2 not being polite

- not polite: **rude** (*adverb* **rudely**), **impolite** (*adverb* **impolitely**), **discourteous**; *nouns* (U): **rudeness, discourtesy** ◦ *It's rude to stare at someone like that.* ◦ *I'd like to apologize for my rudeness.*
- a person who has bad manners and behaves in a rude way is **badly behaved**, (*rather formal*) **ill-mannered** ◦ *I've never seen such badly behaved children.*

- rude, not showing proper respect to sb/sth: **cheeky** (*adverb* **cheekily**); rude behaviour: **cheek** (*noun* U), **nerve** (*noun* U), **disrespect** (*noun* U) ◦ *Don't be so cheeky!* ◦ *'Why don't you do it yourself?' he replied cheekily.* ◦ *She had the nerve to tell me she didn't need me any more.* ◦ *You've got a lot of nerve talking to me like that!* ◦ *I'm sorry – I didn't mean any disrespect.*
- rude and unpleasant: **insolent**; *noun* (U): **insolence** ◦ *insolent behaviour*
- to speak to sb in a rude way: **insult** sb; a rude thing that sb says: **insult**

▷ more on insults ⇨ INSULT

- if you say exactly what you think without being polite or tactful, you are **blunt** (*adverb* **bluntly**), **tactless** (*adverb* **tactlessly**); *nouns* (U): **bluntness, tactlessness** ◦ *It was very tactless of you to tell her she'd put on weight.* ◦ *She told me quite bluntly that I would have to leave.*
- rude and unfriendly, not interested in sb/sth: **offhand** ◦ *She was very offhand with us – she was obviously thinking about something else.*

politics

1 political activity
2 political ideas and political parties
see also GOVERNMENT, PARLIAMENT, ELECTION

1 political activity

- work and ideas that are connected with governing a country, a town, etc: **politics** (*with singular or plural verb*) ◦ *Are you interested in politics?* ◦ *She's very involved in local politics.* ◦ *to go into politics* (= to become a politician)
- connected with politics: **political** (*adverb* **politically**) ◦ *a political party* ◦ *Their decision to close the school is just political.* ◦ *to be politically well informed*

- a person whose job is in politics, especially a Member of Parliament: **politician**
- an important and experienced politician who has earned public respect: **statesman/woman** (*plural* **statesmen/women**)
- a person who is the head of sth or in charge of sth: **leader** ◦ *a political leader*

- the ability to make other people do what you want: **power** (*noun* U) ◦ *Our aim is to reduce the power of central government.*
- the group of people who govern a country: **government** (*with singular or plural verb*)
- when a new government is formed, it **comes* to power, gains power** ◦ *This government came to power in 1979.*
- the people who are ruling a country are **in power, in government, in office** ◦ *The Conservatives have been in office for several years.*
- not governing or ruling a country: **out of power, out of government, out of office**

- a political plan of action or statement of ideas: **policy** (*noun* C/U) ◦ *The government is not explaining its policies well.* ◦ *What is party policy on privatization?*
- a change in sth in order to make it better: **reform** (*noun* C/U) ◦ *a major reform in the system of taxation* ◦ *to be in favour of political reform*
- a person who tries to change society and make it better: **reformer**
- opposing change: **reaction** (*noun* C/U); *adjective*: **reactionary** ◦ *forces of reaction* ◦ *reactionary opinions*
- a person who tries to stop political or social change: **reactionary**

- a group of people who have the same ideas and who want to persuade others that they are right: **movement** ◦ *the anti-abortion movement*
- a public protest or march in which a crowd of people show how they oppose or support sb/sth: **demonstration**; *verb*: **demonstrate** ◦ *to take part in a demonstration against cuts in government spending* ◦ *Thousands of people have been demonstrating against unemployment.*
- a person who takes part in a public protest or march: **demonstrator**
- changing or trying to change the political system by violent action: **revolution** (*noun* C/U) ◦ *to start a revolution* ◦ *the French revolution*

▷ more on protests and demonstrations ⇨ COMPLAIN/PROTEST

2 political ideas and political parties

- a group of people with the same political opinions and who try to win election to parliament: **party** ◦ *A lot of people haven't yet decided which party to vote for in the election.* ◦ *The same party has been in power for nearly twenty years.*
- political actions carried out by or for political parties: **party politics** (*with singular or plural verb*)

- a person who has joined a political party: (**party**) **member** ◦ *a Communist Party member/a member of the Communist Party*
- a person who supports a political party: **supporter** ◦ *a Labour supporter*

- political parties or groups that support social equality, government control of industry, etc: **the Left, the left wing**; *adjectives*: **left-wing** ◦ *The Left is not expected to do well in the general election.* ◦ *the left wing of the Conservative party* ◦ *left-wing policies*
- a person who supports left-wing ideas: **left-winger**
- political parties or groups that support traditional values, private control of industry, etc: **the Right, the right wing**; *adjective*: **right-wing** ◦ *the right wing of the Labour Party* ◦ *right-wing ideology*
- a person who supports right-wing ideas: **right-winger**
- political parties or groups with moderate views: **the centre**; *adjectives*: **centre, centrist** ◦ *a shift of power to the centre* ◦ *a centre party* ◦ *centrist opinions*

- a person's political opinions and beliefs: **politics** (*noun plural*) ◦ *What are her politics?*
- a set of ideas for a political or economic system: **ideology**; *adjective*: **ideological** ◦ *communist ideology*
- a general belief on which ideas or actions are based: **principle** ◦ *socialist principles*

■ political ideas and beliefs

- in favour of existing methods and ideas and only gradual change: **conservative**; a person with conservative opinions: **conservative**; conservative beliefs: **conservatism** (*noun* U) ◦ *I've always been a conservative.*
- in favour of freedom of choice and moderate change: **liberal**; a person with liberal opinions: **liberal**; liberal beliefs: **liberalism** (*noun* U)
- agreeing with modern methods and ideas: **progressive**; a person with progressive opinions: **progressive** ◦ *progressive policies*

- not particularly conservative or progressive: **moderate**; a person with moderate opinions: **moderate**
- not moderate: **extreme**; a person with extreme opinions: **extremist**; extreme beliefs and actions: **extremism** (*noun* U) ◦ *dangerous extremists*

politics *contd.*

- in favour of great political or social change: **radical**; a person with radical opinions: **radical**; radical beliefs: **radicalism** (*noun* U) ◦ *radical solutions to society's problems* ◦ *a famous 19th century radical*
- in favour of changing the political system by violent action: **revolutionary**; a person with revolutionary opinions: **revolutionary**

▷ kinds of political belief, see table below

▷ economic systems ⇨ **ECONOMY**

- the scientific study of government: **politics** (*noun* U), **political science** (*noun* U) ◦ *She's got a degree in politics.*

■ **MORE . . .**

- a person who disagrees in public with the actions or ideas of his/her government: **dissident**
- a person who uses violent action for political purposes: **terrorist**
- a person who is in prison because of his/her political beliefs: **political prisoner**

poor

see also RICH

- having very little money and a low standard of living: **poor**; (*noun* U): **poverty** ◦ *a poor man/family* ◦ *poorer countries*
- very poor: (*formal*) **poverty-stricken**
- a person who is poor can be called **hard up**, **badly off**, **not well off** ◦ *Many old people are very hard up these days.*
- if you have no money at all, you are **penniless**, (*informal*) **broke** ◦ *He said he was broke and asked me to lend him a pound.*
- if you temporarily do not have as much money as you need, you are **short** (**of money**) ◦ *I can't help you I'm afraid – I'm a bit short myself at present.*
- if you have less money than sb else or less money than before, you are **worse off** (**than . . .**); if you have a bit more money than sb else or than you had before, you are **better off** (**than . . .**) ◦ *Paul's got a new job but he seems to be worse off than ever.* ◦ *She's just had a pay rise, so she ought to be a bit better off now.*
- the group of people who have very little money: **the poor** (*with plural verb*)

▷ different groups in society ⇨ **SOCIETY**

■ life without enough money

- suffering caused by being poor: **hardship** (*noun* U), (*more formal*) **deprivation** (*noun* U)
- very dirty and unpleasant conditions of living: **squalor** (*noun* U); *adjective*: **squalid** ◦ *While the fortunate few live in luxury, many people live in squalor.* ◦ *squalid surroundings*
- to ask sb for food, money, etc because you are very poor: **beg**; a person who lives by doing this: **beggar** ◦ *It is sad to see young people begging.*
- with no money, no home and no job: **down and out**; a person who is in this situation: **down and out** ◦ *The centre of the town was full of beggars and down and outs.*
- a person who has no home or job and who moves from place to place: **tramp** (*AmE* **bum**)
- to sleep outside without bedding, etc: **sleep* rough**
- people who have no home are **homeless**; the group of homeless people: **the homeless** (*with plural verb*); the situation of having nowhere to live: **homelessness** (*noun* U)

the idea that...	is called... (*noun* U)	connected with this idea (*adjective*) or a person who believes in this idea (*noun*)
there should be no government or laws in a country	**anarchism**	**anarchist**
the state should control everything and there should be no opposition	**fascism**	**fascist**
the country where you live should form an independent nation; or that your country is better than others	**nationalism**	**nationalist**
people should protect the natural world	**environmentalism, the green movement**	**environmentalist, green**
women should have the same rights as men	**feminism**	**feminist**
some races (especially your own) are better than others	**racism**	**racist**

■ places where poor people live
– an area of a city with dirty buildings and where living conditions are very bad: **slum, the slums** (*noun plural*), (*more formal*) **deprived area** ○ *Many Victorian slums have been cleared from our cities.* ○ *He grew up in one of the most deprived areas of the country.*
– a small town or part of a town where poor people live in bad conditions in badly built huts, etc: **shanty town**

■ help for poor people
– government help given to very poor people: **benefit** (*noun* U), **welfare** (*noun* U)
– food, money, clothes, etc given to people who need it badly: **charity** (*noun* U) ○ *I may be poor but I refuse to live on charity.*

pop/rock

see also MUSIC, SING, DANCE

– the modern music that is most popular among young people: **pop (music)** (*noun* U); one piece of pop music: **pop song**
– a type of pop music with a very strong beat, played on electric guitars, etc: **rock (music)** (*noun* U)
– a type of rock music most popular in the 1950s: **rock and roll** (*noun* U), (*informal*) **rock 'n' roll**
– a type of West Indian popular music with a regular, repeated rhythm: **reggae** (*noun* U)
– a kind of song in which the words are spoken, not sung: **rap** (*noun* U/C)

– a person who sings pop music: **pop singer**
– a famous pop singer or pop musician **rock star, pop star**
– a group of people who play pop music together: **(rock) band, (pop/rock) group**
– the most important singer in a pop/rock group: **lead singer**
– a person who plays the drums: **drummer**
– a person who plays the guitar: **guitarist**

– you can hear live performances of pop music at a **pop/rock concert**
– a series of concerts which are held in one place over a short period of time: **pop/rock festival**

– a pop music record that only has one song on each side is a **single** ○ *Have you heard their new single?*
– a person whose job is to introduce pop songs on the radio or in a disco: **disc jockey, DJ**
– a machine in a café or bar that plays records when you put a coin in: **juke-box**

– the official lists of the most popular records of pop songs: the **charts** (*noun plural*) ○ *a recent release which is already climbing up the charts*
– the ten (or twenty or forty) most popular records in a chart: **the top ten** (or **twenty** or **forty**) ○ *this week's top ten*
– the most popular record at a particular time: **number one** ○ *number one in the charts* ○ *the record at number one*

– a video film that is made to be shown when a particular piece of pop music is played: **pop video** (*plural* **pop videos**)
▷ more on recorded music ⇨ RECORD

popular
– being liked ⇨ LIKE²
– being successful ⇨ SUCCEED/FAIL

population ⇨ PEOPLE

port ⇨ BOAT

position
– where sth is ⇨ PLACE¹
– where sth is in relation to sth else ⇨ PLACE²

positive ⇨ YES/NO

possible¹ possible or probable or certain

1 possible
2 probable
3 certain
4 not certain

1 possible
– if it is possible for sth to happen, or if it is possible that sth is true, it **may, might** or **could** happen or be true ○ *We may be going to Thailand in the summer if we can get some time off work.* ○ *Police think the driver may have been drunk when he crashed the car.* ○ *I might come to the film if I'm not too busy.* ○ *'Where's Peter?' 'He might be upstairs.'* ○ *'What was that bird that just flew past?' 'I'm not sure, but it could have been a robin.'*

possible[1] *contd.*

– if it is not possible for sth to happen, or if it is not possible that sth is true, it **can't** or **couldn't** happen or be true ∘ *They can't have arrived already – the journey takes more than five hours.* ∘ *She can't be forty – I just don't believe it!* ∘ *It couldn't have been an eagle – it was much too small.*

– if sth may happen or be true, it is **possible** ∘ *'Will she get the job?' 'It's possible but not very likely.'*
– a thing that might happen or might be true: **possibility of** sth/**that . . .** (*noun* C/U) ∘ *There's a strong possibility of rain tomorrow.* ∘ *There's no possibility that we'll get there before five.*

– when you are not sure that sth will happen or is true, you can say **perhaps**, **maybe**, **possibly** ∘ *'Why are his cheeks red?' 'Perhaps he's been running.'* ∘ *'Will I see you tomorrow?' 'Maybe.'* ∘ *'Will you be late home tonight?' 'Possibly. It depends on how much work I can get done.'*
– when you do not know if sth will happen or is true, you can say **it's hard to say** ∘ *'Doctor, when do you think I can leave hospital?' 'It's hard to say at the moment, but I'll have a better idea when I've had a look at your X-rays.'*

– the possibility of sth happening (usually sth that you want): **chance of** sth/**that . . .** (*noun* C/U) ∘ *There's a chance of winning a prize.* ∘ *I felt I had little chance of getting the job.*
– to have a chance of doing sth: **stand* a chance** (**of** sth) ∘ *Nobody thought he stood much chance of winning the race.*

– the possibility of sth bad happening: **risk** (*noun* C/U) ∘ *a risk of losing your investment* ∘ *Is there any risk of the bomb exploding?* ∘ *At the risk of boring you, here are all the photos we took on holiday last year.*
– to do sth when you know the result may be bad: **run* the risk of** sth ∘ *If we don't leave now we run the risk of missing the plane.*

2 probable

– if you expect sth to happen or be true, it is **probable** (*adverb* **probably**) ∘ *It's quite probable that she'll get the job instead of me.* ∘ *I'll probably be home at about 6 o'clock depending on the traffic.*
– a thing that will probably happen or be true: **probability** (*noun* C/U) ∘ *There's a strong probability that the match will have to be cancelled if this bad weather continues.* ∘ *There's little probability of a good harvest.*

– if sth is probable or expected, it is **likely**; you can say **it is likely (that) . . .**, or **there is likely to be . . .**, or sb/sth is **likely to** do sth; the state of being likely: **likelihood** (*noun* U) ∘ *the likely result of the inquiry* ∘ *Is it likely that you'll get the job?* ∘ *She's not likely to do anything stupid.* ∘ *There's no likelihood that taxes will go up.*
– very likely: **more than likely**

– to seem probable: **look as if . . .**, **look like . . .** ∘ *It looks as if it's going to rain.* ∘ *It looks like rain.*

– if you think that sth is very likely, you can say that **there must . . .**, or that sb/sth **must . . .**, or you can say (*informal*) **I bet (that) . . .** ∘ *There must be some mistake!* ∘ *You must be joking!* ∘ *He must have been cold without a coat in this weather.* ∘ *I bet she won't phone – she never keeps a promise.*
– if you think that sth is very unlikely, you can say that **there can't/couldn't . . .**, or that sb/sth **can't/couldn't . . .** ∘ *There can't have been ten people in such a small car.* ∘ *You can't be serious!* ∘ *He surely couldn't have forgotten my birthday!*

– to think that sth is likely or probably true: **suppose (that . . .)**, **imagine (that . . .)**, **suspect (that) . . .** ∘ *I imagine you'd like a rest after your long journey.* ∘ *They'll sack me now, I suppose.*
– the feeling that sth is likely: **suspicion** ∘ *I had a slight suspicion that she was not telling the truth.*

– to say that you think sth is probably true, you can say **presumably, no doubt, I expect (that . . .)**, (*especially AmE*) **I guess (that . . .)** ∘ *If the train was late arriving, it will presumably be late leaving too.* ∘ *You are no doubt wondering why I have asked you here.* ∘ *I guess/expect you'd like to have an early night.*

– if sth is probably not true or will probably not happen, it is **improbable**, **unlikely**, **not/hardly likely** ∘ *It seems improbable that house prices will rise.* ∘ *The President's personal telephone number is hardly likely to be in the phone book.*

3 certain

– if sth is definitely the case, it is **certain** (*adverb* **certainly**); you can say **it is certain (that) . . .**, or **there is certain/sure/bound to be . . .**, or sb/sth is **certain/sure/bound to** do sth ∘ *One thing is certain – I'm not going out alone at night again.* ∘ *You certainly did the right thing.* ∘ *It is certain that prices will rise.* ∘ *There are sure to be a lot of accidents in this fog.* ∘ *There's bound to be a long wait at the airport.* ∘ *He's certain to be prime minister one day.* ∘ *The weather's bound to get better in a couple of days.*
– if it is certain that you will get sth, you are **sure of** sth ∘ *Whatever happens, you can be sure of a lot of help and support from your friends and family.*

– fixed and unlikely to change: **definite** ∘ *I have not been given a definite date for my interview yet.*
– showing sth to be true or certain: **conclusive** ∘ *We now have conclusive proof of his guilt.* ∘ *to prove sth conclusively*

– certainly: **definitely**, **undoubtedly**, **for sure/certain** ∘ *She definitely needs hospital treatment.* ∘ *He was undoubtedly drunk – it was obvious to us all.* ∘ *You're going to need a lot of help – that's for sure.*

– something that is certain: **certainty** (*noun* C/U) ○ *It's an absolute certainty that we'll go out of business unless our orders improve.* ○ *There's no certainty that any of us will have a job in six months time.*

– if you believe that sth is certain, you are **sure** (**of** sth), **sure** (**that**) **...**, **certain** (**of** sth), **certain** (**that**) **...** ○ *We must be sure of our facts before we make a decision.* ○ *I feel sure I've met him somewhere before.* ○ *Are you absolutely sure that you know what you're doing?* ○ *I thought I wanted this job, but now I'm not so sure.* ○ *She's not certain it's the same man.*
– completely certain: **positive** (**that**) **...**, **convinced** (**that**) **...** ○ *He was positive that somebody was following him.* ○ *She was convinced he was going to win the race.*
– the state of being sure: **certainty** (*noun* U) ○ *He speaks with such certainty that you feel he must be right.*

4 not certain

– if sth is not definitely the case, it is **uncertain** ○ *The survival of the firm is very uncertain.* ○ *It's very uncertain whether we'll still be here next year.*
– if sth is probably not true or probably will not happen, it is **doubtful**, **unlikely** ○ *It's very doubtful that the president will resign.*

– to give an answer or opinion without being sure of all the facts: **guess** (sth), **speculate** (**about/on** sth); *noun*: **guess** ○ *Can you guess how many people turned up at the meeting?* ○ *I can only speculate what may have happened last night.* ○ *My guess is that she'll agree to it.*

– if you are not sure about sth, you are **uncertain about/of** sth, **unsure** (**about/of** sth), **doubtful** (**about** sth) (*adverb* **doubtfully**) ○ *If you are uncertain of anything, please ask for more details.* ○ *George seemed rather uncertain of his facts.* ○ *I was unsure about inviting a stranger into my house.* ○ *She was doubtful about whether to go on holiday with them or not.* ○ *'Are you sure that's right?' she asked doubtfully.*
– the state of being uncertain: **uncertainty** (*noun* U), **doubt** (*noun* C/U), **question** (*noun* U) ○ *If you have any doubts, we'll discuss the matter again.* ○ *There is no doubt that we have a problem.* ○ *There is no question about it; everything has already been decided.*

– to think that sth probably is not true or will not happen: **doubt** sth ○ *'Do you think it'll rain tonight?' 'I doubt it.'* ○ *She doubted that she would ever see him again.* ○ *I doubt whether I am explaining this very well.*

– to express or feel doubt about sth: **question** sth ○ *Are you questioning my honesty?*
– to doubt whether you can trust sb or believe sth: **suspect** sth ○ *I began to suspect his reasons for being so generous.*

– doubting that sth is true, correct, etc: **sceptical** (*AmE* **skeptical**); a person who doubts a lot: **sceptic** (*AmE* **skeptic**) ○ *The government has made lots of promises, but I'm sceptical about its ability to keep them.*

■ making sure
– to do what is necessary in order to be sure that sth is safe, correct or in good condition: **check** (sth), **make sure/certain** (**that ...**), (*more formal*) **ensure** (*AmE* **insure**) (**that**) **...** ○ *We'd better check what time the train leaves.* ○ *She looked back at the house to make sure that the windows were all closed.* ○ *Please ensure that you have all the necessary papers with you.*

■ **MORE ...**
– when sth is not very likely to happen, but you try to do it anyway, you do it **on the off chance** ○ *I didn't think you'd be at home, but I called in on the off chance.* ○ *I'll speak to her again on the off chance that she has changed her mind.*

---

possible² something can be done

whether sth is possible, probable, etc ⇨ POSSIBLE¹

– to have the skill, time, power, etc to do sth: **be able to** do sth; *opposite*: **be unable to do** sth ○ *The dentist said he'd be able to see me on Thursday morning.* ○ *Will you be able to come to the office party?*
– if sb/sth is able to do sth, they/it **can** do it ○ *Can you drive a car?* ○ *This type of tree can grow to a height of over 30 metres.* ○ *I couldn't understand a word he said.*

– if sth can be done, it is **possible**; *noun* (C/U): **possibility** ○ *It is now possible to fly direct to the island.* ○ *Is there any possibility I can see you at the weekend?* ○ *There is a possibility of promotion after a short time.*
– not possible: **impossible**; *noun* (C/U): **impossibility** ○ *It's impossible to get there on time.* ○ *Getting a pair of trousers that fits both my waist and my leg length seems to be an impossibility.*
– absolutely impossible: **out of the question** ○ *Gary said that marriage was out of the question until he was thirty.*
– what cannot be done: **the impossible** ○ *Don't try to do the impossible.*

– possibly able to do sth or be sth in the future: **potential** (*adverb* **potentially**); *noun* (U): **potential** ○ *Wind power is a potential source of energy.* ○ *a potentially dangerous situation* ○ *Helen has the potential to become an Olympic champion.*

– if sth can be done successfully, it is **feasible**, **practicable** ○ *a feasible plan/solution* ○ *This system is just not practicable. It's too expensive and it takes too long to organize.*

possible[2] *contd.*

- if an idea, plan, etc is sensible or possible to do, it is **practical**; *noun* (U): **practicality** ◦ *I'm not sure of the practicality of the plan.*

■ making sth possible

- to make sth possible: **enable** sb/sth to do sth, **allow** sb/sth **to** do sth ◦ *The master key enables me to unlock any door in the hotel.* ◦ *A week of sunshine allowed the farmers to harvest nearly all the corn.*

- a situation or time when it is possible to do sth that you would like to do: **opportunity** (*noun* C/U) ◦ *an ideal opportunity to acquire a new skill* ◦ *He was at the meeting but there was no opportunity for a chat.*
- to make use of a chance that you have to do sth: **take* the opportunity to** do sth ◦ *While I'm there, I'm going to take the opportunity to see some old friends.*
- (used especially about the work people do) the opportunity to do sth: **scope** (**for** sth), **room** (**for** sth) ◦ *The job offers plenty of scope for creativity.* ◦ *Although your work is not too bad, there is still room for improvement.*

■ **MORE ...**

- if you understand what is or is not possible and you do not try to pretend that things are different, you are **realistic**; *opposite*: **unrealistic**; *noun* (U): **realism** ◦ *It was unrealistic of me to think I could finish this work by the weekend.* ◦ *It's time you showed a bit of realism and accepted that you're not going to get any of your money back.*

post

1 letters and parcels
2 addresses and stamps
3 sending sth through the post

1 letters and parcels

- a written message that you send to sb: **letter**
- a paper cover for a letter: **envelope**
- a card that you write a message on and send to sb: **postcard**
- something that is covered with paper and sent through the post: **parcel** (*AmE also* **package**)
- a general term for letters, parcels, etc that you receive: **post** (*noun* U), (*especially AmE*) **mail** (*noun* U) ◦ *Did we get any post this morning?*

▷ more on letters and parcels ⇨ LETTER[1], PARCEL

2 addresses and stamps

- the number of the house or flat, the name of the street and the name of the town or city in which the person who will receive a letter lives: **address** ◦ *Do you know their address?* ◦ *a change of address*
- to write an address on an envelope: **address** sth (**to** sb) ◦ *Address the envelope to me, and I'll reply with the information you need.*
- a group of letters and numbers which you write after the address: **postcode** (*AmE* **zip code**) ◦ *'What's his postcode?' 'It's SW1 4NP.'*

- a place in a post office where letters are kept until they are collected by the person they have been sent to: **PO Box**, **post office box** ◦ *Sunshine Holidays, PO Box 25, Leeds, Yorkshire*

- the amount of money it costs to send a letter or parcel: **postage** (*noun* U) ◦ *The postage on this parcel will be quite expensive.*
- a small square piece of paper stamp you stick on an envelope in order to show that you have paid for the postage: (**postage**) **stamp** ◦ *Three stamps for Australia please.* ◦ *a first-class stamp* ◦ *Don't forget to stick/put a stamp on the envelope before you post it!*
- the mark that the post office prints over the stamp, showing the date and place where it was posted: **postmark** ◦ *The postmark says it was posted in Manchester on 20 March.*

3 sending sth through the post

- the system for sending letters and parcels: **post**, (*especially AmE* **mail**); *adjective*: **postal** ◦ *a mail van* ◦ *a good postal service*
- a place where you go to buy stamps, send letters and use other postal services: **post office**
- the box in which you put a letter when you send it: **postbox**, **letterbox** (*AmE* **mailbox**)

- to send a letter using the official post system: **send*** sth **by post**; a person who sends a letter: **sender** ◦ *I want to send this by second-class post.*
- to put a letter or parcel in a post box: **send*** sth (**off**), **post** sth, (*especially AmE*) **mail** sth ◦ *If you send it today it should arrive tomorrow.* ◦ *Would you mind posting this letter for me?*
- if you have sent sth, but the person has not received it yet, it is **in the post** ◦ *Your cheque's in the post.*
- if you receive a letter for sb who lived in the house before you, you can write their new address on the envelope and **send* it on**, **forward** it ◦ *Could you forward my mail to my new address please?*
- if you send your reply to a letter immediately, you send it **by return** (**of post**) ◦ *Please reply by return of post.*

- the system for sending letters and parcels by aeroplane: **airmail** (*noun* U); by train and boat: **surface mail** (*noun* U) ◦ *I'd like to send this by airmail.* ◦ *How long will it take if it goes by surface mail?*
- a service which you pay for, where you can receive money if your letter is lost or damaged in the post: **registered post** (*noun* U) ◦ *I'd like to send this by registered post, please.*
- a service which you pay for, where the person who receives your letter must sign a document to say that they have received it: **recorded delivery** (*noun* U)

- to take a letter or parcel to the address which is written on it: **deliver** sth ◦ *The postman delivered a huge parcel this morning.*
- a man/woman whose job is to deliver letters and parcels: **postman/postwoman** (*plural* **postmen/postwomen**) (*AmE* **mail carrier**) ◦ *What time does the postman usually come?*
- the time when letters are taken out of the postbox: **collection** ◦ *The next collection is at 10 am.*
- the time when letters are brought to a place: **delivery**, **post** ◦ *There's usually a delivery at about 9 am.* ◦ *It came in the second post.*

■ **MORE . . .**

- letters that people receive although they have not asked for them, trying to persuade them to buy things, etc: **junk mail** (*noun* U)

- a person who is interested in stamps and makes a hobby of collecting them: **stamp collector**, (*formal*) **philatelist** ◦ *a keen stamp-collector*
- the hobby of collecting stamps: **stamp collecting** (*noun* U), (*formal*) **philately** (*noun* U) ◦ *a book on stamp-collecting*
- a book in which a stamp-collector sticks stamps: (**stamp**) **album**

pot ⇨ CONTAINER

potato

see also FOOD, COOK

- a hard white vegetable with a brown skin, that grows under the ground: **potato** (*plural* **potatoes**) (*noun* C/U), (*informal*) **spud** ◦ *a pound of potatoes* ◦ *potato soup* ◦ *new potatoes* (= potatoes which are cooked when they are still small)

- the brown outer covering of a potato: (**potato**) **skin** (*noun* U)
- to remove the skin from a potato with a knife or other sharp instrument before cooking it: **peel** a potato; the pieces of potato skins that have been removed: **potato peelings** (*noun plural*) ◦ *Shall I peel the potatoes?*
- a special instrument for peeling potatoes: **potato peeler** (picture at COOK)

- you can **boil** potatoes (= cook them in boiling water), **bake** them (= cook them in the oven with the skin on), **roast** them (= cook them in hot oil or fat, in an oven), or **fry** them (= cook them in a small amount of hot oil in a frying pan); *adjectives*: **boiled**, **baked**, **roast**, **fried** ◦ *Do you want boiled potatoes or baked?*
- potatoes which have been cut into long thin pieces and fried in hot oil: **chips** (*AmE* **French fries**)

- very thin pieces of potato that are fried in oil, dried and sold in packets: **crisps** (*AmE* **chips**)

- to mix cooked potatoes (usually with butter and/or milk) until they are soft: **mash** potatoes; potatoes which have been mashed: **mashed potatoes** (*noun plural*), **mash** (*noun* U) ◦ *sausage and mash*
- cold potatoes cut up and mixed with mayonnaise: **potato salad** (*noun* U)

pound

- weight ⇨ WEIGHT
- British money ⇨ MONEY

power

1 physical power
2 power over people and things
political power ⇨ POLITICS, GOVERNMENT
the power needed to make machines work ⇨ MACHINE
see also ORDER², MUST

1 physical power

- the physical ability to move things, lift things, etc: **strength** (*noun* U), **force** (*noun* U); having strength: **strong**, **powerful** ◦ *the strength/force of the wind* ◦ *the force of an explosion* ◦ *The police were ordered not to use force to stop the demonstration.* ◦ *If we can't persuade them peacefully, we shall have to get what we want by force.* ◦ *a strong army* ◦ *powerful muscles*

- to defeat sb because you are too strong for them: **overpower** sb ◦ *Harry was overpowered by the guards and taken to his cell.*
- to use physical strength to do sth or move sth: **force** sth ◦ *We had to force the window open after we had locked ourselves out.*

▷ more on being strong ⇨ STRONG/WEAK

2 power over people and things

- the ability to make other people do what you want: **power** (*noun* U) ◦ *I promised to do everything in my power to help them.*
- having a lot of power: **powerful**, **strong** ◦ *a powerful individual* ◦ *powerful people who control our lives* ◦ *a strong nation*

- the right to do sth: **power** (**to** do sth) (*noun* U) ◦ *Doctors have no power to keep a patient in hospital against their will.*
- the power and right to give orders and make people obey: **authority** (*noun* U) ◦ *I couldn't help him. I had no authority in the matter.*
- to give official permission for sth: **authorize** sth, **authorize** sb **to** do sth ◦ *Who authorized this payment?* ◦ *I don't remember authorizing you to pay this amount.*

- power when it is used indirectly, through example, fear, etc: **influence** (*noun* U); *adjective*: **influential** ◦ *I'm afraid I don't have much influence in this company.* ◦ *I find it very difficult to exert* (= use) *any kind of influence over my children.* ◦ *influential friends*
- a person or thing that affects or changes sb/sth: **influence** (**on** sb/sth) ◦ *My mother was a big influence on my life.*
- to have an influence on sb/sth: **influence** sb/sth ◦ *Who would you say has influenced you most in your life?* ◦ *The fact that she is my friend did not influence my decision at all.*

power *contd.*

- to have strong power or influence over sb/sth: **dominate** sb/sth; *noun* (U): **domination** (**of/over** sb/sth) ∘ *George dominated the discussion and soon got everyone to agree to his plan.*
- having most power or influence: **dominant**; *noun* (U): **dominance** (**of/over** sb/sth) ∘ *the dominant influence in contemporary British art* ∘ *to establish dominance over neighbouring countries*

■ using power
- the ability to organize, direct or guide sb/sth: **control** (**of/over** sb/sth) ∘ *I have been given complete control of the finance department.* ∘ *We have very little control over what happens to the weapons after they have been exported.*
- to have the ability to organize, direct or guide sb/sth: **control** sb/sth, be **in control** (**of** sth), be **in charge** (**of** sb/sth) ∘ *He tries to control every detail of her working life.* ∘ *Who is in control of this organization?* ∘ *Chris was left in charge of the office while Mr Davies was on holiday.*

- to stop sth becoming too much; to take steps to keep sth within limits: **control** sth ∘ *We are trying to control the number of tourists who visit the mountains.*
- to control sth by using rules or laws: **regulate** sth ∘ *There are laws regulating the emission of smoke from factories.*
- something which is done to control sth: **control** (**on/over** sth) ∘ *price controls*

- to control people or a situation: **direct** sth ∘ *The rescue effort was directed by the Chief of Police.*
- to control a business or a country: **run*** sth, **manage** sth; *noun* (U): **management** ∘ *Harry has been running things for ten years now.* ∘ *Kate manages a computer firm.* ∘ *the government's management of the economy*
- to watch sb/sth to make sure they are working properly, etc: **supervise** sb/sth, **oversee*** sb/sth; *noun* (U): **supervision** ∘ *Jenkins' job was to supervise all the building work on the site.* ∘ *The teaching is being overseen by the director of studies.* ∘ *The new pupils will need close supervision for a few days.*

▷ more on management ⇨ **MANAGEMENT**

- to cause sb to do sth that they do not want to do: **force** sb **to** do sth ∘ *She was forced to leave the country.*
- to make sb accept sth that they do not want: **impose** sth (**on** sb) ∘ *I'm worried that some teachers are trying to impose their political views on children.*
- to use power to make sth happen: **enforce** sth ∘ *enforced obedience*
- to try to force sb to do sth: **put* pressure on** sb (**to** do sth) ∘ *Oliver's wife was putting pressure on him to apply for another job.*

- to get or do what you want, although other people may want you to do sth else: **get*/have** your **own way** ∘ *At least I managed to get my own way over the colour of the new wallpaper!*

■ not having power
- having little power: **weak**; *noun* (U): **weakness** ∘ *a weak leader*
- having no power: **powerless**; *noun* (U): **powerlessness** ∘ *We were powerless to act.*
- not having enough power or influence: (*formal*) **impotent**; *noun* (U): **impotence** ∘ *The government is quite impotent in this matter.*
- to accept the power or control of sb/sth: **give* in** (**to** sb/sth), **submit** (**to** sb/sth) ∘ *The government refused to submit to the rebels' demands.*

- impossible to control: **out of control** ∘ *Children who are bored can easily get out of control.*
- not in your control: **out of** your **hands** ∘ *I'm sorry, but the matter is out of my hands.*

■ using power badly
- to use your power in a wrong way: **abuse** sth; *noun* (C/U): **abuse** ∘ *to abuse a position of trust* ∘ *a flagrant abuse of power*

■ getting and losing power
- to come to have control of sb/sth: **take* control/charge** (**of** sb/sth), (in the army, police, etc) **take* command** (**of** sb/sth) ∘ *The department was badly run until she took charge of it.*
- to begin to use power or have a powerful position: **take*** sth **over** ∘ *Hijackers have taken over the plane.*

- to stop having power or a powerful position: **give*** sth **up**, **hand** sth **over**, **surrender** sth ∘ *The military leader has had to hand over power to the people.*
- an occasion, or a cause, of losing power after being very powerful: **downfall** ∘ *His own greed brought about his downfall.*

practise

- for a sport ⇨ **EXERCISE**
- to get a skill ⇨ **SKILL, LEARN**

praise

see also CRITICISM, BLAME

- to say that sb/sth is good and should be admired: **praise** sb/sth (**for** sth); *noun* (U): **praise** ∘ *She was praised for her decision to stay with the children.* ∘ *They might respond better if they were given more praise.* ∘ *His latest novel has received a great deal of praise.*
- to tell sb that sb/sth is good: **recommend** sb/sth (**to** sb) ∘ *Can you recommend anyone for the job?*

- if sth deserves praise, you can call it **admirable**, **impressive** ∘ *an impressive performance*
- if sth deserves a lot of praise, you can call it **brilliant, marvellous, wonderful, excellent, amazing, outstanding**
- if sth deserves praise, but not a lot of praise, you can call it **commendable, creditable** ∘ *a creditable attempt*

- to tell sb that they have done sth well: **congratulate** sb (**on/for** sth), **offer/give*** sb **your congratulations** ∘ *We congratulated her on the birth of her first grandchild.* ∘ *He should be congratulated for the part he has played in our success.*

- when you want to congratulate sb, you can say **Congratulations!** or **Well done!**

- to tell sb politely that they look good, have done sth well, etc: **compliment** sb (**on** sth), **pay*** sb **a compliment**; *adjective*: **complimentary** ◦ *Aren't you going to compliment me on my home-made bread?* ◦ *She's used to getting complimentary remarks.*
- an act of complimenting sb: **compliment** ◦ *You shouldn't have been offended when he said you'd put on weight – I'm sure it was meant as a compliment.*

- to praise sb too much because you want to please them and get some advantage for yourself: **flatter** sb; *noun* (U): **flattery** ◦ *Don't you realize he's just trying to flatter you?* ◦ *Flattery will get you nowhere.*
- to praise your own achievements or qualities with too much pride: **boast** (**about** sth), (*informal*) **blow* your own trumpet**; *adjective*: **boastful** ◦ *Ever since he came first in the exam he's never stopped boasting about it.*

▷ more on praising yourself too much ⇨ PROUD

pray

see also CHRISTIAN, JEW, MUSLIM, RELIGION, CHURCH

- to speak to God in order to give thanks or to ask for sth: **pray** ◦ *He prayed for forgiveness.* ◦ *She prayed for him every day.* ◦ *They prayed to Krishna for help.*
- the act of praying: **prayer** (*noun* U)
- to go down or to be on your knees when you pray: **kneel*** ◦ *She knelt down and closed her eyes.* ◦ *They were kneeling in prayer.*
- the words you use when you pray: **prayer** ◦ *I said a quick prayer.*
- (especially used about children before going to sleep) to pray: **say*** your **prayers** ◦ *His mother reminded him to say his prayers.*
- to pray to and show respect for God: **worship** (God) ◦ *Many people were worshipping in the temple.*
- a person who worships God: **worshipper** ◦ *The temple was crowded with worshippers.*

- to say a special prayer which asks for God's help and protection for sb: **bless** sb ◦ *The Pope blessed the crowd in St Peter's Square.*
- a prayer asking for God's help and protection, often given by a priest: **blessing** ◦ *The congregation knelt for the blessing.*
- a prayer which you say before or after eating a meal: **grace** ◦ *to say grace before a meal*
- the Christian prayer which begins 'Our Father ...': **the Lord's Prayer**
- a short religious service when people come together for prayers: **prayers** ◦ *He has just gone to prayers at the mosque.* ◦ *evening prayers*
- a book containing prayers: **prayer book**
- a string of beads for counting prayers: **rosary**
- a piece of material to kneel on, used by Muslims: **prayer mat**

prefer

see also LIKE²

- to like one thing more than another: **prefer** sth/doing sth (**to** sth/doing sth), **prefer to** do sth ◦ *I prefer my coffee without milk.* ◦ *Do most people prefer watching television to reading books?* ◦ *We prefer to have our main meal in the evening.*
- if you want to have or do one thing rather than another, you **would rather** have/do it, you **would prefer** (**to** have/do) it ◦ *'Would you like some coffee?' 'I'd rather have some tea if there is any, please.'* ◦ *I imagine the children would rather go out and play than stay indoors on a day like this.* ◦ *Would you prefer to spend the night here or to carry on to Plymouth?*
- if you want sb else to do one thing rather than another, you **would rather** they did it, you **would prefer** them **to** do it ◦ *'Do you mind if I smoke?' 'Well, I'd rather you didn't.'* ◦ *Would you prefer me to carry on without you?*

- a liking for one thing more than another: **preference**; if you think that one action would be better than another, you can say that it is **preferable** (*adverb* **preferably**) ◦ *We can have the class on Monday or Tuesday. Does anyone have a preference?* ◦ *I think it would be preferable if we left early.* ◦ *'What time is best for you?' 'Well, preferably the morning.'*
- preferring one person or thing to another: **in preference to** sb/sth else ◦ *I don't understand why they chose her in preference to you – you're much more experienced.*

- the one you like most: **favourite** (*AmE* **favorite**) (*noun, adjective*) ◦ *Which of these pictures is your favourite?* ◦ *Who's your favourite author?*
- giving sb an unfair advantage because you like them more than the rest: **favouritism** (*AmE* **favoritism**) (*noun* U) ◦ *Teachers shouldn't have favourites.* ◦ *'He got the job because his father is a friend of the director.' 'But that's favouritism!'*

- an unfair preference for one thing over sth else: **bias** (*noun* C/U); a person who has a bias is **biased** ◦ *The BBC news is not supposed to show any political bias.* ◦ *You're biased because she's your daughter!*
- if you do not show an unfair preference for one thing over another, you are **unbiased**, **impartial** (*adverb* **impartially**); *noun* (U): **impartiality** ◦ *I'm not sure that the judge was totally impartial.*

pregnant ⇨ SEX²

prejudice

- a kind of opinion ⇨ OPINION
- prejudices against groups of people ⇨ SOCIETY

prepare ⇨ READY

present¹

- something that is given ⇨ GIVE

present² the present time

1 the period we live in
2 now
see also PAST², FUTURE, TIME

1 the period we live in

- the time now: **the present** ◦ *Stop thinking about the past. You must learn to live in the present.*
- the period we live in: **the present day, today** ◦ *a type of craftsmanship that has continued up to the present day* ◦ *British people of today*
- the present time (when compared with the past): **nowadays, these days** ◦ *Nowadays, people pay for things with credit cards.* ◦ *These days, it's very difficult to find a full-time job.*
- of the present or recent period: **modern, present-day, contemporary** ◦ *modern cars* ◦ *present-day attitudes* ◦ *contemporary music*

▷ more on being modern ⇨ MODERN

- that is already there and being used: **existing** ◦ *The existing machines are old and need to be replaced.*
- existing before and likely to continue for some time: **ongoing** ◦ *This is an ongoing problem – we'll have to do something about it soon.*

2 now

■ just now

- existing or happening now: **present, current** ◦ *We would like to stick to the present arrangements.* ◦ *current issues/prices/trends*
- at the present moment: **now, just now, at the moment, at present, currently,** (*especially AmE*) **presently** ◦ *I wonder where they are now.* ◦ *I've got a lot on my mind just now.* ◦ *The prime minister is currently in America.* ◦ *She'll be here presently.*
- at this present moment; as we are speaking now: **right now, at the moment, at this very moment** ◦ *She's not available to see you at the moment but, if you'd like to wait, I'm sure she'll see you soon.*
- at this time, in this place: **here and now** ◦ *I'm afraid it can't wait; I have to speak to you here and now.*

■ just before now

- not long before the present moment: **just now, (just) a moment/minute ago** ◦ *I don't know where she is – she was here just now.*
- during a period between not long ago and now: **recently** ◦ *I only recently started working there.*
- from a period in the past until now: **(up) until/till now, up to now** ◦ *I've been very happy in this job up till now.*

■ just after now

- very soon after the present moment: **in a minute/moment, right away** ◦ *I'll tell you about it in a moment.* ◦ *I'll be there right away.*
- for the present and the immediate future (but likely to change after a while): **for now, for the time being** ◦ *I've got enough bread for the time being, but I'll have to get some more tomorrow.*
- not long after the present time or the time mentioned: **soon** ◦ *We'll be there soon.*

▷ happening soon ⇨ SOON

president ⇨ GOVERNMENT

pretend ⇨ DECEIVE

pretty ⇨ BEAUTIFUL/ATTRACTIVE

prevent ⇨ AVOID/PREVENT

price

1 the price of sth
2 high and low prices
3 changing prices
see also BUY, SELL, PAY¹

1 the price of sth

- the amount of money that you have to pay to buy sth: **price** (*noun* C/U) ◦ *What's the price of petrol now?* ◦ *We can't afford to buy it at that price.* ◦ *to go up in price*
- to have a certain price: **cost*** (sb) sth ◦ *Having my car repaired cost me more than I expected.*
- the amount of money that you have to pay for services such as electricity: **cost** (*noun* U) ◦ *The cost of gas is going up again.*
- the prices of things in general: **cost** (*noun* U) ◦ *the cost of living*
- the amount you have to pay for using sth: **charge** ◦ *Is there a charge for parking here?* ◦ *admission charges at the museum*
- to ask sb to pay a particular amount for sth: **charge** (sb) (sth) (**for** sth) ◦ *She charged me another ten pence for the paper bag.*
- to ask sb to pay more/less than they should: **overcharge/undercharge** (sb) (**for** sth) ◦ *The garage overcharged me for the repairs.*
- to decide the price that people must pay for sth: **price** sth (**at** sth), **ask** sth (**for** sth), **sell** sth **at/for** sth ◦ *Secondhand books priced at 30p each* ◦ *They're asking a ridiculous amount for their house!* ◦ *They're selling the chairs at £20 each.*
- to tell sb what the approximate price of sth is: **quote** (sb) a price, **give*** (sb) **an estimate** ◦ *The garage man quoted me a very reasonable price for my new tyres.* ◦ *Can you give me an estimate of how much the work will cost?*
- a piece of paper showing the prices of a list of things: **price list**

2 high and low prices

- if you think that what you have to pay for sth is a lot, you can call the price **high**; much too high: **extortionate** ◦ *The bill was extortionate.*
- something which has a high price is **expensive**, it **costs* a lot**
- if sth is very expensive, it (*informal*) **costs* the earth/a fortune/a bomb**

- if you think what you have to pay for sth is not much, you can call the price **low** ◦ *The price of petrol is quite low at the moment.*
- something which has a low price is **cheap, inexpensive**, it **doesn't cost much** ◦ *cheap clothes/food/cars* ◦ *an inexpensive holiday/suit/meal*
- very cheap: (*informal*) **dirt cheap**; very cheap, or cheaper than usual: **a bargain** ◦ *It only cost a pound; I think it was a bargain!*
- for a low price: **cheaply, inexpensively**, (*informal*) **cheap** ◦ *You can travel quite cheaply by bus.* ◦ *I bought it cheap.* ◦ *It was going cheap* (= it was being sold for a low price).

- if you think what you have to pay for sth is neither very high nor very low, you can call the price **fair, reasonable**, (*informal*) **not too bad** ◦ *I got them all for a fiver, which I think isn't too bad.*

3 changing prices

- if the price of sth becomes lower, it **comes*/goes* down, falls*** ◦ *House prices are coming down.*
- if the person selling sth makes the price lower, he/she **reduces** it, **brings*** it **down, cuts*** it; *nouns*: **reduction, cut** ◦ *further reductions in the sale* ◦ *price cuts*
- a reduction in the price of sth: **discount** ◦ *Do you give a discount for cash?* ◦ *All staff get a 20% discount.*
- to reduce the price of sth by a certain amount: **knock** sth **off, take*** sth **off** ◦ *He says if I make up my mind today he'll knock another £50 off the price.*
- half the normal price: **half price** ◦ *I got it at half price.*

- if the price of sth becomes higher, it **goes* up, rises***, it is **up** ◦ *Petrol's up again!*
- if the seller makes the price of sth higher, he/she **increases** it, **raises** it, **puts*** it **up**; *nouns*: **increase, rise** ◦ *Why does the government allow them to go on putting up the price of electricity?* ◦ *price increases* ◦ *another rise in the price of cigarettes*

- a situation when most prices continue to go up: **inflation** (*noun* U)
- when the government tries to stop prices going up, it **controls** prices; *noun* (C/U): **price control** ◦ *to impose price controls*
- to stop price rises completely: **freeze*** prices; *noun*: **price freeze**

- if the price of sth does not become less or more, it **remains the same**

■ **MORE ...**

- to argue about the price of sth: **haggle (with** sb) (**about/over** sth), **bargain (with** sb) (**about/over** sth) ◦ *I got it cheap but I had to haggle.* ◦ *They bargained over the price.*

priest

1 different kinds of priest
2 the life and work of a priest

see also CHURCH, CHRISTIAN, JEW, MUSLIM, RELIGION

1 different kinds of priest

- a person who performs religious ceremonies: (especially in the Roman Catholic Church) **priest**, (in the Church of England) **vicar**, (in other Protestant Churches) **minister**
- the group of people who are priests: **clergy** (*noun* U); connected with the clergy: **clerical** ◦ *in clerical dress*
- a member of the clergy: **clergyman** (*plural* **clergymen**)
- a person who gives religious talks in church or elsewhere: **preacher**
- a priest who works in an organization like the army or a school: **chaplain**

- a senior priest who is in charge of all the churches and priests in an area: **bishop**
- a bishop who has authority over other bishops: **archbishop** ◦ *the Archbishop of Canterbury*
- a priest of high rank in the Roman Catholic Church: **cardinal**
- the head of the Roman Catholic Church: **Pope** ◦ *Pope John Paul II*

- the title of a priest: **Reverend** (*written abbreviation* **Rev**), (especially used in the Roman Catholic Church) **Father** ◦ *The Reverend Paul Smith* ◦ *Father Brown*

2 the life and work of a priest

- to make sb a priest: **ordain** sb; the ceremony of making a person a priest: **ordination** (*noun* U/C) ◦ *He was ordained last Saturday.* ◦ *Some churches now accept the ordination of women.*
- the status of being a priest: **the priesthood** (*noun singular*), **the ministry** (*noun singular*) ◦ *to enter the priesthood*
- an area which a priest is in charge of: **parish** ◦ *our local parish priest*

- the house in which the priest in charge of a parish lives: **vicarage**; Roman Catholics use the word **presbytery**
- the official home of a bishop: **palace**

- a long item of clothing worn by some priests: **cassock**
- a piece of stiff cloth that some priests wear round their neck: **dog collar**
- a piece of clothing worn by some priests in church ceremonies: **vestment** (*usually plural*)

- a religious ceremony in a church: **service** ◦ *morning service* ◦ *the eleven o'clock service*
- to speak to God in order to give thanks or to ask for sth: **pray**

▷ more on praying ⇨ PRAY

prince/princess ⇨ KING/QUEEN

print

see also BOOK, PUBLISH

- to put words, pictures, etc onto paper by using a metal or wood surface covered with ink; to make books, newspapers, etc in this way: **print** sth ◦ *Where did you get these leaflets printed?* ◦ *We'll print 1 000 copies.*
- a person or company that prints books, newspapers, etc: **printer** ◦ *It's ready to send to the printer's now.*
- when a book, etc is printed, it **goes* to press** ◦ *The information was correct at the time of going to press.*
- the process of making books, etc using print: **printing** (*noun* U) ◦ *Printing has changed dramatically in the last ten years.*

- the written letters and words found in books, newspapers, etc: **print** (*noun* U) ◦ *The print in this newspaper is so small I can hardly read it.*
- a particular style of print: **font** ◦ *Why don't you try a different font?* ◦ *an italic font*
- the dark, heavy print used for giving some words more importance than others: **bold** (**type**) ◦ *It's best if you put the title in bold.*
- the type of printing when the letters slope forwards: **italics** (*noun plural*)
- a letter, number or sign used in printing: **character** ◦ *count the number of characters and spaces in a line of print*

- a machine which is used to print things: **printing machine**, **printing press**

▷ printing when you are using a computer ⇨ COMPUTER

prison

1 prisons
2 people in prisons
3 going to prison
4 staying in prison
5 leaving prison

see also CRIME, PUNISH

1 prisons

- a building where criminals are kept as a punishment: **prison** (*AmE* **penitentiary**), **jail** (*BrE also* **gaol**) ◦ *a maximum-security prison* (= a special prison for very dangerous prisoners)
- a prison for prisoners of war or political prisoners that has a number of buildings inside a high fence: **prison camp**
- a prison camp where political prisoners are kept in very bad conditions: **concentration camp**
- an underground prison, for example in a castle: **dungeon**

- a small room in a prison or police station where prisoners are locked up: **cell**
- one of the long, thin pieces of metal on the doors and windows of cells that stop prisoners from escaping: **bar**

2 people in prisons

- a person who is being kept in prison: **prisoner**, **inmate**
- a person who has been put in prison because of his/her political views or actions: **political prisoner**
- a soldier who is kept in prison during a war: **prisoner of war**

- a person whose job is to watch over prisoners and stop them from escaping: **prison officer**, (*BrE*) (**prison**) **warder**, (*AmE*) (**prison**) **guard**
- a person who manages or controls a prison: (**prison**) **governor**, (*AmE*) (**prison**) **warden**

3 going to prison

- to put sb in prison: **imprison** sb, **jail** sb, **send*** sb **to prison/jail** ◦ *She was imprisoned for her political beliefs.* ◦ *He was sent to prison for three years.*
- the state of being put or kept in prison: **imprisonment** (*noun* U)
- to be sent to prison: **go* to prison/jail**
- to tell sb who has been found guilty of a crime what his/her punishment will be: **sentence** sb (**to** sth); their punishment: **sentence** ◦ *He was sentenced to ten years with hard labour.* ◦ *He received a long prison sentence.*

- to catch sb and keep them as a prisoner: **capture** sb, **take*** sb **prisoner/captive**; *noun*: **capture** ◦ *He escaped just six weeks after he was captured.* ◦ *Many soldiers were taken prisoner.* ◦ *My uncle often told us the story of his capture during the war.*

4 staying in prison

- if sb is kept in a prison, they are **in prison**, (*informal*) **behind bars**, (*informal*) **inside** ◦ *He's been in prison for five months.* ◦ *I won't be happy until the killer is safely behind bars.* ◦ *Her dad's inside for armed robbery.*
- to spend a period of time in prison as a punishment: **serve ...** ◦ *She is serving six years for attempted murder.*
- the length of time that sb must stay in prison: **term** ◦ *a five-month term*
- staying in prison for a very long time or until you die: **life imprisonment** (*noun* U), **life sentence** ◦ *He was given a life sentence for killing a policeman.*
- a punishment where you stay in a cell on your own and do not meet other prisoners or staff: **solitary confinement**

- to keep sb as a prisoner and not allow them to escape: **hold*** sb **prisoner/captive** ◦ *After being captured by terrorists, she was held prisoner for two months.*

5 leaving prison

- no longer in prison: **free**, **out** ◦ *He'll be free in three weeks.* ◦ *She's been out of prison for three weeks.*
- to allow sb to leave prison: **release** sb, **set*** sb **free**, **free** sb/sth (**from** sth) ◦ *She was released after six months.* ◦ *The judge ordered that the man be set free.*

– the act of freeing sb or being freed: **release** (**from** sth) ○ *The release of the hostages took place last night.*

– to pay money to the court so that sb can be free until the start of a trial: **bail** sb **out**; the money that you pay: **bail** (*noun* U)

– to get free from prison: **escape** (**from** sth), **break* out** (**of** sth); *nouns*: **escape, breakout** ○ *Two prisoners were killed as they tried to escape.* ○ *Twenty men broke out just after midnight; none so far have been recaptured.* ○ *There was a mass breakout by prisoners in section D.*

▷ more on escaping ⇨ **ESCAPE**

■ **MORE ...**

– to release a prisoner before the end of his or her prison sentence on the condition that he/she behaves well: **parole** sb; *noun* (U): **parole** ○ *She was released on parole.*

private

private businesses or companies ⇨ **BUSINESS**

– if a thing belongs to one person or group and should not be used by others, it is **private** (*adverb* **privately**); *opposite*: **public** (*adverb* **publicly**) ○ *You can't park here – this is private property.* ○ *a public library/telephone*

– if you want to keep sth secret or do not want many other people to know about it, it is **private, personal**; *noun* (U): **privacy** ○ *a private letter* ○ *Do you mind if I ask you a personal question?* ○ *I felt that his questions were an attack on my privacy.*

– very private: **intimate** ○ *They told each other their most intimate thoughts and feelings.*

– if sth is not connected with work or business, it is **private, personal** ○ *Harry didn't talk much about his private life.* ○ *The letter was marked 'Personal', so I didn't open it.*

– when you do sth that is not connected with your job, you do it **as a private individual**

– if a lot of people know sth, it is **public** (*adverb* **publicly**) ○ *The Chairman did not make the news public until he had told all members of staff.* ○ *It was public knowledge that the company was losing money.*

– if a thing is intended to be known publicly, it is **official** (*adverb* **officially**); *opposite*: **unofficial** (*adverb* **unofficially**) ○ *She will almost certainly be the new sales manager, although it's not yet official.*

■ doing sth privately

– when one person or a small group of people do sth with nobody else present, they do it **in private, privately**, it is **private**; *opposite*: **in public, publicly** ○ *The meeting was held in private.* ○ *We met privately – we wanted to keep the plans secret.* ○ *a private English lesson* ○ *This is the first time that Sally has spoken about her experiences in public.*

– the state of being alone: **privacy** (*noun* U) ○ *Rachel went upstairs to her room to get some privacy.*

▷ more on being alone ⇨ **ALONE**

probable ⇨ POSSIBLE[1]

problem

1 difficult situations
2 dealing with difficult situations
see also EASY/DIFFICULT

1 difficult situations

– a situation that is difficult to understand or deal with: **problem** ○ *She has a lot of problems at work.* ○ *Unemployment is a serious problem at the moment.* ○ *There's a problem with the photocopier – the paper keeps jamming.* ○ *a big/major problem* ○ *a few small/minor problems*

– something that is difficult to do or understand: **difficulty** (*often plural*) ○ *She's having difficulties with her maths homework.*

– problems: **trouble** (*noun* U) ○ *She's got problems at home and trouble at work.*

– a small temporary problem: **hitch** ○ *There was a technical hitch – the microphone wouldn't work.*

– a small unexpected or hidden problem: **snag** ○ *This paint is really good – the only snag is that it's difficult to wash off your hands.*

– a problem that is difficult to find an answer to: **puzzle** ○ *It's always been a puzzle to me why he left that job.*

– a problem that needs to be discussed or dealt with: **question** ○ *Her resignation raises the question of who will take over the job.*

– a situation in which you have to make a difficult choice between two or more things: **dilemma** ○ *I was in a dilemma: should I go to see her or should I finish my work?*

– (used about problems, difficulties, etc) to begin: **arise*** ○ *The problem would never have arisen if we'd stayed at home.*

– when problems need your attention, they **face** you ○ *The biggest problem facing us is lack of time.*

– if you are in a difficult situation, you are **in difficulty/difficulties, in trouble** ○ *We could see from the shore that the swimmer was in difficulties.* ○ *That boy is always in trouble.*

– to be the reason for a problem: **be the matter** (**with** sb/sth) ○ *I don't know what's the matter with Elizabeth – she never speaks to anyone.*

– not as it should be: **wrong** (**with** sth) ○ *What's wrong with the car this time?* ○ *I think something must be wrong with Rachel – she's looking so worried.*

– if sth is difficult to do or deal with, it is **tricky, awkward** ○ *a tricky situation* ○ *It's been a particularly awkward problem to deal with.*

problem *contd.*

2 dealing with difficult situations

- to do what is necessary when you have a problem: **do* sth about sth, deal* with sth, tackle sth** ◦ *What are you going to do about that leaking pipe?* ◦ *How is Robert dealing with that problem he had at work?* ◦ *The police are trying to tackle the problem of car theft.*
- to see if there is sth you can do to solve a problem: **take* a look (at sth)** ◦ *Could you take a look at my car – it's been giving me a lot of problems.*
- to try hard to find an answer to a problem: **puzzle over sth** ◦ *I've puzzled over this question for ages but I can't seem to find the answer.*
- a piece of information or an idea that helps you find an answer to a problem: **clue** ◦ *The detective was looking for clues to solve the mystery.*
- to deal with a problem successfully: **solve sth, , overcome* sth** ◦ *The council have been trying to solve the problem of traffic congestion.* ◦ *They've finally overcome their financial problems.*
- what you decide to do to solve a problem: **solution (to sth), answer (to sth)** ◦ *long-term solutions* ◦ *There are no easy answers.*
- to think of a solution to a problem: **work sth out, sort sth out, figure sth out** ◦ *We've worked out a compromise solution.* ◦ *I hope they sort it out before Christmas.* ◦ *So you've figured out how to prevent the leak?*
- if events have a successful conclusion, they **work out** ◦ *I'm glad it's all worked out.*

■ **MORE . . .**

- trying different solutions until you find the best one: **trial and error** (*noun* U) ◦ *The only way to solve this problem is by trial and error.*

produce ⇨ MAKE

professional ⇨ WORK, SPORT

profit

- in a business ⇨ **BUSINESS**
- when you sell sth ⇨ **SELL**

progress ⇨ DEVELOP

promise

see also INTEND/PLAN

- to say that you will definitely do sth: **promise (to do sth), promise (sb) (that) . . ., give* sb your word (that . . .)** ◦ *She promised to come early.* ◦ *I promise you I won't forget.* ◦ *I can't pull out now – I've given him my word.*
- an act of making a promise: **promise** ◦ *to make a solemn promise*
- to say that you will definitely give sth to sb: **promise sb sth** ◦ *He promised me a copy of his new book.*
- to agree or promise to do sth: **undertake* to do sth,** (*formal*) **commit yourself to sth/doing sth;** *nouns* (C/U): **undertaking, commitment** ◦ *They undertook to repair it by the end of the week.* ◦ *We've committed ourselves to increasing basic pay for teachers.* ◦ *a firm commitment to improving the environment*
- to promise sb (especially if they are worried) that sth will happen or be true: **assure sb (that) . . .;** *noun*: **assurance** ◦ *She assured me that she wouldn't tell anyone.*
- to make a very serious promise: **swear* that . . ./to do sth** ◦ *He swore that he wouldn't do it again.* ◦ *Do you swear not to tell anyone?*
- a serious and formal promise: **vow** ◦ *marriage vows* ◦ *a vow of silence*

■ keeping and breaking a promise

- to do what you have promised to do: **keep* a/your promise** ◦ *She never keeps her promises.*
- to make sb do what they promised to do: **hold* sb to sth, keep* sb to sth** ◦ *I'll hold you to that!* ◦ *She kept him to his promise.*
- if you do not do what you promised to do, you **break*** a promise, **go* back on** your **word**, the promise is **broken** ◦ *I can't believe he went back on his word!* ◦ *broken promises*

pronoun ⇨ GRAMMAR

pronunciation ⇨ SPEAK

property ⇨ HAVE/POSSESS

protect

1 protecting sb/sth
2 preventing accidents
3 protecting health
see also DANGEROUS, CAREFUL

1 protecting sb/sth

- free from danger or from possible injury, damage, etc: **safe (from sb/sth);** *noun* (U): **safety** ◦ *Don't go out alone at night. It isn't safe.* ◦ *Will my bag be safe if I leave it here?* ◦ *People are worried about their children's safety.*
- to do sth so that a person or thing is safe: **keep* sb/sth safe, protect sb/sth (against/from sb/sth), guard sb/sth (against sb/sth)** ◦ *protecting the environment from atmospheric pollution* ◦ *legislation to protect people at work* ◦ *to guard a country against invasion*
- the action of keeping sb/sth safe: **protection** (*noun* U) ◦ *protection of the environment* ◦ *protection against disease*
- helping to make sb/sth safe: **protective** ◦ *protective clothing*
- to protect or help sb who is weak or ill: **look after sb, take* care of sb** ◦ *I can't go out – there's no one else to look after the children.* ◦ *You will take care of the house while I'm away, won't you?*
- if you feel strongly that you want to protect sb/sth from sb/sth, you are **protective (towards sb/sth)** ◦ *His mother is very protective towards him.*
- things that people do to protect sb/sth from criminals, war, etc: **safety measures** (*noun*

plural), (**safety**) **precautions** (*noun plural*), **security** (*noun* U) ◦ *New safety measures have been introduced on trains.* ◦ *Security was tightened for the Queen's visit.*
- in order to be kept safely: **for safe keeping** ◦ *During the match Jim gave his watch to Derek for safe keeping.*

- to act, especially to fight or to speak, in order to protect sb/sth: **defend** sb/sth (**against** sb/sth) ◦ *He defended himself with a stick.* ◦ *She wants to defend herself against these accusations.*
- the activity of defending sb/sth: **defence** (*AmE* **defense**) (*noun* U) ◦ *We have no defence against increasing violence in society.*
- activity which helps to defend sb/sth is **defensive** ◦ *The troops took up a defensive position.*
- to succeed in defending sb/sth: **save** sb/sth (**from** sth/doing sth) ◦ *to save sb's life* ◦ *to save sb from drowning*
- the activity of defending yourself: **self-defence** (*AmE* **self-defense**) (*noun* U) ◦ *to shoot sb in self-defence*

▷ defending yourself or another person in a fight ➪ FIGHT

- protection from danger or bad weather: **shelter** (*noun* U), **cover** (*noun* U) ◦ *We took shelter in a shop doorway to escape from the rain.* ◦ *The soldiers had no cover and were easy targets.*
- to protect yourself or another person from danger or bad weather: **shelter** (sb) (**from** sb/sth) ◦ *Caroline agreed to shelter her brother from the police.* ◦ *There are now 100 refugees sheltering in foreign embassies.*
- a small building that gives protection or cover from danger or bad weather: **shelter** ◦ *a bus shelter*

- to go with sb to protect them: **escort** sb; a person or a group of people that goes with somebody to protect them: **escort** ◦ *We escorted her to the bus stop.* ◦ *a police escort*

■ people and animals that protect people and things
- a person who protects sb/sth: **protector**
- a person who guards buildings, people, etc: **guard** ◦ *a security guard*
- a man whose job is to protect a building at night: **nightwatchman**
- a person whose job is to protect a person: **bodyguard** ◦ *The president was surrounded by his bodyguards.*
- a person whose job is to protect people from drowning in the sea, in a swimming pool, etc: **lifeguard**

- a dog that is trained to protect a building or place from people: **guard dog**

2 preventing accidents
- a thing that protects sb/sth from danger or accident: **defence** (*AmE* **defense**) ◦ *London has good defences against flooding.*

- to put sth on or in front of sb/sth in order to protect them/it: **cover** sb/sth (**over/up**) (**with** sth) ◦ *I covered the floor with a newspaper before I started painting.*
- a thing that covers sth dangerous or that protects sth: **guard** ◦ *a fireguard* ◦ *mudguards over the wheels of a car*
- a flat, upright surface that is used to hide or protect sb/sth from sb/sth: **screen** ◦ *He stood behind a bullet-proof glass screen.*

- a belt that you wear in a car, aeroplane, etc to protect yourself if there is an accident: **seat belt**, **safety belt** ◦ *Please fasten your seat belts.*
- special glasses that you wear to protect your eyes from water, wind, dust, etc: **goggles**
- a special kind of hard hat that you wear to protect your head: **helmet** ◦ *a motorcycle helmet*

▷ more on accidents ➪ ACCIDENT

3 protecting health
- connected with the protection of health: **sanitary** ◦ *They're trying to improve sanitary conditions in the camps.*
- a system for protecting public health, especially by removing waste: **sanitation** (*noun* U)

▷ protecting health by keeping things clean ➪ CLEAN/DIRTY

- to protect sb from a disease by giving them an injection: **vaccinate** sb (**against** sth), **immunize** sb (**against** sth); an injection of this kind: **vaccination** (*noun* C/U), **immunization** (*noun* C/U) ◦ *plans to vaccinate all children against measles*
- if you are protected against an illness you are **immune** (**from** sth); *noun* (U): **immunity** (**from** sth)

■ MORE ...
- a place where sb/sth can be safe from enemies: **sanctuary**, **refuge** ◦ *a bird sanctuary* ◦ *a refuge for battered women*
- protection that a government gives to people who have left their country for political reasons: **asylum** (*noun* U) ◦ *to seek political asylum*
- to find protection against sth: **take* refuge** (**from** sb/sth) ◦ *We took refuge in an old barn.*

---

protest ➪ COMPLAIN/PROTEST

---

protestant ➪ CHRISTIAN

---

proud

see also PERSONALITY

- if you feel pleased and satisfied about sth that you have done or about sth that you are connected with, you are **proud** (**of** sb/sth), **proud** (**to** do sth) (*adverb* **proudly**); this feeling: **pride** (**in** sb/sth) (*noun* U) ◦ *proud parents* ◦ *They're very proud of their new car.* ◦ *I'm very proud to be here.* ◦ *to smile proudly* ◦ *to feel pride in your achievements*
- if you are very proud of sth that you can do, you **pride** yourself **on** sth/doing sth, **take* pride in** sth/doing sth ◦ *This company prides itself on the quality of its products.* ◦ *He takes great pride in his work.*

proud *contd.*

- the feeling of pride in yourself; the feeling that you are worth sth: **self-respect** (*noun* U), **pride** (*noun* U) ◦ *to lose your self-respect* ◦ *His pride was hurt when they told him that he was too old for the job.*

■ too proud
- too proud: **conceited**, (*informal*) **big-headed** ◦ *He's been very successful, but he's not a bit conceited.* ◦ *Don't get big-headed!*
- too proud of your appearance or of what you can do, etc: **vain**; *noun* (U): **vanity**
- if success makes you conceited, it **goes* to** your **head** ◦ *His success has gone to his head and made him very unpleasant.*

- to talk with too much pride about sth that you own or can do: **boast** (**about** sth), **boast that ...** ◦ *He never stops boasting about his gold medal.* ◦ *She was boasting that her father was a millionaire.*
- to say or do silly things because you are proud of sth that you own or can do: (*informal*) **show off** ◦ *She was driving too fast, to show off.*

- if you feel that you are better than other people, you are **proud**; *noun* (U): **pride** ◦ *She was too proud to admit she was wrong.* ◦ *the sin of pride*
- thinking that you are better and more important than other people and not caring about their feelings: **arrogant** (*adverb* **arrogantly**); *noun* (U): **arrogance** ◦ *He's very charming but I just can't stand his arrogance.*
- if you are pleased with yourself in a way that others find unpleasant, you are **smug** (*adverb* **smugly**), **self-satisfied** ◦ *a smug look* ◦ *'I know what you've been doing,' he said smugly.* ◦ *a self-satisfied smile*

■ not proud
- not having or expressing a high opinion of your own qualities or abilities: **modest**; *noun* (U): **modesty** ◦ *She's very modest about her achievements.*
- not thinking that you are better or more important than other people: **humble**; *noun* (U): **humility** ◦ *You're not perfect. Try to show a little humility!*

prove ⇨ TRUE

provide

see also GIVE, HELP

- to give or lend or sell sth to sb so that they can use it: **provide** sb (**with** sth), **provide** sth (**for** sb), **supply** sb (**with** sth), **supply** sth (**for** sb) ◦ *to provide funding for a project* ◦ *We supply schools with computer software.*
- the act of providing sb with sth: **provision** (*noun* U), **supply** (*noun* U) ◦ *The government is responsible for the provision of health care in Britain.* ◦ *the supply of raw materials to industry*
- a person or company that supplies sth: **supplier**; what they provide: **supply** ◦ *Our electricity supply was cut off because we didn't pay the bill.*
- to provide sb with sth he/she wants, asks for or pays for: **give*** sb sth, **give*** sth **to** sb ◦ *The doctor refused to give me any more of the pills.*
- to provide sb with sth for them to use: **issue** sth (**to** sb) ◦ *All new students are issued with text books.* ◦ *to issue a passport*
- to give or sell things to a number of people: **distribute** sth (**to/among** sb/sth); the act of giving things: **distribution** (*noun singular*/U) ◦ *During the drought, water had to be distributed to households by lorry.* ◦ *the distribution of food parcels to refugees* ◦ *problems of supply and distribution*

- to provide sb/sth with what is needed for a particular purpose: **equip** sb/sth **with** sth; the process of equipping sb/sth with sth: **equipment** (*noun* U) ◦ *All schools have been equipped with new computers.*

■ providing help
- to help sb by giving or paying for all the things that they need: **provide for** sb, **support** sb ◦ *Kevin has to provide for a family of seven.* ◦ *Chris helps to support his mother now that his father has died.*
- to support sb with money: **keep*** sb ◦ *How can you keep a family on £80 a week?*

▷ giving money ⇨ MONEY

public ⇨ KNOW, PRIVATE

publish

see also BOOK, NEWSPAPER/MAGAZINE

- to prepare and print a book, magazine, etc and make it available to the public: **publish** sth ◦ *I work for a company that publishes children's books.*
- the business of producing books: **publishing** (*noun* U) ◦ *a career in publishing*
- a person or a company that publishes books, magazines, etc: **publisher**

- to prepare a book to be published, making sure it is correct, the right length, etc: **edit** sth
- a person who is in charge of editing a book: **editor**
- a book, article, etc that has not yet been printed, and that needs to be checked for mistakes or other changes: **draft** ◦ *a first/final draft*
- to look at a draft of a book, etc to see if any changes need to be made: **proof-read** sth; a person whose job it is to do this: **proof-reader**

- to put words, pictures, etc onto paper by using a metal or wood surface covered with ink; to make books, newspapers, etc in this way: **print** sth
- making books, magazines, etc using a computer: **desktop publishing** (*noun* U) (*abbreviation* **DTP**)

▷ more on printing ⇨ PRINT

- the act of publishing sth: **publication** (*noun* U) ◦ *the publication of his first novel*
- a book, magazine, etc that has been published: **publication** ◦ *a list of publications*

– one example of a book, newspaper, etc which has been published: **copy** ◦ *Do you have a copy of today's Telegraph?*
– when a book, magazine, etc is published, it **appears, comes* out** ◦ *The second part of this story will appear in next month's magazine.* ◦ *When his first book came out, he was still only 22.*

– the form in which a book, newspaper, etc appears; a number of copies of a book, newspaper, etc printed at the same time: **edition** ◦ *There's going to be a new edition of his collected poems next year.*
– one in a series of magazines, newspapers, etc which are published: **issue** ◦ *Have you got last week's issue of this magazine?*
– if a company is still producing a book, the book is **in print**; if it has stopped producing it, the book is **out of print**

– the legal right to be the only person who can print a book, etc: **copyright** (*noun* U); the written symbol is © ◦ *Who owns the copyright to his work?*
– to decide whether a book is suitable to be sold to the public: **censor** sth; (*noun* U): **censorship**

pull/push

see also MOVE

■ towards you
– to move or try to move sb/sth towards you: **pull** sb/sth; *noun*: **pull** ◦ *She pulled the door shut.* ◦ *Paul pulled his son away from the fire.* ◦ *Pull hard.* ◦ *The diver gave a pull on the rope to show when she wanted to go back up to the surface.*

■ away from you
– to move or try to move sb/sth away from you: **push** sb/sth; *noun*: **push** ◦ *He pushed the door open.* ◦ *The engine wouldn't start so we had to give the car a push.*

■ behind you
– to cause sth which is behind you to move in the direction you are moving: **pull** sth ◦ *The car in front of us was pulling a caravan.*
– to pull sth with great effort, because it is heavy: **drag** sth, **haul** sth ◦ *The box was too heavy to lift, so we had to drag it along the ground.* ◦ *It needed eight men to haul the boat onto the beach.*
– to pull a car, lorry, etc by a rope, chain, etc: **tow** sth; *noun*: **tow** ◦ *The lorry was towing a thirty-foot trailer.* ◦ *They had broken down, so we gave them a tow to the nearest garage.* ◦ *a tow bar* (= for pulling a caravan, trailer, etc behind a vehicle)
– to pull sb/sth along with difficulty: **drag** sb/sth ◦ *She dragged the child away from the beach and back to the car.*

■ in a particular direction
– to pull sth in the direction mentioned: **pull** sth (**on, up, across**, etc) ◦ *Pull your socks up!* ◦ *Why don't you pull over a chair and sit down beside me?*
– to push or pull sth that has wheels: **wheel** sth ◦ *I wheeled my bicycle to the top of the hill.*

■ quickly
– to pull sb/sth suddenly and quickly: **jerk** sth; *noun*: **jerk** ◦ *He jerked the chair away just as I was about to sit down.*
– to pull sb/sth hard and quickly: **tug** (sth); *noun*: **tug** ◦ *Susan tugged at her mother's sleeve.* ◦ *Give it a tug and see what happens!*
– to pull sth hard and suddenly: (*informal*) **yank** sth ◦ *He yanked the bedclothes off the bed.*

■ through or against people or things
– to move forward by pushing sb/sth: **push** ◦ *Mary pushed her way through the crowd.* ◦ *Stop pushing!*
– to push with a sudden, rough movement: **shove** (sb/sth); *noun*: **shove** ◦ *The player was sent off the field for shoving the referee.* ◦ *to give sb a shove*

■ into a place
– to push sb/sth into a place where there is not much room: **squeeze** sb/sth **in**, **squeeze** sb/sth **into, through**, etc sth, (*informal*) **jam** sb/sth **in, into, between**, etc sth ◦ *It's almost full but we can probably squeeze you in somewhere.* ◦ *She jammed everything into her suitcase.*

– to push yourself into a place where there is not much room: **squeeze into, through, in between**, etc sb/sth ◦ *I managed to squeeze through the opening in the fence.* ◦ *Can I try and squeeze in between you?*

■ with a finger, stick etc
– to push sb/sth with a finger, stick or other long object: **poke** sb/sth, **prod** sb/sth; *nouns*: **poke, prod** ◦ *Don't poke your finger in your ear.* ◦ *James was prodding the fire with a stick.* ◦ *I gave him a sharp poke in his side to wake him up.*
– to push at sb/sth roughly, often with sth sharp: **jab** (**at** sb/sth) (**with** sth), **jab** sb/sth (**with** sth); *noun*: **jab** ◦ *She jabbed a finger into his chest.*
– to push a pointed object into sb/sth: **stick*** sth **in/into** sb/sth ◦ *She stuck a knife into his back.*

■ to make sth work
– to touch or push sth firmly: **press** sth, **push** sth; *noun*: **push** ◦ *Press this knob to turn the computer on.* ◦ *The car windows opened at the push of a button.*
– the force that is produced when you press sth: **pressure** (*noun* U) ◦ *Don't put so much pressure on the brake or the car will stop too quickly.*

■ pulling a rope, chain, etc
– a very thick, strong cord that is used to pull, tie or lift heavy things: **rope** (*noun* C/U) ◦ *They tied ropes to the boat and dragged it up the beach.*
– a line of metal rings that are joined together which can be used for pulling or lifting heavy things: **chain** (*noun* C/U)
– the condition of being pulled or stretched too tightly: **strain** (*noun* U) ◦ *The rope broke under the strain.*
– when a rope, etc is stretched very tight, it is **taut**

▷ ropes and chains ⇨ STRING/ROPE, LOCK/CHAIN

punctuation

see also WRITE

- the marks that you use to divide up sentences and show meaning in writing: **punctuation** (*noun* U)
- one of the signs that you use to divide up sentences or to show meaning in writing: **punctuation mark**
- to use punctuation marks when you are writing: **punctuate** sth

punctuation mark	name
.	**full stop** (*AmE* **period**)
,	**comma**
;	**semicolon**
:	**colon**
()	**(round) brackets** (*AmE* **parentheses**)
[ ]	**(square) brackets**
?	**question mark**
!	**exclamation mark**
"..." or '...'	**quotation marks, inverted commas**
'	**apostrophe**
/	**slash, oblique**

- the line (–) that you use to show a connection between two parts of a sentence or two sentences: **dash** ◦ *Are you hungry? – If not, we'll eat later.*
- the line (-) that you use to join two words together: **hyphen** ◦ *duty-free* ◦ *a red-hot iron* ◦ *He's twenty-one today.*

punish

1 punishing sb
2 different kinds of punishment

see also TRIAL, LAW

1 punishing sb

- to cause sb to suffer because they have done sth wrong: **punish** sb (**for** sth/doing sth); *noun* (U): **punishment** ◦ *He deserves to be punished for what he did.* ◦ *the fear of punishment* ◦ *physical punishment*
- the way in which sb is punished: **punishment** ◦ *His punishment was thirty days in prison.*
- a crime that you can be punished for is **punishable** (**by** sth) ◦ *This crime is punishable by death.*
- a punishment that is appropriate and right is **fair, just**; *opposites*: **unfair, unjust**
- if a punishment is stronger than usual, it is **heavy, harsh** ◦ *a heavy prison sentence*
- a punishment that is not strict or severe is **lenient, light** ◦ *a lenient prison sentence*
- to punish sb severely to stop other people doing the same thing: **make* an example of** sb ◦ *As a warning to other car thieves, the judge decided to make an example of him and sent him to prison for three years.*

■ being punished lightly or not at all
- to receive little or no punishment for sth: **get* off with** sth, **get* off** (**lightly**) ◦ *Sharon got off with a small fine as it was her first offence.*
- to do sth wrong and not be punished for it: **get* away with** sth ◦ *He's so clever he could get away with anything.*
- to decide not to punish sb for sth: **overlook** sth ◦ *I'll overlook it this time, but don't let it happen again.*

■ punishment according to the law
- a punishment for breaking a rule or law: **penalty**; connected with punishment by law: **penal** ◦ *introduce stiffer penalties for car thieves* ◦ *the death penalty* ◦ *the penal code* (= the system of laws of a country concerning crime and punishment)
- to tell sb who has been found guilty of a crime what their punishment will be: **sentence** sb (**to** sth); their punishment: **sentence** ◦ *He was sentenced to three years in prison and a fine of £1 000.* ◦ *a prison sentence*

■ punishing sb who has hurt you
- something that you do to punish sb who has hurt you: **revenge** (*noun* U) ◦ *I want revenge on the people who attacked my brother.*
- to punish sb for hurting you, your family or friends: **get*/ take*** (your) **revenge** (**on** sb) (**for** sth), (*informal*) **pay*** sb **back** (**for** sth/doing sth) ◦ *I'll pay you back for that mean trick.*
- to hurt or harm sb who has hurt or harmed you: **get* even** (**with** sb)
- to punish sb because you are angry or upset, even though it is not their fault: **take* it out on** sb ◦ *Don't take it out on me. It wasn't me who stole your camera.*

2 different kinds of punishment

■ physical punishments
- to hit a child as a punishment: **smack** sb, **give*** sb **a smack**
- to hit sb/sth many times, usually very hard: **beat*** sb/sth, **give*** sb/sth **a beating** ◦ *I shouted at the man to stop beating his dog.* ◦ *I was soon found out and given a good beating.*
- punishment by hitting sb: **corporal punishment** (*noun* U)

■ punishments often used by schools and employers
- to take sth away from sb as a punishment: **confiscate** sth; *noun* (U): **confiscation** ◦ *The teacher confiscated Harry's computer game after she caught him playing with it in class.*
- to send sb away from their school or job, for a limited period of time: **suspend** sb (**from** sth); *noun* (C/U): **suspension** ◦ *He was suspended from school for two weeks.* ◦ *She faces suspension or dismissal.*

- to force sb to leave a school, country, club, etc as a punishment: **expel** sb (**from** sth); *noun* (C/U): **expulsion** ○ *Two Britons have been expelled from France after causing trouble at a football match.*
- to stop sb from leaving school: **keep*** sb **in**; an act of keeping sb in: **detention** (*noun* U) ○ *Kevin's teacher kept him in after school for not doing his homework.* ○ *The whole class was put in detention.*

■ punishments which are decided by a court of law

- an amount of money that you have to pay for breaking a law: **fine**; to make sb pay a fine: **fine** sb (**for** sth/doing sth), **give*** sb **a fine** ○ *If you don't pay your TV licence, you can be given a £1 000 fine.*
- a building where criminals are kept as a punishment: **prison** (*AmE* **penitentiary**), **jail** (*BrE also* **gaol**)
- being kept in prison: **imprisonment** (*noun* U)
- imprisonment with heavy physical work as punishment: **hard labour** (*AmE* **hard labor**) (*noun* U)

▷ more on prison ⇨ PRISON

- killing sb as an official punishment: **the death penalty** (*noun singular*), **capital punishment** (*noun* U) ○ *A lot of countries have abolished the death penalty.*
- to kill sb as a punishment: **execute** sb; *noun* (C/U): **execution** ○ *The execution was carried out by firing squad.*
- a person who carries out an execution: **executioner**
- to stop or delay an execution: **reprieve** sb; *noun*: **reprieve** ○ *He was given a last-minute reprieve.*
- to change one punishment for another that is not so hard: **commute** sth (**to** sth) ○ *After a big public protest, his death sentence was commuted to life imprisonment.*

- to execute sb by hanging them with a rope round their neck: **hang** sb; *noun* (U/C): **hanging**; a person who does this: **hangman**; the structure used for hanging sb: **gallows** ○ *When were public hangings abolished in this country?*
- to execute sb by shooting them: **shoot*** sb; *noun* (U/C): **shooting**; a group of people who execute sb by shooting: **firing squad**
- to execute sb by using electricity: **electrocute** sb; *noun* (U): **electrocution**; the chair in which this is done: **electric chair**
- to execute sb by injecting them with a poison: **execute** sb **by lethal injection**
- to execute sb by cutting off their head: **behead** sb; *noun* (U/C): **beheading**
- to behead sb using a special machine: **guillotine** sb; *noun* (U/C): **guillotining**; the machine which is used: **guillotine** ○ *Many people were guillotined during the French Revolution.*

■ **MORE ...**

- a situation where a government forgives people who have committed crimes: **amnesty** ○ *Hundreds of political prisoners were released under the general amnesty.*
- protected from punishment: **immune** (**from** sth); *noun* (U): **immunity** (**from** sth) ○ *Young children are immune from prosecution.* ○ *The ambassador and his staff have diplomatic immunity.*

---

purpose ⇨ INTEND/PLAN

---

push ⇨ PULL/PUSH

---

put

putting on clothes ⇨ CLOTHES
see also BRING/TAKE/CARRY, MOVE

- to move sb/sth to a particular place or position: **put*** sb/sth somewhere, **place** sb/sth somewhere ○ *He took the key out of pocket and put it in the drawer.* ○ *We carried the boxes downstairs and put them in the hall.* ○ *The chairs had all been placed in neat rows.*
- to put sth where you usually keep it, for example in a cupboard: **put*** sth **away** ○ *The children put the books away in their desks.*
- to return sth to its place: **put*** sth **back** ○ *Please put it back where you found it.*

- to fix sth to or in sth else: **put*** sth **on/in/into** sth ○ *to put a stamp on an envelope*
- to put sth into sth or between two things: **insert** sth ○ *to insert a coin in a slot*
- to put or fix sth in the right place: **fit** sth **on/in/into** sth ○ *to fit a new engine in a car*

- to put sth in the correct position on or under a surface: **lay*** sth ○ *to lay a carpet/pipe/cable*
- to put sth on sth or in front of sth in order to hide it or protect it: **cover** sth (**up/over**) (**with** sth) ○ *She covered the table with a cloth.*
- to put a soft substance all over a surface: **spread*** A **on** B, **spread*** B **with** A ○ *to spread butter on a piece of bread* ○ *to spread the bread with jam*

- to fix sth to a wall, etc: **put*** sth **up** ○ *When shall we put up the Christmas decorations?*
- to put sth in an upright position: **stand*** sth somewhere ○ *He stood the suitcase by the door while he put on his coat.*

- to put sb/sth that you are holding on a floor, a table, etc: **put*** sb/sth **down** ○ *When the kitten tried to scratch me, I immediately put it down.* ○ *Put me down now, Daddy.*
- to put sb/sth carefully in a particular position, especially on a surface: **lay*** sb/sth somewhere ○ *She laid the child down on the bed.* ○ *He laid the map on the table.*

- to take hold of sb/sth and move them/it to a different position: **lift** sb/sth ○ *Can you help me lift these boxes into the van?*

put *contd.*

– to put sth heavy in sth or on sb/sth: **load** sth ○ *They were still loading the cargo onto the plane.*

▷ more on lifting things ⇨ LIFT

quantity

– large or small quantities ⇨ HOW MUCH / MANY
– some or all of sth ⇨ HOW MUCH / MANY

queen ⇨ KING / QUEEN

question

1 questions
2 answers

questions that you have to think about to find the answer ⇨ PROBLEM
questions in grammar ⇨ GRAMMAR

see also REQUEST

1 questions

– something you say or write that asks for an answer: **question** ○ *Can I ask you a question?* ○ *Why won't you answer my question?* ○ *Have you got any questions on what I've just said?*
– something that you need to be given an answer to: **query** ○ *I have a few other queries.*

– to put a question or questions to sb in order to find out some information: **ask** (sb) (sth), **ask** (sb) (**about** sb/sth), (*formal*) **enquire** (*especially AmE* **inquire**) (**about** sb/sth); *noun* (C/U): **enquiry** (*especially AmE* **inquiry**) ○ *Don't forget to ask which train they're coming on.* ○ *'Are you going to watch the match?' she asked.* ○ *She asked us if/whether we were going to watch the match.* ○ *I'd like to enquire about flights to Nigeria.* ○ *They appear to have made no further enquiry.* ○ *I don't know the answer – I'll have to make some enquiries.*
– to ask for news about sb (their health, etc): **ask after** sb, (*formal*) **enquire** (*especially AmE* **inquire**) **after** sb/sth ○ *Phil asked after you in his letter.*
– a person who asks a question or questions: **questioner**

– to ask questions in order to find out detailed information about sth: **investigate** sth, **look into** sth, (*formal*) **inquire into** sth; this type of activity: **investigation** (**into** sth) (*noun* C/U), **inquiry** (**into** sth) ○ *The police are investigating the crime.* ○ *We're still looking into the causes of the accident.* ○ *a police investigation* ○ *The company is under investigation.* ○ *a public inquiry into safety procedures*
– a person who investigates things: **investigator**
– a list of questions that you ask a lot of people in order to collect information about sth: **questionnaire** ○ *Would you mind filling in this questionnaire?*

– to ask sb questions in order to find out what they did or what they know about sth, for example to find out if they committed a crime: **question** sb, **interrogate** sb; this type of activity: **questioning** (*noun* U), **interrogation** (*noun* C/U) ○ *I was stopped and questioned by the police.* ○ *The three suspects were interrogated repeatedly.* ○ *three days of questioning* ○ *They accused the police of beating them during the interrogations.*
– a person who interrogates people: **interrogator**

– to ask yourself a question in your own mind: **wonder** (sth) ○ *I wonder what time it is.* ○ *I wonder if they'll come.* ○ *We'd been wondering about it for a long time.*

– asking a question or a lot of questions: **questioning** (*adverb* **questioningly**), **inquiring** (*adverb* **inquiringly**) ○ *a questioning look* ○ *an inquiring mind* ○ *She looked at me inquiringly.*
– asking a lot of questions, especially about what other people are doing: **inquisitive**; *noun* (U): **inquisitiveness** ○ *Don't be so inquisitive!*

■ question words

questions about ...	question word
a time or date	**when?**
a place	**where?**
a person	**who?**
a thing, etc	**what?**
the reason for sth	**why?**
the way sth is done	**how?**

Note: these question words can be made stronger to show surprise, anger, etc. You can add **-ever**; for example: **whenever? wherever? whoever? whatever?** Or you can add **on earth**; for example: **where on earth? who on earth? what on earth? why on earth?** ○ *Whatever could have happened to them?* ○ *Why on earth didn't you call?* ○ *How on earth did you find out?*

– if you want to know a thing or person (from a limited group), you say **which?** ○ *Which (one) is yours?*
– if you want to know the person that sth belongs to, you say **whose?** ○ *Whose (car) is that?*
– questions to do with amount (of time, distance, etc) are asked with **how?** ○ *How much is a ticket to Liverpool?* ○ *How much bread did you buy?* ○ *How many people were there?* ○ *How long have you been living here?* ○ *How far is it to Glasgow?* ○ *How old is your sister?* ○ *How often do you go to France?*

2 answers

– to say or write sth to sb after they have asked you a question: **answer** (sb/sth), **reply** (**to** sb/sth) ○ *I asked him a simple question but he couldn't answer.* ○ *Make sure you answer all the questions.* ○ *'What's the time?' 'Four thirty,' she answered.* ○ *'Not just now,' he replied, 'I'm busy at the moment.'*
– to reply to sb in a rude way: (*only used to children*) **answer** (sb) **back** ○ *Don't answer back when I'm talking to you!*

- what you say or write to sb after they have asked you a question: **answer**, **reply** ◦ *She gave a very surprising answer.* ◦ *Bob wasn't satisfied with her reply.* ◦ *Do you want a straight* (= honest and open) *answer?*
- as a reply to sth: **in answer** (**to** sth), **in reply** (**to** sth), **in response** (**to** sth) ◦ *Paul nodded in response to my question.*

■ **MORE ...**

- a clever or amusing question or joke: **riddle** ◦ *Let me ask you a riddle and see if you can solve it.*
- a game or competition in which people have to answer questions: **quiz** ◦ *a general knowledge quiz*
- a question which you ask without expecting an answer: **rhetorical question**

queue ⇨ WAIT

quick ⇨ FAST/SLOW

quiet

see also SOUND, SPEAK

■ quiet

- with very little or no sound: **quiet** (*adverb* **quietly**) ◦ *Be quiet!* ◦ *quiet music* ◦ *a quiet place* ◦ *Not a sound could be heard – the house was absolutely quiet.* ◦ *to talk quietly*
- quiet sounds can be called **soft** (*adverb* **softly**) ◦ *soft singing* ◦ *soft voices* ◦ *to play an instrument softly* ◦ *to speak softly*
- with no sound: **silent** (*adverb* **silently**); *noun* (U/C): **silence** ◦ *a silent film* ◦ *He crept silently into the room.* ◦ *We listened in silence.* ◦ *After a moment's silence, we started to laugh.* ◦ *an awkward silence*

■ loud

- not quiet: **loud** (*adverbs* **loud, loudly**) ◦ *a loud voice* ◦ *Could you speak a little louder?* ◦ *Must you play that stereo so loudly?*
- making too much noise: **noisy** (*adverb* **noisily**) ◦ *noisy people* ◦ *a noisy party* ◦ *The children came noisily into the classroom.*
- (used about music, radios, etc) as loud as possible: (*informal*) **full blast** ◦ *They'd got the radio on full blast.*
- very loud: **deafening** ◦ *a deafening roar*
- extremely loud and painful to hear: **ear-splitting** ◦ *ear-splitting shrieks*

■ quiet behaviour

- a person who does not say much and does not attract much attention is **quiet** ◦ *Although he's a quiet man, he enjoys other people's company.*
- to make sb/sth quiet: **quieten** sb/sth (**down**) ◦ *She quietened the children by giving them sweets.*
- to become quiet: **quieten down** ◦ *Quieten down and get on with your work.*

- not excited, worried, angry, etc: **calm; placid** ◦ *Stay calm – there's no need to panic.* ◦ *a placid temperament*
- to become quiet and calm after some excitement: **settle down, calm down** ◦ *When the wedding was over, we soon settled down again to our usual routine.* ◦ *Calm down now and get back to your work please!*

- when you want other people to be quiet, you can say **sh!** or **shush!** ◦ *Sh! Don't make a noise or you'll frighten the birds away.* ◦ *Shush please! There's far too much noise in here!*

▷ more on being calm ⇨ CALM

■ quiet places and situations

- a state of calm or quiet: **peace** (*noun* U), **peace and quiet** (*noun* U); *adjective*: **peaceful** (*adverb* **peacefully**) ◦ *a moment's peace* ◦ *the peace of a summer evening* ◦ *Leave me in peace!* ◦ *I need some peace and quiet.* ◦ *What a peaceful place!* ◦ *The patient is sleeping peacefully.*

- a place that is made so that no sound can get in or out is **soundproof** ◦ *Please turn your music down – these walls are not soundproof!* ◦ *a soundproof recording studio*

quite ⇨ FAIRLY/VERY

race¹

- a group of people ⇨ PEOPLE

race² a competition

see also SPORT, ATHLETICS

- a competition between people, animals, cars, etc to see which is the fastest: **race** ◦ *to win/lose a race* ◦ *a horse race* ◦ *a boat race* ◦ *a motorcycle race*
- to take part in a race: **be in a race, run*** (**in**) **a race** ◦ *I'm in the next race.* ◦ *to run a marathon* ◦ *Are you running in the 100-metre race?*
- a person who runs in a race: **runner** ◦ *a long-distance/marathon runner*
- to be in a race against a particular person: **race** (**against/with**) sb ◦ *I'll race you to that tree.* ◦ *They'll be racing against each other in the 200 metres.*
- to put an animal or car into a race: **race** sth ◦ *He races horses.*
- an organized event in which people try to win sth: **competition** ◦ *an athletics competition*

▷ more on competitions ⇨ COMPETITION

- a special path, often in a circle, for running races: **track**
- a place where motor races are held: **racetrack**
- a place where horse races are held: **racecourse** (*AmE* **racetrack**)
- one part of the track for a single runner: **lane**
- the place where the race stars from: **start, starting line**
- the place where the race finishes: **finish, finishing line** ◦ *to pass the finishing line*
- once round a track: **lap** ◦ *the first/last lap* ◦ *three laps to go* (= three more laps in this race)

■ the start of a race

- the official person who starts a race: **starter**
- to start a race, the starter says **On your marks,**

race² *contd.*

get set, go! or (this is said to children or by children) **Ready, steady, go!**
– if the runners do not start properly, there is a **false start**

■ during a race
– the position of a runner during a race: **place** ○ *to be in second place*
– if two runners are in the same position in a race, they are **neck and neck** ○ *They were neck and neck as they approached the finishing line.*
– to get in front of sb in a race: **get* ahead (of** sb/sth), **overtake*** (sb/sth)
– to get into the first position in a race: **take* the lead** ○ *Japan has just taken the lead.*
– to be in front of all the others during a race: **lead*, be in the lead**
– to begin to lose a race: **drop back, drop/fall* behind** (sb)

■ the end of a race
– to be the first person to finish in a race: **win*, come* first**; to be second, third, ... last: **come* second, third, ... last**
– a race in which two runners finish first at the same time is a **dead heat**

radio ⇨ TELEVISION/RADIO

railway ⇨ TRAIN

rain

1 rain
2 no rain
3 getting wet in the rain
see also SNOW, WEATHER

1 rain

– water that falls from the sky: **rain** (*noun* U); *verb*: **rain** ○ *It looks like rain again today.* ○ *a long period of rain* ○ *Is it still raining?* ○ *It hardly ever rains in my country.*
– to come down from the sky: **fall*** ○ *The rain was falling steadily.*
– when rain falls slowly off sth like the roof of a building or the leaves of a tree, it **drips** ○ *The rain was dripping down the back of my neck.*
– one small piece of rain: **raindrop**
– a white or grey mass of water in the sky which rain can fall from: **cloud** (*noun* C/U)

▷ more on clouds ⇨ SKY

– if it is raining, the weather is **wet** ○ *a wet day* ○ *a wet summer*
– a period when it rains is **rainy** ○ *a rainy day* ○ *the rainy season*
– a short period of rain: **shower**; when there are showers, the weather is **showery**
– the amount of rain that falls in a certain place within a certain period (for example, a year): **rainfall** (*noun* U) ○ *the average annual rainfall in Brazil*
– water that has fallen as rain: **rainwater** (*noun* U)
– a small pool of rainwater on the ground: **puddle**
– a mixture of earth and water on the ground: **mud** (*noun* U); after it has been raining the ground may be **muddy**

■ just a little rain
– just a little rain: **light** rain; light rain with a lot of small drops: **drizzle** (*noun* U); *verb*: **drizzle** ○ *'Is it still raining?' 'Not really, just drizzling.'*
– a very little rain: a **spot** of rain ○ *I just felt a few spots of rain.*

■ a lot of rain
– a lot of rain: **heavy** rain; very heavy rain: **torrential** rain; hard rain with a strong wind: **driving** rain
– to rain a lot: **rain hard/heavily, pour (with rain), pour down** ○ *It started to rain heavily and we were soon absolutely soaked.* ○ *We can't go out now – it's pouring!*

– a very heavy shower of rain: **downpour**
– a period of heavy rain and strong wind: **storm**; *adjective*: **stormy** ○ *stormy weather*
– (especially after heavy rain) a large amount of water that covers an area that is normally dry: **flood** ○ *Heavy rain has caused floods in low-lying areas.*

▷ more on storms ⇨ STORM

■ when it is very cold
– cold rain that is similar to snow: **sleet** (*noun* U); *verb*: **sleet**
– hard frozen rain that falls as small pieces of ice: **hail** (*noun* U); *verb*: **hail**; a heavy shower of hail: **hailstorm**; a piece of hail: **hailstone**

2 no rain

– when the rain finishes, it **stops raining**
– when it is not raining, it is **dry** ○ *If it's dry tomorrow we can do some gardening.*
– a long period without enough rain: **drought** (*noun* C/U)

– a very dry area where it hardly ever rains: **desert** (*noun* C/U) ○ *the Sahara Desert* ○ *Much of the land is desert.*

3 getting wet in the rain

– when you get very wet in the rain, you get **soaked (to the skin), drenched, soaking wet**
– to get away from the rain: **shelter (from** the rain), **take* shelter**

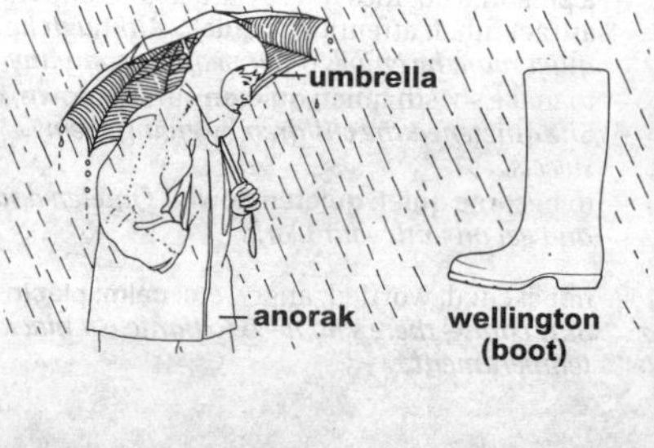

- clothes, watches, etc which are made so that it does not matter if they get wet are **waterproof** ◦ *a waterproof watch/jacket*

▷ coats that you wear in the rain ⇨ COAT

■ **MORE ...**
- a coloured arc of light that sometimes appears in the sky when it is raining lightly: a **rainbow**
- the very heavy rain that falls in tropical countries at certain times of the year: **the monsoon, the rains**

rank

ranks in the army ⇨ ARMY
aristocratic ranks in society ⇨ LORD/LADY
see also SOCIETY

- the level of importance that sb has in an organization or in society: **rank** (*noun* C/U), **position** (*noun* C/U) ◦ *military ranks* ◦ *Several officers of very high rank were present at the meeting.* ◦ *the position of women in society*
- your social or professional position in relation to others: **status** (*noun singular*) ◦ *to achieve a higher social status*
- a word that shows a person's rank or profession: **title** ◦ *He inherited the title of 'Duke' from his father.*
- to have a place in an order of importance: **rank** ◦ *She ranks among the country's top novelists.*
- having a high position in an organization or in society: **high-ranking** ◦ *a high-ranking police officer*

- if you have a higher rank than sb else, you are **above** sb, **senior** (**to** sb), **superior** (**to** sb) ◦ *You need to see the person above me – that's the marketing manager.* ◦ *a senior manager*
- the rank or importance that sb has in an organization: **seniority** (*noun* U) ◦ *in order of seniority*
- a person who is of higher rank than you is your **superior** ◦ *I have to discuss the matter with my superiors.*
- the person of highest rank or of greatest importance in an organization: **head** ◦ *a meeting of European heads of government*

- if you have a lower rank than sb else, you are **below** sb, **subordinate** (**to** sb), **junior** ◦ *a subordinate position* ◦ *a junior office worker*
- of lower social position or importance: **inferior**; *noun* (U): **inferiority**

- to put sb into a higher rank: **promote** sb; *noun* (U/C): **promotion** ◦ *Lieutenant Jones has been promoted to Captain.* ◦ *I was very disappointed not to get my promotion.*
- to put sb into a lower rank: **demote** sb

reach

- arriving at a place ⇨ ARRIVE
- able to touch sth ⇨ TOUCH

read

see also BOOK

- to look at written words and sentences and understand them: **read*** (sth); *noun* (U): **reading** ◦ *Could you be a bit quieter – I'm trying to read.* ◦ *We spent Sunday morning in bed reading the papers.* ◦ *I don't have time to do much reading these days.*
- a person who reads a book, magazine, etc: **reader** ◦ *Many readers wrote to the editor to complain.*

- to read so that you can be heard: **read*** (sth) **aloud/out loud** ◦ *The teacher asked me to read aloud.* ◦ *She read the letter out loud to all the children.*
- to read sth while sb else is listening: **read*** (sth) **to** sb ◦ *Shall I read you a story?*
- to read a message, letter, etc so that other people know what it says: **read*** sth **out** ◦ *She opened the envelope and read out the letter.*
- to continue to read: **read* on** ◦ *I want you all to read on to the end of the chapter.*

■ reading in order to learn sth
- to read a lot about sth so that you learn about it; to make a special study of sth: **read* up on** sth, **read*** sth **up** ◦ *I'll have to read up on management techniques before my interview next week.*
- to read sth very carefully in order to understand and remember the information: **study** (sth)
- printed material on a particular subject: **literature** (*noun* U) ◦ *I'll give you some literature on the subject and you can read about it yourself.*

■ reading sth quickly or incompletely
- to read sth fairly quickly in order to check what has been written, or in order to make a decision: **read*** sth **over**, **read*** sth **through**, **look through** sth ◦ *Could you read over this letter before I send it off please?* ◦ *I read through the proposal and signed it.* ◦ *Look through this catalogue and decide if you want to buy anything.*
- to read sth quickly in order to find a particular piece of information: **scan** sth ◦ *He scanned the newspaper report looking for the name 'Hamilton'.*
- to read sth quickly in order to understand the main idea, without paying attention to detail: **skim** (**through**) sth ◦ *I only had time to skim through the article, but I got the general idea.*
- to read a book, magazine, etc from beginning to end: **read*** sth **from cover to cover** ◦ *The novel was so exciting that I read it from cover to cover without putting it down.*

- to look at a book, magazine, etc without reading every part: **browse** (**through** sth) ◦ *I spent the afternoon browsing in bookshops.* ◦ *She sat in the waiting room browsing through the magazines.*
- to choose parts of a book, article, etc which interest you and read them: **dip into** sth ◦ *I haven't read the whole book, I've just dipped into it.*
- to intentionally miss pages or paragraphs when reading: **skip** sth ◦ *Skip the next section and turn to page 50.*

■ able to read or to be read
- the ability to read and write: **literacy** (*noun* U); *opposite*: **illiteracy** (*noun* U) ◦ *adult literacy classes*

read *contd.*

- a person who can read and write is **literate**; *opposite*: **illiterate** ◦ *Only 35% of the population is literate.*
- if sb's handwriting or other written words are clear enough to be read easily, the writing is **legible** (*adverb* **legibly**); *opposite*: **illegible** (*adverb* **illegibly**) ◦ *Try to write more legibly.* ◦ *The letter was illegible.*
- if sth is easy or enjoyable to read, it is **readable**; *opposite*: **unreadable** ◦ *I find her novels quite unreadable.*

■ **MORE ...**

- a person who has read a lot and knows a lot of things is **well-read** ◦ *George is very well-read – you can ask him about anything and he'll have something to say about it.*
- a problem which makes it difficult for sb to learn to read and write: **dyslexia** (*noun* U); *adjective*: **dyslexic** ◦ *a school for dyslexic children*

ready

planning and organizing ⇨ INTEND / PLAN

- able to do sth or to be used: **ready** (**for** sb/sth), **ready** (**to** do sth) ◦ *Dinner's ready!* ◦ *We have repaired your car and it's ready for you to collect.* ◦ *I'm not really ready for this exam – I just haven't done enough work.* ◦ *Are you ready to go?*
- ready, prepared or likely to do sth: **all set** (**for** sth/**to** do sth) ◦ *I'm all set – let's go!* ◦ *We were all set to leave when the rain started.*
- ready for sth difficult or unpleasant: **prepared for** sth; *opposite*: **unprepared** (**for** sth) ◦ *I certainly wasn't prepared for what happened next!* ◦ *I was quite unprepared for such an experience.* ◦ *I did badly in the exam because I was unprepared.*
- to be ready in case of a problem: **be on the safe side** ◦ *It doesn't look like rain, but let's take an umbrella to be on the safe side.*

■ getting ready

- to become ready: **get* ready** (**for** sth), (*more formal*) **prepare** (**for** sth) ◦ *Why does it take you so long to get ready to go out?* ◦ *The children are getting ready for bed.*
- to make sb/sth ready: **get*** sb/sth **ready** (**for** sth), (*more formal*) **prepare** sb/sth (**for** sth) ◦ *She got the tea ready in five minutes.* ◦ *to prepare a speech* ◦ *to prepare yourself for a shock*
- to make preparations for sth in the future: **arrange** sth, **arrange** (**for** sb/sth) (**to** do sth), **organize** sth ◦ *Have you arranged your holidays yet?* ◦ *She had arranged for a taxi to collect us from the airport.* ◦ *They arranged to meet at six o'clock.*
- the act of getting a thing or person ready: **preparation** (*noun* U) ◦ *He failed the exam because he hadn't done enough preparation.* ◦ *We tidied the spare room in preparation for her visit.*
- done in order to get ready for sth: **preparatory** ◦ *preparatory meetings/talks*
- what you do to get ready for sth: **preparations** (**for** sth) (*noun plural*), **arrangements** (**for** sth) (*noun plural*) ◦ *We'll soon have to start making preparations for the end of term.* ◦ *Preparations for a big celebration have already begun.* ◦ *Will you make the necessary arrangements for my trip to London?*
- the action you take in order to avoid danger or problems: **precaution** (*often plural*) ◦ *to take precautions* ◦ *safety precautions*

real / existing

being alive ⇨ LIVE[1]

- to be real; to live: **exist**; *noun* (U): **existence** ◦ *Scientists say that the earth has existed for about four billion years.* ◦ *Do you think UFOs really exist?* ◦ *All these jobs will cease to exist after April.* ◦ *This is the oldest piece of writing in existence.*
- not existing: **non-existent** ◦ *In those days health care was virtually non-existent.*
- to begin to exist: **come* into being**, **come* into existence** ◦ *The National Health Service in Britain came into being in 1946.* ◦ *This word came into existence around the turn of the last century.*
- to continue to exist: **persist**; *noun* (U): **persistence** ◦ *If these symptoms persist, you'll have to go and see the doctor.* ◦ *the persistence of cholera among the poorest members of the community*
- to continue to exist or to live (often in spite of a dangerous or difficult situation): **survive**; *noun* (U): **survival**; a person or thing that survives: **survivor** ◦ *a traditional way of life that is unlikely to survive in the modern world* ◦ *a long struggle for survival*

■ real or imaginary

- actually existing, not imaginary: **real** (*adverb* **really**); *noun* (U): **reality** ◦ *The story in the film is based on real life.* ◦ *It really was a ghost; I'm absolutely sure of it.* ◦ *Some experts dispute the reality of global warming.*
- life as most people live it, not as in fiction or in films: **real life** (*noun* U) ◦ *Nobody speaks like that in real life.* ◦ *The film is about real-life situations.*
- a description, film, book, etc that shows how people really live is **true to life**, **realistic**; *noun* (U): **realism** ◦ *a true to life portrait of an industrial town* ◦ *a realistic description of the lives of ordinary people in London*
- something that you know has happened or is true: **fact** ◦ *It's a fact that people live longer nowadays.* ◦ *You just have to face facts and accept that she has left you for another man.*
- if sth is based on situations or events that have not yet happened, it is **hypothetical** ◦ *a hypothetical question/situation/event*
- if a person or thing is not real and exists only in the mind, it is **imaginary**; to think of sth that is imaginary: **imagine** sth; the ability to do this: **imagination** (*noun* U) ◦ *an imaginary world in which pain does not exist* ◦ *Imagine what it would be like to have no friends.* ◦ *Her writing shows wonderful originality and imagination.*

▷ more on imagination ⇨ IMAGINATION

■ no longer existing
- if a type of animal or plant no longer exists, it is **extinct**; *noun* (U): **extinction** ◦ *This type of butterfly is almost extinct in some parts of England.* ◦ *to be in danger of extinction*
- to cease to exist: **die out**, **disappear**, **become* extinct** ◦ *This species of tiger has almost died out.* ◦ *disappearing wildlife* ◦ *Thousands of species are becoming extinct every year.*

■ **MORE ...**
- if sth exists only as an idea and not as a real thing, it is **abstract**; *opposite*: **concrete** ◦ *abstract ideas* ◦ *a concrete object*

real / genuine

see also COPY

- natural; not pretending to be something else: **real**, **genuine** ◦ *a real coal fire* ◦ *a genuine leather briefcase*
- a thing that is genuine, not a copy: **the real thing** ◦ *This painting is just a copy. The real thing is in an art gallery in Amsterdam.*
- known to be true or genuine: **authentic**; the quality of being authentic: **authenticity** (*noun* U) ◦ *an authentic Stradivarius violin*

■ not genuine
- if sth is not genuine, it is **artificial**, **false** ◦ *an artificial eye/leg* ◦ *a false moustache*
- something that is artificial but which is intended to look as if it is genuine is **fake**; *noun*: **fake** ◦ *a fake passport* ◦ *The diamond ring you bought is a fake.*
- a copy of a genuine thing: **imitation** ◦ *an imitation leather jacket*

- if sth is not real but it appears to be real, it is **realistic**, **lifelike** ◦ *The model cat was so realistic I thought it was going to move.* ◦ *Those silk flowers look very lifelike.*

rear ⇨ PLACE²

reason

1 reasons and purposes
2 good and bad reasons
3 asking for and giving a reason

see also THINK, CAUSE / EFFECT

1 reasons and purposes
- the cause of sth; sth that explains why sth happens: **reason** (**for ... / why ... / that ...**) (*noun* C/U) ◦ *Does he have a reason for thinking that?* ◦ *There's no reason why you shouldn't come.* ◦ *I sold my car for the simple reason that I could no longer afford to run it.*
- an official reason: **grounds** (*noun plural*) ◦ *He's had to retire on medical grounds.*

- to say why sth happens or exists: **give* a reason** (**for/why ...**), **explain** (sth), **give* an explanation** (**for** sth) ◦ *They asked me to give them three reasons why I wanted to do the course.* ◦ *I asked the mechanic why my engine kept stalling, but he couldn't give me any explanation.*
- to believe that sth is a reason for sth: **attribute** sth **to** sth, **put*** sth **down to** sth ◦ *She attributes her success to hard work and a bit of luck.* ◦ *I put his reaction down to stress.*

▷ more on explanations ⇨ UNDERSTAND

- a reason that supports an idea: **argument** ◦ *She presented some very good arguments for using the new teaching method.*
- to give your opinion about sth and your reasons for what you think: **argue that ...**, **argue for/ against** sth; *noun* (C/U): **argument** ◦ *I argued against the idea of having lessons in the afternoon.* ◦ *What argument is there for raising fees now?*

- the reason for doing or making sth: **purpose** (**of** sth) ◦ *The purpose of this meeting is to discuss next week's timetable.* ◦ *I bought my computer purely for work purposes.*
- a feeling of fear, desire, etc which causes a person to do sth: **motive** (**for** sth) (*noun* C/U) ◦ *The police have been unable to establish a motive for the murder.*
- something which makes people feel they have a good reason for doing sth: **motivation** ◦ *Having foreign friends is a good motivation for learning a foreign language.*
- a good reason for doing sth: **justification** (*noun* C/U), **explanation** (*noun* C/U) ◦ *What justification do you have for such rude behaviour?* ◦ *She didn't have a very good explanation for being late.*
- to give a good reason for doing sth: **justify** sth ◦ *I had to justify my decision to my boss.*

- a reason which may not be the true or real reason for doing sth: **excuse**, (*formal*) **pretext** ◦ *You always find an excuse for not doing your homework!* ◦ *He went home under the pretext of feeling ill.*

2 good and bad reasons
- if there is a good reason for sth, it is **reasonable** (*adverb* **reasonably**), **logical** (*adverb* **logically**), **understandable** (*adverb* **understandably**) ◦ *It's a reasonable assumption that they are tourists.* ◦ *It's quite logical to want to go on holiday after all this hard work.* ◦ *She was understandably angry with him for writing the article.*
- if you think that sb is right in thinking sth or deciding to do sth, you say that their decision **makes* sense**, that it is **sensible**, **justified**, that they acted **rightly**, **sensibly** ◦ *If you're so unhappy there, the only sensible thing to do is to find another job.* ◦ *You were perfectly justified in your choice of candidate. The others were all too inexperienced.* ◦ *You acted rightly in taking the money to the police.*

- if you cannot understand the reason for sth, you say that it is **inexplicable**, **illogical**, **irrational** ◦ *It's illogical to post her present if you're going to see her anyway.* ◦ *I know it's irrational, but I'm really frightened of spiders.*
- if you want sb to do sth without having a good reason, what you want is **unreasonable** ◦ *'My*

reason *contd.*

husband expects me to go out to work, look after the baby, and do the housework.' 'That's so unreasonable!'
- if there is no reason for doing sth, it is **pointless**, **useless** ◦ *It's pointless to look for somewhere to live before you've found a job.*
- if sth is done, or happens, with no clear reason, it is **arbitrary** ◦ *an arbitrary decision*
- if sth is done for no special reason, it is done **at random** ◦ *We looked at the map, chose three places at random, and went to visit them.*

3 asking for and giving a reason
- expressions used for asking for a reason: **why ...**, (*informal*) **how come ...**, **what's the reason ...** ◦ *Why did you do that?* ◦ *How come you're so late?* ◦ *What's the reason for all this noise?*
- expressions used for giving a reason: **because/as/since ...**, **because of ...**, **on account of ...**, **in view of ...**, (*informal*) **seeing as/that ...** ◦ *I didn't go to the party because I was ill.* ◦ *I like this club because of the music.* ◦ *I chose him on account of his experience.* ◦ *In view of the very hot weather, we have decided to cancel afternoon classes.* ◦ *Seeing as it's my birthday, let's go to the pub.*
- if you describe a situation, and you want to show that it is the reason for an action or an opinion, you can say **so**, **therefore** ◦ *I've finished studying, so I'm looking for another job now.* ◦ *He is out of the country and therefore unable to attend the meeting.*

■ **MORE ...**
- if you do sth for no particular reason, or without really thinking about it, you can say that you did it (*informal*) **for the hell of it** ◦ *'Why did you do that?' 'I don't know – just for the hell of it.'*

receive ⇨ GET/OBTAIN

recent ⇨ PAST[2]

recognise ⇨ KNOW

record

1 recording systems
2 making recordings
3 playing recordings

see also MUSIC, POP/ROCK, SING

1 recording systems
- music may be recorded on **CD** (= **compact disc**), on **tape**, or on **record** ◦ *Do you want it on CD or cassette?* ◦ *I've got that song on tape.*

■ CDs
- a flat round shiny piece of plastic on which sound is recorded, and played on a machine using a laser: **CD**, **compact disc** ◦ *a set of classical CDs*
- you play a CD on a **CD player**, **compact disc player** ◦ *a portable CD player*

■ tapes and cassettes
- a small flat plastic case with tape inside: **cassette**, **tape** ◦ *I've got a tape of that.*
- a tape with no recording on it is **blank**; a tape that you buy with a recording on it is **pre-recorded** ◦ *Have you got a blank tape that I could use?*
- you play a tape on a **cassette recorder**, **cassette player**, **tape recorder**

■ records
- a thin round piece of black plastic on which sound is recorded: **record** (*informal* **disc**) ◦ *to make a record* ◦ *She's got a huge record collection.*
- you play a record (disc) on a **record player**
- the flat, round surface that turns when you play a record on it: **turntable**
- a sharp needle which rests on a turning record to produce sounds: **needle**, **stylus**
- a full-size record: **long-playing record** (*abbreviation* **LP**), **album** ◦ *a double album* (= two records)
- the cover of a record: **sleeve**
- a machine in a café or bar that plays records when a coin is put in: **juke box**

■ music systems
- equipment that you use to play CDs, tapes or records: **music system**
- a music system which gives high quality sound and usually consists of several parts: **hi-fi** (**system**) ◦ *hi-fi equipment*
- a system that has two speakers: **stereo** (*noun* C/U) (*plural* **stereos**); when sound is directed through two speakers, it is **in stereo** ◦ *a stereo system* ◦ *a car stereo* ◦ *to listen to the stereo* ◦ *It sounds much better in stereo.*
- the part of a music system that you play records on: (**record**) **deck**
- the part of a music system that plays tapes or cassettes: **tape deck**, **cassette deck**
- to make a sound louder by using electrical equipment: **amplify** sth; *noun* (U): **amplification**; the part of the equipment that makes sounds louder: **amplifier**
- the place where the sound comes out of a record-player, etc: **speaker**
- a record player, etc that can be moved or easily carried is **portable** ◦ *a portable cassette player*
- a small stereo machine that one person can carry and listen to through headphones: **personal stereo** (*plural* **personal stereos**), **Walkman** ◦ *It's not a good idea to listen to your Walkman while riding a bicycle.*

2 making recordings
- to put sounds onto a record, tape, or compact disc: **record** sth, **make* a recording** (**of** sth) ◦ *I don't think they've made a recording of that concerto yet.*

- to record sounds onto a tape: **tape** sth ◦ *I want to tape this evening's Schubert concert.*
- if you remove a recording from a tape, you **wipe** it **off**, (*formal*) **erase** it ◦ *I wiped the last few words off by mistake.*

- one song or piece of music on a record, cassette or CD: **track**
- a small record that has only one song on each side: **single**

3 playing recordings

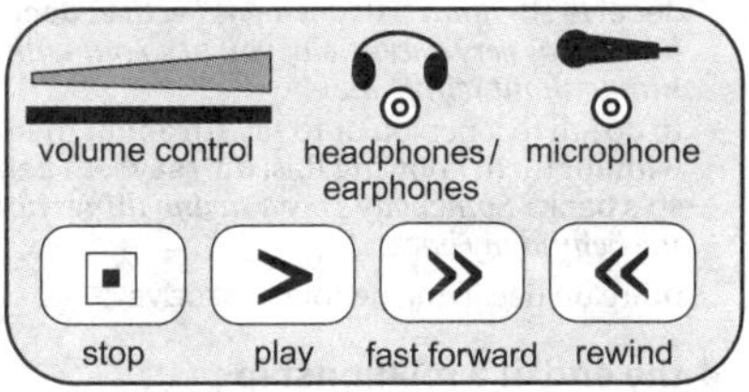

- when you use a record player, etc, you **play** sth (**on** it) ◦ *She spends all day playing loud music on her hi-fi.*
- when you play a recording on a machine, you **put*** it **on** ◦ *Shall I put some music on?*
- if you record something and then want to hear the recording you have made, you **play** it **back** ◦ *Would you like me to play the interview back to you?*

- how loud the sound is: **volume** (*noun* U) ◦ *Do you have to have the volume so high? I'm trying to work!*
- the quality of a sound: **tone** (*noun* U) ◦ *the tone control*
- the high sounds that a machine reproduces: **treble** (*noun* U) ◦ *It's not very clear – try increasing the treble.*
- the low sounds: **bass** (*noun* U) ◦ *too much bass*
- if you increase the volume, the treble, the bass, etc, you **turn** sth **up**; *opposite*: **turn** sth **down** ◦ *Could you turn the volume down a bit please?*
- to change any control: **adjust** sth ◦ *Try adjusting the bass.*

■ **MORE ...**
- a company that makes music recordings: **record company** ◦ *The Beatles formed their own record company.*
- recordings are made in a (**recording**) **studio** (*plural* **studios**)

red
⇨ COLOUR

reduce
⇨ INCREASE/DECREASE

refuse
⇨ WILLING

regret
- sorry for what you have done ⇨ SORRY
- sad about sth ⇨ SAD

relationship

1 different kinds of relationship
2 having relationships
3 personal qualities in relationships
4 the end of a relationship

1 different kinds of relationship
- the way that individual people and groups of people feel about each other and behave towards each other: **relationship**, **relations** (*noun plural*) ◦ *The teachers have a good relationship with the students.* ◦ *My colleagues and I have a good working relationship.* ◦ *diplomatic relations between France and Germany* ◦ *business relations*

- a person that you know and like (not a member of your family): **friend**; *opposite*: **enemy** ◦ *my best friend* ◦ *his worst enemy*
- a person that you enjoy spending time with: **companion**; being with a person: **company** (*noun* U); the enjoyment of being with a person: **companionship** (*noun* U) ◦ *inseparable companions* ◦ *He's great company* (= a nice person to spend time with). ◦ *She's all on her own; she needs some companionship.*
- a person that you know but who is not a close friend: **acquaintance**
- a person that you work with: **colleague** ◦ *one of my colleagues at work*

▷ more on friends and enemies ⇨ FRIEND, ENEMY

▷ other relationships ⇨ FAMILY, MARRY, LOVE, GROUP, WORK, EMPLOYMENT, LIVE[2]

■ describing a relationship
- when a relationship is good, it **goes well**, it is **strong**; not good: **bad**, **poor** ◦ *It looks as if their relationship is going well.* ◦ *Unfortunately, she has a very poor working relationship with her boss.*
- a relationship which is important and special is **serious**; *opposite*: **casual** ◦ *It's just a casual relationship – I don't want it to get serious.* ◦ *a casual acquaintance*
- a relationship between people who know each other well and like or love each other a lot is **close** ◦ *We're not as close as we used to be.*
- when two people know each other very well and/or spend time physically close to each other, their relationship is **intimate**; *noun* (U): **intimacy** ◦ *intimate friends*

2 having relationships
- if you have seen and/or spoken to sb before, you **know*** them, you **have met** them, they are **familiar** (**to** you), (*formal*) you are **acquainted with** them ◦ *'Do you two know each other?' 'Yes, we've met once before at a party.'* ◦ *He looks very familiar, but I can't remember his name.*

- to have a good friendly relationship with sb: **get*** **on**/**along** (**with** sb) ◦ *We're getting along quite well at the moment.* ◦ *to get on well together* ◦ *I don't get on with him.*

relationship *contd.*

– to get on very well with sb: **hit* it off** (**with** sb) ◦ *We met last night for the first time and we really hit it off.*
– to be in a good and friendly relationship with sb: **be on good terms** (**with** sb) ◦ *We're not on very good terms with each other at the moment.*

– to be able to understand how sb feels; to have a good relationship with sb: **relate to** sb ◦ *He's a nice person but I just can't relate to him.*
– if you have the right character or personality to be friends with sb, you are **compatible** (**with** sb); *opposite*: **incompatible** ◦ *I really fancy him, but we're just not compatible – we like totally different things.*

■ getting to know sb
– to tell two or more people who have not met before what each others' names are so that they can get to know each other: **introduce** sb (**to** sb) ◦ *Can you introduce me to your colleague?* ◦ *I'd like to introduce myself – my name's Carol.*
– to be introduced to sb for the first time: **meet*** sb ◦ *Come and meet my husband.*

– to spend time with a person in order to know them better: **get* to know** sb, (*formal*) **get* acquainted** (**with** sb) ◦ *I'd like to get to know him better.* ◦ *to get better acquainted*
– to become a friend of sb's: **make* friends** (**with** sb) ◦ *I haven't been here long but I've already made a few friends.*

▷ meeting people ⇨ MEET

3 personal qualities in relationships

– a person who likes spending time with other people **gets* on well with** people, is **sociable**, **outgoing**; *opposites*: **unsociable, antisocial** ◦ *She's very popular and seems to get on well with everyone.* ◦ *an outgoing personality*

– a person who tries to be kind and pleasant to people is **friendly** (**to/towards** sb); *opposite*: **unfriendly** (**to/towards** sb) ◦ *She seems quite friendly.* ◦ *You could try and be a bit more friendly towards her – she's really very nice.*
– a person you feel able to talk to or able to get to know is **approachable**; *opposite*: **unapproachable** ◦ *You should try and talk to him – he's very approachable.*
– a person who is very honest and is able to talk about himself/herself and his/her feelings is **open** ◦ *a very open individual* ◦ *She was very open with me about her personal life.*

▷ kind and friendly ⇨ KIND/CRUEL

– a person who is honest and does not change in their friendships is **loyal** (**to** sb), **faithful** (**to** sb); *noun* (U): **loyalty** ◦ *a loyal colleague/employee* ◦ *a faithful wife/husband*
– if you know that sb will always do what they say they will do, you can **rely on** them, they are **reliable, trustworthy** ◦ *He's a very good friend – I know I can always rely on him.* ◦ *You can tell her, she's trustworthy.*
– if you are not an honest friend and you change in your relationships, you are **disloyal, unfaithful**; *nouns* (U): **disloyalty, unfaithfulness**
– to be disloyal to sb: **betray** sb ◦ *When I found out he was seeing somebody else, I felt completely betrayed.*
– if you do not give sb the help they expect or you do not do what you promised to do, you **let*** sb **down** ◦ *She said she'd come, but she's let me down again.*

▷ more on being trustworthy ⇨ TRUST

– to make sb think or believe sth that is not true: **deceive** sb; *noun* (U): **deceit**; *adjective*: **deceitful** ◦ *It was very deceitful of you to go out with him without telling me.*
– to do sth to a person or to say sth about them without them knowing this: **do*/say*** sth **behind** sb's **back** ◦ *Somebody's been saying things about me behind my back.*

▷ more on deceiving people ⇨ DECEIVE

4 the end of a relationship

– to change your feelings and decide that you do not like sb: **turn against** sb; to make another person dislike sb: **turn** sb **against** sb ◦ *She hated me and turned her children against me as well.*
– to refuse to speak to sb, or to behave as if they do not exist: **ignore** sb ◦ *I saw him today but he just ignored me.*
– to stop being friends with sb: **turn** your **back** (**on** sb) ◦ *You can't turn your back on her now – she needs you more than ever.*

– when a relationship ends it is **over, finished**, you are **through** (**with** sb) ◦ *We're through – I can't live with you any longer.*
– to end a relationship: **finish** (**with** sb), **break* up** (**with** sb), **split* up** (**with** sb) ◦ *They decided to split up because the relationship just wasn't working.* ◦ *I finished with him last night.*
– to end a relationship and leave sb: **leave*** sb, (*informal*) **ditch** sb, (*informal*) **dump** sb ◦ *I'm leaving you.* ◦ *Did you know that she's dumped her boyfriend?*
– to leave sb because you want to be with another person: **leave*/ditch** sb (**for** sb) ◦ *She ditched me for that rich guy with a Porsche.*
– to leave sb suddenly and go away with another person: **run* off with** sb, **go* off with** sb ◦ *Apparently, she ran off with her best friend's husband.*

■ starting a relationship again
– to decide to work with sb or be friends with sb again: **get* back together** (**with** sb), (*formal*) **be reconciled** (**with** sb); *noun* (U): **reconciliation** ◦ *They've finally got back together again after three years apart.*

relevant ⇨ DISCUSS/ARGUE, MEANING

religion

1 religious beliefs
2 religious practices
3 different religions
see also GOD

1 religious beliefs

- the belief in a god or gods who made the world and can control what happens in it: **religion** (*noun* U)
- connected with religion: **religious** ◦ *religious belief*
- connected with God or with religion: **holy**, **sacred**
- if sth is not connected with religion, it is **secular** ◦ *secular values*

- the part of you that is not physical; your thoughts and feelings, not your body: **spirit**
- the part of a person that is believed to continue to live after the body is dead: **soul**
- connected with the soul or spirit: **spiritual** (*adverb* **spiritually**)

- the place where some people think that God lives and where good people go when they die: **heaven** ◦ *to go to heaven*
- the place where bad people go when they die, according to some religions: **hell**
- the continued existence of a person after death: **life after death**, **afterlife**, **eternal life** ◦ *a belief in the afterlife*
- the belief that after death you are born again: **reincarnation** (*noun* U)

▷ more on spirits ⇨ SPIRIT

- an action which breaks a religious law: **sin** (*noun* C/U) ◦ *He asked for his sins to be forgiven.* ◦ *the sin of envy*
- a person who commits many sins is **sinful**, a **sinner**
- being saved from your sins: **salvation** (*noun* U) ◦ *pray for salvation*

- something that a particular religion teaches: **doctrine** (*noun* C/U), **teaching**; *adjective*: **doctrinal** ◦ *The Christian doctrine of the Trinity* ◦ *the teachings of Islam* ◦ *doctrinal differences*
- to accept a particular religious belief: **believe** (**in** sth); *noun* (U): **belief**; a particular religious idea: **belief** ◦ *to believe in God* ◦ *belief in God* ◦ *strong religious beliefs*
- a feeling of certainty about the truth of religious ideas: **faith** (*noun* U) ◦ *His faith helped him get through a difficult period of his life.*
- a person with religious faith: **believer**

- the writings on which a particular religion is based: **the Scriptures** ◦ *the Hindu Scriptures*
- the main book of the Christian and Jewish scriptures: **the Bible**

2 religious practices

- to take part regularly in the activities connected with your religion: **practise** (sth); a person who does this is **practising** (*only before a noun*) ◦ *It was difficult for people to practise their religion.* ◦ *a practising Catholic*
- a person who believes strongly in a religion and takes part in it is **religious** ◦ *a deeply religious person*
- a person who practises their religion very carefully is **devout** ◦ *a family of devout Muslims*
- a person who is exceptionally pure and good is **holy**; the quality of being holy: **holiness** (*noun* U)
- a man/woman who is believed to be chosen by God to give his message to people: **prophet/prophetess**

- to change your religious beliefs: **convert to** sth ◦ *She told me she had converted to Buddhism.*
- to persuade sb to change their religious beliefs: **convert** sb (**to** sth) ◦ *His friend converted him to Islam.*
- the act of converting (sb) to a religion: **conversion** (*noun* C/U) ◦ *the conversion of St Paul*
- a person who has been converted: **convert**

- a person who performs religious ceremonies: **priest**
- a person who is sent to another country to teach about the Christian religion: **missionary**
- a man who has taken religious vows and usually lives in a religious community: **monk**; a building where monks live: **monastery**; the title given to some monks: **brother**
- a woman who has taken religious vows and usually lives in a religious community: **nun**; a building where nuns live: **convent**
- the title given to a nun: **sister**
- a man/woman who is head of a religious community: **abbot/abbess**

▷ more on priests ⇨ PRIEST

- to speak to God in order to give thanks or to ask for sth: **pray**
- to pray to and show respect for God: **worship** (God)
- a religious talk, especially in church: **sermon**; to give a religious talk, especially in church: **preach** (sth) ◦ *He preached to a large crowd.* ◦ *to preach a sermon*

▷ more on praying ⇨ PRAY

- a formal religious event: **ceremony** ◦ *a wedding ceremony*
- a public celebration of a religious event: **festival** ◦ *the Hindu festival of Diwali*
- to eat no food for a particular period, usually for religious reasons: **fast**; a period of not eating: **fast** ◦ *Some Christians fast during Lent* (= the period of forty days before Easter). ◦ *the Muslim fast of Ramadan*

▷ more on Christian practices ⇨ CHRISTIAN

3 kinds of religion

- a particular system of religious belief and practice: **religion** ◦ *I don't know what her religion is.* ◦ *Eastern religions*
- a religious group that has broken away from a larger group: **sect** ◦ *a small Protestant sect*
- a religious group that is considered unusual: **cult** ◦ *She got involved with a strange cult and did not want to see her family.*

- the traditional religion of India in which there are many gods: **Hinduism** (*noun* U); a person who believes in this religion: **Hindu**; *adjective*: **Hindu**
- a spiritual leader or teacher in the Hindu religion: **guru**

religion *contd.*

– the religion which was started in India by Gautama Buddha: **Buddhism** (*noun* U); a person who believes in this religion: **Buddhist**; *adjective*: **Buddhist**

– a building in which Hindus and Buddhists worship: **temple**

▷ other religions ⇨ **CHRISTIAN, JEW, MUSLIM**

■ **MORE . . .**

– if you follow the traditional practices of certain religions, you are **orthodox** ◦ *an orthodox Jew*
– a person who strictly follows the basic teaching of their religion: **fundamentalist** ◦ *Christian fundamentalists believe in the literal truth of the Bible.*

– to hurt sb or do bad things to sb because of their religion: **persecute** sb; *noun* (C/U): **persecution**; a person who does this: **persecutor** ◦ *victims of religious persecution*

– having hidden spiritual meaning: **mystical** ◦ *a mystical experience*
– a person with deep spiritual knowledge: **mystic**; religion based on this: **mysticism** (*noun* U)
– if sth cannot be explained by the laws of science, it is **supernatural** ◦ *supernatural powers.* ◦ *a supernatural being*

– a person who travels to a holy place for religious reasons: **pilgrim** ◦ *Christian pilgrims in Rome*
– a journey made by a pilgrim: **pilgrimage** ◦ *He has been on the pilgrimage to Mecca.* ◦ *to make a pilgrimage*

remember/forget

1 remembering
2 forgetting
3 using your memory to learn

see also THINK

1 remembering

– to have sth in your mind from the past: **remember** (sth) ◦ *'Where did you park the car?' 'I can't remember!'* ◦ *I just don't remember where I put the key.* ◦ *I remember seeing her at Jo's house.*
– to bring a past event back into your mind: **remember** (sth), **think* of** sth, **recall** (sth) ◦ *I'm trying to remember where I put my umbrella.* ◦ *I can't think of his name.* ◦ *I don't recall giving her any money.*
– your ability to remember things: **memory** ◦ *to have a good/bad memory for faces* ◦ *To the best of my memory* (= as far as I can remember), *he was wearing a red jacket.*

– to cause sb to remember sb/sth: **remind** sb **of** sb/sth, **bring*** sth **back**, **jog** sb's **memory** ◦ *You remind me of my father.* ◦ *The photograph brought back memories of my childhood.* ◦ *Something he said jogged my memory.*
– if sth reminds you of sth, it looks, sounds, etc **familiar**, it **rings* a bell** ◦ *Her name rings a bell – perhaps we met at a party last year?*
– an event or other thing that you remember: **memory** ◦ *memories of childhood* ◦ *I have vivid memories of being pulled out of the water.*
– if sth is easy to remember because of being special, it is **memorable**, **unforgettable** ◦ *a memorable visit* ◦ *an unforgettable experience*

– to remember sth when you have to decide about sth: **bear*/keep*** sth **in mind** ◦ *I hope you will keep me in mind when you decide about the job.*

■ remembering to do sth

– to remember sth so that you do what you were planning to do or were asked to do: **remember** (**to** do sth) ◦ *I must remember to water the plants.*
– to say sth to help a person remember to do sth: **remind** sb (**of/about** sth), **remind** sb **to** do sth ◦ *I'm glad you reminded me about the meeting – I'd forgotten all about it!* ◦ *Remind me to phone Mary.*
– something that makes you remember sth: **reminder** ◦ *We'll send you a reminder* (= a card/letter) *when your next dental appointment is due.*

2 forgetting

– to lose the memory of sth: **forget*** (sth) ◦ *You never forget how to swim.* ◦ *I'd quite forgotten that the time of the meeting had been changed.*
– not to remember to do sth: **forget*** (**to** do sth) ◦ *'Did you remember to post my letter?' 'Oh dear, I completely forgot. I'll do it now.'*
– if you forget sth, it **goes* out of your mind** ◦ *I'm sorry, your name has just gone out of my mind.*
– if you cannot remember anything, your **mind is a blank** ◦ *I remember falling down but after that my mind's a blank.*
– if your memory of sth is not clear, it is **dim** (*adverb* **dimly**) ◦ *I dimly recall meeting him many years ago.*

– if you only remember things that happened recently, you have a **short memory**
– if you often forget things, you are **forgetful**; *noun* (U): **forgetfulness** ◦ *How could I be so forgetful!*
– if you forget things because you are thinking of sth else, you are **absent-minded** (*adverb* **absent-mindedly**)

– to decide to stop thinking about sth: **forget*** sth, **put*** sth **out of** your **mind/head** ◦ *Let's forget about our past disagreements and try to work together.* ◦ *You must try to put that incident out of your head and get on with your life.*

3 using your memory to learn

– to learn sth so that you can remember it exactly: **memorize** sth ◦ *She memorized a lot of dates for her history exam.*
– by remembering exactly: **by heart** ◦ *He knew many of Hardy's poems by heart.*
– if you are able to do sth without looking at anything that is written, you do it **from memory** ◦ *The pianist could play the piece from memory.*

▷ more on learning ⇨ **LEARN**

■ **MORE . . .**

– a feeling of longing and sadness about the past:

nostalgia (*noun* U); *adjective*: **nostalgic** ◦ *nostalgia for the 'good old days'* ◦ *a nostalgic trip to the town of my birth*
- to think about sth in your past life: **look back** (**on** sth) ◦ *She looks back on that period in her life with pride.*
- to make sb remember an earlier period in their life: **take*** sb **back** (**to** sth) ◦ *Seeing his friend took him back to the Vienna of his youth.*

- if you tell sb sth but they quickly forget what you say, it (*informal*) **goes* in one ear and out the other** ◦ *There's no point in telling him – it just goes in one ear and out the other.*
- if you cannot quite remember sth but think that you will remember it soon, it is **on the tip of** your **tongue** ◦ *The name is on the tip of my tongue – I'll remember it in a moment.*

- to keep a special event in people's memories: **commemorate** sth; made for this purpose: **commemorative** ◦ *This statue commemorates the founder of the city.* ◦ *a commemorative stamp*
- a building or statue to make people remember a person or event: **memorial**, **monument** ◦ *a war memorial* ◦ *a monument to Winston Churchill*
- an object that you keep to remind you of a person or special event: **memento** (*plural* **mementoes**) ◦ *They gave him a carving as a memento of his visit.*
- an object that you keep to remind you of a place or event: **souvenir** ◦ *a souvenir of Tahiti*

remind ⇨ REMEMBER/FORGET

remove

removing clothes ⇨ CLOTHES

- to take sb/sth away from a person: **take*** sb/sth **away** (**from** sb), **remove** sb/sth (**from** sb) ◦ *They've taken her driving licence away from her.* ◦ *The children have been removed from their parents.*
- when a doctor or dentist removes a part of your body, such as a tooth, you **have** sth **out** ◦ *The dentist says I've got to have two teeth out.*

- to take sb/sth away from a place: **take*** sb/sth **away** (**from** sth), **remove** sb/sth (**from** sth) ◦ *Can you please remove your car from the staff car park?*
- to take sb/sth out of a place: **take*/get*** sb/sth **out** (**of** sth) ◦ *The rescue workers worked night and day to get the passengers out of the train.*
- to take sb/sth from a surface: **take*/get*** sb/sth **off** sth ◦ *Could you take those papers off the table, please.* ◦ *I can't get the price off this book without tearing the cover!*

- to make sth disappear: **get* rid of** sth, **remove** sth; *noun* (U): **removal** ◦ *How can I get rid of this wine stain?* ◦ *a product for stain removal*
- to remove sth completely: **clear** sth (**from/off** sth), **clear** sth **of** sth, (*formal*) **eliminate** sth (**from** sth); *nouns* (U): **clearance**, **elimination** ◦ *They're clearing the snow from the roads.* ◦ *to clear the paths of snow* ◦ *slum clearance*
- if sth can be removed or is removed, it **comes* off** (sth), **comes* out** (**of** sth) ◦ *This stain won't come off – I shall have to throw the dress away.* ◦ *Unfortunately the cake didn't come out of the tin in one piece.*
- able to be removed: **removable** ◦ *The back seat is removable.*

■ ways of removing things
- to remove sb/sth by lifting or pulling: **lift/pull** sb/sth **off** (sth), **lift/pull** sb/sth **out** (**of** sth) ◦ *The injured passenger was lifted off the boat by helicopter.* ◦ *We had to pull the fallen tree off the road.* ◦ *to pull a tooth out*
- to remove a part of sth by breaking sth: **break*** sth **off** (sth) ◦ *I broke off a square of chocolate.*
- to separate a piece of paper or material from a larger piece of paper or material: **tear*** sth **off** (sth), **tear*** sth **out** (**of** sth) ◦ *She tore off a corner of the paper and wrote her phone number on it.* ◦ *to tear a page out of a book*

- to remove sth using a knife, scissors, etc: **cut*** sth **off** (sth)
- to remove sth with a saw: **saw** sth **off** (sth) ◦ *He sawed a branch off the tree.*
- to remove sth with heat: **burn*** sth **off** (sth) ◦ *Burn off the old paint before repainting the door.*
- to remove sth with a brush: **brush** sth **off** (sth), **brush** sth **away** (**from** sth) ◦ *She brushed the crumbs off the table.*
- to remove sth by moving a sharp edge, for example a knife, across sth: **scrape** sth **off** (sth) ◦ *Scrape the mud off your boots!*

■ throwing things away
- to take sth that you do not want or need and put it in another place: **throw*** sth **away**, **get* rid of** sth, (*formal*) **dispose of** sth; *noun* (U): **disposal** ◦ *Can I throw your old jeans away?* ◦ *I might as well get rid of these clothes – I never use them.* ◦ *the disposal of dangerous chemicals*
- to remove things by tidying sth and throwing away things that you do not want: **clear** sth **out**, (*informal*) **have a clear-out** ◦ *I've decided to clear out the spare room today.* ◦ *We're having a clear-out – do you want any of this stuff?*
- to remove things and put them in cupboards, drawers, etc: **clear** (sth) **away** ◦ *Who's going to offer to clear away the dinner things?*

■ not removing or being removed
- not to remove sth from a place: **leave*** sth **on/in** (sth) ◦ *Leave the baby in his cot for a while and see if he goes to sleep.*
- not to be removed from a place: **stay on/in** (sth) ◦ *The letter stayed on the table for several days before anybody opened it.*

rent

1 renting a house, a flat, etc
2 renting a car, a television, etc
buying a house ⇨ HOUSE

1 renting a house, a flat, etc
- to pay money for the use of a house, a flat or some land: **rent** (sth) (**from** sb) ◦ *The cheapest*

rent *contd.*

way to get somewhere to live is to rent a flat from the council.

– the money you pay each month: **rent** (*noun* C/U) ◦ *It's a lovely flat, but can we afford the rent?* ◦ *an increase in rent*
– a house, flat, etc that you rent from sb is **rented** ◦ *We're living in a rented flat.*
– a person who pays money to the owner of a room, house, etc, so they can live in it: **tenant**

– to offer a house, flat, etc for sb to live in for money: **let*** sth (**to** sb) ◦ *Do you let flats to students?*
– a person who lets a house or room to people for money: **landlord**; a woman who does this can also be called a **landlady**
– a contract (= written agreement) in which a building or land is let to sb for a fixed period of time in exchange for rent: **lease** ◦ *How long is the lease for?*

– a room or rooms in sb's house where you can stay in return for paying rent: **lodgings** (*noun plural*); a person who stays in lodgings: **lodger** ◦ *A lot of the students at the University live in lodgings around the city.* ◦ *Mrs Jones makes a bit of extra money by taking in lodgers.*

2 renting a car, a television, etc

– to pay money for the use of a television, computer, car, etc, usually for a long period of time: **rent** sth (**from** sb); *noun* (U): **rental** ◦ *Is it cheaper to rent a television or to buy one?* ◦ *a car rental company*
– the money you pay regularly for renting sth is the **rental** (*noun* U) ◦ *The rental on a small car is usually not very high.*
– a thing that you rent from sb is **rented** ◦ *a rented flat*
– to pay money for the use of sth for a short period of time: **hire** (*AmE* **rent**) sth (**from** sb); *noun* (U): **hire** (*AmE* **rental**) ◦ *I hired a suit for my sister's wedding.* ◦ *I know a garage which has very cheap car hire.* ◦ *The hire of the suits was £30 for the day.*

– to allow sb to use a car, etc in return for money, for a fairly long period of time: **rent** sth (**out**) (**to** sb)
– to allow sb to use sth in return for money, for a short period of time: **hire** (*AmE* **rent**) sth (**out**) (**to** sb) ◦ *Do you know a shop that hires out pianos?*

repair

see also BREAK, JOIN, SEW

– to work on sth that is broken or damaged to make it whole again, work better, etc: **repair** sth, **mend** sth, (*informal*) **fix** sth ◦ *How much will it cost to repair the car?* ◦ *Can you mend the hole in this jumper for me?* ◦ *Do you think it's possible to get this radio fixed?*
– the work that you do to mend sth that is damaged: **repair** ◦ *This house needs extensive repairs.*
– if sth is not damaged or is working well and does not need to be repaired, it is **in good condition**

– to work on sth that is old to improve its condition: **do*** sth **up**, **restore** sth, **renovate** sth; *nouns* (U): **restoration**, **renovation** ◦ *to restore an old car* ◦ *The restoration of the palace took two years to complete.* ◦ *The hotel was renovated last year.*

– to keep sth in good condition: **maintain** sth; *noun* (U): **maintenance**
– to make sure that a machine (for example, a car) is in good condition and to repair it if necessary: **service** sth; *noun* (C/U): **service** ◦ *Your gas fire should be serviced regularly.* ◦ *I have to take my car in for a service.*
– to look at sth and change or repair it if necessary: **overhaul** sth; *noun*: **overhaul** ◦ *give the car a general overhaul*

– to separate the parts of sth in order to mend it: **take*** sth **to pieces**, **take*** sth **apart**, (*informal*) **take*** sth **to bits**; *opposite*: **put*** sth **back together** ◦ *He's always taking his car to bits.*
– an extra part that is used to replace a similar part that is old or damaged: **spare part**, **spare**

■ people who repair things
– a person who repairs sth: **repairer** ◦ *a shoe/watch repairer*
– a person who repairs cars or other vehicles or other machines: **mechanic**
– a person who puts furniture, pictures and other works of art in good condition: **restorer** ◦ *a picture restorer* ◦ *a furniture restorer*

– the activity of making or repairing things yourself: (*BrE*) **DIY**, **do-it-yourself** ◦ *a DIY enthusiast*

repeat

– doing sth again ⇨ AGAIN
– saying sth again ⇨ SAY

reply

– to a letter ⇨ LETTER[1]
– to a question ⇨ QUESTION

report

– a written account of sth ⇨ INFORMATION
– giving information to sb ⇨ INFORM

reputation

– well known ⇨ FAMOUS
– being thought of in a certain way ⇨ OPINION

request

asking for permission to do sth ⇨ ALLOW
see also QUESTION, ORDER[2]

■ asking for sth
– to ask sb if they will give you sth: **ask** (sb) **for** sth, (*formal*) **request** sth (**from** sb); *noun*: **request** (**for** sth) ◦ *We went into the café and asked for some coffee.* ◦ *I've decided to ask my bank manager for a loan.* ◦ *They've put in a request for more time to finish the project.*

- to speak to sb in order to ask for sth: (*formal*) **approach** sb (**for/about** sth) ◦ *Have you approached your boss about the new job yet?*

- to make a formal request in writing, for example for a job: **apply** (**to** sb) (**for** sth); *noun* (C/U): **application** ◦ *I've applied for several jobs, but I still haven't had any luck.* ◦ *We've received hundreds of applications.* ◦ *an application form*
- a person who applies for sth: **applicant** ◦ *a job applicant*
- to make a formal request for sth that you think you should get: **claim** sth; *noun*: **claim** ◦ *We found this watch in the cloakroom, but no one's claimed it yet.* ◦ *an insurance claim*

- to make a strong request for sth, as if you are giving an order: **demand** sth; *noun*: **demand** ◦ *The men are demanding higher pay.* ◦ *I think it's a reasonable demand.*
- to make a strong and serious request for sth: **appeal** (**to** sb) (**for** sth), **beg** (sb) **for** sth; *noun*: **appeal** ◦ *The Red Cross are appealing to the public for contributions.* ◦ *to beg for forgiveness* ◦ *an urgent appeal for help*

■ asking sb to do sth
- to ask sb if they will do sth for you: **ask** sb (**to** do sth), (*formal*) **request** sb (**to** do sth); *noun*: **request** ◦ *I asked him to help me with my homework.* ◦ *I asked him if he could give me a hand.* ◦ *Customers are requested not to smoke.*
- to ask sb strongly to do sth: **beg** sb (**to** do sth), **urge** sb (**to** do sth), (*formal*) **call on/upon** sb (**to** do sth) ◦ *His mother begged them not to take him away.* ◦ *I urge you to think again.* ◦ *Greenpeace are calling on governments to stop dumping chemical waste in the North Sea.*
- if you do sth because sb has asked you to, you do it **at** sb's **request**, **at the request of** sb ◦ *The letter was sent at my request.*

■ saying yes or no to a request
- to say yes to a request: **agree** (**to** sth), **agree** (**to** do sth), (*formal*) **consent** (**to** sth); *nouns* (U): **agreement, consent** ◦ *Andy has agreed to lend us his car.* ◦ *Her parents refused to consent to the marriage.* ◦ *They can't get married without their parents' consent.*
- to say no to a request: **refuse** (sth), **not agree** (**to** sth), **not agree** (**to** do sth) ◦ *We begged them to lend us the money but they refused.* ◦ *He won't agree to let us out early.*

▷ words for agreeing to a request ⇨ YES/NO

■ some ways of making requests
- the word for making a request more polite: **please**

- to make a request, you can say **Will you ...?** or **Would you** (**kindly**) **...?** or **Can you ...?** or **Could you** (**possibly**) **...?** ◦ *Please will you do me a favour?* ◦ *Would you very kindly bring me that chair?* ◦ *Can you get me a drink, please?* ◦ *Could you possibly go and buy some milk from the shop?*
- to make a very polite request, you can say **Do you mind ...?** or **Would you mind ...?** or **I'm sorry to bother/trouble you, but ...** ◦ *Do you mind waiting a few minutes?* ◦ *Would you mind coming back tomorrow?* ◦ *I'm sorry to trouble you, but would you mind answering a few questions?*

---

rescue ⇨ DANGEROUS, ACCIDENT

---

research ⇨ STUDY

---

rest[1]

- the others (of a group) ⇨ DIFFERENT
- the other part of sth ⇨ PART/WHOLE

---

rest[2] a period of no activity

see also SLEEP

- a period of no activity: **rest** (*noun* C/U) ◦ *Can we stop for a moment? I need a rest.* ◦ *to take a rest* ◦ *The doctor has ordered complete rest for two weeks.*
- to do less or to do nothing after being active: **rest**; to allow a part of your body to rest: **rest** sth ◦ *Do you want to rest here for a while?* ◦ *Your back will not get better unless you rest it.*
- a short period of rest: **break** ◦ *to take/have a break* ◦ *a tea/coffee break* ◦ *They worked for several hours without a break.*
- a short rest or sleep during the day: **nap**, (especially in hot countries) **siesta**

- to rest from physical activity so that your breathing returns to normal: **get*** your **breath back** ◦ *I had to stop climbing several times to get my breath back.*
- to rest and not take an active part in what other people are doing: **sit* back** ◦ *Now that you've finished your share of the work, you can sit back and watch.*

- to become less active and do little: **relax**; *noun* (U): **relaxation** ◦ *You need a holiday to relax after all your hard work.* ◦ *What do you do for relaxation?*
- to relax and stop working or worrying about work: (*informal*) **unwind*** ◦ *It takes me an hour to unwind when I get home from work.*
- to relax and not worry about anything: **take* it easy**, **take* things easy**
- making you feel relaxed and peaceful: **restful**, **relaxing** ◦ *restful music* ◦ *a relaxing drink/massage*

- to relax, usually sitting or lying with your feet supported by sth: **put*** your **feet up**
- to relax in a chair: **sit* back**
- to relax in a horizontal position: **lie* down**; to spend a short time doing this: **have a lie-down** ◦ *She lay down on the bed and fell fast asleep.* ◦ *I'm going to have a lie-down*

- a period of rest from work: **holiday** ◦ *I need a holiday!* ◦ *You should take a holiday.*

▷ more on holidays ⇨ HOLIDAY

restaurant

1 places where you can go for a meal
2 having a meal in a restaurant
see also MEAL, EAT

1 places where you can go for a meal

- a place where you go to buy and eat a meal: **restaurant** ◦ *We went out to an Italian restaurant to celebrate my birthday.*
- a restaurant that serves food that can be eaten quickly or taken away: **fast food restaurant**
- a place where you can buy meals to take away: **take-away** (*AmE* **take-out restaurant**); the food that you buy: **take-away** (*AmE* **take-out**) ◦ *Is there a Chinese take-away near here?* ◦ *We got an Indian take-away.*
- a small restaurant that serves light meals: **caf**
- (in the United States) a small restaurant beside a main road: **diner**

- a restaurant where you collect your food yourself from a counter (= a long flat surface): **self-service restaurant**
- a place in a school, office, factory, etc where people can buy and eat cheap meals: **cafeteria, canteen**
- a flat piece of wood, plastic, metal, etc with raised edges that you use for carrying food, drink, etc: **tray**

- a small place where you can buy sandwiches or other light food: **snack bar, sandwich bar**
- a small place that serves coffee and sometimes light food: **coffee bar**
- (in Britain) a place that serves alcoholic drinks and sometimes food: **pub** ◦ *Pub food has improved a lot recently.* ◦ *pub lunches*
- a place which serves wine and sometimes light food: **wine bar**
- a café at a station, or a place where passengers can buy food and drink on a train: **buffet** ◦ *Is there a buffet car on this train?*

▷ more on pubs ⇨ BAR/PUB

2 having a meal in a restaurant

- to go to a restaurant for a meal: **eat* out, go* out for a meal,** (*formal*) **dine out** ◦ *We're eating out tonight so I don't have to cook.* ◦ *Let's go out for a meal.*

- to ask a restaurant to keep a table for you: **book (a table)** ◦ *I've booked a table for four* (= for four people).
- if there are no free tables, the restaurant will tell you that they are **fully booked, booked up** ◦ *'Can I book a table for eight o'clock tonight?' 'I'm sorry, madam, I'm afraid we're fully booked.'*

- the man/woman who brings you your food: **waiter/waitress**; the most senior (= chief) waiter: **head waiter**
- to ask for food: **order** sth ◦ *Could we order some drinks first?*
- when the waiter/waitress writes down the food that you want, he/she **takes*** your **order** ◦ *I wish the waiter would hurry up and take our order.*
- the waiter/waitress who takes your order and brings you your food **serves** you; *noun* (U): **service** ◦ *We waited ages to get served.* ◦ *I'm not going there again – the service was terrible.*

- the list of food that you can choose from in a restaurant: **menu** ◦ *Could I see the menu, please?* ◦ *What's on the menu today?*
- a type of food prepared in a particular way: **dish** ◦ *an Indian dish*
- if each dish on the menu has its own price, the menu is **la carte**
- the list of wine that you can order in a restaurant: **wine list**

▷ different parts of a meal ⇨ MEAL

■ paying for a meal

- when you want to pay for your meal you ask for the **bill** (*AmE* **check**) ◦ *Can I have the bill please?*
- the extra amount of money you sometimes have to pay for service: **service charge** ◦ *Is the service charge included?*
- extra money that you pay to a waiter, etc to thank them for their work: **tip**; to give sb a tip: **tip** (sb) (some money) ◦ *Shall we leave a tip?* ◦ *How much should I tip the waiter?*

result ⇨ CAUSE/EFFECT

return

- coming back ⇨ COME/GO
- putting sth back ⇨ PUT
- doing sth again ⇨ ACTION

review ⇨ CRITICISM

rhythm ⇨ MUSIC

rice

see also FOOD, COOK

- the grain from a plant that grows in hot wet countries, that people cook and eat: **rice** (*noun* U) ◦ *white rice* ◦ *brown rice* (= rice with its outer covering still on)
- the smallest piece of rice: **grain (of rice)**
- the field where rice is grown: **paddy-field, rice field**

- rice cooked in boiling water: **boiled rice** (*noun* U)
- rice cooked in hot oil: **fried rice** (*noun* U)

- a hot pudding made by cooking rice in milk and sugar: **rice pudding** (*noun* C/U)
- a dish made of rice cooked with pieces of vegetable and meat: **risotto** (*plural* **risottos**) (*noun* C/U)

rich

see also POOR

- having a lot of money or property; not poor: **rich**, **wealthy**; *nouns* (U): **wealth** ◦ *a rich man/family/country* ◦ *She has a lot of wealthy friends.* ◦ *I intend to enjoy my new-found wealth!*
- people, companies or countries that are rich and successful are **prosperous**; (*noun* U): **prosperity** ◦ *Japan has enjoyed a long period of prosperity and economic stability.*

- a person who is rich can be called **well-off**, (*informal*) **loaded**, (*informal*) **rolling in it**, (*informal*) **rolling in money** ◦ *Let Hugh pay; he's loaded.* ◦ *Her parents are rolling in money.*
- a very rich person or a person who has a million pounds (dollars, etc) or more: **millionaire**, **multimillionaire**, **billionaire**
- the group of people with a lot of money or property: **the rich** (*with plural verb*)

▷ different groups in society ⇨ SOCIETY

■ the life of rich people
- wealth, comfort and pleasure: **luxury** (*noun* U); *adjective*: **luxurious** ◦ *a life of luxury* ◦ *living in luxury* ◦ *a luxury hotel* ◦ *a luxurious existence*
- something that is enjoyable and expensive and that you do not really need: **luxury** ◦ *caviar, champagne and other luxuries*
- to have plenty of money and live very comfortably: **live well** ◦ *He's retired from horse-racing and is living very well in Majorca.*

- (used about hotels, aeroplanes, etc) providing the most expensive type of service: **first class** (*adjective, adverb*) ◦ *a first class hotel* ◦ *I always travel first class.*
- smart and expensive: **plush** ◦ *a plush hotel*
- fashionable and expensive: **posh** ◦ *a posh car*

■ becoming rich
- to become successful and rich: **get* rich**, **do* well** (**for** yourself) ◦ *He's done very well for himself in the catering business.*
- to get money, property, etc from sb who has died: **inherit** sth; something that you inherit: **inheritance** ◦ *When my aunt died, I inherited her jewellery.*

■ **MORE ...**
- a rich and powerful person who is successful in business: (*informal*) (**business**) **tycoon**
- a rich man who spends his time enjoying himself and spending money: **playboy**
- the group of rich, successful and fashionable people who travel around the world a lot: the **jet set**

ride ⇨ BICYCLE, MOTORCYCLE, HORSE

ridiculous ⇨ STUPID

right/left

parts and positions of things ⇨ PLACE²

- on or connected with the side of your body that faces east when you are facing north: **right** (*noun, adjective*); *opposite*: **left** (*noun, adjective*) ◦ *I've broken my right arm so I can't do my exams.* ◦ *She's lost her left shoe.*
- on or of the right/left side of sth: **right-hand/left-hand** ◦ *The house is on the left-hand side of the street.* ◦ *Take the right-hand turning.*
- in a direction to the right/left: (**to the**) **right/left** ◦ *Turn right at the crossroads.* ◦ *Could you move a little to the left?*
- in a position to the right/left: **on the right/left** ◦ *Mine is the door on the right as you come out of the lift.* ◦ *to drive on the left*

- a person who most often uses their right/left hand for writing, eating, etc is **right-handed/left-handed** ◦ *Are you left-handed?* ◦ *a left-handed tennis player*

- the side of a ship which is on the right when you are facing towards the front: **starboard**; on the left: **port**

right/wrong¹
- true ⇨ TRUE
- what is needed ⇨ USEFUL/SUITABLE

right/wrong² behaviour

1 right and wrong
2 what is right
3 what is wrong
see also BEHAVIOUR

1 right and wrong
- good and bad behaviour: **right and wrong** ◦ *to learn/know the difference between right and wrong*
- concerned with what is right and wrong: **moral** (*adverb* **morally**); *noun* (U): **morality** ◦ *moral standards/issues* ◦ *to decide something on moral grounds* ◦ *morally right/wrong* ◦ *standards of morality* ◦ *We discussed the morality of the death sentence.*

- a person's standards of good behaviour: **morals** (*noun plural*), **values** (*noun plural*) ◦ *a man without morals* ◦ *traditional values*
- high standards of behaviour for yourself and other people: **ideals** (*noun plural*) ◦ *She finds it hard to live up to her own ideals.*
- willing to listen to and accept ideas about behaviour, etc that are different from your own: **broad-minded** ◦ *His parents are very broad-minded.*

- a person's inner moral strength: **character** (*noun* U) ◦ *a test of character* ◦ *It takes character to admit you're wrong.*
- your own feeling about whether what you are doing is right or wrong: **conscience** (*noun* C/U); to feel bad because you have done sth wrong: **have** sth **on** your **conscience** ◦ *to have a clear/guilty conscience* ◦ *It had been on my conscience for years.*

2 what is right
- if behaviour is good and is fair to other people, it is **right** ◦ *It's not right to tell lies.* ◦ *It was right of him to give the money back.* ◦ *to do the right thing*

right/wrong² *contd.*

- morally right: (*formal*) **ethical** ◦ *Her behaviour was not strictly ethical.*
- fair and right: **just**; fair behaviour or treatment: **justice** (*noun* U) ◦ *a just decision* ◦ *a fight for justice*
- a thing that you have the moral authority to do: **right** (**to** do sth) ◦ *You have no right to hit me.*
- a thing that you must do because people expect you to do it or because you think it is right: **duty** (*noun* C/U) ◦ *It's our duty to protect the weaker members of our society.* ◦ *to do your duty*

▷ more on duty ⇨ **DUTY**

- having high standards of behaviour: **moral** (*adverb* **morally**) ◦ *to lead a moral life* ◦ *a moral person* ◦ *to behave morally*
- a person who behaves in a moral way, or behaviour that is morally right, is **good** ◦ *a good person* ◦ *to lead a good life*
- if you say things that are true and you do not deceive people or steal, you are **honest**; the quality of being honest: **honesty** (*noun* U)

▷ more on being honest ⇨ **HONEST**

3 what is wrong

- if behaviour is bad, unfair to other people, or against the law, it is **wrong** ◦ *to do something wrong* ◦ *You were wrong to laugh at her.* ◦ *It's wrong to steal.*
- if behaviour is bad or wrong according to professional codes of conduct, it is **unethical** ◦ *unethical business practices*
- if behaviour breaks a religious law, it is **sinful**; *noun* (C/U): **sin** ◦ *a sinful life* ◦ *to commit/forgive a sin* ◦ *a life of sin*
- a person or a form of behaviour that is not good is **bad** (*adverb* **badly**), **immoral**; *noun* (U): **immorality** ◦ *a bad man* ◦ *to behave badly* ◦ *He's worse than you think!* ◦ *the worst behaviour you can imagine* ◦ *It's immoral to take another human life.*
- a person or a form of behaviour that is extremely bad can be called **evil**, **wicked**; extremely bad behaviour, or the cause of it: **wickedness** (*noun* U), (*formal*) **evil** (*noun* C/U) ◦ *wicked thoughts* ◦ *to get rid of the evils of poverty and disease* ◦ *There is good and evil in everybody.*
- to use or treat a thing or person badly or wrongly: **abuse** sb/sth; this kind of behaviour: **abuse** (*noun* C/U) ◦ *to be physically abused* ◦ *to abuse sb's friendship* ◦ *an abuse of power* ◦ *a case of sexual abuse* ◦ *drug abuse*
- offending against accepted moral standards of behaviour: **indecent**; this kind of behaviour: **indecency** (*noun* U) ◦ *indecent language* ◦ *to be accused of indecency*
- shockingly indecent: **obscene**; this kind of behaviour or language: **obscenity** (*noun* C/U) ◦ *obscene language* ◦ *an obscene phone call* ◦ *He shouted obscenities at me and drove off.* ◦ *laws against obscenity on television*
- a child who behaves badly is **naughty**; *noun* (U): **naughtiness** ◦ *It was very naughty of you to run away.* ◦ *That is the kind of naughtiness you expect from a five-year-old.*

▷ good and bad behaviour of children ⇨ **CHILD**

■ being unkind or cruel

- if you do not care about how other people feel and you do not do things to help them, you are **unkind**; *noun* (U): **unkindness**
- causing physical or mental pain to sb: **cruel**; *noun* (U): **cruelty** ◦ *a cruel punishment* ◦ *to treat sb with deliberate cruelty*

▷ more on being unkind or cruel ⇨ **KIND / CRUEL**

■ not being honest

- to make sb believe sth that is not true: **deceive** sb
- if you say things that are not true and you deceive people or steal, you are **dishonest**; *noun* (U): **dishonesty** ◦ *dishonest business practices*
- if sb deceives other people or is generally dishonest, they are **deceitful**

▷ more on deceiving people and being dishonest ⇨ **DECEIVE, HONEST**

■ against the law

- against the law: **illegal** (*adverb* **illegally**) ◦ *an illegal act* ◦ *It's illegal to work here without a work permit.* ◦ *She entered the country illegally.*
- behaviour that is against the law: **crime** (*noun* C/U); a person who does this: **criminal** ◦ *to commit a crime* ◦ *a life of crime* ◦ *the crime rate* ◦ *a dangerous criminal*

▷ more on crime and criminals ⇨ **CRIME**

■ being someone who has done sth bad or wrong

- if you are the person who has done sth bad or wrong, you are **responsible** (**for** sth) (*not before a noun*), **to blame** (**for** sth), **at fault**, it is your **fault** ◦ *Who was responsible for the accident?* ◦ *The driver in the second car was at fault for not stopping in time.* ◦ *It's not my fault that you failed your exams.*
- being or feeling responsible for doing sth wrong: **guilty**; *noun* (U): **guilt** ◦ *When I saw how upset she was, I felt terribly guilty.* ◦ *They did not prove her guilt.*
- to think or say that a particular person or thing is responsible for sth bad that has happened: **blame** sb (**for** sth), **blame** sth **on** sb ◦ *The teacher blamed the parents for the child's bad behaviour.* ◦ *The opposition parties blame unemployment on this government's policies.* ◦ *Don't blame me!*

▷ more on blame ⇨ **BLAME**

- if you wish you had not done sth, you are **sorry** (**about** sth), you **regret** sth
- feeling embarrassed and sorry because of sth/sb or because of sth that you have done: **ashamed** (**of** sth/sb/yourself)
- very bad, making people feel ashamed: **shameful** (*adverb* **shamefully**), **disgraceful** (*adverb* **disgracefully**) ◦ *shameful behaviour* ◦ *She was*

shamefully rude. ◦ *Your behaviour has been quite disgraceful.*

▷ more on feeling sorry and ashamed ⇨ SORRY

■ **MORE ...**

- a very kind and good person: **saint**
- an evil spirit: **devil**; the most powerful evil being according to the Christian religion: **the Devil**

ring

- on your finger ⇨ JEWELLERY
- a bell ⇨ BELL

river

1 big and small rivers
2 different parts of rivers
3 the movement of rivers
4 crossing a river
5 using the water in rivers
see also COUNTRY², LAND

1 big and small rivers

- a stream of water that flows down to the sea from higher ground: **river** ◦ *The river is very deep just here.*
- a small river: **stream** ◦ *a shallow stream*
- a man-made channel, like a river, that boats can travel along: **canal**

Note: names of rivers usually have **the River** or simply **the** before them ◦ *the River Thames* ◦ *the Thames.* Sometimes the name comes before the word 'river' ◦ *the Mississippi river*.

- when the two sides of a river are close together, the river is **narrow**; *opposite*: **wide, broad**
- to become more narrow: **narrow**; to become wider: **widen** ◦ *As it nears the coast the river widens.*
- when a river is so full that the water flows over the sides, it **overflows, floods**; when this happens, there is a **flood** ◦ *The fields were flooded when the river burst its banks.*
- when there is no water in a river, it is **dry**
- to become dry: **dry up** ◦ *The animals are dying because all the rivers in the area have dried up.*

2 different parts of rivers

- the side of a river: **bank, river bank** ◦ *We stopped for a picnic on the bank of the river.*
- a wall of earth, stones, etc that is built along the side of a river, especially in a town: **embankment**
- the land on the side of a river: **riverside** ◦ *a riverside restaurant*
- the bottom of a river: **bottom, (river) bed**
- a place where a river falls down a steep cliff or rock: **waterfall, falls** (*noun plural*) ◦ *the Niagara Falls*
- a part of a river where the water flows very fast over rocks: **rapids** (*noun plural*)

- the place where a river starts: **source** (of a river)
- the place where a river flows into the sea: **mouth** (of a river); if the mouth of a river is very wide, it may be called an **estuary** ◦ *the Thames estuary*
- if a river divides into several smaller rivers that flow into the sea, the mouth is called a **delta** ◦ *the Nile delta*

3 the movement of rivers

- when the water in a river moves, the river **runs***, **flows** ◦ *The stream runs through the bottom of the garden.* ◦ *It flows into the sea a few miles up the coast.* ◦ *a fast-flowing river*
- the movement of the water in a river: **current** ◦ *You can't swim here because of the dangerous currents.*
- a very small amount of water moving in a river: **trickle**
- a strong and fast movement of water: **torrent** ◦ *In the winter this river is a torrent, but in the summer it is reduced to just a trickle.*

- the direction that a river takes: **course** ◦ *We followed the course of the river until it reached the sea.*
- if you go along a river in the opposite direction from the sea, you go **up** the river, **up river, upstream** ◦ *I think the bridge is about another hundred yards upstream.*
- if you go towards the sea, you go **down** the river, **down river, downstream**
- when a river has a lot of bends and curves, it **winds***

- a space between hills or mountains where a river runs: **valley**
- a narrow, deep valley with steep, rocky sides: **gorge, ravine**
- a large area of fresh water which a river flows into: **lake** ◦ *Lake Windermere*

4 crossing a river

- to go from one side of a river to the other: **cross** (sth), go **across** (sth)
- to walk through deep water: **wade**; if you cross a river like this, you **wade across** it

- a structure that is built across a river so that people, cars, trains, etc can go across: **bridge**
- a man-made passage that goes under a river so that cars, trains, etc can go across: **tunnel**
- a boat that goes backwards and forwards across a river carrying people, cars, etc: **ferry**
- a place where a road crosses a river through shallow water: **ford**

▷ more on bridges ⇨ BRIDGE

5 using the water in rivers

- a wall that is built across a river to hold back the water and form a lake: **dam**; to make a dam: **dam** sth
- a lake that is made in this way: **reservoir**
- to supply farming land with water by means of pipes, channels, etc: **irrigate** (sth); *noun* (U): **irrigation** ◦ *an irrigation scheme*

road

1 describing roads
2 vehicles on roads
3 people on foot
4 repairing and cleaning roads
see also TRAVEL, TRANSPORT

1 describing roads

– a way between places, with a hard surface, which cars, buses, etc can drive along: **road** ◦ *Is this the road for Charlbury?* ◦ *The government should spend more money on the roads.* ◦ *road safety*

■ big and important roads
– a big road which takes a lot of traffic: **main road**
– a main road between towns: **road**, (*AmE* **highway**) ◦ *a road map of Great Britain*
– a wide road that is specially built for fast traffic: **motorway** (*AmE* **freeway, expressway**)
– a road like a motorway which has a fence or area of grass down the middle to separate the traffic going in different directions: **dual carriageway** (*AmE* **divided highway**)
– a road that traffic can use to go round a town instead of through it: **bypass**; when a road does this, it **bypasses** a town
– a road which is built all round a town: **ring road** (*AmE* **beltway**)
– a system of roads: **road network**

■ where roads meet
– a place where roads join or meet: **junction**; a junction which forms the shape of a T: **T-junction**
– a place where two or more roads cross each other: **crossroads**; a place where two or more main roads or motorways cross each other: **intersection** ◦ *Turn left at the next crossroads.*
– a circular area where several roads meet; you drive around it until you come to the exit you want: **roundabout** (*AmE* **traffic circle**)
– a place where one road joins or leads off from another: **turning, turn-off** ◦ *There's a turn-off on the right just after those trees.*
– when a side road leaves a main road, it **branches off**
– a place where two roads meet: **corner** ◦ *Turn right at the corner of Queen Street.*

■ the shape of roads
– a place where a road turns to the left or to the right: **bend, curve, corner**; to do this: **curve** ◦ *a sharp bend* ◦ *The road curves to the left/right.* ◦ *a blind corner* (= a bend where it is very difficult to see what is coming)
– a very sharp bend in a road: **hairpin bend** (*AmE* **hairpin curve, hairpin turn**)
– a road which does not bend in any direction is **straight**

■ the sides of a road
– the inner part or edge of a road which is furthest from the centre: **inside**; the part nearest the centre: **outside** ◦ *A car drove past me on the inside.*
– the edge of a road: **roadside** ◦ *I saw three hitch-hikers waiting by the roadside.*
– a special place where vehicles can stop on the roadside: **lay-by** (*AmE* **rest stop**)

■ motorways
– one of the two sides of a motorway or dual carriageway on which vehicles travel in one direction: **carriageway**; part of a carriageway for one line of traffic: **lane** ◦ *the northbound carriageway* ◦ *a six-lane motorway*
– a lane for slow traffic: **slow lane, inside lane**; for fast traffic: **fast lane, outside lane**
– a narrow strip of road at the side of a motorway where cars are allowed to stop in an emergency: (*BrE*) **hard shoulder**
– a fence on a motorway, etc that keeps vehicles apart: **crash barrier**
– an area of land between two carriageways on a motorway, etc: (**central**) **reservation** (*AmE* **median**)

– a road that leads onto or off a motorway: **slip road**, (*especially AmE*) **access road**
– a place where you can drive onto or off a motorway: **junction** ◦ *We have to turn off at junction 16.*
– a type of bridge that carries one road over another: **flyover** (*AmE* **overpass**)

■ small roads
– a way across a piece of land that is made or used by people walking: **path, footpath**
– a path or rough road: **track**
– a narrow road in the country: **lane, alley**
– a road which leads from a main road and is less important or busy: **side road, minor road**

■ roads in towns
– a road in a town, etc that has shops, houses, etc on one or both sides: **street**
– the main street of a town, especially as a name: **high street** (*AmE* **main street**)
– a narrow or less important street that usually joins a main road: **side street**
– a wide street, especially one with trees or tall buildings on each side: **avenue**
– a narrow street between buildings: **lane**
– a street that is closed at one end: **cul-de-sac**; if a street does not continue any further, you reach a **dead end**
– a street along which cars can only travel in one direction: **one-way street**
– a private road or path that leads to a house: **drive, driveway**

– a path at the side of a road that is for people to walk on: **pavement** (*AmE* **sidewalk**)
– a line of stones that form the edge of a pavement where it joins the road: **kerb**, (*especially AmE*) **curb**
– a channel between the road and the pavement that carries away rainwater: **gutter**
– a raised area in the middle of the road that you can stand on when you are crossing: (**traffic**) **island** (*AmE* **safety zone**)

■ bridges, etc
- a structure that carries a road across a river, valley, road, railway, etc: **bridge**
- a bridge where people who are on foot can cross a road: **footbridge**
- a passage under the ground, under the sea, etc: **tunnel** ∘ *The road went through a tunnel under the mountains.*
- a road that goes under another road, railway, etc: **underpass**
- a place where a railway line crosses a road: **level crossing** (*AmE* **grade crossing**)
- a shallow place in a river where cars can drive through: **ford**; to use a ford: **ford** sth

▷ more on bridges ⇨ BRIDGE

■ the surface of a road
- the thick, black, sticky material from petroleum that is used on the surface of roads: **tar** (*noun* U), **tarmac** (*noun* U)
- special rounded stones that cover the surface of (old) streets: **cobbles, cobblestones**; a street that is covered with cobblestones is **cobbled**
- a piece of stone used for a path or pavement: **paving stone**

- a road that is difficult to drive on because it is wet, icy, etc is **slippery**
- ice on the road that is very slippery and black in colour: **black ice** (*noun* U)
- a road that has a lot of raised parts in it is **bumpy**; a raised part in a road: **bump** ∘ *a bumpy track* ∘ *We hit a bump.*
- a hole in the surface of a road: **pothole**
- a road that is flat, with no bumps, is **smooth**
- if a road is blocked and you cannot travel on it, it is **impassable** ∘ *The heavy snow has made the roads impassable.*

■ lights and road signs
- a sign that tells drivers where to go, what to do, what not to do, etc: **road sign, traffic sign**
- a sign with two or three coloured lights used for controlling traffic at road junctions: **traffic lights** (*noun plural*) (*AmE* **stoplight**)
- a sign at the roadside that gives information about directions and distances to towns, etc: **signpost** ∘ *Did you see the signpost for Bristol?*

- the lights on a street: **street lights**
- a tall pole with a light on top, often placed on a pavement: **lamp-post**

- a special spot in the road that shines in a car's headlights at night: (*BrE*) **catseye**
- painted marks on the road surface that show drivers where to go, etc: **road markings**

2 vehicles on roads
- to go somewhere in a car: **drive***
- a person who is driving a car or other vehicle: **driver**; a person who drives a car: **motorist**
- the money that you have to pay to drive on some roads or bridges: **toll**

▷ more on driving ⇨ DRIVE

- all the cars, lorries, buses, bicycles, etc using the roads: **traffic** (*noun* U) ∘ *heavy traffic* ∘ *I'm not driving to town today; I can't face all that traffic.* ∘ *traffic police* (= policemen and women who control the traffic)
- a road where there is a lot of traffic is **busy**; *opposite*: **quiet**
- a road with so many vehicles that cars are stopped or are moving slowly is **congested**; *noun* (U): **congestion** ∘ *the problem of traffic congestion*
- if there is no congestion, the road is **clear** ∘ *It was Sunday and the roads were fairly clear.*

- to stop and leave a car, lorry, etc somewhere for some time: **park** (sth); the action of doing this: **parking** (*noun* U)
- a person whose job is to check that cars are not parked in the wrong place: **traffic warden**

- a barrier put across the road by the police or the army to stop traffic: **roadblock**
- to stop traffic from coming down a road: **block** sth **off, close** sth

3 people on foot
- to go somewhere without using a vehicle: **go* on foot**
- a person who is walking in the street: **pedestrian**
- to go from one side of a road to another on foot: **cross the road** ∘ *Please be careful crossing the road!*
- a place where pedestrians can cross the road: (**pedestrian**) **crossing, zebra crossing, pelican crossing** (*AmE* **crosswalk**)
- a man/woman whose job is to help schoolchildren to cross roads: **lollipop man/woman**

4 repairing and cleaning roads
- the work of building or repairing roads; the place where a road is being repaired: **roadworks** (*noun plural*) ∘ *Sorry I'm late. I was held up by the roadworks on the M25.*
- a plastic, (usually orange and white) pointed object that marks off an area where there are roadworks: **cone**
- a vehicle that clears snow off roads: **snowplough** (*AmE* **snowplow**)
- small pieces of stone that are put on the road in icy weather: **grit**; to put grit on the road: **grit** the road

- a person whose job is to clean roads: **road cleaner, road sweeper**

rob ⇨ STEAL

rocket ⇨ SPACE²

roof

other parts of houses or other buildings ⇨ HOUSE, BUILDING

- the part of a building, vehicle, etc, that covers the top of it: **roof** ∘ *a flat roof* ∘ *to climb onto the roof*

roof *contd.*

- a round roof on a building: **dome** ◦ *the dome of St Paul's Cathedral*
- the space inside the roof of a house: **attic**, **loft** ◦ *We have converted our loft into a bedroom for the children.*
- the long metal or plastic pipe that is fixed under the edge of a roof to carry away rainwater: **gutter** ◦ *a blocked gutter*
- smoke from a fireplace in a house goes up above the roof through a **chimney**; the narrow pipe at the top of a chimney: **chimney pot**

▷ picture at HOUSE

■ what roofs are made of

- a piece of baked clay that fits together with others in rows to cover a roof: **tile**; *adjective*: **tiled** ◦ *a tiled roof*
- a type of dark grey rock that can easily be split into thin, flat pieces and used to cover a roof: **slate** (*noun* U); one of these pieces: **slate** ◦ *a slate roof* ◦ *Several of the slates came off in the storm.*
- a roof that is covered with dried straw is **thatched**; the straw that is used for this: **thatch** (*noun* U) ◦ *a thatched cottage*
- a hard, grey metal which is used in sheets that are shaped into folds: **corrugated iron** (*noun* U) ◦ *a hut with a corrugated iron roof*

room

see also BATHROOM, BED, KITCHEN, TOILET, RENT

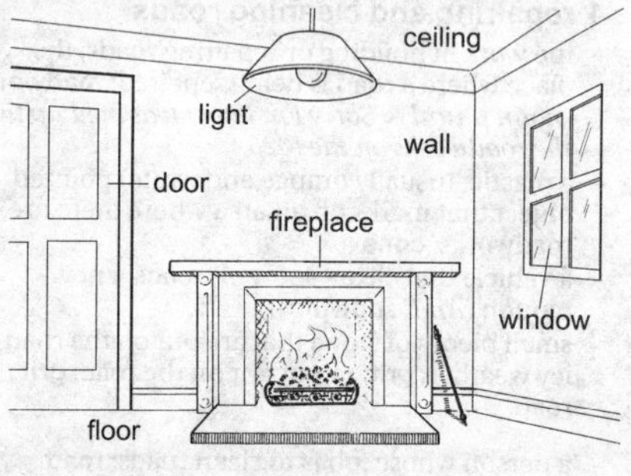

▷ more on doors, floors and windows ⇨ DOOR, FLOOR, WINDOW

- a part of a building that is separated from the rest by its own walls, floor and ceiling: **room** ◦ *a house with four rooms downstairs and three bedrooms* ◦ *Tidy your room – it's a pigsty* (= very untidy)*!*
- a kind of wall or structure that divides a room into parts: **partition** ◦ *A thin partition separated one end of the room from the other.*
- a room that is joined to another is **adjoining** ◦ *We could hear laughter from the adjoining room.*
- a room for one person: **single** (room); for two people: **double** (room) ◦ *Our new house has two double bedrooms and one single.*

■ walls and ceilings

- the mixture that dries to make a smooth, hard surface on the inside walls and ceilings of buildings: **plaster** (*noun* U) ◦ *I'm going to fill these cracks in the plaster.*
- the liquid colour that decorates or protects a wall, ceiling, etc: **paint** (*noun* U); to cover a wall, etc with paint: **paint** sth ◦ *The walls were painted pink.*
- paper that you use to decorate the walls or ceiling of a room: **wallpaper** (*noun* U); to stick wallpaper on a wall: (**wall**)**paper** sth ◦ *Can you help me hang this piece of wallpaper?* ◦ *We spent all weekend wallpapering the hall.*
- a flat piece of baked clay that can be arranged with others to cover a floor, wall or ceiling, etc: **tile**; to stick these to a wall, etc: **tile** sth ◦ *bathroom tiles* ◦ *a tiled kitchen*

▷ more on painting a room ⇨ PAINT[2]

■ different rooms in a house

a room where:	is called a:
you sit and relax	sitting room, living room, lounge
food is cooked	kitchen
you eat meals	dining room
you sleep	bedroom
you wash	bathroom
there is a toilet	toilet, bathroom
you read, write or study at home	study

- a room that is kept for visitors: **spare room**
- a room (usually rented) in which a person lives and sleeps: (*informal*) **bedsitter**, (*informal*) **bedsit**

▷ other parts of a house ⇨ HOUSE

■ rooms in other kinds of building

- a room where many people sleep (for example in a school): **dormitory**
- a room where people sleep in hospital: **ward**
- a room in a school where children have lessons: **classroom**
- a room where business and written work is done: **office**
- a room where you sit and wait for an appointment or a train, etc: **waiting room**
- a room in a hotel or at an airport where you can sit: **lounge**
- a room for a prisoner in a prison: **cell**

■ what you have in a room

- the tables, chairs, etc in a room: **furniture** (*noun* U) ◦ *a lot of expensive furniture*
- to put furniture in a room: **furnish** sth ◦ *Do you like the way it's furnished?*
- the furniture and decoration in a room: **decor** ◦ *Those curtains don't go with the rest of the decor.*
- the way in which colours are arranged in a room: **colour scheme** ◦ *a red and white colour*

scheme ◦ We've decided to change the colour scheme.

▷ more on furniture ⇨ FURNITURE

– to fix a picture, notice, etc on a wall: **hang*** sth, **put*** sth **up** ◦ *The painting was hung over the fireplace.* ◦ *Why haven't you put up any of your wedding photographs?*

■ **MORE ...**

– if a room or building has enough space for a particular number of people, it can **accommodate** them ◦ *The hotel can accommodate about 100 people.*

root ⇨ PLANT

rope ⇨ STRING/ROPE

rough ⇨ SURFACE

round ⇨ CIRCLE, SHAPE

route ⇨ TRAVEL

royal ⇨ KING/QUEEN

rubbish

1 rubbish in your house
2 rubbish in public places
see also ENVIRONMENT

1 rubbish in your house

– things that you do not want any more are **rubbish** (*AmE* **garbage, trash**) (*noun* U), (*formal*) **refuse** (*noun* U) ◦ *When do they collect the rubbish?* ◦ *domestic refuse*
– old, useless things that do not have much value: **junk** (*noun* U) ◦ *We got rid of a lot of junk when we moved house.*

– to get rid of a thing that you do not want: **throw*** sth **away/out**, (*more informal*) **chuck** sth **away/out**, (*formal*) **dispose of** sth; *noun* (U): **disposal** (**of** sth) ◦ *Don't throw that away, I haven't finished with it.* ◦ *Shall I chuck out these old shoes?* ◦ *Please dispose of these batteries safely.*

– a container that you put rubbish in (usually kept in the kitchen): **bin**
– a large container for rubbish (usually kept outside the house): **dustbin** (*AmE* **garbage can, trashcan**)
– a bag that you put inside a dustbin: **dustbin liner, dustbin bag**
– a basket or other container in which you put paper, etc that is to be thrown away: **waste-paper basket, waste-paper bin** (*AmE* **wastebasket, wastebin**)

– a person whose job is to empty dustbins and remove rubbish: **dustman** (*plural* **dustmen**)
– a kind of lorry that is used for collecting rubbish from dustbins: **dustcart** (*AmE* **garbage truck**)
– a place where rubbish is left: (**rubbish**) **tip, rubbish dump, refuse tip** ◦ *We took the old fridge to the tip.*

2 rubbish in public places

– pieces of paper, packets, etc that are dropped in a public place: **litter** (*noun* U)
– if you drop litter, you **litter** a place ◦ *The playground was littered with crisp packets.*
– a person who drops litter in a public place: **litter lout** (*AmE* **litterbug**) ◦ *Don't be a litter lout!*
– a container to put litter in: **litter bin**

■ **MORE ...**

– a material, food, etc that is not needed and is therefore thrown away: **waste** (*noun* U) ◦ *household waste* ◦ *the disposal of radioactive waste* ◦ *waste paper*
– something that you do not want any more but that is made of material that can be used again: **scrap** (*noun* U) ◦ *scrap metal* ◦ *Have you got a piece of scrap paper I can write on?*

– goods that are made to be used once and then thrown away are **disposable** ◦ *a disposable razor* ◦ *disposable nappies*

rude

– not polite ⇨ POLITE
– very rude on purpose ⇨ INSULT

rule

see also LAW

– an official statement that tells you what you can or cannot do, say, etc, in an institution, sport, etc: **rule** ◦ *You can't do that – it's against the rules!* ◦ *the rules of tennis*
– a law or rule that controls how sth is done: **regulation** ◦ *parking regulations* ◦ *a set of rules and regulations*
– a set of rules for behaviour: **code** ◦ *the Highway Code* (= the set of rules for driving a car safely)
– rules of polite and correct behaviour: **etiquette** (*noun* U) ◦ *social etiquette*

– to make rules to control sth: **regulate** sth ◦ *to introduce new measures to regulate the volume of traffic in the city centre*
– an organization that officially regulates sth: **the gas industry regulator**
– to make sure that a rule, law, etc is obeyed: **enforce** sth; when a rule or law is being used, it is **in force**

– a rule that forbids sth: **ban** (**on** sth), **prohibition** (**of** sth) ◦ *to introduce a ban on smoking*
– to make a rule or law which says that sth is not allowed: **ban** sth, **prohibit** sth

– to do what you should according to some rule: **obey** sth, **keep*** **to** sth, **stick*** **to** sth ◦ *The referee warned the players to keep to the rules.* ◦ *Stick to the rules and you won't go wrong.*
– do sth that is against a rule, law, etc: **break*/disobey** a rule, regulation, etc ◦ *If you break the rules you must expect to be punished.*

▷ obeying ⇨ OBEY

– if sth which is made or done follows the rules, it **conforms** (**to** sth) ◦ *This building does not conform to safety regulations.*

rule *contd.*

- something that does not follow a rule: **exception** ◦ *Students are not normally allowed in without an identity card, but I'll make an exception in your case.*

run

see also ATHLETICS, RACE², WALK, MOVE

- to move using your legs, going faster than when you walk: **run*** ◦ *I had to run to catch the bus.* ◦ *She ran across the road.*
- the speed at which you walk, run, etc: **pace** ◦ *Frank was running at such a pace that I couldn't keep up with him.*
- to start running suddenly: **break* into a run** ◦ *The man broke into a run when he saw the police.*

- an occasion of running: **run** ◦ *I go for a five-mile run every morning.*
- a person who runs regularly for pleasure or sport: **runner** ◦ *a long-distance runner*

- a form of exercise in which you run slowly: **jogging** (*noun* U); to do this exercise: **jog, go* jogging**; an occasion of going jogging: **jog**; a person who does this: **jogger** ◦ *to take up jogging* ◦ *to go for a jog*

■ running fast

- to run a short distance very fast: **sprint** ◦ *He sprinted to the station.*
- to run somewhere very fast: **race**, **charge** ◦ *The moment she got off the bus, I raced up the road to give her the news.*
- to run somewhere suddenly and quickly: **dart**, **dash**, **make* a dash** ◦ *A rabbit darted across the field.* ◦ *She dashed outside when she heard the car.* ◦ *She made a dash for the door, but I managed to catch her in time.*
- to increase your speed when running: **speed up**, **put* on a spurt** ◦ *She put on a spurt as she neared the finishing line.*

- to run away because your life is in danger or to escape from sb/sth: **run* for** your **life**, **run* for it** ◦ *When he saw the tiger, Keith ran for his life.* ◦ *The police are coming – run for it!*
- to run after sb/sth in order to catch them: **chase** sb/sth; *noun*: **chase** ◦ *The dog chased the cat up the tree.*

▷ escaping ⇨ ESCAPE

- (used about children and small animals) to run quickly: **scamper** ◦ *The kitten scampered across the room and hid under the sofa.*
- (used about a group of animals or people) to rush in a particular direction in a wild and uncontrolled way: **stampede**; *noun*: **stampede**

▷ ways in which horses run ⇨ HORSE

- breathing quickly after exercise: **out of breath**
- a pain that you sometimes get in your side when you have been running: **stitch** ◦ *I can't go on – I've got a stitch.*

sad

sad because of what you have done ⇨ SORRY
the feeling of sadness that you have when sb dies ⇨ DIE
other emotions ⇨ EMOTION
see also HAPPY

- not happy, or causing you not to be happy: **sad** (*adverb* **sadly**), **unhappy** (*adverb* **unhappily**); *nouns* (U): **sadness, unhappiness** ◦ *to look/feel sad about sth* ◦ *It makes me very unhappy that so few of my friends are willing to help.* ◦ *an unhappy state of affairs*
- to make sb sad: **sadden** sb ◦ *Everyone was saddened by the news of her death.*

- very unhappy, or causing you to feel very unhappy: **miserable** ◦ *a miserable night out*
- unhappy or bored: (*informal*) **fed up** ◦ *I'm fed up with your endless complaints.*
- to make sb unhappy: (*informal*) **get*** sb **down** ◦ *All this talk about illness and death is getting me down.*
- very unhappy, often for a long period: **depressed**, (*informal*) **low**; *noun* (U): **depression** ◦ *This kind of life is enough to make anyone depressed!* ◦ *She's depressed about her exam results.* ◦ *I woke up feeling low.* ◦ *to suffer from depression*
- to make sb feel depressed: **depress** sb; something that depresses you is **depressing** ◦ *That film really depressed me.* ◦ *depressing news*

- worried and unhappy: **upset**; to make sb feel worried and unhappy: **upset** sb; something that upsets you is **upsetting** ◦ *She's feeling a bit upset – I think you should leave her alone for a while.* ◦ *Her sister's death has really upset her.* ◦ *a deeply upsetting experience*
- unhappy and not satisfied: **dissatisfied, discontented**; *nouns* (U): **dissatisfaction, discontent**
- if you are feeling unhappy and angry, you are **in a bad mood**

- sad because sth that you hoped for has not happened: **disappointed**; *noun* (U): **disappointment** ◦ *I hope you won't be too disappointed that you haven't got the job.*
- to make sb feel disappointed: **disappoint** sb; something that disappoints you is **disappointing**, a **disappointment** ◦ *Not getting into university has been a bitter disappointment to her.*

- sad, or causing you to feel sad, because you are not with other people: **lonely**; *noun* (U): **loneliness** ◦ *a lonely existence in a London bedsit* ◦ *Are you often lonely?*
- sad because you are away from home: **homesick**; *noun* (U): **homesickness**
- to feel unhappy because you have not got sth or cannot do sth that you once had or did: **miss** sth ◦ *We miss the house we used to live in.* ◦ *Now I work at home, I miss cycling to the office every day.*
- to feel sad or unhappy because a person is not with you any more: **miss** sb ◦ *Will you miss me?*

■ unhappy about your own troubles
- to feel very unhappy about your own troubles: **feel* sorry for** yourself; this feeling: **self-pity** (*noun* U)
- a situation or feeling of total unhappiness, so that you have no hope that things will get better: **despair** (*noun* U); if you have this feeling, you are **in despair**
- so sad that you might even kill yourself: **suicidal** ◦ *When my business collapsed and I had to sell my house, I was overcome with despair and for a time I was almost suicidal.*

■ showing you are sad
- to produce water from your eyes, and make a noise, because you are unhappy or have hurt yourself: **cry** ◦ *Don't cry. I'm sure things will get better soon.*

▷ more on crying ⇨ CRY

■ sad situations
- if sth happens which you think is bad or unfortunate, you can say that you are **sorry to hear** it, **sorry (that) ...** ◦ *I'm sorry to hear that you'll be leaving soon.* ◦ *I'm sorry you've been so ill.*
- something that you should feel sad or sorry about is (*formal*) **regrettable** (*adverb* **regrettably**) ◦ *a regrettable incident/fact*
- to show that you feel sorry about sth or that sth is a pity, you can say that it is **unfortunate** (*adverb* **unfortunately**) ◦ *It's unfortunate that you missed the meeting.* ◦ *Unfortunately, I can't help you because I haven't got any money either.*
- to want sth that cannot now happen or that probably will not happen: **wish (that) ...** ◦ *I wish you hadn't reminded me of that.* ◦ *I wish I didn't have these exams to revise for!*

▷ more on wishing ⇨ WANT

- an event or situation that causes great sadness: **tragedy** (*noun* C/U); *adjective*: **tragic** (*adverb* **tragically**) ◦ *It's an absolute tragedy that the school has had to be closed.* ◦ *to end in tragedy* ◦ *a tragic accident*

- if you feel sad for another person because of what has happened to them, you are **sorry (for** them)
- to try to stop sb feeling sad: **comfort** sb, **console** sb
- understanding of other people's feelings and problems: **sympathy (for/towards** sb) (*noun* U); *adjective*: **sympathetic** ◦ *She's had a hard time recently and I feel a lot of sympathy for her.* ◦ *a sympathetic look*

▷ more on being sympathetic ⇨ SYMPATHY

safe

- not dangerous ⇨ DANGEROUS
- making sth safe ⇨ PROTECT

sail ⇨ BOAT

salary ⇨ PAY[2]

salt/pepper

see also FOOD, COOK

- the white substance used to flavour food: **salt** (*noun* U): tasting of salt: **salty** ◦ *Can you pass the salt, please?* ◦ *salt water* (= water from the sea or water with salt in it) ◦ *The soup was too salty.*
- the smallest piece of salt: **grain of salt**
- (when you are cooking) a very small amount of salt: **pinch of salt** ◦ *Add a pinch of salt.*
- the container that you put on the table for salt: **salt cellar**

- the hot-tasting black or brown spice often used with salt to flavour food: **pepper** (*noun* U); tasting of pepper: **peppery** ◦ *freshly ground black pepper*
- a pepper seed: **peppercorn**
- a container in which you grind pepper (= make it into a fine powder): **pepper mill**

- (when you are cooking) to add salt, pepper, spices, etc to food: **season** sth; *noun* (U): **seasoning** ◦ *The recipe says 'season well' so you could put in a bit more pepper.* ◦ *I think the soup needs some more seasoning.*

same

1 A = B
2 A is exactly like B
3 A is quite like B
see also DIFFERENT

1 A = B

- exactly the one that was mentioned before; not a different one: **the same ...**, **the identical ...** ◦ *You remember I told you a strange man phoned me up yesterday? Well, the same man phoned me again today.* ◦ *We go to the same hairdresser.* ◦ *This is the identical room we stayed in last year.*

2 A is exactly like B

- exactly like the one already mentioned: **the same (as** sb/sth), **the same that ...**, **identical (to/with** sb/sth) ◦ *Yesterday I was stopped by a policeman and asked to produce my licence, and the same thing happened again today.* ◦ *That car's the same as ours* (= the same model). ◦ *This computer is identical to the one I had before.*
- to be the same as: **correspond (with** sth) ◦ *The two sets of figures did not correspond.*

- when you do the same thing as sb else, you do **likewise** ◦ *I'm leaving before the company goes bankrupt and I advise you to do likwise.*

- to the same degree: **equally, just as, as ... as** sb/sth ◦ *I've got two equally important jobs to do, but only time to do one of them.* ◦ *Her first book was awful, but this one's just as bad.* ◦ *I can swim as fast as you.*

same *contd.*

■ equal in size, number, importance, etc

- the same in size, number or amount: **equal**; *opposite*: **unequal** ○ *a cake divided into six equal pieces* ○ *I think those in favour and those against are about equal.*
- having the same size or weight as sb/sth else: **the same** size/weight (**as** sb/sth), **of equal** size/weight, **equal in** size/weight ○ *She's the same height as her brother.* ○ *They are the same height.* ○ *The two children were of equal height.* ○ *They were equal in height.*
- to be equal in number or amount to sth: **equal** sth ○ *Two plus two equals four.*
- in equal parts: **equally**, **evenly**; *opposites*: **unequally, unevenly** ○ *You'll have to share it equally among the three of you.* ○ *The results are quite evenly distributed.*

■ being as good as something or somebody

- a person or thing equal to oneself in some way: **equal** ○ *She's my equal in size and strength.*
- of the same quality or ability as sb: **just as good as** sb, (*informal*) **every bit as good as** sb ○ *You shouldn't worry – you're every bit as good as the others, if not better.*
- to be as good as sb/sth: **equal** sb/sth (**in** sth) ○ *I can't equal her in intelligence.*
- (used about people in competitions) equal in ability: **even** (*adverb* **evenly**) ○ *The two sides are pretty even – I wonder who'll win.* ○ *to be evenly matched*

▷ equal in society ⇨ SOCIETY

3 A is quite like B

- the same in some ways to sb/sth else, but not completely the same: **similar** (**to** sb/sth), **like** sb/sth ○ *Your skirt's quite similar to mine.*
- two or more people or things that are the same in some way or ways, but not completely the same are **similar**, **alike** (*not before a noun*) ○ *We found that we had similar problems.* ○ *These novels are quite similar in style.* ○ *Those twins are so alike I sometimes don't know which one I'm talking to!*
- the quality of being similar: **similarity** (*noun* U/C), **likeness** (*noun* C/U) ○ *You could see a slight similarity between the two paintings.* ○ *There was almost no similarity between the brothers.* ○ *a strong family likeness*
- very similar: **much the same** ○ *They look much the same. Why not get the cheaper one?*
- of a similar type: **the same sort of ...** ○ *They live in the same sort of house that we do.*

- to be like sb/sth else in appearance: **look like** sb/sth, (*more formal*) **resemble** sb/sth; *noun* (U/C): **resemblance** (**between** A and B) ○ *He looks like your brother.* ○ *They resemble each other a lot.* ○ *I couldn't see much resemblance between them.* ○ *a strong/striking/noticeable resemblance*
- if two or more people are alike in some way, they **share** sth, **have** sth **in common** ○ *We all share the same sense of humour.* ○ *I have nothing in common with her.*
- sb that looks exactly the same as sb else: **the image of** sb/sth ○ *He's the image of his mother.*

- (used about people or things of a different kind or from a different place) similar or equal in value, amount, meaning or importance: **equivalent** (**to** sth); a person or thing that is equivalent to sb/sth else: **equivalent** ○ *an area equivalent to five football pitches* ○ *'Do' and 'make' are not equivalent in meaning.* ○ *The price of British cars is higher than that of equivalent French or German models.*
- to be similar or equal to sth: **correspond** (**to** sth) ○ *'House' corresponds to the word 'casa' in Spanish.* ○ *250 grams or the equivalent in ounces*
- related or similar: **corresponding** ○ *Sales are up by ten per cent on the corresponding period last year*

- to see or show how sb/sth is similar to or different from sb/sth else: **compare** A and B, **compare** A **with/to** B; *noun* (C/U): **comparison** ○ *We have compared the two designs and we prefer this one.* ○ *an interesting comparison*
- similar enough to be compared: **comparable** ○ *How can you say who is worth more? Their jobs are simply not comparable.*

▷ more on comparing people or things ⇨ COMPARE/CONTRAST

■ **MORE ...**

- to make different things the same or similar in quality or form: **standardize** sth; *noun* (U): **standardization** ○ *to standardize measurements/sizes*

satisfy

- making you happy ⇨ HAPPY
- good enough ⇨ GOOD

save

- saving money ⇨ MONEY
- helping sb in a dangerous situation ⇨ DANGEROUS

say

1 saying what you know, think, feel, want, etc
2 choosing the words that you use to say sth
see also INFORM, SPEAK, WRITE, CONVERSATION

1 saying what you know, think, feel, want, etc

- to give information or show in words what you think, feel, want, etc: **say*** sth (**to** sb), **tell*** sb (sth) ○ *He says he doesn't believe you.* ○ *What does it say in the letter?* ○ *'I'll call back later,' she said.* ○ *Did he tell you his new address?* ○ *He wrote to tell us that his father had died.*
- to say or write sth, often formally: **state** sth; *noun*: **statement** ○ *Please state what the problem is in writing.* ○ *a political statement* ○ *You'll have to come to the police station to make a statement.*
- to say sth that there is no doubt what you mean: **make*** sth/yourself **clear/plain** ○ *Have I made myself clear?* ○ *He made it clear that he wouldn't be coming back.*

- to say that sth is (definitely) true: **confirm** sth; *noun* (U): **confirmation** ◦ *Please write to confirm that you will be arriving on 2 May.* ◦ *We're still waiting for confirmation of the news.*
- to say that sth is not true: **deny** sth/doing sth; *noun*: **denial** ◦ *He denied being involved in the fight.* ◦ *The Government issued an official denial.*
- to say what is true: **tell*** (sb) **the truth**
- to say sth which you know is not true: **lie** (**to** sb) (**about** sth), **tell*** (sb) **a lie**
- to say sth which you do not want to be told to any other person: **tell*** (sb) **a secret**

▷ more on telling the truth, a lie, a secret ⇨ **TRUE, LIE[1], SECRET**

- to say what you think or feel: **express** sth; *noun* (C/U): **expression** ◦ *Don't be afraid to express your opinion.* ◦ *I'd like to express my gratitude for all your help.* ◦ *freedom of expression* (= freedom to say what you think)
- to say sth suddenly because of pain, anger, surprise, etc: **exclaim** sth; *noun*: **exclamation** ◦ *'Ouch!' he exclaimed suddenly.* ◦ *an exclamation of surprise*

■ saying sth quickly or briefly

- to say sth about sb/sth, usually briefly: **mention** sb/sth, **refer to** sb/sth; *nouns* (C/U): **mention**, **reference** ◦ *Did he mention what time he would arrive?* ◦ *The next speaker referred to the problem of air pollution, but only briefly.* ◦ *There was no mention of the riots in the paper.* ◦ *The article included reference to several MPs.*

- to say sth, usually briefly, that shows what you think or feel about sth: **remark** (**on/upon** sth), **comment** (**on** sth); an act of saying sth in this way: **remark**, **comment** (*noun* C/U) ◦ *Would you like to comment on what has happened?* ◦ *He made some very unkind remarks about what I was wearing.* ◦ *'Do you like this hat?' 'No comment!'*
- to draw a person's attention to sth: **point** sth **out** ◦ *I think I should point out that if we don't leave soon we'll miss the train.*

- concerning a particular point or topic: (*formal*) **with regard/reference to ...**, (*formal*) **regarding ...** ◦ *And now, regarding your query...*

■ saying sth publicly

- to make sth known publicly, in an official way: **announce** sth ◦ *Mr Stubbs has just announced his resignation.*
- a statement that tells people about sth: **announcement** ◦ *I'd like to make an important announcement.*
- a person who announces things for a government, organization, etc: **spokesman**, **spokeswoman**, **spokesperson**

- if you disagree with what most people think, and say publicly that you think something is bad or wrong, you **speak* out** (**against** sth) ◦ *She spoke out against cruelty to animals.*

■ saying sth strongly or directly

- to say sth clearly and firmly: **declare** sth, **assert** sth; *nouns* (C/U): **declaration**, **assertion** ◦ *the scene where Romeo declares his love for Juliet* ◦ *'I'm going,' she declared.'* ◦ *to assert your innocence* ◦ *He was found guilty despite his repeated assertions that he was innocent.*

- to say sth strongly because you think it is important: **stress** sth, **emphasize** sth; *nouns* (U): **stress**, **emphasis** ◦ *I'd like to stress how important it is to be ready on time.* ◦ *She emphasized the importance of being punctual.*
- to say that sth is bigger, better, worse, etc than it really is: **exaggerate** (sth); *noun* (C/U): **exaggeration** ◦ *She's always exaggerating.* ◦ *His story was full of exaggerations.*

■ saying sth weakly or indirectly

- to say sth in a gentle or indirect way: **hint** (**at**) sth, **suggest** sth, **imply** sth; something that is said in this way: **hint**, **suggestion** (*noun* U), **implication** (*noun* C/U) ◦ *What do you think he was trying to hint at?* ◦ *He implied that he thought I was lying.* ◦ *I thought he would understand what I meant, but he didn't take the hint.* ◦ *There was no suggestion that anyone had acted improperly.* ◦ *I didn't like the implications of what she was saying.* ◦ *He blames me and, by implication, my whole family for his unhappiness.*

■ adding to what you have said

- to say sth more: **add** sth ◦ *'Give my love to Paul,' she added.*
- to say sth again, or to say sth that another person has said: **repeat** sth ◦ *Sorry, I missed that – could you repeat what you just said?* ◦ *Repeat these sentences after me.*

▷ words that show that you are adding sth to what you have said ⇨ **AND/OR/BUT**

2 choosing the words that you use to say sth

- to say sth in a particular way: **express** sth, **word** sth; *noun* (*singular*): **wording** ◦ *You haven't expressed this very clearly.* ◦ *The letter was very carefully worded.* ◦ *The wording of the contract was rather vague.*
- to say sth in a different way, for example to make it easier to understand or to make it sound more polite, etc: **rephrase** sth, **reword** sth, **paraphrase** sth; *noun*: **paraphrase** ◦ *Could you rephrase the question, please?* ◦ *to give a paraphrase of sth*

- as another way of saying the same thing: **in other words** ◦ *'I've looked everywhere and I can't find it.' 'In other words, you've lost it.'*
- as another way of describing or identifying the same thing: **that is, that is to say** ◦ *We live in a democracy – that is, a country with a freely elected government.*
- as a short form of what you have said: **to sum up, to summarize, in short** ◦ *Things couldn't be worse, financially: in short, we're broke.*

say *contd.*

- if you want to give more exact information, you can say **at any rate**, **anyway** ◦ *They said they would come early, or at any rate before eight o' clock.*
- if you want to correct what you have just said, you can say **at least** ◦ *That's the best film I've ever seen, or at least, the best this year.*
- when you think that sb may misunderstood what you have just said, you can say **not that ...** ◦ *This music is very loud. Not that I dislike it. I would just prefer something quieter.*

■ quotation

- to repeat the exact words of sb/sth: **quote** sb/sth; *noun* (U): **quotation** ◦ *He's always quoting Shakespeare.*
- the words that you quote: **quotation**, (*informal*) **quote** ◦ *Make sure you include a few relevant quotations from the text.* ◦ *a quote from the Bible*
- to quote sb/sth wrongly: **misquote** sb/sth ◦ *The bishop complained that he was frequently misquoted in the press.*

- a short well-known sentence which people often quote (for example: 'Don't put all your eggs in one basket.'): **saying, proverb**

scared ⇨ AFRAID

school

1 different kinds of school
2 people in a school
3 places in a school
4 going to school
5 being in school
see also EDUCATION

1 different kinds of schools

- a place where children go to be educated: **school** ◦ *They're building a new school in our village.* ◦ *Which school did you go to?* ◦ *The school was founded* (= started) *in 1962.*
- a place where particular subjects or skills are taught: **school** ◦ *a language school* ◦ *a driving school*

- a school that is owned by the government and in which the education is free: **state school** (*AmE* **public school**)
- a school that is owned privately and in which the education is not free: **private school**, (*BrE also*) **independent school**
- a school (usually private) where pupils live as well as study: **boarding school**
- a school with both boys and girls together in the same class is **co-educational, mixed**

- a school for very young children: **nursery school**
- the first school that children go to (after nursery school): **primary school** (*AmE* **elementary school**)
- the school that children go to after primary school: **secondary school** (*AmE* **high school**)
- (in Britain) a secondary school (not private) for all children: **comprehensive school**
- (in Britain) a secondary school which provides more academic education: **grammar school**
- an institution where you can study after you leave school (but which is not a university): **college** ◦ *a further education college*

2 people in a school

- a boy/girl who goes to school: **schoolboy/schoolgirl**
- a child who goes to school: **schoolchild** (*plural* **schoolchildren**)
- a child in a school: **pupil**
- a person (not a child) who is being taught in a school or college: **student**

- a group of pupils who are taught together: **class** (*with singular or plural verb*) ◦ *The class is going on a visit today.* ◦ *How many people are in the class?*

- a person whose job is to teach in a school: **teacher**, **schoolteacher**; the work or profession of a teacher: **teaching** (*noun* U) ◦ *I've been a teacher for thirty years, but originally I didn't want to go into teaching.*
- the group of teachers who work in a school: **staff** (*noun* C/U, *usually singular, usually with a plural verb*) ◦ *The school has a staff of more than fifty.* ◦ *The staff in the school are very friendly.* ◦ *a new member of staff*
- the person who is in charge of a school: **head teacher** (*AmE* **principal**)

3 places in a school

- a room in a school or college where classes are taught: **classroom**
- a room in a school where teachers can go and work or relax when they are not in class: **staffroom**

- an area of hard ground in a school where children can play: **playground**
- an area of grass in a school where children play games or do sports: **playing field, sports field**
- the whole area which belongs to a school, including the buildings and the playing fields: **school grounds** (*noun plural*) ◦ *Children must not go outside the school grounds.*

4 going to school

- to go regularly to school: **go* to school**, **be at school**, (*formal*) **attend school** ◦ *Her children go to the same school as my son.* ◦ *Are your children at school yet?* (= are they old enough to go to school?) ◦ *All children between the ages of 5 and 16 have to attend school.*
- to go to school on a particular occasion: **go* to school** ◦ *Didn't you go to school today?*
- being present at school: **attendance** (*noun* U) ◦ *His attendance had been very poor due to illness.*

Note: there is no **the** before **school** when you are talking about a teacher or pupil going or being there to teach or learn; **the** is used before **school** if you are talking about going there as a visitor: ◦ *I'm going to the school to see Sara's teacher.*

- the clothes which pupils must wear in some schools: **uniform**
- a bag used by school children for carrying their books, etc: **school-bag**

- to cause sb to go to school: **send*** sb **to school** ◦ *She refuses to send her children to school.*
- not to go to school: **stay away from school** ◦ *We need to know why he's been staying away from school.*
- to cause sb not to go to school: **keep*** sb **away from school** ◦ *His parents were keeping him away from school because of his health.*

- to go to school for the first time: **start school** ◦ *When does she start school?*
- to finish school completely at 16, 18, etc: **leave* school**; a person who has just left school: **school leaver** ◦ *She's just left school and she's looking for a job.* ◦ *There are a lot of school leavers looking for work.*

- to send sb away from school for a short time ususally for doing sth wrong: **suspend** sb; *noun* (U): **suspension** ◦ *She was suspended for smoking in the school grounds.* ◦ *a week's suspension from school*
- to send sb away from school permanently: **expel** sb (**from** sth); *noun* (C/U): **expulsion** ◦ *She has been expelled from a number of schools for attacking other pupils.*

5 being in school

- the time you spend at school; your education: **schooling** (*noun* U) ◦ *His schooling was interrupted by long periods of illness.*

- the school year is divided into three periods of time; each one is called a **term** (*noun* C/U) ◦ *the spring term* ◦ *We've got exams at the end of term.* ◦ *end-of-term examinations* ◦ *There are always lots of things happening during term-time.*
- one of the periods in the year when children are not at school: **holiday** (*often plural*) ◦ *the summer holidays*
- a short holiday halfway through a school term: **half-term** (*noun* C/U) ◦ *We're going away for half-term.*
- a period when the schools are open, usually September to July: **school year**

- a period of time when you learn or teach sth: **lesson, class, period** ◦ *Lessons begin at 9 o'clock.* ◦ *a history class* ◦ *How many periods of maths do you have per week?*
- an area of knowledge that is studied at school, college, etc: **subject** ◦ *My favourite subject at school was biology.*
- a book that teaches a particular subject and that is used especially in schools: **textbook, coursebook**
- a book where students write work which is intended to help them learn or practise sth: **exercise book**

▷ subjects that can be studied at school ⇨ **STUDY**

- a piece of black board that is used for writing on: **blackboard** (*AmE* **chalkboard**); to write on a blackboard, you use **chalk** (*noun* U) ◦ *a piece of chalk*
- a piece of white board that is used for writing on: **whiteboard**; to write on a whiteboard, you use a **marker pen**
- a kind of table that a teacher or pupil sits at in a classroom: **desk**

- a period of time when children at school can stop lessons and relax: **break** (*noun* C/U), **breaktime** (*noun* U)
- a period of time when young children at school stop lessons and go outside to play: **playtime** (*noun* U) ◦ *The bell goes at playtime.*

- to get knowledge or skill: **learn** (sth) ◦ *to learn German* ◦ *to learn how to play the piano*
- to spend time learning about sth: **study** (sth), **do*** sth ◦ *I'm studying very hard at the moment – I've got exams in a couple of weeks.* ◦ *What subjects are you doing next year?*
- to give sb lessons; to show or tell sb sth so that they know about it or how to do it: **teach*** (sb) (sth) ◦ *to teach a child to read* ◦ *to teach chemistry*

- a list of things which have to be taught in a particular subject: **syllabus** ◦ *There's a lot to cover on the history syllabus.*
- the subjects that are taught in a school: **curriculum**

▷ more on learning and teaching ⇨ **LEARN, TEACH**

- something (usually written) that you have to produce in school for a teacher: **work** (*noun* U) ◦ *Did you hand in your work?*
- the work that pupils do in school: **schoolwork** (*noun* U) ◦ *Her schoolwork is very good.*
- the work that teachers give to pupils to do away from school: **homework** (*noun* U) ◦ *I still haven't done my homework.*
- to give a completed piece of work to a teacher: **hand/give*** sth **in** ◦ *When have you got to hand in your essay?*

- a written, spoken or practical test of what you know or can do: **exam**, (*formal*) **examination** ◦ *to sit an exam* ◦ *to pass an exam* ◦ *I think I've failed the history exam.*
- a number or letter given for schoolwork or exams to show how good it is: **grade**, (*BrE*) **mark** ◦ *I got a really good mark for my essay.*
- to look at schoolwork or an exam, show where there are mistakes and give it a number or a letter to show how good it is: **mark** sth ◦ *The teacher marked the essays and gave them back to the pupils.*
- the written statement about the work of a school pupil: (**school**) **report** ◦ *The teachers have to write reports at the end of each term.*

▷ more on exams ⇨ **EXAM**

- a special day when prizes are given to pupils for good work: **prize day**
- a special day when school pupils compete in sports competitions: **sports day**

■ **MORE . . .**

- the things that must or must not be done in a school: (**school**) **rules** ◦ *to break the school rules*

school *contd.*

– not to go to school when you should be in school: **play truant**; *noun* (U): **truancy** ◦ *A lot of the children have been playing truant.* ◦ *Truancy is a serious problem in some schools.*
– an official who visits schools to see that they are working properly: (**school**) **inspector**

science

other areas of knowledge and study ⇨ STUDY

– systematic knowledge about, or study of, the natural world: **science** (*noun* U); *adjective*: **scientific** ◦ *All my friends at university studied science.* ◦ *pure/applied science* ◦ *scientific research/ideas/progress*
– a person who studies science: **scientist**
– the study and use of science for practical purposes in industry, etc: **technology** (*noun* U); *adjective*: **technological** ◦ *to make technological progress*
– the scientific knowledge that is needed in a particular industry: **technology** (*noun* C/U) ◦ *information technology*
– a person who is an expert in technology: **technologist**
– a particular area of science: **science** (*noun* U/C) ◦ *medical science* ◦ *the physical/natural sciences*
– an area of study or knowledge: **field** ◦ *Not many scientists are working in this field.*
– one part of a science: **branch** ◦ *Animal health is a branch of veterinary science.*

▷ more on computers and maths ⇨ COMPUTER, MATHEMATICS

■ doing science
– using the methods of science: **scientific** (*adverb* **scientifically**); *opposite*: **unscientific** (*adverb* **unscientifically**) ◦ *a scientific study of wildlife on the island* ◦ *His methods are rather unscientific.* ◦ *It's hard to prove scientifically.*
– a test which is done by scientists: **experiment**; connected with experiments: **experimental** ◦ *to carry out an experiment* ◦ *experimental research*
– a thin glass tube which is used for doing some experiments: **test tube**
– a group of signs, letter or numbers used for scientific information: **formula** ◦ *The chemical formula for water is H_2O;.*
– a room or building that is used for scientific work or teaching: **laboratory**, (*informal*) **lab**

▷ more on scientific study ⇨ STUDY

screw ⇨ TOOL

sculpture

see also ART

– the art of making shapes and objects from metal, wood, stone, etc: **sculpture** (*noun* U); a work or works of art made in this way: **sculpture** (*noun* C/U) ◦ *a student of painting and sculpture* ◦ *a sculpture by Henry Moore* ◦ *a collector of sculpture*
– a sculpture of a person or an animal, usually put in a public place: **statue** ◦ *a statue of Napoleon* ◦ *a bronze/marble statue*
– a statue of a person's head, shoulders and chest: **bust**
– a building or statue that was built to remind people of a certain person or event: **monument** (**to** sb) ◦ *In the centre of the square there's a monument to Leonardo da Vinci.*
– to put a statue in a particular place: **put* sth up**, (*formal*) **erect** sth ◦ *The statue of Queen Victoria was put up in 1910.*
– the part which supports a statue: **pedestal**

making a sculpture
– a person who makes sculptures: **sculptor**; a female sculptor can also be called a **sculptress**
– to make a sculpture of a person or thing: **do* a sculpture** (**of** sb/sth)

the study of …	**is called (*noun* U) …**	**a person who studies this subject**	**adjective**
natural forces such as light, sound, heat, electricity	**physics**	**physicist**	
machines, buildings, roads, etc	**engineering**	**engineer**	
substances	**chemistry**	**chemist**	**chemical**
living things	**biology**	**biologist**	**biological**
the development of living things	**genetics**	**geneticist**	**genetic**
living things in their surroundings	**ecology**	**ecologist**	**ecological**
plants	**botany**	**botanist**	**botanical**
animals	**zoology**	**zoologist**	**zoological**
the physical world	**geography**	**geographer**	**geographical**
rocks and soil	**geology**	**geologist**	**geological**
the weather	**meteorology**	**meteorologist**	**meteorological**
computers, how they work and how they can be used	**computer science**	**computer scientist**	
numbers, quantities and shapes	**maths** (*AmE* **math**), (*formal*) **mathematics**	**mathematician**	**mathematical**

- to cut wood or stone to make a particular shape: **carve** (sth) (**out of** sth); the work produced is a **carving** ◦ *He carved the figure of a man out of the piece of wood.* ◦ *a woodcarving*
- to stand, sit, etc in a particular position that can be copied for a statue: **pose**; the position that sb sits in for this purpose: **pose** ◦ *It was tiring to hold the same pose for such a long time.*
- if you sit so that an artist can copy you for a statue, you **sit* for** sb ◦ *He only asked the rich and famous to sit for him.*

---

sea

1 seas and oceans
2 movements of the sea
3 where the sea meets the land
4 travelling on the sea
5 working at sea

animals that live in the sea ⇨ FISH[1]

see also LAND, WORLD

1 seas and oceans

- the salty water that covers much of the surface of the earth: **sea** (*noun* U) ◦ *to swim in the sea* ◦ *to live by the sea* ◦ *the deep blue sea* ◦ *a journey by sea*
- a particular area of sea: **sea** ◦ *the Mediterranean sea*
- one of the main areas of sea: **ocean** ◦ *the Atlantic Ocean* ◦ *an ocean voyage*

- an area of sea that is largely enclosed by a curved coastline: **bay** ◦ *the Bay of Bengal*
- an area of sea that is almost surrounded by land: **gulf** ◦ *the Gulf of Mexico*
- a narrow area of sea between two pieces of land: **channel** ◦ *the English Channel*

- the top of the sea: **surface** ◦ *The fish were swimming close to the surface.*
- the bottom of the sea: **seabed, bottom, floor** ◦ *Can you see the bottom?* ◦ *the floor of the ocean*
- the distant line where the sea seems to meet the sky; the furthest point we can see in the distance: **horizon** ◦ *Can you see the ship? It's like a small dot on the horizon.*

- the water in the sea: **sea water** (*noun* U)
- different types of plant which grow in the sea: **seaweed** (*noun* U)
- a light wind by the sea: **sea breeze**

2 movements of the sea

- a raised line of water that moves across the surface of the sea: **wave**
- when a wave falls on the shore, it **breaks*** ◦ *the sound of the waves breaking on the shore*
- when there are a lot of waves, the sea is **rough**; *opposite*: **calm** ◦ *The water's much rougher today.*
- the flow of water in the sea that can make it dangerous to swim: **current** ◦ *You can't swim here because of the dangerous currents.*
- the regular rising and falling of the level of the sea: **tide**; *adjective*: **tidal**
- when the water level is high and the water is closer to the shore, the tide is **in**, it is **high tide**
- when the water level is low and the water is further from the shore, the tide is **out**, it is **low tide**
- when the tide gets higher, it **comes* in**; when it gets lower, it **goes* out**

3 where the sea meets the land

- the land beside or near the sea: **coast**; *adjective*: **coastal**; the shape of the coast: **coastline** ◦ *We could already see the French coast.* ◦ *coastal regions* ◦ *a spectacular coastline*
- the land at the edge of the sea: **shore** (*noun* C/U), **seashore** (*noun* U) ◦ *a few hundred yards from the shore* ◦ *to go on shore* (= to get off a boat and go on to the land) ◦ *We went for a walk along the seashore.*
- a steep, rocky part of the coast: **cliff** ◦ *The hotel is at the top of a cliff.*

- an area on the coast where people go on holiday: **seaside** (*noun singular*) ◦ *a day at the seaside* ◦ *a seaside hotel*
- an area of land by the sea, usually covered with sand or stones, and often covered by the sea at high tide: **beach** ◦ *sunbathing on the beach* ◦ *a sandy/stony beach*

▷ more on beaches ⇨ BEACH

- a piece of land with water all around it: **island** ◦ *a desert island* (= a tropical island where no one lives)
- a piece of land that is almost surrounded by water: **peninsula** ◦ *the Iberian Peninsula*
- a piece of land that sticks out into the sea: **cape** ◦ *Cape Horn* ◦ *The Cape of Good Hope*

4 travelling on the sea

- to go on the sea in a boat: **sail** ◦ *We sailed across the Atlantic.*
- a person who is on the sea in a boat is **at sea** ◦ *They'd been at sea for three months.*
- a journey across an area of sea: **crossing** ◦ *Did you have a pleasant crossing?* ◦ *a transatlantic crossing* (= a journey across the Atlantic Ocean)
- a long journey by sea: (*formal*) **voyage**
- to arrive on land: **land, go* ashore** ◦ *We landed at Southampton.* ◦ *It was such a relief when we finally went ashore.*

- when you feel sick on a boat because of the movement of the waves, you are **seasick**
- an accident at sea in which a ship is destroyed: **shipwreck**
- a person or ship that has suffered such a accident has been **shipwrecked**

▷ more on boats and travelling by sea ⇨ BOAT

- a place on the coast where ships can be tied up to shelter from the sea: **harbour** (*AmE* **harbor**)

sea *contd.*

– an area where ships load and unload goods and passengers: **port**

5 working at sea

– a person who works in boats at sea: **sailor**, **seaman** (*plural* **seamen**)
– a person who sails on the sea in order to catch fish: **fisherman** (*plural* **fishermen**)
– a person who swims underwater wearing special breathing equipment: **diver**; a diver who works in deep water: **deep-sea diver**

– to become a sailor: **go* to sea** ◦ *He went to sea at the age of 16.*

– a special boat that goes out to rescue people who are in danger at sea: **lifeboat**
– a person who works on the coast, watching the sea in order to help people and boats which are in trouble: **coastguard**
– a tower by the sea with a light at the top that guides people in boats and shows them where the land is: **lighthouse**

■ **MORE ...**
– a hard pink or red substance that is found under the sea: **coral** (*noun* U) ◦ *a coral island*
– a line of rocks, coral, etc, on or under the surface of the sea: (**coral**) **reef**

– connected with the sea: **marine**, **maritime** ◦ *marine animals* ◦ *maritime law*

search ⇨ LOOK FOR

season

see also YEAR

– one of the four periods of the year: **season**

■ summer
– the warmest season of the year, between spring and autumn: **summer** (*noun* C/U) ◦ *the summer holidays* ◦ *We went to Spain two summers ago.* ◦ *In summer, I usually spend a lot of time in the garden.*
– the time when it is summer: **summertime** (*noun* U) ◦ *The shop is usually much busier in the summertime when all the tourists are here.*
– if the weather is what you would expect in summer, or if sth is suitable for summer, it is **summery** ◦ *a summery day*
– the time around the middle of summer when the days are long: **midsummer** (*noun* U)

■ autumn
– the season between summer and winter: **autumn** (*AmE* **fall**) (*noun* C/U)
– if the weather is what you would expect in autumn, it is **autumnal**

■ winter
– the coldest time of year, between autumn and spring: **winter** (*noun* C/U) ◦ *a very cold winter* ◦ *We didn't get much snow last winter.* ◦ *winter sports*
– the time when it is winter: **wintertime** (*noun* U) ◦ *The days are shorter in the wintertime.*
– if a winter is particularly cold, it is **hard**; *opposite*: **mild** ◦ *a long hard winter*
– if the weather is what you would expect in winter, it is **wintry** ◦ *wintry showers* ◦ *wintry weather*
– the time around the middle of winter when the days are short: **midwinter** (*noun* U)

■ spring
– the season between winter and summer: **spring** (*noun* C/U)
– the time when it is spring: **springtime** (*noun* U)
– if the weather is what you would expect in spring, it is **springlike** ◦ *a springlike day*

Note: in talking about the seasons we normally do not use **the**, but we may do if we want to talk about a particular winter, summer, etc: ◦ *Winter is not a good time to be in Moscow.* ◦ *I love autumn – it's my favourite season.* ◦ *The winter in Moscow is terrible.* ◦ *I was very ill in April and May but I began to get better as the summer approached.*

secret

1 keeping a secret
2 telling a secret

see also KNOW, INFORM

1 keeping a secret

– something that you do not want anybody else to know: **secret** ◦ *Sorry, I can't tell you – it's a secret!*
– not to be told to other people: **secret**, (*more formal*) **confidential** ◦ *a secret organization* ◦ *a confidential letter* ◦ *This information is strictly confidential.*
– very secret: **top secret** ◦ *a top secret document*

– the state of being a secret, or not letting other people know sth: **secrecy** (*noun* U), **confidentiality** (*noun* U) ◦ *The meeting took place in complete secrecy.*
– something that is done without other people knowing is done **in secret**, **secretly** ◦ *The two leaders met in secret.* ◦ *They met secretly every weekend for several months.*
– if you are told sth, but you are not allowed to give the information to another person, you are told **in** (**strict**) **confidence** ◦ *I was given this information in strict confidence.*

– if you have a secret which you do not tell anybody, you **keep*** (sth) **a secret**, **keep*** sth **secret**, **keep*** sth **to** yourself, **keep*** sth **quiet** ◦ *Can you keep a secret?* ◦ *I hope I can trust you to keep this to yourself.* ◦ *We kept it quiet for as long as we could.*
– if you keep sth secret from a particular person, you **hide*** sth (**from** sb), **keep*** sth (**back**) **from** sb, **conceal** sth (**from** sb); *noun* (U): **concealment** ◦ *He managed to hide his past from her for*

several years. ◦ *I don't trust him – I'm sure he's keeping something (back) from us.* ◦ *She tried to conceal her illness from the children.* ◦ *concealment of the facts*
– to stop people from finding out about sth: **hush** sth **up**, **cover** (sth) **up**; *noun*: **cover-up** ◦ *They managed to hush up the whole affair.* ◦ *The government tried to cover up the mistake.* ◦ *The film suggests that there was a cover-up.*

– the habit of keeping things secret: **secretiveness** (*noun* U); *adjective*: **secretive** ◦ *He's a very secretive person.*

2 telling a secret
– to tell sb a secret on purpose: **reveal** sth (**to** sb), **let*** sb **in on** sth, **let*** sb **into** a **secret**, (*informal*) **let* on** (**about** sth) ◦ *He refused to reveal any more information.* ◦ *Are you going to let Vicky in on the plan?* ◦ *Shall I let you into a secret?* ◦ *Promise not to let on about it!*
– to talk to sb that you trust about sth which is secret or private: **confide in** sb, **confide** sth **to** sb, **take*** sb **into** your **confidence** ◦ *I've got nobody else to confide in.* ◦ *She never confided her worries to me.* ◦ *I'm surprised he took you into his confidence so soon.*
– if you know a secret, you are **in on** sth ◦ *Are you in on their plan?*

– to tell sb a secret accidentally: **let*** sth **out**, **let*** sth **slip**, **give*** sth **away** ◦ *Who let the secret out?* ◦ *Chris let it slip after a few drinks.* ◦ *I made sure I didn't give anything away.*
– to give some information away by speaking suddenly or without thinking: **blurt** sth **out** ◦ *I just blurted it out without thinking.*

– to become known: **come* out**, **leak out** ◦ *The truth finally came out in court.* ◦ *The government didn't want the information to leak out.*
– when a secret has become known, it is **out** ◦ *The secret is out at last!*

■ **MORE ...**
– to tell sb that what you are saying is a secret, you can say **between you and me, between ourselves** ◦ *This is just between ourselves of course.*
– to avoid telling sb a secret: **not breathe a word** (**about** sth) (**to** sb) ◦ *Don't breathe a word about this to anyone!*
– if you refuse to tell someone a secret, your **lips are sealed** ◦ *You can trust me – my lips are sealed!*
– to make a secret public by mistake: (*informal*) **let* the cat out of the bag**

---

secretary ⇨ OFFICE

---

see

1 seeing
2 not able to see well
3 things that help you to see better
4 things that can be seen
5 things that cannot be seen

the other senses ⇨ **FEEL, HEAR, SMELL, TASTE**

see also EYE, LOOK FOR, FIND

1 seeing
– to become aware of sb/sth, using your eyes: **see*** (sb/sth) ◦ *I can't see much without my glasses.* ◦ *I've been looking for my keys but I can't see them anywhere.* ◦ *I can't see what I'm doing in this light.* ◦ *We were able to see clearly by the light of the moon.*
– an act or occasion of seeing sb/sth: **sight** (*noun* U) ◦ *It was love at first sight.* ◦ *He was looking forward to his first sight of home.* ◦ *She always faints at the sight of blood.*

– the ability to see: **sight** (*noun* U), **eyesight** (*noun* U) ◦ *I would rather lose my sense of sight than my sense of hearing.* ◦ *to have poor/good eyesight*
– connected with seeing: **visual** (*adverb* **visually**) ◦ *the visual arts* ◦ *to be visually handicapped* (= partly or completely unable to see)

– to turn your eyes in a particular direction in order to see sb/sth: **look** (**at** sb/sth), **take*/have a look** (**at** sb/sth) ◦ *to look out of the window* ◦ *Look at page four, please.* ◦ *Have a look and see if the post has come.*
– to look at a person doing sth or at sth happening: **watch** (sb/sth) ◦ *I watched the children playing in the garden.*

▷ more on looking at things ⇨ **LOOK AT**

– to see sb/sth and be aware of them/it: **notice** (sb/sth) ◦ *I didn't notice you sitting there.* ◦ *'Was she blonde or dark?' 'I'm afraid I didn't notice her hair.'* ◦ *Did you notice where I put my bag?* ◦ *He noticed that she never smiled.*
– to notice one person or thing among many others; to notice sb/sth when it is not easy to do so: **spot** sb/sth ◦ *I couldn't spot you in the crowd – were you there?* ◦ *Did you spot any mistakes?*
– to see sb/sth for a moment: **glimpse** sb/sth, **catch* a glimpse** (**of** sb/sth), **catch* sight of** sb/sth ◦ *I thought I glimpsed my friend in a passing taxi.* ◦ *We caught a glimpse of the Queen when she arrived at the theatre.* ◦ *I was just going to leave when I caught sight of you in the corner.*
– to be able to see sb/sth, but only with difficulty: **make*** sb/sth **out** ◦ *It was difficult to make the road out in the darkness.*

– quick at noticing things: **observant**; *opposite*: **unobservant** ◦ *She's very observant – she doesn't miss a thing.*

– to know again a person or thing that you have seen before: **recognize** sb/sth ◦ *I'm so sorry, I didn't recognize you.*
– to see sth happen and be able to tell other people about it later: **witness** sth; a person who does this: **(eye)witness** ◦ *to witness a crime* ◦ *There were three witnesses to the accident.* ◦ *The police need an eyewitness.*

2 not able to see well
– unable to see: **blind, visually-impaired**; *noun* (U): **blindness** ◦ *a blind person* ◦ *to go* (=

see *contd.*

become) *blind* ◦ *to be completely/partially blind* ◦ *She's blind in one eye.*
- blind people: **the blind** (*noun plural*) ◦ *a school for the blind*
- unable to identify certain colours: **colour-blind**; *noun* (U): **colour-blindness**
- if you cannot easily see things that are very close to you, you are **long-sighted** (*AmE* **far-sighted**)
- if you cannot easily see things that are far away from you, you are **short-sighted** (*AmE* **near-sighted**)
- to make a person unable to see, for a short time or permanently: **blind** sb ◦ *The car headlights blinded me and I nearly crashed.* ◦ *He was blinded in the war.*

3 things that help you to see better

(a pair of) glasses

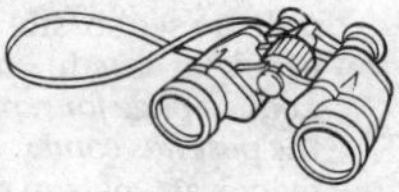

(a pair of) binoculars

telescope

magnifying glass

microscope

▷ more on glasses ⇨ **GLASSES**

- to see sth without the help of a microscope or telescope, etc: see sth **with the naked eye** ◦ *A single cell cannot be seen with the naked eye.*

4 things that can be seen
- something that can be seen is **visible** ◦ *There were no visible signs that a burglar had broken into the house.* ◦ *The house was clearly visible from the road.*
- the amount or distance that you can see in particular light or weather conditions: **visibility** (*noun* U) ◦ *good/poor visibility* ◦ *Visibility was so bad that we had to stop until the fog cleared.*
- if sth can be seen, it **shows** ◦ *Does the hole in my sock show?* ◦ *You can read the letter because the writing shows through the envelope.*
- if sth can be seen easily because of a contrast in colour, it **shows up** ◦ *White shows up well on a black background.*
- to make it possible for other people to see sth: **show** sth **to** sb, **show** sb sth ◦ *She showed her work to me.* ◦ *She showed me her work.* ◦ *Please show me how to do that!* ◦ *I showed him what I had done.*

▷ more on showing things to people ⇨ **SHOW**

- something that is easy to see is **clear** (*adverb* **clearly**), **obvious** (*adverb* **obviously**), **plain** (*adverb* **plainly**) ◦ *The deer left a clear line of footprints in the snow.* ◦ *It was obvious that they had been arguing when I arrived.* ◦ *She plainly wanted us to leave.*
- something that can be noticed is **noticeable** (*adverb* **noticeably**) ◦ *The scar on his face was hardly noticeable any more.* ◦ *She was noticeably anxious about the child's safety.*
- something which is very obvious and easily noticed is **prominent**, **conspicuous**, it **stands* out** ◦ *The article was in a prominent position on the front page.* ◦ *I felt very conspicuous because I was the only person who wasn't wearing black.* ◦ *He's so tall that he always stands out in a crowd.*
- something that can be seen through is **transparent**, (used mainly about clothes) **see-through** ◦ *The material was so old, it had become almost transparent.* ◦ *She was wearing a see-through blouse.*
- something that is near enough to be seen or sb who is near enough to see sth is **(with)in sight (of** sb/sth) ◦ *There wasn't a tree in sight.* ◦ *We were soon within sight of the city lights.*
- your ability to see a particular thing: **view** ◦ *to come into view* ◦ *to disappear from view* ◦ *to be hidden from view* ◦ *They kissed in full view of all the dinner guests!* ◦ *Excuse me – could you please move? You're blocking my view of the stage.*
- to come into sight or arrive: **appear**; *noun* (*singular*): **appearance** ◦ *We waited an hour before they finally appeared.* ◦ *I suppose we ought to put in an appearance at the party.*
- something that is in a place where people can see it is **on show**, **on view** ◦ *The English crown jewels are on show in the Tower of London.*
- what you can see around you in a particular place: **scene** ◦ *a peaceful scene* ◦ *I need a change of scene!*
- what you can see from a particular place: **view** ◦ *Look at the lovely view!* ◦ *There are some wonderful views from the top of the hill.* ◦ *a room with a view*
- to have a view over sth: **overlook** sth, **look out on** sth ◦ *My bedroom overlooks a golf course.*

5 things that cannot be seen
- unable to be seen: **invisible** ◦ *bacteria that are invisible to the naked eye*
- not bright or clear: **dim** (*adverb* **dimly**); *noun* (U): **dimness** ◦ *I could only see a dim shape in the darkness.* ◦ *The room was very dimly lit.*
- something that is too far away to be seen, or sb who is too far away to see sth, is **out of sight (of** sb/sth) ◦ *We watched the plane until it was completely out of sight.*
- if you can just see sth, but not very clearly, it is **faint**, you can see it **faintly** ◦ *I thought I could see a faint light at the end of the tunnel.*
- to become impossible to see or find: **disappear**, **vanish** ◦ *One minute the coin was in the magician's hand and the next, it had disappeared.*

- the act of disappearing or the state of having disappeared: **disappearance** (*noun* C/U) ◦ *They have never solved the mystery of his wife's disappearance.*
- to disappear slowly from sight: **fade** (**away**) ◦ *The sun faded away behind the clouds.*

- to no longer be able to see sb/sth: **lose* sight** (**of** sb/sth) ◦ *We lost sight of them as they went round the corner.*
- without being seen or noticed: **unseen**, **unnoticed** ◦ *She left the room unseen.* ◦ *He had been standing unnoticed by the door for some time.*
- not easily noticed: **inconspicuous** (*adverb* **inconspicuously**) ◦ *to make yourself inconspicuous*
- if sth is in a place where it cannot be seen, it is **hidden** ◦ *From where we stood, the house was hidden from view.*

- to put or keep yourself in a place where you cannot be seen: **hide*** ◦ *Where can I hide?* ◦ *The child was found hiding up a tree.* ◦ *We're hiding from the teacher.*
- to put sb/sth in a place where nobody else can find or see them/it: **hide*** sb/sth ◦ *He had hidden the gun under the floorboards.*

▷ more on hiding sb/sth ⇨ HIDE

seed ⇨ FRUIT, PLANT

select ⇨ DECIDE/CHOOSE

self ⇨ PERSON

sell

1 selling
2 places where things are sold
3 money from selling
4 the work of selling
see also BUY

1 selling

- to give sth to sb who pays for it and is then the owner of it: **sell*** (sb) sth, **sell*** (sth) (**to** sb), (*informal*) **flog** (sth) (**to** sb) ◦ *The fridge you sold me isn't working properly.* ◦ *I'd like to buy his books but he won't sell.* ◦ *Have you managed to flog your guitar yet?*
- the act of selling: **sale** (*noun* U) ◦ *The sale of alcohol to anyone under the age of 18 is forbidden.*
- an occasion when things are sold: **sale** ◦ *a sale of second-hand books* ◦ *a jumble sale* (= an event when people sell old or used things that they do not want any more)

- to offer sth for sale: **sell*** sth ◦ *Are you selling your car?* ◦ *Do you sell stamps?*
- a person who sells sth: **seller** ◦ *a bookseller* ◦ *The seller must ensure that the equipment is safe to use.*
- when sb offers sth for sb to buy, it is **for sale**, **on the market**; things which are being sold in shops are **on sale**

- if people are keen to buy sth, it **sells*** (**well**)
- the amount sold by a shop over a period of time: **sales** (*noun plural*) ◦ *In the week before Christmas sales of toys were very good.*
- to be completely sold, so that no more are available: **sell* out** ◦ *I rushed to the shop but the book had already sold out.*
- to sell all of sth so that there are no more to be bought: **sell* out** (**of** sth) ◦ *He told me they'd sold out of that kind of jacket, but they could order one for me.*

2 places where things are sold

- a building or part of a building where things are bought and sold: **shop** (*AmE* **store**)

▷ more on shops ⇨ SHOP

■ markets
- a regular event at which people come together to buy and sell things: **market**
- the place where a market is held: **market**, **market place**
- the day in the week when a market takes place: **market-day**
- a market where people sell things from the boots of their cars: **car-boot sale**
- a small shop or table where things are sold in a market: **stall**
- a person who buys and sells things, especially in a market: **trader** ◦ *a market trader in the East End of London*

■ auctions
- a public sale at which items are sold to the person who offers the most money: **auction** (*noun* C/U); to sell sth in this way: **auction** sth ◦ *Do you like it? I bought it in an auction.* ◦ *The house will be sold by auction.*
- a place where public sales and auctions are held: **saleroom**
- a person who organizes the selling at an auction: **auctioneer**

3 money from selling

- the amount of money for which sth is sold: **price** (*noun* C/U) ◦ *high/low prices* ◦ *a sudden rise in price*

▷ more on prices ⇨ PRICE

- the money you get as a result of selling sth: **proceeds** (*noun plural*) ◦ *All proceeds will be given to charity.*
- the amount of money that a shop gets in a day, week, etc: **takings** (*noun plural*)
- money that you earn by selling sth for sb: **commission** (**on** sth) (*noun* C/U) ◦ *I get a ten percent commission on all sales.*

- the amount of money made when sth is sold for more than it cost: **profit** (*noun* C/U); *opposite*: **loss** (*noun* C/U) ◦ *We sold our house at a profit.* ◦

sell *contd.*

I made a profit of £10 on my bike. ○ *an increase in annual profits* ○ *We didn't make much profit in the first year or two.*

– to make a profit: **make*** sth (**on** sth) ○ *The firm made £2 million on the deal.*
– if you do not make either a profit or a loss, you **break* even** ○ *I don't think we'll make much on this deal but we ought to break even.*

4 the work of selling

– a man/woman whose job is to sell sth: **salesman/saleswoman** ○ *a door-to-door salesman* (= sb who sells by going to people's houses) ○ *a car salesman* ○ *an insurance salesman*
– a person who buys and sells things, especially of one particular type: **dealer** ○ *a dealer in antiques* ○ *a used-car dealer*

– skill in selling things: **salesmanship** (*noun* U)
– the section of a business that is responsible for selling things: **sales department**
– to put information in a newspaper, on television, etc to persuade people to buy sth: **advertise** (sth)
– a piece of information in a newspaper, on television, etc, intended to persuade people to buy sth or do sth: **advertisement**, (*informal*) **advert**, (*informal*) **ad**
– work that is done to find out what people want to buy: **market research** (*noun* U)

▷ more on advertising ⇨ ADVERTISEMENT

■ packaging

– paper, boxes, etc in which things are packed in order to be sold: **packaging** (*noun* U) ○ *Is it really necessary for food to have so much packaging?*
– a box, bag, etc in which things are packed to be sold in a shop: **packet** (*AmE* **package**) ○ *a packet of sweets/cigarettes/biscuits* ○ *a cigarette packet*

▷ more on packets, etc ⇨ CONTAINER

■ MORE ...

– a person or company that supplies things to a shop: **supplier**, **wholesaler**; connected with selling goods in large quantities (for example, to shops): **wholesale** (*adjective, adverb*) ○ *wholesale prices* ○ *We buy all our paper and office equipment wholesale.*
– a person or shop that sells directly to the public: **retailer**
– connected with selling goods directly to the public: **retail** (*adjective, adverb*) ○ *the retail trade*

– to sell everything you own (your house, your business, etc) in order to move to another place, start a new life, retire, etc: **sell* up** ○ *They sold up and moved to Australia.*

send

– causing sth to be taken to a place ⇨ BRING/TAKE/CARRY
– sending sth by post ⇨ POST

senior ⇨ RANK

sense ⇨ FEEL, HEAR, SEE, SMELL, TASTE

sensible

see also CLEVER

– able to think or act in a reasonable way; showing good judgement: **sensible** (*adverb* **sensibly**) ○ *You were very sensible to call the doctor.* ○ *It wasn't very sensible of her to stay so late at the party.* ○ *a sensible decision* ○ *The sensible thing to do is to phone for a taxi.*
– making sensible decisions and good at dealing with problems: **practical** ○ *We must be practical and find out how much it costs first.*

– (used about an action, decision, etc) taken for good reasons: **reasonable** (*adverb* **reasonably**), **rational** (*adverb* **rationally**) ○ *a reasonable point of view* ○ *to behave rationally*

– the ability to think or act in a reasonable way: **sense** (*noun* U); the ability to do things in a sensible way because of your experience of life, not because of what you have studied: **common sense** (*noun* U) ○ *What a ridiculous thing to do! Have you no sense at all?* ○ *She always talks good sense.* ○ *It's plain common sense to wear a seat belt in a car.* ○ *Use your common sense!*

■ not sensible

– not sensible: **foolish**, **stupid**, **ridiculous** ○ *a foolish course of action* ○ *a really stupid thing to do*

– actions that are not sensible or wise are **inadvisable** ○ *It is inadvisable to carry a lot of cash when you are travelling.*
– if sth has no meaning or purpose, it is **senseless**; *noun* (U): **senselessness** ○ *a senseless killing* ○ *the senselessness of war*
– something that is not based on reason or clear thought is **irrational** (*adverb* **irrationally**) ○ *an irrational fear* ○ *to behave irrationally*

sentence ⇨ GRAMMAR

separate

– not together ⇨ TOGETHER
– making things separate ⇨ DIVIDE

serious

– bad ⇨ BAD
– not funny ⇨ FUNNY
– important ⇨ IMPORTANT
– a problem ⇨ PROBLEM

sew

making clothes by knitting (= using wool) ⇨ WOOL
see also CLOTH, CLOTHES

– cotton for sewing: **thread** (*noun* U), **cotton** (*noun* U) ○ *I need some strong black thread/cotton to sew on a button.*
– the hole in a needle: **eye**

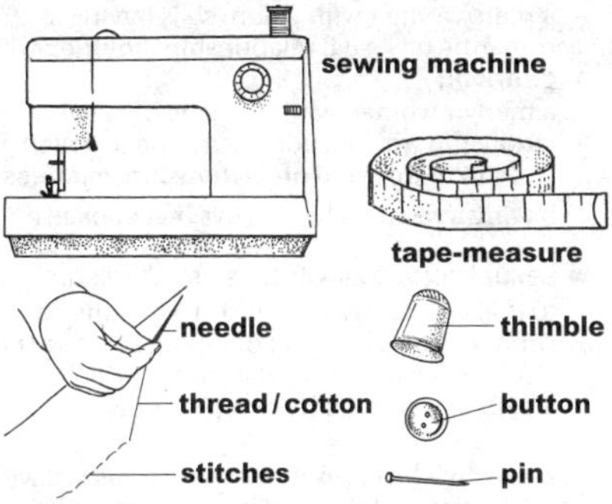

- to put thread through the eye of a needle: **thread** sth ◦ *I need my glasses to thread a needle nowadays.*

- to join pieces of cloth, or to join sth to cloth, using a needle and thread: **sew*** (sth), **stitch** (sth) ◦ *These curtains were sewn by my great-aunt.* ◦ *I'll sew that button on for you.* ◦ *The handle of this bag needs stitching.*
- things which are to be sewn: **sewing** (*noun* U) ◦ *She always has some sewing to do while she watches television.* ◦ *a pile of sewing*

■ making clothes
- the activity of making clothes: **dressmaking** (*noun* U)
- if you sew your own clothes, they are **handmade, made by hand**
- a person whose job is to make clothes for men: **tailor**
- a person who makes dresses and other women's clothes: **dressmaker**

- a piece of paper that shows you how to cut out the materials to the right size: **pattern**
- to join the pattern to the cloth or one piece of cloth to another with pins, you **pin** sth (**to** sth)
- to make the cloth the right size, you **cut*** it (**out**) ◦ *to cut out a dress*
- when you put the needle in the cloth and bring it out again, you make a **stitch** ◦ *Could you put a couple of stitches in my shirt?*

- the bottom edge of a dress/skirt/pair of trousers, where the cloth is folded double: **hem** ◦ *You ought to take the hem up a bit.*
- the smooth cloth which you sew inside a dress or coat: **lining**; *verb*: **line** sth ◦ *It's a wool coat, with a dark green lining.* ◦ *The dress is lined with fine silk.*
- the line of sewing that you make when you sew one piece of cloth to another: **seam** ◦ *to sew up the side seams of a dress*
- to sew stitches on cloth for decoration: **embroider** (sth) ◦ *to embroider your initials on a handkerchief* ◦ *a dress embroidered with red and green flower designs*
- the work of embroidering sth, or sth that has been embroidered: **embroidery** (*noun* U) ◦ *a beautiful piece of embroidery*

■ mending clothes
- to repair clothes by sewing: **mend** sth ◦ *You ought to mend the zip on those trousers before you wear them again.*
- clothes which are to be repaired: **mending** (*noun* U) ◦ *There's a box full of mending, if you want something to do.*

- if there is a hole in a piece of clothing and you mend it by sewing, you **sew*** it **up**; if you put another piece of cloth on top of the hole, you **patch** it, **put* a patch on** it ◦ *She had put patches on both knees of her jeans.*

- if a piece of clothing is too large and you sew new seams to make it smaller, you **take*** it **in**; if you make it bigger, you **let*** it **out** ◦ *'This skirt's getting too tight for me!' 'Why don't you let it out a bit?'*
- if sth is too long, you can **take*** it **up**; if it is too short, you can **let*** it **down**

- to mend a hole in clothes by sewing across it in one direction and then in another: **darn** sth ◦ *These socks have been darned so often that there's not much of the original sock left.*
- a needle used for darning: **darning needle**

---

sex[1] the difference between the sexes

sexual behaviour ⇨ SEX[2]

- the condition of being male or female: **sex** (*noun* U), (particularly referring to social characteristics) (*formal*) **gender** (*noun* C/U) ◦ *They didn't want to know the sex of their baby before it was born.* ◦ *differences of race or gender*
- connected with being male or female: **sexual** ◦ *sexual characteristics*
- the group of either male or female: **sex** ◦ *conflict between the sexes*
- the other sex: **the opposite sex** ◦ *He could never get on with the opposite sex.*

- belonging to the sex that can give birth: **female**
- belonging to the sex that does not give birth: **male**
- if sth is usually associated with women, it is **feminine**; *noun* (U): **femininity** ◦ *She hates looking feminine and always wears trousers.* ◦ *He has a very feminine voice.*
- if sth is usually associated with men, it is **masculine**; *noun* (U): **masculinity** ◦ *masculine pride*

▷ men and women ⇨ MAN, WOMAN

■ attitudes to the different sexes
- treating men and women equally: **sexual equality** (*noun* U)
- not treating men and women equally: (**sexual**) **discrimination** (*noun* U)
- the belief that either men or women are better than the other sex: **sexism** (*noun* U); *adjective*: **sexist** ◦ *I don't agree with you: that's just sexist talk!*
- the belief that men are better than women: **male chauvinism** (*noun* U); a man who has this belief: **male chauvinist**

sex¹ *contd.*

– the belief that women should have the same power, rights and opportunities as men: **feminism** (*noun* U); *adjective*: **feminist**; a person who has such a belief: **feminist** ◦ *the feminist movement*

sex² sexual behaviour

1 sexual activity and relationships
2 sexual feelings
3 sexual parts of the body and their functions
the difference between the sexes ⇨ SEX¹

1 sexual activity and relationships

– the physical act in which the sexual organs of two people touch each other: **sex** (*noun* U), (*formal*) (**sexual**) **intercourse** (*noun* U) ◦ *They don't believe in sex before marriage.* ◦ *to practise safe sex* (= being careful when having sex so as to prevent the spread of disease)
– activities or matters connected with sex: **sex** (*noun* U); *adjective*: **sexual** (*adverb* **sexually**) ◦ *sex education* ◦ *sex and violence on TV* ◦ *sexual behaviour/abuse* ◦ *a sexually explicit film*

– to take part in a sexual act with another person: **have sex** (**with** sb), **go* to bed with** sb, **sleep* with** sb; **make* love** (**to** sb) ◦ *He claimed he'd never had sex with her.* ◦ *Has she ever slept with him?* ◦ *'Let's make love,' she whispered.*
– to stroke or rub your sexual organs in order to get pleasure: **masturbate**; *noun* (U): **masturbation**
– the moment of greatest pleasure in sexual activity: **orgasm, climax**
– to have an orgasm: (*informal*) **come***
▷ kissing and other ways of showing love ⇨ LOVE

– to behave in a way that looks as if you are trying to attract a person: **flirt** (**with** sb) ◦ *She's been flirting with him the whole evening.*
– to talk to sb in order to impress them or ask them for a date: (*informal*) **chat** sb **up** ◦ *I got chatted up in the pub last night.*
– to try to begin a sexual relationship with sb: **make* advances** (**towards** sb), (*informal*) **make* a pass** (**at** sb) ◦ *He started making advances but I quickly told him to stop wasting his time.* ◦ *'Did she make a pass at you?' 'Yes, but I wasn't interested.'*
– to have a sexual experience with sb (usually used by young adults): (*informal*) **get* off with** sb ◦ *They got off with each other at a party.*

– to have sex with many people: (*informal*) **sleep* around** ◦ *He stopped sleeping around when he met her.*
– having sexual relations with many people: **promiscuous**; promiscuous behaviour: **promiscuity** (*noun* U)

– a man/woman with whom sb is having a romantic or sexual relationship: **boyfriend/girlfriend**
– a man or woman who is having a sexual relationship with sb, outside marriage: **lover**; a woman in this kind of relationship: **mistress**
▷ having a relationship ⇨ LOVE, RELATIONSHIP

■ sexual behaviour which is usually illegal
– to make sb have sex with you when they do not want to: **rape** sb; an act of raping sb: **rape** (*noun* C/U) ◦ *a terrible rape* ◦ *the crime of rape*
– a person who is guilty of rape: **rapist**

– a person who earns money by having sex with people: **prostitute**; working as a prostitute: **prostitution** (*noun* U)
– a house where prostitutes work: **brothel**
– the part of a city where prostitutes and brothels can be found: **red-light district**

2 sexual feelings

– the nature of a person's sexual feelings and behaviour: **sexuality** (*noun* U) ◦ *a book on female sexuality*
– a person who is attracted to people of the opposite sex: **heterosexual**; *adjective*: **heterosexual**
– a person who is sexually attracted to people of the same sex: **gay, homosexual**; *adjectives*: **gay, homosexual** ◦ *Most people didn't know he was gay.* ◦ *gay rights* ◦ *a gay bar*
– a homosexual woman: **lesbian**; *adjective*: **lesbian**
– a person who is attracted to both men and women: **bisexual**; *adjective*: **bisexual**
– the state of being attracted to persons of the same sex: **homosexuality** (*noun* U), **gayness** (*noun* U)
– the fact of whether a person is heterosexual or homosexual: (**sexual**) **orientation** (*noun* C/U) ◦ *We do not discriminate on grounds of race, gender or sexual orientation.*

– sexually attractive: **sexy, seductive** ◦ *He looks really sexy.* ◦ *a sexy little dress* ◦ *She was sitting in a very seductive posture.*
– if sb is sexually attractive, they have **sex appeal** (*noun* U) ◦ *She's got lots of sex appeal.*

– causing sexual excitement: **erotic** ◦ *erotic art* ◦ *an erotic novel*
– intending to cause sexual excitement: **provocative** (*adverb* **provocatively**) ◦ *a provocative look* ◦ *She smiled provocatively at him.*
– strong sexual desire: **lust** (*noun* U)
– connected with physical or sexual pleasure: **sensual** (*adverb* **sensually**); *noun* (U): **sensuality** ◦ *a sensual massage* ◦ *a life of sensuality*

– offending against accepted moral standards of behaviour: **indecent**; this kind of behaviour: **indecency** (*noun* U) ◦ *an indecent proposal*
– shocking or disgusting: **obscene**; this kind of behaviour or language: **obscenity** (*noun* C/U) ◦ *an obscene photograph* ◦ *the obscenity laws*

- a person who does not like to see or hear anything connected with sexual activity (used as a term of disapproval): **prude**; *adjective*: **prudish** ◦ *Don't be such a prude!* ◦ *She gave me a rather prudish look.*

- books, films, etc that are intended to create sexual excitement: **pornography** (*noun* U), (*informal*) **porn** (*noun* U); *adjective*: **pornographic** ◦ *a pornographic novel* ◦ *soft porn* (= fairly mild pornography)

3 sexual parts of the body and their functions

- the sex organs on the outside of the body: **genitals** (*noun plural*), **private parts** (*noun plural*)
- the parts of the body which are to do with producing babies: (*formal*) the **reproductive system**
- able to produce children: **fertile**; *noun* (U): **fertility**
- not able to produce children: **infertile**; *nouns* (U): **infertility**

- the time when a child's body is changing and becoming more like that of an adult: **puberty** (*noun* U)
- details about sexual behaviour and how babies are born: **the facts of life** ◦ *Most children seem to learn the facts of life from their school friends.*

■ female
- the inside part of the female sex organ: **vagina**; *adjective*: **vaginal**
- the small part of the female sex organ that becomes larger when a woman is sexually excited: **clitoris**
- the part inside a woman where a baby develops: **womb**, (*formal*) **uterus**
- a small seed that is produced inside a woman: **egg**
- one of the parts inside a woman that produce eggs: **ovary**

- when a woman loses blood from the uterus about once a month, she **has** her **period**, (*formal*) **menstruates**
- the process or time of menstruating: **period**, (*formal*) **menstruation** (*noun* U)
- a pad that women use to soak up blood during menstruation: **sanitary towel** (*AmE* **sanitary napkin**)
- a roll of cotton wool that women place inside their body to soak up blood during menstruation: **tampon**
- the time in a woman's life when she stops menstruating: **menopause**

- having a baby developing inside: **pregnant**; *noun* (U): **pregnancy** ◦ *a pregnant woman* ◦ *six months pregnant*
- to become pregnant: **conceive**; *noun* (U): **conception** ◦ *Unfortunately, she was unable to conceive.*

▷ more on pregnancy and birth ⇨ BIRTH

■ male
- the part of a man's body that he uses for having sex and for passing waste water: **penis**
- the hardening of the penis when a man is sexually excited: **erection** ◦ *to have/get an erection*
- a very small cell that is produced by a man or male animal and that can join with a female egg to create a new life: **sperm**
- the liquid which contains sperm: **sperm** (*noun* U), **semen** (*noun* U)
- to send out semen from the penis: **ejaculate**; *noun* (C/U): **ejaculation**
- one of the two male sex organs that produce sperm: **testicle**

- if a man is not capable of having sexual intercourse, he is **impotent**; *noun* (U): **impotence**

■ contraception
- ways of controlling the number of children in a family: **birth control** (*noun* U), **family planning** (*noun* U) ◦ *a family planning clinic*
- ways of preventing a woman becoming pregnant: **contraception** (*noun* U) ◦ *methods of contraception*
- a particular method of preventing a woman becoming pregnant: **contraceptive**
- a rubber covering that a man wears over his penis: **condom** (*AmE* **rubber**)
- a small piece of plastic or metal that a woman keeps in her womb: **coil, IUD**
- a contraceptive pill that a woman takes regularly: **the pill**; to use this pill: **be on the pill**; to start taking the pill: **go* on the pill**
- to make a person unable to have children: **sterilize** sb; *noun* (U): **sterilization**
- an operation that makes a man unable to have children: **vasectomy**

■ **MORE ...**
- a person (usually female) who has never had sex: **virgin**; the state of being a virgin: **virginity** (*noun* U)
- the state of being without sexual experience by your own choice: **chastity** (*noun* U) ◦ *a vow of chastity*
- the age at which a person can agree to have sex according to the law: **age of consent** ◦ *Do you think that Parliament should lower the age of consent?*

---

shadow ⇨ LIGHT[2]

---

shape

1 describing shapes
2 some common shapes
3 being or becoming or making a shape
the shape of people's bodies ⇨ BODY

1 describing shapes

- the physical outline or outer form of sth: **shape**, (usually used when talking about shapes in art) **form** ◦ *What shape is the room?* ◦ *an unusual shape* ◦ *to change the shape of sth* ◦ *She made a statue in the form of a horse.*

shape *contd.*

- having a certain shape: **shaped** (**like** sth), **in the shape of** sth ◦ *The lake was shaped like an 'S'.* ◦ *a heart-shaped birthday card* ◦ *a cake made in the shape of a house*

- a thing which does not have an attractive or a definite shape is **shapeless** ◦ *a shapeless dress*
- if sth loses its correct shape, it is **out of shape** ◦ *The first time I washed my pullover it went out of shape.*

- if sth is evenly shaped, with equal sides and angles, it is **regular**; *opposite*: **irregular** ◦ *A square is a regular shape.* ◦ *an irregular pattern*
- if sth has two halves, one of which is the mirror image of the other, it is **symmetrical**; *noun* (U): **symmetry** ◦ *a symmetrical design* ◦ *perfect symmetry*
- the area of mathematics concerned with angles, lines, shapes, etc: **geometry** (*noun* U)

- the length, width or height of sth: **dimension** ◦ *What are the dimensions of the room?*
- having two dimensions; flat: **two-dimensional** ◦ *A square is a two-dimensional shape.*
- not flat; having the three dimensions of height, length and width: **three-dimensional**
- an object which has length, width and height (especially in mathematics): **solid** ◦ *A cube is a solid.*

- a line that shows the shape or outside edge of sth: **outline** ◦ *She drew the outline of a horse and then coloured it in.*
- the outline or shape of the outer surface of sth (especially of natural curves): **contour** ◦ *the earth's contours* ◦ *the contours of sb's body*

2 some common shapes

■ shapes with straight lines

	shape	adjective
	square	**square**
	rectangle, oblong	**rectangular, oblong**
	triangle	**triangular**
	parallelogram	
	star	**star-shaped**
	cross	**cross-shaped**
	diamond	**diamond-shaped**

- a shape with 5 straight sides: **pentagon**; *adjective*: **pentagonal**
- a shape with 6 straight sides: **hexagon**; *adjective*: **hexagonal**
- a shape with 7 straight side: **heptagon**; *adjective*: **heptagonal**
- a shape with 8 straight sides: **octagon**; *adjective*: **octagonal**

■ round and curved shapes

	shape	adjective
	circle	**circular, round**
	semicircle	**semicircular**
	oval	**oval**
	crescent	**crescent-shaped**

▷ more on circles ⇨ CIRCLE

■ shapes which have three dimensions

	shape	adjective
	cube	**cube-shaped, cuboid**
	cylinder	**cylindrical**
	pyramid	**pyramidal**
	cone	**conical**
	sphere	**spherical, ball-shaped**

- something that is made into the shape of a cylinder by winding it around itself: **roll** ◦ *a roll of toilet paper* ◦ *a roll of film* ◦ *a roll of cloth*
- a length of rope, wire, etc that has been wound into a round shape: **coil**
- a long curve that moves upwards going round and round a central point: **spiral**

- curved outwards like the outside of a ball: **convex**; *opposite*: **concave**

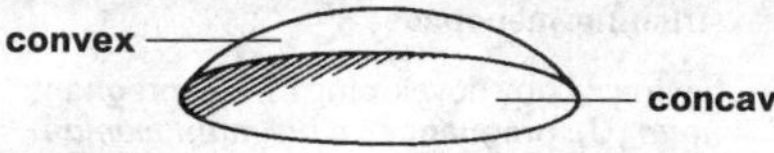

3 being or becoming or making a shape

- to have a particular shape or cause sth to have a shape: **form** sth ◦ *The petals of this flower form a kind of star shape.* ◦ *She took the clay and began to form it into the shape of a head.*
- to make sth into a particular shape: **shape** sth, **make*** sth **in(to) the shape of** sth ◦ *Shape the*

mixture into balls. ∘ *Why don't you make her birthday card in the shape of a cat?*
– to make sth like clay into a particular shape or form: **mould** (*AmE* **mold**) sth, **model** sth ∘ *She moulded the clay into the shape of a head.* ∘ *He modelled the figure of a man from clay.*
– to cut around the outside edge of a shape: **cut*** sth **out** ∘ *The children cut out lots of different shapes and stuck them on the walls.*

– to make sth straight: **straighten** sth (**out**)
– to make sth flat: **flatten** sth (**out**)
– to make sth that was straight into a curved shape: **bend*** sth (**into** sth) ∘ *Bend it back into shape* (= back to its original shape).
– to make sth into a roll: **roll** sth (**up**) ∘ *to roll up a carpet*
– to become the shape of a coil: **coil**; to make sth into this shape: **coil** sth (**up**) ∘ *to coil a piece of rope*
– to become the shape of a curl (= a curved shape): **curl up**; to make sth into this shape **curl** sth ∘ *an old newspaper, curling up at the edges* ∘ *The cat curled up on the sofa.* ∘ *to curl your hair*
▷ straight and not straight ⇨ STRAIGHT

share ⇨ PART/WHOLE

sharp

see also KNIFE/FORK/SPOON, CUT

– having a fine edge or point; that can cut sth or make a hole in sth easily: **sharp**; *opposite*: **blunt** ∘ *a sharp knife* ∘ *sharp teeth/nails/claws*
– the quality of being sharp: **sharpness** (*noun* U)
– to make sth sharp: **sharpen** sth ∘ *to sharpen a pencil/knife*
– to make sth blunt: **blunt** sth
– an instrument that can sharpen sth: **sharpener** ∘ *a pencil sharpener* ∘ *a knife sharpener*

– the sharp part of a knife, etc: **edge** ∘ *a sharp edge*
– the thin sharp end of sth: **point** ∘ *the point of a needle/pencil*
– having a point at one end: **pointed** ∘ *a pointed hat/nose/chin*
– a piece of metal, wood, etc that has a sharp point at one end: **spike** ∘ *On the top of the wall are sharp spikes so that people cannot climb over.*

– to make a small hole in sth or cause sb pain with a sharp point: **prick** sth; the sharp pain that you feel when sth pricks you: **prick** ∘ *She pricked her finger with a needle.* ∘ *She felt a sharp prick as the needle went into her finger.*
– to make a mark on a surface with sth sharp: **scratch** (sb/sth) ∘ *The table was badly scratched.* ∘ *Don't pick up that cat – it'll scratch.*
▷ sharp parts of plants and animals ⇨ PLANT, ANIMAL

sheep

see also ANIMAL, FARM

– an animal that is kept on farms and that is used for its wool and meat: **sheep** (*plural* **sheep**) ∘ *a sheep farm*
– an adult male sheep: **ram**
– an adult female sheep: **ewe**
– a young sheep: **lamb**

– the noise that sheep make: **bleat**, **baa**; *verb*: **bleat**

– a group of sheep: **flock**
– a person who looks after sheep: **shepherd**
– a dog that is trained to control sheep on a farm: **sheepdog**

– the soft hair of sheep, goats, etc: **wool** (*noun* U)
– the skin and the wool of a sheep or a lamb which is used to make coats and rugs: **sheepskin** (*noun* U), **lambskin** (*noun* U) ∘ *a sheepskin rug*

– meat from a sheep: **mutton** (*noun* U)
– meat from a lamb: **lamb** (*noun* U)
▷ more on wool and meat ⇨ WOOL, MEAT

shine ⇨ LIGHT[2]

ship ⇨ BOAT

shirt ⇨ CLOTHES

shoe

see also CLOTHES

– a covering for your foot, usually made of leather or plastic: **shoe** ∘ *I bought a strong pair of shoes to go walking in the hills.* ∘ *I've lost my right shoe*

shoe *contd.*

– have you seen it? ∘ *Those shoes look too small for you.* ∘ *tennis/ballet/gym shoes* ∘ *high-heeled shoes*
- a shoe that covers your foot and ankle, and sometimes part of your leg: **boot** ∘ *walking boots*
- a waterproof boot made of rubber: **wellington**, **wellington boot** (*AmE* **rubber boot**), (*informal*) **welly**
- a light canvas sports shoe: **gym shoe**, (*BrE*) **plimsoll**, (*AmE*) **sneaker**
- a soft shoe that you wear for running or for leisure wear: **trainer**
- an open shoe that you wear in the summer: **sandal**

- the skin of animals, used to make shoes, etc: **leather** (*noun* U) ∘ *Are those boots made of leather or plastic?*
- soft leather which does not have a smooth surface and which feels like cloth: **suede** (*noun* U) ∘ *a pair of suede shoes*

■ wearing shoes
- to have shoes on: **wear*** sth ∘ *She was wearing a pair of red leather shoes with very high heels.*
- to place shoes on your feet: **put*** sth **on** ∘ *I'm coming! – I'm just putting my shoes on.*
- to remove your shoes: **take*** sth **off** ∘ *These boots are very difficult to take off.*
- to fasten your shoes: **do*** sth **up**; (with laces) **lace** sth **up**, **tie** sth ∘ *Do up/Tie your shoelaces.*
- shoe laces which are not fastened are **undone** ∘ *Your shoelaces are undone.*

- if you are not wearing any socks or shoes, you are **barefoot** (*adjective, adverb*) ∘ *barefoot children* ∘ *It's nice to walk barefoot on wet grass.*

■ buying shoes and looking after them
- a shop where you buy shoes: **shoe shop** (*AmE* **shoe store**)
- a person who makes shoes: **shoemaker**

- one of a set of fixed measurements of clothes or shoes: **size** ∘ *What size shoes do you take?* ∘ *Have you got these boots in a size 39?*
- if shoes are the right size for you, they **fit** you ∘ *These boots don't fit properly – my feet are killing me.*
- if shoes are too small for you and hurt you, they **pinch** (you/your toes) ∘ *My new shoes pinch.*

- to make your shoes clean and shiny: **clean** sth, **polish** sth ∘ *Do you ever clean your shoes?* ∘ *well-polished boots*
- a brush that you use for cleaning shoes: **shoe brush**
- a substance that you use to polish shoes: **shoe polish** (*noun* U)

- if your shoes need repairing, you take them to the **shoe-mender's**, **shoe repair shop**
- if the heel has come off, you need to have your shoes **heeled**
- if the sole needs replacing, you need to have your shoes **soled** ∘ *I'd like these shoes soled and heeled please.*

shoot ⇨ GUN

shop

1 big shops, small shops and shopping centres
2 kinds of shop: what they sell or the service they provide
3 parts of shops
4 going shopping
5 managing a shop

see also BUY, SELL

1 big shops, small shops and shopping centres

- a building or part of a building where things are bought and sold: **shop** (*AmE* **store**)

■ big shops
- a large shop that sells food, drink, things for cleaning your house, etc: **supermarket**
- a very large supermarket, usually outside a town: **hypermarket**, **superstore**
- a large shop selling particular kinds of goods: **store** ∘ *a furniture store* ∘ *a DIY store*
- a large shop that is divided into departments selling many different kinds of goods: **department store**

■ small shops
- a small local shop, often situated on a street corner, selling food, drink, etc: **corner shop**
- a very small simple shop selling newspapers, cigarettes, etc: **kiosk**
- a small shop with an open front or a table with things for sale in a market, street, railway station, etc: **stall**

■ shopping areas
- many shops are in the **town centre** or the **city centre**; if you are going to the shops, you can say you are going **into town**

- an area where there are many shops, especially in a large modern building outside the town centre: **shopping centre**
- a special area for shops where cars are not allowed: **shopping precinct**
- an area of shops which is covered (= has a roof): **shopping arcade** (*AmE* **shopping mall**)

2 kinds of shop: what they sell or the service they provide

▷ kinds of shop, see tables on pages 403 and 404

3 parts of shops

- the window of a shop, in which goods are displayed: **window**, **shop window** ∘ *I saw the coat I wanted in the window.*

a shop that sells ...	is called ...	the person who works there is a(n) ...
books, paper		
books	**bookshop** (*AmE* **bookstore**)	**bookseller**
newspapers and magazines	**newsagent's (shop)**	**newsagent**
newspapers, etc at a railway station, etc	**bookstall** (*AmE* **news-stand**)	
pens, pencils, paper, etc (= stationery)	**stationer's**	**stationer**
tapes, CDs, etc	**record shop, music shop**	
food, drink		
bread, cakes, etc	**baker's (shop)**	**baker**
cigarettes, etc (= tobacco)	**tobacconist's (shop)**	**tobacconist**
fish	**fishmonger's**	**fishmonger**
food and other things for the household (= groceries)	**grocer's (shop)**	**grocer**
food which is special or foreign	**delicatessen**	
fruit and vegetables	**greengrocer's (shop)**	**greengrocer**
healthy food	**health food shop**	
meat	**butcher's (shop)**	**butcher**
wine, beer, etc (= alcohol)	**off-licence** (*AmE* **package store**)	
clothes		
clothes	**clothes shop**	
dresses and other women's clothes	**dress shop**	
shoes	**shoe shop**	
for the house		
beds, tables, chairs, etc (= furniture)	**furniture shop**	
flowers	**florist's (shop), flower shop**	**florist**
medicines and toilet things, for example soap	**chemist's (shop), pharmacy** (*AmE* **drugstore**)	**chemist, pharmacist** (*AmE* **druggist**)
old furniture, pictures, etc (= antiques)	**antique shop**	**antique dealer**
paint, nails, tools, etc for improving your house	**DIY store**	
pots and pans and other household things	**hardware shop**	
plants, seeds, garden tools, etc	**garden centre**	
toys	**toyshop**	

- (in a large shop) a part which sells one particular kind of thing: **department** ◦ *the furniture department* ◦ *the electrical goods department*
- a part which is on a particular level: **floor** ◦ *Can you tell me which floor children's wear is on, please?*
- a moving staircase in a large shop: **escalator**
- a machine for moving from one floor to another: **lift** (*AmE* **elevator**)

- the place (a table or other long flat surface) where customers are served: **counter**
- the place in a supermarket where the customers pay for what they buy: **checkout** ◦ *There was a long queue at the checkout.*
- a machine which the shopkeeper uses to keep money in and to add up the amount to be paid: **till**

4 going shopping

- a person in a shop who wants to buy sth: **customer** ◦ *She's a regular customer here* (= she uses this shop often).
- to go out and buy different things in different shops: **go* shopping, shop** ◦ *Let's go shopping together.* ◦ *I spent the morning shopping.*
- to look in several shops for sth to compare prices, etc: **shop around** (**for** sth) ◦ *If you want a bargain, you'd better shop around.*
- to spend time pleasantly, looking round a shop, without a clear idea of what you are looking for: **look, browse** ◦ *'Can I help you madam?' 'It's all right thank you, I'm just browsing.'*
- to go out to look at what is in the shops but not to buy anything: **go* window shopping** ◦ *I've no money to buy anything but I still love going window shopping.*

- a person who sells things in a shop: **shop assistant, sales assistant** (*AmE* **salesclerk** or **clerk**)
- to help a customer: **help** sb, **serve** sb; the help given: **service** (*noun* U) ◦ *Could you help me please, I'm looking for some gloves?* ◦ *'Are you being served?' 'Yes I am, thank you very much.'*
- to put paper round sth to cover it and protect it: **wrap** sth (**up**) ◦ *Could you wrap the flowers for me please?*

a shop where you can ...	is called ...	the person who works there is a(n) ...
arrange a holiday, buy air tickets, etc	**travel agency / agent's**	**travel agent**
arrange to buy or sell a house	**estate agent's**	**estate agent** (*AmE* **realtor, real estate agent**)
have your eyes tested and buy glasses	**optician's**	**optician**
have your face, hands, etc cared for	**beauty parlour / salon**	**beautician**
have your hair cut	**hairdresser's** or (for men) **barber's shop**	**hairdresser**
have your photographs processed	**photographer's, chemist's**	
have photographs taken	**photographer's**	**photographer**
hire or buy video tapes of films	**video shop**	
place a bet on a horse race, etc	**betting shop**	**bookmaker**
take your clothes to be cleaned	**dry-cleaner's**	
wash your clothes in a washing machine	**launderette**	

- (in a clothes shop) to see whether sth will suit you or fit you: **try** sth **on** ◦ *Could I try this on please?*
- if you do not like sth you have bought or if it does not fit, you may want to **take*** it **back**, **return** it ◦ *I don't think this skirt quite suits me; I'll have to take it back.*
- if you take sth back to a shop and get sth else instead, you **change** it (**for** sth), **exchange** it (**for** sth) ◦ *I'd like to change this cardigan for another one in a lighter colour.*
- if you do not want anything else and the shop gives you your money back, you **get*** your **money back**, **get* a refund** ◦ *'If I don't like this, will I be able to get my money back?' 'No, but we'll exchange it for you.'*

- a cart on wheels used by customers in supermarkets for carrying things: **shopping trolley, supermarket trolley**

5 managing a shop
- the person who owns or manages a small shop: **shopkeeper** (*AmE* **storekeeper**)
- the person who manages a large shop: **manager**; a female manager can also be called a **manageress**

- a person who guards things in a shop: **security guard**

■ the things that a shop has for sale
- to keep a particular kind of thing for sale in a shop: **stock** sth, **keep*** sth, **have/keep*** sth **in stock**
- to have sth in the shop at a particular time: **be in/out of stock** ◦ *'Do you have these sweatshirts in a larger size?' 'Yes, normally we do, but I'm afraid we're out of stock at the moment.'*
- if a shop does not have sth which it normally sells, it is **out** (**of** it) ◦ *The supermarket is completely out of bread.*

■ open and shut
- when a shop is selling things, it is **open**; when it is not selling things, it is **closed**, **shut**
- the time when it is normally open: **opening hours** (*noun plural*), **business hours** (*noun plural*)
- the day of the week when some small shops close early, normally at the end of the morning: **early-closing day**

- when a new shop starts in business, it **opens**
- when it finally goes out of business, it **closes** (**down**)

- an event when most things in a shop are sold more cheaply: **sale**; if sth is being sold in this way, it is **in the sale** (*AmE* **on sale**) ◦ *I bought this coat in the sale.*
- the time when many shops reduce their prices: **the sales** (*noun plural*) ◦ *the January sales*

short
- time ⇨ LONG/SHORT[1]
- distance ⇨ LONG/SHORT[2]

shout ⇨ SPEAK

show

1 letting sth be seen
2 showing sb a place
3 giving information
see also SEE

1 letting sth be seen
- to make it possible for a person to see sb/sth: **show*** sb/sth (**to** sb), **show*** sb sb/sth, **let*** sb **see*** sb/sth ◦ *Show me your photos.* ◦ *She showed the picture to him.* ◦ *Please show your ticket at the gate.*
- to show sth so that sb else can examine it: **produce** sth ◦ *You'll have to produce your passport when you check in at the hotel.*

- to use your finger or a stick to make sb see sth: **point** (**at/to** sb/sth) ◦ *She pointed at me and said it was my fault.* ◦ *I pointed to the thing I wanted.*
- to make sb notice sb/sth: **point** sb/sth **out** (**to** sb) ◦ *Can you point him out to me when we get to the party?*
- to use your hands or a part of your body to show sth: **indicate** sth ◦ *The man indicated, with a nod of his head, that he understood.*

- to allow a particular feeling or quality to be seen or expressed: **show*** sth, **display** sth; *noun*: **display** ◦ *Her face showed how happy she was.* ◦ *to show your feelings* ◦ *a display of courage*
- to show sth that was previously hidden: **reveal** sth ◦ *The curtains opened to reveal a stage full of children.*
- to allow sth to be seen: **show*** sth ◦ *This carpet is a good colour – it doesn't show the dirt.*
- to be able to be seen: **show*** ◦ *If you turn the cloth round, the stain won't show.*

■ exhibitions
- to put sth in a place where people will see it: **show*** sth, **display** sth; an arrangement of things for people to see: **display** ◦ *We will show our new dress collection at the beginning of next year.* ◦ *Her work was displayed on the walls of every room.* ◦ *a beautiful display of roses*
- an occasion on which the public can see a display of things: **show, display**; the things are **on show, on display** ◦ *a fashion show* ◦ *a firework display* ◦ *The competition entries are on show in the town hall.*

- a collection of objects, particularly paintings, sculptures, etc that the public can go to see: **exhibition**; one of these objects: **exhibit**; the objects are **on exhibition, on view** ◦ *an art exhibition* ◦ *an exhibition of famous pictures* ◦ *The museum has more than two thousand exhibits.* ◦ *The paintings are on view until next month.*
- to show pictures, sculptures, etc to the public: **exhibit** sth ◦ *Her work has been exhibited all over Europe.*
- a large exhibition of commercial or industrial goods: **fair** ◦ *a trade fair* ◦ *a book fair*

2 showing sb a place
- to take a person to see the different parts of a place: **show*** sb **round/around** (sth); a person who does this as a job: **guide** ◦ *Would you like me to show you round the city?* ◦ *The exhibition is in several rooms – the guides will show you around.*
- to take a person to see the different parts of a building, etc: **show*** sb **over** sth ◦ *I was shown all over the factory.* ◦ *They showed us over the new extension to the hospital.*

- to show a person how to get somewhere: **show*** sb **to** a place, **show*** sb **the way** (**to** a place) ◦ *Could you show me the way out, please?*
- to help a person to find the right way to go: **guide** sb ◦ *She guided me through the narrow streets to the cathedral.*

3 giving information
- to allow a person to see how to do sth: **show*** sth **to** sb, **show*** sb sth, **demonstrate** sth **to** sb; *noun*: **demonstration** ◦ *I showed him how to make a fruit cake.* ◦ *Please show me what to do next.* ◦ *The stewardess demonstrated the emergency procedures.* ◦ *to give a demonstration of how to do sth*
- information about how to do sth: **directions** (*noun plural*) ◦ *Just follow the directions on the packet – they're very clear.*

■ signs
- something that is written or drawn that gives information: **mark** ◦ *A mark on the side of the building indicated where the water had risen to.*
- a machine or device that gives information: **indicator** ◦ *We could see from the indicator that we were getting low in petrol.*
- a sign, etc that shows or points to sth: **indication** ◦ *He gave no indication that he was angry.*

▷ more on signs ⇨ SIGN

---

shut ⇨ OPEN/SHUT

---

shy ⇨ BEHAVIOUR

---

sick ⇨ ILLNESS

---

side ⇨ PLACE²

---

sign

1 signs and their functions
2 some written signs
3 signs we make with movements of the body
see also LANGUAGE, MEANING

1 signs and their functions
- a shape or mark, a movement of the body, or a situation that has a particular meaning: **sign** ◦ *a road sign* ◦ *the signs of the Zodiac* ◦ *He gave a sign and everyone was silent.*
- to be a sign of sth: **mean*** sth, (*formal*) **signify** sth ◦ *If you put up your hand it means you want to say something.* ◦ *What does that red star signify?*

- a picture, object, etc that represents an idea or an aspect of life: **symbol**; *adjective*: **symbolic** ◦ *A cross is the symbol of Christianity.* ◦ *In some cultures, green is symbolic of life.*
- the use of symbols, especially in art and literature: **symbolism** (*noun* U) ◦ *poetry full of religious symbolism*
- to be a symbol of sth: **symbolize** sth, **stand* for** sth, **represent** sth ◦ *The small child in the picture symbolizes youth.* ◦ *The 'P' on this signpost stands for 'parking'.* ◦ *On this map, a cross represents a church.*

- a symbol used by an organization or other group: **emblem** ◦ *The emblem of Ireland is a shamrock.*

sign *contd.*

- a sign used by a business that shows the name of the company in a way which helps people to remember it: **logo** (*plural* **logos**) ◦ *design a new company logo*

■ signs which give information and instructions
- a sign that tells people to do sth: **signal**; to give a signal: **signal** (sth) ◦ *The train stopped at a red signal.* ◦ *The policeman signalled to the driver to stop.* ◦ *He signalled to me that I should finish speaking.*
- a sign at the side of the road that gives information about driving conditions: **road sign**
- a sign at the side of the road that gives information about directions and distances to towns: **signpost** ◦ *The signpost says it's 50 miles to York.*

- a sign that shows where sth is: **marker** ◦ *Motorway marker posts show you where the nearest telephone is.*

- something in a situation that tells you sth: (*formal*) **indication** ◦ *There is some indication that the economy is improving.*
- when a sign gives us information about sth, we say that it **means*** sth, **indicates** sth, (*formal*) is **indicative of** sth ◦ *This sign indicates that the computer is saving your text.* ◦ *A cross means that your answer is wrong; a tick means that it is right.* ◦ *His refusal to help us is indicative of how selfish he is.*
- a sign of illness or sth bad: **symptom** ◦ *You have all the symptoms of a bad cold – headache, sore throat and a cough.*
- a sign that tells us that sth is going to happen in the future: **omen** ◦ *a good/bad omen*

2 some written signs

- a sign (*) which calls attention to sth in a text: **asterisk**
- a sign (⇨) which shows a direction: **arrow**
- a sign (✓) which shows that sth is correct: **tick** (*AmE* **check**)
- a sign (×) which shows that sth is wrong or which shows the position of sth: **cross**

▷ signs for money ⇨ **MONEY**

▷ signs in mathematics ⇨ **NUMBER**

- to mark sth with a tick: **tick** sth (**off**) ◦ *If you finish a job, please tick it off the list.*
- something that is written or drawn which has a meaning: **mark** ◦ *Put a mark in the margin if you notice any problems.*
- a written symbol which helps us to understand a text and divides up sentences: **punctuation mark**

▷ more on punctuation marks ⇨ **PUNCTUATION**

3 signs we make with movements of the body

- a movement of the body which has a particular meaning: **gesture, sign**
- to make this kind of movement: **gesture, make* a gesture, make*/give* a sign** ◦ *He gestured to me to go and speak to him.* ◦ *She made a sign for them to go in.*

- to move your hand from side to side when saying hello or goodbye, or in order to attract sb's attention: **wave, give*** sb **a wave** ◦ *We waved goodbye until we couldn't see them any more.* ◦ *As the train pulled out of the station, she gave me a last wave.*
- to raise your shoulders and drop them again, as a way of showing that you do not know sth or that you do not care about sth: **shrug** (your **shoulders**), **give* a shrug** ◦ *Don't just shrug! Say something!*
- to move your head up and down as a way of showing that you understand or that you agree: **nod** (your **head**), **give* a nod** ◦ *'Don't you think we need to do something about this problem?' I asked. 'Yes,' she nodded.*
- to move your head from side to side as a way of showing that you disagree: **shake*** your **head** ◦ *I waited for an answer. Finally he shook his head and said no.*
- to use your hand or finger to show sb that you want them to follow you or come closer to you: **beckon** (sb) ◦ *He beckoned to me to follow him into his office.*

silence

- no noise ⇨ **QUIET**
- not speaking ⇨ **SPEAK**

silver ⇨ GOLD/SILVER

similar ⇨ SAME

simple

- easy to do or understand ⇨ **EASY/DIFFICULT**
- not complicated in design ⇨ **DESIGN**

since ⇨ TIME

sing

see also MUSIC, POP/ROCK, RECORD

- to make musical sounds with your voice: **sing***; *noun* (U): **singing** ◦ *to sing a song* ◦ *She sang to the children.* ◦ *What lovely singing!* ◦ *singing lessons* ◦ *a singing teacher*
- to sing a tune with your lips closed: **hum** (sth) ◦ *Just hum the tune if you don't know the words.* ◦ *She was humming quietly as she worked.*
- a person who writes songs: **songwriter**

■ songs

- a piece of music which has words that you sing: **song** ◦ *a pop/folk/blues song* ◦ *a love song*
- a single musical sound made by a voice or a musical instrument: **note** ◦ *I can only remember the first few notes of the song.*
- an arrangement of notes to make a pleasant pattern: **tune**, **melody** ◦ *I can never remember the tune of that song.*

- a group of lines that forms one part of a song: **verse**
- the part of a song that is repeated at the end of each verse: **chorus**

- a song which is sung gently in order to help a child to go to sleep: **lullaby**
- a traditional poem for children, often set to music: **nursery rhyme**

- a song sung in churches: **hymn**
- a kind of hymn with words from the Bible: **psalm**
- a song sung at Christmas: **carol**

- the official song of a country, played at public events: **national anthem**
- a song which is often repeated in a film, musical, etc: **theme** (**tune**)

■ singers

- a person who sings: **singer** ◦ *an opera singer* ◦ *a jazz singer*
- a large group of people who sing together: **choir** ◦ *the church choir* ◦ *to sing in a choir*
- a person who sings alone: **soloist**

- the kind of sound that you make when you sing or speak is your **voice** ◦ *What kind of singing voice has she got?* ◦ *a high/low voice*

- a woman, boy or girl with a high singing voice: **soprano** (*plural* **sopranos**)
- a young boy's high singing voice: **treble**
- a woman with a low voice: **contralto** (*plural* **contraltos**)
- a man with a very high voice: **alto** (*plural* **altos**)
- a man who has the highest normal singing voice: **tenor**
- a man with a fairly low voice: **baritone**
- a man with a very low voice: **bass**

■ **MORE ...**

- if people sing exactly the same thing together, they sing **in unison**
- if people sing different notes or tunes that combine together pleasantly, they sing **in harmony**

- a street musician who plays or sings for money: **busker**; what this person does: **busking** (*noun* U) ◦ *He's got no job but he earns a bit from busking.*

single ⇨ ONE

sister ⇨ FAMILY

sit

1 things to sit on
2 sitting in a place
3 ways of sitting
see also STAND, LIE[2]

1 things to sit on

- a thing used for sitting on: **seat**
- a seat with a back, for one person to sit on: **chair**
- a bag filled with soft material that you put on a chair, etc to make it comfortable: **cushion**

▷ more on chairs ⇨ CHAIR

- a long wooden or metal seat for two or more people, often outdoors: **bench**
- a long seat in a church: **pew**
- a seat on a bicycle or motorcycle: **saddle**
- a seat that you put on a horse so that you can ride it: **saddle**

- the flat area that is formed by the upper parts of your legs when you are sitting down: **lap**, **knee** ◦ *The child sat on his mother's lap as she read him a story.* ◦ *Come and sit on my knee.*

2 sitting in a place

- to be in a position (usually on a chair) in which your back is upright and your weight is supported at the bottom of your back: **sit*** ◦ *She was sitting on a chair, reading a book.*
- to put your body into a sitting position: **sit*** (**down**), **take* a seat**, (*more formal*) **be seated** ◦ *Would you like to sit down over here?* ◦ *I took a seat at the front of the hall.* ◦ *Please be seated. The show is about to begin.*
- to move into a sitting position after you have been lying down: **sit* up** ◦ *Jerry woke suddenly and sat up in bed.*
- to sit and do nothing active for a period of time: (*informal*) **sit* about/around** ◦ *I went into the living room where everyone was sitting around watching TV.*

- a place for sb to sit: **seat**, **place** ◦ *Don't sit there. That's Doug's place.* ◦ *Save me a place next to you.*

sit *contd.*

– when a seat has nobody sitting in it, it is **free**; when a seat has sb sitting in it, it is **taken** ◦ *'Is this seat free?' 'No, I'm sorry. It's taken.'*
– to have seats for a particular number of people: **seat . . .** ◦ *This plane seats three hundred people.*

– to lead sb to their seat: **show*** sb **to** their **seat**
– to put sb into a sitting position: **sit*** sb (**down**) ◦ *Margaret sat her baby on the floor.*

■ to stop sitting
– to move into a standing position from your seat: **get* up**, **stand* up**, (*more formal*) **rise*** ◦ *When the performance was over the audience rose from their seats and cheered wildly.*

3 ways of sitting

– the way that a person is sitting: **position** ◦ *She was sitting in a very uncomfortable position on the arm of the chair.*
– to sit with a straight back: sit **upright**
– to relax (in a chair, etc) and not take an active part in what other people are doing: **sit* back** ◦ *Just you sit back and relax while I make the dinner.*
– to put yourself in a comfortable position in a chair: **settle back** ◦ *We settled back in our seats to watch the film.*
– to sit or stand in a lazy way; to relax: **lounge** ◦ *They were lounging on the sofa watching television.*
– to sit without moving: sit **still** ◦ *Sit still, will you? I can't see the screen.*

– to sit down with your feet on the ground and your bottom just above the ground: **squat**
– to sit with your legs on each side of sth: sit **astride** sth ◦ *to sit astride a horse*
– to sit on the floor with your legs pulled up in front of you and with one leg or foot placed over the other: sit **cross-legged**
– to sit on a chair with one leg over the other: **sit* with** your **legs crossed**
– to go down on one or both knees: **kneel*** (**down**)

situation

the place that sth is in ⇨ PLACE[1]

– the things that are happening in a particular place or at a particular time: **situation**, **state of affairs** ◦ *the current situation* ◦ *a changing situation* ◦ *a worrying/difficult state of affairs*

– the facts and events that affect what happens in a particular situation: **circumstances** (*noun plural*) ◦ *the circumstances of sb's death* ◦ *In normal circumstances you would not be allowed in, but we'll make an exception in this case.*
– as a result of a particular situation: **in/under the circumstances** ◦ *Under the circumstances, I think it would be better if you left.*
– facts and events that affect the way that people live, etc: **conditions** (*noun plural*) ◦ *Road conditions were very bad.* ◦ *excellent working conditions*
– the conditions in which you live, work, etc: **environment** ◦ *a pleasant environment in which to work*

– a particular state or situation: **position** ◦ *What would you do in my position?* ◦ *He's put me in a very difficult position.* ◦ *I'm sorry, I'm not in a position to give you that information.*
– a particular situation or a situation of a particular type: **case** ◦ *In some cases, it is possible to get a definite answer immediately.* ◦ *In my case, things were a bit different.*

– the events or place around or within which sth occurs: **background** ◦ *It is against this background that the events of 1968 took place.* ◦ *the cultural/social background to an event*
– the situation in which sth happens and which helps us to understand it: **context** ◦ *the political context of an election* ◦ *in the context of recent social developments*
– the present situation in a particular area of activity: **scene** ◦ *After his injury, he was happy to get back to the football scene again.* ◦ *the fashion scene*

– to emphasize that a particular situation exists, you can say **the fact** (**of the matter**) **is** ◦ *The fact is that the population is getting older.*

size

1 size
2 measurement
3 comparing things of different sizes
4 the right size

1 size

– how big or small sth is: **size** (*noun* C/U) ◦ *the size of a building/person/car* ◦ *They're the same size.* ◦ *This box is four times the size of that one.* ◦ *The batteries you bought weren't the right size.* ◦

They've got this shirt in lots of different sizes. ◦ *an animal the size of a small dog*

- big in size or amount: **big**, **large**; *opposites*: **small**, **little** ◦ *big men/boxes/shoes* ◦ *a large area of desert* ◦ *a small boy* ◦ *a little girl*

▷ being big or small ⇨ **BIG / SMALL**

2 measurement

- to find the size of sb/sth: **measure** sb/sth ◦ *Can you help me measure these curtains?*
- the size or amount that is found by measuring sb/sth: **measurement** ◦ *What are your measurements?* (= all the different measurements of your body)
- to be a certain size: **measure** sth ◦ *The side of the room measures three metres.* ◦ *The garden measures about 30 yards by 95.*

- a hard piece of wood, plastic, etc used for measuring the length of things and drawing straight lines: **ruler**
- a long flexible strip of plastic, metal, etc used for measuring the length of things: **tape measure**

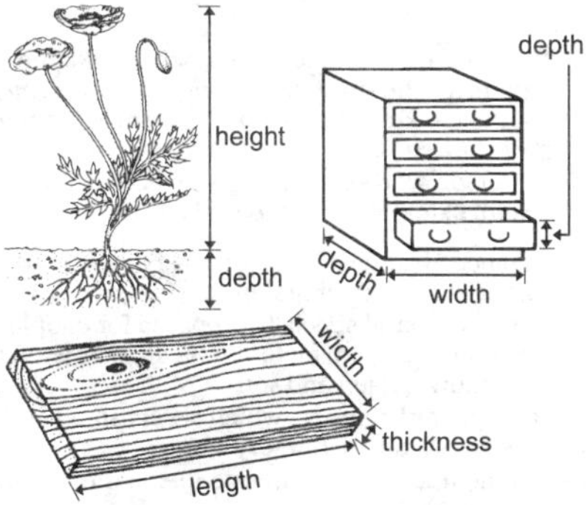

▷ more on height, length, width, thickness ⇨ **HEIGHT, LONG / SHORT[2], WIDE / NARROW, FAT / THIN / THICK**

- the size of the surface of sth: **area** (*noun* C/U) ◦ *The surface area of Great Britain is much less than that of France.* ◦ *You'll need to measure the exact area of the room.* ◦ *The total area of the farm is about 200 hectares.*
- the space that sth contains or occupies: **volume** (*noun* C/U) ◦ *You can find the volume of a box by multiplying its length by its height by its width.*

- a measurement of length, height, width, depth or thickness: **dimension** ◦ *The dimensions of a room are its height, length and width.*

■ units of measurement

- connected with the system of measurements used in most parts of the world: **metric** ◦ *the metric system*

metric measurements	
length	
a unit used for measuring small amounts	**centimetre** (**cm**)
one tenth of a centimetre	**millimetre** (**mm**)
100 centimetres	**metre** (**m**)
1 000 metres	**kilometre** (**km**)
area	
a unit used for measuring small areas	**square centimetre**
10 000 square centimetres (used for measuring areas of buildings)	**square metre**
10 000 square metres (used for measuring small areas of land)	**hectare**
100 hectares (used for measuring large areas of land)	**square kilometre**
volume	
a unit used for measuring small volumes	**cubic centimetre** (**cc**)
1 000 000 cubic centimetres	**cubic metre**

non-metric measurements	
length	
a unit used for measuring small amounts	**inch** (**in**)
twelve inches	**foot** (*plural* **feet**) (**ft**)
three feet	**yard** (**yd**)
1 760 yards	**mile**
area	
a unit used for measuring small areas	**square inch** (**sq in**)
144 square inches	**square foot** (**sq ft**)
9 square feet (used for measuring areas of buildings)	**square yard** (**sq yd**)
4 840 square yards (used for measuring small areas of land)	**acre**
640 square acres (used for measuring large areas of land)	**square mile**
volume	
a unit used for measuring volume	**cubic inch**
1 728 cubic inches	**cubic foot**
27 cubic feet	**cubic yard**

size *contd.*

■ comparing the metric and non-metric systems
- 1 inch = 2.54 centimetres
- 1 foot = 30.48 centimetres
- 1 yard = 0.914 metre
- 1 acre = 0.405 hectare
- 1 mile = 1.609 kilometres

- 1 square inch = 6.45 square centimetres
- 1 square foot = 929.03 square centimetres
- 1 square yard = 0.836 square metre
- 1 square mile = 2.59 square kilometres

- 1 cubic inch = 16.39 cubic centimetres
- 1 cubic foot = 0.028 cubic metre
- 1 cubic yard = 0.765 cubic metre

Note: when you use a measurement in front of a noun, it should not be put in the plural: ◦ *The ruler is six inches long.* ◦ *Have you got a six-inch ruler?* ◦ *We walked for five miles.* ◦ *a five-mile walk* ◦ *Our farm is 1 000 hectares.* ◦ *a 1 000-hectare farm*
Solids are measured either by using units of volume (see above) or by using units of weight: ◦ *a million cubic metres of soil* ◦ *a tonne of sand* ◦ *a pound of jam*

▷ measurement of weight ⇨ **WEIGHT**

▷ measurement of amounts of liquids ⇨ **LIQUID**

3 comparing things of different sizes

- if sth is the same in size as sth else, it is **the same size** (**as** sth), **equal** (**to** sth), the two things are **equal** (**in size**) ◦ *an area equal to England and Wales* ◦ *several items of equal weight*
- if sth is not the same in size as sth else, it is **a different size** (**to** sth), the two things are **unequal** ◦ *unequal in length*
- if things are different in size, they **vary** (**in size**); *noun* (C/U): **variation** ◦ *They're not all the same size – they vary quite a lot.* ◦ *You need to allow for variation in size.*
- two times as big as sb/sth: **double** (**the size**), **twice the size** ◦ *She's almost twice the size of her sister.*

- the relationship between the actual size of sth and its measurement on a map or plan: **scale** ◦ *What scale is the map?* ◦ *This map uses a much larger scale than that one.* ◦ *a large-scale map*
- the same size as the person or thing represented: **full-scale, life-size** ◦ *a full-scale model of a boat* ◦ *They put up a life-size statue of the president.*

▷ more on maps ⇨ **MAP**

4 the right size

- if the size of sth is good for what you need it for, it is the **right size**; *opposite*: **wrong size** ◦ *I'm afraid I bought the wrong size – can I change it?* ◦ *the right size bottle*
- if a piece of clothing is the right size or shape for sb, it **fits**, it is **a good fit** ◦ *It doesn't fit – it's too big.* ◦ *It's not a very good fit.*
- to be the right size or shape to go inside sth or onto sth: **go* in/on** (**to** sth), **fit** ◦ *The plug won't go in to the socket.* ◦ *These chair covers you bought are the wrong size – they don't fit well at all.*

▷ the sizes of clothes ⇨ **CLOTHES**

ski

see also SPORT

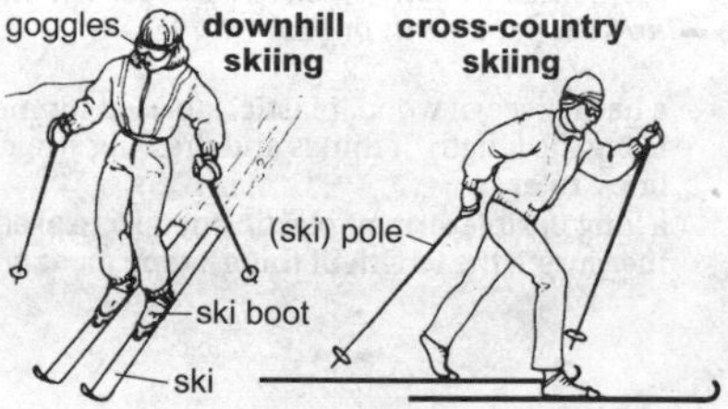

- to move over the ground using skis: **ski**; the name for the sport: **skiing** (*noun* U) ◦ *Do you ski?* (= do you know how to ski?) ◦ *We're going skiing this Christmas.* ◦ *a skiing holiday*
- a person who skis (usually sb who skis quite well): **skier** ◦ *a professional skier*

- a piece of land which people ski down: (**ski**) **slope** ◦ *a steep/gentle slope*
- a piece of land specially prepared for people to ski down: **ski run, piste** ◦ *to ski off piste* (= where the snow is deep and soft)
- a slope for beginners which is very small and easy to ski down: **nursery slope**
- a machine which carries people to the top of a slope: **ski lift**
- a slope without snow which is made of plastic, on which people practise skiing: **dry ski slope, artificial ski slope**

- down a slope from the top to the bottom: **downhill**; across the countryside: **cross-country** ◦ *I prefer cross-country skiing to downhill.* ◦ *a cross-country skier*
- a race along a course in which competitors have to move from side to side between poles: **the slalom** ◦ *to take part in the slalom*
- a platform which skiers jump off (especially in competitions): **ski jump**

- a person who teaches people to ski: **ski instructor**
- a place with hotels, slopes and ski instructors where people go on holiday to ski: **ski resort**

skill

1 kinds of skill
2 having skill
3 acquiring skill

1 kinds of skill

- the ability to do sth well: **skill (in/at** sth/doing sth) (*noun* U), (*formal*) **proficiency (in** sth/doing sth) (*noun* U) ◦ *The job requires considerable skill in dealing with people.* ◦ *his skill at drawing* ◦ *a certificate of proficiency in English*
- an ability that you need in order to do a job or perform an activity: **skill** (*often plural*) ◦ *The job needs good language skills.*
- a particular way of doing sth (often in a job) which requires a particular skill: **technique**
- skill at performing some special task: (*informal*) **knack** (*noun singular*) ◦ *It's easy to make pancakes once you've got the knack.*

2 having skill

- (used about work that is done) requiring skill or showing skill: **skilled**; *opposite*: **unskilled** ◦ *skilled/unskilled work* ◦ *a highly skilled job*

- having skill: **skilled (in/at** sth) ◦ *a skilled dressmaker* ◦ *a cook who is skilled in making bread and pastries*
- having or showing a lot of skill: **good (at** sth), **skilful (in/at** sth) (*adverb* **skilfully**), (*formal*) **proficient (in/at** sth) (*adverb* **proficiently**), **accomplished (in/at** sth) ◦ *He's very good at making bread.* ◦ *She suddenly changed direction, skilfully managing to avoid an accident.* ◦ *to speak a language proficiently* ◦ *an accomplished pianist*

- having as much skill as is needed for a particular job or task: **competent** (*adverb* **competently**); *noun* (U): **competence** ◦ *a very competent teacher* ◦ *showing a high level of competence*

■ natural skill
- the mental or physical power or skill that makes it possible to do sth: **ability** (*noun* C/U); having this kind of skill: **able, capable** ◦ *He has the ability to do well, but he doesn't try very hard.* ◦ *a young woman of considerable abilities* ◦ *a very capable student*
- a natural ability to do sth well: **talent (for** sth) (*noun* C/U), **gift (for** sth), **flair (for** sth) (*noun singular*); having this kind of ability: **talented, gifted** ◦ *She's got a lot of talent.* ◦ *She's got a gift for playing the piano.* ◦ *a flair for storytelling*

- having very great and unusual ability: **brilliant**; *noun* (U): **brilliance** ◦ *a brilliant footballer*
- having many different talents: **talented** ◦ *She's incredibly talented – good cook, fantastic painter, and brilliant at ballroom dancing.*
- good at learning and doing things: **clever** ◦ *a clever child* ◦ *a clever lawyer*
- skilful at making things with your hands: **good with** your **hands**

▷ more on being clever ⇨ CLEVER

■ not having skill
- not good at sth: **no good at** sth, **bad (at** sth), **incompetent** (*adverb* **incompetently**); *noun* (U): **incompetence** ◦ *I'm no good at public speaking.* ◦ *I'm really bad at remembering people's names.* ◦ *He was sacked for incompetence.*

3 acquiring skill

- to get knowledge or skill: **learn** sth, **learn (how) to** do sth ◦ *to learn to play the piano* ◦ *to learn how to sing*
- to learn how to do a job: **train to** do sth, **train (as** sth) ◦ *I'm training to fly jumbo jets.* ◦ *to train as a nurse*
- to do sth many times so that you become good at it: **practise** (*AmE* **practice**) (sth); *noun* (U): **practice** ◦ *You'll never improve if you don't practise.* ◦ *I think I need more practice.*
- if you have not spent much time practising sth recently, you are **out of practice** ◦ *I'd love to come and play tennis, but I'm afraid I'm a bit out of practice.*

▷ more on learning ⇨ LEARN

- to give sb lessons or show sb sth so that they know how to do it: **teach*** (sb **to** do sth) ◦ *She's very good at teaching disabled children to ride.*
- to teach a person to do sth which is difficult or which needs a lot of practice: **train** sb **(for/in** sth), **train** sb **(to** do sth); *noun* (U): **training** ◦ *to train teachers in modern methods* ◦ *to train soldiers to obey orders without thinking* ◦ *a teacher training course*

▷ more on teaching ⇨ TEACH

- if you have done sth for a long time, so that you can now do it well, you are **experienced**; *opposite*: **inexperienced** ◦ *She's a very experienced teacher.*
- a person who has special knowledge or skill: **expert (in/at** sth); *adjective*: **expert**; special knowledge or skill: **expertise** (*noun* U), (*informal*) **know-how** (*noun* U) ◦ *She's been doing it for so long now that she's become a real expert.* ◦ *Get Dan to fix your computer – he's an expert.* ◦ *to do an expert job* ◦ *The work demands considerable expertise.*

■ **MORE ...**
- if you want to say that doing sth repeatedly is the only way to become really good at it, you can say **practice makes perfect** ◦ *They say practice makes perfect, but I've been practising this piece for days and it's far from perfect!*

skill *contd.*

- doing sth in a way that shows skill, training or care: **professional** (*adverb* **professionally**); *noun* (U): **professionalism** ◦ *The builders did not do a very professional job.*
- a person who does things in a professional way: **professional** ◦ *We won't let you down – we're all professionals.*
- a person who can do many different things well (usually sports): **all-rounder**; *adjective* (*only before a noun*): **all-round** ◦ *She's a good all-round sportswoman.*
- changing easily from one skill or occupation to another: **versatile**; *noun* (U): **versatility** ◦ *He's a very versatile teacher – he can teach all levels from beginners to advanced.*

skin

1 skin colour
2 feelings on the skin
3 injuries and marks on the skin
4 looking after your skin
5 animal skins

other parts of the body ⇨ BODY

1 skin colour

- the natural outer covering of a human or animal body: **skin** (*noun* U)
- the natural colour and quality of a person's skin or face: **complexion** ◦ *She has a smooth complexion.*
- light-coloured skin is **fair**; *opposite*: **dark** ◦ *He had very fair skin.*
- the colour of a person's skin, showing their racial type: **colour** (*noun* U); this colour is usually described as **black** or **white** ◦ *laws against discrimination on grounds of colour* ◦ *black/white people*

■ changes in colour

- having less colour than usual: **pale** ◦ *You're looking a bit pale. Are you ill?*
- darker than usual because of spending time in the sun: **brown** ◦ *How did you manage to get so brown?*
- when sb's skin turns red, for example because they are embarrassed, they **blush**
- when sb's skin turns white, for example because they are frightened or ill, they **go*/turn white/pale**

2 feelings on the skin

- a feeling on your skin that makes you want to rub or scratch it: **itch**; to have this feeling: **itch**; *adjective*: **itchy** ◦ *I've got an itch.* ◦ *I'm itching all over.* ◦ *My arm feels itchy.*
- to rub an area of your skin with your fingernails: **scratch** sth ◦ *Can you scratch my back for me?* ◦ *'Stop scratching!' 'I can't; I'm all itchy.'*
- to feel a sensation of sth touching you lightly: **tickle**; to cause this feeling: **tickle** sb/sth ◦ *My nose is tickling.* ◦ *Stop tickling me!*
- feeling painful: **sore**; *noun* (U): **soreness** ◦ *a sore place on your skin*
- a sudden pain that is the result of an insect or plant pushing sth sharp into the skin: **sting**
- the liquid that comes out of your skin when you are hot, ill or afraid: **sweat** (*noun* U), (*formal*) **perspiration**; *verbs*: **sweat**, (*formal*) **perspire** ◦ *I was dripping with sweat.* ◦ *All of us were sweating profusely in the heat of the afternoon sun.*
- wet with sweat: **sweaty**
- small lumps which appear for a short time on your skin when you are ill or frightened: **goose-flesh** (*noun* U), **goose pimples** (*AmE* **goose bumps**) (*noun plural*)

3 injuries and marks on the skin

- to injure your skin because you have rubbed it against sth rough: **graze** sth, **scrape** sth; an injury caused in this way: **graze**, **scrape** ◦ *I grazed my knee when I fell on the pavement.* ◦ *She has a nasty scrape on her arm.*
- a mark on your skin that was made by sth sharp: **scratch**
- a mark that is left on the skin after a cut or wound has healed: **scar**; to leave a scar on sb: **scar** sb/sth ◦ *He was scarred for life in the accident.*
- a small red mark on your skin: **spot**, **pimple**; if you have many of these marks, you are **spotty**, **pimply**
- a small spot with a black centre: **blackhead**
- a large painful spot: **boil**
- a small brown spot: **freckle** (*usually plural*); *adjective*: **freckled** ◦ *covered in freckles* ◦ *a freckled face*
- a small dark spot that never goes away: **mole**
- a small hard lump on your skin: **wart**
- a small painful area on the skin that looks like a bubble and is caused by sunburn, by wearing shoes that are too tight, etc: **blister** ◦ *These boots give me blisters.*
- a place on your skin which hurts a lot because it has become infected: **sore**
- a skin condition that causes a lot of spots on the face and neck: **acne** (*noun* U)
- an area of small red spots that you sometimes get when you are ill or after you have been stung by an insect: **rash**
- if you suddenly become covered in spots, you **come* out in** sth, **break* out in** sth ◦ *She came out in a rash.* ◦ *to break out in spots*
- lines that appear on your face as you get older: **wrinkles**, **lines**; *adjective*: **wrinkled** ◦ *an old man with a wrinkled face*

4 looking after your skin

■ skin qualities

- if your skin has a flat surface with no lumps, it is **smooth**; *noun* (U): **smoothness**
- if your skin is not smooth, it is **rough**; *noun* (U): **roughness**

- if it is pleasant to touch and not rough, it is **soft**; *noun* (U): **softness**
- if it has no marks on it, it is **clear**
- a mark on your skin that spoils your appearance: **blemish**

■ skin treatment
- substances that are used to make the skin look attractive: **cosmetics** (*noun plural*)
- a liquid that you use on your skin: **lotion** (*noun* U) ◦ *body lotion*
- a substance that you put on sore skin to make it heal: **ointment** (*noun* U)

▷ more on cosmetics ⇨ COSMETICS

■ the effect of the sun on skin
- to sit or lie in the sun so that your skin becomes brown: **sunbathe**
- the brown colour which people get on their skin when they sunbathe: **suntan, tan**; *adjective*: **suntanned** ◦ *a good suntan* ◦ *suntanned bodies*
- to become burned by the sun: **burn, catch* the sun** ◦ *I usually don't spend much time in the sun as I burn easily.* ◦ *You really have caught the sun, haven't you?*
- red painful skin that you get by spending too much time in the sun: **sunburn** (*noun* U); suffering from sunburn: **sunburnt**
- if your skin comes off in small pieces, it **peels** ◦ *My neck caught the sun yesterday and now it is starting to peel.*
- an oil or liquid that you put on your skin to reduce the effects of sunburn: **suntan oil/lotion/cream** (*noun* U)

5 animal skins
- the skin of a goat: **goatskin** (*noun* U); of a sheep: **sheepskin** (*noun* U)
- to remove the skin from an animal: **skin** sth
- the skin of an animal before it has been treated: **hide** (*noun* C/U)
- the skin of an animal that has been specially treated: **leather** (*noun* U)
- the soft thick hair that covers the bodies of some animals: **fur** (*noun* U); *adjective*: **furry**
- the outer covering of many fish and reptiles: **scales** (*noun plural*); *adjective*: **scaly**

■ **MORE ...**
- a permanent mark on a person's body, that they were born with: **birthmark**
- a picture or pattern on a person's skin that is made with a needle and coloured liquid: **tattoo**

- a piece of living skin that is moved from one part of the body to another in a medical operation: **graft** ◦ *She needed several skin grafts after being badly burned.*

skirt ⇨ CLOTHES

sky

see also SUN, STAR/PLANET/MOON

- the space which we see above us, and where we see the sun, moon, stars, etc: **sky** (*noun* C/U) ◦ *I saw a plane high up in the sky.* ◦ *a grey/blue sky* ◦ *a starry/starless sky* ◦ *a patch of blue sky*

- a white or grey mass of very small drops of water in the sky which rain can fall from: **cloud** (*noun* C/U) ◦ *The sun disappeared behind the clouds.* ◦ *white/grey/black/dark clouds* ◦ *storm clouds* ◦ *We were flying through thick cloud.*
- when there are clouds in the sky, the weather is **cloudy, dull**, the sky is **grey, overcast**
- when clouds appear in the sky, **it clouds over**, the sun **goes* in** ◦ *We'd better take an umbrella. It's beginning to cloud over.*

- when there are no clouds, the sky is **blue, clear, cloudless**
- when the clouds become less thick so that you can see the sun, the sun **comes* out**
- when the clouds disappear and the sky becomes clear, the weather **clears, clears up, brightens up** ◦ *I hope it clears in time for the wedding.*

- thick, low cloud near the ground which makes it difficult to see: **fog** (*noun* C/U); when there is a fog, the weather is **foggy** ◦ *We often get fogs in the autumn.* ◦ *London was covered in dense fog.* ◦ *a foggy day*
- thin fog: **mist** (*noun* C/U); when there is a mist, the weather is **misty** ◦ *a misty morning* ◦ *misty weather*

- the distant line where the earth and the sky seem to meet; the furthest point we can see in the distance: the **horizon** ◦ *Is that a ship I can see on the horizon?*
- the outline of a city's buildings against the sky: the **skyline** ◦ *I remember being amazed when I saw the Manhattan skyline for the first time.*

sleep

1 falling asleep and not falling asleep
2 being asleep
3 waking up and not waking up
see also BED, TIRED

1 falling asleep and not falling asleep
- if you are very tired and ready to go to sleep, you are **sleepy, dozy, drowsy** ◦ *The wine and the heat made her feel very drowsy.*
- to get into a lying position: **lie* down**

- to begin to sleep: **go* to sleep, fall* asleep**
- to succeed in going to sleep after trying very hard: **get* to sleep** ◦ *I couldn't get to sleep for hours.*
- to fall asleep without meaning to: **doze off, drop off**, (*informal*) **nod off** ◦ *I'm sorry, I must have dozed off.*

sleep *contd.*

- to cry until you fall asleep: **cry*** yourself **to sleep** ◦ *She threw herself on the bed and cried herself to sleep.*
- a night during which you cannot sleep: a **sleepless** night ◦ *I had a sleepless night thinking about the accident.*
- if you cannot relax or lie still to sleep, you are **restless**; *noun* (U): **restlessness**
- if you often find it difficult to sleep, you suffer from **insomnia** (*noun* U), you are an **insomniac**
- a pill that helps you to sleep: **sleeping pill** ◦ *to take a sleeping pill*

2 being asleep

- the condition of rest when your eyes are closed and your mind is not conscious: **sleep** (*noun* U) ◦ *You need to get some sleep.* ◦ *He was talking in his sleep.*
- to be in this state for a period of time: **sleep*, be asleep, have a sleep** ◦ *to sleep well/badly* ◦ *She's upstairs having a sleep.*
- if you are sleeping so well that it is difficult to wake you, you are sleeping **deeply, soundly**, you are **fast asleep, sound asleep**
- to sleep very deeply: **sleep* like a log** ◦ *I was sleeping like a log and didn't hear the crash.*
- a short sleep that you have during the day: **nap**, (*informal*) **snooze**, (*informal*) **kip**; to have a short sleep: (*informal*) **snooze** ◦ *to have/take a nap*
- to sleep lightly and/or for a short time: **doze**; a light, short sleep: **doze** ◦ *He dozed for a while in front of the fire.*
- a short sleep or rest that people take after lunch, especially in hot countries: **siesta** ◦ *to have/take a siesta*
- to breathe noisily through your nose and mouth while you sleep: **snore**
- to see or experience pictures and events in your mind while you sleep: **dream** ◦ *to dream about someone* ◦ *I dreamed that I was flying.* ◦ *Did it really happen, or did I dream it?*
- a series of these pictures or events: **dream** ◦ *It was only a dream.*
- if you always sleep deeply, you are a **heavy sleeper**
- if you are easily woken from your sleep, you sleep **lightly**, you are a **light sleeper**

3 waking up and not waking up

- to stop being asleep: **wake*** (**up**), (*formal*) **awake*** (*usually in the past tense*); when you have woken up, you are **awake** ◦ *I woke up early this morning.* ◦ *to stay awake*
- completely awake: **wide awake**
- to make sb wake up: **wake*** sb (**up**) ◦ *Please wake me up at 6.30.*
- if you are awake and able to see, hear, and feel things, you are **conscious**; *opposite*: **unconscious**

▷ more on being conscious or unconscious ⇨ **CONSCIOUS**

- to sleep longer than you intended to: **oversleep*** ◦ *I'm sorry I'm late. I overslept.*
- to sleep later than usual because you do not need to get up: **sleep* in**, (*informal*) **have a lie-in** ◦ *I'm looking forward to sleeping in on Saturday.*
- to continue to sleep: **sleep* on** ◦ *Let her sleep on – she was so tired yesterday.*
- if you are not woken up by a noise, you **sleep* through** it ◦ *We all slept through the alarm.*

■ **MORE ...**

- a gentle song which you sing to help a child to go to sleep: **lullaby** ◦ *to sing a lullaby*
- when animals spend the winter in a state like deep sleep, they **hibernate**; *noun* (U): **hibernation** ◦ *to go into/come out of hibernation*

slow ⇨ FAST/SLOW

small ⇨ BIG/SMALL

smart

- looking good ⇨ **CLOTHES**
- clever ⇨ **CLEVER**

smell

1 smelling sth
2 the things that you smell
3 good smells
4 bad smells
other senses ⇨ **FEEL, HEAR, SEE, TASTE**
see also NOSE

1 smelling sth

- to notice or identify sth by using your nose: **smell** sth ◦ *I smelled the cakes cooking in the kitchen.* ◦ *Can you smell something burning?*
- to identify or examine sth by using your nose: **smell** sth; to do this by breathing in quickly: **sniff (at)** sth ◦ *She leant forward and smelled the flowers.* ◦ *She sniffed the milk and decided not to use it.* ◦ *The dog sniffed at the food and began to eat.*
- the ability to smell: **sense of smell** ◦ *He has lost his sense of smell.* ◦ *to have a good/bad sense of smell*

2 things that you smell

- what you smell: **smell** ◦ *What's that smell?* ◦ *a sweet/pleasant smell* ◦ *I love the smell of baking bread.*
- the smell and taste of food: **flavour** (*AmE* **flavor**) (*noun* C/U) ◦ *I think a bit of parsley would improve the flavour of this soup.*
- the smell that an animal leaves behind, which can be followed by other animals: **scent** ◦ *to follow a scent*
- to have a particular smell: **smell** + adjective, **smell of** sth, **smell like** sth ◦ *That perfume smells nice.* ◦ *His clothes smell of tobacco.* ◦ *His bedroom smells like a chemist's shop with all those medicines.*

- to send a smell out into the air: **give*** sth **off** ◦ *The rotting vegetables gave off a terrible smell.*
- something which can easily be smelt has a **strong** smell, smells **strongly** ◦ *There was a strong smell of polish in the house.* ◦ *Her breath always smelled strongly of garlic.*
- something which cannot easily be smelt has a **weak** or **faint** smell ◦ *There was a faint smell of disinfectant in the air.*
- something which has no smell is **odourless** ◦ *an odourless gas*

3 good smells

- smelling pleasant, like flowers: **sweet** ◦ *the sweet smell of roses*
- a pleasant, often sweet, smell: **scent** ◦ *the scent of the countryside*
- (often used about food) very good to smell and taste: **delicious** ◦ *That smells absolutely delicious.*

■ making yourself smell nice

- a liquid that people put on their bodies to make them smell nice: **perfume** (*noun* U/C), **scent** (*noun* U/C); *adjectives*: **scented, perfumed** ◦ *What perfume are you wearing?* ◦ *a bottle of perfume* ◦ *a scent bottle* ◦ *scented soap*

▷ other things for making you smell nice ⇨ COSMETICS

4 bad smells

- to have a bad smell: **smell**; *adjective*: (*informal*) **smelly** ◦ *Don't go in that room – it smells.* ◦ *He's got smelly feet.*
- a bad or unpleasant smell: **smell, odour** (*AmE* **odor**) ◦ *There's a smell in here and I don't know where it's coming from.* ◦ *What a smell!*
- the unpleasant smell of a person's body when it is sweating: **body odour** (*noun* U)
- to have a very bad smell: (*informal*) **stink*** (**of** sth) ◦ *She told him that his breath stank of alcohol.*
- a very unpleasant smell: (*informal*) **stink**, (*formal*) **stench** ◦ *the stench of disease and death*
- very unpleasant: **foul** ◦ *a foul smell*
- a chemical which removes bad smells from a room, etc: **air-freshener** (*noun* U)

---

smile ⇨ HAPPY, FACE

---

smoke ⇨ FIRE

---

smooth ⇨ SURFACE

---

snake

see also ANIMAL

- a long thin animal without legs which moves by sliding its body along the ground: **snake** ◦ *a poisonous snake* ◦ *He was bitten by a snake.* ◦ *a snake bite*
- a large snake that kills animals by squeezing them: **python**
- any animal such as a snake or a crocodile that has a scaly skin and lays eggs: **reptile**
- one of the long teeth which a snake uses for biting: **fang**
- the poison that a snake produces when it bites sb/sth: **venom** (*noun* U) ◦ *a cobra's venom*

---

sneeze ⇨ NOSE

---

snow

1 snow
2 when it stops snowing
3 enjoying the snow
see also RAIN, ICE, WEATHER

1 snow

- soft white pieces of frozen rain which fall in winter: **snow** (*noun* U); *verb*: **snow** ◦ *Children love playing in the snow.* ◦ *How long has it been snowing?* ◦ *It doesn't usually snow at this time of year.*
- to come down from the sky: **fall***; *noun*: **fall** ◦ *Three inches of snow fell in the night.* ◦ *a heavy fall of snow*
- a piece of falling snow: **snowflake**
- a short period of snow: **snow shower**
- cold rain which is similar to snow: **sleet** (*noun* U); *verb*: **sleet**
- with a lot of snow: **snowy** ◦ *snowy weather*
- a heavy fall of snow with a strong, cold wind: **snowstorm**; a bad snowstorm: **blizzard**
- a lot of snow pushed by the wind into a particular place: **snowdrift**
- a large amount of snow which slides down the side of a hill or mountain: **avalanche**

▷ more on storms ⇨ STORM

- if you are unable to move from where you are because of the snow, you are **snowed in, cut off** (by the snow) ◦ *It was a terrible winter – we were snowed in for a week.* ◦ *Several villages have been cut off by the snow.*

2 when it stops snowing

- (used about snow and ice) to turn to water because it is not freezing any more: **melt** ◦ *When we got up the snow had already melted.*
- (used about snow or the weather in general) to begin to get warmer so that the snow starts to melt: **thaw**; *noun*: **thaw** ◦ *I think it's beginning to thaw.* ◦ *an unexpected thaw*
- half-melted wet snow: **slush** (*noun* U) ◦ *On the roads the snow was already turning to slush.*

3 enjoying the snow

- to move over snow on long, flat, narrow pieces of wood, metal or plastic (**skis**) that are fastened to boots: **ski**; a person who skis: **skier**
- a type of flat board, often with metal strips underneath, that people use for travelling downhill on snow for fun: **sledge**; *verb*: **sledge** ◦ *Let's go sledging!*
- a lump of snow that is pressed into the shape of a ball and used by children for playing: **snowball** ◦ *a snowball fight*
- the figure of a person made out of snow, usually by children: **snowman** (*plural* **snowmen**)

snow *contd.*

▷ more on skiing ⇨ SKI

■ **MORE . . .**
- a special lorry which clears the snow from the roads: **snowplough** (*AmE* **snowplow**)
- special shoes which are worn over normal shoes to help you walk on the snow: **snowshoes**
- a special vehicle which can travel over snow: **snowmobile**

so

- what makes sth happen ⇨ CAUSE/EFFECT
- giving the reason for sth ⇨ REASON

soap ⇨ CLEAN/DIRTY

socialist ⇨ POLITICS

society

1 society
2 different groups in society
3 the position of groups and individuals in society
4 social attitudes
5 studying people in society

see also PEOPLE, COUNTRY[1]

1 society

- the people in a particular country or area who have the same laws and customs: **society** (*noun* C/U); *adjective*: **social** ◦ *We live in an industrial society.* ◦ *Society's attitude towards sex and marriage has changed a lot since the 1960s.* ◦ *social problems/change* ◦ *a person's social background*
- the customs, ideas, religion, art, music, literature, etc of a particular group or society: **culture** (*noun* C/U); *adjective*: **cultural** (*adverb* **culturally**) ◦ *In this part of Africa you will find many different languages and cultures.* ◦ *similarities of language and culture* ◦ *a culturally distinct region*
- a society which contains and recognizes the cultures of many different groups of people is **multicultural** ◦ *We live in a multicultural society.*
- a society that follows customs and beliefs that have lasted for a long time is **traditional**
- a society that follows recent ideas and ways of behaving is **modern**
- a society that is rich and has a lot of industry is **developed**, **advanced**; *opposite*: **underdeveloped** ◦ *an advanced industrial society*
- the degree to which a society is developed or underdeveloped: **development** (*noun* U) ◦ *a society at an early stage of development*
- having a high level of social and cultural development: **civilized**; *noun* (U): **civilization** ◦ *You don't expect that kind of poverty in a civilized society.* ◦ *a high level of civilization*

▷ customs ⇨ CUSTOM

▷ more on being modern ⇨ MODERN

2 different groups in society

- a number of people who are together or who are connected in some way: **group** (*with singular or plural verb*) ◦ *Pensioners are a group of people who feel that the government is ignoring their needs.*
- a group of people who live in a particular place, area or country or share some interest, quality, etc: **community** (*with singular or plural verb*) ◦ *We are a very close community and we would find it difficult to accept too many newcomers to this area.* ◦ *the gay community*

▷ more on people in groups ⇨ GROUP

■ social class
- a group of people who are at the same social and economic level: (**social**) **class** (*noun* C/U) ◦ *divisions in society caused by class* ◦ *a person's ability to move from one class to another*
- the social class who usually do industrial or physical work: **the working class**; *adjective*: **working-class** ◦ *a working-class area/family*
- the social class that includes professional and business people: **the middle class**; *adjective*: **middle-class** ◦ *They have a comfortable middle-class lifestyle.*
- the highest social class, including very rich people and people who have special titles: **the upper class**; *adjective*: **upper-class**
- without social classes: **classless** ◦ *an attempt to build a classless society*

- people in society who have little money: **the poor** (*noun plural*)
- people in society who have a lot of money: **the rich** (*noun plural*)
- a social group that is considered to be the highest because of its power, money, intelligence, etc: **elite** ◦ *the intellectual elite*

▷ more on being rich or poor ⇨ RICH, POOR

■ race
- one of the groups into which people can be divided according to their skin colour, hair type, etc: **race** (*noun* C/U); *adjective* **racial** (*adverb* **racially**)

▷ different races ⇨ PEOPLE

■ age
- all the people in a group or a country who were born at the same time: **generation** (*with singular or plural verb*) ◦ *My parents' generation were born before the war.* ◦ *the younger generation*
- people of a particular age: **age group** ◦ *the 20-30 age group*

▷ more on age groups ⇨ YOUNG/OLD

3 the position of groups and individuals in society

- the level of importance that sb has in an organization or in society: **rank** (*noun* C/U), **position** (*noun* C/U) ◦ *to be promoted to a higher rank* (= in the army, police, etc) ◦ *Old people have an important position in this community.*

- your social or professional position in relation to others: **status** (*noun singular*) ◦ *a high/low status occupation*
- a person who has the same status or rights in society: **equal** ◦ *to be treated as an equal*

▷ more on rank and position ➪ RANK

- the state of being equal: **equality** (*noun* U); *opposite*: **inequality** (*noun* U) ◦ *racial equality*
- a person's legal right to freedom and equality whatever their sex, race or beliefs: **civil rights/liberties** (*noun plural*)
- the relations between people of different races who live in the same town, country, etc: **race relations** (*noun plural*)

- to join in and become part of a community: **integrate (into/with** sth); to help sb to do this: **integrate** sb (**into/with** sth); *noun* (U): **integration** ◦ *racial integration*
- to separate one group of people from the rest: **segregate** sb (**from** sth); *noun* (U): **segregation**

- work that involves giving help to people in society who have problems because they are poor, ill, etc: **social work** (*noun* U); a person who does this work: **social worker**

4 social attitudes

- the ability or willingness to accept differences between people: **tolerance** (*noun* U); *opposite*: **intolerance** (*noun* U) ◦ *religious intolerance* ◦ *to show intolerance towards another group of people*
- having tolerance: **tolerant**; *opposite*: **intolerant** ◦ *a tolerant society*
- a dislike of a group in society that is not based on reason or experience: **prejudice** (*noun* C/U); a person who has this kind of feeling is **prejudiced** (**against** sb/sth) ◦ *racial prejudice* ◦ *He's prejudiced against foreigners.*
- to treat one group of people worse than others: **discriminate** (**against** sb/sth); *noun* (U): **discrimination** ◦ *It is illegal to discriminate against any ethnic group.* ◦ *racial/religious/sexual discrimination*

- a person who believes that people of other races are not as good as people of their own race: **racist**; *adjective*: **racist**; this kind of belief: **racism** (*noun* U) ◦ *a racist remark* ◦ *an anti-racist demonstration* ◦ *The government is taking measures to stop racism.*

▷ attitudes to the different sexes ➪ SEX[1]

- a person who thinks they are better than sb of a lower class and who admires people of a higher class: **snob**; *adjective*: **snobbish**; *nouns* (U): **snobbishness, snobbery** ◦ *Don't be such a snob!* ◦ *Julia is incredibly snobbish towards her husband's family.*

- a person who is or feels different from other people: **misfit** ◦ *a social misfit*
- a person who is not accepted as a member of a particular group: **outsider**

5 studying people in society

- the study of human societies and social behaviour: **sociology** (*noun* U); *adjective*: **sociological**; a person who studies sociology: **sociologist**
- the study of people, especially of their origins, development, beliefs and customs: **anthropology** (*noun* U); *adjective*: **anthropological**; a person who studies anthropology: **anthropologist**

- an official count of all the people who live in a country, including information about their age, jobs, etc: **census**

---

soft ➪ HARD/SOFT

---

soil ➪ GROUND

---

soldier ➪ ARMY

---

solve ➪ PROBLEM

---

some ➪ HOW MUCH/MANY

---

sometimes ➪ HOW OFTEN

---

son ➪ FAMILY

---

soon

see also FUTURE, TIME

- not long after the present time or the time mentioned: **soon, before long, shortly** ◦ *We'll be home soon.* ◦ *I gave up my job soon after winning the lottery.* ◦ *How soon can you finish it?* ◦ *Before long she was fast asleep.*
- at some time in the future; quite soon: **in due course** ◦ *We'll be leaving in due course.*

- very soon; very quickly: **in a minute/moment, right away, in no time (at all)** ◦ *I'll be with you in a minute.* ◦ *He arrived in no time at all.*
- as quickly as you can: **as soon as possible, the sooner the better** ◦ *'When should I come?' 'The sooner the better.'* ◦ *The sooner they start work the better.*

- without waiting for any time to pass; without delay: **immediately, at once, right/straight away, promptly** ◦ *He expects his orders to be obeyed immediately.* ◦ *You must leave at once.* ◦ *The doctor says he'll be round right away.* ◦ *She replied promptly.*
- an action which is done quickly, without delay, is **immediate, prompt** ◦ *I would appreciate a prompt reply.*

- something which needs to be done very soon is **pressing, urgent** (*adverb* **urgently**) ◦ *a pressing problem* ◦ *This needs to be dealt with urgently.*
- if you need to do sth quickly, you are **in a hurry** ◦ *Can you be quick please – I'm in a hurry.*

▷ doing things quickly ➪ FAST/SLOW

- if you are going to do sth very soon, you are **(just) about to** do sth, (*more formal*) **on the point of** doing sth ◦ *I was on the point of calling you when the phone rang.*

soon *contd.*

– if sth is likely to happen very soon, it is **imminent** ◦ *War seemed imminent in 1938.*
– if sth is likely to happen or appear in the near future, it is **forthcoming** ◦ *You can read about her views on this in her forthcoming book.*

sorry

not happy; sorry because of sth that has happened ⇨ SAD
other emotions ⇨ EMOTION

– if you feel sad because of sth that you have done, you are **sorry ...**, you **feel* bad about** sth, (*more formal*) you **regret** sth ◦ *He was sorry for laughing at her.* ◦ *I'm sorry about that mistake.* ◦ *I'm sorry I upset you. I wish I'd never said anything about it.* ◦ *They were sorry to have to leave.* ◦ *I felt really bad about forgetting her birthday.* ◦ *I deeply regretted what I had done.*
– something that you regret: **regret** ◦ *to have no regrets*

Note: sorry can be followed by **for ...** or **about ...** or **that ...** or **to .... sorry to ...** often expresses polite regret about sth that you have to do: ◦ *I'm sorry to have to say this, but ...*

– if what you have done makes you feel silly or uncomfortable, you are **embarrassed** (**about/at** sth); *noun* (U): **embarrassment** ◦ *He felt embarrassed about arriving so late.*
– causing embarrassment: **embarrassing** ◦ *an embarrassing mistake/remark*
– feeling embarrassed and sorry: **ashamed** (**of** sth/sb/yourself), **ashamed that ...**, **ashamed to** do sth; *noun* (U): **shame** ◦ *I'm thoroughly ashamed of myself for being so rude.* ◦ *too ashamed to admit a mistake*
– if you know that you have done sth wrong and feel sorry about it, you feel **guilty** (*adverb* **guiltily**), **remorseful**; *nouns* (U): **guilt**, **remorse** ◦ *'Do you think you did the right thing?' 'Well, I do feel a bit guilty about it.'*

■ apologizing
– to tell sb that you are sorry for doing sth: **apologize** (**to** sb) (**for** sth); *noun*: **apology**; when you make an apology, you are **apologetic** ◦ *If you did that, you must apologize.* ◦ *She was terribly apologetic but I told her there was nothing to worry about.*
– to admit that sth that you said was wrong: **take*** sth **back** ◦ *I'm sorry – I shouldn't have said that. I take it back.*

– to apologize to sb, you can say **sorry!** (*especially AmE* **excuse me!**) or **I'm so/really/very sorry** ◦ *Sorry! I didn't realize you were there!* ◦ *I'm so sorry – I'll have to ask you to move to another seat.*
– to ask sb not to be angry about sth that you have done, you can say (*formal*) **forgive me** ◦ *Forgive me – I've quite forgotten your name.*

sort ⇨ TYPE

soul ⇨ SPIRIT

sound

1 sound and noise
2 quality of sound
3 kinds of sound
sounds made by animals ⇨ ANIMAL
sound technology ⇨ RECORD
see also HEAR, MUSIC, VOICE, SPEAK

1 sound and noise

– anything that a person or animal can hear: **sound** (*noun* C/U) ◦ *Can you hear that sound?* ◦ *the sound of running water* ◦ *Scientists have identified twenty different sounds that dolphins make* ◦ *light and sound*
– a sound, especially if it is loud, unpleasant or unwanted: **noise** (*noun* C/U) ◦ *I thought I could hear a noise downstairs.* ◦ *Could you ask them to try and make less noise?*

– to make a particular sound: **go*** ◦ *Cats go 'miaow'.* ◦ *The gun went 'bang'.*
– to make a sound as a signal: **go*** ◦ *Has the bell gone yet?*

2 quality of sound

– a sound that can be heard is **audible**; *opposite*: **inaudible** ◦ *the clearly audible sound of a door shutting* ◦ *Her reply was inaudible.*
– if a sound is easy to hear, it is **clear**, you can hear it **clearly**, **loud and clear** ◦ *She has a very clear voice.* ◦ *We can hear you loud and clear.*

– (used particularly about radio, television, etc) the strength of sound: **volume** (*noun* U) ◦ *to turn down/up the volume of the radio*

– the level of a sound: **pitch**
– low in pitch (like a man's voice): **low**, **deep** ◦ *the deep voice of a bass singer*
– high in pitch (like a woman's or a child's voice): **high**, **high-pitched** ◦ *I can't sing the high notes.* ◦ *a high-pitched voice*
– high and unpleasant: **piercing**, **shrill** ◦ *piercing screams* ◦ *a shrill cry*

– with very little or no sound: **quiet** (*adverb* **quietly**) ◦ *Please be quiet, I'm trying to study.*
– having no sound: **silent** (*adverb* **silently**); *noun* (U/C): **silence** ◦ *silent films* ◦ *He silently handed her the package.* ◦ *the silence of the countryside*
– producing a lot of sound: **loud** (*adverbs* **loud**, **loudly**) ◦ *loud music* ◦ *Can you speak a bit louder?* ◦ *She coughed loudly.*
– making a lot of noise: **noisy** (*adverb* **noisily**) ◦ *noisy children* ◦ *a noisy washing machine* ◦ *He blew his nose noisily.*

▷ more on being quiet or loud ⇨ QUIET

3 kinds of sound

■ loud sounds
– a loud unpleasant noise that continues for some time: **din** (*noun singular*), (*informal*) **racket**

(*noun singular*) ◦ *Stop making such a din!* ◦ *I can't hear because of all the racket you're making.*
– a lot of noise and excitement: **uproar** (*noun singular/*U) ◦ *The meeting ended in uproar.*

– a short loud noise: **bang** ◦ *The bomb exploded with an enormous bang.* ◦ *to make a bang*
– a sudden loud noise that sth makes when it breaks, is hit, etc: **crash**; *verb*: **crash** ◦ *We heard a crash and ran outside to see what had happened.*
– the low sound that sth heavy makes when it falls down: **thud**; *verb*: **thud** ◦ *I threw the bag from the window and a moment later I heard it thudding onto the ground.*
– a loud sound that sth makes when it is hit heavily: **thump**; *verb*: **thump** ◦ *The book fell on the floor with a thump.*
– a long low sound like thunder: **rumble**; *verb*: **rumble** ◦ *the distant rumble of thunder*
– a loud deep sound: **boom** (*noun singular*); *verb*: **boom** ◦ *We could hear the guns booming in the distance.*

– the sound of a heavy metal object hitting sth: **clank**; *verb*: **clank** ◦ *the clank of a chain*
– a series of short repeated sounds that hard objects make when they hit against each other: **clatter** (*noun singular*); *verb*: **clatter** ◦ *the clatter of knives and forks* ◦ *We heard their boots clattering down the stairs.*
– a series of short sharp sounds repeated quickly: **rattle**; *verb*: **rattle** ◦ *The windows were rattling all night.*

▷ more on the sounds that are made when things are hit ⇨ **HIT**

– a loud sharp noise that you make when you eat sth or walk on sth like snow: **crunch** ◦ *the crunch of snow under our shoes*
– the noise of wood bending: **creak**; *verb*: **creak**; *adjective*: **creaky** ◦ *The floorboards creaked when I walked across the room.* ◦ *creaky stairs*
– the noise of sth like wood breaking: **crack** ◦ *The wind split the branch from the tree with a sharp crack.*

■ high-pitched sounds
– a high noise that is not very loud: **squeak**; *verb*: **squeak**; *adjective*: **squeaky** ◦ *the squeak of a mouse* ◦ *a squeaky iron gate*
– a loud high noise: **squeal**; *verb*: **squeal** ◦ *the squeal of tyres on the road* ◦ *She squealed with delight.*
– an unpleasant loud high noise: **screech**; *verb*: **screech** ◦ *the screech of a car's brakes* ◦ *jets screeching over the housetops*
– a long high unpleasant noise: **whine**; *verb*: **whine** ◦ *the whine of an aircraft engine* ◦ *The dog whined to go out.*

■ quiet or short sounds
– a short sharp sound like a small explosion: **pop**; *verb*: **pop** ◦ *There was a loud pop as the cork came out of the bottle.* ◦ *The balloon popped.*
– a short ringing noise, for example of glass or metal knocking together: **chink, clink** ◦ *the chink of glasses* ◦ *the clink of coins*
– a short sharp sound, for example of a switch or a lock: **click**; *verb*: **click** ◦ *We heard the click of a switch.* ◦ *The lock clicked open.*
– a short high electronic sound: **beep, bleep**; *verbs*: **beep, bleep** ◦ *The computer gave a bleep.*

▷ the sound of a bell ringing ⇨ **BELL**

■ sounds like water or wind
– a sound like a very long 's': **hiss**; *verb*: **hiss** ◦ *the hiss of escaping steam* ◦ *The goose hissed at me angrily.*
– the sound of food being cooked in very hot fat: **sizzle** (*noun singular*); *verb*: **sizzle** ◦ *the sizzle of eggs in the pan* ◦ *sizzling bacon*
– the sound of sth small dropping into water: **plop**; *verb*: **plop** ◦ *The stone fell into the pond with a plop.*
– the sound of liquid flying about in the air because it has been hit by sth: **splash**; *verb*: **splash** ◦ *He jumped into the pool with a splash.* ◦ *The children were splashing about in the water.*
– the sound of walking in deep wet mud: **squelch** (*noun singular*); *verb*: **squelch** ◦ *She squelched through the mud in her boots.*

– the sound of dry leaves moving together: **rustle** (*noun singular*); *verb*: **rustle** ◦ *the wind rustling through the leaves*
– a hissing sound as sth moves through the air: **swish** (*noun singular*); *verb*: **swish** ◦ *the swish of a horse's tail*

■ human sounds
– a loud high sound that you make by blowing air through your lips: **whistle**; *verb*: **whistle** ◦ *He gave a whistle of surprise.* ◦ *I was walking along in the sunshine, whistling happily.*

– a loud high sound that you make with your voice: **cry**; *verb*: **cry** (**out**) ◦ *a cry of fear/joy* ◦ *to cry out with pain*
– a very loud high cry that you make when you are surprised, afraid or in pain: **scream, shriek**; *verb*: **scream, shriek** ◦ *to give a scream* ◦ *When I saw the burglar, I screamed.* ◦ *They shrieked with delight when the clown came on.*

– to make sounds which show that you are happy or think sth is funny: **laugh** (**at** sb/sth); *noun*: **laugh**; the sound of people laughing: **laughter** (*noun* U) ◦ *to laugh at a joke*
– to produce water from your eyes, and make a noise, because you are unhappy or have hurt yourself: **cry**, (*formal*) **weep*** ◦ *Why are you crying?*
– the sound of breathing air through your nose, especially when you have a cold or are crying: **sniff**; *verb*: **sniff** ◦ *She gave a loud sniff.* ◦ *After a while she stopped sniffing and gave me a big smile.*

▷ more on laughing and crying ⇨ **LAUGH, CRY**

▷ sounds which show pain ⇨ **PAIN**

– the sound of breathing noisily through your nose and mouth when you are asleep: **snore**; *verb*: **snore** ◦ *Your snoring kept me awake.*
– the sound of food or drink passing from your mouth down your throat: **gulp**; *verb*: **gulp** ◦ *He swallowed his beer with loud gulps.*

sound *contd.*

■ **MORE . . .**

- a sound that is repeated by being sent back from the walls of a building, cave, etc: **echo** (*plural* **echoes**); to make an echo: **echo** ◦ *His voice echoed across the valley.*

- the design of a room or building that helps you to hear speech or music: **acoustics** (*noun plural*) ◦ *The acoustics of the new concert hall are wonderful – you can hear perfectly in every seat.*

south ⇨ DIRECTION

space¹

- an area which is empty ⇨ PLACE¹

space² the universe around the earth

see also STAR / PLANET / MOON

- everything that exists, including the earth, the planets, the stars, etc: **the universe**
- the whole area of the universe which surrounds the earth: **space** (*noun* U) ◦ *Do you think there can be life anywhere else in space?*
- the part of the universe which is far away from the earth: **outer space** (*noun* U)

- a piece of rock moving through space: **meteor**
- a piece of rock from space that has landed on earth: **meteorite**
- a meteor which enters the earth's atmosphere and looks like a star moving across the sky: **shooting star**
- a large object like a star with a tail, that moves around the sun and can be seen in the sky: **comet**

■ travelling in space

- travelling outside the earth's atmosphere: **space travel** (*noun* U)
- a journey in space: **voyage** ◦ *a voyage to Mars*

- a vehicle used for travelling in space: **rocket, spaceship, spacecraft**
- a spacecraft which can be used many times to make trips from the Earth into space: **space shuttle**
- a smaller object which is sent into space for a particular purpose, and which moves around the earth without any people on board: **satellite**
- a large satellite used for scientific research, etc in space: **space station**

- a person who travels in space: **astronaut, spaceman, spacewoman**
- a suit of clothes worn by an astronaut: **spacesuit**

- to send a rocket into the sky: **launch** sth; *noun*: **launch** ◦ *The launch is scheduled for twelve o'clock.*
- the place from which a rocket is sent into space: **launch pad**
- the moment that a rocket leaves the ground: **lift-off, blast-off** ◦ *It's ten minutes to lift-off.*
- to say numbers backwards to zero before the launch of a rocket: **count down**; *noun*: **countdown** ◦ *Has the countdown started yet?*
- the organization that controls the flight of a spacecraft: **mission control**

- to go round the earth, the moon, etc in space: **orbit** sth; *noun* (C/U): **orbit** ◦ *The satellite orbits the earth every twenty hours.* ◦ *a space station in orbit around the earth*
- when two spacecraft join together, they **dock** ◦ *The American spaceship docked with the Russian space station.*
- to come back into the earth's atmosphere: **re-enter** sth; *noun*: **re-entry** ◦ *They made their re-entry over the Pacific.*

■ **MORE . . .**

- (in stories and films) a living thing from another planet: **alien**
- a strange object which people see in the sky and think is a spaceship from outer space: **UFO** (= unidentified flying object) (*plural* **UFOs**), (*informal*) **flying saucer**

- (in science) the universe: **the cosmos**; *adjective*: **cosmic**
- endless space: **infinity** (*noun* U)

speak

1 speaking to sb
2 the sounds that your voice makes when you speak
3 speaking loudly or quietly
4 speaking well and clearly
5 speaking a lot
6 not speaking, or stopping speaking
7 speech problems
8 speaking in public

what you say and how you say it ⇨ SAY

see also CONVERSATION, DISCUSS / ARGUE, INFORM, LANGUAGE

1 speaking to sb

- to say things to sb, using your voice: **speak*** (**to** sb), **talk** (**to** sb) ◦ *Can you speak more slowly please?* ◦ *I'd like to speak to the manager.* ◦ *She's just learning to talk.* ◦ *I could hear some people talking.* ◦ *Who do you want to talk to?*
- the act of speaking or the ability to speak: **speech** (*noun* U) ◦ *to lose the power of speech* ◦ *freedom of speech*
- something which is spoken or which involves speech is **oral** (*adverb* **orally**), **verbal** (*adverb* **verbally**) ◦ *an oral examination* ◦ *a verbal warning*

- to speak in a particular language: **speak** (**in**) sth ◦ *They were speaking in Dutch and I didn't understand much of what they said.* ◦ *Do you mind if we speak French? My English is rather poor.*

2 the sounds that your voice makes when you speak

- the way in which sounds are made in a language: **pronunciation** (*noun* C/U); *verb*: **pronounce** sth ◦ *American pronunciation* ◦ *How do you pronounce 'thorough'?*
- a person's way of speaking a language or saying a word: **pronunciation** (*noun* U) ◦ *His pronunciation is so good that people think he's French.*
- to pronounce sth wrongly: **mispronounce** sth ◦ *We've known each other for five years, and she still mispronounces my name!*

- the way in which people from a particular region pronounce the words in their language: **accent** ◦ *to speak with a foreign accent* ◦ *a local accent*
- an accent which is very easy to recognize is **strong**, **broad** ◦ *He's got a broad Scottish accent.*

- the way that your voice rises and falls when you speak: **intonation** (*noun* U)
- the way that sb speaks (for example how loud or high their voice is), which shows how they feel: **tone** (**of voice**) ◦ *From her tone of voice I knew that she was happy.*
- the force that you put on part of a word when you say it: **stress**; *verb*: **stress** sth ◦ *The stress is on the second syllable.* ◦ *The word 'contrast' can be stressed in two different ways.*

▷ the sound of the voice ⇨ **VOICE**

3 speaking loudly or quietly

- if you say sth so that people can hear it, you say it **aloud**, **out loud** ◦ *to read aloud* ◦ *Why don't you say it out loud?*
- to speak more loudly: **speak* up** ◦ *Can you speak up please? I can't hear you.*

- a piece of electrical equipment that is used for making your voice (or other sounds) louder: **microphone**, (*informal*) **mike** ◦ *to speak into a microphone*

- to speak very loudly: **shout** (sth) (**at/to** sb), **shout** (sth) **out**; *noun*: **shout** ◦ *We all shouted goodbye to them from the window.* ◦ *Stop shouting!* ◦ *She shouted out my name.* ◦ *a warning shout* ◦ *to give a loud shout*
- to speak more loudly, especially if you are angry: **raise** your **voice** ◦ *There's no need to raise your voice.*

- to shout very loudly, often because you are angry, excited or in pain: **yell**; *noun*: **yell** ◦ *They were all yelling at me at the same time.* ◦ *a sudden yell of excitement*
- to shout loudly, for example because you are frightened or in pain: **cry** (**out**); *noun*: **cry** ◦ *'Help!' he cried.* ◦ *I fell over and cried out in pain.* ◦ *a cry of pain*
- to speak loudly in order to attract attention to yourself: **call** (**out**); *noun*: **call** ◦ *I could hear someone calling for help.* ◦ *a call for help*
- to cry out very loudly and in a high voice: **scream**; *noun*: **scream** ◦ *'Don't!' she screamed.* ◦ *We often hear screams coming from next door.*

- to speak less loudly: **lower** your **voice**, **keep*** your **voice down** ◦ *Can you lower your voice please?*

- to speak very quietly, using your mouth but not your voice: **whisper** (sth); *noun*: **whisper** ◦ *They sat at the back whispering right through the lesson.* ◦ *I saw her whispering something to Paul.* ◦ *to speak in a whisper*
- to speak in a low voice: **murmur** (sth); *noun*: **murmur** ◦ *murmurs of contentment*

4 speaking well and clearly

- if you speak in a way which is smooth and easy, your speech is **fluent** (*adverb* **fluently**); *noun* (U): **fluency** ◦ *Michael seems able to speak fluently on almost any subject.* ◦ *to speak with fluency*

- a person who can speak very clearly is **articulate** (*adverb* **articulately**), **eloquent** (*adverb* **eloquently**); *noun* (U): **eloquence** ◦ *She's surprisingly articulate for her age.* ◦ *an eloquent speaker* ◦ *Paul's eloquence helped us to win the argument.*
- not articulate: **inarticulate** (*adverb* **inarticulately**)

■ not speaking clearly

- to speak in a low voice which is unclear and difficult to hear: **mumble** (sth) ◦ *Don't mumble – I can't hear what you're saying.* ◦ *Jane mumbled something about leaving.*
- to speak in a low voice, in a way which is not clear or easy to hear, for example if you are angry: **mutter** (sth) ◦ *He just sat in a corner muttering to himself.*

5 speaking a lot

- to talk quickly or for a long time about sth unimportant: **chatter** ◦ *They spent the whole morning chattering.*
- this kind of talk: **chatter** (*noun* U) ◦ *I'm fed up with their constant chatter.*
- a person who talks a lot is **talkative** ◦ *a talkative child*

- to talk for a long time about sth in an uninteresting way: **go* on about** sth, **be on about** sth ◦ *He's always going on about his stamp collection.* ◦ *What's he on about now?*

6 not speaking, or stopping speaking

- quiet, not talking: **silent** (*adverb* **silently**); *noun* (C/U): **silence** ◦ *I asked him a question, but he remained silent.* ◦ *His silence made me nervous.* ◦ *an embarrassing silence*
- a moment when you stop speaking: **pause**; *verb*: **pause** ◦ *She paused for a moment and then went on.*
- a person who does not speak very much or is unwilling to give information is **uncommunicative**, **not communicative** ◦ *I tried talking to her but she wasn't very communicative.*

- to stop talking: (*informal and rather impolite*) **shut* up** ◦ *Shut up and listen!*
- to make sb stop talking: (*informal*) **shut*** sb **up** ◦ *Can't somebody shut him up?*

speak *contd.*

– unable to speak because of surprise, anger, etc: **speechless** ◦ *When he told me I'd been sacked I was absolutely speechless.*

7 speech problems

– to become unable to speak because of a cold or sore throat: **lose* your voice** ◦ *He's got a sore throat and he's lost his voice.*

– a person who is unable to speak is **dumb**
– a person who is unable to hear is **deaf** ◦ *to be deaf and dumb*

▷ more on being deaf ⇨ HEAR

– to speak with difficulty, being unable to say a word without pausing and repeating part of the word: **stammer, stutter**; *nouns*: **stammer, stutter** ◦ *I only stammer when I'm nervous.* ◦ *He's got a terrible stutter.*
– a speech problem which means that a person pronounces the letter 's' as 'th': **lisp**; *verb*: **lisp** ◦ *She speaks with a slight lisp.*

– a person whose job is to help people with serious speech problems: **speech therapist**
– the job of a speech therapist: **speech therapy** (*noun* U)

– a small mistake which you make when you are speaking: **slip of the tongue** ◦ *Don't be angry with him – I'm sure it was just a slip of the tongue.*

8 speaking in public

– to speak about sth publicly to a group of people: **speak* (on/about** sth), **talk (on/about** sth), **make*/give*/deliver** a **speech/talk (on/about** sth) ◦ *I've been invited to speak at the conference.* ◦ *What are you going to talk about?* ◦ *She made an excellent speech.* ◦ *Did you hear the talk he gave on Picasso?*

– a speech on a particular subject, especially to a group of students, etc: **lecture (on/about** sth); *verb*: **lecture (on/about** sth) ◦ *Professor Pinkerton gave an interesting lecture on Eastern philosophy.* ◦ *He usually lectures on nineteenth-century French art.*
– a person who gives a speech, lecture, etc: **speaker, lecturer**

– a religious talk in church: **sermon** ◦ *What was the sermon about?*
– to make a religious speech, usually in a church: **preach (on/about** sth)
– a person who preaches: **preacher**

special ⇨ USUAL

speed ⇨ FAST/SLOW

spend ⇨ MONEY

spice ⇨ COOK

spider

see also INSECT

– a small animal like an insect which has eight legs: **spider** ◦ *She was bitten by a poisonous spider.*
– a type of large hairy spider: **tarantula**

– the net of thin threads in which spiders catch insects: **spider's web, cobweb**
– to make a web, a spider **spins*** a thin thread which it produces from its body

spirit

see also RELIGION

– the part of you that is not physical; your thoughts and feelings, not your body: **spirit** (*noun singular*) ◦ *Despite the illness, her spirit is as strong as ever.*
– connected with the spirit: **spiritual**; *opposites*: **material, physical** ◦ *spiritual needs* ◦ *material possessions* ◦ *the physical world*
– the part of a person that some people believe continues to live after the body is dead: **soul, spirit** ◦ *Christians believe that your soul goes to Heaven when you die.*

– the spirit of a dead person that some people think they can see or hear: **ghost**; *adjective*: **ghostly** ◦ *He thought he'd seen a ghost.* ◦ *There was a ghostly presence in the room.*
– (used about a ghost) to return to a place or person: **haunt** sb/sth ◦ *a haunted house*

– a spiritual being who is a servant of God: **angel**; looking or acting like an angel: **angelic** ◦ *an angelic expression on her face*
– an evil spirit: **devil**; the most powerful evil being according to the Christian religion: **the Devil, Satan**

spoon ⇨ KNIFE/FORK/SPOON

sport

1 sport
2 doing sports
3 watching sport
4 baseball
5 basketball
6 cricket
7 fighting and shooting sports
8 golf
9 hockey
10 indoor sports
11 skating
12 table tennis
13 tennis
14 volleyball
15 water sports

soccer, rugby and American football ⇨ FOOTBALL
catching fish and hunting animals for sport ⇨ FISH[1], HUNT

see also SKI, BICYCLE, BOAT, CLIMB, FLY[2], HORSE

1 sport

- a physical activity that you do for exercise or because you enjoy it: **sport** (*noun* C/U) ◦ *Which sports do you do?* ◦ *winter sports* ◦ *indoor/outdoor sports* ◦ *He does a lot of sport.* ◦ *the importance of sport for health*
- connected with sport: **sports**, **sporting** ◦ *We have excellent sports facilities* (= buildings, equipment, etc) *in this town.* ◦ *the sports page* (in a newspaper) ◦ *a sports star/personality* ◦ *sporting activities* ◦ *a sporting achievement*

- the kinds of sport where people run, jump or throw things: **athletics** (*noun* U)
- a sport which involves playing with a ball: **game** ◦ *to play games* ◦ *the game of tennis*

▷ more on athletics ⇨ **ATHLETICS**

▷ playing games ⇨ **GAME**

2 doing sports

- a man/woman who does sport: **sportsman/woman**
- a person who takes part in a sport for pleasure, not for money: **amateur** ◦ *amateur sports* ◦ *an amateur boxer*
- a person who gets paid to do a sport: **professional**; to stop being an amateur and become a professional: **turn professional** ◦ *a professional footballer* ◦ *She turned professional after the 1996 Olympics.*

- an organized event in which people try to win sth: **competition** ◦ *an athletics competition*
- an occasion of playing a game: **game** ◦ *a game of squash*
- an organized game in a competition: **match** ◦ *a hockey/boxing match*

▷ more on competitions ⇨ **COMPETITION**

Note: you **play** games like tennis, football or golf; you **go* swimming**, **riding**, **skiing**, etc; you **do*** activities like aerobics, karate, judo, and athletic sports such as the high jump or the relay.

- to do sth many times until you are good at it: **practise** (*AmE* **practice**) (sth); *noun* (U): **practice** ◦ *You'll never improve if you don't practise.* ◦ *I've got football practice today.* ◦ *I haven't played tennis for ages – I'm a bit out of practice* (= I haven't practised much recently).
- to practise a sport very hard and in an organized way: **train**; *noun* (U): **training** ◦ *You need to train hard to be a professional.*
- a person who teaches you how to do your sport better: **coach**; this activity: **coaching** (*noun* U); *verb*: **coach** sb ◦ *a tennis coach* ◦ *I'm paying for tennis coaching to improve my game.* ◦ *George is being coached by a professional.*

- use of the body in a way that will keep you healthy: **exercise** (*noun* U) ◦ *I don't get much exercise these days.* ◦ *You should take regular exercise if you want to stay healthy.*

▷ more on exercise ⇨ **EXERCISE**

■ clothes, etc that are needed for sport

- shoes that people wear for doing general sports: **training shoes, trainers** (*AmE* **sneakers**)
- a suit that people wear for sports practice, consisting of loose trousers and a sweater: **tracksuit**
- all the clothes you need to play a particular sport: (**sports**) **kit** (*noun* U), (**sports**) **gear** (*noun* U), (*more formal*) **sportswear** (*noun* U) ◦ *I need to wash my sports gear.* ◦ *They sell all kinds of sportswear.*

- the things that are needed for doing a particular sport: **equipment** (*noun* U)
- a bag used for sports clothes and equipment: **sports bag**

■ places where people do sports

- a large closed area for sports and games with seats for people to watch: **stadium** ◦ *a football stadium* ◦ *a sports stadium*
- part of a stadium with seats for people who are watching: **stand**
- special lights used at sports events which are held at night: **floodlights**

- an area of land used for sports: **sports ground**
- a large field for doing sports or playing on (for example in schools): **playing field**
- a place especially marked out for a particular sport: **pitch**, **court** ◦ *a football/rugby/hockey/cricket pitch* ◦ *a tennis/squash/badminton court*
- a place marked out for particular races: **course**, **track** ◦ a *running track*

- a special centre where people can do all kinds of different sports: **sports centre** (*AmE* **sports center**), **leisure centre** (*AmE* **leisure center**)
- a sports centre where people have to pay to be a member: **sports club**
- a room in a sports centre where people do weight-lifting or gymnastics or other indoor sports: **gym, gymnasium**
- the place in a sports centre where people change their clothes: **changing room** (*AmE* **locker room**); a small box in a changing room where people can keep their things: **locker**

3 watching sport

- a person who watches sport: **spectator**; a person who watches and supports team sports, for example football: **supporter, fan**
- a large group of people watching the sport at a game or a sports competition: **crowd**
- when sb wins or does well, the crowd **cheers**; *noun* (U): **cheering** ◦ *There was cheering and clapping from the crowd when the final whistle went.*

sport *contd.*

– a person who talks about a sport on the television or the radio as it is happening: **commentator**; *verb*: **commentate** (**on** sth) ◦ *a football commentator*
– what a commentator says as he/she is watching a sport: (**running**) **commentary**

4 baseball

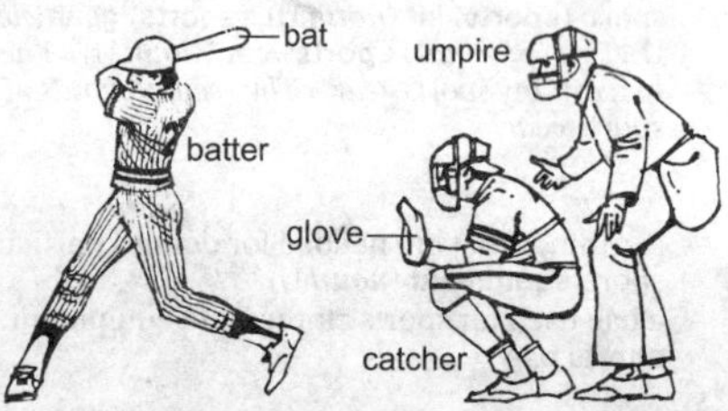

– a game that is popular in the USA, played with a **baseball bat** and **ball** by two teams of nine players. It is played on a baseball **field**. Each player tries to hit the ball and then run round the field, passing four places (**bases**) in order to get a **run**. The player who is trying to hit the ball is the **batter**. The person behind him who tries to catch the ball is the **catcher**. The person who throws the ball is the **pitcher**.

– The batter is **out** if he does not succeed in hitting the ball after three attempts, or if a **fielder** catches the ball or touches him with the ball when he is between bases.

5 basketball

– a game that is played by two teams of five or six players. It is played with a **basketball** on a **basketball court**. A goal (called a **basket**) is scored by throwing the ball into a **net** with an open bottom. A game similar to basketball which is usually played by women is **netball**.

6 cricket

– a game that is played by two teams of eleven players on a grass **pitch**. The teams take it in turns to **bat** (= hit the ball with a **cricket bat**). The **batsman** (= person who is batting) stands at one end of the **wicket** (= strip of grass in the middle of the pitch) and the **bowler bowls** (= throws) the ball towards him and tries to hit the three pieces of wood (also called a **wicket**) which are behind the batsman. If he hits the wicket, the batsman is **out** and a new team member replaces him.

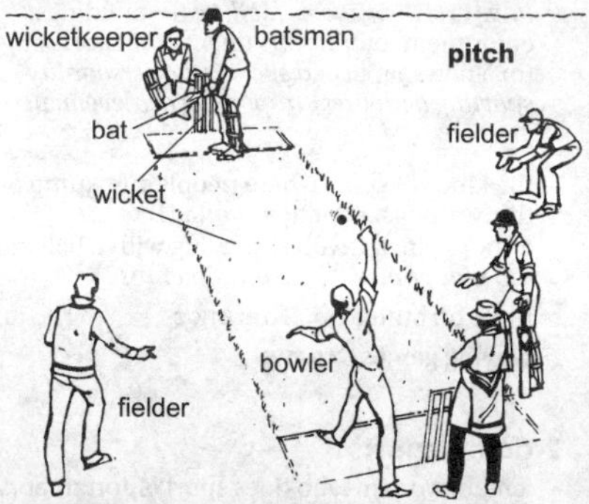

– The batsman tries to hit the ball and **score a run** by running to the other end of the wicket, while the players from the other team (the **fielders**) throw the ball back to the bowler. If one of the fielders catches the ball before it hits the ground, the batsman is **out**. When all the batsmen are out, the other team **comes*** **in to bat**. A person who plays cricket is a **cricketer**.

7 fighting and shooting sports

– the sport in which two people fight by hitting each other with their hands, wearing big gloves: **boxing** (*noun* U); *verb*: **box**; a person who boxes: **boxer**
– a style of fighting, originally from Japan, in which the hands and feet are used as weapons: **karate** (*noun* U)

▷ more on boxing ⇨ BOXING

– a sport in which two people fight and try to throw each other to the ground: **wrestling** (*noun* U); *verb*: **wrestle**; a person who wrestles: **wrestler**
– a sport which is similar to wrestling and is also a form of self-defence: **judo** (*noun* U)
– sports like karate and judo are called **martial arts** (*noun plural*)

– the sport of fighting with swords: **fencing** (*noun* U); to fight with swords: **fence**; a person who fences: **fencer**

– the sport of shooting guns: **shooting**; *verb*: **shoot***; a person who shoots: **shooter**; an object that you aim at (= try to hit) when you practise shooting: **target** ◦ *to shoot at a target*
– the sport of shooting with a bow and arrow: **archery** (*noun* U); a person who does archery: **archer**

▷ picture at WEAPON

8 golf

- a game in which each player uses a **golf club** (= a kind of stick) to hit a **golf ball** (a small hard ball) into a series of nine or eighteen **holes** on a large area of land called a **golf course**. One game of golf is called a **round** (of golf). An act of hitting the ball is a **shot**. The winner is the player who succeeds in going round the course with the smallest number of shots. A person who plays golf is a **golfer**.

9 hockey

- a game (in *AmE* called **field hockey**) played on a **field** by two teams of eleven players each. Each player uses a **hockey stick** (= a kind of curved stick) to hit the **ball** (which is small and hard) into a **goal**. Hockey which is played on ice using **skates** is called **ice hockey** (*AmE* **hockey**). Ice hockey is played with a wooden **puck** instead of a ball.

10 indoor sports

- physical exercises that are done indoors, often using special equipment such as bars and ropes: **gymnastics** (*noun* U); a person who does gymnastics: **gymnast**
- energetic physical exercises (often done to music) that increase the amount of oxygen in your blood: **aerobics** (*noun* U)
lifting heavy objects as an exercise: **weightlifting** (*noun* U); the objects which are lifted: **weights**; a person who does this form of exercise: **weight-lifter**
- a piece of equipment for jumping up and down on: **trampoline**; exercise which is done using this equipment: **trampolining** (*noun* U)

11 skating

- to move over ice wearing boots with thick metal blades (**ice-skates**) on the bottom: **skate**; the name of the activity: **skating** (*noun* U), **ice-skating** (*noun* U); a person who skates: **skater**
- a large area of ice, or a building containing a large area of ice, that is used for skating on: **ice rink**, **skating rink**
- to skate over the ground wearing a type of shoe with small wheels on the bottom (**roller skates** or **Rollerblades**): **roller skate**; the name of the activity: **roller skating** (*noun* U); a person who roller skates: **roller skater**
- to stand on and ride a narrow board with wheels attached to it (a **skateboard**): **skateboard**; a person who skateboards: **skateboarder**

12 table tennis

- a game (also called **ping-pong**) with rules like tennis in which two or four players hit a light plastic **ball** across a **table** with a small light **bat**.

13 tennis

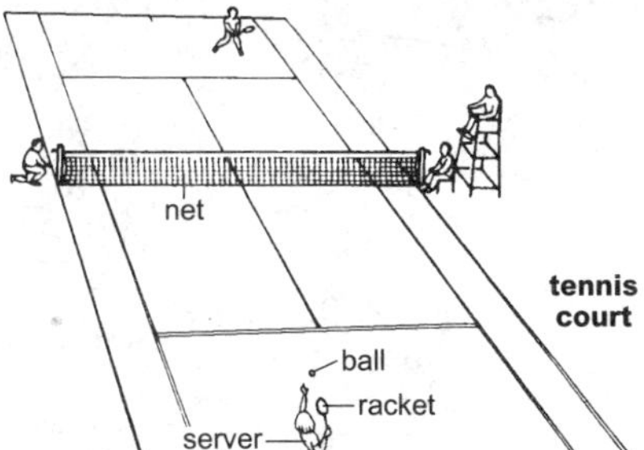

- a game played on a **tennis court** by two or four players who hit a **tennis ball** to each other across a **net** using **tennis rackets**. A game of tennis played by two players is called **singles** and one which is played by four players is called **doubles**. In a game of tennis, players play many

sport *contd.*

games, in which they score **points**; the first player to win six games wins a **set**; three or five sets make a **match**.

- You start play when you **serve** the ball; an act of serving the ball is a **serve** (*formal* **service**); the person who does this is the **server**.
- A score of no points is called **love** (for example, '30 love' means that one player has 30 points and the other player has none). When both players have the same points you say **all** (for example, 'fifteen all' means that both players have fifteen points). When both players have 40 points, the score is called **deuce**.

14 volleyball

- a game that is played on a **volleyball court** by two teams of six players. The players hit a **volleyball** over a high **net** with their hands.

15 water sports

- to move your body through water: **swim***; the name of the activity or sport: **swimming** (*noun* U)
- to jump into the water with your head first: **dive***; an act of diving into water: **dive**;
- the activity or sport of diving into water: **diving** (*noun* U)

▷ more on swimming and diving ⇨ **SWIM**

- to stand or lie on a surfboard and ride on a wave towards the shore: **surf**; the name of the sport: **surfing** (*noun* U); a person who surfs: **surfer** ◦ *good surfing conditions*
- to surf on a board with a sail which is blown by the wind: **windsurf**; the name of the sport: **windsurfing** (*noun* U); a person who windsurfs: **windsurfer** ◦ *to go windsurfing*

- to move across the surface of water standing on water-skis, being pulled by a boat: **water-ski**; the name of the sport: **water-skiing** (*noun* U); a person who does this: **water-skier** ◦ *a water-skiing competition*

spring ⇨ SEASON

square ⇨ SHAPE

stage

- the stage of a theatre ⇨ **THEATRE**
- acting on the stage ⇨ **ACT**[2]

stairs

other parts of houses or other buildings ⇨ **HOUSE, BUILDING**
see also LADDER

- the steps that join different levels inside a building: **stairs** (*noun plural*) ◦ *She went/walked/came down the stairs.* ◦ *to run up the stairs* ◦ *at the top/bottom of the stairs* ◦ *I met her on the stairs.*
- a single step in a set of stairs: **stair** ◦ *the top/bottom stair*

- a set of stairs with a rail at the side that you can hold on to: **staircase**, **stairway**
- a rail for holding on to at the side of a staircase: **banister** (*usually plural*)
- a set of stairs or steps: **flight** ◦ *We had to go up three flights of stairs.*
- the area at the top of a staircase: **landing**
- a moving staircase: **escalator** ◦ *to go up/down an escalator*

- stairs outside a building, usually made of stone or concrete: **steps** (*noun plural*) ◦ *Careful! These steps are rather steep.*
- the rail at the side of steps that you can hold on to: **handrail**
- a sloping path which can be used instead of steps: **ramp** ◦ *She pushed her wheelchair up the ramp.*
- a special staircase which people can escape down if there is a fire: **fire escape** ◦ *Please don't block the fire escape.*

- the floor of a building which is above you is **upstairs** (*adjective, adverb*); the level below you in a building is **downstairs** (*adjective, adverb*) ◦ *an upstairs window* ◦ *to go upstairs/downstairs* ◦ *The bedrooms are upstairs.* ◦ *the downstairs bathroom* ◦ *He fell downstairs and broke a leg.*

stamp ⇨ POST

stand

see also LIE[2]**, SIT**

- to be on your feet with your body upright: **stand*** ◦ *Stand over there, please.* ◦ *I've been standing all day and I'm very tired.*
- to move into a standing position from your seat: **stand* up, get* up** ◦ *When I was at school, we had to stand up when the teacher entered the classroom.* ◦ *Nigel got up and left the room.*

- to suddenly stop standing: **fall*** (**down/over**) ◦ *She slipped on the ice and fell.* ◦ *The clown kept falling over and all the children laughed.*
- to remain steady and upright when you might

expect to fall: **keep*** your **balance**; *opposite*: **lose*** your **balance** ◦ *Kate slipped, but she managed to keep her balance.*
– to stand up after you have fallen: **pick** yourself **up** ◦ *The boxer picked himself up and went on with the fight.*

▷ more on falling ⇨ FALL

■ ways of standing
– standing up tall and upright: **straight**; to move so that you are standing up tall and straight: **straighten** (yourself) **up** ◦ *Stand up straight!*
– to stand, sit or walk in a lazy way, with your head and shoulders hanging down: **slouch**
– a person's way of standing, sitting, etc: **posture** (*noun* U) ◦ *You have very bad posture – you should try to stand up straight.*

– on the ends of your toes, with your heels off the ground: **on tiptoe**; to walk quietly and carefully on tiptoe: **tiptoe** ◦ *I can just reach the top shelf if I stand on tiptoe.* ◦ *Rachel tiptoed down the stairs.*

– when a soldier stands up straight with his/her feet together, he/she **stands*/comes* to attention**
– when a soldier stands in a relaxed way, with his/her feet apart, he/she **stands* at ease**

– to stand doing nothing: **stand* about/around** ◦ *Stop standing about. Go and do some work.*
– to stand without moving your body: **stand* still** ◦ *Stand still, will you, or I won't be able to measure your trousers.*

■ bending
– to move your body forwards and downwards: **bend*** (**over/down**) ◦ *She bent down to pick up the letters.*
– to bend your body towards sb: **lean over**, **lean towards** sb ◦ *He needed a pen so he leaned over and asked the person sitting next to him.*
– to bend your head and shoulders downwards: **stoop** ◦ *The man was so tall, he had to stoop to get through the door.*
– to bend your knees so that your body is close to the ground and leaning forward slightly: **crouch** (**down**) ◦ *She crouched down to look at something on the floor.*
– to bend your body forward or downward as a sign of respect or as a greeting: **bow** (**to** sb); *noun*: **bow** ◦ *He bowed as the president passed.* ◦ *She took a bow* (= bowed to the audience to thank them for their applause) *at the end of the performance.*
– to bend your head forward as a sign of respect, as a greeting or because of sadness: **bow** your **head** ◦ *She bowed her head and looked at the ground.*

star/planet/moon

see also SPACE², SKY, NIGHT, SUN

■ stars
– a large ball of burning gas in space which you can see at night in the sky as a small point of light: **star**
– a group of stars with a name: **constellation**; a very large group of stars: **galaxy**
– the group of stars which includes the sun: **the Milky Way**

– when stars appear in the sky, they **come* out**
– when stars give out light, they **shine*** ◦ *There was no moon but the stars were shining brightly.*
– when stars shine as small points in the sky, they **twinkle**
– when you can see the stars in the sky, they are **out**
– if you can see a lot of stars, it is a **starry** night/sky; *opposite*: **starless**
– the light of the stars: **starlight** (*noun* U); *adjective*: **starlit** ◦ *a beautiful starlit night*

■ planets
– a large object in space which goes around a star, especially the sun: **planet**
– a smaller object which goes around a planet: **moon**

– the sun and the planets that go round it: **the solar system**

the solar system

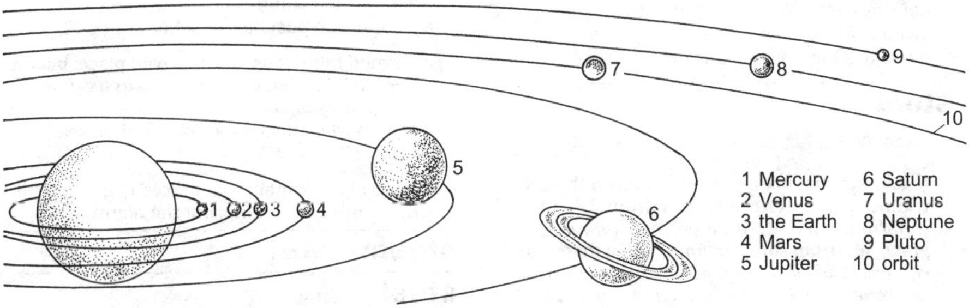

star/planet/moon *contd.*

■ the moon

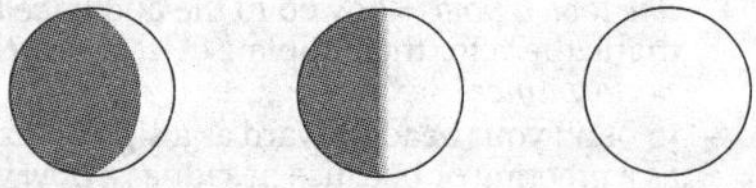

new / crescent moon **half moon** **full moon**

- the round object which moves around the earth and which we can see in the sky at night: **the moon** ◦ *We managed to find our way by the light of the moon.* ◦ *Neil Armstrong was the first person to walk on the moon.*
- connected with the moon: **lunar** ◦ *the lunar calendar* ◦ *a lunar landing*
- the light of the moon: **moonlight** (*noun* U); *adjective*: **moonlit** ◦ *We went for a walk in the moonlight.* ◦ *a beautiful moonlit night*
- when the moon reflects the light of the sun, it **shines*** ◦ *The moon was shining on the water.*
- when the moon appears in the sky, it **comes* out**, **comes* up**, (*formal*) **rises***; when it can be seen in the sky, it is **out** or **up** ◦ *'Is the moon out?' 'No, but I can see some stars.'*

■ the movement of the planets, etc
- to move around a larger object in space: **go* round** sth, **orbit** sth; *noun*: **orbit** ◦ *The moon goes round the earth and the earth goes round the sun.* ◦ *the orbit of Mars around the sun*
- when the earth passes between the sun and the moon so that it throws a shadow on the moon, there is an **eclipse** of the moon, a **lunar eclipse**

■ studying the stars, etc
- the scientific study of the stars, planets, etc: **astronomy** (*noun* U); *adjective*: **astronomical**
- a scientist who studies the stars: **astronomer**
- the belief that the positions and movements of the stars and planets influence what people do and what happens to them: **astrology** (*noun* U)

▷ more on astrology ⇨ ASTROLOGY

start ⇨ BEGIN

station ⇨ TRAIN

statue ⇨ SCULPTURE

stay

- continuing to do sth ⇨ CONTINUE
- visiting sb ⇨ VISIT
- living in a place for a short time ⇨ LIVE²

steal

see also CRIME, DECEIVE

- to take sth that belongs to sb else secretly and without permission: **steal*** sth (**from** sb/sth), (*informal*) **nick** sth (**from** sb/sth), (*informal*) **pinch** sth (**from** sb/sth); *noun* (C/U): **theft** ◦ *My car was stolen last night.* ◦ *Who's pinched my cigarettes?* ◦ *an increase in theft in this neighbourhood* ◦ *People are alarmed at the number of thefts.*
- a person who steals: **thief** (*plural* **thieves**)
- to go away quickly after stealing sth: **make* off with** sth, **run* off with** sth ◦ *Thieves made off with £60 000 worth of jewellery.*
- to enter a building secretly and illegally in order to steal sth from it: **burgle** sb/sth (*AmE* **burglarize** sb/sth); *noun* (C/U): **burglary** ◦ *We've been burgled five times in the last six months!* ◦ *to commit a burglary*
- a person who commits a burglary: **burglar** ◦ *I heard a sound in the middle of the night and I thought it was burglars.*
- to enter a building in order to commit a burglary: **break* into** sth; *noun*: **break-in** ◦ *There was a break-in next door to us only last week, but nothing was taken.*
- the crime of stealing sth from a shop while pretending to be a customer: **shoplifting** (*noun* U)
- a person who steals from shops: **shoplifter**
- to attack a person or a building in order to steal sth, usually money, from them: **rob** sb/sth (**of** sth); *noun* (C/U): **robbery** ◦ *A gang of five men robbed the bank.* ◦ *I was robbed of my handbag in the middle of the street.* ◦ *armed robbery*
- a person who robs sb: **robber** ◦ *a bank robber* ◦ *an armed robber*
- to rob sth using a gun, etc: **hold*** sth **up**; *noun*: **hold-up** ◦ *Four masked men held up a bank in Norwich this morning.*
- to attack sth in order to steal from it: **raid** sth; *noun*: **raid** (**on** sth) ◦ *a bank raid*
- to steal things during a period of fighting: **loot** (sth) ◦ *The riots were followed by looting.*
- to attack and rob sb in the street: **mug** sb; *noun* (C/U): **mugging** ◦ *fear of being mugged*
- a person who mugs sb: **mugger**
- to steal from sb's pocket or bag in a public place: **pick** sb's **pocket**
- a person who picks people's pockets: **pickpocket**
- to drive or ride in a stolen car for fun: **joyride**; *noun* (U): **joyriding**
- a person who does this: **joyrider**
- to stop a lorry, train, etc in order to steal goods from it: **hijack** sth; *noun* (C/U): **hijacking**
- a person who carries out a hijacking: **hijacker**
- to catch or shoot birds, animals or fish on sb else's land without permission: **poach** (sth); *noun* (U): **poaching**
- a person who poaches: **poacher**
- an armed robber, usually in a wild place: **bandit** ◦ *Our bus was hijacked by bandits as we drove through the jungle.*
- a person who attacks and robs ships at sea: **pirate**
- a piece of equipment that makes a loud noise if a thief enters a building: **burglar alarm**

steam ⇨ WATER

steel ⇨ METAL

steep ⇨ HILL/MOUNTAIN

stomach

other parts of the body ⇨ **BODY**
see also EAT

- the front part of your body, below your chest and above your legs: **stomach**, (*informal*) **tummy**, (*formal*) **abdomen**; connected with the abdomen: (*formal*) **abdominal** ◦ *She turned over and lay on her stomach.* ◦ *He showed me the scar on his tummy.* ◦ *abdominal pains*
- the small hollow in the middle of your stomach: **navel**, (*informal*) **tummy button**

- the part of your body where food is digested: **stomach**, (*informal*) **tummy** ◦ *I've got a funny feeling in my tummy.*
- the process that goes on inside your body to change the food you have eaten so that it can be used by the body: **digestion** (*noun* U)

- if you feel ill in your stomach, you **feel* sick** ◦ *I feel sick – it must have been the curry that I ate.*
- a slight illness in your stomach: **upset** ◦ *I haven't quite recovered from that stomach upset I got on holiday.*
- to bring food up from the stomach and out of the mouth: **be sick, throw* up**, (*formal*) **vomit** ◦ *She had eaten too much ice cream and was sick all over the back seat of the car.*
- a pain in your stomach: **stomach-ache** (*noun* C/U), (*informal*) **tummy-ache** (*noun* C/U) ◦ *Have you got a tummy-ache?*
- pain in the stomach that is caused by difficulty in digesting food: **indigestion** (*noun* U) ◦ *I can't eat that cheese – it'll give me indigestion.* ◦ *Have you got any indigestion tablets?*

▷ note on stomach-ache and other aches ⇨ **PAIN**

- to make a noise with your mouth when air comes up from the stomach: **burp**; *noun*: **burp**
- (used about the stomach) to make a deep noise: **rumble** ◦ *I could hear his stomach rumbling.*
- gas that is formed in the stomach: **wind** (*noun* U) ◦ *to suffer from wind*

■ **MORE ...**
- one of the tubes in your body that carries food from your stomach: **intestine**; *adjective*: **intestinal**
- a painful area inside the stomach: **stomach ulcer**

stone

see also GROUND

- a hard, solid substance which is found in the ground: **stone** (*noun* U) ◦ *Most of Edinburgh is built of stone.* ◦ *a stone wall/bridge/building*
- the hard stony part of the earth: **rock** (*noun* U) ◦ *That part of the land is solid rock.*
- very hard grey stone used in building and, in the past, to make fire: **flint** (*noun* U) ◦ *ancient flint axes*
- dark grey stone that can be split into thin flat pieces and is used for making the roofs on some houses: **slate** (*noun* U) ◦ *a slate roof*
- a hard attractive stone often used to make statues and parts of buildings: **marble** (*noun* U) ◦ *a marble statue*
- a soft white rock: **chalk** (*noun* U) ◦ *chalk cliffs*
- a hard often grey rock used in building: **granite** (*noun* U)
- a light yellow coloured rock formed from sand: **sandstone** (*noun* U)

■ big stones and small stones
- a piece of stone or rock: **stone, rock** ◦ *to throw a stone at sb* ◦ *Huge rocks often slip down the side of the mountain and onto the road.*
- having many stones or rocks: **stony, rocky** ◦ *a stony beach* ◦ *rocky islands*

- a very large stone: **boulder**
- a large heavy piece of stone with flat surfaces: **block, slab** ◦ *a block of stone/marble/sandstone* ◦ *huge stone slabs*
- a large piece or area of rock that sticks out of the sea: **rock** ◦ *He swam out to sea and sat on a big rock.* ◦ *The ship crashed against the rocks.*

- a small smooth round stone which is found in or near water: **pebble**; having a lot of pebbles: **pebbly** ◦ *a pebbly beach*
- very small pieces of stone that are used for making roads and pathways: **gravel** (*noun* U) ◦ *a gravel path*
- very small pieces of stone (sometimes put on roads after it has snowed): **grit** (*noun* U)
- to put grit on a road: **grit** sth ◦ *The roads were very icy and hadn't been gritted.*
- a powder made of very small pieces of rock, found on beaches and in the desert: **sand** (*noun* U); having a lot of sand: **sandy** ◦ *a lorryload of sand* ◦ *a sandy beach*

■ using stone
- to form sth (for example a statue) by cutting away material from stone: **carve** sth (**out of/from/in** sth) ◦ *She carved the figure of a horse out of a large block of stone.* ◦ *a beautiful statue carved in marble*
- a person who cuts and prepares stone or builds with stone: **stonemason**
- the art of making shapes and objects from stone, etc: **sculpture** (*noun* U); a person who does this: **sculptor**

▷ more on sculpture ⇨ **SCULPTURE**

- a place where sand and stone are dug out of the ground: **quarry** ◦ *a chalk quarry*

stop

1 movements
2 situations and actions
see also END/FINISH, BEGIN, CONTINUE

stop *contd.*

1 movements

- to finish moving: **stop**; to cause sb/sth to finish moving: **stop** sb/sth ◦ *I stopped for a moment to look in a shop window.* ◦ *I think my watch has stopped.* ◦ *I was stopped in the street by a small boy asking for money.* ◦ *I asked the driver to stop the car.*
- an act of stopping or a state of being stopped: **stop** ◦ *to come to a complete stop* ◦ *Our journey will take eighteen hours, including stops.*

2 situations and actions

- to finish happening: **stop**, (*formal*) **cease** ◦ *Will this rain ever stop?* ◦ *to cease to exist*
- to make sth stop: **stop** sth, **put* an end to** sth ◦ *They stopped the concert to make an urgent announcement.* ◦ *I want to put an end to this discussion now.*
- to make a person stop talking: (*informal*) **shut*** sb **up** ◦ *I asked her to do it herself – that shut her up.*
- to cause sb not to do sth: **stop** sb doing sth, (*more formal*) **prevent** sb (**from**) doing sth ◦ *We must try to stop him working so hard.*

▷ more on preventing things ⇨ AVOID/PREVENT

- to finish doing sth: **stop** (sth/doing sth), (*informal*) **pack** sth **in** ◦ *Stop it! I can't concentrate when you do that.* ◦ *She stopped talking and smiled.* ◦ *Don't stop – I'm enjoying the story.* ◦ *I've packed in my job.*
- to stop suddenly when you are doing sth or speaking: **break* off** ◦ *He began to tell us something, then suddenly broke off.*
- to stop trying to do sth: **give* up** (doing sth) ◦ *Don't give up now – you've almost finished.*
- to give up studying at school or university before you finish your course; to give up taking part in a competition: **drop out** (**of** sth) ◦ *to drop out of college/university* ◦ *to drop out of a competition*
- to leave a job or place: (*especially AmE*) **quit*** sth ◦ *to quit the city* ◦ *to quit your job*
- to stop doing sth that you are used to doing or having: **give*** (sth) **up** ◦ *to give up smoking* ◦ *to give up hope*
- to stop sth before it is finished: **break*** sth **off**, **abandon** sth ◦ *She broke off their engagement without any warning.* ◦ *We abandoned the game when the rain started.*

■ stopping for a short time

- to stop an activity, especially talking, for a short time: **pause**; a short time during which an activity stops: **pause** ◦ *Let's pause for a moment and consider the possibilities.* ◦ *There was a long pause before anyone answered the question.*
- to stop an activity for a period of time in order to do sth else: **break*** (**for** sth); a short period of rest: **break** ◦ *Let's break for lunch and begin again at two o'clock.* ◦ *to have/take a break*
- a break in a performance: **interval** (*AmE* **intermission**) ◦ *We had ice creams during the interval.*

storm

see also RAIN, WIND, SNOW, WEATHER

- a short period of very bad weather, with a lot of wind, rain, snow, etc: **storm** ◦ *a violent storm* ◦ *a storm cloud*
- on a day when there is a storm or several storms, the weather is **stormy**
- when a storm starts, it **breaks*** ◦ *Luckily we got home before the storm broke.*
- when a storm finishes, it **dies down** ◦ *When the storm had died down, we went out to look at the damage.*

■ thunder and lightning

- the loud noise which is heard during some storms: **thunder** (*noun* U); one bit of thunder: a **clap** or **peal** of thunder ◦ *Our dogs are terrified of thunder.*
- the light which appears in the sky before we hear thunder: **lightning** (*noun* U); one bit of lightning: a **flash** or **bolt** of lightning
- when lightning hits sb/sth, it **strikes*** (sb/sth) ◦ *He was struck by lightning when playing golf.*

■ different kinds of storm

- a storm with very heavy rain: **rainstorm**
- a heavy fall of snow with a strong, cold wind: **snowstorm**; a bad snowstorm: **blizzard**
- a storm with hail (= hard frozen rain which falls as small pieces of ice): **hailstorm**
- a storm with thunder and lightning: **thunderstorm**

story

1 different kinds of story
2 telling a story
3 describing a story

see also BOOK, READ, WRITE

1 different kinds of story

- a description of true or invented people and events: **story** ◦ *a detective story* ◦ *a love story* ◦ *a book of fairy/ghost stories* ◦ *He insisted on telling me his entire life story.*
- a book that tells a story about people and events that are not real: **novel**
- a piece of writing that is shorter than a novel: **short story**
- a short story which people tell as part of a conversation: **anecdote** ◦ *Henry's always telling anecdotes about his experiences in the army.*
- an invented story which you tell to make people laugh: **joke**
- a story told with pictures, usually found in newspapers and magazines: **comic strip**, **strip cartoon**
- stories, novels, etc which describe events and people that do not really exist: **fiction** (*noun* U); *adjective*: **fictional** ◦ *Do you read mainly fiction or non-fiction?* ◦ *a fictional account of life on a banana boat*

– fiction which is about what the world may be like in the future: **science fiction** (*noun* U)

– a story which is divided into parts, especially for a magazine or for TV or radio: **serial**; to make a story into a serial: **serialize** sth ◦ *There's a serial about a family during the war on Radio Four every Friday at five.*
– a book or film that is a continuation of a story: **sequel** (**to** sth)

– an old story about sth which may or may not be true: **legend** ◦ *the legend of King Arthur and the Round Table*
– a very old story about gods and heroes: **myth**; *adjective*: **mythical** ◦ *My favourite Greek myth is the one about Narcissus.* ◦ *a mythical hero*
– myths in general: **mythology** (*noun* U); *adjective*: **mythological**
– a story, often with animals as characters, which teaches a lesson about right and wrong actions: **fable** ◦ *Aesop's Fables*
– a story in the Bible, which teaches a lesson about right and wrong actions: **parable** ◦ *the parable of the prodigal son*

2 telling a story

– to say or write the events of a story: **tell*** (sb) a story ◦ *Tell me a story, Grandpa!*
– to tell sb a story by reading to them from a book: **read*** sb a story
– a book which has stories written in it: **story book**
– to tell sb about sth which happened to you: (*formal*) **relate** sth (**to** sb) ◦ *The police asked me to relate the events of the night before.*
– a person who tells a story: **storyteller** ◦ *Old Fred was a great storyteller. You could listen to him for hours.*
– the person who tells the story in a film, book, etc: **narrator**

3 describing a story

– the name of a story: **title**; (used about a story or a book) named: **entitled** ◦ *What's the title of that novel you're reading at the moment?* ◦ *a story entitled 'Italian Adventure'*
– a lot of children's stories begin with the words **once upon a time**

– something which happens in a story: **event, incident** ◦ *The events in this story were all invented by the writer – none of them are true.* ◦ *The narrator relates a number of incidents from his childhood.*
– the important events in a story: **plot** ◦ *a simple/complicated plot* ◦ *to think up a plot*

– a person who takes part in the events of a story: **character** ◦ *There are three main characters in this story, a mother and her two sons.*
– the most important male character in a story: **hero** (*plural* **heroes**); the most important female character: **heroine**

– the place and time at which a story happens: **setting**; to place the action of a story in a particular place and/or time: **set*** sth **in** a place/time ◦ *The story is set in 19th-century Dublin.*
– to describe the time and the place at which the story happened: **set the scene** ◦ *The first chapter of the novel sets the scene in great detail.*

– the part of a story, usually near the end, where we feel most afraid or excited: **climax** ◦ *The climax comes when the professor takes out a gun and turns to face his wife.*
– the last part of a story: **ending** ◦ *Everyone likes a story with a happy ending.*

– what a story is really about: **theme** ◦ *The theme of this story is love and money.*
– the reason for telling a story: **point** ◦ *The point of this story is that if you work hard, you will succeed.* ◦ *I'm afraid I don't get* (= understand) *the point. Why did they steal the car?* ◦ *No! You've missed* (= not understood) *the point completely!*

---

straight

straight lines ⇨ LINE

– something which goes or extends continuously in one direction only, is **straight** ◦ *a straight line* ◦ *straight hair* ◦ *a straight road*
– to become straight: **straighten** (**out**); to make sth straight: **straighten** sth (**out**) ◦ *After a series of bends, the road straightens out.* ◦ *to straighten your hair*

– in the correct position or in a straight line: **straight** (*adjective, adverb*) ◦ *Look at that wall. Do you think it's quite straight?* ◦ *That picture's not quite straight.* ◦ *Stand up straight!* (= with a straight back) ◦ *He couldn't walk straight.*
– standing vertically: **upright** (*adjective, adverb*) ◦ *in an upright position* ◦ *to stand upright*

■ not straight
– to make sth that was straight into a curved shape: **bend*** sth ◦ *She bent her knees.*
– to be or become curved: **bend***; *adjective*: **bent** ◦ *The branch he was on began to bend, but it did not break.* ◦ *a bent fork*
– bent so that it is not straight or level; not in the correct position: **crooked** ◦ *crooked teeth* ◦ *'Is my hat on straight?' 'No, it's a bit crooked.'*

– a part of a road, river, etc that is not straight: **bend** ◦ *The car came around the bend very fast.* ◦ *a bend in the river* ◦ *a sharp bend in the road*
– a line that bends round, gradually changing direction: **curve**; to have the shape of a curve: **curve**; *adjective*: **curved** ◦ *the curves of a person's body* ◦ *the curve of the hill* ◦ *a gentle/smooth curve* ◦ *The road curved gently to the right.* ◦ *a curved line*
– a turn or bend in sth that should be straight: **kink** ◦ *This wire is supposed to be straight but there's a kink in the middle.*

– to curve down in the middle under the weight of sth: **sag** ◦ *The mattress is beginning to sag.*
– to become bent and out of shape, for example because of heat: **warp** ◦ *The door had become warped and wouldn't shut easily.*
– to bend because of heat, force, weakness, etc: **buckle** ◦ *My bike hit a pothole and the front wheel buckled.*

straight *contd.*

– to bend and break or fall down because of pressure or force: **give* way** ◦ *The bench gave way under the weight of all the people.*

■ able to bend

– able to bend easily without breaking: **flexible**; *noun* (U): **flexibility** ◦ *a flexible pipe*
– not easy to bend, or impossible to bend: **inflexible**, **rigid**; *nouns* (U): **inflexibility**, **rigidity** ◦ *safety helmets made from rigid plastic*

■ not upright

– to be in a position that is not straight or upright: **lean**; to cause sth to be in this kind of position: **lean** sth ◦ *The tree was old and had begun to lean to one side.* ◦ *You can lean the bike against the wall.*
– to lean in a particular direction: **slant** ◦ *Her writing slants backwards.*

strange

not strange ⇨ USUAL
see also KNOW

– unusual or unexpected: **strange** (*adverb* **strangely**), **funny** (*adverb* **funnily**), **odd** (*adverb* **oddly**), **peculiar** ◦ *a strange experience* ◦ *to speak in a strange voice* ◦ *to behave strangely* ◦ *He was strangely silent.* ◦ *to feel funny* ◦ *an odd sort of person* ◦ *a peculiar shape/taste*
– the quality of being strange: **strangeness** (*noun* U)
– very strange: **bizarre**, **extraordinary** ◦ *bizarre behaviour* ◦ *I've just had the most extraordinary experience.*
– strange and sometimes frightening: **weird** ◦ *I had a weird dream last night.*

– strange and interesting: **curious** ◦ *What a curious expression! What does it mean exactly?*
– strange and difficult to believe: **fantastic** ◦ *Do you really expect me to believe such a fantastic excuse?*
– strange and different from what is normally expected: **unnatural** ◦ *It's unnatural for a child to be so silent.*
– very strange and seeming to be imagined: **unreal** ◦ *The situation was totally unreal – I had never experienced anything like it before.*

– a thing or person that you cannot understand: **mystery**; *adjective*: **mysterious** (*adverb* **mysteriously**) ◦ *They never solved the mystery of the missing diamonds.* ◦ *It's an absolute mystery.* ◦ *Several people have seen a mysterious figure in the churchyard.*
– a wonderful and extraordinary event that is impossible to explain: **miracle**; *adjective*: **miraculous** (*adverb* **miraculously**) ◦ *Only a miracle can help us now.* ◦ *a miraculous recovery from an illness* ◦ *The policeman miraculously appeared just at the right moment.*

– the unusual or unexpected part of a situation, that seems strange or amusing: **irony** (*noun* C/U); *adjective*: **ironic**, **ironical** (*adverb* **ironically**) ◦ *The irony is that I actually like her, in spite of what she did.* ◦ *It was ironic that his life was saved in an enemy hospital.*
– a statement that seems to be impossible but that is true or may be true: **paradox**; *adjective*: **paradoxical** (*adverb* **paradoxically**) ◦ *Paradoxically, as global warming increases, the winters seem to be getting colder.*

– a person who has strange ideas or who behaves in a strange way: **crank**, **eccentric**; *adjective*: **eccentric** ◦ *He's a bit of a crank, but quite harmless really.* ◦ *She's becoming more and more eccentric in her old age.*

– when you are going to explain how strange sth is, you can begin by saying **funnily/strangely/oddly enough ...** ◦ *Funnily enough, I was thinking about you just before you arrived.*

street ⇨ ROAD

string/rope

see also JOIN

– a long thin flexible material used for joining things, pulling things, etc: **string** (*noun* U), **cord** (*noun* U); a piece of this: **string**, **cord** ◦ *Could you cut the string just here for me?* ◦ *a piece of string* ◦ *beads threaded on a string*
– thick cord or string: **rope** (*noun* U); a piece of this: **rope** ◦ *Can you lend me a rope? My car's got stuck and I want to try and pull it out.*

– to fix sb/sth in position or join people or things together using string, rope, etc: **tie** sb/sth (**to** sth); *opposite*: **untie** sth ◦ *Tie your shoes.* ◦ *The prisoners had been tied to trees.* ◦ *We were tied together and couldn't move.* ◦ *We untied the parcel.*
– to tie or fasten sb/sth with string, etc: **tie** sb/sth **up** ◦ *They found a strong piece of rope and tied him up.*

– a place where two ends or pieces of string, rope, etc have been tied: **knot** ◦ *to tie a knot* ◦ *I can't undo this knot. Can you try?*
– to wrap string, cord, etc round sth: **wind*** sth; *opposite*: **unwind*** sth ◦ *You wind the string round the stick like this, and then you pull it hard.*

– when a piece of string or rope breaks suddenly, it **snaps** ◦ *Don't pull too hard or the string will snap.*
– when a string or a rope is pulled firmly at both ends, it is **taut**; *opposite*: **slack**

strong/weak

1 objects
2 people and animals
power and influence over people ⇨ POWER
strength of character ⇨ PERSONALITY
strong feelings ⇨ EMOTION

1 objects

– not easily broken or damaged: **strong**, **tough**; *nouns* (U): **strength**, **toughness** ◦ *Is this ladder*

strong enough to hold my weight? ◦ *a material chosen for its strength* ◦ *tough fabric/shoes*
– in good condition and not likely to collapse: **solid**, (*more formal*) **sound** ◦ *of solid construction* ◦ *Is the structure sound?*
– to become stronger: **strengthen**; to make sth stronger: **strengthen** sth ◦ *to strengthen a wall*
– to strengthen or support sth: **reinforce** sth; *noun*: **reinforcement** (*noun* U) ◦ *The walls were made with reinforced concrete.* ◦ *The joints need reinforcement or they will soon begin to weaken.*

– not strong; likely to break: **weak**; *noun* (U): **weakness** ◦ *The branch was weaker than I thought and it broke under my weight.*
– not made strongly and therefore easily broken or torn: **flimsy** ◦ *a flimsy bag/cover*
– delicate and easily damaged or broken: **fragile** ◦ *a fragile ornament*
– to become weaker: **weaken**; to make sth weaker: **weaken** sth ◦ *The water has weakened the sides of the canal.*

■ not likely to change or move
– likely to last a long time: **durable**, (especially clothing) **hard-wearing**; *noun* (U): **durability** ◦ *made of particularly durable materials* ◦ *a durable product* ◦ *hard-wearing man-made fibres*
– not easily damaged or affected by sth: **resistant** (**to** sth); *noun* (U): **resistance** (**to** sth) ◦ *plants resistant to frost* ◦ *heat-resistant* ◦ *a high level of resistance to corrosion*
– strong and steady and not likely to change or move: **firm** (*adverb* **firmly**), **secure** (*adverb* **securely**) ◦ *He had a firm grip on her shoulder.* ◦ *to place your feet firmly on the ground* ◦ *a secure foothold* ◦ *We tied the rope securely around the tree.*

2 people and animals

– physically able to lift, carry or push heavy things easily; not easily attacked or hurt: **strong**; *noun* (U): **strength** ◦ *I'm not strong enough to carry both suitcases.* ◦ *strong hands/arms* ◦ *physical strength* ◦ *I didn't have the strength to fight any more.*
– not made weak by cold, painful or difficult conditions: **tough**; *noun* (U): **toughness** ◦ *You have to be tough to survive in this climate.*
– having large and strong muscles: **muscular** ◦ *a muscular body*
– having the strength to do a lot of things in your life: **energetic**; *noun* (U): **energy** ◦ *an energetic businessman* ◦ *I don't know where she gets all her energy from!*
– strong or energetic: **vigorous**
– long-lasting physical or mental energy: **stamina** (*noun* U) ◦ *She can run fast, but she hasn't the stamina to run long distances.*

▷ having a strong, healthy body ⇨ **BODY**

– not being strong or not having energy: **weak** (*adverb* **weakly**); *noun* (U): **weakness** ◦ *to feel weak* ◦ *to be weak with hunger* ◦ *The weakness in her hands spread into her arms.* ◦ *to smile weakly*
– to cause sb to become weak: **weaken** sb ◦ *The illness weakened her terribly.*
– having no strength or energy: **feeble** ◦ *a feeble cry* ◦ *a feeble old man*
– not firm, but moving or shaking: **unsteady** ◦ *an unsteady hand* ◦ *to be unsteady on your feet*
– weak and not very healthy: **frail** ◦ *a frail old woman*
– weak, unhealthy and often ill: **sickly** ◦ *a sickly child*
– a weak person or animal: **weakling**

– easy to attack or hurt: **vulnerable**; *noun* (U): **vulnerability** ◦ *The soldiers were vulnerable to attack.* ◦ *in a vulnerable position*
– unable to defend yourself against attack: **defenceless** ◦ *a poor defenceless child*

student ⇨ LEARN, SCHOOL

study

1 studying sth
2 subjects which are studied
see also LEARN, EDUCATION, SCHOOL, UNIVERSITY

1 studying sth

– to spend time learning about sth: **study** (sth); the act of learning about sth: **study** (*noun* U) ◦ *to study English literature* ◦ *Please be quiet – I'm trying to study!*
– to get information about sth by asking or studying: **find*** sth **out** ◦ *They want to find out why girls do better in some subjects than boys.*
– to study a subject or a problem in detail in order to try and find out more about it: **investigate** sth; *noun* (C/U): **investigation** ◦ *an investigation into the causes of acid rain*
– to read a lot about sth so that you learn about it; to make a special study of sth: **read* up on** sth, **read*** sth **up** ◦ *I'm reading up on the First World War for my exam.*

– an area of knowledge that you study at school or university: **subject** ◦ *Which subject did you study at university?*
– to study a particular subject: **do*** sth ◦ *I did archaeology for two years at university.*
– a (general) area of study or knowledge: **field** ◦ *I'm afraid I don't know much about that – it isn't my field.*

– a person who is studying at a college or university: **student**
– a person who spends a lot of time studying is **studious** (*adverb* **studiously**)
– a person who studies and writes about a subject which they know well: **scholar**; *adjective*: **scholarly** ◦ *a famous Shakespeare scholar* ◦ *a scholarly book*

– a person who has special knowledge or skill: **expert** (**in**/**at**/**on** sth), **specialist** (**in** sth); *adjective*: **expert**; special knowledge or skill which a person has: **expertise** (*noun* U) ◦ *an expert in the field of education* ◦ *a specialist in family law* ◦ *There are a number of people with expertise in this field.*

study *contd.*

– to give most of your attention to one subject: **specialize** (**in** sth); *noun* (U): **specialization** ◦ *She specializes in family law.* ◦ *Family law is her specialization.*

■ research
– careful study of sth to find out more about it: **research** (**into/on** sth) (*noun* U) ◦ *a research project* ◦ *nuclear research* ◦ *research into human biology* ◦ *experimental research*
– to study sth carefully and in detail: **do* research** (**into** sth), **research** sth ◦ *We're doing research into global warming.* ◦ *Scientists are researching the effects of pollution on fish breeding.*
– a piece of scientific research into a particular subject; a book or article that a person writes after studying it: **study** ◦ *He's done a study of modern American society.*
– a study of the behaviour, opinions, etc of a particular group: **survey** ◦ *a government survey of children's attitudes to drugs*
– a person who does research: **researcher**

■ theories
– an idea or set of ideas that try to explain sth: **theory** ◦ *the theory of evolution*
– an idea that is suggested as a possible explanation for sth, but is not yet proved: **hypothesis** (*plural* **hypotheses**); to make a hypothesis: **hypothesize that ...** ◦ *to test/investigate/explore a hypothesis*
– based on theory rather than practical experience: **theoretical** (*adverb* **theoretically**) ◦ *theoretical physics* ◦ *The power of the machine was theoretically limitless.*

■ data
– facts or information used in research: **data** (*noun* U/*plural*) ◦ *We are gathering data on graduates without jobs.* ◦ *data collection*
– information about sth in the form of numbers: **statistics** (*noun plural*) ◦ *He's collected a lot of statistics relating to air pollution.*
– a list of questions used for collecting information about a particular subject: **questionnaire**

■ experiments
– a test which is done by scientists: **experiment**; connected with experiments: **experimental** ◦ *experiments which led to the discovery of penicillin* ◦ *experimental evidence*
– the process of doing experiments: **experiment** (*noun* U) ◦ *The theory needs to be tested by experiment.*
– to do an experiment: **experiment** (**with** sth/**on** sb/sth), **carry** sth **out** ◦ *They never experiment on live animals.* ◦ *to carry out experiments in space*
– a room or building that is used for scientific work or teaching: **laboratory**, (*informal*) **lab** ◦ *The samples were sent to the laboratory for analysis.*

■ results
– to study or think about the different parts or details of sth in order to understand it better: **analyse** (*AmE* **analyze**) sth; *noun* (C/U): **analysis** (*plural* **analyses**) ◦ *I've collected all the data I need and I'm doing the analysis.*
– to come to know sth as a result of doing research: **find*** sth, **discover** sth ◦ *Scientists haven't yet found a cure for colds.*
– the information that you get from doing research: **results** (*noun plural*), **findings** (*noun plural*)
– to make sb believe that sth is true: **prove** sth (**to** sb), **prove** (**that**) ..., **show** (**that**) ... ◦ *to prove a theory* ◦ *We expect to show that fatty diets are associated with high rates of heart disease.*

2 subjects which are studied

– systematic knowledge about, or study of, the natural world: **science** (*noun* U); *adjective*: **scientific** (*adverb* **scientifically**) ◦ *the achievements of modern science*
– the study and use of science for practical purposes in industry, etc: **technology** (*noun* U); *adjective*: **technological** (*adverb* **technologically**) ◦ *science and technology* ◦ *technological advances*

▷ more on science and technology ⇨ SCIENCE

– the study of people and society: **social science** (*noun* U/C) ◦ *Anthropology is one of the social sciences.*
– a person who studies social science: **social scientist**
– subjects of study concerned with human culture, especially literature, language, history and philosophy: **arts** (*noun plural*), **humanities** (*noun plural*) ◦ *an arts subject*

▷ names of subjects ⇨ table on page 435

Note: the name for the subject of study can be used before another noun to talk about sth connected to the whole subject: ◦ *a philosophy student* ◦ *the history department* ◦ *a linguistics exam* ◦ *a sociology textbook*; the adjectives can be used to describe sth concerned with a particular part of the subject of study: ◦ *a philosophical problem* ◦ *a psychological experiment*.

stupid ⇨ CLEVER

style

– in art ⇨ ART
– clothes, etc ⇨ FASHION
– in language ⇨ LANGUAGE
– way of doing sth ⇨ METHOD/MANNER

submarine ⇨ NAVY

succeed/fail

1 succeeding
2 not succeeding
3 wanting to succeed

succeeding in an examination ⇨ EXAM
succeeding in a race or competition ⇨ WIN/LOSE

see also HOPE, LUCK, TRY

the study of ...	is called ...	a person who studies this subject	adjective
social science, economics and law			
human societies and social behaviour	**sociology**	**sociologist**	**sociological**
the mind and the way that people behave	**psychology**	**psychologist**	**psychological**
language	**linguistics**	**linguist**	**linguistic**
human beings, especially of their origins, development, customs and beliefs	**anthropology**	**anthropologist**	**anthropological**
government	**politics, political science**	**political scientist**	**political**
the way money, trade and industry are organized	**economics**	**economist**	**economic**
how to control and manage a business	**business studies**		
the law	**law**		**legal**
arts and humanities			
ideas and beliefs about the meaning of life	**philosophy**	**philosopher**	**philosophical**
ancient Greek and Roman language and literature	**classics**	**classicist**	**classical**
religion	**theology**	**theologian**	**theological**
past events and social, political and economic developments	**history**	**historian**	**historical**
ancient civilizations, based on objects or parts of buildings that are found in the ground	**archaeology**	**archaeologist**	**archaeological**

1 succeeding

- to manage to do what you want: **succeed** (**in** sth/doing sth); *noun* (U): **success** ○ *If you don't succeed the first time, try again.* ○ *She finally succeeded in waking him up.* ○ *We wish you every success in your future career.*
- achieving success: **successful** (**in** sth) (*adverb* **successfully**) ○ *a successful party/ performance*

- to succeed in a particular task or in your job: **make* a success of** sth ○ *George has made a great success of his new job as a theatre director.*
- to succeed in your work, usually earning a lot of money: **do* well for** yourself ○ *Jonathan has done very well for himself since leaving university.*
- to do well in your life, job, etc: **get* on, go* far** ○ *If you want to get on, you have to be prepared to work long hours.*

- to get sth done or gain sth by effort or skill: **achieve** sth; *noun* (U): **achievement**; something which you achieve: **achievement** ○ *I sometimes wonder what I have really achieved in my life.* ○ *a great feeling of achievement* ○ *What a marvellous achievement!*
- to continue to do sth which is difficult, until you have succeeded: **see*** sth **through** ○ *Congratulations on seeing the job through!*

- to be able to do sth or deal with sth: **manage** (sth/**to** do sth) ○ *We finally managed to start the car.*
- to deal successfully with a difficult matter or situation: **cope** (**with** sth) ○ *I just can't cope with the stress of this job.*
- to manage to do sth difficult: (*informal*) **bring*/ carry/pull** sth **off** ○ *We haven't had much time to practise, but I'm sure we'll be able to bring it off.*
- to manage to solve a problem: **work** sth **out** ○ *'I just don't know what to do.' 'Don't worry – we'll work something out.'*
- to manage to do what you want to do, rather than what sb else wants you to do: **get*** your (**own**) **way** ○ *How is it that she always gets her own way?*

- if sth that you plan or do gives you the result that you want, it **goes* right, works, works out** ○ *Things have finally started to go right after all those problems we had.* ○ *I don't think this plan's going to work.* ○ *Things will probably work out all right in the end.*
- if sth produces the result that you want, it is **effective** (*adverb* **effectively**) ○ *a very effective medicine* ○ *to take effective action* ○ *The speaker made his point very effectively.*

2 not succeeding

- to be unsuccessful in sth: **fail** (sth), **fail to** do sth; *noun* (C/U): **failure** ○ *I tried but failed.* ○ *to fail an interview* ○ *Many of us failed to complete the course.* ○ *I felt depressed by constant failure.* ○ *When I lost my job, it just seemed like another failure.*

- (used about a plan or piece of work) to be unsuccessful: **fall* through, go* wrong** ○ *'I thought they were buying this house.' 'No, that fell through.'* ○ *In spite of our preparations, things soon started to go wrong.*
- (used about a business) to fail or break down suddenly or completely: **collapse**; *noun* (U): **collapse** ○ *If the government introduces these new taxes, our business is sure to collapse.* ○ *I'm trying to save the company from collapse.*
- to fail to make any progress: **not get* anywhere** ○ *Look, we're not getting anywhere in this dis-*

succeed/fail *contd.*

cussion – nobody's listening to anyone else's opinion.

– not successful: **unsuccessful** (*adverb* **unsuccessfully**) ◦ *an unsuccessful businessman* ◦ *an unsuccessful journey* ◦ *Edward tried, unsuccessfully, to offer the policeman a bribe.*
– a person or thing that has failed, or that often fails: **failure** ◦ *Everything in my life has gone wrong. I feel like a complete failure.*
– an unsuccessful organized event: **fiasco** (*plural* **fiascos**) ◦ *The dance was a complete fiasco – all the lights went out at 10 pm, and everybody had to go home.*

– not having the effect you want: **futile, ineffective** (*adverb* **ineffectively**); *nouns* (U): **futility, ineffectiveness** ◦ *It's futile trying to help him – he's too proud to accept help from anyone.* ◦ *Some of us made ineffective attempts to stop the water coming into the boat.* ◦ *The futility of the plan soon became obvious.*
– giving no hope of success: **hopeless** (*adverb* **hopelessly**) ◦ *It's hopeless – there's nothing more I can do.* ◦ *We were hopelessly lost.*
– something (for example a plan) which will not work is **unworkable** ◦ *It's an interesting idea, but I'm afraid it's totally unworkable.*

3 wanting to succeed

– a strong desire to be successful: **ambition** (*noun* U); *adjective*: **ambitious** (*adverb* **ambitiously**) ◦ *When he started out in business, he was young and full of ambition.* ◦ *I was very ambitious when I was younger.*
– a particular thing that you want to do: **ambition** ◦ *Her ambition is to climb Everest.*
– likely to succeed in a profession: **promising** ◦ *a promising young musician*

– feeling or showing that you are sure of being successful: **confident** (**of** sth/**that ...**) (*adverb* **confidently**); *noun* (U): **confidence** ◦ *I'm confident that we'll raise the money in time.*
– confident in your own abilities: **self-confident**; *noun* (U): **self-confidence** ◦ *She's very self-confident – she's not afraid to stand up and speak in front of a large audience.*

– the possibility of being successful: **hope** (**of** sth/doing sth), **chance** (**of** sth/doing sth), **prospects** (**of** sth/doing sth) (*noun plural*) ◦ *Unfortunately, they have little hope of completing their journey before winter sets in.* ◦ *'What are our prospects of success?' 'Not very good at present, I'm afraid.'*
– the possibility of not being successful: **risk** ◦ *There is a risk that we might fail.* ◦ *I'm not prepared to take that risk!*
– to have a chance of succeeding in sth: **stand* a ... chance of** doing sth ◦ *I think you stand a good/fair chance of getting that job.*

4 being known and liked

– something that is successful and that a lot of people like: **hit, success**; something that is not successful: **flop** ◦ *That song was a big hit in America.* ◦ *The school play was a great success.* ◦ *His first film was a complete flop.*
– liked by many people or by most people in a group: **popular**; the state of being popular: **popularity** (*noun* U) ◦ *a popular writer/singer/tourist resort*
– to be known by many people as being good: **have a good reputation** ◦ *'Is he a good dentist?' 'Well I've never been to him myself, but he's got a good reputation.'*
– to be as good as people say: **live up to** your **reputation** ◦ *'Well, did the hotel live up to its reputation?' 'Oh, absolutely.'*

success ⇨ SUCCEED / FAIL

sudden(ly) ⇨ FAST / SLOW

suffer

1 pain and suffering
2 experiencing suffering
see also ILLNESS

1 pain and suffering

– the unpleasant feeling that you have when your body has been hurt or when you are ill: **pain** (*noun* C/U); *adjective*: **painful** ◦ *a terrible pain* ◦ *She has to put up with a great deal of pain.* ◦ *a painful operation*
– physical harm: **injury** (*noun* C/U) ◦ *I had serious injuries to my chest and head.*

▷ more on pain and injury ⇨ PAIN, INJURY

– unhappiness that you feel because sth bad has happened or because sb has been unkind to you: **pain** (*noun* U); *adjective*: **painful** ◦ *She experienced a lot of pain as a result of her marriage breaking up.* ◦ *pain and suffering* ◦ *a painful experience*
– physical or mental pain: **suffering** (*noun* U)
– something that hurts your feelings is **hurtful** ◦ *That was a really hurtful thing to say.*

– difficulties or problems, for example because you do not have enough money: **hardship** (*noun* C/U) ◦ *It was not a serious hardship to go without meat for a few days.* ◦ *Anna's had a lot of hardship in her life.*
– great unhappiness or hardship: **misery** (*noun* U)
– a situation which is very unpleasant, painful or miserable: (*informal*) **hell** (*noun* U) ◦ *The weekend was absolute hell.*

– unpleasant or unhappy: **hard** ◦ *a hard life* ◦ *a hard day.*
– too unpleasant or painful for you to accept: **unbearable** (*adverb* **unbearably**), **intolerable** (*adverb* **intolerably**) ◦ *It was an unbearably painful experience.* ◦ *an intolerable situation*

2 experiencing suffering

– to experience sth unpleasant: **suffer** (sth/**from** sth) ◦ *The company has suffered huge losses over the past two years.* ◦ *People are suffering from the effects of atmospheric pollution.*
– to cause sb/sth physical or emotional pain: **hurt*** (sb/sth) ◦ *Stop it – you're hurting me!* ◦ *What he said to me really hurt.*

- to have a difficult or unpleasant experience: **undergo*** sth, **go* through** sth, (*formal*) **endure** sth ◦ *to undergo an operation* ◦ *I hope I never have to go through anything like that again – it was one of the worst experiences of my life.*
- to suffer sth unpleasant and not complain about it: **put* up with** sth ◦ *So I said I'm just not going to put up with it any more.*
- to cause sb to undergo sth difficult or painful: (*informal*) **put*** sb **through** sth ◦ *The treatment is painful – let's hope they don't put him through anything like that.*
- able to put up with sth without complaining or getting angry: **patient**; *noun* (U): **patience** ◦ *He must have had a lot of patience to put up with it for so long.*

- to have difficulties at work or with other people: **have a hard time** ◦ *I've been having a really hard time at work.*
- to make sb's life unhappy: (*informal*) **give*** sb **a hard time** ◦ *His teacher's giving him a bit of a hard time at present.*

- to suffer for a mistake or for sth you have done wrong: **pay* for** sth, **pay* the penalty for** sth ◦ *I knew that I would have to pay for what I'd done.*
- what you suffer in order to obtain sth else: **cost** (*noun* U) ◦ *She took on a difficult job at great cost to her own health.*

- a person or animal that is injured, hurt or killed by sb/sth: **victim** ◦ *victims of racist attacks* ◦ *The victim's body was found in a ditch.*

sugar

see also FOOD

- the sweet substance that we put in or on food: **sugar** (*noun* U) ◦ *Do you take sugar in your tea?* ◦ *a bag of sugar* ◦ *white/brown sugar*
- something used instead of sugar (for example by people who do not want to get fat): (**artificial**) **sweetener** (*noun* U)

- white sugar used in tea and coffee and in cooking: **granulated sugar** (*noun* U)
- fine white sugar used for baking cakes: **castor sugar** (*noun* U)
- light brown sugar which is soft: **soft brown sugar** (*noun* U)
- light brown sugar which has large hard grains: **demerara sugar** (*noun* U)
- very fine white sugar powder used to make icing (= the soft sweet substance put on the top of cakes): **icing sugar** (*noun* U)
- the smallest piece of sugar: **grain** (**of sugar**)

- a small cube of sugar that you put in tea or coffee: **sugar-lump**
- the amount of sugar that can be contained in one spoon: **spoon**(**ful**) (**of sugar**) ◦ *'Do you take sugar?' 'Yes, two spoons, please.'*
- a bowl used for keeping sugar in: **sugar bowl**
- to throw small pieces of sth over a surface: **sprinkle** sth ◦ *Sprinkle sugar over your cornflakes and add milk.*

- something which has sugar in it is **sweet** ◦ *I can't drink this, it's too sweet.*
- to make sth sweet by adding sugar to it: **sweeten** sth
- with sugar added: **sweetened**; *opposite*: **unsweetened** ◦ *unsweetened orange juice*
- something which tastes as if it has a lot of sugar in it is **sugary** ◦ *sugary soft drinks*

▷ sweet food ⇨ SWEET

■ **MORE ...**
- a thick sweet liquid that is made by boiling water with sugar: **syrup** (*noun* U) ◦ *pears in syrup*
- a thick dark sticky liquid that is made from sugar and usually used in cooking: **treacle** (*noun* U)
- a thick light sticky liquid that is made from sugar and sometimes put on bread or used in cooking: **golden syrup** (*noun* U)

suggest ⇨ ADVISE/SUGGEST

suitable ⇨ USEFUL/SUITABLE

summer ⇨ SEASON

sun

1 the sun in the sky
2 the heat of the sun
3 the light of the sun
4 using the energy of the sun

see also WEATHER, SKY, STAR/PLANET/MOON

1 the sun in the sky

- the ball of light which we see in the sky during the day and which gives the earth light and heat: **the sun** ◦ *The weather was terrible – we hardly saw the sun all week.*
- in the morning the sun **rises***, **comes* up**; when it has risen it is **up** ◦ *As soon as the sun was up the whole village came to life.*
- in the evening the sun **sets***, **goes* down** ◦ *The sun rises in the east and sets in the west.*
- the time when the sun rises: **dawn** (*noun* C/U), **sunrise** (*noun* C/U) ◦ *before sunrise* ◦ *at dawn*
- the time when the sun sets: **sunset** (*AmE* **sundown**) (*noun* C/U) ◦ *At sunset, they made camp.*

- when the moon is between the earth and the sun so that it blocks the light, there is an **eclipse** ◦ *a total/partial eclipse of the sun*

2 the heat of the sun

- the light and heat of the sun: **the sun**, **sunshine** (*noun* U) ◦ *I'm exhausted – I've been working out in the sun all day.* ◦ *The thing I miss most about Spain is the sunshine.*
- when the sun can be seen in the sky, it is **out**; when it gives out light, it **shines***, the weather is **sunny**, **bright** ◦ *The sun was shining brightly.* ◦ *It was a lovely sunny day.*
- when the sun appears from behind the clouds, it **comes* out**, **breaks* through**

sun *contd.*

- when it disappears behind the clouds, it **goes* in** ◦ *The sun managed to break through for a few minutes, but now it's gone in again.*

- to lie in the sun: **sunbathe**, **sun** yourself
- the brown colour which people get on their skin when they sunbathe: **tan**, **suntan**
- an illness which people get when they stay in the sun too long: **sunstroke** (*noun* U)

▷ the effect of the sun on your skin ⇨ SKIN

3 the light of the sun

- the light that there is during the day: **daylight** (*noun* U) ◦ *I hope there'll still be some daylight left when we get there.*
- the light seen when the sun is shining: **sunlight** (*noun* U); *adjective*: **sunlit** ◦ *The castle looks beautiful in the evening sunlight.* ◦ *a sunlit street*
- having a lot of light from the sun: **sunny** ◦ *a sunny garden/room/position*
- a line of sunlight shining down (for example into a room): **ray** (of light), **beam** (of light), **sunbeam** ◦ *They stayed outside, enjoying the last rays of the sun.*

- the half-light in the evening around sunset: **dusk** (*noun* U), **twilight** (*noun* U)

- the glasses that people wear to protect their eyes from the sun: **sunglasses** (*noun plural*), **dark glasses** (*noun plural*), (*informal, especially AmE*) **shades** (*noun plural*)
- an area which is not lit by direct sunlight, and which is darker and cooler than areas in the sun: the **shade** (*noun* U); *adjective*: **shady** ◦ *You can go and play; I'll wait here in the shade.* ◦ *This looks like a nice shady place to sit.*
- a dark shape caused by sth blocking the sun and making an area of shade: **shadow** ◦ *Look at the shadows of the trees on the grass.*

4 using the energy of the sun

- something which uses the sun or is connected with the sun is **solar** ◦ *solar energy/ power*
- a machine which is operated using solar power is **solar-powered**
- a piece of equipment, for example on the roof of a house, which is used to collect solar power: **solar panel**

superior

- better quality ⇨ GOOD
- higher rank ⇨ RANK

supermarket ⇨ SHOP

supper ⇨ MEAL

supply ⇨ PROVIDE

support

see also HELP

- to give sb help, money, friendship, etc when they need it: **support** sb; *noun* (U): **support** ◦ *Thank you so much for your support.* ◦ *wholehearted support* (= complete support)
- a person who gives sb support is **supportive** ◦ *When I was ill and short of money, all my friends were wonderfully supportive.*
- to support sb/sth by giving them money: **back** sb/sth; *noun* (U): **backing**

- a person who does not change their support for sb/sth is **faithful**, **loyal**; *nouns* (U): **faithfulness**, **loyalty** ◦ *Ian is a faithful friend.* ◦ *a loyal husband/wife/colleague*
- to say or do sth that shows that you support sb/sth: **stand* up for** sb/sth, (*informal*) **stick* up for** sb/sth ◦ *He was always ready to stand up for his beliefs.*
- to say or write sth to support sb: **defend** sb/sth (**against** sb/sth) ◦ *Mrs. Smith wrote to the newspaper, defending her husband against the criticism.*
- to support sb/sth, especially by saying that sth is true: **back** sb/sth **up** ◦ *Two people backed up his story that he was in Manchester at the time of the murder.*

- when one group of people supports another, they all **stick* together**
- a person or a country that helps and supports you: **ally** ◦ *our political allies*

- to agree with the aims of a person or an organization: **support** sb/sth; the help that you give: **support** (*noun* U); a person who does this: **supporter** ◦ *to support the government* ◦ *to rely on people's support* ◦ *supporters of animal rights*
- to give strong support to a particular person or idea: **champion** sb/sth; a person who does this: **champion** (**of** sth) ◦ *to champion the cause of human rights* ◦ *a champion of free speech*
- to have a particular sports team, etc as your favourite: **support** sb/sth; a person who does this: **supporter**, **fan** ◦ *a Liverpool fan*

■ not supporting sb/sth

- to disagree with sb/sth and try to change or stop them/it: **oppose** sb/sth, **be opposed to** sb/sth; the act of opposing sb/sth: **opposition** (*noun* U) ◦ *Local residents opposed the plan for the bypass.* ◦ *I am opposed to a ban on smoking in the school.* ◦ *to express your opposition to sth*
- the people who oppose sb/sth: **opposition** (*noun* U) ◦ *Mike has joined the opposition.*
- to say in public that you do not like or agree with sth: **come* out against** sth ◦ *The Prime Minister has come out against capital punishment.*

- if you do or say sth that harms sb/sth that you should support, you are **disloyal** (**to** sb/sth); *noun* (U): **disloyalty**
- to stop supporting sb/sth and start opposing them/it: **turn against** sb/sth ◦ *Public opinion has turned against the President.*

- if you do not want to show your support for one person rather than another, you do not **take* sides** ◦ *It has been a long and involved argument, and I refuse to take sides.*

– if you do not support any side in an argument or a war, etc, you are **neutral**; *noun* (U): **neutrality** ◦ *to remain neutral*

sure ⇨ POSSIBLE[1]

surface

1 surfaces
2 flat or bumpy surfaces
3 smooth or rough surfaces
4 covering a surface

1 surfaces

– the outside part of sth: **surface** ◦ *to land on the surface of the moon* ◦ *a work surface in a kitchen* ◦ *a flat/bumpy surface* ◦ *a rough/smooth surface* ◦ *a polished/shiny surface*
– any of the flat outer surfaces of an object: **side** ◦ *the sides of a pyramid*
– the size of a surface: **area** ◦ *The room is about 45 square metres in area.*
– something that is only on the surface is **superficial** ◦ *He only had superficial injuries.* ◦ *There were some scratches on the paintwork but they were only superficial.*

▷ the different sides of an object ⇨ PLACE[2]

2 flat or bumpy surfaces

– (used about the surface of sth) having no parts that are raised above the rest: **flat**, **level**, **even** ◦ *The countryside round here is very flat.* ◦ *a flat roof* ◦ *a flat surface* ◦ *a level teaspoon of sugar* ◦ *level ground* ◦ *The game must be played on an even surface.*
– to make sth flat: **flatten** sth, (used especially about the ground) **level** sth ◦ *She drove the car over his ball and flattened it.* ◦ *The ground will need to be levelled before we can build on it.*

– a surface that is not flat is **uneven** ◦ *uneven ground*
– a part of a flat surface that is raised above the rest: **bump**; *adjective*: **bumpy** ◦ *There were lots of bumps in the road.* ◦ *The road was really bumpy.*
– a sea which is not smooth can be called **rough**, **choppy**

– an outward curve on sth that is usually flat, perhaps because there is sth underneath: **bulge**; to form a bulge: **bulge** (**out**) ◦ *She had a huge bulge in her pocket.*
– an outward curve or swelling on sth (especially on the body or on flat surfaces): **lump**; *adjective*: **lumpy** ◦ *He had a big lump on his forehead where he'd knocked his head.* ◦ *I hardly slept at all – the bed was really lumpy.*

3 smooth or rough surfaces

– having an even surface with no lumps or holes: **smooth**; *noun* (U): **smoothness** ◦ *smooth skin* ◦ *a smooth lawn* ◦ *the smooth surface of the material* ◦ *the smoothness of her complexion*
– smooth and nice to touch: **soft** ◦ *soft smooth sheets*

– not smooth: **rough**; *noun* (U): **roughness** ◦ *rough skin/hands* ◦ *a rough road* ◦ *The material was a nice colour but it felt very rough against the skin.*
– consisting of large pieces; rough: **coarse** ◦ *coarse cloth*
– very rough and broken objects and materials, with sharp points, can be called **jagged** ◦ *a jagged edge* ◦ *jagged rocks*

■ making something smooth
– to make sth smooth: **smooth** sth (**back**, **down**, **out**, etc) ◦ *He looked in the mirror and smoothed down his hair.*
– strong paper with sand on it, that is used for rubbing surfaces in order to make them smoother: **sandpaper** (*noun* U)
– to make sth smooth by rubbing sandpaper across it firmly: **rub** sth (**down**), **sand** sth (**down**)

4 covering a surface

– a thickness of material that is laid over a surface: **layer** ◦ *I had to remove several layers of old wallpaper.*
– a thin layer of sth that covers a surface: **coating** ◦ *There was a coating of dust over all the furniture when we came back from our holiday.*

– to put sth over a surface so that it touches it partly or completely: **cover** sth (**with** sth) ◦ *I think I'll cover this old chair with some new material.*
– if a surface has sth over it which touches it partly or completely, it **is covered in/with** sth ◦ *The floors were covered with expensive carpets.*
– something which covers a surface: **cover**, **covering** ◦ *I've bought new covers for the chairs.* ◦ *There was a thin covering of snow on the ground.*

surprise

1 different feelings of surprise
2 what you do and say when you are surprised

1 different feelings of surprise

– something that you did not expect, or the feeling that you have when this happens: **surprise** (*noun* C/U) ◦ *I want my birthday present to be a surprise.* ◦ *He looked up in surprise when I spoke.* ◦ *To our surprise, she had already gone when we arrived.*
– something that causes a feeling of surprise is **surprising** (*adverb* **surprisingly**), it **surprises** you ◦ *It's surprising that nobody has asked that question before.* ◦ *Not surprisingly, she got pretty angry.* ◦ *It wouldn't surprise me if it rained this afternoon.* ◦ *Let's surprise her by giving her a party.*
– when sth happens which you did not expect, you are **surprised** ◦ *I was surprised to see so many people there.* ◦ *She was surprised at his behaviour.*
– if sth that you were not expecting happens to you, it **takes*** you **by surprise** ◦ *His answer took me by surprise.*

surprise *contd.*

- something that you did not expect is **unexpected** (*adverb* **unexpectedly**) ◦ *an unexpected guest* ◦ *to arrive unexpectedly*
- happening unexpectedly and quickly: **suddenly**, **all of a sudden**, **all at once**; *adjective*: **sudden** ◦ *Everything happened so suddenly that it's difficult to remember the details.* ◦ *All of a sudden, she burst out laughing.* ◦ *a sudden noise/movement*

■ very surprising
- very surprising: **amazing**, **incredible**, **astonishing** ◦ *an amazing trick* ◦ *an astonishing success*
- if sth is very surprising, it **amazes** you, **astonishes** you, you are or feel **amazed/astonished** (**at/by** it) ◦ *You amaze me.* ◦ *She has astonished us all by her decision.* ◦ *I'm amazed at the prices here.*
- a feeling of great surprise: **amazement** (*noun* U), **astonishment** (*noun* U) ◦ *to stare in amazement* ◦ *Her eyes opened wide in astonishment.*

■ bad surprises
- something which is surprising and bad or unpleasant is **shocking**, a **shock**, it **shocks** you, you feel **shocked** ◦ *Conditions in the camps are shocking.* ◦ *His death was a terrible shock to everyone.* ◦ *She's suffering from the shock of the news.* ◦ *The pictures may shock you.*
- if sth surprises and perhaps frightens you, it is **startling**, it **startles** you, you feel **startled** ◦ *You startled me when you came into the room so quietly.* ◦ *a startled look*
- a sudden shock or disappointment: **blow** ◦ *His death was a terrible blow to the whole family.* ◦ *My exam results were a bit of a blow.*

■ strange and surprising
- strange and surprising: **funny** ◦ *That's funny – why have the lights gone out?*
- to say that sth is strange and surprising, you can begin **funnily** (**enough**) ◦ *Funnily enough, I had a similar experience to yours last week.*
- very surprising and therefore rather difficult to believe: **incredible** (*adverb* **incredibly**) ◦ *What an incredible story!*
- two or more things happening at the same time by chance: **coincidence** (*noun* C/U) ◦ *What a coincidence! I had just mentioned your name when you came in the door.* ◦ *By coincidence, we had bought our hats from the same shop.*

2 what you do and say when you are surprised

- to make a sudden movement because of surprise or fear: **jump** ◦ *I wish you would knock on the door before you come in – you made me jump.*
- very surprised and therefore unable to speak for a moment: **speechless**, **stunned**, **taken aback** ◦ *Her answer left him speechless.* ◦ *a stunned silence* ◦ *We were stunned by the news.* ◦ *She was completely taken aback by his question and couldn't think of a thing to say.*
- to say sth suddenly because you are surprised, angry, etc: **exclaim**; what you say: **exclamation** ◦ *'What a lovely surprise!' he exclaimed.* ◦ *There were exclamations of delight as the children opened their presents.*
- to express surprise, you can say (**oh**) **really?** or (**good**) **heavens!** or **gosh!** or **wow!** ◦ *Really? How did you find this out?* ◦ *Good heavens! Is that really the time? I must go!* ◦ *Gosh! I don't know what to say! Thank you!* ◦ *Wow! That's fantastic!*
- to emphasize that sth is surprising, you can use **even** ◦ *I was in such a hurry that I didn't even have time for breakfast.* ◦ *Even the Prime Minister was present.*

■ MORE ...
- an unexpected and unpleasant piece of news: **bombshell** ◦ *The announcement came as a bombshell.*
- if sth is completely unexpected, you can say that it happens (**right**) **out of the blue** ◦ *The job offer came right out of the blue, from a company I had never even heard of.*

swear

- when you are angry ⇨ ANGRY
- bad language ⇨ LANGUAGE
- making a promise ⇨ PROMISE

sweet

see also TASTE

- tasting like sugar: **sweet** ◦ *sweet tea* ◦ *sweet white wine*
- something which tastes as if it has a lot of sugar in it is **sugary**

▷ making sth sweet by adding sugar, etc ⇨ SUGAR

■ not sweet
- having a sharp taste like that of a lemon: **sour** ◦ *These apples are rather sour.*
- having a sharp unpleasant taste: **bitter** ◦ *bitter coffee*
- flavoured with salt or spices, not sugar: **savoury** (*AmE* **savory**) ◦ *a savoury dish at the end of the meal*

■ sweet things to eat
- sweet food that is often served at the end of a meal: **sweet**, **pudding**, (*more formal* or *AmE*) **dessert** ◦ *'Would you like a sweet?' 'No thanks, just coffee please.'* ◦ *'What's for pudding today?' 'Apple pie.'*
- a small piece of boiled sugar, chocolate, etc, that children like to eat: **sweet** ◦ *I bought a packet of sweets.*

▷ more on sweets ⇨ SWEETS

- if you like sugar and sweet things a lot, you **have a sweet tooth** ◦ *She has a sweet tooth – she loves cakes and sweets.*

sweets

other sweet things to eat ⇨ CAKE, SUGAR

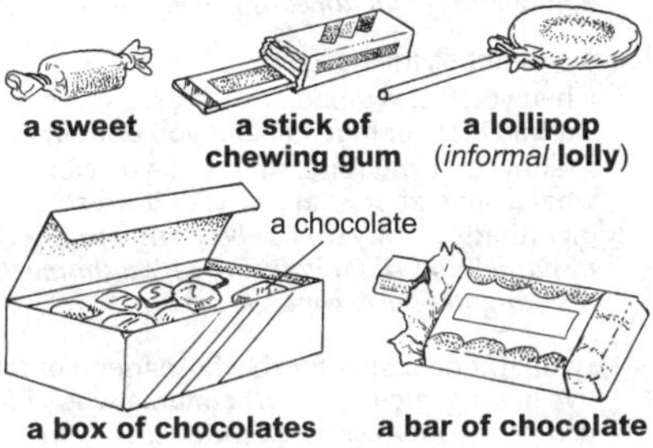

- a small piece of boiled sugar, chocolate, etc, that children like to eat: **sweet**, (*AmE*) **candy** (*noun* C/U) ◦ *Would you like a sweet?* ◦ *a packet/bag of sweets* ◦ *a sweet wrapper* (= a piece of paper covering a sweet) ◦ *a piece of candy*
- a hard sticky sweet made with boiled sugar and butter: **toffee** (*noun* C/U)
- a sweet (usually white or green) with the flavour of peppermint: **peppermint**, **mint**
- a coloured sweet made of boiled sugar which you usually suck: **boiled sweet**
- a sweet sticky substance that you chew but do not swallow: **chewing gum** (*noun* U)
- a type of hard sweet made in long sticks and usually sold at the seaside: **rock** (*noun* U) ◦ *a stick of rock*

- chocolate which is light in colour and sweet: **milk chocolate** (*noun* U); chocolate which is darker in colour and more bitter: **plain chocolate** (*noun* U)

- when you eat a sweet, you can **chew** it (= break it up with your teeth before you swallow it), **suck** it (= hold it in your mouth and pull liquid out of it slowly) or **lick** it (= move your tongue across it) ◦ *Suck it slowly – don't chew it.* ◦ *She was happily licking her lollipop.*

- the shop where you buy sweets: **sweetshop** (*AmE* **candy store**)
- the general word for all sweets, cakes and chocolate: **confectionery** (*noun* U)

swim

see also SPORT, SEA

- to move your body through water: **swim***; the name of this activity or sport: **swimming** (*noun* U) ◦ *Can you swim?* ◦ *Swimming's my favourite sport.*
- to swim for pleasure: **go* swimming**; a particular occasion of swimming: **swim** ◦ *I'm going swimming tomorrow.* ◦ *I had a swim this morning.* ◦ *Are you coming for a swim?*
- a person who is swimming or who swims regularly: **swimmer**
- to swim in the sea, a lake or river: **bathe**; the name of the activity: **bathing** (*noun* U) ◦ *The sea was beautiful, but it was too cold to bathe.* ◦ *This beach is not suitable for bathing.*
- a quick swim: **dip** ◦ *Shall we go for a dip?* ◦ *to take a dip*

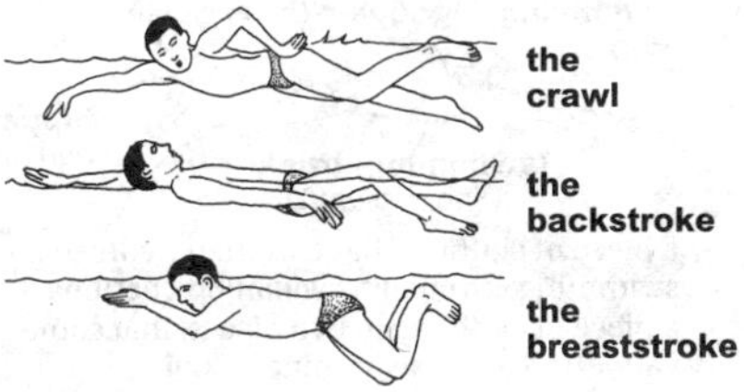

- one of the movements you make when you are swimming: **stroke**
- to stay on the surface of the water, without making swimming strokes: **float** ◦ *to float on your back*
- to keep your body floating by moving your legs under you: **tread* water** ◦ *I had to tread water for thirty minutes before a boat came and picked me up.*
- if you cannot swim and you go below the surface of the sea, you **go* under** ◦ *She went under three times before the lifeguard pulled her out.*
- to die in water because you cannot breathe: **drown**, **be drowned**

- if you are in water that is too deep for you to stand up in, you are **out of your depth** ◦ *Enjoy your swim, but take care not to go out of your depth.*
- below the surface of water: **underwater** (*adjective, adverb*) ◦ *an underwater camera* ◦ *I love swimming underwater.*

■ diving
- to jump into the water with your head first: **dive***; the act of diving into water: **dive** ◦ *Larry dived into the river.* ◦ *a diving competition*
- the activity or sport of diving into water: **diving** (*noun* U)
- a person who swims underwater: **diver**
- to dive, fall, jump, etc into water suddenly and with force: **plunge** (**into** sth) ◦ *She plunged into the icy water.*
- to come to the surface of the water from below: **surface**, **come* up** ◦ *He surfaced after two minutes underwater.*
- a sport where a person swims underwater with special breathing equipment: **scuba-diving** (*noun* U), **skin-diving** (*noun* U)
- a swimmer who works underwater wearing special rubber clothes and using breathing equipment: **frogman** (*plural* **frogmen**)

■ swimming pools
- a pool that is built especially for people to swim in: (**swimming**) **pool** ◦ *an indoor/outdoor pool* ◦ *The pool is two metres deep.*
- a public swimming pool, usually indoors: **swimming bath**, (**swimming**) **baths** (*noun plural*)

swim *contd.*

- a board at the side of a swimming pool from which a person can dive into the water: **diving board**

■ things people wear when they are swimming

- a piece of clothing that a woman wears to go swimming: **swimsuit, swimming costume**
- a piece of clothing, in two pieces, that some women wear for swimming: **bikini**

- a short tube that a swimmer can use to breathe through when swimming below the surface of the water: **snorkel**
- a rubber suit that covers the whole of the body, used by underwater swimmers and people doing water sports: **wetsuit**

■ safety
- a ring that floats and that you throw to a person who has fallen in the water to stop them going underwater: **lifebelt, lifebuoy**
- a person at a beach or swimming pool whose job is to rescue people who are in difficulties in the water: **lifeguard**

sword ⇨ WEAPON

sympathy

see also EMOTION

- understanding of other people's feelings and problems: **sympathy** (**for/towards** sb) (*noun* U); to have sympathy for sb: **sympathize** (**with** sb/sth); *adjective*: **sympathetic** (*adverb* **sympathetically**) ◦ *I know I won't get any sympathy from you.* ◦ *I sympathize with you/your problems, but there's nothing I can do.* ◦ *a sympathetic attitude* ◦ *I spoke to Tom as sympathetically as I could.*
- thinking about what other people feel, want, need, etc: **thoughtfulness** (*noun* U); *adjective*: **thoughtful** (*adverb* **thoughtfully**) ◦ *It was so thoughtful of you to remember me – I know how busy you are.*
- sadness for other people's suffering: **pity** (*noun* U); to feel pity for sb: **pity** sb, **feel* sorry** for sb; to help sb who is in trouble or suffering, because you feel sorry for them: **take* pity on** sb ◦ *I can't feel pity for a person who treats animals like that.* ◦ *I don't want you to feel sorry for me.*
- if you do sth because you feel sorry for sb, you do it **out of pity** (**for** them)
- caring about how other people feel and doing things to help them: **kindness** (*noun* U); *adjective*: **kind** (*adverb* **kindly**) ◦ *We were treated with wonderful kindness.* ◦ *Be kind to her!*

▷ being kind to people ⇨ KIND/CRUEL

- something that causes you to feel sad or sympathetic is **moving, touching**; if you have this feeling, you are **moved** (**by** sth), **touched** (**by** sth) ◦ *a moving performance* ◦ *a touching moment* ◦ *to be deeply moved* ◦ *to be moved to tears*
- asking for help and support: **appealing** (*adverb* **appealingly**) ◦ *an appealing look*

■ sympathetic things to say
- when you feel sympathetic towards sb, you can say **bad luck!** or **hard luck!** or **you poor thing!**
- to show that you think sth is sad, you can say **what a shame!** or **what a pity!** or **it's a shame/pity (that) ...** ◦ *'My cat has been run over!' 'What a shame! How did it happen?'* ◦ *It's a shame that his daughter never comes to see him.*

- sympathetic wishes for sb whose friend or relative has just died: (*formal*) **condolences** ◦ *Please accept my condolences on the death of your brother.* ◦ *to express your condolences*
- if sb has experienced sth bad (for example if a friend is very ill or if a member of the family has died), you can say **I'm so/very sorry**

■ not sympathetic
- not sympathetic: **unsympathetic** (*adverb* **unsympathetically**), **hard-hearted**
- not thinking about what other people feel, want, need, etc: **thoughtless** (*adverb* **thoughtlessly**); *noun* (U): **thoughtlessness** ◦ *a thoughtless action/attitude*

table

using a table for meals ⇨ MEAL
see also FURNITURE, CHAIR

- a piece of furniture with a flat top and one or more legs: **table** ◦ *The food's on the table!* ◦ *We sat round the table and discussed what to do.* ◦ *to sit at table* (= for a meal)

- a table used for preparing food, eating meals, etc: **kitchen table**
- a table used for eating meals in a dining room: **dining table, dining-room table**
- a small low table that is usually in a living room: **coffee table**
- a table that you sit at to write or work: **desk**
- a small table that stands next to a bed: **bedside table**
- a table that you stand at in order to make things: (**work**)**bench**

- the most important end of a table is its **head** ◦ *She always sat at the head of the table.*

tail ⇨ ANIMAL

take

- bringing or taking sth ⇨ BRING/TAKE/CARRY
- getting sth ⇨ GET/OBTAIN
- catching and holding sth ⇨ HOLD/CATCH
- taking sth away ⇨ REMOVE

talk ⇨ SPEAK

tall ⇨ HEIGHT

tap ⇨ WATER

tape-recorder ⇨ RECORD

taste

the other senses ⇨ **FEEL, HEAR, SEE, SMELL**
see also FOOD, DRINK

- to have a particular taste: **taste** + adjective, **taste of** sth, **taste like** sth ◦ *That fish didn't taste very nice, did it?* ◦ *The wine tasted of strawberries.* ◦ *What does it taste like?*
- the flavour of a particular food or drink: **taste** ◦ *This cheese has a strange taste.* ◦ *a slight taste of garlic*

- the smell and taste of food: **flavour** (*AmE* **flavor**) (*noun* C/U) ◦ *'What flavours have you got?' 'Strawberry or vanilla.'* ◦ *Do you think a little salt would improve the flavour?*
- to add sth to food to give it a particular flavour: **flavour** (*AmE* **flavor**) sth ◦ *I flavoured the soup with lemon and parsley.* ◦ *a strawberry-flavoured milk shake*
- sth that is added to food or drink to give it a particular flavour: **flavouring** (*AmE* **flavoring**)

- to eat or drink a small amount of sth to see what it tastes like: **taste** sth ◦ *Can you just taste this and tell me if it's OK?*
- to be able to recognize the taste of food or drink: **taste** sth ◦ *I can't taste it – I've got a cold.*
- the ability to recognize the flavour of sth: **taste** (*noun* U) ◦ *Taste is one of the five senses.*

■ different kinds of taste

- having a taste like sugar: **sweet**
- having a sharp taste like that of a lemon: **sour**
- having a sharp unpleasant taste; not sweet, like coffee: **bitter** ◦ *The wine left a bitter taste in my mouth.*

▷ sweet things ⇨ **SWEET**

- if sth tastes good, it is **tasty**, **good** ◦ *a very tasty meal* ◦ *good wine*
- if sth tastes very good, it is **delicious**
- if sth has no flavour or taste, it is **tasteless**
- if sth tastes very bad, it is **disgusting**, **revolting**, **horrible** ◦ *The restaurant looked nice, but the meal was disgusting.*
- if sth tastes bad because it is old, it is **bad**, **off** (*not before a noun*) ◦ *That milk tastes a bit off – somebody must have forgotten to put it in the fridge.*
- if a taste is powerful or intense, it is **strong**; *opposite*: **mild** ◦ *a strong taste of onions* ◦ *a mild chocolate flavour*

■ words used about particular types of food

- types of food that are made with a lot of spices or pepper are **hot**, **spicy**; *opposite*: **mild** ◦ *The curry was too hot.* ◦ *spicy Mexican food* ◦ *mild mustard/cheese*
- if a drink is made with very little water or a lot of alcohol, it is **strong**; *opposite*: **weak** ◦ *strong coffee* ◦ *strong beer* ◦ *weak tea*
- tasting like fish, nuts, sugar, pepper, salt, etc: **fishy**, **nutty**, **sugary**, **peppery**, **salty**, etc

▷ salt and pepper ⇨ **SALT / PEPPER**

tax

1 different kinds of tax
2 paying taxes
3 collection of taxes by the government
see also GOVERNMENT, PAY[2]

1 different kinds of tax

- the money you have to pay to the government so that it can provide public services: **tax** (*noun* C/U) ◦ *a new tax on fuel* ◦ *How much tax do you pay?*
- a tax (in Britain and Europe) which is paid on goods and services which are bought and sold: **VAT** (**value added tax**) (*noun* U) ◦ *Does the price of this computer include VAT?*
- a tax paid on goods imported into a country: **customs duty** (*noun* C/U), **import duty** (*noun* C/U) ◦ *We had to pay £1 000 duty on the car we imported from Germany.*

- a tax that you pay on the money that you earn: **income tax** (*noun* U)
- a tax (in Britain) that you pay to your local council for local services: **council tax** (*noun* U)
- a tax (in Britain) that working people and their employers pay so that the government can help people who are ill, unemployed, retired, etc: **National Insurance** (*noun* U)

2 paying taxes

- if sth can be taxed, it is **taxable** ◦ *Only half my income is taxable.*
- the amount of tax (%) that has to be paid: **rate** ◦ *In Britain, the higher rate of income tax is 40%.*
- if you do not pay tax on sth, it is **tax-free**, **duty-free** ◦ *I bought these cigarettes at the airport duty-free shop.*

- a person who pays tax: **taxpayer**
- to give information about goods or income on which you have to pay tax: **declare** sth ◦ *You must declare all your income for the year.*
- a statement to the government's tax department about your income: **tax return** ◦ *I haven't completed my tax return for this financial year yet.*
- money which is taken away from the total amount that you earn is **deducted**; the amount that is taken away: **deduction** (**from** sth) ◦ *How much have they deducted for tax?* ◦ *I have very little of my wages left after deductions.*
- if you are employed, the main way of paying income tax is by **PAYE** (**Pay As You Earn**)
- your income before tax is your **pre-tax** income

- avoiding paying tax, usually illegally: **tax evasion** (*noun* U)

tax *contd.*

3 collection of taxes by the government

- the system by which a government takes money from people so that it can pay for services: **taxation** (*noun* U) ◦ *direct/indirect taxation* ◦ *high/low taxation* ◦ *The government promised to reduce taxation but now says it is going to increase it.*
- to raise money through taxation: **tax** sth ◦ *Luxury goods are taxed very highly.*
- to make a new tax: **impose** a tax (**on** sb/sth); *noun*(U):**imposition** ◦ *Many British people have complained about the imposition of VAT on books.*

- (in Britain) a government department which collects taxes: **the Inland Revenue**
- the period of twelve months for which taxes are calculated: **financial year** ◦ *In Britain the financial year begins in April.*

taxi

see also BUS, CAR

- a car with a driver whose job it is to take you somewhere for money: **taxi**, (*especially AmE*) **cab**
- a person who uses a taxi: **passenger**
- a place where taxis park while they are waiting for passengers: **taxi rank** (*AmE* **cab stand**)
- a person who drives a taxi: **taxi driver** (*AmE* **cab driver**)

- the money you pay for a journey by taxi: **fare** ◦ *Can you tell me roughly how much the fare will be to the airport?*
- a machine in a taxi which shows you how much money you have to pay: **meter**
- a small amount of money you give to a taxi driver to thank him/her: **tip**; *verb*: **tip** sb (sth) ◦ *I gave him a big tip because he was so helpful with my luggage.* ◦ *How much should I tip the taxi driver?*

- to call or wave to a taxi to get it to stop for you: **hail** a taxi
- to telephone a taxi company and ask them to send a taxi to you: **phone for a taxi**, **call a taxi** ◦ *Would you like me to call a taxi for you?*
- to travel in a taxi: **take* a taxi**, **get* a taxi**, **go* by taxi** ◦ *We missed the bus and had to get a taxi.*

tea ⇨ COFFEE/TEA

teach

see also LEARN

■ teaching
- to give sb lessons; to show or tell sb sth so that they know about it or how to do it: **teach*** (sb) (sth), **teach*** sb **to do** sth, **teach*** sb **about** sth ◦ *I must go – I'm teaching this morning.* ◦ *Will you teach me to drive?* ◦ *She teaches history in the local school.* ◦ *Children are taught to read and write when they first go to school.*
- to tell sb when they are making a mistake and to show them the correct answer: **correct** sb; *noun* (U): **correction** ◦ *Our teacher never corrects our mistakes.*

- a person whose job is to teach, especially in a school or college: **teacher**; the work or profession of a teacher: **teaching** (*noun* U) ◦ *He left university and went into teaching.*

- a teacher who teaches one person or a very small group: **tutor**
- a talk or speech to a group of people on a particular subject (especially in a university): **lecture** (**on/about** sb/sth) ◦ *She gave a lecture on the American political system.* ◦ *This morning we had a lecture on chaos theory.*
- to give a lecture or lectures on a particular subject: **lecture** (**on/about** sb/sth)
- a person who teaches at a university or college: **lecturer**

▷ more on teaching in schools and universities ⇨ SCHOOL, UNIVERSITY

■ training
- to teach sb to do sth which is difficult or which needs lots of practice: **train** sb (**in/for** sth), **train** sb (**to** do sth); *noun* (U): **training** ◦ *You don't need any past experience – they train you on the job.* ◦ *teacher training* ◦ *language training*
- to train or teach sb, especially to compete in a sport or pass an examination: **coach** sb (**in** sth); *noun* (U): **coaching** ◦ *Their son is having extra maths coaching.*

- a person who teaches (usually not in a school): **instructor** ◦ *a driving instructor*
- a person who trains people: **trainer** ◦ *a basketball trainer* ◦ *a teacher trainer*

■ education
- to teach or train sb, especially in a school, university, etc: **educate** sb; *noun* (C/U): **education**; *adjective*: **educational** ◦ *Where were you educated?* ◦ *They sacrificed everything to give their son a good education.* ◦ *educational technology*

▷ more on education ⇨ EDUCATION

■ the organization of teaching
- a period of time when you learn or teach sth: **lesson**, **class** ◦ *a history lesson* ◦ *We don't have classes on Wednesday afternoons.*

- a complete series of lessons: **course** ◦ *Which courses are you doing this term?* ◦ *an English language course*
- to teach and organize a course in sth: **run*** sth ◦ *We're planning to run several new courses this summer.*
- a list of things which have to be taught in a particular subject: **syllabus** ◦ *There's a lot to cover in this syllabus.*
- the way in which sth is taught: **method** ◦ *a new teaching method*
- an area of knowledge that is studied at school, college, etc: **subject** ◦ *Which subjects do you teach?*

- a book that is used to teach a particular subject: **textbook** ○ *We're going to use a new geography textbook next term.*
- a piece of work that is intended to help you learn sth: **exercise, task** ○ *If everybody understands then we'll try doing exercise 4 on the next page.*

team

see also GAME, SPORT

- a group of people who play a game or sport together against another group: **team**
- either one of two teams taking part in a game or sport: **side** ○ *Whose side are you on?*

- a person in a team: **member** ○ *a member of the Irish team* ○ *two team members*
- a position in a team: **place** ○ *He got a place on the school team.*
- a person who is a member of a team is **in/on the team, plays for** a team ○ *Which team are you on?* ○ *He plays for England.*
- to choose a team, or to choose sb to be in a team: **pick** sb, **select** sb ○ *They've finished picking the team – I'm afraid you're not in it.* ○ *She hasn't been selected.*
- to decide not to have sb as a team member any longer: **drop** sb ○ *She's been dropped from the England team.*

- a person who is in the same team as you: **team-mate**
- the person who leads the team: (**team**) **captain**; *verb*: **captain** sth
- an extra member of a team who plays if sb is ill or hurt: **reserve, substitute** ○ *'Are you in the team?' 'I'm just a reserve.'*
- to replace one member of a team with another: **substitute** sb ○ *He was substituted in the second half.*
- an occasion of substituting sb: **substitution** ○ *to make a substitution*

- the particular job or place that sb has on a team: **position** ○ *'What position does he usually play in?' 'Goalkeeper.'*
- the way that a team works together: **teamwork** (*noun* U) ○ *a display of good teamwork*
- the feeling that you should act for the good of the team rather than for yourself: **team spirit** (*noun* U)

telephone

1 telephones
2 making a telephone call

1 telephones

- the thing you use to speak to sb who is in another house, town, country, etc: **telephone, phone**
- the link between two telephones: **line** ○ *There's no answer from his number. Perhaps there's a problem on the line.*

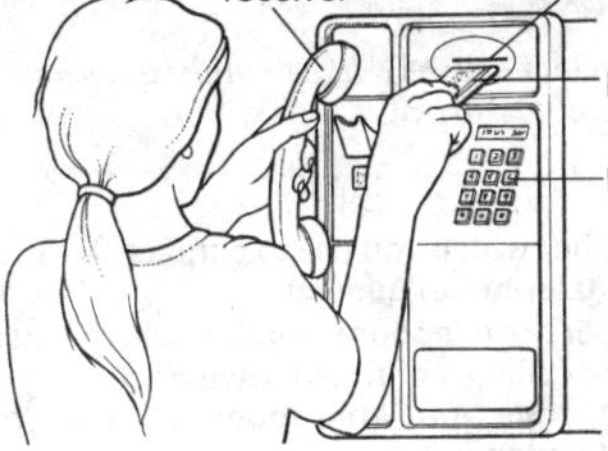

telephone

- a phone which you can find in the street, a shop, a café, etc: **public telephone/phone, payphone**
- a phone which you can use in a car: **car phone**
- a phone which you can carry, and which you can use outside: **mobile phone**
- a phone which does not have a wire: **cordless telephone/phone**

- a place where you can use a public telephone in the street: **telephone/phone box, call box** (*AmE* **telephone/phone booth**)
- a card which you use to make some public telephones work: **phonecard**

- a machine which answers the telephone and records messages from callers: **answering machine, answerphone**
- a machine that is used for sending written messages using the telephone line: **fax** (**machine**)

▷ sending a message using a fax machine ⇨ LETTER[1]

2 making a telephone call

- to use the telephone: **make* a telephone/phone call**
- to contact a particular person by using the telephone: **telephone/phone** sb, **call** sb (**up**), **ring*** sb (**up**), **give*** sb **a call/ring** ○ *I'll call you when I get home this evening.* ○ *I'll give you a call as soon as I get in.*
- to telephone a person who has already called you: **call/ring*** sb **back** ○ *Shall I ask him to call you back when he comes home?*

- if you call somebody, their phone **rings***; when they go to the telephone to see who is calling, they **answer the phone**
- when people hear the telephone ringing, they sometimes say **I'll get it** (= I'll answer the phone)
- a person who is making a call is **on the phone** ○ *See who's at the door, will you – I'm on the phone.*

■ types of telephone call
- a call to a person who is a long way away is a **long distance** call
- a call to a person who is in the same town or area as you is a **local** call ○ *It won't cost much, it's only a local call.*
- if you need to make a telephone call but do not have any money, you can **reverse the charges** (*AmE* **call collect**) (= ask the person you are calling to pay); the call is a **reverse charge call**

telephone *contd.*

(*AmE* **collect call**) ◦ *I'd like to make a reverse charge call to Australia.*

■ preparing to make a call

– the number which you use to contact sb by telephone: **(telephone) number**
– the part of the telephone number which you use if you are calling a different town or country: **(dialling) code** (*AmE* **area code**) ◦ *The code for central London is 0171.*
– to press the buttons on a telephone in order to call a number: **dial** (sth) ◦ *Insert your card, and then dial the number.*
– the sound that you hear which tells you that you can dial a number: **dialling tone** (*AmE* **dial tone**)

– a book which has lists of the names, addresses and telephone numbers of the people who live in a certain town or area: **telephone directory, phone book** ◦ *'What's Susan's number?' 'I don't know. Have a look in the phone book.'*
– the service that you can call if you need to know a person's telephone number: **directory enquiries** (*noun singular*)

■ making contact

– to be able to speak to sb on the telephone: **contact** sb, **get* through** (**to** sb), **reach** sb ◦ *I've been trying to contact James all day, but he hasn't been answering the phone.* ◦ *Is there something wrong with his telephone? I can't get through.* ◦ *If you need to speak to me, you can reach me on 303403.*
– to have made contact with a person on the telephone: **be through** ◦ *Hello, am I through to the Sales Department?*
– if a person, for example a secretary, makes contact with sb for you, they **put*** you **through, connect** you ◦ *Can you put me through to the English Department, please?* ◦ *Just a moment please, while I try to connect you.*
– to wait for the person you want to speak to come to the phone: **hold* the line, hold* on,** (*informal*) **hang* on** ◦ *Hold the line, please; Mr Parker will speak to you in a moment.* ◦ *'I'm afraid the manager's line is busy.' 'I'll hold on if that's okay.'*

– the line between the main telephone in a company and the telephone in sb's office: **extension** ◦ *Hello. Could I speak to Mr Carter on extension 206, please?*

■ problems

– if you cannot contact sb because they are already using their telephone, the line is **engaged** (*AmE* **busy**) ◦ *I tried to call him, but the line was engaged.* ◦ *I'm afraid his number is busy. Can you call back later?*
– if you suddenly cannot hear the other person who you are speaking to on the telephone, you have been **cut off** ◦ *She was just telling me the changed time of her flight when suddenly we were cut off.*
– if the line is not working at all, it is **dead** ◦ *She ran to the phone to call the police, but the line was dead.*
– to make a mistake and call sb who you did not want to speak to: **have/dial the/a wrong number** ◦ *Oh, I'm sorry, I think I've got the wrong number.*
– if you have difficulties in making a call, you can dial a number and ask for help from the **operator**

■ finishing the call

– to put down the receiver when you have finished making your call: **hang* up, ring* off** ◦ *There was no answer so I hung up.* ◦ *I said goodbye and rang off.*

■ **MORE ...**

– communications by telephone, radio, etc: **telecommunications** (*noun plural*) ◦ *the telecommunications industry*

– a place where telephone calls are connected: **telephone exchange**
– a machine which is used by a person who works in a company or public organization to connect telephone calls: **switchboard**; a person who uses this machine: **switchboard operator**

– to call a large organization (usually a television or radio station) in order to say or ask sth: **phone in** (*AmE* **call in**) ◦ *After the programme, many people phoned in to complain.*
– a television or radio programme where people are invited to call the TV or radio station in order to give their opinion or ask a question: **phone-in** (*AmE* **call-in**) ◦ *Next week we have a phone-in on the government's new education policy.*

television/radio

1 watching television
2 listening to the radio
3 controlling a television or radio
4 television and radio programmes
5 broadcasting

see also FILM, CINEMA

1 watching television

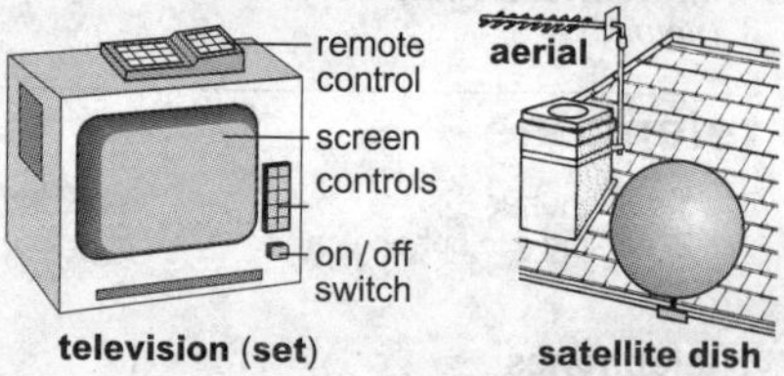

– a piece of electrical equipment which receives televised pictures and sound: **television, television set, TV,** (*BrE informal*) **telly,** (*BrE informal*) **the box** ◦ *'Where's Mary?' 'Watching the telly.'* ◦ *What's on the box tonight?*

- a television which shows pictures in colour: **colour television/TV**; a television which shows pictures in black and white: **black and white television/TV**

- what you see on your television: **picture** ◦ *a good/bad picture*
- the quality of the pictures received on a television: **reception** (*noun* U) ◦ *Reception here is very poor.*

- an individual who watches the television: **viewer**
- if you watch a programme, film, etc from beginning to end, you **see*** it; if you do not see a programme, you **miss** it ◦ *Did you see the news last night?* ◦ *I missed last night's episode.*
- if you record a television programme onto a tape, you **video** it ◦ *If you can't watch it now, why not video it and watch it later?*

▷ more on video ⇨ **VIDEO**

- when a picture is coming from a television set, it is **on**; *opposite*: **off** ◦ *Make sure the TV's off before you go to bed.*
- one of the sets of programmes that you can choose to watch on television: **channel**, (*especially AmE*) **station** ◦ *Which channel do most people watch?* ◦ *There's an interesting programme on Channel 4 this evening.* ◦ *local TV stations*

2 listening to the radio

- a piece of electrical equipment which receives sounds: **radio** (*plural* **radios**) ◦ *Have you got a radio?* ◦ *a car radio*
- when sound is coming from a radio, it is **on**; *opposite*: **off** ◦ *Please leave the radio on so that I can get the next programme.*

- when you want to hear a radio programme, you **listen to** it ◦ *Be quiet, I'm trying to listen to the news.*
- a person who listens to the radio: **listener**

- a company or system that provides radio programmes: **station** ◦ *a local radio station*
- a measurement of radio waves; this tells you where to find a particular station on the radio: **frequency**, **wavelength**
- a set of radio waves of similar length: **band**, **waveband** ◦ *the FM band*
- frequencies are divided up into **short wave**, **medium wave** and **long wave** ◦ *broadcast on long wave* ◦ *a short-wave radio*
- the part of a radio that you can adjust to pick up the signals that you want to receive: **tuner**
- if you adjust the controls of a radio so that you can receive a particular station, you **tune in** (**to** sth)

- the quality of the signals a radio receives: **reception** (*noun* U)
- the noise (which may be caused by bad weather or other radio stations) that prevents the clear reception of radio programmes: **interference** (*noun* U) ◦ *There's too much interference to hear exactly what they're saying.*

3 controlling a television or radio

- to start a television or radio, you **turn** it **on**, **switch** it **on**, **put*** it **on**
- to stop a television or radio, you **turn** it **off**, **switch** it **off**, **put*** it **off**
- to change the channel or station, you **switch** (it) **over** (**to** sth), **switch channels/stations** ◦ *Do you mind if I switch over to Radio 3?*
- to make the television or radio louder or quieter, you **turn** it **up/down**, (*formal*) **adjust the volume**
- to make the television picture darker or brighter, you **adjust the brightness**

4 television and radio programmes

- a show which you can watch on a television set or hear on the radio: **programme** (*AmE* **program**)
- the programmes that you can see on television: **television** (*noun* U), (*informal*) **TV** ◦ *He spends far too much time watching television.* ◦ *a TV addict*
- programmes that you can hear on the radio: **the radio** (*noun* U) ◦ *to listen to the radio* ◦ *What's on the radio?*
- a programme or person that can be seen on the television or heard on the radio is **on** ◦ *My favourite show isn't on any more.*
- when a programme begins on the television or radio, it **comes* on** ◦ *The news comes on at nine o'clock.*
- all the people who listen to a programme on the radio or watch a programme on television: **audience**

- if sth is broadcast at the same time as it actually happens, it is **live** (*adjective, adverb*) ◦ *a live appearance by the President* ◦ *This report is coming live from Moscow.*
- a programme which has been shown before: **repeat**
- a piece of film which advertises sth during and in between other programmes: **advertisement**, **commercial**, (*informal*) **ad**, (*BrE informal*) **advert**

▷ more on advertisements ⇨ **ADVERTISEMENT**

- to introduce and give information about programmes: **announce** sth; a person who does this: **announcer**
- to introduce each part of a programme: **present** sth; a person who does this: **presenter**
- to organize the making of a programme: **produce** sth; a person who does this: **producer**
- to describe and explain an event that is happening: **commentate** (**on** sth); a person who does this: **commentator** ◦ *a football commentator*
- a person who speaks regularly on the radio or television: **broadcaster** ◦ *a popular broadcaster*

■ news and weather
- a programme which shows the latest news regularly: **the news**; a short news report: (**news**) **bulletin**
- a person who reads the news: **newsreader**
- a programme which tells you what the weather will be like: **weather forecast**

television/radio *contd.*

- the person who presents a weather forecast: **weatherman** (*plural* **weathermen**), **weathergirl**, (*formal*) **weather forecaster**

■ information and talk
- a programme (or part of one) which has a presenter who asks sb questions about their opinions, life, etc: **interview**; to ask questions in an interview: **interview** sb; a person who interviews sb: **interviewer**
- a programme which is made up of informal interviews with well-known people: **chat show**, (*especially AmE*) **talk show**; a person who asks the questions on a chat show: **chat-show host**, (*especially AmE*) **talk-show host**
- a programme which includes telephone calls from members of the public: **phone-in** (*AmE* **call-in**)
- a programme which gives facts and information about a particular subject: **documentary**

■ stories and plays
- a number of programmes which have the same main characters and each tell a complete story: **series** (*plural* **series**); a series where the characters get into funny situations: **situation comedy**, (*informal*) **sitcom**
- a number of programmes which tell a single story in a number of parts over a period of time: **serial**; one part of a serial: **episode**
- a serial about the lives and problems of a particular group of people: **soap opera**, (*informal*) **soap**

■ games
- a programme which has a presenter who organizes people in a game or competition: **game show**; a person who presents a game show: **game-show host**
- a programme which has people trying to answer questions so that they can win prizes: **quiz show**

5 broadcasting
- the system and business of producing television/radio programmes: **television** (*noun* U), **radio** (*noun* U) ◦ *She works in television.*
- to send out television or radio programmes: **broadcast*** (sth); a programme which is sent out in this way: **broadcast** ◦ *The Olympics will be broadcast live by satellite.* ◦ *a party political broadcast*
- the system of broadcasting which makes money by broadcasting advertisements: **commercial television/radio** (*noun* U)
- the equipment that sends out television or radio signals: **transmitter**
- a system which uses cables (= wires) to carry television programmes: **cable television/TV** (*noun* U) ◦ *You can get Spanish television on cable TV.*
- a system which uses a satellite to send television pictures: **satellite television/TV** (*noun* U)◦ *Have you got satellite TV?*
- a kind of television system which operates inside a shop, bank or building, etc: **closed-circuit television**
- to show an event on television: **televise** sth ◦ *to televise a football match* ◦ *a televised performance*
- television pictures are made with a **television camera**
- a room or building where television or radio programmes are usually made: **studio** (*plural* **studios**) ◦ *a television studio*
- television, radio and newspapers are called the (**mass**) **media** (*noun plural*) ◦ *He tried to keep the story out of the media.* ◦ *the political power of the mass media*

■ MORE ...
- music that is regularly used to introduce a particular programme: **signature tune** ◦ *He switched the radio on just in time to hear the signature tune of his favourite programme.*
- noises which are supposed to sound like the real thing (the wind, for example) in a programme: **sound effects**
- a system that provides news and other information in written form on television: **teletext**
- the official piece of paper that you must buy in Britain in order to receive television pictures legally: **television/TV licence**
- the cost of a television licence: **licence fee**

tell
- giving sb some information ⇨ INFORM
- how you say sth ⇨ SAY
- telling a story ⇨ STORY

temperature ⇨ HOT

ten ⇨ NUMBER

tennis ⇨ SPORT

tense ⇨ GRAMMAR

tent ⇨ CAMP

test
- trying sth ⇨ TRY
- a kind of exam ⇨ EXAM

thank

polite behaviour ⇨ POLITE

- to tell sb that you are happy about sth that they have given you or sth that they have done for you: **thank** sb (**for** sth) ◦ *I'm writing to thank you for the book you sent me.*
- when you feel happy about sth that sb has given you or sth that they have done for you, you are **grateful** (*adverb* **gratefully**); *noun* (U): **gratitude** ◦ *I'd be very grateful if you could give me some advice.* ◦ *I can't tell you how grateful I am.* ◦ *She was full of gratitude for all the support she was given.* ◦ *He never shows me any gratitude for anything I do.*

- not grateful: **ungrateful**; *noun* (U): **ingratitude**

- to feel grateful for sth: **appreciate** sth; *noun* (U): **appreciation**; *adjective*: **appreciative** (**of** sth) ◦ *I really appreciate your help.* ◦ *I'm sending you a small present as a sign of my appreciation.* ◦ *She was appreciative of my support.*
- to express gratitude for sth: **say* thank you** (**for** sth), (*formal*) **acknowledge** sth; an act of saying thank you: **thanks** (*noun plural*), **acknowledgement** (*noun* U) ◦ *They never acknowledged my help.* ◦ *I'd like to express my thanks to everyone at the hospital.* ◦ *I didn't get any acknowledgement for the work I had done.*

■ ways of thanking people
- to thank sb for sth, you can say **Thank you** (**very/so much**) or (*more informal*) **Thanks** (**a lot**) or (*informal*) **Cheers** or (*informal*) **Ta** ◦ *'Will you join us for lunch?' 'Thank you very much!'* (= yes) ◦ *Thank you so much for the beautiful gift!* ◦ *'How are you feeling?' 'Much better, thanks.'* ◦ *'Good luck with the test.' 'Thanks a lot!'*
- to refuse sth politely, you can say **No, thank you** or (*more informal*) **No, thanks** ◦ *'Would you like a coffee?' 'No, thanks.'*
- to reply when sb thanks you for sth, you can say **You're welcome!** or **Not at all!** or **Don't mention it!**

■ **MORE ...**
- hard work which nobody appreciates or thanks you for is **thankless** ◦ *a thankless task*

theatre

1 inside a theatre
2 going to the theatre
3 working in a theatre
see also PLAY[1], CINEMA, ENTERTAINMENT

1 inside a theatre
- a building where you go to see plays, musicals, etc: **theatre** (*AmE* **theater**)
- the part of a theatre where the actors perform: **stage**

- a kind of lamp used to light up the stage: **spotlight**
- the furniture, painted cloth, etc that are used on the stage: **scenery** (*noun* U)
- the area at the sides of the stage where an actor cannot be seen by the audience: **the wings** (*noun plural*) ◦ *waiting in the wings*
- the area in front of the stage in a theatre where an orchestra sits: **orchestra pit**

- a room where actors change their clothes: **dressing room**
- behind the stage, where the dressing rooms, etc are: **backstage** (*adjective/adverb*) ◦ *We were invited backstage by the star of the show.*

theatre

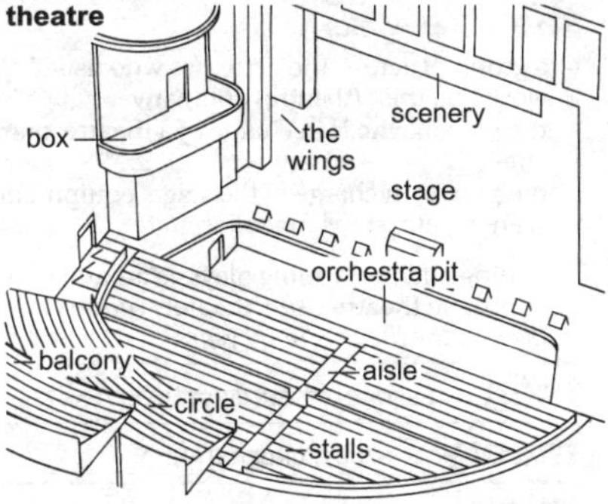

- the entrance hall of a theatre: **foyer** ◦ *I'll meet you in the foyer.*
- the place where the audience can leave their coats: **cloakroom**

2 going to the theatre
- a story which is performed in a theatre: **play**
- a performance with singing, dancing, acting, etc: **show** ◦ *For her birthday, he took her to see a show.*
- a show, play, etc that can be seen at the moment is **on** ◦ *What's on at the King's this week?* ◦ *It's on for another week.*
- an occasion when a play, show, etc is performed: **performance**
- an afternoon performance: **matinée** ◦ *We're taking the children to the Saturday matinée.*

- when a performance is going to begin, the curtain **goes* up**
- a short break between parts of a play, when the curtain is closed: **interval** ◦ *We had a drink in the interval.*

▷ more on plays ⇨ PLAY[1]

- if you go to see a play, you **go* to the theatre**
- the group of people who go to see a particular performance of a play, concert, etc: **audience**
- the place where you sit in the theatre: **seat** ◦ *Try to get good seats for the show tonight.* ◦ *a seat in the stalls*
- a man/woman who shows people to their seats: **usher**, **usherette**
- a person who often goes to the theatre: **theatregoer** (*AmE* **theatergoer**)

▷ more on audiences ⇨ AUDIENCE
- when you pay to go into a theatre, you buy your **ticket**
- the place where you buy theatre tickets: **box office**, **booking office**

▷ more on getting a ticket ⇨ TICKET

3 working in a theatre
- to perform a part (= pretend to be a different person) in a play or film: **act**; *noun* (U): **acting**; a man/woman who acts in a play or film: **actor**; a female actor can also be called an **actress**

theatre *contd.*

- a group of actors and actresses who usually work together: (**theatre**) **company**
- the person who is in charge of a theatre: **manager**
- the person in charge of the stage, equipment, scenery, etc: **stage manager**

- writing and performing plays as art and entertainment: **theatre** (*AmE* **theater**) (*noun* U) ◦ *He's been in the theatre for 30 years.*

then ⇨ BEFORE/AFTER, FIRST/NEXT/LAST

theory ⇨ STUDY, UNDERSTAND

thick ⇨ FAT/THIN/THICK

thing

things that happen ⇨ HAPPEN
things that are true ⇨ TRUE

- any object, quality, state, event, fact, etc that you do not give a name to: **thing** ◦ *I've put that thing you wanted on your desk.* ◦ *Did you see that thing on the television last night about flying foxes?* ◦ *And another thing: don't forget to mention your experience as a teacher in Malaysia.*
- a thing that you can see and touch: **object** ◦ *There was a very strange object in the middle of the floor.* ◦ *objects of all shapes and sizes*
- a thing that is usually part of a set: **article** ◦ *an article of clothing* ◦ *articles of climbing equipment*
- a single thing on a list or in a collection: **item** ◦ *the third item on the list* ◦ *What's the first item on the agenda?*

- small things of different kinds: **bits and pieces** ◦ *'What did you find in the box?' 'Just bits and pieces.'*
- small things that are not very important or valuable: (*informal*) **odds and ends** ◦ *a box full of odds and ends*
- your clothes, personal possessions or necessary equipment: **things** (*noun plural*) ◦ *Hold on a minute, I've just got to get my things.*

- things that you need for doing a particular activity, for example, a sport: **equipment** (*noun* U) ◦ *climbing equipment*
- a thing that can be used for making or doing sth: **material** (*noun* C/U) ◦ *the cost of raw materials* ◦ *building material*
- a solid or liquid material: **substance** ◦ *dangerous substances* ◦ *What's that substance they put on frying pans to stop the food from sticking?*
- a substance, thing or group of things: (*informal*) **stuff** (*noun* U) ◦ *What's that white stuff on top of the car?* ◦ *Don't offer her sweet sherry – I happen to know she hates the stuff.*

▷ more on materials ⇨ MATERIAL

- a group of people or things that have the same quality or qualities: **type**, **sort**, **kind** ◦ *an unusual type of plastic material* ◦ *I just can't stand those sort of people.* ◦ *This is just the kind of thing I've been looking for.*

▷ more on types ⇨ TYPE

- each thing or all things: **everything** ◦ *He lost everything in the fire.*
- one thing (of any kind): **anything**; not anything: **nothing** ◦ *Isn't there anything to eat in this house?* ◦ *'I'd better just check that we haven't left anything in the wardrobe.' 'It's OK, I've looked. There's nothing.'*

■ **MORE ...**
- a thing that you cannot think of the right word for: (*informal*) **thingummy**, (*informal*) **thingumajig**, (*informal*) **what-do-you-call-it** ◦ *I need one of those green string thingummies which hold pieces of paper together.*

think

1 thinking about sth
2 what you think: ideas
3 reason: thinking in a systematic way

thinking that sth is true ⇨ TRUE
thinking that sth is possible or probable ⇨ POSSIBLE[1]
thinking about the future ⇨ FUTURE
intending to do sth and making plans ⇨ INTEND/PLAN
good at thinking ⇨ CLEVER

see also KNOW, MIND, UNDERSTAND

1 thinking about sth

- to use your mind for a purpose, for example to find an answer to a problem: **think*** (**about** sth) ◦ *Shut up! I'm trying to think.* ◦ *He thought hard for a moment and then left without saying anything.* ◦ *What are you thinking about?*
- the act of thinking about sth: **thought** (*noun* U), **thinking** (*noun* U) ◦ *I need to give this problem more thought.* ◦ *I've been doing some serious thinking and I've finally come to a decision.*
- to ask yourself a question: **wonder ...** ◦ *I wonder what she would have done if she hadn't got the job.*

- if you are quiet and serious because you are thinking about sth, you are **thoughtful** (*adverb* **thoughtfully**) ◦ *He was looking quite thoughtful when I came into the room.*
- to say your thoughts out loud as they come into your mind: **think* aloud** ◦ *I'm just thinking aloud about what to do.*

■ thinking before you take a decision
- to think about a possibility: **think* about** sth, **look at** sth ◦ *We need to think very carefully about what to do next.* ◦ *I've been thinking about your suggestion.* ◦ *She agreed to look at my proposal.*
- to think about sth before taking a decision: **think*** sth **over**, (*informal*) **have a think** (**about** sth), (*more formal*) **consider** sth ◦ *I need to go away and think it over before I agree.* ◦ *I'll go and have a think about what you've told me.* ◦ *We should consider other possibilities.*
- to carefully consider all the details of a plan, idea, etc: **think*** sth **out** ◦ *If they had thought it*

out properly in the first place, these problems might not have arisen.
- to think carefully before deciding to do sth: **think* twice** (**about** sth) ∘ *You'd better think twice before you agree to that.*

- to think about sth when you take a decision: **think* of** sth ∘ *There are so many things to think of before we can decide.*
- to consider an extra piece of information, etc when you take a decision: **take*** sth **into consideration, take*** sth **into account** ∘ *The committee will certainly take the report into consideration.* ∘ *His views were never taken into account.*

■ thinking carefully about sth
- to think hard about a particular thing: **concentrate** (**on** sth); *noun* (U): **concentration** ∘ *You really must concentrate if you want to pass the exam.*
- to think carefully and deeply about sth: **reflect on** sth ∘ *He's had plenty of time in prison to reflect on his past mistakes.*
- to keep thinking about sth: **keep*** your **mind on** sth ∘ *She can't keep her mind on any topic for more than five minutes.*
- if sth is giving you a lot to think about or is worrying you, it is **on** your **mind** ∘ *She's got a lot on her mind at the moment.*

- when you are thinking about an answer or trying to remember sth, you say **Let me see** or **Let's see** ∘ *Let me see, I'm sure he said he would meet us outside the station.*

■ the result of thinking about sth
- to think about several possibilities and choose one: **decide** (**on/against** sb/sth), **decide** to do sth, **conclude that . . .**; what you have decided: **decision** ∘ *Have you decided on a pudding?* ∘ *The government has decided to raise the higher rate of tax.* ∘ *I think it was a very stupid decision that she made.*

▷ more on making a decision ⇨ DECIDE/CHOOSE

■ thinking again
- to think a second time about sth: **think* again** (**about** sth), **reconsider** sth ∘ *Please think again about John's suggestion.* ∘ *We shall have to reconsider our strategy.*
- to change an opinion or decision: **change** your **mind** (**about** sb/sth) ∘ *Won't you change your mind and come for a drink with us?*
- when you change your mind about sth, you can say **on second thoughts, on reflection** ∘ *On second thoughts, I don't think it's such a good idea.*

■ stopping people from thinking about things
- to take a person's attention away from sth: **distract** sb (**from** sth); something that distracts you: **distraction** ∘ *Don't distract him – he's trying to work out how much we've spent!* ∘ *It's difficult trying to work at home – there are too many distractions.*
- to give sb sth else to think about or do when they are worried about sth: **take*** sb's **mind off** sb/sth ∘ *Talking to you has helped to take my mind off my problems.*

2 what you think: ideas
- something that you think: **idea** (*noun* C/U) ∘ *I've got an idea for a new novel.* ∘ *My idea of perfect happiness is two weeks on a Caribbean island.* ∘ *I've no idea what I shall do next.*
- an idea or opinion: **thought** ∘ *What are your thoughts on the matter?*
- a picture in your mind: **image** ∘ *What image do you have in your mind of the Antarctic?*
- to form a picture in your mind: **imagine** sth ∘ *Imagine that you are in London.*

▷ more on imagining ⇨ IMAGINATION

- to create an idea in your mind: **think* of** sth ∘ *I tried hard to think of an answer.* ∘ *Think of a number; then double it.*
- to think of sth for the first time: **think*** sth **up**, **invent** sth ∘ *Whatever will they think up next?* ∘ *She invented a fantastic story to account for her absence.*

▷ more on inventing ⇨ INVENT

- to think of an idea unexpectedly: **hit* on** sth ∘ *He hit on the idea of everyone contributing a pound.*
- when an idea comes into your mind, it **occurs to** you, **crosses** your **mind** ∘ *Has it ever occurred to you that I might be right?*

- to give sb an idea: **put*** sth **into** sb's **head/mind** ∘ *Was it you who put this crazy idea of going to Australia into her head?*
- when you start thinking about an idea, it **enters** your **head/mind** ∘ *It didn't enter my mind to phone Sue.*

3 reason: thinking in a systematic way
- the ability to think and make sensible decisions: **reason** (*noun* U); to use this ability: **reason** ∘ *I've tried to make him change his mind but he just won't listen to reason.* ∘ *Animals lack the capacity to reason.*
- the process of thinking: **reasoning** (*noun* U) ∘ *What's the reasoning behind his decision to leave?*
- based on reason: **rational** (*adverb* **rationally**); *opposite*: **irrational** (*adverb* **irrationally**) ∘ *a rational decision* ∘ *to behave irrationally*

- the power of the mind to think and learn: **intellect** (*noun* U); connected with the intellect: **intellectual** (*adverb* **intellectually**) ∘ *to develop your intellect* ∘ *You'll find it's not a very intellectually demanding course.*
- the use of reason: **logic** (*noun* U); in a way that uses reason: **logical** (*adverb* **logically**); *opposite*: **illogical** (*adverb* **illogically**) ∘ *There is no logic in your argument.* ∘ *an illogical suggestion/reply/argument*

- a person who thinks deeply about important things: **thinker**
- a person who is interested in ideas: **intellectual**

- the study of ideas and beliefs about the meaning of life: **philosophy** (*noun* U); connected with philosophy: **philosophical** (*adverb* **philosophically**)
- a person who has developed a set of ideas and beliefs about the meaning of life: **philosopher**

think *contd.*

- a particular set of ideas and beliefs about knowledge, the meaning of life, etc: **philosophy** ◦ *the philosophy of Wittgenstein*
- the ideas or ways of thinking which belong to a person, a group or a subject: **thought** (*noun* U) ◦ *the thought of Karl Marx* ◦ *modern political thought*

thirsty ⇨ DRINK

thousand ⇨ NUMBER

three ⇨ NUMBER

through ⇨ MOVE

throw

see also ATHLETICS

- to send sth through the air by pushing it out of your hand: **throw*** sth ◦ *to throw a ball* ◦ *Throw me the towel, will you?*
- an act of throwing sth: **throw** ◦ *a brilliant throw*
- the distance that sth is thrown: **throw** ◦ *a throw of more than 100 metres*
- to return sth by throwing it: **throw*** sth **back**
- to throw sth in a careless way, not using all your strength: **toss** sth, (*informal*) **chuck** sth ◦ *Chuck me over the car keys, will you?*
- to throw sth with force: **hurl** sth, **fling*** sth ◦ *I was so angry that I flung the book at him.*

- to take hold of sth that is moving, usually with your hands: **catch*** sth ◦ *One man threw the sacks from the lorry; another man caught them and stacked them in the store.*
- to come down from the air: **land** ◦ *Charlie threw his ball over the wall and it landed in our neighbour's swimming pool.*

▷ more on catching things ⇨ HOLD/CATCH

thunder ⇨ STORM

ticket

tickets for travelling by bus, train, etc ⇨ TRAVEL

- the place where you buy a ticket (for any kind of event): **ticket office**, **booking office**; in a theatre, cinema, etc: **box office**
- the amount you pay for a ticket: **price** ◦ *What's the price of a ticket for the Scotland-England match?*

- to wait in a line of people to buy a ticket: **queue** (**up**) (**for** sth)/(**to** do sth) ◦ *Queue here for the 1.30 performance.*
- a line of people who are waiting: **queue** (*AmE* **line**) ◦ *Is this the queue for 'The Jungle Book'?*

- to arrange to buy a ticket in advance: **book** a ticket; *noun* (C/U) **booking** ◦ *Did you book those tickets for the opera on Thursday?* ◦ *a booking in the name of McDonald* ◦ *Booking for the show doesn't start until next Monday.*
- if all tickets have been sold, sth is **fully booked**, **booked up**, **sold out** ◦ *We can't take the children to the pantomime this year – it's already fully booked.*
- a ticket that can be used repeatedly for a fixed period of time: **season ticket** ◦ *Some football fans buy season tickets to watch their club's home games.*

- a ticket that is cheaper for certain groups of people such as students or old people: **concession** ◦ *Do you have concessions for students?*
- a free ticket: **complimentary ticket**

tidy

see also CLEAN/DIRTY

- a room, house, etc where everything is in its right place is **tidy** (*adverb* **tidily**); *noun* (U): **tidiness** ◦ *a tidy house* ◦ *Let's put the toys away tidily.*
- a person who likes things to be neat and in good order is **tidy** ◦ *I'm not a tidy person.* ◦ *Do you think you could be a little tidier?*
- clean, tidy and well-dressed, wearing fairly formal clothes: **smart** ◦ *I wear a lot of casual clothes, but I like to look smart for work.*

▷ more on clothes ⇨ CLOTHES

■ making things tidy

- to make a place or person tidy: **tidy** (sb/sth/yourself) (**up**); to put a thing out of sight: **tidy** sth **away** ◦ *Please tidy your room.* ◦ *It's time to tidy up.* ◦ *I need to tidy my hair.* ◦ *Tidy yourself up before you go to see the boss.* ◦ *Could you tidy all those clothes away?*
- to arrange things and make them tidy: **put*** sth **in order** ◦ *Please put these papers in order so that we can find what we need.*

- to put a thing in the place where you usually keep it (in a cupboard, drawer, etc): **put*** sth **away** ◦ *I'm sure I put my cheque book away.*
- to tidy things and put them away: **clear** (sth) **up** ◦ *Please clear up before you leave.*
- to arrange a room, etc or a group of things tidily: **put*** sth **straight** ◦ *Put the tables and chairs straight after using them.*
- to clean and tidy a place: **clean** (sth) **up** ◦ *We'll have to clean up the kitchen before Mum and Dad get back.*
- to tidy a place and throw away things that you do not want: **clear** sth **out**; *noun*: **clear-out** ◦ *I'm going to clear out the hall cupboard.* ◦ *It's about time we had a thorough clear-out – we have far too much stuff.*

■ untidy

- not tidy: **untidy**; *noun* (U): **untidiness** ◦ *You can't find anything on an untidy desk.*
- an untidy or dirty state: **mess**; to cause a mess: **mess** sth **up** ◦ *What a mess the children have made!* ◦ *Let's clear up this mess!* ◦ *I spent all day cleaning the house, and then the children came home and messed it all up again.*

- a state of untidiness and confusion: **muddle** (*noun* U) ◦ *These papers are all in a muddle. I can't find the letter I need.*
- not to put sth away in its correct or usual place: **leave*** sth **lying about** ◦ *Why do you leave your money lying about?*

- a room or house that is very dirty or untidy: (*informal*) **tip**, (*informal*) **pigsty** ◦ *How can you live in such a tip?* ◦ *His flat is a real pigsty.*

---

tight

1 fitting very closely
2 stretched or pulled hard
3 firm and difficult to move

1 fitting very closely

- fitting very closely: **tight** (*adverbs* **tight**, **tightly**) ◦ *This skirt is a bit tight around the waist.* ◦ *tight-fitting trousers/shoes*
- so full of things or people that there is no spare space: **tight** (*adverb* **tightly**) ◦ *We can get one more person in, but it's a bit of a tight fit.*

Note: before a past participle use **tightly**, not **tight**: ◦ *a tightly packed box* ◦ *a box packed tight with priceless jewels*

- not fitting closely: **loose** (*adverbs* **loose**, **loosely**) ◦ *He's lost so much weight that all his clothes are loose on him.* ◦ *a loose-fitting blouse* ◦ *His clothes hung loosely from his body.*
- (used about clothes) very loose: **baggy** ◦ *She was wearing jeans and a baggy T-shirt.*

- (used about clothes) very tight: **skintight** ◦ *a pair of skintight jeans*
- fitting closely without being tight: **close-fitting** ◦ *This dress should be close-fitting but not tight.*

- to go into or through a place where there is not much space: **squeeze into/through** sth, **squeeze in/through/past**; to make sb/sth do this: **squeeze** sb/sth **into** sth, **squeeze** sb/sth **in** ◦ *The shoes were a bit small and I could hardly squeeze into them.* ◦ *There were a lot of people in the corridor but I managed to squeeze through.* ◦ *It's quite full but they may be able to try and squeeze one more person in.*
- shoes that are too tight and hurt you **pinch** (you/your toes) ◦ *I think I need a larger size, they're pinching a little bit.*

2 stretched or pulled hard

- stretched or pulled hard: **tight** (*adverbs* **tight**, **tightly**) ◦ *a tight belt/rope* ◦ *Pull the rope tight!*
- stretched very tight: **taut**

- not stretched or pulled hard: **loose**, **slack** (*adverb* **loosely**) ◦ *When people get old, their skin starts to become looser.* ◦ *The belt was loose around his waist.*
- to become looser: **loosen**, **slacken**; to make sth looser: **loosen** sth, **slacken** sth ◦ *The rope slackened when they let go of it.*

3 firm and difficult to move

- firm and difficult to move: **tight** (*adverb* **tight**, **tightly**) ◦ *I can't open the drawer – it's too tight.*
- to become tighter: **tighten**; to make sth tighter: **tighten** sth ◦ *to tighten a nut/screw/lid*

- not firmly fixed: **loose** (*adverb* **loosely**) ◦ *Be careful, the door handle is loose – it'll come off if you pull too hard.* ◦ *a loose knot* ◦ *to tie sth loosely*
- to make sth less tight: **loosen** sth ◦ *Can you loosen the lid on the jar?*

- to take or keep hold of sth firmly or tightly: **grip** sth; *noun*: **grip** ◦ *to grip sth tightly* ◦ *You must keep a tight grip on the rope – don't let it slip out of your hand.*
- something that stops air, liquid, etc getting in or out of sth: **seal**; *verb*: **seal** sth (**up**) ◦ *to seal up a box/package/window*

---

till ⇨ TIME

---

time

1 periods of time
2 the passing of time
3 points in time
4 how often sth happens
5 happening at the same time
6 organizing and using time

1 periods of time

- an amount of time: **time** (*noun* U/C) ◦ *They allowed her some extra time to finish.* ◦ *During that time he organized many different events.* ◦ *The weather was hotter today than at any time in the last ten years.* ◦ *a long/short time ago*

- the time now: **the present**
- the time before the present: **the past**
- the time that will come after the present: **the future**

- a form of a verb which shows whether sth happens in the past, present or future: **tense**

▷ more on the present, past and future ⇨ PRESENT², PAST², FUTURE

▷ more on tenses ⇨ GRAMMAR

- a length of time: **period** ◦ *The English language has developed over a long period of time.* ◦ *a further period of a week* ◦ *There have been some bad periods in my life.*
- a period in the development of sth: **phase**, **stage** ◦ *Just ignore him, he's going through a difficult phase.* ◦ *University is the final stage of the education system.*
- a short period of time: **spell** ◦ *a short spell of rain* ◦ *He had a spell in politics.*
- the whole of a period of time: **all ...** (*with singular noun*), **the whole** (**of**) ... (*with singular noun*) ◦ *I've spent all week trying to finish my work.* ◦ *I think about it all day long.* ◦ *the whole day/the whole of the day*

time *contd.*

- a period of time in history that is special for some reason: **age**, **era** ○ *The Bronze Age* ○ *the post-war era*

▷ periods of time in history ⇨ **HISTORY**

- a period of time between two events: **interval** ○ *There will be an interval between Act 2 and Act 3.*
- a period of time when no activity takes place: **gap** ○ *There was a gap of three years between my first visit to France and my second.*
- in the time between two things happening: **in the meantime**, **meanwhile** ○ *We can't discuss this until he arrives. In the meantime, I suggest we get on with something else.*

■ hours, days, years, etc

- a period of sixty minutes: **hour** ○ *The film lasts three hours.* ○ *a two-hour drive*
- happening or done every hour: **hourly** (*adjective, adverb*) ○ *There's an hourly bus service to the town centre.* ○ *The label on the bottle says you should take it hourly.*

- a period of thirty minutes: **half-hour**, **half an hour** ○ *The bus goes every half-hour.* ○ *a half-hour lecture* ○ *I'll be back in half an hour.*
- a period of fifteen minutes: **quarter of an hour** ○ *I'll be there in about three quarters of an hour* (= 45 minutes). ○ *It took me an hour and a quarter to get home last night.*

- one of the sixty parts which make an hour: **minute** ○ *She will be here in about ten minutes.* ○ *at five minutes past three*
- one of the sixty parts which make a minute: **second** ○ *Twenty seconds to go!* ○ *In 1991 Carl Lewis set a world record of 9.86 seconds for the 100m sprint.*

this period of time ...	is a ...
24 hours	**day**
7 days	**week**
about 4 weeks	**month**
12 months	**year**
10 years	**decade**
100 years	**century**

▷ more on days, weeks, months and years ⇨ **DAY, WEEK, YEAR**

2 the passing of time

- the passing of minutes, hours, days, etc: **time** (*noun* U) ○ *As time passed, we could see changes in her appearance.* ○ *Only time will tell* (= we'll have to wait and see what happens). ○ *It's time we made some changes around here.*

- (used about time) to move forward: **pass**, **go* by**, (*formal*) **elapse** ○ *Five months have passed, and I still haven't heard from them.* ○ *Time is going by very quickly.*
- as time passes: **day by day** ○ *Things gradually improved day by day.*
- often during a period of time: **day after day**, **day in day out**, **year after year**, etc ○ *I go to work day in day out and I never seem to have anything to show for it.*

- to need or require a certain amount of time: **take*** ... ○ *How long does it take to get there?* ○ *It takes five hours by road.* ○ *I don't know what she's doing – she's taking ages.*
- to use up time: **take* up time** ○ *I'm sorry to take up your time, but I really need your help.*

- to measure how long sb/sth takes: **time** sb/sth ○ *He timed her as she ran round the track.*
- a person or machine that measures time: **timer** ○ *an egg timer*

- needing a lot of time: **time-consuming** ○ *a time-consuming job*
- to seem to last a long time; to be boring: **drag** (**on**) ○ *The days and weeks dragged on until finally the term came to an end.*
- to seem to pass very quickly: **fly* by/past** ○ *The two weeks of the holiday flew by.*

- (used about a period of time) finished: **up** ○ *When the time was up, we all had to stop writing and hand in our papers.* ○ *Time's up, everybody.*
- (used about a period of time) still remaining for sth to happen: **to go** ○ *Only a week to go until Christmas!*

■ duration

- to describe a period of time, you can use **from ... to** ○ *I had to wait from two o'clock to about half past three.* ○ *I lived there from 1990 to 1995.*
- to continue for a period of time: **last** (**for**) ..., **go* on** (**for**) ... ○ *How long does the film last?* ○ *It went on for two hours.*
- to express the length of time that sth lasts you say **for ...** ○ *That bell has been ringing for more than an hour!* ○ *How long must I wait here for?*
- for a period of time, or within a period of time: **during ...** ○ *I was very happy during my stay in Britain.* ○ *I stayed at home during the day, and then went out later on.*
- for the whole of a period of time, from beginning to end: **throughout ...** ○ *Passengers must stay in their seats throughout the flight.*

- continuing over a long period of time: **long**; *opposite*: **short** ○ *a long holiday* ○ *a short prison sentence*
- the time that sth lasts: (*formal*) **duration** ○ *You must stay in your seats for the duration of the performance.*

▷ more on long or short periods of time ⇨ **LONG/SHORT[1]**

- to make sth last longer: **extend** sth, **prolong** sth ○ *Stopping smoking can prolong your life.*
- strong and able to last a long time: **durable** ○ *a very durable material*

■ continuing situations

- from a point in the past up to the present: **since ...** ○ *I haven't seen her since we went to the*

States in 1963. ◦ *We saw her a few weeks ago, but we haven't seen her since.*
- to emphasize the whole of a period of time, from beginning to end, you say **ever since . . .** ◦ *Ever since I can remember, I've wanted to go to Russia.*
- from the beginning: **all along** ◦ *I knew she was lying all along.*

- up to the time or the event mentioned: **until . . ., till . . ., up to . . .** ◦ *I waited until the end, then I left.* ◦ *Let's not go till we absolutely have to.* ◦ *Up to now, I've been working in London, but I'm moving to Paris very soon.*

- (used to talk about sth that started at an earlier time) continuing until now or until the time you are talking about: **still**; not continuing: **no longer, not any longer, not any more** ◦ *'Have you finished yet?' 'No, I'm still working on it.'* ◦ *Because of her accident she can no longer enjoy swimming as she used to.* ◦ *He doesn't live here any more.*

3 points in time
- the time of speaking; the present time: **now** ◦ *She's leaving the house right now, and she'll be here in a few minutes.* ◦ *He now lives in Stockholm.*
- not at the time of speaking; at some other time; after sth else: **then** ◦ *I finish my degree in June and I hope I'll be able to get a good job then.* ◦ *First I'll read it at a normal speed; then I'll read it more slowly.*

- a particular length of time before now: **ago** ◦ *We bought this house exactly a year ago.* ◦ *'When did you last see her?' 'About a week ago.'*
- not long ago: **recently**; *adjective*: **recent** ◦ *'Have you been living here long?' 'No, we moved quite recently.'* ◦ *We have been badly affected by the recent floods.* ◦ *the recent past*

- not long after the present time or the time mentioned: **soon, before long, shortly** ◦ *I soon realized that he was not going to agree.*
- not far in time from now: **near, close**; *opposites*: **distant, remote** ◦ *in the near future* ◦ *The day of the wedding was close.* ◦ *in the distant future* ◦ *in the distant past* ◦ *Those days seem very remote now.*

▷ more on things happening soon ⇨ **SOON**

- before the usual or expected time: **early** (*adjective, adverb*) ◦ *I'll have to get up early tomorrow.*
- after the usual or expected time: **late** (*adjective, adverb*) ◦ *I handed in my essay two days late.*

▷ more on being early or late ⇨ **EARLY/LATE**

- before now, or before the time you are talking about: **already**; not before now, or not before the time you are talking about: **not yet** ◦ *I've already been to the shops once today; I don't want to go again.* ◦ *Have you done the washing-up already? That was quick.* ◦ *'Have you finished that letter?' 'Not yet.'* ◦ *I don't expect they will have arrived yet.*

■ which day, week, month, year?
- a particular day of the month or the year: **date** ◦ *'What's the date today?' 'It's Wednesday, April 12th.'*

▷ giving the date ⇨ **DATE**

▷ mentioning a particular day, week, month, year ⇨ **DAY, WEEK, YEAR**

Note: the prepositions that are used
with months and years: **in** ◦ *in January* ◦ *in 1999*
with days of the week: **on** ◦ *on Wednesday*
with times of the day: **at** ◦ *at midnight* ◦ *at three o'clock*
with a point of time in the future: **in** ◦ *I'll see you in a minute.* ◦ *It'll be finished in a few weeks.*
not later than a point of time in the future: **by** ◦ *I was promised a reply by the end of the week.*

■ what time of day?
- when in the day sth happens: **time** ◦ *What time does the plane arrive in Madrid?* ◦ *I've no idea what the time is.*
- to be able to say what time it is: **tell* the time** ◦ *I'm teaching the children to tell the time.*
- an instrument to tell you what time it is (usually found on the wall of a house or building): **clock**
- an instrument worn on the wrist, used to tell you what time it is: **watch**

▷ more on clocks and watches ⇨ **CLOCK/WATCH**

- to ask sb what the time is, you say **What's the time?** or **What time is it?** or **Have you got the time?** or **Do you know the time?** or (*formal*) **Can you tell me the time, please?** ◦ *'Have you got the time?' 'Yes, it's just after half past three.'*

- you say times like this:

10.00: **ten o'clock**
10.05: **five past ten, ten o five**
10.10: **ten past ten, ten ten**
10.15: **a quarter past ten, ten fifteen**
10.20: **twenty past ten, ten twenty**
10.25: **twenty-five past ten, ten twenty-five**
10.30: **half past ten, ten thirty**
10.35: **twenty-five to eleven, ten thirty-five**
10.40: **twenty to eleven, ten forty**
10.45: **a quarter to eleven, ten forty-five**
10.50: **ten to eleven, ten fifty**
10.55: **five to eleven, ten fifty-five**
10.22: **twenty-two minutes past ten, ten twenty-two**
10.38: **twenty-two minutes to eleven, ten thirty-eight**

time *contd.*

- the middle part of the day; 12 o'clock: **midday** (*noun* U) ○ *at midday*
- the middle part of the night; 12 o'clock: **midnight** (*noun* U) ○ *It was almost midnight.*
- between midnight and midday: **am**; between midday and midnight: **pm** ○ *The meeting adjourned at three pm.*

- at the time when the new hour starts: **on the hour** ○ *The buses leave every hour, on the hour* (= the buses leave at four o'clock, five o'clock, six o'clock etc).
- not later than; no more than: **only** ○ *It's only six o'clock; I thought it was later.*
- a long time before or after: **well before/after** ○ *The party went on until well after midnight.*
- a little more or less than: **about**, **around** ○ *'What's the time?' 'It's about five.'*
- a little less than: **nearly** ○ *The time is nearly six o'clock.*
- approximately: **-ish** ○ *'What time shall I come?' 'About sevenish?'*

- the time mentioned, neither earlier nor later: **exactly**, **sharp**, **on the dot** ○ *It's exactly six o'clock.* ○ *It's six o'clock sharp.* ○ *We left the house at six o'clock on the dot.*

4 how often sth happens

- a particular time when sth happens: **time** ○ *How many times have you been to America?* ○ *I've been there three times.* ○ *This is the first time I've been here.*
- a situation or event in which sth happens: **occasion** ○ *I've met him on several occasions.*
- happening many times: **often**, **frequently**; *adjective*: **frequent** ○ *How often do you come here?* ○ *I met her frequently when she was a student.* ○ *frequent interruptions*
- how often sth happens: **frequency** (*noun* U) ○ *happening with increasing frequency*

▷ more on how often things happen ⇨ **HOW OFTEN**

5 happening at the same time

- at the same time: **while ...**, **at the same time (as ...)**, **meanwhile** ○ *The kids were watching television while their parents were doing the washing-up.* ○ *I was trying to make the dinner at the same time as answering the phone.* ○ *I was waiting for her outside the restaurant. Meanwhile, she was waiting for me on the other side of town.*
- during the same time that sb was doing sth or that sth was happening: **all the time** ○ *I looked everywhere for my keys, and all the time they were in my bag.*

- to happen at the same time as sth else: **coincide (with** sth), **clash with** sth ○ *The meeting coincided with my appointment at the doctor's.*
- happening at exactly the same time: **simultaneous** (*adverb* **simultaneously**) ○ *The two things happened simultaneously.*

■ not happening at the same time

- happening one after the other: **consecutive** (*adverb* **consecutively**) ○ *I've been away for three consecutive weekends.*
- the order in which things happen: **sequence** ○ *The police were trying to work out the exact sequence of events.*
- arranged in the order in which the events happened: **chronological** ○ *in chronological order*

▷ one thing happening before/after another ⇨ **BEFORE/AFTER**

6 organizing and using time

- to arrange a time when sth will be done: **fix** a time, **set*** a time ○ *Let's fix a time to meet.* ○ *We need to set a date for the next committee meeting.*
- to allow sb a period of time for sth: **give*** sb sth ○ *I'll give you five days to finish the job.*
- to give time for sth: **spare** time ○ *Can you spare a bit of time to see her?*
- to give time for sth when you are very busy: **find*** time, **make*** time ○ *I'll try and find a few minutes tomorrow to discuss it with you.* ○ *She said if I hadn't got time to do it, I'd have to make time.*

- a time during which sth must be done: **time limit** ○ *Hurry up! There's a time limit of three hours.*
- a time or date before which sth must be done: **deadline** ○ *Friday's the deadline for finishing this piece of work.* ○ *to meet a deadline* (= to do sth within a certain time)
- to succeed in doing a task in time: **meet*/make* a deadline** ○ *I can't come out – I've got a deadline to meet.*
- to fail to complete a task in time: **miss a deadline**

- to choose or plan the time that sth happens: **time** sth ○ *They timed the wedding very carefully, so that everything would run smoothly.* ○ *If you time it right, you'll arrive just in time for the party.*
- your skill at choosing or arranging when sth will happen: **timing** ○ *The timing of each event was perfect.* ○ *His timing wasn't very good – his talk went on for much longer than it should have.*

- a list that shows the times when sth happens: **timetable** (*AmE* **schedule**) ○ *a school timetable* ○ *a train timetable*
- a plan of things that will happen or of things that need to be done: **schedule**, **programme** (*AmE* **program**); *verbs*: **schedule** sth, **programme** sth ○ *a television schedule* ○ *a programme of the day's events* ○ *The concert is scheduled for nine o'clock tonight.* ○ *We've programmed your lecture for nine o'clock on the first evening.*

- if you need to do sth quickly, you are **in a hurry**, **pushed for time** ○ *Can you be quick please – I'm*

in a hurry. ◦ *Can you hurry up a bit, I'm a bit pushed for time.*
- if you do not have to hurry, you can **take* your time** ◦ *Take your time, there's no rush.*

- to use your time for a particular purpose: **spend*** time ◦ *I spent my holiday lying on the beach.* ◦ *He spends most of his time in the library.*
- to find things to do so that the time passes quickly: **pass the time** ◦ *He's a bit bored in hospital – can you take something for him to pass the time?*
- to avoid spending time doing sth that is not necessary: **save** time; *noun*: **saving** ◦ *Going to work by train instead of by car saves me half an hour.* ◦ *a considerable saving of time*
- to spend time doing sth that is not necessary: **waste** time; *noun*: **waste** ◦ *I wasted the whole day, waiting for them at the airport.* ◦ *What a dreadful waste of time that was!*

- time that is not used for work is **spare**, **free** ◦ *What do you do in your spare time?* ◦ *Have you got a spare half-hour to help me with my project?* ◦ *I don't have much free time these days.*

tired

no longer interested in sth ⇨ INTERESTING

- when you feel that you need to rest or sleep, you are **tired**, (*formal*) **weary** (*adverb* **wearily**) ◦ *I feel tired.* ◦ *You look tired.* ◦ *She asked wearily if I needed any more help.*
- to begin to feel tired: **tire**; to make sb else feel tired: **tire** sb ◦ *She's very old and tires easily.*
- things that make you feel tired are **tiring**; the feeling of being tired: **tiredness** (*noun* U) ◦ *a long, tiring walk* ◦ *a tiring day*

- extremely tired: **exhausted**, **worn out**, **tired out** ◦ *I was exhausted after running all the way home.* ◦ *She was simply worn out from doing everything herself.*
- the feeling of being very tired: **exhaustion** (*noun* U); things that make you feel like this are **exhausting** ◦ *to be in a state of exhaustion* ◦ *I've had an exhausting morning.* ◦ *an exhausting job*

- when you feel tired and ready to go to sleep, you are **sleepy** (*adverb* **sleepily**) ◦ *He looked up sleepily and asked what time it was.*
- very sleepy: **drowsy**; this feeling: **drowsiness** (*noun* U) ◦ *The heat in here is making me drowsy.* ◦ *Do these tablets cause drowsiness?*
- if you feel tired and generally unhealthy because you are too busy, you are **run down** ◦ *She needs a holiday – she's looking terribly run down.*

- if you are tired because you have travelled a long way by plane to a place where the local time is different, you are **jet-lagged**; this kind of tiredness: **jet lag** (*noun* U) ◦ *Do you feel jet-lagged at all?* ◦ *to suffer from jet lag*

■ what you do if you are tired
- to open your mouth and breathe in deeply when you are tired or bored: **yawn**; this action: **yawn** ◦ *Stop yawning!*
- if you let out a long, deep breath that shows that you are tired, sad, etc, you **sigh**; *noun*: **sigh** ◦ *That was a big sigh – what's the matter with you?*

- a period of no activity: **rest** (*noun* C/U) ◦ *I need a rest.* ◦ *She's having a rest.* ◦ *Try to get some rest.*
- to do less or to do nothing after being active: **rest**; to allow a part of your body to rest: **rest** sth ◦ *Rest here for a while.* ◦ *If you rest your eyes, your headache will probably go away.*
- an evening when you go to bed earlier than usual: **early night** ◦ *I'm exhausted – I think I'll have an early night.*

▷ resting and sleeping ⇨ REST², SLEEP

to

- to a place ⇨ MOVE
- up to a time ⇨ TIME

tobacco ⇨ CIGARETTE

today ⇨ DAY

toe ⇨ LEG/FOOT

together

1 together
2 people together
3 things together
4 not together; separate

meeting sb ⇨ MEET
having a meeting ⇨ MEETING
working together ⇨ WORK
coming together or putting things together ⇨ JOIN

1 together

- with each other: **together** ◦ *Can we have lunch together?* ◦ *Keep together while we are going round the museum.* ◦ *Put your feet together.* ◦ *Mix the egg, flour and milk together.* ◦ *Add these numbers together to get the total.*
- a number of people or things that are together: **group**; to put sb/sth together into one or more groups: **group** sb/sth ◦ *A group of us went to see a film last night.* ◦ *The children were grouped according to their age.*

▷ groups of people ⇨ GROUP

- two people, animals or things that are closely connected or belong together: **pair** ◦ *The teacher asked the students to get into pairs to do the exercise.* ◦ *A pair of hawks are nesting in the woods near our house.* ◦ *a pair of gloves*

- if several different types of people or things are together, they are **mixed**, **miscellaneous**; *noun*: **mixture** ◦ *mixed nuts* ◦ *a miscellaneous collection of photographs* ◦ *a mixture of nationalities*
- a number of things which are different from each other, mixed: **variety** (**of** sth) (*noun singular*); *adjective*: **various** ◦ *A wide variety of goods*

together *contd.*

were on display. ◦ *The college offers various kinds of courses.*

▷ being the same or different ⇨ SAME, DIFFERENT

2 people together

– being with a person: **company** (*noun* U) ◦ *I really enjoy his company* (= I like being with him).
– a person or animal that you spend a lot of time with: **companion** ◦ *a travelling companion* ◦ *Her dog is her only companion.*
– two people who are married or living together: **couple** ◦ *the couple who live next door*

– to spend time and go to places regularly with sb: **go* round/around/about with** sb, **go* around together** ◦ *I don't like the people you are going around with.*
– to be with and talk to other people: **associate with** sb, **mix with** sb ◦ *I don't associate with people from work.* ◦ *Her father thought she was mixing with the wrong sort of people.*
– always together: **inseparable** ◦ *inseparable friends*

– to go with sb to a place: **go*** (**along**) **with** sb, **accompany** sb ◦ *I went along to the post office with Carmen.* ◦ *The students were accompanied by their teacher.*

▷ taking sb to a place ⇨ BRING/TAKE/CARRY

– (used about two people) holding each other's hands: **hand in hand**; with your arm linked together with sb else's arm: **arm in arm** ◦ *They were walking along arm in arm.*
– if people are beside each other they are **side by side** ◦ *We sat side by side on a wall.*

3 things together

– a number of things that belong together: **set** ◦ *a set of furniture* ◦ *a chess set* ◦ *a set of mathematical problems*
– a number of objects of a particular type that have been brought together: **collection** ◦ *There was a large collection of papers on the table.* ◦ *a stamp collection*
– to bring together a number of objects of a particular type over a period of time because they interest you: **collect** sth; a person who does this: **collector** ◦ *He has managed to collect together a large number of books and papers connected with the life of his famous uncle.*

– a number of things of the same type, joined together or growing together: **bunch** ◦ *a bunch of flowers/bananas*
– a number of things that are tied or wrapped together: **bundle** ◦ *a bundle of clothes* ◦ *a bundle of letters with an elastic band around them*
– a number of things lying on top of one another or in a large mass: **pile** ◦ *a pile of books* ◦ *a pile of sand*
– an untidy pile: **heap** ◦ *All his clothes are in a heap on the floor.*
– to put things in a pile or heap: **pile** sth (**up**), **heap** sth (**up**) ◦ *Where shall we pile all this sand?* ◦ *They heaped all the boxes in the corner.*

4 not together; separate

– things which are not together are **separate** (*adverb* **separately**) ◦ *We sat at separate tables.* ◦ *Do you think they look better together or separately?*
– separately; away from sb/sth or each other: **apart** (**from** sb/sth) ◦ *They're always arguing, so it's best to keep them apart.* ◦ *Our two houses are only about five miles apart.* ◦ *She sat apart from the rest of the group, apparently absorbed in her own thoughts.*

– without any other person: **alone** ◦ *I live alone.*
– without another person or thing: (**all**) **on** your **own**, (**all**) **by** yourself

▷ more on being alone ⇨ ALONE

– not together; at different times or in different places: **one by one**, **individually**, **separately** ◦ *We'll have to see them one by one.* ◦ *Put the glasses carefully into the box, one by one.* ◦ *We went in to the interview room one by one.* ◦ *We talked to them all individually.*

■ becoming separate

– to stop being together: **separate**, **split* up**; to make people or things separate: **separate** sb/sth (**from** sb/sth); *noun* (C/U): **separation** ◦ *We separated outside the station and went our different ways.* ◦ *The rocket separated into two parts.* ◦ *Separate the whites of the eggs from the yolks.* ◦ *a painful separation* ◦ *separation from family and friends*

– to separate sth from what it is joined to: **detach** sth (**from** sth) ◦ *The collar had become detached from my shirt.*
– to separate from sth else by force: **break* off**; to cause sth to separate from sth else by force: **break*** sth **off** ◦ *Part of the wing broke off, causing the pilot to lose control of the plane.* ◦ *He broke off another piece of chocolate and gave it to the child.*
– something which can be detached is **detachable** ◦ *a detachable bicycle lamp*

– to break or separate into parts: **divide** (**into** sth); to break or separate sth into parts: **divide** sth (**up**) (**into** sth); *noun* (U): **division**
– a thing that separates sb/sth: **division** (**between** sth **and** sth) ◦ *There is a deep division in this country between rich and poor.*

▷ more on dividing things ⇨ DIVIDE

toilet

see also BATHROOM, BODY

– a large bowl that you use when you want to get rid of waste from your body: **toilet**, (*BrE informal*) **loo**, (*more formal*) **lavatory**

– a room that contains a toilet: **toilet**, (*BrE informal*) **loo**, (*formal*) **lavatory** (*AmE* **bathroom**) ◦ *Where's the toilet, please?* ◦ *I'm going to the loo.*

– a toilet in a public place: **public toilet**, (*formal*) **public convenience**
– usually people will say (for men) **the Gents**, (for women) **the Ladies**, (*AmE*) **the restroom**,

(*AmE*) **the washroom** ◦ *Is there a public toilet near here?* ◦ *Can you tell me where the Ladies is?*

■ using the toilet
- to get rid of waste from the body: **go* to the toilet**, (*informal*) **go* to the loo**
- the waste water that you pass out of your body when you go to the toilet: **urine**, (*informal*) **pee**
- to get rid of urine from the body: (*informal*) **pee**, (*informal*) **have a pee**, (*formal*) **urinate**

- the part of a toilet that you sit on: (**toilet**) **seat**
- the tissue paper that you use to clean yourself in a toilet: **toilet paper** (*noun* U)
- a roll of toilet-paper: **toilet roll**

- when you pull the handle on a toilet to clean it, you **flush** the toilet
- when water flows to clean the toilet, the toilet **flushes** ◦ *What's wrong with the toilet – it isn't flushing properly.*

- a bowl that children sit on when they are too small to use a toilet: **potty**

▷ more on babies ➪ BABY

■ **MORE ...**
- a large underground pipe that carries away the waste from toilets: **sewer**; the waste from toilets: **sewage** (*noun* U)

tomorrow ➪ DAY

ton / tonne ➪ WEIGHT

tongue ➪ MOUTH

too
- also ➪ AND / OR / BUT
- too much ➪ FAIRLY / VERY

tool

see also MACHINE, CUT, GARDEN

- a piece of equipment that can help you do a particular job: **tool** ◦ *a set of garden tools* ◦ *power tools* (= tools that run on electricity)
- a tool used especially for delicate or scientific work: **instrument** ◦ *surgical instruments*
- a tool or machine: **device**, (*informal*) **gadget** ◦ *a kitchen full of electrical gadgets*
- a tool used for outdoor work: **implement** ◦ *farm implements*

- all the things, such as tools, machines, clothing, that are needed for a particular activity: **equipment** (*noun* U), **gear** (*noun* U) ◦ *camping equipment/gear* ◦ *a piece of climbing equipment*

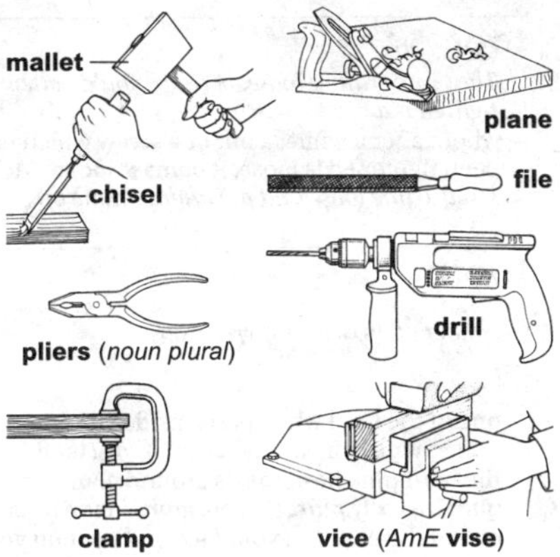

- a number of tools which are used for a certain purpose: **set**, **kit** ◦ *a set of spanners* ◦ *a bicycle-repair kit*

- to use a chisel: **chisel** sth (**into** sth) ◦ *lettering chiselled into the stone*
- to use a file: **file** sth
- to use a plane: **plane** sth ◦ *to plane sth smooth*
- to make a hole with a drill: **drill** sth ◦ *You need to drill another hole just here.*
- to hold sth with a clamp: **clamp** sth (**to** sth)
- a table that you can work on, attach tools to, etc: **workbench**

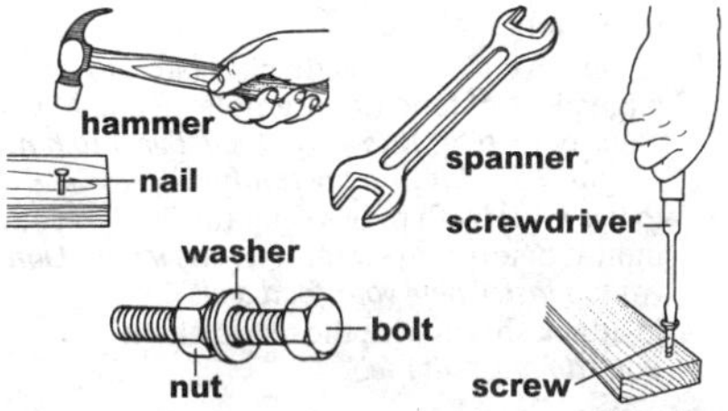

- a heavy wooden hammer: **mallet**
- a very large and heavy kind of spanner: **wrench**

- to hit sth with a hammer: **hammer** sth ◦ *to hammer a nail into a piece of wood*
- the activity of using a hammer, or the sound of one being used: **hammering** ◦ *the noise of hammering*
- to join two things together with a nail: **nail** sth (**to** sth), **knock** a nail (**in/into** sth) ◦ *to nail two bits of wood together* ◦ *to knock a nail in the wall*

- to connect sth to sth else with a screw or screws; to join two or more things with a screw or screws: **screw** sth (**into/onto** sth); *opposite*: **unscrew** sth ◦ *to screw a lock onto the door* ◦ *The shelves were screwed into the wall.*
- to turn a screw, etc until it cannot turn any more: **tighten** sth; *opposite*: **loosen** sth ◦ *I can't tighten this screw any more.*
- if sth has been tightened, it is **tight**; *opposite*: **loose** ◦ *Can you check that the screws are tight?* ◦

tool *contd.*

That nut's rather loose; perhaps you'd better tighten it a bit.
- when, after a while, a nut or a screw which had been tightened is loose, it **comes* loose** ◦ *A screw came loose and the handle came off.*

tooth

other parts of the body ⇨ BODY

- one of the hard white parts inside your mouth that you use for eating: **tooth** (*plural* **teeth**)
- the hard pink flesh that is around your teeth: **gum** (*usually plural*) ◦ *sore gums* ◦ *gum disease*
- one of the bones in your face that contain your teeth: **jaw** ◦ *the upper/lower jaw*
- one of the large teeth at the back of your mouth: **molar**
- one of four teeth at the back of your mouth that appear when you are about 20 years old: **wisdom tooth** (*plural* **wisdom teeth**)
- one of the first set of teeth in young children: **milk tooth** (*AmE* **baby tooth**) (*plurals* **milk/baby teeth**)
- when a baby is starting to grow its first teeth, it is **teething**
- having no teeth: **toothless** ◦ *The old man gave me a toothless grin.*

■ using your teeth
- to cut sth with your teeth: **bite*** (sth); to cut a large piece of food (for example an apple) with your teeth: **bite* into** sth ◦ *Ouch! I've bitten my tongue!* ◦ *She bit into the sandwich.*
- to use your teeth to break up the food in your mouth before you swallow it: **chew** sth ◦ *Don't eat too fast. Chew your food well.*
- to attack sb/sth with the teeth: **bite*** sb/sth ◦ *Your dog just bit me!*

▷ eating ⇨ EAT

■ cleaning your teeth
- to remove food particles from your teeth with a brush: **clean** your **teeth**, **brush** your **teeth**
- the object that is used for brushing your teeth: **toothbrush** ◦ *Brush your teeth after meals and before you go to bed.*
- the substance that you use on a toothbrush to clean your teeth: **toothpaste** (*noun* U) ◦ *a tube of toothpaste*
- a small pointed piece of wood for removing food from between your teeth: **toothpick**; to use a toothpick: **pick** your **teeth**
- soft thread that you use to remove food from between your teeth: **(dental) floss** (*noun* U)

■ problems with teeth
- pain in a tooth: **toothache** (*noun* U/C) ◦ *I've got toothache.*
- when a tooth causes pain, it **aches**
- if a tooth becomes bad, it **decays**; the process is called **tooth decay** (*noun* U)
- a hole in one of your teeth caused by decay: **hole**, (*formal*) **cavity** ◦ *The dentist said I had several cavities that needed filling.*
- if a tooth is not firmly fixed in your mouth, it is **loose**

▷ note on toothache and other aches ⇨ PAIN

- a person whose job is to look after people's teeth: **dentist**
- connected with teeth and looking after teeth: **dental** ◦ *She's had a lot of dental problems.* ◦ *dental treatment*
- to remove a tooth: **take*** sth **out**
- to have a tooth removed by a dentist: **have** sth **out** ◦ *I've just had a tooth out.*
- artificial teeth: **false teeth, dentures**

▷ going to the dentist ⇨ DENTIST

■ MORE ...
- a long, sharp tooth of a dog, a poisonous snake, etc: **fang**

top ⇨ PLACE[2]

touch

see also FEEL

- to put a part of your body, usually your fingers, on sb/sth: **touch** (sb/sth); an act of doing this: **touch** ◦ *Don't touch!* ◦ *Simply touch this switch and the machine will start.* ◦ *My knee hurts when I touch it.* ◦ *Her touch was light and gentle.*
- to learn about sth by touching it with your hands: **feel*** sth ◦ *Feel how soft this material is.* ◦ *She felt the child's forehead to find out if he had a temperature.*

- (used about two or more things) to have physical contact: **touch** ◦ *A bell rings when the wires touch.* ◦ *You must remove one stick without touching any of the others.* ◦ *Make a space between the desks so that they aren't touching.*
- the state of two surfaces, etc being together with no space between: **contact**; to come together: **come* into contact** (**with** sth) ◦ *physical contact* ◦ *The two metal parts should not come into contact with each other.*

- to touch and move sth with your hands: **handle** sth ◦ *Fragile – handle with care!* ◦ *The workers wear gloves when handling chemicals.*
- to touch or feel sth with your fingers: **finger** sth ◦ *She fingered the dress and wondered whether she should buy it.*

- to touch or hit sb/sth quickly and gently with your hand: **tap** sb/sth; *noun*: **tap** ◦ *to tap a person on the shoulder* ◦ *to feel a tap on your back*
- to hit sb/sth very gently with a flat hand: **pat** sb/sth; *noun*: **pat** ◦ *to pat a dog* ◦ *a pat on the hand*
- to move your hand gently over sth: **stroke** sth ◦ *He stroked his beard thoughtfully.* ◦ *to stroke an animal*
- to move your hand backwards and forwards while pressing sth: **rub** sth; *noun*: **rub** ◦ *Polish the brass by rubbing it hard.* ◦ *She rubbed her*

arm where it hurt. ◦ *Give the stain a quick rub with mild soap.*
- to touch or push sb with your elbow: **nudge** sb; *noun*: **nudge** ◦ *My friend gave me a nudge when it was my turn to speak.*
- to push sb/sth with a finger or a long, thin object: **poke** sb/sth; *noun*: **poke** ◦ *I nearly poked my eye out putting on my make-up.* ◦ *He gave the fire a poke to keep it burning.*
- to touch sb lightly so that they laugh: **tickle** sb; *noun*: **tickle** ◦ *The baby likes to be tickled under the chin.*

- too far away to touch: **out of reach**; not too far away to touch: **within reach** ◦ *Keep all medicines out of reach of children.*
- not to touch sth: **leave*** sth **alone**, (*informal*) **keep*** your **hands off** sth ◦ *If you leave the wound alone, it will heal quickly.* ◦ *Eat your own dinner and keep your hands off mine!*
- if you want to order sb not to touch sth, you can say **Hands off!**

tourist ⇨ TRAVEL

town

1 towns, cities and villages
2 parts of towns
3 the government of towns
the countryside ⇨ COUNTRY²

1 towns, cities and villages

- a place with many streets and buildings: **town** ◦ *a university town* ◦ *a small market town*
- a large and important town: **city** ◦ *the city of Birmingham*
- the town or city where the government of a country is: **capital**, **capital city** ◦ *The capital of Sweden is Stockholm.*
- connected with a town or a city: **urban** ◦ *problems of urban development* ◦ *the urban environment*

- a person who lives in a town or city: **inhabitant**, (*formal*) **citizen**
- the people who live in a town: **the people of** somewhere, **the** (**whole**) **town** ◦ *the people of Glasgow* ◦ *The whole town was on the streets, waving flags and cheering.*
- the town where you live or where you feel you belong: **home town**

- land which is away from towns and cities: **the country** (*noun singular*)
- a group of houses with a school, church, etc in the country: **village**; a person who lives in a village: **villager**
- connected with the countryside: **rural** ◦ *rural communities*

2 parts of towns

- the centre of a town/city: **town/city centre**
- the main part of a town where the shops, offices, pubs, cinemas, etc are: **town** (*noun* U, *only after a preposition*) ◦ *My sister goes into town every Saturday to do the shopping.* ◦ *They live right in the centre of town.*
- to or in the centre of a city: (*especially AmE*) **downtown** (*adverb, adjective*) ◦ *We're moving downtown.* ◦ *downtown Manhattan*

- an area of a town: **district**, **part of town** ◦ *Which part of town do you live in?*
- a particular part of a town and the people who live there: **neighbourhood** (*AmE* **neighborhood**) ◦ *It's a nice, friendly neighbourhood.*

- an area of a town where people live, outside the centre: **suburb** ◦ *Most people live in the suburbs and travel to work in the centre of town.*
- the parts of a town or city that are farthest from the centre: **the outskirts** (*noun plural*) ◦ *I live on the outskirts of Bradford.*

- an area of a city where living conditions are very bad and the buildings have not been repaired for a long time: **slum** ◦ *The slums were cleared and replaced with blocks of flats.*
- a very poor area on the outside of a town: **shanty town**

- an open space in a town or city that has buildings all around it: **square** ◦ *Trafalgar Square* ◦ *We lived on the other side of the square.*
- a public garden with grass, trees and open spaces: **park**

■ roads etc
- a road in a town, etc that has shops, houses, etc on one or both sides: **street** (*written abbreviation* **St**) ◦ *Oxford Street* ◦ *to walk along the street*
- the path at the side of the road that is for people to walk on: **pavement** (*AmE* **sidewalk**)
- a path under a busy road or railway that is for people who are walking: **subway**
- a road that goes around a city so that cars do not need to go through the centre: **ring road** (*AmE* **beltway**)
- an underground railway system in a town: **underground** (*AmE* **subway**) (*noun singular*); the London underground is often called **the tube** ◦ *to travel by underground*

▷ more on streets and railways ⇨ ROAD, TRAIN

■ shops etc
- an area where there are many shops, especially in a large modern building outside the town centre: **shopping centre**
- a special area for shops where cars are not allowed: (*BrE*) **shopping precinct**, (*BrE*) **pedestrian precinct**; if the area of shops is covered (= has a roof), it is called a **shopping centre**, (*especially AmE*) (**shopping**) **mall**

- a place in a town where people go to buy and sell things, often in the open air: **market**, **market place**, **market square** ◦ *I'll meet you in the market place at half past eleven.*

▷ different kinds of shops ⇨ SHOP

▷ more on markets ⇨ SELL

town *contd.*

3 the government of towns

- a group of people who are elected to manage the affairs of a town/city: **(town/city) council**; a member of a council: **councillor**
- the person who leads a council: **mayor**

- connected with the government of a town: **municipal** ◦ *the municipal offices* ◦ *municipal transport*
- a large building that contains the town/city council offices: **town/city hall**

toy

see also PLAY, GAME[2]

- a thing that children play with: **toy** ◦ *children's toys* ◦ *toy soldiers* ◦ *a toy car* ◦ *to play with toys*
- a shop which sells toys: **toyshop** (*AmE* **toy store**)

- a toy (for example, sth like an animal) that is made of fur or a soft material: **soft toy, cuddly toy**
- a toy that a baby can shake to make a noise: **rattle**
- operated by a small machine which works when you turn a key: **clockwork** ◦ *a clockwork train*
- needing batteries (= devices which supply electricity): **battery-operated** ◦ *a battery-operated racing car*

- a toy which uses small computer parts to work or which you play on a computer: **computer game**

trade

- buying and selling ⇨ SELL, BUSINESS
- the economy of a country ⇨ ECONOMY

traffic ⇨ DRIVE, ROAD

train

1 different kinds of train
2 parts of trains
3 travelling on trains
4 the movement of trains

see also TRANSPORT, TRAVEL

1 different kinds of train

- a number of carriages or wagons that are pulled by an engine along a railway line: **train** ◦ *a diesel/electric/steam train* ◦ *a fast/slow train*
- a train that carries people: **passenger train**
- a train that carries goods: **goods train**, (*especially AmE*) **freight train**

- a slow train that stops at a lot of places: **local train, stopping train**
- a fast train that only stops at big or important places: **intercity (train), express (train)**
- a train that has compartments where passengers can sleep: **sleeper**

2 parts of trains

- one of the separate parts of a train where people sit: **carriage, coach** ◦ *'Which coach are we in?' 'F, I think.'*
- one of the separate sections into which some train carriages are divided: **compartment** ◦ *a non-smoking compartment*
- a place where you can sit in a train: **seat** ◦ *Hurry up or you won't get a seat!*
- a place above the seats where luggage can be put: **luggage-rack**
- a passage between the rows of seats in a train: **aisle**
- a long, narrow passage along one side of a carriage: **corridor**

- a type of carriage where there are places for people to sleep: **sleeping car**
- a type of carriage where food and drinks can be bought: **buffet car**
- a type of carriage where meals are served: **restaurant car**

- a machine that pulls a train: **engine, locomotive**
- an open truck used for transporting goods: **goods truck, goods wagon** (*AmE* **freight car**)

3 travelling on trains

- using a train or trains to travel: **by train, on the train, by rail** ◦ *Will you go by car or by train?* ◦ *We came up on the train.* ◦ *Travel by rail can be cheaper than by car.*
- to travel to a place by train: **take* a/the train, catch* a/the train, get* a/the train** ◦ *I don't think I'll fly to London. It's cheaper to take the train.* ◦ *We drove to Norwich and then caught the train to York.*
- a person who travels on a train but does not drive it or work on it: **passenger**

- to arrange to get a seat on a train: **reserve a seat, make* a reservation**; a seat that has been reserved is a **reserved** seat ◦ *The train was crowded and unfortunately I hadn't reserved a seat.*
- a seat that sb is already using is **taken** ◦ *Excuse me, is this seat taken?*
- a seat with nobody in it is **empty** ◦ *All the empty seats were reserved.*

- the money you pay to travel from one place to another on a train: **fare** ◦ *How much is the fare to Cambridge?*

- a piece of paper that shows that you have paid for your journey: **ticket**
- a ticket to travel to a place and back again: **return** (**ticket**) ○ *a day return* (= that allows you to return on the same day)
- a ticket to travel to a place but not back again: **single** (**ticket**)
- a ticket that allows you to make a particular journey by train as often as you like and for a fixed period of time: **season ticket** ○ *a three-month season ticket*
- a special card that allows you to buy train tickets more cheaply if you are an old person, a student, etc: **railcard**
- the best and most expensive type of seat on a train: **first-class**; the second best type of seat: **second-class**, (*BrE*) **standard class** ○ *a first-class ticket to Glasgow*

- to climb onto a train: **get* on** (sth), (*formal*) **board** sth ○ *We only just got on before the train left.*
- to succeed in getting onto a train before it leaves the station: **catch*** sth; *opposite*: **miss** sth ○ *'Did they catch their train?' 'No, they just missed it.'*
- to leave a train: **get* off** ○ *Which stop do you get off at?*

- to get off one train and get onto another: **change** (**trains**) ○ *You can catch a later train if you want, but you'll have to change at Crewe.*
- a train on which you can reach your destination without changing to another train: **through train** ○ *Is the 12.30 a through train or will I have to change somewhere?*
- a train that leaves soon after another arrives and that takes you on to the next part of your journey: **connection** ○ *We arrive at Leeds at ten, and there's a connection to Blackpool fifteen minutes later.*

- the person who is in charge of a train: **guard**, (*especially AmE*) **conductor**
- the person who drives a train: **train driver** (*AmE* **engineer**)
- a person who checks and collects tickets on a train: **ticket collector**
- a person who carries luggage at a railway station: **porter**

■ stations
- a building where trains stop so that passengers can get on and off: (**railway**) **station**, **train station**
- any place where a train normally stops: **stop** ○ *The next stop will be Doncaster.*
- the place at a station where you buy a ticket to travel by train: **ticket office**
- a written notice, a book or a computer screen which gives the times when trains arrive and depart from a station: **timetable** (*AmE* **schedule**)
- the place at a station where you can sit and wait for a train: **waiting room**

- a raised flat surface at a railway station where people get on and off trains: **platform** ○ *'What platform does the Leeds train leave from?' 'Platform 4.'*
- the place where you may have to wait before going onto the platform and where you show your ticket: **barrier**
- the person you show your ticket to at the barrier: **ticket collector**

4 the movement of trains
- the metal bars that the wheels of a train go on: **rails** ○ *The train came off the rails.*
- the path which the rails follow: **track**
- a track which trains go on between one place and another: **railway** (*AmE* **railroad**), (*BrE*) (**railway**) **line** ○ *the trans-Siberian railway* ○ *There are engineering works on the line to Plymouth.* ○ *a main line* ○ *a branch line*
- a place where a railway line goes underground, under the sea, etc: **tunnel** ○ *the Channel Tunnel* (= between England and France)

- a place where several railway lines meet: **junction**
- a place where a railway line and a road cross each other: **level crossing** (*AmE* **grade crossing**)
- a set of lights which give information to train drivers: **signals** (*noun plural*)

- the system of railway lines and the system which organizes travel by train: **railway** (*often plural*) (*AmE* **railroad**) ○ *He used to work on the railways.*
- an underground railway system in a town: **underground** (*AmE* **subway**) (*noun singular*); the London underground is often called **the tube** ○ *to travel by underground* ○ *an underground station/ train* ○ *We left the car near Paddington and took the tube to Oxford Street.*

- the trains which run on a railway: (**train**) **service** ○ *The service is quite good on weekdays, but on Sundays there's only one train every two hours.*
- if a train keeps to its proper time, it is **on time**; if it does not do so, it is **late**, it is **running late** ○ *The trains are running late today because of an accident near Reading.*

- a train crash in which a train comes off the track: **derailment**; when a train comes off the track, it is **derailed**

translate ⇨ LANGUAGE

transport

particular means of transport by road ⇨ **BICYCLE, BUS, CAR, LORRY, MOTORCYCLE, TAXI**
transport by rail, air and sea ⇨ **TRAIN, PLANE, BOAT**
see also TRAVEL

- to move people/things from one place to another in a train, bus, lorry, aeroplane, etc: **transport** sth; *noun* (U): **transport** ○ *The animals are transported to the docks by lorry.* ○ *road/rail/ air/sea transport* ○ *transport by road/rail/air/sea* ○ *public transport* (= transport that anybody can use)

transport *contd.*

– something, for example a car or a bus, that transports people and things from place to place, especially on land: (*formal*) **vehicle** ◦ *Every year there are more and more vehicles on the roads.*

■ transporting goods

– things that are carried by lorries, trains, aeroplanes, etc: **goods** (*noun plural*), **freight** (*noun* U) ◦ *a goods vehicle* ◦ *a freight train*
– goods that are carried in a ship or aircraft: **cargo** (*noun* C/U), (*plural* **cargoes**, *AmE* **cargos**) ◦ *a cargo plane* ◦ *a ship carrying a cargo of coal*
– something (heavy) that is being transported or that is going to be transported: **load** ◦ *a lorry with a heavy load* ◦ *a load of bricks/sand*
– a load that is being carried, especially by a ship: **shipment** ◦ *A further shipment of grain is expected to arrive in a few days.*

– a large metal box that is used for transporting goods by sea, road or rail: **container** ◦ *a container ship/ lorry* (= a ship/lorry that transports containers)
– a large box in which goods are transported or stored: **crate** ◦ *We had to pack everything into crates when we moved house.*
– a wooden box that you put things into to be transported or stored: **packing case**

– to transport sth by some means: **send*** sth ◦ *Would it be cheaper to send the books by rail or by road?*
– to transport sth, especially by ship: **ship** sth
– to transport many people and things by air, especially in an emergency: **airlift** sth; *noun*: **airlift** ◦ *Food and medical supplies were airlifted into the city*.

– to put things into boxes, etc so that they are ready to be transported: **pack** (sth)
– to put a load or a large quantity of sth in or on a lorry, ship, train, etc: **load** sth (**onto/into** sth) ◦ *Crates of fish were loaded on to the plane.*
– to take a load or large quantity of sth off a lorry, ship, train, etc: **unload** (sth) ◦ *to unload bricks from a lorry* ◦ *Vehicles may only park here when loading or unloading.*

travel

1 travelling
2 means of transport
3 tickets, passports, money, etc
4 starting a journey, moving and arriving

luggage and packing ⇨ BAG
accidents and crashes ⇨ ACCIDENT
travelling in space ⇨ SPACE²

see also HOLIDAY, HOTEL, CAMP

1 travelling

– to go to a place, or different places, usually over a long distance: **travel**; *noun* (U): **travel** ◦ *She has to travel a lot in her job.* ◦ *She's planning to travel by train across Canada.* ◦ *air travel* ◦ *foreign travel* ◦ *a travel book*
– a person who is travelling or who often travels: **traveller** ◦ *My aunt is a great traveller: she's been to every country in Europe.*
– a person who travels with you: (**travelling**) **companion**
– an act of travelling from one place to another: **journey** ◦ *I hope you have a good journey.* ◦ *a four-hour journey* ◦ *a twenty-mile journey to work* ◦ *a journey across America* ◦ *a difficult/easy/ smooth journey*
– a journey that you make for pleasure during which you visit many places: **tour**; to make a journey like this: **go*/be on a tour**, **tour** (sth) ◦ *Peter and Louise are on a tour of the Italian lakes.* ◦ *We toured round the United States last summer.*
– a journey during which you visit a place and return: **trip** ◦ *How was your trip to Brussels?* ◦ *a business trip*

– to travel around a place in order to learn about it: **explore** (sth); *noun* (U): **exploration**; a person who explores a place: **explorer** ◦ *We left our hotel and set out to explore.*

– to travel to another country: **go* abroad** ◦ *We went abroad for our holidays last year.*
– to travel to another country across the sea, usually to stay for a long time: **go* overseas** ◦ *Will you be going overseas in your new job?*

– the business of providing holidays for people: **tourism** (*noun* U) ◦ *The island's economy is heavily dependent on tourism.*
– a person who travels for pleasure: **tourist** ◦ *a party of tourists* (= a group of tourists) ◦ *the tourist industry*
– a person who is away from home on holiday: **holidaymaker**

– a short visit round a famous building, city, etc: **tour** ◦ *a guided tour of Buckingham Palace*
– an organized trip with a group of people: **excursion** ◦ *On Sunday, we went on an excursion to the mountains.*
– places of interest that are visited by tourists: **sights** (*noun plural*), **tourist attractions** (*noun plural*)
– to visit the places of interest in a city, etc as a tourist: **go* sightseeing, see* the sights**; a person who visits the sights of a city as a tourist: **sightseer**

■ travelling to work

– to travel a long distance from home to work every day: **commute**; a person who travels a long distance to work every day: **commuter**
– a time each day when traffic is very busy because people are travelling to or from work: **the rush hour**

2 means of transport

– using a car, bus, lorry, etc to travel: **by road, car, bus,** etc, **on the bus/coach**
– to go somewhere in a car: **drive***; a journey in a car or other vehicle: **drive** ◦ *We're driving up to Scotland this summer.*
– to travel by getting free rides in other people's cars, lorries, etc: **hitch-hike**, (*informal*) **hitch**; a

person who does this: **hitch-hiker** ◦ *We hitched down to Devon.* ◦ *I picked up two hitch-hikers on the way home from Bath.*

- using a bicycle or motorcycle: **by bike, by motorcycle**, etc
- to travel on a motorcycle: **ride*** (sth)
- to travel on a bicycle: **ride*** (sth), **cycle** ◦ *to ride along cycle tracks in the New Forest* ◦ *I usually cycle to work.*

- using a train or trains: **by train**, **on the train**, **by rail**
- (used about long journeys) by road or rail: **overland** ◦ *We travelled overland to Delhi and then flew on to Singapore.*

- using an aeroplane: **by air**, **by plane**
- to travel somewhere by plane: **fly***; a journey by plane: **flight**

- using a boat: **by sea**, **by boat**
- to travel somewhere in a boat: **sail**; a long journey by sea: **voyage**
- to travel by boat, visiting a number of places, as a holiday: **cruise**; *noun*: **cruise** ◦ *to go cruising in the Mediterranean* ◦ *a river cruise*

- without using a vehicle: **on foot**
- to go somewhere on foot: **walk**

- to travel to somewhere by train, bus, plane, etc: **take*** sth, **catch*** sth, **get*** sth ◦ *I decided to take the train.* ◦ *We caught the train to Leeds and then got a bus to where she lives.*
- a person who travels in a bus, train, aeroplane, etc but who does not drive or work on it: **passenger**

▷ more on different means of transport ⇨ **BICYCLE, BUS, CAR, LORRY, MOTORCYCLE, PLANE, TAXI, TRAIN**

▷ more on walking ⇨ **WALK**

3 tickets, passports, money, etc

- a piece of paper that shows you have paid for a journey: **ticket** ◦ *a train ticket* ◦ *an air ticket*
- a ticket to travel to a place and back again: **return** (**ticket**), (*AmE* **round-trip ticket**)
- a ticket to travel to a place but not back again: (on a bus or train) **single** (**ticket**), (on a plane) **one-way ticket**
- a ticket that allows you to make a particular journey by bus, train, etc as often as you want for a fixed period of time: **season ticket** ◦ *a three-month season ticket from Edinburgh to London*
- when your ticket can be used or accepted legally at a certain time, it is **valid** ◦ *Your season ticket isn't valid after the end of this week.*

- the money you pay for a journey by bus, train or taxi: **fare** ◦ *How much is the return/single fare to New York?*

- to buy a ticket in advance for a train or bus journey, you go to a **ticket office**, **booking office**; for an air ticket you go to a **travel agent**
- when you arrange to buy a ticket in advance, you **book** (a ticket) ◦ *You need to book weeks in advance if you want to travel on Christmas Eve.*
- to make sure you will have somewhere to sit on a bus or train, you can sometimes **reserve** a seat, **make* a reservation**

▷ tickets for travelling on buses or trains ⇨ **BUS, TRAIN**

- an official document that shows who you are and which you sometimes have to show when you enter or leave a country: **passport**
- a mark in your passport which shows that you have permission to enter or leave a country: **visa**
- the place where you have to stop and show your passport when you enter or leave a country: **passport control**

- a type of cheque you can change into foreign money while travelling abroad: **traveller's cheque** (*AmE* **traveler's check**)
- the money of a foreign country: **foreign currency** (*noun* U)
- a place where you can change your money into a different currency: **bureau de change**

▷ more on money ⇨ **MONEY**

4 starting a journey, moving and arriving

■ starting to travel

- to begin travelling to a place: **leave*** (**for** a place), **set* off** (**for** a place), **set* out** (**for** a place) ◦ *We're leaving for Italy in the morning.* ◦ *When are you setting off on your travels?* ◦ *We set out at three o'clock.*
- to go with sb to a station, airport, etc and say goodbye to them as they leave: **see*** sb **off** ◦ *Mr and Mrs White saw their daughter off at the station.*
- to leave a hotel at the end of your stay: **check out** (**of** sth) ◦ *When do we have to check out by?*

▷ more on leaving a place ⇨ **LEAVE**

■ moving from one place to another

- the place where you are going: **destination** ◦ *We reached our final destination at midnight.*
- the path or line along which a person or vehicle is moving: **direction** ◦ *We've been travelling in the same direction for hours.*
- to travel towards sth: **make* for** a place, **head for** a place ◦ *We headed for the town centre.*

- the way you follow to get from one place to another: **route**, **way** ◦ *We've got plenty of time – shall we take the tourist route?* ◦ *a bus route* ◦ *the coastal route* ◦ *Can you tell me the way to Trafalgar Square?* ◦ *Which way shall we go?*
- a different route which you decide to take or have to take: **detour** ◦ *We decided to make a detour to Florence before going on to Pisa.*
- a quicker, easier, or more direct route to get somewhere: **short cut** ◦ *Sheila took a short cut through the park.*
- on the way to somewhere: **en route** (**from** a place) (**to** a place) ◦ *We stopped off in Paris en route to Nice.*
- a plan of a journey, route, etc: **itinerary** ◦ *The travel agent suggested some changes to my itinerary.*

travel *contd.*

- a book or drawing that shows road routes across a country: **road map**

- an object (especially a building) that can be seen from a distance: **landmark** ◦ *One of the most famous landmarks in London is Nelson's Column.*
- to explain to sb how to get to a place: **direct** sb, **give*** sb **directions**
- to help sb find the right way or direction to go: **guide** sb ◦ *She guided us through the busy streets down to the harbour.*
- to find out where you are and in which direction you should be going: **find*** your **way**
- not to know where you are or in which direction you should be going: **be/get* lost, lose*** your **way** ◦ *I lost my way and had to ask for directions from a policeman.*

▷ more on finding your way ⇨ **DIRECTION**

- a person whose job it is to show cities, museums, etc to tourists: **guide** ◦ *a tour guide*
- a book for tourists that gives information about interesting places: **guidebook, guide** ◦ *a guide to Prague*

- to be travelling: (*informal*) **be on the move** ◦ *We had been on the move for twenty-four hours and were absolutely exhausted.*
- to continue travelling forward: **go* on** ◦ *Who thinks we should stop? Who wants to go on?*
- to continue travelling forward (despite difficulties): **push on, keep* going** ◦ *The explorers pushed on through the snow.*
- to start to go back to the place you began travelling from: **turn back** ◦ *It was getting dark, so we decided to turn back.*

- to get off one train, bus, plane, etc during a journey and get onto another: **change** (sth) ◦ *We changed trains at Manchester.*
- an aeroplane, train, bus, etc that leaves soon after another arrives and that takes you on to the next part of your journey: **connection** ◦ *If this train is late, we may miss our connection.*
- a short stop on a journey: **stopover**; *verb*: **stop over** ◦ *We made a stopover at Frankfurt on the way to Tokyo.* ◦ *Sheila decided to stop over in St Louis to see her parents.*
- to stop your journey for a time in order to do sth else: **break*** your **journey** ◦ *They decided to break their journey in Paris.*

- the amount of space between two points: **distance** (*noun* C/U) ◦ *It's only a short distance from here to the sea.*
- to go a certain distance: **travel ..., cover ..., do* ...** ◦ *How far have we travelled today?* ◦ *We covered fifty miles on our bikes yesterday.* ◦ *We did 20 miles before lunch and another 20 by the time we stopped for the night.*
- the amount of distance travelled by sb or sth: **mileage** (*noun* U/C) ◦ *The cost of the hired car includes unlimited mileage.*
- to travel at a certain speed: **go* at ..., do* ...** ◦ *That car was doing more than eighty miles an hour.*

- feeling ill because of the movement of the car, bus, etc you are travelling in: **travel sickness** (*AmE* **motion sickness**); feeling this way in a car: **carsick**; in a boat: **seasick** ◦ *I began to feel seasick as soon as we left port.*

■ arriving
- to come to the place you were travelling to: **arrive** (**at/in** a place), **reach** (a place); *noun*: **arrival** ◦ *The train arrives at ten past four.* ◦ *We reached Birmingham at six o'clock.* ◦ *Our arrival was delayed because of the storm.*
- to arrive somewhere in time for sth: **make*** somewhere, **make* it to** somewhere ◦ *Do you think we can make it to Heathrow on time?*
- to go to a place and wait for sb to arrive: **meet*** sb ◦ *I'll come to meet you at the airport.*
- to go to a hotel, airline, etc desk and say you have arrived: **check in** (**at** sth)

▷ more on arriving at a place ⇨ **ARRIVE**

■ **MORE ...**
- a special journey which is made to a holy place: **pilgrimage** (*noun* C/U); a person who makes this kind of journey: **pilgrim** ◦ *to go on a pilgrimage* ◦ *The church was crowded with pilgrims.*

- a person who does not live in one place and travels with his/her group to find grass for their animals: **nomad**; *adjective*: **nomadic**
- a member of a race of people who spend their lives travelling around from place to place, living in caravans: **gypsy** (*plural* **gypsies**), **traveller**

tree

1 parts of a tree
2 different kinds of tree
3 places where trees grow
4 using trees
see also PLANT

1 parts of a tree

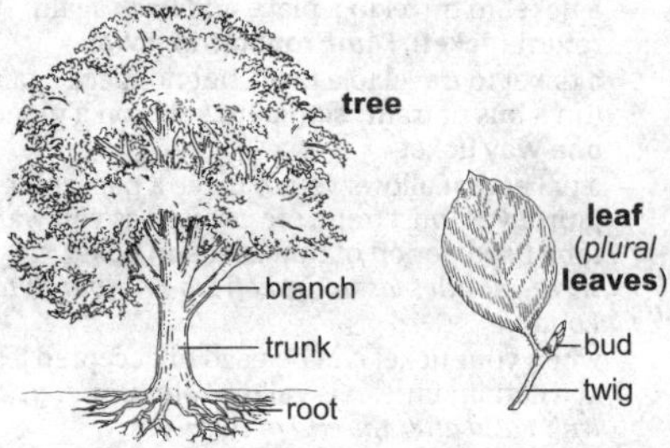

- the hard outer covering of a tree: **bark** (*noun* U)
- the liquid in a plant or tree: **sap** (*noun* U)
- one of the parts of a tree that grows under the ground: **root**
- a small thin branch: **twig**
- a new leaf or flower on a tree before it opens: **bud**
- a flower or a mass of flowers on a fruit tree: **blossom** (*noun* C/U)

- part of a tree that is left in the ground after it has been cut down: **(tree) stump**

2 different kinds of tree

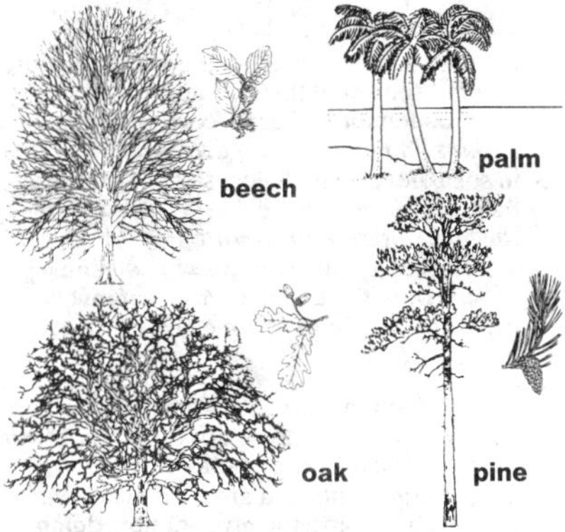

- a kind of small tree with many branches: **bush**
- a tree that produces fruit: **fruit tree**
- a tree that produces apples, pears, plums, etc: **apple tree, pear tree, plum tree**, etc

- a tree that is covered in green leaves all year round is **evergreen**; *noun*: **evergreen** ○ *Pine trees are evergreen.*
- a tree that loses its leaves in winter is **deciduous** ○ *Apple trees are deciduous.*

3 places where trees grow

- an area of land with a lot of trees: **wood, woodland** (*noun* U) ○ *a beech wood* ○ *woodland flowers*
- a large area of land covered in trees: **forest** (*noun* C/U) ○ *a tropical forest* ○ *Much of the land is covered in dense forest.*
- a thick forest in a tropical part of the world: **rain forest, jungle** ○ *the Amazon jungle*
- an area of land covered in woods or forests is **wooded, forested** ○ *densely wooded areas*
- a small area without trees in the middle of a wood or forest: **clearing**

- a field or part of a garden where fruit trees grow: **orchard** ○ *an apple orchard*
- a large piece of land used for growing trees for their wood: **plantation** ○ *a conifer plantation* (= of trees like pines)

4 using trees

- to put a very young tree in the ground so that it will grow: **plant** sth
- to cut a tree at the bottom so that it falls down: **cut*** sth **down, chop** sth **down, fell** sth ○ *A lot of trees will have to be cut down when they build the new road.*
- a tool which has a long metal blade with sharp teeth, and is used to cut wood: **saw**
- a tool with a wooden handle and a metal blade, used for cutting wood: **axe** (*AmE* **ax**)

▷ pictures of saw and axe ⇨ CUT

- the hard material that the trunk and branches of trees are made of: **wood** (*noun* U) ○ *Put some more wood on the fire.* ○ *It looks as if it's made of wood but in fact it's plastic.*
- wood that is going to be used for building: **timber** (*noun* U)
- a thick piece of wood that has been cut from a tree: **log**
- a factory where logs are cut for building: **sawmill**

▷ more on wood ⇨ WOOD

trial

1 different kinds of trials and courts
2 parts of courts and people in courts
3 what happens in a trial
see also LAW, CRIME, PRISON, PUNISH

1 different kinds of trials and courts

- a formal process in which people decide if sb has broken a law: **trial** (*noun* C/U) ○ *He was on trial for murder.*
- something that has to be decided in a trial: **case** ○ *a court case* ○ *They threatened to take the case to court.*
- a case that is about a crime is a **criminal** case; a case that is about the rights of ordinary people, for example property rights, divorce, etc, is a **civil** case

- a place where trials take place to decide if sb has broken a law: **court** (*noun* C/U), **law court** ○ *The judge ordered everyone in the court to be silent.* ○ *I'm due to appear in court on Wednesday.*
- a court used for serious civil cases: **the High Court**
- a court used for serious crimes: **crown court**
- a court used for less serious crimes: **magistrates' court**
- the highest court in some countries: **the Supreme Court**
- a special court used for particular types of case: **tribunal** ○ *an industrial tribunal*
- a court that you can go to when you want to prove that the decision of another court was wrong: **court of appeal, appeal court**

2 parts of courts and people in courts

- the people in a court: **the court** ○ *He told the court that he was sorry for what he had done.*
- a person who controls things in a court and decides what punishment to give to sb who is guilty of a crime: **judge**
- a judge who deals with less serious crimes: **magistrate** (*AmE also* **attorney**)
- a person who has studied law and whose job is to give advice about the law: **lawyer**
- a lawyer (in Britain) who gives legal advice, prepares documents and usually speaks in less serious court cases: **solicitor**
- a lawyer (in Britain) who usually speaks in more serious court cases: **barrister**

- a person who is said to have broken a law: **defendant, the accused** (*plural* **the accused**) ○ *The accused was brought into the court by two policemen.*

trial *contd.*

- the part of the court where the accused sits or stands: the **dock** ◦ *The prisoner stood in the dock.*
- a person who appears in a trial to say what he/she has seen, heard or knows about a crime: **witness**
- the part of a court where witnesses stand or sit: the **witness box** (*AmE* **witness stand**)
- a group of people who listen to the facts about a crime and decide if sb is guilty or not: **jury** ◦ *The jury took only one hour to reach their decision.* ◦ *trial by jury*
- a member of a jury: **juror**; the chief member of a jury: **foreman/woman** (**of the jury**)
- the part of a court where the jury sits: the **jury box**

3 what happens in a trial

■ before the trial

- a person who is thought to have done sth wrong: **suspect** ◦ *Following the shooting, the police have arrested two suspects.*
- to say that sb has done sth against the law: **accuse** sb (**of** sth)
- when the police accuse sb officially of doing sth against the law, they **charge** sb (**with** sth); *noun*: **charge** ◦ *to be charged with murder* ◦ *He was arrested on a charge of theft.* ◦ *What are the charges against me?*
- an order to go to a court to be at a trial: **summons**; *verb*: **summons** sb ◦ *They've served a summons on me to appear in court next Friday.* ◦ *He was summonsed for speeding.*
- to pay money to the court so that sb can be free until the start of a trial: **bail** sb **out**; the money that you pay: **bail** (*noun* U) ◦ *Fortunately, John's already been bailed out by his lawyer.* ◦ *Bail was set at fifty thousand pounds.* ◦ *Thirteen of the fans were freed on bail.*

■ going to court

- to say that sb committed a crime and try to prove it in a court: **prosecute** sb (**for** sth), **put*** sb **on trial** (**for** sth); *noun* (C/U): **prosecution** ◦ *to be prosecuted for dangerous driving* ◦ *The ex-minister was put on trial for taking bribes.* ◦ *He was threatened with prosecution if he didn't pay his council tax.*
- if a case is dealt with in court, it **goes*/comes* to court** ◦ *If the case does go to court, it won't be heard until next year at the earliest.* ◦ *The case will never come to court.*
- to examine sb in a court to find out if they are guilty of a crime or not: **try** sb (**for** sth); a person who is being tried is **on trial** (**for** sth) ◦ *She was tried for shooting a policeman.* ◦ *Frank is on trial for burglary.*
- to listen to evidence and reach a decision in a trial: **hear* a case, conduct a trial** ◦ *Their case will be heard tomorrow afternoon.* ◦ *The trial was conducted before a special tribunal.*
- to say at the beginning of a trial that you did a crime or did not do a crime: (*formal*) **plead** (**guilty/not guilty**); *noun*: **plea** ◦ *The judge turned to the prisoner and asked: 'How do you plead to the charges against you?'* ◦ *They all decided to plead guilty.* ◦ *a plea of guilty/not guilty*

■ the two sides in a trial

- the person or group of people who prosecute sb (= try to show that they committed the crime): **the prosecution** ◦ *The prosecution claimed that Jenkins had fired the gun deliberately.*
- to speak for sb who is accused of a crime: **defend** (sb) ◦ *She was being defended by one of the top lawyers in the country.*
- a person or group of people who defend a person in court: **the defence** (*AmE* **defense**) ◦ *The defence asked for more time to prepare its case.* ◦ *a defence lawyer*
- an argument that is used to defend sb in court: **defence** (*AmE* **defense**) ◦ *His defence was that the gun went off by accident.*
- a set of arguments that are used to accuse/defend sb in court: **the prosecution/defence case, the case for the prosecution/defence** ◦ *What are the main points of the defence case?*
- to ask sb a lot of questions to find out the truth: **question** sb, **cross-examine** sb; *noun* (C/U): **cross-examination** ◦ *The witness was cross-examined for three hours by the defence.*
- to describe in a few words the main points of an argument: **sum** (sth) **up** ◦ *Mr Laughton summed up for the prosecution.*
- to show that sth is true: **prove** sth; a piece of information that shows that sth is true: **proof** ◦ *They weren't able to prove that he had been in the area at the time.* ◦ *I think he did it but do we have any proof?*

■ the witnesses

- to have promised the court to tell the truth: **be on/under oath** ◦ *The judge reminded the witness that he was under oath and that he must tell the whole truth.*
- something that you say or show in court to make people believe your explanation of how sth happened: **evidence** (*noun* U) ◦ *Pictures taken by a security camera were shown as evidence that she was in the shop at the time of the robbery.* ◦ *The evidence against him was overwhelming.* ◦ *an important piece of evidence*
- to say in court what you know or what you have seen or heard about a crime, etc: **give* evidence, testify** (**that ...**) ◦ *The witness testified that she had seen the accused running away from the bank just after the robbery.*
- a statement by sb that they were in another place at the time of a crime and so could not have done it: **alibi** ◦ *All the suspects had perfect alibis.*

■ the result of a trial

- a speech in which a judge sums up what has been said in a trial: **summing-up** ◦ *The judge began his summing-up.*
- to decide that sb has broken a law: **find*** sb **guilty** (**of** sth), **convict** sb (**of** sth); an act of con-

victing sb: **conviction** ○ *He was found guilty of murder.* ○ *She was convicted of kidnapping the child.* ○ *He had three previous convictions for violence.*

– to decide that sb has not broken the law: **find*** sb **not guilty**, **clear** sb (**of** sth), (*formal*) **acquit** sb (**of** sth); an act of acquitting sb of sth: **acquittal** ○ *All the defendants were found not guilty.* ○ *She was cleared of the murder of her husband.*
– if sb has not done sth that is wrong or illegal, they are **innocent** ○ *The accused had always said he was innocent.*

■ the decision of the court
– the decision at the end of a trial: **verdict** ○ *The jury returned a unanimous verdict of 'not guilty'.*

– a punishment given by a judge: **sentence** ○ *a prison sentence*
– to say what punishment a person is to have: **sentence** sb (**to** sth), **pass sentence** (**on** sb) ○ *He was found guilty and sentenced to three months in prison.*
– to make sb go to prison as a punishment: **send*** sb **to prison**
– an amount of money that you have to pay for breaking a law: **fine**; to make sb pay a fine: **fine** sb (**for** sth) ○ *He was fined one thousand pounds for not paying his television licence.*

– to ask a court to change a verdict against you: **appeal** (**to** sb) (**against** sth); *noun*: **appeal** ○ *He appealed to the high court against his conviction.* ○ *She was given twenty days to make an appeal.*

– a decision, etc that is fair is **just**; fair behaviour or treatment in a court: **justice** (*noun* U) ○ *a just punishment* ○ *Justice was finally done when the killer was sent to prison for life.*
– a decision, etc that is unfair is **unjust**; an unfair decision, or unfair behaviour or treatment: **injustice** (*noun* C/U) ○ *an unjust sentence* ○ *People thought that his short prison sentence was a great injustice.* ○ *Amnesty International fights against injustice all over the world.*

■ **MORE ...**
– to go to a court and ask for money from sb because they have done sth bad to you or said sth bad about you: **sue** (sb) (**for** sth), **take*** sb **to court** (**for** sth) ○ *If the work is left unfinished, we'll sue the builders.* ○ *I took the garage to court for the damage they had done to my car.*

– money that you can claim from sb if they hurt you or damage your property: **damages** (*noun plural*)
– an amount of money that a court decides to give to sb: **award**; to decide that sb must be given an award: **award** sth (**to** sb) ○ *June was awarded one hundred thousand pounds in compensation for her loss of earnings.*

– money that you have to pay for the cost of a trial: **costs** (*noun plural*) ○ *a £250 fine and £100 costs*
– help that you can get from the government to pay your costs: **legal aid** (*noun* U)

– a military court or a trial that takes place in a military court: **court-martial**; *verb*: **court-martial** ○ *He was court-martialled for desertion.*

triangle ⇨ SHAPE

trouble

1 kinds of trouble
2 causing trouble

1 kinds of trouble
– problems, difficulties, worries, etc: **trouble** (*noun* C/U) ○ *She was sure all her troubles would soon be over.* ○ *I've been having trouble with my car.*
– trouble or difficulty: **bother** (*noun* U) ○ *We decided it would be too much bother to drive back into town.*
– a person, thing or situation that annoys you or that causes you trouble: **nuisance** ○ *I hope I'm not being a nuisance.* ○ *It's such a nuisance that this bank is closed on Saturday mornings.*

– a difficult situation that you must deal with: **problem**; a continuing problem: (*informal*) **headache** ○ *Shortage of money is a real problem for many students.* ○ *social problems such as unemployment and drug abuse* ○ *It's a real headache trying to decide which school to send our children to.*
– causing difficulty or discomfort: **inconvenient**; *noun* (C/U) **inconvenience** ○ *Five o'clock is a bit inconvenient for me – could we make it earlier?* ○ *the inconvenience of not having a car*

– to experience trouble: **be in trouble**, **have trouble**, **run* into trouble**, (*informal*) **hit* trouble** ○ *The Government's in serious trouble.* ○ *I've had nothing but trouble with this computer.* ○ *The plane ran into trouble over the Atlantic and had to make a crash landing in the sea.*
– if you manage not to have trouble, you **avoid** trouble, **stay out of** trouble ○ *I want you to be a good boy and stay out of trouble while I'm away.*

▷ worries and problems ⇨ WORRY, PROBLEM

2 causing trouble
– to cause difficulties, problems, inconvenience, etc for yourself or for another person: **cause trouble** (**to/for** sb), **get*** (sb) **into trouble** ○ *If he goes on causing trouble, he'll be expelled from the school.* ○ *I'm sorry – I really didn't mean to get you into trouble.*
– a person who often causes trouble for other people: **troublemaker**
– if you do sth that is likely to cause you trouble, you are (*informal*) **asking for trouble** ○ *If you buy that old car you're asking for trouble.*

– to make sb rather angry, worried, etc: **annoy** sb, **bother** sb ○ *Does this noise annoy you?* ○ *I'm sorry to bother you with my problems.*
– to interrupt and annoy sb while they are doing sth: **disturb** sb, **bother** sb ○ *Don't disturb him while he is working.* ○ *Don't bother your mother now – she's busy.*

trouble *contd.*

▷ things that annoy you ⇨ ANGRY

– to cause trouble to a process or a system: **disrupt** sth; *noun* (C/U): **disruption**; *adjective*: **disruptive** ◦ *The strike did not succeed in causing any serious disruption.* ◦ *The teacher sent the boy out of the classroom because of his disruptive behaviour.*

– to cause sb trouble or annoyance, especially continuously or on many different occasions: **harass** sb; *noun* (U): **harassment** ◦ *The court ordered him to stop harassing his ex-wife.* ◦ *Marion accused her boss of sexual harassment.*

trousers

see also CLOTHES

– a piece of clothing that covers both legs, from waist to ankles: **trousers** (*AmE* **pants**) (*noun plural*) ◦ *I like those trousers you're wearing.* ◦ *tight trousers* (= fitting closely to the body) ◦ *baggy trousers* (= hanging loosely on the body)

▷ picture at CLOTHES

Note: because **trousers** is plural, we cannot say, for example, 'a trouser'. Instead, we must say 'some trousers' or 'a pair of trousers'. The same is the case with all the different kinds of trousers listed below. Before another noun, we use **trouser** ◦ *I think I left the keys in my trouser pocket.*

– short trousers that end above your knee: **shorts** (*AmE* **short pants**) ◦ *tennis shorts*
– strong trousers, usually blue, made of denim: **jeans** ◦ *a pair of blue jeans*
– soft thin stretchy trousers, usually worn by women, which fit tightly, from waist to ankles: **leggings**
– thick loose trousers worn for sport: **tracksuit bottoms** ◦ *He went jogging in tracksuit bottoms and a T-shirt.*
– a piece of clothing, similar to trousers, but covering your chest as well as your legs, with straps that go over your shoulders: **dungarees**

– trousers and a jacket made of the same cloth: **suit**

– one leg of a pair of trousers: **trouser leg**
– the middle part of a trouser leg: **knee** ◦ *The knees of my jeans need patching.*
– the line that you put down the front of a trouser leg when you iron it: **crease**
– a small place inside your clothes that you can put things in: **pocket** ◦ *I put my keys in my back pocket.*
– the front fastening of a pair of trousers: **flies** (*noun plural*) ◦ *George, your flies are undone.*
– the metal fastening at the front of a pair of trousers: **zip** ◦ *Do your zip up.* ◦ *I can't undo this zip.*

– a long thin piece of leather, etc that you wear around your waist: **belt** ◦ *I have to wear a belt with these trousers to stop them falling down.*

– a pair of straps that fasten onto the tops of your trousers and go over your shoulders, to keep the trousers up: **braces** (*AmE* **suspenders**) (*noun plural*)

true

1 true
2 not true
3 believing that sth is true
4 not believing that sth is true
5 showing that sth is true
6 saying what you believe to be true
what you think about sth ⇨ OPINION

1 true

– if sth is correct and agrees with the facts, it is **true** ◦ *Is it true that they're going to get married?* ◦ *That's simply not true!* ◦ *a true story*
– the state or quality of being true: **truth** (*noun* U) ◦ *Why can't you just tell me the truth?* ◦ *The truth is that I don't have enough money to pay for it.* ◦ *There is a lot of truth in old proverbs.*

– actually existing; not imagined: **real** ◦ *It's a real life story about a family who emigrated to America in the last century.*
– actually true, not what may appear to be true: **real** (*adverb* **really**); *noun* (U): **reality** ◦ *She said she didn't want a holiday, but the real reason is she can't afford one.* ◦ *Is that really your car?* ◦ *He tells people he's a writer, but in reality he's unemployed.*

▷ more on things really existing ⇨ REAL/EXISTING

■ facts
– something that you know has happened or is true: **fact** ◦ *a scientific fact* ◦ *Is that a fact? I am surprised!* ◦ *Do you know that for a fact?* ◦ *You must face facts and accept the situation.*
– true things: **fact** (*noun* U) ◦ *This story is based on fact.*
– a fact or idea that is true, especially one connected with science or religion: **truth** ◦ *scientific truths*
– based on or containing facts: **factual** (*adverb* **factually**) ◦ *a factual account of the events* ◦ *His statement was factually incorrect.*
– facts that are heard, told or discovered about sth: **information** (**on/about** sb/sth) ◦ *I'm collecting information on the causes of the strike.* ◦ *Do you have any information about tours to Loch Ness?*

▷ more on information ⇨ INFORMATION

– true or having no mistakes: **right**, **correct** (*adverb* **correctly**) ◦ *You're right!* ◦ *If you want to argue about something, you have to get your facts right first.* ◦ *What's the correct answer?* ◦ *Only one child answered correctly.*
– absolutely correct: **exact** (*adverb* **exactly**) ◦ *I can't remember the exact cost, but it is more or less £250.* ◦ *It's an exact copy of the original.* ◦ *Can you tell us exactly what happened?*

▷ more on being absolutely correct ⇨ EXACT/APPROXIMATE

■ obviously true

- if sth is easily seen or understood, it is **clear** (*adverb* **clearly**), **obvious** (*adverb* **obviously**) ◦ *Is that clear?* ◦ *Well, clearly, it will have to be done again.* ◦ *It's rather obvious that she isn't interested in you!* ◦ *We obviously can't do anything about it now.*
- clearly true: **undeniable** (*adverb* **undeniably**) ◦ *Well, it's undeniable that he's very good at his job, but he is not easy to work with.* ◦ *undeniably true*
- fairly obvious: **evident, apparent** ◦ *Her unhappiness was evident to anyone who knew her.*
- if you do not need to prove or explain sth, it is **self-evident** ◦ *a self-evident truth*

■ generally true

- true in most cases: **generally** (**speaking**), **in general, on the whole** ◦ *Generally speaking, northern Europeans are taller than southern Europeans.* ◦ *On the whole, he had done very well in his exams.*
- to speak in general about sth: **generalize** (**about** sth); *noun*: **generalization** ◦ *You can't really generalize about this kind of situation.* ◦ *to make generalizations*

2 not true

- if sth is not true, it is **false** (*adverb* **falsely**), **untrue** ◦ *Mount Everest is the tallest mountain in the world: true or false?* ◦ *That's totally untrue. I never said anything of the kind.*
- not true; not correct: **wrong** (*adverb* **wrongly**), **incorrect** (*adverb* **incorrectly**) ◦ *You were wrong about her name. It's Jane not Jean.* ◦ *Wrong! Try again.* ◦ *I'm afraid your information is incorrect.* ◦ *The sentence had been incorrectly translated.*
- sth that is wrong or not correct: **mistake** (*noun* C/U); *adjective*: **mistaken** ◦ *to make a mistake* ◦ *a mistaken idea/opinion/conclusion*

▷ more on mistakes ⇨ **MISTAKE**

■ making sb believe what is not true

- to say or write sth that you know is not true: **lie** (**about** sth) ◦ *I had to lie about what I had been doing because it was a surprise for her birthday.* ◦ *Don't lie to me. What really happened?*
- a statement that sb makes but which they know is not true: **lie** ◦ *Don't tell lies!*
- to make sb think or believe sth that is not true: **deceive** sb (**into thinking/believing** sth), **mislead*** sb (**into thinking/believing** sth); the act of deceiving sb: **deceit** (*noun* U), **deception** (*noun* U) ◦ *You've been deliberately deceiving me!* ◦ *I was shocked by this deception.*
- to seem to do sth or to be sth in order to deceive sb: **pretend** (**to** do sth), **pretend** (**that**) ... ◦ *Oh, don't believe him. He's just pretending!* ◦ *They pretended to be soldiers on a secret mission.*

▷ more on telling lies and deceiving people ⇨ **LIE**[1], **DECEIVE**

- to make sth seem larger, better, more important, more exciting, etc than it really is: **exaggerate** (sth); *noun* (C/U): **exaggeration** ◦ *He exaggerated when he said we climbed a mountain – it was only a hill!* ◦ *Don't listen to her – she always exaggerates.* ◦ *It's a bit of an exaggeration to say that all politicians are dishonest.*

3 believing that sth is true

- to think that sb is telling the truth or that sth is true: **believe** sb/sth; *noun* (C/U): **belief** ◦ *I'm sorry; I just don't believe you.* ◦ *When the news was first announced, nobody could believe it.* ◦ *He gave me the letter in the mistaken belief that it was addressed to me.*
- if you believe sth very strongly, you are **sure/certain of** it; *noun* (C/U): **certainty**
- if you have facts which tell you that sth is true, you **know*** it; *noun* (U): **knowledge**
- if you think that sth is probably not true, you **doubt** it; *noun* (C/U): **doubt**; *adjective*: **doubtful**

▷ knowing sth ⇨ **KNOW**

▷ doubt and certainty ⇨ **POSSIBLE**[1]

- the reasons you have for believing that sth is true: **grounds for** sth ◦ *What grounds do you have for suspecting him?*
- to accept sth as being true: **take*** sth **for granted** ◦ *I take it for granted that you've read the course handbook.*

- to feel sure that sb/sth exists or is true: **believe in** sb/sth; *noun* (C/U): **belief** (**in** sb/sth) ◦ *I believe in God.* ◦ *You don't really believe in astrology, do you?* ◦ *belief in ghosts* ◦ *a strong belief in Buddhism/socialism*

▷ believing in God and religion ⇨ **RELIGION**

▷ political beliefs ⇨ **POLITICS**

- to believe that sth is true even though you cannot prove it: **assume** sth; *noun*: **assumption** ◦ *I assumed that he had gone to London.* ◦ *to make a false/mistaken/reasonable assumption*
- to make sb see that sth is true: **convince** sb (**of** sth), **convince** sb **that** ... ◦ *We are not convinced of his honesty.* ◦ *She convinced me that she would do the job well.*
- a person or thing that can make sb believe sth is **convincing** (*adverb* **convincingly**) ◦ *convincing arguments* ◦ *He spoke very convincingly about his policies.*

- if sth is easy to believe, it is **credible** (*adverb* **credibly**), **believable**; *noun* (U): **credibility** ◦ *a credible explanation/story* ◦ *the credibility of the witness*
- something that sounds true is **reasonable, plausible** ◦ *a reasonable excuse* ◦ *He came up with a very plausible story to explain his absence.*

■ false belief

- if you believe things too easily, you are **credulous, gullible**; *noun* (U): **credulity** ◦ *credulous people who believe what advertisements say* ◦ *I'm afraid he's very gullible and may be persuaded to hand over the money.*
- if you are too ready to believe what other people say because you are not experienced enough, you are **naive** (*adverb* **naively**); the quality of being naive: **naivety** (*noun* U) ◦ *I think her behaviour showed a lot of naivety.*

true *contd.*

- a belief in things like magic, ghosts, etc that cannot be explained by reason or science: **superstition** (*noun* C/U); *adjective*: **superstitious** ◦ *There's a superstition that black cats are lucky.* ◦ *a superstitious belief*

4 not believing that sth is true

- to think that sb is not telling the truth or that sth is not true: **disbelieve** sb/sth; *noun* (U): **disbelief** ◦ *There's no reason to disbelieve her story.* ◦ *He stared at me in disbelief.*
- difficult to believe: **unlikely** ◦ *an unlikely explanation*

- surprising and difficult to believe: **incredible** (*adverb* **incredibly**), **unbelievable** (*adverb* **unbelievably**) ◦ *an incredible escape* ◦ *Incredibly, she has managed to persuade him.*
- impossible to believe: **inconceivable** ◦ *It's inconceivable that he could have found the money.*
- if you find it very difficult to believe sth, you are **incredulous**; *noun* (U): **incredulity** ◦ *I stared at him in incredulity.*

5 showing that sth is true

- to investigate or look at sth in order to be sure that sth is true or correct: **check** (sth) ◦ *The editor asked her to check that the story was true.*

- to make sb believe that sth is true: **prove*** sth (**to** sb), **prove*** (**that ...**) ◦ *Can you prove that he stole the money?*
- to make sth clear: **show*** sth, (*more formal*) **demonstrate** sth ◦ *She couldn't find the receipt, so she wasn't able to show that she'd bought the jumper in their shop.* ◦ *These figures demonstrate that standards in schools are rising.*
- a piece of information that shows that sth is true: **proof** (*noun* U) ◦ *They asked me if I had any proof of who I was.* ◦ *That may be your opinion, but where is the proof?* ◦ *I now have conclusive* (= definite) *proof that he stole the picture.*
- information that helps to show whether sth is true or not: **evidence** (*noun* U) ◦ *The police did not have enough evidence to be able to arrest him.*

- to prove that sth is not true: **disprove*** sth ◦ *No one has succeeded in disproving Einstein's theory of relativity.*

6 saying what you believe to be true

- to say only things which you believe to be true: **tell* the truth** ◦ *She says she doesn't know him, but I don't think she's telling the truth.*
- a person who tells the truth is **honest** (*adverb* **honestly**); the quality of being honest: **honesty** (*noun* U) ◦ *She's a very honest person.* ◦ *At least he had the honesty to admit that he broke it.*
- if sb or sth gives the truth about sth, they are **truthful** (*adverb* **truthfully**) ◦ *She gave a truthful account of what had happened.*

▷ more on being honest ⇨ **HONEST**

- to say that you are sure sth is true or will happen: **assure** sb (**that**) ..., **swear** (**that**) ...; *noun*: **assurance** ◦ *I swear I've never met her before.* ◦ *He gave me his personal assurance that the information was true.*
- to say that sth is true, even if you are not able to prove it: **claim that ...**, **claim to** do/be sth; *noun*: **claim** ◦ *He claimed that he had done it many times before.* ◦ *They claimed to be the original owners of the land.*
- to say or show that sth is true or right: **confirm** sth, **confirm that ...**; *noun* (C/U): **confirmation** ◦ *The doctor confirmed that she was pregnant.* ◦ *I need confirmation that those dates are correct.*
- to say very strongly that sth is true: **insist that ...**; *noun* (U): **insistence** ◦ *He insisted that he had completed the work and that he had not been paid for it.*

- to think the same thing as another person: **agree** (**with** sb) (**on/about** sth), **agree with** sth; *noun* (U): **agreement** ◦ *I don't agree with you that we should build more roads.* ◦ *She doesn't agree with experiments on animals.* ◦ *Managers and workers found it hard to reach agreement.*

▷ agreeing or not agreeing with sb ⇨ **DISCUSS/ARGUE**

- to say that sth is not true: **deny** sth, **deny that ...**; *noun*: **denial** ◦ *He accused me of taking the money. I denied it.* ◦ *You can't deny that you have met this man.* ◦ *No one believed his denials.*
- to say sth which means that sth else is not true: **contradict** (sb/sth) ◦ *This contradicts your earlier statement.*

- to emphasize that sth is true, you can say **in** (**actual**) **fact**, **as a matter of fact**, **actually**, **the fact is** (**that**) ... ◦ *In actual fact we're having the party on Friday, not Saturday.* ◦ *I thought the film would be boring but in fact it was great.* ◦ *As a matter of fact she's here.* ◦ *What I actually said was that no one deserved a pay increase.* ◦ *The fact is that you have made a mistake and you won't admit it.*
- according to what people say (but which may not be true): **apparently** ◦ *Apparently, he owns more than half of the company.*

■ **MORE ...**

- if sth is obviously true, you can say **it goes without saying** (**that ...**) ◦ *It goes without saying, of course, that taking legal advice is going to cost you a lot of money.*
- to be obviously true: **speak* for** itself ◦ *The figures speak for themselves. We can't afford to buy it.*
- if something is probably not entirely true or accurate, you **take*** it **with a pinch of salt** ◦ *You should take everything he says with a pinch of salt – he loves to exaggerate.*

- based only on facts and not influenced by personal opinion or emotion: **objective** (*adverb* **objectively**); *opposite*: **subjective** (*adverb* **subjectively**) ◦ *We tried to give an objective account of what had happened.* ◦ *Look at the facts objectively.* ◦ *a very subjective view*

- to officially or formally state that sth is correct or true: **certify** sth, **certify that ...** ◦ *The inspector* *certified that the work had been done properly and that it met the required standard.*

trust

see also HONEST

– to believe that sb will do sth that they promised to do, or that they will not harm you: **trust** sb (**to** do sth); *nouns* (U): **trust** (**in** sb), **faith** (**in** sb); *adjective*: **trusting** ◦ *Do you think we can trust Eddie to look after the children while we are away?* ◦ *I have complete trust in him.* ◦ *I have little faith in him.* ◦ *She is a very trusting child.*

– to trust sb/sth to work or behave well or to give you help when you need it: **rely on** sb/sth, **depend on** sb/sth; *noun* (U): **reliance** (**on** sb/sth) ◦ *Can we rely on you not to be late?* ◦ *If you need any help, you know you can depend on me.*
– to feel that you can always depend on sb/sth: **have confidence in** sb/sth, **trust in** sb/sth
– a person or a thing that you can trust is **reliable**, **dependable**, (used mainly about people) **trustworthy**; *noun* (U): **reliability** ◦ *a reliable car* ◦ *Do you think he's trustworthy?* ◦ *a dependable bus service*
– if you can trust sb to behave well and sensibly, they are **responsible** ◦ *Children must be accompanied by a responsible adult.*

– if you do not change in your friendships or beliefs, you are **loyal** (**to** sb/sth), **faithful** (**to** sb/sth); *nouns* (U): **loyalty**, **faithfulness** ◦ *Tom has always been a faithful friend to me.* ◦ *loyalty to your friends*

■ lack of trust
– not to trust sb/sth: **distrust** sb/sth, **mistrust** sb/sth; *nouns* (U): **distrust** (**of** sb/sth), **mistrust** (**of** sb/sth); *adjective*: **distrustful** ◦ *I distrust him because he lied to me once before.* ◦ *I always mistrust what politicians say.* ◦ *There was a strong feeling of distrust between the two countries.*
– if you start to distrust sb/sth, you **lose* trust in** them ◦ *After Robert had missed three important meetings, I began to lose trust in him.*

– a person or a thing that you cannot trust is **unreliable**, (used mainly about people) **untrustworthy**; *noun* (U): **unreliability** ◦ *an unreliable car* ◦ *an untrustworthy accountant*
– if you cannot trust sb to behave well and sensibly, they are **irresponsible**; *noun* (U): **irresponsibility** ◦ *She's totally irresponsible; I would never trust her to look after my children.*

– to make sb think or believe sth that is not true: **deceive** sb (**into thinking/believing** sth); *noun* (U): **deceit**; *adjective*: **deceitful** ◦ *He deceived his mother into believing that he had bought the radio, not stolen it.* ◦ *a deceitful child*

▷ deceiving people ⇨ DECEIVE

■ harming people who trust you
– if sb trusts you and you do not do what they expect you to do, you **let*** them **down** ◦ *You've really let me down this time!*
– if you say or do sth against sb who you should support, you are **disloyal**; *noun* (U): **disloyalty** ◦ *disloyal behaviour* ◦ *an act of disloyalty*

– to harm a person or an organization that trusts you: **betray** sb/sth; *noun* (U): **betrayal**; a person who does this: **traitor** ◦ *to betray your country* ◦ *Mike was really hurt by his son's betrayal.*
– if sb that you trust harms you, they are **treacherous**; *noun* (U): **treachery** ◦ *a treacherous plot* ◦ *an act of treachery*
– the act of causing harm to your country by betraying it: **treason** (*noun* U) ◦ *He was put on trial for treason.*

try

1 making an effort to do sth
2 testing sth

1 making an effort to do sth

– to do what you can to achieve sth: **try** (**to** do sth), (*informal*) **try and** do sth ◦ *How do you know you can't make a cake if you haven't even tried?* ◦ *I tried to lift the box, but I wasn't strong enough.* ◦ *Try and be on time tonight, won't you?*
– to try to do sth which is difficult: **attempt** (**to** do) sth ◦ *Are you really going to attempt that drive in these icy conditions?*
– to do sth in order to find out if you can do it: (*informal*) **have a go/shot** (**at** sth), (*informal*) **try your hand at** sth ◦ *I think I'm going to have a go at skiing this winter.*
– an occasion when you make an effort to do sth: **try**, **attempt** ◦ *Good try! Better luck next time!* ◦ *That was a rather poor attempt!*

– to manage to do what you want or are trying to do: **succeed** (**in** sth/doing sth); *opposite*: **fail** (**in** sth), **fail to** do sth ◦ *I finally succeeded in making him smile!* ◦ *Unfortunately we failed in our attempt to revive the patient.*
– to stop trying to do sth: **give* up** ◦ *I give up. What's the answer?*

▷ more on succeeding and failing ⇨ SUCCEED/FAIL

■ trying hard
– to make a great effort to do sth: **try hard** (**to** do sth)
– to try very hard to do sth: **make* an** (**all-out**) **effort** (**to** do sth), **go* to a lot of trouble to do** sth, (*informal*) **go* all out** (**for** sth/**to** do sth) ◦ *You'll never succeed in your ambitions if you don't make an effort.* ◦ *They were so kind – they went to a lot of trouble to ensure that we were happy and comfortable.*
– to try very hard to do sth, even when others are trying to stop you: **fight*** (**for** sth/**to** do sth), **struggle** (**for** sth/**to** do sth); *nouns*: **fight**, **struggle** ◦ *to fight for freedom* ◦ *the struggle for democracy*

– to do sth as well as you possibly can: **do*** your **best** (**to** do sth), **do*** sth **to the best of** your **ability**, **try** your **best/hardest** (**to** do sth) ◦ *I didn't win, but at least I know I did my best.* ◦ *Just do it*

try *contd.*

to the best of your ability – I'll understand if it's not perfect.

2 testing sth

- to do sth in order to see if it helps you to deal with a problem: **try** sth, **try** doing sth ◦ *Have you tried this new kind of tin-opener?* ◦ *Have you still got a headache? Try taking another aspirin.*
- to see if sth works or is all right by using it: **try** sth **out** (**on** sb) ◦ *Can I try my new card trick out on you?*
- to use or test sth in order to find out if you like it: **try** sth, **sample** sth ◦ *Would you like to sample some of our cheeses?*
- if sth has been used by many people and has always been successful, it is **well-tried** ◦ *a well-tried method*
- if nobody has used sth yet, it is **untried** ◦ *This solution is as yet untried, but we are confident that it will be successful.*

- to try, use or examine sth in order to find out if it is working properly or how good it is: **test** sth ◦ *It was tested before it left the factory, so it should work.*
- an occasion when you test sth: **test**, **trial** ◦ *We did a test to find out everybody's level of English.* ◦ *These new drugs have been through careful trials.*
- trying different ways of doing sth until you find the best one: **trial and error** ◦ *We found the answer by trial and error.*
- a scientific test that is done in order to prove sth or to learn sth new: **experiment** ◦ *experiments on heat-resistant materials*

▷ more on experiments ⇨ STUDY

tune ⇨ MUSIC, SING

turn

1 things turning in a circle
2 changing position
3 changing direction while you are moving

see also MOVE

1 things turning in a circle

- to move round in the kind of way that a wheel does: **turn**, **go* round**, (*more formal and scientific*) **rotate**, **revolve**; *nouns*: **rotation**, **revolution** ◦ *The wheels were turning faster and faster.* ◦ *The blades of the helicopter slowly began to rotate.* ◦ *This wheel revolves when you turn the engine on.* ◦ *A single rotation of the earth takes twenty-four hours.* ◦ *a thousand revolutions per minute*
- to make sth go round: **turn** sth; *noun*: **turn** ◦ *She turned the handle of the door.* ◦ *I gave the screw one more turn.*
- to move round sth in the way that the earth moves around the sun: **go* round** (sth), **revolve** (**round/around** sth) ◦ *The earth takes a year to revolve around the sun.*
- to turn round quickly: **spin***; to make sth turn quickly: **spin*** sth; a spinning movement: **spin** (*noun* U) ◦ *The engine had stopped but the wheels of the machine were still spinning.* ◦ *Kevin spun the coin in the air.* ◦ *to put spin on a ball*
- to move by turning over and over: **roll** ◦ *The ball rolled off the pavement and under the car.*
- to make sth move in this way: **roll** sth ◦ *The children were rolling rocks down the hill into the river.*

- to turn sth in a particular direction: **twist** sth ◦ *I managed to twist the lid off the jam jar.*
- to make sth move or work by turning a handle, etc: **wind*** sth ◦ *He wound down the window and shouted to the other driver.*

2 changing position

- to change the position of sb/sth: **turn** (sb/sth) **over/round** ◦ *Wendy picked up the vase and turned it over to look at the bottom.* ◦ *If it doesn't fit, try turning it round.*
- with the top part turned to the bottom: **upside-down** ◦ *Turn the printer upside-down and insert the cable in the socket.*

■ changing the position of your body

- to change your position so that you are looking in a different direction: **turn** (**round/around**); to do this very quickly: **spin* round** ◦ *He turned to face me.* ◦ *Turn around and go back the way you came.* ◦ *Brian spun round when he heard me call him.*
- to change your position when you are lying down, for example in bed: **turn over**, **roll over** ◦ *Terry turned over and went back to sleep.* ◦ *The dog rolled over and put its legs in the air.*

3 changing direction while you are moving

- to change direction when you are moving: **turn**; an act of changing direction: **turn** ◦ *turn left/right* ◦ *The car turned the corner.* ◦ *a left/right turn* ◦ *a sharp turn*
- to change direction suddenly: **swerve** ◦ *I swerved to avoid the dog that was in the middle of the road.*

▷ changing direction when driving a car, etc ⇨ DRIVE

▷ the turning movements of roads, etc ⇨ ROAD

two

1 two people or things
2 one thing with two parts
3 two times the size or amount

other numbers ⇨ ONE, HUNDRED, NUMBER

1 two people or things

- the number 2: **two**
- number 2 in position: **second** ◦ *I didn't win – but I came second.*
- two people or things: (*informal*) **a couple** ◦ *I'd like a couple of pounds of apples please.* ◦ *I spoke to a couple of people about it.* ◦ *'How many were there?' 'Just a couple.'*

- two times: **twice** ◦ *The film was so good, I went to see it twice.* ◦ *twice a week*

- the two; the one as well as the other: **both (of)** ... ◦ *Both my brothers are coming to visit.* ◦ *Both of us like golf.* ◦ *We both like golf.* ◦ *Put both in the water at the same time.*
- one or the other of two; it does not matter which: **either (of)** ... ◦ *I'll have either of them, I don't mind which.* ◦ *One of us has to go – it's either you or me.*
- (used about two people or things) not one and not the other: **neither (of)** ... ◦ *Neither of us will be there.* ◦ *I asked John and then I asked Mary, but neither wanted to help me.* ◦ *In my view, neither team was really any good.*

- two people or animals that are closely connected with each other: **pair** ◦ *a pair of naughty children* ◦ *a pair of blackbirds on the lawn*
- two people who are married, living together, etc: **couple** ◦ *a married couple* ◦ *I think they're a couple.*
- two together: **in pairs, in twos** ◦ *You can't go on your own – you have to go in pairs.* ◦ *You can only buy these batteries in twos.*
- first two and then another two: **two by two** ◦ *The couples went into the building two by two.*

■ two which are the same
- two things that are almost the same and that are used together: **pair** ◦ *a pair of shoes/socks/gloves*
- being one of a pair from which the other is missing: **odd** ◦ *You've got odd socks on!*
- one of a pair of things that are the same or very similar: **twin** ◦ *a plane with twin engines*

- one of two children or animals that are born to the same mother at the same time: **twin** ◦ *They must be twins, they look exactly the same.* ◦ *This is my twin sister.*

2 one thing with two parts
- a thing that consists of two parts that are joined together: **pair** ◦ *a pair of scissors* ◦ *an old pair of trousers*

- one of two equal parts of sth: **half** (*plural* **halves**) ◦ *Two halves make a whole.* ◦ *Half of this is mine.* ◦ *Half the farm belongs to my brother. The other half belongs to me.* ◦ *the second half of a football match* ◦ *a half portion of food* ◦ *to be half-finished*
- to divide sth into two equal parts: **halve** sth, **cut***, **fold**, **divide**, etc sth in **half/two** ◦ *Halve the pumpkin with a knife.* ◦ *Cut it in half and share it between you.*

- having two equal or similar parts or aspects: **double, dual** ◦ *double yellow lines* ◦ *to have dual nationality*
- made for or used by two people or things: **double** ◦ *a double bed* ◦ *a double garage*

3 two times the size or amount
- a number or amount that is two times as big as another one is **twice** ..., **double** ... ◦ *Why should you earn twice what I do?* ◦ *She took double the proper amount of medicine.*
- two times as big, happy, etc: **twice as** ... ◦ *She's twice as big as her brother.*
- to make sth twice the size or amount of sth else: **double** sth ◦ *You'll have to double the amounts they say in the recipe book because we're cooking for double the number of people.*

■ **MORE** ...
- two people performing sth together (especially music): **duo** (*plural* **duos**) ◦ *a comedy duo* ◦ *a musical duo*
- a piece of music for two people: **duet** ◦ *a piano duet*
- a comedy act of two people: **double act**

---

type

1 types
2 being typical
see also COMPARE/CONTRAST

1 types
- a group of people or things that share certain qualities: **type, sort, kind** ◦ *A word processor is a type of computer.* ◦ *different kinds of automatic camera* ◦ *What kind of music would you like to be played at your wedding?*
- a particular type of sth or way of doing sth: **form** ◦ *Swimming is an excellent form of exercise.*

- many different types of people or things: **all sorts of** ..., **all kinds of** ... ◦ *There were all kinds of shops in the new shopping mall.*

- the name of a product that is made by a particular company: **brand** ◦ *a new brand of washing powder*
- the name of a company that produced sth: **make** ◦ *a popular make of car*
- the way that sth is made, done, built, etc; the fashion, shape or design of sth: **style** (*noun* C/U) ◦ *a new style of painting* ◦ *a management style* ◦ *a hairstyle* ◦ *different styles of clothes* ◦ *a church built in the Gothic style*

■ types of animals, plants, etc
- a group of animals or plants that are very similar to each other and can reproduce together: **species** (*plural* **species**) ◦ *different species of ants*
- a smaller group within a species: **variety** ◦ *a variety of rose*
- a type of a particular species of animal: **breed** ◦ *a breed of cattle* ◦ *What breed is your dog?*
- a group of species, languages, etc that have some similarities: **family** ◦ *the Indo-European family of languages* ◦ *Lions belong to the cat family.*

■ putting things into groups
- to put sb/sth into a group with other people or things of a similar type: **classify** sb/sth, **categorize** sb/sth; *nouns* (U): **categorization, classification** ◦ *The books are classified according to subject.*
- a group into which people or things are classified: **class, category** ◦ *Vehicles in this class are taxed more highly.* ◦ *a social class* ◦ *These books*

type *contd.*

are divided into categories according to their subject matter.

- to put things into different groups so that they are properly organized: **sort** sb/sth (**into** sth) ◦ *I'm just sorting these papers into their proper files.* ◦ *Have you finished sorting your CDs?*
- to be included in a particular group, section, etc: **come* under** sth ◦ *Bed and breakfast places might come under 'Hotels' in the phone book.*

2 being typical

- showing the usual qualities of a particular type: **typical** (**of** sb/sth), **characteristic** (**of** sb/sth); *opposite*: **uncharacteristic** ◦ *This is a typical problem with this kind of computer.* ◦ *uncharacteristic behaviour*
- something that is typical of a particular group: **characteristic** ◦ *One important characteristic of mammals is that the mothers feed their babies on milk from their bodies.*
- of a similar type: **related**; *opposite*: **unrelated** ◦ *physics and other related areas of science*

- belonging to one particular person, place, etc: **peculiar** (**to** sb/sth) ◦ *a tree peculiar to north-eastern Europe*
- typical of a single person or thing: **individual** ◦ *an individual style of teaching*
- not like anyone/anything else: **unique** (**to** sb/sth) ◦ *a unique system of government* ◦ *a type of folk dancing that is unique to this part of the country*

■ **MORE...**

- a fixed idea about a type of person or thing that is often not true: **stereotype**; *adjective*: **stereotypical** ◦ *She's nothing like the stereotype of a successful businesswoman.*

typewriter ⇨ WRITE

tyre ⇨ WHEEL

ugly ⇨ BEAUTIFUL/ATTRACTIVE

uncle ⇨ FAMILY

under ⇨ PLACE[2]

understand

1 understanding
2 not understanding
3 explaining

see also DESCRIBE, KNOW, LEARN, MEANING, REASON

1 understanding

- to know what sth means or the reason for sth: **understand*** (sth), **see*** (sth) ◦ *Did you understand that lecture?* ◦ *I think I understand now – you want me to leave.* ◦ *Do you see what I mean?*
- to hear or understand sth: **get*** it, **get*** sth ◦ *Ah yes, I get it. You want me to lend you some money.* ◦ *Did you get the joke?*
- when you begin to understand sth completely, it **sinks* in** ◦ *The news finally sank in and she started crying.*

- to know and understand that sth is true or that sth has happened: **realize** (**that**) ... ◦ *Of course I do realize that the situation has changed.* ◦ *I suddenly realized that I'd forgotten my keys.*
- to understand or find sth out from sb/sth: **gather** (**that**) ... ◦ *I gather that you're not very happy with my work.*

- to understand an explanation or a story: **follow** (sth) ◦ *I'm sorry. I don't follow.*
- to understand a difficult idea: **grasp** sth ◦ *I've never really grasped how computers work.*
- to understand information that is not very clear: **make*** sth **out** ◦ *Could you make out what he was trying to say in his letter?*
- to understand what you see, hear or read: **take*** sth **in** ◦ *We found it hard to take in everything the teacher said.*
- to understand how sth works: **get* the hang of** sth ◦ *You'll soon get the hang of this computer program.*
- to understand a difficult situation or a problem: (*formal*) **appreciate** sth; *noun* (U/*singular*): **appreciation** ◦ *I don't think you really appreciate the difficulty of the situation.*

- the way you think that sth is meant: **understanding** (*noun* U) ◦ *My understanding of his letter is that he wants to leave immediately.*
- the ability to understand sth: **comprehension** (*noun* U) ◦ *How he managed to get the job is beyond my comprehension.*

■ possible or easy to understand

- if sth can be understood, it is (*formal*) **intelligible** (**to** sb), (*formal*) **comprehensible** (**to** sb); *noun* (U): **intelligibility** ◦ *easily intelligible, even to small children* ◦ *His new book is only comprehensible to experts in his field.*
- if sth can be understood easily, it is **clear** (*adverb* **clearly**), **plain** (*adverb* **plainly**); the quality of being easy to understand: **clarity** (*noun* U) ◦ *a clear explanation* ◦ *plain English* ◦ *Speak plainly!* ◦ *clarity of expression*

- if it is possible to understand the reason for sth, it is **understandable**, it **makes*** (**good**) **sense** ◦ *It is understandable that she should wish to be alone for a while.* ◦ *understandable objections* ◦ *What does this mean? It just doesn't seem to make sense.*

2 not understanding

- not to know what sth means or the reason for sth: **not understand**, **fail to understand** ◦ *I didn't understand a word she said.* ◦ *I fail to understand why she didn't come.*
- to understand sb/sth wrongly: **misunderstand*** sb/sth ◦ *He misunderstood the girl's smile.* ◦ *Don't misunderstand me – I wish I could help you.*
- an act of misunderstanding: **misunderstanding** (*noun* C/U) ◦ *I'm afraid there's been some misunderstanding.* ◦ *a slight misunderstanding*

- to misunderstand completely what has been said: (*informal*) **get* (hold of) the wrong end of the stick** ◦ *He got hold of the wrong end of the stick and thought he'd been insulted.*

- if you completely fail to understand what sth means or what is happening, you are **confused**, **puzzled**, **baffled** ◦ *She looked confused by all the shouting.* ◦ *I'm baffled by his attitude.*

■ not possible or easy to understand
- if sth cannot be understood, it is **unintelligible**, **incomprehensible** ◦ *an unintelligible reply* ◦ *Her sudden departure was incomprehensible to all her friends.*
- if sth is difficult to understand, it **makes* no/little sense** (**to** you) ◦ *The excuse he gave made little sense.*
- if sth is not very clear and you cannot understand it, you **cannot make it out** ◦ *I can't make out what he's trying to signal to us.*
- if sth is too difficult to understand, it is **beyond** you, **above/over** your **head** ◦ *'What do you think it means?' 'It's beyond me.'* ◦ *Anything to do with computer programming is way above my head.*

- if sth is very difficult for you to understand, it is **confusing**, **puzzling** ◦ *a confusing situation* ◦ *a puzzling decision*
- a situation which is difficult to understand or deal with: **problem** ◦ *to try to solve a problem*
- a thing that you cannot understand or explain: **mystery** ◦ *It's a mystery to me why she ever bothered to come.*

▷ more on problems ⇨ PROBLEM

3 explaining
- to give the meaning of sth or the reason for sth, so that sb can understand it: **explain** (sth), **explain** sth **to** sb, **explain** (**to** sb) **that . . .**; *noun* (C/U): **explanation** ◦ *I don't understand the question – can you explain?* ◦ *She couldn't explain why the money was missing.* ◦ *She explained her plan to the rest of the team.* ◦ *That's not a very satisfactory explanation.* ◦ *This requires more detailed explanation.*
- to succeed in making people understand sth: **get*** sth **across/over** (**to** sb) ◦ *He's not very good at getting his ideas across.* ◦ *She managed to get her meaning over to the audience.*

- to explain or understand the meaning of sth: **make* sense of** sth, **interpret** sth (**as** sth); *noun* (C/U): **interpretation** ◦ *I've read your letter twice and am still trying to make sense of it.* ◦ *How do you interpret her comments?* ◦ *a new interpretation of Darwin's theory*

- to make sth clear and easy to understand: (*formal*) **clarify** sth; *noun* (U): **clarification** ◦ *I hope that helps to clarify the situation.* ◦ *We'll have to ask for further clarification.*
- to look at some facts carefully in order to understand or explain them: **analyse** sth; *noun* (C/U): **analysis** ◦ *I now have to analyse the results of the questionnaire.* ◦ *an analysis of the causes of the riots* ◦ *Further analysis will be needed before we can understand this properly.*

- something which gives an explanation is **explanatory** ◦ *explanatory notes at the back of a book*
- something which does not need to be explained because it is clear is **self-explanatory** ◦ *The instructions should be self-explanatory.*
- something which can be explained is **explicable**; *opposite*: **inexplicable** ◦ *inexplicable behaviour*
- an idea that explains sth: **theory** ◦ *theories that explain how children learn to talk* ◦ *My theory is that he fell while trying to save his companion.*

■ **MORE . . .**
- if you understand what sb really means, even though it is not said openly, you **read* between the lines** ◦ *Reading between the lines, she could see that something was wrong.*

- to understand two completely different opinions: **see* both sides of** sth ◦ *I'm trying hard to see both sides of the argument.*

---

unhappy ⇨ SAD

unite ⇨ JOIN

university

1 structure and organization
2 teaching and research
3 studying at a university
4 getting a degree

see also EDUCATION, LEARN, TEACH

1 structure and organization
- an educational institution of the highest level: **university** ◦ *the University of Edinburgh* ◦ *the Open University* ◦ *a university student*
- an institution where you can study after you leave school which is not a university: **college** ◦ *a further education college* ◦ *a technical college* ◦ *a teacher training college*
- education at a university: **higher education** (*noun* U) ◦ *The government wants to make it possible for more people to go on to higher education.*

- (at some universities) an independent institution which has its own teachers, students and buildings: **college** ◦ *He went to Oxford University but I don't know which college he was at.*
- the area of land where the main building of a university is: **campus** (*noun* C/U) ◦ *Do you live on campus?*

- the head of a university: **vice-chancellor** (*AmE* **chancellor**), **principal**
- the head of some colleges: **president**

- one of the parts into which a university is divided: **department**; *adjective*: **departmental**; a person who runs a department in a university: **head of department** ◦ *the Department of Sociology* ◦ *a departmental meeting*
- a group of related departments in a university: **faculty**; the head of a faculty: **dean** ◦ *the Faculty*

university *contd.*

of Science and Engineering ◦ *the dean of the Arts Faculty*
– the teaching staff of a faculty: **faculty** (*noun* U, *with singular or plural verb*) ◦ *a meeting of faculty*
– the teaching staff of the whole university: (*AmE*) **faculty** (*noun* U, *with singular or plural verb*)

– the part of a year at university when students have classes and exams: **academic year** ◦ *The academic year begins in October.*
– one of three parts that the academic year is divided into in some countries: **term** (*noun* C/U) ◦ *the Autumn/Spring/Summer term* ◦ *end-of-term examinations*
– one of two parts that the academic year is divided into in some countries: **semester**
– one of the parts of the university year when there are no classes: **vacation** ◦ *the Easter vacation* ◦ *the long vacation* (= the summer vacation)

2 teaching and research

– a person who teaches at a university or college: **lecturer**; the position of a lecturer: **lectureship** ◦ *They're advertising a lectureship in the Sociology Department.*
– a senior person who teaches at a university: **professor**; the position of a professor: **chair**, **professorship** ◦ *She's just been appointed to the Chair of European History.*
– a person who teaches and/or does research at a university: **academic**

– a talk to a group of people on a particular subject: **lecture** (**on/about** sth) ◦ *Did you go to his lecture on Brecht?* ◦ *to give a lecture*
– to give a lecture or lectures on a particular subject: **lecture** (**on/about** sth)
– a room which is used for giving lectures: **lecture room, lecture theatre**

– a person who teaches a small group of students: **tutor**
– a lesson given by a tutor to one student or a small group of students: **tutorial**
– a class in which a small group discuss or study a subject with a teacher: **seminar**; a talk which is given for a seminar: **seminar paper** ◦ *All the students have to give a seminar paper at least once during the term.* ◦ *a seminar room*
– a teacher at a university who makes sure that students are doing their work properly: **supervisor**; to work as a supervisor: **supervise** sb; *noun* (U): **supervision** ◦ *Her dissertation is being supervised by Professor Holroyd.* ◦ *I'm not happy with the supervision I'm getting.*

– a detailed and careful study of sth to find out more about it: **research** (**into/on** sth) (*noun* U) ◦ *What's his research on?* ◦ *a research project* ◦ *a research student*
– to study sth carefully and in detail: **do* research** (**into/on** sth), **research** sth ◦ *She's doing some research into animal behaviour.* ◦ *She's researching her new book.*
– a room or building that is used for scientific work, research or teaching about science: **laboratory**
– a place where you can go to read, work and borrow books: **library**

▷ more on research ⇨ STUDY
▷ libraries ⇨ LIBRARY

3 studying at a university

– a person who is studying at a college or university: **student** ◦ *a university student*
– a student who has not yet taken his or her first degree: **undergraduate** ◦ *an undergraduate course*
– a student who is studying for a second degree at a university: **postgraduate** ◦ *new computer facilities for the postgraduates in the department* ◦ *a postgraduate student*

– to attend university regularly as a student: **go* to university**, **be at university** ◦ *She's planning to spend a year abroad before she goes to university.* ◦ *I'm at London University.*
– an opportunity to study at university: **place** ◦ *I got a place at Manchester University.*

– a university building where some students live: **hall (of residence)**
– to live in a hall of residence: **live in hall**
– a society which all students can join: **student union**

– to spend time learning about sth: **study** (sth); the act of learning about sth: **study** (*noun* U) ◦ *George is studying German literature.* ◦ *What's his field of study?*
– an area of knowledge that is studied at school, university, etc: **subject** ◦ *What subjects will you take when you go to university?*

▷ more on studying ⇨ STUDY

– a complete series of lessons or classes: **course** (**in/on** sth); a part of a course: **module** ◦ *Which courses are you doing this term?* ◦ *How's your course going?* ◦ *The course consists of six modules.*
– a part of a course that a student has completed and that appears on his/her record: **credit** ◦ *I need another four credits to complete this course.*
– a written, spoken or practical test of what you know or can do: **exam**, (*formal*) **examination** ◦ *to take a maths exam*

▷ more on exams ⇨ EXAM

– a short piece of writing on one subject: **essay** ◦ *to write an essay on sth* ◦ *to hand in an essay*
– a piece of work that you are given to do by university teachers which counts towards your final degree: **assignment** ◦ *You need to do well in your assignments as well as in the exam.*
– a long piece of writing on sth which you have studied or researched, especially as part of a university degree: **dissertation, thesis** (*plural* **theses**) ◦ *to write a thesis*

– to give a completed piece of work to a person in authority: **hand** sth **in** ◦ *When have you got to hand in your essay?*
– a number or letter given for schoolwork or exams to show how good it is: **mark, grade** ◦

What mark did you get? ◦ *a high mark* ◦ *a good grade*

4 getting a degree

- an examination that you have passed or a course of study that you have successfully completed: **qualification** ◦ *a teaching qualification*
- a qualification gained by successfully completing an academic course at a university or college: **degree** ◦ *My daughter's at Harvard doing a degree in Political Science.* ◦ *I've got a degree in psychology.*
- a qualification of a lower level than a degree: **diploma** ◦ *a diploma in hotel management*
- to study sth as your main subject at college or university: (*AmE*) **major in** sth ◦ *I'm majoring in English.*

- a person who holds a (first) degree from a university: **graduate** ◦ *a graduate in engineering* ◦ *a history graduate*
- to get a first degree from a university: **graduate** (**in** sth) (**from** sth); *noun* (U): **graduation** ◦ *I graduated in History from Sussex University.* ◦ *After graduation, I plan to do a postgraduate degree.*
- a ceremony in which degree certificates are given to people who have graduated from a university: **graduation**

■ different kinds of degree

- a first university degree in an arts subject (= history, languages, etc): **BA** (= Bachelor of Arts)
- a first degree in a science subject: **BSc** (= Bachelor of Science)
- (in Britain) grades for a university degree: **first** (**class**), (**upper**) **second** (**class**), **third** (**class**) ◦ *She got an upper second in politics from Surrey University.* ◦ *a first-class honours degree*

- a degree taken after a first degree in an arts subject: **MA** (= Master of Arts)
- a degree taken after a first degree in a science subject: **MSc** (= Master of Science)
- the highest university degree: **PhD, DPhil** (= Doctor of Philosophy), **doctorate** ◦ *to get a PhD* ◦ *to work for a doctorate*

■ **MORE ...**

- money that is given (by the government) to help pay for a university or college education: (**student**) **grant**
- money that is borrowed by a student from the government to help pay for university education: (**student**) **loan**
- an amount of money that is given to a person who has passed an exam or won a competition in order to help pay for their studies: **scholarship** ◦ *She's won a scholarship to study music.*

- a loose piece of clothing worn by students when they graduate: **gown**

- to leave university without finishing your studies: **drop out** (**of** sth) ◦ *He started university but dropped out after two years.*

unlucky ⇨ LUCK

until ⇨ TIME

unusual ⇨ USUAL

up ⇨ MOVE

use

1 using sth
2 sth being used
3 using sth wrongly

1 using sth

- to do sth with sth for a purpose: **use** sth ◦ *They use their spare bedroom as a study.* ◦ *I only use the car for taking the children to school.*
- to use sth for a particular purpose: **make* use of** sth, (*formal*) **utilize** sth ◦ *You ought to make more use of the library.* ◦ *We're not utilizing our resources economically.*
- the act of using sth: **use** (*noun* U) ◦ *People are worried by the increasing use of drugs by schoolchildren.*
- a person who uses sth: **user** ◦ *Users are requested to turn off the lights when they leave the laboratory.*

- to use natural resources, for example energy or food: **consume** sth; *noun* (U): **consumption** ◦ *The meat was declared unfit for human consumption.*
- to use sth again: **reuse** sth ◦ *to reuse an old envelope*
- to put sth (for example paper, glass) through a process that enables you to use it again: **recycle** sth ◦ *Save your paper for recycling.*

- to use sth in order to see if it works or how well it works: **try** sth **out** ◦ *Take it home, try it out, and if you don't like it you can bring it back.*
- to use one person or thing instead of another: **replace** A (**with** B), **substitute** B (**for** A); *nouns* (U): **replacement**, **substitution** ◦ *They want to replace him with a younger person.* ◦ *If she leaves, we'll have to advertise for a replacement.* ◦ *the substitution of one thing for another*
- a person or thing that is used instead of another: **replacement** (**for** sb/sth), **substitute** (**for** sb/sth) ◦ *to use margarine as a substitute for butter*

- if you no longer need to use sb/sth, you **stop using** them/it, (*formal*) **dispense with** them/it ◦ *I've stopped using my typewriter – I use a computer instead.* ◦ *We've entirely dispensed with security staff. We now rely on closed circuit TV.*

■ using sth until it is finished

- to use sth until there is nothing left: **use** sth **up**, **exhaust** sth ◦ *You've used up all my envelopes!* ◦ *By the end of the journey we had almost exhausted our supplies.*
- if sth has been used so much that it breaks or is no longer usable, it **wears* out**; to use sth so much that it breaks or is no longer usable: **wear*** sth **out** ◦ *These trousers have worn out – I'll have to throw them away.*

use *contd.*

2 sth being used

- the purpose for which sth is used: **use**, **function** ◦ *a penknife with lots of different uses* ◦ *For most people, the main function of a computer is as a word processor.*
- to be used as sth: **serve as** sth ◦ *This box can serve as a table until we buy some furniture.*
- if sth helps you or you can use it, it is **useful**; *noun* (U): **usefulness** ◦ *a useful tool* ◦ *Medical experts are questioning the usefulness of this treatment.*
- something which can be used is **usable** ◦ *It's very old and no longer usable.*

▷ being useful ⇨ USEFUL / SUITABLE

- being used at the moment: **in use**, (used about a system) **operational**, **in operation**, (used about a rule or arrangement) **in effect** ◦ *The room is in use at the moment – come back in five minutes.* ◦ *The new factory is now fully operational.*
- to start using sth: **bring*** sth **into use / operation / effect**; to begin to be used: **come* into use / operation / effect** ◦ *When did fax machines come into use?* ◦ *The new timetable comes into effect on the 1 May.*

- available for you to use: **at** your **disposal**, (used about a room, a seat, etc) **free** ◦ *You will have a small office at your disposal while you're working for us.* ◦ *'Is this seat free?' 'No, I'm afraid it's taken.'*
- easy to use: **user-friendly** ◦ *a user-friendly computer program*
- designed to be thrown away after you have used it: **disposable** ◦ *disposable nappies* ◦ *a disposable razor*

■ not used

- if sth is not being used or cannot be used because it is broken it is **out of use** ◦ *My car's been out of use for two months now.*
- not yet used: **unused** ◦ *an unused envelope*
- no longer used: **abandoned**, (used about buildings) **disused**, **derelict** ◦ *We saw several abandoned cars at the side of the road.* ◦ *a disused warehouse* ◦ *a derelict house*

3 using sth wrongly

- to use sth in a way that it is not intended to be used: **misuse** sth; *noun* (U): **misuse** ◦ *I'm worried about the possible misuse of this equipment.*
- to use a person or thing wrongly, and in a way which may damage them/it: **abuse** sb/sth; *noun* (C/U): **abuse** ◦ *to suffer physical and mental abuse* ◦ *an abuse of power*
- to use sb/sth selfishly, wrongly or unfairly: **exploit** sb/sth; *noun* (U): **exploitation** ◦ *I felt I was being exploited.* ◦ *To work so hard for so little money sounds like exploitation.*

- to use sth in a careless or unnecessary way: **waste** sth; *adjective*: **wasteful** (*adverb* **wastefully**) ◦ *He wastes his money gambling.* ◦ *It seems wasteful to spend so much money at Christmas.*
- if you think that it is a pity that sb/sth good or useful is not being used, you can say that it is **a waste** ◦ *a waste of valuable resources*

useful / suitable

> 1 useful
> 2 suitable
>
> things that are not useful and that you throw away ⇨ RUBBISH

1 useful

- if sth helps you or you can use it, it is **useful**, **helpful**; *noun* (U): **usefulness** ◦ *This bag is really useful.* ◦ *That's a useful idea.* ◦ *The map you drew was very helpful in finding this place.*
- if sth is useful or easy to use, it is **handy** ◦ *This is a very handy little book that lists all the tourist information offices.*
- if sb/sth is very useful, it is **valuable**; *noun* (U): **value** ◦ *valuable advice*

- to be useful: **be of use** (**to** sb) ◦ *If this old bike is of any use to you, you can have it.*
- to be possibly useful at some time: **come* in useful**, **come* in handy** ◦ *I keep all my old newspapers – you never know when they might come in handy.*
- if sth is useful or satisfying enough to be worth the cost or effort, it is **worthwhile**, **worth** your/sb's **while**, (*informal*) **worth it** (*not before a noun*) ◦ *Before you buy that printer it might be worth your while to have a look at some other models.*

■ not useful

- not useful: **useless**, (**of**) **no use**, **no good**; *noun* (U): **uselessness** ◦ *I felt so useless while my wife was giving birth.* ◦ *Throw out that chair – it's no use to anyone.* ◦ *This heater's no good. I'll have to buy a new one.*
- an action or event which is not useful: **waste of time** ◦ *I thought the course was a complete waste of time – I learnt absolutely nothing.*

- if you do sth that has no effect or result it is **futile**, **ineffective**; *noun* (U): **futility** ◦ *Our attempts to stop the ants coming into the house were futile.*
- if sth has no purpose, it is **pointless**, **useless**, there is **no point in** it ◦ *This is a pointless argument.* ◦ *It's useless to argue with her.* ◦ *There's no point in waiting here. Let's go home.*

- if a thing is not used because it is out of date, it is **obsolete** ◦ *Typewriters are becoming obsolete now that more and more people have personal computers.*
- no longer needed: **redundant** ◦ *This machine is redundant now that we have bought a new one.*

2 suitable

- right for a particular purpose, occasion or person: **right** (**for** sth/sb), **suitable** (**for** sth/sb) (*adverb* **suitably**), **appropriate** (**for** sth/sb) (*adverb* **appropriately**) ◦ *I don't think this actor is right for the part.* ◦ *I'm afraid this isn't the right place to talk about it.* ◦ *Is this a suitable card to give to*

your mother? ◦ *I think the police acted very appropriately.*
– the quality of being right or suitable: **suitability**

– suitable according to normal customs and ideas: **correct** (*adverb* **correctly**) ◦ *correct behaviour/manners/dress*
– suitable, right or correct: **proper** (*only before a noun*) (*adverb* **properly**) ◦ *You should wear proper walking boots when you go hillwalking.* ◦ *If you don't sit properly you'll get a bad back.*

– not suitable: **wrong** (**for** sth/sb), **unsuitable** (**for** sth/sb) (*adverb* **unsuitably**), **inappropriate** (**to/for** sth/sb) (*adverb* **inappropriately**) ◦ *This is the wrong course for me – I want something more practical.* ◦ *His clothes were quite unsuitable for a formal reception.* ◦ *an inappropriate speech for a wedding*
– a person or thing that does not belong in a particular situation is **out of place** ◦ *My father looked terribly out of place at the pop concert.*

– if sth gives you the result that you want, it **works**, it is **effective** ◦ *'Have you got something to clean the oven?' 'Yes, but it doesn't work very well.'* ◦ *This cream is very effective against mosquito bites.*
– suitable for a particular purpose: **practical**, **functional** ◦ *Plastic tablecloths are very practical, but they don't look very nice.*
– suitable for many different uses: **all-purpose** (*only before a noun*) ◦ *an all-purpose knife*

– good enough for some purpose: **fit for** sth/sb, **fit to** do sth; *opposite*: **unfit for** sth/sb, **unfit to** do sth ◦ *With so little experience, I don't think he is really fit for the job.* ◦ *This food is unfit to be eaten.*
– if sth is what you need, it **serves** its **purpose** ◦ *It's an old television but it serves its purpose.*
– to be good enough to be used: **do*** (**for/as** sth) ◦ *I haven't got a screwdriver – will this knife do?*

– suitable to be used together or to live together: **compatible**; *opposite*: **incompatible** ◦ *Is my computer compatible with yours?* ◦ *Although they shared some interests, they were basically incompatible.*
– the quality of being compatible: **compatibility** (*noun* U); *opposite*: **incompatibility** (*noun* U)

– suitable or practical for a particular purpose; not causing difficulty: **convenient** (*adverb* **conveniently**); *opposite*: **inconvenient** (*adverb* **inconveniently**) ◦ *When would it be convenient to phone?* ◦ *Have I called at an inconvenient moment?*
– to be convenient for sb/sth: **suit** (sb/sth) ◦ *Would three o'clock on Monday suit you?*
– the quality of being convenient: **convenience** (*noun* U); *opposite*: **inconvenience** (*noun* U)

■ the right size, colour, etc
– to be the right size or shape for sb/sth: **fit** (sb/sth) ◦ *These shoes don't fit properly – they're too tight.* ◦ *Do you think this rug would fit in our sitting room?*
– to be the same colour as sth else: **match** (sth) ◦ *That skirt matches your blouse very nicely.*
– to look good on sb: **suit** sb ◦ *Those trousers really suit you.*
– to look or taste good with sth else: **go* with** sth, **go* together** ◦ *I think green curtains would go well with the carpet.* ◦ *Do those pictures really go together?*

---

usual

1 usual
2 unusual
3 very unusual

1 usual

– happening or used most often: **usual** ◦ *Please pay for your drinks at the bar in the usual way.* ◦ *'Who was at the meeting?' 'Oh, the usual people.'*
– often found or experienced: **common** ◦ *It's quite common for one person to have two different jobs.* ◦ *a common experience*
– not different from others of its type: **normal**, **ordinary** (*AmE* **regular**), **typical** (**of** sb/sth) ◦ *It's impossible to live a normal life if you work nights.* ◦ *an ordinary person* ◦ *We were a typical family: father, mother and two children.* ◦ *That sort of attitude is typical of the people here.*
– of the normal type; without anything special or extra: **standard** ◦ *I wrote to complain but they just sent their standard reply.*

– a fixed and usual way of doing things: **routine**; *adjective*: **routine** ◦ *Once you get used to your new routine, you'll find things easier.* ◦ *routine activities*
– as part of a routine: **routinely**, **as a matter of routine** ◦ *Managers routinely attend meetings to assess their progress.*
– happening at the same time each day, week, etc: **regular** (*adverb* **regularly**); *noun* (U): **regularity** ◦ *We pay our parents a regular visit at the weekend.* ◦ *We meet regularly once a month.* ◦ *I was fed up with the monotonous regularity of my life.*

– following usual and generally accepted behaviour, methods, etc: **conventional** (*adverb* **conventionally**) ◦ *We use conventional methods here – we believe they are the best.* ◦ *a rather conventional style of writing*
– suitable according to normal customs and ideas: **correct** (*adverb* **correctly**), **right** ◦ *What's the correct way to address the teacher – as Ken or Mr Marsh?*
– usual and known well or known by many people: **familiar** ◦ *That's a familiar tune!*
– usual or normal; what you would expect: **natural** (*adverb* **naturally**) ◦ *It's only natural to feel nervous before an interview.*

– a way of behaving which a particular group has had for a long time: **custom** ◦ *It's the custom in Britain to give presents on 25 December.*
– something that sb does often: **habit** ◦ *I always have a short rest after lunch. It's a habit I got into when I lived in South America.*
– to have the habit of doing sth; to think it is a good thing to do sth: **like to** do sth ◦ *I like to have my main meal in the middle of the day.*

usual *contd.*

– to happen or do sth usually or often: **tend to do** sth, **have a tendency** (**to** do sth) ◦ *It tends to rain at this time of year.* ◦ *He has a tendency to arrive late.*

▷ more on customs and habits ⇨ **CUSTOM, HABIT**

– in a way that is usual; most often: **usually, generally, normally, as a rule** ◦ *I usually get up at about 8 o'clock.* ◦ *We generally stay in on Monday nights.* ◦ *As a rule, I prefer to catch the bus up to London, rather than catching the train.* ◦ *He's normally home by now.*
– often: **commonly** ◦ *This type of plant is commonly found in mountainous areas.*
– in a way that has often happened before: **as usual** ◦ *'Where's George?' 'Late, as usual.'*

– mostly: **generally, for the most part** ◦ *It is generally felt that his work is not good enough.* ◦ *They are, for the most part, happy.*
– without looking at details or exceptions: **on the whole, by and large, in general** ◦ *On the whole, things have been quite good.* ◦ *By and large, we've had quite a successful year.*

2 unusual

– not usual or ordinary: **unusual** (*adverb* **unusually**) ◦ *What an unusual ring! Where did you get it?* ◦ *It's quite unusual for me to be at home on a Saturday night.* ◦ *It's unusually hot for the time of year, isn't it?*
– not happening or found very often: **uncommon** (*adverb* **uncommonly**) ◦ *25°C isn't uncommon here, even in winter!*
– different in a way that is worrying or unpleasant: **abnormal** (*adverb* **abnormally**); *noun*: **abnormality** ◦ *She was told that her child might be abnormal.* ◦ *He's abnormally tall for his age.*
– not considered normal; wrong: **unnatural** ◦ *It always feels a bit unnatural spending Christmas away from my family.*

– unusual or unexpected: **strange** (*adverb* **strangely**) ◦ *It's very strange that no one came to meet us at the station.* ◦ *That's strange – I wasn't expecting any visitors this evening.* ◦ *Don't you think Jeremy was acting rather strangely last night?*

▷ more on being strange ⇨ **STRANGE**

– interesting, different: **out of the ordinary** ◦ *I feel like doing something out of the ordinary today.*
– different from usual, important: **special** ◦ *Is the party for a special occasion?* ◦ *This bracelet is very special to me.*

– more than usual: **particular, special, extra** ◦ *I made a particular effort to go and see her this time.*
– to a greater degree than others mentioned: **in particular, particularly, especially** ◦ *I don't like any of their children; the youngest in particular.* ◦ *I hate waiting for buses, especially in the rain.*

3 very unusual

– very unusual: **extraordinary** (*adverb* **extraordinarily**), **remarkable** (*adverb* **remarkably**) ◦ *He said that? How extraordinary!* ◦ *extraordinarily interesting* ◦ *He's exceptionally talented.* ◦ *a remarkable fact* ◦ *You're looking remarkably well!*
– extremely unusual and almost impossible: **miraculous** (*adverb* **miraculously**) ◦ *He made a miraculous recovery.* ◦ *Miraculously, he arrived on time.*

– somebody or something which is very unusual and goes against a rule: **exception** ◦ *Most of the children were not happy at the school, but Paul was an exception.* ◦ *an exception to the rule*
– very uncommon: **rare** (*adverb* **rarely**); a person or thing which is rare: **rarity** ◦ *a rare type of fossil* ◦ *Women pilots are still quite a rarity.*
– different from all others: **unique** ◦ *a unique occasion*

– only belonging to a particular person or found in a particular place: **peculiar** (**to** sb/sth) ◦ *a species of bird peculiar to New Zealand*
– only for a selected person or group of people: **exclusive** (*adverb* **exclusively**) ◦ *an exclusive night club* ◦ *The party is open exclusively to the people on our course.*

valley ⇨ HILL/MOUNTAIN

value

1 value in money
2 usefulness and importance
see also PRICE

1 value in money

– the amount of money that sth can be bought or sold for: **value** (*noun* C/U) ◦ *The stolen property had a total value of over £1 000.* ◦ *What's the value of this house now?* ◦ *of little/great value*
– having a particular value: **worth ...** ◦ *Our new house is worth far more than we paid for it.* ◦ *£300 for that picture? It's not worth it!*

– worth a lot of money: **valuable** ◦ *This ring is so valuable that I never wear it.*
– rare and worth a lot of money: **precious** ◦ *precious metals* (= gold and silver)
– extremely valuable: **priceless** ◦ *a priceless painting*
– so special or valuable that you could not find another one the same: **irreplaceable** ◦ *Please be careful with that vase – it's irreplaceable.*

– to become more valuable: **increase/rise* in value**, (*formal*) **appreciate** ◦ *We're waiting for the house to rise in value before we try to sell it.*
– the process of becoming more valuable: **increase/rise in value**, (*formal*) **appreciation** (*noun* U) ◦ *a further increase in the value of agricultural land* ◦ *the appreciation of the franc against the pound* (= the amount by which the value of the franc has risen when you compare it with the pound)
– to decide how much sth is worth: **value** sth (**at ...**); *noun*: **valuation** ◦ *Her collection of jewels was valued at over a million pounds.* ◦ *I'm going to take this bracelet to the jeweller's for a valuation.*

■ having no value or less value

– having no value: **worthless, valueless** ◦ *I've just found out that this necklace is completely worthless.*
– to become less valuable: **depreciate, fall* (in value)**; *noun* (C/U): **depreciation** ◦ *You shouldn't keep your car for too long – they depreciate so quickly.* ◦ *a further depreciation in the value of the currency*
– to reduce the value of money in one country compared to the value of money in other countries: **devalue** sth; *noun* (C/U): **devaluation** ◦ *The pound was devalued yesterday for the second time this year.* ◦ *a further devaluation of the dollar*

2 usefulness and importance

– the usefulness or importance of sth: **value** (*noun* U), **worth** (*noun* U) ◦ *I'm not sure that this exercise has any value at all.* ◦ *Since joining the company last year he has definitely proved his worth.*

– very useful or important: **valuable, invaluable** ◦ *It was a very valuable experience for all of us.* ◦ *Thank you, your advice has been invaluable.*
– (used about things that people do) helpful, useful or interesting: **worth** doing, **worth** your/sb's **while**, **worthwhile** ◦ *Is that play worth going to?* ◦ *It would be worth your while to check the prices in a few shops before you decide to buy.* ◦ *You should visit this museum – it's quite expensive but it's really worthwhile.*

– not helpful, useful or interesting: **worthless** ◦ *Some people think that watching TV is a worthless activity.*

– to decide on the value or usefulness of sth: **evaluate** (sth), **assess** sth; *nouns* (C/U): **evaluation, assessment** ◦ *Each new course offered by the university has to be evaluated.* ◦ *An assessment of your work will be carried out by an external examiner.*
– to say how good you think sb/sth is: **rate** sth, **rank** sb/sth ◦ *This car was rated 'Car of the Year' by Motor Magazine.* ◦ *She's ranked among the best women golfers of all time.*
– if people say that sth is better or more important than it really is, it is **overrated** ◦ *That restaurant is overrated – the food's not actually very good.*

– to have a private or personal value for sb: **mean*** sth **to** sb ◦ *I know it's not worth a lot of money, but it means a lot to me.*
– to understand and enjoy the value of sb/sth: **appreciate** sb/sth ◦ *Ask John what he thinks – he appreciates good wines.*
– to give value and importance to an idea, person or thing: **believe in** sb/sth ◦ *I believe in living life for the moment, and not worrying too much about the future.*

▷ being useful or important ⇨ USEFUL/SUITABLE, IMPORTANT

various ⇨ DIFFERENT

vary ⇨ CHANGE

vegetable

see also FOOD, FRUIT, COOK

– a plant that you eat as food: **vegetable**, (*informal*) **veg** (*noun* U) ◦ *What vegetables would you like?* ◦ *vegetable soup* ◦ *fruit and veg*
– the seeds of certain plants that are eaten as vegetables: **beans** ◦ *broad beans* ◦ *French bean* ◦ *a tin of baked beans*

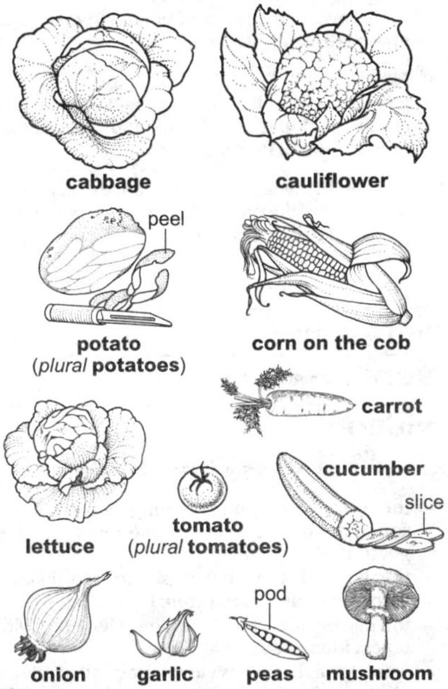

Note: bean and **pea** are countable; **corn on the cob** is uncountable; the other words can be either countable or uncountable: ◦ *a fresh lettuce* ◦ *a salad made with lettuce, cucumber and tomato.*

▷ more on potatoes ⇨ POTATO

– some vegetables can be **dried** (= have all the water taken out) ◦ *dried peas/beans*

■ cooking and eating vegetables

– vegetables that are not frozen or bought in tins are **fresh** ◦ *Sorry, we haven't got any fresh peas – only frozen.*
– vegetables that have not been cooked are **raw** ◦ *You should eat plenty of raw vegetables.*
– a mixture of vegetables, usually uncooked and eaten cold: **salad** (*noun* U/C) ◦ *Anyone want more salad?* ◦ *I'd like to order a salad with my main course, please.*

vegetable *contd.*

- the outer covering of some vegetables: **skin** (*noun* U) ◦ *onion/potato/tomato skin*
- to prepare vegetables to eat, you can **wash** them (= clean them with water), **peel** them (= remove the skin with a knife), **chop** them (= cut them into pieces), **slice** them (= cut them into flat slices) ◦ *Don't forget to wash the lettuce.* ◦ *Have you peeled the potatoes?* ◦ *chopped onion* ◦ *sliced tomatoes*

- to cook vegetables, you can **boil** them (= cook in boiling water) or **fry** them (= cook in hot fat); *adjectives*: **boiled, fried** ◦ *boiled cabbage* ◦ *stir-fried beans and mushrooms*
- to remove all the water after cooking vegetables: **strain** sth, **drain** sth

■ buying vegetables
- a person who sells fruit and vegetables: **greengrocer**; a shop that sells fruit and vegetables: **greengrocer's (shop)**

- you can buy vegetables in a **bag, packet, tin** (*especially AmE* **can**) or **jar** ◦ *a bag of potatoes* ◦ *a packet of frozen peas* ◦ *a tin of tomatoes* ◦ *a jar of pickled onions*

▷ pictures at CONTAINER

verb ⇨ GRAMMAR

very ⇨ FAIRLY/VERY

video

see also TELEVISION/RADIO, FILM, RECORD

- the system for keeping moving pictures and sound on magnetic tape: **video** (*noun* U) ◦ *We've got that film on video.*
- the magnetic tape that is used to record video pictures: **(video)tape** (*noun* U)
- the plastic box which contains a length of videotape: **video cassette**
- a machine that plays videotapes: **video** (*plural* **videos**), **video recorder**, (*especially AmE*) **VCR** (= video cassette recorder)
- something that has been recorded on videotape: **video** (*plural* **videos**) ◦ *Shall we watch a video?*

■ operating a video recorder
- to make a video begin working: **start** sth
- to stop the tape moving for a moment: **pause** sth
- to move the tape forwards quickly: **fast-forward** (sth)
- to move the tape backwards quickly: **rewind** (sth)
- to put TV pictures on videotape: **record** (sth)
- to remove a videotape from the machine: **eject** sth
- to make the video recorder record a programme automatically at a later time: **programme** (*AmE* **program**) sth ◦ *Have you programmed the video to record that documentary?*
- to operate a switch (= **button**) on a video: **press** sth ◦ *to press play* (= the button which starts the film) ◦ *to press pause/fast-forward/rewind/eject*
- a small box that you hold in your hand, with buttons that you press to control a video recorder or television: **remote control**

▷ picture at TELEVISION/RADIO

■ making video pictures
- a camera that makes video films: **(video) camera**; a camera which records sound as well as pictures: **camcorder**
- to film sth with a video camera: **video** sth ◦ *We videoed the school play last year.*
- to cut and arrange parts of a film in a particular order: **edit** (sth) ◦ *This video's too long – it needs editing.*

■ renting video films
- when a film that has been shown at the cinema becomes available on videotape, it **comes* out on video**
- a shop where you can rent a videotape to watch: **video shop**

violent ⇨ FIGHT

violin ⇨ MUSIC, ORCHESTRA

visit

1 going to visit a person or a place
2 staying in a place
3 looking after a visitor
see also TRAVEL

1 going to visit a person or a place

- to go to see a person or place and to spend some time there: **visit** sb/sth, **go* and see** sb/sth ◦ *Did you visit the British Museum when you were in London?* ◦ *I'm going to go and see my sister and her family this weekend.*
- a short stay with sb in a particular place: **visit** ◦ *We're only planning a short visit.* ◦ *to pay sb a visit*
- a person who visits sb/sth: **visitor** ◦ *We're having visitors on Sunday.*

- to visit a person or place for a short time: **call (in)** (**on** sb/**at** a place), **call round** (**at** a place), **pay a call on** sb ◦ *Jim called round when you were out.* ◦ *Let's call in on John on our way home.*
- to make a short visit to a place or person as you pass: (*informal*) **call by, stop by** ◦ *I'll call by on my way home from work.* ◦ *I'll stop by later for a drink.*
- a person who pays a short visit: **caller** ◦ *You had a caller today, but she didn't say who she was.*

- to visit sb informally, or without having told them you were coming: **drop by/in, drop in on** sb ◦ *We were just starting dinner when George dropped by.* ◦ *We dropped in on Cathy when we were in London.*
- to arrive unexpectedly at a place to visit: **turn up** ◦ *Guess who's turned up! It's your grandmother!*
- to visit sb's home, usually a short distance away: **go* round/over** (**to** a place), **come* round/over** (**to** a place), **pop round/over** (**to** a place) ◦ *I'm going round to Diane's place for dinner tonight.* ◦ *I'm going over to see Penny.* ◦ *Can you come*

round for drinks on Friday night? ◦ *I'm just popping over to Simon's house to watch football.*
– to go to a place (for example a restaurant or a bar) often: (*formal*) **frequent** sth ◦ *When he was in Paris he used to frequent all the expensive restaurants and night-clubs.*

■ visiting people on business
– to visit sb in order to receive a service: **go* to** sb ◦ *I'm going to the dentist this afternoon.* ◦ *They went to an accountant for financial advice.*
– to have a meeting with a doctor, dentist, lawyer, etc: **see*** sb ◦ *You should see a doctor about that cold.*

– to take a person into an office, a doctor's waiting room, etc: **show** sb **into** a place, **show** sb **in** ◦ *Will you show the next patient in please?*
– to take a person out of an office, etc: **see*** sb **out** (**of** a place), **show** sb **out** (**of** a place) ◦ *If you're ready to go, I'll show you out.*

2 staying in a place

– to remain somewhere (for a day or more) as a visitor or a guest: **stay** (**in** a place) (**with** sb) ◦ *We are going to stay with friends in Italy.* ◦ *to stay at a hotel*
– to arrive at a place to stay: **come* to stay** ◦ *Your mother's coming to stay.*
– to stay somewhere for a night: **spend* the night** somewhere ◦ *It was after eight o'clock and we still didn't know where we were going to spend the night.*

▷ hotels ⇨ HOTEL

3 having sb to stay

– to ask sb to come to your home: **invite** sb (**over/round**), **have** sb **round** ◦ *Shall we invite Brian and Pilar round for a meal next Thursday?* ◦ *We haven't had anyone round for ages.*
– to invite sb to stay at your house: **have** sb **to stay**
– to give sb food and a place to stay: **put*** sb **up** ◦ *It's very late. Why don't you stay here? We can easily put you up for the night.*

– a person that you invite to your home or to a party, etc: **guest** ◦ *wedding guests* ◦ *an uninvited guest*
– a man/woman who receives and entertains visitors: **host/hostess** ◦ *Our host looked after us very well.*

▷ more on inviting people ⇨ INVITE

– to say hello to sb who is arriving somewhere, for example at your house: **welcome** sb, **greet** sb; *nouns*: **welcome, greeting** ◦ *The whole family came to the door to welcome us.*
– to ask sb to come into your house: **ask** sb **in**, **invite** sb **in** ◦ *I had to wait for ages before she finally asked me in.*

▷ things you say when you welcome sb ⇨ GREET

– when you are happy to see sb, they are **welcome**; *opposite*: **unwelcome** ◦ *Remember you're always welcome.* ◦ *an unwelcome guest*
– to welcome sb in a friendly way: **make*** sb (**feel**) **welcome** ◦ *They'd never met us before but they made us feel very welcome.*

■ **MORE ...**
– if you stay in sb's house longer than you should, so that they are waiting for you to leave, you **outstay/overstay** your **welcome** ◦ *Do you think we outstayed our welcome?*

voice

see also SPEAK, LANGUAGE

– the sound that you make when you speak or sing: **voice** ◦ *I'm sure I heard voices outside.* ◦ *Shh! Keep your voice down!* ◦ *He's got a sore throat and he's lost his voice.* ◦ *She's got a beautiful voice.*
– connected with the voice: **vocal** ◦ *vocal music*

– a voice that you can hear easily because the person makes a lot of noise is **loud** ◦ *to speak in a loud voice*
– a voice that is not loud is **quiet, low, soft** ◦ *She has a very quiet voice and it was difficult to hear what she said.*
– the way a person speaks (for example how loud or soft their voice is), which shows how they feel: **tone** (**of voice**) ◦ *He spoke in an angry tone of voice.*
– to make your voice quieter: **lower** your **voice**; to make it louder: **raise** your **voice**

– a child's or a woman's voice is **high**; a man's voice is **deep**
– when a boy's voice becomes deep like a man's, it **breaks*** ◦ *His voice still hasn't broken.*

– if your voice is rough and quiet, for example because you have a cold or a dry throat, it is **hoarse** (*adverb* **hoarsely**), **husky** (*adverb* **huskily**); *noun* (U): **hoarseness** ◦ *speaking in a hoarse whisper*
– if your voice is weak, for example because you are nervous, it **shakes***, **trembles** ◦ *His voice shook with excitement.*

▷ the different voices of singers ⇨ SING

vote ⇨ ELECTION

wait

see also EARLY/LATE

– to remain in a particular place, or delay doing sth, until sb arrives or sth happens: **wait** (**for** sb/sth) (**to** do sth), (*formal*) **await** sb/sth ◦ *Wait a moment! Don't start without me!* ◦ *What are you waiting for?* ◦ *'How long will we have to wait?' 'Well, we're expecting him to arrive in about ten minutes.'* ◦ *She's still waiting for him to phone.* ◦ *a prisoner who is awaiting trial*
– a period of waiting: **wait** (*noun singular*) ◦ *to have a long/short wait*

– a period of waiting for sth that should already have happened: **delay** (*noun* U/C) ◦ *We need the money without delay.* ◦ *Long delays are expected at the airport.*
– to be left or delayed until a later time: **wait** ◦ *Can this matter wait until tomorrow?*

wait *contd.*

– to tell sb to wait for a short time, you can say (*informal*) **hold on**, (*informal*) **hang on, just a minute, just a moment** ◦ *Can you hang on a minute? I'm just coming.*

■ different kinds of waiting

– to pause to think a moment longer before doing sth: **hesitate**; *noun* (U): **hesitation** ◦ *She hesitated before opening the door.* ◦ *a moment's hesitation* ◦ *He answered without hesitation.*
– to wait and find out what will happen before doing anything: **wait and see** ◦ *The match might be cancelled if it rains – we'll just have to wait and see.*

– to stay in a place doing nothing but waiting: **wait about/around, hang* about/around** ◦ *They kept me waiting around all morning before my interview.* ◦ *I hung around in the shopping centre until the time of my appointment.*
– to make sb wait for you: **keep*** sb **waiting** ◦ *I'm sorry to have kept you waiting.*

– to stay at home because you are expecting sb: **wait in** ◦ *I waited in all evening but he didn't come.*
– not to go to bed because you are waiting for sb to come home: **wait up** (**for** sb) ◦ *Don't wait up – I'll probably be quite late.*
– to stay after other people have left: **wait behind** ◦ *The manager asked me to wait behind at the end of the meeting.*
– to wait in a hiding place in order to surprise sb: **lie* in wait** (**for** sb/sth)

■ waiting with other people

– a line of people that are waiting to do sth: **queue** (*AmE* **line**) ◦ *a bus queue* ◦ *to join a queue*
– to form a line with other people who are waiting: **queue** (**up**) (**for** sth/**to** do sth), (*AmE* **stand in line**) ◦ *Three hours before the sale started, people were already queuing up outside the shop.* ◦ *You'll have to queue to get a good seat.*
– to go to the front of a queue instead of the back: **jump the queue**

– a room where people can sit and wait: **waiting room**
– a list of people who are waiting for sth that will be available in the future: **waiting list** ◦ *Could you put my name on the waiting list?*

■ **MORE ...**

– able to remain calm and not get angry, especially when there is a difficulty or you are waiting: **patient** (*adverb* **patiently**); *opposite*: **impatient**; the quality of being patient: **patience** (*noun* U); *opposite*: **impatience** (*noun* U) ◦ *Please try to be patient – I'm doing this as quickly as I can.* ◦ *to wait patiently* ◦ *to lose patience with sb/sth*

wake up ⇨ SLEEP

walk

1 different ways of walking
2 difficulty in walking
3 walking for pleasure
4 walking in the street
5 walking with another person

see also RUN, STAND, MOVE

1 different ways of walking

– to move along on foot at a fairly slow speed: **walk**
– to walk somewhere, rather than go by car, bus, etc: **go*/come* on foot** ◦ *They made the long journey over the mountains on foot.*
– the speed at which you walk or run: **pace** ◦ *to walk at a brisk pace* (= quite fast) ◦ *to walk at a leisurely pace* (= quite slow) ◦ *at a walking pace* (= slowly, at the speed of sb walking)

– an act of lifting one foot and putting it down in a different place: **step**; *verb*: **step** ◦ *She took a couple of steps and then fell over.* ◦ *Please step forward when I call your name.*
– the distance that you move when you take one step: **pace** ◦ *Take two paces forward and then stop.*
– the sound of sb walking, or the step that you take when walking: **footstep** ◦ *I could hear footsteps outside the window.*
– the mark that a person leaves when walking: **footprint** ◦ *to leave footprints in the snow*

– to put your foot accidentally on sb/sth: **tread* on** sb/sth, **step on** sb/sth ◦ *Ow! You just trod on my foot.* ◦ *Look out! You've just stepped on my toe.*
– to walk on sb/sth and hurt or damage them: **trample** (**on**) sb/sth ◦ *The boys trampled on the flowers.* ◦ *The cows trampled the corn.*

■ walking with long or regular steps

– to walk with long steps: **stride**; a long step: **stride** ◦ *Robert strode up to the desk and demanded to see the manager.*
– to walk with regular steps (like a soldier): **march**; a journey made by marching: **march** ◦ *The General saluted his men as they marched past.* ◦ *She marched in and demanded an explanation.* ◦ *The soldiers were tired after their long march.*

■ walking slowly

– to walk slowly for pleasure: **stroll, wander**; *noun*: **stroll** ◦ *In the evening we strolled up to the castle.* ◦ *We went for a stroll along the river after lunch.*
– to walk with slow, heavy steps: **tramp** ◦ *We had a miserable afternoon tramping across the moors in pouring rain.*
– to walk slowly by sliding your feet along instead of lifting them from the ground: **shuffle** ◦ *The old man shuffled across the room in his slippers.*

- at a very slow speed: **at a snail's pace** ◦ *The queue was moving at a snail's pace – I got fed up and left.*

■ walking carefully or quietly
- to move very quietly and carefully, often with your body in a low position so that nobody will notice you: **creep*** ◦ *He crept down the stairs hoping that nobody would wake.*
- on your hands and legs: **on all fours** ◦ *The children went through the tunnel on all fours.*
- to move slowly with your body on or close to the ground: **crawl** ◦ *Has the baby started to crawl yet?*
- to walk or move quietly, in a suspicious way: **prowl** (**about/around**) ◦ *Someone was prowling about outside the house, so I called the police.*

■ walking in water
- to walk with bare feet in shallow water: **paddle**
- to walk with difficulty through deep water, mud, etc: **wade** ◦ *The soldiers jumped out of the boat and waded ashore.*

2 difficulty in walking
- to walk in an unsteady way as if you could fall at any moment: **stagger** ◦ *The man staggered out of the pub and called a taxi.*
- to hit your foot against sth when you are walking and almost fall over: **stumble** (**over** sth), **trip** (**over** sth, **up**) ◦ *He stumbled over a tree root.* ◦ *Be careful you don't trip over this rug.*
- to walk in an uneven way because you have hurt your leg or foot: **limp**; *noun*: **limp** ◦ *He fell and twisted his ankle and limped home in great pain.* ◦ *Her leg's getting better but she's still got a bit of a limp.* ◦ *to walk with a limp*
- a person who cannot walk properly because their legs or back have been injured is **disabled** ◦ *This cinema now has better facilities for disabled people.*
- to walk, move or travel to places (especially after being ill): **get* about/around** ◦ *She has difficulty getting about with her bad leg.*
- an animal that is not able to walk properly because of an injury to the leg is **lame** ◦ *The horse went lame.* ◦ *a lame horse*
- a long, thin piece of wood that you lean on if you have difficulty walking: (**walking**) **stick**
- a type of stick that you put under your arm to help you walk when you have hurt your leg or foot: **crutch** ◦ *I had plaster on my leg and was walking on crutches.*
- a chair with large wheels that can be used by people who are unable to walk: **wheelchair**

3 walking for pleasure
- to walk for pleasure, exercise, etc: **go* for a walk, have/take* a walk**; an occasion of doing this: **walk** ◦ *I'm just going for a walk – are you coming?* ◦ *Does anyone feel like a walk?*
- to get up and go for a walk after sitting down for a long time: **stretch** your **legs**
- to go for a long walk in the country: **hike, go* hiking, go* on a hike**; a person who goes hiking: **hiker** ◦ *We spent our holidays hiking in the Lake District.* ◦ *a ten-mile hike*
- to go on a walking holiday carrying your clothes, food, etc in a bag on your back: **backpack** ◦ *We're planning to go backpacking in New Zealand at Easter.*
- to go from place to place with no particular purpose: **wander/roam/walk around/about** (a place) ◦ *Sarah had a pleasant afternoon wandering around the old market.* ◦ *Hundreds of football fans were roaming around the city centre following the match.* ◦ *She walked about the old walled city, peering into the shops.*

- a path or route that is used for walking for pleasure: **walk** ◦ *There's a lovely walk along the river from here that takes you to the village.*

4 walking in the street
- a person who is walking in the street: **pedestrian**; of or for pedestrians: **pedestrian** ◦ *a pedestrian subway* ◦ *a pedestrian precinct*
- a person who is walking past you or sth (by chance): **passer-by** (*plural* **passers-by**) ◦ *The journalist asked a passer-by if he had seen what had happened.*

▷ roads and paths ⇨ ROAD

5 walking with another person
- to go with sb to a place: **accompany** sb, **go*** (**along**) **with** sb ◦ *Children must be accompanied by an adult.* ◦ *I went along with him to the post office.*
- to go with sb/sth to protect them or as an honour: **escort** sb ◦ *The film star was escorted by two bodyguards.*

- with your arm linked together with sb else's: **arm in arm** ◦ *The couple walked arm in arm along the promenade.*

▷ picture at HAND

- next to each other or close together: **side by side** ◦ *The three men walked side by side along the pavement.*
- moving/not moving your feet at the same time as other people when you are marching, dancing, etc: **in/out of step** (**with** sb) ◦ *Look at that soldier. He's completely out of step with the others.*

- to walk more slowly than sb/sth else: **lag behind** (sb/sth) ◦ *Damian always lags behind when we are walking in the mountains.*
- to reach sb who is ahead of you: **catch*** sb **up**, **catch* up** (**with** sb) ◦ *I'm just going to post a letter. You go on and I'll catch you up in a minute.*

■ **MORE ...**
- a number of people, vehicles, etc that move slowly in a line: **procession** ◦ *to walk in procession* ◦ *a wedding procession*
- an occasion when a group of people stand or walk in a procession so that people can look at them: **parade** ◦ *a fashion parade*

wall/fence/hedge

the walls of a room ⇨ **ROOM**
making a wall ⇨ **BUILD**
see also DOOR, BUILDING

– a solid, upright structure made of stone, brick, etc that forms one of the sides of a building or room, or is used to enclose or protect sth: **wall** ◦ *a garden wall* ◦ *the wall of the house* ◦ *a picture on the wall* ◦ *The land was divided into two by a low wall.* ◦ *the city walls*

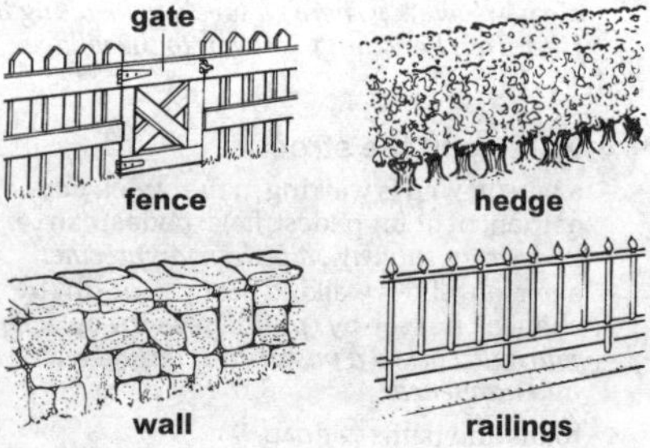

– material which is made of long pieces of metal twisted together, with spaces between them, which is used for fences, etc: **wire-netting** (*noun* U)
– a kind of wire which has sharp pointed spikes close together and which is used for fences and as an obstruction during a war: **barbed wire** (*noun* U) ◦ *a barbed wire fence*

– to surround an area with a fence/wall: **fence/ wall** sth (**in**); if you use a fence to keep a small area separate from the rest of the land, you **fence** the area **off** ◦ *The play area in the park has been fenced off to make it safer for young children.*
– a line of metal bars that are joined to form a kind of fence: **railing** (*usually plural*) ◦ *We jumped over the railings and ran across the road.*

– an empty space in sth or between two things: **gap** ◦ *The sheep got through a gap in the fence.*
– a wooden step which you climb to get to the other side of a wall or fence in the countryside: **stile**

want

1 wanting sth
2 wanting sth very much
3 not wanting sth
see also WILLING

1 wanting sth

– to feel that you would like to have sth or do sth: **want** sth, **want** (sb) **to** do sth, (*formal*) **wish** (sb) **to** do sth ◦ *They want this work done by the weekend.* ◦ *We want you to come and stay with us.* ◦ *Do you wish me to forward your letters?*
– a feeling of wanting sth: **wish** ◦ *I've made my wishes clear.* ◦ *I have no wish to go back to that hospital.* ◦ *So you've got your wish at last* (= what you wanted has happened).
– wanted by many people: **desirable** ◦ *a desirable area to live in*

– to want sth to happen or be true: **hope for** sth, **hope to** do sth, **hope** (**that**) ... ◦ *We're hoping for good weather on holiday.* ◦ *She's hoping to study biology at university.* ◦ *I really hope I pass my exam!*

▷ more on hoping ⇨ **HOPE**

– to like the idea of having or doing sth: **feel* like** sth/doing sth ◦ *I feel like an egg for breakfast.* ◦ *What do you feel like doing today?*
– to want sth and try hard to get it or do it: **be after** sth, **be out for** sth ◦ *He's after Peter's job.* ◦ *She's out for whatever she can get.*
– if you want or need sth, you **would like** it, (*formal*) you **desire** it, (*informal*) you **could do with** it ◦ *Would you like some tea?* ◦ *They have everything they could possibly desire.* ◦ *I could do with a drink right now.*

■ wishing
– to want sth that cannot now happen or that probably will not happen: **wish** (**that**) ... ◦ *I wish I had listened to my father's advice.* ◦ *I wish I could help you.* ◦ *She said she wished she were dead.*
– to wish that sth had not happened: **regret** sth ◦ *I regret not saying goodbye to him.*
– an unlikely event that you very much want to happen: **dream** ◦ *My dream is to go and live on a tropical island.*
– to express a strong wish, you can say **if only** ... ◦ *If only I could be there when he comes.*
– ideas that are based on what you would like, not on reality: **wishful thinking** (*noun* U) ◦ *That's just wishful thinking.*

■ wanting what sb else has
– to want sth that sb else has: **envy** sb sth ◦ *She has always envied him his success.*
– feeling or showing that you want sth that sb else has: **jealous** (**of** sb/sth), **envious** (**of** sb/sth); *nouns* (U): **jealousy, envy** ◦ *She's jealous of me because I got the job and she didn't.* ◦ *I'm very envious of your new computer!* ◦ *I'm filled with envy every time I see their beautiful house.* ◦ *to show envy of sb*
– causing or capable of causing envy: **enviable** ◦ *an enviable reputation*

2 wanting sth very much

– to want sth very much: **want** sth **badly, long for** sth, **be dying for** sth ◦ *I badly wanted to get out of London and see the countryside.* ◦ *They're longing for a holiday.* ◦ *I'm dying for a cigarette.*
– the feeling of wanting sth very much: **desire** ◦ *an overwhelming desire for peace*
– wanting sth very much: **eager** (**for** sth) (*adverb* **eagerly**), **anxious for** sth (*adverb* **anxiously**) ◦ *The students are all eager to finish the course.* ◦ *Your report is eagerly awaited.* ◦ *We're anxious to finish the work as soon as possible.*

- wanting more of sth than you really need: **greedy**; *noun* (U): ◦ *Don't be so greedy! You've had three cakes already!*
- wanting sth to happen soon: **impatient** (**for** sth/**to** do sth) (*adverb* **impatiently**) ◦ *They're impatient to see the results.* ◦ *Everyone's impatient for the summer to come.*

- a strong desire to be successful: **ambition** (*noun* U); *adjective*: **ambitious** ◦ *an ambitious politician*
- a particular thing that you want very much to have or do: **ambition** ◦ *My ambition is to go up in a hot air balloon.*
- if you have decided to succeed in sth you want, you are **determined** (**to** do sth); *noun* (U): **determination** ◦ *She was determined to win.*

- wanting sth very much: **desperate** (**for** sth/**to** do sth) ◦ *I'm desperate to get out of this place.*
- a strong desire that you cannot control: **compulsion**, **urge** ◦ *He felt a compulsion to smash everything in sight.* ◦ *I had an urge to tell him what I thought of him.*
- caused by a strong desire that you cannot control: **compulsive** ◦ *This book makes compulsive reading – you just can't put it down.*
- unable to stop taking sth (for example a drug) or doing sth: **addicted**; *noun* (C/U): **addiction** ◦ *Gerry's addicted to fast cars.*

3 not wanting sth

- not wanting to do sth: **unwilling** ◦ *He's unwilling to give us any more money.*
- not eager or interested: **unenthusiastic** ◦ *I offered him my own car in exchange, but he didn't seem very enthusiastic.*

▷ more on being unwilling ⇨ WILLING

- not wanted: **unwanted** ◦ *unwanted Christmas presents*
- not desirable or pleasant: **undesirable** ◦ *This drug has no undesirable side-effects.*

■ **MORE ...**

- to do what you want without worrying about other people's opinions: **please yourself**, **do* as** you **please** ◦ *'I'm sure my idea is the best one.' 'Okay, please yourself.'* ◦ *Whatever I tell him, he'll still do as he pleases.*

- a sudden wish to do sth without thinking of the results: **impulse** ◦ *She had an impulse to rush straight out of the room.*
- a person who does things without thinking of the results is **impulsive** (*adverb* **impulsively**)

- the power of the mind to make things happen: **will** (*noun* C/U) ◦ *the will to live*
- strength of mind: **willpower** (*noun* U) ◦ *It takes a lot of willpower to give up smoking.*

war

1 wars
2 armed forces
3 starting a war
4 fighting a war
5 winning and losing
6 not at war (peace)

see also FIGHT

1 wars

- a situation of fighting between countries, groups, etc: **war** (*noun* C/U) ◦ *to fight a war* ◦ *to go to war* ◦ *nuclear war* ◦ *a prisoner of war*
- ways of fighting a war: **warfare** (*noun* U) ◦ *biological/chemical/atomic warfare* ◦ *conventional warfare* (= warfare in which nuclear weapons are not used)
- before a war: **pre-war**; after a war: **post-war** ◦ *the pre-war period* ◦ *post-war economic recovery*

- a war that involves many countries: **world war** ◦ *the Second World War*
- a war between groups of people inside the same country: **civil war**
- a war in which small groups of fighters make surprise attacks on the enemy: **guerrilla war**, **guerrilla warfare**; a person who fights in a guerrilla war: **guerrilla**
- fighting against the government: **rebellion** (*noun* C/U); a person who fights against his/her government, etc: **rebel**

- the army or country that your country is fighting against: (**the**) **enemy** (*with singular or plural verb*) ◦ *The enemy is attacking on four fronts.* ◦ *an enemy warplane*
- a country that supports your country in a war: **ally**; *adjective*: **allied** ◦ *The allied attack succeeded in pushing the enemy over the river.*

▷ more on enemies ⇨ ENEMY

2 armed forces

- the military forces of a country that are trained to fight on land: **army**; a member of an army: **soldier**
- the military forces of a country that are trained to fight at sea: **navy**; *adjective*: **naval**; a member of a navy: **sailor** ◦ *a naval officer*
- the military forces of a country that are trained to fight in the air: **air force**; a member of an air force: (*BrE*) **airman** (*plural* **airmen**)
- all the soldiers, sailors and airmen of a country; their organization and their equipment: **the armed forces**, **the armed services**, **the military**; *adjective* (*only before a noun*): **military** ◦ *military action* ◦ *military service* ◦ *a military disaster*

■ weapons

- an object that is used for fighting or killing people: **weapon**
- weapons used in war: **arms** (*noun plural*)
- a weapon that is used for shooting: **gun**
- a container that is filled with material that will explode if you throw it, drop it, etc: **bomb**

war *contd.*

▷ more on guns, bombs and other weapons ⇨ **GUN, BOMB, WEAPON**

– a large heavy military vehicle covered in armour and armed with guns, that moves on special wheels: **tank**
– a type of ship used for war: **warship**
– a type of aeroplane used for war: **warplane**

▷ more on armies and their weapons ⇨ **ARMY**

▷ more on navies and their weapons ⇨ **NAVY**

▷ more on air forces and their weapons ⇨ **AIR FORCE**

3 starting a war

– to say publicly and officially that your country is at war with another country: **declare war** (**on/against** sb/sth) ◦ *Britain declared war on Germany in September 1939.*
– the beginning of a war: **outbreak** ◦ *at the outbreak of war*
– to enter a country with an army in order to attack it: **invade** (a country); *noun*: **invasion**; a person or country that does this: **invader** ◦ *They invaded with tanks, warplanes and thousands of ground forces.* ◦ *troops sent to guard against invasion*
– an act of starting a fight or war without a good reason: **aggression** (*noun* U); a person or country that does this: **aggressor** ◦ *an act of aggression*

4 fighting a war

– a country that is fighting a war is **at war** ◦ *We are at war with a larger and more powerful country.*
– a period when there is a war: **wartime** (*noun* U) ◦ *life in wartime Britain*
– a fight between armies during a war: **battle** ◦ *the battle of Waterloo*
– a place where armies fight each other: **battlefield**
– a line or area where fighting takes place during a war: **front** ◦ *The soldiers were sent to the Eastern front.*

– fighting, especially during a war: **combat** (*noun* U), **action** (*noun* U) ◦ *He was wounded in combat.* ◦ *My grandfather saw action in Norway during the war.*

– to try to defeat a person, country, etc by using force: **attack** (sb/sth); *noun*: **attack** (**on** sb/sth), (*formal*) **offensive** ◦ *The enemy attacked at night.* ◦ *Rebel forces launched* (= began) *an attack on the parliament building.* ◦ *attacking forces* ◦ *They're planning another offensive.*
– connected with or used for attacking: **offensive** ◦ *offensive weapons*

– to make a surprise attack on a place: **raid** a place; *noun*: **raid** (**on** sth) ◦ *a dawn raid*
– an attack by warplanes: **air raid, air strike**
– to drop bombs onto a place from warplanes: **bomb** a place; *noun* (U): **bombing** ◦ *They bombed all the main industrial cities.* ◦ *a bombing raid*

– to fight a person, country, etc to protect sb/sth: **defend** sb/sth (**against** sb/sth); *noun* (U): **defence** (*AmE* **defense**) (**of** sb/sth) (**against** sth) ◦ *Would you fight to defend your country?* ◦ *the defence of our country against its enemies*
– to attack the enemy after the enemy has attacked you: **counter-attack**; *noun*: **counter-attack** ◦ *The counter-attack caught the enemy by surprise.*

– a planned series of attacks in a war: **campaign** ◦ *Napoleon's Russian campaign*
– an organized plan of attack in a war: **operation** ◦ *an operation to capture a bridge*
– the skilful use of your army to win a battle, etc: **tactics** (*noun plural*); *adjective*: **tactical** ◦ *a tactical success*
– a plan to win a battle, get sth, etc: **strategy** (*noun* C/U); *adjective*: **strategic** ◦ *a successful strategy* ◦ *military strategy*

– to surround a place with an army: **besiege** a place; an act of besieging a place: **siege** ◦ *The town was under siege and no supplies were allowed in.*
– to take control of a building, town, country, etc by force: **occupy** a place; *noun* (U): **occupation** ◦ *Rebel forces have occupied the TV station.*
– to take or win sth from your enemy by force: **capture** sth ◦ *The town has been captured by rebel troops.*

– to go round a town, building, etc to make sure there is no trouble: **patrol** (a place); a person or group of people that patrol: **patrol**; patrolling a place: **on patrol** ◦ *The army makes hourly patrols of this area.* ◦ *a night patrol* ◦ *We were on patrol near the docks.*

– extra soldiers, etc that are sent to make an army stronger: **reinforcements** (*noun plural*) ◦ *to send reinforcements*

■ killing and injuring people

– to injure sb with a weapon: **wound** sb; the injury which a person receives: **wound** ◦ *He was wounded in the leg.* ◦ *an old war wound*
– to kill a large number of people: **massacre** people; *noun*: **massacre** ◦ *The entire village was massacred.* ◦ *a terrible massacre*
– to kill a large number of people, especially in a cruel way: **slaughter** people; *noun* (U): **slaughter** ◦ *The soldiers entered the village and slaughtered the women and children.*

– people who have been wounded in fighting: **the wounded** (*noun plural*)
– people who have been killed in fighting: **the dead** (*noun plural*)
– a person who is killed or wounded in a war, accident, etc: **casualty** ◦ *Both sides suffered heavy casualties.* ◦ *the casualty list*

5 winning and losing

– to be successful in a war, battle, etc: **win*** (sth) ◦ *They had won the battle but not the war.*
– to win a war, battle, etc against sb/sth else: **defeat** sb/sth, **beat*** sb/sth; *noun* (C/U): **defeat** (**of** sb/sth) ◦ *The Scots defeated the English at Bannockburn.*

- success in winning sth: **victory** (*noun* C/U) ◦ *to be confident of victory*
- to take control of an area by winning a war: **conquer** a place; *noun*: **conquest** ◦ *the Spanish conquest of central America*
- a person who conquers: **conqueror**

- not to be successful in a war, battle, etc: **lose*** (sth), **be defeated/beaten** (**by** sb/sth); *noun* (C/U): **defeat** (**by** sb/sth) ◦ *They were shocked by their defeat.* ◦ *The rebels would not accept defeat.*
- (used about a town) to be defeated or captured by the enemy: **fall***; *noun* **fall** ◦ *The town fell after a three week siege.* ◦ *the fall of Troy*
- to move away in order to leave a battle: **retreat**; *noun* (C/U): **retreat** ◦ *The troops retreated along the river.* ◦ *Napoleon's retreat from Moscow.* ◦ *no possibility of retreat*

- to stop fighting and admit that you have lost: **surrender** (**to** sb), **lay* down** your **arms**; *noun* (C/U): **surrender** ◦ *The general ordered his men to lay down their arms.* ◦ *the surrender of the city*

▷ more on winning and losing ⇨ WIN/LOSE

6 not at war (peace)

- the state of not being at war: **peace** (*noun* U) ◦ *Europe has been at peace for fifty years.*
- a period of peace: **peacetime** (*noun* U) ◦ *a peacetime economy*
- a written agreement between two countries not to continue to fight each other: **peace treaty** ◦ *to sign a peace treaty*
- to stop enemies from fighting each other: **keep* the peace**; a person or country that does this: **peacekeeper**; *adjective*: **peacekeeping** ◦ *United Nations troops were sent in to keep the peace.* ◦ *a peacekeeping force*

■ **MORE ...**

- a country that decides not to fight on either side in a war is **neutral**; the state of being neutral: **neutrality** (*noun* U)

- a person who refuses to join the army because he/she believes that war and fighting are wrong: **conscientious objector**
- the belief that all wars are wrong and you should not fight in them: **pacifism** (*noun* U)
- a person who believes in pacifism: **pacifist**

- the international organizations that give medical assistance to soldiers, etc: **the Red Cross**, **the Red Crescent**

warm ⇨ HOT

warn

see also ADVISE/SUGGEST, DANGER, CAREFUL

- to tell sb about sth bad which might happen, and to advise them to be careful: **warn** sb (**of/about** sth), **warn** sb **against** sth/doing sth, **warn** sb **not to** do sth, **warn** sb **that...**; *noun* (C/U): **warning** ◦ *I tried to warn him of the danger, but he wouldn't listen.* ◦ *Did you warn her about the snakes?* ◦ *I warn you strongly against trying to change your money on the black market.* ◦ *I warned her not to cross the park alone at night.* ◦ *They had warned me that it might be very hot.* ◦ *He's been given plenty of warnings.* ◦ *He was sacked without any warning.*

- to warn sb that you will do sth bad to them if they do not do what you tell them to do: **threaten** sb (**with** sth); *noun* (C/U): **threat** ◦ *They threatened to kill us.* ◦ *She was threatened with dismissal.* ◦ *Do you think they would carry out their threat?*
- in a way which threatens: **threatening** (*adverb* **threateningly**) ◦ *threatening behaviour* ◦ *He raised his knife threateningly.*

- to warn sb of a particular danger: **alert** sb (**to** sth); *noun*: **alert** ◦ *Have they been alerted to the possible dangers?* ◦ *a bomb alert*
- to give a warning sound or signal: **raise the alarm** ◦ *Fortunately he was quick to raise the alarm.*

- a warning that turns out to be unnecessary: **false alarm** ◦ *We heard that there might be another power cut, but it turned out to be a false alarm.*
- not to take any notice of a warning: **ignore a warning** ◦ *We told him the brakes weren't reliable, but he ignored all our warnings.*

- a machine that warns you about sth bad with a bell or other loud noise: **alarm** ◦ *The fire alarm went off* (= sounded). ◦ *a smoke alarm* ◦ *a burglar alarm*
- a machine, for example on an ambulance, fire engine or police car, that makes a loud noise to warn you about sth: **siren**
- when sth happens which starts an alarm, it **sets*** the alarm **off** ◦ *I burnt the toast and set off the smoke alarm.*

■ different ways of warning sb

- to tell sb to be careful of sth, you can tell them to **look out** (**for** sth), **watch out** (**for** sth), **mind out** (**for** sth), **mind** sth, **watch** sth ◦ *Look out for ice on the roads.* ◦ *Watch out for pickpockets.* ◦ *Mind your head.* ◦ *Mind the step.* ◦ *Watch what you say.*

- to give a warning, you can say **(Be) careful!** or **Look out!** or **Watch out!** or **Mind out!** ◦ *Careful! There's ice on the road.* ◦ *Look out! There's a car coming.* ◦ *Watch out! There are thieves about.* ◦ *Mind out! These boxes are heavy!*

- written warnings say **Beware** (**of** sth) or **Caution!** ◦ *Beware of the dog!* ◦ *Caution! Main road ahead.*

■ **MORE ...**

- a sign that sth good or bad is going to happen in the future: **omen** ◦ *a bad/good omen*
- a sign or warning of future danger or trouble: **threat** (*noun* U/*singular*) ◦ *the threat of rain*
- something which suggests that sth bad is going to happen is **threatening**, **ominous** ◦ *a very threatening situation* ◦ *ominous black clouds*

warn *contd.*

– if you warned sb about a danger, but they ignored your warning, afterwards you can say (*informal*) **I told you so!**

wash

1 washing and drying
2 washing yourself or another person
3 washing clothes
4 washing dishes
other ways of making things clean ⇨ CLEAN/DIRTY

1 washing and drying

– to make sth clean by using water: **wash** sth ◦ *to wash the car/the floor/the dog*
– to wash the inside of sth: **wash** sth **out** ◦ *You had better wash that jug out thoroughly – I've been using it for flowers.*
– to leave sth in water for some time in order to clean it: **soak** sth; to be left in water to get clean: **soak** ◦ *Leave the saucepans to soak for a while.*

– a substance which you use with water to wash yourself or to clean things: **soap** (*noun* U); a piece of soap: **bar of soap**; full of soap: **soapy** ◦ *to wash with soap* ◦ *Wash in plenty of warm, soapy water.*

– to clean sth with soap and water by rubbing it hard, often with a brush: **scrub** sth; an act of scrubbing: **scrub** ◦ *I scrubbed my hands but I couldn't get the ink off.* ◦ *I'm going to give the floor a good scrub – it's filthy.*
– to remove sth by scrubbing: **scrub** sth **off** ◦ *They scrubbed off all the writing on the walls.*
– a small brush used for scrubbing: **scrubbing-brush**

– a small piece of material used for cleaning things: **cloth**; a piece of old cloth that is used for cleaning things: **rag**
– a cloth for washing the floor: **floorcloth**
– a bunch of thick strings or a sponge with a long handle which is used for washing floors: **mop**; if you use one of these, you **mop** the floor
– a piece of plastic or other material with many small holes which soaks up water, used for cleaning things or washing: **sponge**

– to wash sth in clean water: **rinse** sth; to remove soap or dirt from sth with water: **rinse** sth **out**; *noun*: **rinse** ◦ *Rinse your hair thoroughly.* ◦ *Rinse the soap out carefully.* ◦ *Give the glasses a good rinse.*
– to clean an object by rubbing it with a wet cloth, a piece of paper, etc: **wipe** sth ◦ *Would you wipe the table please?*

– to remove all the liquid from sth: **dry** sth; to become dry: **dry** ◦ *Dry your hands.* ◦ *The washing is drying in the sunshine.*

2 washing yourself or another person

– the room in a house where you wash: **bathroom**
– to clean yourself or part of yourself with water: **have a wash, wash** (sth) ◦ *I'll have a quick wash, then I'll join you downstairs.* ◦ *Have you washed yet?* ◦ *to wash your hands*
– to stand and wash under running water: **have/take* a shower, shower** ◦ *I'm going to have a quick shower and get changed.*

▷ picture at BATHROOM

– to wash yourself in a bath: **have/take* a bath**
– when you climb into a bath, you **get* in, get* into** it ◦ *I had just got in the bath when the phone rang.*
– when you are having a bath, you are **in the bath** ◦ *I could hear him singing in the bath.*
– when you climb out of a bath, you **get* out** (**of** it) ◦ *Get out quickly and dry yourself before you get cold.*
– if you wash sb in a bath, you **bath** them, **give*** them **a bath** ◦ *It's your turn to bath the children.*

– to wash and make yourself look clean and tidy: **freshen** (yourself) **up** ◦ *I'd like a minute to freshen up before the interview.*

– a small, square towel that you use for washing your face: **face cloth, flannel**
– a piece of rubber or plastic or a natural material that has many small holes and which soaks up water: **sponge**; to use a wet sponge to clean sb/sth: **sponge** sb/sth ◦ *He sponged himself from head to foot.*
– a small brush for cleaning your fingernails: **nail brush**
– a piece of cloth or paper that you use for drying yourself: **towel** ◦ *a hand towel* ◦ *paper towels*
– a liquid that you use for washing your hair: **shampoo** (*noun* U); when you use this, you **shampoo** your hair ◦ *a shampoo for greasy hair*
– to wash your teeth: **clean/brush** your **teeth**
– to remove hair with a razor: **shave** sth (**off**), (used about a man shaving his face) **shave, have a shave**

▷ cleaning your teeth ⇨ TOOTH
▷ shaving ⇨ HAIR

– a bag in which you keep soap, toothpaste, etc, when you are travelling: **sponge bag**

3 washing clothes

– to clean clothes, etc with water: **wash** sth ◦ *to wash the sheets*
– the clothes, etc that need washing: **washing** (*noun* U), **laundry** (*noun* U) ◦ *Don't leave your dirty washing on the floor.* ◦ *a laundry basket*
– if you wash all the clothes, etc that need to be washed, you **do* the washing**
– the powder that is used for washing clothes: **washing powder** (*noun* U), **soap powder** (*noun* U), **detergent** (*noun* U) ◦ *a box/packet of soap powder.*
– an electric machine for washing clothes: **washing machine**
– a machine that dries clothes by moving them about in hot air: **tumble-dryer**

- a machine that turns wet clothes, etc very quickly to force water out of them: **spin-dryer**; to use this machine to get the water out of the washing: **spin-dry** sth
- if you wash clothes, etc in a bowl, not in a machine, you wash them **by hand**

- a place where you can pay to wash clothes, etc in a washing machine: **launderette**
- a place where you send clothes, etc to be washed: **laundry**
- to clean clothes, etc using special chemicals and no water: **dry-clean** sth
- a shop where clothes can be taken to be dry-cleaned: (**dry-**)**cleaner's**

- a thin rope that you can hang clothes on so that they can dry: **clothes line**, **washing line**
- the small wooden or plastic object that you use to fasten clothes to a clothes line: (**clothes-**)**peg** (*AmE* **clothes-pin**)
- to hang washing on a clothes line in the open air: **hang*** sth **out** ◦ *I hung the sheets out in the garden and the wind dried them quickly.*
- to twist and squeeze wet cloth to remove water from it: **wring*** sth (**out**) ◦ *When you have wrung the clothes out, hang them out to dry.*

- to remove creases from clothes, etc with heat: **iron** (sth)

▷ more on ironing ⇨ IRONING

4 washing dishes

- to wash plates, cups, knives and forks, etc: **wash** (sth) **up**, **do* the washing-up**, **do*/wash the dishes**
- liquid soap for washing dishes: **washing-up liquid** (*noun* U)
- a cloth for washing plates, knives and forks, etc: **dishcloth**
- an electric machine that washes plates, cups, knives and forks, etc: **dishwasher** ◦ *Put everything in the dishwasher.*

- to rub dishes with a cloth to make them dry: **dry** (sth) **up**, **do* the drying up**
- to do the drying up, you use a **tea towel**

waste

- things that are not wanted ⇨ RUBBISH
- using sth carelessly ⇨ USE

watch

- looking at sth ⇨ LOOK AT
- something that tells the time ⇨ CLOCK/WATCH

water

1 water and its different forms
2 being in water
3 water in the home and garden
4 water in the street and countryside
see also LIQUID

1 water and its different forms

- the clear liquid that falls as rain and is in seas, rivers and lakes: **water** (*noun* U) ◦ *a glass of water* ◦ *rainwater* ◦ *sea water* ◦ *deep/shallow water*
- a very small rounded mass of water (or other liquid): **drop** ◦ *a raindrop* ◦ *a drop of rain* ◦ *a teardrop*
- water in very small drops on a surface or in the air: **moisture** (*noun* U)

- water that is clean and not mixed with anything else is **pure** ◦ *pure water*
- water with salt in: **salt water**
- salt water from the sea: **sea water**
- water that is not sea water: **fresh water**; living in fresh water: **freshwater** ◦ *freshwater fish*

■ dirty water
- if water is not easy to see through, it is **murky**; *opposite*: **clear** ◦ *The water in the pond was very murky and we could not see the bottom.* ◦ *the clear blue sea*
- if water is not flowing and is dirty, with an unpleasant smell, it is **stagnant**
- soft, wet earth: **mud** (*noun* U); *adjective*: **muddy** ◦ *muddy water*
- a dirty or unpleasant substance on the surface of a liquid: **scum** (*noun* U) ◦ *The river was covered in scum caused by waste from a local factory.*

■ water for drinking
- water that is safe to drink: **drinking water**
- water for drinking that contains natural minerals: **mineral water** ◦ *I'll have a mineral water please.*
- water containing bubbles of gas: **sparkling/fizzy/carbonated water**; *opposite*: **still water**
- water from the tap rather than a bottle: **tap water**

■ movement of water
- to move in a continuous way: **flow**, **run*** ◦ *a fast-flowing river* ◦ *This stream runs into the Thames.*
- a raised line of water moving on the surface of water, especially the sea: **wave**
- a very small wave or movement on the surface of the water: **ripple** ◦ *There were tiny ripples of water where the fish had come to the surface.*

▷ more on the movement of water and other liquids ⇨ LIQUID

▷ the sea ⇨ SEA

■ water at different temperatures
- to reach a high temperature where bubbles rise to the surface and the liquid changes to a gas: **boil**; to heat a liquid until it boils: **boil** sth ◦ *Water boils at 100° Celsius.* ◦ *boiling water* ◦ *The water here is not clean and you should boil it before you drink it.*
- the temperature at which a liquid boils: **boiling point**
- the hot gas that water changes into when it boils: **steam** (*noun* U) ◦ *We stopped the car because there was steam coming out of the engine.*

water *contd.*

- water that is very cold and has become solid: **ice** (*noun* U)
- to change from water into ice: **freeze***; *adjective*: **frozen**
- the temperature at which water freezes: **freezing point**

▷ more on ice ⇨ ICE

- the small drops of liquid that form when steam or warm air touches a cold surface: **condensation** (*noun* U) ◦ *When we woke up in the morning, there was condensation on the windows.*
- to change from a liquid into steam or a gas and disappear: **evaporate**; *noun* (U): **evaporation** ◦ *If you boil liquid, the water evaporates and the liquid gets thicker.*
- small drops of water that form on plants, etc during the night: **dew** (*noun* U)

▷ adjectives to describe hot or cold water or other liquids ⇨ LIQUID

2 being in water

- water that goes a long way down is **deep**; *opposite*: **shallow** ◦ *a deep puddle* ◦ *the shallow end of the swimming pool*
- how deep sth is: **depth** (*noun* C/U)

▷ more on depth ⇨ DEEP

- to die in water because you cannot breathe: **drown, be drowned**; to kill sb/sth in this way: **drown** (sb/sth) ◦ *She fell over the edge of the boat and drowned/was drowned.*
- in, and covered by, water: **under water** ◦ *The divers stayed under water for several minutes.*
- existing or happening under water: **underwater** (*adjective, adverb*) ◦ *an underwater tunnel* ◦ *to swim underwater*
- to go under water: **submerge**; to make sth do this: **submerge** sth; *adjective*: **submerged** ◦ *We could see the submarine submerging.* ◦ *Several streets were completely submerged by the floods.*
- to go down to the bottom of the water: **sink***; to make sth go down: **sink*** sth ◦ *Many ships have sunk in this part of the channel.* ◦ *They sank their boat quite deliberately.*

- to stay on or at the surface of a liquid: **float** ◦ *We could see something floating on the surface of the pond.*
- on the surface of the water; not sinking: **afloat** (*not before a noun*) ◦ *They tried to keep the boat afloat as the water started to come in.*

- to move your body through water: **swim***
- sports that people do in the water: **water sports**

▷ more on swimming and other sports ⇨ SWIM, SPORT

- to walk with bare feet in shallow water: **paddle** ◦ *We went paddling in the sea – it was too cold to swim.*
- to walk with difficulty through fairly deep water, mud, etc: **wade** ◦ *He waded into the river to try and rescue the dog.*

- covered in a liquid, especially water: **wet** ◦ *soaking wet clothes*
- completely wet: **soaked** ◦ *I got absolutely soaked in the rain.*
- to make sth completely wet: **soak** sth (**in** sth)
- material (especially for clothes) that does not let water go through is **waterproof** ◦ *a waterproof jacket/watch*

▷ more on being wet ⇨ WET/DRY

3 water in the home and garden

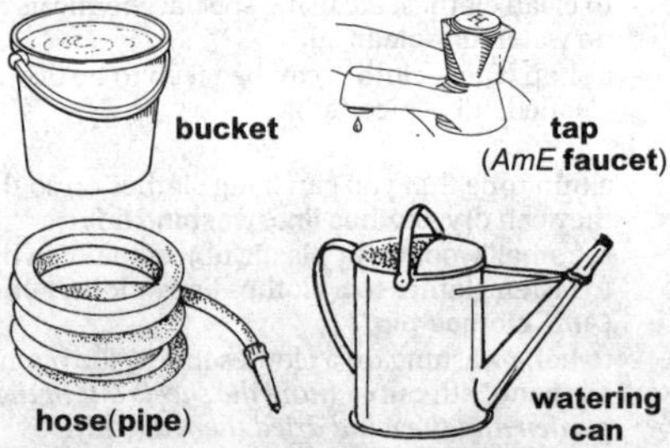

- to move the top part of a tap so that water comes out: **turn** the tap **on**; *opposite*: **turn** the tap **off**
- to cause water to flow: **run*** sth ◦ *If you run the tap for a few seconds, the water will get hot.*
- water which is available from a tap or which is coming out of a tap is **running** (water) ◦ *We stayed in a horrible hotel which had no running water.*

- to clean sb/sth or yourself using water and usually soap: **wash** (sb/sth); *noun*: **wash** ◦ *I'll give my face a quick wash and then we'll go.*

▷ more on washing ⇨ WASH

▷ the room where you wash ⇨ BATHROOM

- to give water to plants (using a watering can or hosepipe, for example): **water** sth ◦ *Don't forget to water the plants.* ◦ *The tomatoes need watering.*

■ systems which bring water to your house

- a hollow tube that carries gas or liquid: **pipe** ◦ *a water pipe* ◦ *the hot-water pipe*
- a large pipe that carries water to a building: **water main, mains** (*with singular or plural verb*) ◦ *If you want to replace that pipe, you'll have to turn the water off at the mains.*
- a container for holding water (often kept at the top of the house or in the roof): (**water**) **tank**
- a metal container used for supplying hot water in a house: **boiler, hot-water tank**

- all the pipes, water tanks, etc in a building: **plumbing** (*noun* U) ◦ *We need to get somebody to look at the plumbing.*
- a person whose job it is to put in and repair pipes, baths, sinks etc: **plumber**

▷ more on pipes ⇨ PIPE

- the system of providing and storing water: **water supply** ◦ *to turn on/off the water supply*

- to stop the supply of water to sb: **cut*** sb/sth **off** ○ *They cut us off, because we hadn't paid our water bill.*
- a situation where there is not enough water: (water) **shortage**

■ dirty water which leaves the house
- a pipe or hole that dirty water goes down to be carried away: **drain** ○ *to go down the drain* ○ *a blocked drain*
- to flow away: **drain** (**away**); to make a liquid flow away: **drain** sth ○ *I've pulled out the plug but the water isn't draining away.*
- a pipe which goes down the side of a building, especially one that carries water from the roof to a drain: **drainpipe**
- a system used for draining water away, especially from land: **drainage** (*noun* U) ○ *drainage channels*

▷ waste water from toilets ⇨ TOILET

4 water in the street and countryside
- a stream of water that flows down to the sea from higher ground: **river** ○ *The river flows through the centre of the town.*
- a small river: **stream** ○ *A small stream ran along the side of the field.*
- a long narrow hole that has been dug into the ground, especially along the side of a road or field for water to flow through: **ditch** ○ *a muddy ditch*
- a channel that is cut through land so that boats and ships can travel along it or so that water can flow to an area where it is needed: **canal** ○ *the Panama Canal*

▷ more on rivers ⇨ RIVER

- a large area of water that is surrounded by land: **lake** (*in Scotland* **loch**)
- a small area of water (often in a park or a garden): **pond** ○ *They had a fish pond in their back garden.*
- a small shallow area of water: **pool** ○ *The children played in the rock pools on the beach.*
- a small amount of water (especially rain that has gathered on the ground): **puddle**
- an area of soft wet land: **swamp, marsh, bog**; *adjectives*: **swampy, marshy, boggy** ○ *marshy land* ○ *a boggy field*

- a stream of water that falls down from a cliff or rock: **waterfall**
- an ornament (in a garden or in a town) that shoots a stream of water into the air: **fountain**

- a place where water comes up naturally from under the ground: **spring**
- a deep hole in the ground from which water is obtained: **well** ○ *to draw water from a well*
- a place in the desert where there is water and where plants grow: **oasis** (*plural* **oases**)

- (especially after heavy rain) a large amount of water that covers an area that is normally dry: **flood** ○ *There have been terrible floods all over the country.*
- to be filled with a very large amount of water: **flood**; to cause this to happen: **flood** sth ○ *If the rain continues, the rivers will flood.* ○ *Large areas of farmland have been flooded.*
- when the amount of water (in a flood, for example) becomes less, the water **subsides** ○ *After a few days, the floods subsided.*

- a large lake where water is stored: **reservoir**
- a wall built across a river to hold back the water and form a lake or a reservoir: **dam**

- a machine that is used for forcing a gas or a liquid in a particular direction: **pump** ○ *a water pump*
- to force a gas or liquid to go in a particular direction: **pump** sth ○ *Our drinking water is pumped directly from the river.*
- to supply land and crops with water by means of pipes, channels, etc: **irrigate** sth; the system of supplying water in this way: **irrigation** (*noun* U) ○ *irrigated land* ○ *an irrigation channel*

■ **MORE...**
- (used about an animal or plant) living in water: **aquatic** ○ *aquatic plants*

---

way
- how to get to a place ⇨ DIRECTION
- how far sth is ⇨ DISTANCE
- a method of doing sth ⇨ METHOD/MANNER

---

weak ⇨ STRONG/WEAK

---

weapon

see also FIGHT, WAR

- an object that is used for fighting or killing people: **weapon**
- weapons used in war: **arms** (*noun plural*) ○ *arms control/reduction*
- equipped with arms: **armed** ○ *heavily armed* ○ *armed forces* ○ *an armed man*
- weapons and military equipment: **armaments** (*noun plural*)

- weapons that use the energy produced by splitting an atom: **nuclear weapons, nuclear arms**
- weapons that use harmful chemicals to damage or destroy people or things: **chemical weapons**
- weapons that use living things to injure or kill people: **biological weapons**
- weapons that are not nuclear, chemical or biological: **conventional weapons**

■ guns and bombs
- a weapon that is used for shooting: **gun**
- a container that is filled with material that will explode if you throw it, drop it, etc: **bomb**
- a powerful exploding weapon that can travel long distances through the air: **missile**
- the bullets, bombs, etc that people need when they use a weapon: **ammunition** (*noun* U)

▷ more on bombs and guns ⇨ BOMB, GUN

weapon *contd.*

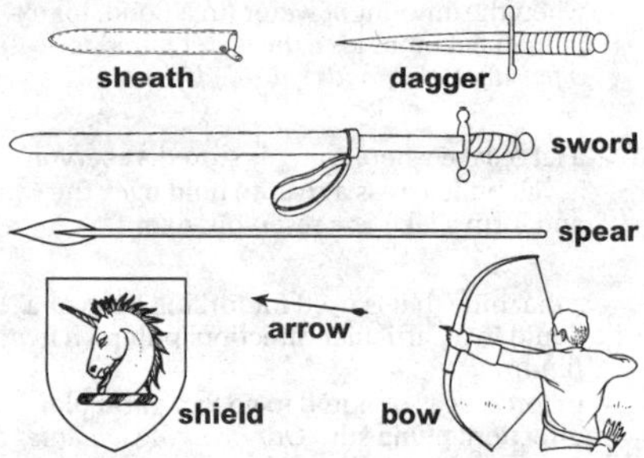

■ knives
- to hold a knife so that it is facing sb: **point** a knife **at** sb ◦ *He pointed the knife right at me and I dropped my bag.*
- to push a knife hard and deep into sb/sth: **stab** sb/sth; *noun*: **stab** ◦ *She came up behind him and stabbed him in the back.* ◦ *a stab wound*

■ gas
- gas that hurts your eyes: **tear gas** (*noun* U) ◦ *The police used tear gas to control the crowd.*
- a poisonous gas that affects the nerves: **nerve gas** (*noun* U)
- if you want to protect yourself from poisonous gas, you can wear a **gas mask**
- to kill or injure somebody with gas: **gas** sb ◦ *He was gassed in the First World War.*

■ getting or reducing weapons
- to prepare a person or country to fight by supplying weapons: **arm** (yourself/sb/sth)
- to take weapons away from sb: **disarm** sb
- (used about a country) to reduce the number of weapons that it has: **disarm**; *noun* (U): **disarmament** ◦ *nuclear disarmament*
- (used about a country) to increase, once again, the number of weapons that it has: **rearm**; *noun* (U): **rearmament**
- a situation during peacetime where countries try to have as many weapons as their enemies: **arms race**

- a person or company that makes weapons: **arms manufacturer**
- a person or company that sells weapons: **arms dealer**

wear ⇨ CLOTHES

weather

> **1** What's the weather like?
> **2** what the weather is normally like in a place
> **3** saying what the weather will be like
>
> **see also** RAIN, SNOW, STORM, WIND

1 What's the weather like?
- how hot or cold, wet or dry it is, and how much sun, wind, rain, etc there is at a certain time in a certain place: the **weather** ◦ *We had a lovely holiday even though the weather wasn't very good.* ◦ *windy/rainy/stormy/sunny weather*

■ good or bad weather
- if the weather is very good, you can say it is **lovely**, **beautiful**, **glorious**
- if the weather continues to be good, it **keeps* up** ◦ *I hope this weather keeps up for the weekend.*
- if the weather is very bad, you can say it is **awful**, **terrible**, **horrible**
- when people think they are likely to have bad weather, they say they are **in for** sth ◦ *It looks like we're in for another hard winter.*

■ bright or dull weather
- when the sun can be seen in the sky, it is **out**; when it gives out light, it **shines***, the weather is **sunny**, **bright** ◦ *The sun was shining.* ◦ *a bright, sunny day*
- bright and sunny; not raining: **fine** ◦ *Fortunately, the weather stayed fine and we had a lovely picnic.*
- when there are no clouds, the sky is **blue**, **clear**, **cloudless**

▷ more on the sun ⇨ SUN

- when there are clouds in the sky, the weather is **cloudy**, **dull**, the sky is **grey**, **overcast** ◦ *It's a rather dull, grey day.* ◦ *The sky was overcast.*

- thick, low cloud near the ground which makes it difficult to see: **fog** (*noun* C/U); when there is a fog, the weather is **foggy** ◦ *Drive carefully – there's a thick fog tonight.* ◦ *patches of fog* ◦ *foggy weather*
- thin fog: **mist** (*noun* C/U); when there is a mist, the weather is **misty** ◦ *The mist came down so fast we couldn't find our way back.* ◦ *a misty day*
- if it is foggy and you cannot see very far so that it is dangerous to drive fast, there is poor **visibility** (*noun* U)

■ warm or cold weather
- not cold; quite hot but not very hot: **warm** ◦ *a warm evening*
- warmer than expected (for example, in winter) **mild** ◦ *a mild winter*
- very warm: **hot**
- very hot: (*informal*) **boiling**, (*informal*) **boiling hot**, (*informal*) **scorching**
- a period of very hot weather: **heatwave**

- when the air is heavy and there is no wind, for example before a storm, the weather is **close** ◦ *It's very close – I think there's going to be a storm.*

- not warm: **cold**; rather cold, but not very cold: **cool**
- very cold, with the temperature below zero: (*informal*) **freezing**, (*informal*) **freezing cold**, **bitterly cold**, **icy** ◦ *a freezing cold day* ◦ *bitterly cold weather*
- the weather conditions when the temperature falls below freezing-point: **frost** (*noun* C/U) ◦ *There was a heavy frost last night.*
- a very thin layer of small thin pieces of ice on the ground, the trees, etc: **frost** (*noun* U)

- very cold, with frost: **frosty** ◦ *The car windows were covered in frost.* ◦ *a frosty morning*
- pleasantly cold: **crisp**, **fresh** ◦ *a fresh crisp morning in January*
- unpleasantly cold: **chilly**; *noun (singular)*: **chill** ◦ *Wrap up well, there's a chill in the air.*
- the measurement of how hot or cold sth is: **temperature** ◦ *The temperature will fall to ten degrees below zero in some places tonight.*

▷ measuring temperature ⇨ HOT

■ wet or dry weather

- having a lot of rain: **wet** ◦ *a wet day* ◦ *wet weather*
- wet weather: **the wet** ◦ *Don't go out in the wet or you'll catch a cold.*
- when there is a lot of water in cold air, it is **damp**
- when there is a lot of water in warm air, it is **humid** ◦ *The air feels really humid today.*
- too warm and humid: **muggy**, **sticky**
- small drops of water which form on plants or grass in the early morning: **dew** (*noun* U) ◦ *The grass was covered in dew this morning.*
- when it is not raining, it is **dry** ◦ *a dry day*

2 what the weather is normally like in a place

- the normal weather conditions of a particular country: **climate** ◦ *What's the climate like in your country?* ◦ *a hot/warm/cold/cool/dry/wet climate*
- the hot, wet climate of countries close to the Equator is a **tropical** climate
- the cool climate of Europe, etc is a **temperate** climate
- in a temperate climate there are four **seasons**: **spring**, **summer**, **autumn**, **winter**

▷ more on the seasons ⇨ SEASON

- how hot it usually is in a place: (**the**) **heat** (*noun* U); *adjective*: **hot** ◦ *I don't think I'd like to live in Africa – I couldn't stand the heat.*
- how cold it usually is: (**the**) **cold** (*noun* U) ; *adjective*: **cold** ◦ *getting used to a cold climate*
- how wet the air is (in a usually warm place): (**the**) **humidity** (*noun* U) ; *adjective*: **humid** ◦ *We never got used to the humidity of the coast.*
- how wet the air is (in a usually cold place): (**the**) **damp** (*noun* U); *adjective*: **damp** ◦ *the damp of the Highlands in winter*
- the amount of rain that falls in a certain place within a certain period (for example, a year): **rainfall** (*noun* U) ◦ *an average annual rainfall of 10 cm*

3 saying what the weather will be like

- the radio or television broadcast that tells you what the weather will be like today, tomorrow, or for the next few days: **weather forecast** ◦ *Have you heard the weather forecast for tomorrow?*
- the person who presents a weather forecast: **weatherman**, **weathergirl**, (*formal*) **weather forecaster**
- a map or chart that shows the weather forecast: **weather map**, **weather chart**
- to study the weather and say what it will be like: **forecast** sth ◦ *They're forecasting strong winds and rain.*
- the study of the weather: **meteorology** (*noun* U); *adjective*: **meteorological** ◦ *abnormal meteorological conditions*
- a person who studies the weather: **meteorologist**
- a piece of equipment which is used to forecast the weather by measuring the air pressure: **barometer**

■ **MORE ...**

- when you get used to a new climate, you **acclimatize** ◦ *I don't think I ever really acclimatized to the cold and damp of that place.*

---

wedding

1 people at a wedding
2 what happens at a wedding
see also MARRY

1 people at a wedding

- the woman who gets married at a wedding: **bride**
- the man who gets married at a wedding: **groom**, **bridegroom**
- the two people being married: the **couple**, the **bride and groom** ◦ *What a beautiful couple!*
- the man who helps the groom at a wedding: **best man**
- a girl who stands behind the bride during a wedding: **bridesmaid**; a boy who does this: **page** (**boy**)
- a person who is invited to a wedding: **wedding guest**

2 what happens at a wedding

- the ceremony in which a man and a woman are officially joined as husband and wife: **wedding** ◦ *I've been invited to a wedding on Saturday.* ◦ *a wedding invitation* ◦ *the wedding dress* (= the dress worn by the bride)
- the day when a man and woman get married is their **wedding day**
- a wedding in a church: **church wedding** ◦ *We want to have a church wedding.*
- a place where people get married if they do not get married in a church: **registry office**
- the religious part of a wedding: (**marriage/wedding**) **ceremony**, (**marriage**) **service**
- to give a woman to her new husband formally during the wedding ceremony (this is usually done by the bride's father): **give*** sb **away** ◦ *The bride's father gave her away.*
- the formal promises that you make to sb in a wedding ceremony: (**marriage**) **vows**
- a ring that the bride or groom gives to the other during the wedding ceremony: **wedding ring** ◦ *He put the ring on her finger.*
- a party after a wedding ceremony: (**wedding**) **reception** ◦ *The wedding reception's being held in a hotel near the church.*

wedding *contd.*

- to talk in front of all the guests: **make* a speech**; what is said: **speech** ◦ *The bride's father made a speech.* ◦ *The best man's speech was very funny.*
- to hold up your glass and wish success and happiness to sb, before you drink: **toast** sb, **drink* to** sb/sth; *noun*: **toast** ◦ *Let us drink to their future happiness.* ◦ *I'd like to propose a toast to the bride and groom – may they find health and happiness.*
- a cake made especially for a wedding: (**wedding**) **cake**

- the holiday that a man and woman take just after they have got married: **honeymoon** ◦ *Where did you go for your honeymoon?* ◦ *They're on their honeymoon.*
- a room in a hotel for two people who have just been married: **bridal suite**

■ **MORE ...**
- the day of a wedding which is celebrated every year: **wedding anniversary**
- the celebration of 25 years of marriage: **silver wedding**; of 50 years of marriage: **golden wedding**; of 60 years of marriage: **diamond wedding** ◦ *They are celebrating their golden wedding this year.*

week

see also DAY, YEAR

- a period of seven days: **week** ◦ *We're going away for a couple of weeks.* ◦ *It was a full two weeks before they replied to my letter.* ◦ *I hope to finish this job in about a week.*
- happening once a week: **weekly** (*adjective, adverb*) ◦ *a weekly magazine* ◦ *Wages are paid weekly.*

- the week after this: **next week**
- the week before this: **last week**
- the week after next week: **the week after next**
- the week before last week: **the week before last**
- a week from today: **a week today**
- a week from tomorrow: **a week tomorrow**, **tomorrow week**
- a week from Monday, etc: **Monday**, etc **week, a week on Monday**, etc ◦ *It's my birthday a week on Tuesday.*
- seven days before yesterday, last Monday, etc: **a week yesterday, a week last Monday**, etc

- the seven days of the week: **Sunday, Monday, Tuesday, Wednesday, Thursday, Friday, Saturday**
- abbreviations for the names of the weeks: **Sun, Mon, Tue, Wed, Thur, Fri, Sat**

- a period of two weeks: **fortnight** ◦ *We're going to Greece for a fortnight.* ◦ *a fortnight's holiday*
- happening once a fortnight: **fortnightly** (*adjective, adverb*) ◦ *a fortnightly meeting* ◦ *We meet fortnightly.*

- the part of the week when you usually go to work: **week** ◦ *I work a 40-hour week.*
- any day of the week except Saturday and Sunday: **weekday**
- Saturday and Sunday: **weekend** ◦ *I get up early during the week but at the weekend I laze around in bed.* ◦ *What are you doing this weekend?*

weight

1 being heavy or light
2 weighing sb/sth
3 lifting and moving heavy things
lifting heavy objects in sport ⇨ SPORT

see also SIZE, BIG/SMALL

1 being heavy or light

- how heavy sb/sth is: **weight** (*noun* U) ◦ *The weight of the bag is 20 kg.* ◦ *5 kg in weight*
- to have a certain weight: **weigh ...** ◦ *How much do you weigh?* ◦ *This suitcase weighs rather a lot! What on earth have you got in it?* ◦ *She weighed three kilos at birth.*

- a person or thing that weighs a lot and is difficult to lift or move is **heavy** ◦ *a heavy load* ◦ *heavy machinery* ◦ *This suitcase is too heavy to carry.*
- to be extremely heavy: (*informal*) **weigh a ton** ◦ *I can't lift this, it weighs a ton.*
- (used about a person) weighing too much: **overweight** ◦ *He's very overweight – he should go on a diet.*

▷ being fat ⇨ FAT/THIN/THICK

- a person or thing that does not weigh a lot is **light** ◦ *Why is your bag so much lighter than mine?* ◦ *a light cotton shirt*
- extremely light: (*informal*) **as light as a feather** ◦ *I can lift her up – she's as light as a feather.*

■ changing your body weight
- to get fatter: **put* ... on, put* on weight** ◦ *I've put on a few pounds recently.* ◦ *She's really put on weight since she gave up smoking.*
- to become thinner: **lose* ..., lose* weight** ◦ *I lost over a kilo when I was ill last month.*
- to do a lot of exercise in order to lose weight: **work** sth **off** ◦ *I'm going to the gym to try and work off some of this fat.*

▷ more on exercise ⇨ EXERCISE

2 weighing sb/sth

- a machine used for weighing people or things: **scales** (*noun plural*) ◦ *kitchen scales* ◦ *weigh yourself on the bathroom scales*
- to find the weight of sb/sth: **weigh** sb/sth ◦ *Have you weighed yourself recently?*
- to measure a quantity of sth (especially food): **weigh** sth **out** ◦ *Weigh out all the ingredients before you start cooking.*

■ measurements of weight

metric measurements	
a unit used to measure small amounts of sth, for example food	**gram (g)**
1 000 grams	**kilo, kilogram (kg)**
1 000 kilograms	**tonne**

non-metric measurements	
a unit used for measuring small amounts of sth, for example food	**ounce (oz)**
16 ounces	**pound (lb)**
14 pounds (used for weighing people)	**stone**
2 240 pounds	**ton**

■ comparing the metric and non-metric systems
- 1 ounce = 28.35 grams
- 1 pound = 0.454 kilogram
- 1 stone = 6.356 kilograms
- 1 ton = 1.016 tonnes

3 lifting and moving heavy things
- something heavy which is carried or supported: **load** ◦ *These lorries carry very heavy loads.*
- a heavy load which has to be supported: **weight** (**of** sth) ◦ *I don't think that chair can support his weight.* ◦ *The shelf collapsed under the weight of the books.*
- to support the weight of sth: **carry** sth, **hold*** sth ◦ *How many people does this lift carry?* ◦ *How much weight do you think it can hold?*
- the weight of sth pressing on sth else: **pressure** (*noun* U) ◦ *If you stand on it you'll put too much pressure on it and it'll break.*

- to pull sth heavy along with difficulty: **drag** sth ◦ *We dragged the boat down to the sea.*
- to put sth heavy down in a careless way: **dump** sth (**down**) ◦ *We dumped our bags in the hall and rushed upstairs.*
- the noise of sth heavy dropping: **thud** ◦ *The man fell to the ground with a thud.*

welcome ⇨ VISIT

west ⇨ DIRECTION

wet/dry

see also WATER, RAIN, WEATHER

■ wet
- covered in a liquid, especially water: **wet** ◦ *You'd better take an umbrella or you'll get wet.* ◦ *to feel cold and wet*
- to make sth wet: **wet** sth ◦ *Wet the cloth a bit before you wipe the table.*

- very wet: **soaking wet**, **wet through** ◦ *to get soaking wet* ◦ *soaking wet shoes/trousers* ◦ *You can't wear these trousers, they're wet through.*
- completely wet; dripping with water: **soaked** (**to the skin**), **drenched** ◦ *They went sailing in the rain and got soaked to the skin.* ◦ *We went for a walk in the rain and came back absolutely drenched.*

- to become completely wet, usually by being in water for a long time: **soak** (**in** sth); to make sth completely wet in this way: **soak** sth (**in** sth); *noun*: **soak** ◦ *Put the clothes in cold water and just let them soak.* ◦ *Soak very dirty dishes in hot soapy water.* ◦ *I'm going to have a long soak in the bath.*

- (used about water or other liquids) to pass into or through sth: **soak into/through** sth, **soak in** ◦ *Quick, mop up that wine before it soaks into the carpet.* ◦ *The water soaked through my bag and onto my books.*
- to draw a liquid into sth: **soak** sth **up** ◦ *We put down newspapers to soak up the water on the floor.*

- slightly wet: **moist** ◦ *moist lips* ◦ *a moist cake*
- to cause sth to become slightly wet: **moisten** sth ◦ *Moisten your fingertips to turn the pages.* ◦ *to moisten your lips*
- slightly wet, making you feel uncomfortable: **damp** ◦ *damp clothes/hair*
- water in small drops on a surface or in the air: **moisture** (*noun* U) ◦ *It's the moisture in the air which makes biscuits go soft.*

- to fly about in drops and make sb/sth wet: **splash** (**on/over/onto**) sb/sth; to cause a liquid to do this: **splash** sth **on/over/onto** sb/sth, **splash** sb/sth (**with** sth) ◦ *The car went through a puddle and splashed rainwater all over my trousers.* ◦ *I splashed my face with cold water.*
- an act or sound of splashing: **splash** ◦ *The dog jumped into the water with a big splash.*

- (used about a surface or object) difficult to move over or to hold because it is wet: **slippery** ◦ *Be careful, the floor's a bit slippery.*

■ dry
- without liquid in it or on it: **dry** ◦ *dry clothes/hair* ◦ *to keep sth dry*
- completely dry: **bone dry**, (**as**) **dry as a bone** ◦ *The clothes have been in the sun, so they're bone dry.*
- food or plants that have had the water removed are **dried** ◦ *dried milk/fruits*

■ drying wet things
- to become dry: **dry**; to cause sth to become dry: **dry** sth ◦ *If you hang the clothes outside, they'll dry in the sun.* ◦ *to dry your hair with a towel*

wet / dry *contd.*

- to become completely dry or too dry: **dry out**; to cause this to happen: **dry** sth **out**
- (used about a river, for example) to have no more water in it: **dry up** ◦ *The river dried up during the hot summer.* ◦ *The food was in the oven for so long that it completely dried up.*

- a piece of cloth or paper that you use to dry sb/sth: **towel** ◦ *a bath towel* ◦ *a paper towel*
- a piece of cloth that you use to dry dishes: **tea towel**
- a machine that you use for drying hair: **hair-dryer**

▷ washing and drying ⇨ **WASH**

wheel

see also CAR, BICYCLE

- a circular object that moves round and makes it possible for a car, bicycle, etc to move; a similar object in a machine: **wheel**
- the outside edge of a wheel: **rim**
- the round, central part of a wheel: **hub**
- one of the thin pieces of metal that join the rim to the hub on some types of wheel: **spoke**
- a bar that joins a pair of wheels on a vehicle: **axle**
- a curved cover over a wheel on a bicycle, car, etc: **mudguard**

▷ picture at **BICYCLE**

- when a wheel moves, it **goes*** **round**, **turns**, (*more formal*) **revolves**; to make a wheel go round: **turn** sth; *nouns*: **turn**, **revolution** ◦ *Slowly the wheels of the train began to turn.* ◦ *a single turn of the wheel* ◦ *100 revolutions per minute*
- to turn fast: **spin***; to cause sth to spin fast: **spin*** sth

- to push or pull sth that has wheels: **wheel** sth ◦ *I wheeled my bike up the hill.*

- a deep track that a wheel makes in soft ground: **rut**

■ tyres
- a thick rubber ring that fits around the outside of a wheel: **tyre** (*AmE* **tire**)
- the material used to make tyres: **rubber** (*noun* U)
- the raised pattern on the outside surface of a tyre: **tread** (*noun* C/U) ◦ *I think the tread on that tyre is getting a bit thin.*
- the hollow rubber tube inside a tyre: **inner tube**
- a device that controls the flow of air in an inner tube or tyre: **valve**

■ repairing a tyre
- when a tyre has no air in it, it is **flat**
- a flat tyre: (*especially AmE*) **flat**
- a hole in a tyre or inner tube: **puncture** ◦ *I'm sorry we're late – we had a puncture on the M4.* ◦ *to mend a puncture*
- when a tyre or inner tube breaks open suddenly and violently because it has too much air inside or because it gets a hole in it, it **bursts***, **punctures**; *adjective*: **burst**

- to fill a tyre with air, you **pump** it **up**, **blow*** it **up**, (*formal*) **inflate** it
- a machine that you use to pump up a tyre: **pump** ◦ *a bicycle pump* ◦ *a foot pump* (= a pump that you operate with your feet)
- a piece of rubber that you use to put over a puncture: **patch**
- to replace a wheel that has a puncture with a another wheel: **change a wheel**
- a tool that you use to lift a car, etc so that you can change a wheel: **jack**
- to lift a car, etc with a jack: **jack** sth **up**
- an extra wheel that you keep in your car so that you can replace a wheel that has a puncture: **spare (wheel)**

when ⇨ TIME

where ⇨ PLACE[1]

white ⇨ COLOUR

whole ⇨ PART/WHOLE

wide / narrow

see also SIZE, LONG / SHORT[2]

- large in size from one side to the other: **wide**, **broad**; *opposite*: **narrow** ◦ *The curtains weren't wide enough for the window.* ◦ *a broad expanse of desert* ◦ *broad shoulders/hips* ◦ *a broad smile* ◦ *a narrow path*
- as wide or as open as possible: **wide** (*adverb*) ◦ *Her eyes opened wide in amazement.* ◦ *a wide open door* ◦ *with legs wide apart*

Note: wide and **broad** mean the same, but **wide** is much more frequently used when you are talking about the distance between one side of something and the other. **Broad** is often used to talk about parts of the body and sometimes about geographical features like valleys and mountain ranges.

- the measurement of sth from one side to the other: **width** (*noun* C/U), **breadth** (*noun* C/U) ◦ *It was about the width of the palm of my hand.* ◦ *five metres in width*
- having a certain width: **wide** ◦ *The new swimming pool is 50 metres long and 10 metres wide.*
- a measurement that is equal to the width of sth: **width** ◦ *Today Sally managed to swim a complete width of the pool.* ◦ *Dress material comes in different widths.*

- to become wider: **widen** (**out**), **broaden** (**out**); to make sth wider: **widen** sth, **broaden** sth ◦ *As it nears the sea, the river broadens considerably.* ◦ *They want to widen the road.*
- to become more narrow: **narrow** ◦ *At this point, the path narrows.*

wife ⇨ MARRY

wild

- plants and animals ⇨ **PLANT, ANIMAL**

– wild countryside ⇨ **COUNTRY²**

willing

1 willing
2 not willing
saying yes or no ⇨ **YES / NO**
see also WANT

1 willing

– if you agree that you will do sth, you are **willing** (**to** do sth) (*not before a noun*), **ready** (**to** do sth) (*not before a noun*), **prepared** (**to** do sth) (*not before a noun*); *noun* (U): **willingness** ◦ *I'm not willing to work on Sundays.* ◦ *'Would you be prepared to lend us the van next week?' 'Yes, of course.'* ◦ *Thanks for your willingness to help.*
– very willing to do sth: **eager** (**to** do sth), **keen** (**to** do sth), **keen on** doing sth ◦ *eager volunteers* ◦ *keen supporters* ◦ *I'm quite keen to get involved in the project.* ◦ *Are you really keen on joining the army?*

– willing to help: **helpful** ◦ *I wish he would try and be more helpful.*
– happy to help: **willing** (*adverb* **willingly**) ◦ *willing assistants* ◦ *He offered his services willingly.*
– willing to do what sb wants: **cooperative**
– if you do sth without being forced or asked, you do it **of** your **own accord** ◦ *I didn't have to ask him. He did it entirely of his own accord.*

– to show that you are willing to do sth, you can use **will**, **would** ◦ *I'll phone her now if you want.* ◦ *I won't accept their offer.* ◦ *He said he wouldn't help me.*
– to say that you are willing to do sth: **agree to** sth ◦ *Eric's agreed to lend us his car for the weekend.*
– willing to leave things the way they are or as others want them: **content** (**to** do sth), **content** (**with** sth) ◦ *He's content to stay at home and look after the children.* ◦ *I'm quite content with my life at the moment.*

2 not willing

– not ready to do sth: **unwilling** (*adverb* **unwillingly**); *noun* (U): **unwillingness** ◦ *She's unwilling to help.* ◦ *Chris went to school unwillingly.* ◦ *his unwillingness to get involved*
– not willing to do what sb wants; not being helpful: **uncooperative** ◦ *She's being very uncooperative about the move.*
– very unwilling: **grudging** (*adverb* **grudgingly**) ◦ *grudging thanks* ◦ *He grudgingly agreed to give me the money.*

– to be unwilling to do sth because you are not sure if it is right: **hesitate** (**to** do sth), **hold* back** (**from** doing sth) ◦ *She hesitated to accept his offer.* ◦ *They held back until they had more information about the project.*
– not willing and therefore slow to agree to do sth: **reluctant** (*adverb* **reluctantly**); *noun* (U): **reluctance** ◦ *I was reluctant to lend him the car because he's such a fast driver.* ◦ *I'm not surprised at your reluctance to go and see him.*

■ refusing
– to say or show that you do not want to do, give, accept, etc sth: **refuse** (sth), **refuse to** do sth; noun (C/U): **refusal** ◦ *I offered him a lift but he refused.* ◦ *She refused to believe that he had gone for good.* ◦ *They refused to help us.* ◦ *We were surprised at his refusal to accept the job.*

– to refuse to accept sb/sth: **reject** sb/sth; *noun* (C/U): **rejection** ◦ *Our offer has been rejected.*
– to refuse to allow sb to go into a place: **turn** sb **away** ◦ *We were turned away from the night club.*
– to refuse to accept sb who has applied for a job: **turn** sb **down**
– to refuse to accept an offer or suggestion: **turn** sth **down** ◦ *My suggestion was turned down.*

– not wanting to do what other people want you to do: **stubborn** (*adverb* **stubbornly**); *noun* (U): **stubbornness** ◦ *She's too stubborn to apologize.* ◦ *He stubbornly refused to let her go.*

■ **MORE ...**
– to refuse directly without any discussion: **refuse point-blank** ◦ *I asked him to let me go but he refused point-blank.*
– to refuse to change your mind: **stand* firm** ◦ *We should stand firm by our decision.*
– to refuse to listen to what sb is saying: **turn a deaf ear** (**to** sb/sth) ◦ *I tried to convince him that my plan was sensible but he turned a deaf ear to me.*

win / lose

see also FIGHT, WAR, ATHLETICS, COMPETITION, GAME, RACE², SPORT

– to be first, second, third, ... last in a competition: **come* first**, **second**, **third**, **... last** ◦ *She came second in the chess competition.*
– the person who comes second: **runner-up**

■ winning
– to be the best, the first or the most successful in sth: **win*** (sth) ◦ *to win a match/race/battle* ◦ *I never win at cards.* (= I never win when I play cards)
– an act of winning: **win**, (*more formal*) **victory** ◦ *They had a convincing win.* ◦ *a decisive/overwhelming victory for the visiting team*
– a great success in a competition: (*formal*) **triumph** ◦ *It was a great triumph for such a young competitor.*
– a person who wins: **winner**, (*more formal*) **victor**; *adjective*: **victorious** ◦ *a victorious army*

– to receive sth for winning a competition, race, etc: **win*** sth ◦ *to win a prize/medal*

– to win a game, fight, vote, etc against sb/sth, or to be better than sb: **defeat** sb/sth, **beat*** sb/sth, **get* the better of** sb/sth ◦ *They were defeated in the first match of the season.* ◦ *Ann usually beats John at chess.* ◦ *Our team was soundly beaten in the quiz.*
– to defeat sb because you are stronger than they are: **overpower** sb

win/lose *contd.*

– if you have not been beaten, you are **unbeaten**, **undefeated**
– if you cannot be beaten, you are **unbeatable** ◦ *This team haven't lost for sixteen matches; they seem completely unbeatable.*

■ losing
– not to win sth: **lose*** (sth) ◦ *I've never lost at badminton with George* (= I've never lost when playing badminton with George). ◦ *to lose a battle/war*
– to lose a battle, war, competition, etc: **be beaten/defeated** (**by** sb/sth) ◦ *We were badly beaten by the other team.*
– an act of losing a fight, war, competition, etc: **defeat** (*noun* C/U) ◦ *They refused to admit defeat and kept fighting.*
– a person or a group that loses: **loser**

– to stop trying to win: **give* up** ◦ *Chelsea gave up after Leeds had scored their third goal.*
– to accept that you have been defeated: **give* in** (**to** sb/sth) ◦ *The rebels gave in after losing half their men in ten days of fighting.*
– to stop fighting and admit that you have lost: **surrender** (**to** sb); *noun* (C/U): **surrender** ◦ *They put their hands up and surrendered.* ◦ *to wave a white flag in surrender*

■ equal
– to finish a competition with the same result as someone else: **draw*** (**with** sb), **tie** (**with** sb); *nouns*: **draw**, **tie** ◦ *We tied for first place.* ◦ *The match ended in a draw.*
– a competition in which two winners are equally good is a **dead heat**
– a competition where the difference between first place and second place is very small is **close** ◦ *It was very close – the judges found it difficult to decide.* ◦ *a close contest*

wind

movement of air in a room or building ⇨ AIR
see also WEATHER

– the movement of air across the earth: **wind** (*noun* C/U) ◦ *a cold/warm wind* ◦ *a tree blown over by the wind* ◦ *There was a lot of wind and rain all day.*
– with a lot of wind: **windy** ◦ *windy weather* ◦ *a windy night*
– a wind which comes from the north/south/east/west: **north/south/east/west wind**

– when it is windy, the wind **blows*** ◦ *The wind is blowing harder than ever.*
– to fly away because of the wind: **blow* away, be blown away** ◦ *All his papers blew away.* ◦ *The roof of the house had been blown completely away.*
– to fall off sth because of the wind: **blow* off, be blown off** ◦ *My hat blew off in the wind.*
– to fall down because of the wind: **blow* over, be blown over** ◦ *The wind was so strong I was nearly blown over.*

■ strong wind
– a wind that is blowing hard is a **strong** wind
– a very strong wind: **gale**, **hurricane**; different kinds of strong circular wind: **cyclone**, **tornado**, **typhoon**, **whirlwind**
– a short period of strong wind and heavy rain or snow: **storm**; *adjective*: **stormy** ◦ *a violent storm* ◦ *stormy weather*
– a strong sudden movement of wind: **gust** ◦ *gusts of wind up to 100 mph*
– when a strong wind makes a noise, it **howls**, **whistles** ◦ *We could hear the wind whistling through the trees.*

▷ more on storms ⇨ STORM

■ wind which is not strong
– a wind that is not strong is **light**, **gentle** ◦ *a light south-westerly wind*
– a light wind: **breeze**; when there is a breeze, the weather is **breezy** ◦ *a gentle breeze* ◦ *a sea breeze* ◦ *a breezy day*
– a small amount of gentle wind: **breath** of wind ◦ *There was not even a breath of wind.*

■ cold wind
– a very cold wind is **biting**, **freezing**, **icy** ◦ *a biting north wind*

■ when the wind stops
– when the wind stops, it **drops**, **dies down**, (*formal*) **subsides**
– when there is no wind, the weather is **calm**, **still** ◦ *The wind died down and everything was still.*

■ **MORE ...**
– the most common wind direction in a particular place: **prevailing wind** ◦ *The prevailing wind is from the west.*

– a tall building with long arms (**sails**) that stick out from it and turn in the wind; used for grinding corn, producing electricity, etc: **windmill**
– a place where there are several windmills used for producing electricity: **wind farm**

window

see also HOUSE, BUILDING, ROOM, DOOR

– an opening in a building, car, etc that you can see through and which lets light in: **window** ◦ *the upstairs/downstairs windows* ◦ *She was leaning out of the window and waving at us.* ◦ *a window seat on a train/aeroplane* ◦ *a wide open window* ◦ *All the windows were shut.* ◦ *I sat looking out of the window.* ◦ *I've seen what I want in the window* (= a shop window). ◦ *My bedroom window overlooks the park.*
– a small, round window in a ship: **porthole**

▷ car windows ⇨ CAR

– the material that windows are made of: **glass** (*noun* U); one piece of glass in a window: **pane** ◦ *a pane of glass* ◦ *a window pane*
– the arrangement of two layers of glass in a window: **double-glazing** (*noun* U); a window or building that uses this system is **double-glazed** ◦ *Has your house got double-glazing?*

- a person whose job is to clean windows: **window cleaner**

- the wood or metal that goes round the outside of a window: (**window**) **frame**
- a long thin piece of wood or stone that is underneath a window (either inside or outside the building): **window sill**
- a box on an outside window sill containing flowers: **window box**

- a wooden or metal cover that is fixed on the outside of a window and that can be open or shut: **shutter**
- one of several thin, straight pieces of metal in front of a window or door: **bar** ◦ *There were bars at the window to stop thieves breaking into the house.*

- a piece of material that can be moved sideways to cover a window: **curtain** ◦ *to draw* (= open or close) *the curtains*
- a piece of material that can be pulled down to cover a window: **blind** ◦ *Can you pull down the blinds?*
- a kind of blind that is made from horizontal strips of plastic: **venetian blind**

■ opening and shutting a window
- to move a window so that air can enter a building, car, etc: **open** sth; *opposite*: **close** sth, **shut** sth ◦ *May I open the window?* ◦ *Would you mind closing the window?*
- to close and lock a window: **fasten** sth ◦ *Make sure your doors and windows are securely fastened.*

▷ more on opening and closing doors, windows, etc ⇨ **OPEN/SHUT, LOCK/CHAIN**

wine

see also ALCOHOL

- an alcoholic drink made from grapes: **wine** (*noun* U/C) ◦ *Shall we have wine with our meal?* ◦ *South African wines* (= types of wine) ◦ *A large red wine* (= glass of wine), *please.*

- wine that has more sugar is **sweet**; *opposite*: **dry** ◦ *dry white wine*
- pale yellow wine is called **white** (**wine**); dark red wine is called **red** (**wine**); between white and red: **ros** (*noun* U/C) ◦ *Shall we have red wine or white?* ◦ *I bought a bottle of rosé for supper.*
- wine that has air bubbles: **sparkling wine** (*noun* U/C)

- a strong wine, originally from Spain, that is usually drunk before a meal: **sherry** (*noun* U/C) ◦ *Would you like another sherry?*
- a strong wine, originally from Portugal, that is usually drunk after a meal: **port** (*noun* U/C)
- an expensive sparkling wine from Champagne in France: **champagne** (*noun* U/C) ◦ *Everybody celebrated with a glass of champagne.*

- wine which is cheap and of poor quality: (*informal*) **plonk** (*noun* U)

- wine that is normally served by a particular restaurant: **house wine** ◦ *We'll have a carafe* (= a kind of bottle) *of the house red.*

■ drinking wine
- a glass that you drink wine from: **wineglass**; a glass with wine, etc in it: **glass of** sth ◦ *I'll have a glass of wine.*
- a bottle in which wine is sold: **wine bottle**; a bottle with wine, etc in it: **bottle of** sth ◦ *You can take your empty wine bottles to the bottle bank.* ◦ *We celebrated with a bottle of champagne.*
- the thing which stops the wine from coming out of the bottle: **cork**
- to remove the cork: **open** sth, **uncork** sth ◦ *Shall I open the wine now?*
- the thing that you use to take the cork out: **corkscrew**

▷ picture at **CONTAINER**

- a special bar where people go to drink wine: **wine bar**
- a shop where wine and other alcoholic drinks can be bought: **off-licence** (*AmE* **package store**)

▷ more on bars and pubs ⇨ **BAR/PUB**

■ making wine
- the fruit that wine is made from: **grape** ◦ *white/black grapes*
- the plant on which grapes grow: **vine**
- an area of land where vines grow and the place where wine is made: **vineyard**
- an underground room where wine is kept: **cellar**
- when the sugar in grapes, etc turns to alcohol, it **ferments**; *noun* (U): **fermentation**

■ **MORE...**
- a person or a business that sells wine: **wine merchant**
- an event when a group of people try different wines: **wine tasting** ◦ *Are you going to the wine tasting this evening?*

- the solid pieces at the bottom of a bottle of wine: **the dregs** ◦ *'Is there any wine left?' 'Just the dregs, I'm afraid.'*

wing

- of a bird ⇨ **BIRD**[1]
- of an aeroplane ⇨ **PLANE**
- flying ⇨ **FLY**

winter ⇨ SEASON

wire

uses of wire ⇨ **ELECTRICITY, WALL/FENCE/HEDGE**

- a long, thin piece of metal that can bend, that is used for carrying electricity, making fences, etc: **wire** (*noun* C/U) ◦ *birds sitting on the telephone wires* ◦ *a piece of copper wire* ◦ *a wire coat hanger*
- a set of wires covered with plastic, etc that carry electricity or signals: **cable** (*noun* C/U) ◦ *overhead power cables*

wire *contd.*

– a tool for cutting wire: **wire-cutters** (*noun plural*), **pliers** (*noun plural*) ◦ *a pair of wire-cutters* ◦ *Have you got some pliers?*

wise ⇨ CLEVER

wish

– wanting sth very much ⇨ WANT
– saying that you hope sb will have sth ⇨ HOPE

woman

women in families ⇨ FAMILY
the two sexes ⇨ SEX[1]
see also CHILD, MAN

– an adult female person: **woman** (*plural* **women**), (*formal*) **lady** (*plural* **ladies**) ◦ *Is there a lady here called Mrs. Richards?*
– a young adult woman: **young woman**
– what you call a woman when you talk to her: (*formal*) **madam** (*AmE* **ma'am**) ◦ *Excuse me, madam.*

– a person who has the physical characteristics of a woman or girl is **female**; *noun*: **female** ◦ *the female sex*
– being or behaving like a woman: **feminine**; *noun* (U): **femininity** ◦ *feminine behaviour*

■ titles before a woman's name
– used as a title before a married woman's name: **Mrs**
– used as a title before the name of a woman who is not married: **Miss**
– used as a title before a married or single woman's name: **Ms** ◦ *Dear Ms Anderson . . .*
– the title for sb who is a doctor: **Dr** (short for Doctor)
– a title for a woman who has a high social position (usually with a lot of money or property): **Lady** ◦ *Lady Bracknall*

■ women in relationships
– the person that a man is married to: **wife** (*plural* **wives**)
– the person that sb lives with, as if they were married: **partner**
– if a man has formally promised to marry a woman, she is his **fianc e**
– a woman with whom a man has a romantic and/or sexual relationship; a female friend of another woman: **girlfriend**
– a woman or man who is having a sexual relationship with sb, outside marriage: **lover**; a woman in this kind of relationship: **mistress**

– a woman who is not married is **single, unmarried**
– a woman who is divorced (= was married but is no longer married): **divorcee**
– a woman whose husband has died: **widow**

– a woman who is sexually attracted to other women: **lesbian, gay**; *adjectives*: **lesbian, gay**

▷ love, sex and marriage ⇨ LOVE, SEX[2], MARRY

wood

see also TREE

– a hard material that forms the trunk or branches of a tree, and is used for burning or for making objects: **wood** (*noun* U) ◦ *Most furniture is made of wood.*
– made of wood: **wooden** ◦ *wooden furniture* ◦ *wooden toys*
– wood from an oak tree, pine tree, etc: **oak** (*noun* U), **pine** (*noun* U), etc ◦ *a solid oak table*

– wood that is going to be used for building: **timber** (*noun* U)
– the trunk or a large branch of a tree that has been cut down: **log** ◦ *The logs are transported from the forests to the sawmills in large trucks.*
– a long flat piece of wood that is used for making for floors, etc: **plank**

– a short, thin piece of wood, often from the branch of a tree: **stick** ◦ *I'm going to look for some sticks to start the fire.*
– a very small, sharp piece of wood: **splinter** ◦ *I've got a splinter in my finger!*

– wood that is used for burning on a fire: **firewood** (*noun* U)
– a piece of wood for a fire: **log** ◦ *Could you put another log on the fire?*

▷ more on fires and burning ⇨ FIRE

■ working with wood
– a person whose job is to make and repair wooden objects: **carpenter**; the work of a carpenter: **carpentry** (*noun* U)
– to cut wood (or stone) in order to make an object or to put a pattern or writing on it: **carve** sth; *noun* (U): **carving**; a person who does this: **carver** ◦ *a wood carving*
– something, usually made of wood, which has been carved: **carving** ◦ *a carving of a lion*

– a tool that is used to cut wood: **saw**
– a saw that is driven by a motor and has teeth on a moving chain: **chainsaw**
– to cut wood using a saw: **saw*** sth
– to cut a piece of wood into pieces using a saw: **saw*** sth **up** ◦ *We had to saw up the furniture to use as firewood.*
– to remove a piece of wood or a branch from a tree using a saw: **saw*** sth **off**
– very small pieces of wood that fall like powder when you are sawing: **sawdust** (*noun* U)

▷ picture at CUT

– a tool with a wooden handle and a metal blade, used for cutting wood: **axe** (*AmE* **ax**)
– to cause sth such as a tree to fall by using an axe: **cut*/chop** sth **down** ◦ *to cut down a tree* ◦ *I'll chop some more wood for the fire.*

▷ picture at CUT

▷ other tools used with wood ⇨ TOOL

- strong paper with a rough surface that is used to rub wood to make it smoother: **sandpaper** (*noun* U)
- to make the surface of sth smooth by using sandpaper: **sand** sth (**down**) ◦ *Sand down the window frames before painting.*

- a clear liquid that you put onto wood and other hard surfaces to protect them and make them shine: **varnish** (*noun* U); to put varnish on sth: **varnish** sth
- a special cream which is used for cleaning and protecting things, especially wood: **polish** (*noun* U); to make sth shine using polish: **polish** sth

■ **MORE ...**
- if wood becomes old and starts to decay, it **rots**, it becomes **rotten** ◦ *Some of these floorboards are rotten and will have to be replaced.*
- if a piece of wood becomes bent or twisted, especially because of heat or damp, it **warps**, it becomes **warped**

wool

see also CLOTH, CLOTHES

- the soft hair of sheep, goats, etc: **wool** (*noun* U)
- wool that has been made into a long thread to make clothes with: **wool** (*noun* U) ◦ *a ball of wool*
- something that is made of wool is **woollen** (*AmE* **woolen**), **woolly** (*AmE* **wooly**), **wool** ◦ *woollen gloves* ◦ *a woolly hat* ◦ *a wool blanket*
- something that feels like wool is **woolly** (*AmE* **wooly**) ◦ *The dog had a thick woolly coat.*
- artificial wool can be made of **acrylic** (*noun* U) or **nylon** (*noun* U); *adjectives*: **acrylic**, **nylon** ◦ *an acrylic jumper*
- a thick woollen cloth: **tweed** (*noun* U)

- a fine, soft wool which comes from very young sheep: **lambswool** (*noun* U)
- two very soft, fine kinds of wool: **cashmere** (*noun* U), **mohair** (*noun* U)

■ knitting

- to make sth (for example, a piece of clothing) out of wool using two needles that you hold in your hands: **knit** (sth); something made in this way is **knitted** ◦ *a knitted scarf*
- thin, pointed pieces of metal, plastic or wood used in knitting: (**knitting**) **needles**
- one of the small pieces of wool that you put around a needle when knitting: **stitch**
- a machine used for knitting: **knitting machine**
- something that is being knitted: **knitting** (*noun* U) ◦ *Where have I put my knitting?*
- clothing which is knitted: **knitwear** (*noun* U)
- a set of instructions that explains how to knit sth yourself: **pattern** ◦ *a knitting pattern*

- a way of making clothes, cloth, etc by using wool or cotton and one needle with a hook at the end: **crochet** (*noun* U); *verb*: **crochet** (sth)

■ **MORE ...**
- to make thread for knitting, etc from a mass of wool: **spin** (sth)

word

1 different kinds of words
2 sounds and letters
3 information about words
words that belong to particular varieties of language ⇨ LANGUAGE
the meaning of words ⇨ MEANING

1 different kinds of word

- a sound or letter, or a group of sounds or letters, with a particular meaning: **word** ◦ *What's the Spanish word for table?* ◦ *I don't know what this word means.* ◦ *That word is not spelt correctly.*
- relating to words, especially spoken words: **verbal** ◦ *verbal skills*

- all the words in a language, or the number of words that a person knows: **vocabulary** ◦ *By the end of this course, you should have a vocabulary of 2000 words.*
- a word or group of words that relates to a particular subject: **term** ◦ *'What's the term for someone who collects stamps?' 'A philatelist.'*
- the special words and expressions which are used by people who know a lot about a particular subject: **terminology** (*noun* U), **jargon** (*noun* U) ◦ *scientific terminology* ◦ *legal/computer jargon*

- the short form of a word: **abbreviation**; we say that an abbreviation is **short for** the complete form of the word ◦ *The abbreviation for 'Monday' is 'Mon'.* ◦ *'Dr' is short for 'Doctor'.*
- to use a short form of a word: **abbreviate** sth ◦ *'Telephone' is usually abbreviated to 'phone' in the spoken language.*
- a word which consists of two words put together in order to make them easier to pronounce: **contraction** ◦ *There are two possible contractions of the phrase 'it is not': 'it's not' and 'it isn't'.*

- a word or group of letters that you add on to the beginning/end of a word to change its meaning: **prefix/suffix** ◦ *'Pre-' is a prefix which means 'before'.* ◦ *'-ly' is a suffix used to make an adjective into an adverb.*

■ groups of words
- a number of words that go together to express a particular meaning: **expression** ◦ *a slang expression* ◦ *Try to think of a more informal expression.*
- an expression with a meaning that you cannot guess from the meanings of the individual words: **idiom** ◦ *'To fall out with' in 'He's fallen out with his girlfriend' is an idiom.*

word *contd.*

2 sounds and letters

- to say a word, paying attention to the way the sounds are made: **pronounce** sth ◦ *I never know how to pronounce the word 'data'.*
- the way in which a word is pronounced: **pronunciation** (*noun* C/U) ◦ *I need to practise my pronunciation.* ◦ *There are several possible pronunciations of the word 'garage'.*
- one of the sounds that you make with your lips and teeth open; one of the sounds represented in English by the letters 'a', 'e', 'i', 'o' and 'u': **vowel** ◦ *a difficult vowel sound*
- one of the other sounds in a language: **consonant** ◦ *The sounds represented by the letters 'b', 'c', 'd', 'f', etc are consonants.*
- a word or part of a word which contains one vowel sound: **syllable** ◦ *There are three syllables in the word 'computer'.*

- the force that you put on part of a word when you say it: **stress**; *verb*: **stress** sth ◦ *In the word 'consultant', the stress is/falls on the second syllable.* ◦ *You stress the first syllable in the word 'Italy'.*
- the parts of a word that you say with more force than the other parts are **stressed**; *opposite*: **unstressed** ◦ *In 'teacher', the second syllable is unstressed.*

- the technique of using words which have the same sound as each other, especially at the ends of lines: **rhyme** (*noun* U); a word that has the same sound as another word: **rhyme**; if words have the same sound, they **rhyme** ◦ *Does 'poor' rhyme with 'law'?*

- one of the symbols representing a sound, that forms part of a written word: **letter** ◦ *'A' is the first letter of the alphabet.*
- to write or say the letters of a word in the correct way: **spell** (sth); *noun* (U): **spelling** ◦ *Many English words are difficult to spell because there are a lot of silent letters.* ◦ *I'm not very good at spelling.*
- the way a word is spelt: **spelling** (*noun* C/U) ◦ *Remember to check your spellings.* ◦ *the difficulties of English spelling*
- to spell a word wrongly: **misspell** sth ◦ *You've misspelt my name!*

▷ more on letters ⇨ LETTER[2]

3 information about words

- to give an exact explanation of the meaning of a word: **define** sth ◦ *'Can you define 'slim'?' 'Yes, it means "thin in an attractive way".'*
- a book that contains lists of words and their meanings or words with the same or similar meaning in another language: **dictionary** ◦ *a Spanish-English dictionary*
- to look for a word in a dictionary: **look** sth **up** (**in** sth) ◦ *'What does this word mean?' 'I don't know – look it up in the dictionary.'*
- a list of words, often at the end of a book, that gives the meanings of some of the more difficult words in the text: **glossary**

■ **MORE ...**

- if you do not think that a particular word should be used to speak about sb/sth, you can use the expression **so-called** before you say the word ◦ *This so-called Socialist Party wants to privatize public services!*

- the historical origin of a word: **derivation** (*noun* C/U) ◦ *English has many words of Latin derivation.*

- a word from which you can make another word by changing the position of the letters in it: **anagram** ◦ *'Meat' is an anagram of 'team'.*
- a joke that is made using a word with two meanings or different words that sound the same: **pun** ◦ *to make a pun*
- a word that is made from the first letters of a group of words: **acronym** ◦ *'Ecu' is an acronym for 'European Currency Unit'.*

work

1 kinds of work
2 working
3 controlling your own or other people's work
4 working with other people
5 not working
6 workers

going to work ⇨ TRAVEL

1 kinds of work

- the use of mental or physical effort to do sth: **work** (*noun* U) ◦ *I've still got a lot of work to do to finish this job.* ◦ *to start/stop work*

- a piece of work that has to be done: **job**, **task** ◦ *My parents give me various jobs around the house to do during the school holidays.* ◦ *a boring/difficult task*
- the tasks that you do when you are at work: **duty** (*noun* C/U) ◦ *What exactly are my duties as safety officer?* ◦ *to be on night duty*
- small and varied jobs that have to be done: **odd jobs** (*noun plural*) ◦ *I do a lot of odd jobs for the neighbours, like gardening, painting fences and washing their car.*

- to give work to sb and pay them for doing it: **employ** sb ◦ *She's employed as a security officer.*
- the state of being employed, or the act of employing sb: **employment** (*noun* U)
- the work that you do for sb else, who pays you: **job**, **work** (*noun* U), (*formal*) **occupation** ◦ *Have you got a job?* ◦ *I start my new job next week.* ◦ *He managed to find work as a tour guide for the summer holidays.* ◦ *Do I need to state my occupation on the registration form?*
- to do a job in order to earn money: **work** (**for** sb) ◦ *Who do you work for?*

▷ being employed ⇨ EMPLOYMENT

- the way in which you earn money: **living** (*noun singular*) ◦ *What do you do for a living?*
- a type of job or area of work that needs sb who is well-educated and highly-trained: **profession**; a person who works in a profession: **professional**;

adjective: **professional** ◦ *the legal/medical/teaching profession* ◦ *a professional musician*

- work that requires a lot of effort: **hard work**; *opposite*: **light work**
- work that you do using your body: **physical work**
- work that you do using your hands: **manual work**
- work that requires a lot of physical effort: **heavy work**
- work that requires considerable knowledge and training: **skilled work**; *opposite*: **unskilled work**

2 working

- to do work: **work** ◦ *I've been working on the computer all afternoon.* ◦ *I can't come out – I've got to work.*
- to do a particular job: **do*** sth ◦ *Do you think you could do it by this afternoon?* ◦ *I haven't done all the typing yet.*
- to do a lot of work on a particular job: **work at/on** sth ◦ *I worked at it all night to try and get it done.* ◦ *Scientists have been working on this problem for years.*
- to do a piece of work, especially work that has been planned or agreed to: **carry** sth **out**, (*formal*) **perform** sth ◦ *The surgeon performed the emergency operation this morning.*
- to start doing sth that you have planned to do: **go* ahead** ◦ *Shall I just go ahead and do what I can?*

- doing or having work: **working** ◦ *a working lunch* ◦ *Working parents can find it difficult to look after young children.*
- visiting another place and doing some work there as part of your job: **on business** ◦ *She's away on business at the moment. Can I help you?*
- when doctors, nurses, policemen, firemen, etc are working, they are **on duty**

■ how well you do your work

- the way that you do a task or your job: **performance** (*noun* U) ◦ *The boss was not very satisfied with the performance of some of his staff.*
- to do sth, particularly some task, well/badly: **make* a good/poor job (of** sth**)**, **do* a good/poor job** ◦ *I haven't made a very good job of it, have I?*
- to finish or complete sth well, or to get the result you wanted, especially after a lot of hard work: **achieve** sth; *noun* (C/U): **achievement** ◦ *We've achieved some really good results this year.* ◦ *That's a great achievement!* ◦ *a great sense of achievement*

- to achieve part of the work you have to do: **make* progress (with/on** sth**)**, **get* on (with** sth**)** ◦ *I'm afraid I haven't made much progress with it so far.* ◦ *How are you getting on?*
- if work is being done now, it is **in progress** ◦ *The work of entering the data is already in progress.*
- to continue doing sth, particularly after you have been interrupted: **get* on (with** sth**)** ◦ *I can't spend all day chatting. I must get on with this or I'll never get it done.*
- to do extra work in order to finish sth, especially when you have been away: **catch* up on** sth ◦ *She had a lot of work to catch up on after she got back from holiday.*

- the time by which sth must be finished or done: **deadline** ◦ *I've still so much to do. I'll never make the deadline!*

■ working hard

- if you have a lot of work to do, you are **busy** ◦ *I'm sorry, I'm rather busy at the moment. Could you call me back?*
- a period in which you have a lot of work to do is **busy**; very busy: **hectic** ◦ *It's been a busy day today.* ◦ *I've had a really hectic day at the office. I didn't even have time for lunch!*
- to work as fast as you possibly can without a break: **work flat out** ◦ *They're working flat out over the weekend to get it finished in time for Monday.*

- to accept or agree to do sth: **take*** sth **on** ◦ *He's taken on more work than he can cope with.*
- working too much: **overwork** (*noun* U); *adjective*: **overworked** ◦ *I was made ill by overwork.* ◦ *The staff feel overworked and underpaid.*

- to work less hard: **slow down**, **take* it easy**, **take* things easy** ◦ *Her doctor advised her to slow down and not try to do so much.* ◦ *Relax! Take it easy! There's still plenty of time to get it all finished.*

- to focus your attention on a task: **concentrate (on** sth**)**; *noun* (U): **concentration** ◦ *How can I possibly concentrate with all this noise?*
- to prevent sb from concentrating on their work: **distract** sb **(from** sth**)**; *noun* (C/U): **distraction** ◦ *I can't work here – I keep getting distracted by people walking in and out.* ◦ *Let's go and do this somewhere else. There are too many distractions here.*

3 controlling your own or other people's work

- if you have to do sth, or look after sb/sth, you are **responsible (for** sb/sth**)** ◦ *Managers are responsible for the way their staff work.* ◦ *You can't hold me responsible for that. It's not my job to do it.*
- the state of being responsible for sb/sth: **responsibility** (*noun* U) ◦ *It's not my responsibility.* ◦ *to take/have responsibility for sth*
- if you are responsible for sb/sth, can give orders, etc, you are **in charge (of** sb/sth**)** ◦ *Who's in charge here?*

- to be in charge of a company or other organization: **run*** sth, **manage** sth; *noun* (U): **management**
- a person whose job is to give orders to other people at work: (*informal*) **boss**
- to make sure that work is done properly, or that people are doing their work properly: **supervise** sb/sth; *noun* (U): **supervision**; a person who does this: **supervisor** ◦ *The maintenance work must be supervised to make sure that it is being done thoroughly.* ◦ *Trainees should not be left to work without supervision.*

▷ more on management ⇨ **MANAGEMENT**

work *contd.*

4 working with other people

- to help sb to do sth: **give*** sb **a hand** (**with** sth), (*formal*) **assist** sb; *noun* (U): **assistance** ◦ *Can you give me a hand with this suitcase?* ◦ *If someone could give me some assistance with these letters, I would be very grateful.*
- a person who helps sb of a higher rank, or who sells things in a shop: **assistant** ◦ *a personal assistant* ◦ *the assistant manager*
- a person who works with you: **colleague**

- to work with sb else in order to do sth: **cooperate** (**with** sb/sth), **collaborate** (**with** sb); *nouns* (U): **cooperation, collaboration** ◦ *Our company will be cooperating with a German firm on this new project.* ◦ *work done in collaboration with another research team*
- a person who is willing to cooperate is **cooperative** ◦ *cooperative colleagues*

- a group of people who work together in order to achieve the same thing: **team** ◦ *They had a team of top lawyers.*
- to join up with other people to form a team: **team up** (**with** sb) ◦ *We teamed up with another group to do a project on Europe.*
- the work done by a team: **teamwork** (*noun* U) ◦ *It was great teamwork that helped get the job done on time.*

■ doing sb else's work

- to do sb else's job while they are absent: **fill in** (**for** sb), **stand* in** (**for** sb), **cover for** sb ◦ *They got a temporary secretary to fill in for her while she was off sick.* ◦ *Could you cover for me while I go to the meeting?*
- doing sb else's job for a short period of time until they return or until sb is appointed to do the job officially: **acting** (*only before a noun*) ◦ *This is Mr Stuart – our acting head teacher.*
- to take over the position of sb for a temporary period: **act as** sth ◦ *She's acting as manager for the next couple of months.*
- to replace sb in a job, etc: **take* the place** (**of** sb) ◦ *Who will take his place when he leaves?*
- to take the responsibility for sth or to continue where sb else has finished: **take*** (sth) **over from** sb ◦ *The morning shift takes over from the night shift at 9am.*

5 not working

- a short time when you stop work (especially in order to have some coffee, tea, sth to eat, etc): **break** ◦ *a lunch break* ◦ *a tea break* ◦ *I'm getting tired. Let's take a break for ten minutes.*
- to finish doing some work: (*informal*) **knock off** ◦ *They normally knock off work about 5.30pm and go off to the pub.*

- a period of time when you relax or sleep after working: **rest** (*noun* C/U) ◦ *I need a rest.* ◦ *Okay. You get some rest, and I'll take over.*
- a period of time when you do not go to work, and often travel to another place or country to relax: **holiday** ◦ *I'm sorry she's not in the office. She's on holiday this week.*

▷ not working when you are employed ⇨ **EMPLOYMENT**

▷ more on having a rest or taking a holiday ⇨ **REST²**, **HOLIDAY**

- the time when you do not have to work: **spare time** (*noun* U), **leisure** (*noun* U) ◦ *What do you do in your spare time?* ◦ *Shorter working hours mean that people have more leisure.*
- when you are not busy, or you are not doing any work at the moment, you are **free** ◦ *When are you free?*
- when doctors, nurses, policemen, firemen, etc are not working, they are **off duty**

6 workers

- a person who works, especially sb who does a particular type of job: **worker** ◦ *an office worker* ◦ *a manual worker* ◦ *factory workers*
- a person who does heavy manual work, especially on building sites: **workman** (*plural* **workmen**), **labourer**
- a person who does administrative work rather than manual work, and usually works in offices: **white-collar worker**
- the group of people in an industrialized society who do manual work: **the working class**: *adjective*: **working class**

- if you have the knowledge or ability to do sth, because you have done it before, you are **experienced**; *opposite*: **inexperienced** ◦ *a highly experienced pilot* ◦ *They were rather inexperienced for this kind of work.*
- the quality of being experienced: **experience** (*noun* U); *opposite*: **inexperience** (*noun* U) ◦ *He'd had a lot of experience of this kind of problem.* ◦ *All these mistakes are because of his relative inexperience in this area.*

- if you have studied for and passed all the necessary examinations and conditions for sth, you are **qualified**; *opposite*: **unqualified** ◦ *a qualified accountant* ◦ *Is he sufficiently qualified for this position?*
- the examinations that you have passed, the courses that you have completed, etc: **qualifications** ◦ *List your qualifications on the application form.*
- the ability to do sth well because you have been trained: **skill** (*noun* U) ◦ *a job requiring a great deal of skill*
- having a lot of skill in a particular area: **skilled**; *opposite*: **unskilled** ◦ *skilled/unskilled workers*

▷ more on skill ⇨ **SKILL**

- a person who works hard is **hardworking**; *opposite*: **lazy**
- a person who is good at what they do is **competent**; *opposite*: **incompetent** ◦ *Though lacking experience, he soon became very competent at his job.*
- a person who is able to do their job quickly, without making mistakes and wasting time, is **efficient** (*adverb* **efficiently**); *opposite*: **inefficient** (*adverb* **inefficiently**) ◦ *an efficient secretary* ◦ *to work efficiently*
- the quality of being efficient: **efficiency** (*noun* U); *opposite*: **inefficiency**

- showing care and attention to details in the work you do: **careful** (*adverb* **carefully**); *noun* (U): **care**
- a person who does things carefully, paying attention to detail to make sure that it is right, is **thorough**; *noun* (U): **thoroughness**
- a person who takes care to do things well is **conscientious** (*adverb* **conscientiously**); *noun* (U): **conscientiousness**

▷ more on being careful ⇨ **CAREFUL**

■ **MORE ...**
- work that you do because you want to do it, and not because you have to, or work that you are not paid to do, is **voluntary** ◦ *A lot of retired people do voluntary work.* ◦ *You don't have to do it, it's voluntary.*
- a person who does voluntary work: **volunteer**
- a person who is not able to stop working: **workaholic**

world

1 the whole world
2 different parts of the world
3 studying the world

countries ⇨ **COUNTRY[1]**
the countryside ⇨ **COUNTRY[2]**
protecting the environment ⇨ **ENVIRONMENT**
north, south, east, west ⇨ **DIRECTION**

see also AIR, LAND, SEA, HILL/MOUNTAIN, RIVER

1 the whole world
- the planet where we live, and its surface: **earth**, **the earth** (*also* **the Earth**) ◦ *The moon goes round the earth, and the earth goes round the sun.* ◦ *life on earth*
- the earth, including all the countries, people, etc: **world** (*often* **the world**) ◦ *Which is the largest city in the world?* ◦ *She's saving up to travel round the world.* ◦ *English is a world language.*
- all over the world: **worldwide** (*adjective, adverb*) ◦ *Pollution is a worldwide problem.* ◦ *Scotch whisky is popular worldwide.*
- affecting the whole world: **global**, **universal** ◦ *global warming* ◦ *universal trends*
- everything that exists, including the earth, the planets, the stars, etc: **the universe**

2 different parts of the world

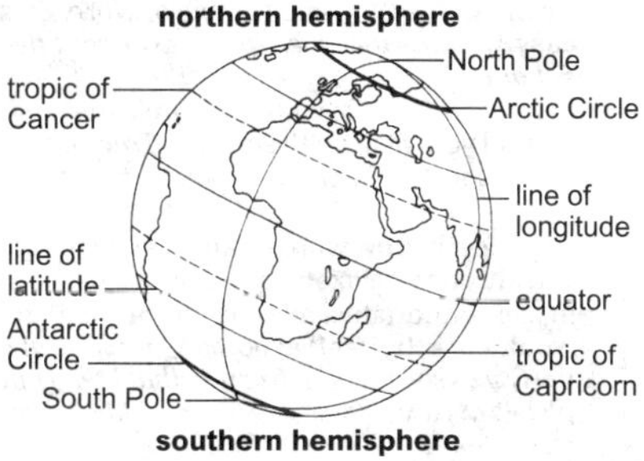

- latitude and longitude are measured in **degrees** ◦ *The equator is at 0° (zero degrees) latitude.*
- one of the main areas of land in the world (Europe, Asia, Africa, North/South America, Australia, the Antarctic): **continent**; *adjective*: **continental**
- one of the main areas of sea in the world (the Atlantic, the Pacific, etc): **ocean**
- a piece of land with water all around it: **island**
- the part of the world near the equator: **the tropics** (*noun plural*); *adjective*: **tropical** ◦ *I can't stand the cold – I'd much rather live in the tropics.* ◦ *tropical fruit* ◦ *the tropical rain forest*
- connected with the area around the equator: **equatorial**
- connected with the North or South pole: **polar** ◦ *the polar regions* ◦ *a polar bear*
- a part of the world where the time is the same: **time zone** ◦ *You'd better change your watch because we're entering a different time zone.*
- a part of the world: **world** ◦ *the western world* ◦ *the English-speaking world* ◦ *America used to be known as the New World.*
- the poorer countries of Africa, Asia, and South America: **the Third World**
- the countries of Western Europe, North America, etc: **the West**
- the countries of Asia: **the East** ◦ *the Far East* (= countries such as China and Japan) ◦ *the Middle East* (= the group of countries that are situated where Europe, Africa and Asia meet)
- the main part of Europe, not including the British Isles: **the Continent**; *adjective*: **continental** ◦ *We're thinking of going to the Continent.* ◦ *a continental holiday* ◦ *a continental breakfast*

3 studying the world
- the study of the world, including its natural and man-made features (seas, mountains, countries, cities, etc): **geography** (*noun* U); *adjective*: **geographical** ◦ *geographical features on a map, such as hills, rivers and valleys*
- a person who studies geography: **geographer**
- the study of the rocks, etc, which form the surface of the earth: **geology** (*noun* U); *adjective*: **geological**
- a person who studies geology: **geologist**

■ pictures of the world
- a drawing or plan of the world or a part of the world: **map**
- a book of maps: **atlas**
- a model of the earth in the shape of a ball: **globe**

▷ more on maps ⇨ **MAP**

worry

1 worrying
2 stopping worrying
3 not worrying or causing worry

see also EMOTION

1 worrying
- to feel anxious and unhappy about bad things that might happen: **worry** (**about** sth), **feel*/be**

worry *contd.*

worried (**about** sth); to cause sb to worry: **worry** sb ◦ *What are you worried about?* ◦ *I'm worried about my overdraft!*

- the state of being worried: **worry** (*noun* U); something that worries you: **worry**; *adjective*: **worrying** ◦ *She's got so many worries!* ◦ *He's had a worrying time lately.*
- very worrying: **nerve-racking** ◦ *'How did you get on in your driving test?' 'It was nerve-racking!'*

- if you are worried and afraid, you are **anxious** (*adverb* **anxiously**); *noun* (U): **anxiety**; something that makes you feel anxious: **anxiety** ◦ *It was already dark and I was beginning to get anxious.* ◦ *I have a slight anxiety about his state of health.*
- a state of constant worry about the problems of everyday life: **stress** (*noun* U); *adjective*: **stressed** ◦ *to be under a lot of stress* ◦ *to suffer from stress* ◦ *I'm feeling rather stressed at the moment.*

- if you worry about a particular problem, you are **troubled**, **disturbed**, **concerned**; the problem **troubles** you, **disturbs** you, **causes** you **concern**; it is **disturbing** ◦ *The doctor said he was rather concerned about Tom's condition.* ◦ *What's troubling you?* ◦ *a disturbing event*
- if you feel slightly worried about sth and therefore not relaxed, you are/feel **nervous** (*adverb* **nervously**), **uneasy** (*adverb* **uneasily**); *nouns* (U): **nervousness**, **unease** ◦ *Harry kept looking nervously at his watch. 'Where is she?' he asked.* ◦ *She was still not back. I was beginning to feel uneasy.*

- if you are ashamed or made worried by a situation or by your own or another person's behaviour, you are **embarrassed**; *noun* (U): **embarrassment** ◦ *Karen turned red with embarrassment when she met him unexpectedly.*
- to cause sb to be embarrassed: **embarrass** sb; something that causes you to be embarrassed is **embarrassing** ◦ *My children often embarrass me in public.* ◦ *an embarrassing incident*
- feeling or causing worry or embarrassment: **uncomfortable** (*adverb* **uncomfortably**) ◦ *Official occasions always make me feel uncomfortable.* ◦ *My question made him shift uncomfortably in his seat.*

- worried about sth bad that may happen: **afraid** (**that** .../**of** doing sth) (*not before a noun*), **frightened** (**at** sth/**that** .../**of** doing sth) ◦ *She was afraid that we would say no.* ◦ *Don't be afraid of making your views known.* ◦ *All of us were frightened at the possibility of another attack.*
- very frightened and worried: **alarmed**; the state of being alarmed: **alarm** (*noun* U); to make sb frightened and worried: **alarm** sb ◦ *The whole country was in a state of alarm.*
- very frightening and worrying: **alarming** ◦ *an alarming idea*
- if you are in a very emotional state of worry, you are **frantic** (*adverb* **frantically**) ◦ *frantic cries for help* ◦ *frantic with worry*
- to have a great fear about sth that will happen in the future: **dread** sth; *noun* (*singular*/U): **dread** ◦ *She dreaded going to see the doctor.* ◦ *a secret dread of what might happen* ◦ *to be filled with dread*
- if you are worried about another person or thing, you **fear for** them ◦ *He feared for his wife's safety.*

▷ more on being afraid ⇨ AFRAID

2 stopping worrying

- to cause a person to stop worrying about sth: **set*** sb's **mind at rest**
- to cause a person to feel less worried: **reassure** sb; this help: **reassurance** (*noun* U); *adjective*: **reassuring**
- the feeling that you have when you stop worrying: **relief** (*noun* U); if you are happy because you can stop worrying, you are **relieved** ◦ *a sigh of relief* ◦ *She was relieved to hear they had arrived home safely.*

- to tell a person not to worry, you can say **never mind** ◦ *Never mind, it's not important.*
- to show happiness and relief when you stop being worried, you can say **thank God!** or **thank goodness!** or **what a relief!** ◦ *Thank God you're safe!*

- to become less worried, frightened, etc: **relax** ◦ *Once I got home, I began to relax.*
- to make sb feel less nervous, worried, etc: **put*** sb **at** (their) **ease** ◦ *She began her speech with a couple of jokes and this helped to put everyone at their ease.*
- to start to feel comfortable and relaxed in a place: **make*** yourself **at home** ◦ *Just make yourself at home while I finish getting ready. I won't be long.*
- to do sth or say sth to make sb feel relaxed, especially when you meet them for the first time or at the start of a party: **break* the ice** ◦ *The arrival of the couple with the baby helped to break the ice.*

3 not worrying or causing worry

- not causing you worry, difficulty, etc: **comfortable** ◦ *Do you feel comfortable in large groups of people?*
- a person or thing that helps you when you are sad or worried: **comfort** ◦ *It was a great comfort to know that you'd be waiting for me.*
- if something causes no trouble or worry, it is **easy** ◦ *an easy life* ◦ *I felt quite easy about the situation.*
- to feel comfortable with the people or things around you: **fit in** (**with** sb/sth) ◦ *Tracy has really fitted in well at her new school.*

- if you feel happy, with nothing to worry about, you are **calm**, **relaxed** ◦ *a relaxed outlook on life*
- to feel comfortable, relaxed, etc: **be/feel* at** (your) **ease**, **be/feel* at home** ◦ *Everyone at the party was so kind and friendly that I felt completely at ease.* ◦ *After a week or so, Mark began to feel at home in his new office.*

- to relax and not work too hard or worry: **take* it/things easy** ◦ *I'm planning to take things easy for a few days.*

- if you do not feel worried about sth, you are **unconcerned** (**about** sth), you **don't care** (**about** sth) ◦ *She doesn't care what other people think.*

▷ more on being calm ⇨ **CALM**

■ **MORE ...**
- nervous and worried in a way that is not normal: **neurotic** (*adverb* **neurotically**)
- a person who continually worries about their health: **hypochondriac**

worse/worst ⇨ BAD

wound ⇨ INJURY

write

1 putting words on paper, etc
2 spelling, punctuation and grammar
3 listening and copying
4 things which people write
5 writing something
see also SAY, READ, SPEAK

1 putting words on paper, etc
- to put words or letters on paper, using a pen, pencil, etc: **write*** (sth) ◦ *to be able to read and write* ◦ *I can't write neatly with a biro.* ◦ *Can you write your name and address here, please?*
- to write information on a form: **fill in** a form ◦ *I had to fill in an application form for this job.*

- material that is used for writing and drawing on: **paper** (*noun* U) ◦ a sheet/piece of paper
- a number of sheets of paper, joined together at one side, often used for making notes: **pad (of paper)**, **notepad**, **notebook**
- paper used for writing letters: **notepaper** (*noun* U), **writing paper** (*noun* U)

▷ more on paper ⇨ **PAPER**

- a table that you sit at when writing or studying: **desk** ◦ He was sitting at his desk writing letters.

■ writing with a pen, pencil, etc
- instruments that you can use for writing: **pen**, **pencil** ◦ *I write my notes in pencil.*
- a hard, white substance used for writing on a blackboard: **chalk** (*noun* U) ◦ *a piece of chalk*
- a small piece of material that you use to remove pencil marks: **rubber** (*especially AmE* **eraser**)
- to remove pencil marks using a rubber: **rub** sth **out** (*especially AmE* **erase**) ◦ *Rub it out and try again.*

▷ more on pens, pencils, etc ⇨ **PEN/PENCIL**

- the way that you write by hand: **handwriting** (*noun* U), **writing** (*noun* U) ◦ *Your handwriting is terrible! It'd be better if you typed your work.*
- something that is written by hand, not typed, is **handwritten** ◦ *a handwritten message*

- to write letters which are not joined together, as in a book: **print** sth ◦ *Print your name please, with one letter in each box.*
- your name, written by hand in a special way so that nobody else can copy it: **signature** ◦ *Do you need my signature on this form?*
- to put your signature on sth: **sign** (sth) ◦ *Sign here, please.*

- if sb's handwriting or other words are clear enough to be read easily, the writing is **legible** (*adverb* **legibly**); *opposite*: **illegible** (*adverb* **illegibly**) ◦ *to write legibly* ◦ *I prefer to type my essays – my handwriting's virtually illegible.*
- to write in a very untidy way: **scribble** (sth), **scrawl** (sth); *nouns* (C/U) : **scribble, scrawl** ◦ *He scribbled something on a piece of paper.* ◦ *What a horrible scrawl! How am I supposed to read that?*

■ using a machine for writing
- a machine used for writing: **typewriter**; to write using a typewriter: **type** (sth); a person whose job is to type letters, reports, etc: **typist** ◦ *to type a report* ◦ *I need to learn to type.*
- a kind of small computer used for writing: **word processor**; knowledge of how to use a word processor: **word processing** (*noun* U) ◦ *Can you use a word processor?*

▷ computers ⇨ **COMPUTER**

■ being able to write
- the ability to read and write: **literacy** (*noun* U); *opposite*: **illiteracy** (*noun* U)
- a person who can read and write is **literate**; *opposite*: **illiterate**

2 spelling, punctuation and grammar
- to write or say the letters of a word in the correct way: **spell** (sth)
- the way that a word is spelt; the act of spelling or the ability to spell: **spelling** (*noun* C/U) ◦ *How do you spell your surname?* ◦ *I can't spell.* ◦ *Can you spell that for me, please?* ◦ *Your ideas are good but you need to improve your spelling.* ◦ *The teacher gave the children a list of spellings to learn.*
- to spell sth wrongly: **misspell** sth

▷ more on letters and words ⇨ **LETTER[2], WORD**

- the marks that you use in writing to show divisions in sentences or to show meaning: **punctuation** (*noun* U); one piece of punctuation: **punctuation mark** ◦ *You need a punctuation mark here – a dash or a semicolon.*
- a row of words on a page: **line** ◦ *You should start a new line here.*
- the empty space at the side of a page: **margin** ◦ *I've made some notes in the margin.*
- to put a line under a word or group of words to show that they have a particular importance: **underline** sth ◦ *Don't forget to underline the title of the book or journal you used.*

▷ more on punctuation ⇨ **PUNCTUATION**

- a group of words that expresses a statement, a question, etc: **sentence**
- the way in which words, sentences, etc are formed and used in a language: **grammar** (*noun* U); if sth that you say or write follows the rules

write *contd.*

of grammar correctly, it is **grammatical**; *opposite*: **ungrammatical**
- a section of writing which covers a particular idea: **paragraph**
- the words in a book, not the pictures, etc: **text**

▷ more on grammar ⇨ **GRAMMAR**

3 listening and copying
- to say or read aloud a letter, a message, etc, while sb else writes it down: **dictate** sth; *noun* (U): **dictation** ◦ *to dictate a letter* ◦ *to take dictation*
- to write down words at the same time as sb says them: **take*** sth **down** ◦ *Could you take down this letter, please.*
- a system for writing words and sentences in short forms, so that you can write things very quickly: **shorthand** (*noun* U) ◦ *to take sth down in shorthand*

- a test in which you have to write down sth that is said aloud: **dictation** (*noun* C/U)
- to write down words which are written on a blackboard, screen, etc: **copy** sth **down** ◦ *He wrote the vocabulary on the board and the students copied it down.*
- to write down words which are written in a book: **copy** sth (**out**), **copy** sth **out of** sth ◦ *Copy out the questions on page 15.* ◦ *This isn't your own work – it's all copied out of a book!*

4 things that people write
- a number of sheets of paper, with words printed or written on them, fastened in a cover: **book**
- novels, poems and plays, which are considered to be of high quality and an important part of a country's culture: **literature** (*noun* U)

▷ different kinds of book ⇨ **BOOK**

▷ literature ⇨ **LITERATURE, PLAY[1], POEM**

- a short piece of writing on one subject: **essay** ◦ *I'm writing an essay on Shakespeare's sonnets.*
- a long piece of writing which you may have to write as part of a university degree: **dissertation, thesis** (*plural* **theses**) ◦ *Have you decided what your dissertation's going to be about yet?*
- a shortened form of a piece of writing that contains only the most important information: **précis, summary**

- a piece of writing that describes sth that happened: **report** (**of/on** sth); *verb*: **report** (**on**) sth ◦ *I've been asked to write a report about my business trip to Spain.* ◦ *The trial was reported in detail in all the newspapers.*
- a book in which you write down what has happened to you each day: **diary** ◦ *I've started writing a diary since my baby was born.* ◦ *You should keep a diary of your trip to Australia.*
- a short written account of what has happened: **record**; *verb*: **record** sth ◦ *Can you write down what you talked about at the meeting? – just so that we have a record for next time.* ◦ *I've recorded all the details of the meeting.*
- something that you have recorded is **on record** ◦ *It's all on record, so don't worry if you forget anything.*

- a written message which you send to sb: **letter** ◦ *Did you get my letter this morning?*

▷ more on letters and other written messages ⇨ **LETTER[1]**

- a number of words written one after another, often used to help you remember sth: **list** ◦ *a shopping list*
- a piece of paper on which you write some information and which you stick on the wall for people to read: **notice** ◦ *The lecture's been postponed till next week – didn't you see the notice?*
- a large notice, often with a picture, giving information about concerts, etc: **poster** ◦ *There are posters up all over the university advertising next week's concert.*

5 writing something
- to create a book, story, report, etc and write it on paper: **write*** sth ◦ *I must write some letters this afternoon.*
- the act of writing: **writing** (*noun* U) ◦ *I've got a lot of writing to do this term.*

- a person who writes, especially one who writes books: **writer** ◦ *'What does he do?' 'He's a writer.'*
- a person who has written a particular book: **author** ◦ *She's the author of several well-known children's books.*
- a piece of writing by a particular author: **work** ◦ *a new work by Kazuo Ishiguro* ◦ *the complete works of W.B. Yeats*

- to write concerning a particular subject: **write*** (sth) **about/on** sb/sth ◦ *I wrote a poem about winter.*
- to produce a piece of writing using careful thought: (*formal*) **compose** sth ◦ *I need your help to compose a letter to my bank manager.*

- to write some particular piece of information on to a page: **write*** sth **down, get*** sth **down** ◦ *Write the number down so you don't forget it.* ◦ *Could you repeat that? – I didn't have time to get it down.*
- to write sth in a particular place: **write*/put*** sth ... ◦ *Write the answer here.* ◦ *Put your name at the top of the page.*
- to quickly write a few words to help you to remember sth: **jot** sth **down, note** sth **down** ◦ *I jotted the address down on a piece of paper but I've no idea where I put it.*

- the name of a book, story, etc: **title** ◦ *What's the title of the book you're reading?*
- the title of a section in a book, article, etc: **heading** ◦ *This paragraph needs a heading.*

- the words you use to say sth: **wording** (*noun singular*) ◦ *I think you need to change the wording of this sentence.*
- the way that sb usually writes; a recognized way of writing: **style** ◦ *a clear, economical style* ◦ *in the style of Jane Austen*

- the ideas, information, etc that a piece of writing contains: **content**

▷ different styles of language ⇨ **LANGUAGE**

■ planning and changing what you write

- a piece of writing that is unfinished and that can still be changed: **draft**; *verb*: **draft** sth ○ *I've written the first draft of my dissertation.* ○ *Have you drafted that report yet?*
- to read a document, report, essay, etc, to check for spelling mistakes, style, etc: **read*** sth **over/through** ○ *Could you read over that, please, and tell me what you think of it?*

- to read sth that you have written and correct it: **revise** sth ○ *to revise an article before publication*
- to write sth again: **rewrite*** sth ○ *I read what I had written the night before, and decided to rewrite the whole thing.*
- to change the way in which sth is written: **reword** sth ○ *Can you reword this sentence? It sounds awkward.*

- to take out sth that has been written or printed: **delete** sth, **cut*** (sth **out**) ○ *I think it's best if you delete this paragraph – people won't understand it.* ○ *My essay is too long – I'll have to cut it.*
- to put a line through sth that you have written: **cross** sth **out** ○ *I crossed out his name and wrote yours above it.*

- to write sth in a complete and final form, often using notes that you have made: **write*** sth **up** ○ *If you've corrected all the mistakes, you can write it up now.*

■ **MORE . . .**

- to start writing sth: **put* pen to paper** ○ *It took me a long time to decide what to write, but as soon as I put pen to paper, the words came easily.*

- a name of a writer which is not his/her real name: **pseudonym, pen-name** ○ *Ruth Rendell sometimes writes under the pseudonym of Barbara Vine.*

wrong

- not true ⇨ **TRUE**
- a mistake ⇨ **MISTAKE**
- morally wrong ⇨ **RIGHT/WRONG**²

year

see also DAY, WEEK

- a period of 365 days; a period of twelve months: **year** ○ *The diploma course takes a full year.* ○ *The house is over 200 years old.* ○ *I'm hoping to finish my book in another year, or a year and a half.* ○ *We last saw them about a year ago.*
- the year from January to December: **year** ○ *I can't remember which year my grandfather was born in.* ○ *the year 2000*
- a year which has 366 days: **leap year**

- a period of 10 years: **decade**
- a period of 100 years: **century** ○ *in the 18th century*
- the period between 1920 and 1929: **the twenties**; between 1930 and 1939: **the thirties**; etc ○ *Do you like sixties music?*

- a celebration of sth that happened 100 years ago: **centenary** (*AmE* **centennial**)
- a celebration of sth that happened 200 years ago: **bicentenary** (*AmE* **bicentennial**)

- one of the twelve periods into which the year is divided; a period of about four weeks: **month** ○ *at the beginning/end of the month* ○ *I waited a full month before I decided to phone them.* ○ *I normally see her about once a month.* ○ *We'll be meeting again in a month.* ○ *'How old is she now?' 'She's nearly six months.'*

- the twelve months of the year: **January, February, March, April, May, June, July, August, September, October, November, December** ○ *I'm going to France in June.* ○ *on 23rd January*
- abbreviations for the names of the months: **Jan, Feb, Mar, Apr, May, Jun, Jul, Aug, Sept, Oct, Nov, Dec**

- happening every year: **yearly** (*adjective, adverb*), **annual** (*adverb* **annually**) ○ *an annual sales conference* ○ *The exhibition is held annually.*
- every six months: **half-yearly** (*adjective, adverb*) ○ *at half-yearly intervals* ○ *We get a full report half-yearly.*
- a period of three months: **quarter**; happening every three months: **quarterly** (*adjective, adverb*) ○ *I pay my telephone bill quarterly.*
- once a month: **monthly** (*adjective, adverb*) ○ *a monthly magazine* ○ *I'm paid monthly.*
- in the middle of (a month, year, etc): **mid** (*only before a noun*) ○ *I'm leaving my job in mid-April.*

- the month/year before this one: **last month/year**
- the month/year after this one: **next month/year**
- two months/years before this one: **the month/year before last**
- two months/years after this one: **the month/year after next**

- one of the four periods into which the year is divided: **season**; happening or existing at a particular time of the year: **seasonal** ○ *seasonal work* ○ *Many jobs in the tourist industry are only seasonal.*

▷ more on the seasons ⇨ **SEASON**

yellow ⇨ COLOUR

yes/no

asking and answering questions ⇨ **QUESTION**
requests, offers and invitations ⇨ **REQUEST, OFFER, INVITE**
giving and refusing permission ⇨ **ALLOW**
agreeing and disagreeing ⇨ **DISCUSS/ARGUE, OPINION**
saying that sth is or is not true ⇨ **TRUE**

yes/no *contd.*

– to show that you agree with sb or accept what sb has said, you say **yes**, (*informal*) **yeah**
– stronger ways of expressing agreement: **exactly**, **absolutely**, **definitely** ◦ *'I'd rather drive there than go by train, wouldn't you?' 'Oh, absolutely.'*
– to show that you agree with sb but you are not sure or happy about it, you can say **yes and no**, **up to a point**, **I suppose so**

– to politely accept an offer or invitation, you can say **yes please**
– to agree to a request, you can say **OK**, **all right**, **right**
– to agree happily to a request, you can say **of course**, **sure**, **certainly**, **by all means**

– to show that you do not agree with sb, accept sth, etc, you say **no**
– stronger ways of saying no: **certainly not**, (*informal*) **not likely**, (*informal*) **no way** ◦ *'Are you a Manchester United supporter?' 'Certainly not!'* ◦ *'Would you volunteer to join the army?' 'Not likely!'*

– to politely say no to a request, invitation, etc, you can say **I'm afraid ... not** or **(I'm) sorry, but ...** ◦ *'Can you come?' 'I'm afraid I can't.'* ◦ *'Have you spoken to her yet?' 'I'm afraid not.'* ◦ *'Do you think you could lend me ten pounds?' 'I'm sorry, but I'm a bit short myself just now.'*

– to say that a second thing is the case, you say **so** ◦ *'Are you a member of this club?' 'Yes, and so is my wife.'*
– to say that a second thing is not the case, you say **neither** or **nor** ◦ *'Does your wife play tennis?' 'No, she doesn't, and neither/nor do I.'*

– to move your head up and down as a way of saying yes: **nod** (your **head**); *noun*: **nod** ◦ *When I asked her if she was going out, she just nodded.* ◦ *a nod of approval*
– to move your head from side to side as a way of saying no: **shake*** your **head** ◦ *He just shook his head without saying anything.*

– meaning 'yes': (*formal*) **affirmative** (*noun, adjective*) ◦ *to answer in the affirmative* ◦ *an affirmative answer*
– meaning 'no': **negative** (*noun, adjective*) ◦ *to answer in the negative* ◦ *a negative sentence*

yesterday ⇨ DAY

young/old

1 how old?
2 young
3 old

new and old things ⇨ NEW/OLD
the stages of a person's life (childhood, adulthood, etc) ⇨ LIFE

1 how old?

– the length of time that sb has lived: **age** (*noun* C/U) ◦ *He died at the age of 88.* ◦ *I shouldn't be doing things like this at my age.* ◦ *suitable for people of all ages*
– of a particular age: **old**, **aged ...** ◦ *I'm 27 years old.* ◦ *How old do you think she is?* ◦ *He's got a three-year-old son.* ◦ *This keep-fit class is intended for anyone aged fifty or over.*
– to ask sb their age, you say **How old are you?**

– if you are aged between 20 and 29, you are **in** your **twenties**; between 30 and 39: **in** your **thirties**, etc ◦ *She's in her early forties* (= between forty and forty-four).
– if you do not know sb's exact age, you can say that they are **thirty-odd**, **thirty-something**, etc ◦ *'How old is he?' 'I don't know, seventy-odd I should guess.'*

– younger than a particular age: **under** sth ◦ *a toy for children under five*
– people younger than a particular age: **under-16s**, etc ◦ *games for under-fives*
– older than a particular age: **over** sth ◦ *She must be over sixty.*
– people older than a particular age: **over-50s**, etc ◦ *a club for the over-60s*
▷ older and younger members of a family ⇨ FAMILY

– people of a particular age: **age group** ◦ *These holidays are very popular with the 20-30 age group.*
– all the people in a group or country who were born at about the same time: **generation** ◦ *People of my grandparents' generation have very different views on life from people my age.* ◦ *the older/younger generation*

2 young

– not having lived for a long time: **young** ◦ *when I was young* ◦ *young people* ◦ *young plants/animals*
– the state of being young: **youth** (*noun* U) ◦ *Her youth gives her an advantage over the other runners.*
– young people when you are thinking about them as a group: **young people**, **the young**, **the youth of** sth ◦ *The young are often blamed for the social problems of today.* ◦ *the youth of China/today*
– young animals: **young** (*noun plural*) ◦ *We watched the lioness with her young.*

– the period of time in your life when you are young, especially the time between being a child and an adult: **youth** (*noun* U) ◦ *She was very badly behaved in her youth.*
▷ children ⇨ CHILD

3 old

– having lived a long time; not young: **old**, (*more formal and polite*) **elderly** ◦ *old men and women* ◦ *an elderly person*
– the state of being old: **old age** (*noun* U) ◦ *extreme old age*

- to become old: **get* old**, (*informal*) **be getting on (a bit)** ◦ *She's getting on a bit now – she's over eighty.*
- to become old or look old: **age**; *adjective*: **ageing** ◦ *In the last few months he has aged a great deal.* ◦ *the problems of an ageing population*
- old people when you are thinking about them as a group: **old people, the old** ◦ *Even the old and the sick were caught up in the fighting.*

■ **MORE . . .**

- to seem or look as old as you really are: **look** your **age** ◦ *The last few years have been very difficult for him – you can see he's beginning to look his age.*
- a small line on the skin of the face which you get as you grow older: **wrinkle**; *adjective*: **wrinkled** ◦ *to have wrinkles* ◦ *old and wrinkled*
- old, but still fit and healthy: **going strong** ◦ *He's 90 and still going strong.*
- confused, unable to remember things or to look after yourself properly because of old age: **senile**; *noun* (U): **senility** ◦ *She's gone a bit senile.*

- the oldest or youngest age at which you can be allowed to do sth: **age limit** ◦ *There is no age limit for entry to the course.*
- not old enough by law to do sth: **under age**

zero ⇨ NUMBER

zip ⇨ CLOTHES

zodiac ⇨ ASTROLOGY

Irregular verbs

This list shows the irregular forms that are to be used when a verb is marked * in the dictionary.

Infinitive	Past tense	Past participle
arise	arose	arisen
awake	awoke	awoken
babysit	babysat	babysat
bear	bore	borne
beat	beat	beaten
become	became	become
begin	began	begun
bend	bent	bent
bet	bet, betted	bet, betted
bid	bid	bid
bite	bit	bitten
bleed	bled	bled
blow	blew	blown
bottle-feed	bottle-fed	bottle-fed
break	broke	broken
breastfeed	breastfed	breastfed
breed	bred	bred
bring	brought	brought
broadcast	broadcast	broadcast
build	built	built
burst	burst	burst
buy	bought	bought
cast	cast	cast
catch	caught	caught
choose	chose	chosen
cling	clung	clung
come	came	come
cost	cost	cost
creep	crept	crept
cut	cut	cut
deal	dealt	dealt
dig	dug	dug
disprove	disproved	disproved (*AmE* disproven)
dive	dived (*AmE* dove)	dived
do	did	done
draw	drew	drawn
drink	drank	drunk
drive	drove	driven
eat	ate	eaten
fall	fell	fallen
feed	fed	fed
feel	felt	felt
fight	fought	fought
find	found	found
fling	flung	flung
fly	flew	flown
forbid	forbade	forbidden
forecast	forecast, forecasted	forecast, forecasted
foresee	foresaw	foreseen
forget	forgot	forgotten
forgive	forgave	forgiven
freeze	froze	frozen
get	got	got (*AmE* gotten)
give	gave	given
go	went	gone
grind	ground	ground
grow	grew	grown
hang	hung	hung
have	had	had
hear	heard	heard
hide	hid	hidden
hit	hit	hit
hold	held	held
hurt	hurt	hurt
keep	kept	kept
kneel	knelt (*esp AmE* kneeled)	knelt (*esp AmE* kneeled)
know	knew	known
lay	laid	laid
lead	led	led
leap	leapt, leaped	leapt, leaped
leave	left	left
lend	lent	lent
let	let	let
lie	lay	lain
light	lighted, lit	lighted, lit
lose	lost	lost
make	made	made
mean	meant	meant
meet	met	met
mislead	misled	misled
mistake	mistook	mistaken
misunderstand	misunderstood	misunderstood
mow	mowed	mown, mowed
outgrow	outgrew	outgrown
overcome	overcame	overcome
overeat	overate	overeaten
overhear	overheard	overheard
overrun	overran	overrun
oversee	oversaw	overseen
oversleep	overslept	overslept
overtake	overtook	overtaken
overthrow	overthrew	overthrown
panic	panicked	panicked
pay	paid	paid
prove	proved	proved (*AmE* proven)
put	put	put
quit	quit, quitted	quit, quitted
read	read	read
rebuild	rebuilt	rebuilt
repay	repaid	repaid
rewind	rewound	rewound
rewrite	rewrote	rewritten
ride	rode	ridden
ring	rang	rung
rise	rose	risen
run	ran	run
saw	sawed	sawn (*AmE* sawed)

Infinitive	Past tense	Past participle
say	said	said
see	saw	seen
seek	sought	sought
sell	sold	sold
send	sent	sent
set	set	set
sew	sewed	sewn, sewed
shake	shook	shaken
shine	shone	shone
shoot	shot	shot
show	showed	shown, showed
shrink	shrank	shrunk
shut	shut	shut
sing	sang	sung
sink	sank	sunk
sit	sat	sat
sleep	slept	slept
slide	slid	slid
slit	slit	slit
sow	sowed	sown, sowed
speak	spoke	spoken
speed	sped	sped
spend	spent	spent
spin	spun	spun
spit	spat (*AmE* *also* spit)	spat (*AmE* *also* spit)
split	split	split
spread	spread	spread
stand	stood	stood
steal	stole	stolen
stick	stuck	stuck

Infinitive	Past tense	Past participle
sting	stung	stung
stink	stank, stunk	stunk
strike	struck	struck
swear	swore	sworn
sweep	swept	swept
swell	swelled	swollen, swelled
swim	swam	swum
swing	swung	swung
take	took	taken
teach	taught	taught
tear	tore	torn
tell	told	told
think	thought	thought
throw	threw	thrown
tread	trod	trodden, trod
undergo	underwent	undergone
understand	understood	understood
undertake	undertook	undertaken
undo	undid	undone
unwind	unwound	unwound
upset	upset	upset
wake	woke	woken
wear	wore	worn
weave	wove	wove
weep	wept	wept
win	won	won
wind	wound	wound
withdraw	withdrew	withdrawn
wring	wrung	wrung
write	wrote	written

Geographical names

This list shows the English spelling of geographical names. If a country has a different word for the adjective and the person from the country, both are given, (eg **Denmark**; **Danish**, **Dane**).

To make the plural of a word for a person from a particular country, add **-s**, except for **Swiss** and words ending in **-ese** (eg *Japanese*), which stay the same, and for words that end in **-man** or **-woman**, which change to **-men** or **-women** (eg *three Frenchmen*).

Afghanistan; Afghan, Afghani, Afghanistani
Africa; African
Albania; Albanian
Algeria; Algerian
America ⇨ (the) United States (of America)
America; American
Andorra; Andorran
Angola; Angolan
Antarctica; Antarctic
Antigua and Barbuda; Antiguan, Barbudan
(the) Arctic Ocean; Arctic
Argentina, the Argentine; Argentinian, Argentine
Armenia; Armenian
Asia; Asian
Australia; Australian
Austria; Austrian
Azerbaijan; Azerbaijani, Azeri
(the) Bahamas; Bahamian
Bahrain, Bahrein; Bahraini, Bahreini
Bangladesh; Bangladeshi
Barbados; Barbadian
Belarus; Belorussian
Belgium; Belgian
Belize; Belizean
Benin; Beninese
Bhutan; Bhutani, Bhutanese
Bolivia; Bolivian
Bosnia-Herzegovina; Bosnian
Botswana; Botswanan, *also* Tswanan
Brazil; Brazilian
Britain ⇨ Great Britain
Brunei Darussalam; Brunei, Bruneian
Bulgaria; Bulgarian
Burkina; Burkinese
Burundi; Burundian
Cambodia; Cambodian
Cameroon; Cameroonian
Canada; Canadian
(the) Cape Verde Islands; Cape Verdean
(the) Caribbean Sea; Caribbean
Central African Republic
Chad; Chadian
Chile; Chilean
China; Chinese
Colombia; Colombian
Comoros; Comoran
Congo; Congolese
Costa Rica; Costa Rican
Côte d'Ivoire
Croatia; Croatian
Cuba; Cuban
Cyprus; Cypriot
(the) Czech Republic; Czech
Denmark; Danish, Dane
Djibouti; Djiboutian
Dominica; Dominican
(the) Dominican Republic; Dominican
Ecuador; Ecuadorian
Egypt; Egyptian
El Salvador; Salvadorean
England; English, Englishman, Englishwoman (the English)
Equatorial Guinea; Equatorial Guinean
Eritrea; Eritrean
Estonia; Estonian
Ethiopia; Ethiopian
Europe; European
Fiji; Fijian
Finland; Finnish, Finn
France; French, Frenchman, Frenchwoman
Gabon; Gabonese
(the) Gambia; Gambian
Georgia; Georgian
Germany; German
Ghana; Ghanaian
Gibraltar; Gibraltarian
Great Britain; British, Briton (the British)
Greece; Greek
Grenada; Grenadian
Guatemala; Guatemalan
Guinea; Guinean
Guinea-Bissau
Guyana; Guyanese
Haiti; Haitian
Holland ⇨ (the) Netherlands
Honduras; Honduran
Hungary; Hungarian
Iceland; Icelandic
India; Indian
Indonesia; Indonesian
Iran; Iranian
Iraq; Iraqi
(the Republic of) Ireland; Irish, Irishman, Irishwoman (the Irish)
Israel; Israeli
Italy; Italian
Jamaica; Jamaican
Japan; Japanese
Jordan; Jordanian
Kazakhstan; Kazakh

Kenya; Kenyan
Kirgyzstan; Kirgyz
Kiribati
Korea; North Korea, North Korean; South Korea, South Korean
Kuwait; Kuwaiti
Laos; Laotian
Latvia; Latvian
Lebanon; Lebanese
Lesotho; Sotho, (person: Mosotho, people: Basotho)
Liberia; Liberian
Libya; Libyan
Liechtenstein; Liechtenstein, Liechtensteiner
Lithuania; Lithuanian
Luxembourg; Luxembourg, Luxembourger
Madagascar; Madagascan, Malagasy
Malawi; Malawian
Malaysia; Malaysian
(the) **Maldives**; Maldivian
Mali; Malian
Malta; Maltese
Mauritania; Mauritanian
Mauritius; Mauritian
Mexico; Mexican
Moldova; Moldovan
Monaco; Monacan, Monégasque
Mongolia; Mongolian, Mongol
Montserrat; Montserratian
Morocco; Moroccan
Mozambique; Mozambiquean
Myanmar
Namibia; Namibian
Nauru; Nauruan
Nepal; Nepalese
(the) **Netherlands**; Dutch, Dutchman, Dutchwoman
New Zealand; New Zealand, New Zealander
Nicaragua; Nicaraguan
Niger; Nigerien
Nigeria; Nigerian
Northern Ireland; Northern Irish (*adjective only*)
Norway; Norwegian
Oman; Omani
Pakistan; Pakistani
Panama; Panamanian
Papua New Guinea; Papuan
Paraguay; Paraguayan
Peru; Peruvian
(the) **Philippines**; Philippine, Filipino
Poland; Polish, Pole
Portugal; Portuguese
Qatar; Qatari
Romania; Romanian
Russia; Russian
Rwanda; Rwandan
San Marino; San Marinese
Sao Tomé and Principe
Saudi Arabia; Saudi, Saudi Arabian
Scotland; Scottish, Scot, Scotsman, Scotswoman (the Scots)
Senegal; Senegalese
(the) **Seychelles**; Seychellois
Sierra Leone; Sierra Leonean
Singapore; Singaporean
Slovakia; Slovak
Slovenia; Slovene, Slovenian
(the) **Solomon Islands**
Somalia; Somali
(the Republic of) South Africa; South African
Spain; Spanish, Spaniard
Sri Lanka; Sri Lankan
St Kitts and Nevis
St Lucia
St Vincent and the Grenadines
Sudan; Sudanese
Surinam; Surinamese
Swaziland; Swazi
Sweden; Swedish, Swede
Switzerland; Swiss
Syria; Syrian
Tajikistan; Tajik
Tanzania; Tanzanian
Thailand; Thai
Togo; Togolese
Tonga; Tongan
Trinidad and Tobago; Trinidadian, Tobagan, Tobagonian
Tunisia; Tunisian
Turkey; Turkish, Turk
Turkmenistan; Turkmen
Tuvalu; Tuvaluan
Uganda; Ugandan
Ukraine; Ukrainian
(the) United Arab Emirates
(the) United Kingdom; British, Briton (the British)
(the) United States (of America); American
Uruguay; Uruguayan
Uzbekistan; Uzbek
Vanuatu
(the) Vatican City
Venezuela; Venezuelan
Vietnam; Vietnamese
Wales; Welsh, Welshman, Welshwoman (the Welsh)
(the) West Indies; West Indian
Western Samoa; Samoan
Yemen Republic; Yemeni
Yugoslavia; Yugoslavian, Yugoslav
Zaïre; Zairean
Zambia; Zambian
Zimbabwe; Zimbabwean

图书在版编目(CIP)数据

牛津英语联想词典/(英)洛马斯(Trappes-Lomax, H.)编.
—北京:商务印书馆,2003
ISBN 7-100-03904-5

I. 牛... II. 洛... III. 英语-词典 IV. H316

中国版本图书馆 CIP 数据核字(2003)第 073437 号

NIÚJĪN YĪNGYǓ LIÁNXIǍNG CÍDIǍN

牛津英语联想词典

英 语 版

出版:商务印书馆
(北京王府井大街 36 号 邮政编码 100710)
牛津大学出版社(中国)有限公司
(香港鲗鱼涌英皇道 979 号太古坊和域大厦东翼十八楼)
国内总发行:商务印书馆
国外以及香港、澳门、台湾地区总发行:牛津大学出版社(中国)有限公司
印刷:北京冠中印刷厂
ISBN 700-100-03904-5/H·979

2003 年 12 月第 1 版 开本 880×1230 1/32
2003 年 12 月北京第 1 次印刷 印张 16⅞
印数 20 000 册

定价:33.00 元